THE
ALL ENGLAND
LAW REPORTS

1993

Volume 1

Editor
PETER HUTCHESSON LL M
Barrister, New Zealand

Assistant Editor
BROOK WATSON
of Lincoln's Inn, Barrister
and of the New South Wales Bar

Consulting Editor
WENDY SHOCKETT
of Gray's Inn, Barrister

London
BUTTERWORTHS

UNITED KINGDOM	Butterworth & Co (Publishers) Ltd, 88 Kingsway, **London** WC2B 6AB and 4 Hill Street, **Edinburgh** EH2 3JZ
AUSTRALIA	Butterworths Pty Ltd, **Sydney, Melbourne, Brisbane, Adelaide, Perth, Canberra** and **Hobart**
BELGIUM	Butterworth & Co (Publishers) Ltd, **Brussels**
CANADA	Butterworths Canada Ltd, **Markham** and **Vancouver**
IRELAND	Butterworth (Ireland) Ltd, **Dublin**
MALAYSIA	Malayan Law Journal Pte Ltd, **Kuala Lumpur**
NEW ZEALAND	Butterworths of New Zealand Ltd, **Wellington** and **Auckland**
PUERTO RICO	Butterworths of Puerto Rico Inc, **Hato Rey**
SINGAPORE	Butterworths Asia, **Singapore**
USA	Butterworth Legal Publishers, **Austin**, Texas, **Clearwater**, Florida, **Orford**, New Hampshire, **St Paul**, Minnesota and **Salem**, New Hampshire

ISBN for the complete set of volumes: 0 406 85159 X
for this volume: ISBN 0 406 01666 6

Typeset, printed and bound in Great Britain by William Clowes Limited, Beccles and London

House of Lords

The Lord High Chancellor of Great Britain: Lord Mackay of Clashfern

Lords of Appeal in Ordinary

Lord Keith of Kinkel
Lord Bridge of Harwich
Lord Templeman
Lord Griffiths
Lord Goff of Chieveley
Lord Jauncey of Tullichettle

Lord Lowry
Lord Browne-Wilkinson
Lord Mustill
Lord Slynn of Hadley
Lord Woolf

Court of Appeal

The Lord High Chancellor of Great Britain

The Lord Chief Justice of England: Lord Taylor of Gosforth
(President of the Criminal Division)

The Master of the Rolls:
Sir Thomas Henry Bingham
(President of the Civil Division)

The President of the Family Division: Sir Stephen Brown

The Vice-Chancellor: Sir Donald James Nicholls

Lords Justices of Appeal

Sir Tasker Watkins VC
(Deputy Chief Justice)
Sir Francis Brooks Purchas
(retired 10 January 1993)
Sir George Brian Hugh Dillon
Sir Anthony John Leslie Lloyd
Sir Brian Thomas Neill
Sir Martin Charles Nourse
Sir Iain Derek Laing Glidewell
Sir Alfred John Balcombe
Sir Ralph Brian Gibson
Sir Thomas Patrick Russell
Dame Ann Elizabeth Oldfield Butler-Sloss
Sir Murray Stuart-Smith
Sir Christopher Stephen Thomas Jonathan
Thayer Staughton
Sir Michael Mann
Sir Donald Henry Farquharson

Sir Anthony James Denys McCowan
(Senior Presiding Judge for England
and Wales)
Sir Alexander Roy Asplan Beldam
Sir Andrew Peter Leggatt
Sir Michael Patrick Nolan
Sir Richard Rashleigh Folliott Scott
Sir Johan Steyn
Sir Paul Joseph Morrow Kennedy
Sir David Cozens-Hardy Hirst
Sir Simon Denis Brown
Sir Anthony Howell Meurig Evans
Sir Christopher Dudley Roger Rose
Sir Leonard Hubert Hoffmann
Sir John Douglas Waite
(appointed 11 January 1993)
Sir John Ormond Roch
(appointed 11 January 1993)

High Court of Justice

The Lord High Chancellor of Great Britain
The Lord Chief Justice of England
The President of the Family Division
The Vice-Chancellor
The Senior Presiding Judge for England and Wales
The puisne judges of the High Court

Chancery Division

The Lord High Chancellor of Great Britain

The Vice-Chancellor

Sir John Evelyn Vinelott
Sir Jean-Pierre Frank Eugene Warner
Sir Peter Leslie Gibson
Sir David Herbert Mervyn Davies
  (retired 10 January 1993)
Sir Jeremiah LeRoy Harman
Sir John Leonard Knox
Sir Peter Julian Millett

Sir Robert Andrew Morritt
  (Vice-Chancellor of the County Palatine
  of Lancaster)
Sir William Aldous
Sir John Frank Mummery
Sir Francis Mursell Ferris
Sir John Murray Chadwick
Sir Jonathan Frederic Parker
Sir John Edmund Fredric Lindsay

Queen's Bench Division

The Lord Chief Justice of England

Sir Haydn Tudor Evans
Sir Ronald Gough Waterhouse
Sir Frederick Maurice Drake
Sir Barry Cross Sheen
Sir Christopher James Saunders French
Sir Iain Charles Robert McCullough
Sir Hamilton John Leonard
Sir John Stewart Hobhouse
Sir Oliver Bury Popplewell
Sir William Alan Macpherson
Sir Philip Howard Otton
Sir Michael Hutchison
Sir Mark Oliver Saville
Sir Swinton Barclay Thomas
Sir Richard Howard Tucker
Sir Robert Alexander Gatehouse
Sir Patrick Neville Garland
Sir John Ormond Roch
  (appointed Lord Justice of Appeal
  11 January 1993)
Sir Michael John Turner
Sir Harry Henry Ognall
Sir John Downes Alliott
Sir Konrad Hermann Theodor Schiemann
Sir John Arthur Dalziel Owen
Sir Denis Robert Maurice Henry
Sir Francis Humphrey Potts
Sir Richard George Rougier
Sir Ian Alexander Kennedy
Sir Nicholas Addison Phillips
Sir Robin Ernest Auld

Sir Malcolm Thomas Pill
Sir Stuart Neill McKinnon
Sir Mark Howard Potter
Sir Henry Brooke
Sir Thomas Scott Gillespie Baker
  (transferred from Family Division
  1 January 1993)
Sir Igor Judge
Sir Edwin Frank Jowitt
Sir Michael Morland
Sir Mark Waller
Sir Roger John Buckley
Sir Anthony Brian Hidden
Sir John Michael Wright
Sir Charles Barrie Knight Mantell
Sir John Christopher Calthorpe Blofeld
Sir Peter John Cresswell
Sir Anthony Tristram Kenneth May
Sir John Grant McKenzie Laws
Dame Ann Marian Ebsworth
Sir Simon Lane Tuckey
Sir David Nicholas Ramsay Latham
Sir John William Kay
Sir Christopher John Holland
Sir Richard Herbert Curtis
Sir Stephen John Sedley
Dame Janet Hilary Smith
Sir Anthony David Colman
Sir Anthony Peter Clarke
  (appointed 11 January 1993)

Family Division

The President of the Family Division

Sir Alfred Kenneth Hollings
Sir John Kember Wood
Sir Thomas Michael Eastham
  (died 4 March 1993)
Dame Margaret Myfanwy Wood Booth
Sir Anthony Bruce Ewbank
Sir John Douglas Waite
  (appointed Lord Justice of Appeal
  11 January 1993)
Sir Anthony Barnard Hollis
Sir Mathew Alexander Thorpe
Sir Edward Stephen Cazalet

Sir Alan Hylton Ward
Sir Thomas Scott Gillespie Baker
  (transferred to Queen's Bench Division
  1 January 1993)
Sir Robert Lionel Johnson
Sir Douglas Dunlop Brown
Sir Donald Keith Rattee
Dame Joyanne Winifred Bracewell
Sir Michael Bryan Connell
Sir Jan Peter Singer
  (appointed 11 January 1993)

CITATION

These reports are cited thus:

[1993] 1 All ER

REFERENCES

These reports contain references to the following major works of legal reference described in the manner indicated below.

Halsbury's Laws of England

The reference 26 *Halsbury's Laws* (4th edn) para 577 refers to paragraph 577 on page 296 of volume 26 of the fourth edition of *Halsbury's Laws of England*.

The reference 7(1) *Halsbury's Laws* (4th edn reissue) para 267 refers to paragraph 267 on page 177 of reissue volume 7(1) of the fourth edition of *Halsbury's Laws of England*.

Halsbury's Statutes of England and Wales

The reference 40 *Halsbury's Statutes* (4th edn) 734 refers to page 734 of volume 40 of the fourth edition of *Halsbury's Statutes of England and Wales*.

The reference 19 *Halsbury's Statutes* (4th edn) (1990 reissue) 499 refers to page 499 of the 1990 reissue of volume 19 of the fourth edition of *Halsbury's Statutes of England and Wales*.

The Digest

(formerly *The English and Empire Digest*)

The reference 37(2) *Digest* (Reissue) 424, 2594 refers to case number 2594 on page 424 of the reissue of green band volume 37(2) of *The Digest*.

The reference 27(1) *Digest* (2nd reissue) 330, 2849 refers to case number 2849 on page 330 of the second reissue of green band volume 27(1) of *The Digest*.

Halsbury's Statutory Instruments

The reference 17 *Halsbury's Statutory Instruments* 305 refers to page 305 of volume 17 of the grey volumes series of *Halsbury's Statutory Instruments*.

The reference 14 *Halsbury's Statutory Instruments* (1991 reissue) 195 refers to page 195 of the 1991 reissue of volume 14 of the grey volumes series of *Halsbury's Statutory Instruments*.

Cases reported in volume 1

Digest of cases reported in volume 1

House of Lords petitions

This list, which covers the period 16 December 1992 to 18 March 1993, sets out all cases which have formed the subject of a report in the All England Law Reports in which an Appeal Committee of the House of Lords has, subsequent to the publication of that report, refused leave to appeal. Where the result of a petition for leave to appeal was known prior to the publication of the relevant report a note of that result appears at the end of the report.

R v International Stock Exchange of the UK and the Republic of Ireland Ltd, ex p Else (1982) Ltd [1993] 1 All ER 420, CA. Leave to appeal refused 25 February 1993 (Lord Keith, Lord Griffiths and Lord Mustill)

CORRIGENDA

[1993] 1 All ER

p 1. **R v Gomez.** Line *g* 5 should read 'Held (Lord Lowry dissenting)—A person could be . . .'

p 42. **Pepper (Inspector of Taxes) v Hart.** Line *b* 1: for '4 February 1991' read '4 November 1991'.

p 155. **R v Secretary of State for the Home Dept, ex p Doody.** Line *e* 3 should read 'appellant Pierson' and not 'appellants Doody and Pierson'. Page 160: Line *j* 3 should read '17 years *after* the date of his sentence . . .'

p 317. **Dale v British Coal Corp.** Between the title of this case and the catchwords there should appear the words: 'COURT OF APPEAL, CIVIL DIVISION   DILLON, STUART-SMITH AND STEYN, LJJ   17 JUNE 1992'.

R v Gomez

HOUSE OF LORDS

LORD KEITH OF KINKEL, LORD JAUNCEY OF TULLICHETTLE, LORD LOWRY, LORD BROWNE-
WILKINSON AND LORD SLYNN OF HADLEY

20, 21, 22 JULY, 3 DECEMBER 1992

*Criminal law – Theft – Appropriation – Owner consenting to property being taken –
Owner induced by fraud, deception or false representation to consent to or authorise
taking of goods – Payment made for goods by stolen cheque – Owner induced by deception
to accept cheque as good – Cheque dishonoured on presentation – Whether appropriation
of goods if possession obtained with consent of owner – Whether transaction amounting to
theft – Theft Act 1968, ss 1, 15.*

The respondent, who was employed as the assistant manager of an electrical goods
shop, was approached by B, who asked to be supplied with quantities of electrical
goods from the shop in exchange for two stolen building society cheques which
were worthless. The respondent agreed and asked the shop manager to authorise
the supply of the goods against the cheques. The manager told him to find out
from the bank whether the cheques were acceptable and the respondent later
pretended to have done so and told him that the cheques were 'as good as cash'.
The cheques were then used for the purchase of goods to the value of over
£16,000 and were later dishonoured on presentation. The respondent was jointly
charged with B and another with theft. At his trial it was submitted that there
was no case to answer, on the ground that the electrical goods were sold to B
pursuant to a contract of sale between B and the shop (the owners of the goods)
and although it was conceded that the contract had been induced by the fraudulent
misrepresentation of the respondent and that the manager would not have agreed
to the removal of the goods had he known the truth, the manager had expressly
authorised the goods to be removed and therefore there had been no 'appropriation'
within s 1(1)ᵃ of the Theft Act 1968. The judge rejected that submission and the
respondent then pleaded guilty. He appealed on the ground that the judge's
ruling was wrong. The Court of Appeal held that there had been no appropriation
and accordingly it allowed the respondent's appeal and quashed his conviction.
The Crown appealed to the House of Lords.

Held (Lord Lowry dissenting) – A person could be guilty of theft, contrary to s 1(1)
of the 1968 Act, by dishonestly appropriating goods belonging to another if the
owner of the goods was induced by fraud, deception or a false representation to
consent to or authorise the taking of the goods, since it was the actual taking of the
goods, whether with or without the consent of the owner, in circumstances where
it was intended to assume the rights of the owner that amounted to the 'appropriation'
and the fraud, deception or false representation practised on the owner made the
appropriation dishonest. It was irrelevant that the taking of the goods in such
circumstances could also constitute the offence of obtaining property by deception
under s 15(1)ᵇ of the 1968 Act. It followed that the respondent had been properly

---

a   Section 1(1), is set out at p 4 *j*, post
b   Section 15(1) is set out at p 5 *a*, post

convicted. The Crown's appeal would therefore be allowed and the conviction restored (see p 9 *h*, p 12 *j*, p 13 *b g h*, p 39 *c* and p 40 *j*, post).

Lawrence v Comr of Police for the Metropolis [1971] 2 All ER 1253 applied.

Dobson v General Accident Fire and Life Assurance Corp plc [1989] 3 All ER 927 considered.

Dictum of Lord Roskill in *R v Morris* [1983] 3 All ER 288 at 292–293 disapproved.

R v Skipp [1975] Crim LR 114 and *R v Fritschy* [1985] Crim LR 745 overruled.

Decision of the Court of Appeal [1991] 3 All ER 394 reversed.

Notes

For what amounts to theft, see 11(1) *Halsbury's Laws* (4th edn reissue) para 541, for what amounts to appropriation, see ibid para 543, and for cases on the subject, see 15 *Digest* (Reissue) 1262–1264, 1282, 10824–10832, 11029–11030.

For the Theft Act 1968, ss 1, 15, see 12 *Halsbury's Statutes* (4th edn) (1989 reissue) 485, 496.

Cases referred to in opinions

A-G's Reference (No 2 of 1982) [1984] 2 All ER 216, [1984] QB 624, [1984] 2 WLR 447, CA.

Anderton v Wish (1980) 72 Cr App R 23, CA.

Belmont Finance Corp Ltd v Williams Furniture Ltd [1979] 1 All ER 118, [1979] Ch 250, [1978] 3 WLR 712, CA.

Black-Clawson International Ltd v Papierwerke Waldhof-Aschaffenburg AG [1975] 1 All ER 810, [1975] AC 591, [1975] 2 WLR 513, HL.

Dobson v General Accident Fire and Life Assurance Corp plc [1989] 3 All ER 927, [1990] 1 QB 274, [1989] 3 WLR 1066, CA.

Lawrence v Comr of Police for the Metropolis [1971] 2 All ER 1253, [1972] AC 626, [1971] 3 WLR 225, HL; *affg* [1970] 3 All ER 933, [1971] 1 QB 373, [1970] 3 WLR 1103, CA.

Lewis v Averay [1971] 3 All ER 907, [1972] 1 QB 198, [1971] 3 WLR 603, CA.

Phillips v Brooks Ltd [1919] 2 KB 243, [1918–19] All ER Rep 246.

R v Ball [1951] 2 KB 109, CCA.

R v Fisher (1921) 16 Cr App R 53, CCA.

R v Fritschy [1985] Crim LR 745, CA.

R v Gallagher (orse Hemingway) (1929) 21 Cr App R 172, CCA.

R v Kassim [1991] 3 All ER 713, [1992] 1 AC 9, [1991] 3 WLR 254, HL.

R v Kilham (1870) LR 1 CCR 261.

R v Lovell (1881) 8 QBD 185, CCR.

R v McDonnell [1966] 1 All ER 193, [1966] 1 QB 233, [1965] 3 WLR 1138, Assizes.

R v McHugh (1988) 88 Cr App R 385, CA.

R v McPherson [1973] Crim LR 191, CA.

R v Morris, Anderton v Burnside [1983] 3 All ER 288, [1984] AC 320, [1983] 3 WLR 697, HL; *affg* [1983] 2 All ER 448, [1983] QB 587, [1983] 2 WLR 768, CA.

R v Philippou (1989) 89 Cr App R 290, CA.

R v Roffel [1985] VR 511, Vict SC.

R v Shuck [1992] Crim LR 209, CA.

R v Skipp [1975] Crim LR 114, CA.

Salomon v A Salomon & Co Ltd [1897] AC 22, [1895–99] All ER Rep 33, HL.

Smith v Desmond [1965] 1 All ER 976, [1965] AC 960, [1965] 2 WLR 894, HL.

Tesco Supermarkets Ltd v Nattrass [1971] 2 All ER 127, [1972] AC 153, [1971] 2 WLR 1166, HL.

Walters v Lunt [1951] 2 All ER 645, DC.

Whitehorn Bros v Davison [1911] 1 KB 463, [1908–10] All ER Rep 885, CA.
a *Wimpey (George) & Co Ltd v British Overseas Airways Corp* [1954] 3 All ER 661, [1955] AC 169, [1954] 3 WLR 932, HL.

Appeal

The Director of Public Prosecutions appealed with the leave of the Court of Appeal granted on 14 October 1991 against the decision of the Court of Appeal
b (Lord Lane CJ, Hutchison and Mantell JJ) ([1991] 3 All ER 394, [1991] 1 WLR 1334) on 22 April 1991 allowing the appeal of the respondent, Edwin Peter Gomez, and quashing his conviction on two counts of theft, to one of which the respondent had pleaded guilty on 20 April 1990 and on the other of which he was found guilty on 24 April 1990 in the Crown Court at Isleworth before Mr Recorder K Bassingthwaighte and a jury. On 14 October 1991 the Court of Appeal (Lord
c Lane CJ, Roch and Auld JJ) certified under s 33(2) of the Criminal Appeal Act 1968 that a point of law of general public importance (set out at p 4 *g h*, post) was involved in the decision to allow the appeal. The facts are set out in the opinion of Lord Keith.

d Michael Austin-Smith QC and *Philip Shorrock* (instructed by the *Crown Prosecution Service*) for the Crown.
Anthony Hacking QC and *James Pavry* (instructed by *Vassallo & Dillon*) for the respondent.

Their Lordships took time for consideration.

e 3 December 1992. The following opinions were delivered.

LORD KEITH OF KINKEL. My Lords, this appeal raises the question whether two decisions of your Lordships' House upon the proper construction of certain provisions of the Theft Act 1968 are capable of being reconciled with each
f other, and, if so, in what manner. The two decisions are *Lawrence v Comr of Police for the Metropolis* [1971] 2 All ER 1253, [1972] AC 626 and *R v Morris* [1983] 3 All ER 288, [1984] AC 320. The question has given rise to much debate in subsequent cases and in academic writings.

The facts of this case are that the respondent, Edwin Gomez, was employed as assistant manager at a shop trading by retail in electrical goods. In September
g 1987 he was asked by an acquaintance called Jit Ballay to supply goods from the shop and to accept payment by two stolen building society cheques, one for £7,950 and the other for £9,250, which were undated and bore no payee's name. The respondent agreed, and prepared a list of goods to the value of £7,950 which he submitted to the manager, Mr Gilberd, saying that it represented a genuine order by one Johal and asking him to authorise the supply of the goods in return
h for a building society cheque in that sum. Mr Gilberd instructed the respondent to confirm with the bank that the cheque was acceptable, and the respondent later told him that he had done so and that such a cheque was 'as good as cash'. Mr Gilberd agreed to the transaction, the respondent paid the cheque into the bank, and a few days later Ballay took possession of the goods, the respondent helping him to load them into his vehicle. Shortly afterwards a further
j consignment of goods to the value of £9,250 was ordered and supplied in similar fashion (apart from one item valued at £1,002·99 which was not delivered), against the second stolen building society cheque. Mr Gilberd agreed to this transaction without further inquiry. Later the two cheques were returned by the bank marked 'Orders not to pay. Stolen cheque'.

The respondent, Ballay and another employee of the shop, named Rai, were arrested and later tried on an indictment the fourth and fifth counts in which

charged all three with theft contrary to s 1(1) of the Theft Act 1968 in respect of
the two transactions. After evidence had been led for the prosecution, counsel for   *a*
the respondent submitted that there was no case to answer on the theft charges
because the manager of the shop had authorised the transactions, so that there
had been no appropriation within the meaning of s 1(1) of the 1968 Act. The trial
judge rejected this submission, whereupon the respondent pleaded guilty to
count 4, but defended himself on count 5 on the basis that he had acted under
duress. The jury, however, convicted him on this count, and he was sentenced to   *b*
two years' imprisonment on each count to run concurrently. The respondent
appealed to the Court of Appeal, Criminal Division (Lord Lane CJ, Hutchison and
Mantell JJ), which on 22 April 1991 quashed the convictions (see [1991] 3 All ER
394, [1991] 1 WLR 1334). Lord Lane CJ, delivering the judgment of the court,
after considering *Lawrence v Comr of Police for the Metropolis* [1971] 2 All ER 1253,   *c*
[1972] AC 626 and *R v Morris* [1983] 3 All ER 288, [1984] AC 320, said:

> 'What in fact happened was that the owner was induced by deceit to agree
> to the goods being transferred to Ballay. If that is the case, and if in these
> circumstances the [respondent] is guilty of theft, it must follow that anyone
> who obtains goods in return for a cheque which he knows will be dishonoured
> on presentation, or indeed by way of any other similar pretence, would be   *d*
> guilty of theft. That does not seem to be the law. *R v Morris* decides that
> when a person by dishonest deception induces the owner to transfer his entire
> proprietary interests that is not theft. There is no appropriation at the
> moment when he takes possession of the goods because he was entitled to do
> so under the terms of the contract of sale, a contract which is, it is true,   *e*
> voidable, but has not been avoided at the time the goods are handed over ...
> We therefore conclude that there was a de facto, albeit voidable, contract
> between the owners and Ballay, that it was by virtue of that contract that
> Ballay took possession of the goods, that accordingly the transfer of the goods
> to him was with the consent and express authority of the owner and that
> accordingly there was no lack of authorisation and no appropriation.' (See   *f*
> [1991] 3 All ER 394 at 398, 400, [1991] 1 WLR 1334 at 1338–1340.)

The court later granted a certificate under s 33(2) of the Criminal Appeal Act 1968
that a point of law of general public importance was involved in the decision,
namely:

> 'When theft is alleged and that which is alleged to be stolen passes to the   *g*
> defendant with the consent of the owner, but that consent has been obtained
> by a false representation, has, a) an appropriation within the meaning of
> s. 1(i) of the Theft Act 1968 taken place, or, b) must such a passing of property
> necessarily involve an element of adverse [interference] with or usurpation
> of some right of the owner?'   *h*

The Crown now appeals, with leave granted here, to your Lordships' House.
  The provisions of the 1968 Act principally relevant are these:

> '**1.**—(1) A person is guilty of theft if he dishonestly appropriates property
> belonging to another with the intention of permanently depriving the other
> of it; and "thief" and "steal" shall be construed accordingly ...   *j*
> **3.**—(1) Any assumption by a person of the rights of an owner amounts to
> an appropriation, and this includes, where he has come by the property
> (innocently or not) without stealing it, any later assumption of a right to it
> by keeping or dealing with it as owner ...
> **4.**—(1) "Property" includes money and all other property, real or personal,
> including things in action and other intangible property ...

a
7. A person guilty of theft shall on conviction on indictment be liable to imprisonment for a term not exceeding ten years . . .

15.—(1) A person who by any deception dishonestly obtains property belonging to another, with the intention of permanently depriving the other of it, shall on conviction on indictment be liable to imprisonment for a term not exceeding ten years . . .'

b It is to be observed that by s 26 of the Criminal Justice Act 1991 the maximum sentence for theft was reduced from ten to seven years. The s 15(1) penalty was left unchanged.

The facts in *Lawrence v Comr of Police for the Metropolis* [1971] 2 All ER 1253 at 1254, as set out in the speech of Viscount Dilhorne, were these:

c
'. . . the appellant was convicted on 2nd December 1969 of theft contrary to s 1(1) of the Theft Act 1968. On 1st September 1969 a Mr Occhi, an Italian who spoke little English, arrived at Victoria Station on his first visit to this country. He went up to a taxi driver, the appellant, and showed him a piece of paper on which an address in Ladbroke Grove was written. The appellant said that it was very far and very expensive. Mr Occhi got into the taxi, took
d £1 out of his wallet and gave it to the appellant who then, the wallet being still open, took a further £6 out of it. He then drove Mr Occhi to Ladbroke Grove. The correct lawful fare for the journey was in the region of 10s. 6d. The appellant was charged with and convicted of the theft of the £6.'

The conviction was upheld by the Court of Appeal, Criminal Division, which in
e granting leave to appeal to your Lordships' House certified the following questions as involving a point of law of general public importance:

'(1) Whether Section 1(1) of the Theft Act, 1968, is to be construed as though it contained the words "without the consent of the owner" or words to that effect.

f (2) Whether the provisions of Section 15(1) and of Section 1(1) of the Theft Act, 1968, are mutually exclusive in the sense that if the facts proved would justify a conviction under Section 15(1) there cannot lawfully be a conviction under Section 1(1) on those facts.'

Viscount Dilhorne, whose speech was concurred in by Lord Donovan, Lord Pearson, Lord Diplock and Lord Cross of Chelsea, after stating the facts, and
g expressing some doubts as to what Mr Occhi had meant when he said that he 'permitted' the taxi driver to take the £6, continued ([1971] 2 All ER 1253 at 1254–1255, [1972] AC 626 at 631–633):

'The main contention of the appellant in this House and in the Court of Appeal ([1970] 3 All ER 933, [1971] 1 QB 373) was that Mr Occhi had
h consented to the taking of the £6 and that, consequently, his conviction could not stand. In my opinion, the facts of this case to which I have referred fall far short of establishing that Mr Occhi had so consented. Prior to the passage of the Theft Act 1968, which made radical changes in and greatly simplified the law relating to theft and some other offences, it was necessary to prove that the property alleged to have been stolen was taken "without the
j consent of the owner" (Larceny Act 1916, s 1(1)). These words are not included in s 1(1) of the Theft Act 1968, but the appellant contended that the subsection should be construed as if they were, as if they appeared after the word "appropriates." Section 1(1) provides: "A person is guilty of theft if he dishonestly appropriates property belonging to another with the intention of permanently depriving the other of it; and 'thief' and 'steal' shall be construed accordingly." I see no ground for concluding that the omission of the words

'without the consent of the owner" was inadvertent and not deliberate, and
to read the subsection as if they were included is, in my opinion, wholly   a
unwarranted. Parliament by the omission of these words has relieved the
prosecution of the burden of establishing that the taking was without the
owner's consent. That is no longer an ingredient of the offence. Megaw LJ,
delivering the judgment of the Court of Appeal ([1970] 3 All ER 933 at 935,
[1971] 1 QB 373 at 376), said that the offence created by s 1(1) involved four
elements: "(i) a dishonest (ii) appropriation (iii) of property belonging to   b
another (iv) with the intention of permanently depriving the owner of it." I
agree. That there was appropriation in this case is clear. Section 3(1) states
that any assumption by a person of the rights of an owner amounts to an
appropriation. Here there was clearly such an assumption. That an
appropriation was dishonest may be proved in a number of ways. In this case   c
it was not contended that the appellant had not acted dishonestly. Section
2(1) provides, inter alia, that a person's appropriation of property belonging
to another is not to be regarded as dishonest if he appropriates the property
in the belief that he would have the other's consent if the other knew of the
appropriation and the circumstances of it. A fortiori, a person is not to be
regarded as acting dishonestly if he appropriates another's property believing   d
that with full knowledge of the circumstances that other person has in fact
agreed to the appropriation. The appellant, if he believed that Mr Occhi,
knowing that £7 was far in excess of the legal fare, had nevertheless agreed
to pay him that sum, could not be said to have acted dishonestly in taking it.
When Megaw LJ said that if there was true consent, the essential element of
dishonesty was not established, I understand him to have meant this. Belief   e
or the absence of belief that the owner had with such knowledge consented
to the appropriation is relevant to the issue of dishonesty, not to the question
whether or not there has been an appropriation. That may occur even though
the owner has permitted or consented to the property being taken. So proof
that Mr Occhi had consented to the appropriation of £6 from his wallet   f
without agreeing to paying a sum in excess of the legal fare does not suffice
to show that there was not dishonesty in this case. There was ample evidence
that there was. I now turn to the third element "property belonging to
another". Counsel for the appellant contended that if Mr Occhi consented to
the appellant taking the £6, he consented to the property in the money
passing from him to the appellant and that the appellant had not, therefore,   g
appropriated property belonging to another. He argued that the old
distinction between the offence of false pretences and larceny had been
preserved. I am unable to agree with this. The new offence of obtaining
property by deception created by s 15(1) of the Theft Act 1968 also contains
the words "belonging to another". "A person who by any deception
dishonestly obtains property belonging to another with the intention of   h
permanently depriving the other of it . . ." commits that offence. "Belonging
to another" in s 1(1) and in s 15(1) in my view signifies no more than that, at
the time of the appropriation or the obtaining, the property belonged to
another with the words "belonging to another" having the extended meaning
given by s 5. The short answer to this contention on behalf of the appellant
is that the money in the wallet which he appropriated belonged to another,   j
to Mr Occhi. There was no dispute about the appellant's intention being
permanently to deprive Mr Occhi of the money. The four elements of the
offence of theft as defined in the Theft Act 1968 were thus clearly established
and, in my view, the Court of Appeal was right to dismiss the appeal.'

In the result, each of the certified questions was answered in the negative.

It will be seen that Viscount Dilhorne's speech contains two clear pronounce-
a ments, first that it is no longer an ingredient of the offence of theft that the taking
should be without the owner's consent and, second, that an appropriation may
occur even though the owner has permitted or consented to the property being
taken. The answer given to the first certified question was in line with those
pronouncements, so even though Viscount Dilhorne was of opinion that the
evidence fell short of establishing that Mr Occhi had consented to the taking of
b the £6 it was a matter of decision that it made no difference whether or not he
had so consented.

R v Morris [1983] 3 All ER 288, [1984] AC 320 involved two cases of price label
switching in a supermarket. In the first case the defendant had removed the price
label from a joint of meat and replaced it with a label showing a lesser price which
c he had removed from another joint. He was detected at the checkout point before
he had paid for the joint and later convicted of theft contrary to s 1(1) of the 1968
Act. In the second case the defendant had in similar manner switched price labels
on goods in a supermarket but was not arrested until after he had passed the
checkout point and paid the lesser prices for the goods. He was charged with two
counts of theft contrary to s 1(1) and one count of obtaining property by deception
d contrary to s 15(1). The jury convicted him on the counts of theft, but by direction
of the recorder returned no verdict on the s 15(1) count. Appeals against
conviction by both defendants were dismissed by the Court of Appeal, Criminal
Division and by this House. Lord Roskill, in the course of a speech concurred in
by Lord Fraser of Tullybelton, Lord Edmund-Davies, Lord Brandon of Oakbrook
and Lord Brightman, referred to *Lawrence*'s case with apparent approval as having
e set out the four elements involved in the offence of theft and as having rejected
the argument that there could not be theft within s 1(1) if the owner of the
property had consented to the defendant's acts (see [1983] 3 All ER 288 at 292,
[1984] AC 320 at 331). He observed that in *Lawrence*'s case the House did not
have to consider the precise meaning of 'appropriation' in s 3(1) and continued
f ([1983] 3 All ER 288 at 292–293, [1984] AC 320 at 331–333):

> 'Counsel for the appellants submitted that the phrase in s 3(1) "any
> assumption by a person of *the rights* of an owner amounts to an appropriation"
> must mean any assumption of "*all* the rights of an owner". Since neither
> appellant had at the time of the removal of the goods from the shelves and of
> the label switching assumed *all* the rights of the owner, there was no
g > appropriation and therefore no theft. Counsel for the prosecution, on the
> other hand, contended that *the* rights in this context only meant *any* of the
> rights. An owner of goods has many rights: they have been described as "a
> bundle or package of rights". Counsel for the prosecution contended that on
> a fair reading of the subsection it cannot have been the intention that every
> one of an owner's rights had to be assumed by the alleged thief before an
h > appropriation was proved and that essential ingredient of the offence of theft
> established. My Lords, if one reads the words "the rights" at the opening of
> s 3(1) literally and in isolation from the rest of the section, the submission of
> counsel for the appellants undoubtedly has force. But the later words "any
> later assumption of a right" . . . seem to me to militate strongly against the
j > correctness of the submission. Moreover the provisions of s 2(1)(*a*) also seem
> to point in the same direction. It follows therefore that it is enough for the
> prosecution if they have proved in these cases the assumption by the
> defendants of *any* of the rights of the owner of the goods in question, that is
> to say, the supermarket concerned, it being common ground in these cases
> that the other three of the four elements mentioned in Viscount Dilhorne's
> speech in *Lawrence*'s case had been fully established. My Lords, counsel for

the prosecution sought to argue that any removal from the shelves of the
supermarket, even if unaccompanied by label-switching, was without more   *a*
an appropriation. In one passage in his judgment in *Morris's* case [1983] 2 All
ER 448 at 454, [1983] QB 587 at 596 Lord Lane CJ appears to have accepted
the submission, for he said: ". . . It seems to us that in taking the article from
the shelf the customer is indeed assuming one of the rights of the owner, the
right to move the article from its position on the shelf to carry it to the checkout . . ." With the utmost respect, I cannot accept this statement as correct. If   *b*
one postulates an honest customer taking goods from a shelf to put in his or
her trolley to take to the check-point there to pay the proper price, I am
unable to see that any of these actions involves any assumption by the shopper
of the rights of the supermarket. In the context of s 3(1), the concept of
appropriation in my view involves not an act expressly or impliedly
authorised by the owner but an act by way of adverse interference with or   *c*
usurpation of those rights. When the honest shopper acts as I have just
described, he or she is acting with the implied authority of the owner of the
supermarket to take the goods from the shelf, put them in the trolley, take
them to the check-point and there pay the correct price, at which moment
the property in the goods will pass to the shopper for the first time. It is with   *d*
the consent of the owners of the supermarket, be that consent express or
implied, that the shopper does these acts and thus obtains at least control if
not actual possession of the goods preparatory, at a later stage, to obtaining
the property in them on payment of the proper amount at the check-point.
I do not think that s 3(1) envisages any such act as an "appropriation",
whatever may be the meaning of that word in other fields such as contract or   *e*
sale of goods law. If, as I understand all your Lordships to agree, the concept
of appropriation in s 3(1) involves an element of adverse interference with or
usurpation of some right of the owner, it is necessary next to consider
whether that requirement is satisfied in either of these cases. As I have already
said, in my view mere removal from the shelves without more is not an
appropriation. Further, if a shopper with some perverted sense of humour,   *f*
intending only to create confusion and nothing more, both for the
supermarket and for other shoppers, switches labels, I do not think that that
act of label-switching alone is without more an appropriation, though it is
not difficult to envisage some cases of dishonest label-switching which could
be. In cases such as the present, it is in truth a combination of these actions,
the removal from the shelf and the switching of the labels which evidences   *g*
adverse interference with or usurpation of the right of the owner. Those acts,
therefore, amount to an appropriation and if they are accompanied by proof
of the other three elements to which I have referred, the offence of theft is
established. Further, if they are accompanied by other acts such as putting
the goods so removed and relabelled into a receptacle, whether a trolley or   *h*
the shopper's own bag or basket, proof of appropriation within s 3(1) becomes
overwhelming. It is the doing of one or more acts which individually or
collectively amount to such adverse interference with or usurpation of the
owner's rights which constitute appropriation under s 3(1) and I do not think
it matters [whether] there is more than one such act in which order the
successive acts take place, or whether there is any interval of time between   *j*
them. To suggest that it matters whether the mislabelling precedes or
succeeds removal from the shelves is to reduce this branch of the law to an
absurdity.' (Lord Roskill's emphasis.)

The answer given to the question certified by the Court of Appeal was ([1983] 3
All ER 288 at 295, [1984] AC 320 at 335):

a
'. . . there is a dishonest appropriation for the purposes of the Theft Act 1968 where by the substitution of a price label showing a lesser price on goods for one showing a greater price, a defendant either by that act alone or by that act in conjunction with another act or other acts (whether done before or after the substitution of the labels) adversely interferes with or usurps the right of the owner to ensure that the goods concerned are sold and paid for at that greater price.'

b
In my opinion Lord Roskill was undoubtedly right when he said in the course of the passage quoted that the assumption by the defendant of any of the rights of an owner could amount to an appropriation within the meaning of s 3(1), and that the removal of an article from the shelf and the changing of the price label on it constituted the assumption of one of the rights of the owner and hence an c appropriation within the meaning of the subsection. But there are observations in the passage which, with the greatest possible respect to Lord Roskill, I must regard as unnecessary for the decision of the case and as being incorrect. In the first place, it seems to me that the switching of price labels on the article is in itself an assumption of one of the rights of the owner, whether or not it is accompanied by some other act such as removing the article from the shelf and placing it in a d basket or trolley. No one but the owner has the right to remove a price label from an article or to place a price label upon it. If anyone else does so, he does an act, as Lord Roskill puts it, by way of adverse interference with or usurpation of that right. This is no less so in the case of the practical joker figured by Lord Roskill than in the case of one who makes the switch with dishonest intent. The practical e joker, of course, is not guilty of theft because he has not acted dishonestly and does not intend to deprive the owner permanently of the article. So the label switching in itself constitutes an appropriation and so to have held would have been sufficient for the dismissal of both appeals. On the facts of the two cases it was unnecessary to decide whether, as argued by counsel for the prosecution, the mere taking of the article from the shelf and putting it in a trolley or other f receptacle amounted to the assumption of one of the rights of the owner, and hence an appropriation. There was much to be said in favour of the view that it did, in respect that doing so gave the shopper control of the article and the capacity to exclude any other shopper from taking it. However, Lord Roskill expressed the opinion that it did not, on the ground that the concept of appropriation in the context of s 3(1) 'involves not an act expressly or impliedly g authorised by the owner but an act by way of adverse interference with or usurpation of those rights'. While it is correct to say that appropriation for purposes of s 3(1) includes the latter sort of act, it does not necessarily follow that no other act can amount to an appropriation and in particular that no act expressly or impliedly authorised by the owner can in any circumstances do so. Indeed, Lawrence's case is a clear decision to the contrary since it laid down unequivocally h that an act may be an appropriation notwithstanding that it is done with the consent of the owner. It does not appear to me that any sensible distinction can be made in this context between consent and authorisation.

In the civil case of Dobson v General Accident Fire and Life Assurance Corp plc [1989] 3 All ER 927, [1990] 1 QB 274 a Court of Appeal consisting of Parker and j Bingham LJJ considered the apparent conflict between Lawrence's case and R v Morris and applied the former decision. The facts were that the plaintiff had insured property with the defendant company against, inter alia, 'loss or damage caused by theft'. He advertised for sale a watch and ring at the total price of £5,950. A rogue telephoned expressing an interest in buying the articles and the plaintiff provisionally agreed with him that the payment would be by a building society cheque in the plaintiff's favour. The rogue called on the plaintiff the next

day and the watch and the ring were handed over to him in exchange for a
building society cheque for the agreed amount. The plaintiff paid the cheque into   *a*
his bank, which informed him that it was stolen and worthless. The defendant
company denied liability under its policy of insurance on the ground that the loss
of the watch and ring was not caused by theft within the meaning of the 1968
Act. The plaintiff succeeded in the county court in an action to recover the
amount of his loss, and the decision was affirmed by the Court of Appeal. One of
the arguments for the defendants was that there had been no theft because the   *b*
plaintiff had agreed to the transaction with the rogue and reliance was placed on
Lord Roskill's statement in *R v Morris* [1983] 3 All ER 288 at 293, [1984] AC 320
at 332 that appropriation 'involves not an act expressly or impliedly authorised
by the owner but an act by way of adverse interference with or usurpation of
those rights'.   *c*
    In dealing with this argument Parker LJ said ([1989] 3 All ER 927 at 931,
[1990] 1 QB 274 at 281):

> 'The difficulties caused by the apparent conflict between the decision in
> *Lawrence's* case and *R v Morris* have provided, not surprisingly, a basis for
> much discussion by textbook writers and contributors of articles to law   *d*
> journals. It is, however, clear that their Lordships in *R v Morris* did not
> regard anything said in that case as conflicting with *Lawrence's* case for it was
> specifically referred to in Lord Roskill's speech, with which the other
> members of the Appellate Committee all agreed, without disapproval or
> qualification. The only comment made was that, in *Lawrence's* case, the
> House did not have to consider the precise meaning of "appropriation" in   *e*
> s 3(1) (see [1983] 3 All ER 288 at 292, [1984] AC 320 at 331). With respect, I
> find this comment hard to follow in the light of the first of the questions
> asked in *Lawrence's* case and the answer to it, the passages from Viscount
> Dilhorne's speech already cited, the fact that it was specifically argued that
> "'appropriates' is meant in a pejorative, rather than a neutral, sense in that   *f*
> the appropriation is against the will of the owner" (see [1972] AC 626 at 631
> arg), and finally that dishonesty was common ground. I would have supposed
> that *the* question in *Lawrence's* case was whether appropriation necessarily
> involved an absence of consent.' (Parker LJ's emphasis.)

Parker LJ then said that he found other difficulties in Lord Roskill's speech in *R v*   *g*
Morris, and after setting out the facts of the case and quoting a long passage from
that speech (see [1983] 3 All ER 288 at 293, [1984] AC 320 at 332) and also the
answer to the certified question he continued ([1989] 3 All ER 927 at 932–933,
[1990] 1 QB 274 at 283–284):

>   *h*
> 'In the first passage Lord Roskill, as it seems to me, impliedly envisages
> that mere label-switching could be an appropriation and that this is so is
> confirmed by the answer to the certified question which specifically uses the
> words "either by that act alone". What then is it which would make label-
> switching alone something which adversely affects or usurps the right of the
> owner? In that passage it appears to be envisaged that it will depend on the   *j*
> question whether the label-switching was dishonest and coupled with the
> other elements of the offence of theft or was due to a perverted sense of
> humour. This, however, appears to run together the elements of dishonesty
> and appropriation when it is clear from *Lawrence's* case that they are separate.
> That the two elements were indeed, at any rate to some extent, run together

a
is plain from the fact that the answer to the certified question begins with the words "there is a dishonest appropriation". Moreover, on general principles, it would in my judgment be a plain interference with or usurpation of an owner's rights by the customer if he were to remove a label which the owner had placed on goods or put another label on. It would be a trespass to goods and it would be usurping the owner's rights, for only he would have any right to do such an act and no one could contend that there was any implied consent or authority to a customer to do any such thing.

b
There would thus be an appropriation. In the case of the customer with a perverted sense of humour there would however be no theft for there would probably be no dishonesty and certainly no intent permanently to deprive the owner of the goods themselves. The case of the customer who simply removes goods from the shelves is of course different because the basis on which a supermarket is run is that customers certainly have the consent of the owner to take goods from the shelves and take them to the checkout point, there to pay the proper price for them. Suppose, however, that there were no such consent, in, for example, a shop where goods on display were to be taken from the shelves only by the attendant. In such a case a customer who took from the shelves would clearly be usurping the right of the owner.

c

d
Indeed he would be doing so if he did no more than move an item from one place on a shelf to another. The only difference appears to be that in the one case there is consent and in the other there is not. Since, however, it was held in *Lawrence's* case that consent is not relevant to appropriation there must, one would have supposed, be no difference between the two cases on that aspect of the offence. There are further matters in *R v Morris* [1983] 3 All ER 288, [1984] AC 320 in which I find difficulty. I mention only two. The first is the observation made on *R v McPherson* [1973] Crim LR 191. That was a case in which the defendant took two bottles of whisky from the shelves and put them in her shopping bag. The sole question in issue was whether there had been an appropriation. It was held in the Court of Appeal that there had been. As to this Lord Roskill said ([1983] 3 All ER 288 at 294, [1984] AC 320 at 333): "That was not, of course, a label-switching case, but it is a plain case of appropriation effected by the combination of the acts of removing the goods from the shelf and of concealing them in the shopping bag. *R v McPherson* is to my mind clearly correctly decided as are all the cases which have followed it. It is wholly consistent with the principles which I have endeavoured to state in this speech." Reference to the transcript of the judgment in that case however reveals that the decision did not turn on concealment in the shopping bag but was expressly on the ground that the goods were appropriated when they were taken from the shelves. This indeed was recognised in *Anderton v Wish* (1980) 72 Cr App R 23 at 25, where Roskill LJ said: "The Court of Appeal . . . held . . . they were guilty of theft because when the bottles were taken there was a dishonest appropriation. If that decision is right and, with respect, it seems to me plainly right . . ." Furthermore in *R v Morris* [1983] 3 All ER 288 at 294, [1984] AC 320 at 334 Lord Roskill said: ". . . I understand all your Lordships to agree that *Anderton v Wish* was rightly decided for the reasons given."'

e

f

g

h

j
Later Parker LJ quoted this passage from the speech of Lord Roskill in *R v Morris* [1983] 3 All ER 288 at 294, [1984] AC 320 at 334:

"'. . . without going into further detail I respectfully suggest that it is on any view wrong to introduce into this branch of the criminal law questions whether particular contracts are void or voidable on the ground of mistake

or fraud or whether any mistake is sufficiently fundamental to vitiate a
contract. These difficult questions should so far as possible be confined to *a*
those fields of law to which they are immediately relevant and I do not regard
them as relevant questions under the 1968 Act." After anxious consideration
I have reached the conclusion that whatever *R v Morris* did decide it cannot
be regarded as having overruled the very plain decision in *Lawrence's* case
that appropriation can occur even if the owner consents and that *R v Morris*
itself makes it plain that it is no defence to say that the property passed under *b*
a voidable contract.' (See [1989] 3 All ER 927 at 934, [1990] 1 QB 274 at 285.)

On this ground Parker LJ dismissed the appeal.

Bingham LJ plainly took the view that a customer in a supermarket assumes
some of the rights of an owner when he takes goods into his possession and
exercises control over them by putting them in a basket or trolley, and thus *c*
appropriates them (see [1989] 3 All ER 927 at 936, [1990] 1 QB 274 at 287). Later
he mentioned that in Lord Roskill's speech in *R v Morris* no reference was made
to Viscount Dilhorne's ruling in *Lawrence's* case that appropriation might occur
even though the owner has permitted or consented to the property being taken,
and continued ([1989] 3 All ER 927 at 937, [1990] 1 QB 274 at 289): *d*

> 'I do not find it easy to reconcile this ruling of Viscount Dilhorne, which
> was as I understand central to the answer which the House of Lords gave to
> the certified question, with the reasoning of the House in *R v Morris*. Since,
> however, the House in *R v Morris* considered that there had plainly been an
> appropriation in *Lawrence's* case, this must (I think) have been because the *e*
> Italian student, although he had permitted or allowed his money to be taken,
> had not in truth consented to the taxi driver taking anything in excess of the
> correct fare. This is not a wholly satisfactory reconciliation, since it might be
> said that a supermarket consents to customers taking goods from its shelves
> only when they honestly intend to pay and not otherwise. On the facts of the
> present case, however, it can be said, by analogy with *Lawrence's* case, that *f*
> although the plaintiff permitted and allowed his property to be taken by the
> rogue, he had not in truth consented to the rogue becoming owner without
> giving a valid draft drawn by the building society for the price. On this basis
> I conclude that the plaintiff is able to show an appropriation sufficient to
> satisfy s 1(1) of the 1968 Act when the rogue accepted delivery of the articles.'

g

It was argued for the respondent in the present appeal that *Dobson's* case was
wrongly decided. I disagree, and on the contrary find myself in full agreement
with those parts of the judgment of Parker LJ to which I have referred. As regards
the attempted reconciliation by Bingham LJ of the reasoning in *R v Morris* with
the ruling in *Lawrence's* case it appears to me that the suggested basis of *h*
reconciliation, which is essentially speculative, is unsound. The actual decision in
R v Morris was correct, but it was erroneous, in addition to being unnecessary for
the decision, to indicate that an act expressly or impliedly authorised by the
owner could never amount to an appropriation. There is no material distinction
between the facts in *Dobson's* case and those in the present case. In each case the
owner of the goods was induced by fraud to part with them to the rogue. *j*
Lawrence's case makes it clear that consent to or authorisation by the owner of the
taking by the rogue is irrelevant. The taking amounted to an appropriation
within the meaning of s 1(1) of the 1968 Act. *Lawrence's* case also makes it clear
that it is no less irrelevant that what happened may also have constituted the
offence of obtaining property by deception under s 15(1) of the 1968 Act.

a In my opinion it serves no useful purpose at the present time to seek to construe the relevant provisions of the Theft Act by reference to the report which preceded it, namely the eighth report of the Criminal Law Revision Committee, *Theft and Related Offences* (Cmnd 2977 (1966)). The decision in *Lawrence's* case was a clear decision of this House upon the construction of the word 'appropriates' in s 1(1) of the 1968 Act, which had stood for 12 years when doubt was thrown upon it by obiter dicta in *R v Morris*. *Lawrence's* case must be regarded as authoritative and
b correct, and there is no question of it now being right to depart from it.

It is desirable to say a few words about *R v Skipp* [1975] Crim LR 114 and *R v Fritschy* [1985] Crim LR 745. In the first case the defendant, posing as a haulage contractor, was instructed to collect consignments of goods from three different places and deliver them to a certain destination. He collected the goods and made
c off with them. The Court of Appeal, on his appeal against his conviction for theft upon one count covering all three consignments, on the ground that the count was bad for duplicity in that there were three separate appropriations, held that there had been no appropriation until the last of the goods were loaded, or probably until the defendant deviated from the route to the proper destination. In the second case the defendant was instructed by the owner to collect a quantity
d of krugerrands in London and deliver them to a safe deposit in Switzerland. Although the short report is not very clear on the matter, it seems that the defendant, having collected the coins, took them to Switzerland and there made away with them. The trial judge directed the jury that if at the time he collected the coins the defendant had formed the dishonest intention of keeping them for himself he was guilty of theft. The Court of Appeal overturned the resultant
e conviction for theft on the ground, following *R v Morris*, that there had been no appropriation in England because the defendant had there taken possession of the krugerrands with the owner's authority. In my opinion both these cases were inconsistent with *Lawrence's* case and were wrongly decided.

There were cited to your Lordships a number of cases involving the abstraction
f of moneys from a limited company by a person who was in a position to give the consent of the company to the abstraction. It is sufficient to say that I agree with what my noble and learned friend Lord Browne-Wilkinson has to say about these cases in the speech to be delivered by him, and that in my opinion a person who thus procures the company's consent dishonestly and with the intention of permanently depriving the company of the money is guilty of theft contrary to
g s 1(1) of the 1968 Act.

My Lords, for the reasons which I have given I would answer branch (a) of the certified question in the affirmative and branch (b) in the negative, and allow the appeal.

LORD JAUNCEY OF TULLICHETTLE. My Lords, I have had the
h advantage of reading in draft the speeches of my noble and learned friends Lord Keith of Kinkel and Lord Browne-Wilkinson and for the reasons which they give I agree that the appeal should be allowed and the questions answered in the way in which my noble and learned friend Lord Keith of Kinkel proposes.

LORD LOWRY. My Lords, this is an appeal brought by the Director of Public
j Prosecutions with the leave of the Court of Appeal, Criminal Division from a decision of that court on 22 April 1991 allowing the appeal of the present respondent, Edwin Gomez, against his convictions on 20 and 24 April 1990 in the Crown Court at Isleworth on two counts of theft, for which he received concurrent sentences of two years' imprisonment, and quashing those convictions.

The facts are as follows. Gomez was the assistant manager of the Ealing branch (the shop) of a chain of retail electrical goods shops trading as 'Bennetts Retail'. On 14 September 1989 an acquaintance, Jit Ballay, asked Gomez, and Gomez *a* agreed, to supply goods from the shop in exchange for two undated building society cheques for £7,950 and £9,250, which both Ballay and Gomez knew to be stolen and worthless cheques. Gomez then prepared and submitted to the manager of the shop, Mr Gilberd, a list of goods to the value of £ 7,950, telling him that the list represented a bona fide order placed by one Johal and asking him to authorise the supply of the goods against a building society cheque for that *b* amount. On being told by the manager to check with the bank, he pretended to have done so and assured the manager that the cheque was 'as good as cash', whereupon the manager authorised the transaction. On 20 September Gomez paid the cheque into his employers' bank and on 28 September Ballay took possession of the listed goods. Gomez helped to load the goods into Ballay's van. *c* A further consignment of goods was ordered and supplied against the second stolen cheque, Mr Gilberd having agreed to the transaction without further inquiry.

The judge's note of Mr Gilberd's evidence when he was cross-examined at the trial included the following:

'I was involved in both transactions. Exceptionally high orders. I would *d* expect to be consulted as I was. I authorised discount. I authorised release. I expressly authorised this.'

The manager at all times believed that the stolen cheques were genuine. On 5 October 1989, however, both cheques were returned by the bank marked 'Orders not to pay. Stolen cheque.' *e*

Gomez, Ballay and Jatinder Rai, another employee of Bennetts Retail, were arrested and jointly tried on an indictment alleging two counts of handling the stolen cheques against Ballay (counts 1 and 2), one count of conspiracy (count 3, which was not proceeded with) and two counts of theft of the electrical goods against all the defendants (counts 4 and 5). All three were found guilty as charged, *f* save that Gomez had pleaded guilty to count 4 after a ruling against him on a legal submission. He had continued to plead not guilty in respect of count 5, but the only defence made after the legal ruling was the defence of duress, which was rejected by the jury and with which the Court of Appeal was not concerned.

Under the law before 1968 the facts of this case would have led to charges, to which there would have been no defence, of obtaining goods by false pretences. *g* Since the passing of the Theft Act 1968 the accused could equally well have been prosecuted successfully for obtaining property by deception contrary to s 15 of that Act. Under the old law they could not have been found guilty of larceny, because the seller agreed to transfer the property in the goods to Ballay, and the fact that the seller's agreement was obtained by a fraud does not affect that conclusion. Indeed, if the seller's consent could have been vitiated in that way, *h* Parliament would never have needed to create the statutory offence of obtaining by false pretences. The accused in this case, however, were prosecuted for theft under s 1(1) of the 1968 Act and were convicted notwithstanding the submission of counsel for the defence to the effect that the crime for which the accused were indicted did not amount to theft because the seller had consented to sell the property, albeit consent had been obtained by fraud, as alleged. When Gomez *j* appealed, the Court of Appeal upheld that submission and quashed his convictions. In order to restore those convictions, the Crown must say that the Theft Act 1968 has altered the law in such a way (among others) that anyone who, by a false representation such as a worthless cheque, induces an owner to sell property is thereby guilty of stealing.

Section 1(1) of the 1968 Act provides:

a

'A person is guilty of theft if he dishonestly appropriates property belonging to another with the intention of permanently depriving the other of it; and "thief" and "steal" shall be construed accordingly.'

This appeal turns on the meaning in that subsection of the word 'appropriates' and will involve the consideration, among other things, of conflicting statements

b in this House, which I shall come back to at a later stage. One was by Viscount Dilhorne in *Lawrence v Comr of Police for the Metropolis* [1971] 2 All ER 1253 at 1255, [1972] AC 626 at 632, where, having noted the absence from the subsection of the words 'without the consent of the owner', he said:

'Parliament by the omission of these words has relieved the prosecution of

c the burden of establishing that the taking was without the owner's consent. That is no longer an ingredient of the offence.'

Lord Roskill, on the other hand, in *R v Morris* [1983] 3 All ER 288 at 293, [1984] AC 320 at 332 said:

'In the context of s 3(1), the concept of appropriation in my view involves

d not an act expressly or impliedly authorised by the owner but an act by way of adverse interference with or usurpation of those rights.'

The certified question in this appeal is:

'When theft is alleged and that which is alleged to be stolen passes to the

e defendant with the consent of the owner, but that consent has been obtained by a false representation, has, a) an appropriation within the meaning of s. 1(i) of the Theft Act 1968 taken place, or, b) must such a passing of property necessarily involve an element of adverse [interference] with or usurpation of some right of the owner?'

f I can say now that I would answer (a) No and (b) No, because such a passing of property does not involve an appropriation.

Since the question turns on the meaning of the word 'appropriates' in s 1(1) of the 1968 Act, the problem is therefore one of statutory interpretation and it will be helpful to start by setting out the immediately relevant provisions of that Act:

Definition of "Theft"

g **1.**—(1) A person is guilty of theft if he dishonestly appropriates property belonging to another with the intention of permanently depriving the other of it; and "thief" and "steal" shall be construed accordingly.

(2) It is immaterial whether the appropriation is made with a view to gain, or is made for the thief's own benefit.

h (3) The five following sections of this Act shall have effect as regards the interpretation and operation of this section (and, except as otherwise provided by this Act, shall apply only for purposes of this section).

2.—(1) A person's appropriation of property belonging to another is not to be regarded as dishonest—(*a*) if he appropriates the property in the belief that he has in law the right to deprive the other of it, on behalf of himself or

j of a third person; or (*b*) if he appropriates the property in the belief that he would have the other's consent if the other knew of the appropriation and the circumstances of it; or (*c*) (except where the property came to him as trustee or personal representative) if he appropriates the property in the belief that the person to whom the property belongs cannot be discovered by taking reasonable steps.

(2) A person's appropriation of property belonging to another may be dishonest notwithstanding that he is willing to pay for the property.   *a*

3.—(1) Any assumption by a person of the rights of an owner amounts to an appropriation, and this includes, where he has come by the property (innocently or not) without stealing it, any later assumption of a right to it by keeping or dealing with it as owner.

(2) Where property or a right or interest in property is or purports to be transferred for value to a person acting in good faith, no later assumption by   *b* him of rights which he believed himself to be acquiring shall, by reason of any defect in the transferor's title, amount to theft of the property.

4.—(1) "Property" includes money and all other property, real or personal, including things in action and other intangible property.

(2) A person cannot steal land, or things forming part of land and severed   *c* from it by him or by his directions, except in the following cases, that is to say—(*a*) when he is a trustee or personal representative, or is authorised by power of attorney, or as liquidator of a company, or otherwise, to sell or dispose of land belonging to another, and he appropriates the land or anything forming part of it by dealing with it in breach of the confidence reposed in him; or (*b*) when he is not in possession of the land and appropriates   *d* anything forming part of the land by severing it or causing it to be severed, or after it has been severed; or (*c*) when, being in possession of the land under a tenancy, he appropriates the whole or part of any fixture or structure let to be used with the land. For purposes of this subsection "land" does not include incorporeal hereditaments; "tenancy" means a tenancy for years or any less period and includes an agreement for such a tenancy, but a person who after   *e* the end of a tenancy remains in possession as statutory tenant or otherwise is to be treated as having possession under the tenancy, and "let" shall be construed accordingly . . .

5.—(1) Property shall be regarded as belonging to any person having possession or control of it, or having in it any proprietary right or interest (not being an equitable interest arising only from an agreement to transfer   *f* or grant an interest) . . .

6.—(1) A person appropriating property belonging to another without meaning the other permanently to lose the thing itself is nevertheless to be regarded as having the intention of permanently depriving the other of it if his intention is to treat the thing as his own to dispose of regardless of the   *g* other's rights; and a borrowing or lending of it may amount to so treating it if, but only if, the borrowing or lending is for a period and in circumstances making it equivalent to an outright taking or disposal.

(2) Without prejudice to the generality of subsection (1) above, where a person, having possession or control (lawfully or not) of property belonging to another, parts with the property under a condition as to its return which   *h* he may not be able to perform, this (if done for purposes of his own and without the other's authority) amounts to treating the property as his own to dispose of regardless of the other's rights . . .

Fraud and blackmail   *j*

15.—(1) A person who by any deception dishonestly obtains property belonging to another, with the intention of permanently depriving the other of it, shall on conviction on indictment be liable to imprisonment for a term not exceeding ten years.

(2) For purposes of this section a person is to be treated as obtaining

a
property if he obtains ownership, possession or control of it, and "obtain" includes obtaining for another or enabling another to obtain or to retain.

(3) Section 6 above shall apply for purposes of this section, with the necessary adaptation of the reference to appropriating, as it applies for purposes of section 1.

b
(4) For purposes of this section "deception" means any deception (whether deliberate or reckless) by words or conduct as to fact or as to law, including a deception as to the present intentions of the person using the deception or any other person.'

To be guilty of theft the offender, as I shall call him, must act dishonestly and must have the intention of permanently depriving the owner of property. Section 1(3) shows that in order to interpret the word 'appropriates' (and thereby to define c theft), ss 1 to 6 must be read together. The ordinary and natural meaning of 'appropriate' is to take for oneself, or to treat as one's own, property which belongs to someone else. The primary dictionary meaning is 'take possession of, take to oneself, especially without authority', and that is in my opinion the meaning which the word bears in s 1(1). The act of appropriating property is a one-sided d act, done without the consent or authority of the owner. And, if the owner consents to transfer property to the offender or to a third party, the offender does not appropriate the property, even if the owner's consent has been obtained by fraud. This statement represents the old doctrine in regard to obtaining property by false pretences, to which I shall advert presently.

The references in ss 2, 3 and 4 qualify but do not impair the meaning of the e words 'appropriates' and 'appropriation', as they are used in s 1. Section 2(1) does not change the meaning of appropriation but it tells us when appropriation is not to be regarded as dishonest (and so does not amount to stealing). Paragraphs (a), (b) and (c) of the subsection all describe unilateral, though honest, acts of the appropriator, who takes the property for himself and treats it as his own. For the benefit of those who would suggest that s 2(1)(b) shows that appropriation is f something which can be done with the consent of the owner, I would paraphrase that provision by saying 'if he appropriates the property in the belief that he would have the other's consent if the other knew what he had done and the circumstances in which he did it'. The opportunity for confusion arises from the use of the word 'appropriates' in a clearly unilateral sense followed by the word 'appropriation' (describing what the appropriator has unilaterally done) hypotheti-g cally linked to the idea of consent.

Coming now to s 3, the primary meaning of 'assumption' is 'taking on oneself', again a unilateral act, and this meaning is consistent with sub-ss (1) and (2). To use the word in its secondary, neutral sense would neutralise the word 'appropriation', to which assumption is here equated, and would lead to a number of strange results. Incidentally, I can see no magic in the words 'an owner' in sub-s h (1). Every case in real life must involve the owner or the person described in s 5(1); 'the rights' may mean 'all the rights', which would be the normal grammatical meaning, or (less probably, in my opinion) 'any rights': see R v Morris [1983] 3 All ER 288 at 293, [1984] AC 320 at 332. For present purposes it does not appear to matter; the word 'appropriate' does not on either interpretation acquire the j meaning contended for by the Crown. Still looking at s 3(1), I point out that 'any later assumption of a right to it' (that is a right to the property) amounts to an appropriation of a right to it and that normally 'a right to it' means a right to the property and not a right in it. Section 3(2) protects an innocent purchaser from an accusation of theft when, having bought in good faith from someone with a defective title, he later treats the property as his own.

Section 4(2) lists three exceptions to the general proposition that a person cannot steal land etc. The word 'appropriates' in paras (a), (b) and (c) is thoroughly consistent with unilateral action.

Section 6(1) introduces a deemed intention of permanently depriving the owner of his property when the person appropriating the property 'for the time being', as one might say, intends 'to treat the thing as his own to dispose of regardless of the other's rights'. Here again the offender's act is unilateral and the same can clearly be said of s 6(2).

Mr Hacking QC, for the respondent, also drew attention to ss 24(4) and 28(6) of the 1968 Act, which can be required only on the basis that s 15, in at least some respects, is not dealing with theft. He also pointed out the amendment in s 26 of the Criminal Justice Act 1991 (effective from 1 October 1992) reducing the maximum term of imprisonment for theft from ten to seven years, thereby distinguishing theft from obtaining by deception, the maximum term for which remains at ten years.

Accordingly, reading ss 1 to 6 as a whole, and also taking into account ss 24(4) and 28(6) and the 1991 amendment, the ordinary and natural meaning of 'appropriates' in s 1(1) is confirmed. So clear is this conclusion to my mind that, notwithstanding anything which has been said in other cases, I would be very slow to concede that the word 'appropriates' in s 1(1) of the 1968 Act is in its context ambiguous. But, as I have indicated, the Crown case requires that there must be ambiguity and further requires that the ambiguity must be resolved against the ordinary meaning of the word and in favour of the neutral meaning preferred and required by the Crown's argument. Therefore, my Lords, I am willing for the purpose of argument to treat the word 'appropriates' as ambiguous in its context and, on that basis, following the principles enunciated in *Black-Clawson International Ltd v Papierwerke Waldhof-Aschaffenburg AG* [1975] 1 All ER 810, [1975] AC 591 and the example of Lord Ackner in *R v Kassim* [1991] 3 All ER 713 at 718, [1992] 1 AC 9 at 16, where the construction of s 20(2) of the Theft Act 1968 was the question at issue, I turn, for such guidance as it may afford, to the eighth report of the Criminal Law Revision Committee, *Theft and Related Offences* (Cmnd 2977 (1966)).

While the report may not completely resolve the question for your Lordships, it provides in the first place a very useful summary of the state of the law in 1966. It also discusses in some detail the shortcomings of the law in regard to theft and kindred offences, as they appeared to the committee, and it proposes remedies. A reading of the 1968 Act, which was based on the draft Bill annexed to the report, leads me to the conclusion that, when using the very words of the draft, Parliament intended to implement the committee's thinking. Of course, if the words of the 1968 Act clearly achieve a different result from that which seemed to be intended by the Criminal Law Revision Committee, it is the words which must prevail and strained constructions must not be adopted in order to give effect to the report.

In para 15 the committee discuss the 'chief defects in the existing law of larceny', including its failure to deal with certain kinds of dishonesty. In para 16 they point out that the defects stem from regarding larceny as a violation of possession and not of rights of ownership, with the offence depending on a *taking* of the property. The notion of taking had been extended both judicially and by statute and examples of statutory extension by way of ss 17(1)(b) (embezzlement) and 20(1)(iv) (fraudulent conversion) of the Larceny Act 1916 are given in para 17. The committee observed at para 18 that the fact that misappropriation of property was dealt with under the three separate heads of larceny, embezzlement and fraudulent conversion inevitably made for difficulty and complication. Paragraph

a 19 introduces what will be seen as a specially relevant topic:

> 'In addition to the division of misappropriation into three main offences
> the distinction between larceny and obtaining by false pretences contrary to
> 1916 s. 32 is sometimes very subtle. A person commits the latter offence if
> he "by any false pretence . . . with intent to defraud, obtains from any other
>
> *b* person any chattel, money, or valuable security, or causes or procures any
> money to be paid, or any chattel or valuable security to be delivered to
> himself or to any other person for the use or benefit or on account of himself
> or any other person". The essential difference between this offence and
> larceny is that in larceny the victim does not part with the ownership but in
> obtaining by false pretences he does. But since "obtaining the possession by
>
> *c* any trick" amounts to a taking for the purpose of larceny, it is notoriously
> difficult to draw any logical distinction between larceny by a trick and
> obtaining by false pretences and to decide whether a particular case amounts
> to the one offence or the other. The matter is made worse by the fact that the
> two offences are construed as being mutually exclusive; and the resulting
> difficulties are not entirely overcome by the provisions in 1916 [Act] s. 44 as
>
> *d* to the verdicts open to the jury when they find that the accused committed
> an offence different from that charged (cf. paragraph 90).'

Paragraph 21 exposes a gap, pointing out that an innocent acquisition followed
by a dishonest decision to keep or dispose of the property was in general not
larceny and that larceny by finding was committed only where *at the time of the*

e *finding* the finder believed that the owner could be discovered by taking reasonable
steps. After discussing various loopholes in the law of theft the committee
proceeded in what may be seen as a key paragraph:

> '30. The essence of the offence of fraudulent conversion under 1916
> s. 20(1)(iv) (referred to in paragraph 17) is misappropriation of property by a
>
> *f* person who has possession on behalf of somebody else. The offence was
> created by the Larceny Act 1901 (c. 10) in order to provide for cases of
> dishonest misappropriation which were not covered by larceny (in particular
> because there was no taking) or embezzlement (because the offender was not
> a clerk or servant) or by other statutory offences of fraudulent conversion
>
> *g* which depended on the offender being in a special position, for example a
> trustee. The language of s. 20(1)(iv)(*b*) is wide enough to cover larceny by a
> bailee or part owner and embezzlement; but it is a matter of dispute whether
> it does so or whether it is limited to those types of misappropriation,
> originally not criminal, for which the 1901 Act was intended to provide.
> Whichever is the true view, the general offence of fraudulent conversion has
>
> *h* proved valuable, covering as it does in clear language a wide range of
> circumstances in which property may be misappropriated. As will be seen
> (paragraph 35), the idea contained in the words "fraudulently converts to his
> own use or benefit, or the use or benefit of any other person" corresponds to
> what we propose should be the essence of the new offence of theft.'

j Paragraph 33 states an important conclusion:

> 'The committee generally are strongly of opinion that larceny, embezzle-
> ment and fraudulent conversion should be replaced by a single new offence
> of theft. The important element of them all is undoubtedly the dishonest
> appropriation of another person's property—the treating of "tuum" as

"meum"; and we think it not only logical, but right in principle, to make
this the central element of the offence. In doing so the law would concentrate   *a*
on what the accused dishonestly achieved or attempted to achieve and not on
the means—taking or otherwise—which he used in order to do so. This
would avoid multiplicity of offences. Accordingly clause 1(1) of the draft Bill
provides that—"A person is guilty of theft if he dishonestly appropriates
property belonging to another with the intention of permanently depriving
the other of it; and 'thief', 'steals' and 'stolen' shall be construed accordingly."   *b*
This will be the main provision in the definition of theft, replacing the
definition in 1916 s. 1(1). There are ancillary definitions in clause 1 and in
clauses 2–5 which are referred to in the notes. The more important elements
of the definition of the new offence are referred to in paragraphs 34–58.'

This conclusion, in order to create a single comprehensive offence in place of   *c*
larceny, embezzlement and fraudulent conversion, makes 'appropriation' (the
treating of 'tuum' as 'meum') the key element in place of taking, and it is the
activity expressed by the word 'appropriation' which dispenses with the need for
the phrase 'without the consent of the owner', which preceded the words 'takes
and carries away' in the old definition of larceny in s 1(1) of the 1916 Act. The   *d*
opening lines of para 34 further elucidate the committee's thinking:

'We hope, and believe, that the concept of "dishonest appropriation" will
be easily understood even without the aid of further definition. But there is
a partial definition of "appropriates" in clause 3(1), which is included partly
to indicate that this is the familiar concept of conversion but also for particular   *e*
reasons later to be mentioned. Clause 3(1) provides that—"Any assumption
by a person of the rights of an owner amounts to an appropriation . . ." It
seems to us natural to refer to the act of stealing in ordinary cases as
"appropriation". We see no reason why the word should seem strange for
more than a short time. It is moreover not a new word to use in connection
with theft. Sir James Fitzjames Stephen (afterwards Stephen J.), in his   *f*
"General View of the Criminal Law" (1st edn, 1863, p 129), suggested as a
definition of theft:—"To steal is unlawfully, and with intent to defraud, by
taking, by embezzlement, by obtaining by false pretences, or in any other
manner whatever to appropriate to the use of any person any property
whatever real or personal in possession or in action, so as to deprive any other
person of the advantage of any beneficial interest at law or in equity, which   *g*
he may have therein". Sir F. Stephen added:—"The effect of adopting this
definition would be to include under one description all the cognate offences
which at present make up the crime of theft. Its terms would include larceny,
embezzlement, false pretences, larceny by bailees, fraudulent breaches of
trust, and offences by factors, agents, and bankers, and thus five or six useless   *h*
and intricate distinctions between cognate crimes would be abolished."'

(I digress for a moment to point out that, while this proposal would have included
obtaining by false pretences within the definition of stealing, that was not the
option preferred by the committee, as your Lordships will have noted.)
    The next four paragraphs are important in the committee's scheme of things   *j*
and I must ask your Lordships' indulgence while I quote them in full:

'35. The idea of dishonest appropriation which underlies the new offence
of theft corresponds, as mentioned in paragraph 30, to the idea in the words
"fraudulently converts to his own use or benefit, or the use or benefit of any
other person" in the definition of fraudulent conversion under 1916

a

s. 20(1)(iv). The new offence will in fact consist of the present offence of fraudulent conversion without the requirement that the offender should, at the time of the conversion, be in possession of the property either in the circumstances mentioned in s. 20(1)(iv) or at all. With the removal of this requirement the offence will extend to ordinary stealing by taking property from another's possession. The effect will be as if fraudulent conversion were

b

widened to include the whole of larceny and embezzlement; the new offence will indeed include conduct which may not be criminal under the present law such as the dishonest appropriation by a parent of things taken and brought home by a child under the age of criminal responsibility (cf. *Walters v. Lunt* ([1951] 2 All ER 645)). The expression "dishonestly appropriates" in clause 1(1) means the same as "fraudulently converts to his own use or

c

benefit, or for the use or benefit of any other person" in 1916 s. 20(1)(iv); but the former expression is shorter and, we hope, clearer. There is an argument for keeping the word "converts" because it is well understood. But it is a lawyers' word, and those not used to legal language might naturally think that it meant changing something or exchanging property for other property. "Appropriates" seems altogether a better word.

d

36. The offence will also cover cases of dishonest retention or disposal after an innocent acquisition such as are mentioned in paragraphs 21–5. This result is probably implicit in the concept of appropriation (or "conversion"); but it is made explicit by the provision in clause 3(1) that a person's assumption of the rights of an owner "includes, where he has come by the property (innocently or not) without stealing it, any later assumption of a

e

right to it by keeping or dealing with it as owner". It seems natural to regard dishonestly keeping or dealing with the property as theft (as it is now in the case of bailees). This has the advantage that the cases referred to will be brought within the single concept of dishonest appropriation. If taking were to be kept as the basis of the offence, it would be necessary to create a separate

f

offence of dishonest retention or disposal in order to deal with these cases.

37. We propose however that there should be a special exception for one case. A person may buy something in good faith, but may find out afterwards that the seller had no title to it, perhaps because the seller or somebody else stole it. If the buyer nevertheless keeps the thing or otherwise deals with it as owner, he could, on the principles stated above, be guilty of theft. It is

g

arguable that this would be right; but on the whole it seems to us that, whatever view is taken of the buyer's moral duty, the law would be too strict if it made him guilty of theft. Clause 3(2) accordingly ensures that a later assumption of ownership in such circumstances will not amount to theft.

38. The sub-committee for a considerable time proposed that the general offence of theft should be made to cover the present offence of obtaining by

h

false pretences under 1916 s. 32(1). It might seem appropriate to extend theft in this way in order to make it cover as many ways as possible of getting property dishonestly. But in the end the sub-committee gave up the idea (to the regret of some members), and the full committee agreed. In spite of its attractions, it seemed to the majority of the committee that the scheme would be unsatisfactory. Obtaining by false pretences is ordinarily thought

j

of as different from theft, because in the former the owner in fact consents to part with his ownership; a bogus beggar is regarded as a rogue but not as a thief, and so are his less petty counterparts. To create a new offence of theft to include conduct which ordinary people would find difficult to regard as theft would be a mistake. The unnaturalness of including obtaining by false pretences in theft is emphasized by the difficulty of drafting a satisfactory definition to cover both kinds of conduct. The examination by Mr. Griffith-Jones's sub-sub-committee, mentioned in paragraph 3, showed also that it *a* would be difficult to frame an indictment charging theft by false pretences.'

The committee's proposed remedies for the defects of the law as they found it appear clearly from the foregoing paragraphs. 'Fraudulent conversion' is accepted as the starting point for the new and comprehensive definition of theft and 'dishonest appropriation' is chosen as a synonym. Both expressions embody the *b* notion of an adverse unilateral act done to the prejudice of the owner and without his authority; indeed, fraudulent conversion can have no other meaning. Paragraph 38 shows that the committee considered the idea, once recommended by Sir James Fitzjames Stephen, of making 'theft' cover the offence of obtaining by false pretences. But that idea was ultimately abandoned for the reasons there mentioned.   *c*

The committee's philosophy with regard to obtaining by false pretences and its near relation, larceny by a trick, is expounded in paras 86 to 90 of the report. Draft cl 12 was enacted as s 15 (which I have reproduced above) and s 16 of the 1968 Act and has got rid of some defects and difficulties which had arisen from s 32 of the 1916 Act and from judicial interpretations of that section. The false pretence (or 'deception', to use the new term) was no longer confined to pretence *d* about an existing fact and no longer excluded a misrepresentation as to the offender's intention. An important point, with a view to interpreting the 1968 Act and understanding comments, both judicial and academic, which have been made about it, is the fusion in cl 12 and s 15 of larceny by a trick and obtaining by false pretences. I refer to para 90 of the report: *e*

'On the other hand clause 12(1) provides that "a person is to be treated as obtaining property if he obtains ownership, possession or control of it . . ." This is a departure from the present law, which requires that ownership should be obtained (*Kilham* ((1870) LR 1 CCR 261), mentioned in paragraph 89; *Ball* ([1951] 2 KB 109). The extension of the offence to include obtaining *f* possession or control will have the result that if Kilham, although pretending that he only wanted to borrow the horse, had in fact intended to deprive the owner permanently, he would be guilty under the clause, because he obtained possession of the horse. The extension will also have the effect that the offences of theft and criminal deception will overlap and that conduct which under the present law is larceny by a trick and that which is obtaining by *g* false pretences will be the same offence of criminal deception. In practice, if there is any doubt whether it is appropriate to charge theft or obtaining property by deception, it will be natural to charge the latter; and in our opinion it would be wise to do so, because this will be a much easier offence to establish than is the present offence of obtaining by false pretences, as it will be unnecessary to show that the owner was deceived into intentionally *h* passing the ownership but sufficient to show that he was tricked into parting with the possession. Theft could be charged only in very clear cases. The new law will have the advantage that the prosecution will not be in the present difficulty (referred to in paragraph 19) of deciding which of two mutually exclusive offences to charge. The existing difficulties in this respect are considerably reduced by the provision in 1916 s. 44(3) that a person charged *j* with larceny may be convicted of obtaining by false pretences and the provision in s. 44(4) that a person charged with obtaining by false pretences may be convicted of this offence even if the evidence proves larceny. But these provisions are not entirely satisfactory. If a person is rightly charged with larceny, but the jury in reliance on 44(3) mistakenly convict him of

obtaining by false pretences, the Court of Criminal Appeal cannot substitute
a   a verdict of guilty of larceny under s. 5(2) of the Criminal Appeal Act 1907
(c. 23); for the verdict implies an acquittal of larceny, so that it cannot
"[appear] to the Court of Criminal Appeal that the jury must have been
satisfied of facts which proved him guilty of [larceny]" (*Fisher* ((1921) 16 Cr
App R 53)). Again, a person charged with attempted larceny cannot be
convicted of attempting to obtain by false pretences (*Gallagher* ((1929) 21 Cr
b   App R 172)). The provision in s. 44(4) has been criticized on the ground that
it is wrong in principle that a person should be found guilty of an offence
which the jury find that he did not commit. It seems to us that the Bill would
be open to criticism if it had to rely on provisions such as those in 1916 [Act]
s. 44(3) and (4). But it does not have to do so. *Difficulties of the kinds provided
c   for by those subsections will not arise, because the overlapping of the two offences
under the Bill will have the result that the accused can be convicted of whichever
offence is charged.* It also seems right that the offence under clause 12(1), as
well as applying to obtaining possession or control without ownership, should
apply to obtaining ownership without possession or control. For ownership
enables a person to pass the title to another in fraud of the person from whom
d   the property is obtained, and this may make it difficult or impossible for the
latter to recover the property.' (My emphasis.)

(I am not entirely clear about the wording of the sentence which I have
emphasised, but I think the sense is that the accused can be convicted of obtaining
by deception, whether the offence has taken the form of larceny by a trick or
e   obtaining by false pretences.) It can be seen that the committee continues to
recognise the difference between obtaining *possession* by a trick (that is, 'by
deception' in its new wide sense) and obtaining *ownership* by false pretences (again,
'by deception') but the committee intended, and it seems that Parliament has
adopted the same approach in s 15, that, for the purpose of finding the accused
guilty, it would cease to matter whether the victim was deceived into transferring
f   ownership or into handing over possession. But the distinction continues to
matter to an innocent third party who has purchased directly or indirectly from
the offender.

My Lords, as I would submit, the report contains a great deal which confirms
and nothing which contradicts the interpretation of the word 'appropriates' which
I have preferred, and a comparison of the 1968 Act with the draft Bill gives no
g   support to the contrary view. Clauses 1, 2 and 4 and the corresponding sections
exhibit very minor drafting differences. Section 6 is new and I refer to it below.
Sections 11 and 14 are new. They need not concern your Lordships, but, with s 6,
their presence explains why cl 12 corresponds to s 15. Clause 12(1) is matched by
s 15(1) and (2). The provisions of cl 12(2) and (3) are subsumed in a new s 16.
h   'Deception' is identically defined in cl 12(4) and s 15(4). Section 15(3) is new:

'Section 6 above shall apply for purposes of this section, with the necessary
adaptation of the reference to appropriating, as it applies for purposes of
section 1.'

This provision stems logically from the new s 6, on which I commented earlier,
j   and the necessary adaptation of the reference to appropriating is made by inserting
a reference to obtaining property.
The conclusion from this comparison of the draft Bill and the 1968 Act is that
Parliament has in all material respects adopted the committee's approach and has
thereby indorsed the committee's point of view. While not forgetting the
observations in *Black-Clawson International Ltd v Papierwerke Waldhof-Aschaffenburg*

AG [1975] 1 All ER 810 at 814, 828, 835, [1975] AC 591 at 614, 629, 637 of
Lord Reid, Lord Wilberforce and of Lord Diplock, where he wisely warned   *a*
against departing from the plain and natural meaning in favour of a strained
construction, I am much impressed by the more adventurous but very logical
pronouncements of Viscount Dilhorne and Lord Simon of Glaisdale (see [1975] 1
All ER 810 at 824, 842–843, [1975] AC 591 at 622–623, 646). In particular, after
stating the principles and citing authority, Viscount Dilhorne said ([1975] 1 All
ER 810 at 823, [1975] AC 591 at 623):   *b*

> 'While I respectfully agree that recommendations of a committee may not
> help much when there is a possibility that Parliament may have decided to
> do something different, where there is no such possibility, as where the draft
> bill has been enacted without alteration, in my opinion it can safely be
> assumed that it was Parliament's intention to do what the committee   *c*
> recommended and to achieve the object the committee had in mind. Then,
> in my view the recommendations of the committee and their observations
> on their draft bill may form a valuable aid to construction which the courts
> should not be inhibited from taking into account.'

Before going on to consider the cases and some of the observations which the   *d*
academic writers have made on s 1, I should like to say something more about
s 15. According to the Crown's argument, this provision seems to be unnecessary
and must have been included in the 1968 Act (and presumably also in the draft
Bill) as a mere matter of convenience. A possible alternative theory is that the
committee, the responsible government department and the learned Parliamentary draftsmen all thought that s 15 (cl 12) was needed, which turns out to be a   *e*
mistaken view when s 1 is properly understood. I call this an alternative theory
because it seems obvious to me that the committee *did* think that cl 12 was
necessary—and I am not simply referring to the definition of 'deception'. The
Crown says that s 15 merely describes a particular type of theft and that all
stealing by means of deception can be prosecuted under s 1 just as well as under
s 15. I would point out that s 15 covers what were formerly two offences,   *f*
obtaining by false pretences (where the ownership of the property is transferred
by the deceived victim) and theft (or larceny) by a trick (where the possession of
the property passes, but not the ownership). In the former case, according to the
interpretation which I prefer, the offender does not *appropriate* the property,
because the ownership (in colloquial terms, the property) is transferred with the   *g*
owner's consent, albeit obtained by deception. In the latter case the offender does
appropriate the property because, although the owner has handed over *possession*
by consent (which was obtained by deception), he has not transferred the property
(that is the ownership) and the offender, intending to deprive the owner
permanently of his property, appropriates it, not by taking possession, but by the
unilateral act, adverse to the owner, of treating as his own and taking to himself   *h*
property of which he was merely given *possession*. Thus, the kind of obtaining by
deception which amounts to larceny by a trick and involves appropriation *could*
be successfully prosecuted under s 1, but the old false pretences type of obtaining
by deception could not. Of course, unless the facts were absolutely clear, it would
be foolish to prosecute under s 1 an offence of obtaining by deception, since
something which at first looked like larceny by a trick might turn out to have   *j*
involved a transfer of the ownership, in which case only s 15 would meet the
prosecution's needs, if I am right. Some theft cases can be prosecuted under s 15,
but it is fallacious, having regard to what I perceive as the true meaning of
appropriation, to say that *all* cases of obtaining by deception can be prosecuted
under s 1.

There are only three cases which I need to look at in detail, *Lawrence, Morris*
a and *Dobson v General Accident Fire and Life Assurance Corp plc* [1989] 3 All ER 927,
[1990] 1 QB 274, a decision of the Court of Appeal in a case where a policy holder
was insured against 'loss or damage caused by theft'. In the Court of Appeal,
Criminal Division in *Lawrence* [1970] 3 All ER 933, [1971] 1 QB 373 the main
contention of the defence, noted by Megaw LJ, who delivered the judgment of
the court, was that there must be implied into s 1(1) of the 1968 Act a requirement
b that the dishonest appropriation must be without the consent of the owner of the
property. Megaw LJ then said ([1970] 3 All ER 933 at 935–936, [1971] 1 QB 373
at 377):

> 'In our view, no such implication is justified. The words contained in the
> former definition of larceny, in s 1 of the Larceny Act 1916, "without the
c > consent of the owner", have been omitted, and, we have no doubt, deliberately
> omitted from the definition of theft in the 1968 Act. If the owner does not
> resist the taking of his property, or actually hands it over, because of, e g
> threats of violence, in one sense it could be said that there is "consent"; yet
> the offence of robbery, as defined in s 8(1) of the 1968 Act involves, as one of
> its elements, theft. Again, the former offences of larceny by a trick and
d > obtaining property by false pretences, although technically distinct offences
> under the old law, both involved what in one sense could be described as
> "consent" by the victim. It was conceded by counsel for the appellant,
> necessarily and rightly, that the old offence of larceny by a trick is covered by
> s 1(1) of the 1968 Act, as well as by s 15(1) to which we shall refer later,
e > despite what may be called the apparent consent of the victim. Of course,
> where there is true consent by the owner of property to the appropriation of
> it by another, a charge of theft under s 1(1) must fail. This is not, however,
> because the words "without consent" have to be implied in the new definition
> of theft. It is simply because, if there is such true consent, the essential
> element of dishonesty is not established. If, however, the apparent consent is
f > brought about by dishonesty, there is nothing in the words of s 1(1), or by
> reason of any implication that can properly be read into those words, to make
> such apparent consent relevant as providing a defence. The prosecution have
> to prove the four elements already mentioned, and no more. No inference to
> the contrary is to be drawn from the words of s 2(1)(b), already quoted. That
> reference does no more than show that the essential element of dishonesty
g > does not exist if the defendant when he appropriates the property believes
> that the owner would consent if he knew the circumstances. "The
> circumstances" are, of course, all the relevant circumstances. "The belief" is
> an honest belief. That paragraph does not give rise to the inference that an
> appropriation of property is not theft when there is a "consent"—if it can be
> rightly so described—which is founded on the dishonesty of the defendant.
h > The primary submission on behalf of the appellant, therefore, fails.'

My respectful view, for reasons which your Lordships will have noted, is that
both the contention of the defence and the court's refutation of it were
misconceived: the absence of consent on the part of the owner is already inherent
in the word 'appropriates', properly understood, and therefore the argument for
j the defence got off on the wrong foot and the counter-argument that the words
specified by the defence cannot be read into s 1(1) did not assist the prosecution.
And the observation, without further discussion, that the omission of the words
'without the consent of the owner' is deliberate seems to have led directly to the
erroneous conclusion that a supposed appropriation *with* the consent of the owner
is one of the four ingredients which are required (and which suffice) to constitute

theft. I do not propose to restate the facts of *Lawrence*. It is enough to recall that the Court of Appeal, accepting the defence submission on that point, regarded it *a* as an example, according to the old law, of obtaining by false pretences (see [1970] 3 All ER 933 at 936, [1971] 1 QB 373 at 378). But the court did not accept the legal conclusion which the defence sought to draw from that fact, since Megaw LJ continued ([1970] 3 All ER 933 at 936–937, [1971] 1 QB 373 at 378):

> 'The court sees no ground for saying that, for present purposes, it makes *b* the slightest difference whether under the old law the offence would have been false pretences or larceny by a trick. The old and unsatisfactory distinction is not to be perpetuated unnecessarily where the language of the Theft Act 1968 does not require it. There is no magic in the word "property" in s 1(1) in view of the definition in s 4(1) of the Act. In either case, the fact that a charge could have been brought under s 15(1), which covers both, in *c* no way operates to prevent the charge being validly laid as theft under s 1(1) if the prosecution can prove what they must prove, as previously described, under that subsection. This is conceded in respect of an offence which would once have been larceny by a trick. It applies equally to what would once have been obtaining by false pretences, if, as is here the case, the requirements of *d* s 1(1) are also satisfied. That submission also fails. It may be that the result of our decision is that in any case where the facts would establish a charge under s 15(1) they would also establish a charge under s 1(1). The alternative, however, involves the writing back into s 1(1) of words which the legislature, no doubt deliberately omitted, and the reintroduction into the criminal law of the distinction between larceny by a trick and obtaining by false pretences.' *e*

It is true that it would make no difference whether under the old law the offence would have been false pretences or larceny by a trick, provided the charge was laid under s 15(1). It was, indeed, with the object of getting over that difference that the Criminal Law Revision Committee proposed their cl 12(1). But the 'old and unsatisfactory distinction' continues to operate if the charge is *f* laid under s 1(1) and this is due to the true meaning in that subsection of the word 'appropriates'. That is why s 15(1) is needed and why it is best to prosecute under that provision in cases where deception is alleged to have been practised. It can be seen that the entire reasoning of the passage I have just quoted is based on a misconception of the meaning of the word 'appropriates', and that misconception springs from the misconceived argument and counter-argument of the judgment *g* (see [1970] 3 All ER 933 at 936, [1971] 1 QB 373 at 377).

Turning back to the earlier extract which I have quoted, I note that Megaw LJ gives two examples in order to show that theft may be committed, although the (so-called) appropriation is made by the offender with the consent of the owner, (1) in the case of robbery and (2) where there has been larceny by a trick.

As to the former, before 1968 robbery was a felony at common law and, *h* according to *Archbold's Criminal Pleading Evidence and Practice* (36th edn, 1966) para 1761, consisted 'in the felonious taking of money or goods of any value from the person of another, or in his presence, against his will, by violence or putting him in fear'. The old authorities, Coke, Hale, Hawkins and Blackstone are cited in *Smith v Desmond* [1965] 1 All ER 976 at 980–983, [1965] AC 960 at 980–985 by *j* Lord Morris of Borth-y-Gest. Section 8(1) of the Theft Act 1968 was modelled on cl 7(1) of the draft Bill and provides:

> 'A person is guilty of robbery if he steals, and immediately before or at the time of doing so, and in order to do so, he uses force on any person or puts or seeks to put any person in fear of being then and there subjected to force.'

(I can see no sign of any intention to change the common law, as declared in *Smith*
a *v Desmond.*) When, in response to the highwayman's threat, 'Your money or your
life', the victim delivered up his money, he did so *against his will* and there was no
question of consent. The highwayman was guilty of an aggravated form of
stealing and did not obtain even a voidable title. The same holds good today and
it would be idle to suggest that the victim of a robbery consents in any way to
hand over his property, much less to transfer its ownership, to the robber.
b   In the case of larceny by a trick, as I explained earlier, the owner consents to
hand over possession but he does not consent to transfer ownership of his property,
unlike the victim of what was formerly known as false pretences, who *does* indeed
consent to transfer his ownership. That is the difference which makes it irrelevant
and misleading to say that both larceny by a trick and obtaining by false pretences
c involved 'consent' by the victim, because what is involved is consent to two
different things (see [1970] 3 All ER 933 at 936, [1971] 1 QB 373 at 377).
      The reference to 'true consent' (see [1970] 3 All ER 933 at 936, [1971] 1 QB 373
at 377) calls for a further observation which will also be apt when I consider
Dobson. The victim of false pretences does truly consent and acts of his own
volition, although his consent to transfer his property to another has been obtained
d by fraud. I refer again to *Archbold* (36th edn, 1966), this time at para 1479:

> 'Where the owner, of his own free will, parts not only with the possession
> but also with the *property* in the goods taken, the person taking the goods
> cannot be guilty of larceny, however fraudulent were the means by which
> the delivery of the goods was procured . . .' (Archbold's emphasis.)

e At para 1497 it is stated that in larceny the owner of the thing stolen has no
intention to part with his property therein to the person taking it, although he
may intend to part with the possession; in false pretences the owner does intend
to part with his property in the money or chattel, but it is obtained from him by
fraud. Of the nine cases cited for this proposition I refer to just one, *Whitehorn*
f *Bros v Davison* [1911] 1 KB 463, [1908–10] All ER Rep 885, a decision of the Court
of Appeal to the effect that the false pretences rule concerning the passing of a
good title to an innocent purchaser applied when the owner had been induced by
false pretences to deliver goods to the buyer on sale or return. Buckley LJ said
([1911] 1 KB 463 at 479, [1908–10] All ER Rep 885 at 893):

> 'It is, I think, obtaining goods by false pretences where the owner, being
g > induced thereto by a trick, voluntarily parts with the possession, and either
> intends to pass the property, or intends to confer a power to pass the property.
> If he gives, and intends to give, that power, and the power is exercised, the
> person who takes under the execution of the power obtains the property, not
> against, but by the authority of, the original owner, *and none the less because*
h > *the authority was obtained by fraud.*' (My emphasis.)

Paragraph 1499 deals with larceny by intimidation (which has much in common
with one branch of robbery):

> 'Where a man, having the *animus furandi* (see ante, para. 1469), obtains
> possession of goods by frightening the owner, as by threatening him with
j > temporary imprisonment unless he delivers up his goods, and the owner does
> deliver them under the influence of the fear inspired by his threat, this is
> considered such a taking (although there is a delivery in fact) as to constitute
> larceny: *R. v. Lovell* ((1881) 8 QBD 185).'

I have cited these passages in order to illustrate the difference between larceny
by a trick and obtaining by false pretences and the important, if obvious, fact that

the owner's consent to transfer the property prevents the offender from being
guilty of larceny, although the consent was obtained by fraud and, in the words *a*
of Megaw LJ, is not a 'true consent'. I say 'obvious' because, if this proposition did
not prevail, the property would not pass and the offender would be guilty of
larceny, now described as theft. Accordingly, the statement of the judgment in
the Court of Appeal (see [1970] 3 All ER 933 at 936, [1971] 1 QB 373 at 377) to
the effect that, if the apparent consent of the owner is brought about by
dishonesty, there is nothing in the words of s 1(1) to make such apparent consent *b*
relevant as providing a defence is, with respect, erroneous in relation to a charge
of theft (which was the relevant charge) if the word 'appropriates' bears the
meaning which the Criminal Law Revision Committee (rightly, in my opinion)
has deliberately given it.

In *Law of Theft* (6th edn, 1989) ch 2 Professor J C Smith discusses the difference *c*
between larceny by a trick and obtaining by false pretences and continues (para
38):

> 'It may of course be perfectly proper for the court to put on the Act an
> interpretation different from that intended by the framers of it. The question
> is one of the proper interpretation of the words enacted by Parliament and it
> could be that the Act does what the Committee thought was not practicable *d*
> and what they did not intend to do. It is submitted, however, that the right
> interpretation of the Act is that intended by the Committee.'

His further comment at is also valuable, in my opinion (para 39):

> 'There is, however, a considerable degree of doubt about this matter, *e*
> because of the case of *Lawrence*. The Court of Appeal in that case thought
> that the distinction between larceny by a trick and obtaining by false
> pretences depended on the presence in the Larceny Act of the words, "without
> the consent of the owner", and, as these words do not appear in the definition
> of theft, the distinction is gone; all cases of obtaining by deception, contrary
> to s. 15, are also theft. This argument, however, appears to give insufficient *f*
> weight to the notion of "appropriation" and to the words "property *belonging
> to another*".' (Professor Smith's emphasis.)

The report of the argument in this House in *Lawrence* (see [1972] AC 626 at
628–631) shows that the appellant, understandably from his own point of view,
again approached the case as one of false pretences. That basis would provide *g*
grounds for an acquittal of the charge of theft if the word 'appropriates' in s 1(1)
connotes an absence of consent by the owner, and the appellant presented his
argument on the meaning of that subsection in the same way as in the Court of
Appeal and with the same unsuccessful result (see [1972] AC 626 at 630). But that
was not all. Viscount Dilhorne, when reviewing the evidence ([1971] 2 All ER
1253 at 1254, [1972] AC 626 at 631), expressed the opinion that the facts of the *h*
case fell far short of establishing that Mr Occhi, the Italian student who was the
victim of the taxi driver, had consented to the acquisition by the appellant of the
£6 (as argued at [1972] AC 628). On that footing the taxi driver could have been
guilty of larceny by a trick (in old-fashioned terms), so as to be guilty of theft
under any interpretation of s 1(1). It has to be said, however, that the way in
which Mr Occhi left the taxi at the end of the journey without further question *j*
seems more consistent with his having accepted that £7 in all was the fare to be
charged and that he had been induced by the driver's false representations to part
out and out with all the money which he had passively allowed the taxi driver to
take from his wallet. It is of no assistance, however, to your Lordships in the
present appeal to debate the finer points of *Lawrence* with a view to deciding

whether the decision in this House (although not that of the Court of Appeal) can
a be justified on the special facts. What is important is the unequivocal, but in my
respectful opinion wrong, statement of the law made by Viscount Dilhorne (to
which I referred at the outset of my speech) that Parliament by omitting the
words 'without the consent of the owner' from s 1(1) of the Theft Act 1968 'has
relieved the prosecution of the burden of establishing that the taking was without
the owner's consent' (see [1971] 2 All ER 1253 at 1255, [1972] AC 626 at 632). He
b added: 'That is no longer an ingredient of the offence' (scil 'of theft'). The
reasoning which follows is based on the opinion, already inseparable from what
has been said, that appropriation is a neutral expression and does not convey the
sense of taking property for oneself without the owner's authority. As in the
Court of Appeal, the defence argument was primarily directed towards implying
c words into s 1(1), a difficult task at best, and only secondarily towards the meaning
of 'appropriates' (see [1972] AC 626 at 631 arg). But the only speech delivered did
not consider this second point and the summary treatment of the appellant's
argument is reflected in the opinion expressed that the point certified and argued
was scarcely worthy of their Lordships' attention (see [1971] 2 All ER 1253 at
1256, [1972] AC 626 at 633). My Lords, I have found nothing in *Lawrence* which
d affects my view of the present appeal. The crucial statement (apart from what was
said about the omission of the words 'without the consent of the owner') was:
'[Appropriation] may occur even though the owner has permitted or consented
to the property being taken' (see [1971] 2 All ER 1253 at 1255, [1972] AC 626 at
632). If 'taken' there signifies a permitted change of ownership, I respectfully
cannot agree.
e   In *Morris*, the label-switching case, the facts to be considered by the jury and
subsequently by the Court of Appeal ([1983] 2 All ER 448, [1983] QB 587) were,
like those of many supermarket frauds, more complex than those of the present
case. There would have been no defence (just as in *Lawrence*) if the charge had
been laid under s 15(1) and, as in *Lawrence* and the present case, it was the Crown's
f resort to s 1(1) which alone gave rise to a legal problem. Lord Lane CJ expounded
the main points on each side ([1983] 2 All ER 448 at 451, [1983] QB 587 at 593):

> 'As to the meaning of the word "appropriation", there are two schools of
> thought. The first contends that the word "appropriate" has built into it a
> connotation that it is some action inconsistent with the owner's rights,
> something hostile to the interests of the owner or contrary to his wishes and
g > intention or without his authority. The second school of thought contends
> that the word in this context means no more than to take possession of an
> article and that there is no requirement that the taking or appropriation
> should be in any way antagonistic to the rights of the owner. Support can be
> found for each of those two points of view both in the authorities and also
h > amongst the textbook writers.'

He then reviewed a number of cases, concluding with *Lawrence*, and, referring to
Viscount Dilhorne, said ([1983] 2 All ER 448 at 454, [1983] QB 587 at 597):

> 'He stated tersely in terms ([1971] 2 All ER 1253 at 1256, [1972] AC 626
> at 633): "The first question posed in the certificate was: 'Whether section 1(1)
j > of the Theft Act, 1968, is to be construed as though it contained the words
> "without having the consent of the owner" or words to that effect.' In my
> opinion, the answer is clearly No." That being the emphatic view of their
> Lordships, it would, we think, be quite wrong in effect to reimport into the
> offence the necessity of proving what amounts to absence of consent on the
> part of the owner by saying that the word "appropriates" necessarily means

some action contrary to the authority or interests of the owner and that that
is one of the requirements which the prosecution must prove.'   a

Here again (understandably, since *Lawrence* was a decision of this House) the
misconceived argument and refutation, which were related to the possibility of
implying words into s 1(1), took precedence. I am much attracted, as indeed the
Court of Appeal may have been, by counsel's argument for the appellant which
Lord Lane CJ summarised (see [1983] 2 All ER 448 at 456, [1983] QB 587 at 599).   b
His comment was significant:

> 'Whilst appreciating the simplicity of this approach, we think, for the
> reasons already set out, that the wording of the Act, coupled with the decision
> in *Lawrence v Comr of Police for the Metropolis* [1971] 2 All ER 1253, [1972] AC
> 626, does not allow us to adopt this solution.'   c

This House, having granted leave to appeal, affirmed the Court of Appeal's
decision in *Morris*, but reached its conclusion by a different route, as explained in
the speech of Lord Roskill, to which I have already referred. I would respectfully
agree with his description, in relation to dishonest actions, of appropriation as
involving an act by way of adverse interference with or usurpation of the owner's
rights, but I believe that the less aggressive definition of appropriation which I   d
have put forward fits the word as used in an honest sense in s 2(1) as well as
elsewhere in the 1968 Act. The important feature, of course, which our definitions
have in common is that the appropriation must be an act done without the
authority or consent, express or implied, of the owner. I do not consider that it
would help towards the solution of your Lordships' present problem for me to   e
discuss further the points which arose in *Morris* (including the question whether
it really is an example of *theft*) or in the many other cases on s 1(1) which have
occupied the anxious attention of the courts and the academic writers. I must,
however, look at *Dobson*, which I referred to above. That was the case in which
the owner, Mr Dobson, sold his gold watch and diamond ring in return for a
building society cheque which turned out to be a stolen cheque and worthless.   f
When he tried to recover his loss, the insurers denied liability on the ground that,
whereas his policy insured him against 'loss or damage caused by theft', the
circumstances did not disclose a theft within the meaning of the 1968 Act. The
owner sued the insurers and obtained judgment in the county court for £5,199·30.
The insurers appealed to the Court of Appeal, contending that there had been no
appropriation of the property by the buyer but that the owner had transferred   g
the ownership of the property to the buyer, who had obtained a voidable title.
The insurers also sought to distinguish *Lawrence* by contending that in that case
the student's money had not passed to the taxi driver and that the student had not
conferred on the taxi driver the rights of an owner. Furthermore, they contended,
Morris should be preferred to *Lawrence*, in so far as those cases were in conflict.   h
The respondent relied on *Lawrence* to show that an appropriation could occur,
even if the owner consented.

The Court of Appeal, dismissing the insurers' appeal, simply followed the
Lawrence approach. Parker LJ said correctly that on the basis of that case—

> 'the facts of the present case appear to establish that the rogue assumed all   j
> the rights of an owner when he took or received the watch and ring from the
> plaintiff.' (See [1989] 3 All ER 927 at 930, [1990] 1 QB 274 at 279.)

Having discussed certain arguments relating to the time when the property
passed (which were relevant to an additional and unsound argument put forward
by the insurers), he continued ([1989] 3 All ER 927 at 930–931, [1990] 1 QB 274
at 280):

a
'Having regard to the terms of the contract, the conduct of the parties and the circumstances of the case, I have no doubt that the property was not intended to pass in this case on contract but *only in exchange for a valid building society cheque*, but even if it may be regarded as intended to pass in exchange for a false, but believed genuine, building society cheque it will not in my view avail the insurers.' (My emphasis.)

b I would respectfully join issue with this statement on two grounds. (1) No doubt everyone who sells property in exchange for a cheque intends to sell only in exchange for a valid cheque. But the buyer has induced the owner to sell by the false pretence that the cheque is good. Unless the owner stipulates to the contrary, the property passes on delivery, if it has not already passed, and the buyer obtains a voidable title. (2) On any hypothesis, unless the statement in *Lawrence* is right,
c there was no theft, because the property passed with the fraudulently obtained consent of the owner and the buyer was guilty of obtaining by deception in the false pretences sense.

Dealing with a further argument of the insurers as to *when* the property passed, Parker LJ said ([1989] 3 All ER 927 at 931, [1990] 1 QB 274 at 280–281):

d
'If [the argument] were right, then the result would merely be that the making of the contract constituted the appropriation. It was by that act that the rogue assumed the rights of an owner and at that time the property did belong to the plaintiff.'

This observation merely perpetuates what I would call the *Lawrence* fallacy and
e disregards the unilateral meaning of appropriation.

Parker LJ then turned to the argument derived from *Morris* and said ([1989] 3 All ER 927 at 931, [1990] 1 QB 274 at 281):

'The difficulties caused by the apparent conflict between the decision in *Lawrence*'s case and *R v Morris* have provided, not surprisingly, a basis for
f much discussion by textbook writers and contributors of articles to law journals. It is, however, clear that their Lordships in *R v Morris* did not regard anything said in that case as conflicting with *Lawrence*'s case for it was specifically referred to in Lord Roskill's speech, with which the other members of the Appellate Committee all agreed, without disapproval or qualification. The only comment made was that, in *Lawrence*'s case, the
g House did not have to consider the precise meaning of "appropriation" in s 3(1) (see [1983] 3 All ER 288 at 292, [1984] AC 320 at 331). With respect, I find this comment hard to follow in the light of the first of the questions asked in *Lawrence*'s case and the answer to it, the passages from Viscount Dilhorne's speech already cited, the fact that it was specifically argued that
h "'Appropriates' is meant in a pejorative, rather than a neutral, sense in that the appropriation is against the will of the owner" (see [1972] AC 626 at 631 arg), and finally that dishonesty was common ground. I would have supposed that *the* question in *Lawrence*'s case was whether appropriation necessarily involved an absence of consent. Lord Roskill's comment on *Lawrence*'s case is, however, not the only difficulty presented by his speech in *R v Morris*, but
j before I consider other difficulties it is necessary to set out in short form the facts of the two cases considered in that speech.' (Parker LJ's emphasis.)

Then, having stated the facts, he criticised in some detail the reasoning in *Morris* (see [1989] 3 All ER 927 at 932–934, [1990] 1 QB 274 at 282–285) and considered *R v Skipp* [1975] Crim LR 114 and *R v Fritschy* [1985] Crim LR 745. It is true that *Morris* contains no disapproval or qualification of *Lawrence*, but, in my view, the

main statements of principle in these cases cannot possibly be reconciled and the
later case therefore must not be regarded as providing any support for the earlier. *a*
  Coming back to *Dobson*, Parker LJ rightly observed that the insurers' main
arguments were negatived by *Lawrence* and concluded ([1989] 3 All ER 927 at
935, [1990] 1 QB 274 at 286):

> 'I am fully conscious of the fact that in so concluding I may be said not to
> be applying *R v Morris*. This may be so, but in the light of the difficulties *b*
> inherent in the decision, the very clear decision in *Lawrence's* case and the
> equally clear statement in *R v Morris* that the question whether a contract is
> void or only voidable is irrelevant, I have been unable to reach any other
> conclusion. I would therefore dismiss the appeal.'

Bingham LJ, when considering the meaning of s 1(1), attached importance to the
omission of the words 'without the consent of the owner'. I have already *c*
commented on this point. Having adverted briefly to supermarket offences, he
then said ([1989] 3 All ER 927 at 936, [1990] 1 QB 274 at 287–288):

> 'This analysis appears to me to have been authoritatively adopted by the
> House of Lords in *Lawrence v Comr of Police for the Metropolis* [1971] 2 All ER
> 1253, [1972] AC 626. The first question certified was: "Whether Section 1(1) *d*
> of the Theft Act, 1968 is to be construed as though it contained the words
> 'without the consent of the owner' or words to that effect." The House
> answered the question with an emphatic No, requiring no argument from
> the prosecutor and expressing surprise that the Court of Appeal had certified
> the question as fit for the consideration of the House. Although it appears *e*
> that the Italian student who was the victim in the case permitted or allowed
> the taxi driver to take £6 from his wallet, Viscount Dilhorne (with whose
> speech the other members of the House agreed) was in no doubt that there
> had been an appropriation. He said ([1971] 2 All ER 1253 at 1255, [1972] AC
> 626 at 632): "Belief or the absence of belief that the owner had with such
> knowledge consented to the appropriation is relevant to the issue of *f*
> dishonesty, not to the question whether or not there has been an appropriation.
> That may occur even though the owner has permitted or consented to the
> property being taken."'

Turning to *Morris*, Bingham LJ said ([1989] 3 All ER 927 at 937, [1990] 1 QB 274
at 289):   *g*

> 'Reference was not made to Viscount Dilhorne's ruling that appropriation
> may occur even though the owner has permitted or consented to the property
> being taken. I do not find it easy to reconcile this ruling of Viscount Dilhorne,
> which was as I understand central to the answer which the House of Lords
> gave to the certified question, with the reasoning of the House in *R v Morris*. *h*
> Since, however, the House in *R v Morris* considered that there had plainly
> been an appropriation in *Lawrence's* case, this must (I think) have been
> because the Italian student, although he had permitted or allowed his money
> to be taken, had not in truth consented to the taxi driver taking anything in
> excess of the correct fare. This is not a wholly satisfactory reconciliation, since
> it might be said that a supermarket consents to customers taking goods from *j*
> its shelves only when they honestly intend to pay and not otherwise. On the
> facts of the present case, however, it can be said, by analogy with *Lawrence's*
> case, that although the plaintiff permitted and allowed his property to be
> taken by the rogue, he had not in truth consented to the rogue becoming
> owner *without giving a valid draft* drawn by the building society for the price.

On this basis I conclude that the plaintiff is able to show an appropriation
a sufficient to satisfy s 1(1) of the 1968 Act when the rogue accepted delivery
of the articles.' (My emphasis.)

I consider that Bingham LJ's rationalisation of the failure of *Morris* to disapprove
of *Lawrence* is of some significance. I have already commented, when discussing
the judgment of Parker LJ, on the seller's expectation that he would receive a
b valid cheque. In short, *Dobson* follows the erroneous interpretation which was
endowed with authority by *Lawrence* and was therefore, in my respectful opinion,
wrongly decided. I would refer with respectful approval to Professor Smith's
commentary on *Dobson* (see [1990] Crim LR at 273–274).

The judgment in the Court of Appeal in this case, which was delivered by
Lord Lane CJ, puts the matter clearly ([1991] 3 All ER 394 at 398, [1991] 1 WLR
c 1334 at 1338):

'What in fact happened was that the owner was induced by deceit to agree
to the goods being transferred to Ballay. If that is the case, and if in these
circumstances the appellant is guilty of theft, it must follow that anyone who
obtains goods in return for a cheque which he knows will be dishonoured on
d presentation, or indeed by way of any other similar pretence, would be guilty
of theft. That does not seem to be the law. *R v Morris* decides that when a
person by dishonest deception induces the owner to transfer his entire
proprietary interests that is not theft. There is no appropriation at the
moment when he takes possession of the goods because he was entitled to do
so under the terms of the contract of sale, a contract which is, it is true,
e voidable, but has not been avoided at the time the goods are handed over.'

Exception has been taken by some commentators to the words '*R v Morris*
decides', but the proposition which is stated in the judgment of the court follows
inevitably from Lord Roskill's statement as to the meaning of appropriation.
Having reviewed the judgment in *Dobson*, Lord Lane CJ said ([1991] 3 All ER
f 394 at 399–400, [1991] 1 WLR 1334 at 1339–1340):

'We do not consider that the judgment in *Dobson*'s case requires or allows
us to disregard what we have earlier in this judgment sought to extract as the
ratio of the decision in *R v Morris*. We therefore conclude that there was a de
facto, albeit voidable, contract between the owners and Ballay, that it was by
g virtue of that contract that Ballay took possession of the goods, that
accordingly the transfer of the goods to him was with the consent and express
authority of the owner and that accordingly there was no lack of authorisation
and no appropriation. In the absence of any charge under s 15 of the 1968
Act, this appeal must therefore be allowed and the conviction quashed.'

h I respectfully agree.

My Lords, to sum up, every indication seems to me to point away from
adopting a neutral meaning of the word 'appropriation'. I would reinforce that
view by recalling that in *George Wimpey & Co Ltd v British Overseas Airways Corp*
[1954] 3 All ER 661 at 672–673, [1955] AC 169 at 191 Lord Reid stated that if
the arguments are fairly evenly balanced (not that I believe they are in this case),
j that interpretation should be chosen which involves the least alteration of the
existing law. *Maxwell on Interpretation of Statutes* (12th edn, 1969) p 116 states:

'Few principles of statutory interpretation are applied as frequently as the
presumption against alterations in the common law. It is presumed that the
legislature does not intend to make any change in the existing law beyond

that which is expressly stated in, or follows by necessary implication from, the language of the statute in question.'   *a*

If the change in the law of theft which is signalled by decisions such as that reached in *Dobson* has in reality occurred, the position of insurers in that field has in the result been prejudiced by legislation the effect of which was far from clear.

I come back to the word 'assumption' in s 3(1). If it is said that that word is capable of a neutral meaning, my answer is that, in order to read s 3(1)   *b* harmoniously with s 1(1) in its natural sense, 'assumption' must receive a unilateral meaning. So to limit the interpretation of the word would follow the principle that words in a statute which have, or can have, a general meaning may have to be given a specialised and narrower meaning in order to make sense of the legislation and to avoid the conclusion that changes have been made to the   *c* existing law which cannot have been intended by Parliament. This principle must be stronger when, as in the present case, the specialised and narrower meaning is also the primary meaning.

Not only *Lawrence* and *Morris*, but a large number of cases on s 1(1), have furnished the material for animated and often penetrating academic discussion. I am encouraged to have seen that submissions based on such discussion are   *d* increasingly made by counsel and entertained by the courts and your Lordships have in the present appeal benefited from counsel's industry in this respect. I could not possibly do justice in this speech to all that has been written on the subject, but I hope that I have profited from the many articles which I have read since the hearing. Perhaps because his view on the main point is the same as mine, but certainly because I consider it to be a clear exposition, I here reproduce   *e* the statement of Professor J C Smith in *Law of Theft* (6th edn, 1989) ch 2, para 31 on which Mr Hacking QC strongly relied:

'The Larceny Act 1916 required that the taking and carrying away should be "without the consent of the owner". The absence of the owner's consent was an essential feature of the trespassory taking which had to be proved.   *f* The omission of these words from the definition of theft lends some support to the argument that an act may amount to an appropriation although it is done with the consent of the owner. The omission of the words is, however, sufficiently accounted for by the fact that they were part of the definition of the trespassory taking which it was a principal object of the 1968 Act to   *g* abolish. It is not a reason for giving to the word "appropriate" a meaning narrower than it would naturally bear. The Larceny Act itself provided for an alternative form of stealing—larceny by a bailee who "fraudulently converts" the bailed goods. The section did not say "converts without the consent of the owner". That would have been absurd because the word "converts", itself implied that the bailee had done something with the bailed   *h* goods which was not authorised by the terms of the bailment. Similarly, fraudulent conversion, contrary to s. 20(1)(iv) of the Larceny Act, required an act inconsistent with the terms on which the property was received. Section 20(1)(iv) was the model for the definition of theft and "appropriate" was intended to bear the same meaning. If "converts" in the 1916 Act implied an unauthorised act, notwithstanding its proximity to the definition   *j* of larceny with its requirement of the absence of the owner's consent, there is, a fortiori, no reason why the word "appropriates" in the Theft Act should not be similarly construed. In *Morris* the House of Lords held that "In the context of s. 3(1), the concept of appropriation ... involves not an act

a
expressly or impliedly authorised by the owner but an act by way of adverse
interference with or usurpation of [the owner's] rights." This statement by
Lord Roskill, with whom all their Lordships agreed, was probably an *obiter
dictum* since there was no doubt in that case that the act was done without the
consent of the owner. It is submitted that it is correct in principle. It is in
accord with the legal meaning of "converts", and with the natural meaning
of "appropriates" which suggests "helping oneself" to the property of another.

b
A person does not "assume" the rights of an owner if the owner has conferred
those rights on him.'

To the same effect is Professor Smith's comment on *R v Shuck* [1992] Crim LR
209 at 211–213. Referring to *Lawrence*, he says (ch 2, para 32):

c
'One of the questions of law of general public importance which the House
was required to answer was—"Whether s. 1(1) of the Theft Act 1968 is to be
construed as though it contained the words 'without having the consent of
the owner' or words to that effect." Viscount Dilhorne, with whom the whole
House concurred, dealt with the matter with extreme brevity. He said, "In
my opinion, the answer is clearly No." The answer to the question played no

d
part in the actual decision. Viscount Dilhorne had already decided that the
appeal should be dismissed before he turned to it. The certificate asked the
wrong question and merited the short shrift which it received. The expression
"appropriates without the consent of the owner", would have been just as
inept as "converts without the consent of the owner".'

e
I also found helpful Professor Smith's further comment (para 41) on *Lawrence*.
I would in addition commend to your Lordships an article by Giles and Uglow,
'Appropriation and manifest criminality in theft' (1992) 56 J Cr L 179, which is
distinguished by its regard for principle and the absence of undue deference to
dubious judicial pronouncements.

f
My Lords, I think I have in passing taken account of most of the points made
in the pro-*Lawrence* academic contributions to the debate. I feel no qualms about
taking sides against these contributions, nearly all of which seem to me to
disregard the Criminal Law Revision Committee report and to neglect to analyse
the meaning in its context of the word 'appropriate'. Moreover, they choose to
disregard the ordinary law governing the transfer of title, calling it the civil law,

g
as if to contrast it with the criminal law and thus render it surplus to requirements.
At least Bingham LJ refused to fall in with this idea, saying in *Dobson* [1989] 3 All
ER 927 at 937, [1990] 1 QB 274 at 289:

'But whether, in the ordinary case to which s 5 of the 1968 Act does not
apply, goods are to be regarded as belonging to another is a question to which

h
the criminal law offers no answer and which can only be answered by
reference to civil law principles.'

Accordingly, it is both proper and rational to rely on such cases as *Phillips v
Brooks Ltd* [1919] 2 KB 243, [1918–19] All ER Rep 246 and *Lewis v Averay* [1971]
3 All ER 907 at 912, [1972] 1 QB 198 at 207.

j
My Lords, having drafted this speech, I then had the pleasure and advantage of
reading in draft the speech to be delivered by my noble and learned friend
Lord Browne-Wilkinson and concluded that I ought to refer to the company
fraud cases which were canvassed before your Lordships, lest it be thought that
the *Morris* statement of principle is inconsistent with a proper approach to such

cases. I fully agree with Lord Browne-Wilkinson's observation that the dictum in
Morris has led to confusion and complication where those in de facto control have   *a*
been charged with theft from a company and I, too, consider, on the basis (which
he assumes only for the sake of argument) that the *Morris* dictum is correct, that
it would be wrong, when a person who by virtue of his position in the company
constitutes 'the directing mind and will of the company' is accused of stealing
from the company, to acquit that person on the ground that, in his capacity as the
company, he has consented to the taking (by himself) of the company's property,   *b*
with the result that no appropriation, and therefore no theft, has occurred. The
reason why acquittal would be wrong is explained by Lord Browne-Wilkinson:

> 'Where a company is accused of a crime the acts and intentions of those
> who are the directing minds and will of the company are to be attributed to   *c*
> the company. That is not the law where the charge is that those who are the
> directing minds and will have themselves committed a crime against the
> company . . .'

(I refer, on this point, to *A-G's Reference (No 2 of 1982)* [1984] 2 All ER 216 at 223,
[1984] QB 624 at 640.) Of course, if the principle enunciated in *Lawrence* is   *d*
followed, the error identified above cannot possibly arise, because the question
whether the company has consented to the taking of its property ceases to matter,
so long as the property is taken dishonestly with the intention of permanently
depriving the company of it. But the fact that the *Morris* principle can be
misapplied to a company theft case (and that the *Lawrence* principle cannot be so
misapplied) is not an argument for saying that the *Morris* dictum is wrong and   *e*
the *Lawrence* dictum right. The mistake is to say that a 'directing mind' accused
is to be treated as having validly consented on behalf of the company to his own
dishonest taking of the company's property. Provided that mistake is avoided, the
Morris principle poses no threat to a just outcome in company theft cases.

The company and the person (or persons) constituting the directing mind are   *f*
two (or more) separate persons: *Salomon v A Salomon & Co Ltd* [1897] AC 22,
[1895–99] All ER Rep 33. That fact should be easily appreciated when the
company is the victim of the other person (or persons). The 'directing mind',
when taking the company's property, does a unilateral act, to the prejudice of the
company, which the company does not authorise or consent to. My Lords, if I
may revert to the proposition that a person cannot consent to the theft of property   *g*
from himself, it is absurd to suppose that a company consents to the theft of its
own property, merely because the thief is for most purposes of the company its
directing mind. The act of the directing mind is here unilateral and not consensual
and bilateral.

In *A-G's Reference (No 2 of 1982)*, where the trial judge had directed an acquittal,
the following question was referred for the opinion of the Court of Appeal: *h*

> 'Whether a man in total control of a limited liability company (by reason
> of his shareholding and directorship) is capable of stealing the property of the
> company; and whether two men in total control of a limited liability
> company (by reason of their shareholdings and directorships) are (while   *
> acting in concert) capable of jointly stealing the property of the company.'   *j*

Kerr LJ, delivering the court's affirmative answer, mentioned the Crown's
arguments, which had included reliance on *Lawrence*, and the defendants'
concessions that appropriation had occurred and (in the light of *Lawrence*) that the
absence of the owner's consent was no longer an essential ingredient of theft. But

the court rejected the submissions that, as the sole owners of the property, the
a defendants could not steal from themselves and that they were bound to succeed
under s 2(1)(*b*) (appropriation in the belief that the taker would have the owner's
consent). In these respects, as your Lordships can see, the *Lawrence* principle was
not essential to the reasoning. *Tesco Supermarkets Ltd v Nattrass* [1971] 2 All ER
127, [1972] AC 153 merely showed that—

b   'in situations like the present the defendants "are" the company in the
          sense that any offences committed by them in relation to the affairs of the
          company would be capable of being treated as offences committed by the
          company itself. The decision has no bearing on offences committed against
          the company.' (See [1984] 2 All ER 216 at 223, [1984] QB 624 at 640.)

c Then, having referred to the need for belief under s 2(1)(*b*) to be an honest belief,
Kerr LJ, delivering the opinion of the court, said ([1984] 2 All ER 216 at 224,
[1984] QB 624 at 642):

          'Second, we do not consider that in circumstances such as those alleged in
          the present case s 2(1)(*b*) has any application or that it can provide the basis
          for any defence. The essence of the defendants' argument is the alleged
d   identity, in all respects, and for every purpose, between the defendants and
          the company. It is said, in effect, that their acts are necessarily the company's
          acts, that their will, knowledge and belief are those of the company and that
          their consent necessarily implies consent by the company. But how then can
          the company be regarded as "the other" for the purposes of *this* provision?
          One merely has to read its wording to see that it cannot be given any sensible
e   meaning in a context such as the present, where the mind and will of the
          defendants are also treated in law as the mind and will of "the other". It is for
          this reason that in such cases there can be [no] conspiracy between the
          directors and shareholders on the one hand and the company on the other:
          see *R v McDonnell* [1966] 1 All ER 193, [1966] 1 QB 233.' (Kerr LJ's emphasis.)

f Accordingly, *A-G's Reference* (*No 2 of 1982*) does not depend on *Lawrence* for the
undoubted validity of its conclusions and is consistent with *Morris*. Again, *R v
Philippou* (1989) 89 Cr App R 290 was correctly decided by the Court of Appeal.
For the reasons which I have given above I do not think the court in *R v Philippou*
were justified in reconciling *Morris* with *Lawrence*, but they were correct in
following *A-G's Reference* (*No 2 of 1982*) and could have reached their conclusion
g without relying on *Lawrence*.
    R v Philippou disapproved of the decision in *R v Roffel* [1985] VR 511, where a
husband and wife ran a small clothing manufacturing business. They then
formed a limited company of which they became the sole directors and
shareholders and sold the business to the company. The price remained unpaid.
h The company's premises were destroyed by fire and the proceeds of insurance
were paid into the company's bank account. The company's debts exceeded the
proceeds of the insurance. The husband drew cheques on the company's account
and was prosecuted for theft from the company and convicted. The Supreme
Court of Victoria by a majority quashed the conviction on appeal, holding that,
under the Crimes Act 1958 (which in its amended form corresponded closely
j with the 1968 Act), the necessary element of appropriation required proof of
adverse interference with or usurpation of some right or rights of the owner
(*Morris*). As the company was a separate legal entity, and in the particular
circumstances (through its directing mind and will) had consented to the
husband's drawing the cheques, it could not be said that he had appropriated the
company's property. The decision must, with respect, be regarded as a

misapplication of *Morris*, since the majority relied on *Tesco Supermarkets Ltd v Nattrass* for the directing mind doctrine and refused to apply *A-G's Reference (No 2 of 1982)*, insisting that the transaction between the husband and the company was 'consensual'. Brooking J, on the other hand, accepted *A-G's Reference (No 2 of 1982)* and would have upheld the conviction, even assuming that *Morris* should be followed (at 526–527). In fairness I must add that he indorsed the *Lawrence* principle. The lesson, however, is, in my opinion, that the company cases can be satisfactorily and justly resolved without discrediting the *Morris* dictum.

In my opinion, any attempt to reconcile the statements of principle in *Lawrence* and *Morris* is a complete waste of time. And certainly reconciliation cannot be achieved by the unattractive solution of varying the meaning of 'appropriation' in different provisions of the 1968 Act. It is clear that, whether they succeeded or not, both the committee and the draftsman must have intended to give the word one meaning, which would be the same in the Act as in the report.

To simplify the law, where possible, is a worthy objective but, my Lords, I maintain that the law, as envisaged in the report, is simple enough: there is no problem (and there would have been none in *Lawrence, Morris* and the present case) if one prosecutes under s 15 all offences involving obtaining by deception and prosecutes theft in general under s 1. In that way some thefts will come under s 15, but no 'false pretences' will come under s 1.

The respondent can already count himself lucky to have received only a two-year sentence, having regard to the amount involved and to the position of trust which he held. He will be even more fortunate if he has his conviction quashed, since there was against him an open and shut case under s 15. But, if I am right in my analysis, one cannot simply be content to say that, if his conviction is restored, the respondent will have suffered no injustice. The right legal answer, based on the true meaning of the 1968 Act, must be found and applied.

If my submissions are correct, the question finally remains whether your Lordships are bound by the doctrine of precedent to follow and apply the statements in *Lawrence* [1971] 2 All ER 1253 at 1255, [1972] AC 626 at 632 that Parliament, by omitting the words 'without the consent of the owner' from s 1(1) of the 1968 Act, has 'relieved the prosecution of the burden of establishing that the taking was without the owner's consent' and that '[appropriation] may occur even though the owner has permitted or consented to the property being taken'. I suggest not. In the first place, Viscount Dilhorne had already expressed the opinion that the facts of the case fell far short of establishing that the victim had consented to the acquisition by the appellant of the money he was alleged to have stolen. This line of reasoning (though not the approach of the Court of Appeal in *Lawrence*) supports a conviction for theft under s 1(1) on any view of the law and enables your Lordships to regard the statements as obiter dicta. Secondly, it follows that *Dobson*, the only case of authority on the point which is at the heart of this appeal (which case in any event is not binding on your Lordships), applied the obiter dicta in *Lawrence* to reach an erroneous conclusion. Thirdly, Lord Roskill's statement in *Morris*, while it may be obiter, contradicts Viscount Dilhorne's.

Lastly, let me assume that Viscount Dilhorne's statements have the character of a 'decision' as that word is used in the practice statement on judicial precedent (see *Note* [1966] 3 All ER 77, [1966] 1 WLR 1234), which intimated that this House would depart from a previous decision 'when it appears right to do so'. Your Lordships might then so elect. The statement referred to 'the especial need for certainty as to the criminal law', but there is ample proof that both before and after *Morris* certainty has been lacking. The cases on the practice statement are conveniently found in 26 *Halsbury's Laws* (4th edn) para 577. A previous decision

should not be departed from merely because the House considers it to be wrong
a and only rarely should questions of construction be reconsidered. But the precise
meaning of s 1(1) has not received serious judicial attention before. Furthermore,
your Lordships may feel that it is inconvenient and undesirable for the criminal
law as enunciated in *Lawrence* and *Dobson* to be in conflict with the law affecting
the title to money and other kinds of property.

b   Accordingly, for the reasons already given, I would dismiss the Crown's appeal.

LORD BROWNE-WILKINSON. My Lords, I have read the speech of my
noble and learned friend Lord Keith of Kinkel, with which I agree. I only add a
few words of my own out of deference to the contrary view expressed by my
noble and learned friend Lord Lowry and to consider the cases on thefts from
companies to which we were referred in the course of argument.
c   In *Lawrence v Comr of Police for the Metropolis* [1970] 3 All ER 933 at 935, [1971]
1 QB 373 at 376 Megaw LJ in the Court of Appeal analysed the constituent
elements of the offence created by s 1(1) of the Theft Act 1968 as being '(i) a
dishonest (ii) appropriation (iii) of property belonging to another (iv) with the
intention of permanently depriving the owner of it.' This analysis was adopted
d and approved by this House (see [1971] 2 All ER 1253, [1972] AC 626) and I do
not intend to cast any doubt on it. But it should not be overlooked that elements
(i) and (ii) (unlike elements (iii) and (iv)) are interlinked: element (i) (dishonest) is
an adjectival description of element (ii) (appropriation). Parliament has used a
composite phrase 'dishonest appropriation'. Thus it is not every appropriation
which falls within the section but only an act which answers the composite
e description.
    The fact that Parliament used that composite phrase 'dishonest appropriation'
in my judgment casts light on what is meant by the word 'appropriation'. The
views expressed (obiter) by this House in *R v Morris* [1983] 3 All ER 288 at 293,
[1984] AC 320 at 332 that 'appropriation' involves an act by way of adverse
interference with or usurpation of the rights of the owner treats the word
f 'appropriation' as being tantamount to 'misappropriation'. The concept of adverse
interference with or usurpation of rights introduces into the word 'appropriation'
the mental state of both the owner and the accused. So far as concerns the mental
state of the owner (did he consent?), the 1968 Act expressly refers to such consent
when it is a material factor: see ss 2(1)(b), 11(1), 12(1) and 13. So far as concerns
g the mental state of the accused, the composite phrase in s 1(1) itself indicates that
the requirement is dishonesty.
    For myself, therefore, I regard the word 'appropriation' in isolation as being an
objective description of the act done irrespective of the mental state of either the
owner or the accused. It is impossible to reconcile the decision in *Lawrence* (that
the question of consent is irrelevant in considering whether this has been an
h appropriation) with the views expressed in *Morris*, which latter views in my
judgment were incorrect.
    It is suggested that this conclusion renders s 15 of the 1968 Act otiose since a
person who, by deception, persuades the owner to consent to part with his
property will necessarily be guilty of theft within s 1. This may be so though I
venture to doubt it. Take for example a man who obtains land by deception. Save
j as otherwise expressly provided, the definitions in ss 4 and 5 of the 1968 Act apply
only for the purposes of interpreting s 1 of that Act: see s 1(3). Section 34(1)
applies ss 4(1) and 5(1) generally for the purposes of the 1968 Act. Accordingly
the other subsections of ss 4 and 5 do not apply to s 15. Suppose that a fraudster
has persuaded a victim to part with his house: the fraudster is not guilty of theft
of the land since s 4(2) provides that you cannot steal land. The charge could only

be laid under s 15, which contains no provisions excluding land from the
definition of property. Therefore, although there is a substantial overlap between *a*
s 1 and s 15, s 15 is not otiose.

Turning to the company cases, the dictum in *Morris* has led to much confusion
and complication where those in de facto control of the company have been
charged with theft from it. The argument which has found favour in certain of
the authorities runs as follows. There can be no theft within s 1 if the owner
consents to what is done: *Morris*. If the accused, by reason of being the controlling *b*
shareholder or otherwise, is 'the directing mind and will of the company' he is to
be treated as having validly consented on behalf of the company to his own
appropriation of the company's property. This is apparently so whether or not
there has been compliance with the formal requirements of company law
applicable to dealings with the property of a company and even to cases where
the consent relied on is ultra vires: see *R v Roffel* [1985] VR 511 and *R v McHugh* *c*
(1988) 88 Cr App R 385.

In my judgment this approach was wrong in law even if the dictum in *Morris*
had been correct. Where a company is accused of a crime the acts and intentions
of those who are the directing minds and will of the company are to be attributed
to the company. That is not the law where the charge is that those who are the *d*
directing minds and will have themselves committed a crime against the
company: see *A-G's Reference (No 2 of 1982)* [1984] 2 All ER 216, [1984] QB 624
applying *Belmont Finance Corp Ltd v Williams Furniture Ltd* [1979] 1 All ER 118,
[1979] Ch 250.

In any event, your Lordships' decision in this case, re-establishing as it does the
decision in *Lawrence*, renders the whole question of consent by the company *e*
irrelevant. Whether or not those controlling the company consented or purported
to consent to the abstraction of the company's property by the accused, he will
have appropriated the property of the company. The question will be whether
the other necessary elements are present, viz was such appropriation dishonest
and was it done with the intention of permanently depriving the company of
such property? In my judgment the decision in *R v Roffel* and the statements of *f*
principle in *R v McHugh* (1988) 88 Cr App R 385 at 393 are not correct in law and
should not be followed. As for *A-G's Reference (No 2 of 1982)*, in my judgment
both the concession made by counsel (that there had been an appropriation) and
the decision in that case were correct, as was the decision in *R v Philippou* (1989)
89 Cr App R 290.

I am glad to be able to reach this conclusion. The pillaging of companies by *g*
those who control them is now all too common. It would offend both common
sense and justice to hold that the very control which enables such people to extract
the company's assets constitutes a defence to a charge of theft from the company.
The question in each case must be whether the extraction of the property from
the company was dishonest, not whether the alleged thief has consented to his *h*
own wrongdoing.

LORD SLYNN OF HADLEY. My Lords, I agree with my noble and learned
friend Lord Keith of Kinkel, whose draft speech I have had the opportunity to
read, that, for the reasons he gives, the appeal should be allowed and the questions *j*
answered in the way he proposes.

Appeal allowed. Conviction restored.

Mary Rose Plummer   Barrister.

a
Practice Note

COURT OF APPEAL, CRIMINAL DIVISION
LORD TAYLOR OF GOSFORTH CJ, POPPLEWELL AND LAWS JJ
16 DECEMBER 1992

b Crown Court – Distribution of court business – Serious and complex fraud cases – Places of trial – Supreme Court Act 1981, s 75(1) – Criminal Justice Act 1987, s 51(1).

LORD TAYLOR OF GOSFORTH CJ gave the following direction at the sitting of the court.

1. With the concurrence of the Lord Chancellor and pursuant to s 75(1) of the
c Supreme Court Act 1981 I make with effect from 1 January 1993 the following direction with regard to the place of trial for cases of serious and complex fraud transferred to the Crown Court under the Criminal Justice Act 1987.

2. The proposed place of trial specified in the notice of transfer under s 5(1) of the Criminal Justice Act 1987 shall be one of the following Crown Court centres:

d Circuit	Centres	Circuit	Centres
Midland and Oxford	Birmingham	Wales and Chester	Cardiff
	Leicester		Chester
	Northampton		Mold
	Nottingham		Swansea
	Oxford		Warrington
e	Stafford		
	Wolverhampton	Western	Bristol
			Exeter
North Eastern	Bradford		Plymouth
	Leeds		Portsmouth
	Newcastle		Southampton
f	Sheffield		Winchester
	Teesside		
Northern	Liverpool		
South Eastern	Aylesbury		
	Central Criminal Court		
g	Chelmsford		
	Guildford		
	Isleworth		
	Knightsbridge		
	Maidstone		
h	Middlesex Guildhall		
	Norwich		
	Snaresbrook		
	Southwark		
	Wood Green		

j 3. The Practice Direction of 2 October 1990 (see *Practice Note* [1990] 3 All ER 320, [1990] 1 WLR 1310) is hereby revoked.

N P Metcalfe Esq   Barrister.

Pepper (Inspector of Taxes) v Hart and related appeals

HOUSE OF LORDS

LORD BRIDGE OF HARWICH, LORD GRIFFITHS, LORD EMSLIE, LORD OLIVER OF AYLMERTON
AND LORD BROWNE-WILKINSON

4 FEBRUARY 1991

LORD MACKAY OF CLASHFERN LC, LORD KEITH OF KINKEL, LORD BRIDGE OF HARWICH,
LORD GRIFFITHS, LORD ACKNER, LORD OLIVER OF AYLMERTON AND LORD BROWNE-
WILKINSON

8–11, 17–18 JUNE, 26 NOVEMBER 1992

Income tax – Emoluments from office or employment – Benefits derived by directors and higher-paid employees from employment – Cash equivalent of benefit – Cost of providing benefit – Concessionary fees scheme operated by school for sons of teaching staff – Whether cost of benefit limited to additional costs directly incurred by school in providing benefit – Finance Act 1976, ss 61(1), 63(1)(2).

Statute – Construction – Hansard – Reference to proceedings in Parliament as an aid to construction – Ambiguous or obscure legislation – Whether court may look at parliamentary history of legislation or Hansard as aid to interpretation – Whether use of Hansard contravening Bill of Rights – Whether use of Hansard breach of parliamentary privilege – Bill of Rights (1688), s 1, art 9.

The taxpayers were nine masters and the bursar at an independent boys' school. Under a concessionary fees scheme operated by the school for members of its teaching staff the taxpayers' sons were educated at the school for one-fifth of the fees ordinarily charged to members of the public. The concessionary fees more than covered the additional cost to the school of educating the taxpayers' sons and since in the relevant years the school was not full to capacity their admission did not cause the school to lose full fees which would otherwise have been paid by members of the public for the places so occupied. The education of the taxpayers' sons at reduced fees was a taxable benefit under s 61(1)[a] of the Finance Act 1976 and the taxpayers were assessed to income tax on the 'cash equivalent' of that benefit on the basis that they were liable for a rateable proportion of the expenses in running the school as a whole for all the boys, which proportion was roughly equal to the amount of the ordinary school fees. By s 63(1)[b] of the 1976 Act the cash equivalent of the benefit was 'an amount equal to the cost of the benefit' and by s 63(2) the cost of the benefit was 'the amount of any expense incurred in or in connection with its provision'. The taxpayers appealed against the assessments, claiming that since all the costs of running the school generally would have had to be incurred in any event the only expense incurred by the school 'in or in connection' with the education of their sons was the small additional or marginal cost to the school caused by the presence of their sons, which was covered by the fees they paid, and so the 'cash equivalent of the benefit' was nil. The Crown contended that the 'expense incurred in or in connection with' the provision of education for the taxpayers' sons was exactly the same as the expense incurred in or in connection with the education of all other pupils at the school and accordingly the expense of educating any one child was a proportionate part of the cost of running the whole school. The Special Commissioner allowed the taxpayers' appeals, holding that since the taxpayers' sons occupied only surplus

---

a   Section 61(1) is set out at p 53 j, post
b   Section 63, so far as material, is set out at p 54 a b, post

a places at the school at the school's discretion and the fees paid by the taxpayers fully covered and reimbursed the cost to the school of educating the taxpayers' sons no tax was payable by the taxpayers. The judge allowed an appeal by the Crown and his decision was affirmed by the Court of Appeal. The taxpayers appealed to the House of Lords, where it became apparent that an examination of the proceedings in Parliament in 1976 which led to the enactment of ss 61 and 63 might give a clear indication whether Parliament intended that the cost of the *b* benefit, ie 'the amount of any expense incurred in or in connection with its provision', in s 63(2) meant the actual expense incurred by the school in providing the benefit or the average cost of the provision of the benefit, the latter being very close to a market value test. The House then heard submissions on the questions whether it would be appropriate to depart from previous authority prohibiting the courts from referring to parliamentary materials in construing statutory *c* provisions and whether the use of Hansard in such circumstances would be an infringement of s 1, art 9^c of the Bill of Rights (1688) or a breach of parliamentary privilege.

Held – (1) (Lord Mackay LC dissenting) Having regard to the purposive approach *d* to construction of legislation the courts had adopted in order to give effect to the true intention of the legislature, the rule prohibiting courts from referring to parliamentary material as an aid to statutory construction should, subject to any question of parliamentary privilege, be relaxed so as to permit reference to parliamentary materials where (a) the legislation was ambiguous or obscure or the literal meaning led to an absurdity, (b) the material relied on consisted of *e* statements by a minister or other promoter of the Bill which lead to the enactment of the legislation together if necessary with such other parliamentary material as was necessary to understand such statements and their effect and (c) the statements relied on were clear. Furthermore, the use of parliamentary material as a guide to the construction of ambiguous legislation would not infringe s 1, art 9 of the Bill of Rights since it would not amount to a 'questioning' of the freedom of speech *f* or parliamentary debate provided counsel and the judge refrained from impugning or criticising the minister's statements or his reasoning, since the purpose of the courts in referring to parliamentary material would be to give effect to, rather than thwart through ignorance, the intentions of Parliament and not to question the processes by which such legislation was enacted or to criticise anything said *g* by anyone in Parliament in the course of enacting it (see p 49 *b f* to *j*, p 50 *b* to *d*, p 51 *j*, p 52 *a d e*, p 53 *b c*, p 64 *d e j*, p 66 *b c*, p 67 *e j*, p 68 *b c j* to p 69 *a e*, p 73 *d* and p 74 *e f*, post); dictum of Lord Reid in *Warner v Metropolitan Police Comr* [1968] 2 All ER 356 at 367, *Pickstone v Freemans plc* [1988] 2 All ER 803 and *Brind v Secretary of State for the Home Dept* [1991] 1 All ER 720 applied; *Church of Scientology of California v Johnson-Smith* [1972] 1 All ER 378 distinguished; dicta of *h* Lord Reid in *Beswick v Beswick* [1967] 2 All ER 1197 at 1202, of Lord Reid and Lord Wilberforce in *Black-Clawson International Ltd v Papierwerke Waldhof-Aschaffenburg AG* [1975] 1 All ER 810 at 814–815, 828 and of Lord Scarman in *Davis v Johnson* [1978] 1 All ER 1132 at 1157 not followed; dictum of Dunn LJ in *R v Secretary of State for Trade, ex p Anderson Strathclyde plc* [1983] 2 All ER 233 at 239 overruled.
j (2) (Per Lord Keith, Lord Bridge, Lord Griffiths, Lord Ackner, Lord Oliver and Lord Browne-Wilkinson) Section 63(2) of the 1976 Act was clearly ambiguous because the 'expense incurred in or in connection with' the provision of in-house benefits could be interpreted as being either the marginal cost caused by the provision of the benefit in question or a proportion of the total cost incurred in

---

c   Section 1, art 9 is set out at p 55 *j*, post

providing the service both for the public and for the employee (the average cost). However, the parliamentary history of the 1976 Act and statements made by the Financial Secretary to the Treasury during the committee stage of the Bill made it clear that Parliament had passed the legislation on the basis that the effect of ss 61 and 63 was to assess in-house benefits, and particularly concessionary education for teachers' children, on the marginal cost to the employer and not on the average cost of the benefit. Accordingly (per curiam, Lord Mackay LC so construing the section in any event and Lord Griffiths resolving the ambiguity in the taxpayers' favour) s 63 should be given that meaning (see p 46 *e* to *h*, p 47 *a*, p 49 *b d* to *f*, p 50 *c g h*, p 51 *g* to *j*, p 52 *a j* to p 53 *b*, p 66 *h j*, p 69 *f g*, p 70 *d*, p 71 *c* to *f j* and p 73 *b c*, post).

(3) (Per Lord Keith, Lord Bridge, Lord Griffiths, Lord Ackner, Lord Oliver and Lord Browne-Wilkinson) Since the Crown had not identified or specified the nature of any parliamentary privilege going beyond that protected by the Bill of Rights, there was no defined privilege as to the existence and validity of which the House in its judicial capacity would otherwise have been entitled to make a determination, and it would therefore not be right to withhold from the taxpayers the benefit of a decision to which, in law, they were entitled. Accordingly (Lord Mackay LC concurring) the appeal would be allowed (see p 47 *b*, p 49 *b f j*, p 50 *c*, p 51 *h j*, p 52 *a*, p 53 *b*, p 71 *j* and p 74 *c d*, post).

Decision of the Court of Appeal [1991] 2 All ER 824 reversed.

Notes
For the tax treatment of cash equivalent of benefits to employees, see 23 *Halsbury's Laws* (4th edn reissue) paras 729, 735.

For statutory construction where statute ambiguous, see 44 *Halsbury's Laws* (4th edn) paras 858, 901, and for cases on the subject, see 45 *Digest* (Reissue) 405–409, 3898–3966.

For proceedings in Parliament as aids to the construction of statutes, see 44 *Halsbury's Laws* (4th edn) para 901, and for cases on the subject, see 45 *Digest* (Reissue) 315–316, 2720–2732.

For freedom of speech, debates and proceedings in Parliament, see 34 *Halsbury's Laws* (4th edn) para 1486, and for the privileges of Parliament generally, see ibid paras 1482–1506, and for cases on the subject, see 36(2) *Digest* (2nd reissue) 231–240, 1787–1888.

For the Bill of Rights (1688), s 1, art 9, see 10 *Halsbury's Statutes* (4th edn) 46.

In relation to tax for the year 1988–89 and subsequent years of assessment ss 61 and 63 of the Finance Act 1976 were replaced by ss 154 and 156 of the Income and Corporation Taxes Act 1988. For ss 154 and 156 of the 1988 Act, see 44 *Halsbury's Statutes* (4th edn) 201, 203.

Cases referred to in opinions
Ash v Abdy (1678) 3 Swan 664, 36 ER 1014.
Assam Railways and Trading Co Ltd v IRC [1935] AC 445, [1934] All ER Rep 646, HL.
Beswick v Beswick [1967] 2 All ER 1197, [1968] AC 58, [1967] 3 WLR 932, HL.
Black-Clawson International Ltd v Papierwerke Waldhof-Aschaffenburg AG [1975] 1 All ER 810, [1975] AC 591, [1975] 2 WLR 513, HL.
Brind v Secretary of State for the Home Dept [1991] 1 All ER 720, [1991] 1 AC 696, [1991] 2 WLR 588, HL.
Church of Scientology of California v Johnson-Smith [1972] 1 All ER 378, [1972] 1 QB 522, [1971] 3 WLR 434.

Davis v Johnson [1978] 1 All ER 1132, [1979] AC 264, [1978] 2 WLR 553, HL.
a *Eastman Photographic Materials Co Ltd v Comptroller-General of Patents Designs and Trade-marks* [1898] AC 571, HL.
Factortame Ltd v Secretary of State for Transport [1989] 2 All ER 692, [1990] 2 AC 85, [1989] 2 WLR 997, HL.
Fothergill v Monarch Airlines Ltd [1980] 2 All ER 696, [1981] AC 251, [1980] 2 WLR 696, HL.
b *Hadmor Productions Ltd v Hamilton* [1981] 2 All ER 724, [1981] 1 AC 191, [1981] 3 WLR 129, CA; *rvsd* [1982] 1 All ER 1042, [1983] 1 AC 191, [1982] 2 WLR 322, HL.
Mew and Thorne, Re (1862) 31 LJ Bcy 87.
Millar v Taylor (1769) 4 Burr 2303, [1558–1774] All ER Rep 119, 98 ER 201.
Note [1966] 3 All ER 77, [1966] 1 WLR 1234, HL.
c *Owens Bank Ltd v Bracco* [1992] 2 All ER 193, [1992] 2 AC 443, [1992] 2 WLR 621, HL.
Pickstone v Freemans plc [1988] 1 All ER 803, [1989] AC 66, [1988] 3 WLR 265, HL.
R v Secretary of State for Trade, ex p Anderson Strathclyde plc [1983] 2 All ER 233, d DC.
Salkeld v Johnson (1848) 2 Exch 256, 154 ER 487.
Warner v Metropolitan Police Comr [1968] 2 All ER 356, [1969] 2 AC 256, [1968] 2 WLR 1303, HL.

Consolidated appeals

e Dr D M Penter, Messrs H J Campbell-Ferguson, M J P Knott, J P Knee, B B White, W J Denny, J T Hart, T Southall and A J Hunter and the personal representatives of Mr C Nicholls deceased (the taxpayers) appealed with leave of the Court of Appeal from the decision of that court (Slade, Nicholls and Farquharson LJJ) [1991] 2 All ER 824, [1991] Ch 203) on 13 November 1990 dismissing their appeal from the decision of Vinelott J ([1990] STC 6, [1990] 1 WLR 204) dated 24 f November 1989 whereby he allowed an appeal by the Crown by way of case stated (set out at [1990] STC 7–17) by the Commissioner for the Special Purposes of the Income Tax Acts in respect of his decision that the expense incurred in educating and maintaining the taxpayers' sons at the school at which the taxpayers were employed did not add to the general costs of the school but was equal to the direct additional costs involved in so doing. Following a hearing on 4 November g 1991 the Appellate Committee decided to invite further argument on the question whether the House should depart from previous authority of the House which forbade reference to parliamentary proceedings leading to the enactment of a statute for the purpose of construing ss 61 and 63 of the Finance Act 1976. The case was thereupon relisted for further hearing before a freshly constituted h committee of seven Lords of Appeal in ordinary, four of whom had sat on the original committee. The facts are set out in the opinion of Lord Browne-Wilkinson.

Stephen Oliver QC and *Jeremy Woolf* (instructed by *Kenwright & Cox*, agents for *Jagger Son & Tilley*, Birmingham) for the taxpayers at the first hearing.
j *Alan Moses QC* and *Timothy Brennan* (instructed by the *Solicitor of Inland Revenue*) for the Crown at the first hearing.
Anthony Lester QC, Jeremy Woolf and *Clive Sheldon* (instructed by *Kenwright & Cox*, agents for *Jagger Son & Tilley*, Birmingham) for the taxpayers at the further hearing.

The *Attorney General (The Rt Hon Sir Nicholas Lyell QC), Alan Moses QC, Timothy*
Brennan and *Rabinder Singh* (instructed by the *Solicitor of Inland Revenue*) for the *a*
Crown at the further hearing.

Their Lordships took time for consideration.

26 November 1992. The following opinions were delivered.
                                                                                    b
LORD MACKAY OF CLASHFERN LC. My Lords, I have had the advantage
of reading in draft the speech of my noble and learned friend Lord Browne-
Wilkinson. I respectfully adopt his narrative of the proceedings in this appeal and
his account of the statutory provisions by reference to which it falls to be decided.
    A fact which I regard as crucial to the decision of these appeals is stated by the
Special Commissioner as follows ([1990] STC 6 at 11): 'On the facts, the taxpayers' *c*
sons occupied only surplus places at the college and their right to do so was
entirely discretionary.' I regard it as important in considering the benefit which
is to be subject to taxation that the benefit should be identified. The benefit which
the taxpayers in this case received was the placing of their children in surplus
places at the college, if as a matter of discretion the college agreed to do so. As I *d*
read the stated case there was no question of the taxpayers being entitled to have
their children educated at the school. They were in a similar position to the
person coming along on a standby basis for an airline seat as against the passenger
paying a full fare, and without the full rights of a standby passenger, in the sense
that the decision whether or not to accommodate them in the college was entirely
discretionary. If one regards the benefit in this light I cannot see that the cost *e*
incurred in, or in connection with, the provision of the benefit can properly be
held to include the cost incurred, in any event, in providing education to fee-
paying pupils at the school who were there as a right in return for the fees paid in
respect of them. The expenses incurred by the college were all incurred necessarily
in order properly to provide for these pupils. No further expense over and above
that was incurred in, or in connection with, the provision of surplus places to the *f*
taxpayers' children. Although the later words of s 63(2) of the Finance Act 1976
provide that the expense incurred in, or in connection with, the provision of a
benefit includes a proper proportion of any expense relating partly to the benefit
and partly to other matters, I consider that the expenses incurred in provision of
places for fee-paying pupils were wholly incurred in order to provide those places.
The benefit conferred on the taxpayers was one which logically followed only *g*
when it was determined that there were surplus places and the authorities of the
college in their discretion agreed to admit the taxpayers' children to these places.
This decision was the decision to provide the benefit to the taxpayers' children
and this decision involved no further expense on the college. I conclude that
looking at the matter from the point of view of expense incurred and not from *h*
the point of view of loss to the employer no expense could be regarded as having
been incurred as a result of the decision of the authorities of the college to provide
this particular benefit to the taxpayer.
    Notwithstanding the views that have found favour with others I consider this
to be a reasonable construction of the statutory provisions and I am comforted in
the fact that, apart from an attempt to tax airline employees, which was taken to *j*
the Special Commissioners, who decided in favour of the taxpayer, this has been
the practice of the Revenue in applying the relevant words where they have
occurred in the Income Tax Acts for so long as they have been in force, until they
initiated the present cases.

At the very least it appears to me that the manner in which I have construed

a the relevant provisions in their application to the facts in this appeal is a possible construction and that any ambiguity there should be resolved in favour of the taxpayer.

For these reasons I would allow these appeals. I should perhaps add that I was not a member of the committee who heard these appeals in the first hearing, since I became involved only when your Lordships who sat in the first hearing

b suggested a second hearing under my chairmanship and accordingly I have not been asked to consider this matter apart from the discussion of the extracts from Hansard which have been put before us in this appeal. However, this is the conclusion that I would have reached apart altogether from considering Hansard.

But much wider issues than the construction of the Finance Act 1976 have

c been raised in these appeals and for the first time this House has been asked to consider a detailed argument on the extent to which reference can properly be made before a court of law in the United Kingdom to proceedings in Parliament recorded in Hansard.

For the taxpayers Mr Lester QC submits that it should now be appropriate for the courts to look at Hansard in order to ascertain the intention of the legislators

d as expressed in the proceedings on the Bill which has then been enacted in the statutory words requiring to be construed. This submission appears to me to suggest a way of making more effective proceedings in Parliament by allowing the court to consider what has been said in Parliament as an aid to resolving an ambiguity which may well have become apparent only as a result of the attempt to apply the enacted words to a particular case. It does not seem to me that this

e can involve any impeachment, or questioning, of the freedom of speech and debates or proceedings in Parliament; accordingly I do not see how such a use of Hansard can possibly be thought to infringe s 1, art 9 of the Bill of Rights (1688) and I agree with my noble and learned friend's more detailed consideration of that matter.

f The principal difficulty I have on this aspect of the case is that in Mr Lester's submission reference to parliamentary material as an aid to interpretation of a statutory provision should be allowed only with leave of the court and where the court is satisfied that such a reference is justifiable (a) to confirm the meaning of a provision as conveyed by the text, its object and purpose, (b) to determine a meaning where the provision is ambiguous or obscure or (c) to determine the meaning where the ordinary meaning is manifestly absurd or unreasonable.

g I believe that practically every question of statutory construction that comes before the courts will involve an argument that the case falls under one or more of these three heads. It follows that the parties' legal advisers will require to study Hansard in practically every such case to see whether or not there is any help to be gained from it. I believe this is an objection of real substance. It is a practical

h objection, not one of principle, and I believe that it was the fundamental reason that Lord Reid, for example, considered the general rule to be a good one as he said in the passage my noble and learned friend has cited from *Beswick v Beswick* [1967] 2 All ER 1197 at 1202, [1968] AC 58 at 74. Lord Reid's statement is, I think, worthy of particular weight since he was a parliamentarian of great experience as well as a very distinguished judicial member of your Lordships'

j House. It is significant that in the following year, in his dissenting speech in *Warner v Metropolitan Police Comr* [1968] 2 All ER 356 at 366–367, [1969] 2 AC 256 at 279, he, while agreeing with the general rule, was prepared to consider an exception from it although the time was not right to do so. But the exception he contemplated was in respect of a particular type of statute, namely a statute creating criminal liability in which the question was whether or not a guilty intention was required to create liability. Now that type of exception would mean *a* that the practical difficulties to which he referred would not arise except in the comparatively few cases that arise of the particular type. The submission which Mr Lester makes on the other hand is not restricted by reference to the type of statute and indeed the only way in which it could be discovered whether help was to be given is by considering Hansard itself. Such an approach appears to me to involve the possibility at least of an immense increase in the cost of litigation in *b* which statutory construction is involved. It is of course easy to overestimate such cost but it is I fear equally easy to underestimate it. Your Lordships have no machinery from which any estimate of such cost could be derived. Two inquiries with such machinery available to them, namely that of the Law Commission and the Scottish Law Commission, in their joint report on *Interpretation of Statutes* *c* (Law Com no 21; Scot Law Com no 11(1969)), and the Renton Committee report on *Preparation of Legislation* (Cmnd 6053 (1975)) advised against a relaxation on the practical grounds to which I have referred. I consider that nothing has been laid before your Lordships to justify the view that their advice based on this objection was incorrect.

In his very helpful and full submissions Mr Lester has pointed out that there is *d* no evidence of practical difficulties in the jurisdictions where relaxations of this kind have already been allowed, but I do not consider that, full as these researches have been, they justify the view that no substantial increase resulted in the cost of litigation as a result of these relaxations, and, in any event, the parliamentary processes in these jurisdictions are different in quite material respects from those in the United Kingdom.   *e*

Your Lordships are well aware that the costs of litigation are a subject of general public concern and I personally would not wish to be a party to changing a well-established rule which could have a substantial effect in increasing these costs against the advice of the Law Commissions and the Renton Committee unless and until a new inquiry demonstrated that that advice was no longer valid.

I do not for my part find the objections in principle to be strong and I would *f* certainly be prepared to agree the rule should no longer be adhered to were it not for the practical consideration to which I have referred and which my noble and learned friend agrees to be of real substance. Reference to proceedings in Parliament has already been allowed in *Pickstone v Freemans plc* [1988] 2 All ER 803, [1989] AC 66 without, I think, any argument on whether or not it was *g* permissible for ascertaining the purpose of subordinate legislation and also in other cases for ascertaining the purpose for which a power to make subordinate legislation was used. I believe that such statements are likely to be readily identified in parliamentary proceedings and the cases in which they are relevant will be determined by the nature of the subject matter. Allowing reference to Hansard in such cases does not have the large practical consequences to which I *h* have referred. If reference to parliamentary material is permitted as an aid to the construction of legislation which is ambiguous, or obscure or the literal meaning of which leads to an absurdity, I believe as I have said that in practically every case it will be incumbent on those preparing the argument to examine the whole proceedings on the Bill in question in both Houses of Parliament. Questions of construction may be involved on what is said in Parliament and I cannot see how *j* if the rule is modified in this way the parties' legal advisers could properly come to court without having looked to see whether there was anything in the Hansard report on the Bill which could assist their case. If they found a passage which they thought had a bearing on the issue in this case, that passage would have to be construed in the light of the proceedings as a whole.

I fully appreciate and feel the force of the narrowness of the distinctions which
a are taken between what is admissible and what is not admissible, but the exception
presently proposed is so extensive that I do not feel able to support it in the present
state of our knowledge of its practical results in this jurisdiction. For these reasons,
I agree that these appeals should be allowed, although I cannot agree on the main
issue for the discussion of which this further hearing was arranged.

b **LORD KEITH OF KINKEL**. My Lords, for the reasons set out in the speech
to be delivered by my noble and learned friend Lord Browne-Wilkinson, which I
have had the opportunity of considering in draft and with which I agree, I would
allow this appeal.

c **LORD BRIDGE OF HARWICH**. My Lords, I was one of those who were in
the majority at the conclusion of the first hearing of this appeal in holding the
opinion that s 63 of the Finance Act 1976, construed by conventional criteria,
supported the assessments to income tax made by the Revenue on the taxpayers
which had been upheld by Vinelott J (see [1990] STC 6, [1990] 1 WLR 204) and
the Court of Appeal (see [1991] 2 All ER 824, [1991] Ch 203). If it were not
d permissible to take account of the parliamentary history of the relevant legislation
and of ministerial statements of its intended effect, I should remain of that
opinion. But, once the parliamentary material was brought to our attention, it
seemed to me, as, I believe, to others of your Lordships who had heard the appeal
first argued, to raise an acute question as to whether it could possibly be right to
give effect to taxing legislation in such a way as to impose a tax which the
e Financial Secretary to the Treasury, during the passage of the Bill containing the
relevant provision, had, in effect, assured the House of Commons it was not
intended to impose. It was this which led to the appeal being reargued before the
Appellate Committee of seven which now reports to the House.

Following the further arguments of which we have had the benefit, I should
f find it very difficult, in conscience, to reach a conclusion adverse to the taxpayers
on the basis of a technical rule of construction requiring me to ignore the very
material which in this case indicates unequivocally which of the two possible
interpretations of s 63(2) of the 1976 Act was intended by Parliament. But, for all
the reasons given by my noble and learned friend Lord Browne-Wilkinson, with
whose speech I entirely agree, I am not placed in that invidious situation.

g It should, in my opinion, only be in the rare cases, where the very issue of
interpretation which the courts are called on to resolve has been addressed in
parliamentary debate and where the promoter of the legislation has made a clear
statement directed to that very issue, that reference to Hansard should be
permitted. Indeed, it is only in such cases that reference to Hansard is likely to be
of any assistance to the courts. Provided the relaxation of the previous exclusionary
h rule is so limited, I find it difficult to suppose that the additional cost of litigation
or any other ground of objection can justify the court continuing to wear blinkers
which, in such a case as this, conceal the vital clue to the intended meaning of an
enactment. I recognise that practitioners will in some cases incur fruitless costs in
the search for such a vital clue where none exists. But, on the other hand, where
Hansard does provide the answer, it should be so clear to both parties that they
j will avoid the cost of litigation.

I would allow the appeal.

LORD GRIFFITHS. My Lords, I have long thought that the time had come to
change the self-imposed judicial rule that forbade any reference to the legislative
history of an enactment as an aid to its interpretation. The ever-increasing volume

of legislation must inevitably result in ambiguities of statutory language which
are not perceived at the time the legislation is enacted. The object of the court in *a*
interpreting legislation is to give effect so far as the language permits to the
intention of the legislature. If the language proves to be ambiguous I can see no
sound reason not to consult Hansard to see if there is a clear statement of the
meaning that the words were intended to carry. The days have long passed when
the courts adopted a strict constructionist view of interpretation which required
them to adopt the literal meaning of the language. The courts now adopt a *b*
purposive approach which seeks to give effect to the true purpose of legislation
and are prepared to look at much extraneous material that bears on the
background against which the legislation was enacted. Why then cut ourselves
off from the one source in which may be found an authoritative statement of the
intention with which the legislation is placed before Parliament. I have had the
advantage of reading the speech of my noble and learned friend Lord Browne- *c*
Wilkinson and, save on the construction of the 1976 Act without recourse to
Hansard, I agree with all he has to say. In summary, I agree that the courts should
have recourse to Hansard in the circumstances and to the extent he proposes.
I agree that the use of Hansard as an aid to assist the court to give effect to the true
intention of Parliament is not 'questioning' within the meaning of s 1, art 9 of *d*
the Bill of Rights (1688). I agree that the House is not inhibited by any
parliamentary privilege in deciding this appeal.

I cannot agree with the view that consulting Hansard will add so greatly to the
cost of litigation that on this ground alone we should refuse to do so. Modern
technology greatly facilitates the recall and display of material held centrally.
I have to confess that on many occasions I have had recourse to Hansard, of course *e*
only to check if my interpretation had conflicted with an express parliamentary
intention, but I can say that it does not take long to recall and assemble the
relevant passages in which the particular section was dealt with in Parliament,
nor does it take long to see if anything relevant was said. Furthermore if the
search resolves the ambiguity it will in future save all the expense that would
otherwise be incurred in fighting the rival interpretations through the courts. *f*
We have heard no suggestion that recourse to parliamentary history has
significantly increased the cost of litigation in Australia or New Zealand and I do
not believe that it will do so in this country.

As to the question of statutory construction I should myself have construed the
section in favour of the taxpayers without recourse to Hansard. The crucial
question is the meaning of the words 'the cost of a benefit is the amount of any *g*
expense incurred in or in connection with its provision'. Do these words refer to
the actual expense incurred by the school in providing the benefit or do they refer
to the hypothetical expense incurred by the school arrived at by the formula of
dividing the total cost of running the school by the number of pupils attending it
or, to put it more shortly, do they refer to the additional or the average cost of the *h*
provision of the benefit?

I concede at once the language is ambiguous and I see the strength of the
linguistic argument in favour of the average cost construction. Nevertheless I
could not believe that Parliament intended such a construction because it will
produce what I regard as such unfair and absurd results.

If what I will call the hypothetical cost test is adopted it will come very close to *j*
a market value test. In the case of independent schools which for the most part
are not run as independent profit-making institutions and which set the fees to
raise enough money to cover the cost of running the school, the test is virtually
indistinguishable from a market value test. In the case of passenger transport

undertakings such as railways and airlines which allow free travel to employees
a the test would provide mind-boggling difficulties of calculation and when the
undertaking was running at a loss would result in a charge to tax that exceeded
the fare charged to the general public; this would also be the case where school
fees were heavily subsidised by endowments. I could not believe that this was the
intention of Parliament. Nor could I believe that it was the intention to bring in
at a single stroke a charge to tax that would be calculated to interrupt the
b education and expectations of so many parents and children, for it is surely
common knowledge that the provision of free or subsidised education for the
children of those teaching in independent schools was part of their usual terms of
employment and that the salaries paid would be wholly insufficient to meet a
charge to tax based on the full fees of the school. By the same token, bearing in
mind that the salary level at which the tax bit was £5,000 a year, it will put the
c travel facilities attached to their employment out of the reach of many airline and
rail employees. Probably the most universally provided 'perk' is the company car.
Parliament has introduced taxation of this 'perk' but on a gradually increasing
scale—still short of the true value of the use of the car—no doubt because to have
introduced it at its full value would have been seen as an unfair and unacceptable
d increase in the burden of taxation in one year on those who enjoyed the perk and
of course the future of the British motor industry would be taken into account. It
is against this background that I approached the construction and which led me
to prefer the interpretation which bases the assessment to tax on the actual cost to
the employer rather than the hypothetical cost arrived at by dividing the number
of pupils into the total cost of providing full facilities.
e   I should make it clear that my construction did not depend on the children of
the staff taking up surplus places in the sense that if there were sufficient fee-
paying pupils the staff's children would not be given a place. The crucial question,
as I see it, is whether accepting the staff children involved the school in extra
expenditure. Absorbing the few staff children only involves the school in small
extra costs such as food and laundry. All the main facilities of the school such as
f staff, buildings, playing fields and so forth are already provided for the fee-paying
pupils and no additional expenditure is incurred in respect of these costs by
accepting a few children of the staff. This, as I understand it, is now the
construction accepted by the majority of your Lordships in the light of the
parliamentary history.
g   On this question of construction I was in a judicial minority of one at the end
of the first hearing of this appeal. It was as a result of the discovery that the
parliamentary history of the legislation gave conclusive support to the construction
I preferred that your Lordships agreed that the matter should be reargued to
determine whether it was permissible to use the parliamentary history as an aid
to the interpretation of the legislation. In my view this case provides a dramatic
h vindication of the decision to consult Hansard; had your Lordships not agreed to
do so the result would have been to place a very heavy burden of taxation on a
large number of persons which Parliament never intended to impose.
     I agree that this appeal should be allowed.

LORD ACKNER. My Lords, I entirely agree that for the reasons set out in the
j speech of my noble and learned friend Lord Browne-Wilkinson, which I have had
the advantage of reading in draft, this appeal should be allowed.

LORD OLIVER OF AYLMERTON. My Lords, I have had the advantage of
reading in draft the speech prepared by my noble and learned friend Lord Browne-

Wilkinson. I agree with it in its entirety and would, in the ordinary way, be
content to do no more than express my concurrence both in the reasoning and in *a*
the result. I venture to add a few observations of my own only because I have to
confess to having been a somewhat reluctant convert to the notion that the words
which Parliament has chosen to use in a statute for the expression of its will may
fall to be construed or modified by reference to what individual members of
Parliament may have said in the course of debate or discussion preceding the
passage of the Bill into law. A statute is, after all, the formal and complete *b*
intimation to the citizen of a particular rule of the law which he is enjoined,
sometimes under penalty, to obey and by which he is both expected and entitled
to regulate his conduct. We must, therefore, I believe, be very cautious in opening
the door to the reception of material not readily or ordinarily accessible to the
citizen whose rights and duties are to be affected by the words in which the
legislature has elected to express its will.   *c*

But experience shows that language—and, particularly, language adopted or
concurred in under the pressure of a tight parliamentary timetable—is not always
a reliable vehicle for the complete or accurate translation of legislative intention;
and I have been persuaded, for the reasons so cogently deployed in the speech of
my noble and learned friend, that the circumstances of this case demonstrate that *d*
there is both the room and the necessity for a limited relaxation of the previously
well-settled rule which excludes reference to parliamentary history as an aid to
statutory construction.

It is, however, important to stress the limits within which such a relaxation is
permissible and which are set out in the speech of my noble and learned friend.
It can apply only where the expression of the legislative intention is genuinely *e*
ambiguous or obscure or where a literal or prima facie construction leads to a
manifest absurdity and where the difficulty can be resolved by a clear statement
directed to the matter in issue. Ingenuity can sometimes suggest ambiguity or
obscurity where none exists in fact, and, if the instant case were to be thought to
justify the exercise of combing through reports of parliamentary proceedings in
the hope of unearthing some perhaps incautious expression of opinion in support *f*
of an improbable secondary meaning, the relaxation of the rule might indeed
lead to the fruitless expense and labour which has been prayed in aid in the past
as one of the reasons justifying its maintenance. But so long as the three conditions
expressed in the speech of my noble and learned friend are understood and
observed, I do not, for my part, consider that the relaxation of the rule which he
has proposed will lead to any significant increase in the cost of litigation or in the *g*
burden of research required to be undertaken by legal advisers.

So far as the merits of the instant appeal are concerned, I, like my noble and
learned friends Lord Bridge and Lord Browne-Wilkinson, was in favour of
dismissing the appeal at the conclusion of the first hearing. Were it not for the
material in the reports of Hansard to which your Lordships have been referred, I *h*
too would still be of that view, for, although I recognise that in popular parlance
the provision to one individual of a service which is, in any event, being provided
for reward to many others may be said to cost the provider little or nothing, 'cost'
in accountancy terms is merely a computation of outgoing expenditure without
reference to receipts. Where, however, the cost of providing a service is balanced
or overtopped by amounts received for the service from others to whom it is *j*
provided, the man in the street might well, and probably would, say that the
provider had incurred no expense in providing the particular benefit under
consideration. Certainly he incurs no additional cost or expense. I accept,
therefore, that, in referring to 'the cost of the benefit' and the 'expense incurred
in . . . its provision', s 63(1) and (2) of the Finance Act 1976 introduced an element

of ambiguity. That is underlined by the absurdity which would result from a
a literal construction of the word 'cost' in the case of a loss-making concern such as
British Rail or a heavily endowed institution, where the employee's benefit would
have to be valued at a figure in excess—indeed, it may be many times in excess—
of the market price of the service provided. The references to Hansard which are
set out in the speech of my noble and learned friend Lord Browne-Wilkinson put
it beyond doubt that that could not have been the intention of Parliament in
b enacting the section.

Accordingly, I too would allow the appeal. I would add only that I find myself
quite unable to see how referring to the reports of parliamentary debates in order
to determine the meaning of the words which Parliament has employed could
possibly be construed as 'questioning' or 'impeaching' the freedom of speech or
c debate or proceedings in Parliament or as otherwise infringing the provisions of
art 9 of s 1 of the Bill of Rights (1688).

LORD BROWNE-WILKINSON. My Lords, the underlying subject matter
of these tax appeals is the correct basis for valuing benefits in kind received by the
taxpayers, who are schoolmasters. However, in the circumstances which I will
d relate, the appeals have also raised two questions of much wider importance. The
first is whether in construing ambiguous or obscure statutory provisions your
Lordships should relax the historic rule that the courts must not look at the
parliamentary history of legislation or Hansard for the purpose of construing such
legislation. The second is whether, if reference to such materials would otherwise
be appropriate, it would contravene s 1, art 9 of the Bill of Rights (1688) or
e parliamentary privilege so to do.

The facts are fully set out in the judgments of Vinelott J at first instance (see
[1990] STC 6, [1990] 1 WLR 204) and of the Court of Appeal (see [1991] 2 All ER
824, [1991] Ch 203). Shortly stated, the taxpayers are nine masters and the bursar
employed by Malvern College (the school). For many years the school has run a
concessionary scheme under which members of the staff are entitled to have their
f children educated at the school on payment of only one-fifth of the sum charged
to members of the public. In the relevant tax years, 1983–84, 1984–85 and 1985–
86, children of one or more of the taxpayers were educated at the school on
payment of the concessionary fees only. It is common ground that the
concessionary fees more than covered the additional cost to the school of educating
the taxpayers' children.
g
The school had a capacity to accept 625 boys but in the relevant years the school
was not full to capacity. The admission of the taxpayers' children to the school
therefore did not involve the school in losing full fees which would otherwise
have been paid by members of the public for the places which the taxpayers'
children occupied.
h It is common ground that the education of the children at reduced fees was a
taxable benefit under s 61(1) of the Finance Act 1976, which provides:

> 'Subject to section 63A where in any year a person is employed in director's
> or higher-paid employment and—(a) by reason of his employment there is
> provided for him, or for others being members of his family or household,
> *j* any benefit to which this section applies; and (b) the cost of providing the
> benefit is not (apart from this section) chargeable to tax as his income, there
> is to be treated as emoluments of the employment, and accordingly chargeable
> to income tax under Schedule E, an amount equal to whatever is the cash
> equivalent of the benefit.'

The crucial question relates to the amount which is to be treated as an

emolument, ie what is 'the cash equivalent of the benefit'. These words are
defined by s 63(1) and (2) as follows: *a*

'(1) The cash equivalent of any benefit chargeable to tax under section 61
above is an amount equal to the cost of the benefit, less so much (if any) of it
as is made good by the employee to those providing the benefit.
(2) Subject to the following subsections, the cost of a benefit is the amount
of any expense incurred in or in connection with its provision, and (here and *b*
in those subsections) includes a proper proportion of any expense relating
partly to the benefit and partly to other matters.'

The taxpayers contend that the only expense incurred by the school 'in or in
connection' with the education of their children is the additional, or marginal,
cost to the school. The school was, in any event, up and running so as to provide
its educational facilities for 625 boys. All the costs of running the school (staff *c*
salaries, provision of buildings and grounds etc) would have had to be incurred in
any event; the admission of the taxpayers' children did not increase these basic
expenses in any way. The only expense attributable to the education of the
taxpayers' children (additional food, laundry, stationery etc) was fully covered by
the one-fifth concessionary fee paid by the taxpayers. Therefore 'the cash *d*
equivalent of the benefit' is nil.

The Revenue on the other hand contend that the 'expense incurred in or in
connection with' the provision of education for the children of the taxpayers was
exactly the same as the expense incurred in or in connection with the education
of all other pupils at the school and accordingly the expense of educating any one
child is a proportionate part of the cost of running the whole school. *e*

These provisions regulate the taxation of all benefits in kind. As Nicholls LJ
pointed out in the Court of Appeal, for present purposes such benefits can be of
two kinds (see [1991] 2 All ER 824 at 827, [1991] Ch 203 at 210). First, the benefit
may be of a kind bought in from outside the employer's business, such as a car or
medical insurance (external benefits). Second, the benefit may consist of the
enjoyment by the employee of services or facilities which it is part of the *f*
employer's business to sell to the public, for example concessionary travel for
railway or airline employees or concessionary education for the children of
schoolteachers (in-house benefits). In both cases the benefit falls to be quantified
by reference to the expense of providing the benefit. In the case of external
benefits this does not normally raise any major problems because such cost is an *g*
isolated expenditure. But in the case of in-house benefits there is an obvious
problem, since the employer is, for the purpose of selling the facility to the public,
incurring the cost of running the train, airline or school the use of which is
provided on a concessionary basis to the employee. What then is the cost to the
employer of providing the in-house benefit for the employee? Is it only the
additional or marginal cost to the employer of providing the service for the *h*
employee, or is it a proportionate part of the total costs incurred by the employer
in providing the facility to be used both by the public and by the employee?

The Special Commissioner held in favour of the taxpayers (see [1990] STC 7–
17). That decision was reversed by Vinelott J, whose decision was affirmed by the
Court of Appeal. The taxpayers appeal to your Lordships' House.

The case was originally argued before a committee of five of your Lordships *j*
without reference to any parliamentary proceedings. After the conclusion of the
first hearing, it came to your Lordships' attention that an examination of the
proceedings in Parliament in 1976 which led to the enactment of ss 61 and 63 of
the 1976 Act might give a clear indication which of the two rival contentions

represented the intention of Parliament in using the statutory words. Your
a Lordships then invited the parties to consider whether they wished to present
further argument on the question whether it was appropriate for the House
(under *Note* [1966] 3 All ER 77, [1966] 1 WLR 1234) to depart from previous
authority of this House which forbids reference to such material in construing
statutory provisions and, if so, what guidance such material provided in deciding
the present appeal. The taxpayers indicated that they wished to present further
b argument on these points. The case was listed for rehearing before a committee
of seven members not all of whom sat on the original committee.

At the start of the further hearing, the Attorney General, who appeared for the
Crown, drew our attention to a letter addressed to him by the Clerk of the House
of Commons suggesting that any reference to Hansard for the purpose of
c construing the 1976 Act might breach the privileges of that House. Until 31
October 1980 the House of Commons took the view that any reference to Hansard
in court proceedings would constitute a breach of its privileges and required a
petition for leave to use Hansard to be presented in each case. On 31 October
1980 the House of Commons resolved as follows:

d   'That this House, while re-affirming the status of proceedings in Parliament
      confirmed by article 9 of the Bill of Rights, gives leave for reference to be
      made in future court proceedings to the Official Report of Debates and to the
      published Reports and evidence of Committees in any case in which, under
      the practice of the House, it is required that a petition for leave should be
      presented and that the practice of presenting petitions for leave to refer to
e   Parliamentary papers be discontinued.'

The letter of 5 June 1992 from the Clerk of the House of Commons starts by
saying:

      'My attention has been drawn to the fact that the House of Lords may be
      asked to hear argument in this case based on the meaning or significance of
f   words spoken during proceedings on a Bill in the House of Commons.'

The letter then sets out the text of the resolution of 31 October 1980, and
continues:

      'In my opinion, the use proposed for the Official Report of Debates in this
      case is beyond the meaning of the "reference" contemplated in the Resolution
g   of October 1980. If a court were minded in particular circumstances to
      permit the questioning of the proceedings of the House in the way proposed,
      it would be proper for the leave of the House to be sought first by way of
      petition so that, if leave were granted, no question would arise of the House
      regarding its Privileges as having been breached.'

h   The reference in that letter to 'questioning' the proceedings of the House of
Commons plainly raised the issue whether the proposed use of parliamentary
materials without the leave of the House of Commons would breach s 1, art 9 of
the Bill of Rights, which provides:

      'That the freedome of speech and debates or proceedings in Parlyament
j   ought not to be impeached or questioned in any court or place out of
      Parlyament.'

The Attorney General, while submitting that such use of parliamentary
material would breach art 9, accepted that it was for the courts to determine the
legal meaning and effect of art 9. However, the Attorney General warned your

Lordships that, even if reference in this case to parliamentary materials did not
infringe art 9, the House of Commons might take the view the House enjoyed *a*
some wider privilege which we would be infringing and might well regret that
its views on the point had not been sought before a decision was reached by your
Lordships. Whilst strictly maintaining the privileges of the House of Commons,
the Attorney General used the parliamentary materials in this case as an illustration
of the dangers of so doing. Moreover, in order to assist us, whilst still maintaining
the privileges of the House of Commons, he made submissions as to the effect of *b*
such material on the construction of s 63 if, contrary to his contentions and
advice, we decided this appeal with the assistance of such material.

In the result, the following issues arise. (1) Should the existing rule prohibiting
any reference to Hansard in construing legislation be relaxed and, if so, to what
extent? (2) If so, does this case fall within the category of cases where reference to
parliamentary proceedings should be permitted? (3) If reference to parliamentary *c*
proceedings is permissible, what is the true construction of the statutory
provisions? (4) If reference to the parliamentary proceedings is not permissible,
what is the true construction of the statutory provisions? (5) If the outcome of
this case depends on whether or not reference is made to Hansard, how should
the matter proceed in the face of the warnings of the Attorney General that such *d*
references might constitute a breach of parliamentary privilege?

I will consider these issues in turn, but first I must set out the parliamentary
history of ss 61 and 63 by reference to which the case was argued before us.

The parliamentary material   *e*
For reasons which will appear it is necessary first to refer to the legislation
affecting the taxation of benefits in kind before 1975. Under s 39(1) of the Finance
Act 1948, directors and employees of bodies corporate earning more than £2,000
per annum were taxed under Sch E on certain benefits in kind. The amount
charged was the expense incurred by the body corporate 'in or in connection with
the provision' of the benefit in kind. By s 39(6) it was provided that references to *f*
expenses 'incurred in or in connection with any matter includes a reference to a
proper proportion of any expense incurred partly in or in connection with that
matter'. Employment by a school or charitable organisation was expressly
excluded from the charge (see ss 41(5) and 44). These provisions were re-enacted
in the Income and Corporation Taxes Act 1970.

Those provisions covered in-house benefits as well as external benefits. We *g*
were told that after 1948 the Revenue sought to tax at least two categories of
employees in receipt of in-house benefits. Higher-paid employees of the railways
enjoy free or concessionary travel on the railways. The Revenue reached an
agreement that such employees should be taxed on 20% (later 25%) of the full
fare. Airline employees also enjoy concessionary travel. We were told that in the
1960s the Revenue sought to tax such employees on that benefit on the basis of *h*
the average cost to the airline of providing a seat, not merely on the marginal
cost. The tax commissioners rejected such claim; the Revenue did not appeal.
Therefore in practice from 1948 to 1975 the Revenue did not seek to extract tax
on the basis of the average cost to the employer of providing in-house benefits.

In 1975 the government proposed a new tax on vouchers provided by an *j*
employer to his employees which could be exchanged for goods or services. Clause
33(1) of the Finance (No 2) Bill 1975 provided that the employee was to be treated,
on receipt of a voucher, as having received an emolument from his employment
of an amount 'equal to the expense incurred by the person providing the voucher
in or in connection with the provision of the voucher and the money, goods or

services for which it is capable of being exchanged'. The statutory wording of the
a Bill was therefore similar to that in the 1948 Act and in s 63(2) of the Finance Act
1976. In the standing committee on the Bill, the Financial Secretary was asked
about the impact of the clause on railwaymen. He gave the following answer (HC
Official Report, SC H (Finance (No 2) Bill), 1 July 1975, col 666):

> 'Similarly, the railwayman travelling on his normal voucher will not be
> *b* taxable either. The clause deals with the situation where a number of firms
> produce incentives of various kinds. In one or two instances, there is likely
> to be some liability concerning rail vouchers of a special kind, but in general,
> the position is as I have said and they will not be taxable.'

He was then asked to explain why they would not be taxable and replied:

> *c*   'Perhaps I can make clear why there is no taxable benefit in kind, because
> the provision of the service that he provides falls upon the employer. Clearly,
> the railways will run in precisely the same way whether the railwaymen use
> this facility or not, so there is no extra charge to the Railways Board itself,
> therefore there would be no taxable benefit.'

d   Later he explained that by the words 'no extra charge' he meant 'no extra cost'.
Clause 33(1) of the Bill was enacted as s 36(1) of the Finance (No 2) Act 1975.

The Finance Bill 1976 sought to make a general revision of the taxation of
benefits in kind. The existing legislation on fringe benefits was to be repealed.
Clause 52 of the Bill as introduced eventually became s 61 of the 1976 Act and
imposed a charge to tax on benefits in kind for higher-paid employees, i e those
e paid more than £5,000 per annum. Clause 54 of the Bill eventually became s 63
of the 1976 Act. As introduced, cl 54(1) provided that the cash equivalent of any
benefit was to be an amount equal to 'the cost of the benefit'. Clause 54(2)
provided that, except as provided in later subsections, 'the cost of a benefit is the
amount of any expense incurred in or in connection with its provision'. Crucially,
f cl 54(4) of the Bill sought to tax in-house benefits on a different basis from that
applicable to external benefits. It provided that the cost of a benefit consisting of
the provision of any service or facility which was also provided to the public (i e
in-house benefits) should be the price which the public paid for such facility or
service. Employees of schools were not excluded from the new charge.

Thus if the 1976 Bill had gone through as introduced, railway and airline
g employees would have been treated as receiving benefits in kind from
concessionary travel equal to the open market cost of tickets and schoolmasters
would have been taxed for concessionary education on the amount of the normal
school fees.

After second reading, cl 52 of the Bill was committed to a committee of the
whole House and cl 54 to Standing Committee E. On 17 May 1976 the House
h considered cl 52 and strong representations were made about the impact of cl 52
on airline and railway employees. At the start of the meeting of Standing
Committee E on 17 June 1976 (before cl 54 was being discussed) the Financial
Secretary to the Treasury, Mr Robert Sheldon, made an announcement in the
following terms (HC Official Report, SC E (Finance Bill), 17 June 1976, cols 893–
895):
j
> 'The next point I wish to make concerns services and deals with the position
> of employees of organisations, bodies, or firms which provide services, where
> the employee is in receipt of those services free or at a reduced rate. Under
> Clause 54(4) the taxable benefit is to be based on the arm's length price of the
> benefit received. At present the benefit is valued on the cost to the employer.

Representations have been made concerning airline travel and railway employees ... It was never intended that the benefit received by the airline *a* employee would be the fare paid by the ordinary passenger. The benefit to him would never be as high as that, because of certain disadvantages that the employee has. Similar considerations, although of a different kind, apply to railway employees. I have had many interviews, discussions and meetings on this matter and I have decided to withdraw Clause 54(4). I thought I would mention this at the outset because so many details, which would normally be *b* left until we reach that particular stage, will be discussed with earlier parts of the legislation. I shall give some reasons which weigh heavily in favour of the withdrawal of this provision. The first is the large difference between the cost of providing some services and the amount of benefit which under the Bill would be held to be received. There are a number of cases of this kind, *c* and I would point out that air and rail journeys are only two of a number of service benefits which have a number of problems attached to them. But there is a large difference between the cost of the benefit to the employer and the value of that benefit as assessed. It could lead to unjustifiable situations resulting in a great number of injustices and I do not think we should continue with it ... The second reason for withdrawing Clause 54(4) is that *d* these services would tend to be much less used. The problem would then arise for those who had advocated the continuation of this legislation that neither the employer nor the employee nor the Revenue would benefit from the lesser use of these services. This factor also weighed with me. The third reason is the difficulty of enforcement and administration, which both give rise to certain problems. Finally, it was possible to withdraw this part of the *e* legislation as the services cover not only a more difficult area, but a quite distinct area of these provisions, without having repercussions on some of the other areas ... [*A member*:] I, too, have talked to many airline employees about this matter, and I am not completely clear as to the purport of my hon. Friend's remarks. Is he saying that these benefits will remain taxable but that *f* the equivalent cost of the benefit will be calculated on some different basis? Or is he saying that these benefits will not be taxable at all? [*Financial Secretary*:] The existing law which applies to the taxation of some of these benefits will be retained. The position will subsequently be unchanged from what it is now before the introduction of this legislation.'

The Financial Secretary was then asked to elucidate the impact of this on airline *g* employees. He is reported as saying (col 930):

'There is a difference between the provision of services to an employee earning less than £5,000 and an employee earning more than £5,000, or one who is a director. The position is quite clear. What we are withdrawing is the arms-length valuation of benefit under Clause 54(4) where an employer *h* is providing services to the employee at a cost which may be very little. The employee earning more than £5,000 or the director will be assessed on the benefit received by him on the basis of the cost to the employer rather than the price that would generally be charged to the public. That is the position that we have now brought in, as opposed to the original one in the Bill where it would be assessed on the cost to a member of the public. That position *j* now is the same as it stands before this legislation is passed.'

After being further pressed, the Financial Secretary (cols 931–932) said:

'The position is as I have enunciated it. If a company provides a service to the kind of employee which we have been talking about, and the company _a_ subsidises that service, the benefit assessable on the employee is the cost to the employer of providing that service. This was to have been changed by Clause 54(4) under which the benefit received was to be assessed at the arm's length price which an ordinary member of the public would have paid for that service. Some companies provide services of a kind where the cost to them is very little. For example, an airline ticket, allowing occupation of an empty seat, costs an airline nothing—in fact, in such a case there could be a _b_ negative cost, as it might be an advantage to the airline to have an experienced crew member on the flight. The cost to the company, then, would be nothing, but the benefit assessable under Clause 54(4) could be considerable. We are reverting to the existing practice.'

He further said (col 931):

_c_
'If the company provides services to such people at a subsidised rate, the employee will be assessed on the benefit received on the basis of the cost to the employer. That is the position as it was before this Bill and as it will be if the whole of the Bill is passed, because subsection (2) only re-states the existing position. It does not produce anything new.'

_d_ Simultaneously with the announcement to the standing committee, a press release was issued announcing the withdrawal of cl 54(4) (see Finance Bill Changes, HM Treasury Press Release of 17 June 1976). It referred to the same matters as the Financial Secretary had stated to the committee and concluded: 'The effect of deleting this sub-clause will be to continue the present basis of taxing of services, namely the cost to the employer of providing the service.'
_e_ The point was further debated in committee on 22 June 1976. A member is reported as saying that 'like many others, I welcome the concession that has been made to leave out the airline staff and the railway employees and all the others that are left out by the dropping of Clause 54(4)' (see HC Official Report, SC E (Finance Bill), 22 June 1976, col 1013). Another member, after referring to the _f_ particular reference in the Financial Secretary's statement to airline and railway employees, asked whether the same distinction applied to services provided by hotel companies to their employees—that is to rooms which are freely available for the general public in hotels being offered at a concessionary rate to employees of the hotel group (col 1023). In response, the Financial Secretary said of the position of such employees (col 1024):

_g_
'The position is, as he probably expected, the same as that which, following my announcement last week about the withdrawal of Clause 54(4), applies to other employees in service industries: the benefit is the cost to the employer. It is a good illustration of one of the reasons why I withdrew this subsection, in that the cost to the employer in this instance could be much less than the _h_ arms-length cost to the outside person taking advantage of such a service.'

The question of the taxation of merchant seamen in respect of travel concessions to their families on their employers' ships was raised by another speaker and an amendment (No 299) was tabled to meet their position. The Financial Secretary (col 1100) said:

_j_
'Perhaps I may discuss a closely allied problem under Amendment No. 299, to which a number of hon. Gentlemen spoke. This proposal concerns the employee of a company and his wife, or the spouse, and the concession of a free passage or voyage in a company ship "once in each calendar year" according to the amendment. I think that I can satisfy the hon. Gentlemen that these voyages will not now be subject to tax as a result of the withdrawal

of subsection (4) apart from the nominal charge for food which is normally made and which would be assessable. The current position more than meets *a* the amendment. As I understand the matter, there could be a fair number of such voyages, but the only basis for charge would be on the cost to the employer, and in the example that we are considering that would be very small.'

The very question which is the subject matter of the present appeal was also *b* raised. A member said (cols 1091–1092):

'I should be grateful for the Financial Secretary's guidance on these two points . . . The second matter applies particularly to private sector, fee-paying schools where, as the Financial Secretary knows, there is often an arrangement for the children of staff in these schools to be taught at less than the commercial fee in other schools. I take it that because of the deletion of *c* Clause 54(4) that is not now caught. Perhaps these examples will help to clarify the extent to which the Government amendment goes.'

The Financial Secretary responded to this question as follows (col 1098):

'He mentioned the children of teachers. The removal of Clause 54(4) will *d* affect the position of a child of one of the teachers at the child's school, because now the benefit will be assessed on the cost to the employer, which would be very small indeed in this case.'

Thereafter, cl 54 was not the subject of further debate and passed into law as it now stands as s 63 of the 1976 Act.

The position can therefore be summarised as follows. The 1976 Bill as *e* introduced sought by cl 54(4) to tax in-house benefits on a different basis from other benefits, ie not on the cost of the in-house benefit to the employer but on the open market price charged to the public. On the deletion of cl 54(4), in-house benefits were to be taxed on the same basis as external benefits, ie on the cost to the employer of providing the benefit. Numerous inquiries were made of the *f* Financial Secretary to elucidate the resulting effect of the Bill on in-house benefits, ie concessionary travel for airline, railway and merchant navy employees, on benefits for hotel employees and on concessionary education for the children of teachers. In responding to each of these requests for information (save that relating to teachers), the Financial Secretary stated that the effect of the Bill would be to leave their position unchanged from the previous law. He explained that in *g* each case (including that of teachers) the charge would be on the cost to the employer of providing the services and that in each case that cost would either be nil or very small. After these statements were made by the Financial Secretary the Bill passed into law without further discussion on this aspect of the matter.

Against that background I turn to consider the various issues which I have identified. *h*

I. SHOULD THE RULE PROHIBITING REFERENCES TO PARLIAMENTARY PRIVILEGE BE RELAXED?

Under present law, there is a general rule that references to parliamentary material as an aid to statutory construction is not permissible (the exclusionary rule) (see *Davis v Johnson* [1978] 1 All ER 1132, [1979] AC 264 and *Hadmor* *j* *Productions Ltd v Hamilton* [1981] 2 All ER 724, [1983] 1 AC 191). This rule did not always apply but was judge-made. Thus, in *Ash v Abdy* (1678) 3 Swan 664, 36 ER 1014 Lord Nottingham LC took judicial notice of his own experience when introducing the Bill in the House of Lords. The exclusionary rule was probably

first stated by Willes J in *Millar v Taylor* (1769) 4 Burr 2303 at 2332, 98 ER 201 at
a 217. However, *Re Mew and Thorne* (1862) 31 LJ Bcy 87 shows that even in the
middle of the last century the rule was not absolute: in that case Lord Westbury
LC in construing an Act had regard to its parliamentary history and drew an
inference as to Parliament's intention in passing the legislation from the making
of an amendment striking out certain words.

    The exclusionary rule was later extended so as to prohibit the court from
b looking even at reports made by commissioners on which legislation was based
(see *Salkeld v Johnson* (1848) 2 Exch 256 at 273, 154 ER 487 at 495). This rule has
now been relaxed so as to permit reports of commissioners, including Law
Commissioners, and white papers to be looked at for the purpose solely of
ascertaining the mischief which the statute is intended to cure but not for the
c purpose of discovering the meaning of the words used by Parliament to effect
such cure (see *Eastman Photographic Materials Co Ltd v Comptroller-General of Patents
Designs and Trade-marks* [1898] AC 571 and *Assam Railways and Trading Co Ltd v
IRC* [1935] AC 445 at 457–458, [1934] All ER Rep 646 at 655). Indeed, in
Factortame Ltd v Secretary of State for Transport [1989] 2 All ER 692, [1990] 2 AC
85 your Lordships' House went further than this and had regard to a Law
d Commission report not only for the purpose of ascertaining the mischief but also
for the purpose of drawing an inference as to parliamentary intention from the
fact that Parliament had not expressly implemented one of the Law Commission's
recommendations.

    Although the courts' attitude to reports leading to legislation has varied, until
recently there was no modern case in which the court had looked at parliamentary
e debates as an aid to construction. However, in *Pickstone v Freemans plc* [1988] 2
All ER 803, [1989] AC 66 this House, in construing a statutory instrument, did
have regard to what was said by the minister who initiated the debate on the
regulations. Lord Keith after pointing out that the draft regulations were not
capable of being amended when presented to Parliament, said that it was 'entirely
legitimate for the purpose of ascertaining the intention of Parliament to take into
f account the terms in which the draft was presented by the responsible minister
and which formed the basis of its acceptance' (see [1988] 2 All ER 803 at 807,
[1989] AC 66 at 112). Lord Templeman also referred to the minister's speech,
although possibly only by way of support for a conclusion he had reached on
other grounds (see [1988] 2 All ER 803 at 814, [1989] AC 66 at 121–122).
g Lord Brandon and Lord Jauncey agreed with both those speeches. This case
therefore represents a major inroad on the exclusionary rule (see also *Owens Bank
Ltd v Bracco* [1992] 2 All ER 193, [1992] 2 AC 443).

    Mr Lester QC, for the taxpayers, did not urge us to abandon the exclusionary
rule completely. His submission was that where the words of a statute were
ambiguous or obscure or were capable of giving rise to an absurd conclusion it
h should be legitimate to look at the parliamentary history, including the debates
in Parliament, for the purpose of identifying the intention of Parliament in using
the words it did use. He accepted that the function of the court was to construe
the actual words enacted by Parliament so that in no circumstances could the
court attach to words a meaning that they were incapable of bearing. He further
accepted that the court should only attach importance to clear statements showing
j the intention of the promoter of the Bill, whether a minister or private member;
there could be no dredging through conflicting statements of intention with a
view to discovering the true intention of Parliament in using the statutory words.

    In *Beswick v Beswick* [1967] 2 All ER 1197 at 1202, [1968] AC 58 at 74 Lord Reid
said:

'For purely practical reasons we do not permit debates in either House to be cited: it would add greatly to the time and expense involved in preparing *a* cases involving the construction of a statute if counsel were expected to read all the debates in Hansard, and it would often be impracticable for counsel to get access to at least the older reports of debates in select committees of the House of Commons; moreover, in a very large proportion of cases such a search, even if practicable, would throw no light on the question before the court . . .'   *b*

In *Black-Clawson International Ltd v Papierwerke Waldhof-Aschaffenburg AG* [1975] 1 All ER 810 at 814–815, [1975] AC 591 at 613–615 Lord Reid said:

'We often say that we are looking for the intention of Parliament, but that is not quite accurate. We are seeking the meaning of the words which *c* Parliament used. We are seeking not what Parliament meant but the true meaning of what they said . . . I have more than once drawn attention to the practical difficulties . . . but the difficulty goes deeper. The questions which give rise to debate are rarely those which later have to be decided by the courts. One might take the views of the promoters of a Bill as an indication of the intention of Parliament but any view the promoters may have had *d* about questions which later come before the court will not often appear in Hansard and often those questions have never occurred to the promoters. At best we might get material from which a more or less dubious inference might be drawn as to what the promoters intended or would have intended if they had thought about the matter, and it would, I think, generally be dangerous to attach weight to what some other members of either House *e* may have said . . . in my view, our best course is to adhere to present practice.'

In the same case Lord Wilberforce said ([1975] 1 All ER 810 at 828, [1975] AC 591 at 629):

'The second [reason] is one of constitutional principle. Legislation in *f* England is passed by Parliament, and put in the form of written words. This legislation is given legal effect on subjects by virtue of judicial decision, and it is the function of the courts to say what the application of the words used to particular cases or individuals is to be . . . it would be a degradation of that process if the courts were to be merely a reflecting mirror of what some other interpretation agency might say.'   *g*

In *Fothergill v Monarch Airlines Ltd* [1980] 2 All ER 696 at 705, [1981] AC 251 at 279 Lord Diplock said:

'The constitutional function performed by courts of justice as interpreters of the written law laid down in Acts of Parliament is often described as *h* ascertaining "the intention of Parliament"; but what this metaphor, though convenient, omits to take into account is that the court, when acting in its interpretative role, as well as when it is engaged in reviewing the legality of administrative action, is doing so as mediator between the state in the exercise of its legislative power and the private citizen for whom the law made by Parliament constitutes a rule binding upon him and enforceable by the *j* executive power of the state. Elementary justice or . . . the need for legal certainty, demands that the rules by which the citizen is to be bound should be ascertainable by him (or, more realistically, by a competent lawyer advising him) by reference to identifiable sources that are publicly accessible.'

In *Davis v Johnson* [1978] 1 All ER 1132 at 1157, [1979] AC 264 at 350
a Lord Scarman said:

> '. . . such material is an unreliable guide to the meaning of what is enacted.
> It promotes confusion, not clarity. The cut and thrust of debate and the
> pressures of executive responsibility, the essential features of open and
> responsible government, are not always conducive to a clear and unbiased
b > explanation of the meaning of statutory language. And the volume of
> parliamentary and ministerial utterances can confuse by its very size.'

Thus the reasons put forward for the present rule are, first, that it preserves the
constitutional proprieties, leaving Parliament to legislate in words and the courts
(not parliamentary speakers) to construe the meaning of the words finally enacted,
c second, the practical difficulty of the expense of researching parliamentary
material which would arise if the material could be looked at, third, the need for
the citizen to have access to a known defined text which regulates his legal rights
and, fourth, the improbability of finding helpful guidance from Hansard.

The Law Commissions of England and Scotland in their joint report on
Interpretation of Statutes (Law Com no 21; Scot Law Com no 11 (1969)) and the
d Renton Committee on *Preparation of Legislation* (Cmnd 6053 (1975)) both
recognised that there was much to be said in principle for relaxing the rule but
advised against a relaxation at present on the same practical grounds as are
reflected in the authorities. However, both bodies recommended changes in the
form of legislation which would, if implemented, have assisted the court in its
search for the true parliamentary intention in using the statutory words.

e Mr Lester submitted that the time has come to relax the rule to the extent
which I have mentioned. He points out that the courts have departed from the
old literal approach of statutory construction and now adopt a purposive approach,
seeking to discover the parliamentary intention lying behind the words used and
construing the legislation so as to give effect to, rather than thwart, the intentions
of Parliament. Where the words used by Parliament are obscure or ambiguous,
f the parliamentary material may throw considerable light not only on the mischief
which the Act was designed to remedy but also on the purpose of the legislation
and its anticipated effect. If there are statements by the minister or other promoter
of the Bill, these may throw as much light on the 'mischief' which the Bill seeks
to remedy as do the white papers, reports of official committees and Law
Commission reports to which the courts already have regard for that purpose. If
g a minister clearly states the effect of a provision and there is no subsequent
relevant amendment to the Bill or withdrawal of the statement it is reasonable to
assume that Parliament passed the Bill on the basis that the provision would have
the effect stated. There is no logical distinction between the use of ministerial
statements introducing subordinate legislation (to which recourse was had in
h Pickstone's case [1988] 2 All ER 803, [1989] AC 66) and such statements made in
relation to other statutory provisions which are not in fact subsequently amended.
Other common law jurisdictions have abandoned the rule without adverse
consequences. Although the practical reasons for the rule (difficulty in getting
access to parliamentary materials and the cost and delay in researching it) are not
without substance, they can be greatly exaggerated: experience in Commonwealth
j countries which have abandoned the rule does not suggest that the drawbacks are
substantial, provided that the court keeps a tight control on the circumstances in
which references to parliamentary material are allowed.

On the other side, the Attorney General submitted that the existing rule had a
sound constitutional and practical basis. If statements by ministers as to the intent

or effect of an Act were allowed to prevail, this would contravene the constitutional rule that Parliament is 'sovereign only in respect of what it expresses by the words *a* used in the legislation it has passed' (see the *Black-Clawson* case [1975] 1 All ER 810 at 836, [1975] AC 591 at 638 per Lord Diplock). It is for the courts alone to construe such legislation. It may be unwise to attach importance to ministerial explanations which are made to satisfy the political requirements of persuasion and debate, often under pressure of time and business. Moreover, in order to establish the significance to be attached to any particular statement, it is necessary *b* both to consider and to understand the context in which it was made. For the courts to have regard to parliamentary material might necessitate changes in parliamentary procedures to ensure that ministerial statements are sufficiently detailed to be taken into account. In addition, there are all the practical difficulties as to the accessibility of parliamentary material, the cost of researching it and the use of court time in analysing it, which are good reasons for maintaining the rule. *c* Finally, to use what is said in Parliament for the purpose of construing legislation would be a breach of s 1, art 9 of the Bill of Rights as being an impeachment or questioning of the freedom of speech in debates in proceedings in Parliament.

My Lords, I have come to the conclusion that, as a matter of law, there are sound reasons for making a limited modification to the existing rule (subject to *d* strict safeguards) unless there are constitutional or practical reasons which outweigh them. In my judgment, subject to the questions of the privileges of the House of Commons, reference to parliamentary material should be permitted as an aid to the construction of legislation which is ambiguous or obscure or the literal meaning of which leads to an absurdity. Even in such cases references in court to parliamentary material should only be permitted where such material *e* clearly discloses the mischief aimed at or the legislative intention lying behind the ambiguous or obscure words. In the case of statements made in Parliament, as at present advised I cannot foresee that any statement other than the statement of the minister or other promoter of the Bill is likely to meet these criteria.

I accept Mr Lester's submissions, but my main reason for reaching this *f* conclusion is based on principle. Statute law consists of the words that Parliament has enacted. It is for the courts to construe those words and it is the court's duty in so doing to give effect to the intention of Parliament in using those words. It is an inescapable fact that, despite all the care taken in passing legislation, some statutory provisions when applied to the circumstances under consideration in any specific case are found to be ambiguous. One of the reasons for such *g* ambiguity is that the members of the legislature in enacting the statutory provision may have been told what result those words are intended to achieve. Faced with a given set of words which are capable of conveying that meaning it is not surprising if the words are accepted as having that meaning. Parliament never intends to enact an ambiguity. Contrast with that the position of the courts. The courts are faced simply with a set of words which are in fact capable of bearing *h* two meanings. The courts are ignorant of the underlying parliamentary purpose. Unless something in other parts of the legislation discloses such purpose, the courts are forced to adopt one of the two possible meanings using highly technical rules of construction. In many, I suspect most, cases references to parliamentary materials will not throw any light on the matter. But in a few cases it may emerge that the very question was considered by Parliament in passing the legislation. *j* Why in such a case should the courts blind themselves to a clear indication of what Parliament intended in using those words? The court cannot attach a meaning to words which they cannot bear, but if the words are capable of bearing more than one meaning why should not Parliament's true intention be enforced rather than thwarted?

A number of other factors support this view. As I have said, the courts can now

a look at white papers and official reports for the purpose of finding the 'mischief' sought to be corrected, although not at draft clauses or proposals for the remedying of such mischief. A ministerial statement made in Parliament is an equally authoritative source of such information; why should the courts be cut off from this source of information as to the mischief aimed at? In any event, the distinction between looking at reports to identify the mischief aimed at but not to find the

b intention of Parliament in enacting the legislation is highly artificial. Take the normal Law Commission report which analyses the problem and then annexes a draft Bill to remedy it. It is now permissible to look at the report to find the mischief and at the draft Bill to see that a provision in the draft was *not* included in the legislation enacted (see *Factortame v Secretary of State for Transport* [1989] 2

c All ER 692, [1990] 2 AC 85). There can be no logical distinction between that case and looking at the draft Bill to see that the statute as enacted reproduced, often in the same words, the provision in the Law Commission's draft. Given the purposive approach to construction now adopted by the courts in order to give effect to the true intentions of the legislature, the fine distinctions between looking for the mischief and looking for the intention in using words to provide

d the remedy are technical and inappropriate. Clear and unambiguous statements made by ministers in Parliament are as much the background to the enactment of legislation as white papers and parliamentary reports.

The decision in *Pickstone v Freemans plc* [1988] 2 All ER 803, [1989] AC 66 which authorises the court to look at ministerial statements made in introducing regulations which could not be amended by Parliament is logically indistinguish-

e able from such statements made in introducing a statutory provision which, though capable of amendment, was not in fact amended.

The judicial antipathy to relaxing the rule has been far from uniform. Lord Reid, who in the passage I have quoted from the *Black-Clawson* case [1975] 1 All ER 810 at 814–815, [1975] AC 591 at 613–615 supported the maintenance of the rule, in his dissenting speech in *Warner v Metropolitan Police Comr* [1968] 2

f All ER 356 at 367, [1969] 2 AC 256 at 279 said:

> '... the layman may well wonder why we do not consult the Parliamentary debates for we are much more likely to find the intention of Parliament there than anywhere else. The rule is firmly established that we may not look at Hansard, and in general I agree with it for reasons which I gave last year in
> *g* *Beswick* v. *Beswick* ([1967] 2 All ER 1197 at 1202, [1968] AC 58 at 73–74). This is not a suitable case in which to reopen the matter, but I am bound to say that this case seems to show that there is room for an exception where examining the proceedings in Parliament would almost certainly settle the matter immediately one way or the other.'

h Lord Wilberforce (whose words I have also quoted) had second thoughts in an extra-judicial capacity at a seminar in Canberra where he referred to a case in which the minister on two occasions during the passage of a Finance Bill stated expressly that the provision was not intended to tax a particular class of beneficiary. Yet subsequently beneficiaries of that class were sought to be taxed under the statutory provision. Lord Wilberforce suggested that there should be a relaxation

j of the exclusionary rule so that, where a minister promoting a Bill makes an explicit and official statement as to the meaning or scope of the provision, reference should be allowed to that statement.

Textbooks often include reference to explanations of legislation given by a minister in Parliament, as a result of which lawyers advise their clients taking account of such statements and judges when construing the legislation come to know of them. In addition, a number of distinguished judges have admitted to breaching the exclusionary rule and looking at Hansard in order to seek the *a* intention of Parliament. When this happens, the parties do not know and have no opportunity to address the judge on the matter. A vivid example of this occurred in *Hadmor Productions Ltd v Hamilton* [1981] 2 All ER 724, [1983] 1 AC 191, CA; [1982] 1 All ER 1042, [1983] 1 AC 191, where Lord Denning MR in the Court of Appeal relied on his own researches into Hansard in reaching his conclusions; in the House of Lords, counsel protested that there were other *b* passages to which he would have wished to draw the court's attention had he known that Lord Denning MR was looking at Hansard (see [1982] 1 All ER 1042 at 1056, [1983] 1 AC 191 at 233). It cannot be right for such information to be available, by a sidewind, for the court but the parties be prevented from presenting their arguments on such material.

Against these considerations, there have to be weighed the practical and *c* constitutional matters urged by the Attorney General, many of which have been relied on in the past in the courts in upholding the exclusionary rule. I will first consider the practical difficulties.

It is said that parliamentary materials are not readily available to, and understandable by, the citizen and his lawyers, who should be entitled to rely on *d* the words of Parliament alone to discover his position. It is undoubtedly true that Hansard and particularly records of committee debates are not widely held by libraries outside London and that the lack of satisfactory indexing of committee stages makes it difficult to trace the passage of a clause after it is redrafted or renumbered. But such practical difficulties can easily be overstated. It is possible to obtain parliamentary materials and it is possible to trace the history. The *e* problem is one of expense and effort in doing so, not the availability of the material. In considering the right of the individual to know the law by simply looking at legislation, it is a fallacy to start from the position that all legislation is available in a readily understandable form in any event: the very large number of statutory instruments made every year are not available in an indexed form for well over a year after they have been passed. Yet, the practitioner manages to deal *f* with the problem, albeit at considerable expense. Moreover, experience in New Zealand and Australia (where the strict rule has been relaxed for some years) has not shown that the non-availability of materials has raised these practical problems.

Next, it is said that lawyers and judges are not familiar with parliamentary *g* procedures and will therefore have difficulty in giving proper weight to the parliamentary materials. Although, of course, lawyers do not have the same experience of these matters as members of the legislature, they are not wholly ignorant of them. If, as I think, significance should only be attached to the clear statements made by a minister or other promoter of the Bill, the difficulty of knowing what weight to attach to such statements is not overwhelming. In the *h* present case, there were numerous statements of view by members in the course of the debate which plainly do not throw any light on the true construction of s 63. What is persuasive in this case is a consistent series of answers given by the minister, after opportunities for taking advice from his officials, all of which point the same way and which were not withdrawn or varied prior to the enactment of the Bill. *j*

Then it is said that court time will be taken up by considering a mass of parliamentary material and long arguments about its significance, thereby increasing the expense of litigation. In my judgment, though the introduction of further admissible material will inevitably involve some increase in the use of

time, this will not be significant as long as courts insist that parliamentary material
a should only be introduced in the limited cases I have mentioned and where such
material contains a clear indication from the minister of the mischief aimed at, or
the nature of the cure intended, by the legislation. Attempts to introduce material
which does not satisfy those tests should be met by orders for costs made against
those who have improperly introduced the material. Experience in the United
States of America, where legislative history has for many years been much more
b generally admissible than I am now suggesting, shows how important it is to
maintain strict control over the use of such material. That position is to be
contrasted with what has happened in New Zealand and Australia (which have
relaxed the rule to approximately the extent that I favour): there is no evidence of
any complaints of this nature coming from those countries.

There is one further practical objection which, in my view, has real substance.
c If the rule is relaxed legal advisers faced with an ambiguous statutory provision
may feel that they have to research the materials to see whether they yield the
crock of gold, ie a clear indication of Parliament's intentions. In very many cases
the crock of gold will not be discovered and the expenditure on the research
wasted. This is a real objection to changing the rule. However, again it is easy to
d overestimate the cost of such research: if a reading of Hansard shows that there is
nothing of significance said by the minister in relation to the clause in question,
further research will become pointless.

In sum, I do not think that the practical difficulties arising from a limited
relaxation of the rule are sufficient to outweigh the basic need for the courts to
give effect to the words enacted by Parliament in the sense that they were intended
e by Parliament to bear. Courts are frequently criticised for their failure to do that.
This failure is due not to cussedness but to ignorance of what Parliament intended
by the obscure words of the legislation. The courts should not deny themselves
the light which parliamentary materials may shed on the meaning of the words
Parliament has used and thereby risk subjecting the individual to a law which
Parliament never intended to enact.
f   Is there, then, any constitutional objection to a relaxation of the rule? The
main constitutional ground urged by the Attorney General is that the use of such
material will infringe s 1, art 9 of the Bill of Rights as being a questioning in any
court of freedom of speech and debates in Parliament. As I understood the
submission, the Attorney General was not contending that the use of parliamentary
g material by the courts for the purposes of construction would constitute an
'impeachment' of freedom of speech since impeachment is limited to cases where
a member of Parliament is sought to be made liable, either in criminal or civil
proceedings, for what he has said in Parliament, eg by criminal prosecution, by
action for libel or by seeking to prove malice on the basis of such words. The
submission was that the use of Hansard for the purpose of construing an Act
h would constitute a 'questioning' of the freedom of speech or debate. The process,
it is said, would involve an investigation of what the minister meant by the words
he used and would inhibit the minister in what he says by attaching legislative
effect to his words. This, it was submitted, constituted 'questioning' the freedom
of speech or debate.

Article 9 is a provision of the highest constitutional importance and should not
j be narrowly construed. It ensures the ability of democratically elected members
of Parliament to discuss what they will (freedom of debate) and to say what they
will (freedom of speech). But, even given a generous approach to this construction,
I find it impossible to attach the breadth of meaning to the word 'question' which
the Attorney General urges. It must be remembered that art 9 prohibits

questioning not only 'in any court' but also in any 'place out of Parliament'. If the
Attorney General's submission is correct, any comment in the media or elsewhere *a*
on what is said in Parliament would constitute 'questioning' since all members of
Parliament must speak and act taking into account what political commentators
and others will say. Plainly art 9 cannot have effect so as to stifle the freedom of
all to comment on what is said in Parliament, even though such comment may
influence members in what they say.

In my judgment, the plain meaning of art 9, viewed against the historical *b*
background in which it was enacted, was to ensure that members of Parliament
were not subjected to any penalty, civil or criminal, for what they said and were
able, contrary to the previous assertions of the Stuart monarchy, to discuss what
they, as opposed to the monarch, chose to have discussed. Relaxation of the rule
will not involve the courts in criticising what is said in Parliament. The purpose
of looking at Hansard will not be to construe the words used by the minister but *c*
to give effect to the words used so long as they are clear. Far from questioning the
independence of Parliament and its debates, the courts would be giving effect to
what is said and done there.

Moreover, the Attorney General's contentions are inconsistent with the practice
which has now continued over a number of years in cases of judicial review. In *d*
such cases, Hansard has frequently been referred to with a view to ascertaining
whether a statutory power has been improperly exercised for an alien purpose or
in a wholly unreasonable manner. In *Brind v Secretary of State for the Home Dept*
[1991] 1 All ER 720, [1991] 1 AC 696 it was the Crown which invited the court
to look at Hansard to show that the minister in that case had acted correctly (see
[1991] 1 AC 696 at 741). This House attached importance to what the minister *e*
had said (see [1991] 1 All ER 720 at 724, 729–730, [1991] 1 AC 696 at 749, 755–
756). The Attorney General accepted that references to Hansard for the purposes
of judicial review litigation did not infringe art 9. Yet reference for the purposes
of judicial review and for the purposes of construction are indistinguishable. In
both types of case, the minister's words are considered and taken into account by
the court; in both, the use of such words by the courts might affect what is said in *f*
Parliament.

As to the authorities, in *Church of Scientology of California v Johnson-Smith* [1972]
1 All ER 378, [1972] 1 QB 522 the plaintiff sued the defendant, a member of
Parliament, for an alleged libel on television and sought to introduce evidence of
what the defendant had said in the House of Commons as proof of malice.
Browne J held, rightly in my view, that such use would breach art 9 as questioning *g*
the motives and intentions of a member of the House. To the extent that he went
further so as to suggest that in no circumstances could the speeches be looked at
other than for the purposes of seeing what was said on a particular date, his
remarks have to be understood in the context of the issues which arose in that
case. Those issues included an allegation that the defendant acted improperly in *h*
Parliament in saying what he did in Parliament. That plainly would amount to
questioning a member's behaviour in Parliament and infringe art 9.

In *R v Secretary of State for Trade, ex p Anderson Strathclyde plc* [1983] 2 All ER
233 an applicant for judicial review sought to adduce parliamentary materials to
prove a fact. The Crown did not object to the Divisional Court looking at the
materials but the court itself refused to do so on the grounds that it would *j*
constitute a breach of art 9 (at 237, 239 per Dunn LJ). In view of the Attorney
General's concession and the decision of this House in *Brind's* case, in my judgment
Ex p Anderson Strathclyde plc was wrongly decided on this point.

Accordingly in my judgment the use of clear ministerial statements by the court as a guide to the construction of ambiguous legislation would not contravene

a art 9. No doubt all judges will be astute to ensure that counsel does not in any way impugn or criticise the minister's statements or his reasoning.

The Attorney General raised a further constitutional point, namely that for the court to use parliamentary material in construing legislation would be to confuse the respective roles of Parliament as the maker of law and the courts as the interpreter. I am not impressed by this argument. The law, as I have said, is to be

b found in the words in which Parliament has enacted. It is for the courts to interpret those words so as to give effect to that purpose. The question is whether, in addition to other aids to the construction of statutory words, the courts should have regard to a further source. Recourse is already had to white papers and official reports not because they determine the meaning of the statutory words but because they assist the court to make its own determination. I can see no

c constitutional impropriety in this.

Finally on this aspect of the case, the Attorney General relied on considerations of comity: the relaxation of the rule would have a direct effect on the rights and privileges of Parliament. To the extent that such rights and privileges are to be found in the Bill of Rights, in my judgment they will not be infringed for the

d reasons which I have given. I deal below with any other parliamentary privileges there may be (see 5. Parliamentary privilege, post).

I therefore reach the conclusion, subject to any question of parliamentary privilege, that the exclusionary rule should be relaxed so as to permit reference to parliamentary materials where: (a) legislation is ambiguous or obscure, or leads to an absurdity; (b) the material relied on consists of one or more statements by a

e minister or other promoter of the Bill together if necessary with such other parliamentary material as is necessary to understand such statements and their effect; (c) the statements relied on are clear. Further than this, I would not at present go.

f 2. DOES THIS CASE FALL WITHIN THE RELAXED RULE?

(a) *Is s 63 ambiguous?*

I have no hesitation in holding that it is. The 'expense incurred in or in connection with' the provision of in-house benefits may be either the marginal cost caused by the provision of the benefit in question or a proportion of the total cost incurred in providing the service both for the public and for the employee

g (the average cost).

In favour of the marginal cost argument, it is submitted by the taxpayers that there has to be a causal link between the benefit in kind taxed under s 61(1) and its 'cash equivalent': s 63(1) defines the cash equivalent of the benefit as being an amount equal to the cost of the benefit. Therefore, it is said, one is looking for the

h actual cost of providing that benefit for the employee. The basic expense of providing and running the school would have been incurred in any event; therefore that expenditure is not caused by the provision of the benefit for the employee. The test is whether the cost would have been incurred but for the provision of the benefit. Therefore, when one comes to s 63(2) one is looking for the additional expense incurred in or in connection with the provision of the

j benefit.

The taxpayers' contention is supported by certain unfair consequences which could ensue if the cost of the benefit is to be taken as the average cost. Take a railway running at a loss: the average cost of providing concessionary travel would be a sum greater than the fare charged to the public. In the case of a heavily endowed school, the fees charged to the public may be less than sufficient to cover the total cost of running the school, the shortfall being made good by the *a* endowment. On the average cost basis, the taxpayer would be treated as receiving a benefit greater than the amount charged to the public.

On the other side, the Revenue contend that, once one has identified the benefit under s 61, s 63 contains a code for establishing its cash equivalent. Section 63(1) defines the cash equivalent as the cost of the benefit and s 63(2) defines 'the cost of a benefit' as being the expense 'incurred in or in connection with' its provision. *b* The benefit in this case consists of the enjoyment of the facilities of the school. What is the cost of providing those facilities? It must be the total cost of providing the school. However, the total cost of providing the school is incurred not only in connection with the provision of the benefit to the employee but also in providing the school with fee-paying boys. This provision is expressly covered by the final words of s 63(2) 'and includes . . . a proper proportion of any expense relating *c* partly to the benefit and partly to other matters'. Therefore, says the Revenue, the cost of the benefit is a proportion of the total cost of providing the services. The Revenue has no answer to the anomalies which arise when the cost of providing a loss-making facility means that the average cost basis results in the taxpayer being treated as receiving a sum by way of benefit greater than the cost *d* of buying that benefit on the open market.

I find these arguments nicely balanced. The statutory words are capable of bearing either meaning. There is an ambiguity or obscurity.

(b) *Are the words of the Financial Secretary clear?*

It is necessary by way of preface to emphasise that in no circumstances can in- *e* house benefits give rise to no taxable benefit or only a small taxable benefit if that benefit is to be assessed on an average cost basis. The average cost basis means that the cost will approximate to the open market charge (less any profit element) and therefore must in all circumstances be substantial.

The Finance Bill 1976 as introduced proposed to charge in-house benefits on a *f* different basis from that applicable to external benefits, ie on the open market price charged to the public (see cl 54(4)). Once the government announced its intention to withdraw cl 54(4) a number of members were anxious to elucidate what effect this would have on classes of taxpayers who enjoyed in-house benefits: concessionary transport for railwaymen, airline employees and merchant seamen; concessionary accommodation for hotel employees; concessionary education for *g* the children of teachers. In answer to these inquiries the Financial Secretary gave similar answers in relation to each class, namely (1) that in all the cases (except that of the teachers' concessionary education) the benefits would be taxed on the same basis as under the existing law and (2) that in all cases the amount of the charge would be nil, small or, in the case of the schoolteachers, 'very small indeed'. In my view these repeated assurances are quite inconsistent with the minister *h* having had, or communicated, any intention other than that the words 'the expense incurred in or in connection with' the provision of the benefit would produce a charge to tax on the additional or marginal cost only, not a charge on the average cost of the benefit.

It may be said that the Financial Secretary's reference to the taxpayers being liable to tax as under the pre-existing law (ie under the Finance Act 1948, s 39, as *j* re-enacted by the Income and Corporation Taxes Act 1970) shows that he was saying that the position was unchanged: nothing the minister said could affect the proper construction of legislation already on the statute book. To this contention there are, in my judgment two answers. First, the old Acts were repealed by the 1976 Act; the provisions were re-enacted in different language,

albeit that the phrase 'incurred in or in connection with the provision of the
a benefit' appeared in both statutes. In this case the court is concerned to construe
the 1976 Act; what is relevant is the ministerial statement as to the effect of that
Act. Second, the existing practice of the Revenue under the pre-1976 law was not
to tax benefits in kind on the average cost basis and those who were asking
questions on behalf of their constituents would have been well aware of this fact.
For example, in the case of the airline employees the Revenue had sought to tax
b concessionary travel on the average cost basis but their claim had failed before the
commissioners and they had not persisted in that claim. The minister's answer in
Parliament that the cost to the airlines of providing concessionary travel for airline
employees would be nothing was exactly what in practice had been happening
under the old law.

c The question then arises whether it is right to attribute to Parliament as a
whole the same intention as that repeatedly voiced by the Financial Secretary. In
my judgment it is. It is clear from reading Hansard that the committee was
repeatedly asking for guidance as to the effect of the legislation once cl 54(4) was
abandoned. That Parliament relied on the ministerial statements is shown by the
fact that the matter was never raised again after the discussions in committee,
d that amendments were consequentially withdrawn and that no relevant
amendment was made which could affect the correctness of the minister's
statement.

Accordingly, in my judgment we have in this case a clear statement by the
responsible minister stating the effect of the ambiguous words used in what
became s 63 of the 1976 Act which the parliamentary history shows to have been
e the basis on which that section was enacted.

3. IF REFERENCE TO HANSARD IS PERMISSIBLE, WHAT IS THE TRUE CONSTRUCTION?
In my judgment there can be no doubt that, if parliamentary privilege does
not prohibit references to Hansard, the parliamentary history shows that
f Parliament passed the legislation on the basis that the effect of ss 61 and 63 of the
1976 Act was to assess in-house benefits, and particularly concessionary education
for teachers' children, on the marginal cost to the employer and not on the average
cost. Since the words of s 63 are perfectly capable of bearing that meaning, in my
judgment that is the meaning they should be given.

I have had the advantage of reading in draft the speech of my noble and learned
g friend on the Woolsack. In construing the 1976 Act without reference to the
parliamentary proceedings, he treats it as decisive that in this case the taxpayers'
children were only occupying surplus accommodation and that it lay in the
discretion of the school whether to grant such benefit to the taxpayers. This
approach draws a distinction which is not reflected in the parliamentary
proceedings. Concessionary travel for railwaymen is not discretionary nor is it
h dependent on there being surplus seats on any train. Similarly, in many cases the
education of teachers' children at concessionary rates is neither discretionary nor
dependent on there being surplus capacity. Yet in both cases in Parliament the
section was put forward as providing that only the marginal cost would be treated
as taxable. I can therefore find no ground for drawing the narrow distinction and
would hold that in the case of all in-house benefits the same test applies, viz the
j cost of the benefit to the employer is the additional or marginal cost only.

Therefore if reference to Hansard is permissible, I would allow the appeal.

4. IF REFERENCE TO HANSARD IS NOT PERMISSIBLE, WHAT IS THE TRUE CONSTRUCTION?
Having once looked at what was said in Parliament, it is difficult to put it out
of mind. I have the advantage that, after the first hearing and before seeing the

parliamentary materials, I had reached the conclusion, in agreement with
Vinelott J and the Court of Appeal, that the Revenue's submissions were correct. *a*
If it is not permissible to take into account what was said by the Financial
Secretary, I remain of the same view.

My reasons are the same as those given by the Court of Appeal. I accept
Mr Lester's submission that there must be a causal link between the benefit
provided for the taxpayers and the cost of the benefit referred to in s 63(1). But in
my judgment s 63(2) provides a statutory formula for quantifying such cost: it *b*
requires one to find 'the amount of any expense incurred in or in connection
with' the provision of the benefit, such expense to include 'a proper proportion of
any expense relating partly to the benefit and partly to other matters'.

To apply s 63(2) it is first necessary to identify 'the benefit'. It has throughout
been common ground that the benefit in this case to each taxpayer is that 'his son
is allowed to participate in all the facilities afforded by the school to boys who are *c*
educated there'. These facilities are exactly the same as those afforded to every
boy in the school, whether his parents are paying the full or concessionary fees.
Therefore the relevant question is: what is the expense incurred in or in connection
with providing those facilities? On the literal meaning of the words, the expense
to the school of providing those facilities is exactly the same for each boy in the *d*
school, i e a proportion of the total cost of running the school.

Even if it could be said that, because the school would have incurred the basic
expense of running the school in any event, such expense was not incurred 'in'
providing the facilities for the taxpayer's child, on the literal meaning of the
words such expense was in any event incurred 'in connection with' the provision
of such facilities. The words 'in connection with' have the widest connotation and *e*
I cannot see how they are to be restricted in the absence of some context
permitting such restriction.

The strongest argument in favour of the taxpayers is the anomaly which would
arise if the employer's business were running at a loss or was subsidised by
endowment: as I have explained, in such a case the adoption of the literal meaning
of the statutory words would lead to a result whereby the taxpayer is assessed at *f*
an amount greater than that charged by the employer to the public for the same
service. The Crown has no answer to this anomaly as such. But there are other
anomalies which arise if the taxpayers' argument is correct. For example, if,
unlike the present case, the school could have been filled with boys paying the
full fee, the school would have lost the fee income from the places occupied by
the children of the taxpayers for whom only the concessionary fee was payable. *g*
Without deciding the point, it seems to me arguable that, on the taxpayers'
argument, such loss or part of it would be an expense incurred by the school in
providing the concessionary places. If so, the amount on which the taxpayer
would be assessed to tax would vary from year to year depending on the success
of the school in attracting applicants. To my mind such a variation on a year-by- *h*
year basis by reference to an extraneous factor would be a most anomalous result,
and would involve great difficulties in quantifying the cost to the employer in
each case.

In the circumstances, if I could detect from the statute any statutory purpose or
intention pointing to one construction rather than the other, I would certainly
adopt it. But the statute yields no hint. The basic problem is this. What is taxable *j*
is the benefit to the employee and one would have expected the quantum of that
benefit to be assessed by reference to the value of the benefit to the employee. But
the statutory formula does not seek to value the benefit to the employee as such,
but requires the quantum of the benefit to be fixed by reference to the cost to the

a employer in providing it. Given this dislocation between the benefit which is assessable to tax and the basis on which its value is to be assessed it is impossible to gain any guidance in the statute as to the parliamentary intention. In the circumstances there is in my judgment no option but to give effect to the literal meaning of the words as did the Court of Appeal. In the result, the Revenue's argument should succeed and the appeal should be dismissed.

b
5. PARLIAMENTARY PRIVILEGE

It follows from what I have said that in my view the outcome of this appeal depends on whether or not the court can look at parliamentary material: if it can, the appeal should be allowed; if it cannot, the appeal should be dismissed. For the reasons I have given, as a matter of pure law this House should look at Hansard *c* and give effect to the parliamentary intention it discloses in deciding the appeal. The problem is the indication given by the Attorney General that, if this House does so, your Lordships may be infringing the privileges of the House of Commons.

For the reasons I have given, in my judgment reference to parliamentary *d* materials for the purpose of construing legislation does not breach s 1, art 9 of the Bill of Rights. However, the Attorney General courteously but firmly warned your Lordships that this did not conclude the question. He said that art 9 was an illustration of the right that the House of Commons had won by 1688 to exclusive cognisance of its own proceedings. He continued:

e   'I remain convinced ... that the House of Commons would regard a decision by your Lordships to use Hansard to construe a statute as a grave step and that the House of Commons may well regret that its views were not sought on such an important matter before your Lordships reached a decision.'

My Lords, this House and the courts have always been, and I trust will always *f* continue to be, zealous in protecting parliamentary privileges. I have therefore tried to discover some way in which this House can fulfil its duty to decide the case before it without trespassing on the sensibilities of the House of Commons. But I can find no middle course. Although for a considerable time before the resumed hearing it was known that this House was to consider whether to permit Hansard to be used as an aid to construction, there was no suggestion from the *g* Crown or anyone else that such a course might breach parliamentary privilege until the Attorney General raised the point at the start of the rehearing. Even then, the Attorney General did not ask for an adjournment to enable the House of Commons to consider the matter. Your Lordships therefore heard the case through to the end of the argument.

h Although in the past the courts and the House of Commons both claimed the exclusive right to determine whether or not a privilege existed, it is now apparently accepted that it is for the courts to decide whether a privilege exists and for the House to decide whether such privilege has been infringed (see *Erskine May Parliamentary Practice* (21st edn, 1989) pp 147–160). Thus, *Erskine May* p 150 says:

j   'In the 19th century, a series of cases forced upon the Commons and the courts a comprehensive review of the issues which divided them, from which it became clear that some of the earlier claims to jurisdiction made in the name of privilege by the House of Commons were untenable in a court of law: that the law of Parliament was part of the general law, that its principles

were not beyond the judicial knowledge of the judges, and that it was the
duty of the common law to define its limits could no longer be disputed.'   *a*

Again it is said (p 154):

> 'Though events have revealed no single doctrine by which all issues of
> privilege arising between Parliament and the courts may be resolved, many
> of the problems of earlier years which are dealt with above have been
> substantially solved. Neither House is by itself entitled to claim the supremacy   *b*
> over the courts of law enjoyed by the undivided medieval High Court of
> Parliament. Since neither House can by its own declaration create a new
> privilege, privilege may be considered to be capable of being ascertained and
> thus judicially known to the courts.'

Accordingly, if the nature of the privilege going beyond the Bill of Rights had   *c*
been identified, your Lordships could have determined whether or not such
privilege exists, although it would be for the House of Commons to determine
whether or not there was an infringement of any privilege found to exist. In fact,
neither the letter from the Clerk of the Commons nor the Attorney General has
identified or specified the nature of any privilege extending beyond that protected
by the Bill of Rights. In the absence of a claim to a defined privilege as to the   *d*
validity of which your Lordships could make a determination, it would not in
my view be right to withhold from the taxpayers a decision to which, in law, they
are entitled. I would therefore allow the appeal.

I trust that, when the House of Commons comes to consider the decision in
this case, it will be appreciated that there is no desire to impeach its privileges in   *e*
any way. Your Lordships are motivated by a desire to carry out the intentions of
Parliament in enacting legislation and have no intention or desire to question the
processes by which such legislation was enacted or of criticising anything said by
anyone in Parliament in the course of enacting it. The purpose is to give effect to,
not thwart, the intentions of Parliament.

Appeals allowed.   *f*

Mary Rose Plummer   Barrister.

a
R v Naillie
R v Kanesarajah

COURT OF APPEAL, CRIMINAL DIVISION
WATKINS LJ, SWINTON THOMAS AND GARLAND JJ
b 21, 24 FEBRUARY, 14 APRIL 1992

Immigration – Assisting illegal entry into United Kingdom – Illegal entry – Asylum seeker – Asylum seeker using false documents to leave country of origin – Asylum claimed immediately on arrival in United Kingdom – False documents not used to gain entry into United Kingdom – Whether asylum seeker 'illegal entrant' – Immigration Act 1971,
c ss 11, 25.

The two appellants, N and K, were separately charged with facilitating the illegal entry of others into the United Kingdom contrary to s 25(1)[a] of the Immigration Act 1971. N, a Kenyan national of Somali origin, arranged for two Somali women and six Somali children, who had entered Kenya from Somalia, to book a flight
d from Kenya to the United Kingdom using forged Tanzanian passports. N and the Somalis then travelled from Kenya to the United Kingdom on the same flight, in the course of which the aircrew took possession of the women's passports because the crew became aware that they were asylum seekers. On arrival in the United Kingdom the Somalis disembarked separately from N and after being interviewed
e by immigration officers were given temporary admittance as asylum seekers. N was meanwhile arrested and charged with facilitating the illegal entry of the Somalis into the United Kingdom. At his trial N submitted that no case to answer had been made out because, inter alia, it had not been established that the Somalis were illegal entrants within the terms of the 1971 Act when they had disembarked in the United Kingdom, since the Somalis, although using their forged passports
f to deceive the Kenyan authorities, had not used the passports to attempt to gain entry into the United Kingdom. The judge rejected the submission of no case to answer and N was convicted. He appealed. K, a British national born in Sri Lanka, took his wife's passport with him to Sri Lanka, where it was altered with his knowledge to enable another woman and her child and two strangers to use it to deceive the Sri Lankan authorities into allowing them to leave Sri Lanka. K, the
g woman and her child and the two strangers then flew to London using airline tickets which had been purchased in K's name for himself, the woman and her child and the two strangers. During the flight K retrieved his wife's passport, leaving the woman and the two strangers with no passports. On disembarkation in the United Kingdom and before going through immigration control the woman and the strangers sought political asylum and were given temporary
h admittance as asylum seekers. K was arrested in possession of the forged passport and documents relating to the Sri Lankans and charged with facilitating their illegal entry into the United Kingdom. At his trial K submitted that no case to answer had been made out because it had not been shown that the woman was an illegal entrant, but that submission was rejected and K was convicted. He
j appealed.

Held – Illegal entrants were those who either entered clandestinely or obtained leave to enter by themselves using fraud or deceit or a materially false document.

---

a   Section 25(1), so far as material, is set out at p 80 *h*, post

A person, such as an asylum seeker, who disembarked without a right of entry
had not in fact 'entered' the country merely by disembarking from the mode of a
transport which brought him to the United Kingdom, since entry was not to be
equated with disembarkation, the distinction between the two being clearly
recognised in s 11[b] of the 1971 Act. Accordingly, persons who arrived in the
United Kingdom without a right of entry were not automatically illegal entrants.
Since the asylum seekers in question had not entered clandestinely or by means
of deception by proffering forged documents to immigration officers as being b
genuine they were not illegal entrants for the purposes of s 25(1) of the 1971 Act
and an essential element of the offence with which N and K had been charged
had not been made out. The appeals would therefore be allowed (see p 82 h to
p 83 e j to p 84 c g to j and p 85 b, post).

Khawaja v Secretary of State for the Home Dept [1983] 1 All ER 765 and R v c
Immigration Officer, ex p Chan [1992] 2 All ER 738 applied.

Notes

For illegal entry into the United Kingdom, see 4(2) Halsbury's Laws (4th edn
reissue) para 118, and for cases on the subject, see 2 Digest (Reissue) 199–200,
1153–1154.   d
For the Immigration Act 1971, ss 11, 25, see 31 Halsbury's Statutes (4th edn) 64,
77.

Cases referred to in judgment

Khawaja v Secretary of State for the Home Dept [1983] 1 All ER 765, [1984] AC 74,
    [1983] 2 WLR 321, HL.   e
R v Immigration Officer, ex p Chan [1992] 2 All ER 738, [1992] 1 WLR 541, CA.
Vilvarajah v Secretary of State for the Home Dept [1990] Imm AR 457, CA.

Cases also cited or referred to in skeleton arguments

Air-India v Wiggins [1980] 2 All ER 593, [1980] 1 WLR 815, HL.
Board of Trade v Owen [1957] 1 All ER 411, [1957] AC 602, HL.   f
Bugdaycay v Secretary of State for the Home Dept [1987] 1 All ER 940, [1987] AC
    514, HL.
Mokuolu v Secretary of State for the Home Dept [1989] Imm AR 51, CA.
R v Secretary of State for the Home Dept, ex p Jayakody [1982] 1 All ER 461, [1982]
    1 WLR 405, CA.
R v Secretary of State for the Home Dept, ex p Patel [1986] Imm AR 515, CA.   g
R v Singh (Amar Jit), R v Meeuwsen [1973] 1 All ER 122, [1972] 1 WLR 1600, CA.
Zamir v Secretary of State for the Home Dept [1980] 2 All ER 768, [1980] AC 930,
    HL.

Appeal against conviction
R v Naillie   h

Yabu Hurerali Naillie appealed against his conviction on 7 August 1991 in the
Crown Court at Isleworth before Judge Simon Evans and a jury of facilitating
illegal entry into the United Kingdom contrary to s 25(1) of the Immigration Act
1971 for which he was sentenced to 18 months' imprisonment. The facts are set
out in the judgment of the court.   j

R v Kanesarajah

Rajaratnam Kanesarajah appealed against his conviction on 18 November 1991 in
the Crown Court at Croydon before Judge Sir David Hughes-Morgan and a jury

---

b   Section 11, so far as material, is set out at p 80 f g, post of facilitating illegal entry into the United Kingdom contrary to s 25(1) of the

a Immigration Act 1971 for which he was sentenced to 15 months' imprisonment. The facts are set out in the judgment of the court.

The appeals were heard together by consent.

b *Anthony Scrivener QC* and *Michel G A Massih* (assigned by the *Registrar of Criminal Appeals*) for the appellant Naillie.
Martin Griffith (instructed by the *Crown Prosecution Service*) for the Crown in *R v Naillie*.
Frances Webber (assigned by *Registrar of Criminal Appeals*) for the appellant Kanesarajah.

c *Timothy R Spencer* (instructed by the *Crown Prosecution Service*) for the Crown in *R v Kanesarajah*.

Cur adv vult

14 April 1992. The following judgment of the court was delivered.

d
WATKINS LJ. We heard these appeals together by consent of the appellants because they raise similar issues as to the meaning of the phrase 'illegal entrant' in s 25(1) of the Immigration Act 1971, the status of persons entering the United Kingdom without permission who claim to be asylum seekers or political refugees and the offence committed by anyone who assists an illegal entrant to enter.

e   On 7 August 1991 Yabu Naillie, then 41 years of age, in the Crown Court at Isleworth before Judge Simon Evans was convicted of facilitating illegal entry into the United Kingdom contrary to s 25(1). He was sentenced to 15 months' imprisonment. He appeals on a point of law against conviction and applies for leave to appeal against sentence.

f   On 18 November 1991 Rajaratnam Kanesarajah in the Crown Court at Croydon before Judge Sir David Hughes-Morgan was convicted of facilitating illegal entry contrary to s 25(1). He was sentenced to 15 months' imprisonment. He appeals against conviction by leave of the single judge. An application with regard to sentence has been referred to this court.

     The facts in Naillie's case are that on 3 March 1991 two Somali women,

g Mrs Ahmadi and Mrs Said, who are half sisters, together with six children landed at Gatwick Airport in a Gulf Air aeroplane which had come from Nairobi, Kenya. The appellant was on the same aeroplane. The women had with them during the flight forged Tanzanian passports. They had left their homes in Somalia and travelled to Nairobi, where they purchased the forged passports. There was no evidence, certainly no direct evidence, that Naillie had been involved in that but

h at some time or other he must have met the two women or someone concerned with them because he purchased their air tickets, and either had the Tanzanian passports in his possession then or knew the women possessed them. He is himself of Somali parentage but is a Kenyan national and has a valid Kenyan passport.

     On Saturday, 2 March 1991 Naillie went into the offices of Haidery Tours in Nairobi. He purchased nine tickets for a flight from Nairobi to London for

j himself, the two women and the six children, saying that three children belonged to each woman. In fact one of the women was the mother of all the children. He told the salesman that he had a Kenyan passport and the women had Tanzanian passports. It was essential that onward tickets to London should be booked because otherwise the women would be treated as Tanzanians seeking entry to Kenya. Naillie paid for the tickets and described himself as the group leader.

They travelled on the Gulf Air aeroplane which left Nairobi on 2 March. On *a* the first leg of the journey, to Muscat, Naillie sat with the women and the children. On the second leg to Gatwick he did not. The Crown alleged that he deliberately distanced himself from them. In the course of that journey the crew on the aeroplane took possession of the women's passports because they became aware from what the women said that they were asylum seekers. When the aeroplane arrived at Gatwick the women and the children on the one hand and *b* Naillie on the other disembarked separately and stayed apart. The women and the children were directed to the transit lounge, where they were interviewed by immigration officers who were in possession of the women's passports by then. Had they been Tanzanians on a visit to this country they would have presented their passports at the usual place on their way out of the airport. As a result of the interview the women, and the children, were given temporary admittance to the *c* United Kingdom as asylum seekers pending an inquiry and decision by the Home Secretary as to whether they were or were not genuine political refugees and whether they should be allowed to remain in this country or be deported. It was part of Naillie's case at the trial, and on this appeal, that whilst the forged passports had been used to deceive the Kenyan authorities before departure from Nairobi, they had not been used to gain entry into the United Kingdom and the women *d* had made it clear it was never their intention that they would be. In any event, so it was contended, the acts complained of were committed outside the jurisdiction of the United Kingdom.

The Crown's case against Naillie was that he bought the tickets in Nairobi having the forged passports in his possession. He travelled with the two women and then deliberately distanced himself from them. He was acting as the group *e* leader throughout. There was a plan to deceive the United Kingdom Immigration Service and Naillie was a party to that plan. After his arrest for having contravened s 25(1) he told a number of lies to the immigration officers.

At the outset of his trial, which commenced on 29 July, and at the close of the Crown's case counsel for Naillie submitted that no case to answer had been made out, inter alia because it had not been established that the two women were illegal *f* entrants as defined by the 1971 Act. Counsel for the Crown contended that the women were illegal entrants when they disembarked at Gatwick Airport and it was irrelevant for the purposes of s 25(1) that they did not thereafter attempt to go through immigration control using the forged passports.

The judge rejected the submission of no case to answer. He also rejected *g* Mr Spencer's submission for the Crown as to the meaning of the words 'illegal entrant' in s 25(1). He said that he would direct the jury as follows: (1) the Crown must prove that there was a plan that the false passports be used to allow Mrs Ahmadi and Mrs Said to enter the United Kingdom; (2) Naillie knew or had reasonable cause to believe the passports were to be used to secure their entry and (3) Naillie took part in carrying out those arrangements by travelling to the *h* United Kingdom with them. In summing up the judge said:

'The main question of fact for you to decide—and there are a number of questions of fact really which I will come to in a moment—before reaching a verdict is: are we sure that that was part of a plan to deceive the United Kingdom Immigration Service? If you are sure it was part of a plan, then you *j* may and probably will—but it will be a matter for you as all matters of fact are—find the defendant guilty, if you have found the other ingredients which I will come to in a moment.'

He summarised those ingredients as follows:

a '(1) Was there a plan that false passports be used to allow the ladies to enter the United Kingdom? If "Yes" to (1), (2) are we sure [that Naillie] knew or had reasonable cause to believe that the false passports were to be used to secure their entry? If "Yes" to that . . . (3) did he take part, that is "become concerned" as you can see there, in that plan and the carrying out of that plan by travelling to the United Kingdom?'

b In Kanesarajah's case there was little, if any, dispute of the following facts. On 9 March 1991 Kanesarajah, born in Sri Lanka but a British national, travelled to Sri Lanka. He took his wife's passport with him. It was indorsed with particulars of their three children. Whilst he was there his wife's passport was altered, with his knowledge, by removing the photograph of his wife and inserting the photograph of another woman and her child. On 25 April four airline tickets *c* were purchased in the name of Kanesarajah, to be used by him, the woman and child and two others who were strangers to him. The forged passport belonging to Kanesarajah's wife was used to deceive the immigration authorities in Sri Lanka to allow all except Kanesarajah, who possessed his own passport, to leave that country and to obtain access to a flight between Colombo and London via Dubai. *d* In the course of the journey Kanesarajah retrieved his wife's passport. Accordingly, on arrival, the woman and the others had no passports of any description in their possession and no other documents.

On disembarkation at Gatwick and before going through immigration the woman and the strangers sought asylum and said they were political refugees. Kanesarajah was arrested. He had in his possession the forged passport and *e* documents relating to the woman and the two strangers. They were given temporary admittance as asylum seekers to await the decision of the Home Secretary.

Kanesarajah was unquestionably a party to deceiving the authorities in Sri Lanka. That fact by itself does not, of course, make him guilty of any offence in this country.

f At the close of the Crown's case counsel for Kanesarajah submitted that there was no case to answer because it had not been shown that the woman was an illegal entrant. The judge rejected that submission. After reciting the brief facts, he said in his summing up:

g 'Here was this lady and she was going to come into the United Kingdom with this passport. I have used what I hope is going to be a neutral expression "come into the United Kingdom" because what Miss Joseph has been saying to you is that the passport was only used to get out of Sri Lanka and that on arrival in the United Kingdom the passport was not used. That seems to be the position from what we have heard. I was reminded when Miss Joseph was talking about using the passport only to get out and not into England of *h* the old contemplation that is suggested ought to be carried out by Zen Buddhists, namely you sit for five or six years concentrating upon the sound of one hand clapping. That occurred to me because I am wondering whether there is not a danger that Miss Joseph has been concentrating in her submissions to you upon a door with only one side, a side labelled exit. However, that door not only has one side it has two sides. You go through *j* the door to get out of Sri Lanka and when you are through the door you enter into the United Kingdom. It is a matter for you to decide . . . the evidence is all one way here that the lady did not have a valid passport. She apparently demanded entry on the basis that she was a political refugee. She sought political asylum. We have further been told that there is nothing in

the law—in so far as I am the judge of the law I have to tell you there is
nothing in the law—which says that anybody can demand entry, legal entry, *a*
by claiming political asylum. You remain an illegal entrant if you satisfy this
definition in other words if you have not got a passport or some other proper
document.'

The two main questions which arise on these appeals are: (1) was it established
that the persons in both cases (we shall call them henceforward as they claimed to *b*
be 'asylum seekers') upon arriving in the United Kingdom were illegal entrants
and (2) if not what was their status when actually claiming to seek asylum in
relation to an alleged offence by another under s 25(1)?

The relevant legislation under the 1971 Act and the Statement of Changes in
Immigration Rules (HC Paper (1989–90) no 251), including, in particular,
references to the Convention and Protocol relating to the Status of Refugees *c*
(Geneva, 28 July 1951; TS 39 (1954); Cmd 9171 and New York, 31 January 1967;
TS 15 (1969); Cmnd 3906) to which the United Kingdom is a signatory, is as
follows.

The 1971 Act   *d*

'... **3.**—(1) Except as otherwise provided by or under this Act, where a
person is not a British citizen—(a) he shall not enter the United Kingdom
unless given leave to do so in accordance with this Act ...

4.—(1) The power under this Act to give or refuse leave to enter the United
Kingdom shall be exercised by immigration officers, and the power to give *e*
leave to remain in the United Kingdom, or to vary any leave under section
3(3)(a) ...

11.—(1) A person arriving in the United Kingdom by ship or aircraft shall
for purposes of this Act be deemed not to enter the United Kingdom unless
and until he disembarks, and on disembarkation at a port shall further be
deemed not to enter the United Kingdom so long as he remains in such area *f*
(if any) at the port as may be approved for this purpose by an immigration
officer; and a person who has not otherwise entered the United Kingdom
shall be deemed not to do so as long as he is detained, or temporarily admitted
or released while liable to detention, under the powers conferred by Schedule
2 to this Act.

(2) In this Act "disembark" means disembark from a ship or aircraft, and *g*
"embark" means embark in a ship or aircraft; and, except in subsection (1)
above ...

25.—(1) Any person knowingly concerned in making or carrying out
arrangements for securing or facilitating the entry into the United Kingdom
of anyone whom he knows or has reasonable cause for believing to be an *h*
illegal entrant shall be guilty of an offence ...

(5) Subsection (1) above shall apply to things done outside as well as to
things done in the United Kingdom where they are done—(a) by a British
citizen, a British Dependent Territories citizen, or a British Overseas citizen;
(b) by a person who under the British Nationality Act 1981 is a British subject;
or (c) by a British protected person (within the meaning of that Act) ... *j*

33.—(1) ... "entrant" means a person entering or seeking to enter the
United Kingdom, and "illegal entrant" means a person unlawfully entering
or seeking to enter in breach of a deportation order or of the immigration
laws, and includes also a person who has so entered ...'

Schedule 2 deals with, inter alia, the powers and duties of immigration officers.
a Section 26 makes it an offence for someone without reasonable excuse to fail to
comply with a number of its provisions. The relevant paragraphs of Sch 2 are as
follows:

'2.—(1) An immigration officer may examine any persons who have
arrived in the United Kingdom by ship or aircraft (including transit
b passengers, members of the crew and others not seeking to enter the United
Kingdom) for the purpose of determining—(*a*) whether any of them is or is
not a British citizen; and (*b*) whether, if he is not, he may or may not enter
the United Kingdom without leave . . .

4.—(1) It shall be the duty of any person examined under paragraph 2 or
3 above to furnish to the person carrying out the examination all such
c information in his possession as that person may require for the purpose of
his functions under that paragraph.

(2) A person on his examination under paragraph 2 or 3 above by an
immigration officer shall, if so required by the immigration officer—(*a*)
produce either a valid passport with photograph or some other document
satisfactorily establishing his identity and nationality or citizenship . . .'
d

The immigration rules
The relevant rules are as follows:

'7 A person must, on arrival in the United Kingdom, produce on request
e by the immigration officer a valid national passport or other document
satisfactorily establishing his identity and nationality. Everyone arriving in
the United Kingdom is liable to be examined and must furnish the
immigration officer with such information as may be required for the
purpose of deciding whether he requires leave to enter and, if so, whether
and on what terms leave should be given . . .

f 21 Where a person is a refugee full account is to be taken of the provisions
of the Convention and Protocol relating to the Status of Refugees [Cmd 9171
and Cmnd 3906]. Nothing in these rules is to be construed as requiring
action contrary to the United Kingdom's obligations under these instruments
. . .

75 Special considerations apply where a person seeking entry claims
g asylum in the United Kingdom, or where it appears to the immigration
officer as a result of information given by that person that he may be eligible
for asylum in the United Kingdom. Every such case is to be referred by the
immigration officer to the Home Office for decision regardless of any
grounds set out in any provision of these rules which may appear to justify
refusal of leave to enter. The Home Office will then consider the case in
h accordance with the provisions of the Convention and Protocol relating to
the Status of Refugees. Asylum will not be refused if the only country to
which the person could be removed is one to which he is unwilling to go
owing to a well-founded fear of being persecuted for reasons of race, religion,
nationality, membership of a particular social group or political opinion . . .

j 140 A person may apply for asylum in the United Kingdom on the ground
that, if he were required to leave, he would have to go to a country to which
he is unwilling to go owing to a well-founded fear of being persecuted for
reasons of race, religion, nationality, membership of a particular social group
or political opinion. Any such claim is to be carefully considered in the light

of all the relevant circumstances . . .

161 Where a person is a refugee full account is to be taken of the provisions *a*
of the Convention and Protocol relating to the Status of Refugees. Nothing
in these rules is to be construed as requiring action contrary to the United
Kingdom's obligations under these instruments . . .

173 In accordance with the provisions of the Convention and Protocol
relating to the Status of Refugees, a deportation order will not be made
against a person if the only country to which he can be removed is one to *b*
which he is unwilling to go owing to well-founded fear of being persecuted
for reasons of race, religion, nationality, membership of a particular social
group or political opinion . . .'

We have heard submissions for the Crown by Mr Griffith and Mr Spencer, who
appeared separately in the two trials—we shall regard their submissions as having *c*
been made more or less jointly—and from Mr Scrivener QC for Naillie and
Miss Webber for Kanesarajah, neither of whom appeared in the trials.

The Crown submitted that the asylum seekers upon arriving in the United
Kingdom from Kenya and Sri Lanka were seeking to enter in breach of the
immigration laws. In *Khawaja v Secretary of State for the Home Dept* [1983] 1 All
ER 765, [1984] AC 74 it was held that the expression 'illegal entrant' in s 33(1) *d*
included any person who had obtained leave to enter the United Kingdom by
practising fraud or deception in contravention of the 1971 Act and was not
limited to persons who had entered the country clandestinely. *Khawaja's* case was
considered by this court in *R v Immigration Officer, ex p Chan* [1992] 2 All ER 738,
[1992] 1 WLR 541. The appellant had entered the United Kingdom from Hong *e*
Kong with a forged work permit, but the fact that it was a forgery was unknown
to him. Neill LJ quoted a passage at the conclusion of the speech of Lord Bridge
of Harwich in *Khawaja's* case [1983] 1 All ER 765 at 787, [1984] AC 74 at 118 and
said ([1992] 2 All ER 738 at 744, [1992] 1 WLR 541 at 548):

'. . . it seems to me to be clear that he [Lord Bridge] did not intend at that *f*
stage to extend the categories of illegal entrants beyond those who had
entered clandestinely or who had obtained leave to enter by themselves
practising fraud or deception in contravention of s 26(1)(c) [of the 1971 Act].'

Neill LJ then posed the question as to whether there are any categories of illegal
entrants other than those specifically recognised in *Khawaja's* case. He answered
that question by saying that if, as in that case, leave to enter the United Kingdom *g*
was obtained by a materially false document then that person was not given leave
to enter in accordance with the 1971 Act and that accordingly he entered in
breach of the immigration laws and was an illegal entrant.

Thus illegal entrants are those who (a) enter clandestinely or (b) obtain leave to
enter by themselves practising fraud or deceit or by the use of a materially false *h*
document. Therefore, unless it can be said that the asylum seekers in these cases
actually entered the United Kingdom when they disembarked from the aeroplane,
they clearly could not have offended in any of those ways.

Mr Griffith and Mr Spencer in submitting that the asylum seekers upon arrival
in the United Kingdom had sought to enter in breach of the immigration laws
said that they should be regarded as having entered the United Kingdom when *j*
they disembarked from the aircraft. Seeing that they had no passports then they
were inevitably illegal entrants. We cannot agree with that. A person is required
under the immigration rules to produce a passport to an immigration officer
before, or at, or after immigration control if so required by that officer. The
asylum seekers arriving in the United Kingdom in these cases had not been so

required. None of them at any time produced a forged passport within this
a country or attempted to go through immigration control using a false passport or
any other false document.

The submission that the asylum seekers were illegal entrants when they
disembarked from their aircraft involved the proposition that they left the
country of embarkation with forged passports and thus could not be legal entrants
to this country. Accordingly, it followed that because they were not legal entrants
b they were illegal entrants. Leaving on one side their claimed status of asylum
seekers, that submission makes the assumption that on disembarkation a person
must either be a legal entrant or an illegal entrant. It leaves out of the calculation
the vital question as to whether such a person is an illegal entrant as defined in
the 1971 Act.

Quite clearly, in our view, these asylum seekers on the facts were not persons
c who had sought to enter in breach of the immigration laws and had not so
entered. They were not people who had entered clandestinely or by practising
fraud or deception by means of materially false documents or otherwise. Entry
cannot, we think, be equated with disembarkation. The distinction between
entry into the United Kingdom and disembarkation from a ship or aircraft is
d quite clearly recognised in s 11, where disembarkation and entry are contrasted,
and specific provision is made for the area which exists at the airport between the
two where persons are deemed not to enter the United Kingdom. The sidenote to
that section reads: 'Construction of references to entry, and other phrases relating
to travel.' The section in terms recognises that there is an area at the airport where
people wait before making entry into the United Kingdom as defined in the 1971
e Act.

It cannot be the law, in our view, on any proper construction of the relevant
sections of the 1971 Act that disembarkation is to be equated with entry, or that
persons who disembark without a right of entry are automatically illegal entrants.

Lord Donaldson MR's observations in *Vilvarajah v Secretary of State for the Home*
f *Dept* [1990] Imm AR 457 at 459–460 are in that respect very much in point. He
said:

> '. . . those who are or claim to be refugees and who arrive in this country
> seeking asylum may well have to arrive armed with false documents and
> false passports. It may be that there is no other way in which they can leave
> *g* the country from which they have come and come to this country. That is
> quite understandable, and if the Secretary of State had relied in any way upon
> that fact he would in my judgment have been wrong. That is one thing. A
> refugee arrives with a forged passport and says to the immigration officer, "I
> am a refugee. I claim to be a refugee. I have arrived with forged documents
> because there was no other way of my coming here. Here are the documents.
> *h* They are forged." Nobody could hold that against him. It is quite a different
> matter where a refugee or somebody claiming to be a refugee arrives with
> forged documents and proffers them to the immigration authorities as being
> genuine. That is entirely different.'

j In these two cases the asylum seekers upon arrival in the United Kingdom
immediately claimed refuge and did not proffer any forged documents to
immigration officers as being genuine. If the contention put forward by the
Crown is correct almost all asylum seekers or political refugees would inevitably
be illegal entrants from the moment they disembarked from ship or aircraft.
Such a construction has never, so far as we know, previously been suggested and

there is no authority to support it. In our judgment it cannot be a correct construction of the relevant sections of the 1971 Act.

Mr Spencer contended, with regard to s 11(1), that the phrase 'a person who has not otherwise entered the United Kingdom shall be deemed not to do so as long as he is detained, or temporarily admitted or released while liable to detention' means that the asylum seekers upon arrival in the United Kingdom had not otherwise entered the United Kingdom and so were accordingly not deemed not to do so. It is clear, in our judgment, that the part of s 11 to which we have referred relates to those who have not disembarked as set out in the first part of the section, for example persons who have arrived clandestinely and were then detained or temporarily admitted or released while liable to detention. That part of s 11 cannot turn persons, such as these asylum seekers, who are in a designated area in a transit lounge, for example, approved by the immigration officer, into illegal entrants. Accordingly in both these cases it was not shown on the Crown's evidence that the asylum seekers who arrived in the United Kingdom were illegal entrants for the purposes of the offence created by s 26(1) of the 1971 Act.

We turn to the second issue with the observation that signing the Convention and Protocol relating to the Status of Refugees has undoubtedly caused serious problems for immigration control and the Home Secretary.

Ever since then those who claim asylum pursuant to the convention and protocol form a special and different category of persons when arriving in the United Kingdom. Once the claim has been made, the Home Secretary will investigate the claim and either allow the claimant to remain or deport him. It was not suggested by the Crown that any of the claims put forward by these asylum seekers were other than, apparently anyway, genuine. It does not follow, of course, that the Home Secretary will so regard them, after investigation, and allow the asylum seekers to remain in the United Kingdom. It is, therefore, clear, so it seems to us, that special considerations apply to persons seeking asylum and a valid passport is not a prerequisite. As Lord Donaldson MR pointed out in the passage which we have quoted from *Vilvarajah*'s case, it is unlikely that the asylum seeker will have a valid passport.

Nevertheless it was submitted on behalf of the Crown that, despite the provisions of the rules relating to the protocol, a refugee, unless he has valid documentation on arrival in the United Kingdom, is an illegal entrant. We do not agree. In the light of the authorities which we have quoted and the relevant sections of the 1971 Act and the rules, so long as a person leaving an aircraft is an asylum seeker and does not attempt otherwise to seek entry or to obtain entry by fraud such as by the use of false documents or without any documentation at all, but remains within a designated area when he claims asylum, he is not, in our view, an illegal entrant. He does not fall within s 33(1).

For those reasons we are driven to hold, being only too conscious of the awful problems a flood of asylum seekers would create for the immigration authorities and the Home Secretary, that the asylum seekers in the present cases were not illegal entrants. Therefore an essential ingredient of the offences laid under s 25(1) was not made out against either appellant. It follows that the submissions made by counsel for each of the appellants at the close of the Crown's case at trial should have been allowed.

Mr Scrivener made a further submission on behalf of Naillie. It was to the effect that Naillie had not committed any act within the United Kingdom which was in any sense of relevance. All such acts as he had committed were performed outside the jurisdiction. Accordingly, seeing that he is a Kenyan he does not come within any of the categories of persons in s 25(5) and is not, therefore, caught by

the words: 'Subsection (1) shall apply to things done outside as well as things done
a in the United Kingdom.'

The Crown disagreed with this proposition and, inter alia, contended that there
need be no overt act committed in this country to establish an offence under
s 25(1). The subsection is aimed at any plan or conspiracy no matter where
formed to secure or facilitate the entry and so forth of anyone known or believed
to be an illegal entrant.

b Having regard to the reasons we have provided for allowing, as we do, these
appeals and quashing the convictions, we do not have to resolve the central issues
arising from the arguments of counsel in this interesting context. Suffice it to say
that our tentative opinion is that the Crown's contention is probably sound.
Whether that be so or not it seems to us that if the two Somali women had
somehow got past immigration control and become illegal entrants the jury on
c the whole of the facts would have been entitled to convict Naillie on the basis that
he was their shepherd so to speak in a strange land, guiding them through a
barrier they had no right to penetrate.

Appeals allowed. Convictions quashed.

d
10 June. *The court refused leave to appeal to the House of Lords but certified, under
s 33(2) of the Criminal Appeal Act 1968, that the following point of law of general public
importance was involved in the decision: whether a person seeking political asylum who
disembarks from a ship or aircraft at a port in the United Kingdom without a valid
passport or other document satisfactorily establishing his identity and nationality is on
e disembarkation an illegal entrant for the purposes of the Immigration Act 1971.*

Kate O'Hanlon Barrister.

Ex parte Coventry Newspapers Ltd   *a*

COURT OF APPEAL, CRIMINAL DIVISION
LORD TAYLOR OF GOSFORTH CJ, SIMON BROWN AND ROCH JJ
25, 26 JUNE, 24 JULY 1992

Discovery – Privilege – Production contrary to public interest – Documents in possession ***b***
of Police Complaints Authority – Evidence given to internal police disciplinary investigation
– Defendant successfully appealing against conviction on ground that police officers had
fabricated admissions – Notes of police interviews with defendant subsequently removed
from court file – Police Complaints Authority inquiring into disappearance of notes of
police interviews – Newspaper alleging interview notes removed by police officers to
prevent them being tested for fabrication – Police officers bringing action for libel against ***c***
newspaper – Newspaper applying for disclosure of documents in possession of Police
Complaints Authority – Whether public interest in disclosure of documents to newspaper
to defend libel action outweighing prima facie public interest immunity.

On 15 July 1989 the appellant, who had been convicted of unlawful wounding,
made a written complaint that a police officer from the serious crime squad who ***d***
had interviewed him in relation to the offence had fabricated admissions in the
interview record. On 28 July the police officer and another officer visited the
Crown Court centre where the appellant's trial had taken place and were permitted
unsupervised inspection of the court file concerning the appellant's case. On 3
August officers pursuing inquiries into the appellant's complaint on behalf of the ***e***
Police Complaints Authority also visited the Crown Court centre and found that
the original interview notes regarding the appellant's case were missing from the
court file. The two police officers were then suspended and the Police Complaints
Authority commenced an inquiry into the disappearance of the notes, but the
investigation produced no evidence that the officers had removed anything from
the court file and they were cleared of suspicion and returned to duty. On 17 ***f***
April 1991 the applicants, the publishers of a local newspaper, published an article
which referred to the suggestion that the interview notes had been removed by
two officers from the serious crime squad and suggested that allegations about
tampering with files could never be proved because the vital evidence contained
in the file had disappeared. The two police officers issued a writ against the
applicants for libel. In the meantime the appellant's case was referred to the Court ***g***
of Appeal by the Home Secretary and on 9 July 1991 the Lord Chief Justice
ordered that all witness statements and documents in the possession of the Police
Complaints Authority relating to the appellant's appeal should be disclosed to the
appellant. The appellant's appeal was successful and the applicants immediately
applied for disclosure to them of documents disclosed by the Police Complaints ***h***
Authority under the order of 9 July for use in the criminal appeal, so that the
applicants could use them in the libel action.

Held – Notwithstanding that documents in the possession of the Police
Complaints Authority were prima facie subject to public interest immunity, that
had to be balanced against the public interest in preventing allegedly corrupt ***j***
police officers from successfully suing the press for damages while the courts
disabled their adversaries from an effective defence by withholding the documents
from them. Accordingly, the court would permit the documents disclosed by the
Police Complaints Authority by order of the court for use in the appellant's
criminal appeal to be disclosed by the appellant to the applicants for the purpose

of defending the libel proceedings arising out of the appeal since it was in the
a public interest to permit such disclosure (see p 95 *d* to *f j* and p 96 *b* to *f*, post).

Makanjuola v Comr of Police of the Metropolis (1989) [1992] 3 All ER 617
distinguished.

Notes

b For discovery of documents, see 13 *Halsbury's Laws* (4th edn) paras 1–7, and for
cases on the subject, see 18 *Digest* (2nd reissue) 7–9, 1–36, 571–575, 624–652.

Cases referred to in judgment

Bibby Bulk Carriers Ltd v Cansulex Ltd, The Cambridgeshire [1988] 2 All ER 820,
    [1989] QB 155, [1989] 2 WLR 182.
c
Crest Homes plc v Marks [1987] 2 All ER 1074, [1987] AC 829, [1987] 3 WLR 293,
    HL.

Derby & Co Ltd v Weldon (1988) Times, 20 October.

Derby & Co Ltd v Weldon (No 3) (1988) Times, 15 November.

Hehir v Comr of Police of the Metropolis [1982] 2 All ER 335, [1982] 1 WLR 715,
d   CA.

Home Office v Harman [1982] 1 All ER 532, [1983] 1 AC 280, [1982] 2 WLR 338,
    HL.

Makanjuola v Comr of Police of the Metropolis (1989) [1992] 3 All ER 617, CA.

Neilson v Laugharne [1981] 1 All ER 829, [1981] QB 736, [1981] 2 WLR 537, CA.

Peach v Comr of Police of the Metropolis [1986] 2 All ER 129, [1986] QB 1064, [1986]
e   2 WLR 1080, CA.

R v Governor of Brixton Prison, ex p Osman (No 1) [1992] 1 All ER 108, [1991] 1
    WLR 281, DC.

R v Parchment (17 July 1989, unreported), CA.

f ### Cases also cited

A-G v Guardian Newspapers Ltd (No 2) [1988] 3 All ER 545, [1990] 1 AC 109,
    Ch D, CA and HL.

A-G v Newspaper Publishing plc [1987] 3 All ER 276, [1988] Ch 333, Ch D and CA.

Burmah Oil Co Ltd v Bank of England (A-G intervening) [1979] 3 All ER 700, [1980]
    AC 1090, HL.

g *Sankey v Whitlam* (1978) 42 CLR 1, Aust HC.

Thorpe v Chief Constable of the Greater Manchester Police [1989] 2 All ER 827, [1989]
    1 WLR 665, CA.

Application

h Coventry Newspapers Ltd (CNL), publishers of the Coventry Evening Telegraph,
applied to the Court of Appeal, Criminal Division, to vary an implied undertaking
given by Michael Thomas Bromell, the defendant in earlier criminal proceedings,
whose conviction of unlawful wounding had been quashed by the Court of
Appeal on 22 June 1992, so as to enable documents disclosed by the Police
Complaints Authority (the PCA) in those proceedings to be used by CNL in
j defending a libel action brought by two police officers. The facts are set out in the
judgment of the court.

Desmond Browne QC and *Mark Warby* (instructed by *Oswald Hickson Collier & Co*)
    for CNL.

Stephen Richards (instructed by the *Treasury Solicitor*) for the PCA.

24 July 1992. The following judgment of the court was delivered.

Cur adv vult

LORD TAYLOR OF GOSFORTH CJ. This is an application by Coventry Newspapers Ltd (CNL), the publishers of the Coventry Evening Telegraph, who are defendants in a libel action. It is an unusual application to come before this court. Its practical object is to gain access to certain documents disclosed by the Police Complaints Authority (the PCA) by order of this court for use in a criminal appeal, so that CNL may use them in the libel action.

The background to it is this. On 22 June 1992 this court heard and allowed an appeal on a Home Secretary's reference pursuant to s 17(1)(a) of the Criminal Appeal Act 1968. The appellant was Michael Thomas Bromell, who had been convicted on 16 October 1987 in the Crown Court at Warwick of unlawful wounding and had been sentenced to seven years' imprisonment. His original appeal against conviction, pursuant to s 1 of the Criminal Appeal Act 1968, was dismissed by this court on 14 October 1988.

The Home Secretary's reference was made following complaints by the appellant of police malpractice, an investigation by the PCA and the quashing of convictions in other cases involving one of the officers of whose conduct the appellant complained.

So far as is relevant, the sequence of events was as follows. Following the failure of his appeal, the appellant wrote on 15 July 1989 complaining that Det Con Woodley, who had interviewed him in relation to the offence of which he was convicted, had fabricated admissions in the record of interview.

On 17 July 1989 an appeal against conviction in *R v Parchment* (unreported) succeeded in this court. It was the first case in which electrostatic depression analysis evidence had exposed police malpractice by analysis of the interview notes. The success of the appeal would therefore have been alarming news for any officer who had tampered with the original notes of interview in any other case.

On 26 July the appellant's official complaint arrived at West Midlands Police Headquarters and Supt Fancott was asked to conduct inquiries.

On 28 July Det Con Woodley and another officer named Clifford visited Warwick Crown Court and were permitted unsupervised inspection of the court file concerning the appellant's case.

On 3 August officers pursuing inquiries on behalf of the PCA also visited Warwick Crown Court and found that the original interview notes regarding the appellant's case were missing from the court file.

On 11 August, on being informed of this, the chief constable, Mr Geoffrey Dear, suspended the officers Woodley and Clifford and ordered an inquiry to be supervised by the PCA.

On 9 February 1990 it was announced by the deputy chief constable that the investigation had produced no evidence that the officers Woodley and Clifford had removed anything from the court file. Det Con Woodley was cleared of suspicion and he and Clifford were returned to duty.

On 17 April 1991 CNL published in the Coventry Evening Telegraph an article headlined 'Why the Chief cracked down on his crime staff'. The article referred to the suggestion that the interview notes had been removed by two officers from the serious crime squad and suggested that allegations about tampering with files could never be proved because the vital evidence contained in the file had disappeared.

On 7 June the two officers Woodley and Clifford issued a writ against CNL for

libel. Meanwhile, on 10 May, the appellant's case was referred to this court by the
a Home Secretary. On 9 July Lord Lane CJ ordered that all witness statements and
documents in the possession of the PCA relating to the appellant's appeal should
be disclosed to him. That was done and counsel for the appellant told us that the
disclosed documents had proved vital to the presentation of the appellant's case.

As already stated, that appeal succeeded in this court on 22 June 1992. There
immediately followed the hearing of the present application, argued most ably
b before us by Mr Browne QC for CNL and by Mr Stephen Richards for the PCA.

Before describing more precisely the nature of the application and the difficult
and important questions of public interest which it raises, it is convenient first to
indicate why CNL say that they now need to see these documents for justice to be
done in the libel proceedings.

c The essential basis of the police officers' claim in those proceedings is that the
article complained of carried the clearly defamatory innuendo that their
vindication by the PCA and the deputy chief constable was worthless. Each of the
officers, we are told, has already recovered in total over £40,000 damages in
settlement of similar claims brought variously against the Independent, the
Guardian and the BBC. This is the one action remaining.

d Thus far CNL have been unable to plead justification in defence to the claim.
And, without such plea, none of the background to the case to which we have
briefly alluded can ever be placed before the jury: the only issues arising would
be whether or no the publication was defamatory and, if so, what should the
damages be. Now, however, having regard to what was learned by CNL's counsel
whilst sitting in court during the successful appeal, they are for the first time in a
e position to raise a plea of justification. But they would greatly prefer to do so with
the benefit of seeing the actual documents. Only then will they be able to plead
the defence both with full particularity and in the expectation that admissible
evidence will become available to support the plea at trial. Mr Bromell, in a
sentence, represents CNL's only possible source of the documents at this stage.
And he, let it be said at once, is anxious to co-operate.

f CNL's altogether less satisfactory course would be to plead a defence of
justification as best they can in the hope that at some later date the documents
may be obtained in response to a subpoena duces tecum issued to the PCA itself.
That course would doubtless prompt an application by the PCA to set aside the
subpoena on grounds of public interest immunity. Thus would be decided
whether or not CNL should ever see the documents. If upon the hearing of such
g setting aside application CNL were to succeed, the PCA were then to co-operate
by handing over the documents before (rather than at) trial, CNL could start
using the material to prepare their evidence for trial—albeit by then, of course,
the trail would have cooled still further. If, however, CNL were to fail, they
would have exposed themselves to the additional financial perils involved in
h advancing an insupportable plea of justification. CNL have, theoretically, one
other alternative: they could at this late stage, without benefit of the PCA
documents, mount their own unaided inquiry into the police officers' conduct
and thus seek independently to obtain all the same evidence that the PCA so
painstakingly uncovered some three years ago. But that, as they suggest, is a well-
nigh impossible task at this distance in time.

j That then is the context in which this application arises. What is its precise
nature and why is it before this court?

In form it is an application at the suit of CNL as a third party for the court to
release the appellant from his implied undertaking pursuant to which discovery
of the PCA documents was given under the court's order of 9 July 1991—released
that is to the extent of permitting him to disclose the documents to CNL, they

for their part undertaking to the court to hold them for the strictly limited purpose of defending the libel proceedings brought against them by Woodley *a* and Clifford. But for such proposed order the appellant would clearly be unable to hand over the documents: he would be subject to an implied undertaking, analogous to that arising on discovery in civil proceedings, not to use the disclosed documents otherwise than for the purposes for which discovery was given, here the pursuance of the criminal appeal which is now, of course, successfully concluded. The PCA assert the undertaking and CNL acknowledge it. What is in *b* issue here is whether it should now be varied.

The issue of public interest immunity arises because, quite apart from the considerations underlying the implied undertaking, the particular class of documents here in question is clearly recognised on authority to be subject to such a claim. The PCA invoke this immunity as perhaps their main reason for *c* asserting that the implied undertaking should not be varied in this case. In short, therefore, public interest immunity arises as an issue ancillary to the implied undertaking. Thus the question raised by the application is whether we should vary Bromell's implied undertaking and free the documents for limited further disclosure having regard not only to the public interest underlying the implication of the undertaking in the first place, but also the public interest giving rise to the *d* recognised immunity generally attaching to this class of documents.

As to why the application is before this court, that quite simply is because it was to this court that the implied undertaking was given; we alone, therefore, have power to vary it. Whilst, however, it clearly follows that we have jurisdiction to entertain this application, it is a good deal less clear that we should be prepared to do so. There are obvious disadvantages in such a course. Not merely is the *e* Criminal Division of the Court of Appeal hardly the most suitable tribunal to determine complex questions of civil law—the pressures on the court's time aside—but the very fact that this *is* the Criminal Division carries with it the consequence that whatever we decide cannot be the subject of appeal: see s 33 of the Criminal Appeal Act 1968.

Nevertheless, having recognised and explored those disadvantages, we have *f* thought it right not only de bene esse to hear this application, but now to decide it. As explained, this is CNL's only hope of acquiring these documents at the present stage. And at least this court has one advantage over others: we know the extent to which disclosure of the PCA documents was made during the course of the appeal hearing. True, the extent of public disclosure is but one of the *g* considerations in play—and, as we shall shortly indicate, not in our judgment the most material one in the circumstances of this case. But clearly it is another factor that would make it the less satisfactory for us simply to refuse the application without more. That said, however, the decisive reason why we now think it right to determine this application on its substantive merits is that we have all three of us arrived at a very clear conclusion upon the case and, moreover, a conclusion *h* reached with particular regard to the very special facts of the case. This is not a case where we need decide difficult questions of law or lay down principles of general application. If it were, our decision ought obviously to be amenable to appeal.

We come therefore, to the substantive application and to note first the legal principles governing the public interest immunity attaching to this class of *j* documents.

That such immunity exists is plain. It was established by the Court of Appeal in *Neilson v Laugharne* [1981] 1 All ER 829, [1981] QB 736 and, despite a number of subsequent expressions of judicial regret and reservation—see particularly

Hehir v Comr of Police of the Metropolis [1982] 2 All ER 335, [1982] 1 WLR 715 and
a *Peach v Comr of Police of the Metropolis* [1986] 2 All ER 129, [1986] QB 1064—has
not since been doubted. The most recent authority in point is the decision of the
Court of Appeal in *Makanjuola v Comr of Police of the Metropolis* (1989) [1992] 3 All
ER 617 and this provides a useful starting point for consideration of the precise
nature of the public interest here in question. Mrs Makanjuola was suing the
police for damages for alleged sexual assault and buggery and to that end was
b seeking discovery of all relevant documents resulting from an investigation under
s 49 of the Police Act 1964 and the police disciplinary proceedings which followed.
Her application was refused, the Court of Appeal regarding the case as effectively
determined by *Neilson v Laugharne*. Lord Donaldson MR said (at 620):

c   'Although it was submitted that the balancing operation had to be
     conducted in each case and that accordingly we were not bound by *Neilson v
     Laugharne*, I consider that it at least binds us to start from the position that in
     a similar case public interest immunity will apply and that any re-balancing
     should only be undertaken if there are additional factors which need to be
     taken into account.'

d Bingham LJ stated (at 622): '. . . we in this court must apply the ratio of *Neilson's*
case to any case not distinguishable from it in principle', and summarised as
follows the public interest which the court in *Neilson's* case had accepted as
justifying the immunity:

     '. . . the maintenance of an honourable, disciplined, law-abiding and
e   uncorrupt police force. The protection of that public interest required that
     allegations of improper or criminal conduct by police officers should be
     investigated and appropriate action taken. To that end it was necessary that
     members of the public or other police officers should be encouraged to give
     any relevant information they had to the appropriate authority without fear
     of harassment, intimidation or use of any statement in any other proceedings.
f   It was therefore desirable in the public interest that statements made to the
     appropriate authority investigating a complaint against a police officer should
     not be liable to be produced or disclosed or referred to in any proceedings
     save disciplinary or criminal proceedings officially brought against the police
     officer in question. To hold otherwise would frustrate the statutory purpose
     of an investigation under the Act.'

g
Rejecting the plaintiff's argument that the s 49 statements had lost their
confidentiality following two disciplinary hearings which she herself had
attended, Bingham LJ added (at 623):

     'The public interest which the court upheld in *Neilson's* case was not based
h   on confidentiality . . . but on the need to reassure informants that statements
     would not be usable for any but s 49 purposes. This need remains as strong
     after disciplinary proceedings as before, perhaps even stronger. Statements
     do not in my view lose the immunity upheld in *Neilson's* case simply because
     proceedings contemplated when the statements were made in fact occur.'

j
The court recognised, however, that circumstances may arise which require
not merely the carrying out of a fresh balancing exercise but the disclosure of
documents within this otherwise immune class because of some yet more potent
countervailing public interest. The public interest in establishing innocence in
criminal proceedings is classically recognised as one such. But no one, and
certainly not Mr Richards in argument before us, suggests that there cannot be

others. He does, however, urge that disclosure orders ought only to be made in
the most exceptional circumstances lest otherwise the public interest underlying *a*
the immunity be insidiously destroyed. And that submission we would accept:
as Bingham LJ observed in *Makanjuola's* case (at 623–624):

> '... such occasions [when a judge may properly rule that a document
> ordinarily immune in the public interest should in the public interest be
> disclosed] will be exceptional and the fluctuating fortunes of parties in *b*
> litigious combat will rarely justify a judge in disturbing an immunity firmly
> rooted in the public interest.'

The first ground on which CNL here seek to escape the rigour of the principle
established in *Neilson's* case and so firmly reiterated in *Makanjuola's* case is by
invoking the decision of the Court of Appeal in *Peach v Comr of Police of the*
Metropolis [1986] 2 All ER 129, [1986] QB 1064. The plaintiff there was claiming *c*
damages for her son's death brought about, she alleged, by a blow from a police
truncheon. Discovery of s 49 documents was granted; *Neilson's* case was
distinguished on the basis that the dominant purpose of the s 49 inquiry in *Peach's*
case was to investigate a violent death that was a matter of public concern and in
circumstances where it was apparent from the beginning that an inquest would *d*
be held and a prosecution might follow. Fox and Stephen Brown LJJ noted that
the relevant statements were not taken on the basis that they were merely 'to be
used for a private investigation to see if the police had acted improperly in any
way' (one of the two main reasons for Lord Denning MR's decision in *Neilson's*
case, the other being that the plaintiff there was merely 'fishing') (see [1986] 2 All
ER 129 at 138, 144, [1986] QB 1064 at 1080, 1089). Purchas LJ observed that the *e*
s 49 investigation had started during the course of a full Criminal Investigation
Department investigation already in train and had become co-terminous with it
and in no way dominant. His conclusion was ([1986] 2 All ER 129 at 144, [1986]
QB 1064 at 1089):

> 'In my judgment, in the class of documents with which we are now faced, *f*
> there is an overwhelming bias in favour of the public interest being served
> by the disclosure of these documents and that, therefore, there is no
> justification for creating a new class of privileged documents, which would
> be the effect of extending the class in respect of which *Neilson v Laugharne*
> remains an authority to the class of documents with which the court is
> concerned in this appeal.' *g*

The only reference to that decision in *Makanjuola's* case was Bingham LJ's
description of it as a case where statements were made 'for a hybrid purpose' so
that 'a different rule' applied (see [1992] 3 All ER 617 at 622).

Mr Browne's first contention is that the PCA documents in the present case fall
into essentially the same category as those in *Peach's* case and are thus strictly *h*
outside the class of documents attracting public interest immunity as decided in
Neilson's case. His arguments for such a conclusion are, first, the narrow one that
Bromell's complaint of 15 July 1989 was about the police officers' fabricating the
interview notes—whereas the inquiry was principally into the possibility of their
having, following his complaint, removed them from Crown Court. Second that,
as in *Peach's* case, the inquiry into Bromell's complaint was simply part of a *j*
substantially wider investigation, in this instance into the practices of the West
Midland serious crime squad, a matter of the very gravest public concern.

(At one stage of the argument Mr Browne suggested that the investigation here
was not under the provisions of s 85 of the Police and Criminal Evidence Act

1984 (the analogue of s 49) but rather under s 88. That, however, proved to be a misunderstanding based upon a somewhat elliptical written parliamentary answer. There was indeed a s 88 investigation here, carried out by Mr Shaw, an assistant chief constable of West Yorkshire Police, but that was separate from, although no doubt assisted by, the investigation into Bromell's complaint. Both investigations were supervised by the PCA under the provisions of s 89.)

Neither of Mr Browne's arguments can we accept. The first we reject because it is unrealistically narrow—the inquiry into the possible removal of the interview notes from Warwick Crown Court being a necessary consequence of Bromell's initial complaint and, as it seems to us, integral to it; the second, because the parallel investigations into other complaints against the West Midlands Police (no fewer than 103 we were told), and Mr Shaw's broader inquiry into the general integrity of the squad and its practices, cannot alter the fundamental nature of Supt Fancott's inquiry. That was and remained an investigation into Bromell's complaint of misconduct by the individual officers involved in his prosecution, there being no other 'dominant' purpose for it. We furthermore accept Mr Richards's submission that the gravity of the misconduct under investigation cannot be the determinative factor as to whether public interest immunity attaches to the documents—*Makanjuola's* case itself is an indication of that.

It follows that in our judgment CNL cannot successfully bring themselves within the ratio of *Peach's* case so to escape the prima facie claim to immunity which this class of documents ordinarily attracts. It does not, however, follow that the obvious public concern felt about the conduct of the West Midlands serious crime squad is irrelevant to the balancing operation which this court is now required to undertake, and to that we shall return.

Mr Browne's next argument centres upon the extent to which these documents are now, as he contends, already in the public domain following the hearing of Bromell's criminal appeal. His submission in this regard is that they have now been 'read to or by the Court, or referred to, in open court' within the meaning of RSC Ord 24, r 14A (introduced with effect from 1 October 1987 following *Home Office v Harman* [1982] 1 All ER 532, [1983] AC 280 as part of the friendly settlement resulting from Miss Harman's successful application before the European Commission of Human Rights). In these circumstances, he submits, relying principally upon the judgments of Browne-Wilkinson V-C in *Derby & Co Ltd v Weldon* (1988) Times, 20 October and *Derby & Co Ltd v Weldon (No 3)* (1988) Times, 15 November, r 14A provides that the implied undertaking lapses. So, submits Mr Browne, inviting analogy first between discovery in civil and in criminal proceedings, and then between the implied undertaking on the one hand and public interest immunity on the other, this court should now conclude that the immunity too has lapsed: in other words that there no longer remains any public interest in withholding these documents from further dissemination.

This submission appears to us unsound on several grounds. First, because r 14A in any event expressly provides for the court to order otherwise if appropriate. More fundamentally, however, because the suggested analogy at once breaks down when it is recognised that the public interest immunity presently in question is not (or at least not principally) confidentiality based. Rather, as was pointed out in *Makanjuola's* case, it is intended to reassure informants that their statements will only be used for the investigation of complaints and for such criminal or disciplinary proceedings as directly follow.

It is accordingly unnecessary to address the fine points of interpretation which r 14A undoubtedly raises in the context of civil discovery for, even if Mr Browne's arguments upon them are correct, that cannot avail him here.

Nor, for the same reason, can he succeed upon his broader submission that the publicity now given to these documents has so eroded their privacy that the a public interest in their future non-disclosure should be found to have evaporated. Publication of the disclosed material during the recent criminal appeal hearing, even had it been total, would no more rid it of its prima facie immunity than had it been aired in disciplinary or criminal proceedings brought against the police officers concerned, the situation expressly envisaged in Makanjuola's case.

In short, all depends upon the precise nature of the public interest sought to be b protected and this is not one of those cases—unlike, for example, R v Governor of Brixton Prison, ex p Osman (No 1) [1992] 1 All ER 108, [1991] 1 WLR 281—where the extent to which the documents have entered the public domain will critically affect the question whether immunity from further disclosure should be held to survive. It is accordingly unnecessary to indicate the actual extent of disclosures c made at the appeal hearing or the consequences that that might have had upon a differently based immunity claim.

Once again, however, that is not to say that the public's post-appeal awareness of the essential contents of the PCA documents must be regarded as wholly immaterial to the balancing exercise this court is now required to perform and to that too we shall return. d

Mr Browne's third main argument focuses upon what he maintains is the urgent need for the disclosure of these documents in the interests of justice for the fair and proper disposal of the libel proceedings between these possibly corrupt police officers and CNL. This, too, Mr Browne submits, represents an important public interest—indeed, he contends, the pre-eminent public interest arising here. e

Before dealing with this submission, which seems to us a powerful one indeed, it is necessary to consider shortly the added dimension to this case brought about by Bromell's implied undertaking.

Mr Browne's arguments upon this part of the case are a fortiori to those he advances with regard to public interest immunity, more particularly with regard to the impact of the recent use of the documents in open court upon public f interest immunity. It is the argument founded upon analogy with r 14A and it seems to us in this context a little stronger. The reason is this. Rule 14A appears clearly to postulate confidentiality as the central consideration underlying the implication of the undertaking in the first place. Once that confidentiality is dissipated by the use of the documents in open court, prima facie the undertaking g lapses. But the argument still cannot carry Mr Browne all the way. Because even if the element of confidentiality in the documents is entirely lost, the rule nevertheless clearly caters to other considerations: it expressly empowers the court 'for special reasons' to order the undertaking to continue. Even, therefore, were the r 14A analogy exact, the future of this undertaking remains in the court's discretion. h

We turn to Mr Richards's argument. Essentially it is this: that only very exceptionally should the implied undertaking be varied to permit disclosed documents to be used for ulterior purposes, not least when the application is made by a third party and for the purposes of proceedings wholly unconnected with those in which discovery was ordered. He invites our attention in particular to Home Office v Harman [1982] 1 All ER 532, [1983] 1 AC 280, Crest Homes plc v j Marks [1987] 2 All ER 1074, [1987] AC 829 and Bibby Bulk Carriers Ltd v Cansulex Ltd, The Cambridgeshire [1988] 2 All ER 820, [1989] QB 155.

This court, submits Mr Richards, with impressive citation from those high authorities, should think long and hard before waiving Bromell's undertaking

merely so as to improve CNL's position in their libel action. The fortuitous
a intervention of a criminal appeal during the course of those proceedings ought
not, he contends, to persuade us to permit any departure from the usual strict
approach taken rightly to implied undertakings.

Mr Richards's argument would, we accept, be formidable indeed had the
implied undertaking with which we are concerned been one given in the usual
way in civil proceedings. Certainly nothing that we decide in the present case is
b intended in the least degree to diminish the high importance rightly recognised
to attach to the concept of the implied undertaking as a necessary way of
underpinning the integrity of the discovery process. But characterisations of
discovery such as that of Lord Keith in *Harman's* case [1982] 1 All ER 532 at 540,
[1983] 1 AC 280 at 308 as 'a very serious invasion of the privacy and confidentiality
c of a litigant's affairs', although of the clearest application to discovery given in
private civil litigation, appear to us altogether less obviously apt in relation to an
order such as that made by this court in Bromell's appeal. Orders for discovery
rarely are made in criminal appeals and, when made, generally go, if not to the
prosecution, then, as here, to a statutory body. Such bodies surely need little in
the way of encouragement before making full and frank disclosure.

d In short, we have reached the conclusion that the public interest underlying
this particular implied undertaking adds little, if anything, to that giving rise to
the basic immunity claim attaching to these documents. If that immunity ought
properly to be overridden in light of the countervailing public interest arising,
then in our view that countervailing interest will outweigh too such limited value
as still attaches to the implied undertaking.

e How strong then is the countervailing public interest arising here in favour of
allowing CNL to make use of these documents? If, as both CNL and the wider
public now have every reason to suspect, these documents appear to point clearly
towards corruption on the part of named police officers, it is surely not to be
tolerated that those same officers should continue to mulct the press in damages
whilst the courts disable their adversaries from an effective defence by withholding
f the documents from them. That we believe would be repugnant alike to justice,
to the public, and, we would suggest, to those who gave their co-operation to the
PCA—CNL's intended witnesses—the very people whose interest is said to
underlie the immunity.

We recognise, of course, the general reluctance of those invited to assist in the
g investigation of police complaints to be drawn into proceedings beyond those
which strictly flow from the complaint itself. We understand indeed from Mr
Richards that reassurance is nowadays routinely given to those whose co-operation
is sought: they are told that their statements will not ordinarily be used otherwise
than for the investigation of the complaint and for any disciplinary or criminal
proceedings that may follow. It is, of course, to reinforce that reassurance and, in
h turn, to win the co-operation of potential witnesses, that this public interest
immunity exists.

All that we recognise. But what we cannot accept is that those who have been
prepared to co-operate thus far with the PCA, now knowing as a result of this
court's widely publicised recent judgment of the grave suspicions presently
surrounding the police officers concerned, would truly prefer to remain
j anonymous and watch these officers prosper in their libel action, than that their
statements should be disclosed to CNL with a view to their being proofed and, if
necessary, called as witnesses in defence. As was suggested in argument, that
would indeed be to swallow the elephant and strain at the gnat.

Nor can we believe that were we to allow this application, potential future

witnesses would be deterred from co-operating in investigations yet to come or
the police feel inhibited from giving future reassurance as to the consequences of *a*
such co-operation in the selfsame terms as at present. That reassurance, be it
noted, expressly admits of exceptions. What better case for an exception than
this? And it is, moreover, a different case from those in which disclosure of this
class of document is generally sought. The documents here are proposed for use
not as a sword but as a shield; this is hardly a floodgate situation.

We summarise our reasoning thus. Given the central objective of this category *b*
of public interest immunity as 'the maintenance of an honourable, disciplined,
law-abiding and uncorrupt police force', given the grave public disquiet
understandably aroused by proven malpractice on the part of some at least of
those who served in the now disbanded West Midlands serious crime squad, given
the extensive publicity already attaching to the documents here in question *c*
following Bromell's successful appeal, it seems to us nothing short of absurd to
suppose that those who co-operated in this investigation—largely other police
officers and court officials—will regret that co-operation (or that future generations
of potential witnesses will withhold it) were this court now to release the
documents to CNL to enable them to defeat if they can an allegedly corrupt claim
in damages. *d*

We accordingly vary Bromell's undertaking to allow him to hand over to CNL
those PCA documents that were incorporated in his appeal bundle, CNL for their
part undertaking to use those documents only for the purposes of defending the
libel proceedings currently being pursued against them.

We add only this. This court is in no way prejudging any defence of justification
which may hereafter be raised in those libel proceedings. All that we are *e*
concerned to ensure is that the present applicants have a proper opportunity of
obtaining the evidence they seek so that the grave allegations which they make—
the very same allegations that troubled this court sufficiently to allow Bromell's
appeal—can be properly tested in the courts. Justice in our judgment demands
no less. This, we conclude, is the imperative public interest in the case. *f*

Application granted.

N P Metcalfe Esq   Barrister.

Page v Hull University Visitor

HOUSE OF LORDS
LORD KEITH OF KINKEL, LORD GRIFFITHS, LORD BROWNE-WILKINSON, LORD MUSTILL AND LORD SLYNN OF HADLEY
6–9, 13 JULY, 3 DECEMBER 1992

University – Academic staff – Dismissal – Jurisdiction – Jurisdiction of court to grant judicial review of decision to dismiss member of academic staff – Lecturer appointed on terms that employment could be terminated by either party on three months' notice – Appointment subject to university statutes – Statutes providing that academic staff could be removed for good cause – Lecturer dismissed on ground of redundancy by three months' notice – Visitor deciding that dismissal within powers of university and refusing to intervene – Lecturer challenging visitor's decision by application for judicial review – Whether court having power to review visitor's decision as to construction of university's statutes – Whether lecturer's employment properly terminated.

In 1966 the appellant was appointed to a university lectureship on terms that his appointment was subject to the statutes of the university, that he was obliged to vacate his post as lecturer on reaching the retirement age of 67 and that his appointment could be terminated by either party by three months' written notice. In 1988 the appellant was given three months' written notice terminating his employment on the ground of redundancy. No criticism was made about him personally or professionally. The appellant petitioned the visitor of the university, claiming that the university was not entitled to dismiss him on the ground of redundancy because under the university's statutes it could not dismiss him before retirement except for good cause, which related to immoral conduct of a disgraceful nature or to incapacity, and by giving him three months' written notice. The visitor rejected the petition, holding that the university was entitled to dismiss the appellant either without notice for good cause as defined in the statutes or by three months' notice. The appellant applied for judicial review of the visitor's decision. The questions arose whether the High Court had jurisdiction to grant judicial review of the visitor's decision as to the construction of the university's statutes and, if so, whether the visitor's decision should be quashed. The Divisional Court held that judicial review could be granted to challenge the decision of the visitor as to the construction of the statutes of the university, granted a declaration that on the true construction of the statutes the university did not have power to dismiss the appellant on the ground of redundancy and quashed the the visitor's decision. The visitor and the university appealed to the Court of Appeal, which allowed the appeal on the grounds that, although the decision of the visitor was amenable to the supervisory jurisdiction of the High Court by way of judicial review when it amounted to an abuse of the visitor's powers and that to misconstrue the statutes of the university would be such an abuse, on the true construction of the statutes and the appellant's letter of appointment the university had been entitled to terminate his appointment by proof of good cause with or without notice or on the ground of redundancy by giving him three months' notice in writing without specifying the reason for the dismissal. The appellant appealed to the House of Lords on the question of construction and the visitor and the university cross-appealed from that part of the decision which held that the decision of the visitor was amenable to judicial review.

Held (Lord Mustill and Lord Slynn dissenting) – Because a university was an

eleemosynary charitable foundation and the visitor was the sole judge of the law
of the foundation, which was its peculiar or domestic law rather than the general *a*
law of the land, the visitor had exclusive jurisdiction to determine disputes arising
under the domestic law of the university and the proper application of those laws
to those persons within his jurisdiction. Accordingly, the court had no jurisdiction
to determine those matters or to review a decision made by the visitor on
questions of either fact or law, whether right or wrong, provided his decision was
made within his jurisdiction (in the narrow sense of acting within his power *b*
under the regulating documents to enter into the adjudication of the dispute) and
in accordance with the rules of natural justice. However, judicial review would
lie against the visitor if he acted outside his jurisdiction (in the narrow sense) or if
he abused his powers in a manner wholly incompatible with his judicial role or
acted in breach of the rules of natural justice. It followed that the Divisional Court *c*
had had no jurisdiction to review the visitor's construction of the university
statutes. In any event (Lord Mustill and Lord Slynn concurring), no error of law
had been shown in the visitor's decision. The appeal would therefore be dismissed
and the cross-appeals allowed (see p 99 *h j*, p 104 *e f*, p 106 *c d*, p 108 *d e*, p 109
b c j to p 110 *c* and p 116 *h*, post).

Per Lord Griffiths. A judge who makes what an appellate court later regards to *d*
be a mistake of law does not thereby abuse his powers but rather exercises his
powers to the best of his ability, albeit some other court thinks he was mistaken
(see p 100 *g*, post); dictum of Lord Griffiths in *Thomas v University of Bradford*
[1987] 1 All ER 834 at 850 explained.

Decision of the Court of Appeal sub nom *R v Hull University Visitor, ex p Page*
[1991] 4 All ER 747 affirmed.   *e*

Notes
For court's control over visitors, see 5 *Halsbury's Laws* (4th edn) paras 885–889,
and for cases on the subject, see 8(1) *Digest* (2nd reissue) 649–650, 5221–5235.

f

Cases referred to in opinions
Anisminic Ltd v Foreign Compensation Commission [1969] 1 All ER 208, [1969] 2 AC
    147, [1969] 2 WLR 163, HL.
Appleford's Case (1672) 1 Mod Rep 82, 86 ER 750.
Associated Provincial Picture Houses Ltd v Wednesbury Corp [1947] 2 All ER 680,
    [1948] 1 KB 223, CA.   *g*
Bently v Bishop of Ely (1729) 1 Barn KB 192, 94 ER 132.
Buller, Ex p (1855) 1 Jur NS 709, Bail Ct.
Chichester (Bishop) v Harward and Webber (1787) 1 Term Rep 650, 99 ER 1300.
Council of Civil Service Unions v Minister for the Civil Service [1984] 3 All ER 935,
    [1985] AC 374, [1984] 3 WLR 1174, HL.
Czarnikow v Roth Schmidt & Co [1922] 2 KB 478, [1922] All ER Rep 45, CA.   *h*
O'Reilly v Mackman [1982] 3 All ER 1124, [1983] 2 AC 237, [1982] 3 WLR 1096,
    HL.
Patel v University of Bradford Senate [1978] 3 All ER 841, [1978] 1 WLR 1488; *affd*
    [1979] 2 All ER 582, [1979] 1 WLR 1066, CA.
Pearlman v Keepers and Governors of Harrow School [1979] 1 All ER 365, [1979] QB
    56, [1978] 3 WLR 736, CA.   *j*
Philips v Bury (1694) Holt KB 715, 2 Term Rep 346, [1558–1774] All ER Rep 53,
    90 ER 1294.
R v Bishop of Chester (1747) 1 Wm Bl 22, 96 ER 12.
R v Bishop of Ely (1788) 2 Term Rep 290, [1775–1802] All ER Rep 70, 100 ER 157.
R v Bishop of Ely (1794) 5 Term Rep 475, 101 ER 267.
R v Bland (1740) 7 Mod Rep 355, 87 ER 1287.

R v Dunsheath, ex p Meredith [1950] 2 All ER 741, [1951] 1 KB 127, DC.

a *R v Independent Television Commission, ex p TSW Broadcasting Ltd* (1992) Independent, 27 March, HL.

R v Northumberland Compensation Appeal Tribunal, ex p Shaw [1952] 1 All ER 122, [1952] 1 KB 338, CA.

R v St John's College Cambridge (1673) 4 Mod Rep 233, 87 ER 366.

b *Racal Communications Ltd, Re* [1980] 2 All ER 634, [1981] AC 374, [1980] 3 WLR 181, HL.

South East Asia Fire Bricks Sdn Bhd v Non-Metallic Mineral Products Manufacturing Employees Union [1980] 2 All ER 689, [1981] AC 363, [1980] 3 WLR 318, PC.

Thomas v University of Bradford [1987] 1 All ER 834, [1987] AC 795, [1987] 2 WLR 677, HL.

c
Appeal

Edgar Page appealed with leave of the Court of Appeal from the decision of that court (Lord Donaldson MR, Staughton and Farquharson LJJ) ([1991] 4 All ER 747, [1991] 1 WLR 1277) on 31 July 1991 allowing the appeal of the Lord President of the Privy Council, acting on behalf of the Queen as visitor of the University of Hull, and the university from the decision of the Divisional Court of the Queen's

d Bench Division (Taylor LJ and Rougier J) on 27 March 1991 granting the appellant's application for judicial review by way of an order of certiorari to quash the decision of the Lord President on 28 September 1989 whereby, on the advice of Lord Jauncey of Tullichettle, he rejected a petition by the appellant to set aside his dismissal by the university from his post as lecturer by reason of redundancy,

e and declaring that on the true construction of the statutes of the university, the university had no power to dismiss the appellant by reason of redundancy and that his purported dismissal was without effect. The visitor and the university cross-appealed with leave of the Court of Appeal from its decision that it had jurisdiction to supervise the decision of the visitor on the construction of the

f university statutes. The facts are set out in the opinion of Lord Browne-Wilkinson.

Jeffrey Burke QC and *Brian Langstaff* (instructed by *Robin Thompson & Partners*) for the appellant.

Michael Beloff QC and *Hubert Picarda QC* (instructed by *Nabarro Nathanson*, agents for *Nabarro Nathanson*, Hull) for the university.

g *Philip Havers* (instructed by the *Treasury Solicitor*) for the visitor.

Their Lordships took time for consideration.

3 December 1992. The following opinions were delivered.

h
LORD KEITH OF KINKEL. My Lords, for the reasons set out in the speech to be delivered by my noble and learned friend Lord Browne-Wilkinson, which I have had the opportunity of considering in draft and with which I agree, I would dismiss this appeal and allow the cross-appeals.

j
LORD GRIFFITHS. My Lords, I have had the advantage of reading the judgment of my noble and learned friend Lord Browne-Wilkinson, with which I agree and I would dismiss this appeal on the ground that certiorari is not available to challenge the decision of a visitor on the ground of an error of law within his jurisdiction. I add a few words of my own only because of the difference of opinion between your Lordships on this question and because what I said about the availability of certiorari in my speech in *Thomas v University of Bradford* [1987]

1 All ER 834, [1987] AC 795 has been interpreted to include an error of law by the Divisional Court and the Court of Appeal which was not what I had intended. *a*

It is in my opinion important to keep the purpose of judicial review clearly in mind. The purpose is to ensure that those bodies that are susceptible to judicial review have carried out their public duties in the way it was intended they should. In the case of bodies other than courts, in so far as they are required to apply the law, they are required to apply the law correctly. If they apply the law incorrectly they have not performed their duty correctly and judicial review is available to *b* correct their error of law so that they may make their decision upon a proper understanding of the law.

In the case of inferior courts, that is courts of a lower status than the High Court, such as the justices of the peace, it was recognised that their learning and understanding of the law might sometimes be imperfect and require correction by the High Court and so the rule evolved that certiorari was available to correct *c* an error of law of an inferior court. At first it was confined to an error on the face of the record but it is now available to correct any error of law made by an inferior court. But despite this general rule Parliament can if it wishes confine a decision on a question of law to a particular inferior court and provide that the decision shall be final so that it is not to be challenged either by appeal or by judicial *d* review. Such a case was *Pearlman v Keepers and Governors of Harrow School* [1979] 1 All ER 365, [1979] QB 56, in which the dissenting judgment of Geoffrey Lane LJ was approved by the majority of the House of Lords in *Re Racal Communications Ltd* [1980] 2 All ER 634, [1981] AC 374.

The common law has ever since the decision in *Philips v Bury* (1694) Holt KB 715, 90 ER 1294 recognised that the visitor acting as a judge has exclusive *e* jurisdiction and that his decision is final in all matters within his jurisdiction. The common law courts have through three centuries consistently resisted all attempts to appeal decisions of the visitor. The courts have however been prepared to confine the visitor to his proper role as a judge of the internal affairs of the foundation by the use of the writs of prohibition and mandamus.

When I said in *Thomas*'s case [1987] 1 All ER 834 at 850, [1987] AC 795 at 825: *f*

'... I have myself no doubt that in the light of the modern development of administrative law, the High Court would have power, upon an application for judicial review, to quash a decision of the visitor which amounted to an abuse of his powers'

I used the words 'an abuse of his powers' advisedly. I do not regard a judge who *g* makes what an appellate court later regards as a mistake of law as abusing his powers. In such a case the judge is not abusing his powers: he is exercising them to the best of his ability albeit some other court thinks he was mistaken. I used the phrase 'abuse of his powers' to connote some form of misbehaviour that was wholly incompatible with the judicial role that the judge was expected to *h* perform. I did not intend it to include a mere error of law.

The decision in the *Racal* case shows that Parliament can by the use of appropriate language provide that a decision on a question of law whether taken by a judge or by some other form of tribunal shall be considered as final and not be subject to challenge either by way of appeal or judicial review. For three centuries the common law courts have recognised the value of the visitor acting *j* as the judge of the internal laws of the foundation and have refused to trespass upon his territory. I do not believe that it would be right to reverse this long line of authority and declare that certiorari should now lie to reverse the decision of a visitor on a question of law. The value of the visitorial jurisdiction is that it is swift, cheap and final. These benefits will be largely dissipated if the visitor's

decision can be challenged by way of judicial review. Many decisions may turn
a upon the interpretation of the statutes and other decisions of a more factual nature
can all too easily be dressed up as issues of law under the guise of *Wednesbury*
principles (see *Associated Provincial Picture Houses Ltd v Wednesbury Corp* [1947] 2
All ER 680, [1948] 1 KB 223). The learning and ingenuity of those members of
the foundation who are likely to be in dispute with the foundation should not be
lightly underestimated and I believe to admit certiorari to challenge the visitor's
b decision on the grounds of error of law will in practice prove to be the introduction
of an appeal by another name.

The visitor either is a person holding a high judicial office or is advised on
questions of law by such a person, in whose decision on matters of law it is
reasonable to repose a high degree of confidence. I say this not because any holder
of judicial office should ever regard it as an affront to be overruled by an appellate
c court but merely to emphasise that as a practical matter the chances are that the
visitor probably will get it right.

If it is thought that the exclusive jurisdiction of the visitor has outlived its
usefulness, which I beg to doubt, then I think that it should be swept away by
Parliament and not undermined by judicial review.

d I would add that in the present case I am satisfied that the decision of the visitor
was correct.

LORD BROWNE-WILKINSON. My Lords, the appellant, Mr Page, was
appointed a lecturer in the department of philosophy at the University of Hull by
a letter dated 13 June 1966. The letter stated: 'The appointment may be
e terminated by either party on giving three months' notice in writing expiring at
the end of a term or of the long vacation.' As a lecturer, Mr Page became a
member of the university which is a corporate body regulated by royal charter.
Section 34 of the statutes made under the charter provides:

> '1. The Vice-Chancellor and all Officers of the University including
f Professors and members of the Staff holding their appointments until the age
> of retirement may be removed by the Council for good cause . . .
>
> 3. Subject to the terms of his appointment no member of the teaching
> research or administrative staff of the University (including the Vice-
> Chancellor) shall be removed from office save upon the grounds specified in
> paragraph 2 of this Section and in pursuance of the procedure specified in
g Clause 1 of this Section.'

Section 34(2) defines the meaning of 'good cause'.

On 30 June 1988 Mr Page was given three months' notice terminating his
appointment on the grounds of redundancy. It is common ground that there was
no 'good cause' within the meaning of section 34; the university was relying on
h the three months' notice term contained in the letter of appointment coupled
with the provision in section 34(3) that Mr Page's tenure was to be subject to the
terms of the appointment.

Mr Page took the view that on the true construction of section 34 of the statutes
the university had no power to remove him from office and terminate his
employment save for good cause. Your Lordships were told that Mr Page started
j an action in the Queen's Bench Division for wrongful dismissal which action was
struck out on the grounds that the matter fell within the exclusive jurisdiction of
the visitor of the university, Her Majesty the Queen. Mr Page then petitioned the
visitor for a declaration that his purported dismissal was ultra vires and of no
effect. The petition was considered by the Lord President of the Council, on behalf
of Her Majesty. He sought advice from Lord Jauncey of Tullichettle, who advised

that on the true construction of the statutes the dismissal was valid and intra vires.
On that advice, the petition was dismissed by the visitor.

Mr Page then applied by way of judicial review for an order quashing the
visitor's decision. Before the Divisional Court (Taylor LJ and Rougier J) two issues
arose: first, did the Divisional Court have jurisdiction to review the visitor's
decision and, if so, second, was the visitor's construction of the statutes correct?
The Divisional Court held that it had jurisdiction to review the visitor's decision
and that the visitor's decision was wrong in law. They made an order quashing
the decision and made a declaration that 'upon a true construction of the statutes
of the University of Hull the University has and had no power to dismiss Edgar
Page by reason of redundancy and his purported dismissal is without effect'.

The university and the visitor appealed to the Court of Appeal (Lord Donaldson
MR, Staughton and Farquharson LJJ) which upheld the Divisional Court's decision
on jurisdiction but reversed its decision on construction taking the view that the
visitor's construction of the statutes was correct (see [1991] 4 All ER 747, [1991] 1
WLR 1277).

Mr Page appeals to your Lordships' House against the decision of the Court of
Appeal on the construction of the statutes: the university and the visitor cross-
appeal against the decision on jurisdiction. I will deal first with the question of
jurisdiction.

As the argument was refined in the course of the hearing, it emerged that the
rival contentions came down to a narrow but difficult issue. It is established that,
a university being an eleemosynary charitable foundation, the visitor of the
university has exclusive jurisdiction to decide disputes arising under the domestic
law of the university. This is because the founder of such a body is entitled to
reserve to himself or to a visitor whom he appoints the exclusive right to
adjudicate upon the domestic laws which the founder has established for the
regulation of his bounty. Even where the contractual rights of an individual (such
as his contract of employment with the university) are in issue, if those contractual
rights are themselves dependent upon rights arising under the regulating
documents of the charity, the visitor has an exclusive jurisdiction over disputes
relating to such employment.

Those propositions are all established by the decision of this House in *Thomas v
University of Bradford* [1987] 1 All ER 834, [1987] AC 795 which held that the
courts had no jurisdiction to entertain such disputes which must be decided by
the visitor. However *Thomas*'s case was concerned with the question whether the
courts and the visitor had concurrent jurisdictions over such disputes. In that
context alone it was decided that the visitor's jurisdiction is 'exclusive'. *Thomas*'s
case does not decide that the visitor's jurisdiction excludes the supervisory
jurisdiction of the courts by way of judicial review. On the contrary, Lord Griffiths
said ([1987] 1 All ER 834 at 849–850, [1987] AC 795 at 825):

'Finally, there is the protection afforded by the supervisory, as opposed to
appellate, jurisdiction of the High Court over the visitor. It has long been
held that the writs of mandamus and prohibition will go either to compel
the visitor to act if he refused to deal with the matter within his jurisdiction
or to prohibit him from dealing with a matter that lies without his
jurisdiction ... Although doubts have been expressed in the past as to the
availability of certiorari, I have myself no doubt that in the light of the
modern development of administrative law, the High Court would have
power, upon an application for judicial review, to quash a decision of the
visitor which amounted to an abuse of his powers.'

a Lord Ackner said that the case fell within the exclusive jurisdiction of the visitor 'subject always to judicial review' (see [1987] 1 All ER 834 at 852, [1987] AC 795 at 828).

Under the modern law, certiorari normally lies to quash a decision for error of law. Therefore, the narrow issue in this case is whether, as Mr Page contends and the courts below have held, certiorari lies against the visitor to quash his decision *b* as being erroneous in point of law notwithstanding that the question of law arises under the domestic law of the university which the visitor has 'exclusive' jurisdiction to decide.

It is necessary first to consider in some detail the nature of the visitor's jurisdiction. After some earlier doubts on the matter, the exclusivity of the visitor's jurisdiction was finally confirmed in *Philips v Bury* (1694) Holt KB 715, *c* 90 ER 1294, where the reported dissenting judgment of Holt CJ was eventually adopted by this House. In that case, the visitor of Exeter College, Oxford, had deprived Bury of his office as rector. The new rector appointed in his place had leased a house to the plaintiff Philips, who had been evicted by Bury. Philips brought an action in ejectment against Bury. Accordingly the issue in the case was whether the removal of Bury by the visitor was valid or not. Holt CJ held *d* that two questions arose: first, did the visitor have jurisdiction to remove Bury; if so, second, was the visitor's decision correct? He held that the visitor did have jurisdiction and that 'having that power, the justice thereof is not examinable in a Court of Law, upon any action concerning the [visitor's] power'. He contrasted private charitable bodies with public corporations and said (Holt KB 715 at 723–726, 90 ER 1294 at 1299–1300):

e

'And I think the Sufficiency of the Sentence is never to be called in Question, nor any Enquiry to be made here into the Reasons of the Deprivation. If the Sentence be given by the proper Visitor, created so by the Founder, or by the Law, you shall never enquire into the Validity, or Ground of the Sentence. And this will appear, if we consider the Reason of a Visitor, *f* how he comes to be supported by Authority in that Office ... But private and particular Corporations for Charity, founded and endowed by private Persons, are subject to the private Government of those who erect them; and therefore if there be no Visitor appointed by the Founder, I am of Opinion that the Law doth appoint the Founder and his Heirs to be Visitors. The *g* Founder and his Heirs are Patrons, and not to be guided by the Common known Laws of the Kingdom. But such Corporations are, as to their own Affairs, to be governed by the particular Laws and Constitutions assigned by the Founder ... But you'll say, this Man hath no Court. It is not material whether he hath a Court or no; all the Matter is, whether he hath a *h* Jurisdiction; if he hath Conusance of the Matter and Person, and he gives a Sentence, it must have some Effect to make a Vacancy, be it never so wrong. But there is no Appeal, if the Founder hath not thought fit to direct an Appeal; that an Appeal lieth in the Common Law Courts is certainly not so. This is according to the Government settled by the Founder; if he hath directed all to be under the absolute power of the Visitor, it must be so ... As *j* to the Matter of there being no Appeal from an arbitrary Sentence; it is true, the Case is the harder, because the Party is concluded by one Judgment, but it doth not lessen the Validity of the Sentence, nor doth it in any Way prove that you shall find out some Way to examine this Matter at Law in a Judicial Proceeding .'

Later, Holt CJ said (Holt KB 715 at 727–728, 90 ER 1294 at 1301):

'I know no Difference between this Case and that of a *Mandamus*. In that
Case of *Appleford* ((1672) 1 Mod Rep 82, 86 ER 750) there was a *Mandamus*
brought, to restore him to his Fellowship: It was returned, that by the Statutes
of the College, for Misdemeanour they had a Power to turn him out; and
that the Bishop of *Winchester* was Visitor, and that he was turned out *pro
crimine enormi*, and had appealed to the Bishop, who confirmed the Expulsion;
and the particular Cause was not returned: I was of Counsel for the College,
and we omitted the Cause in the Return for that Reason, because *indeed it was
not so true as it should have been*. It was insisted, that we ought to shew the
Cause in the Return, to bring it within the Statutes. It was answered, here
was a local Visitor, who has given a Sentence; and be it right, or be it wrong,
the Party is concluded by it; and you must submit to such Laws as the
Founder is pleased to put upon you. And Mr. *Appleford* was not restored.
This is an express Authority to guide our Judgment in this Case. Here is a
local Visitor hath given a Sentence, he hath declared the Rector to be actually
deprived of his Place. When shall we know when a Deprivation is good? If
not upon a *Mandamus*, why in an Ejectment?' (Holt LJ's emphasis.)

The decision of Holt CJ in *Philips v Bury* is the locus classicus of the law of
visitors. It has been repeatedly applied for the last 300 years, most recently in
Thomas v University of Bradford. For present purposes it is important for three
reasons. (1) It shows that the court can and will inquire whether the visitor has
jurisdiction to determine the question, ie to enter into the matter. (2) If the
visitor has such jurisdiction, the court has no power to ignore it or review it by
way of mandamus or in any other way. (3) The reason for such lack of jurisdiction
to review in the court is that an eleemosynary corporation is governed by a system
of private law which is not of 'the common known laws of the kingdom' but the
particular laws and constitutions assigned by the founder.

As to the first of those points, the ability of the courts to control the visitor by
the prerogative writs has been established by many cases. Thus, the court has by
mandamus required a visitor to exercise his jurisdiction: see *R v Bishop of Ely*
(1794) 5 Term Rep 475, 101 ER 267 and *R v Dunsheath, ex p Meredith* [1950] 2 All
ER 741 at 744, [1951] 1 KB 127 at 134. The court will also grant prohibition to
restrain a visitor from acting outside his jurisdiction: *Bishop of Chichester v Harward
and Webber* (1787) 1 Term Rep 650, 99 ER 1300. In one case, the court indicated
that it would intervene to prevent a breach by the visitor of the rules of natural
justice: see *Bently v Bishop of Ely* (1729) 1 Barn KB 192, 94 ER 132.

As to the second point, there are numerous cases in which attempts have been
made to induce the courts to review or ignore decisions of the visitor acting
within his jurisdiction, all of which have been unsuccessful. For some technical
reason certiorari used not to be available in such cases; but the aggrieved party
applied for mandamus to require the other parties to act on the footing that the
visitor's decision was invalid. Thus in the case referred to by Holt CJ, *Appleford's
Case* (1672) 1 Mod Rep 82, 86 ER 750, the plaintiff sought an order directed to
the master and fellows of a college to reinstate him as a fellow, the visitor having
already adjudicated that he had been rightly removed. Mandamus was refused.

In *R v Bishop of Chester* (1747) 1 Wm Bl 22, 96 ER 12 the bishop as visitor had
removed the applicant as a canon. The applicant sought mandamus directed to
the visitor to restore him. The order was refused. Lee CJ said (1 Wm Bl 22 at 26,
96 ER 12 at 14): 'There is no precedent, where a *mandamus* has gone to a visitor,
to reverse his own sentence.' Wright J agreed, saying: 'Visitors have an absolute

power; the only absolute one I know of in England.' Denison J said: 'This Court
a cannot control visitors.'

Similarly in *R v Bishop of Ely* (1794) 5 Term Rep 475, 101 ER 267 the applicant
had been removed as a fellow of Jesus College, Cambridge and had appealed
unsuccessfully to the bishop as visitor. He then applied for a mandamus directed
to the visitor to hear an appeal on the grounds that the earlier appeal to the visitor
had been no true appeal at all. His counsel admitted that, by reason of *Philips v*
b *Bury*, the court had no power to order the visitor to correct his decision however
erroneous. Lord Kenyon CJ said (5 Term Rep 475 at 477, 101 ER 267 at 268–
269):

> 'It was settled in *Philips v. Bury*, in which determination the profession has
> ever since acquiesced, that this court has no other power than that of putting
c > the visitatorial power in motion, (if I may use the expression,) but that if the
> judgment of the visitor be ever so erroneous, we cannot interfere in order to
> correct it. Now here the visitor received the appeal; each party disclosed his
> case to him; the whole merits of the case were before him; and he has
> exercised his judgment upon the whole. If therefore we were to interfere, it
> would be for the purpose of controlling his judgment. But any interference
d > by us to control the judgment of the visitor, would be attended with the
> most mischievous consequences, since we must then decide on the statutes
> of the college, of which we are ignorant, and the construction of which has
> been confided to another forum.'

Grose J said (5 Term rep 475 at 477, 101 ER 267 at 269):
e
> 'If the bishop had not exercised his judgment at all, we would have
> compelled him: but it is objected that he has not exercised it rightly; to this I
> answer that we have no authority to say how he should have decided.'

This case seems to me clear authority that the court has no jurisdiction to
review the decision of a visitor made within his jurisdiction.
f In *Ex p Buller* (1855) 1 Jur NS 709 the applicant had been expelled from his
fellowship by the provost and fellows of King's College, Cambridge. His appeal
to the visitor had been dismissed. He sought mandamus directed not to the visitor
but to the provost and fellows to reinstate him on the grounds that the provost
and fellows had breached the rules of natural justice. Coleridge J held, quoting
the judgment of Lord Kenyon CJ in *R v Bishop of Ely*, that the court had no power
g to compel the visitor 'to correct or alter his decision although that decision may
be erroneous'. He said that mandamus would not go to the provost and fellows
because 'a member of a college puts himself voluntarily under a peculiar system
of law, and assents to being bound by it, and cannot thereafter complain that such
a system is not in accordance with that adopted by the common law.' Mandamus
h was therefore refused because the visitor's determination provided a complete
answer to the complaint of breach of natural justice by the provost and fellows.

As to the third point (the reason why the court lacks jurisdiction to review), the
views of Holt CJ are supported by the passages I have already quoted from *R v*
Bishop of Ely (inability to decide on the statutes of the college 'of which we are
ignorant and the construction of which has been confided to another forum') and
j *Ex p Buller* ('a peculiar system' which is not required to be in accordance with
common law). In *Thomas v University of Bradford* [1987] 1 All ER 834, [1987] AC
795 this House had to decide whether the jurisdiction of the visitor was founded
on membership of the university or (as the House held) on the fact that a separate
system of law was applicable. Lord Griffiths referred to the visitor's jurisdiction
stemming from the power of the founder—

'to provide the laws under which the object of charity was to be governed and to be *sole* judge of the interpretation and application of those laws either by himself or by such person as he should appoint as a visitor.' (See [1987] 1 All ER 834 at 842, [1987] AC 795 at 814–815; my emphasis.)

He also referred to the laws as being 'domestic' and 'the internal laws of the foundation' (see [1987] 1 All ER 834 at 842, 843, [1987] AC 795 at 815, 816). Lord Ackner referred to the function of the visitor as being the supervision 'of the internal rules of the foundation so that it is governed in accordance with those private laws which the founder has laid down ...' (see [1987] 1 All ER 834 at 851, [1987] AC 795 at 827).

In my judgment this review of the authorities demonstrates that for over 300 years the law has been clearly established that the visitor of an eleemosynary charity has an exclusive jurisdiction to determine what are the internal laws of the charity and the proper application of those laws to those within his jurisdiction. The court's inability to determine those matters is not limited to the period pending the visitor's determination but extends so as to prohibit any subsequent review by the court of the correctness of a decision made by the visitor acting within his jurisdiction and in accordance with the rules of natural justice. This inability of the court to intervene is founded on the fact that the applicable law is not the common law of England but a peculiar or domestic law of which the visitor is the sole judge. This special status of a visitor springs from the common law recognising the right of the founder to lay down such a special law subject to adjudication only by a special judge, the visitor.

How then is it contended that the courts have power to review the visitor's decision as to the effect of the domestic law of the university in this case? The Divisional Court and the Court of Appeal did not consider in any detail the old authorities to which I have referred. They started from the position, in my judgment incorrectly, that the references in *Thomas*'s case to the visitor's jurisdiction being exclusive meant simply that the court did not have concurrent jurisdiction with him. Then, since this House in *Thomas*'s case had accepted that judicial review by way of certiorari did lie to the visitor at least to restrain an abusive process, they held that there was jurisdiction to correct errors of law since 'illegality' is one of the accepted heads of judicial review.

Before your Lordships, Mr Burke QC refined this argument. He relied upon the great development that has recently taken place in the law of judicial review whereby the courts have asserted a general jurisdiction to review the decisions of tribunals and inferior courts. He points to the way in which the law has developed from a maze of individual sets of circumstances in which one or other of the prerogative writs would lie to a general principle under which courts will review decisions on the three grounds of illegality, irrationality and procedural impropriety: see *Council of Civil Service Unions v Minister for the Civil Service* [1984] 3 All ER 935 at 950, [1985] AC 374 at 410 per Lord Diplock. Mr Burke submits that, if judicial review lies at all, then it is not possible to pick and choose between Lord Diplock's three categories: it must lie on all three grounds or not at all. As to illegality, recent developments in the law have shown that any relevant error of law made by the decision maker, whether as to his powers or as to the law he is to apply, may lead to his decision being quashed. In the present case, since the decision in *Thomas*'s case shows that judicial review does lie against the visitor, so his decision is capable of being reviewed on any one of Lord Diplock's three grounds, including illegality. If, therefore, the visitor has made an error in construing the statutes of the university, his decision can be quashed on judicial review.

I accept much of Mr Burke's submissions. Over the last 40 years the courts
a have developed general principles of judicial review. The fundamental principle
is that the courts will intervene to ensure that the powers of public decision
making bodies are exercised lawfully. In all cases, save possibly one, this
intervention by way of prohibition or certiorari is based on the proposition that
such powers have been conferred on the decision maker on the underlying
assumption that the powers are to be exercised only within the jurisdiction
b conferred, in accordance with fair procedures and, in a *Wednesbury* sense (see
Associated Provincial Picture Houses Ltd v Wednesbury Corp [1947] 2 All ER 680,
[1948] 1 KB 223), reasonably. If the decision maker exercises his powers outside
the jurisdiction conferred, in a manner which is procedurally irregular or is
Wednesbury unreasonable, he is acting ultra vires his powers and therefore
unlawfully: see Wade *Administrative Law* (6th edn, 1988) p 39ff. The one possible
c exception to this general rule used to be the jurisdiction of the court to quash a
decision taken within the jurisdiction of the decision taker where an error of law
appeared on the face of the record: *R v Northumberland Compensation Appeal
Tribunal, ex p Shaw* [1952] 1 All ER 122, [1952] 1 KB 338.

In my judgment the decision in *Anisminic Ltd v Foreign Compensation Commission*
d [1969] 1 All ER 208, [1969] 2 AC 147 rendered obsolete the distinction between
errors of law on the face of the record and other errors of law by extending the
doctrine of ultra vires. Thenceforward it was to be taken that Parliament had
only conferred the decision making power on the basis that it was to be exercised
on the correct legal basis: a misdirection in law in making the decision therefore
rendered the decision ultra vires. Professor Wade considers that the true effect of
e the *Anisminic* case is still in doubt: see *Wade* p 299ff. But in my judgment the
decision of this House in *O'Reilly v Mackman* [1982] 3 All ER 1124, [1983] 2 AC
237 establishes the law in the sense that I have stated. Lord Diplock, with whose
speech all the other members of the committee agreed, said that the decision in
the *Anisminic* case—

f   'has liberated English public law from the fetters that the courts had
        theretofore imposed upon themselves so far as determinations of inferior
        courts and statutory tribunals were concerned, by drawing esoteric distinctions
        between errors of law committed by such tribunals that went to their
        jurisdiction, and errors of law committed by them within their jurisdiction.
        The breakthrough that *Anisminic* made was the recognition by the majority
g   of this House that if a tribunal whose jurisdiction was limited by statute or
        subordinate legislation mistook the law applicable to the facts as it had found
        them, it must have asked itself the wrong question, ie one into which it was
        not empowered to inquire and so had no jurisdiction to determine. Its
        purported "determination", not being "a determination" within the meaning
h   of the empowering legislation, was accordingly a nullity.' (See [1982] 3 All
        ER 1124 at 1129, [1983] 2 AC 237 at 278.)

Therefore, I agree with Mr Burke that in general any error of law made by an
administrative tribunal or inferior court in reaching its decision can be quashed
for error of law.

j   At this point I must notice an argument raised by Mr Beloff QC for the
university. He suggests that the recent decision of this House in *R v Independent
Television Commission, ex p TSW Broadcasting Ltd* (1992) Independent, 27 March
has thrown doubt on the proposition that all errors of law vitiate the decision. In
my judgment this is a misreading of that authority. This House was asserting
that the mere existence of a mistake of law made at some earlier stage does not

vitiate the actual decision made: what must be shown is a relevant error of law, ie
an error in the actual making of the decision which affected the decision itself. *a*
This is demonstrated by Lord Templeman's quotation from the well-known
judgment of Lord Greene MR in the *Wednesbury* case [1947] 2 All ER 680 at 682–
683, [1948] 1 KB 223 at 229 (including the passage 'a person entrusted with a
discretion must, so to speak, direct himself properly in law') and the manner in
which thereafter he applied those principles to the facts of the case before the
House.   *b*

Although the general rule is that decisions affected by errors of law made by
tribunals or inferior courts can be quashed, in my judgment there are two reasons
why that rule does not apply in the case of visitors. First, as I have sought to
explain, the constitutional basis of the courts' power to quash is that the decision
of the inferior tribunal is unlawful on the grounds that it is ultra vires. In the
ordinary case, the law applicable to a decision made by such a body is the general *c*
law of the land. Therefore, a tribunal or inferior court acts ultra vires if it reaches
its conclusion on a basis erroneous under the general law. But the position of
decisions made by a visitor is different. As the authorities which I have cited
demonstrate, the visitor is applying not the general law of the land but a peculiar,
domestic law of which he is the sole arbiter and of which the courts have no   *d*
cognisance. If the visitor has power under the regulating documents to enter into
the adjudication of the dispute (ie is acting within his jurisdiction in the narrow
sense) he cannot err in law in reaching this decision since the general law is not
the applicable law. Therefore he cannot be acting ultra vires and unlawfully by
applying his view of the domestic law in reaching his decision. The court has no
jurisdiction either to say that he erred in his application of the general law (since *e*
the general law is not applicable to the decision) or to reach a contrary view as to
the effect of the domestic law (since the visitor is the sole judge of such domestic
law).

The second reason is closely allied to the first. In *Pearlman v Keepers and
Governors of Harrow School* [1979] 1 All ER 365, [1979] QB 56 a statute provided
that the decision of the county court as to whether works constituted an   *f*
'improvement' within the meaning of the Act should be 'final and conclusive'. A
tenant claimed that the installation of a central heating system constituted an
'improvement'. The county court judge ruled that it did not. The tenant then
applied to the Divisional Court by way of judicial review to quash the judge's
decision. The majority of the Court of Appeal held that it had jurisdiction to
quash the judge's order. However, Geoffrey Lane LJ dissented. He held that the   *g*
judge had done nothing which went outside the proper area of his inquiry. The
question was not whether the judge had made a wrong decision but whether he
had inquired into and decided a matter which he had no right to consider.
Therefore he held that the court had no jurisdiction to review the decision of the
county court judge for error of law.   *h*

This dissenting judgment of Geoffrey Lane LJ has been approved by the Privy
Council in *South East Asia Fire Bricks Sdn Bhd v Non-Metallic Mineral Products
Manufacturing Employees Union* [1980] 2 All ER 689 at 692, [1981] AC 363 at 370
and by a majority in this House in *Re Racal Communications Ltd* [1980] 2 All ER
634 at 639, 644–645, [1981] AC 374 at 384, 390–391. In the latter case,
Lord Diplock pointed out that the decision in *Anisminic* applied to decisions of *j*
administrative tribunals or other administrative bodies made under statutory
powers: in those cases there was a presumption that the statute conferring the
power did not intend the administrative body to be the final arbiter of questions
of law. He then contrasted that position with the case where a decision, making
power had been conferred on a court of law. In that case no such presumption

could exist; on the contrary where Parliament had provided that the decision of
a an inferior court was final and conclusive the High Court should not be astute to
find that the inferior court's decision on a question of law had not been made
final and conclusive, thereby excluding the jurisdiction to review it.

In my judgment, therefore, if there were a statutory provision that the decision
of a visitor on the law applicable to internal disputes of a charity was to be 'final
and conclusive', courts would have no jurisdiction to review the visitor's decision
b on the grounds of error of law made by the visitor within his jurisdiction (in the
narrow sense). For myself, I can see no relevant distinction between a case where
a statute has conferred such final and conclusive jurisdiction and the case where
the common law has for 300 years recognised that the visitor's decision on
questions of fact and law are final and conclusive and are not to be reviewed by
c the courts. Accordingly, unless this House is prepared to sweep away long-
established law, there is no jurisdiction in the court to review a visitor's decision
for error of law committed within his jurisdiction.

Mr Burke urged that the position of a visitor would be anomalous if he were
immune from review on the grounds of error of law. He submitted that the
concept of a peculiar domestic law differing from the general law of the land was
d artificial since in practice the charter and statutes of a university are expressed in
ordinary legal language and applied in accordance with the same principles as
those applicable under the general law. He pointed to the important public role
occupied by universities and submitted that it was wrong that they should be
immune from the general law of the land: 'There must be no Alsatia in England
where the King's writ does not run': see *Czarnikow v Roth Schmidt & Co* [1922] 2
e KB 478 at 488, [1922] All ER Rep 45 at 50 per Scrutton LJ. He further suggested
that to permit review of a visitor's decision for error of law would not impair the
effectiveness of the visitor's domestic jurisdiction.

I accept that the position of the visitor is anomalous, indeed unique. I further
accept that where the visitor is, or is advised by, a lawyer the distinction between
f the peculiar domestic law he applies and the general law is artificial. But I do not
regard these factors as justifying sweeping away the law which for so long has
regulated the conduct of charitable corporations. There are internal disputes
which are resolved by a visitor who is not a lawyer himself and has not taken legal
advice. It is not only modern universities which have visitors: there are a
substantial number of other long-established educational, ecclesiastical and
g eleemosynary bodies which have visitors. The advantages of having an informal
system which produces a speedy, cheap and final answer to internal disputes has
been repeatedly emphasised in the authorities, most recently by this House in the
Thomas v University of Bradford [1987] 1 All ER 834 at 850, [1987] AC 795 at 825
per Lord Griffiths; see also *Patel v University of Bradford Senate* [1978] 3 All ER 841
at 852, [1978] 1 WLR 1488 at 1499–1500. If it were to be held that judicial
h review for error of law lay against the visitor I fear that, as in the present case,
finality would be lost not only in cases raising pure questions of law but also in
cases where it would be urged in accordance with the *Wednesbury* principle that
the visitor had failed to take into account relevant matters or taken into account
irrelevant matters or had reached an irrational conclusion. Although the visitor's
position is anomalous, it provides a valuable machinery for resolving internal
j disputes which should not be lost.

I have therefore reached the conclusion that judicial review does not lie to
impeach the decisions of a visitor taken within his jurisdiction (in the narrow
sense) on questions of either fact or law. Judicial review does lie to the visitor in
cases where he has acted outside his jurisdiction (in the narrow sense) or abused
his powers or acted in breach of the rules of natural justice. Accordingly, in my

judgment the Divisional Court had no jurisdiction to entertain the application
for judicial review of the visitor's decision in this case.   *a*

In those circumstances, it is unnecessary to express any view on the proper
construction of the charter and statutes beyond saying that I have heard nothing
which persuades me that the views of Lord Jauncey of Tullichettle and the Court
of Appeal were wrong. I would dismiss the appeal and allow the cross-appeals,
with costs.

b

LORD MUSTILL. My Lords, because I consider that the decision of the visitor
was right I concur in the order proposed by your Lordships that this appeal should
be dismissed. I have however found it difficult to subscribe to the opinion
preferred by the majority of your Lordships that the appeal should be dismissed
because the decision of a visitor is not susceptible to judicial review for an error of   *c*
law, and had prepared a judgment setting out in summary my reasons for this
difficulty. Subsequently, I have had the advantage of reading in draft the speech
to be delivered by my noble and learned friend Lord Slynn of Hadley, in which
he concludes that the decision is indeed reviewable and does so on grounds which
I venture to find convincing. Accordingly, I need say no more than that, with due
respect to the majority of your Lordships, I agree with my noble and learned   *d*
friend in both his conclusions and his reasoning.

LORD SLYNN OF HADLEY. My Lords, Mr Page was appointed as a lecturer
in philosophy in the University of Hull with effect from 1 October 1966. By
letter dated 30 June 1988 his appointment was terminated on 2 October 1988.   *e*
The reason for terminating his appointment was that the university felt it
necessary to reduce the number of staff in the philosophy department by one and
he was the oldest member. Mr Page began proceedings in the Queen's Bench
Division to establish that the university was not entitled to dismiss him. Those
proceedings were struck out on the basis that his claim fell within the exclusive
jurisdiction of the visitor of the university and so he petitioned the visitor, Her   *f*
Majesty the Queen. Having received from Lord Jauncey of Tullichettle advice
that the dismissal was valid, the Lord President of the Council on behalf of Her
Majesty dismissed the petition.

Mr Page applied for judicial review of that decision. The Divisional Court held
that it had power to review the visitor's decision and that upon a proper
construction of the university statutes the university had no power to dismiss   *g*
Mr Page. The Court of Appeal likewise held that the visitor's decision could be
reviewed but held that the visitor's decision was correct in law.

On this appeal questions as to the court's jurisdiction and as to the proper
construction of the university's statutes have been raised.

The jurisdiction issue seems to me to divide into two parts. First, does judicial   *h*
review by way of certiorari ever lie to review error of law where there is no issue
as to excess of jurisdiction or breach of natural justice? If it does not, it cannot in
any event lie against a visitor on that basis. If it does, the second question is
whether certiorari can lie in respect of the decision of a visitor.

As to the first question it is clear that views as to the availability and scope of
certiorari together with its actual use have varied from time to time. In particular   *j*
distinctions were drawn between errors of law going to jurisdiction and errors of
law within jurisdiction and between errors of law on the face of the record and
other errors on law which in neither case went to jurisdiction.

For my part and despite the advice of the Privy Council in *South East Asia Fire
Bricks Sdn Bhd v Non-Metallic Mineral Products Manufacturing Employees Union*

a [1980] 2 All ER 689, [1981] AC 363, I would now follow the opinion of Lord Diplock in *Re Racal Communications Ltd* [1980] 2 All ER 634, [1981] AC 374 (with which Lord Keith of Kinkel agreed) and in *O'Reilly v Mackman* [1982] 3 All ER 1124, [1983] 2 AC 237 (with which the other members of the Appellate Committee agreed). In the former case Lord Diplock said ([1980] 2 All ER 634 at 638–639, [1981] AC 374 at 382–383):

b   'The breakthrough made by *Anisminic* was that, as respects administrative tribunals and authorities, the old distinction between errors of law that went to jurisdiction and errors of law that did not was for practical purposes abolished.'

In the latter case Lord Diplock said that the decision in *Anisminic Ltd v Foreign*
c *Compensation Commission* [1969] 1 All ER 208, [1969] 2 AC 147—

'has liberated English public law from the fetters that the courts had theretofore imposed upon themselves so far as determinations of inferior courts and statutory tribunals were concerned, by drawing esoteric distinctions between errors of law committed by such tribunals that went to their
d   jurisdiction, and errors of law committed by them within their jurisdiction. The breakthrough that the *Anisminic* case made was the recognition by the majority of this House that if a tribunal whose jurisdiction was limited by statute or subordinate legislation mistook the law applicable to the facts as it found them, it must have asked itself the wrong question, ie one into which it was not empowered to inquire and so had no jurisdiction to determine. Its
e   purported "determination", not being a "determination" within the meaning of the empowering legislation, was accordingly a nullity.' (See [1982] 3 All ER 1124 at 1129, [1983] 2 AC 237 at 278).

I accordingly accept that certiorari is now available to quash errors of law in a decision albeit those errors do not go to the jurisdiction of the tribunal.
f   The second part of this issue is therefore whether the decision of a visitor can be reviewed for error of law.

It is common ground between the parties, and, on the basis of earlier cases, rightly so, that the visitor to a university may be given an exclusive jurisdiction, eg to decide disputes arising under the statutes of the university, as may visitors to such eleemosynary foundations as schools, colleges and dioceses. It has long
g been accepted that this exclusive jurisdiction prevents the courts of the land from dealing initially with issues falling to be decided by the visitor, and prevent an appeal from the visitor to those courts.

As early as 1694 in *Philips v Bury* Holt KB 715, 90 ER 1294 this House accepted as correct the dissenting judgment of Holt CJ where it was sought to challenge the removal of a rector by the visitor of Exeter College by an action in ejectment.
h   Holt CJ held that the visitor did have jurisdiction to deprive the rector of his office and that 'having that power, the justice thereof is not examinable in a Court of Law, upon any action concerning the [visitor's] power' (see Holt KB 715 at 719, 90 ER 1294 at 1297). He asked (Holt KB 715 at 723, 90 ER 1294 at 1299):

j   'First, Whether the Sufficiency of the Sentence, as to the Cause, be examinable in the Common Law Courts? And, Secondly, whether the Truth of that cause, suppose it to be sufficient to ground the Sentence, if true, can be inquired into here?'

In vigorous terms he stated the position (Holt KB 715 at 723–725, 90 ER 1294 at 1299–1300):

'If the Sentence be given by the proper Visitor, created so by the Founder,
or by the Law, you shall never enquire into the Validity, or Ground of the *a*
Sentence . . . private and particular Corporations for Charity, founded and
endowed by private Persons, are subject to the private Government of those
who erect them . . . if [the visitor] hath Conusance of the Matter and Person,
and he gives a Sentence, it must have some effect to make a Vacancy, be it
never so wrong. But there is no Appeal, if the Founder hath not thought fit
to direct an Appeal; that an appeal lieth in the Common Law Courts, is *b*
certainly not so. This is according to the Government settled by the Founder;
if he hath directed all to be under the absolute Power of the Visitor, it must
be so.'

The reason for the rule was explained further in the same year in *R v St John's
College Cambridge* (1693) 4 Mod Rep 233 at 241, 87 ER 366 at 371): *c*

'THE VISITOR is made by *the founder*, and is the proper judge of the private
laws of the college; he is to determine offences against those laws. But where
the law of the land is disobeyed, this court will take notice thereof
notwithstanding THE VISITOR . . .'

To the same effect was *R v Bland* (1740) 7 Mod Rep 355, 87 ER 1287 and in *d*
1794 in *R v Bishop of Ely* 5 Term Rep 475, 101 ER 267 Lord Kenyon CJ regarded
what had been said by Holt CJ as settled law. In 1855 Coleridge J accepted the
same principle in *Ex p Buller* (1855) 1 Jur NS 709:

'It has been decided, and is now admitted, that where a visitor has acted in
his visitatorial capacity, this Court has no power to compel him to correct or *e*
alter his decision, although that decision may be erroneous. All that we can
do is to set the visitor in motion; but having done so, we cannot review his
decision. In *Rex* v. *The Bishop of Ely* Lord Kenyon refused the rule upon this
ground, and says, "It was settled in *Philips* v. *Bury* ((1694) 2 Term Rep 346,
[1558–1774] All ER Rep 53), in which determination the Profession has ever *f*
since acquiesced, that this Court has no other power than that of putting the
visitatorial power in motion, (if I may use the expression); but that if the
judgment of the visitor be erroneous, we cannot interfere in order to correct
it. Now, here the visitor received the appeal, each party disclosed his case to
him, the whole merits of the case were before him, and he has exercised his
judgment upon the whole. If, therefore, we were to interfere, it would be *g*
for the purpose of controlling his judgment; but any interference by us to
control the judgment of the visitor would be attended with the most
mischievous consequences, since we must then decide upon the statutes of
the college, of which we are ignorant, and the construction of which has been
confided to another forum."'

On the other hand, the court will order by mandamus a visitor to exercise his *h*
jurisdiction if he refuses or fails to do so since, if he does not, no one else can.

In *R v Bishop of Ely* (1788) 2 Term Rep 290, [1775–1802] All ER Rep 70 and
again in *R v Bishop of Ely* (1794) 5 Term Rep 475, 101 ER 267 the court recognised
this principle. In the latter case Grose J said (5 Term Rep 475 at 477, 101 ER 267 *j*
at 269):

'If the bishop had not exercised his judgment at all, we would have
compelled him: but it is objected that he has not exercised it rightly; to this I
answer that we have no authority to say how he should have decided.'

a Conversely, it has been accepted that the court may inquire as to whether a visitor intends to act outside his jurisdiction and in a proper case to grant a writ or order of prohibition to restrain him: *Bishop of Chichester v Harward and Webber* (1787) 1 Term Rep 650, 99 ER 1300; see also *Bently v Bishop of Ely* (1729) 1 Barn KB 192, 94 ER 132.

b Thus, despite the rule in *Philips v Bury*, some control over the exercise of jurisdiction was well recognised. The position is summarised in *R v Bishop of Chester* (1747) 1 Wm Bl 22 at 25, 96 ER 12 at 13–14 by Lee CJ: 'Certainly, if a visitor is in his jurisdiction, his acts are not to be inquired into; if out of it, his acts are void.'

c There is thus no doubt that on the older authorities the courts have refused to review by way of certiorari the decision of a visitor even though they were prepared to grant mandamus to require him to act or to prohibit him from acting in excess of jurisdiction.

d More recently in *Thomas v University of Bradford* [1987] 1 All ER 834, [1987] AC 795 Lord Griffiths (with whom Lord Bridge of Harwich, Lord Brandon of Oakbrook and Lord Mackay of Clashfern agreed) confirmed that the courts have no concurrent or appellate jurisdiction in respect of matters referred to a visitor by the special regulations of a university and emphasised the advantages of the visitorial procedure. Lord Griffiths concluded ([1987] 1 All ER 834 at 849–850, [1987] AC 795 at 825):

e 'Finally, there is the protection afforded by the supervisory, as opposed to appellate, jurisdiction of the High Court over the visitor. It has long been held that the writs of mandamus and prohibition will go ... Although doubts have been expressed in the past as to the availability of certiorari, I myself have no doubt that in the light of the modern development of administrative law, the High Court would have power, on an application for judicial review, to quash a decision of the visitor which amounted to an abuse of his powers.'

f Lord Ackner said ([1987] 1 All ER 834 at 852, [1987] AC 795 at 828):

g 'The *source* of the obligation on which Miss Thomas relies for her claim is the domestic laws of the university, its statutes and its ordinances. It is her case that the university has failed either in the proper interpretation of its statutes or in their proper application. Miss Thomas is not relying on a contractual obligation other than an obligation by the university to comply with its own domestic laws. Accordingly, in my judgment, her claim falls within the exclusive jurisdiction of the visitor, subject always to judicial review.' (Lord Ackner's emphasis.)

h It is thus clear on the basis of all these authorities that at the present time universities can create a jurisdiction for the visitor which excludes the concurrent and appellate jurisdiction of the courts. I do, however, respectfully agree with Lord Griffiths that certiorari would go to quash a decision of the visitor which amounted to an abuse of his power. The question in the present case is a different question: does certiorari go beyond quashing for abuse of power and allow judicial review for errors of law within jurisdiction? I do not think that this question was *j* resolved in *Thomas*'s case by what was said by Lord Griffiths though Lord Ackner's reference to judicial review is in general terms.

It is obviously not necessary to cite cases for the proposition that there has been a considerable development in the scope of judicial review in the second half of this century. It is more than enough to refer to the analysis of Sir William Wade in *Administrative Law* (6th edn, 1988). The old cases which I have cited have to be read subject to that development and not least to what was said in *Thomas*'s case.   *a*

With deference to the contrary view of the majority of your Lordships, in my opinion if certiorari can go to a particular tribunal it is available on all the grounds which have been judicially recognised. I can see no reasons in principle for limiting the availability of certiorari to a patent excess of power (as where a visitor has decided something which was not within his remit) and excluding review on other grounds recognised by the law. If it is accepted, as I believe it should be   *b* accepted, that certiorari goes not only for such an excess or abuse of power but also for a breach of the rules of natural justice there is even less reason in principle for excluding other established grounds. If therefore certiorari is generally available for error of law not involving abuse of power (as on the basis of Lord Diplock's speeches I consider that it is so available) then it should be available   *c* also in respect of a decision of a visitor.

I am not persuaded that the jurisdiction of the visitor involves such exceptional considerations that this principle should be departed from and that some grounds be accepted and others held not to be available for the purposes of judicial review.

The submissions made to your Lordships on the basis of the history of eleemosynary corporations do not seem to me to justify the drawing of such a   *d* distinction at the present time once it is accepted that certiorari can be available (as in *Thomas*'s case) on some grounds. Nor do I accept that all the questions referred to a visitor involve such arcane learning that only those intimately aware of university affairs can begin to understand it, the judges of the land not being able to appreciate the issues. The fact that Lords of Appeal in Ordinary and other senior judges are invited to advise the visitor show that this cannot be assumed.   *e* Moreover, issues of law may be referred to the visitor which are wholly analogous to questions decided by the courts. The present is such a case in which, if there had been no referral to a visitor, the matter would have come before the tribunals and courts on a clearly recognisable employment law question.

Nor am I impressed by the floodgates argument—it is said that the Divisional Court would be overwhelmed by applications to review visitors' decisions. In the   *f* first place many references to the visitor in student or staff disputes with university authorities do not involve questions of law at all. It will quickly be recognised that on matters of fact and challenges to the exercise of discretion leave to apply for judicial review will be refused. Moreover where the issue really does raise a question of esoteric university 'lore' the courts are unlikely to override the decision   *g* of the visitor, informed as he will be by the university authorities.

If there is a real question of law, particularly if it involves matters analogous to or the same as issues of the general law, I can see no reasonable justification for refusing judicial review. If the individual's rights are affected he should be entitled to the same protection by the courts as he would be in respect of the decision of a wide range of other tribunals and bodies to whom decisions involving   *h* a question of law are assigned.

I do not accept the intervener's argument that it is in some way undignified for the decision of a visitor on the basis of advice from an eminent judge to be subject to judicial review and that if certiorari is held to be available senior judges will not wish to give such advice. In most cases their advice will either be right in law or be in an area where the courts will wish to leave alone the exercise of the   *j* visitor's discretion. If there is an important and difficult question of law, however, I do not anticipate that senior judges will either feel 'demeaned' or take umbrage at the possibility of the courts looking at the question again on fuller argument.

The suggested analogies relied on with ecclesiastical courts and military courts which apply wholly distinct areas of law do not seem to me to be helpful or valid.

I therefore consider that certiorari does lie to review the construction placed
a upon the statutes by the visitor and that the cross-appeals should be dismissed.

The question then arises as to whether an error of law has been shown in the
present case.

The notice inviting applications for an appointment as senior lecturer/lecturer
in philosophy contained the following paragraph:

b   'TENURE   The appointments will date from the 1st October, 1966 and will
be subject to the Statutes of the University for the time being in force and to
any conditions prescribed by the Council at the time of the appointments.
The Senior Lecturer or Lecturer shall vacate his office on the 30th day of
September following the date on which he attains the age of 67 years, unless
it is specially extended by resolution of Council . . . The appointments may
c   be terminated on either side by three months' notice in writing expiring at
the end of a term or of the long vacation.'

On 13 June 1966 the registrar wrote to offer Mr Page, subject to the formal
approval of senate and council, an appointment as a lecturer with effect from 1
October 1966—

d   'on the terms and conditions set out below: The appointment may be
terminated by either party on giving three months' notice in writing expiring
at the end of a term or of the long vacation.'

On 14 June 1966 Mr Page replied: 'I am pleased to accept the appointment and
have taken note of the terms laid down in your letter.'
e There were interviews of which oral evidence was given in the inquiry ordered
by the visitor but these were found by Lord Jauncey of Tullichettle to be neutral
so far as the question at issue falls to be considered.

If the letters of offer and acceptance are looked at alone then it is clear that the
university was entitled to terminate the appointment on three months' notice.

It is said, however, that if regard is had to the statutes of the university, referred
f to in the notice inviting applications, on the basis of which the contract was
clearly made even if the statutes were not referred to in the letter, the university
had no such right.

By section 11 of the statutes the council shall appoint such other officers as may
be deemed necessary—

g   'with such duties at such remuneration and upon such terms and conditions
as the Council shall deem fit provided that no Academic Officer shall be
appointed except after consideration of a Report from the Senate.'

The statutes also include the following provisions:

h   'SECTION 34
REMOVAL OF MEMBERS OF THE TEACHING RESEARCH AND ADMINISTRATIVE
STAFF AND VACATION OF OFFICE

1. The Vice Chancellor and all Officers of the University including
Professors and members of the Staff holding their appointments until the age
of retirement may be removed by the Council for good cause . . .
j   2. "Good Cause" in this Statute means: [four categories are then specified
including certain convictions, incapacity rendering unfit to perform the
duties of the office, conduct of an immoral, scandalous or disgraceful nature
rendering unfit to perform the duties of the office].
3. Subject to the terms of his appointment no member of the teaching
research or administrative Staff of the University (including the Vice-

Chancellor) shall be removed from office save upon the grounds specified in
paragraph 2 of this section and in pursuance of the procedures specified in
Clause 1 of this Section.

SECTION 35

RETIREMENT OF MEMBERS OF THE ACADEMIC AND ACADEMIC-RELATED
STAFF OF THE UNIVERSITY.

The Vice-Chancellor and all Professors, Readers, Lecturers and other
salaried Officers of the University shall vacate their office on the 30th day of
September following the date on which they attain the age of 65 years unless
the Council . . . shall request any such Officer to continue in office for such
period as it shall from time to time determine provided that in the case of
such persons holding office on 30th September, 1977 the date shall be that
on which they attain the age of 67 years.'

Essentially the argument of Mr Page is that any member of the academic staff
who is appointed until a determined retiring age (in his case 67) can only be
removed before that date for good cause as defined in section 34(2) of the statutes.
The provision as to three months' notice has to be read with the limitation that
there can only be dismissal for good cause. It follows that, except in a case where
either the common law or statute allows instant dismissal (eg for gross
misconduct), a lecturer can only be dismissed for good cause after being given
three months' notice (though the lecturer can terminate the agreement on three
months' notice without any reason being assigned). A distinction is sought to be
drawn between the staff included in section 34(1) (being those also falling within
section 35 and who are appointed until a fixed age) and staff not so appointed to
whom section 34(3) applies and who may be dismissed on the notice period
specified in their letter of appointment.

I do not accept this. Although the drafting of the statutes leaves much room
for argument (as this case has shown) it seems to me that reading the statutes as a
whole 65 is fixed as the retiring age for a member of the academic staff. It is the
age beyond which a member of staff may not continue; they 'shall vacate their
Office' (section 35). That provision in itself does not guarantee continuance in
post until age 65. Whether members of staff can so continue depends on the other
terms and conditions of the appointment. Those terms in this case include
provision for termination for good cause under section 34(1) and on three months'
notice as one of the terms of the appointment under section 34(3). This result
could have been spelled out more clearly in the statutes but it seems to me to
follow from the provisions of the statutes as they stand and, contrary to the
argument of Mr Page, to be no more curious than the alternative for which he
contends.

It follows in my view that no error of law has been shown in the decision of
the visitor and for that reason I consider that this appeal like the cross-appeals
should be dismissed.

Appeal dismissed ; cross-appeals allowed.

Mary Rose Plummer   Barrister.

a

Farmer (Valuation Officer) and another v Buxted Poultry Ltd

HOUSE OF LORDS

LORD TEMPLEMAN, LORD OLIVER OF AYLMERTON, LORD GOFF OF CHIEVELEY, LORD MUSTILL AND LORD SLYNN OF HADLEY

b

11 NOVEMBER, 10 DECEMBER 1992

Rates – Exemption – Buildings occupied together with agricultural land and used solely in connection with agricultural operations thereon – Buildings occupied together with buildings used for keeping and breeding of livestock – Occupied together with – Provender
c *mill and poultry processing factory – Mill and factory providing feed and processing plant for broiler houses on 67 farms situated up to 120 miles away – Whether mill and factory 'occupied together with' broiler houses on farms – Whether distance relevant factor – General Rate Act 1967, s 26(1) – Rating Act 1971, ss 1(1), 2(1)(b).*

The ratepayer company owned and occupied two hereditaments in the same
d village for the purposes of its poultry business. The first hereditament comprised a provender mill used for the production of pelleted feed for turkeys and chickens housed in broiler houses on 67 farms owned and occupied by the company and situated between a quarter of a mile and 120 miles in distance from the mill. The second hereditament comprised a separate poultry processing factory used for the slaughter and processing of turkeys and chickens from the company's broiler
e houses and ancillary buildings. The company made proposals to delete both hereditaments from the valuation list for rating on the ground that the buildings on the hereditaments were 'agricultural buildings' as defined by s 2(1)(b) and (3)(a)[a] of the Rating Act 1971 and were therefore exempted from rating by s 26(1)[b] of the General Rate Act 1967 as applied to 'agricultural buildings' by s 1(1)[c] of the
f 1971 Act inasmuch as the provender mill and the poultry processing factory were buildings 'occupied together with' buildings (the broiler houses) used for the keeping or breeding of livestock, within s 2(1)(b), since they were both occupied by the same person, they were both so occupied during the same period and they both took part in one continuous process of rearing, slaughtering and preparing poultry for sale so that a test of functional unity was satisfied. It was accepted that
g the broiler houses were agricultural buildings within s 2(1)(b) of the 1971 Act. The local valuation court agreed to the proposals and deleted both entries from the list. The valuation officer and the council appealed to the Lands Tribunal, which dismissed the appeals, holding that the geographical test, ie the distance between the hereditments and the farms, was not a relevant consideration and that the provender mill and the factory were 'occupied together with' the broiler
h houses. The council appealed to the Court of Appeal, which allowed the appeal, holding that the Lands Tribunal had applied the wrong test in determining whether the provender mill and factory were occupied together with the broiler houses on the farms, and remitted the case to the tribunal. The company appealed to the House of Lords.

j **Held** – For a building to be 'occupied together with' another for the purposes of the 1967 Act the buildings had to be in the same occupation and the activities

---

a   Section 2, so far as material, is set out at p 119 *j* to p 120 *c*, post

b   Section 26(1) is set out at p 119 *f*, post

c   Section 1(1), so far as material, provides: 'In section 26 of the General Rate Act 1967 ... (*a*) the expression "agricultural buildings" shall include any building which is an agricultural building by virtue of section 2 ... of this Act ...'

carried on in both had to be jointly controlled or managed. Moreover, the two buildings or, as the case might be, the buildings and agricultural land had to be *a* so occupied and the activities so controlled or managed at the same time, so as to form in a real sense a single agricultural unit. Although there was no conclusive geographical test for the purpose of deciding whether buildings were occupied together for rating purposes, the distance between them was a relevant factor, since contiguity or propinquity might go far to show that they were so occupied whereas separation might indicate that they were not and the greater the distance *b* the less likely they were to be one agricultural unit. On the facts it was impossible to say that each farm or broiler house was occupied together with all the other broiler houses as one unit or that the factory was occupied as one unit together with all of the farms since the farms were separate and distinct agricultural units. The appeal would accordingly be dismissed (see p 119 *b* to *d* and p 123 *b* to *e j* to *c* p 124 *b*, post).

Decision of the Court of Appeal sub nom *Hambleton DC v Buxted Poultry Ltd* [1992] 2 All ER 70 affirmed.

Notes

For exemption from rating of agricultural land and buildings, see 39 *Halsbury's* *d* *Laws* (4th edn) paras 62–64, and for cases on the subject, see 38 *Digest* (Reissue) 335–338, 2296–2307.

For the General Rate Act 1967, s 26, see 36 *Halsbury's Statutes* (4th edn) 656.

For the Rating Act 1971, ss 1, 2, see ibid 798, 799.

Cases referred to in opinions   *e*

Eastwood (W & J B) Ltd v Herrod (Valuation Officer) [1970] 1 All ER 774, [1971] AC 160, [1970] 2 WLR 775, HL; *affg* [1968] 3 All ER 389, [1968] 2 QB 923, [1968] 3 WLR 593, CA.

Handley (Valuation Officer) v Bernard Matthews plc [1988] RA 222, Lands Trib.

Hilleshogg Sugar Beet Breeding Co Ltd v Wilkes (Valuation Officer) [1971] RA 275, Lands Trib.   *f*

Midlothian Assessor v Buccleuch Estates Ltd 1962 SC 453, LVAC.

Taylor (Maurice E) (Merchants) Ltd v Comr of Valuation [1981] NI 236, NI CA.

Appeal

Buxted Poultry Ltd appealed with the leave of the Appeal Committee of the House of Lords given on 15 January 1992 from the decision of the Court of *g* Appeal (Purchas, Glidewell LJJ and Sir John Megaw) (sub nom *Hambleton DC v Buxted Poultry Ltd* [1992] 2 All ER 70, [1992] 1 WLR 330) on 19 July 1991 allowing the appeals of the first respondent, Hambleton District Council, by way of case stated from the decision of the Lands Tribunal (C R Mallett and T Hoyes) given on 24 November 1989 dismissing appeals by the first respondent and the second respondent, W N Farmer (the valuation officer), from the decision of a *h* local valuation court for North Yorkshire given on 12 May 1987 determining that the hereditaments described as the provender mill and premises situate at Nitrovit Ltd, Dalton Airfield, Eldmire Lane, Topcliffe and the poultry processing factory and premises situate at Site No 1, Dalton, Thirsk, both owned and occupied by the appellant be exempt from rating. The facts are set out in the opinion of Lord *j* Slynn.

Peter Curry QC and Malcolm Davis-White (instructed by Stephens & Scown, Exeter) for the appellant.

Christopher Cochrane QC and Simon Bird (instructed by Sharpe Pritchard, agents for C Spencer, Northallerton) for the council.

Their Lordships took time for consideration.

a

10 December 1992. The following opinions were delivered.

LORD TEMPLEMAN. My Lords, I have had the advantage of reading in draft the speech prepared by my noble and learned friend Lord Slynn of Hadley. I agree with it, and for the reasons given, I too would dismiss the appeal.

b

LORD OLIVER OF AYLMERTON. My Lords, I have had the advantage of reading in draft the speech prepared by my noble and learned friend Lord Slynn of Hadley. I agree with it, and for the reasons given, I too would dismiss the appeal.

c **LORD GOFF OF CHIEVELEY.** My Lords, I have had the advantage of reading in draft the speech prepared by my noble and learned friend Lord Slynn of Hadley. I agree with it, and for the reasons given, I too would dismiss the appeal.

d **LORD MUSTILL.** My Lords, I have had the advantage of reading in draft the speech prepared by my noble and learned friend Lord Slynn of Hadley. I agree with it, and for the reasons given, I too would dismiss the appeal.

LORD SLYNN OF HADLEY. My Lords, the underlying question at issue in this appeal is whether a poultry processing factory owned, occupied and operated *e* by the appellant is an 'agricultural building' within the meaning of s 26 of the General Rate Act 1967 and ss 1 and 2 of the Rating Act 1971, so as to be exempt from rates.

The local valuation court (to whom an application was made by the appellant contesting the decision of the second respondent) and the Lands Tribunal held that it was an 'agricultural building' and was exempt. The Court of Appeal held *f* that the Lands Tribunal had misdirected itself in law and remitted the question to the Lands Tribunal (see [1992] 2 All ER 70, [1992] 1 WLR 330).

By s 26(1) of the General Rate Act 1967: 'No agricultural land or agricultural buildings shall be liable to be rated or included in any valuation list or in any rate.' By sub-s (4):

g   'In this section the expression "agricultural buildings"—(*a*) means buildings (other than dwellings) occupied together with agricultural land or being or forming part of a market garden, and in either case used solely in connection with agricultural operations thereon; and (*b*) includes a building which is used solely in connection with agricultural operations carried on on agricultural land and which is occupied either—(i) by the occupiers of all that *h*   land; or (ii) by individuals who are appointed by the said occupiers for the time being to manage . . .'

By s 1 of the Rating Act 1971, the definition of 'agricultural buildings' in s 26 of the 1967 Act is extended for purposes of derating. The extensions include:

j   '**2.** *Livestock buildings.*—(1) Subject to subsections (2) to (4) of this section, each of the following is an agricultural building by virtue of this section— (*a*) any building used for the keeping or breeding of livestock; and (*b*) any building (other than a dwelling) which is occupied together with one or more buildings falling within paragraph (*a*) above and is used in connection with the operations carried on in that building or those buildings. (2) A building used as mentioned in subsection (1)(*a*) of this section is not

an agricultural building by virtue of this section unless either—(a) it is solely
so used; or (b) it is occupied together with agricultural land (as defined in the   a
principal section) and used also in connection with agricultural operations on
that land, and that other use together with the use mentioned in subsection
(1)(a) of this section is its sole use.

(3) A building occupied and used as mentioned in subsection (1)(b) of this
section is not an agricultural building by virtue of this section unless either—
(a) it is solely so used; or (b) it is occupied also together with agricultural land   b
(as defined in the principal section) and used also in connection with
agricultural operations on that land and that other use together with the use
mentioned in subsection (1)(b) of this section is its sole use.

(4) A building is not an agricultural building by virtue of this section
unless it is surrounded by or contiguous to an area of agricultural land (as
defined in the principal section) which amounts to not less than two hectares   c
...'

But for the purpose of deciding whether a building is so surrounded by or
contiguous to an area of agricultural land certain items are to be disregarded.

The Lands Tribunal found that the objects of the appellant company included
the breeding, rearing, slaughtering, processing, packing, selling and distributing   d
of turkeys and chickens for human consumption. For this purpose it owned and
occupied 67 poultry breeding and rearing farms situated between a quarter of a
mile and 120 miles from the hereditaments in question at Dalton, Thirsk, North
Yorkshire, where the appellant owned and occupied a provender mill and
premises and a separate processing factory and premises.   e

The mill produced and supplied to the 67 farms pelleted feed for consumption
by the poultry but it also supplied 6% to 8% of its total production (amounting to
between 162 and 216 tonnes per week) to farms occupied by independent turkey
rearers. The Lands Tribunal accepted that the provender mill was both occupied
together with the farms and used solely in connection with them. The Court of
Appeal rejected both of these contentions. The 6% to 8% supplied to other farmers   f
prevented the supply from being the sole use in connection with the appellant's
farms and even if the de minimis rule applied (which as a matter of construction
the Court of Appeal found that it did not) this quantity was not de minimis.
There has been no appeal to your Lordships' House from that decision.

The factory received the substantial production (though not the entire
production) of poultry from 48 of the farms, again scattered over a very large   g
area. Poultry was not received from other farms. The poultry was processed at
the factory and either frozen or sold fresh to depots. The Court of Appeal, like
the Lands Tribunal, accepted that the factory itself was used solely in connection
with the operations carried on at the 48 broiler rearing houses on the farms. The
Court of Appeal, however, regarded the Lands Tribunal's decision, that the   h
ancillary buildings (a sales office, shop and maintenance workshop) were so linked
to the factory that they could be regarded as solely used for the same purposes, as
one of fact and degree which could not be set aside. There is no appeal from that
part of the Court of Appeal's decision.

The sole question, therefore, is whether the factory can be said to have been
'occupied together with' buildings used for the keeping or breeding of livestock   j
so as to satisfy the requirements of s 2(1)(b) of the 1971 Act.

The appellant's case is that the factory was occupied together with those
buildings since they were both occupied by the same person, they were both so
occupied during the same period and they both took part in one continuous
process of rearing, slaughtering and preparing poultry for sale so that a test of
functional unity was satisfied. There is no requirement that the relevant building

should be contiguous or adjacent to the farms. The absence of contiguity in the
a present case was not found by the Lands Tribunal to prevent the factory being
'occupied together with' the broiler houses. That is a question of fact and degree
which cannot be interfered with on appeal.

The Lands Tribunal in the present case found that the distance of the factory
from the farms did not appear to weaken the functional link between the factory
and the farms, nor prevent the company from occupying those distant farms
b 'together with' their buildings at Dalton. They concluded:

> 'For these reasons we do not think that a geographical test has merit in
> these cases and we find that the provender mill and the factory are, as a
> matter of fact, "occupied together with" the farms in the occupation of the
> Company.'
c

In the Court of Appeal Glidewell LJ, with whom Sir John Megaw agreed,
considered that not to treat the geographical test of propinquity as a relevant
consideration was an error of law. Purchas LJ was of the same view and considered
that the Lands Tribunal misdirected themselves in so far as they ignored the
d geographical relationship between the factory and the agricultural building in
coming to the conclusion that it was 'occupied together with' those buildings.

Glidewell LJ was of the opinion, with which the other members of the Court
of Appeal agreed, that—

> 'a building can be said to be occupied together with another building used
> for the breeding or keeping of livestock, provided, firstly, that they have a
e > single occupier, secondly, that the activities carried on in both are jointly
> controlled or managed and, thirdly, that the physical communication
> between the two buildings is, by reason either of physical nearness or some
> other factor, so close and convenient that they can properly be regarded as
> being occupied as parts of the same enterprise.' (See [1992] 2 All ER 70 at 79,
f > [1992] 1 WLR 330 at 339.)

The phrase 'occupied together with' has been considered in a number of cases
arising either under the 1967 Act or under the 1971 Act and different approaches
have been adopted. Thus in *Hilleshog Sugar Beet Breeding Co Ltd v Wilkes (Valuation
Officer)* [1971] RA 275 the question was whether a plant research centre was
g occupied together with a number of widely scattered plots of land, some of which
were up to 40 miles away from the centre. There men and machines were sent
out from the centre to work on the plots of land in order to plant out seed beds
with a view to producing an improved type of beet. Sir Michael Rowe QC,
President of the Lands Tribunal, quoted (at 284) the proposition in *Ryde on Rating*
(12th edn, 1968) p 289 that '"Occupied together with" seems to imply a functional
h rather than a geographical connection'. He accepted that the centre was occupied
together with the plots of land.

In *Handley (Valuation Officer) v Bernard Matthews plc* [1988] RA 222 the
hereditament was used for the production of pelleted feed for turkeys on 29 farms
owned and occupied by the company and situated between 9 and 74 miles from
the hereditament. Mr V G Wellings QC concluded (at 229):
j

> 'On the facts, I find that the appeal hereditament at all material times was
> and is occupied together with the livestock buildings on all the 29 farms. I
> am not impressed by any geographical test, at all events in the present case.
> If it is desired to ascribe a specific meaning to the words "occupied together
> with", it appears to me that the most likely meaning is "occupied at the same
> time as": see Stroud, *Judicial Dictionary* (5th edn, 1986) . . .'

In *Maurice E Taylor (Merchants) Ltd v Comr of Valuation* [1981] NI 236 a company
carried on business as a shipper of seed and ware potatoes. Some of the land on
which the potatoes were grown was 10 to 20 miles from the buildings in question
which consisted of a shed, where the potatoes were graded and bagged, and a
store. Gibson LJ could see—

> 'no principle of rating law which would suggest that, once it has been
> proved that the land and buildings are in common occupation, their physical
> relationship should determine whether the buildings are to be treated as
> agricultural or not. I would accept the view stated in *Ryde on Rating* ((13th
> edn, 1976) p 300) that "occupied together with" seems to imply a functional
> rather than a geographical connection.' (See [1981] NI 236 at 348.)

Lord Lowry CJ rejected the proposition that the buildings and the land must
be contiguous or adjacent (at 251) and said (at 252):

> 'In any case there is really no reason why the words "together with" should
> connote more than the occupation of buildings and land by the same person,
> since the need for a functional connection is ensured by the words "and used
> solely in connection with, etc.".'

Finally on the English cases reference must be made to *W & J B Eastwood Ltd v
Herrod (Valuation Officer)* [1970] 1 All ER 774, [1971] AC 160 where again the
rearing, killing and preparing of poultry for sale were at issue. The case turned
on whether the buildings in question were used 'solely in connection with the
agricultural operations on the land', it being conceded that all the buildings were
occupied together with the 1,150 acres of land. Viscount Dilhorne expressed
suprise that that should be so. He said ([1970] 1 All ER 774 at 788, [1971] AC 160
at 180):

> 'But for this concession I do not think I should have found it easy to
> conclude that the packing station in Gainsborough nine miles or so away was
> occupied together with the agricultural land in the sense in which those
> words are used in the definition, and it may be that I would have had
> difficulty in coming to that conclusion in relation to the five layer houses at
> Norton Brisney some six miles away and some of the other buildings. In its
> context "occupied together with agricultural land" may connote more than
> common ownership. My impression on reading the definition of "Agricul-
> tural buildings" is that it was an attempt by the draftsman to define a farm
> in statutory language and that it was intended to include buildings used and
> occupied together with the land for the purpose of farming the land, not
> buildings far distant and not used in connection with an operation on the
> land, even though owned by the same person.'

In *Midlothian Assessor v Buccleuch Estates Ltd* 1962 SC 453 the Lands Valuation
Appeal Court in Scotland was concerned with woodlands, comprising several
scattered areas of land, and sawmills on separate sites. The majority decision was
that sawmills other than one sawmill contiguous to the woodlands were not part
of agricultural land. They were not 'buildings thereon'. Both Lord Sorn, who
dissented, and Lord Kilbrandon approached the matter on the basis that the
relevant question was what was: the unit or unum quid for rating purposes? Lord
Kilbrandon said (at 465):

> 'It has never yet been admitted that you can have a unit of valuation
> consisting of widely scattered heritable subjects connected only by some

functional or commercial *nexus*, and I do not see why it should be. I do not
think one is being merely old-fashioned or obscurantist in insisting, in the
conception of *unum quid*, upon a fairly close physical relationship between
what might be considered as parts of a commercial unit; one is, after all,
attempting to value not a business but heritable subjects, and it may be that
the precedents, which all insist upon such a physical relationship, indicate a
determination to preserve that essential distinction.'

I agree with Glidewell LJ that for one building to be 'occupied together with'
another for the purposes of this Act they must be in the same occupation and the
activities carried on in both must be jointly controlled or managed. I also consider
that the buildings must be so occupied and the activities so controlled and
managed at the same time. These are necessary conditions to be satisfied but to
satisfy each of them separately or together is not sufficient to establish that one
building is 'occupied together with' another for rating purposes. Nor is there any
geographical test which gives a conclusive answer—though the distance between
the buildings is a relevant consideration, as the Court of Appeal held.

It is not, however, sufficient to ask generally whether the buildings or buildings
and land in question are all part of the same business enterprise. What it is
necessary to show is that the two buildings, or as the case may be, the buildings
and agricultural land, are occupied together so as to form in a real sense a single
agricultural unit. Contiguity or propinquity may go far to show that they are.
Thus farm buildings surrounded by land which is farmed with other land nearby
though not contiguous or even land in another neighbouring village may well as
a matter of fact be found to be 'occupied together with' each other. On the other
hand separation may indicate that they are not and the greater the distance the
less likely they are to be one agricultural unit.

In view of the extension in the 1971 Act to derate further hereditaments, it is
not right now to ask whether the two premises constituted one 'farm' in the
ordinary sense but Viscount Dilhorne, in the passage quoted above, in my view
indicates the right direction. Though I consider that the actual decision in the
case is to be treated as one on its special facts and the correctness of which may in
any event be debatable, the sense of 'togetherness' referred to by Sir Michael Rowe
QC in *Hilleshog*'s case perhaps equally shows that the important question is
whether the two buildings or the buildings and land are worked together so as to
form one agricultural unit.

The Rating and Valuation (Apportionment) Act 1928, which was the forerunner
of the 1967 Act, gives a similar indication since it distinguished 'agricultural
hereditaments' from other hereditaments and defined 'agricultural buildings' as
meaning—

> 'buildings (other than dwelling-houses) occupied together with agricultural
> land or being or forming part of a market garden, and in either case used
> solely in connection with agricultural operations thereon.'

That again gives the impression of an agricultural unit.

In the present case there are 48 farms with their broiler houses and each broiler
house must be surrounded by at least two hectares of land to qualify. They are
kept separate and distinct, in part, in order to prevent or reduce the spread of
disease. Yet it is an inescapable finding that they are separate and distinct farms
and are to be treated as such for rating purposes since it has not been suggested
that any two or more of the broiler houses are in reality run as a single unit. It
seems to me that it is quite impossible on the findings of the Lands Tribunal to
say that each farm or broiler house is occupied together with all of the other

broiler houses as one unit or that the factory is occupied as one unit together with
all of the farms, some of which are 100 miles away.

Applying the test as to whether the several buildings are worked together as
one agricultural unit, and having regard to their physical separation, as part of
this test, it seems to me that the Lands Tribunal could not possibly conclude that
the 48 farms are 'occupied together with' the factory for the purposes of the Act.

I take the view therefore that the appeal should be dismissed, that there is no
point in referring the matter back to the Lands Tribunal and that it be ordered
that the appellant's processing factory and premises at Dalton, Thirsk, North
Yorkshire, should be reinstated in the valuation list, it being agreed that the
appropriate rating valuation is £20,150.

Appeal dismissed.

Mary Rose Plummer   Barrister.

Zucker and others v Tyndall Holdings plc

COURT OF APPEAL, CIVIL DIVISION
DILLON, NEILL AND STAUGHTON LJJ
6, 7 MAY 1992

*Practice – Pre-trial or post-judgment relief – Mareva injunction – Jurisdiction – Claim
for specific performance of option in share agreement – Action pending in Swiss courts to
determine whether option validly exercised – Circumstances giving rise to valid exercise
of option not yet arising – Whether threatened breach of term of contract sufficient cause
of action to support Mareva injunction.*

The plaintiffs were minority shareholders in a Swiss company. Under a
shareholders' agreement made between themselves and the majority shareholders
the plaintiffs were entitled to exercise an option to sell their shares. The agreement,
which was governed by Swiss law, provided for the option to be exercised by the
plaintiffs sending their share certificates to a subsidiary of the defendants, the
English holding company of the Swiss company. Thereafter the defendants had a
period of three months in which to issue and deliver the shares. The plaintiffs
purported to exercise their option on 23 March 1992, and therefore under the
terms of the agreement the expiry date for the delivery of the shares was 24 June
1992. On 25 March the plaintiffs commenced proceedings in Switzerland seeking
a declaration that they had validly exercised their option and an order that the
defendants pay them the sum of 6m Swiss francs, which they claimed represented
the aggregate value of the shares in the company. On 30 March the plaintiffs
issued a writ in England claiming, in effect, specific performance of the agreement
for the sale of the shares, and on the same day they obtained ex parte a Mareva
injunction against the defendants. The injunction was discharged on the ground
that since the relief sought was merely declaratory the court had no jurisdiction
to grant Mareva relief. The plaintiffs appealed.

Held – The court had no jurisdiction to grant a Mareva injunction unless there
was a pre-existing cause of action which could be enforced immediately against a
defendant arising out of an invasion, actual or threatened, of a legal or equitable
right of the plaintiff. A cause of action would not arise where there was only a
threatened breach of some term of a contract which was not presently enforceable

a or performable. Since the plaintiffs' claim was for specific performance of a term of a contract which was not presently enforceable because at the time the Mareva injunction was granted the due date for performance was six weeks away and since the question whether the plaintiffs had a valid claim under the agreement had yet to be determined by the Swiss courts, it followed that the threatened breach of contract on which the plaintiffs founded their claim could not constitute a cause of action on which the grant of Mareva relief could be based and therefore

b the court had no jurisdiction to grant a Mareva injunction. The appeal would accordingly be dismissed (see p 129 *b*, p 131 *c d g* to p 132 *b d j* and p 133 *a* to *c h*, post).

Dictum of Lord Diplock in *Siskina (cargo owners) v Distos Cia Naviera SA, The Siskina* [1977] 3 All ER 803 at 824 and *Ninemia Maritime Corp v Trave*
c *Schiffahrtsgesellschaft mbH & Co KG, The Niedersachsen* [1984] 1 All ER 398 applied.

Notes
For Mareva injunctions, see 37 *Halsbury's Laws* (4th edn) para 362, and for cases on the subject, see 28(4) *Digest* (2nd reissue) 197–214, 5326–5392.

For the jurisdiction of the Court of Appeal, see 10 *Halsbury's Laws* (4th edn)
d paras 899–900 and 37 *Halsbury's Laws* (4th edn) para 678, and for cases on the subject, see 16 *Digest* (Reissue) 241–244, 2359–2388 and 37(3) *Digest* (Reissue) 144–150, 3692–3735.

Cases referred to in judgments
Gubisch Maschinenfabrik KG v Palumbo Case 144/86 [1987] ECR 4861.
e *Hasham v Zenab* [1960] AC 316, [1960] 2 WLR 374, PC.
Ninemia Maritime Corp v Trave Schiffahrtsgesellschaft mbH & Co KG, The Niedersachsen [1984] 1 All ER 398, [1983] 1 WLR 1412, [1983] 2 Lloyd's Rep 600, CA; *affg* [1984] 1 All ER 398.
North London Rly Co v Great Northern Rly Co (1883) 11 QBD 30, CA.
f *Siporex Trade SA v Comdel Commodities Ltd* [1986] 2 Lloyd's Rep 428.
Siskina (cargo owners) v Distos Cia Naviera SA, The Siskina [1977] 3 All ER 803, [1979] AC 210, [1977] 3 WLR 818, HL.
South Carolina Insurance Co v Assurantie Maatschappij 'de Zeven Provincien' NV [1986] 3 All ER 487, [1987] AC 24, [1986] 3 WLR 398, HL.
Steamship Mutual Underwriting Association (Bermuda) Ltd v Thakur Shipping Co Ltd
g [1986] 2 Lloyd's Rep 439, CA.
Veracruz Transportation Inc v VC Shipping Co Inc, The Veracruz I [1992] 1 Lloyd's Rep 353, CA.

Case also cited
Marks v Lilley [1959] 2 All ER 647, [1959] 1 WLR 749.
h

Interlocutory appeal
The plaintiffs, Willard Ira Zucker, Sylviane Francine Zucker, Eric Alain Zucker, Paul Francis Zucker and Phillipe Grossglauser, appealed from a decision of Morland J made on 6 April 1992 on an application made ex parte by the defendants, Tyndall Holdings plc (Tyndall Holdings), whereby he discharged the
j order of Potter J made on 30 March 1992 restraining Tyndall Holdings from removing from the jurisdiction or disposing of any of their assets within the jurisdiction save in so far as the unencumbered value of those assets exceeded 8,300,000 Swiss francs or the sterling equivalent thereof, an undertaking in the terms of the injunction having been given by Tyndall Holdings pending appeal. The appellants' intended action was for a declaration that they were entitled under

a shareholders' agreement dated 2 June 1989 to exercise their option to sell all
their shares in a company, Tyndall Trust SA, the majority of the shares in which   *a*
were held by a wholly-owned subsidiary of Tyndall Holdings. The facts are set
out in the judgment of Neill LJ.

Martin Mann QC (instructed by *Jay Benning & Levine*) for the appellants.
John Thomas QC and *David Foxton* (instructed by *Turner Kenneth Brown*) for Tyndall   *b*
  Holdings.

NEILL LJ (delivering the first judgment at the invitation of Dillon LJ). This is
an appeal by the plaintiffs, Mr Willard Zucker and three other members of the
Zucker family and Mr Grossglauser (who I will refer to as 'the appellants'), from
the order of Morland J dated 6 April 1992 whereby he discharged a Mareva   *c*
injunction granted by Potter J on an application made to the court ex parte on
30 March 1992. The application to discharge was made ex parte on notice. I
understand that pending the hearing of this appeal the defendants have given an
undertaking in the terms of the injunction.

By an agreement dated 2 June 1989 the appellants were allotted 25% of the
shares in a Swiss company called Tyndall Trust SA. The other 75% of the shares   *d*
in Tyndall Trust were allotted to Tyndall International Holdings Ltd save in so far
as they already owned shares which they agreed to retain. Tyndall International
is a company incorporated in Bermuda and is a wholly-owned subsidiary of an
English company, Tyndall Holdings plc (Tyndall Holdings), the defendants.

The parties to the agreement of 2 June 1989 were the appellants, Tyndall
Holdings (the defendants and the present respondents) and Tyndall International.   *e*

At the time of the agreement the share capital of Tyndall Trust was substantially
increased, and the purpose of the agreement (which I shall call 'the shareholders'
agreement') was to enable Mr Willard Zucker and his companies to join forces
with another larger group (the Tyndall Group) and to enable the Tyndall Group,
headed by Tyndall Holdings, to obtain access to the Swiss market and to have the   *f*
benefit of the services of Mr Zucker and of Mr Grossglauser, who is the fifth
appellant. At the time of the shareholders' agreement Mr Zucker was the founder
and managing director of a company which I can refer to as 'Serfid'. The shares in
Serfid were owned as to 100% by Mrs Sylviane Zucker, the second appellant. Mr
Grossglauser, for his part, was an executive director of Serfid. At the time both
Serfid and its wholly-owned subsidiary (a company called CSF Investments Ltd of   *g*
Hamilton, Bermuda) were active in investment management and in providing
other financial services to both private and corporate clients. For its part the
Tyndall Group were also interested on a worldwide scale in the provision of a
range of financial services.

It was a term of the shareholders' agreement that if the control of Tyndall Trust
should ever pass out of the hands of Tyndall International then the appellants   *h*
would be entitled to exercise a put option to sell their shares. I should refer shortly
to art 4 of the shareholders' agreement, having first referred to two parts in the
definition section in art 4 which define 'The minority shareholder(s)' as meaning
the appellants and a 'Put option' as being the right of the minority shareholders
to sell the shares at a defined price. It was provided in section B of art 4 of the
shareholders' agreement as follows: *j*

'(a) If, on or before 30th June, 1992: (i) TIH, without the consent of the
minority shareholders, either sells all of TT's shares to any third party or
disposes of all of TT's assets, [and then follow the important words] or sells or
otherwise disposes of a controlling interest in TT's shares [or certain other
events which it is not necessary to refer to], then the holders of the ᴢᴜᴄᴋᴇʀ

a   shares jointly and/or the holders of the GROSSGLAUSER – shares will have the right to exercise their respective put option, in respect of all their shares in TT, against TIH, at any time after such event, but no later than 30th September 1992.'

It was then provided that in that case the minority shareholders would be entitled to receive from Tyndall International the greater of either what was described as *b*   'the formula price per share', which was defined, or what was also defined as 'the floor price per share'.

Section C of art 4 of the shareholders' agreement contained provisions for the issue in satisfaction of either the floor price or the formula price due to the appellants as minority shareholders of a number of new fully paid ordinary shares in Tyndall Holdings which were to be calculated in a manner there set out. It was *c*   further provided in this section (in order that the minority shareholders would get marketable securities if they exercised the put option) that Tyndall Holdings undertook to apply for listing on the London Stock Exchange of the Tyndall shares which were to be issued and that in the meantime they would retain sufficient outstanding capital to make the necessary allotments to fulfil their *d*   obligations if required.

It was further provided in art 4 that the put option could be exercised by any or all of the minority shareholders by sending a letter to Tyndall International by telefax or by registered mail, and that on receipt of such a notice Tyndall International, when they got the notification letter and the certificates representing the Tyndall Trust shares from the minority shareholders, would then proceed to *e*   determine the exact and final amount of Tyndall shares to be issued and that within three months they would issue and deliver the relevant Tyndall shares to the minority shareholders.

Finally, I think the only other part of the agreement to which it is necessary to refer is art 14, which provided that the agreement should be governed by Swiss law and that any disputes (save one which it is not necessary to trouble with) *f*   which arose in connection with the agreement should be submitted—

> 'to the non-exclusive competence of the Courts of the Canton of Geneva, Switzerland, subject to an appeal to the Federal Tribunal, in Lausanne . . .'

On 26 or 27 September 1991 Tyndall Holdings was taken over by another company, Jupiter Tarbutt Merlin Holdings plc (Jupiter). It is apparent that that *g*   take-over caused some concern to the appellants. It came to their attention that the services of a number of senior executives had been dispensed with and that certain subsidiaries of the Tyndall Group had been disposed of. It was a development that had not been anticipated by the appellants, and one of the effects of the takeover was that the shares in Tyndall Holdings were no longer *h*   going to be listed on the London Stock Exchange. So the appellants took the opinion of a Swiss lawyer, and in an opinion dated 18 February 1992 Professor Dr Frank Vischer expressed the opinion that as a result of the take-over of Tyndall Holdings by Jupiter the appellants had become entitled to exercise the put option contained in the shareholders' agreement. He expressed his final conclusion in these words by way of summary:

j
> 'By the take-over of Tyndall Holdings PLC by Jupiter Tarbutt Merlin Holdings PLC on August 31, 1991, Tyndall Holdings PLC has directly disposed of its controlling interest in Tyndall International Holdings Limited and therefore has indirectly disposed of its controlling interest in Tyndall Trust SA. Consequently, the right to exercise the put option by the minority shareholders according to art. 4 lit. B lit. a of the shareholders agreement of June 2, 1989 has to be admitted. The formula price per share as stated in the

shareholders' agreement today cannot be applied stricto sensu in the case of
the said take-over. It seems justified to calculate the formula price on the *a*
basis of the date of the take-over.'

Dr Vischer at that time was treating the date of the take-over as being 31 August,
but it was in fact 26 or 27 September 1991. For present purposes nothing turns
on that point.

On 23 March 1992, following the obtaining of that opinion in February, the *b*
appellants exercised the put option and sent their share certificates to Tyndall
International, and I understand that it is accepted that if there was a valid exercise
of the option the three months' period for the issue of the Tyndall shares will
expire on 24 June next (24 June 1992).

On 25 March 1992 proceedings were commenced by the appellants in the court
of first instance in Geneva. In these proceedings the appellants claimed first a *c*
declaration that they had validly exercised their right to 'put' the shares as foreseen
in art 4 of the shareholders' agreement, and secondly an order that Tyndall
Holdings and Tyndall International should jointly and severally pay to them the
amount of 6m Swiss francs with interest at 8% from 24 June 1992. Certain other
relief was claimed to which it is unnecessary to refer.

It seems that the sum claimed was calculated on the basis that it was no longer *d*
possible for the appellants to obtain marketable securities by way of shares by the
issue to them of shares in Tyndall Holdings and that the sum claimed represented
the aggregate value of the shares in Tyndall Trust.

On 30 March the writ of summons was issued in the present proceedings and
it was on that day that the appellants obtained an order ex parte from Potter J. In *e*
the writ the appellants claim various declarations, including a declaration that the
option was validly exercised by the notice of 23 March. It has been conceded,
however, that in the present proceedings the declarations in these terms are not
being sought in England from the English court but are being sought from the
Swiss court. The effective relief sought in the English proceedings is a claim for
specific performance of the agreement for the sale of the shares constituted by the *f*
giving of the notice.

The question which arises for consideration in this case is whether the court
has any jurisdiction to grant a Mareva injunction to the appellants in the present
circumstances. When the matter came on inter partes before Morland J on
6 April, it being inter partes in the sense that both sides were heard, the judge was
referred to a number of authorities. He came to the conclusion that in the *g*
circumstances the nature of the action for specific performance was such that the
order that might be obtained until or before 24 June 1992 would be an order of a
merely declaratory nature. In those circumstances he concluded on the authorities
that the court had no jurisdiction to grant a Mareva injunction. It is in relation to
that decision that the present appeal arises. It is directed solely to the question of *h*
jurisdiction.

The power of the High Court to grant an injunction is now contained in s 37
of the Supreme Court Act 1981, which is derived from s 45 of the Supreme Court
of Judicature (Consolidation) Act 1925 and earlier from the Supreme Court of
Judicature Act 1873. Section 37(1) provides:

> 'The High Court may by order (whether interlocutory or final) grant an *j*
> injunction or appoint a receiver in all cases in which it appears to the court to
> be just and convenient to do so.'

Those words, on the face of it, are very wide indeed. But, as Lord Brandon
explained in *South Carolina Insurance Co v Assurantie Maatschappij 'de Zeven
Provincien' NV* [1986] 3 All ER 487 at 495, [1987] AC 24 at 40:

a 　'... although the terms of s 37(1) of the 1981 Act and its predecessors are very wide, the power conferred by them has been circumscribed by judicial authority dating back many years.'

In particular the power to grant an interlocutory injunction can, in the words of Lord Diplock in *Siskina (cargo owners) v Distos Cia Naviera SA, The Siskina* [1977] 3 All ER 803 at 824, [1979] AC 210 at 256, only be exercised 'in protection or
b assertion of some legal or equitable right which it has jurisdiction to enforce by final judgment'. A little earlier in his speech Lord Diplock said ([1977] 3 All ER 803 at 824, [1979] AC 210 at 256):

　　'A right to obtain an interlocutory injunction is not a cause of action. It cannot stand on its own. It is dependent upon there being a pre-existing
c 　cause of action against the defendant arising out of an invasion, actual or threatened by him, of a legal or equitable right of the plaintiff for the enforcement of which the defendant is amenable to the jurisdiction of the court. The right to obtain an interlocutory injunction is merely ancillary and incidental to the pre-existing cause of action. It is granted to preserve the status quo pending the ascertainment by the court of the rights of the parties
d 　and the grant to the plaintiff of the relief to which his cause of action entitles him, which may or may not include a final injunction.'

In a passage in the same speech when drawing attention to the wording of s 45(1) of the Supreme Court of Judicature (Consolidation) Act 1925, which was the
e forerunner to s 37 of the Supreme Court Act 1981, Lord Diplock said ([1977] 3 All ER 803 at 823, [1979] AC 210 at 254):

　　'That subsection, speaking as it does of interlocutory orders, presupposes the existence of an action, actual or potential, claiming substantive relief which the High Court has jurisdiction to grant and to which the interlocutory
f 　orders referred to are but ancillary. This factor has been present in all previous cases in which Mareva injunctions have been granted.'

On the basis of that speech, the principle laid down in *The Siskina* has been applied in a very large number of more recent cases. It is sufficient to refer for present purposes to a passage in the judgment of Bingham J in *Siporex Trade SA v*
g *Comdel Commodities Ltd* [1986] 2 Lloyd's Rep 428 at 436 where he summarised the law in these words:

　　'I take it to be clear law, both on principle and authority, that a *Mareva* injunction will not be granted to an applicant who has no cause of action
h 　against the defendant at the time of application ...'

That sentence was cited with approval by Beldam LJ in *Veracruz Transportation Inc v VC Shipping Co Inc, The Veracruz I* [1992] 1 Lloyd's Rep 353 at 358.
　　Mr Mann QC, however, who appears on behalf of the appellants, has submitted that on a proper analysis the appellants have a cause of action both in Swiss law
j and in English law. Therefore they are able to satisfy the condition which he recognises is a condition which has to be satisfied if a Mareva injunction is to be granted.
　　For the position in Swiss law he relies on passages in the affidavits of Mr Halperin, who is acting for the appellants in the proceedings in Geneva. Mr Halperin is the current President of the Geneva Bar Association. In para 8 of an affidavit sworn by him on 1 April 1992 he said:

'In my opinion the Minority Shareholders have a right to demand
immediately payment of the appropriate sum in three months' time. They *a*
may therefore ask the Court as soon as the right to payment in due course
has arisen to confirm and enforce that right and declare that the right has
been validly exercised.'

He returned to the same theme in a later affidavit sworn on 9 April, when he said
in para 4 in relation to the exercise of the put option on 23 March: *b*

'This created an immediate right in the minority shareholders to receive
the greater of the floor price or the formula price. The fact that Tyndall
Holdings Plc undertook to deliver the shares of Tyndall Holdings Plc within
three months, did not postpone the creation of a right to receive compensation
until the end of a three month period. There is nothing that I see in the   *c*
Shareholders' Agreement which provides for a suspensive condition for three
months. The defendants in the UK proceeding are mistaken in confusing the
creation of a right and the date after which Tyndall Holdings Plc would
clearly be in default of its obligation to satisfy that right.'

d

For the position in English law Mr Mann relies on the rule of equity which
entitles, for example, a purchaser of property to sue for specific performance
before the time for performance has occurred. He referred us in particular to the
decision of the Privy Council in *Hasham v Zenab* [1960] AC 316 at 329, where in
dealing with the submissions made on behalf of the defendant, Lord Tucker, who
delivered the judgment of the Privy Council, said: *e*

'Their Lordships are of opinion that the fallacy of the submissions consists
in equating the right to sue for specific performance with a cause of action at
law. In equity all that is required is to show circumstances which will justify
the intervention by a court of equity. The purchaser has an equitable interest
in the land and could get an injunction to prevent the vendor disposing of *f*
the property. The order for specific performance often falls into two parts.
The first can be of a declaratory nature and the second contain consequential
directions.'

Then Lord Tucker referred to the form set out in *Seton's Forms of Judgments and* *g*
Orders (7th edn, 1912) vol 3, p 2136 and said (at 330):

'[That form] is clearly suitable to a case where the time for performance
may not have arrived even at the date of the order, but in such a case, in the
event of subsequent non-performance the court would not require the issue
of a fresh writ before making the consequential directions for performance.' *h*

So, says Mr Mann, if you look at the matter from the point of view of whether
a right of action has arisen the answer is plainly, 'Yes, a right of action has arisen
here', and the earlier cases, which were decided on the limits of a Mareva
injunction, are all distinguishable. In particular, in relation to the decision in
Ninemia Maritime Corp v Trave Schiffahrtsgesellschaft mbH & Co KG, The Niedersachsen *j*
[1984] 1 All ER 398, [1983] 1 WLR 1412, which was a case which involved the
delivery of a ship where the court held that no Mareva injunction was to be
granted because the time for performance had not yet arisen and therefore no
breach had occurred, he said that that case was not really authority to the contrary
because the possibility of obtaining an order for specific performance had not

a been canvassed and therefore what would have been the position if it had been is not clear.

One of the difficulties which arises in these cases is the fact that the phrase or expression 'cause of action' can be used in different contexts and in different senses. In a case which was before a division of the court in which I was sitting a week or so ago we had our attention drawn to a passage *Gubisch Maschinenfabrik*
b *KG v Palumbo* Case 144/86 [1987] ECR 4861 at 4875 (para 15) to the effect that, for the purpose of art 21 of the Convention on Jurisdiction and the Enforcement of Judgments in Civil and Commercial Matters (Brussels, 27 September 1968; EC 46 (1978); Cmnd 7395), proceedings were based on the same cause of action if they were based on the same contractual relationship. That was for the purpose of art 21 of that convention.

c In the present context, however, one has to consider what is meant by the phrase 'cause of action'. As I understand the present law, it is that a Mareva injunction cannot be granted unless there is an existing cause of action which can be immediately enforced. An order for specific performance which is granted before the time of performance has arrived is, as pointed out by Lord Tucker, really in two parts: first of all the declaratory part and secondly the part where
d consequential directions might be given.

To come back to the facts of this case, there has been no failure to pay the sum of 6m Swiss francs. It is quite true that, as Mr Thomas QC has very frankly conceded, the attitude taken by the respondent company is that the circumstances which would give rise to the valid exercise of the put option have not arisen. But it is not suggested that there has been any failure to pay the money at this stage
e when 24 June is still six weeks away and there has been no repudiatory breach. The appellants have the right to be paid, but, in the words of Lord Diplock, there has been no invasion of that right. The word 'invasion' is the word used by Lord Diplock in *The Siskina* [1977] 3 All ER 803 at 824, [1979] AC 210 at 256. In the earlier case to which Lord Diplock referred, *North London Rly Co v Great Northern Rly Co* (1883) 11 QBD 30, Cotton LJ referred to a legal or equitable right 'being
f interfered with'.

It seems to me that, as the law stands at present, for the purpose of a Mareva injunction it is necessary to demonstrate that a legal or equitable right has been interfered with or invaded or that such an invasion or interference is threatened, though it is certainly true, as Mr Mann has demonstrated in the course of his
g argument, that interlocutory relief can be obtained in certain circumstances to protect an equitable interest even before the time for performance under a contract has arisen.

For my part, I see great force in the submissions Mr Mann has put forward, and it is to be noted that in some of the Australian cases courts exercising a jurisdiction similar to the Mareva jurisdiction have regarded the matter as a matter of
h discretion and have held that in certain circumstances exceptions can be made to the general principle that a cause of action must exist which is independent of the right to a Mareva injunction. But, in my judgment, on the facts of the present case, it is not open to this court to grant an injunction. It has no jurisdiction to do so.

There is, in fact, a further reason why I have come to that conclusion. Under
j the terms of the shareholders' agreement the right of the appellants was to obtain the issue of a determinable number of shares. They are bringing proceedings in Switzerland for an order that in lieu of such shares a payment of a sum of money amounting approximately to 6m Swiss francs should be made. But that is a matter which has not yet been determined by the Swiss court, and unless and until the Swiss court makes a declaration it seems to me that there is on any view

no present right in the appellants to claim a sum of money to which a Mareva
injunction would be attached.	*a*

For these reasons I, for my part, would dismiss this appeal.

STAUGHTON LJ. I agree that this appeal should be dismissed. I also agree
that, as Neill LJ has said, the apparently unlimited discretion in s 37(1) of the
Supreme Court Act 1981 to grant an injunction, whether interlocutory or final,
is subject to the exceptions which the law imposes. Those are, as it seems to me,	*b*
conveniently and accurately set out in the speech of Lord Diplock in *Siskina (cargo
owners) v Distros Cia Naviera SA, The Siskina* [1977] 3 All ER 803 at 824, [1979] AC
210 at 256:

'A right to obtain an interlocutory injunction is not a cause of action. It
cannot stand on its own. It is dependent upon there being a pre-existing	*c*
cause of action against the defendant arising out of an invasion, actual or
threatened by him, of a legal or equitable right of the plaintiff.'

The question for us is not, I think, whether the appellants have a cause of
action. The question is whether they have a cause of action arising out of the
invasion, actual or threatened, of a legal or equitable right of theirs. So we do not	*d*
need to consider whether a right to sue for specific performance before the
completion date arrives is or is not by itself a cause of action. I happily leave that
for others to determine. What we have to decide is whether there is here a cause
of action arising out of the invasion, actual or threatened, of a legal or equitable
right.

Actual invasion of such a right is plain enough. In a contract case the plaintiff	*e*
must not only show that there is a relevant term of the contract, he must also
show that the defendant has broken it. The plaintiff can then obtain an
interlocutory injunction in support of his claim in the action. In an appropriate
case, that can be a prior restraint injunction, preventing the defendant from
removing or dissipating his assets.

But what of threatened invasion? That must cover a threat to break a contractual	*f*
obligation which is presently performable. But does it cover a threatened breach
of some term of a contract which is not presently performable? It appears from
Veracruz Transportation Inc v VC Shipping Co Inc, The Veracruz 1 [1992] 1 Lloyd's
Rep 353, *Steamship Mutual Underwriting Association (Bermuda) Ltd v Thakur Shipping
Co Ltd* [1986] 2 Lloyd's Rep 439, *Ninemia Maritime Corp v Trave Schiffahrtsgesellschaft	*g*
mbH & Co KG, The Niedersachsen* [1984] 1 All ER 398, [1983] 1 WLR 1412 and
Siporex Trade SA v Comdel Commodities Ltd [1986] 2 Lloyd's Rep 428 that it does
not cover such a threat. One example that has occurred is what I call the poisoned
pill case, where the plaintiff is bound by his contract to pay money to the
defendant against delivery of a chattel, and accompanies his cheque with a Mareva
injunction granted a day or two earlier, anticipating that the chattel, when	*h*
delivered, will be defective in breach of contract. That is not permitted.

If there was no actual breach at the date when the injunction was granted, and
no threatened breach of an obligation which was then presently performable,
there should be no injunction. In this case, there has been no actual breach and
no threat to break a term which is presently performable. If there has been any
threat at all, which is challenged, it is a threat to break a term which is not yet	*j*
presently performable.

In my judgment Morland J was right to discharge the injunction, and I would
dismiss this appeal.

DILLON LJ. I see this case on a narrower basis than that on which it was decided
a by the judge in the court below. It is clear beyond dispute that a Mareva
injunction can only be granted by the English court in support of a cause of action
which the English court has jurisdiction to entertain (see the speech of Lord
Diplock in *Siskina (cargo owners) v Distos Cia Naviera SA, The Siskina* [1977] 3 All
ER 803 at 824, [1979] AC 210 at 256, a passage which has been cited by Neill and
Staughton LJJ in their judgments). Moreover, the particular cause of action which
b the Mareva is to support must be complete at the time when the application for
the Mareva is made (see *Ninemia Maritime Corp v Trave Schiffahrtsgesellschaft mbH
& Co KG, The Niedersachsen* [1984] 1 All ER 398 at 401 per Mustill J, [1984] 1 All
ER 398 at 414, [1983] 1 WLR 1412 at 1416 per Kerr LJ in relation to the first
application for Mareva relief made by the buyers in that case).

c   In the present case what the appellants are claiming is said to be specific
performance of a contract arising out of the exercise of their put options under
the shareholders' agreement. But under the shareholders' agreement, which is
governed by Swiss law, the put options were to be exercisable on the happening
of certain specified events, none of which have in precise terms happened.
Moreover, the consideration for the transfer of the appellants' shares in the Swiss
d company, Tyndall Trust SA, under the put options was to be satisfied by the issue
to the appellants of shares in Tyndall Holdings plc, the present defendants, which
would be quoted on the London Stock Exchange. But that is no longer possible,
since the quotation has been withdrawn on the takeover of Tyndall Holdings by
the purchaser company.

     The appellants accordingly seek in the Swiss courts firstly to establish that they
e have validly exercised the put options, although not in the precise circumstances
envisaged in the shareholders' agreement, and secondly, and for present purposes
more relevantly, that they are entitled, as a result of the withdrawal of the
quotation, not to shares in Tyndall Holdings but to a money payment as being in
effect the purchase price or value of the shares as assessed by the Swiss court under
f its own procedure. It is a form of relief which may, I know not, be valid and
available in Switzerland in the circumstances of this case, but it goes, it seems to
me, very much further than the English courts have gone, for instance, in cases
where the parties have agreed on a sale of property at a price to be fixed by
valuation and machinery agreed on between the parties for making the valuation
has broken down.

g   The Mareva relief is sought in aid of the appellants' claim for that money
payment. But the jurisdiction of the court to award the money payment depends
on Swiss law and the Swiss courts and the English court has no jurisdiction to
award it, nor is it asked to. Therefore the claim for Mareva relief, in aid of the
claim for the money payment, must be premature until the Swiss court has made
its determination. Therefore, as in *The Niedersachsen*, the application for Mareva
h relief is premature.

     To talk generally of claims for specific performance does not assist. The key
step is not part of the working out of a previous specific performance order by the
English court. It is a step for the Swiss court. Therefore I too would dismiss this
appeal for want of jurisdiction.

j *Appeal dismissed. Leave to appeal to the House of Lords refused.*

Carolyn Toulmin   Barrister.

Securities and Investments Board v Pantell SA and others (No 2)

COURT OF APPEAL, CIVIL DIVISION

NEILL, SCOTT AND STEYN LJJ

1, 2 APRIL, 12 JUNE 1992

Investment business – Restitution order – Liability to make restitution – Person contravening Act – Carrying on investment business in contravention of Act – Person 'knowingly concerned' in contravention of Act – Solicitors acting for client allegedly carrying on unauthorised investment business – Swiss companies carrying on investment business in United Kingdom without authority – English solicitors alleged to be knowingly concerned in companies' breaches of Act – Whether person knowingly concerned in contravention of Act can be ordered to repay to investors moneys lost – Whether solicitors could be ordered to repay to investors sums paid to companies – Financial Services Act 1986, ss 6(2), 61(1).

The Securities and Investments Board (the SIB) brought an action against two overseas companies alleging that they had carried on investment business in the United Kingdom selling unmarketable and worthless shares in a Utah corporation when they were not authorised to do so and had made misleading statements and unsolicited calls and issued investment advertisements in the United Kingdom contrary to the provisions of the Financial Services Act 1986. The claim was later amended to join the English solicitors acting for the companies as defendants, alleging that they had knowledge of the nature of the companies' business and the fact that the companies were operating in contravention of the 1986 Act and that accordingly the solicitors were 'knowingly concerned' in the companies' breaches of that Act in that they operated the companies' bank account in the United Kingdom, assisted in the distribution of advertisements and paid cheques from United Kingdom investors into the companies' bank account. The SIB claimed that the solicitors could therefore be held to account under ss 6(2)[a] and 61(1)[b] of the 1986 Act, which empowered the court to make an order against a person carrying on unauthorised investment business (the contravener) or a person knowingly concerned in a contravention of that Act requiring him to remedy that contravention by taking steps to restore the parties to a share transaction to their former positions. The SIB further alleged that investors had suffered loss and damage as a result of the companies' breaches of the 1986 Act in which the solicitors were knowingly concerned. The solicitors denied the allegations and applied to strike out the claims made against them on the grounds that on the true construction of ss 6(2) and 61(1) of the 1986 Act the SIB was not entitled to the relief claimed because the SIB's claim against them was not for restitution, since none of the payments made by the investors had been made to the solicitors, but for compensation for loss suffered by investors in the companies, which only a contravener could be ordered to pay and which was not relief available under ss 6(2) and 61(1). The judge dismissed the summons to strike out. The solicitors appealed.

Held – The court could make an order under s 6(2) of the 1986 Act imposing on a person carrying on investment business in the United Kingdom without

a   Section 6(2) is set out at p 138 *a*, post

b   Section 61(1), so far as material, is set out at p 139 *e f*, post

authorisation (the contravener) and, in default of payment by the contravener, on
a a person or persons, such as the contravener's solicitors, who were 'knowingly
concerned' in the contravener's breaches of the 1986 Act, liability to repay to an
investor the purchase price of the shares comprised in a particular investment
transaction, provided the order stipulated that payment was to be made against
the delivery up by the investor of the share certificates, since the purpose of the
order had to be the restoration of all parties to the transaction to their former
b positions and the steps directed by the order had to be reasonably capable of doing
so. It was irrelevant that a person against whom an order was sought had received
nothing under the transaction resulting from or constituting the contravention.
Similarly, an order could be made under s 61(1) against a person 'knowingly
concerned' in the contravener's breaches of the 1986 Act directing him to take
steps which were reasonably capable of remedying the contravention of the Act
c alleged, but the purpose of the order had to be the remedying of the contravention
and not some other purpose. In the circumstances there was no ground for
striking out the SIB's claim. The appeal would therefore be dismissed (see p 143 c
to p 144 a d f, p 145 c to e, p 146 b, p 148 j to p 149 f and p 150 d to g, post).
    Decision of Browne-Wilkinson V-C [1991] 4 All ER 883 affirmed.

d
Cases cited or referred to in skeleton arguments
Alati v Kruger (1955) 94 CLR 216, Aust HC.
Gorton v Champneys, Coventry v Champneys (1823) 1 Bing 287, 130 ER 116.
Northern Bank Finance Corp Ltd v Charlton [1979] IR 149, Ir HC and Ir SC.
Salaman v Warner (1891) 65 LT 132, CA.

e
Notes
For restrictions on carrying on investment business, see 32 *Halsbury's Laws* (4th
edn) para 326.
    For the Financial Services Act 1986, ss 6, 61, see 30 *Halsbury's Statutes* (4th edn)
f (1991 reissue) 173, 233.

Appeal
The third, fourth and fifth defendants (the solicitors) appealed with leave of the
judge from the decision of Browne-Wilkinson V-C ([1991] 4 All ER 883, [1991] 3
WLR 857) on 29 July 1991 whereby he dismissed their application by summons
dated 15 March 1991 to strike out the claims made against them in an action
g brought by the plaintiff, the Securities and Investments Board (the SIB), against
two Swiss companies, Pantell SA and Swiss Atlantic Holdings Ltd, and the
solicitors. The facts are set out in the judgment of Scott LJ.

Jonathan Sumption QC and *Leslie Kosmin* (instructed by *Barlow Lyde & Gilbert*) for
h   the solicitors.
David Oliver QC and *Thomas Lowe* (instructed by *Booth & Blackwell*) for the SIB.
The first and second defendants did not appear.

Cur adv vult

j 12 June 1992. The following judgments were delivered.

SCOTT LJ (giving the first judgment at the invitation of Neill LJ). This is an
appeal from the refusal of Browne-Wilkinson V-C to strike out the relief claimed
in the action by the plaintiff, the Securities and Investments Board (the SIB),
against the third, fourth and fifth defendants. The appeal, brought with the leave

of Browne-Wilkinson V-C, raises a question as to the nature and extent of the
restitutionary relief that may be obtained by the SIB under ss 6(2) and 61(1) of the a
Financial Services Act 1986 against a firm of solicitors who acted for a person
carrying on an unauthorised investment business.

For the purposes of the striking-out application the facts alleged by the SIB in
its statement of claim must be assumed to be correct. For present purposes, the
assumed facts are relatively straightforward.

From about April 1988 to March 1989 the first defendant, Pantell SA, a b
company incorporated under the laws of Switzerland, carried on an unauthorised
investment business in the United Kingdom. It was neither an authorised person
under Ch III of the 1986 Act nor an exempted person under Ch IV. In the course
of carrying on this investment business Pantell SA distributed a series of
advertisements in order to persuade persons in the United Kingdom to purchase c
shares in European American Corp Inc (Euramco), a company incorporated in
Utah, USA. These advertisements contained a number of false and misleading
statements. In addition, salesmen acting for Pantell SA made unsolicited telephone
calls to persons in the United Kingdom in order to persuade them to purchase
Euramco shares. As a result of these misleading advertisements and unsolicited
telephone calls a number of individuals in the United Kingdom over the period d
July 1988 to March 1989 purchased Euramco shares. The allegations in the
statement of claim do not make it clear who was the vendor of the Euramco
shares that were purchased by the United Kingdom investors. The vendor may
have been Pantell SA. The vendor may have been Swiss Atlantic Holdings Ltd, a
United Kingdom company, on whose behalf Pantell SA was, under an agreement
dated 1 March 1988, authorised to sell Euramco shares to the investing public on e
a commission basis. Or the vendor may have been the second defendant, also
called Swiss Atlantic Holdings Ltd, a company incorporated in the British Virgin
Islands on 23 September 1988 and to which company all the assets of the United
Kingdom Swiss Atlantic Holdings Ltd had, following an agreement of 26 October
1988, been transferred. Or it may have been that the shares were not purchased
but were subscribed for and were issued to the investors by Euramco. The f
statement of claim does not make clear the route or routes by which the United
Kingdom investors acquired their shares. This uncertainty is of relevance to some
of the issues that arise on this appeal.

The fifth defendants are a firm of solicitors. The third defendant is, or was the
partner in charge of the fifth defendants' London office. The fourth defendant is, g
or was, an assistant solicitor at the fifth defendants' London office. It is alleged in
the statement of claim that at all material times since in or about 1988 the fifth
defendants were retained and acted for, inter alia, Pantell SA and both of the Swiss
Atlantic Holdings Ltd companies.

The carrying on by Pantell SA of an unauthorised investment business in the
United Kingdom was a contravention of s 3 of the 1986 Act. The publishing of h
misleading advertisements was a contravention of s 47 of that Act. Moreover the
advertisements had not been approved by an authorised person. This was a
contravention of s 57 of the 1986 Act. The purchase or sale or issue to subscribers
of shares in consequence of unsolicited telephone calls was a contravention of s 56
of that Act.

The 1986 Act not only imposes criminal sanctions for contraventions of its j
various provisions but also provides remedies for investors who enter into share
transactions as a result of the contraventions. The remedies provided by the 1986
Act fall into three categories. There are provisions enabling investors to recover
loss they have suffered as a result of entering into the share transactions. There
are provisions enabling the contravener to be stripped of the profit made out of

the transactions and for the profit to be distributed among the investors. And
a there are provisions of a restitutionary character designed to restore the respective
parties to the share transactions to their former positions.

The present case is concerned with the restitutionary provisions contained in
the 1986 Act. But it is necessary to refer also to the provisions dealing with the
recoupment of losses and the disgorging of profits in order to enable the
restitutionary provisions to be construed in the context of that Act as a whole.

b Section 5 of the 1986 Act provides remedies for individual investors who have
entered into investment agreements with persons carrying on unauthorised
investment businesses.

Subsection (1) provides that any such agreement—

c   'shall be unenforceable against the other party [i e the investor]; and that
party shall be entitled to recover any money or other property paid or
transferred by him under the agreement, together with compensation for
any loss sustained by him as a result of having parted with it.'

The subsection combines, therefore, a restitutionary remedy and a compensatory
remedy.

d Subsection (3) gives the court a discretion to refuse to allow restitution if certain
specified conditions are satisfied. Subsections (4) and (5) provide as follows:

     '(4) Where a person elects not to perform an agreement which by virtue of
this section is unenforceable against him or by virtue of this section recovers
money paid or other property transferred by him under an agreement he
shall repay any money and return any other property received by him under
e   the agreement.

     (5) Where any property transferred under an agreement to which this
section applies has passed to a third party the references to that property in
subsections (1), (3) and (4) above shall be construed as references to its value
at the time of its transfer under the agreement.'

f The restitutionary and compensatory provisions of s 5 do not in terms identify
the person or persons against whom the remedies are available. But it is difficult
to see how the s 5 restitutionary remedy could be available against anyone other
than the other party to the transaction in question or the party to whom, under
the transaction in question, the investor's money or property had been paid or
g transferred. Whether the compensatory remedy available 'together with' the
restitutionary remedy, could be obtained against an accomplice who was neither
a party to the transaction nor a person to whom money or property of the investor
had been transferred is equally doubtful. These difficulties do not, however, have
to be resolved on this appeal.

The second comment to be made on s 5 is that sub-s (5), in allowing financial
h restitution to be substituted in certain circumstances for restitution in specie,
indicates that, in general, restitution in specie is contemplated. It would not, in
my opinion, be open to an investor to retain the purchased shares and, under s 5,
to claim back the purchase money less the financial value of the retained shares.

Section 6 of the 1986 Act provides remedies which may be invoked by the
Secretary of State or, by delegation from the Secretary of State, by the SIB. The
j section is dealing with contraventions or apprehended contraventions of s 3, i e
the carrying on of an unauthorised investment business.

Subsection (1) enables the Secretary of State, or the SIB, to obtain an injunction
to restrain apprehended contraventions of s 3.

Subsection (2) contains the critical provision so far as the present case is
concerned. It provides a restitutionary remedy in the following terms:

'If, on the application of the Secretary of State, the court is satisfied that a
person has entered into any transaction in contravention of section 3 above
the court may order that person and any other person who appears to the
court to have been knowingly concerned in the contravention to take such
steps as the court may direct for restoring the parties to the position in which
they were before the transaction was entered into.'

A number of comments may be made on this provision. First, the restitutionary
remedy is expressed to be available not only against 'that person', i e the
contravener of s 3 or perhaps an associate of the contravener, but also against 'any
other person . . . knowingly concerned in the contravention'. The criteria to be
applied in order to determine whether a person was 'knowingly concerned' are
not specified.

Second, the discretion of the court, '. . . such steps as the court may direct for
restoring the parties . . .' etc, is conferred in very wide terms. Contrast the more
restricted remedy given to investors by s 5.

Third, although sub-s (2) gives a very wide discretion to the court on the 'steps'
to be taken, the purpose of any order must be 'for restoring the parties to the
position in which they were before the transaction was entered into'. It seems
clear to me that the expression 'the parties' means all the parties to the 'transaction
in contravention of section 3' and does not simply mean 'the investors'. The
purpose of any order under sub-s (2) must, in my opinion, be to restore all of the
parties to their former positions. It would not be a proper exercise of the sub-s (2)
power to make an order simply directed to the repayment to the investors of their
money.

Fourth, sub-s (2) is contemplating orders directed to reversing specific
transactions: note the reference to 'the position in which they were before *the
transaction* was entered into'.

Subsections (3), (4) and (5) of s 6 enable the Secretary of State, or the SIB, to
obtain orders against 'a person . . . carrying on investment business in
contravention of section 3' requiring that person to disgorge profits thereby made
(sub-ss (3)(a) and (4)(a)) or to compensate investors for losses they have suffered
(sub-ss (3)(b) and (4)(b)).

Subsection (6) deals with the distribution among the investors of sums recouped
from contraveners under sub-ss (4) and (5). Subsection (7) gives the court power
to require the contravener to furnish accounts or other information for the
purposes of applications made under sub-s (3).

The significance of the statutory provisions in sub-ss (3) to (7) is in the contrast
to be drawn with the provisions of sub-s (2). The disgorgement of profits and
compensatory remedies provided by sub-ss (3) to (7) are available only against the
contravener. They cannot be invoked against persons 'knowingly concerned in
the contravention'. Second, the ancillary provisions of sub-ss (6) and (7) are only
available for the purposes of the disgorgement of profits and compensatory
remedies. They are rot available for the purposes of the sub-s (2) restitutionary
remedy. This feature emphasises the point already made, namely that the sub-s
(2) remedy is directed to the reversal of specific transactions and, unlike the sub-ss
(3) to (7) remedies, does not contemplate orders made for the benefit of investors
as a class.

In this action the SIB is seeking a remedy against the third, fourth and fifth
defendants under s 6(2). It is alleged that the solicitors were 'knowingly concerned'
in Pantell SA's contravention of s 3.

Section 47 of the 1986 Act prohibits the making of misleading statements for
the purpose, inter alia, of inducing persons to purchase shares. Section 56 prohibits

persons carrying on an investment business from entering into agreements for,
a inter alia, the sale of or subscription for shares 'in the course of or in consequence
of an unsolicited call' (sub-s (1)). Section 57 imposes restrictions on the contents
of advertisements inviting, inter alia, the purchase of or subscription for shares.
Sections 61 and 62 of the 1986 Act provide remedies for contraventions of these,
and other, statutory prohibitions and regulations.

b Section 62 provides a remedy in damages for investors who suffer 'loss as a
result of the contravention' (sub-s (1)). An action under s 62 is, like an action
under s 5, a private action brought by the investor against the contravener.

Section 62 does not give the investor any right of rescission. The investor's
right of action under s 62 is confined to an action for damages. However, an
investor would, under the general law, have a right of rescission if induced to
c enter into a transaction by a misleading statement. A statutory right of rescission
of a transaction brought about by a breach of s 47 was not, therefore, necessary.
And both s 56 (unsolicited calls) and s 57 (restrictions on the contents of
advertisements) contain express provisions enabling individual investors to bring
actions for restitution and compensation. These restitutionary provisions are in
the same terms as the corresponding provisions of s 5.

d Section 61 provides remedies which can be sought by the Secretary of State or,
by delegation, the SIB.

Subsection (1) enables injunctions to be granted to restrain apprehended
contraventions but enables also remedial steps to be ordered. The contents of
sub-s (1) that relate to the remedial steps are as follows:

e   'If on the application of the Secretary of State the court is satisfied—(a) that
there is a reasonable likelihood that any person will contravene any provision
of—(i) rules or regulations made under this Chapter; (ii) sections 47, 56, 57
or 59 above . . . (iv) . . . (c) that any person has contravened any such provision
or condition and that there are steps that could be taken for remedying the
contravention, the court may grant an injunction restraining the contraven-
f tion . . . or, as the case may be, make an order requiring that person and any
other person . . . knowingly concerned in the contravention to take such steps
as the court may direct to remedy it.'

Subsections (3) to (7) of s 61 enable the Secretary of State, or the SIB, to apply
for disgorgement of profits orders or compensation for loss orders for the benefit
g of investors as a class. The terms of these subsections are exactly the same mutatis
mutandis as the terms of sub-ss (3) to (7) of s 6.

In this action the SIB is seeking a remedy against the third, fourth and fifth
defendants under s 61(1). It is alleged that the solicitors were 'knowingly
concerned' in Pantell SA's contraventions of ss 47, 56 and 57 of the 1986 Act.
h The third, fourth and fifth defendants deny that they were 'knowingly
concerned' in Pantell SA's contraventions of that Act, whether under s 3 or under
ss 47, 56 and 57. But they contend that, even if they were, the SIB is not, on the
true construction of ss 6(2) and 61(1), entitled to the relief claimed against them
in the statement of claim.

It is convenient, I think, at this point to go to the statement of claim and
j examine the relief claimed against the solicitors and the basis on which it is
claimed. The statement of claim has been amended and reamended. I will refer
to it in its reamended form.

Paragraph 23 of the statement of claim alleges the breaches by Pantell SA of
ss 3, 47, 56 and 57. Paragraph 24 alleges that the Euramco shares are 'unmarketable
and accordingly effectively worthless . . .' and that, as a result of Pantell SA's

breaches of the 1986 Act, investors in the United Kingdom have suffered loss. A
schedule attached to the statement of claim gives the names and, in most cases, *a*
the addresses of the investors of whom the SIB is aware and the sums of money
they are believed to have paid for their Euramco shares. As I have already
remarked, no details are given of the other party or parties to the transactions
entered into by these investors. Nor are details given of the number of Euramco
shares that the respective investors purchased or subscribed for. These details may
not, as yet, be known to the SIB.   *b*

There is no allegation that any part of the money paid by the investors for the
Euramco shares was paid to or received by the solicitors.

Paragraph 29 of the statement of claim alleges that the third and fourth
defendants and through them, the fifth defendant were 'knowingly concerned' in
the breaches of ss 3, 47, 56 and 57 in four specified respects, namely: (i) in
authorising the transfer of a sum of $US250,000 out of an account in the name of *c*
the second defendant into which investors' money had been paid; (ii) in making
arrangements during the postal strike in September 1988 for the collection from
investors of their cheques and for the distribution of advertisements inviting
investment in Euramco; (iii) in paying investors' cheques into Pantell SA's bank
account; and (iv) in attempting to set up an account at Barclays Bank's Holborn *d*
branch for another company, also called Pantell SA.

The striking-out application did not involve any close examination of para 29
of the statement of claim. The question whether the involvement of the solicitors
in the manner pleaded in the four sub-paragraphs is sufficient to make them
'knowingly concerned' for the purposes of ss 6(2) or 61(1) of the 1986 Act has not
been addressed. We must assume, for present purposes, that the factual allegations *e*
pleaded in para 29 are true and that the solicitors were, as a result, 'knowingly
concerned' as alleged.

Paragraph 30 of the statement of claim in its original form pleaded that
investors who had purchased Euramco shares had suffered loss as a result of the
breaches of the 1986 Act by Pantell SA in which the solicitors had been knowingly
concerned. The paragraph reads like a prelude to a claim that the solicitors be *f*
made responsible for the loss. But under ss 6 and 62 of the 1986 Act compensatory
claims can be brought only against the contravener. Compensation for loss
cannot, under the 1986 Act, be claimed against persons 'knowingly concerned' in
the breaches of that Act. So it is not surprising to find the original para 30 deleted
by amendment and the substitution of new paras 30 and 31 in its place. The new *g*
paras 30 and 31 are in these terms:

> '30. From about July 1988 to March 1989 inclusive the First Defendant
> entered into transactions with members of the UK investing public who paid
> out money thereunder in return for shares in EURAMCO as appears from the
> entries for that period in the Schedule annexed hereto. The said transactions
> and each of them were so entered into:—(i) in the course of the First *h*
> defendant's contravention of section 3 of the Act for the period (July 1988 to
> March 1989) when the Third to Fifth Defendants were knowingly concerned
> therein and/or (ii) as a result of contraventions of sections 47 and 57 in which
> the Third to Fifth Defendants were knowingly concerned.
>
> 31. Further the Third to Fifth Defendants were also knowingly concerned *j*
> in investment transactions entered into by the First Defendant with members
> of the UK investing public in the course of and/or as a result of the aforesaid
> contraventions of the Act by the First Defendant in which the Third to Fifth
> Defendants were knowingly concerned in the respects set out in paragraph
> 29 herein. Pending discovery and/or the administration of interrogatories

the best particulars the Plaintiff is able to give of such transactions is that the
Third to Fifth Defendants were knowingly concerned in each and every
transaction of which the following payments and each of them represent the
proceeds of such transactions namely . . .'

There then follow particulars of the payments. It is apparent from these particulars
that in relation to some of the payments the SIB does not know the identity of the
investors.

The relief sought against the third, fourth and fifth defendants is set out in
paras 10 to 13 (inclusive) of the prayer for relief. Paragraphs 10 and 12 seek
declarations that these defendants were 'knowingly concerned' in the alleged
contraventions of the 1986 Act.

Paragraph 11 seeks:

'An order under section 6(2) requiring the Third, Fourth and Fifth
Defendants to pay such sum as the Court thinks fit to the Plaintiffs or
alternatively into Court or alternatively to each and every investor who was
a party to a transaction referred to in paragraph 30 or, alternatively, to each
and every investor who was a party to a transaction referred to in paragraph
31 in such manner as the Court may direct for the purpose of restoring
persons who entered into transactions with the First Defendant in the course
of contravention of section 3 by the First Defendant to the position in which
they were before the transactions were entered into.'

Paragraph 13 seeks:

' An order under section 61(1) that the Third, Fourth and Fifth Defendants
and each of them pay such sum as the Court thinks fit to the Plaintiffs or
alternatively into Court or alternatively to each and every investor who was
a party to a transaction referred to in paragraph 30 or alternatively to each
and every investor who was a party to a transaction referred to in paragraph
31 in such manner as the Court may direct or alternatively that they take
such other steps as the Court may direct for the purpose of remedying the
contravention by the First Defendant of sections 47 and 57.'

By summons, issued on 15 March 1991, the third, fourth and fifth defendants
asked, first, for an order that the action be struck out against them on the ground
that it disclosed no reasonable cause of action or, alternatively, that paras 11 and
13 of the prayer be struck out. In the alternative the summons sought an order
that the court had no power under s 6(2) or s 61(1) of the 1986 Act to make the
orders sought in paras 11 and 13 of the prayer.

The summons came before Browne-Wilkinson V-C. He gave judgment on 29
July 1991 dismissing the summons but granting leave to appeal (see [1991] 4 All
ER 883, [1991] 3 WLR 857).

The case for the third, fourth and fifth defendants before this court, as before
Browne-Wilkinson V-C, is based upon the undisputed fact that none of the
payments made by the investors was made to these defendants. It is contended
that a restitutionary order under s 6(2) can only be made against a party to the
transaction in question who has, or had, something to restore. A compensatory,
as opposed to a restitutionary, order cannot be made under sub-s (2), but only
under sub-ss (3), (4) and (5), and only against the contravener. A person 'knowingly
concerned' in a transaction entered into in contravention of s 3 can only be
subjected to a restitutionary order under sub-s (2) if and to the extent that the
person received money or property under the transaction in question. Similar
submissions are made regarding orders under s 61(1).

Browne-Wilkinson V-C was not prepared to accept these submissions. He accepted that neither s 6(2) nor s 61(1) gave power to order the payment of compensation for loss (see [1991] 4 All ER 883 at 889, [1991] 3 WLR 857 at 863), and agreed that both s 6(2) and s 61(1) were aimed at the statutory rescission of unlawful transactions (see [1991] 4 All ER 883 at 890, [1991] 3 WLR 857 at 864). He concluded, however, that it was not a necessary precondition of a restitutionary order under s 6(2) or of a remedial order under s 61(1) that the person against whom the order was made, whether the contravener or the person 'knowingly concerned' in the contravention, should have received the money or property ordered to be restored to the investor. So he declined to strike out paras 11 and 13 of the prayer or to make the alternative orders that were sought.

Mr Sumption QC, counsel for the third, fourth and fifth defendants, has re-newed before us the same arguments as he addressed to Browne-Wilkinson V-C. He has concentrated on the limitations on the compensatory orders that can be sought by the SIB under s 6 and under s 61. These compensatory orders can only be obtained against the contravener who, for s 6 purposes, has been carrying on the unauthorised investment business, or who, for s 61 purposes, has contravened one or other of the statutory provisions referred to in s 61(1)(a). The statutory remedy does not, where compensation for loss is to be sought, impose any liability on those 'knowingly concerned' in the contravention. It follows that, if what is being sought in this action against the third, fourth and fifth defendants is compensation for the loss suffered by the investors arising out of their purchases of or subscription for Euramco shares, the action cannot be sustained. With all of this I agree, as did Browne-Wilkinson V-C.

The next step in Mr Sumption's argument is the difficult one. An order requiring the third, fourth and fifth defendants, who were not parties to any Euramco transaction and who did not receive anything under any Euramco transaction, to repay the investors the money paid for the Euramco shares is, he submits, a compensatory order, not a restitutionary one. It is not restitutionary because these defendants have received nothing from the investors and so have nothing that they can restore. This submission is the kernel of the appellants' case.

The legislative policy that led to persons 'knowingly concerned' being made liable to restitutionary orders but not liable to compensatory orders is very difficult to discern. Nothing in Professor Gower's report *Review of Investor Protection* (Cmnd 9125), the recommendations of which were carried into effect by the 1986 Act, elucidates why the distinction was made. But we must take the legislation as we find it. While I agree that orders made under ss 6(2) and 61(1) must be restricted to their proper restitutionary purpose, it is not, in my opinion, right to emasculate the restitutionary remedy available against persons 'knowingly concerned' on the ground that they are not liable to be subjected to compensatory remedies. After all, in many cases and, perhaps, in the case of Euramco transactions, a restitutionary remedy and a compensatory remedy will cover the same ground. If the only loss of an investor whose shares are worthless is his purchase money, it will be a matter of indifference to him whether his money is restored by a restitutionary order or by a compensatory order. Both would involve payment to him of the same sum of money. The scope of the restitutionary remedy depends upon the statutory language used and it is, to my mind, immaterial that the restitutionary remedy and the compensatory remedy may overlap.

Mr Sumption, in arguing that the restitutionary remedy under ss 6(2) and 61(1) did not permit an order against a non-recipient, submitted that the effect of the statutory provisions was simply to provide machinery whereby the SIB could

enforce the rescission to which investors, either under the 1986 Act or under the
a general law, were entitled. Browne-Wilkinson V-C described this submission as
'plainly ill-founded' and said that it was 'no answer to SIB's claim against the
solicitors that an individual investor would have no right of action against the
solicitors' (see [1991] 4 All ER 883 at 890, [1991] 3 WLR 857 at 864). I respectfully
agree. Individual investors, unlike the SIB, are given no statutory right of action
against third parties 'knowingly concerned'. The ss 6(2) and 61(1) remedies are
b more than mere machinery.

In considering the various questions of construction that arise in this case it is
convenient, in my opinion, to consider ss 6(2) and 61(1) separately. The purpose
of each is different and the scope of each, in relation to the pleaded facts of the
present case, is also different.

c
Section 6(2)

The precondition of an order under s 6(2) is that 'a person has entered into [a]
transaction in contravention of section 3'. The purpose of an order under s 6(2)
must be to restore the parties to the transaction to the position in which they were
before the transaction was entered into. So an order ought not, in my opinion, to
d require a contravener to repay to an investor the purchase price of shares sold to
the investor unless there is also provision for the return of the shares by the
investor. Rescission under s 6(2), as under the general law, must go both ways.
Otherwise only one of the parties is being restored to his former position.

In my judgment, provided the specified precondition is met, the only
limitations on the type of order that can be made under s 6(2) that are justified by
e the statutory language are that the order must be intended to restore all the parties
to the transaction to their respective former positions and that the steps directed
by the order to be taken must be reasonably capable of doing so. An order
requiring the contravener to repay the purchase price of the shares would not be
capable of restoring the parties to their respective former positions unless the
obligation to repay were made conditional on the tender of the share certificates.
f So an order confined to directing the repayment of the price would not, in my
judgment, be a proper order for the SIB to seek or for the court to make under
s 6(2).

Subject, however, to the limitations to which I have referred I do not see why
any restriction should be placed on the type of order that could be made under
g s 6(2). The width of the statutory language, 'such steps as the court may direct' is
striking and there is, in my opinion, no good reason why it should be restricted.
Nor, in my opinion, does the statutory language warrant any distinction between
the type of order that can be made against the contravener and the type of order
that can be made against a person 'knowingly concerned' in the contravention.
The circumstances of a particular case may, as a matter of discretion, justify a
h more stringent order against a contravener than would be justified against a
person 'knowingly concerned', but that is not the point.

In particular, the fact that a person 'knowingly concerned' has not himself
received anything under the transaction in question does not, in my judgment,
restrict the power of the court to make a s 6(2) order against that person. It may
be that the contravener himself has not received anything under the transaction
j in question. It is not hard to construct a case in which a contravener induces an
investor to enter into a share purchase transaction with a third party associate
under which the price for the shares is paid to the third party. The court has
power under s 6(2) to order the contravener to 'take such steps as the court may
direct' to restore the parties to the transaction to their former position.
Mr Sumption's argument would, if right, be as applicable to the contravener as to

a person 'knowingly concerned'. The contravener could not be made liable under
s 6(2) except to the extent of the money or property he had himself received from *a*
the investor. I am unable to accept this argument, whether it is applied to the
contravener himself or to persons 'knowingly concerned'.

The points I have endeavoured to make regarding the scope of orders that can
be made under s 6(2) have implications for the present case. Thus, the remedy
the SIB can seek under s 6(2), whether against the contravener or anyone else,
ought, in my opinion, to be directed to specific transactions. A class recovery, *b*
such as that possible under sub-ss (3) to (7) is not available under sub-s (2). The
reason for this lies in the limitations to which I have already referred. An order
for payment of money or for the transfer of assets cannot be an order intended to
restore parties to transactions to their former positions unless it is known in
relation to each transaction in question (a) who the parties were, (b) what the *c*
nature of the transaction was and (c) what assets or money each party to the
transaction had paid or transferred to the others. This seems to me to be the
minimum information necessary if the order is to be capable of restoring the
parties to their former positions.

A second point is that each investor must, in my opinion, be willing that there
should be a rescission of the investment transaction in question and be willing to *d*
return any shares or money he has received under the transaction. The present
case is an example of why this requirement is necessary. It is not pleaded that
Euramco has gone into liquidation. The shares in Euramco are not, apparently,
marketable. But it is at least possible that one or more of the investors might
want to keep the shares for whatever remote speculative value the shares might
have. It would be wrong, in my judgment, to order under sub-s (2) the repayment *e*
of the price of the shares unless it were known that the investor was willing to
give up the shares. If an investor wants to keep the shares acquired under the
transaction in question but to recover the difference in value between the shares
and the price paid, the remedy to achieve this is not, in my judgment, a
restitutionary one but is compensatory and cannot be obtained under sub-s (2). *f*

Section 61(1)

Similar points arise in relation to s 61(1) as those which I have made regarding
s 6(2). But the implications for the present case are not entirely the same.

There are two relevant preconditions before an order 'to take . . . steps' etc can
be made under s 61(1). One is that a person has contravened one or other of the *g*
statutory provisions referred to in sub-s (1)(a). In the present case it is alleged that
Pantell SA has contravened ss 47, 56 and 57. The second precondition is that
'there are steps that could be taken for remedying the contravention'. The court
is empowered, if these two preconditions are satisfied, to make an order for 'such
steps as the court may direct to remedy [the contravention]' to be taken. The steps
directed by the order to be taken must, therefore, be intended to remedy and be *h*
reasonably capable of remedying the contravention. Otherwise the order would
not be a proper one to be made.

The alleged contraventions of s 47 consist of the making of misleading
statements for the purpose of inducing persons to enter into investment
transactions. Entering into investment transactions that have been induced by
misleading statements is not a contravention of s 47 but the result of a *j*
contravention. Can the reversal of the result of the contravention be regarded as
a step taken to remedy the contravention? Can an order for repayment to an
investor of money paid by the investor pursuant to an investment transaction
induced by a contravention of s 47 be described as an order to take steps to remedy

the contravention? I have doubts about this but, even if it can, the order could
a not, in my opinion, be made without the consent of the investor and the return
by the investor of the purchased shares.

The alleged contraventions of s 57 consist of the publication of investment
advertisements whose contents had not been approved as required by the 1986
Act. Where that has happened an order may be made under s 61(1) directing
steps to be taken to remedy the contravention. I do not follow how an order for
b the repayment of money to investors could ever be described as an order for a step
to be taken to remedy a contravention of s 57.

Section 56 is breached by entering into an investment transaction in the course
of or as a consequence of an unsolicited call. Unlike ss 47 and 57 where, at best,
the entry into the investment transaction may be a result of the contravention
c but will not be the contravention itself, the contravention of s 56 does consist of
the entry into the transaction. So the reversal of the transaction can reasonably be
regarded as a step to remedy the contravention.

As a general proposition, however, orders cannot, in my judgment, be made
under s 61(1) unless they direct the taking of steps which, if taken, are reasonably
capable of remedying the contravention in question. The purpose of the order
d must be the remedying of the contravention.

But, subject to the limitations as to purpose and effect that I have mentioned,
there is no reason, in my opinion, to place any further limitations on the steps
that, under s 61(1), can be directed to be taken. Nor is there, in my opinion, any
difference between the type of orders that can be made against the contravener
and the type of orders that can be made against persons 'knowingly concerned in
e the contravention'. The fact that a person against whom an order is sought has
received nothing under the transaction resulting from or, as the case may be,
constituting the contravention may be relevant to discretion but is not, in my
judgment, relevant to the power of the court to make the order.

I must now examine the case that has been pleaded against the third, fourth
f and fifth defendants in the light of the analysis of ss 6(2) and 61(1) that I have
attempted.

(1) It is not in my judgment, a valid objection to the SIB's pleaded case that
these defendants have not themselves received any of the money of the investors
that it is proposed that they should be ordered to repay. On the main point on
this appeal the appellants, in my judgment, fail.

g (2) It is, however, in my judgment, a valid objection to the s 6(2) order sought
by para 11 of the prayer that it appears to be directed to restoring only the
investors to their former positions. The paragraph should, in my judgment, be
amended so as to make clear that what is being sought is an order for steps to be
taken restoring all the parties to the respective transactions to their former
position.

h (3) Paragraph 11 is objectionable also, in my opinion, in that it appears to
contemplate the possibility of a class remedy. A s 6(2) order should be directed to
individual transactions with payment being directed to be made to individual
investors upon the individual investors retransferring their Euramco shares or
delivering up their Euramco share certificates.

j (4) While it is, in my opinion, possible for a restitutionary order to be made in
order to remedy a breach of s 56, such an order could not, in my opinion, be
regarded as remedying a contravention of s 57. Whether it could be regarded as
remedying a contravention of s 47 I regard as doubtful. This point did not,
however, form part of the attack on the pleadings below and does not have to be
decided on this appeal.

(5) To the extent that restitutionary orders can be made under s 61(1), however, the objections referred to under paras 2 and 3 above apply also to the s 61(1) order *a* sought by para 13.

None of these objections to which I have referred is, in my opinion, a present ground for striking out. None was the basis of the application below and none figures in the notice of appeal. So I think the SIB should have an opportunity of reconsidering the form of restitutionary or remedial order it will seek against these defendants. *b*

The only striking-out ground urged upon us was the ground referred to under para 1 above. On that point I am against the appellants and, accordingly, would dismiss this appeal.

Since I have, on the one hand, declined to accept that non-recipients such as the third, fourth and fifth defendants are necessarily free from liability under ss 6(2) *c* and 61(1) and, on the other hand, have criticised the form of order sought by the SIB under paras 11 and 13 of the prayer, I ought, I think, to give an indication of what, in my opinion, would be a permissible form of order that could be sought against a non-recipient.

An order could, in my opinion, be sought imposing on the contravener and, in default of payment by the contravener, on the person or persons 'knowingly *d* concerned' liability to repay to the investor the purchase price of the shares comprised in a particular investment transaction, with payment to be made against the delivery up by the investor of the share certificates and, if necessary, a signed form of transfer. The carrying out of such an order would, I think, have to be adjourned to chambers and procedure similar to specific performance procedure could then be employed. If the contravener paid up there would be no *e* liability on the persons knowingly concerned. If not, the persons 'knowingly concerned' would have to pay and, on payment, would become subrogated to the primary claim against the contravener. There would be a variety of variations in the order that the circumstances of a particular transaction might require. Financial restitution, if restitution in specie were not possible, could be provided *f* for by the s 6(2) order (cf s 5(5)). A lien over the shares to be restored by the investor could be granted to persons 'knowingly concerned' in order to secure their right to be reimbursed by the person primarily liable to repay the investor. I would repeat that, in my opinion, the only limitations on the type of order that can be made are those imposed by its statutory purpose and intended effect.

g

STEYN LJ. In the process of interpreting a statute there is one consideration which overshadows all others in importance. That is the need to consider the words of the statute, and the contending interpretations, in the light of the contextual scene or setting. In a difficult case that setting will include the genesis of the statutory provision, countervailing considerations of policy and public interest and the common law and statutory framework in which the provision *h* will operate. These propositions are self-evident. But they merit special emphasis in the approach to be adopted to the construction of a statute, such as the Financial Services Act 1986, which in some respects introduced radical new solutions for old problems.

The main issue is a question of principle regarding the correct interpretation of s 6(2) of the 1986 Act. The question is in what circumstances the court may, on *j* the application of the Securities and Investments Board (the SIB), order persons who were knowingly concerned in the unauthorised carrying on of investment business under s 3 of that Act to take steps to restore the parties to the transaction to the position in which they were before the transaction was entered into.

a The genesis of these provisions was the widespread belief that the operations of share-pushers were damaging to the integrity of the markets, and contrary to the public interest. It was argued that the law should do more to ensure, not fairness, but honesty, in the carrying on of investment business in the United Kingdom. That view is reflected in a government White Paper which was published in January 1985: *Financial Services in the United Kingdom: A New Financial Framework for Investor Protection* (Cmnd 9432). The White Paper argued that the existing

b investor protection laws were outdated and incomplete. Many facets of the problem had to be addressed. But two points were of particular importance. First, in the context of share-pushing there was the reality that the share-pusher was often beyond the reach of English law. But it was equally clear that the share-pushing operations were often made possible only because of the assistance of third parties such as bankers, accountants and solicitors.

c Secondly, share-pushing raised in acute form a problem which bedevils much of civil law. That is the fact that the cost and expense of legal proceedings against a share-pusher will often be beyond the pockets of individual investors. The civil law provides a framework for the redress of individual grievances. But it also fulfils a wider social purpose in setting standards for the markets and in

d discouraging aberrant behaviour. But if resort to civil remedies is impracticable for most individual investors the sanctions of the civil law cannot play their proper role.

A central provision of the 1986 Act is s 3, which provides that no person shall carry on investment business in the United Kingdom unless he is an authorised person or an exempted person as defined. The importance which the legislature

e attached to the observance of the regulatory system is demonstrated by s 4, which makes a contravention of s 3 an offence, punishable on conviction on indictment by a term of two years imprisonment or a fine or both.

But the prohibition on the carrying on of unauthorised investment business is also underpinned by new civil remedies. Section 5 renders an agreement made

f with an unauthorised person unenforceable at the option of the innocent party. Section 6(1) empowers the court to restrain by injunction apprehended breaches of s 3. Section 6(2) is for present purposes the critical provision. It reads as follows:

> 'If, on the application of the Secretary of State, the court is satisfied that a person has entered into any transaction in contravention of section 3 above the court may order that person and any other person who appears to the
g > court to have been knowingly concerned in the contravention to take such steps as the court may direct for restoring the parties to the position in which they were before the transaction was entered into.'

Subsection (3) creates remedies for the recovery of profits and compensation for loss, and sub-ss (4) to (7) contain procedural provisions applicable to the remedies

h under sub-s (3).

Under s 6 the new civil remedies may be granted by the court on the application of the SIB. Proceedings by the SIB under s 6(2) is a type of representative action for the benefit of investors. The decision whether to bring such proceedings is a matter for the discretion of the SIB. The advantage of the new representative action is that action can be taken on behalf of the body of investors, large and

j small, at the expense of the SIB. Investor protection is therefore buttressed by a potentially powerful new procedure.

Section 6(2) must now be examined in some detail. Browne-Wilkinson V-C held, and both sides accept, that s 6(2) created a form of statutory rescission and restitution. I respectfully agree. On the other hand, a comparison with rescission and restitution at common law or in equity should not necessarily lead one to approach the construction of s 6(2) with the a priori disposition that the legislature *a* wished to reproduce exactly the rules governing rescission and restitution at common law or in equity.

Section 6(2) empowers the court to order a person who has entered into a transaction in contravention of s 3 to take such steps as the court may direct for restoring 'the parties' (that is the contravener and the investor) to the position in which they were before the transaction was entered into. This part of s 6(2) is not *b* in issue in the present case. It is not in doubt that as against Pantell SA the court has jurisdiction to make an order under s 6(2) for the restoration of the status quo ante. It was, however, argued that at common law and in equity rescission can only be granted if full restitution can be made by both parties. It was suggested that this 'principle' is only subject to minor qualification: see Goff and Jones *Law of Restitution* (3rd edn, 1986) pp 169–171. I express no view on this point. But, in *c* so far as it may be relevant, I do not accept that the independent new remedy under s 6(2) is so confined. Under consideration are transactions entered into in the course of carrying on unauthorised investment business. The definition of 'investment business' is to be found in s 1(2) of the 1986 Act, read with Schs 1 and 2 to that Act. The transactions covered are in broad terms financial agreements. *d* It seems to me that the purpose of an order under s 6(2) is to restore the parties to the financial position in which they were before the transaction was entered into. The mere fact, for example, that the investor had sold on the shares would not by itself render the statutory remedy of rescission inapplicable. In such a case the counter-restitution could be achieved by a financial adjustment based on the value of the shares. Rescission will only be impossible when financial adjustment is *e* obstructed by circumstances going beyond the difficulty of valuation of investments which have been sold on: see Birks *Introduction to the Law of Restitution* (1985) p 423. Having heard argument on this point, I have briefly recorded my view. But the matter is strictly irrelevant at this stage since there is no factual basis for saying that in the present case restoration will be impossible or even difficult. *f*

That brings me to the real issue, namely the circumstances in which an order under s 6(2) can be made against third parties who were knowingly concerned in the contravention, that is the unauthorised carrying on of investment business. 'Knowingly concerned' is not defined. In my judgment it is clear that proof of actual knowledge is essential but not enough. Mere passive knowledge will not *g* be sufficient: actual involvement in the contravention must be established. By way of shorthand I will refer to third parties who, with the requisite knowledge, were concerned in the carrying on of unauthorised investment business as responsible third parties.

The question is whether, apart from the requirement of proof that the third party was knowingly concerned in the contravention, there is any jurisdictional *h* restriction on the court's power to make an order under s 6(2) against responsible third parties. No doubt in the exercise of its discretion a court may take into account a number of factors, such as for example the conduct and wishes of individual investors, which might in a given case militate against the making of an order. But the issue to be decided on this appeal is one relating to the jurisdiction of the court. *j*

The starting point must be the ordinary meaning of the words of s 6(2). The language is general. It provides that the court may make an order against both the contravener and responsible third parties for the restoration of 'the parties' (that is the contravener and the investor) to the status quo ante. Apart from proof that the third party was knowingly concerned in the contravention, I find no

further expressed restriction in s 6(2) on the jurisdiction of the court to make an
a order against a responsible third party. If s 6(2) is interpreted in this way, the
liability of the contravener can be regarded as a primary liability; the liability of
the responsible third party is an accessory liability. On this view s 6(2) empowered
the court to impose an order against both the contravener and the responsible
third party, the effect of which is to make them jointly and severally liable. In
my judgment the language of s 6(2) is wide enough to create such a jurisdiction.
b Moreover, it is right to take into account that one mischief sought to be addressed
by legislation was the fact that third parties often assisted share-pushing operations.
Giving effect to the full width of the ordinary meaning of the words therefore
promotes the purpose of the legislation.

But it is necessary to examine the arguments advanced on behalf of the
c solicitors. First, it was emphasised that ex hypothesi the responsible third parties—
and in particular the solicitors in this case—were not themselves contraveners. So
be it. But if they were knowingly involved in the carrying on of unauthorised
investment business that provides the rationale for orders against them under
s 6(2).

Secondly, it was emphasised that ex hypothesi the responsible third parties—
d and in particular the solicitors in this case—were not parties to the transaction
and received nothing under it. It was suggested that, because the third parties
received nothing under the transaction, it would be unworkable to make an order
requiring them to restore 'the parties' (that is the contravener and the investor) to
the status quo ante. I disagree. Let us suppose that the contravener sold to an
investor 1000 shares at a price of £100,000. Let us further assume that the shares
e were and are worth only £50,000. It would be perfectly proper in an appropriate
case to order the contravener to pay £100,000 to the investor, subject to the
investor restoring the shares to the contravener, together with an order that the
responsible third party should on a joint and several basis pay £50,000 to the
investor. For the avoidance of doubt I make clear that the investor would not be
entitled to recover more than £100,000. Such an order would restore 'the parties'
f to the financial position in which they were before the transaction was entered
into. And there may be other ways in which in practice composite orders against
a contravener and a third party, on a joint and several basis, can be structured.
I am satisfied that it cannot be said that s 6(2) is unworkable if the words of that
provision are given their wide general meaning.

g The third argument was that it would be unfair, if a responsible third party
was compelled to make payment under an order pursuant to s 6(2) without a
right of indemnity or contribution against the contravener. I do not propose to
consider whether there might be an implied right of this nature, or whether a
court order under s 6(2) may deal with reimbursement as between a third party
and the contravener. After all, if there is no such right of indemnity, and none
h may be created by order of the court, there may be a sound policy reason for it,
namely that the court will not aid somebody who was knowingly involved in
carrying on unauthorised investment business.

Fourthly, it was pointed out that under s 6(3) no order can be made against
third parties. Like Browne-Wilkinson V-C I find that puzzling. A possible
explanation may be that the remedies under s 6(3) may be wider than the remedy
j under s 6(2). Section 6(2) contemplates restoration of what was received, or the
value of it; sub-ss (3)(*a*) *and* (4)(*a*) contemplate restoration of the value surviving;
and sub-ss (3)(*b*) and (4)(*b*) are wide enough to cover in principle compensation in
respect of loss of an opportunity to make a profit. But the fact that the legislature
refrained where creating a jurisdiction to make orders against a third party under
s 6(3) and (4) does not justify a cutting down of the ordinary meaning of s 6(2).

Fifthly, it was emphasised that the procedural provisions in sub-ss (4), (5) and (6) do not apply to the remedy under sub-s (2). The remedy under sub-s (2) will *a* usually be a narrower one, and usually there will be less scope for dispute. That may explain why procedural provisions regarding the operation of sub-s (2) are not spelled out. In any event, this point cannot possibly justify departing from the clear import of the language of the statute.

One is entitled to ask what sensible purpose the provision for orders against third parties could serve if there is not a jurisdiction to make orders against the *b* solicitors in this case. On behalf of the solicitors Mr Sumption QC argued that the power to make orders under s 6(2) was extended to persons concerned in the contravention because money ordered to be repaid, or contracts or securities ordered to be delivered up, or guarantees ordered to be cancelled may be in the hands of third parties, such as agents, assignees or chargees. It was further said *c* that the reason for limiting the application of sub-s (2) to those third parties who are knowingly concerned in the contravention is that an order addressed directly to a third party (as opposed to the contravener acting by his servants or agents) would only be necessary where the third party had an interest of his own in the subject matter of the order. This interpretation emasculates the remedy against third parties almost completely. The emphasis is on restoration of things in specie *d* and physical things. This narrow interpretation may be ingenious but in my judgment it flies in the face of the ordinary meaning of the language and of the purpose of the statute. That is particularly so if one bears in mind that the transactions in question are financial agreements, and that the manifest aim of s 6(2) is to restore the parties in financial terms to the status quo ante.

For my part I am satisfied that there exists a jurisdiction to make orders under *e* s 6(2) against the solicitors, if they were knowingly concerned in the alleged contraventions.

I am in respectful agreement with the reasoning of Scott LJ on the brief submissions which were made on s 61(1) of the 1986 Act. I have nothing to add on that aspect of the case. I also agree with Scott LJ's observations about the form *f* of order that would be proper to be made.

In my view the appeal should be dismissed.

NEILL LJ. I agree that this appeal should be dismissed for the reasons given by Scott and Steyn LJJ.

I also agree with the guidance given by Scott LJ as to the forms of order which *g* it is permissible to make where an order is sought against a person or persons 'knowingly concerned'.

Appeal dismissed. Leave to appeal to the House of Lords refused.

Raina Levy   Barrister.

a
R v Secretary of State for the Home Department, ex parte Doody and other appeals

COURT OF APPEAL, CIVIL DIVISION
b GLIDEWELL, STAUGHTON AND FARQUHARSON LJJ
24–27, 30–31 MARCH, 6 MAY 1992

Prison – Release on licence – Life sentence – Mandatory or discretionary life sentence – Tariff period – Procedure for fixing tariff period – Judiciary invited to advise on period that should be served for purposes of retribution and deterrence – Secretary of State
c *taking account of judicial recommendation in reaching decision on appropriate tariff period – Whether Secretary of State entitled to set tariff period differing from that recommended by judiciary – Criminal Justice Act 1967, s 61(1).*

Prison – Release on licence – Life sentence – Mandatory or discretionary life sentence –
d *Tariff period – Principles of natural justice – Secretary of State deciding tariff period – Date for first review of prisoner's sentence set according to tariff period – Whether prisoner entitled to make written representations to Secretary of State before tariff period set – Whether Secretary of State required to inform prisoner of tariff period recommended by judiciary and other opinions expressed by judiciary relevant to decision on tariff – Whether Secretary of State required to give reasons if he departs from judicial view of*
e *tariff period.*

The four applicants were separately convicted of murder and received mandatory sentences of life imprisonment. Under the procedure adopted by the Secretary of State for the exercise of his discretionary power under s 61(1)[a] of the Criminal Justice Act 1967 to decide the date on which a person serving a mandatory life
f sentence for murder or a discretionary life sentence for other offences could be released on licence, the trial judge and the Lord Chief Justice were invited to express their views at the earliest possible opportunity after conviction and sentence on the period that the prisoner should serve for the purposes of retribution and deterrence (the tariff period). The Secretary of State's policy was that if the tariff period was less than 20 years the date for the first review by the
g Parole Board of a prisoner's sentence was 3 years before the end of the tariff period and if it was 20 years or more the first review was always 17 years after sentence. If a discretionary life sentence was passed, the minister of state in charge of the prison department, not the Secretary of State himself, set the date for the first review strictly in accordance with the views of the judiciary; in the case of a
h mandatory life sentence for murder the minister of state took the judicial view into account but did not necessarily adopt it as the tariff period. The prisoner was then informed of the date of the first review but he was not told what recommendation the judiciary had made. The four applicants had each been told the date of the first review and considered that the minister of state had increased the tariff periods recommended by the judiciary. They applied for judicial review,
j seeking declarations that the Secretary of State was required to adopt the judicial view of the tariff period, that the prisoner had the right to make representations before the Secretary of State set the date for the first review and, for that purpose, to be told of any information on which the Secretary of State would make his

---

a Section 61(1), so far as material, is set out at p 156 *h j*, post

decision which was not in the prisoner's possession, and that the prisoner was
entitled to be told the judicial view of his tariff period, the reasons for the *a*
recommendation by the judiciary and for any departure from that recommendation. The Divisional Court refused to grant the relief sought and the applicants
appealed. The questions for the Court of Appeal were (i) whether the decision on
the period which a life sentence prisoner was obliged to serve for the purposes of
retribution and deterrence was required to be made by the Secretary of State
personally or whether that task could be performed by a junior minister on his *b*
behalf, (ii) whether the Secretary of State was obliged to adopt the judicial view of
the tariff period, (iii) whether a life sentence prisoner was entitled to make
representations before his tariff period was set by the Secretary of State,
(iv) whether the Secretary of State was required to tell the prisoner what tariff
period the judiciary had recommended he should serve and (v) whether, if a *c*
prisoner was entitled to be told the judicial view of his tariff period, the Secretary
of State was obliged to give reasons if he departed from it.

Held – (1) Although the power to release a life prisoner on licence was conferred
by s 61(1) of the 1967 Act on the Secretary of State, the decisions leading to that
release, including the decision as to the period to be served by the prisoner for the *d*
purposes of retribution and deterrence, could properly and lawfully be made by a
junior minister in the Home Office (see p 162 *c d*, p 178 *d e* and p 184 *e f*, post);
dicta of Lord Greene MR in *Carltona Ltd v Comrs of Works* [1943] 2 All ER 560 at
563 and of Lord Donaldson MR in *R v Secretary of State for the Home Dept, ex p
Oladehinde* [1990] 2 All ER 367 at 381 applied.
(2) In accordance with s 61(1) of the 1967 Act the ultimate decision on the *e*
period of imprisonment which a prisoner serving a life sentence, whether
mandatory or discretionary, should serve for the purposes of retribution and
deterrence was that of the Secretary of State, who although required to take into
account the advice of the judiciary, was entitled as a matter of law if he had good
reason for doing so to set a tariff period different from that recommended by the *f*
judges. However, in the case of prisoners serving discretionary life sentences it
was unlikely that the Secretary of State could depart from his policy of accepting
the judicial recommendation on the tariff period in all cases, having regard to the
fact that he had probably created a legitimate expectation that he would continue
to apply the policy (see p 166 *h j* to p 167 *a*, p 175 *a b j* to p 176 *b* and p 182 *c d*,
post); *R v Secretary of State for the Home Dept, ex p Handscomb* (1987) 86 Cr App *g*
R 59 overruled in part.
(3) The principles of natural justice endowed a prisoner serving a mandatory
life sentence with the right to make representations in writing to the Secretary of
State as to the period he should serve for the purposes of retribution and deterrence
before the date for the first review of his sentence and, before giving him the
opportunity to make such representations, the Secretary of State was also required *h*
to inform the prisoner of the period recommended by the judiciary as the tariff
period and of any other opinion expressed by the judiciary which was relevant to
the Secretary of State's decision as to the appropriate tariff period, although (per
Staughton and Farquharson LJJ) the prisoner was not entitled to see comments,
summaries and advice provided to the Secretary of State by officials in his
department. If the Secretary of State set a tariff period which exceeded that *j*
recommended by the judiciary he was under no obligation to give reasons for
departing from the judicial view, but, if there was a considerable disparity
between the two periods and the Secretary of State failed to give any reasons for
his decision, his decision might well be open to challenge by way of judicial
review as being irrational. It followed that the decisions made by the Secretary of
State as to the length of the tariff period for each of the applicants would be

quashed and the decisions referred back to him for reconsideration. The appeals
a would therefore be allowed (see p 169 *f* to p 170 *a*, p 171 *h*, p 172 *f g*, p 179 *g* to *j*,
p 180 *b*, p 183 *g* to *j* and p 184 *c d*, post); dicta of Lord Reid in *Wiseman v Borneman*
[1969] 3 All ER 275 at 277, of Lord Bridge in *Lloyd v McMahon* [1987] 1 All ER
1118 at 1161 and *R v Civil Service Appeal Board, ex p Cunningham* [1991] 4 All ER
310 applied; *Payne v Lord Harris of Greenwich* [1981] 2 All ER 842 considered.

b

Notes

For the powers of the Secretary of State to release on licence prisoners serving life
sentences, see 37 *Halsbury's Laws* (4th edn) para 1190, and for a case on the subject,
see 37(3) *Digest* (Reissue) 406, 5341.
c   For the Criminal Justice Act 1967, s 61, see 34 *Halsbury's Statutes* (4th edn) 699.
      As from 1 October 1992 new arrangements for the early release of prisoners,
including those serving sentences of life imprisonment, were made by s 33 to 37
of the Criminal Justice Act 1991, s 101(2) of which and Sch 13 to which repealed,
inter alia, s 61 of the 1967 Act.

d **Cases referred to in judgments**

Associated Provincial Picture Houses Ltd v Wednesbury Corp [1947] 2 All ER 680,
  [1948] 1 KB 223, CA.
Bushell v Secretary of State for the Environment [1980] 2 All ER 608, [1981] AC 75,
  [1980] 3 WLR 22, HL.
Carltona Ltd v Comrs of Works [1943] 2 All ER 560, CA.
e *Cooper v Wandsworth Board of Works* (1863) 14 CBNS 180, 143 ER 414.
Council of Civil Service Unions v Minister for the Civil Service [1984] 3 All ER 935,
  [1985] AC 374, [1984] 3 WLR 1174, HL.
Findlay v Secretary of State for the Home Dept [1984] 3 All ER 801, [1985] AC 318,
  [1984] 3 WLR 1159, CA and HL.
f *Kanda v Government of Malaya* [1962] AC 322, [1962] 2 WLR 1153, PC.
Leech v Parkhurst Prison Deputy Governor [1988] 1 All ER 485, [1988] AC 533,
  [1988] 2 WLR 290, HL.
Lloyd v McMahon [1987] 1 All ER 1118, [1987] AC 625, [1987] 2 WLR 821, HL.
London Export Corp Ltd v Jubilee Coffee Roasting Co Ltd [1958] 1 All ER 494, [1958]
  1 WLR 271; *affd* [1958] 2 All ER 411, [1958] 1 WLR 661, CA.
g *Lonrho plc v Secretary of State for Trade and Industry* [1989] 2 All ER 609, [1989] 1
  WLR 525, HL.
Minister for Aboriginal Affairs v Peko-Wallsend Ltd (1986) 162 CLR 24, Aust HC.
Payne v Lord Harris of Greenwich [1981] 2 All ER 842, [1981] 1 WLR 754, CA.
Public Service Board of New South Wales v Osmond (1986) 159 CLR 656, [1987] LRC
  (Const) 681, Aust HC.
h *R v Brixton Prison Governor, ex p Enahoro* [1963] 2 All ER 477, [1963] 2 QB 455,
  [1963] 2 WLR 1260, DC.
R v Civil Service Appeal Board, ex p Cunningham [1991] 4 All ER 310, CA.
R v Commission for Racial Equality, ex p Hillingdon London BC [1982] AC 779, [1982]
  3 WLR 159, HL.
R v Flemming [1973] 2 All ER 401, CA.
j *R v Gaming Board for GB, ex p Benaim* [1970] 2 All ER 528, [1970] 2 QB 417, [1970]
  2 WLR 1009, CA.
R v Hull Prison Board of Visitors, ex p St Germain [1979] 1 All ER 701, [1979] QB
  425, [1979] 2 WLR 42, CA.
R v Parole Board, ex p Wilson [1992] 2 All ER 576, [1992] QB 740, CA.
R v Secretary of State for the Home Dept, ex p Benson (1988) Independent,
  16 November, DC.

R v Secretary of State for the Home Dept, ex p Handscomb (1987) 86 Cr App R 59, DC.
R v Secretary of State for the Home Dept, ex p Oladehinde [1990] 2 All ER 367, [1991] **a**
    1 AC 254, [1990] 2 WLR 1195, CA; *affd* [1990] 3 All ER 393, [1991] 1 AC 254,
    [1990] 3 WLR 797, HL.
R v Secretary of State for the Home Dept, ex p Walsh (1991) Independent,
    17 December, DC.
Raymond v Honey [1982] 1 All ER 756, [1983] 1 AC 1, [1982] 2 WLR 465, HL.
Russell v Duke of Norfolk [1949] 1 All ER 109, CA.   **b**
Thynne, Wilson and Gunnell v UK (1990) 13 EHRR 666, E Ct HR. .
Wiseman v Borneman [1969] 3 All ER 275, [1971] AC 297, [1969] 3 WLR 706, HL.

Cases also cited or referred to in skeleton arguments   **c**
Air Canada v Secretary of State for Trade (No 2) [1983] 1 All ER 910, [1983] 2 AC
    394, HL.
Alexander v Home Office [1988] 2 All ER 118, [1988] 1 WLR 968, CA.
Amand v Secretary of State for Home Affairs [1942] 2 All ER 381, [1943] AC 147,
    HL.
Board of Education v Rice [1911] AC 179, [1911–13] All ER Rep 36, HL.   **d**
Brind v Secretary of State for the Home Dept [1991] 1 All ER 720, [1991] 1 AC 696,
    HL.
Campbell and Fell v UK (1984) 7 EHRR 165, E Ct HR.
CREEDNZ Inc v Governor General [1981] 1 NZLR 172, NZ CA.
de Freitas v Benny [1976] AC 239, PC.
Derbyshire CC v Times Newspapers Ltd [1992] 3 All ER 65, [1992] QB 770, CA.   **e**
Dunlop, Secretary of Labor v Bachowski (1974) 421 US 560, US SC.
Golden Chemical Products Ltd, Re [1976] 2 All ER 543, [1976] Ch 300.
Golder v UK (1975) 1 EHRR 524, E Ct HR.
Hague v Deputy Governor of Parkhurst Prison [1991] 3 All ER 733, [1992] 1 AC 58,
    HL.   **f**
K (H) (an infant), Re [1967] 1 All ER 226, [1967] 2 QB 617, DC.
Liversidge v Anderson [1941] 3 All ER 338, [1942] AC 206, HL.
McInnes v Onslow Fane [1978] 3 All ER 211, [1978] 1 WLR 1520.
Newman and Myers, Re (1979) 1 Cr App R (S) 252, CA.
Nottinghamshire CC v Secretary of State for the Environment [1986] 1 All ER 199,
    [1986] AC 240, HL.   **g**
O'Reilly v Mackman [1982] 3 All ER 1124, [1983] 2 AC 237, HL.
Pearlberg v Varty (Inspector of Taxes) [1972] 2 All ER 6, [1972] 1 WLR 534, HL.
Pergamon Press Ltd, Re [1970] 3 All ER 535, [1971] Ch 388, CA.
R v Army Board of the Defence Council, ex p Anderson [1991] 3 All ER 375, [1992] 1
    QB 169, DC.
R v Blandford Magistrates' Court, ex p Pamment [1991] 1 All ER 218, [1990] 1 WLR **h**
    1490, CA.
R v Chiswick Police Station Superintendant, ex p Sacksteder [1918] 1 KB 578, CA.
R v Commission for Racial Equality, ex p Cottrell & Rothon (a firm) [1980] 3 All ER
    265, [1980] 1 WLR 1580, DC.
R v Gould [1968] 1 All ER 849, [1968] 2 QB 65, CA.
R v Housing Appeal Tribunal [1920] 3 KB 334, DC.   **j**
R v Lancashire CC, ex p Huddleston [1986] 2 All ER 941, CA.
R v Parole Board, ex p Bradley [1990] 3 All ER 828, [1991] 1 WLR 134, DC.
R v Secretary of State for the Home Dept, ex p G (1990) Times, 26 June, [1990] CA
    Transcript 555.

R v Secretary of State for the Home Dept, ex p Gunnell (1984) Times, 7 November,
[1984] CA Transcript 391.

R v Spencer [1985] 1 All ER 673, [1985] QB 771, CA.

R v Sutton London BC, ex p Hamlet (26 March 1986, unreported), QBD.

Ridge v Baldwin [1963] 2 All ER 66, [1964] AC 40, HL.

Weeks v UK (1987) 10 EHRR 293, E Ct HR.

Williams v Home Office [1981] 1 All ER 1151.

Appeals

Stephen Doody, Kenneth Stephen Pegg, John David Pierson and Elfed Wayne
Smart appealed from the decision of the Divisional Court of the Queen's Bench
Division (Mann LJ and Macpherson J) made on 18 January 1991 whereby the
court refused their applications for judicial review of decisions of the Secretary of
State for the Home Department as to the length of the tariff period each should
remain in prison as punishment for the offence of murder and consequently the
dates on which their cases should first be reviewed for release on licence by the
Parole Board. The principal grounds for the appeals were that the Divisional
Court had erred in rejecting the appellants' submissions that the Home Secretary
was bound to adopt the judicial view of the tariff period to be served and that the
nature of the decision called for the application of the principles of natural justice
to enable the appellants to make informed representations on the factual basis
which the Home Secretary proposed to adopt in fixing the tariff. The facts are set
out in the judgment of Glidewell LJ.

Stephen Sedley QC and *Edward Fitzgerald* (instructed by *B M Birnberg & Co*) for the
appellant Doody and (instructed by *Graham Withers & Co*, Shrewsbury) for the
appellant Pierson.

Anthony Scrivener QC and *Richard Gordon* (instructed by *Bindman & Partners*) for
the appellant Pegg.

Geoffrey Nice QC and *Gregory Treverton-Jones* (instructed by *Cartwrights Adams &
Black*, Cardiff) for the appellant Smart.

David Pannick and *Robert Jay* (instructed by the *Treasury Solicitor*) for the Secretary
of State.

Cur adv vult

6 May 1992. The following judgments were delivered.

GLIDEWELL LJ. In these appeals we are concerned with issues arising out of
the procedure by which the Secretary of State for the Home Department decides,
in the exercise of his power under s 61 of the Criminal Justice Act 1967, the date
on which a person serving a sentence of imprisonment for life may be released on
licence. Messrs Doody, Pierson, Smart and Pegg appeal against a decision of the
Divisional Court (Mann LJ and Macpherson J) given on 18 January 1991 refusing
them the relief claimed in their applications for judicial review of decisions made
in relation to each of them by the Secretary of State for the Home Department.

The same issues arise in all four appeals and it is therefore convenient to
consider them in one judgment. However, Mr Pegg raises a point which relates
only to his own appeal, to which I shall refer later.

This court does not have jurisdiction to determine these appeals if they are
appeals in a 'criminal cause or matter' within s 18(1) of the Supreme Court Act
1981. Counsel for all the appellants and for the respondent were unanimous in

their view that the appeals are not in a criminal cause or matter, and on a brief consideration of the relevant authorities I agree. I note that in two of the main *a* authorities to which we have been referred on the substantive issues, *Payne v Lord Harris of Greenwich* [1981] 2 All ER 842, [1981] 1 WLR 754 and *Findlay v Secretary of State for the Home Dept* [1984] 3 All ER 801, [1985] AC 318, it seems to have been assumed without argument that this court had jurisdiction.

Messrs Doody, Pierson, Smart and Pegg have all been convicted of murder, and each in consequence is serving a sentence of imprisonment for life. This is of *b* course the mandatory sentence for a person convicted of murder. Before setting out such facts relating to the sentences on the individual offenders as are material for the purposes of these appeals, it is necessary first to describe the procedure followed by the Secretary of State in exercising his power under s 61, and the steps by which he came to adopt that procedure.

c

The statutory background

Section 1(1) of the Murder (Abolition of Death Penalty) Act 1965 abolished the death penalty for murder and substituted for it imprisonment for life. By s 27(1) of the Prison Act 1952 the Secretary of State was already empowered—

> 'at any time if he thinks fit [to] release on licence a person serving a term *d* of imprisonment for life subject to compliance with such conditions, if any, as the Secretary of State may from time to time determine.'

Section 1(2) of the 1965 Act provided:

> 'On sentencing any person convicted of murder to imprisonment for life *e* the Court may at the same time declare the period which it recommends to the Secretary of State as the minimum period which in its view should elapse before the Secretary of State orders the release of that person on licence under section 27 of the Prison Act 1952 . . .'

Moreover, s 2 of the 1965 Act imposed a restraint on the power of the Secretary *f* of State to release on licence a person convicted of murder, by providing that no such person should be released—

> 'unless the Secretary of State has prior to such release consulted the Lord Chief Justice of England . . . together with the trial judge if available.'

Presumably this provision had the effect of discouraging the Secretary of State *g* from releasing a convicted murderer on licence at a date earlier than the judiciary thought appropriate.

The provisions of s 27 of the 1952 Act and s 2 of the 1965 Act were repealed by the Criminal Justice Act 1967, and replaced by s 61 of that Act. Section 61(1) provides:

> 'The Secretary of State may, if recommended to do so by the Parole Board, *h* release on licence a person serving a sentence of imprisonment for life . . . but shall not do so in the case of a person sentenced to imprisonment for life . . . except after consultation with the Lord Chief Justice of England together with the trial judge if available.'

This subsection applies both to mandatory life sentences for murder and to *j* discretionary life sentences for other offences for which such a sentence may lawfully be imposed.

Section 62 of the 1967 Act deals with the revocation of licences, a subject which has aroused much controversy but with which we are not concerned in any of these appeals.

It will be seen that s 61(1) does not *require* the Secretary of State to release any
a person serving a sentence of imprisonment for life on licence, but imposes two
conditions which must be satisfied before he may do so, namely that the release
must first be recommended by the Parole Board (a body which was itself
constituted by s 59 of the 1967 Act) and that the Secretary of State may not release
on licence except after consultation with the Lord Chief Justice of England
together with the trial judge if available.
b

The procedure adopted

Section 61 of the 1967 Act does not specify any procedure by which the
Secretary of State should decide whether and when to release a prisoner serving a
life sentence. The choice of an appropriate procedure is therefore a matter within
his discretion. However, since he may not release a prisoner unless and until he is
c recommended to do so by the Parole Board, the stage in an individual prisoner's
sentence at which the board considers whether to make a recommendation for
his release is therefore very important.

The wording of s 61(1) apparently envisages that, if and when the Parole Board
(or a local review committee) recommends release, the judiciary will then be
d consulted.

For some years after the 1967 Act came into force, the majority of life sentences
were reviewed by local review committees seven years after the sentences were
imposed. A small number were reviewed earlier, usually after four years. In
many cases the local review committee at the seven-year review considered it too
early to set a release date, which no doubt dashed the hopes of the prisoners whose
e sentences were under review.

A new procedure was introduced in 1973. A joint committee of members of
the Parole Board and officials of the Home Office was formed, which included
the vice-chairman of the board, a High Court judge. This committee scrutinised
the case of each prisoner serving a life sentence in order to set the date for the first
review, which might be more than seven years after the date of sentence. It was
f not the committee's function to recommend release, but inevitably the committee
would attempt to set a date at which there would be a reasonable prospect that
the local review committee and then the Parole Board might be able to
recommend release.

This procedure remained in force for ten years, until on 30 November 1983
g the then Secretary of State, the Rt Hon Leon Brittan MP, made a statement in a
parliamentary answer about the release of prisoners on parole licences (see 49 HC
Official Report (6th series) written answers cols 505–507). The first part of the
statement announced a specific policy relating to prisoners serving determinate
sentences of over five years for offences of violence or drug trafficking. The second
part related to prisoners serving life sentences. It read as follows:
h

> '*Life Sentence Prisoners*
> The release of life sentence prisoners is at the discretion of the Home
> Secretary, subject to a favourable recommendation by the Parole Board and
> to consultation with the Lord Chief Justice and, if he is available, the trial
> judge. Taking account again of the public concern about violent crime, in
> *j* future I intend to exercise my discretion so that murderers of police or prison
> officers, terrorist murderers, sexual or sadistic murderers of children and
> murderers by firearm in the course of robbery can normally expect to serve
> at least 20 years in custody; and there will be cases where the gravity of the
> offence requires a still longer period. Other murders, outside these categories,
> may merit no less punishment to mark the seriousness of the offence. At

present I look to the judiciary for advice on the time to be served to satisfy
the requirements of retribution and deterrence and to the Parole Board for *a*
advice on risk. I shall continue to do so. The Joint Parole Board/Home Office
committee was established in 1973 to give initial consideration, usually after
a life sentence prisoner had been detained for about three years in custody, to
the date for the first formal consideration of the case by the Parole Board
machinery. The Lord Chief Justice has agreed with me that this is the
appropriate time to obtain an initial judicial view on the requirements of *b*
retribution and deterrence. In future, therefore, I will decide the date of the
first reference of a case to a local review committee following the initial
consultation with the judiciary. The joint committee has therefore been
disbanded. The first local review committee will normally take place three
years before the expiry of the period necessary to meet the requirements of
retribution and deterrence. This would give sufficient time for preparation *c*
for release if the Parole Board recommended it, having considered risk. The
judiciary will also be consulted when release is an actual possibility to meet
fully the requirements of section 61 of the Criminal Justice Act 1967. These
new procedures will separate consideration of the requirements of retribution
and deterrence from consideration of risk to the public, which always has *d*
been, and will continue to be, the pre-eminent factor determining release.
They will enable the prison and other staff responsible for considering and
reporting on life sentence cases, the local review committees and the Parole
Board, to concentrate on risk. The judiciary will properly advise on
retribution and deterrence. But the ultimate discretion whether to release
will remain with me.' *e*

I need not read the remainder of the statement.

So far as I am aware, this was the first occasion on which it was made clear that
the period which elapses before a prisoner serving a life sentence is released is
determined by consideration of two factors, namely: (i) the period necessary to
satisfy retribution and deterrence, which has come to be called 'the tariff'; and *f*
(ii) a possible further period if it is thought by the Parole Board and/or the
Secretary of State that the prisoner would pose an unacceptable risk of danger to
the public were he to be released at the end of his tariff period.

In further parliamentary answers given in March and October 1985, the
Secretary of State made it clear (i) that if the tariff was to be 20 years or more there
would be a local review committee review after 17 years and (ii) that the procedure *g*
announced by Mr Brittan in November 1983 applied to discretionary as well as to
mandatory life sentences.

On 2 March 1987 the Divisional Court gave its decision in *R v Secretary of State
for the Home Dept, ex p Handscomb* (1987) 86 Cr App R 59. Mr Handscomb and the
other applicants for judicial review were serving discretionary life sentences.
They challenged the procedure announced in Mr Brittan's November 1983 *h*
statement. The court granted declarations to the following effect: (a) that the
Secretary of State is not entitled in relation to prisoners serving discretionary life
sentences to postpone consultation with the judiciary to a date later than the
earliest possible date after the imposition of the sentence; and (b) that in relation
to all the applicants the Secretary of State should fix the date of the first review by *j*
the local review committee and the Parole Board strictly in accordance with the
period of detention recommended by the judiciary as necessary to meet the
requirements of retribution and deterrence.

Following that decision, on 23 July 1987 the then Secretary of State, the Rt
Hon Douglas Hurd MP, made a further statement in a parliamentary answer (see

120 HC Official Report (6th series) written answers cols 347–349). After reviewing
a the procedure which had been in force since 1983, he referred to the decision of
the Divisional Court in *Ex p Handscomb* and said that he accepted the conclusion
of that court—

> 'that there are strong arguments for carrying out this consultation exercise
> as soon as practicable following the imposition of a discretionary life sentence.'

b The Secretary of State then continued:

> 'Following consultation with the Lord Chief Justice it has been agreed that
> the most satisfactory way of obtaining the judicial view is to ask the trial
> judge to write to me, through him, in every case where a discretionary life
> sentence is passed giving his view on the period necessary to meet the
> requirements of retribution and deterrence. This view will be related to the
c determinate sentence that would have been passed but for the element of
> mental instability and/or public risk which led the judge to pass a life
> sentence and will also take account of the notional period of the sentence
> which a prisoner might expect to have been remitted for good behaviour had
> a determinate sentence been passed. The date of the first formal review by
d the Parole Board machinery will then be fixed in accordance with the judicial
> view on the requirements of retribution and deterrence; and the review will,
> as before, normally take place three years before the expiry of that period. I
> have agreed with the Lord Chief Justice that this new procedure will be
> introduced with effect from 1 October 1987. Arrangements have also been
e made to consult the judiciary about those discretionary life sentence cases
> where the first formal review has not yet been set, with a view to fixing the
> date as soon as possible. In addition, I will arrange for a review to be
> undertaken of all discretionary life sentence cases with a first formal review
> date of January 1988 or later. Where account has been taken of factors other
> than the judicial view on the requirements of retribution and deterrence in
f fixing the date, the date will be adjusted to bring it into line with the judicial
> view. Although the issues before the Divisional Court related only to
> prisoners serving discretionary life sentences, I have decided that the date of
> the first formal review of the cases of prisoners serving mandatory life
> sentences should also be fixed as soon as practicable after conviction and
> sentence. The procedure under which the views of the trial judge and the
g Lord Chief Justice about the requirements of retribution and deterrence are
> obtained will be the same as that proposed for discretionary life sentence
> cases, and will be introduced at the same time. A similar exercise will also be
> carried out to fix the first review date in outstanding mandatory life sentence
> cases where this has not already been done. In view of the large number of
> cases involved (around 750) this will inevitably take some time. In cases of
h prisoners serving life sentences for murder, where the sentence is not at the
> discretion of the court, the question of the notional equivalent determinate
> sentence does not arise. I shall continue to take into account the view of the
> judiciary on the requirements of retribution and deterrence in such cases as a
> factor amongst others (including the need to maintain public confidence in
j the system of justice) to be weighed in the balance in setting the first review
> date. I shall ensure that the timing of the first formal review in such cases is
> fixed in accordance with my overall policy for ensuring that the time served
> by prisoners serving sentences for the worst offences of violence fully reflects
> public concern about violent crime. As indicated in the November 1983
> statement, the setting of the first review date under these arrangements will

enable a life sentence prisoner to be released [within] three years of that date
if the parole board so recommends, subject to the policy announced in reply *a*
to a question by the right hon. and learned Member for Warrington South
(Mr. Carlisle) on 1 March 1985 that no life sentence prisoner will be detained
for more than 17 years without a formal review of his case even where the
period thought necessary to meet the requirements of retribution and
deterrence exceeds 20 years. Ministers will continue to review every case
where a life sentence prisoner has been detained for 10 years. However, as *b*
was made clear by the Divisional court, the release of a life sentence prisoner
is solely at my discretion and it is for me to decide, after receiving the Parole
Board's recommendation and after consulting the judiciary as required by
section 61(1) of the Criminal Justice Act 1967, when actual release should
take place.'
c

This statement defined the procedure which has been followed since October
1987, and which has been applied in the case of all four applicants. The trial judge
and the Lord Chief Justice express their views as to the proper period to be served
by the prisoner for the purposes of retribution and deterrence voluntarily, in
accordance with the agreement made by the Lord Chief Justice with the Home
Secretary. They are not the statutory consultations required by s 61(1) of the 1967 *d*
Act, but are added to that consultation at an earlier stage.

From the parliamentary answers to which I have referred, and from the other
evidence before us in these appeals, it is clear that the procedure now followed
can be summarised as follows. (i) When a prisoner is sentenced to imprisonment
for life, within a short time the trial judge and the Lord Chief Justice are invited *e*
by the Secretary of State to express their views on the period he should serve for
the purposes of retribution and deterrence. It is not said on the form containing
the request that the judicial view will be treated as confidential, but it has always
been so regarded by the Lord Chief Justice and the judges. In *Ex p Handscomb*
(1987) 86 Cr App R 59 at 75 Watkins LJ said that the advice given by the
judiciary— *f*

'is a matter of confidence between him [the Home Secretary] and the
judiciary which we have not sought to breach because such consultation truly
lies in my view within the realm of confidence, *i.e.* privilege.'

(ii) The minister of state in charge of the Prison Department (not the Secretary of *g*
State himself) then sets the date for the first review by the local review committee.
(iii) If the tariff is less than 20 years, the date for the first review is 3 years before
the end of the tariff. If the tariff is 20 years or more, the first review is always
17 years after sentence. (iv) If a discretionary life sentence is passed, the minister
of state sets the date for the first review strictly in accordance with the views of
the judiciary, thus following the decision in *Ex p Handscomb* and Mr Hurd's 1987 *h*
statement. In the case, however, of a mandatory life sentence for murder (into
which category all the present appeals fall) the minister of state takes the judicial
view into account but does not necessarily adopt it as the tariff. The evidence
shows that in many cases the minister of state has set a date for the first review
later than would have been the case if he had adopted the views expressed by the
judiciary. (v) The prisoner is then informed of the date for the first review, and *j*
that this is 3 years less than the tariff if the first review is to be held less than
17 years after the date of his sentence. Thus a prisoner with a tariff less than
20 years can immediately calculate the length of his tariff. He is not told what
recommendation the judiciary have made. (vi) If the date for the first review is
fixed 17 years after sentence, the prisoner is told that this does not necessarily

mean that the period for retribution and deterrence has been set at 20 years.

a However, it is apparently the practice that if the prisoner inquires in such a case whether the tariff has been set at 20 years he will be told if it has been set at that period, but not if it has not. (vii) In every case it is made clear to the prisoner from the information supplied to him that he may not be recommended for release at the end of his tariff period at the first or any subsequent review. Release will depend upon whether he is thought to pose a danger to the public and

b therefore should be detained beyond the end of his tariff period. (viii) The prisoner may make representations to the local review committee before the first review. In the case of a prisoner whose tariff does not exceed 20 years, these representations will not be relevant to the tariff but only to the question whether he should be detained beyond the end of his tariff period because of the danger he

c is thought to pose.

The tariffs set for these appellants

Mr Doody was convicted and sentenced on 29 July 1987. The first review of his possible release is to take place in October 1998. I assume that in each case time in custody before trial is counted as part of the period before the first review.

d His first review date therefore implies a tariff of about 15 years.

Mr Pierson was convicted and sentenced on 8 July 1985. The first review is to take place in September 2001. When he applied for judicial review he did not know whether his tariff exceeded 20 years, but on 10 April 1990 his solicitors were informed by the Home Office that it did not.

Mr Smart was convicted and sentenced on 31 October 1986. The first review is

e to take place in April 1995, which implies a tariff of about 12 years.

Mr Pegg was convicted and sentenced on 25 March 1985. The first review is to take place in August 1993, which implies a tariff of about 11 years.

The relief sought

f For the most part the relief sought by each of these four appellants in their procedures for judicial review is the same, though somewhat differently expressed. They all seek declarations to the following effect: (a) that as a matter of law in the case of a prisoner serving a mandatory life sentence the Secretary of State is required to set a period for retribution and deterrence which does not exceed the tariff recommended by the judiciary; (b) that the Secretary of State is required by

g law to tell the prisoner what period the judiciary have recommended, and the reasons for that recommendation, and also if he has departed from that recommendation to tell the prisoner his reason for doing so; (c) that the prisoner is entitled to be given the opportunity to make representations to the Secretary of State before the tariff is set, and for this purpose to be told of any information upon which the Secretary of State will make his decision which is not in his, the

h prisoner's, possession. This in particular goes back to the issue of being told what the judiciary have recommended.

All the appellants seek orders that, because of the Secretary of State's failure to comply with what are said to be the requirements as I have set them out, the decisions made in relation to each of the appellants as to their respective tariffs should be quashed.

j On Mr Pegg's behalf, a further more detailed submission is made to which I shall refer later.

The issues

I summarise the issues which have been argued before us on these appeals as follows. (1) Is the Secretary of State obliged to make the decision on the period which a life sentence prisoner should serve for the purposes of retribution and deterrence personally, or may this task be performed by a junior minister on his behalf? I shall describe this issue as 'delegation'. (2) Is the Secretary of State obliged to adopt the judicial view of the period to be served for retribution and deterrence by a prisoner serving a mandatory life sentence? (3) Is a prisoner serving a life sentence entitled to make representations before his tariff is set by the Secretary of State? (4) Is the Secretary of State required to tell the prisoner what period the judiciary have recommended he should serve for the purposes of retribution and deterrence? (5) If a prisoner is to be told the judicial view of his tariff, is the Secretary of State obliged to give reasons for departing from it if he does?

Delegation

I have had the advantage of reading in draft the judgment of Staughton LJ. I agree with his conclusion that, although the power to release a life prisoner on licence is conferred by s 61(1) on the Secretary of State, the decisions leading to that release, including the decision as to the period to be served by the prisoner for the purposes of retribution and deterrence, may properly and lawfully be made by a junior minister in the Home Department. I also agree with, and adopt, the reasoning which leads Staughton LJ to this conclusion, and I therefore need say no more about this subject.

General principles of decision-making

Before expressing my views about the remaining issues, I think it helpful to set out shortly the general principles of law which are applicable to the Secretary of State's decision-making process. The Secretary of State may only exercise his power under s 61(1) of the 1967 Act to release on licence a prisoner serving a life sentence if (a) the Parole Board has recommended he should do so and (b) he has consulted with the Lord Chief Justice and the trial judge if available. Subject to these constraints, the wording of the section gives the Secretary of State an unfettered discretion in deciding whether to release any particular prisoner and, if so, when.

However, it is a commonplace that a decision-maker who is given an apparently unfettered discretion must still exercise his power within the limits imposed by the law. The principles within which the Secretary of State must operate, which in my view are relevant to these appeals, are as follows. (1) He must not reach a decision which is irrational, i e 'so outrageous in its defiance of logic or of accepted moral standards that no sensible person who had applied his mind to the question to be decided could have arrived at it': see Lord Diplock in *Council of Civil Service Unions v Minister for the Civil Service* [1984] 3 All ER 935 at 951, [1985] AC 374 at 410. (2) If a decision-maker establishes a procedure or practice for the making of decisions which gives advantages to those affected by them, he creates a legitimate expectation that he will follow that procedure or practice in relation to any particular case, unless or until he gives notice of intention to change the procedure and an opportunity for those affected to make representations: see again Lord Diplock in *Council of Civil Service Unions v Minister for the Civil Service* [1984] 3 All ER 935 at 949, [1985] AC 374 at 408. (3) A decision-maker is required to adopt a procedure for decision-making which is fair in all the circumstances. In a case very different on its facts, *R v Commission for Racial Equality, ex p Hillingdon London BC* [1982] AC 779 at 787, Lord Diplock said:

'Where an Act of Parliament confers upon an administrative body functions which involve its making decisions which affect to their detriment the rights *a* of other persons or curtail their liberty to do as they please, there is a presumption that Parliament intended that the administrative body should act fairly towards those persons who will be affected by their decision.'

What is a fair procedure in relation to any particular decision depends upon all the circumstances, including the subject matter of the decision, its importance to the person particularly affected and the interests of the public in general.

b That this principle applies even to a person convicted of murder and sentenced to life imprisonment seems to me to emerge clearly from the decision in this court in *R v Hull Prison Board of Visitors, ex p St Germain* [1979] 1 All ER 701, [1979] QB 425, referred to by Lord Wilberforce in *Raymond v Honey* [1982] 1 All ER 756 at 759, [1983] 1 AC 1 at 10 when he said:

c
'. . . under English law, a convicted prisoner, in spite of his imprisonment, retains all civil rights which are not taken away expressly or by necessary implication.'

The judgment of Shaw LJ in *Ex p St Germain* was quoted with approval by Lord *d* Bridge of Harwich in *Leech v Parkhurst Prison Deputy Governor* [1988] 1 All ER 485 at 490, [1988] AC 533 at 554.

I remind myself, however, that in seeking to apply these principles we must not overstep them. Thus we must not, if we think that some other procedure than that adopted by the Secretary of State would be better or fairer, therefore conclude that the procedure he did adopt is necessarily unfair. Moreover, it is not *e* our function to form a view in relation to any one of these appellants of the proper period for him to serve for the purposes of retribution and deterrence, and then if we disagree with the Secretary of State's tariff say that the Secretary of State was wrong and quash his decision. We could only do so if in our view he was so clearly and outrageously wrong that his decision could properly be said to be irrational.

f With these general observations I now turn to consider the remaining issues.

Is the Secretary of State required by law to adopt the judicial view of the tariff?

I start by observing that, if the Lord Chief Justice does not agree with the view *g* expressed by the trial judge as to the proper period to be served for retribution and deterrence, there are two judicial views. Nevertheless, it has not been argued that the Secretary of State's decision on the tariff could properly be challenged if he adopted the opinion of the Lord Chief Justice where this differed from that of the trial judge. Where there is such a difference, therefore, 'the judicial view' means that expressed by the Lord Chief Justice.

h The argument for the appellants on this issue, expressed somewhat differently by their respective counsel, can be summarised as follows. Since November 1983 the Secretary of State has sought the advice of the Lord Chief Justice and the trial judge on the period necessary for retribution and deterrence. The judges are, by their training and experience, the persons best equipped to form an opinion on this issue. Neither the Secretary of State, nor his minister of state, nor any of their *j* officials, have the judges' unique expertise in this respect. Therefore it must necessarily be irrational, ie 'Wednesbury unreasonable' (see *Associated Provincial Picture Houses Ltd v Wednesbury Corp* [1947] 2 All ER 680, [1948] 1 KB 223), for the Secretary of State to set a tariff period longer than that recommended by the judiciary.

The argument is supported by reference to the decision of the Divisional Court in *Ex p Handscomb* (1987) 86 Cr App R 59. In that case the court was considering *a* applications for judicial review by four prisoners serving sentences of imprisonment for life imposed in the discretion of the trial judges for offences other than murder (manslaughter by reason of diminished responsibility, false imprisonment of and sexual offences with boys, and arson by two of the appellants). There were two main issues before the court. The first arose out of the practice announced in Mr Brittan's statement of 30 November 1983 of seeking the views of the judiciary *b* on the tariff for a prisoner when he had been detained in custody for about three years. The court decided that the adoption by the Secretary of State of this general policy, which had the result that the judicial views were not sought at the earliest opportunity after conviction and sentence, was unlawful. As I have said, this decision was accepted by the then Secretary of State, Mr Douglas Hurd, in his *c* statement of 23 July 1987. This issue does not arise in the present case.

The second issue in *Ex p Handscomb* is, however, directly relevant to our decision. All four applicants in that case sought a declaration that the Secretary of State was not entitled to set a date for the first review of his case on the basis of the requirements of retribution and deterrence. The court rejected this proposition, but went on to consider whether the Secretary of State could *d* justifiably depart from the judicial view on tariff. As to this, Watkins LJ (in a judgment with which the other members of the court agreed) said (86 Cr App R 59 at 82):

'If, as I am in no doubt, the inference must be from Mrs. Murray's affidavit that the Home Secretary is not obliged to accept the judicial view of tariff *e* and may, as I have also said, impose his own view as to this, a prima facie case of irrationality and *Wednesbury* unreasonableness must surely arise. If the Home Secretary is not to be guided by the judges on retribution and deterrence, where else can he look for guidance? Mr. Atkinson's letter suggests that the initial judicial view is the only view on tariff which he thinks is relied upon for fixing the date of the first review.' *f*

He added, in relation to Mr Handscomb (at 83):

'According to present arrangements, he will not be considered by anyone outside the prison service or the Home Office until 1991. So an interval of 10 years will have gone by without his situation being looked at by the local review committee or the parole board. That fact standing alone might be *g* regarded as a not unjust consequence of the Home Secretary's policy. But it must stand alongside other factors, the principal one of which is that the date of his first review should, in my view, relate strictly to the judicial view of the tariff. If it does not—and Mrs. Murray states quite clearly that it does not—then I would regard the Home Secretary as having acted contrary to his *h* policy. The implication of it relating strictly to tariff involves an assumption that the tariff advised was 17 years' detention as punishment for retribution and deterrence. In a case of manslaughter with diminished responsibility, this is something I am not prepared to assume. Handscomb has served the equivalent of a 15-year notional determinate sentence now, a sentence which, as I have already pointed out, is well in excess of the maximum fixed-term *j* sentence passed for this offence in recent years. I do not see how relief can be denied to Handscomb in consequence of this as well as other declaratory relief which will be later formulated.'

In a later decision of the Divisional Court, *R v Secretary of State for the Home Dept, ex p Benson* (1988) Independent, 16 November, Lloyd LJ said:

'As for the *Handscomb* case, the ratio decidendi was that a sentence of 27 years was so far beyond anything which the judiciary could have recommended as the appropriate tariff that the decision to postpone the first review until 1991 was one which no reasonable Secretary of State could have reached. The case does not decide that the Secretary of State is obliged to accept the judicial review on tariff; if it did so decide, I would respectfully disagree.'

Nolan J expressed no view on this, but said:

'It must be remembered, however, that *Handscomb* was principally concerned with the fixing of the date at which the period of the detention should be reviewed . . .'

It seems, however, that Lloyd LJ had not seen the relevant declaration granted by the court in *Ex p Handscomb*, which was:

'In respect of all the applicants, a declaration that in carrying out his announced policy under and in relation to section 61(1) of the Criminal Justice Act 1967 in respect of persons serving sentences of life imprisonment imposed in the discretion of the trial judge, the Secretary of State for the Home Department, in determining for how long such a person ought to be detained for punitive purposes, should fix the date of the first review by the Local Review Committee and the Parole Board strictly in accordance with a period of detention (that is to say, the notional determinate sentence less one-third remission) recommended by the judiciary as necessary to meet the requirements of retribution and deterrence.'

There was no appeal against the decision in *Ex p Handscomb*, so the Secretary of State was bound by this declaration, at least in relation to prisoners serving discretionary life sentences. In his statement on 23 July 1987 Mr Douglas Hurd therefore announced that for prisoners serving discretionary life sentences:

'The date of the first formal review by the Parole Board machinery will then be fixed in accordance with the judicial view on the requirements of retribution and deterrence . . .'

He also said that for prisoners serving mandatory life sentences for murder:

'I shall continue to take into account the view of the judiciary on the requirements of retribution and deterrence in such cases as a factor amongst others (including the need to maintain public confidence in the system of justice) to be weighed in the balance in setting the first review date.'

Counsel for the appellants argue that the Secretary of State is not entitled to make this distinction. If he is bound by the judicial view in relation to the date of the first review for prisoners serving discretionary life sentences, he is also so bound in relation to those serving mandatory life sentences.

In his judgment in the Divisional Court in the present case, Mann LJ giving the judgment of the court rejected this argument:

'In our judgment there is an important distinction to be drawn between discretionary and mandatory life sentences. In the case of the discretionary sentence there is always a notional equivalent determinate sentence which could be imposed in accord with established sentencing practice but for the current mental state of the defendant which makes him a danger to the public. There is truly a tariff. As Mr Secretary Hurd pointed out in his

written answer, there is no equivalent determinate sentence for murder. So
soon as that is appreciated the force of the suggested analogy falls away. Its *a*
collapse does no violence to the decision in *Handscomb*. That was a case
concerning discretionary life sentences and the remarks in the case must be
read in that context. Watkins LJ said (86 Cr App R 59 at 82): "If, as I am in
no doubt, the inference must be from Mrs. Murray's affidavit that the Home
Secretary is not obliged to accept the judicial view of tariff and may, as I have
also said, impose his own view as to this, a prima facie case of irrationality *b*
and *Wednesbury* unreasonableness must surely arise. If the Home Secretary is
not to be guided by the judges on retribution and deterrence, where else can
he look for guidance?" We do not read that passage with its use of "prima
facie" as requiring that the Secretary of State must adopt the judicial view in
all cases. What was decided in regard to the applicant Handscomb was that, *c*
where the first review date predicated an equivalent determinate sentence
well in excess of that which could have been imposed under established
sentencing practice, there was impugnable unreasonableness. We do not
think that the decision bears any wider interpretation, and that it does not
was also the view of Lloyd LJ in *R v Secretary of State for the Home Dept, ex p
Benson.'*   *d*

For my part, I think it is clear that the court in *Ex p Handscomb* did decide what
Mr Douglas Hurd understood it decided, namely that, in setting the tariff for
prisoners serving discretionary life sentences, the Secretary of State is obliged to
adopt the judicial view.

If we were bound by the decision in *Ex p Handscomb*, I would see force in the *e*
argument that this principle should apply equally to mandatory life sentences.
Of course, when sentencing for murder, a judge does not have any established
guidelines to appropriate ranges of determinate sentences for similar offences.
Since the sentence is mandatory, there is no such tariff (using the word in its true
sense). But when the judge, and the Lord Chief Justice, express their views on the
period a particular prisoner should serve for the purposes of retribution and *f*
deterrence, they are involved in part of the same consideration as they would be
when deciding a proper determinate sentence for a serious offence other than
murder. I am therefore not convinced that the distinction is a sufficient basis for
concluding that the Secretary of State is bound by the judicial view for one class
of case but not for the other.

If, as Lloyd LJ suggested in *Ex p Benson*, the decision in *Ex p Handscomb* had *g*
been that detention for a period equivalent to a determinate sentence of 27 years
exceeded by such a wide margin any determinate sentence passed in recent years
for the offence of manslaughter by reason of diminished responsibility, and was
thus in the absence of reasons irrational, I would not disagree. But the proposition
that it was not lawful for the Secretary of State to adopt a tariff which differed
from that of the judges was in my opinion wrong. The ultimate decision on the *h*
period a life sentence prisoner should serve for the purposes of retribution and
deterrence is that of the Secretary of State. In making his decision, he seeks the
advice of the judiciary, but, if he has good reason for doing so, he is, as a matter
of law, entitled to set a tariff period different from that recommended by the
judges. I would therefore hold that in this respect *Ex p Handscomb* was wrongly *j*
decided.

Nevertheless, since Mr Hurd's July 1987 statement the Secretary of State has,
for discretionary life sentence prisoners, adopted a policy of accepting the judicial
view on tariff. He has probably thus created a legitimate expectation that he will
continue to apply this policy. Since the same policy is now given statutory

expression in s 34 of the Criminal Justice Act 1991, which will come into force
a on 1 October 1992, he will presumably not seek to depart from this policy in the
meantime.

Procedural fairness

It is convenient to consider the third and fourth issues—has the prisoner the
right to make representations before the Secretary of State sets the date for the
b first review, and has he a right to be told the judicial view of his tariff ?—together.
As has frequently been said, the right to be heard or to make representations is
worth little unless the person making the representations knows, at least in
general terms, the case he has to meet: see, for example, Lord Denning in *Kanda
v Government of Malaya* [1962] AC 322 at 337.

c Mr Pannick, for the Secretary of State, reminds us that a prisoner serving a
sentence of life imprisonment has no right to be released on licence; he has at best
a hope that the Secretary of State will release him in the exercise of his discretion
under s 61(1). Moreover, in the case of a prisoner who has been released on licence
under s 61, if his licence is revoked he is entitled under s 62(3) to make
representatons in writing with respect to his recall and to be informed of the
d reasons for it. No such rights are provided by s 61. Thus Parliament clearly did
not intend that a life sentence prisoner should have such rights in relation to the
consideration of his release on licence.

The answer to this, at least in part, is that, over the years since the 1967 Act
came into force, the relatively elaborate procedure to which I have referred has
been created. A life prisoner cannot be certain that he ever will be released on
e licence, but he can be certain that he will be considered for release, at latest
17 years after his sentence and periodically thereafter. Moreover, he is told that
the date of the first review is related to the length of time the Secretary of State
decides he must serve for retribution and deterrence, and that the judicial view as
to this period is a factor taken into account in making the decision.

f The classic origin of the requirement to hear a party alleged to be in default
before reaching a decision is in *Cooper v Wandsworth Board of Works* (1863) 14
CBNS 180, 143 ER 414. The board demolished a partly built house without
giving any opportunity to the builder to be heard in opposition to the demolition.
Willes J said (14 CBNS 180 at 190, 143 ER 414 at 418):

g 'I apprehend that a tribunal which is by law invested with power to affect
the property of one of Her Majesty's subjects, is bound to give such subject
an opportunity of being heard before it proceeds: and that that rule is of
universal application, and founded upon the plainest principles of justice.'

Byles J said (14 CBNS 180 at 194, 143 ER 414 at 420):

h '. . . a long course of decisions . . . establish, that, although there are no
positive words in a statute requiring that the party shall be heard, yet the
justice of the common law will supply the omission of the legislature.'

In *Russell v Duke of Norfolk* [1949] 1 All ER 109 at 118 Tucker LJ said:

j 'There are, in my view, no words which are of universal application to
every kind of inquiry and every kind of domestic tribunal. The requirements
of natural justice must depend on the circumstances of the case, the nature
of the inquiry, the rules under which the tribunal is acting, the subject-
matter that is being dealt with, and so forth. Accordingly, I do not derive
much assistance from the definitions of natural justice which have been from
time to time used, but, whatever standard is adopted, one essential is that the

person concerned should have a reasonable opportunity of presenting his case.'

In *Wiseman v Borneman* [1969] 3 All ER 275 at 277, [1971] AC 297 at 308 Lord Reid said:

'For a long time the courts have, without objection from Parliament, supplemented procedure laid down in legislation where they have found that to be necessary for this purpose. But before this unusual kind of power is exercised it must be clear that the statutory procedure is insufficient to achieve justice and that to require additional steps would not frustrate the apparent purpose of the legislation.'

Lord Guest said ([1969] 3 All ER 275 at 279, [1971] AC 297 at 310):

'It is reasonably clear on the authorities that where a statutory tribunal has been set up to decide final questions affecting parties' rights and duties, if the statute is silent on the question, the courts will imply into the statutory provision a rule that the principles of natural justice should be applied. This implication will be made on the basis that Parliament is not to be presumed to take away parties' rights without giving them an opportunity of being heard in their interest. In other words, Parliament is not to be presumed to act unfairly. The dictum of BYLES, J., in *Cooper* v. *Wandsworth Board of Works* ((1863) 14 CBNS 180 at 194, 143 ER 414 at 420) is clear to this effect and has been followed in many subsequent cases.'

On the application of the duty on a decision-maker to adopt a fair procedure, Lord Denning MR said in *R v Gaming Board for GB, ex p Benaim* [1970] 2 All ER 528 at 533, [1970] 2 QB 417 at 430:

'It is not possible to lay down rigid rules as to when the principles of natural justice are to apply; nor as to their scope and extent. Everything depends on the subject-matter . . .'

More recently, in *Lloyd v McMahon* [1987] 1 All ER 1118 at 1161, [1987] AC 625 at 702–703 Lord Bridge of Harwich said:

'My Lords, the so-called rules of natural justice are not engraved on tablets of stone. To use the phrase which better expresses the underlying concept, what the requirements of fairness demand when any body, domestic, administrative or judicial, has to make a decision which will affect the rights of individuals depends on the character of the decision-making body, the kind of decision it has to make and the statutory or other framework in which it operates. In particular, it is well established that when a statute has conferred on any body the power to make decisions affecting individuals, the courts will not only require the procedure prescribed by the statute to be followed, but will readily imply so much and no more to be introduced by way of additional procedural safeguards as will ensure the attainment of fairness.'

In *Payne v Lord Harris of Greenwich* [1981] 2 All ER 842, [1981] 1 WLR 754 this court decided that, when a prisoner serving a mandatory life sentence for murder had not been recommended for release by the local review committee or the Parole Board, before his next review he was not entitled to be told the reasons for the board's decision. The members of the court (Lord Denning MR, Shaw and Brightman LJJ) all took the view that the Criminal Justice Act 1967 and the Local

Review Committee Rules 1967, SI 1967/1462, which governed the work of that
a body, imposed no obligation to give such reasons, that in reaching their decision
on whether to recommend release the Parole Board and the local review
committee were under a duty to act fairly, but that the scope of that duty did not
include a requirement to give reasons for their recommendation. In reaching that
last conclusion, however, the members of the court differed in their own
reasoning, though all took the view that the interests of society as a whole—
b public policy—outweighed the prisoner's interest in being given reasons.

As I have said, since the decision in *Payne v Lord Harris of Greenwich* the present
procedure by which the Secretary of State decides whether and when to release a
prisoner serving a life sentence has been created. Mr Brittan's statement of
November 1983 made clear the division of the decision-making process into two
c parts, the 'tariff' period to meet the purposes of retribution and deterrence which
the Secretary of State decides on the advice of the judges, a review towards the
end of that period by the local review committee and after the end of the tariff
period a possible further period if the Secretary of State on the advice of the local
review committee and the Parole Board decides that the prisoner's continued
detention is necessary because of the danger he might pose if released, and to
d maintain public confidence in the system. In *Payne v Lord Harris of Greenwich* the
court was concerned with the process of making the second decision (though the
division into the two periods of detention was not then clear). We are concerned
with the Secretary of State's decision as to the first period, the 'tariff'. Nothing I
say hereafter is intended to relate to the second decision.

There are no statutory rules governing the procedure for deciding a prisoner's
e tariff. In my view, we should, to adapt Lord Bridge's phrase, imply some
additional procedural safeguards to ensure what I believe fairness in the making
of this decision requires.

The decision as to the length of the prisoner's tariff period is obviously of great
importance to him. It sets the earliest date at which he can hope to regain his
freedom. On the other hand, it would be wrong to imply any procedure which
f might improperly fetter the Secretary of State in reaching his decision.

Taking both these factors into account, I conclude that a prisoner serving a
mandatory life sentence should be given the opportunity to make representations
in writing to the Secretary of State about the length of his tariff period before it is
set. I also conclude that, to enable him to make such representations, he should
g be given such relevant information as he does not already have. However, the
scope of such information is limited. The prisoner has been at his own trial and
he already knows, or has had access to, all the evidence and all that was said. He
has heard his counsel, under the procedure now generally adopted, making
submissions to the judge after his conviction about the recommendation the
judge will make as to the tariff period. Thus the only relevant facts he does not
h know are what period the judiciary have recommended as the tariff, and what
further comments the judges have made which will affect the Secretary of State's
decision on the tariff. Such comments would include, for example, any opinions
that the trial judge has expressed, in a case where there was more than one
defendant, as to the respective parts each played and thus as to the culpability of
each for the offence. In my view, the prisoner should be given this information
j before he writes any representation he may wish to make.

The addition to the present procedure of a requirement that the prisoner be
given this information, and thereafter be entitled to make written representations
before his tariff is set, would in my opinion satisfy Lord Reid's test in *Wiseman v
Borneman* [1969] 3 All ER 275, [1971] AC 297. The present procedure is in my

opinion insufficient in these respects to achieve justice, and there is nothing in what I propose which would frustrate the apparent purpose of the legislation.   *a*

Until now the judiciary have expressed their views about the tariff period, tacitly if not expressly, in confidence. However, I do not regard this problem as insuperable. I suspect that the confidentiality is largely that of the Secretary of State, and am confident that in acceptance of our decision he will not seek to maintain a claim to such confidentiality. For the future, the judges can be asked to express their views on the basis that their recommendations (in effect that of   *b* the Lord Chief Justice) will be communicated to the prisoner. We must not, of course, seek to guess how individual judges will respond. A judge, however, perhaps more than any other person, is accustomed to making and announcing his decisions in public. I note also that of the judges who expressed opinions to the House of Lords Select Committee on Murder and Life Imprisonment about   *c* this issue a majority favoured immediate disclosure of the judges' recommendation as to the tariff. If, therefore, prisoners are in future to be told the judicial recommendation as to the tariff period, many judges may think it appropriate to announce their own recommendations publicly in court when passing sentence.

For those prisoners like the present appellants currently serving life sentences, I appreciate that the fact that the judicial recommendation was made in confidence   *d* presents a practical problem. The Secretary of State will have to consider what steps to take to overcome it. Presumably he will ask the Lord Chief Justice (and trial judges where possible) if they object to their recommendations as to the tariff period and other material expressions of view now being revealed to the prisoner.

The duty to give reasons   *e*

The precise question here under consideration is: if the Secretary of State does not adopt the judicial view of the tariff, is he obliged to give reasons for departing from it? I agree with Mr Sedley, for Messrs Doody and Pierson, that the decision of this court in *Payne v Lord Harris of Greenwich* [1981] 2 All ER 842, [1981] 1 WLR 754 does not bind us to conclude that the Secretary of State is not obliged to   *f* give reasons in this respect. As I have already made clear, the issue in that case concerned the second decision which the Secretary of State has to make, whether to release the prisoner at the end of his tariff period or to detain him in custody. The factors relevant to the giving of reasons by the Parole Board or a local review committee are not the same as those relevant to the Secretary of State's giving reasons for not accepting the judicial view of the tariff.   *g*

The leading authority on this subject is now *R v Civil Service Appeal Board, ex p Cunningham* [1991] 4 All ER 310, a decision of this court. A prison officer who had been dismissed from the prison service appealed against his dismissal to the Civil Service Appeal Board, which held that his dismissal was unfair. The board assessed his compensation at a substantially lower figure than he would have been awarded by an industrial tribunal had he been able in law to appeal to such a   *h* tribunal. The board refused to give reasons for its award. This court held that the board was required to give reasons for the way in which it had reached its award, and that in the absence of such reasons its award was prima facie irrational. The applicant was therefore entitled to a judicial review of the award.

In his judgment, Lord Donaldson MR considered some of the authorities on the requirement that a decision-making body should give reasons for its decision,   *j* including a decision of the High Court of Australia in *Public Service Board of New South Wales v Osmond* (1986) 159 CLR 656. He concluded that there was neither a general rule of the common law nor a principle of natural justice that a public law authority should always or even usually give reasons for its decisions. He said, however (at 316):

a
'In fairness to the board it must be emphasised that it is not being unco-operative. It has been advised, mistakenly as I think, that to attempt any justification of a particular award, however surprising that award might be, would be to concede the right of every claimant to reasons. As I have sought to show, this is not so. The principles of public law will require that those affected by decisions are given the reasons for those decisions in some cases,
b
but not in others. A classic example of the latter category is a decision not to appoint or not to promote an employee or office holder or to fail an examinee. But, once the public law court has concluded that there is an arguable case that the decision is unlawful, the position is transformed. The applicant may still not be entitled to reasons, but the court is.'

c
McCowan LJ said (at 322):

'As Mr Pannick says, it cries out for some explanation from the board. As I would put it, not only is justice not seen to have been done but there is no way, in the absence of reasons from the board, in which it can be judged whether in fact it has been done. I find that a thoroughly unsatisfactory situation, in which this court should hold, if it properly can do so, that the
d
board ought to give reasons for its recommendation.'

Leggatt LJ said (at 326):

'Since the board has elected as a matter of practice not to give reasons, and has given none to Mr Cunningham, it has been bound by its own logic not to attempt to justify for the benefit of the court the figure awarded. In default
e
of explanation Mr Cunningham's award was so far below what, by analogy with the award of an industrial tribunal, he was entitled to expect as in my judgment to compel the inference that the assessment was irrational, if not perverse. Because there was no general duty to give reasons, the absence of reasons does not by itself entitle the court to hold that the award was not
f
supportable. But the unexplained meagreness of the award does compel that inference. As Lord Keith said in *Lonrho plc v Secretary of State for Trade and Industry* [1989] 2 All ER 609 at 620, [1989] 1 WLR 525 at 539: "The only significance of the absence of reasons is that if all other known facts and circumstances appear to point overwhelmingly in favour of a different decision, the decision-maker who has given no reasons cannot complain if
g
the court draws the inference that he had no rational reason for his decision."'

I would apply that decision and those dicta, and in particular the passage from the judgment of Leggatt LJ, in the present case. In my judgment the Secretary of State, if he sets a tariff period which exceeds that recommended by the judiciary, is not under an absolute obligation to give reasons for departing from the judicial
h
view. Nevertheless, if the disparity between the two periods is considerable and he gives no reasons, it may well be that his decision will be open to challenge by way of judicial review as being irrational. That in my view is the appropriate sanction.

Mr Pegg's separate point
j
Mr Pegg was convicted on 25 March 1985 before Caulfield J and a jury of the murder of one Peter Goddard by stabbing him with a knife. The prosecution case was that the murder was premeditated, the evidence of the premeditation being, as the prosecutuion suggested, that Mr Pegg had returned to his home to fetch the knife before setting out to meet Goddard. The defence was self-defence. Mr Pegg denied that he had returned to his home to fetch the knife, and alleged that he

had seized it from Goddard during the struggle between them. There were two
bases on which he could have been convicted, either that the jury accepted that *a*
he had fetched the knife from his home or, alternatively, that he had obtained
the knife during the struggle but that they were satisfied that the essentials of
self-defence were not made out.

After the Secretary of State, having received judicial advice, had set the date for
the first review of Mr Pegg's sentence in August 1993, and thus set his tariff, in
January 1989 Mr Pegg submitted a petition to the Secretary of State. The petition *b*
refers to nine separate matters which, it is alleged, tend to establish that the attack
on Goddard was not premeditated. Mr Pegg believes that his tariff may have been
set on the basis that the attack was premeditated, and thus that the tariff period
should be reduced. He complains that the Secretary of State has not taken his
petition properly into account. *c*

According to an affidavit sworn on behalf of the Secretary of State by Mr
Anthony David Burgess on 5 April 1990, the Secretary of State did consider the
points raised in the affidavit and 'concluded that the submissions raised in it were
not of sufficient substance to justify referring the same to the judiciary or altering
the first review date'. I should say that Mr Pegg had earlier appealed to the Court
of Appeal, Criminal Division, but his appeal against his conviction had been *d*
dismissed. In my view, a number of the points raised in his petition are matters
which could have been raised at the appeal. As to the other matters, in my view
the Secretary of State's decision not to alter the review date having considered the
petition was one which was entirely a matter for the exercise of his discretion. I
therefore cannot find that in this respect the procedure adopted by the Secretary
of State was challengeable in any way. *e*

Conclusion

I conclude that the court should grant declarations in the following terms. (1)
The Secretary of State is required to afford to a prisoner serving a mandatory life
sentence the opportunity to submit in writing representations as to the period he *f*
should serve for the purposes of retribution and deterrence before the Secretary
of State sets the date of the first review of the prisoner's sentence. (2) Before giving
the prisoner the opportunity to make such representations, the Secretary of State
is required to inform him of the period recommended by the judiciary as the
period he should serve for the purposes of retribution and deterrence, and of any
other opinion expressed by the judiciary which is relevant to the Secretary of *g*
State's decision as to the appropriate period to be served for these purposes.

It follows that the decisions made by the Secretary of State as to the length of
the tariff for each of these appellants should be quashed, and the decisions
reconsidered in accordance with the procedure to which I have referred.

To that extent I would allow these appeals. *h*

STAUGHTON LJ.

(1) *Irrationality*

It is said for the appellants that the decisions of Home Office ministers fixing *i*
their tariff periods were irrational, in public law terms, because they must have
exceeded those recommended by the trial judge and the Lord Chief Justice.

When capital punishment for murder was abolished by s 1 of the Murder
(Abolition of Death Penalty) Act 1965, it was provided (by sub-s (2)) that the court
may—

'declare the period which it recommends to the Secretary of State as the *a* minimum period which in its view should elapse before the Secretary of State orders the release of that person on licence . . .'

There were no recommendations by the judges under that section in the cases with which we are now concerned. Evidently that power was intended to act as a restraint on undue leniency by the Secretary of State. It provided for a minimum but no maximum. By contrast the present cases arise because Home Office *b* ministers are thought to have increased the periods recommended by the judiciary, in a process of consultation which is extra-statutory. It is not excessive leniency which is sought to be restrained now, but punishment which exceeds the judicial view of what is appropriate.

The statutory power to recommend a minimum period might, in practice, have been used to create a tariff among the judges for all murders, so that the *c* recommended minimum came to be regarded as the appropriate period of detention, subject only to the question whether the prisoner was a danger to the public when it expired. But that did not happen. It was said in *R v Flemming* [1973] 2 All ER 401 at 403 that no recommendation under the Act should be for less than 12 years. Possibly for that reason, and certainly for others, minimum recommendations came to be made in only a small proportion of cases. We were *d* told that in 1988, when life sentences for murder were passed in 150 cases, only 10 minimum recommendations were made.

The 1965 Act also contained, in s 2, a provision that no person convicted of murder should be released on licence unless the Secretary of State had prior to such release consulted the Lord Chief Justice, together with the trial judge if *e* available. That section was repealed and replaced by s 61(1) of the Criminal Justice Act 1967, which applied to all life prisoners and not merely those convicted of murder.

There is in my opinion nothing whatever in s 61(1) to suggest that the Secretary of State is bound by the advice of the Lord Chief Justice or the trial judge. On the contrary, it remains for him to decide. To adapt what was said by Lloyd LJ in *R v* *f* *Secretary of State for the Home Dept, ex p Benson* (1988) Independent, 16 November, the duty is to consult, not to obey.

The question is whether that has changed since the statement in the House of Commons of Mr Leon Brittan QC as Home Secretary in 1983. This said that he would look to the judiciary, as in the past, for advice on the time to be served to satisfy the requirements of retribution and deterrence. After he had done that, he *g* would decide the date of the first reference of the case to a local review committee.

The minimum period which a prisoner can be expected to serve in order to satisfy the requirements of retribution and deterrence has become known as the tariff period. Presently it is fixed by a Home Office minister after consultation with the judiciary. It can be deduced by the prisoner, if his local review committee *h* date is less than 17 years after he was first detained, by adding 3 years to the period that he will have served at that date. In other cases the prisoner will know only that it is 20 years or more, although if he asks and if it is no more than 20 years he will, as I understand it, be given that information.

At this point I must consider what is meant by 'tariff' in this context. There has been a tariff among the judges since the latter part of the nineteenth century. *j* Its object was to reduce disparity in sentences of imprisonment, and to remove the difficulty which judges faced when Parliament had told them no more than the maximum sentence for a particular crime: see Professor Sir Rupert Cross's *Child & Co* lecture in 1980, *Reflections on the English Sentencing System*. The judges' tariff is now publicly available, from the law reports (including in particular guideline cases on sentencing for particular crimes) and the *Encyclopaedia of Current Sentencing Practice*. But it does not follow that one can predict with

complete accuracy the sentence that a judge will pass in a given case. At most the
tariff information will provde a range or bracket. Dr Thomas in *Principles of*
Sentencing (2nd edn, 1979) p 9 writes:

> '. . . the application of tariff principles requires the sentencer to find the
> sentence which most accurately reflects the offender's culpability, a process
> which involves relating the gravity of the offence to the established pattern
> of sentences for offences of that kind, and then making allowance for such
> mitigating factors as may be present which tend to reduce the offender's
> culpability.'

That is, I think, the task which the Home Secretary expects judges to perform
when he asks for their advice on the requirements of retribution and deterrence,
and the task which the judges do perform.

Naturally the judges' tariff is not writ in stone; it may and does change over
time, so that sentences passed in 1900 are of little or no value in ascertaining the
tariff in 1992.

When a discretionary life sentence is passed, for an offence other than murder
because of the danger to the public from the convicted person, there is no undue
difficulty in ascertaining the determinate sentence which would otherwise be
appropriate according to the judges' tariff. The practice has been for the judge to
deduct a period for remission which might be earned, and to advise the Home
Secretary that what remains is the requirement of retribution and deterrence. In
the nature of things, experienced judges are those best qualified to perform this
task. But I would suppose that the Home Office has at least some information as
to the judges' tariff, and probably a great deal. The inhabitants of prisons may
also be expected to know it.

For the offence of murder a life sentence is mandatory. Consequently there are
no cases in our books which show what the appropriate determinate sentence is
specifically for that offence. In some cases the judge can look at sentences for
manslaughter, and make an appropriate adjustment. In others he will have
virtually no guidance, beyond looking at the relatively few determinate sentences
for attempted murder and considering what adjustment should be made for the
fact that death ensued. This lack of an established pattern has been recognised.
Thus in *R v Secretary of State for the Home Dept, ex p Handscomb* (1987) 86 Cr App
R 59 at 79 Watkins LJ said: 'There are no precedents or guidelines to assist the
judge in forming that view.'

In the 1987 statement Mr Douglas Hurd said (120 HC Official Report (6th
series) written answers col 349):

> 'In cases of prisoners serving life sentences for murder, where the sentence
> is not at the discretion of the court, the question of a notional equivalent
> determinate sentence does not arise.'

And in the present case Mann LJ said in the Divisional Court:

> '. . . we cannot part from the argument without expressing our belief that
> some trial judges would be troubled if they were told that their view,
> unguided as it is by any established practice and expressed in confidence, was
> to be determinate of the period to be served by a prisoner.'

Thus far I have been careful to refer to 'the judges' tariff', for such it is. The
Home Secretary, in fixing the period which he regards as necessary to meet the
requirements of retribution and deterrence, not infrequently exceeds the judicial
view. He is often said to be fixing a 'tariff' period; and there is no harm in using
that expression provided that one realises that it is the Home Secretary's tariff, not

the judges' tariff. But is it lawful for the Home Secretary to have a different tariff
a from the judges?

In my judgment it is lawful. Section 61(1) makes it clear that the decision as to
release on licence is for the Home Secretary, although he is obliged to consult the
judiciary. There was nothing in the 1983 statement to alter that; as Lloyd LJ put
it in *Benson's* case, Mr Brittan said that he would look to the judges for advice, not
orders. Nor was there any change so far as mandatory life sentences were
b concerned in the 1987 statement. I shall consider later what was then said by Mr
Hurd about discretionary life sentences. *Findlay v Secretary of State for the Home
Dept* [1984] 3 All ER 801, [1985] AC 318 accepts, as it seems to me, that it is
legitimate for the Home Secretary to form his own view. Lord Scarman there
said, after discussing the constitution of the Parole Board ([1984] 3 All ER 801 at
c 826, [1985] AC 318 at 333):

> 'The emphasis is on the need for the board to include among its members
> persons with the skills and experience required to assess the risk of early
> release. But the Secretary of State has clearly to consider other aspects of the
> early release of a prisoner serving a sentence of imprisonment. Deterrence,
> retribution and public confidence in the system are factors of importance.
d > The Parole Board, through its judicial and other members, can offer advice
> on these aspects of the question. But neither the board nor the judiciary can
> be as close, or as sensitive, to public opinion as a minister responsible to
> Parliament and to the electorate. He has to judge the public acceptability of
> early release and to determine the policies needed to maintain public
e > confidence in the system of criminal justice. This must be why Parliament
> saw as necessary the duality of the parole system: without the advice and
> recommendation of a body capable of assessing the risk of early release the
> Secretary of State was not to act; but, having received such advice and
> recommendation, he was to authorise early release only if he himself was
> satisfied that it was in the public interest that he should.'

f
That brings me to the decision in the *Handscomb* case. Watkins LJ asked where
else the Home Secretary could look for guidance as to retribution and deterrence,
if not to the judges (see (1987) 86 Cr App R 59 at 82). And he expressed the view
that, in discretionary life sentence cases, the period fixed by the Home Secretary
should 'relate strictly to the judicial view of the tariff' (at 83). I am afraid that I
g cannot accept the reasoning which has led subsequent Divisional Courts to limit
the ambit of that decision (*Benson's* case, the Divisional Court in the present case
and *R v Secretary of State for the Home Dept, ex p Walsh* (1991) Independent, 17
December). After all, there was in *Handscomb's* case a declaration that—

> 'the Secretary of State for the Home Department, in determining for how
h > long . . . a person ought to be detained for punitive purposes, should fix the
> date of the first review by the Local Review Committee and the Parole Board
> strictly in accordance with a period of detention . . . recommended by the
> judiciary as necessary to meet the requirements of retribution and deterrence.'

Since there was no appeal, in my opinion the Home Secretary was bound to
change his policy for discretionary life sentence cases as he did in 1987.
j However, I am bound to say that in my judgment *Handscomb's* case was
wrongly decided on that issue. The Home Secretary is in my opinion entitled and
bound to reach his own tariff decision, after having regard both to the judges'
tariff and to the factors such as public confidence in the administration of justice
which Lord Scarman mentioned. I have already accepted that the judges are the
best persons to say what the judges' tariff is, as Watkins LJ implied, at any rate in

discretionary life sentence cases. But the Home Secretary is, for good reason, entrusted with the final decision. Judges have a lively perception of public *a* opinion on sentences; from time to time they receive letters from disgruntled members of the public, and they read criticism of their decisions in the newspapers. But the Home Secretary has a wider view, and he is answerable to Parliament and public opinion.

I therefore reject the argument on behalf of the prisoners in this case, that the Home Secretary is obliged to follow the judges' views as to the requirements of *b* retribution and deterrence in mandatory life sentence cases, even though it allowed some exceptions. I would also hold that he was not obliged to do so in discretionary life sentence cases. We need not decide today whether, in consequence of the 1987 statement, prisoners have a legitimate expectation that he will do so, or whether that expectation can be dispelled for the future. In the *c* light of the changes effected by the Criminal Justice Act 1991 and its transitional provisions, the problem may never arise.

It is argued by Mr Scrivener QC that the Home Secretary has acted unfairly or irrationally in treating discretionary and mandatory cases differently. But, even if the *Handscomb* decision were fully accepted, I consider that he was entitled to make a distinction; the difficulty of assessing the requirements of retribution and *d* deterrence from the judges' tariff in a murder case was a sufficient ground for his reserving the decision in mandatory life sentence cases to himself. The European Court of Human Rights accepted the distinction in *Thynne, Wilson and Gunnel v UK* (1990) 13 EHRR 666 at 693 (para 74). Furthermore, since I disagree with the view of the Divisional Court on this point in *Handscomb*'s case, but the Home Secretary was obliged for the time being to follow it, there is little logic in saying *e* that he should have extended it to mandatory cases.

(2) *Delegation*

Section 61(1) of the 1967 Act confers power to release a life prisoner on the Secretary of State. It is argued for the prisoners that fixing a tariff period is part of *f* that power, and must be done by the Secretary of State himself, rather than by a junior minister or official.

There is evidence that, at least in some of the cases before us, the tariff period was fixed by a minister of state or a parliamentary under-secretary of state. That this is the practice commonly adopted appears from the Report of the Select Committee on Murder and Life Imprisonment (HL Paper (1988–89) 78-I) para *g* 155.

This issue was not raised on behalf of the prisoners before the proceedings reached this court. Mr Pannick, for the Secretary of State, did not object to it being raised here; but he observed that we have no evidence from the department on the topic.

Parliament frequently confers powers on a minister who is the political head *h* of a department. Much less frequently it confers powers on an official of a particular description or grade. I know of no instance, and counsel were not able to find one, where power is conferred on a junior minister. But it is absurd to suppose that every power which is conferred on the political head of a department must be exercised by him and him alone. It is in general sufficient that the power is exercised by a junior minister or an official on his behalf. *j*

The classic statement of that principle is to be found in *Carltona Ltd v Comrs of Works* [1943] 2 All ER 560 at 563 by Lord Greene MR:

'In the administration of government in this country the functions which are given to ministers (and constitutionally properly given to ministers *a*   because they are constitutionally responsible) are functions so multifarious that no minister could ever personally attend to them. To take the example of the present case no doubt there have been thousands of requisitions in this country by individual ministries. It cannot be supposed that this regulation meant that, in each case, the minister in person should direct his mind to the matter. The duties imposed upon ministers and the powers given to ministers are normally exercised under the authority of the ministers by responsible

b   officials of the department. Public business could not be carried out if that were not the case. Constitutionally, the decision of such an official is, of course, the decision of the minister. The minister is responsible. It is he who must answer before Parliament for anything that his officials have done under his authority, and, if for an important matter he selected an official of such junior standing that he could not be expected competently to perform

c   the work, the minister would have to answer for that in Parliament. The whole system of departmental organisation and administration is based on the view that ministers, being responsible to Parliament, will see that important duties are committed to experienced officials. If they do not do that, Parliament is the place where complaint must be made against them.'

d   However, in *Minister for Aboriginal Affairs v Peko-Wallsend Ltd* (1986) 162 CLR 24 at 38 Mason J said of the *Carltona* principle:

'The cases in which the principle has been applied are cases in which the nature, scope and purpose of the function vested in the repository made it

e   unlikely that Parliament intended that it was to be exercised by the repository personally because administrative necessity indicated that it was impractical for him to act otherwise than through his officers or officers responsible to him.'

Mason J went on to explain the reasons why, in that case, the minister's function

f   was to be exercised by him personally.

Some such limitation on the *Carltona* doctrine is also to be found in English cases. Thus in *R v Brixton Prison Governor, ex p Enahoro* [1963] 2 All ER 477 at 481, [1963] 2 QB 455 at 465 Lord Parker CJ said:

'It is well settled that certainly no person made responsible for a judicial

g   decision can delegate his responsibility. Equally, in certain cases of administrative decisions there is no power to delegate . . .'

The latest case on the topic is *R v Secretary of State for the Home Dept, ex p Oladehinde* [1990] 2 All ER 367, [1991] 1 AC 254. In the Court of Appeal Lord Donaldson MR held that there might be express or implied limitations on the

h   right to devolve in the statute, and that otherwise a decision to devolve could be attacked if it was irrational in administrative terms (see [1990] 2 All ER 367 at 381, [1991] 1 AC 254 at 282). In the House of Lords, Lord Griffiths found no express or implied limitation in the statute, and no objection to devolution under the *Carltona* principle provided that the decisions to be taken by officials were 'suitable to their grading and experience' (see [1990] 3 All ER 393 at 402, [1991]

j   1 AC 254 at 303).

In the present case, there is no express or implied requirement in the 1967 Act that a decision fixing the tariff period—or for that matter a decision to release a prisoner on licence—must be taken by the Secretary of State personally. Is it then irrational for the Secretary of State, by devolution, to allow such decisions to be taken by a minister of state or parliamentary under-secretary of state?

Mr Scrivener points out that, in the days of capital punishment, it was the practice for the Home Secretary personally to decide whether to recommend a *a* reprieve; and political memoirs record how seriously that responsibility was regarded. The fixing of a tariff period for life prisoners is likewise of great importance to the individuals affected. But so, no doubt, is the exercise of a great many other powers which are entrusted to the Secretary of State for the Home Department. Parliament must be well aware of the great burden that is imposed on senior ministers, who not only take charge of their departments but also speak *b* for them in Parliament, attend meetings of the Cabinet and its committees, and see to their constituency affairs if they are members of the House of Commons.

A footnote in the Report of the Select Committee on Murder and Life Imprisonment (p 41 para 147, n 1) records that there were 2,927 mandatory life sentence cases in a period of slightly more than 23 years, an average of 127 a year. *c* On 7 May 1991 the Minister of State (Earl Ferrars) said that 274 mandatory life sentence cases were considered in 1990, possibly because there was still a backlog from pre-*Handscomb* days (see 528 HL Official Report (5th series) written answers col 39). Every such case demands serious consideration, and the burden of considering them all must be substantial. I can see nothing irrational in the Secretary of State devolving the task upon junior ministers. They too are appointed *d* by the Crown to hold office in the department, they have the same advice and assistance from departmental officials as the Secretary of State would have and they too are answerable to Parliament. There is in my judgment no objection to the decisions attacked in this case on the ground that they were or may have been taken by junior ministers rather than by the Secretary of State.

e

(3) *Natural justice/procedural impropriety*

It is now clear that the fixing of the period of detention required by retribution and deterrence is of fundamental importance to the prisoner. It will determine, in many cases, the earliest date at which his release can even be considered by the local review committee or the Parole Board, subject only to an overriding *f* discretion of the Home Secretary. There is a powerful argument for saying that, in general, it should be subject to the rules of administrative law. Many years ago, there was a statutory provision that, in the event of an appeal to the Court of Criminal Appeal, the trial judge could write a letter to that court which was not disclosed to the appellant. Although defended by Diplock J in *London Export Corp* *g* *Ltd v Jubilee Coffee Roasting Co Ltd* [1958] 1 All ER 494 at 500, [1958] 1 WLR 271 at 281, the practice was discontinued shortly afterwards.

The first requirement of natural justice is the right of the prisoner to make representations. He has that already, since any prisoner can petition the Secretary of State.

The second requirement is that he should know what is said against him. *h* Unless he does, the right to make representations is of little value: see *Kanda v Government of Malaya* [1962] AC 332 at 337.

Much of the material on which the Home Secretary is likely to base his decision will have been available to the prisoner at his trial: the evidence, both for and against him, any reports considered by the court and remarks in mitigation made on his behalf (as is now the practice). All that will be considered by the judge and *j* the Lord Chief Justice in making their recommendations. Since those recommendations are now made shortly after the trial, there will no longer be additional material such as reports on the prisoner's subsequent behaviour, which would in any event be irrelevant to the requirements of retribution and deterrence.

However, there will also be in some cases the judge's view of the relative
a culpability of the prisoner and co-defendants. In my judgment natural justice
requires that the prisoner be told what the judges have recommended, and
anything the trial judge has said about relative culpability, in such time that he
can make representations before the Home Secretary fixes the tariff period. That
period is to all intents and purposes part of the sentence, and he ought to know
everything that is said about him before it is fixed.

b There is, however, a difficulty. The evidence is that communications from the
judiciary to the Home Secretary on this topic are confidential; and I accept that
there is at least a tacit agreement that neither side will disclose them without the
consent of the other. I would hope that this tacit agreement will be rescinded for
the future, and if the judges then take the view that they will disclose their
c recommendations (with reasons) in open court, in mandatory as well as
discretionary cases, so be it. But that will still leave a problem for existing cases.
The Home Secretary will no doubt give his consent, if otherwise the decisions of
junior ministers are liable to be quashed on judicial review. It is not for me to say
whether the judges or the Lord Chief Justice should or will consent. But, if they
do not, I am inclined to think that it would be open to the Divisional Court, in an
d appropriate case, to order production of the document in judicial review
proceedings despite the confidentiality. No doubt the Divisional Court would
often wish to read the document first before ordering its disclosure wholly or in
part.

There is other material which may reach the Home Office. There may be
letters from the victim's relations, from members of Parliament, from the general
e public (whether directed at a particular case or at penal policy in general), or from
the Howard League or the National Association for the Care and Rehabilitation
of Offenders. None of this material need in my opinion be disclosed to the
prisoner. If it is directed to his particular case, the Home Secretary should
disregard it at this stage unless it was evidence at the trial; if directed to penal
policy in general, it is merely a small part of his information as to public opinion.
f The same is true of newspaper comment.

It was suggested that the prisoner is entitled to see comments, summaries and
advice which officials provide to the minister. I do not agree, for the department
is to be treated as a whole: see Lord Diplock in *Bushell v Secretary of State for the
Environment* [1980] 2 All ER 608 at 613, [1981] AC 75 at 95. If a prisoner has or
g knows the material which reaches the department, that is sufficient. Nor do I
consider that any in-house tariff which may exist in the Home Office need be
disclosed.

Lastly under this head come the minister's reasons. There is no general
obligation to give reasons for administrative decisions: see *R v Civil Service Appeal
Board, ex p Cunningham* [1991] 4 All ER 310 at 317. In the particular case of a
h minister's decision fixing the tariff period for a life sentence prisoner, there is not
in my opinion a requirement that reasons should always be given. The prisoner
should have seen or known the information that was available to the minister, to
the extent that I have indicated, and had an opportunity to make representations.
The minister will generally have to decide only whether the period required for
retribution and deterrence is that recommended by the judge, or by the Lord
j Chief Justice, or is some lesser or greater period. I can see no need to give reasons
for that decision.

There will, however, be some cases where the minister's decision is more
complex, and requires some explanation. The court may then find that, if
unexplained, it is irrational. To avoid that possibility it would be right to give
reasons in complex cases.

(4) Conclusion

These four cases are among a great number where ministers have in the past *a* fixed a tariff period on material that was not available to the prisoner, and which in my opinion ought to have been available to him. I would not afford the remedy of judicial review in all those cases—far from it. But in these four cases there are features that require the decision, which was relatively recent, to be reconsidered after what I consider to be a proper procedure. I would therefore quash the decisions by ministers fixing the tariff period, and make the declarations proposed *b* by Glidewell LJ. There is no need to order discovery, at any rate at this stage.

FARQUHARSON LJ. Each of the four applicants—now the appellants—has been individually convicted of murder and sentenced to life imprisonment. The offences were of varying degrees of gravity and the appellants have been given *c* different release dates under the statutory provisions which have been under examination in these appeals. It has for long been the task of the Secretary of State for the Home Department either in the exercise of the prerogative of mercy or more recently on a statutory basis to determine, in the case of prisoners sentenced to life imprisonment, how much of that sentence should be served.

After the abolition of the death penalty in 1965 there was plainly some anxiety *d* by the legislature as to how prisoners sentenced to life imprisonment for murder should be dealt with. This was reflected in the Criminal Justice Act 1967, which by s 61(1) provides:

'The Secretary of State may, if recommended to do so by the Parole Board, release on licence a person serving a sentence of imprisonment for life . . . *e* but shall not do so . . . except after consultation with the Lord Chief Justice of England together with the trial judge if available.'

The Secretary of State was thus granted a discretionary power to release a person serving a sentence of life imprisonment subject to two conditions: (1) he must be recommended so to do in a particular case by the Parole Board (which was constituted by s 59 of the same Act) and (2) he shall not do so except after *f* consultation with the Lord Chief Justice together with the trial judge if available. While it appears that the application to the Parole Board can only be made by the Secretary of State, he has no power to release a prisoner on licence until he receives the board's recommendation to do so.

The Secretary of State's duty so far as the Lord Chief Justice and the trial judge *g* are concerned is only to 'consult'. The Act does not specify at what stage, or how often or in what form, the consultation is to take place, but the subsection implies that it should be after the Secretary of State has received the recommendation of the Parole Board. The words of the subsection also imply that the judges are intended by Parliament to act as a form of brake upon any overeagerness on the part of a Home Secretary when exercising the power of release. *h*

On 30 November 1983 the then Secretary of State made a statement to Parliament explaining how he proposed thereafter to exercise his powers under the subsection (see 49 HC Official Report (6th series) written answers cols 505–507). There was to be an additional consultation with the two judges which would take place after the prisoner had served three years of his sentence, so that the Secretary of State could receive at that stage their advice on the total period *j* which should be served to satisfy the requirements of retribution and deterrence. The period advised by the judges has become known as 'the judicial tariff'.

The first reference to the local review committee or the Parole Board would normally take place three years before the expiry of the tariff period. The Secretary

of State made it clear that after the first application to the local review committee
a there should, before he ordered release, be a further consultation with the judges
'to meet fully the requirements of [s 61]'.

Under this procedure the prisoner could discover what his tariff was as set by
the judges, by simply adding three years to the date of the first reference to the
local review committee. At the same time the Secretary of State gave notice that
for certain categories of crime where life sentences had been passed the offenders
b could expect to spend at least 20 years in prison. It was made clear in a further
policy statement that in those cases where the tariff was 20 years or more the
reference to the local review committee would be made after 17 years had been
served, though a warning was given that this did not imply that any particular
period had been set for the prisoner's tariff. Those in the 20 years or more category
c remained unaware of their tariff or of any possible release date.

In 1986 *R v Secretary of State for the Home Dept, ex p Handscomb* 86 Cr App R 59
came before the Divisional Court. There has been some difference of opinion as
to what that case decided, but there is no dispute that the court held that the
postponement of the consultation process with the Lord Chief Justice and the   •
trial judge until three years after sentence was unlawful, and that it should take
d place as soon as possible after conviction. Watkins LJ dealt with the status of the
judges' advice in these terms (at 82):

> 'If, as I am in no doubt, the inference must be from Mrs Murray's affidavit
> that the Home Secretary is not obliged to accept the judicial view of tariff
> and may, as I have also said, impose his own view as to this, a prima facie case
> of irrationality and *Wednesbury* unreasonableness must surely arise. If the
e Home Secretary is not to be guided by the judges on retribution and
> deterrence, where else can he look for guidance?'

Handscomb was a case involving a discretionary life sentence, and on 23 July 1987
the Secretary of State made a further policy statement explaining some
modifications to the procedure (see 120 HC Official Report (6th series) written
f answers col 347). In future the advice of the Lord Chief Justice and the trial judge
was to be obtained immediately after sentence, whether the life sentence was
mandatory or discretionary, but in the latter case the judicial view of the tariff
was to determine the date of the first review by the Parole Board machinery. The
Secretary of State emphasised that—

g > 'the release of a life sentence prisoner is solely at my discretion and it is for
> me to decide, after receiving the Parole Board's recommendation and after
> consulting the judiciary as required by section 61(1) of the Criminal Justice
> Act 1967, when actual release should take place.'

This policy statement made for the first time in this context a distinction in the
h Secretary of State's approach to mandatory life sentences on the one hand and
discretionary life sentences on the other. The latter no longer present so serious a
cause of complaint compared with the mandatory sentences because of the
provisions of s 34 of the Criminal Justice Act 1991. This section, which will come
into force on 1 October 1992, introduces a new procedure whereby the prisoner
may require the Secretary of State to refer his case to the board, in certain specified
j circumstances.

The effect of consultation

The observations of Watkins LJ already cited concerning the duty of the
Secretary of State when receiving advice from the judiciary on the tariff has been

the subject of judicial comment. For example, Lloyd LJ in *R v Secretary of State for the Home Dept, ex p Benson* (1988) Independent, 16 November said:

'The case [*Handscomb*] does not decide that the Secretary of State is obliged to accept the judicial view on tariff; if it did so decide, I would respectfully disagree.'

Lloyd LJ was evidently basing this comment on the terms of s 61(1). The subsection creates an obligation to *consult* the judiciary, not to be governed by their opinion, which amounts to no more than advice. If the decision of the Secretary of State as to the correct tariff after going through the consultation process is so out of touch with reality that it is irrational then, as in *Ex p Handscomb*, that decision could be the subject of judicial review.

Apart from that situation the Secretary of State is not in my judgment bound to accept the advice of the judges. They may be the best equipped to identify the tariff for retribution and deterrence in a particular case but they may also be wrong. Other considerations of a public character may be present in the mind of the Secretary of State which persuade him to take a different view from the judges. I would reject the argument advanced before us that a failure to follow the judicial advice on tariff, save in exceptional cases, is in itself irrational.

The position of the judges

Submissions were made that a life prisoner whose case is being referred to the judges under the 'first' consultation procedure ought to be allowed to make representations to the judges with the object of limiting his tariff, and further that the material to be placed before the judges should also be available for examination by the prisoner. So far as the present procedure is concerned, I would reject those submissions. As already observed, the judges are not called upon under the consultation procedure to make any decisions. Their task is simply to give advice. The decision-maker is the Secretary of State. No rights under public law arise at the stage the judges' advice is given. There cannot be judicial review of an opinion. Moreover, as pointed out by Watkins LJ in *Ex p Handscomb* (1987) 86 Cr App R 59 at 75 the advice given by the judges to the Secretary of State on tariff is given in confidence.

The present procedure when a judge is about to pass a life sentence for murder is for him to invite defending counsel to make submissions on what advice the judge should give to the Secretary of State on the appropriate tariff. Unless the judge makes a recommendation under s 1(2) of the Murder (Abolition of Death Penalty) Act 1965 as to the minimum period of imprisonment a person convicted of murder should serve—and this is now done infrequently—he does not say what advice he proposes to give the Secretary of State. For my part, I do not see why the trial judge should not at that stage state in open court what that advice will be. All the facts of the case will be fresh in his mind and he will have just heard the mitigation of counsel. He will thus be better equipped to give an informed opinion than under the present procedure, when the papers are returned to him some months later through the Lord Chief Justice. Furthermore, there would be no question of the judge, before giving his advice, seeing documents which have not been available to the prisoner. Both would have seen all the relevant documents either before or during the course of the trial.

As the law stands at present, however, even if the trial judge reveals at the time of sentencing what advice he proposes to give to the Secretary of State, it will still be necessary for the latter to consult the Lord Chief Justice and the trial judge at a later stage. It may be that on such a consultation the Lord Chief Justice will take a   a different view from that of the trial judge, but under the present procedure the prisoner will be unaware of any variation of the trial judge's original advice.

The present appellants argue that every life prisoner should be informed of the advice on tariff given by the judges to the Secretary of State. If the prisoner is not aware of the judge's advice he is not able to present to the Secretary of State a reasoned case for a lower figure.

b   This argument, which is based on grounds of natural justice and procedural fairness, is resisted by counsel for the Secretary of State, partly because the statutory structure does not require that the information should be given and partly in reliance on the decision of this court in *Payne v Lord Harris of Greenwich* [1981] 2 All ER 842, [1981] 1 WLR 754. In that case the appellant, who was, and is, serving a mandatory sentence of life imprisonment for murder, sought a declaration against the Parole Board and the Secretary of State that he was in effect
c   entitled to know the reasons for refusing to release him on licence. The appeal was dismissed, Lord Denning MR saying ([1981] 2 All ER 842 at 846, [1981] 1 WLR 754 at 759):

d   'In the end I think the problem comes down to this: what does public policy demand as best to be done? To give reasons or to withhold them? This is more a matter for the Secretary of State than for the courts. But, so far as I can judge of the matter, I should think that in the interests of the man himself, as a human being facing indefinite detention, it would be better for him to be told the reasons. But, in the interests of society at large, including the due administration of the parole system, it would be best not to give
e   them. Except in the rare case when the board themselves think it desirable, as a matter of fairness, to ask one of the members to interview him. That member may then think it appropriate to tell him. This is not a case for any declaration. I would dismiss the appeal.'

f   This basis of deciding the case is not very satisfactory in the current climate. More than a balancing exercise is required and the decision has not been followed in another case before this court: see *R v Parole Board, ex p Wilson* [1992] 2 All ER 576, [1992] QB 740. In any case *Payne v Lord Harris of Greenwich* is not dealing with the Secretary of State's decision on tariff.

For my part, I conclude that the life prisoner should be informed of the judge's advice on tariff, together with any comments the judges, or either of them, may
g   have made about the responsibility of the prisoner for the crime compared with that of any co-defendant tried with him. If a prisoner serving a mandatory life sentence is to be given the opportunity to make representation to the Secretary of State concerning the length of his tariff, as in my judgment he should be, then, for those representations to be effective, he ought to be made aware beforehand of the nature of the judge's advice. I recognise that at present this advice is given
h   in confidence but, like Glidewell LJ, I would foresee little difficulty in the Secretary of State asking to be released from that confidence in pending cases.

Counsel for the appellants further submit that the life prisoner should also be informed of any advice given to the Secretary of State by the officials of his department.

j   I would reject this argument as calculated to undermine the proper administration of a department of state. The minister in charge must be able to seek the advice of his subordinates without having to publish what he has been told. The minister is to be regarded as head, and part of, his department, and his decision represents its collective wisdom. Procedural fairness does not require him to identify his advisers or the advice they give to him.

Should the Secretary of State be compelled to give reasons for his decision to refuse the prisoner's release? Mr Sedley QC for two of the appellants argues that, *a* because of the quasi-judicial nature of the Secretary of State's task, it comes at that end of the spectrum of tribunal decisions which require reasons to be given. We have been taken through a number of English and Australian authorities, but none I think are determinative of the Secretary of State's position.

The most recent case, a decision of this court, is *R v Civil Service Appeal Board, ex p Cunningham* [1991] 4 All ER 310. In his judgment Lord Donaldson MR said *b* that, in deciding whether a tribunal was under a duty to give reasons for its decision, one considered, first, the character of the decision-making body and, secondly, the framework in which it operated (at 318–319). One then posed the question whether fairness required any additional procedural safeguards. It is clear in the present case that the statute makes no express or implied requirement *c* that the Secretary of State should state his reasons for refusing a prisoner's release.

Is the 'character' of the decision-maker, ie the Secretary of State, and the framework in which he operates, such that additional procedural safeguards are required in the interests of fairness? As already indicated in this judgment, I think that some additional safeguards are necessary, namely that the prisoner should be informed of the advice given by the judges to the Secretary of State, *d* and also have the opportunity to make representations to the Secretary of State before he makes his decision about the prisoner's date of release. It is not necessary that the prisoner should be further protected by compelling the Secretary of State to give the reasons for his decision. Any challenge to the rationality of the decision can be sufficiently based on the disclosed material.

A further point was taken by Mr Scrivener QC that the decisions referred to in *e* the subsection can only be made by the Secretary of State personally and that he may not delegate or transfer the power to make the decision to a minister of state, as happened in the case of Pegg. For the reasons set out in the judgment of Staughton LJ, I would reject that contention.

I agree that the appeal should be allowed and that declarations should be made *f* in the terms appearing at the end of the judgment of Glidewell LJ.

Appeals allowed. Declarations granted in favour of applicants and Secretary of State's decisions quashed. Leave to appeal to the House of Lords granted to Secretary of State.

3 November 1992. The Appeal Committee of the House of Lords gave Mr Doody leave to *g* *cross-appeal.*

L I Zysman Esq   Barrister.

a

Haniff v Robinson

COURT OF APPEAL, CIVIL DIVISION
LORD DONALDSON OF LYMINGTON MR, WOOLF AND LEGGATT LJJ
9 JUNE 1992

b *Rent restriction – Statutory tenant – Termination of tenancy – Landlord obtaining order for possession – Tenant applying to set aside order – Landlord applying for warrant of execution and forcibly evicting tenant before warrant executed by court bailiff – Whether tenant a statutory tenant at time of eviction – Whether eviction unlawful – Rent Act 1977, s 2(1)(a) – Protection from Eviction Act 1977, ss 3(1), 8(1) – Housing Act 1988, s 27 – CCR Ord 26, r 17(1).*

c

The landlord let premises to the tenant under a residential tenancy for a period of six months expiring on 5 June 1989. When the contractual tenancy ended the tenant remained in possession as a statutory tenant under s 2(1)(a)[a] of the Rent Act 1977. The landlord brought proceedings for possession in the county court,
d wrongly claiming that he was a resident landlord. The tenant was out of the country at the time and did not become aware of the proceedings until her return in November 1989. In her absence a possession order was made against her to take effect on 28 November 1989. On 27 November the tenant, having learnt of the order, applied to have it set aside. The landlord, aware of the application to set aside the possession order, applied for a warrant of execution but before the
e warrant could be executed by the court bailiff the landlord forcibly ejected the tenant on 24 December 1989. The possession order was subsequently set aside and the tenant obtained damages for unlawful eviction under s 27[b] of the Housing Act 1988. The landlord appealed, contending that the tenant had ceased to be a statutory tenant for the purposes of s 2(1)(a) of 1977 Act either when the possession order was made or when it took effect or when the landlord applied for
f a warrant of execution and therefore he had been entitled personally to evict her.

Held – A statutory tenant remained a statutory tenant for the purposes of s 2(1)(a) of the 1977 Act so long as he occupied the dwelling house as his residence, although once an order for possession was made the extent of his right as a statutory tenant could and would be curtailed. However, since the defendant's
g tenancy was neither a statutory protected tenancy within s 8(1)[c] of the Protection from Eviction Act 1977 nor an excluded tenancy she was not precluded from claiming the protection of that Act and under s 3[d] thereof she was protected from eviction until the court bailiff executed the warrant for possession in accordance with CCR Ord 26, r 17(1)[e]. It followed that the landlord had had no right to
h resort to self-help to take possession of the premises before the warrant had been executed by the bailiff and in doing so he was guilty of unlawful eviction. The tenant was therefore entitled to damages under s 27 of the 1988 Act. The appeal would therefore be dismissed (see p 188 *f*, p 190 *h*, p 191 *b c* and p 192 *e f*, post).

---

j *a* Section 2(1), so far as material, is set out at p 188 *e*, post
   b Section 27, so far as material, is set out at p 187 *g* to *j*, post
   c Section 8(1), so far as material, provides: 'In this Act "statutorily protected tenancy" means—(a) a
      protected tenancy within the meaning of the Rent Act 1977 . . .'
   d Section 3, so far as material, is set out at p 190 *j*, post
   e Rule 17(1) is set out at p 191 *d*, post

Brown v Draper [1944] 1 All ER 246 and *American Economic Laundry Ltd v Little*
[1950] 2 All ER 1186 considered.   *a*

Per curiam. Where an order for possession has been made against a statutory
tenant the landlord is not entitled to re-enter, even peaceably, between the date of
the order and its execution by the court bailiff (see p 192 *c d f*, post).

Notes   *b*
For termination of a statutory tenancy, see 27 *Halsbury's Laws* (4th edn) para 599,
and for cases on the subject, see 31(3) *Digest* (2nd reissue) 480–492, 11922–11994.
    For the Rent Act 1977, s 2, see 23 *Halsbury's Statutes* (4th edn) (1989 reissue)
522.
    For the Protection from Eviction Act 1977, ss 3, 8, see ibid 307, 316.
    For the Housing Act 1988, s 27, see ibid 454.   *c*

Cases referred to in judgments
Aglionby v Cohen [1955] 1 All ER 785, [1955] 1 QB 558, [1955] 2 WLR 730.
American Economic Laundry Ltd v Little [1950] 2 All ER 1186, [1951] 1 KB 400, CA.
Brown v Draper [1944] 1 All ER 246, [1944] KB 309, CA.
Clifton Securities Ltd v Huntley [1948] 2 All ER 283.   *d*
Keeves v Dean, Nunn v Pellegrini [1924] 1 KB 685, [1923] All ER Rep 12, CA.
Kyriacou v Pandeli [1980] CLY 1648, Cty Ct.

Case also cited
Jessamine Investments Co v Schwartz [1976] 3 All ER 521, [1978] QB 264, CA.   *e*

Appeal
The plaintiff, Hassan Haniff (the landlord), appealed out of time with the leave of
Mr Registrar Adams given on 14 November 1991 from the judgment of Judge
Roger Cox given on 5 August 1991 in the Edmonton County Court whereby he   *f*
gave judgment for the defendant, Susan Robinson (the tenant) on her counterclaim
for £24,751·59, after taking account of a set-off for arrears of rent and mesne
profits, in respect of her claim for unlawful eviction under s 27 of the Housing
Act 1988 and general damages and consequential loss together with interest of
£3,550·24, making a total of £28,301·83, in an action brought by the landlord
claiming possession of a ground-floor maisonette at 36 Ferndale Road, Tottenham,   *g*
London N15, arrears of rent and mesne profits, of which the defendant was the
tenant. The facts are set out in the judgment of Woolf LJ.

Ita Marshall (instructed by *Craigen Wilders & Sorrell*) for the landlord.
David Watkinson and *Hilary Beechey* (instructed by *Norton & Co*) for the tenant.
                                                                                                              h

WOOLF LJ (delivering the first judgment at the invitation of Lord
Donaldson MR). This appeal raises a single issue as to whether a landlord who has
obtained an order for possession in the county court against the statutory tenant
is entitled to resort to self-help and take possession of the premises himself without
involving the bailiff in executing the order for possession.   *j*
    The issue arises on this appeal because, on 25 May 1991, Judge Roger Cox in
the Edmonton County Court determined this issue against the plaintiff landlord
and awarded the defendant, his former statutory tenant, the sum of £28,300-odd,
including interest, in her counterclaim, partly in respect of her claim for unlawful
eviction under s 27 of the Housing Act 1988.

a The facts so far as relevant are not in dispute, the judge having rejected the evidence of the former landlord, the plaintiff, Mr Haniff, and accepted the evidence of the former tenant, the defendant, Miss Susan Robinson. The landlord owned 36 Ferndale Road, London N15. On 6 December 1988 he entered into a tenancy agreement with Miss Robinson under which she was entitled to occupy the premises for a period of six months. The contractual tenancy therefore came to an end by effluxion of time on 5 June 1989. After 5 June 1989 the tenant

b remained in possession. The landlord served an invalid notice to quit which does not affect the situation. In September 1989 the tenant visited the United States, returning in November 1989. Without her knowledge, in August 1989 the landlord had issued proceedings, wrongly contending that he was a resident landlord. The proceedings did not come to the tenant's notice until after she

c returned from the United States. In her absence a possession order was made on 31 October 1989 to take effect on 28 November 1989. The day before it was due to take effect, the tenant, having learnt of the order, made an application to set aside the order for possession and the judgment which had resulted in that order. The landlord was aware of the fact that she had made that application but, notwithstanding that, on 4 December 1989 he applied for execution. On

d 24 December 1989 he forcibly ejected the tenant. On 22 January 1990 the possession order which had been made was set aside.

For the purposes of this appeal, it is not necessary to take account of the implications which arise or could arise as a result of the possession order being set aside. However, the facts of this case do illustrate the injustice which could arise if Miss Marshall is correct in the admirable submissions which she has advanced

e on behalf of the landlord, to the effect that in this case he was entitled to resort to self-help.

As regrettably is often the case where Rent Act issues are involved, the answer to the issue identified at the beginning of this judgment requires an undesirably tortuous journey through a number of statutory provisions. It is convenient to

f start at the end of that journey and work backwards from the provisions dealing with unlawful eviction which resulted in the order for damages being made in the court below. The starting point is s 27 of the Housing Act 1988. Subsection (1) of that section provides:

> 'This section applies if, at any time after 9th June 1988, a landlord (in this section referred to as "the landlord in default") or any person acting on behalf

g of the landlord in default unlawfully deprives the residential occupier of any premises of his occupation of the whole or part of the premises.'

I emphasise the word 'unlawfully' in that subsection and the words 'residential occupier'. Subsection (2) contains a similar provision to that contained in sub-s (1), which it is not necessary to cite. Subsection (3) is important and provides:

h
> 'Subject to the following provisions of this section, where this section applies, the landlord in default shall, by virtue of this section, be liable to pay to the former residential occupier in respect of his loss of the right to occupy the premises in question as his residence, damages assessed on the basis set out in section 28 below.'

j I draw attention to the words 'right to occupy'. Subsection (4) indicates that the liability for damages shall be in the nature of a liability in tort. Subsection (9)(*a*) contains a definition of residential occupier, the relevant words being:

> '"residential occupier" in relation to any premises, has the same meaning as section 1 of the 1977 Act [ie the Protection from Eviction Act 1977].'

Section 1(1) of that Act states:

> '..."residential occupier", in relation to any premises, means a person *a*
> occupying the premises as a residence, whether under a contract or by virtue
> of any enactment or rule of law giving him the right to remain in occupation
> or restricting the right of any other person to recover possession of the
> premises.'

The important words so far as this appeal is concerned are the words 'any *b*
enactment or rule of law ... restricting the right of any other person to recover
possession of the premises'. 'Any other person' in this context would apply to the
landlord. Section 28 sets out the measure of damages. It is not necessary to refer
to the terms of that section.

We can leave the 1988 Act and proceed to the Rent Act 1977, bearing in mind *c*
that the issue in this case was whether there was a person, namely the landlord,
who was restricted in his right to recover possession of the premises by virtue of
any enactment or rule of law. Section 1 of the Rent Act 1977 provides:

> 'Subject to this Part of this Act, a tenancy under which a dwelling-house
> ... is let as a separate dwelling is a protected tenancy for the purposes of this
> Act ...'   *d*

Section 2(1)(a) provides:

> 'Subject to this Part of this Act—(a) after the termination of a protected
> tenancy of a dwelling-house the person who, immediately before that
> termination, was the protected tenant of the dwelling-house shall, if and so *e*
> long as he occupies the dwelling-house as his residence, be the statutory
> tenant of it ...'

Applying ss 1 and 2 to the facts of this appeal, the position is that for the first
six months (the period of the original letting) the tenant was a protected tenant.
Thereafter, she became a statutory tenant under s 2(1)(a), and giving the words of
that subsection their natural meaning, it would appear that she was by that Act to *f*
remain a statutory tenant so long as she continued in occupation of the dwelling
house.

Miss Marshall contends, however, that that is not the effect of the subsection.
She contends that the tenant ceased to be a statutory tenant for the purposes of
the subsection when the possession order was made in the county court or, *g*
alternatively, when the possession order took effect or, alternatively, when her
client applied for the warrant of execution. She submits that she obtains support
for that approach from two decisions. The first of those decisions is *Brown v
Draper* [1944] 1 All ER 246, [1944] KB 309 and the second of those decisions is
American Economic Laundry Ltd v Little [1950] 2 All ER 1186, [1951] 1 KB 400. It
is only necessary to refer to the second of those cases, which were decisions of this *h*
court, because in the judgments in the second of those cases, reference is made
back to *Brown v Draper*. In the *American Economic Laundry* case a final order for
possession had been made but that order for possession had been suspended.
During the period of suspension the tenant died. The tenant having died, his
daughter sought to rely on the provisions which would give her the right to
succeed to the statutory tenancy. Reading from the headnote ([1951] 1 KB 400), *j*
it was held—

> 'that, although, by the indulgence of the court, a statutory tenant might
> be permitted to continue to occupy premises after the making of an order for
> possession, he was not, during such a period of occupation, a statutory tenant

a with all the rights to protection conferred by the Rent Restriction Acts which he had enjoyed before the order for possession was made; and, consequently, the daughter could not claim protection as a "tenant" under s. 12, sub-s. 1(*g*) [of the Increase of Rent and Mortgage Interest (Restrictions) Act 1920].'

As Lord Donaldson MR pointed out during the course of argument, there is a difference between saying that 'a person is not a statutory tenant' from saying that *b* 'a person is not a statutory tenant with all the rights to protection' such a tenant can possess. When one comes to look at the judgments in the *American Economic Laundry* case, it appears clear that the approach which the court was adopting in that case was to regard the tenant against whom a possession order had been made as a statutory tenant who did not have *all* the rights to protection conferred by the Rent Restriction Acts. Somervell LJ said ([1951] 1 KB 400 at 403–404, cf *c* [1950] 2 All ER 1186 at 1187–1188):

'The question as stated at the beginning of his argument by Mr. MacDermot was whether a tenant against whom a final order for possession has been made is a tenant within s. 12, sub-s 1(*g*). That definition of "tenant" like all the definitions in the Act of 1920, is to be read as applying except where the *d* context otherwise requires. The judge decided that the defendant was within that definition and could remain in possession. In a long and careful judgment he said, and I agree with him, that the point is not free from difficulty. He referred first, to two statements in *Brown* v. *Draper* ([1944] 1 All ER 246 at 248, [1944] KB 309 at 312), where Lord Greene, M.R., used more than once words to this effect: "the only ways in which [a tenant] can *e* be deprived of the protection of the Acts are (a) by giving up possession, in which case no order for recovery of possession against him is required; (b) having an order for recovery of possession made against him". Those words, read literally, might be taken to indicate that the order for possession in itself deprived him of the protection of the Act. On the other hand, the county court judge referred to this statement by Scrutton, L.J., in *Keeves* v. *Dean* *f* ([1924] 1 KB 685 at 694, [1923] All ER Rep 12 at 17): "I take it that [the tenant] has a right as against all the world to remain in possession until he is turned out by an order of the court". The difference between the literal meanings of those two statements of the law is illustrated by this case. I agree with the county court judge, in that I do not think that Lord Greene had in *g* mind what we have to consider here, namely, the position of a tenant, a person who has been a statutory tenant (I am not begging the question by using the word "tenant" but it is a convenient expression) between the time when the order for possession is made and the time when it falls to be executed having regard to a suspension granted under s. 5, sub-s. 2, of the Act of 1920. I do not think that that point was in the mind of either Lord *h* Greene or Scrutton, L.J., but the former in the words above quoted, expressed something with which I respectfully agree, and which seems plain, namely, that an absolute order for possession made against a tenant fundamentally alters the position.'

Somervell LJ said later in his judgment ([1951] 1 KB 400 at 404, cf [1950] 2 All *j* ER 1186 at 1188–1189):

'I agree with [Jenkins LJ's] observation, made in the course of the argument, that the position of someone against whom an order for possession has been made, and then suspended at common law or under s. 5, sub-s. 2, of the Rent Act of 1920 is sui generis. I do not think that the problem which we have to solve is really assisted by considering in what respect his position is the same quoad the landlord as it was before the order was made. It is obviously fundamentally different in this respect, that, whereas before, he was entitled to the protection of the Act until successful proceedings were taken, he is now in the position that proceedings have been taken and that an order for possession has been made. All that he has is a right to apply for postponement under s. 5, sub-s. 2. In my opinion a tenant in that position, that is to say where an absolute order for possession has been made against him, notwithstanding that it may be suspended, is not a tenant for the purposes of s. 12, sub-s. 1(g). That I think is in accordance with a common-sense application of the paragraph. It would be an illogical result, I think, if the paragraph gave a protection to a widow which the court had expressly taken away from her deceased husband, on whose tenancy she relies, that tenancy having been brought to a suspended end by the order for possession.'

What Jenkins LJ said was ([1951] 1 KB 400 at 406–407, cf [1950] 2 All ER 1186 at 1190):

'The tenant here died after the date of the order for recovery of possession against him but before the expiration of the last of a series of extensions which had been made by way of postponement of the date on which the order was to be complied with. What, then, was his position? It is said that, notwithstanding the order for possession, he was still a statutory tenant. To say that seems to me really to beg the question. It may well be that he could be described as a statutory tenant; but that description would not itself accurately define his precise position, for he was a statutory tenant against whom a final order had been made, under which possession was to be delivered up on a fixed date, April 3, 1950, he having died on the previous March 8. During the intervening period between the date of such an order and the date fixed for delivery of possession it may very well be, and indeed obviously must be, that the statutory tenant has certain rights and certain obligations. For instance he would have to pay the equivalent of the rent during the period of his occupation between the date of the order and the date of giving up possession. But that is not to say, and it obviously cannot be the case, that he is still the statutory tenant for all purposes, so as to be in the same position as if the order had never been made. He has nothing left but the limited interest granted to him by what may perhaps be described as the indulgence of the court under s. 5, sub-s. 2, of the Act of 1920. In effect he has a period of grace.'

I therefore do not regard those authorities as affecting what I would conclude was the clear language of s 2(1)(a) of the Rent Act 1977, that a statutory tenant remains a statutory tenant so long as he occupies the dwelling house as his residence. However, I do accept that once an order for possession is made, the extent of his right as a statutory tenant can and will be curtailed. If that is the position, it is necessary to consider s 3 of the Protection from Eviction Act 1977. Section 3(1) of that Act states:

'Where any premises have been let as a dwelling under a tenancy which is neither a statutorily protected tenancy nor an excluded tenancy and—(a) the tenancy (in this section referred to as the former tenancy) has come to an end, but (b) the occupier continues to reside in the premises or part of them, it shall not be lawful for the owner to enforce against the occupier, otherwise than by proceedings in the court, his right to recover possession of the premises.'

a Unless the tenant here was a statutorily protected tenant, as the premises were not let to her on an excluded tenancy she is entitled to the benefit of that protection. Section 8(1) of the same Act contains a definition of a statutorily protected tenancy. That definition makes it clear that a statutory tenant is not the holder of a statutorily protected tenancy. Accordingly, the tenant whom we are here considering was entitled to the protection of s 3. The reason that a protected tenancy, for example, does not fall within s 3 is because there is a separate regime of protection provided for such tenants.

b

Having come to the conclusion that the tenant is entitled to the protection of s 3, the next question is, when does that protection cease? The section provides that it was to continue and to prevent the owner from enforcing against the occupier a right to possession otherwise than by proceedings in court. The words 'otherwise than by proceedings in court' do not clearly indicate what is to be treated as being included in the proceedings. However, I have no doubt that, in the context of the statutory tenancies with which we are here concerned, what is intended to be the effect of s 3 is that it should continue to provide protection until there has actually been execution in the ordinary way by the court's bailiff in accordance with the requirement of the County Court Rules. CCR Ord 26, r 17(1) provides:

c

d

> 'A judgment or order for the recovery of land shall be enforceable by warrant of possession.'

e The rules indicate no other way of enforcement. The table of procedure presupposes that after an order is made, that will be followed by a request for execution in due course by the person in whose favour the order has been made, followed by the execution by the court bailiff. The actual warrant for possession of land which is issued in consequence of the request under CCR Ord 26, r 17 makes the position clear. It is addressed to the registrar and bailiffs of the court, and it presupposes that the bailiff, having obtained possession, will deliver that possession to the plaintiff.

f

The position is clarified by the effect of s 100 of the Rent Act 1977. Section 100 deals with the extent of discretion of the courts in respect of claims for possession of residential dwellings where the Rent Act applies. Subsection (2) states:

g

> 'On the making of an order for possession of such a dwelling-house, or at any time before the execution of such an order . . . the court, subject to subsection (5) below, may—(a) stay or suspend execution of the order, or (b) postpone the date of possession, for such period or periods as the court thinks fit.'

As that subsection gives the court a discretion to stay or suspend execution of the order, it cannot be the position that it was intended that the landlord could take *h* the matter into his own hands. When there is a stay or a suspension of execution, he cannot rely on the order for possession as giving him a right to possession. There is also the problem, if Miss Marshall is correct, that you would have a situation arising where, once a statutory tenancy had ceased to exist on an order for possession being made, it would be revived if the court were to exercise the powers which are contained in s 100(4), which provides:

j

> 'If any such conditions as are referred to in subsection (3) above are complied with, the court may, if it thinks fit, discharge or rescind any such order as is referred to in subsection (2) above.'

There is a passage in *Megarry on the Rent Acts* (11th edn, 1987) vol 1, p 386 which leaves the position open. It says:

'Again, a landlord who has obtained an order for possession may still be
entitled to re-enter peaceably without invoking the assistance of the sheriff,   *a*
even during a stay of execution; but this may now be confined to cases where
nobody is lawfully in residence.'

The passage refers to two authorities, *Aglionby v Cohen* [1955] 1 All ER 785, [1955]
1 QB 558 and *Clifton Securities Ltd v Huntley* [1948] 2 All ER 283. We have been
referred to those authorities. They dealt with cases which did not involve statutory   *b*
tenants. They did not deal with situations where the Protection from Eviction
Act 1977 could apply and, in my judgment, they are of no assistance here. Indeed,
the passage in *Megarry* is wrong, in so far as it suggests that there may be a right
in a landlord to re-enter peaceably, in the circumstances of this sort of case,
between an order for possession and execution of the order by the bailiff. In that
regard *The Supreme Court Practice 1991* vol 1, para 45/3/3 is correct, in so far as it   *c*
states in relation to RSC Ord 45, r 3:

'In relation to a dwelling-house, whether it is a protected tenancy or not,
the plaintiff may not enter into possession himself, even peaceably, and he
can only enter into possession under a writ of possession (Protection from
Eviction Act 1977, s. 3) negativing to this extent *Aglionby* v. *Cohen* ([1955] 1   *d*
All ER 785, [1955] 1 QB 558).'

It also follows that the county court decision in *Kyriacou v Pandeli* [1980] CLY
1648 was correctly decided.

The position here is that the landlord, although he had obtained an order of
possession, had no right to resort to self-help to take possession of the premises in   *e*
question. By doing so he was guilty of unlawful eviction and, accordingly, the
judge in the court below was right to conclude that this was a case in which the
tenant, on her counterclaim, was entitled to damages under s 28 of the Housing
Act 1988. I would dismiss this appeal.

LORD DONALDSON OF LYMINGTON MR. I agree.   *f*

LEGGATT LJ. I also agree.

Appeal dismissed.

Mary Rose Plummer   Barrister.

a # R v Master of the Rolls, ex parte McKinnell

QUEEN'S BENCH DIVISION

LORD TAYLOR OF GOSFORTH CJ, SIMON BROWN AND ROCH JJ

2, 24 JULY 1992

b *Solicitor – Disciplinary proceedings – Appeal – Restoration of name to roll of solicitors – Application for restoration of name to roll of solicitors – Application granted by Solicitors Disciplinary Tribunal – Whether Law Society having locus standi to appeal against tribunal's order to restore struck-off solicitor's name to roll – Solicitors Act 1974, ss 47(1)(b), 49(1)(a).*

c In 1975 the applicant was ordered to be struck off the roll of solicitors by the Solicitors Disciplinary Tribunal because he had breached the Solicitors' Accounts Rules and misused clients' money. In 1976 he was convicted of obtaining money dishonestly while in the employment of a local authority and was sentenced to 12 months' imprisonment suspended for two years. In 1988 he started working for another local authority and applied under s 47(1)(b)[a] of the Solicitors Act 1974 to

d have his name restored to the roll of solicitors. After a hearing by the Solicitors Disciplinary Tribunal at which the application was opposed by the Law Society, the tribunal granted the application and ordered that the applicant's name be restored to the roll subject to a recommendation that any practising certificate granted to the applicant should restrain him from practising other than in approved supervised employment. The Law Society sought to appeal under

e s 49(1)(a)[b] of the 1974 Act to the Master of the Rolls against the tribunal's order but at the hearing before the Master of the Rolls the applicant objected that the Law Society had no locus standi to appeal under s 49 since s 49(2) permitted an appeal at the instance of the applicant, the complainant (which had no relevance in the case of an application to restore because there was no one who could be

f described as the complainant) or the person with respect to whom the application or complaint was made but did not allow for an appeal by a respondent such as the Law Society when it opposed an application to restore. The Master of the Rolls ruled that the Law Society had locus standi. The applicant applied for judicial review of that ruling, seeking an order of certiorari to quash it on the ground that it was wrong in law.

g **Held** – The Law Society could appeal under s 49(1)(a) of the 1974 Act to the Master of the Rolls from a decision of the Solicitors Disciplinary Tribunal to restore a former solicitor to the roll since prior to the enactment of the 1974 Act, which was a consolidating statute, the Solicitors Act 1954 had provided for an

h appeal against an order made on an application to restore to the roll or against the refusal of such an application 'by any of the parties to the application'. Accordingly, the Law Society had had power under the 1954 Act to appeal against a decision of the tribunal to restore, and it was to be presumed that in enacting the consolidating 1974 Act Parliament had not intended to remove the Law Society's right of appeal from orders restoring the names of struck-off solicitors to the roll. It followed that

j the applicant's application for judicial review would be dismissed (see p 196 *j* to p 197 *c h* to p 198 *d*, post).

---

a   Section 47(1), so far as material, provides: 'Any application . . . (b) by a former Solicitor whose name has been struck of the roll to have his name restored to the roll, shall be made to the [Solicitors Disciplinary Tribunal] . . .'

b   Section 49, so far as material, is set out at p 195 *g* to *j*, post

Notes

For jurisdiction in respect of disciplinary proceedings under the Solicitors Act   a
1974, see 44 *Halsbury's Laws* (4th edn) para 290, and for cases on the subject, see
44 *Digest* (Reissue) 484–486, 5238–5249.

For the right of appeal from the Solicitors Disciplinary Tribunal, see 44
Halsbury's Laws (4th edn) para 318, and for cases on the subject, see 44 *Digest*
(Reissue) 507–509, 5578–5598.

For appeals from the Solicitors Disciplinary Tribunal to the Master of the Rolls,   b
see 44 *Halsbury's Laws* (4th edn) para 321.

For the Solicitors Act 1974, ss 47, 49, see 41 *Halsbury's Statutes* (4th edn) 56, 61.

Application for judicial review

Anthony George McKinnell applied, with the leave of the Divisional Court of the
Queen's Bench Division (Mann LJ and Hidden J) given on 19 June 1991, for   c
judicial review of a decision of the Master of the Rolls whereby he ruled on
18 December 1990 that the Law Society did have locus standi and was entitled,
pursuant to s 49(1)(a) of the Solicitors Act 1974 to appeal to him against the order
of the Solicitors Disciplinary Tribunal, which on 30 August 1990 granted the
application of Mr McKinnell to be restored to the roll of solicitors. The facts are   d
set out in the judgment of the court.

Ian Croxford (instructed by *Colin Watson & Co*, Warrington) for Mr McKinnell.
Michael Briggs (instructed by *Michael Hoyle,* Kendal) for the Law Society.
The Master of the Rolls did not appear.

e
Cur adv vult

24 July 1992. The following judgment of the court was delivered.

LORD TAYLOR OF GOSFORTH CJ. On 19 December 1975 the Solicitors   f
Disciplinary Tribunal ordered that Anthony George McKinnell be struck off the
roll of solicitors. Mr McKinnell, who is now 56 years of age, had been admitted
as a solicitor in 1960. The reason for his being struck off was that he had breached
the Solicitors' Accounts Rules and used clients' money.

Following his being struck off Mr McKinnell obtained employment with a
local authority. In 1976, in the course of that employment, Mr McKinnell   g
obtained various sums of money dishonestly, by deception and forgery. He
disclosed those criminal offences to the police voluntarily and on 2 November
1977 he was convicted of six counts of obtaining money by deception or by means
of forged instruments and was sentenced to 12 months' imprisonment suspended
for two years.

In 1980 Mr McKinnell obtained employment with Newark District Council as   h
a management assistant. Three years later, in September 1983, he moved to the
legal department of that district council. In early 1988 Mr McKinnell commenced
work for High Peak District Council.

On 16 November 1988 Mr McKinnell made application under s 47 of the
Solicitors Act 1974 to have his name restored to the roll of solicitors. No doubt   j
one reason for that application was an observation made by the Solicitors
Disciplinary Tribunal on 19 December 1975, namely:

'That the respondent may be encouraged to rehabilitate himself by
continuing in employment within the law subject to such consents as may
be necessary, and they believe that in due course the time may come when

a an application on his part that his name should be restored to the roll might
be favourably considered.'

The hearing of Mr McKinnell's application for restoration to the roll of solicitors
took place before the tribunal on 19 May 1990. The matter was listed under Case
No 5544/1989, which was a new and different case number from that given to
the 1975 disciplinary proceedings. The Law Socieity appeared and opposed the
b application. The findings and order of the tribunal refer to the Law Society as 'the
respondent to the application'. Throughout those findings and order Mr
McKinnell is referred to as 'the applicant' and the Law Society as 'the respondent'.
The tribunal gave their decision on 30 August 1990 in these terms:

c 'The Tribunal are prepared to grant this application and Order that
Anthony George McKinnell . . . . be restored to the Roll of Solicitors and they
further Order that he do pay the costs of and incidental to this application,
such costs to be taxed by one of the Taxing Masters of the Supreme Court.
The Tribunal recommend to the Law Society that any Practising Certificate
granted to the applicant should restrain him from practising other than in
approved supervised employment.'

d
The Law Society sought to bring an appeal before the Master of the Rolls
against the order of the tribunal under s 49(1)(a) of the 1974 Act. Counsel for Mr
McKinnell before the Master of the Rolls took a preliminary point of law, namely
that the Law Society had no locus standi to appeal under that section. The Master
of the Rolls ruled on 18 December 1990 that the Law Society did have locus
e standi and was entitled, pursuant to s 49(1)(a) of the 1974, Act, to appeal to him
against the order of the tribunal restoring the applicant to the roll of solicitors.
An application for judicial review of that ruling was made on behalf of the
applicant on 18 April 1991. The relief sought was certiorari to quash the ruling
on the grounds that it was wrong in law. That application was refused on the
papers by Otton J on 10 May 1991, but granted at an oral hearing before Mann LJ
f and Hidden J on 19 June 1991.
The issue is whether on an application by a former solicitor to have his name
restored to the roll under s 47(1)(b) of the 1974 Act, where the tribunal makes an
order for such restoration, an appeal from the tribunal lies at the instance of the
Law Society under s 49(1)(a) to the Master of the Rolls.
Section 49 of the 1974 Act, so far as it is material, provides:
g
'(1) An appeal from the Tribunal shall lie—(a) in the case of an order on
an application under section 43(3) or 47(1)(b) or the refusal of any such
application, to the Master of the Rolls; (b) in any other case, to the High
Court.

h (2) Subject to subsection (3), an appeal shall lie at the instance of the
applicant or complainant or of the person with respect to whom the
application or complaint was made.
(3) An appeal against an order under section 43(2) shall lie only at the
instance of the person with respect to whom the application was made.
(4) The High Court and the Master of the Rolls shall have power to make
j such order on an appeal under this section as they may think fit . . .'

Subsection (6) of s 49 provides that the decision of the Master of the Rolls on an
appeal under this section shall be final and sub-s (7) enables the Master of the Rolls
to make regulations about appeals to him under the section.
Mr Croxford, counsel for Mr McKinnell, submitted that the application to the
tribunal under s 47(1)(b) was a fresh proceeding in which Mr McKinnell was the

applicant and the Law Society were the respondents. Mr Croxford relied upon the 1989 case number and the terminology adopted by the tribunal in their 'finding and order'. He argued that the forms in the schedule to the Solicitors (Disciplinary Proceedings) Rules 1985, SI 1985/226, and the terminology of rr 11 to 15 are consistent with the application to restore being fresh proceedings distinct from the proceedings which had led to the solicitor's name being removed from the roll and with the Law Society being respondents to such fresh proceedings. Mr Croxford pointed out that the applicant or complainant in the original disciplinary proceedings did not have to be the society, although in this case the society had brought the complaint against Mr McKinnell.

If those propositions were sound, argued Mr Croxford, then s 49(2) was mandatory and did not allow for an appeal by a respondent. Section 49(2) permitted an appeal at the instance of the applicant, the complainant (which had no relevance in the case of an application to restore where there is no one who can be described as the complainant) or the person with respect to whom the application or complaint was made. Again this last category was unnecessary in the case of applications to restore and was included only because s 49(2) dealt with appeals to the High Court in other situations, as well as appeals to the Master of the Rolls under s 49(1)(a). Thus it was necessary to have these words to allow for an appeal by a solicitor who had been suspended from practice under s 47(2)(b) or who had been ordered to pay a financial penalty under s 47(2)(c). In such cases the words 'or of the person with respect to whom the application or complaint was made' were necessary so that the solicitor concerned, who would not be the 'applicant or complainant', would have the right to appeal.

The words of s 49(2) should, said Mr Croxford, be given their ordinary and natural meaning. If this is done, he says, it is clear that Parliament has not provided the Law Society or any objector under rr 15 and 16 of the 1975 rules with the power to appeal against an order that a solicitor's name be restored to the roll.

Mr Briggs, for the Law Society, began his submission by pointing out that under the Solicitors Act 1957, as amended by the Solicitors Act 1965, when Parliament first gave the Solicitors Disciplinary Committee power to direct the Society to restore to the roll the name of a former solicitor whose name had been removed from or struck off it (s 47(2)(bb) of the 1954 Act), it had provided for an appeal against an order made on such an application or against the refusal of such an application 'by any of the parties to the application'. The appeal was to be direct to the Master of the Rolls, who was to have the power to confirm or rescind the order made or confirm the refusal to restore the name to the roll or to make such other order as he might think fit. Section 48(3) of the Solicitors Act 1957 (a provision inserted in the 1957 Act by the 1965 Act) established this system of appeals and also provided that the Master of the Rolls could make regulations relating to the manner in which such appeals were to be presented.

The evidence indicates that since the 1965 Act it has been the practice of the Society to oppose applications to restore, made by solicitors whose names have been struck off the roll for misconduct, and to appeal against orders by the tribunal that such solicitors' names be restored to the roll. This is to enable the Master of the Rolls to exercise his supervisory jurisdiction over the solicitors' profession.

The correct approach, submits Mr Briggs, to the construction of s 49(2) is that it should be assumed Parliament did not intend to remove the Law Society's right of appeal against orders restoring the names of struck off solicitors to the roll. That it was not Parliament's intention in s 49(2) to effect so fundamental a change can be gathered from the remaining subsections of s 49 and also from the wording of sub-s (2) itself. Thus s 49(1)(a) states that an appeal from the tribunal shall lie

both against the refusal of an application to restore and the making of an order on
a such an application. Where the tribunal makes an order under s 43(2) that no
solicitor shall, except in accordance with the permission in writing granted by the
society for such period and subject to such conditions as the society may think fit,
employ or remunerate in connection with his practice as a solicitor a solicitor's
clerk, s 49(3) provides that an appeal against the order shall lie only at the instance
of the person with respect to whom the application was made. Thus, argues Mr
b Briggs, where it is intended that only one side to an application before the tribunal
is to have a right of appeal against the tribunal's order, Parliament so provides in
express terms.

Finally, Mr Briggs submits that the language of s 49(2) makes it clear that
Parliament intended both sides to any application or complaint to have the right
to appeal. That emerges from the use of the words 'at the instance of the applicant
c or complainant' referring to the person initiating the proceeding on the one hand,
and the words 'or of the person with respect to whom the application or complaint
was made' referring to the respondent to the application or complaint on the
other hand. If Parliament had intended each term to be read disjunctively, the
subsection would have read 'at the instance of the applicant or of the complaint
d or of the person with respect to whom the application or complaint was made'.

In reply Mr Croxford submitted, first, that the addition of a lay member or
members to the Solicitors Disciplinary Tribunal explained why Parliament had
removed the society's right of appeal against an order restoring the name of a
solicitor to the roll. The lay element provided the necessary safeguard on behalf
of the public against inappropriate restoration.

e Secondly, Mr Croxford argued that the provision for an appeal against an order
made under s 47(1)(*b*) was not inconsistent with only the applicant having a right
of appeal because he might wish to appeal about costs or against a condition or
recommendation in an order made in his favour which he considered to be unfair.
Section 47(2) of the 1974 Act gave the tribunal power to make such order as it
might think fit. In the present case the tribunal had added a recommendation
f which was acceptable to Mr McKinnell, but it was not difficult to envisage a
recommendation being added which would effectively deprive the solicitor of the
benefit of having his name restored to the roll.

In our view these two arguments, although ingenious, involve strained and far-
fetched explanations of the statutory purpose.

g Finally, the presence of s 49(3) in the 1974 Act was explained as being part of
special provisions for the control of employed clerks, where the employed clerk
was not directly amenable to the jurisdiction of the disciplinary tribunal and any
jurisdiction had to be exercised by the making of orders binding on solicitors,
either prohibiting them from employing the individual clerk or requiring the
solicitor to employ such a person on special conditions. The existence of s 49(3)
h could not justify an interpretation of s 49(2) which did not give the words used
their ordinary and natural meaning.

The conclusion we have reached is that the submissions made on behalf of the
Law Society (and which found favour with the Master of the Rolls) are to be
preferred. The Solicitors Act 1974 is a consolidating statute so that there is a
presumption, albeit rebuttable, that Parliament did not intend to make changes
j to the existing law. In our judgment the wording used in s 49(2) is not such as to
displace that presumption when the words are read in the context of s 49 as a
whole and in the general context of the 1974 Act. True, s 49(3) indicates
Parliament's clear intention to introduce change in the rights of appeal against a
s 43(2) order—depriving the Law Society of the right it had previously enjoyed
under s 48(3) of the 1957 Act (as amended in 1965) to appeal against an order
(then under s 38(2A)) prohibiting the employment of a named solicitor's clerk.

But in our judgment no such clear intention is shown in regard to the rights of
appeal against orders under s 47(1)(b) (restoration to the roll), or under s 43(3) *a*
(revocation of a s 43(2) order at the suit of either the clerk or the Law Society). On
the contrary, all the indications are the other way. The very fact that ss 43(3) and
47(1)(b) find no mention in s 49(3) is surely eloquent of Parliament's intention. In
short the wording of sub-s (2) of s 49, read against the wording of sub-s (3), in our
judgment makes it clear that appeals from the tribunal, other than appeals against
orders made under s 43(2), are to lie at the instance of either side to the application *b*
or complaint. Indeed, that this was Parliament's intention is abundantly clear also
from the wording of s 49(1), which expressly allows for an appeal equally from
the making of an order that a solicitor's name be restored to the roll as from the
refusal of an application. It may be that the Parliamentary draftsman did not
consider it necessary to alter or add to the wording of s 49(2), which in effect re-
enacted the terms of s 48(1) of the 1957 Act, because he considered an application *c*
by a solicitor to restore his name to the roll was a continuation of the original
application or complaint to strike him off the roll for misconduct. Be that as it
may, however, the language of the subsection is capable of sustaining that
construction and is consistent both with the presumption arising from
consolidating legislation and Parliament's clear intention. We so construe it. *d*

Consequently we uphold the ruling of Lord Donaldson MR, given on
18 December 1990 and refuse the relief sought by the applicant.

Application dismissed.

N P Metcalfe Esq   Barrister. *e*

Hillingdon London Borough Council v H
f

FAMILY DIVISION
JOHNSON J
21 MAY, 11 JUNE 1992

*Family proceedings – Orders in family proceedings – Reasons for order – Appeal –
Justices providing additional reasons for their decision under appeal – Whether court will*
have regard to subsequent findings and reasons provided by justices – Family Proceedings *g*
Courts (Children Act 1989) Rules 1991, r 21(6).

*Family proceedings – Costs – Order for costs made by justices – Order for costs against
local authority – Local authority opposing application for residence order and then
withdrawing opposition – Father awarded costs against local authority – Whether order* *h*
*for costs against local authority justified – Duty of party seeking order for costs to provide
detailed statement of costs prepared with proper care – Family Proceedings Courts
(Children Act 1989) Rules 1991, r 22.*

In May 1991 a care order was made committing two children of divorced parents
into the care of the local authority and they were removed from the mother's care *j*
and placed with friends of the family. The father proposed that the children
should live with him and his new partner but the local authority informed the
father that the question of whether the children should go to live with him would
be reviewed in six months' time. Shortly afterwards, the children were moved to
foster parents pending the local authority's assessment of the suitability of the
father. On 22 November 1991 the father, who was dissatisfied with the local

authority's progress in carrying out an assessment of the prospect of the children
_a_ making their permanent home with him and his new partner, applied to the
family proceedings court for a residence order under the Children Act 1989,
which would have had the effect of revoking the care order. Initially, the local
authority opposed the father's application and proposed instead that the children
be placed with long-term foster parents. On 3 January 1992 the father's solicitors
indicated that, whatever the outcome of the forthcoming hearing, they would be
_b_ asking the court to consider the question of costs. The guardian ad litem appointed
on behalf of the children prepared a report which was critical of the local authority
and recommended that the father's application for a residence order be granted.
On 22 January the local authority, having considered the report of the guardian
ad litem, changed its view and informed all the parties that it no longer intended
to oppose the application. After a two-day hearing the family proceedings court
_c_ granted the residence order and, after stating that it adopted the guardian ad
litem's view of the local authority's actions, ordered the local authority to pay the
father's costs of £7,171 under r 22ᵃ of the Family Proceedings Courts (Children
Act 1989) Rules 1991. The local authority appealed to the High Court against the
costs order. Prior to the hearing the justices provided additional reasons for their
_d_ decision and the question arose whether, in the light of r 21(6)ᵇ of the 1991 rules,
which provided that when making an order under the 1989 Act justices were
required to state and record any findings of fact and the reasons for their decision,
it was appropriate for the court to have regard to the additional findings and
reasons provided by the justices.

_e_ **Held** – (1) On an appeal to the High Court under the 1989 Act the only findings
of fact and the only reasons that could be relied on to support a decision of a
family proceedings court under appeal were those announced by the justices in
accordance with r 21(6) of the 1991 rules, which required them to record the facts
which they judged to be significant in the making of their decision and also the
salient considerations which had led to their conclusion. The court would not
_f_ have regard to any subsequent findings and reasons provided by the justices. On
the facts, the findings and reasons given by the justices at the time they announced
their decision were wholly insufficient to sustain their order, but even if their
additional findings and reasons were taken into account the order could still not
be sustained because the justices had been plainly wrong in their conclusion that
the father had been forced into legal proceedings by the local authority's attitude
_g_ since, the children having already been committed to the care of the local
authority by the 1991 care order, he would in any event have had to apply to the
justices if he wished for a residence order since such orders were not available
simply by way of agreement of the parties (see p 204 _d e_, p 206 _j_ and p 207 _d_,
post); _G v G_ [1985] 2 All ER 225 applied.

_h_   (2) In the absence of any provision as to the mechanism for assessing costs in
proceedings under the 1989 Act, it was the duty of a party seeking an order for
costs under r 22 of the 1991 rules to provide the court with a detailed statement
of those costs prepared with proper care and to make that statement available to
all parties well in advance of the hearing so that the claim could be properly
considered. On the facts, it was clear that the solicitors' claim had not been
_j_ prepared with proper care and was inaccurate, and since the parents were legally
aided it was impossible for the solicitors to make an accurate assessment of the
remuneration which they would receive from the Legal Aid Board. Moreover,
the local authority had properly carried out its statutory function and ought not

---

_a_   Rule 22 is set out at p 204 _f g_, post
_b_   Rule 21(6) is set out at p 204 _a_, post

to be penalised for its change of mind in withdrawing its opposition to the father's
application. In those circumstances the appeal would be allowed and the order   a
for costs made against the local authority would be set aside (see p 204 h to p 205
a e and p 207 f to j, post); R v Tottenham Justices, ex p Joshi [1982] 2 All ER 507 and
Gojkovic v Gojkovic (No 2) [1992] 1 All ER 267 applied.

Notes
For residence orders with respect to children, see Supplement to 24 Halsbury's   b
Laws (4th edn) para 541A.
     For the Children Act 1989, see 6 Halsbury's Statutes (4th edn) (1992 reissue) 387.
     For the Family Proceedings Courts (Children Act 1989) Rules 1991, rr 21, 22,
see 4 Halsbury's Statutory Instruments (1992 reissue) 338, 339.

Cases referred to in judgment   c
B v Derbyshire CC [1991] 1 FLR 538.
Bolton Metropolitan BC v B and H [1980] 2 FLR 349.
G v G [1985] 2 All ER 225, [1985] 1 WLR 647, HL.
G (a minor) (wardship: costs), Re [1982] 2 All ER 32, [1982] 1 WLR 438, CA.
Gojkovic v Gojkovic (No 2) [1992] 1 All ER 267, [1992] Fam 40, [1991] 3 WLR 621,   d
     CA.
Havering London BC v S [1986] 1 FLR 489.
R v Tottenham Justices, ex p Joshi [1982] 2 All ER 507, [1992] 1 WLR 631, DC.
Scherer v Counting Instruments Ltd [1986] 2 All ER 507, [1982] 1 WLR 615, CA.

Cases also cited   e
Leary v Leary [1987] 1 All ER 261, [1987] 1 WLR 72, CA.
R v North Yorkshire CC, ex p M [1989] 1 All ER 143, [1989] QB 411.
R v Salisbury and Tisbury and Mere Combined Juvenile Court, ex p Bull (1985) 149 JP
     346, DC.

Appeal   f
Hillingdon London Borough Council appealed under s 94 of the Children Act
1989 from an order made by the justices sitting in the Hillingdon area Family
Proceedings Court at Uxbridge on 28 January 1992 whereby, having granted the
respondent father's application for a residence order relating to the two children
of the marriage, the justices ordered that his costs of £7,171 be paid by the local
authority pursuant to r 22 of the Family Proceedings Courts (Children Act 1989)   g
Rules 1991, SI 1991/1395. The appeal was heard and judgment was given in
chambers. The case is reported by permission of Johnson J. The facts are set out
in the judgment.

Judith Parker QC (instructed by F Craig Pile, Uxbridge) for the appellant.   h
Lord Meston and Susan Castle (instructed by W H Matthews & Co, Staines) for the
respondent.

11 June 1992. The following judgment was delivered.

JOHNSON J. This is an appeal to the High Court from an order of justices   j
sitting in the Hillingdon area Family Proceedings Court. The order is an unusual
one in that in proceedings under the Children Act 1989 the justices ordered that
the local authority involved in those proceedings should pay to another party the
costs of that party in the sum of no less than £7,171.
     The factual background is as follows. The proceedings concern two children
now aged seven and eight. The marriage of their parents had ended by separation
in September 1989 and subsequently in divorce. After the separation the children

had lived with the mother and her new man friend. Social workers became
a involved, as later did the National Society for the Prevention of Cruelty to
Children. Eventually it became necessary for a place of safety order to be made
and for care proceedings to be instituted. The final hearing of those proceedings
was on 15 May 1991. As had been proposed to the court, both by the NSPCC and
by the guardian ad litem appointed by the court to act on behalf of the children,
the court made a full care order. At that time the guardian's report had spoken of
b the intense conflict between the mother and the father and the consequent effect
upon the children of that conflict.

Before the justices on that occasion the local authority had proposed that
further attempts be made to improve the ability of the mother to care adequately
for the children so that their future could be with her. The submission of the
father had been to the effect that the court should leave open the opportunity for
c him to apply for custody of the children in the divorce proceedings then pending.
By its order then made the court clearly rejected that possibility, and moreover
rejected the submission of the local authority, to which I have referred.

The day following the hearing of 15 May the local authority social worker
concerned with the children wrote to the father a letter which referred to periodic
d reviews taking place and concluded:

> 'These reviews will be held every six months. During these meetings we
> must have a serious look at whether the children should be coming home to
> live with you in the future.'

On 17 July 1991 the children were removed from the care of the mother and
e placed with friends of the family. Unhappily, in August 1991, those friends
informed the social worker that they no longer felt able to care for the children.
The consequence was that the local authority had to consider the situation of the
children, including carrying out an assessment of the prospect of the children
making their permanent home with their father, who, by now, had a new
partner.
f In my view, this local authority has shown itself throughout conscious of its
duty to keep an open mind about the future of these children and to consider all
the potential options in what was often an extremely difficult and fraught
situation. Notwithstanding the making of the care order on 15 May 1991 and the
implications of that order, the local authority, in my view, continued to have in
mind the possibility of placing the children within their natural family, and
g specifically with the father and his new partner.

The father, however, was dissatisfied with what he thought to be the inadequacy
of the local authority's endeavours in this regard and he instructed solicitors. By a
letter of 17 October 1991 those solicitors asked the local authority to keep them
informed about the progress of the assessment that was being undertaken of the
h father and his partner. Most unhappily and regrettably there was no answer to
that letter. One must be conscious of the pressures under which local authority
social workers operate, particularly in boroughs such as that with which this case
is concerned, but nonetheless one might have hoped that the letter would have
received at least some acknowledgment.

My impression, and without a full inquiry such as might be carried out by the
j social service inspectorate it can be little more, is that the assessment of the father
and his partner had scarcely advanced. What is, however, a matter of concern is
that within days of receiving and failing to reply to that letter, namely on 23
October 1991, the local authority moved the children from the family friends
with whom they had lived since 17 July 1991 and placed them with foster parents.
I was told that the local authority was still maintaining an open mind about the
possibility of placing the children with the father and that the choice of foster
parents made in October was intended to cover the possibility of the children

being returned to the father, but also to cover the possibility of a need for the children to be with foster parents for some longer time, in the event of the *a* assessment of the father proving unsatisfactory.

The father found out what had happened and on 22 November 1991 issued an application in the local family proceedings court asking for a residence order, the effect of which would be to revoke the care order. In response to that application the local authority social worker filed a statement opposing the father's application and proposing instead that the children be placed with long-term foster parents. *b*

It is to be borne in mind that the children had not lived with their father since September 1989. The social worker's reasons were set out in a statement extending to some 12 pages which concluded:

> 'Given the acrimony between the parents who both vie for the children's affection and blacken each other's characters and motives in the process, I am *c* of the view that the children have become pawns in their game of hurt and ascendency. I believe that this application for a residence order is yet another step in this game and that neither parent has been able or willing to see matters from the children's point of view or in terms of their feelings, experiences and level of understanding. I feel that these difficulties have gone *d* on too long for there to be a realistic prospect of change in time for these children and given their improvement whilst in foster care, where they are not brought up in their parents' conflict, it is not in the children's interests for them to go and live with the father and that they need to be placed in an environment with permanent substitute parents, who can meet the boys' physical, emotional, educational and social needs.' *e*

On 23 December 1991 the directions hearing contemplated by the new Children Act procedure was held in the family proceedings court and the hearing of the father's application fixed for 27 and 28 January 1992. Both the court and the father's solicitors were aware that the principal social worker involved on behalf of the local authority would be on leave and unable to play any significant *f* part in the preparation of the hearing before 20 January 1992.

On 3 January 1992 the father's solicitors, apparently taking exception to something stated by the local authority's solicitor in correspondence, wrote to the local authority giving notice that they would be asking the court to consider the question of costs, whether their client was successful or not. Meanwhile, the guardian ad litem appointed on behalf of the children was preparing her report. *g* That became available to the parties on 19 January. By that report the guardian ad litem recommended that a residence order be made in favour of the father and her report contained passages critical of the local authority. I have read that report now on several occasions and I have its contents fully in mind, but I quote for the purposes of my judgment the following from the guardian's report: *h*

> 'In October 1991, when the local authority negotiated a long-term foster home placement it seems reasonable to suppose then they had already embarked on a plan to move towards adoption. There are inevitably tensions and pressures created for social workers who are responsible for making long-term plans for children which may include separation from parents when *j* working with natural parents. However, to suggest to a parent that an assessment should start at the same point in time as the children are prepared for removal to a long-term placement, does not enable an open and honest working relationship.'

I have already referred to the fact that the need to move the children had been precipitated by the announcement by the friends of the family with whom the children were staying that they could not keep the children any longer. In the

light of that report the local authority carried out what has been referred to as a
a radical re-examination of the position. The principal social worker involved
having returned from leave, on 22 January 1992 the local authority informed all
the parties by telephone that it no longer intended to oppose the father's
application. On 24 January the local authority confirmed that decision in writing.
Moreover, it informed the parties of its decision to place the children with the
father forthwith, in advance of the hearing. The 24 January was a Friday and the
b hearing was due to begin on the following Monday.

It seems that the guardian ad litem expressed some reservations about that
decision to move the children in advance of the hearing, but by a letter of 24
January the father's solicitors said that it seemed to them that the view of the
guardian ad litem was 'quite wrong as a matter of law'. They insisted that the
c children be transferred as had been previously suggested by the local authority.

The hearing began on 27 January 1992. Mrs Castle, in opening the case on
behalf of the father, no doubt acting under compelling instructions, indicated
that at the conclusion of the proceedings she would be pressing the justices to
make an order for costs against the local authority. It is to be borne in mind that
the justices were no mere rubber stamp. The father's solicitors appear to have
d thought perhaps otherwise and that the hearing on 27 January would be nothing
more than a formality. That, of course, is not the case. Justices who exercise this
delicate jurisdiction are under a statutory duty to carry out the inquiry expected
of them by the Children Act 1989. That is a mandatory duty imposed upon the
justices and one that the law does not permit them to relinquish albeit the parties
appearing before them are in agreement as to the order that shall be made. The
e responsibility for the order is that of the justices.

By s 1(3) Parliament has required a court exercising this jurisdiction to have
regard to a number of considerations and by sub-s (5) has directed the court to
make no order, notwithstanding an agreement between the parties, unless it
considers that doing so would be better for the child than making no order at all.
f Moreover, in this particular case the justices were hearing this application on 27
January 1992 against the background which included the making of a full care
order on 15 May 1991, an order which, as I have already indicated, was made
after hearing submissions by the guardian ad litem and by the local authority
which might seem to be in marked distinction to the submissions being made
now, only a few months later.

g The hearing occupied the justices on 27 and 28 January 1992, the second day
being occupied largely with a consideration of the mother's application for a
contact order. On 28 January 1992 a residence order was made, with the order
for costs which is the subject of this appeal.

Before me the argument has covered three main areas. The first area is one that
was raised by me rather than by counsel. It relates to the reasons given for the
h justices' decision. Prior to the 1989 Act coming into operation on 14 October
1991 the practice was for justices to announce their decision in the most simple
terms, saying that they made a care order or a custody order, as the case might be.
They were required to give no detailed reasons and seldom did so. If, however,
that order was the subject of an appeal to the Divisional Court, then the practice
was that they thereafter drafted reasons, usually in quite considerable detail.

j Now, of course, the practice is entirely different. The 1989 Act and the
regulations made under that Act have imposed upon the justices a new and very
substantial burden and one which I am aware is sometimes causing difficulty, as
justices are not accustomed to giving a judgment or a detailed explanation of
their findings and their reasons.

The matter is now covered by the Family Proceedings Courts (Children Act
1989) Rules 1991, SI 1991/1395, r 21 of which imposes upon justices the following
duty. I read only the words which are material to this appeal:

'... (5) Before the court makes an order ... the justices' clerk shall record in writing ... (b) ... the reasons for the court's decision and any findings of fact.

(6) When making an order ... the court, or one of the justices constituting the court by which the decision is made, shall state any findings of fact and the reasons for the court's decision ...'

In this case the findings of the justices and their reasons, so far as concerns the making of the order for costs, were announced by them in the following terms:

'We adopt the guardian ad litem's view of the local authority's actions and order the father's full costs to be paid by the local authority, assessed at £7,171.'

As I have said I have now read the report of the guardian ad litem and such information as I have which would indicate her view of the local authority's actions on several occasions and I have to say that I do not understand what findings the justices believed that they were making or what reasons they were giving for their decision in that brief statement, which I have just quoted in full.

In accordance with the former practice but, as I hold, contrary to what should now be the practice under the 1989 Act, the justices have provided further reasons extending to three pages. I raised with counsel the question whether, on an appeal such as this, it was appropriate or permissible for me to have regard to those additional findings and reasons. I hold that on an appeal to the High Court under the 1989 Act the only findings of fact and the only reasons that may be relied on to support the decision of the justices under appeal are those announced by the justices in accordance with the rule to which I have referred.

Undoubtedly in applying this rule the High Court will seek to avoid undue rigidity and technicality. Nonetheless, it seems to me that the rules require the justices to record and to announce the facts which they judged to be significant in the making of their decision and also the salient considerations which have led them to their conclusion.

Orders for costs

There is provision in the rules for justices to make an order for costs. Rule 22 provides:

'(1) In any relevant proceedings, the court may, at any time during the proceedings in that court, make an order that a party pay the whole or any part of the costs of any other party.

(2) A party against whom the court is considering making a costs order shall have an opportunity to make representations as to why the order should not be made.'

Before me there was an analysis of the arrangements that are available in other jurisdictions exercised by justices for the making of costs orders and for the assessment of those costs. The conclusion of counsel, with which I agree, was that in this jurisdiction no mechanism has been provided for the assessment of costs and the matter seems to be left to the justices themselves. Justices, of course, are accustomed, as part of their day-to-day work, to assessing costs of comparatively small amounts. However, a claim for costs of £7,171.50 was, I suspect, outside the experience of most justices. Indeed, I have to say that I doubt whether a judge, either of the High Court or of the county court, would have regarded himself as qualified to make an assessment of so substantial a claim. Accordingly, it was the duty of the solicitors who were instructing counsel to make this claim and who, in correspondence, had evinced an intention to seek an order for costs against the local authority because of the supposed failure of the local authority to discharge

its duty properly, to provide for the court a detailed statement of those costs;
a moreover, to prepare that statement with proper care. It would, I think, be
appropriate for that detailed statement to be made available to the other parties
well in advance of the hearing, to enable the claim and the detail of it to be
considered.

Here it is plain that the solicitors' claim was not prepared with proper care. For
example, it included costs which ought more properly to have been included in
b their bill relating to the divorce proceedings, in which they were acting for the
father. That, I was told, led to their claim, by agreement, being reduced now
from £7,171 to £6,439, but, moreover, the claim that they put forward took no
account of the fact that the second day of the hearing was occupied in consideration
of the mother's claim for a contact order as to which no possible complaint could
c be made against the local authority.

In a case in which a solicitor is privately instructed, the solicitors would, of
course, be able to assess the profit costs and if counsel had been engaged then, of
course, the brief fee and other fees would have been agreed in advance of the
hearing. However, in proceedings under the 1989 Act it is almost always the case
that the parents are represented by virtue of a legal aid certificate. Such was the
d case here. The Legal Aid Act 1988 provides that solicitor and counsel may receive
their remuneration only from the fund. The extent of that remuneration can be
known only when the assessment has been carried out that is provided by the
legal aid scheme. In such an assessment, of course, some items are the subject of
fixed costs, but many and usually the most significant, are the subject of a
discretion. Accordingly, in the present case it would have been, I think, impossible
e for the solicitors, however careful they had been, to make an assessment which
accurately reflected the remuneration which would have been paid to them and
to counsel after the matter had been considered under the arrangements provided
by the Legal Aid Board.

I think from this unhappy tale there are a number of lessons to be learnt. It is,
f of course, unusual for an order for costs to be made in proceedings such as this. I
have been helpfully referred to a number of authorities relating to costs, beginning
with the decision of the Court of Appeal in *Scherer v Counting Instruments Ltd*
[1986] 2 All ER 529 at 535–536, [1986] 1 WLR 615 at 621, Buckley LJ set out a
number of considerations. Undoubtedly, there will be cases under the Children
Act in which it is appropriate for orders for costs to be made. By way of example
g I was referred to the decision of Bush J in *Havering London BC v S* [1986] 1 FLR
489 at 491, where he said:

> 'I accept that the local authority and the social workers behaved in the way
> in which they did in error, but it is an important constitutional matter, and
> to mark the position, and so that local authorities shall not be under any
h > misapprehension about their powers, I order that the costs of this application
> be paid by the local authority.'

Similarly, in *Bolton Metropolitan BC v B and H* [1989] 2 FLR 349 Ewbank J
ordered a local authority to pay the costs of the Official Solicitor to mark his
disapprobation of the delay on the part of the local authority in appointing a social
j worker, a delay which he described as 'inexcusable and deplorable'.

More recently in *Gojkovic v Gojkovic (No 2)* [1992] 1 All ER 267 at 270, [1992]
Fam 40 at 56 Butler-Sloss LJ asked:

> 'What are the principles governing costs in applications for financial relief
> in the Family Division and, in particular, in cases where open offers and
> *Calderbank* offers are made? In particular, what is the starting point of
> entitlement to costs?'

She then referred to RSC Ord 62 and continued ([1992] 1 All ER 267 at 271,
[1992] Fam 40 at 57):   *a*

> 'However, in the Family Division there still remains the necessity for some
> starting point. That starting point, in my judgment, is that costs prima facie
> follow the event . . . but [that principle] may be displaced much more easily
> than, and in circumstances which would not apply, in other divisions of the
> High Court. One important example is, as the judge pointed out, that it is   *b*
> unusual to order costs in children cases.'

In reading the bundle of documents relating to this appeal, both before, during
and since the hearing before me, I have wondered whether attention was not
focused almost as much on the father's wish to obtain an order for costs against
the local authority as upon the important question of making for these children
the best decision that was available. I wish to echo the words of Sir Stephen Brown   *c*
P in *B v Derbyshire CC* [1992] 1 FLR 538 at 546 where he said:

> 'On 14 October 1991 the Children Act 1989 is going to become effective
> and, when that takes place, I very much hope that the adversarial approach
> to care proceedings will disappear to a very large extent. What has happened
> in this case is symptomatic of the adversarial approach, where technical   *d*
> points are taken in order to secure a particular result. What will become
> more apparent from 14 October 1991 is that what the court is concerned
> with is the whole welfare of the child and that its task is to investigate, in an
> inquisitorial manner if necessary, the interests of the child.'

As I have already indicated, it is undoubtedly the case that there may be   *e*
circumstances in which it is appropriate for a court to make an order for costs in
a case relating to children. Moreover, in an appeal to the High Court relating to
such an order, the principle to be adopted is that set out by Lord Lane CJ in *R v
Tottenham Justices, ex p Joshi* [1982] 2 All ER 507, [1982] 1 WLR 631. In effect, the
principle is the same as that laid down in *G v G* [1985] 2 All ER 225, [1985]   *f*
1 WLR 647.

Finally, I was referred to the judgment of Ormrod LJ in *Re G (a minor)
(wardship: costs)* [1982] 2 All ER 32 at 36, [1982] 1 WLR 438 at 443–444, where
he said:

> 'Where the proceedings are between the parents, both of whom are acting
> bona fide in the interests of the child, it is not uncommon to make no order   *g*
> as to the costs of the proceedings. Where a local authority has initiated the
> proceedings there seems to be no reason to approach the question of costs in
> any special way . . . If this judgment is less helpful than the parties hoped, as
> it almost certainly is, the reason lies in the terms of the statute, which places
> the discretion so unequivocally on the trial judge that it leaves little or no   *h*
> room for an appellate court to lay down principles or even guidelines.'

I turn then to consider whether this order for costs made by the justices was
justified and whether it is one with which this court can interfere, having regard
to the familiar principals of *G v G*. I have already referred to the findings and the
reasons given by the justices at the time that they announced their decision on 28
January. Those findings, such as they be, and those reasons such as they be, are in   *j*
my judgment wholly insufficient to sustain their order.

If, however, I were to consider the more elaborate findings and reasons which
they gave subsequently, then again I would hold their findings and their reasons
to be unsustainable. By way of illustration I refer to the following. The submission
of the father's counsel is recorded as follows:

a

'In summary she submitted that the local authority should bear the costs of the application of the father because at the time of his application the local authority either had access to all the information or it had access to all the information available to the guardian. She also submitted that either the social worker had assessed him or ought to have assessed him. The local authority's decision to agree to his application was an admission that it had been wrong all the time.'

b

In their elaborated reasons the justices expressed their conclusion in the following terms:

c

'At the time the respondent made his application to the court the local authority had decided that it was in the best interests of the children that they be placed with long-term foster parents. The respondent was forced to go to law to seek a residence order.'

That was, of course, plainly wrong. The children had been committed to the care of the local authority by the order made by the justices on 15 May 1991. If the father wished there to be a residence order and thus revocation of the care order it was, of course, necessary for him to have that order from the justices. It

d was not an order that was available simply by way of agreement. Moreover, as I indicated earlier in my judgment, there were reasons why the justices might be particularly cautious in considering the proposal agreed between all the parties that there should now be the fundamental reversal of the future of these children, so soon after the making of the care order in 1991.

I have considered the grounds advanced before me on behalf of the father in

e the notice. In effect, the suggestion is that the sudden change of mind on the part of the local authority after receipt of the guardian's report in January 1992 constituted an admission that its previous decision about the children was wholly wrong and, moreover, it is suggested that it has mismanaged its care of these children in specific regards. I have considered each of those submissions and I

f reject each of them.

There have been a number of changes of mind since May 1991 on the part not only of the local authority. Moreover, it seems to me that a local authority is to be commended for a decision such as this, made in the light of the report of an independent person of the qualification and experience of the guardian ad litem. It would be a sad day if it was thought that a change of mind on the part of a local

g authority in any question relating to children was an admission of past error. In almost every case relating to children, and certainly in this particular case, circumstances change, often frequently. Far from condemning this local authority I hold that it behaved properly and that its exercise of its difficult statutory role was properly performed. It seems to me that when one looks at the brief findings and reasons of the justices given at the conclusion of the hearing, or even if one

h were to look at the more elaborate reasons which they have compiled subsequently for the purpose of this appeal, then their decision was plainly wrong. It is certainly not a decision that is justified by their findings and their reasons.

I have considered whether this is a case which I should remit for hearing before the justices. It seems to me that that would be wholly inappropriate, it would

j involve further analysis of the history relating to the local authority's care of these children and that, I think, can be in the interests of no one, certainly not of the children. Accordingly, I allow the appeal and set aside the order.

Appeal allowed.

Bebe Chua   Barrister.

Re St Chad's Churchyard, Bishop's Tachbrook

COVENTRY CONSISTORY COURT

CHANCELLOR WILLIAM M GAGE QC

16 NOVEMBER 1991

Ecclesiastical law – Monument – Headstone in churchyard – Headstone with gilded lettering – Diocesan regulations providing that gilded lettering 'undesirable' – Petitioner seeking to erect headstone with gilded lettering – Whether incumbent having power to licence monument not complying with regulations – Whether consistory court should grant faculty to permit erection of headstone with gilded lettering.

The petitioner sought to erect a headstone to the grave of his late wife. In accordance with a wish expressed by his wife during her lifetime, the petitioner proposed to use gilded lettering for the inscription on the headstone. In that area of the churchyard in which the petitioner's wife was buried some 28 headstones had gilded lettering, but in the churchyard as a whole only a comparatively small number of headstones had gilded lettering. The regulations for the erection of monuments in churchyards that had been promulgated by the diocesan advisory committee stated that the gilding of lettering was 'undesirable', but it was not specifically proscribed. The incumbent refused to consent to the use of gilded lettering on the ground that if he made an exception in the case of the petitioner he would be breaking faith with others whom he had persuaded to comply with the regulations. The petitioner applied to the consistory court for a faculty for the erection of a headstone with gilded lettering.

Held – Those who were buried in churchyards were buried in consecrated ground, which was land belonging to the church and which was open to the public, and it was the church's responsibility to see that what was placed on the land was fitting and appropriate, both for the time being and for the future. It followed that those who sought to exercise the right to place memorials on consecrated ground had to accept that they did so by licence and had to conform to conditions imposed by the church. Although proposed monuments which came within the diocesan regulations could be licensed by an incumbent, an incumbent had no power to license those which were outside the regulations and anyone who sought such a monument had to apply for a faculty from the chancellor. So long as such regulations existed it was important that they were adhered to, and the fairest system for all was one which was known and seen to apply to all. It would therefore only be in exceptional circumstances that the consistory court would grant a faculty for a monument which breached those rules. In all the circumstances, no sensible purpose would be served by a further exception allowing the petitioner to erect a headstone with gilded lettering, and accordingly the petition would be refused (see p 211 *g h* and p 212 *a* to *c e g*, post).

Notes

For faculties for the erection of monuments in churchyards, see 14 *Halsbury's Laws* (4th edn) para 1316, and for cases on the subject, see 19 *Digest* (Reissue) 449–450, 3549–3553.

Case referred to in judgment

St Peter, Kineton, Re [1967] WLR 347, Con Ct.

Petition for faculty

a By a petition dated 19 March 1991 Geoffrey Basil Walker sought a faculty for the erection of a headstone to the grave of his late wife, Mrs Florence Catherine Walker, who was interred in the churchyard of St Chad's church in the parish of Bishop's Tachbrook, Warwickshire, in the diocese of Coventry. The petition was opposed by the Rev W Roy Large, the vicar of the parish, and Mr E Fox and Mr P Sankey, the two churchwardens. The facts are set out in the judgment.

b

The petitioner and the parties opponent appeared in person.

THE CHANCELLOR. This is a petition by Geoffrey Walker, who seeks a
c faculty for the erection of a headstone to the grave of his late wife, Florence Catherine Walker. She died on 5 October 1990 and is buried in the churchyard of St Chad, Bishop's Tachbrook in Warwickshire. She lived together with Mr Walker for some years in the parish of St Chad, Bishop's Tachbrook and Mr Walker seeks a faculty in respect of the headstone. It is to be of simple design, made of grey granite and polished only on one side. On the side on which it is
d polished Mr Walker proposes that there shall be placed an inscription in gilded lettering. When he approached the monumental masons, B Astill Memorials, they sought permission from the vicar, the Rev W Roy Large. It then transpired that there was to be, as Mr Walker wishes, an inscription in gilded lettering. The result has been that Mr Large has refused his consent; there has been a petition for a faculty and Mr Large and his two churchwardens have objected. Their
e objections relate solely to the gilded lettering. The nub of their objection is that the gilded lettering does not conform to the spirit of the diocesan advisory committee's regulations for the erection of monuments in churchyards.

I have heard evidence in this matter from Mr Walker, from Mr Large, the incumbent, and from the two churchwardens, Mr Sankey and Mr Fox. I can
f summarise their evidence comparatively shortly. First, Mr Walker told me that he had lived in the parish for some nine years. He had always worked for the Church of England, starting by being in the choir at the age of 7. He has been a licensed reader for 32 years and his wife, when they lived in this parish, used to attend services regularly and was one of those who polished the brass. He himself served on the parochial church council and became secretary in 1987. He was
g secretary until he resigned in January 1989. He told me that he was thoroughly conversant with the diocesan advisory committee regulations relating to graveyards and he knew, as indeed is clear from a visit round the churchyard, that previous incumbents had not placed restrictions on the colouring on headstones.

After his wife died he instructed B Astill Memorials to make him a memorial headstone and as I say, in due course, they approached the vicar. Mr Large, when
h he learnt of this matter, sent out a letter which he told me was a standard letter which he sends out on such occasions. It said:

> 'I am happy to approve the proposed memorial provided that the polished section is where the inscription is, and that the inscription is not gilded. This is in keeping with diocesan rules and guidelines.'

j
Mr Walker told me that, when they received that letter, Astill's got in touch with him and as a result he wrote to Mr Large a letter dated 2 February 1991:

> 'With reference to your letter of Jan. 13th to B. Astill Memorials., I have counted thirty-four Headstones which are either all-black or grey granite of the type I have ordered. All of these, without exception, have gilded lettering.

The majority (28) are located at the North end of the churchyard where my
wife is interred. Diocesan regulations require that memorials shall be in a
keeping with those already there, and although the regulations state that
gilded lettering is to be discouraged it is not specifically proscribed. I have
therefore told the monumental masons to proceed as originally instructed.'

If he will allow me to say so it was a little peremptory in tone, but he explained
that he did not in fact instruct the monumental masons to go ahead. b

The next thing that happened was that the matter was raised at a meeting of
the parochial church council on 18 March 1991. Mr Walker was not then himself
a member of the parochial church council but he sent a letter to all members of
the council seeking, in effect, their support for his petition for a faculty to grant
him the right to have a memorial with gilded lettering. The matter was taken by
the council under 'Any other relevant business' and I have a copy of the minutes, c
which stated:

'A letter was received from Mr G Walker with regard to his erecting a grey
granite headstone with gilded inscription as a memorial to his late wife. The
policy set out by the Diocesan Regulation discourage the use of gildings. The
PCC were unable to support his application for a faculty.' d

No resolution was in form put to the meeting but there is some evidence that
the matter was put to the meeting by way of a show of hands with the majority
not supporting the application for faculty, although I think it was Mr Sankey who
told me that there might have been some dissenters.

Thereafter the matter took its formal course with Mr Walker applying by e
petition for a faculty. Regrettably the citation was delayed. It should not have
been delayed. Mr Large gave me his reasons for doing so. I dare say he acted from
the best of motives but I should make it quite clear that citations should not be
delayed. I do not, however, think that that goes to the heart of this particular
matter. Mr Walker has told me that the reason that he wants gilded lettering is
because he believes that his wife would have wanted it, she having expressed f
some wish during her lifetime for gilded lettering. He himself prefers gilded
lettering, but he feels very strongly that it should be in keeping with other
memorials in the particular area of the churchyard where she is buried. There
are, as he has pointed out to me on our visit round the graveyard, quite a large
number of headstones with gilded lettering on them. He also said that his
daughter—there has been some apparent misunderstanding between him and g
Mr Large about this—did not support him in this. She was not against it but she
did not think it was a matter of major importance.

The incumbent, Mr Large, gave evidence. He told me that he came to the
parish in May 1988 and not long afterwards he began to receive the usual requests
from monumental masons for approval to erect monuments and cremation h
tablets. He was not, at that stage, very familiar with the diocesan advisory
committee regulations but he soon became so. He took the view that, so far as
possible, those regulations should be complied with. They had been promulgated
in 1981 but he realised soon that, particularly in the matter of gilded lettering,
they had not recently been followed. He said that he did not discuss it with the
parochial church council. It did not really come up because whenever anybody j
asked for a headstone with gilded lettering or which in some other way did not
conform with the diocesan advisory committee regulations he would discuss it
with them. Up until Mr Walker's case it was resolved amicably. He gave me
three instances when people had applied for memorials which do not comply

a with the regulations. In two of those instances he refused his permission and the matter was resolved amicably. In one case, where it involved the addition of a gilded inscription on an existing black monument where there was already a gilded inscription, he thought that he should give his permission because different coloured lettering would look out of place. I have seen that particular memorial and it is in the book form, which itself is contrary to the diocesan advisory committee regulations. He accepted that Mr Walker had given much service to

b the Church and had been very helpful to him personally when he had first come to the parish. He said that the matter presented him with a considerable problem. If he were to make an exception in Mr Walker's case he would, to some extent, if not completely, be breaking faith with others whom he had persuaded to comply with the regulations. For that reason he decided that he should not give his permission. He said that on receipt of Mr Walker's letter of 2 February 1991 he

c went to discuss the matter with Mr Walker but it was not resolved at that meeting. He said that he had not brought up the matter of the diocesan advisory committee regulations at previous parochial church council meetings because it did not really arise and, as I have said, he had mostly managed to resolve these matters amicably.

d   I heard evidence from the two churchwardens, who supported the incumbent. Mr Fox in particular said that Mr Walker was aware of the regulations and still went ahead and he, Mr Fox, thought that there really was not much point in having regulations if they were not adhered to. In addition, Mr Hawkes, chairman of the diocesan advisory committee, gave evidence about the policy that lay behind the diocesan advisory committee regulations. He said that what the

e diocesan advisory committee do is to provide guidelines so that our churchyards should be preserved in a fit state for posterity. So far as gilded lettering is concerned the regulations read in the part that is applicable: 'The gilding of lettering is undesirable.' Mr Hawkes made the point that 'undesirable' is not perhaps a word which allows for certainty and when considering the regulations again the diocesan advisory committee will probably change that. What is clear

f is that its view as a committee is that, on the whole, gold lettering is visually intrusive to English country churchyards, which is why that passage is in the regulations. They do not propose in the future to soften their attitude on that particular aspect.

The question that I have to resolve is one of an exercise of my discretion. The principle which it seems to me I should adopt is this. Those who are buried in

g churchyards are buried in consecrated ground. The land belongs to the church and it is open to the public. It is the church's responsibility to see that what is placed on the land is fitting and appropriate, and fitting and appropriate not only to today, but for the future. It follows that those who seek to exercise the rights to place memorials on consecrated ground must accept that they will do so by

h licence and must conform to conditions imposed by the church. Mr Hawkes pointed out that a former chancellor of this diocese said that we all bear a responsibility to keep the churchyards fit for posterity (see *Re St Peter, Kineton* [1967] 1 WLR 347 at 348 per Chancellor Judge Gage). That is the reason why the diocesan advisory committee regulations for the erection of monuments have been promulgated. This diocese like all dioceses has laid down certain standards

j by regulation and there are three objectives of such regulations. First, they are there to produce general rules as to what may be regarded as fitting for monuments within this diocese. Second, they are there to ensure that it is widely known throughout the diocese by incumbents, by parochial church councils and by all who may be concerned with Christian burial what are the standards required of churchyards in this diocese so that there may be some uniformity. And third, although it does not really apply in this case, and is not of such importance, it is to make churchyards easier to be maintained and cared for.

Monuments that are proposed which come within the regulations can be licenced by an incumbent. Those that are outside the regulations an incumbent has no power to license and anyone who seeks such a monument must, as Mr Walker has done, apply for a faculty from the chancellor.

I want to make it quite clear in this case that in my judgment so long as there exist such rules and regulations I regard it as important that they be adhered to. As Mr Fox has said, what is the point of having rules if you do not adhere to them? In my judgment the fairest system of all is one which is known and seen to apply to all. It will therefore only be in exceptional circumstances that I shall grant a faculty for monuments which breach these rules. And so we come to the present position. On the one hand Mr Walker says, with some considerable force, that the regulations have not been adhered to in this graveyard for some time. There are a number of monuments with gilded lettering on them. In the particular area where his wife is buried they are, if I may use the expression, thickest on the ground. What difference will one further monument with gilded lettering make upon it? On the other hand Mr Large and the churchwardens say what has happened was in the past. We are now seeking to obey the regulations. Mr Large in particular has persuaded other people to conform. How is he to face them if he had allowed this particular application and so broken faith with them? That is the dilemma which the court finds itself in and I have to balance those two arguments and decide what the right answer is.

I have very considerable sympathy with Mr Walker's point of view but I regret that I have to come to the conclusion that the petition must be rejected. It seems to me, as I have said earlier, that the greater good is served by the rules being enforced. I take a little comfort, although Mr Walker may not think it so, from the fact that I detect from what he said to me that he does not personally have very strong views about the gilded lettering being in keeping with the other memorials in that particular area. On the other hand it seems to me that, looked at as a whole, there are a comparatively small number of headstone with gilded lettering on them by comparison with all the headstones in the churchyard. It seems to me that to make a further exception now would serve no sensible purpose and accordingly I do not propose to do so. I appreciate that my decision may cause Mr Walker very considerable pain and for that I can only say he has my sympathy but I hope for that for the reasons that I have outlined he will understand that the greater good is served by them being enforced rather than breached. For those reasons I reject the petition.

Petition refused.

N P Metcalfe Esq   Barrister.

a
Cresstock Investments Ltd v Commons Commissioner

CHANCERY DIVISION
JUDGE PAUL BAKER QC SITTING AS A JUDGE OF THE HIGH COURT
8, 11 MAY 1992

b

Commons – Registration – Claim to rights of common – Appeal – Land conveyed with cottage registered by neighbour as common land – Whether land 'ancillary to a dwelling-house' – Whether land forming part of 'garden' – Common Land (Rectification of Registers) Act 1989, s 1(2)(3).

c
In 1964 the appellant, which was a company controlled by B, a businessman who was based mainly abroad, bought a cottage which stood in some four and a half acres of land comprising lawn, flowerbeds and to the north approximately one acre of shrubbery and woodland. In 1968 a neighbouring owner registered the appellant's area of woodland and shrubbery as common land under the Commons
d Registration Act 1965, which provided that any person could provisionally register a piece of land thought to be common land. In the absence of objections the registration became final in October 1970. At the time B was abroad and he did not become aware of the registration until 1986. In 1991 the appellant lodged with the registration authority an objection under the Common Land (Rectification of Registers) Act 1989, s 1(2) and (3)[a] of which provided for the
e removal from the commons register of land if it could be shown that the land was 'ancillary to a dwellinghouse', that the ancillary land was, inter alia, a 'garden' and that the ancillary land had existed as such since 1945. The basis of the objection was that the registered land was part of the cottage garden, and thus ancillary to the cottage. The appellant adduced evidence of a conveyance of the cottage together with the land as far back as 1933. The commons commissioner,
f after finding that a 'garden' meant an enclosed piece of ground devoted to the cultivation of flowers, fruit or vegetables and used as a place of recreation, held that the appellant had failed to show that the land in question had been used and enjoyed as a garden before 1964 or that it was a garden. The appellant appealed to the High Court, contending that the commissioner had misconstrued the meaning of 'garden' for the purposes of s 1(3) of the 1989 Act and that he had
g erred in not accepting that the conveyance of the land together with a dwelling house at all times since 1945 was evidence that it was land ancillary to a dwelling house within s 1(2) of that Act.

Held – Where a unit of land was conveyed together with a dwelling house and
h ownership of the land and dwelling house was established, there was a presumption that the land was ancillary to the house and thus part of its garden, provided that the grounds were not so extensive as to rebut the presumption that they were ancillary and provided there was no evidence of any agricultural or other commercial use. Furthermore, for the purposes of s 1(3) of the 1989 Act the meaning of 'garden' was not to be narrowly construed since the purpose of the
j Act was not the preservation and promotion of horticulture, but the remedying of inadvertent expropriation or dedication of land to public use, and objectors ought not to be required to show that the land in question had been in continuous cultivation since 1945. It followed that there was insufficient evidence to displace

---

a   Section 1, so far as material, is set out at p 215 *c d*, post

the presumption arising from the proof of title since before 1945 that the
appellant's land had throughout been held with the dwelling house as part of its   *a*
garden. Accordingly, the appeal would be allowed and the registration cancelled
(see p 217 *e f* and p 218 *b c g h*, post).

Notes
For removal of land from a commons register, see 6 *Halsbury's Laws* (4th edn
reissue) para 682.   *b*
   For the Commons Registration Act 1965, see 6 *Halsbury's Statutes* (4th edn)
(1992 edn) 1214.
   For the Common Land (Rectification of Registers) Act 1989, s 1, see ibid 1232.

Case stated   *c*
Cresstock Investments Ltd appealed by way of a case stated by the Commons
Commissioners (Mr Martin Roth) in respect of his decision dated 18 July 1991
whereby he dismissed the objection registered under the Common Land
(Rectification of Registers) Act 1989 to the inclusion in the register of land owned
by the appellant. The facts are set out in the judgment.

                                                                                    d
Samuel Parrish (instructed by *Thomson Snell & Passmore*, Tunbridge Wells) for the
appellant.
The commissioner did not appear.

JUDGE PAUL BAKER QC. This is an appeal by way of case stated from the
decision of Mr Martin Roth sitting as a Commons Commissioner. It arises under   *e*
the Common Land (Rectification of Registers) Act 1989. The purpose of the 1989
Act is to provide for the removal from the register maintained under the
Commons Registration Act 1965 land on which there is a dwelling house or
which is ancillary to a dwelling house. It was passed to correct a deficiency in the
1965 Act which had led to injustices being suffered by a number of houseowners.
Under the 1965 Act any citizen could provisionally register a piece of land thought   *f*
to be common land. The applications frequently, but unjustifiably, included
dwellings. The registrations became absolute in some cases without the owner
being aware of the application. Hence the need for this short remedial 1989 Act,
to which I must now turn. Section 1(1) reads:

   'Within three years of the passing of this Act any person may, by notice in   *g*
   writing given to the registration authority maintaining a register of common
   land and of town and village greens under the Commons Registration Act
   1965, object to the inclusion on either of the registers of the whole or part of
   any land in respect of which the requirements specified in subsection (2)
   below are satisfied.'
                                                                                    h
So from that subsection one sees that the right to give notice is temporary.
There is apparently under consideration a more wide-ranging review of the
working of the 1965 Act. I now go, missing for the moment sub-ss (2) and (3), to
sub-ss (4) to (6) of s 1:

   '(4) On the receipt of a notice under subsection (1) of this section the   *j*
   registration authority shall refer the matter to a Commons Commissioner
   who shall inquire into the matter and, if he considers that the requirements
   specified in subsection (2) above are satisfied in the case of the land to which
   the objection relates or in the case of any part of it, he shall give notice of his
   decision to the registration authority who shall modify the register so as to
   exclude that land or, as the case may be, that part of it.
   (5) Where the register is modified under this section so as to exclude any

a land the registration authority shall also cancel the registration of any person as the owner of that land.

(6) Section 17(2) of the said Act of 1965 (procedure of Commons Commissioners) shall apply to a matter referred to a Commissioner under this section as it applies to a matter referred under that Act.'

b That provision shows the procedure. It explains the involvement of the Commons Commissioners and brings in the same rights of appeal as are provided for under the 1965 Act. I now come to the critical subsections for the purposes of this appeal, the requirements to be satisfied in order to obtain the relief under the 1989 Act. Returning to sub-ss (2) and (3) of s 1:

c '(2) Those requirements are—(*a*) that—(i) there is a dwellinghouse on the land and, if and so far as the land is not the site of that dwellinghouse, it is ancillary to that dwellinghouse; or (ii) the land is ancillary to a dwellinghouse which is not on the land; and (*b*) that the requirements of paragraph (*a*) above have been satisfied at all times since 5th August 1945.

d (3) For the purposes of subsection (2) above land ancillary to a dwellinghouse means a garden, private garage or outbuildings used and enjoyed with the dwellinghouse; and in that subsection "dwellinghouse" includes a building consisting of two or more separate dwellings.'

I am not concerned in this case with that last phrase. But as for the rest of it there are three points one notices about it. First of all, one sees that the land has *e* to be the site of a dwelling house or, what is important in this case, it has to be ancillary to a dwelling house. Secondly, ancillary land is limited to a garden, private garage or outbuildings used and enjoyed with a dwelling house. Thirdly, the ancillary land has to have existed as such since 5 August 1945. The reason for that date seems to be that it is 20 years before the passing of the 1965 Act.

I now come to the facts. The appellant here is a private company owned and *f* controlled by a Mr Mark Bostock, who, though British, has spent most of his working life in Sri Lanka making only occasional visits to this country. In 1964 Mr Bostock contracted to purchase a dwelling house and land known as Spring Cottage in Crowborough, Sussex. On 10 August 1964 it was conveyed to the appellant company by direction of Mr Bostock. In 1987, without any intervening change of ownership, the title was registered at HM Land Registry under no ESX *g* 134876. The whole of the land so registered is said to be some four and a half acres. It was a triangular site. One long side was bounded on the west by Lordswell Lane. The site fell into two parts. In the south, within the base of the triangle was Spring Cottage, a substantial old dwelling surrounded by a well-cultivated lawn and flower beds. To the north of this was an area of shrubbery and woodland going up into the apex of the triangle. That part of the land, in no way fenced off *h* from the other and consisting of rather more than an acre, was registered as common land on the application dated 26 June 1968 of a neighbouring owner, a registration which became final on 1 October 1970. As I have just been reminded, the land registered is what I have described as both the area of shrubbery and the woodland going up into the apex of the triangle.

j Mr Bostock, being absent, was unaware of this until 1986. It is that land which was the subject of the company's objection. It is claimed that it is part of the garden of Spring Cottage and hence falls within s 1(2)(*a*)(ii) of the 1989 Act that is to say land ancillary to a dwelling house which is not on the land.

The commissioner heard the objection on 28 June 1991 and then visited the site apparently accompanied by a large number of people. On the site visit the commissioner found the greater part of the land to be overgrown woodland. The description of what he found on the site visit continues as follows:

'The most northerly section is impenetrable, the remainder largely
wilderness. There are many fallen trees. Traces of the acts of gardening   *a*
described by Mr Bostock may be seen in the area closest to Spring Cottage;
for example, there are a number of hydrangeas and the area around the pond
shows signs of having been cleared. There are also rhododendrons of
considerable size. The western boundary of the unit land is unfenced
throughout its length. It is open to Lordswell Lane as far as the entrance to
Spring Cottage, and then open to the bridle path that proceeds south to   *b*
Crowborough Common. In this southerly section I saw traces of the barbed
wire described by Mr Bostock as having been cut after he had put it up. I
found the precise boundaries far less clear on the land than they are on the
plans. The bridle path leads direct from the unit land to Crowborough
Common. I found no clear division between the two.'
                                                                          c
The commissioner then referred to two dictionary definitions of 'garden'. The
first is in the *Oxford English Dictionary*, which has as its first meaning the following
for the word 'garden': 'An enclosed piece of ground devoted to the cultivation of
flowers, fruit, or vegetables.' Then he went on to the first meaning in the *Concise
Oxford Dictionary* (8th edn, 1990) which was: *d*

'a piece of ground, usu. partly grassed and adjoining a private house, used
for growing flowers, fruit, or vegetables, and as a place of recreation.'

Then, having noted that the objector (the appellant) accepted that the burden
of proof was on the objector to prove that at all times since August 1945 the land
was a garden used and enjoyed with Spring Cottage, the commissioner reached   *e*
the following conclusions:

'I do not have to find that in order to constitute a garden within the
meaning of the 1989 Act the land must necessarily be enclosed. On the other
hand the fact that it is unenclosed is consistent with its having been waste   *f*
land. Assuming that the unit land were waste land, then, being in an urban
district, the public would have rights of access for air and exercise under
section 193 of the Law of Property Act, 1925. There was ample evidence
before me that members of the public exercised such rights, at least before
the devastation caused by the storm of October 1987.'
                                                                          g
He then went on in a section he called 'Conclusion':

'Whilst I do not consider that the unit land can properly be described as a
garden, the deciding factor is not what it is like today, but the lack of evidence
as to what it was like before Mr Bostock's Company acquired it in 1964.
There was no evidence that before 1964 the unit land was used and enjoyed   *h*
as a garden or that it was a garden. Such evidence as is before me is entirely
to the contrary. Accordingly the Objector has failed to show that the
requirements specified in Section 1(2) of the Act of 1987 have been satisfied
at all times since 5th August 1985.'

The appellant was dissatisfied with that conclusion of the commissioner and it   *j*
asked the commissioner, as it was entitled to do under the Common Land
(Rectification of Registers) Regulations 1990, SI 1990/331, to state a case, which
the commissioner duly did.
    After the formal parts of the case stated and, of course, incorporating his written
decision, parts of which I have already read out, the commissioner stated the point
of law (and it is only on points of law that an appeal lies to this court) thus:

'The question of law for the decision of this Honourable Court is whether on the facts found by me I erred in law in holding that the requirements specified in section 1(2) of the Act of 1989 were not satisfied in respect of any part of the land to which this Objection related.'

He was persuaded by the appellant, through its solicitors, to add the following questions:

'(i) Whether in finding that there was no evidence that before 1964 the unit land was used and enjoyed as a garden or that it was a garden I misconstrued the word garden as used in sub-section (3) of Section 1 of the 1989 Act.

(ii) Whether I erred in law in requiring direct evidence that the unit land had at all times since 1945 been land ancillary to a dwellinghouse within sub-sections (2)(a)(ii) and (3) of Section 1 of the 1989 Act.

(iii) Whether I erred in law in not accepting that the fact that the unit land was conveyed together with a dwellinghouse at all times since 1945 was evidence that it was land ancillary to a dwellinghouse within the said sub-sections of the 1989 Act.

(iv) Whether I was correct in holding that the fact that the land was in the ownership of the specified person had no bearing on whether or not it was land capable of being manorial waste.'

The appellant challenges the commissioner's decision on two main grounds. First it is said that the commissioner defined the word 'garden' too narrowly by applying the dictionary definitions. Secondly, it is submitted that the ownership of the land together with the house (established since 1933) raises a presumption that it was ancillary to the dwelling and part of its garden. There was no evidence that it had ceased to be so.

The commissioner has not appeared here. That is perfectly understandable, but it has this consequence: that I had no opposing argument. It is therefore with some diffidence that I reach my conclusion that Mr Parrish's submissions are correct. My reasons are as follows.

On 23 September 1933 Spring Cottage was conveyed by the executors of Wilson Stuckey, who had owned it for many years previously, to Florence Schwind in the following terms:

'All that messuage or dwellinghouse formerly called "Spring Cottage" but then called "Spring Cotton Cottage" garage and other outbuildings with the appurtenances thereto belonging and several pieces or parcels of land adjoining and enjoyed therewith situate at Crowborough all which property intended to be thereby conveyed was more particularly delineated in the plan drawn thereon and thereon edged pink.'

The plan shows that land amounting to nearly six acres was conveyed. It included the whole of the land subsequently conveyed to the appellant together with two acres or thereabouts of land which was later conveyed away. There was nothing in the description to suggest that the land was other than land ancillary to the dwelling house. Of course it may be that the grounds associated and held with a house are so extensive that they could not be said to be ancillary to it rather than the other way about, but these grounds, or at least those now owned by the appellant, are not in that category.

This was a substantial residence dating from a period when large gardens were commoner than they are today. Similarly there is no indication in the description of any agricultural or other commercial use which would preclude their being described as ancillary to the house. The other feature required by the statute is that the ancillary land has to be a garden, private garage or outbuildings used and enjoyed with the dwelling house.

Both of the definitions upon which the commissioner relied referred to its use for the cultivation of flowers, fruit and vegetables. In my judgment this places two narrow a meaning on the word 'garden' as used in the 1989 Act. The purpose of this Act is not the preservation and promotion of horticulture but the remedying of inadvertent expropriation or dedication to public use. It cannot be that an objector is required to show that the land has been cultivated continuously since 1945 any more than he would be required to show that the dwelling house has been occupied throughout that period. Frequently parts of a large garden are left wild and uncultivated. They remain available for cultivation and use and form part of the garden.

Accordingly, the land conveyed by the conveyance of 1933 was prima facie a conveyance of a dwelling house and land ancillary to it as defined in the 1989 Act. I must however look at the contrary evidence before the commissioner, starting with the correspondence in 1948 together with the newspaper cuttings. It suggests that the subject land was part of the manorial waste. It is, however, inconclusive. The letter of 9 March 1948 suggests that the then owner would acknowledge the right of common if he could be satisfied that it was manorial waste. The letter of 22 August 1949 shows that the right of the owner to fence was still unresolved. In any event, as the commissioner observed, he had no jurisdiction to determine whether the subject land was correctly registered as common land.

There was evidence before the commissioner that members of the public exercised rights of access at least before the devastation caused by the storm of October 1987 which rendered the northern part of the land impenetrable. He also observed on the site visit that the land was largely, if not wholly, unfenced. As against that, he accepted that there had been some cultivation of the southern portion by Mr Bostock after the purchase of the land in 1964 and the building of an artificial pool there. There was also the absence of Mr Bostock leading to his inability to monitor the activities of others on his land.

On the definition of 'garden' which the commissioner adopted, his conclusion that there was no evidence before 1964 that the land had been used and enjoyed as a garden could not be faulted. But, having regard to the features which I consider to be material, the land held with the house is a garden and outbuildings, and there is no sufficient evidence to displace the presumption arising from the proof of the title since before 6 August 1945 that the land was throughout held with the dwelling house and part of its garden.

In holding that view I will therefore reverse the decision of the commissioner and answer the questions. The initial question I answer Yes. The supplementary questions I answer as follows: (i) Yes; (ii) I am not clear to what that question is directed and I propose to return no answer to that question; (iii) Yes; (iv) as I understand that question my answer to it would be Yes.

I think it falls for me therefore to direct that the registration be cancelled.

Order accordingly.

Hazel Hartman   Barrister.

a # R v Bow Street Stipendiary Magistrate and another, ex parte South Coast Shipping Co Ltd and others

QUEEN'S BENCH DIVISION

b LLOYD LJ AND WATERHOUSE J

9, 10, 13 APRIL 1992

Criminal law – Proceedings – Duties of Director of Public Prosecutions – Institution of proceedings – Private prosecution – Criminal proceedings to which Director's duty to take over conduct does not apply – Director deciding not to institute proceedings –
c *Whether decision of Director precluding private prosecution – Prosecution of Offences Act 1985, ss 3(2)(b), 6.*

Where the Director of Public Prosecutions could have instituted proceedings against a person under s 3(2)(b)[a] of the Prosecution of Offences Act 1985 on the ground that it appeared to him to be appropriate that he do so having regard to
d the importance and difficulty of the case but he has decided not to bring proceedings, any other person may institute a private prosecution in respect of the same matter, since on the true construction of ss 3(2)(b) and 6(2)[b] of the 1985 Act a person is only precluded by s 6(1) of that Act from bringing a private prosecution in respect of those proceedings set out in s 3(2)(a), (c) and (d) which the Director is under a duty to take over, and there is nothing in s 6(1) to preclude
e the bringing of a private prosecution in respect of proceedings under s 3(2)(b). However, the Director may take over proceedings instituted by a private prosecutor which he might otherwise have instituted himself and having done so he may then discontinue them under s 23 of the 1985 Act if the evidence is insufficient or if the proceedings would be contrary to the public interest or to
f avoid duplication of proceedings or for any other good reason or, if it is too late to discontinue, he may offer no evidence or the Attorney General can enter a nolle prosequi (see p 222 *b* to *d* and p 225 *c*, post).

Notes

g For the duties of the Director of Public Prosecutions with respect to initiating criminal proceedings, see 11(1) *Halsbury's Laws* (4th edn reissue) paras 639, 646.
    For the Prosecution of Offences Act 1985, ss 3, 6, see 12 *Halsbury's Statutes* (4th edn) (1989 reissue) 936, 939.

h ### Cases referred to in judgments

Associated Provincial Picture Houses Ltd v Wednesbury Corp [1947] 2 All ER 680, [1948] 1 KB 223, CA.
Connelly v DPP [1964] 2 All ER 401, [1964] AC 1254, [1964] 2 WLR 1145, HL.
DPP v Humphrys [1976] 2 All ER 497, [1977] AC 1, [1976] 2 WLR 857, HL.
R v Horseferry Road Magistrates' Court, ex p Stephenson (1989) Times, 25 January,
j   DC.
R v Telford Justices, ex p Badhan [1991] 2 All ER 854, [1991] 2 QB 78, [1991] 2 WLR 866, DC.

---

a   Section 3, so far as material, is set out at p 221 *f g*, post
b   Section 6 is set out at p 221 *j* to p 222 *a*, post

Cases also cited or referred to in skeleton arguments

Blue Metal Industries Ltd v Dilley [1969] 3 All ER 437, [1970] AC 827, PC.　　　　**a**
Chief Constable of West Midlands Police v Gillard [1985] 3 All ER 634, [1986] AC
　442, HL.
Luke v IRC [1963] 1 All ER 655, [1963] AC 557, HL.
Metropolitan Police Comr v Curran [1976] 1 All ER 162, [1976] 1 WLR 87, HL.
R v Bow Street Stipendiary Magistrate, ex p Cherry (1990) 91 Cr App R 283, DC.
R v Chief Constable of the Merseyside Police, ex p Calveley [1986] 1 All ER 257, [1986]　**b**
　QB 424, CA.
R v Crown Court at Derby, ex p Brooks (1985) 80 Cr App R 164, DC.
R v Cuthbertson [1980] 2 All ER 401, [1981] AC 470, HL.
R v Stafford Justices, ex p Customs and Excise Comrs [1991] 2 All ER 201, [1991] 2
　QB 339, DC.
　　　　c

Application for judicial review

South Coast Shipping Co Ltd, Robert Henry Samuel, Peter Malcolm Butcher,
Frederick Brian Darwell and George Edward Greenwood (the defendants) applied,
with the leave of Popplewell J given on 19 December 1991, for judicial review by
way of (i) an order of certiorari to quash the decisions of the first respondent, Sir　**d**
David Hopkin, the Chief Stipendiary Magistrate at Bow Street Magistrates' Court,
on 12 November 1991 in which he ruled that the second respondent, Ivor Glogg,
had locus to bring a private prosecution for manslaughter against the defendants
and on 21 November 1991 in which he ruled that the charges of manslaughter
did not amount to an abuse of the process of the court, (ii) an order of prohibition
to prevent the magistrates' court from inquiring into the charges and (iii) an order　**e**
of mandamus requiring the magistrates' court to stay the proceedings. The
Director of Public Prosecutions was joined as third respondent to the application
under RSC Ord 53, r 9. The facts are set out in the judgment of Lloyd LJ.

Michael Hill QC and *Michael Wood* (instructed by *Hill Taylor Dickinson*) for the
　defendants.　　　　**f**
Michael Mansfield QC and *Sally Bradley* (instructed by *Christian Fisher & Co*) for Mr
　Glogg
R Alun Jones QC (instructed by the *Crown Prosecution Service*, Headquarters) for the
　Director of Public Prosecutions.
The first respondent did not appear.
　　　　g

LLOYD LJ. These proceedings arise out of a collision on the River Thames on
20 August 1989 when the Bowbelle, a dredger owned and operated by South
Coast Shipping Co Ltd, ran down a pleasure boat, the Marchioness. The
Marchioness sank and 51 people lost their lives. Among them was Mrs Ruth
Hadden. On 17 July 1991 her husband, Mr Ivor Glogg, brought a private　**h**
prosecution against the owners of the Bowbelle and four of the company's
employees. I shall refer to them all as 'the defendants'. They are charged with
manslaughter. On 12 November 1991 there was an application to stay the
prosecution. It came before Sir David Hopkin, the Chief Stipendiary Magistrate
at Bow Street Magistrates' Court.
　There were two grounds for the application. The first was that Mr Glogg is not　**j**
entitled to bring a private prosecution; he has no locus standi. The second ground
was that the prosecution is an abuse of the process of the court. Sir David Hopkin
decided both points in favour of Mr Glogg. The defendants now apply for an
order of certiorari to quash his decision. The committal proceedings which were

a due to start on 6 January 1992 have been adjourned to await the outcome of this application.

I take each of the two points in turn.

Locus standi

b On 26 April 1990 the Director of Public Prosecutions announced that Captain Henderson, the master of the Bowbelle, would be charged with an offence under s 32 of the Merchant Shipping Act 1988 of failing to keep a proper lookout. He also announced that no other charges would be brought.

On 30 October 1990 there was an application to the Divisional Court to challenge the Director's decision not to bring other charges. That application failed. On 3 April 1991 Captain Henderson's trial began. The jury was unable to
c reach a verdict. There was a retrial in July 1991 but the jury again failed to reach a verdict, whereupon Captain Henderson was discharged.

In those circumstances, Mr Michael Hill QC for the defendants submits that there is no room for further criminal proceedings arising out of the same casualty. It might have been different if the Director had brought no proceedings at all. But here the Director brought proceedings against Captain Henderson and
d decided not to bring proceedings against these defendants. Parliament cannot have intended to leave it open for a private prosecutor to bring proceedings which the Director has decided not to bring, especially when the case is one of difficulty and importance.

I see the force of Mr Hill's argument. Parliament might well have legislated so
e as to exclude the private individual's right to prosecute in those circumstances. But the question is whether it has in fact done so. The answer depends on two sections of the Prosecution of Offences Act 1985. Section 3 defines the functions of the Director. Section 3(2) provides:

f 'It shall be the duty of the Director, subject to any provisions contained in the Criminal Justice Act 1987—(*a*) to take over the conduct of all criminal proceedings, other than specified proceedings, instituted on behalf of a police force (whether by a member of that force or by any other person); (*b*) to institute and have the conduct of criminal proceedings in any case where it appears to him that—(i) the importance or difficulty of the case makes it appropriate that proceedings should be instituted by him; or (ii) it is otherwise
g appropriate for proceedings to be instituted by him; (*c*) to take over the conduct of all binding over proceedings instituted on behalf of a police force (whether by a member of that force or by any other person); (*d*) to take over the conduct of all proceedings begun by summons issued under section 3 of the Obscene Publications Act 1959 (forfeiture of obscene articles) . . .'

h It will be noticed that s 3(2)(*a*), (*c*) and (*d*) each provide for the Director to take over the conduct of certain kinds of proceedings. By contrast, s 3(2)(*b*) provides for the Director to *institute* certain other kinds of proceedings where it appears to him to be appropriate, having regard to the importance and the difficulty of the case. The difference in language is not, in my view, accidental. It becomes of crucial importance when one turns to s 6, which deals with private prosecutions.
j Section 6 provides:

'(1) Subject to subsection (2) below, nothing in this Part shall preclude any person from instituting any criminal proceedings or conducting any criminal proceedings to which the Director's duty to take over the conduct of proceedings does not apply.

(2) Where criminal proceedings are instituted in circumstances in which the Director is not under a duty to take over their conduct, he may nevertheless do so at any stage.'

The effect of s 6(1) is to preclude a person from bringing a private prosecution in cases covered by s 3(2)(*a*), (*c*) and (*d*) but not in the residuary category of cases covered by s 3(2)(*b*). So far as s 3(2)(*b*) cases are concerned, there is nothing to preclude a private prosecution.

Mr Hill submits that s 6 must be read subject to an implied limitation so as to preclude more than one prosecution in any one case whether against the same defendant or another defendant. I can see no basis for reading in any such limitation, especially when one has regard to s 6(2).

Section 6(2) is clearly intended to cover s 3(2)(*b*) cases, ie cases where the Director has a duty to institute proceedings as distinct from his duty to take over their conduct. Section 6(2) therefore contemplates that the Director may take over the conduct of proceedings instituted by a private prosecutor which he might otherwise have instituted himself. Having taken over the conduct of those proceedings, he may then discontinue them under s 23 of the 1985 Act if the evidence is insufficient, or if the proceedings would be contrary to the public interest, or to avoid duplication, or for any other good reason. If it is too late to discontinue, he may offer no evidence or the Attorney General can enter a nolle prosequi.

So read, ss 3(2) and 6 make a coherent and consistent framework in which the right of the private citizen to bring a prosecution is preserved but subject always to the Director's right to intervene at any stage. It provides a useful and effective safeguard against 'improper inaction' by the prosecuting authority (I quote from the Report of the Royal Commission on Criminal Procedure (Cmnd 8092 (1981)), p 161, para 7.50 under Sir Cyril Philips).

In the course of the hearing, it occurred to us that the Director might himself be affected by the result of this application and ought therefore to have been given the opportunity to be heard. Mr Alun Jones QC has appeared this morning on behalf of the Director and addressed us in opposition to Mr Hill's application. We gave leave for him to be joined under the provisions of RSC Ord 53, r 9. We are grateful for Mr Jones's attendance. We do not however think it necessary to give separate consideration to his arguments, which echo in every respect those advanced by Mr Mansfield.

On 2 August 1991 the Director indicated that he did not intend to intervene at that stage of the proceedings. But it will be open to him to reconsider that decision if the prosecution goes ahead.

For the above reasons, which are substantially those given more shortly by Sir David Hopkin, I would reject Mr Hill's first ground of attack on Sir David's decision.

Abuse of process

I now turn to the second ground of application. Under this head, Mr Hill advances three main arguments. The first goes to Mr Glogg's motive. It is said that he is manipulating or misusing the prosecution because what he really wants is a full scale public inquiry. Deprived of the opportunity afforded by a public inquiry, he is now using the prosecution as a platform to ventilate his grievances.

Mr Hill's second argument is that the delay in launching the prosecution has been so prolonged that a fair trial is no longer possible.

Mr Hill's third argument is that the publicity generated by Mr Glogg's solicitors has been so great that any jury is likely to be prejudiced against the defendants. Again, I will take each of those three points in turn.

Manipulation or misuse of the prosecution process

a   I do not doubt that Mr Glogg wanted a full scale public inquiry instead of the limited investigation carried out in private by the Marine Accident Investigation Bureau under the new procedure introduced by s 33 of the Merchant Shipping Act 1988 and the Merchant Shipping (Accident Investigation) Regulations 1989, SI 1989/1172. Those regulations came into force only a fortnight before the casualty. No doubt the members of the so-called Marchioness Action Group who

b   have lost relatives in the disaster also wanted a public inquiry. I can well understand their anxiety, frustration and sense of grievance when a public inquiry was not announced. I should add that Mr Glogg was not himself a member of the Marchioness Action Group but he is represented by the same firm of solicitors.

Does it then follow from Mr Glogg's desire for a public inquiry that he had some indirect or improper motive in launching the prosecution? I do not think

c   it does. At the start, Mr Glogg's state of mind may well have been that he wanted *both* a public inquiry *and* a prosecution for manslaughter. The fact that a public inquiry has been ruled out does not mean that his motive in instituting the prosecution should now be regarded as improper. If there is evidence that a defendant has been guilty of an offence, then a desire to see him prosecuted and,

d   if found guilty, punished is not an improper motive, especially where the prosecutor is one of the bereaved. Even if Mr Glogg's motives were mixed, the court should be slow to halt a prosecution unless the conduct of the prosecution is truly oppressive (see *Connelly v DPP* [1964] 2 All ER 401 at 409, [1964] AC 1254 at 1301 per Lord Morris and *DPP v Humphrys* [1976] 2 All ER 497 at 527, [1977] AC 1 at 46 per Lord Salmon). The law was correctly stated on this point by Mann

e   LJ in *R v Telford Justices, ex p Badhan* [1991] 2 All ER 854 at 862–863, [1991] 2 QB 78 at 90. Dealing with the power of the justices to prevent an abuse of process, he said:

> 'They have no power to refuse to embark on an inquiry because they think that a prosecution should not have been brought because it is, for example,
f   mean-minded, petty or animated by hostility. It is for this reason that the powers of the justices are said to be "very strictly confined" . . .'

Mr Hill referred us to *R v Horseferry Road Magistrates' Court, ex p Stephenson* (1989) Times, 25 January. But that was a very different case on its facts. There was no evidence at all which could possibly have grounded a prosecution for

g   blackmail; it was a mere device to embarrass the impending conference. In the present case it has not been argued that there is no evidence to support the manslaughter charge, although Mr Hill has made no admission to that effect.

An alternative line of argument under this head was as follows. In the course of the summer of 1991 the Director was pressing Mr Glogg's solicitors to hand over any fresh material available to Mr Glogg so that he could make up his mind

h   whether or not to take over the conduct of the prosecution. Mr Glogg's solicitors declined to hand over the evidence until after the committal. It is said that Mr Glogg's purpose was to bring to bear on the Director such intense pressure of publicity that he would be unable to take over and discontinue the prosecution.

I do not accept that it would necessarily be wrong for a private prosecutor to attempt to dissuade the Director from taking over the conduct of the prosecution

j   by force of publicity. I suspect he is made of sterner stuff. But, even if it were wrong, it does not show that the prosecutor's purpose here in bringing the prosecution was oppressive or improper.

Finally, it is said that, if I am right in thinking that Mr Glogg had a sufficient locus standi to bring the prosecution, that must be because there is an unforeseen or unintended lacuna in the 1985 Act. Mr Hill contends that it is an abuse of process to take advantage of that lacuna. It is sufficient to say that I do not agree.

Delay

Mr Hill argues that the delay since the date of the casualty, or at least since 27 **a**
October 1989 when Mr Glogg's solicitors indicated in a letter that they had
enough evidence in their possession to prove wilful misconduct on the part of the
owners of the Bowbelle, was such as to cause serious prejudice to the defendants.

The questions to be asked in these cases, where delay is relied on as an abuse of
process of the court, are, first, whether the delay on the part of the prosecution is
unjustifiable and, secondly, whether, if so, the prejudice to the defendant is such **b**
that a fair trial can no longer be held. I would answer both those questions in
favour of Mr Glogg. It was entirely reasonable for him to wait as he did until after
the completion of the second trial of Captain Henderson before serving his
summonses on the defendants on 31 July 1991. There has been little, if any, delay
since then. There are, it is true, cases in which it has been held that what is called
'mere delay' may suffice. But these cases should be regarded as highly exceptional. **c**

Nor has there been, in my view, any substantial prejudice to the defendants.
No specific prejudice is alleged. This is not a case where prejudice should be
inferred since the trial will not depend on eye-witness accounts of fast-moving
events. It is the mens rea of the company which will be mainly in issue. It is
therefore to be expected that the trial will depend largely on documents. But, in **d**
so far as it will depend on the memory of witnesses, the defendants will have had
every reason to have these events very much in mind since the day of the casualty.
I am not persuaded that a fair trial in this case is no longer possible.

Publicity

I can deal with this question even more shortly without, I hope, doing injustice **e**
to Mr Hill's very careful argument on behalf of the defendants. That argument
was that there has been so much adverse publicity in the past in this case and
there is likely to be so much further adverse publicity in the future that the jury
is bound to be prejudiced against the defendants. I do not agree. Sir David Hopkin
was taken through the publicity page by page and paragraph by paragraph. What
he had to say was this: **f**

'It is quite clear, by anyone's standard, that this incident was of the greatest
public interest and concern and it appears to me, reading the publicity as it
has been put before me, that the reporting was mainly restricted to those
matters which were matters of public interest and concern. It is my view
that the main subject of publicity were the Ministry of Transport for their **g**
laxity in licensing unsuitable vessels and their refusal to mount a public
inquiry. Another subject was the question of compensation. Yet another was
the general question of corporate liability, which was dealt with in a general
way and emphasised the difficulties involved. The final target was the
Director of Public Prosecutions when he threatened to intervene in the
private prosecution. Then, of course, followed his withdrawal from that **h**
stance which also attracted publicity. Only on a very few occasions was it
even specifically suggested that this company, or any of its directors, would
be prosecuted for manslaughter.'

That was a view which Sir David Hopkin was entitled to take. It is a view with
which I agree, although I do not pretend to have the same familiarity with the **j**
publicity material as he had.

Mr Hill's case, as it turned out in reply, does not depend on showing that Mr
Glogg's solicitors were personally responsible for generating the publicity or that
they were party to a concerted campaign. It is right to say, however, that the
material which Mr Mansfield put before us this morning gives me the opposite

impression, that Mr Glogg's solicitors were doing their best to avoid adverse
a publicity which might affect the conduct of the present proceedings once the
summonses had been served. Whether that impression be correct or not, I am
quite unable to hold that a fair trial is no longer possible on the ground that a
jury, however carefully directed, is likely to be prejudiced against these defendants
or because there is even a risk that the jury would be so prejudiced. In my view,
Sir David Hopkin reached the right view on all the points before him. Mr Hill
b has fallen far short of showing that we ought to interfere on *Wednesbury* grounds
(see *Associated Provincial Picture Houses Ltd v Wednesbury Corp* [1947] 2 All ER 680,
[1948] 1 KB 223). I would therefore dismiss the application.

WATERHOUSE J. I agree and there is nothing that I can usefully add.

c
Application dismissed.

Dilys Tausz   Barrister.

d

R v Shepherd

HOUSE OF LORDS
LORD GRIFFITHS, LORD EMSLIE, LORD ROSKILL, LORD ACKNER AND LORD LOWRY
e 11 NOVEMBER, 16 DECEMBER 1992

*Criminal evidence – Document – Computer print-out – Admissibility – Statement in
document produced by computer – Evidence as to functioning of computer – Who may
give evidence – Till rolls – Till rolls linked to computer – Evidence of store detective as to
how tills operated, what computer did and computer's reliability – Whether person*
f *familiar with operation of computer can give evidence that computer was operating
properly at material time – Whether fact that computer was operating properly may be
proved without calling computer expert – Police and Criminal Evidence Act 1984,
s 69(1)(b), Sch 3, para 8(d).*

g The appellant was arrested at her home on suspicion of theft. In her car were
goods from a department store to the value of £78·36 consisting of various items
of food, including a joint of beef priced at £12·57 and five items of clothing, for
which she had no receipt. When interviewed the appellant stated that she had
bought the items at a branch of the department store that day and that on
returning to her car the bags had split and she had transferred the items to a bag
h of her own; she said that she never kept receipts and denied stealing the goods.
At her trial the principal evidence for the Crown was given by a store detective
employed at the branch store, who stated that she had removed all the till rolls
for the day in question from the tills, which were linked to a central computer,
and examined all of them, that there was no trace on them of the unique product
code for the clothing found in the appellant's car and no record of an item of food
j costing £12·57 and nor was there any group of prices matching the items of food
found in the car. In the course of her evidence she described how the tills
operated, what the central computer did, that there had been no trouble with the
computer and how she had also examined all the till rolls, which showed no
evidence of malfunction either by the tills or the central computer. The appellant
objected to the admission of that evidence, contending that it did not satisfy the

provisions of s 69(1)(b)[a] of the Police and Criminal Evidence Act 1984 since oral
evidence that the computer was operating properly at the material time was not   *a*
admissible unless it was given by a person who was qualified to sign the certificate
for the purpose of providing proof of the matters contained in s 69(1) in
accordance with para 8(d)[b] of Sch 3 to the 1984 Act, ie by a person responsible for
the operation of the computer. The judge having ruled that the evidence was
admissible, the appellant was convicted. The Court of Appeal upheld her
conviction and she appealed to the House of Lords.   *b*

Held – If the prosecution wished to rely on a document produced by a computer
they had to comply with s 69 of the 1984 Act in all cases; the operation of s 69
was not limited to cases falling within s 24 of the Criminal Justice Act 1988
relating to hearsay evidence. However, for the purposes of s 69(1) of the 1984
Act, proof that a computer was reliable could be provided by calling a witness   *c*
who was familiar with its operation in the sense of knowing what the computer
was required to do and who could say that it was doing it properly, and such a
witness need not be someone responsible for the operation of the computer
within para 8(d) of Sch 3 to the 1984 Act or a computer expert. Accordingly,
since the store detective had been fully familiar with the operation of the store's   *d*
computer, she had been fully qualified to give the evidence required by s 69 and
in the light of her evidence the till rolls were properly admitted as part of the
Crown's case. The appeal would therefore be dismissed (see p 228 *h* to p 229 *a* and
p 230 *d f* to p 231 *a d* to *j*, post).
    R v Minors, R v Harper [1989] 2 All ER 208 considered.
    R v Spiby (1990) 91 Cr App R 186 overruled.   *e*

Notes
For the admissibility of statements produced by computers, see 17 *Halsbury's Laws*
(4th edn) para 59.
    For the Police and Criminal Evidence Act 1984, s 69, Sch 3, para 8, see 17   *f*
Halsbury's Statutes (4th edn) 209, 222.

Cases referred to opinions
R v Ewing [1983] 2 All ER 645, [1983] QB 1039, [1983] 1 WLR 1, CA.
R v Minors, R v Harper [1989] 2 All ER 208, [1989] 1 WLR 441, CA.
R v Neville [1991] Crim LR 288, CA.
R v Spiby (1990) 91 Cr App R 186, CA.   *g*
R v Wood (1982) 76 Cr App R 23, CA.
Sophocleous v Ringer [1988] RTR 52, DC.

Appeal
Hilda Shepherd appealed with the leave of the Appeal Committee of the House   *h*
of Lords given on 15 June 1992 against the decision of the Court of Appeal,
Criminal Division (Lloyd LJ, Leonard and Blofeld JJ) (93 Cr App R 139) on
18 January 1991 dismissing her appeal against her conviction in the Crown Court
at St Albans on 27 October 1989 before Judge Hickman and a jury on a charge of
theft contrary to s 1(1) of the Theft Act 1968, for which she was sentenced to six
months' imprisonment suspended for two years. The Court of Appeal certified   *j*
under s 33(2) of the Criminal Appeal Act 1968 that a point of law of general
public importance (set out at p 227 *c d*, post) was involved in the decision but

_a_   Section 69, so far as material, is set out at p 228 *b* to *d*, post
_b_   Paragraph 8 is set out at p 228 *e* to *g*, post.

refused leave to appeal to the House of Lords. The facts are set out in the opinion
a of Lord Griffiths.

Christopher Llewellyn-Jones QC and *Robert Leonard* (instructed by *Ellis & Hancock,*
Watford) for the appellant.
Brian Barker QC and *Esther Kayman* (instructed by the *Crown Prosecution Service*)
for the Crown.
b

Their Lordships took time for consideration.

16 December 1992. The following opinions were delivered.

c **LORD GRIFFITHS.** My Lords, the Court of Appeal has certified the following
point of law of general public importance:

'Whether a party seeking to rely on computer evidence can discharge the
burden under section 69(1)(*b*) of the Police and Criminal Evidence Act 1984
without calling a computer expert, and if so how?'

d The point of law falls to be considered against the following background of
fact. The appellant was arrested at her home at Maple Cross, Rickmansworth at
about 5.30 pm on 17 March 1989. In her car were goods from Marks & Spencers
worth £78·36. The goods consisted of various items of food, including a joint of
beef priced at £12·57 and five items of clothing. The appellant had no receipt. In
an initial interview on 17 March 1989 she declined to answer questions. She was
e interviewed again on 29 April 1989 when she said that she had bought the goods
at Marks & Spencers at St Alban's. When she returned to her car the bags had split
so she transferred the shopping to a bag of her own. She said she never kept
receipts and denied stealing the goods.

The principal evidence for the prosecution was given by a store detective
employed by Marks & Spencers at their St Alban's branch. She said that at 10 am
f on the morning of 18 March she removed all the till rolls from the tills and
recovered a further two till rolls from a cupboard which bore the date 17 March.
She explained that the tills were connected to a central computer which fed in the
date, time, customer number and till number on each of the till rolls.

She further explained that each item of clothing has upon it a seven-figure
numbered label known as a unique product code or UPC. The UPC numbers are
g unique to clothing of a particular type, size and colour. The till operator punches
in the UPC number on the till, which then registers the appropriate price.

In the case of food each item of food has a price upon it and the operator
punches in the price of each item on the till. She said they had had no trouble
with the operation of the central computer.

h She carried out an examination of all the till rolls which she had recovered
from the tills which would have been those in use on 17 March and stamped as
such by the central computer and she also examined the two till rolls also stamped
and dated 17 March which had been placed in the cupboard where all used till
rolls were kept. She thus examined all the tills rolls in use on 17 March.

She said that there was no trace on the till rolls of the UPCs for the clothing
j found in the appellant's car. She said there was no record on any of the till rolls of
an item of food costing £12·57, the price of the beef. Nor was there any group of
prices matching the items of food found in the car.

It was quite apparent from the store detective's evidence that she was thoroughly
familiar with the operation of these tills and of the computer, albeit she did not
pretend to any technical understanding of the operation of the computer.

The appellant did not herself give evidence and no evidence was called on her behalf. The jury convicted her. If the till rolls were properly admitted in evidence *a* this is hardly surprising for they provided the most powerful evidence of guilt.

It is however submitted that the till rolls should not have been admitted in evidence because the store detective's evidence did not satisfy the provisions of s 69 of the Criminal Evidence Act 1984, which provides:

'(1) In any proceedings, a statement in a document produced by a *b* computer shall not be admissible as evidence of any fact stated therein unless it is shown—(a) that there are no reasonable grounds for believing that the statement is inaccurate because of improper use of the computer; (b) that at all material times the computer was operating properly, or if not, that any respect in which it was not operating properly or was out of operation was not such as to affect the production of the document or the accuracy of its *c* contents; and (c) that any relevant conditions specified in rules of court under subsection (2) below are satisifed.

(2) Provision may be made by rules of court requiring that in any proceedings where it is desired to give a statement in evidence by virtue of this section such information concerning the statement as may be required by the rules shall be provided in such form and at such time as may be so *d* required.'

No rules have yet been made under sub-s (2) but it is also necessary to note Pt II of Sch 3:

'PROVISIONS SUPPLEMENTARY TO SECTION 69 *e*

8. In any proceedings where it is desired to give a statement in evidence in accordance with section 69 above, a certificate—(a) identifying the document containing the statement and describing the manner in which it was produced; (b) giving such particulars of any device involved in the production of that document as may be appropriate for the purpose of showing that the document was produced by a computer; (c) dealing with *f* any of the matters mentioned in subsection (1) of section 69 above; and (d) purporting to be signed by a person occupying a responsible position in relation to the operation of the computer, shall be evidence of anything stated in it; and for the purposes of this paragraph it shall be sufficient for a matter to be stated to the best of the knowledge and belief of the person stating it.

9. Notwithstanding paragraph 8 above, a court may require oral evidence *g* to be given of anything of which evidence could be given by a certificate under that paragraph . . .'

The object of s 69 of the Act is clear enough. It requires anyone who wishes to introduce computer evidence to produce evidence that will establish that it is safe to rely on the documents produced by the computer. This is an affirmative duty *h* emphatically stated (sub-s (1)):

'. . . a statement in a document produced by a computer shall not be admissible as evidence of any fact stated therein *unless it is shown* . . .'

Such a duty cannot be discharged without evidence by the application of the *j* presumption that the computer is working correctly expressed in the maxim omnia praesumuntur rite esse acta as appears to be suggested in some of the cases. Nor does it make any difference whether the computer document has been produced with or without the input of information provided by the human mind and thus may or may not be hearsay. If the document produced by the computer is hearsay it will be necessary to comply with the provisions of s 24 of the Criminal *a* Justice Act 1988, the successor to s 68 of the Police and Criminal Evidence Act 1984, before the document can be admitted as evidence and it will also be necessary to comply with the provisions of s 69 of the 1984 Act. I see no warrant for an interpretation of the 1984 Act which limits the operation of s 69 to cases that fall within s 68 of that Act or s 24 of the Criminal Justice Act 1988. This however was the construction of the 1984 Act adopted by the Court of Appeal in *R v Minors, R v Harper* [1989] 2 All ER 208, [1989] 1 WLR 441 and which has

b been followed in a number of subsequent cases most notably *R v Spiby* (1990) 91 Cr App R 186 and *R v Neville* [1991] Crim LR 288.

In *R v Minors* [1989] 2 All ER 208 at 212, [1989] 1 WLR 441 at 446 it is stated in the judgment:

c '. . . to the extent to which a computer is merely used to perform functions of calculation, no question of hearsay is involved and the requirements of ss 68 and 69 do not apply: see *R v Wood* (1982) 76 Cr App R 23 and *Sophocleous v Ringer* [1988] RTR 52.'

d I do not think that these authorities give any support to the proposition that s 69 does not apply. *R v Wood* deals with the circumstances in which the contents of a computer print-out are to be regarded as real rather than hearsay evidence. It naturally does not touch upon the requirements of s 69 as the 1984 Act had not yet been enacted. In *Sophocleous v Ringer* the accused was charged with driving after consuming so much alcohol that the proportion of it in his breath exceeded the prescribed limit. Evidence was given against him by an analyst who had

e analysed a specimen of his blood through a technology known as gas chromatography for which a computer is used. She was permitted to refresh her memory by looking at the graph produced by the computer during the course of her work. The graph was not put in evidence by the prosecution nor did the defence require it to be exhibited. As the graph had not been put in evidence the court rightly pointed out that s 69 had no application on the facts of that case. I

f would add that if the graph had been made an exhibit in that case, the analyst would have been well-qualified to give the necessary evidence under s 69 (as will appear from later passages in my speech).

In a later passage of the judgment the court said ([1989] 2 All ER 208 at 212, [1989] 1 WLR 441 at 446):

g 'In the courts below it was assumed by all concerned that s 69 constitutes a self-contained code governing the admissibility of computer records in criminal proceedings. Undoubtedly, that is a legislative technique which Parliament could have adopted. The question is whether Parliament *did* adopt it.' (The court's emphasis.)

h The court then gave as its reason for confining the operation of s 69 to cases falling within s 68 the fact that in *R v Ewing* [1983] 2 All ER 645, [1983] QB 1039 a computer print-out of an appellant's bank account was held admissible under s 1 of the Criminal Evidence Act 1965 which was the forerunner of s 68 of the 1984 Act from which the court drew the inference that Parliament must therefore have intended s 69 to apply only to computer documents falling within the

j meaning of s 68. I cannot accept this reasoning. When *R v Ewing* was decided the safeguards later introduced by s 69 had not yet been enacted and I see no reason to suppose that because of the decision in *R v Ewing* Parliament intended the language of s 69 which is in general terms to be read in a restricted sense. It is surely every bit as important that a document produced by a computer and tendered as proof of guilt should be reliable whether or not it contains hearsay.

In *R v Spiby* (1990) 91 Cr App R 186 the accused was charged with smuggling
drugs into this country. As a part of the proof of his guilt the prosecution wished *a*
to show he was in touch with an accomplice in France. They invited the jury to
draw this inference from a computer print-out that recorded a number of
telephone calls made from a hotel in Cherbourg at which the accomplice was
staying to the accused's home in England. The computer did not record the
contents of the conversations but it did show the date, the time, the number of
the hotel room from which the call was made, the number to which the call was *b*
made in England; not, the duration and the cost. It seems to me as important to
have an assurance that the computer was recording this information accurately as
it would if the computer had also recorded the conversation. The important link
in the chain of evidence was not what these men said to each other but the fact
that they were in constant touch with one another and for this the prosecution
was relying solely on the reliability of the computer record. In such circumstances *c*
evidence to satisfy s 69 is required and in so far as *R v Spiby* holds to the contrary
it should not be followed; furthermore affirmative evidence is required and it is
not sufficient to rely on the presumption expressed in the Latin phrase omnia
praesumuntur rite esse acta. In fact there was satisfactory evidence given by the
sub-manager of the hotel who was familiar with the operation of the computer *d*
and could speak to its reliability.

I therefore approach this question upon the basis that if the prosecution wish
to rely upon a document produced by a computer they must comply with s 69 in
all cases.

The principal argument for the appellant starts with the proposition that the
store detective was not 'a person occupying a responsible position in relation to *e*
the operation of the computer' within the meaning of para 8(*d*) of Sch 3 and
therefore was not qualified to sign a certificate for the purpose of providing proof
of the matters contained in s 69(1). This I accept. Although the store detective
understood the operation of the computer and could speak of its reliability she
had no responsibility for its operation.

I cannot however accept the next step in the appellant's argument, which is *f*
that oral evidence is only acceptable if given by a person who is qualified to sign
the certificate. The appellant does not go so far as to submit that evidence must
be given by a computer expert but insists that it must be someone who has
responsibility for the operation of the computer, either the operator or someone
with managerial responsibility for the operation of the computer.

Proof that the computer is reliable can be provided in two ways: either by *g*
calling oral evidence or by tendering a written certificate in accordance with the
terms of para 8 of Sch 3, subject to the power of the judge to require oral evidence.
It is understandable that if a certificate is to be relied upon it should show on its
face that it is signed by a person who from his job description can confidently be
expected to be in a position to give reliable evidence about the operation of the *h*
computer. This enables the defendant to decide whether to accept the certificate
at its face value or to ask the judge to require oral evidence which can be
challenged in cross-examination. A defendant seeing a certificate signed by a store
detective would not necessarily assume that such a person was familiar with the
operation of the computer or had any responsibility for it and might well
challenge the certificate. It does not however follow that the store detective cannot *j*
in fact give evidence that shows she is fully familiar with the operation of the
store's computer and can speak to its reliability.

The appellant's argument requires one to read into s 69(1) after the words
'unless it is shown' the following words lifted from para 8 of Sch 3: 'by [the oral

evidence of] a person occupying a responsible position in relation to the operation
a of the computer'.

These words do not appear in the section. They are, for the reasons I have
given, contained in Sch 3 as a necessary qualification to sign a certificate but I can
see no reason to read them into s 69(1) when oral evidence will be open to
challenge by cross-examination.

Documents produced by computers are an increasingly common feature of all
b business and more and more people are becoming familiar with their uses and
operation. Computers vary immensely in their complexity and in the operations
they perform. The nature of the evidence to discharge the burden of showing
that there has been no improper use of the computer and that it was operating
properly will inevitably vary from case to case. The evidence must be tailored to
suit the needs of the case. I suspect that it will very rarely be necessary to call an
c expert and that in the vast majority of cases it will be possible to discharge the
burden by calling a witness who is familiar with the operation of the computer
in the sense of knowing what the computer is required to do and who can say
that it is doing it properly.

The computer in this case was of the simplest kind printing limited basic
d information on each till roll. The store detective was able to describe how the tills
operated, what the computer did, that there had been no trouble with the
computer and how she had also examined all the till rolls, which showed no
evidence of malfunction either by the tills or the central computer.

In these circumstances I agree with the Court of Appeal that she was fully
qualified to give the evidence required by s 69 and that in the light of her evidence
e the till rolls were properly admitted as part of the prosecution case.

I therefore answer the certified question by saying that s 69(1) of the Police and
Criminal Evidence Act 1984 can be satisfied by the oral evidence of a person
familiar with the operation of the computer who can give evidence of its
reliability and such a person need not be a computer expert.

For these reasons I would dismiss this appeal.
f

LORD EMSLIE. My Lords, I have had the advantage of reading in draft the
speech of my noble and learned friend Lord Griffiths. I entirely agree with him
and for the reasons which he gives I, too, would dismiss this appeal.

g **LORD ROSKILL.** My Lords, I have had the advantage of reading in draft the
speech of my noble and learned friend Lord Griffiths. I agree with him and for
the reasons which he gives I, too, would dismiss this appeal.

LORD ACKNER. My Lords, I have had the advantage of reading in draft the
speech of my noble and learned friend Lord Griffiths. I agree with it and, for the
h reasons given by my noble and learned friend, I, too, would answer the certified
question in the way that he has done and would dismiss the appeal.

LORD LOWRY. My Lords, I have had the advantage of reading in draft the
speech of my noble and learned friend Lord Griffiths. I agree with it and, for the
reasons given by my noble and learned friend, I, too, would answer the certified
j question in the way that he has done and would dismiss the appeal.

Appeal dismissed.

Mary Rose Plummer   Barrister.

Re Elgindata Ltd (No 2)   a

COURT OF APPEAL, CIVIL DIVISION
NOURSE, STOCKER AND BELDAM LJJ
9, 10, 11 JUNE 1992

Costs – Order for costs – Discretion – Disallowing costs of successful plaintiff – Principles b
on which discretion to award costs to be exercised – Petitioning shareholders successful in
obtaining order for purchase of shares by another shareholder – Judge deciding that for
most part petitioners' case failing – Judge ordering petitioners to pay three-quarters of
defendant's costs and defendant to pay one-quarter of petitioners' costs – Whether judge's
order erroneous.

c

The petitioners were successful in obtaining an order under s 459 of the
Companies Act 1985 that P, another shareholder in the company, purchase their
shares. The judge found that for the most part the petitioners' case had failed but
that there was some conduct on the part of P that constituted unfairly prejudicial
conduct and ordered, inter alia, that three-quarters of P's costs should be paid by
the petitioners and one-quarter of the petitioners' costs should be paid by P. The d
petitioners' costs were estimated at £120,000 and those of P at £200,000 so that
the petitioners would have to bear costs of some £240,000. The petitioners
appealed against the order for costs.

Held – The principles on which costs were to be awarded were (i) that costs were e
in the discretion of the court, (ii) that costs should follow the event except when
it appeared to the court that in the circumstances of the case some other order
should be made, (iii) that the general rule did not cease to apply simply because
the successful party raised issues or made allegations that failed, but that he could
be deprived of his costs in whole or in part where he had caused a significant
increase in the length of the proceedings, and (iv) that where the successful party f
raised issues or made allegations improperly or unreasonably the court could not
only deprive him of his costs but could also order him to pay the whole or part of
the unsuccessful party's costs. The fourth principle implied, moreover, that a
successful party who neither improperly nor unreasonably raised issues or made
allegations which failed ought not to be ordered to pay any part of the unsuccessful
party's costs, and because the judge had disregarded that principle his order could g
not stand. In the circumstances the costs ought to follow the event except to the
extent that the award of costs to the petitioners should be diminished by the
amount of time and expense taken up by the allegations that failed. Accordingly,
the petitioners would not be ordered to pay any part of P's costs but they would
be deprived of half of their costs payable by P (see p 237 *d* to *h*, p 239 *j*, p 240 *b c j* h
to p 241 *a* and p 242 *c d*, post).

Notes
For the court's discretion not to award costs to a successful party, see 37 *Halsbury's*
Laws (4th edn) paras 714, 717, and for cases on the subject, see 37(3) *Digest*
(Reissue) 240–247, 249–255, 4350–4399, 4413–4446.   j
    For the Companies Act 1985, s 459, see 8 *Halsbury's Statutes* (4th edn) (1991
reissue) 531.

Cases referred to in judgment
Alltrans Express Ltd v CVA Holdings Ltd [1984] 1 All ER 685, [1984] 1 WLR 394,
    CA.

Bird Precision Bellows Ltd, Re [1984] 3 All ER 444, [1984] Ch 419, [1984] 2 WLR
869; *affd* [1985] 3 All ER 523, [1986] Ch 658, [1986] 2 WLR 158, CA.
Elgindata Ltd, Re [1991] BCLC 959.
Gupta v Klito [1989] CA Transcript 89.
Maxwell v Keun [1928] 1 KB 645, CA.

Case also cited

Tramountana Armadora SA v Atlantic Shipping Co SA [1978] 2 All ER 870.

Appeal

The petitioners, Derek Rowland and Glenys Margaret Rowland, appealed with
the leave of the judge against the order for costs made by Warner J on 5 July 1991
following a substantive judgment ([1991] BCLC 959) on the hearing of a petition
brought under s 459 of the Companies Act 1985 seeking an order against the
respondents, Elgindata Ltd (the company), Richard John Purslow and Christine
Ann Purslow on the ground that the affairs of the company had been conducted
in a manner unfairly to the interests of the petitioners who were minority
shareholders in the company. The facts are set out in the judgment of Nourse LJ.

Timothy Lloyd QC and *Gordon Nurse* (instructed by *Shindler & Co*) for the petitioners.
David Chivers (instructed by *Robbins Olivey*, Woking) for the respondents.

NOURSE LJ. This is an appeal relating only to costs. It is brought with the leave
of the judge below, which means that the restriction on an appeal imposed by
s 18(1)(*f*) of the Supreme Court Act 1981 does not apply. However, we can only
allow the appeal if, in making his order, the judge erred in principle or if there is
some other ground on which a decision made by a judge in the exercise of his
discretion can be reviewed: cf *Alltrans Express Ltd v CVA Holdings Ltd* [1984] 1 All
ER 685, [1984] 1 WLR 394. In this instance we have had to investigate and
identify the principles on which a successful party may be deprived of costs or
may even be ordered to pay costs to the unsuccessful party.

The proceedings in which the order was made was a petition under s 459(1) of
the Companies Act 1985 seeking relief from the court on the ground that the
affairs of a small private company called Elgindata Ltd (the company) were being
or had been conducted in a manner which was unfairly prejudicial to the interests
of the petitioners, Mr Derek Rowland and his wife, Mrs Glenys Margaret Rowland,
who are the joint holders of 33% of its issued share capital. The respondents to
the petition were the company itself and Mr Richard John Purslow and his wife,
Mrs Christine Ann Purslow, who hold 56% and 11% respectively of the issued
share capital. The trial of the petition before Warner J extended over the whole
or some part of 43 days between 1 October and 29 November 1990. The judge's
reserved judgment was delivered on 28 January 1991, when he made an order
that Mr Purslow should purchase the petitioners' shares at a price to be fixed by
the court (see *Re Elgindata Ltd* [1991] BCLC 959). On 5 July 1991, having heard
argument as to the costs of the petition, the judge ordered (1) that Mrs Purslow's
costs should be paid by the petitioners, (2) that three-quarters of Mr Purslow's
costs should be paid by the petitioners, (3) that one-quarter of the petitioners' costs
should be paid by Mr Purslow and (4) that the costs of the company should be
paid as to one-quarter by Mr Purslow and as to three-quarters by the petitioners.
The petitioners now appeal against the second, third and fourth of those orders.

It may be assumed that the costs of Mrs Purslow and the company were trivial
in amount, but those of the petitioners and Mr Purslow have been estimated on a
standard basis at around £120,000 and £200,000 respectively. If they were to be
taxed in those amounts, the result would be that the petitioners, albeit that they

succeeded in obtaining the relief which they sought, would have to bear total costs of £240,000 against a total of £80,000 borne by Mr Purslow. The price to *a* be paid by Mr Purslow for the petitioners' shares has now been fixed by agreement at no more than £24,600. These figures are enough to show that, if the judge's order for costs stands, the petitioners' victory will, as Beldam LJ observed in argument, have become worse than pyrrhic. In purely monetary terms it will have proved to be an annihilating defeat. I should make it clear that none of the figures were before the judge when he gave his decision on costs and that they *b* cannot have any influence on anything which we have to decide on this appeal. I refer to them only in order to demonstrate the great importance of our decision to the parties in the suit.

The reserved judgment of Warner J on the petition is reported (see [1991] BCLC 959). For present purposes it is not necessary to give even a brief résumé of the facts. I will refer to the judgment only so far as is necessary to understand the *c* present dispute as to costs. The judge stated the questions to be determined at that stage as being ([1991] BCLC 959 at 961):

> '(1) whether the affairs of the company have been conducted in a manner which is unfairly prejudicial to the interest of Mr and Mrs Rowland; (2) if so, whether the appropriate remedy is to order Mr Purslow, or Mr and Mrs *d* Purslow to purchase their shares; and (3) if so, on what basis the price for the shares should be arrived at.'

He added that it had been agreed between counsel that he should not at that stage hear the evidence of the valuers on the footing that that would be necessary only if he ordered a purchase. *e*

The judge came to the petitioners' case on the first question. He divided their complaints of unfairly prejudicial conduct into four categories. He accepted that that was his own classification and not counsel's, but it is easy to see why he thought it necessary to make it. He expressed the four categories as follows (at 983): *f*

> 'First, Mr Rowland had, after the execution of the 1986 agreements, if not a legal right, at least a legitimate expectation that he would be consulted about and participate in the policy-making decisions of the company, but in fact he was not consulted about those decisions and was excluded from participation in them. Secondly, in certain specific instances the affairs of the company were conducted in a manner which was unfairly prejudicial to the *g* interests of Mr and Mrs Rowland. Among those instances were the late payment of the dividend of £9,900, the failure to disclose the ASEM approach and Mr Purslow's service agreement. Thirdly, Mr Purslow was neglectful of and incompetent in the management of the company's business. Fourthly, Mr Purslow used assets of the company for his personal benefit and the benefit of his family and friends.' *h*

Shortly stated, the judge's conclusions as to the first three categories of complaints were as follows. As to the first, he thought that the petitioners' case was thin but not non-existent (see [1991] BCLC 959 at 989, 1004). As to the second, he thought it thinner still, but likewise not non-existent in so far as it rested on the late payment of the dividend (at 1004). As to the third, he found that there had been *j* instances both of neglect of management and of bad management on the part of Mr Purslow and he thought that that conduct was prejudicial to the petitioners. However, he held that it was not unfairly prejudicial to them. The conduct was of a kind of which Mr Rowland took the risk when he invested in the company (at 1000).

As to the fourth category of complaints, the judge was satisfied that Mr Purslow
_a_   had been unscrupulous in the use of the company's money, that he had indeed
used it for his personal benefit and for the benefit of his family and friends and
that his conduct in that respect had been unfairly prejudicial to the interests of
the petitioners, albeit to an extent that was difficult to quantify (at 1003). Later
he said that this conduct had resulted in a diminution in value of the petitioners'
shares only to a very limited and unquantifiable extent. The reason why he had
_b_   concluded that it was conduct unfairly prejudicial to the petitioners' interests was
that it was inherently so (at 1004–1005).

The judge started his consideration of the second question with these words (at
1005):

_c_   'The petitioners' case has for the most part failed. Ought I none the less to
order Mr Purslow, or Mr and Mrs Purslow, to purchase Mr and Mrs Rowland's
shares? I have, after a great deal of hesitation, come to the conclusion that I
should. The decisive factor to my mind is Mr Purslow's propensity for using
the company's assets for his personal benefit and the benefit of his family and
friends. I accept Mr Nurse's submission that, having regard to the evidence
about that, it would be unfair to Mr and Mrs Rowland for the court to leave
_d_   them "locked in" as minority shareholders in the company.'

Later the judge said that he thought, to use an expression that was more familiar
in the Family Division, that it was a case for a clean break. He then held that the
purchase order should be made against Mr Purslow alone and not against Mr and
Mrs Purslow jointly.

_e_   Lastly, the judge came to the third question. That gave rise to four sub-
questions, which were mainly questions of law. I need not go into them in detail.
Three were decided in favour of Mr Purslow and one in favour of the petitioners.
Of those decided in favour of Mr Purslow the most important was that the shares
should be valued as at the date of the order and not at some earlier date, when
they would without doubt have been considerably more valuable.
_f_   I now come to the judgment of Warner J on costs. Having referred to the
general rule that a successful plaintiff is entitled to his costs notwithstanding that
he may have failed on some issues, he said that he had to look at the realities of
the case. The essence of the petitioner's case had been that there had been unfairly
prejudicial conduct in all four categories which had resulted in a substantial
diminution in value of their shares, entitling them to be bought out at their value
_g_   before that diminution had occurred. In the event that case had failed and what
had succeeded was a case of a different magnitude and a different nature. There
had been unfairly prejudicial conduct in the fourth category only, which had not
diminished the value of the shares to any significant or quantifiable extent and
had led only to an order that the price be fixed as at the date of the order. For
_h_   those reasons he did not think that the general rule ought to be applied.
The judge continued by recording a suggestion by Mr Chivers for the
respondents that Mr Purslow should not have to pay any of the petitioners' costs
and moreover that they should have to pay seven-eighths of his costs. That did
not seem to the judge to be right either. He then considered and rejected three
reasons suggested by Mr Chivers for depriving the petitioners of all their costs. (I
_j_   interpose to emphasise that those were not advanced as reasons for ordering the
petitioners to pay seven-eighths of Mr Purslow's costs. Mr Chivers has confirmed
that he did indeed advance separate arguments, first, for depriving the petitioners
of all their costs and, secondly, for making them pay seven-eighths of Mr Purslow's
costs.) Having disposed of Mr Chivers's three points under his first argument, the
judge continued:

'The consequence of the petitioners' case having for the most part failed is, as I have already indicated, that in my view this is not simply a case where *a* the petitioners have succeeded and are, therefore, entitled to all their costs. But, it is not that they should have no part of their costs. The real question here seems to me to be how the burden of the costs of the petition should, in all fairness, be divided between Mr Purslow and the petitioners. Leaving aside for the moment certain specific items of costs which were mentioned by counsel in their submissions, it seems to me that one cannot do more in a *b* situation such as this than make a rough and ready apportionment of the costs of the proceedings.'

Next the judge rejected the notion of an order based on Mr Chivers's detailed analysis of the issues and the evidence, saying that it was not a realistic approach if only because it ignored all the time spent on general and background matters *c* and on issues that were not pursued. Then he expressed his decision thus:

'Thinking back about the trial and the issues, it seems to me that as fair a basis as any for apportioning the costs would be the four categories into which I placed the petitioners' complaints against Mr Purslow, and, looking at it broadly (and particularly looking at the reason why in the end I decided *d* that Mr Purslow should buy the petitioners' shares), it seems to me that the petitioners should receive one quarter of their costs from Mr Purslow and should pay three-quarters of Mr Purslow's costs.'

Finally, the judge considered a number of specific points raised by counsel, but concluded that none of them required any alteration in the orders that he had *e* proposed.

The judge's decision on costs can be summarised as follows. (1) For the reasons he stated, the general rule that a successful plaintiff is entitled to his costs notwithstanding that he may have failed on some issues ought not to be applied. (2) On the other hand, the reasons advanced for depriving the petitioners of all their costs having been considered and rejected, it would not be right that they *f* should have no part of their costs and, on a rough and ready apportionment based on the parties' respective degrees of success in regard to the four categories of complaints of unfairly prejudicial conduct, that part ought to be one quarter. (3) On the same rough and ready apportionment, but for reasons not stated, the plaintiffs ought to pay three-quarters of Mr Purslow's costs.
g
Mr Lloyd QC, whose argument for the petitioners in this court has been notable for its steadiness in not putting any point higher than it can sensibly be put, accepts that if the judge's decision had stopped at (2), it would not have been one with which this court could have interfered. The position would have been that the judge had departed from the general rule by depriving the successful parties of part of their costs in recognition of their having failed on issues or allegations *h* which had taken up a substantial part of the trial. That would have been in accordance with an established practice and well within the judge's discretion. Mr Lloyd would have said that the deprivation of three-quarters was too high. But he would not have been able to say that it was so high as to be outside the ambit of reasonable disagreement. However, on coming to the third element of the judge's decision, Mr Lloyd submits that here he has made a further departure *j* from the general rule and, moreover, a very unusual one which, in the absence of any suggestion that the allegations were unreasonably or improperly pursued (and no such suggestion has been made), necessarily involved an error in principle on his part.

I have to say that I have been very puzzled as to how the judge came to the
a third element of his decision. On any footing it is such an unusual order to make,
both in form and in substance. When contrasted with his full consideration of
the matter at the first and second stages, the judge's omission to give any reasons
at the third and most crucial stage is very remarkable. This has caused me to ask
myself whether he assumed that the only way in which the rough and ready
apportionment that he had in mind could be implemented was by making the
b two cross-orders that he did. Bearing in mind how difficult these questions of
costs often are and how easy it is to overlook the practical consequences of any
proposed order, I think it possible that he did not fully appreciate that, on the
assumption that the costs on both sides were equal (the only assumption that
could be made at that stage), his order was equivalent to one giving Mr Purslow,
c the unsuccessful party, half his costs or, if you prefer, to one ordering the
petitioners, the successful parties, to pay three-quarters of the costs as a whole.

It is out of deference to the judge that I have thought it right to speculate a
little as to his processes of thought. But in the end we have to take his judgment
as it stands. Taking it thus, I am in no doubt that he erred in principle. Mr
Chivers strove to persuade us to the contrary. In order to support the judge's
d decision, he sought again to rely on the detailed analysis which the judge himself
had not found helpful. His arguments wholly failed to convince me that the
orders made were open to the judge. At every stage they ignored the import of
the petitioners' success in the proceedings, a success which consisted in establishing
a right to have their shares purchased by Mr Purslow, a right which he had at all
times denied them and in order to establish which they had to go to judgment.

e In order to show that the judge erred I must state the principles which ought
to have been applied. They are mainly recognised or provided for (it matters not
which) by s 51 of the Supreme Court Act 1981 and the relevant provisions of RSC
Ord 62, in this case rr 2(4), 3(3) and 10. They do not in their entirety depend on
the express recognition or provision of the rules. In part they depend upon
f established practice or implication from the rules. The principles are these. (1)
Costs are in the discretion of the court. (2) They should follow the event, except
when it appears to the court that in the circumstances of the case some other
order should be made. (3) The general rule does not cease to apply simply because
the successful party raises issues or makes allegations on which he fails, but where
that has caused a significant increase in the length or cost of the proceedings he
g may be deprived of the whole or a part of his costs. (4) Where the successful party
raises issues or makes allegations improperly or unreasonably, the court may not
only deprive him of his costs but order him to pay the whole or a part of the
unsuccessful party's costs. Of these principles the first, second and fourth are
expressly recognised or provided for by rr 2(4), 3(3) and 10 respectively. The third
depends on well-established practice. Moreover, the fourth implies that a
h successful party who neither improperly nor unreasonably raises issues or makes
allegations on which he fails ought not to be ordered to pay any part of the
unsuccessful party's costs. It was because of his disregard of that principle that the
judge erred in this case.

Although we have been referred to a number of authorities, it is only in two of
them that there are observations which bear directly on these principles. That no
j doubt is because, being axiomatic, it is only rarely that they rise to the surface of
judicial expression. In *Re Bird Precision Bellows Ltd* [1984] 3 All ER 444, [1984] Ch
419; *affd* [1985] 3 All ER 523, [1986] Ch 658 this court also delivered a judgment
on costs which does not appear in the report. That was another case under the
then equivalent of s 459(1) in which there had been a consent order that the

respondent majority should purchase the petitioning minority's shares at such price as the court should determine. After a trial extending over some 13 days, three of which were taken up with valuation evidence, I determined that the price should be one in excess of that for which the majority had contended but below that for which the minority had contended. On an erroneous supposition that the outcome of the valuation dispute had been a draw, I deprived the successful minority of 15% of their costs. However, this court held that I had erred in principle and made an order giving them the whole of their costs.

One of my reasons for referring to that decision is that it is another example of a case where the trial judge had overlooked or failed to apply basic principles as to costs. It was another case where the petitioners had to go to judgment in order to establish their right, in that case the right to obtain the price which they were in fact awarded. But I refer to it primarily for some observations of Oliver LJ, which expressly supports the third of the principles I have stated and impliedly supports the fourth. Having expressed the view that it was clearly a case in which on any normal view the petitioners would have been entitled to the costs of proving their case, Oliver LJ continued:

> 'I can see a ground, if the learned judge had been of this view, for depriving them of perhaps part of the costs of the valuation on the footing that the evidence as to valuation had been so extreme that it had wasted part of the time or something of that sort. But that is not this case and he has treated the matter simply on the basis that there was a draw and decided to deprive the respondents of all the costs of the valuation. That, as it seems to me, must on the stated reason that this was a draw be wrong. It was not a draw. It was a victory for the [petitioners]. In those circumstances it seems to me that the discretion was plainly wrongly exercised in this case and in my judgment the [petitioners] are entitled to the whole of the costs of the hearing below.'

Further support for the fourth principle is to be found in these words of Mustill LJ in *Gupta v Klito* [1989] CA Transcript 89 where he said:

> 'In those circumstances it seems to me that this is not a case where there was anything for which Mrs Ferguson deserved such criticism as to justify the extreme sanction of ordering her to pay the costs of her unsuccessful opponents. I would therefore be of the opinion that so far as the question of costs is concerned, the learned judge must be taken to have erred in principle and that therefore the case is one where this court should substitute its own opinion.'

There has been some debate in argument as to what was the 'event' of the proceedings for the purposes of Ord 62, r 3(3), and what were the issues in it. For my part I agree with Mr Lloyd that the event was the judge's order that Mr Purslow should purchase the shares of the petitioners. Moreover, I would say that there were at the most the three issues or questions identified by the judge at the beginning of his judgment. Mr Chivers sought to treat the four categories of complaints of unfairly prejudicial conduct as separate issues and even to go further and subdivide them into the individual allegations made in the petition. I wholly reject that approach. But, however you look at the case, it was not one in which there was any justification for separating out part of the subject matter and making a special order for costs in respect of that part.

On the footing that the learned judge erred in principle, we in this court must exercise an original discretion of our own. Here Mr Lloyd's formal position is that we should award the petitioners the whole of their costs. However, he correctly recognised that we would be bound under the third principle to deprive

them of a substantial part of their costs. He said that that part should not be more
a than half; at the very most it should be three-quarters.

For a long time I was of the view that we could not properly award the
petitioners more than one-quarter of their costs. That, it would seem, is the
fraction that would have been adopted by the judge if he had applied the correct
principles. It seemed to me that we could not properly go behind his assessment
of the effect of the petitioners making allegations which have failed. However,
b on reflection I have come to a clear view that we should award the petitioners half
of their costs. I will explain my reasons as briefly as I can.

It is to be noted that in making his rough and ready apportionment on the
basis of the parties' respective degrees of success in regard to the four categories of
complaints, the judge did not express any estimate of the time and costs of which
c they had respectively been the cause. Moreover, he did not say that that was the
only fair basis for an apportionment. He said that it was as fair a basis as any
other. In my judgment the only fair basis for deciding the part of their costs of
which the petitioners should be deprived is to ask how much time and expense
was taken up in dealing only with the allegations on which they failed. I
acknowledge the difficulties with which we are confronted in answering that
d question. An apportionment made by us is bound to be even more rough and
ready than one made by the judge. But we must do the best we can.

Mr Lloyd has submitted that it is too facile and superficial to look only at the
four categories of complaints. That approach, he says, would be an oversimplifi-
cation which ignored both the time taken up in establishing matters of general
relevance and the facts, first, that the petitioners were not wholly unsuccessful in
e regard to the first and second categories and, secondly, that the judge found that
in regard to the third category Mr Purslow's management was prejudicial, albeit
not unfairly so.

I agree with those submissions, in particular the last of them, which leads on to
the most telling of Mr Lloyd's submissions. He pointed to the judge's 'great deal
of hesitation' under the second question in ordering Mr Purslow to purchase the
f petitioners' shares. The judge said that to his mind the decisive factor was Mr
Purslow's propensity for using the company's assets for his personal benefit and
the benefit of his family and friends. But that cannot have been the only factor
which affected his thinking. At that stage he was, as he himself said, considering
whether the petitioners should be locked in as minority shareholders in the
g company. That inquiry necessarily involved looking at the extent of the
breakdown in mutual confidence between the parties and the causes for it. At
that stage the failure of communication between Mr Rowland and Mr Purslow,
the late payment of the dividend and in particular the prejudicial mismanagement
of Mr Purslow were also important matters for consideration. Even if the judge
did not consider them, and I am quite sure that he did, they were certainly
h matters which the petitioners were entitled to submit for his consideration. It is
that which is the acid test on a question of costs.

So in the end I have not found an assessment based only on the four categories
of complaints to be at all helpful. Looking at the case as a whole and taking
account, for what they are worth, of the specific points raised by Mr Chivers
before the judge and raised again before us under a respondent's notice, I am
j satisfied that the fair and proper order for us to make is to deprive the petitioners
of half their costs and no more. I would only add, so that it should not be thought
that the petitioners have been prejudiced by Mr Lloyd's not asking for more, that
I am quite certain that if he had asked for more they would not have got it.
Indeed, I suspect that their case has been positively assisted by the moderation of
his stance.

Finally, I must deal with the company's costs. In a normal case of this kind it would be right that the company itself should not have to bear any of its costs, *a* because otherwise the value of the successful party's shares might be correspondingly diminished. But here the price for the petitioners' shares has now been agreed and cannot be further affected. In the circumstances, there is no necessity for any order as to the company's costs.

I would allow this appeal, discharge the second, third and fourth of the judge's orders as to costs and order instead that half of the petitioners' costs down to the *b* foot of the order entered on 31 October 1991 should be paid by Mr Purslow.

STOCKER LJ. I agree, and I agree with the orders which have been proposed by Nourse LJ for the reasons which he has given.

BELDAM LJ. I, too, agree that, notwithstanding the spirited defence of the *c* judge's exercise of his discretion, this appeal succeeds. The petitioners' application under Pt IV of the Companies Act 1985 was contested every step of the way in detail and at length. In the end they succeeded in showing that the respondent had conducted the affairs of the company in a manner unfairly prejudicial to their minority holding in which they had invested the substantial sum of £40,000. *d* But it took them 43 days of hotly contested evidence to obtain an order that the respondent should buy their one-third holding eventually valued at just £24,600. Their own costs, as Nourse LJ has said, were estimated at about £120,000 and the respondent's at £200,000. In the event, the judge's order for costs effectively means that they not only bear the full amount of their own costs but have to pay a similar sum to the unsuccessful respondent. As Nourse LJ has said, in *Gupta v* *e* *Klito* [1989] CA Transcript 89 this court regarded such an order as an extreme sanction. Yet the judge made no finding that the petitioners had been guilty of improper or unreasonable conduct in the proceedings or were deserving of any penalty. His order was based solely on the ground that they had failed to establish some of the factual matters which they had alleged or in some cases had failed to show that the acts of mismanagement which they did establish were of a sufficient *f* degree to warrant the statutory description of unfairly prejudicial conduct.

If a penal order of this severity could be so justified, few litigants would recover any damages. It would add a hazard to the pursuit of justice which few, if any, would be prepared to risk. As Atkin LJ said of the exercise of a judicial discretion in a different context in *Maxwell v Keun* [1928] 1 KB 645 at 653: *g*

'I quite agree the Court of Appeal ought to be very slow indeed to interfere with the discretion of the learned judge on such a question as an adjournment of a trial, and it very seldom does do so; but, on the other hand, if it appears that the result of the order made below is to defeat the rights of the parties altogether, and to do that which the Court of Appeal is satisfied would be an *h* injustice to one or other of the parties, then the Court has the power to review such an order, and it is, to my mind, its duty to do so.'

The effect of the judge's order, though it did not deprive the petitioners of their right altogether, would clearly have such an adverse effect on the right they were forced by the respondent to establish in proceedings as to make it valueless and its pursuit ruinous. In the absence of any finding by the judge of improper or *j* oppressive conduct, I am bound to conclude that the exercise of the discretion was based on a wrong principle or at least that the injustice to the successful petitioners is so manifest that the court ought to review it. I am satisfied, therefore, that there was no justification in this case for ordering the successful petitioners to pay

any part of the respondent's costs. The only question to my mind is what
a proportion of their costs should the petitioners recover? Naturally it was urged
that the trial judge, having listened to the evidence for eight weeks, was in a far
better position to judge where responsibility for the costs of the petition should
fall and that this court should at least accept that in his view the petitioners only
deserved to receive a small proportion of their costs, if any proportion.

I am only prepared to acknowledge the judge's advantage to the extent that I
b accept that he formed the view that the respondent should not be required to pay
the costs of all the matters pursued by the petitioners in the evidence and that any
order for costs of the successful petitioners should reflect that view to a significant
extent. I say that because the learned judge divided the issues in the trial into four
groups of issues of fact. He had previously set out at the outset of his judgment,
c as Nourse LJ has said, the three real or substantial issues in the case, namely:
whether the affairs of the company had been conducted in a manner which was
unfairly prejudicial to the petitioners' interests; secondly, if so, whether the
appropriate remedy was to order that the respondent should purchase the
petitioners' shares; and, thirdly, if so, on what basis the price of the shares should
be arrived at. It was no doubt convenient for the judge to consider the factual
d issues in four groups, but by concluding on a purely numerical basis that costs
should be borne in the proportion three-quarters to one-quarter the judge
apparently assumed, firstly, that the costs of the groups of issues would all be
equal and, secondly, he made no allowance for the fact that proof of some of the
facts in the groups of issues on which he had deprived the petitioners of all costs
was essential to establish the petitioners' right to an order that the respondent buy
e their shares. In my view it is only if it is possible so to isolate an issue in the case
that it can properly be said that it is unnecessarily pursued as having no bearing
on the real questions in the suit that it would be proper to deprive the successful
party of all costs of that issue. Otherwise a more general assessment should be
made.

f To illustrate my point I would like to take three examples from this case. The
first group of complaints considered by the judge was based on a failure of the
respondent to consult the petitioners about significant policy decisions. There
was no doubt that some lack of consultation was proved, though the judge
described the case on this ground as thin. Even though not itself sufficient to
justify an order, nevertheless the lack of consultation clearly contributed to the
g breakdown in confidence in the respondent's management of the affairs of the
company. Nor in my view would it be right to regard that aspect of the case in
isolation when the main ground established was the respondent's propensity to
treat the assets of the company as his own without regard to or consideration of
the petitioners' interests. So, in my view, what was established on the first
category of the learned judge went to the first real issue in the case. The complaint
h of lack of consultation, though thin, was neither immaterial nor could it be said
to be irrelevant. It may have been exaggerated, but that in itself is no ground for
depriving the party making the allegation of all the costs. The second instance I
would take is in the treatment of the respondent's service agreement which caused
the company to enter into the agreement without consultation. It formed part of
the second category of complaints considered by the learned judge. The petitioner
j succeeded in showing and convinced the judge that this service agreement should
be ignored when a valuation of the petitioners' shares was made. It may only have
had a small influence on the value of the shares. Nevertheless, it cannot be said to
be irrelevant or inconsequential and it went to the third real issue in the case
which the judge had earlier identified. The third instance is in the findings which

he made in the third category of issues which included complaints of mismanagement. As the judge held in his judgment, mismanagement may amount to conduct unfairly prejudicial and it may be so even if those responsible for the mismanagement suffer equally with the minority shareholders the same or even greater prejudice (see [1991] BCLC 959 at 993). The judge held that the matters which he found established were prejudicial. He said prejudicial they were, but not unfairly so. That therefore went to the first real issue which he had identified.

I cite these instances only to show that in some respects the petitioners succeeded in the issues of which they were deprived of all costs and that the matters established were obviously relevant when the court came to consider whether to make an order under s 461. In the result I was satisfied by Mr Lloyd QC's commendably moderate analysis that the apportionment which gave the successful petitioners only one-quarter of their costs would not be just in the circumstances of this case. Accepting, as the learned judge obviously concluded, that it was appropriate to deprive the petitioners of a significant part of their costs, having regard to the length of the proceedings which he must have regarded as unjustified, I agree with the assessment which Nourse LJ has made and with the order proposed that the petitioners should receive one-half of their costs and with the further orders which he has made.

Appeal allowed with costs not to be enforced without leave of the court. Leave to appeal to the House of Lords refused.

Raina Levy   Barrister.

National Westminster Bank plc v Skelton and another

COURT OF APPEAL, CIVIL DIVISION
SLADE LJ AND ANTHONY LINCOLN J
23, 25, 26 MAY 1989

Mortgage – Order for possession of mortgaged property – Counterclaim – Mortgagee bringing action for possession against mortgagor – Counterclaim by mortgagor for unliquidated damages – Counterclaim alleged to exceed amount of debt due – Mortgagor claiming equitable set-off – Whether mortgagee entitled to possession notwithstanding counterclaim – Whether counterclaim a defence to mortgagee's claim to possession.

By a legal mortgage dated 25 October 1985 the defendant mortgagors charged their home as security to the bank in respect of all present, future, actual and/or contingent liabilities owed by a company to the bank. Clause 11 of the mortgage agreement provided that the defendants were deemed to stand charged with the liabilities secured 'as if they were primarily due from the Mortgagor'. In February 1988 the bank issued proceedings seeking possession of the mortgaged property. The defendants filed a defence and counterclaim alleging, inter alia, that the company was entitled to recover unliquidated damages against the bank for an alleged breach of duty and that, since the sum claimed would exceed the amount of the arrears, that claim could be set off against the sums owing by the company to the bank, thus extinguishing the company's debt and discharging the mortgage over the defendants' home. The bank applied to strike out the defence on the ground that it disclosed no reasonable defence to the bank's claim against the

defendants to possession of the property. The judge struck out the defence and
a ordered the defendants to deliver immediate possession of the property. The
defendants appealed, contending that the principle that a legal mortgagee's right
to possession of the mortgaged property could not be defeated by a cross-claim on
the part of the mortgagor was not applicable where the cross-claim would give
the mortgagor rights by way of an equitable set-off or where the mortgage was
merely by way of guarantee intended to afford security for the debts of a third
b party.

Held – The general rule that, subject to contractual or statutory limitations, a
mortgagee under a legal charge was entitled to seek possession of the mortgaged
property at any time after the mortgage was executed and that the existence of a
cross-claim, even if it exceeded the amount of the mortgage debt, would not by
c itself defeat the right to possession enjoyed by the mortgagee was applicable both
where the cross-claim was a mere counterclaim and where it was a cross-claim for
unliquidated damages which, if established, would give rise to a right by way of
equitable set-off. Furthermore, any right to a set-off to which the defendants
might be entitled as sureties was excluded by virtue of cl 11 of the mortgage
d agreement since the mortgage was deemed to be a primary security and the
defendants were deemed to be in the position of primary debtors rather than
guarantors. It followed that there was no defence to the bank's claim to immediate
possession of the property. The appeal would therefore be dismissed (see p 247 *d
e*, p 248 *b c*, p 249 *b c f j*, p 251 *e* to *h* and p 253 *e f h*, post).
Dicta of Russell LJ in *Samuel Keller (Holdings) Ltd v Martins Bank Ltd* [1970] 3 All
e ER 950 at 952, 953 followed.
Mobil Oil Co Ltd v Rawlinson (1981) 43 P & CR 221 applied.
Cellulose Products Pty Ltd v Truda (1970) 92 WN (NSW) 561 considered.

Notes
For right to possession of the mortgaged property, see 32 *Halsbury's Laws* (4th
f edn) paras 672–707, and for cases on the subject, see 35 *Digest* (Reissue) 245–261,
2036–2148.

Cases referred to in judgments
Barclays Bank plc v Tennet [1984] CA Transcript 242.
Birmingham Citizens Permanent Building Society v Caunt [1962] 1 All ER 163, [1962]
g Ch 883, [1962] 2 WLR 323.
British Anzani (Felixstowe) Ltd v International Marine Management (UK) Ltd [1979] 2
All ER 1063, [1980] QB 137, [1979] 3 WLR 451.
Cellulose Products Pty Ltd v Truda (1970) 92 WN (NSW) 561, NSW SC.
Citibank Trust Ltd v Ayivor [1987] 3 All ER 241, [1987] 1 WLR 1157.
h *Covino v Bandag Manufacturing Pty Ltd* [1983] 1 NSWLR 237, NSW CA.
Fourmaids Ltd v Dudley Marshall (Properties) Ltd [1957] 2 All ER 35, [1957] Ch
317, [1957] 2 WLR 931.
Hyundai Shipbuilding and Heavy Industries Co Ltd v Pournaras [1978] 2 Lloyd's Rep
502, CA.
Indrisie v General Credits Ltd [1985] VR 251, Vict SC.
j *Keller (Samuel) (Holdings) Ltd v Martins Bank Ltd* [1970] 3 All ER 950, [1971] 1
WLR 43, CA.
Mobil Oil Co Ltd v Rawlinson (1981) 43 P & CR 221.
Royal Trust Co of Canada v Markham [1975] 3 All ER 433, [1975] 1 WLR 1416,
CA.
Western Bank Ltd v Schindler [1976] 2 All ER 393, [1977] Ch 1, [1976] 3 WLR 341,
CA.

Williams & Humbert Ltd v W & H Trade Marks (Jersey) Ltd, Rumasa SA v Multinvest
    (UK) Ltd [1986] 1 All ER 129, [1986] AC 368, [1986] 2 WLR 24, HL.   **a**
Wilson v Mitchell [1939] 2 All ER 869, [1939] 2 KB 869.

Appeal

The defendants, Robert Charles Skelton and Wendy Linda Skelton, appealed with
the leave of Judge Head given on 6 January 1989 from the judgment of Judge **b**
Phelan sitting in the West London County Court on 14 December 1988 ordering
the defendants to deliver to the plaintiff, National Westminster Bank plc (the
bank), immediate possession of the property at 4 Moorcroft Way, Pinner,
Middlesex. The facts are set out in the judgment of Slade LJ.

Jonathan Brock (instructed by *Lock & Marlborough*) for the defendants.   **c**
Anthony Mann (instructed by *Wilde Sapte*) for the bank.

SLADE LJ. This is an appeal by Mr Robert Charles Skelton and Mrs Wendy
Linda Skelton, the defendants in a mortgagee's action, from a judgment given by
Judge Phelan in the West London County Court on 14 December 1988. The **d**
proceedings arise out of a legal mortgage made on 25 October 1985 by the
defendants in favour of National Westminster Bank plc (the bank). The bank was
the plaintiff in the proceedings and is the respondent to this appeal.

By cl 1(a) of the mortgage the defendants charged by way of legal mortgage the
property, 4 Moorcroft Way, Pinner, which I understand to be their home—

> 'as a continuing security to the Bank for the discharge on demand by the **e**
> Bank on the Mortgagor of all present future actual and/or contingent
> liabilities of:—LEAMINGTON CONSTRUCTION COMPANY LIMITED (the Debtor) to
> the Bank whether on account of moneys advanced bills of exchange
> promissory notes guarantees indemnities interest commission banking
> charges and whether incurred solely severally and/or jointly and all legal and **f**
> other expenses (on a full indemnity basis) howsoever incurred by the Bank
> in connection therewith . . .'

The mortgage included, inter alia, the following further provisions:

> '3   Section 103 of the Law of Property Act 1925 shall not apply to this
> Mortgage and the statutory power of sale and other powers shall be exercisable **g**
> at any time after demand . . .
> 6   At any time after the power of sale has become exercisable the Bank or
> any Receiver appointed hereunder may enter and manage the Mortgaged
> Property or any part thereof and provide such services and carry out such
> repairs and works of improvement reconstruction addition or completion
> (including the provision of plant equipment and furnishings) as deemed **h**
> expedient . . .'

On 9 February 1988 the bank issued proceedings seeking possession of the
mortgage premises. In its particulars of claim it asserted that it had written to the
two defendants respectively, formally calling up the mortgage on the property
and requiring payment of the sum of £98,480·02 as the principal and interest **j**
calculated to that date. It asserted that the precise amount due and owing to it,
inclusive of interest at the date of the particulars of claim, was £104,957 and that
interest continued to accrue at present at a daily rate of £36·68. It further asserted,
as I understand to be common ground, that the property is a dwelling house
occupied by the defendants within the meaning of Pt IV of the Administration of
Justice Act 1970.

On 30 March 1988 the defendants filed a defence and counterclaim. The nature
of the defence appears from paras 4 to 12 thereof, which I should read:

'4. If, which is not admitted, the Defendants charged the property of the
Plaintiff, such charge was to secure the indebtedness of Leamington
Construction Limited ("The Company") to the Plaintiff.

5. [At] the material times, the Company was a customer of the Plaintiff
bank and, in particular, the Company [had] an account with the Plaintiff at
its Ickenham Road Corner branch, Ruislip Middlesex.

6. It was an implied term of the contract between the Plaintiff as banker
and the Company as customer and/or the Plaintiff as banker owed a duty to
the Company as customer not to disclose to any third party unless authorised
so to do by the Company information as to the affairs of the Company which
had been imparted by the Company to the Plaintiff in confidence.

7. In or around September 1986, a Mr David Buckby an employee of the
Plaintiff and the Plaintiff's manager of the Ickenham Road Corner branch, in
breach of the said implied term and in breach of the said duty, communicated
to a Mr R Bailey an employee of the Company, information as to the financial
position of the company so as to inform Mr Bailey or so as to give Mr Bailey
the impression that the Company was in financial difficulties and further,
Mr Buckby advised Mr Bailey that Mr Bailey should cease his involvement
with the Company.

8. As a consequence of the matters set out in paragraph 7 thereof,
Mr Bailey:—(1) Removed from the premises at Frome Wiltshire which were
occupied by the Company, timber and a stock of knobs knockers laminated
boards wax and stainers screws nails and fittings and other stock which was
the property of the Company; (2) Removed from the said premises at Frome
machinery and equipment which included two single-phrase radio arm saws,
one three-phase radio arm saw, one green mortiser (free standing), one plane
and thicknesser, one bench saw, a selection of hand tools and drills, two hand
planes, one rooter and two free standing rooters, two jigsaws, one blue
compressor and other equipment, the property of the Company; (3) Began
to trade in a business which was similar to the business carried on by the
Company at the said premises in Frome and in competition therewith; (4)
[Induced] employees of the Company to determine their employment with
the Company and to become employees of Mr Bailey.

9. By reason of the matters aforesaid, the Company lost stock machinery
equipment and profit as aforesaid and in January 1987 was compulsorily
wound up.

10. The damages recoverable by the Company from the Plaintiff when set
off against any sums otherwise due from the company to the Plaintiff
extinguished the same so that there is no sum remaining due from the
Company to the Plaintiff.

11. By reason of the matters aforesaid, any charge over the property in
favour of the Plaintiff has been discharged alternatively the Defendants are
entitled to redeem the same.

12. By reason of the matters aforesaid, the Plaintiff is not entitled to
alternative, ought not to be granted the relief sought herein.'

There followed a counterclaim in which the defendants repeated their defence
and sought:

'Insofar as the same may be necessary, an order for redemption of any
charge over the property in favour of the Plaintiff, on such terms (if any) as
may be just . . .'

On 20 June 1988 the bank filed a reply and a defence to counterclaim, which it subsequently amended on 6 December 1988.

Meantime, however, on 31 October 1988 the bank (perhaps not as promptly as it should have done) had given notice of an application pursuant to CCR Ord 13, r 5 seeking the following relief:

'(1) Paragraphs 7 to 12 of the Defence and as repeated in the Counterclaim be struck out; (2) The Plaintiffs have leave to enter judgment against the Defendants herein . . .'

The relevant provisions of Ord 13, r 5 are as follows:

'(1) The court may at any stage of the proceedings in an action order the whole or any part of any pleading to be struck out or amended on the ground that—(a) it discloses no reasonable cause of action or defence, as the case may be . . . and may order the action to be stayed or dismissed or judgment to be entered accordingly, as the case may be.'

The learned judge concluded that paras 7 to 12 of the defence disclosed no reasonable defence as a matter of law. He had before him an affidavit sworn on behalf of the bank deposing to the indebtedness of the defendants alleged in the particulars of claim, the notice requiring payment and the other matters alleged in the bank's pleading. By his order of 14 December 1988 he accordingly ordered that the defendants deliver to the bank on or before 10 January 1989 possession of the property and that paras 7 to 12 inclusive of the defence be struck out. On 6 January 1989 Judge Head granted the defendants leave to appeal from the order and a stay of execution pending appeal.

Neither of the counsel who have appeared before us appeared in the court below and we can only guess at the course which the hearing then took. However, it would appear that the matter may have been argued before Judge Phelan much less fully than it has been argued in this court. A number of matters have been canvassed extensively in argument on this appeal which are not expressly referred to in the judge's judgment at all. I mention, for example, the principles governing a mortgagee's right to take possession of the mortgaged property, the construction of this particular mortgage, the relevance, if any, of the fact that this was a mortgage by way of guarantee and s 36 of the Administration of Justice Act 1970. In the course of a very brief extempore judgment acceding to the bank's application, the judge apparently regarded the all-important proposition, conclusive of the case, as being: '. . . a mortgagor cannot appropriate a counterclaim, even if admitted, in discharge of the debt.' As authority for this proposition he cited three cases, namely *Samuel Keller (Holdings) Ltd v Martins Bank Ltd* [1970] 3 All ER 950, [1971] 1 WLR 43, *Mobil Oil Co Ltd v Rawlinson* (1981) 43 P & CR 221 and *Citibank Trust Ltd v Ayivor* [1987] 3 All ER 241, [1987] 1 WLR 1157.

In the *Samuel Keller* case [1970] 3 All ER 950 at 953, [1971] 1 WLR 43 at 51, which Judge Phelan described as 'the major case', Russell LJ expressly approved a passage from the judgment of Megarry J in the court below, in the course of which it was said:

'A doctrine of the discharge of a mortgage debt by the existence of unilateral appropriation of an unliquidated claim is one to which I gave no countenance; I regard it as neither convenient nor just. Even where there is a claim which is both liquidated and admitted, and it exceeds the mortgage debt in amount, it may be to the interest of one party or the other, or both, that the mortgage and the mortgage debt should continue in existence.'

The learned judge apparently regarded this as the principle governing and conclusive of the case. However, as a further ground for his conclusion, he

expressed the view that the allegations made in paras 7 to 12 of the defence would
a be for the company (not the defendants) to argue. He observed, by reference to
Wilson v Mitchell [1939] 2 All ER 869, [1939] 2 KB 869, that the counterclaim in
the action could not be maintained in the absence of the principal debtor.

In this court we have had the benefit of very full and careful argument on both
sides. The course of this argument has shown that the case involves some points
of law which are by no means entirely easy. In these circumstances, Mr Brock for
b the defendants has rightly reminded us that in general the court will exercise its
striking-out jurisdiction only in plain and obvious cases. He submitted that this
was not on any footing an appropriate case for the learned judge to exercise it.
I have borne in mind that general principle. However, as Mr Mann for the bank
has reminded us, the decision of the House of Lords in *Williams & Humbert Ltd v
W & H Trade Marks (Jersey) Ltd, Rumasa SA v Multinvest (UK) Ltd* [1986] 1 All ER
c 129 esp at 139, [1986] AC 368 esp at 436 per Lord Templeman shows that on a
striking-out application it may be proper for the court, at least in special
circumstances, to hear argument and adjudicate upon even difficult points of law
if it is satisfied that their resolution may obviate the necessity for a trial.

In the present case the bank's submission is that as a matter of law paras 7 to 12
d of the defendants' pleading would disclose no defence to the bank's claim to
immediate possession of the property, even if the allegations of fact made therein
were shown to be well founded. I should say straight away that, after hearing full
argument, I am, in agreement with the judge, of the view that this submission of
law is correct. I am also of the opinion that in the circumstances it was not
incumbent on the judge to require the bank to go to the expense and delay of
e proceeding to a full trial in order to establish the validity of this submission.

Before turning to the legal issues, I propose to list a number of assumptions
which I will make in favour of the defendants for present purposes. This being a
striking-out application, not based on evidence, I will assume first that, if the case
were to go to trial, the defendants would be able to prove all the matters of fact
asserted in paras 7 to 12 of their defence. I make that assumption in their favour,
f even though I am bound to say that the prospects of their being able to prove that
the events alleged in para 8(1) and (2) of the pleading (referring to the removal by
Mr Bailey of large numbers of items from the business premises of the company
at Frome, Wiltshire) occurred as a consequence of the matters set out in para 7
would on any footing seem to me somewhat slender. I also make the assumption,
g favourable to the defendants, that if the case were allowed to go to trial proof of
the facts alleged in their defence would reveal the existence of a claim by the
company against the bank exceeding in amount the sums claimed by the bank
from the defendants. Again the assumption may perhaps not be a very realistic
one, but I make it in the defendants' favour.

I make one further assumption in their favour, which is one of law. Mr Mann
h for the bank submitted that any claim by the company would be one by way of
ordinary cross-claim rather than by way of set-off. The borderline between cross-
claims which will give rise to a right of equitable set-off and those which will not
is a thin one, particularly now that it is established that one can have a set-off even
though claim and cross-claim do not arise out of the same contract: see e g *British
Anzani (Felixstowe) Ltd v International Marine Management (UK) Ltd* [1979] 2 All ER
j 1063, [1980] QB 137. However, from the latter decision it appears that in deciding
whether or not to allow a set-off the court will be much influenced by what it
regards as the essential requirements of justice. In the present case, it seems to me
that, if it were to conclude that the alleged breaches of the bank's duties to the
company were established, and that these breaches had caused the company the
injury alleged, the court might consider that it would be unjust to allow the bank
to enforce payment against the company without taking into account the cross-
claim—in other words, that it might allow a set-off.

In these circumstances, I will assume in favour of the defendants—without, of course, deciding the point—that, if the case were allowed to proceed to trial, they *a* would or might be able to establish that at all material times the company was entitled to a claim for unliquidated damages by way of set-off against the bank in an amount which equalled or exceeded the debts said by the bank to be secured by cl 1 of the mortgage. Even on these assumptions, however, I think that neither paras 7 to 12 nor indeed any other paragraphs of the defendants' pleading afford any ground in law by way of defence to the bank's claim to immediate possession *b* of the property.

In explaining my reasons, I begin by stressing that the bank's claim is one simply for possession, not payment. The general rule established by long-standing authority is that, except in so far as his rights are limited by contract or statute, a mortgagee by way of legal charge is entitled to seek possession of the mortgage *c* property at any time after the mortgage is executed: see e g *Mobil Oil Co Ltd v Rawlinson* (1981) 43 P & CR 221, *Barclays Bank plc v Tennet* [1984] CA Transcript 242 and *Citibank Trust Ltd v Ayivor* [1987] 3 All ER 241, [1987] 1 WLR 1157.

In *Birmingham Citizens Permanent Building Society v Caunt* [1962] 1 All ER 163 at 168, [1962] Ch 883 at 890 Russell J cited with approval a passage from the judgment of Harman J in *Fourmaids Ltd v Dudley Marshall (Properties) Ltd* [1957] *d* 2 All ER 35 at 36, [1957] Ch 317 at 320 in which he put the matter thus:

> '... I said [in an earlier case] and I repeat, that the right of the mortgagee to possession in the absence of some specific contract has nothing to do with default on the part of the mortgagor. The mortgagee may go into possession before the ink is dry on the mortgage unless by a term expressed or necessarily *e* implied in the contract he has contracted himself out of that right. He has the right because he has a legal term of years in the property. If there is an attornment clause, he must give notice. If there is a provision express or to be implied that, so long as certain payments are made he will not go into possession, then he has contracted himself out of his rights. Apart from that, possession is a matter of course.' *f*

The mortgage in the present case contains no attornment clause and no express provision restricting the bank's right to take possession. Does it contain any implied provision? Having regard to the particular clauses in the mortgage instrument in *Caunt's* case, Russell J implied a provision restricting the mortgagee's right to possession until there was default on the part of the mortgagor. However, *g* the court will not readily imply any such restriction. As Buckley LJ said in *Western Bank Ltd v Schindler* [1976] 2 All ER 393 at 396, [1977] Ch 1 at 9:

> 'A legal mortgagee's right to possession is a common law right which is an incident of his estate in the land. It should not, in my opinion, be lightly treated as abrogated or restricted.' *h*

Mr Brock, in the course of his forceful argument, drew our attention particularly to cl 1(a) of the mortgage in the present case, which expressed the security to be '... a continuing security to the Bank for the discharge on demand by the Bank on the Mortgagor' of the liabilities of the company. This provision in his submission by implication showed an intention to limit the bank's right to take possession so that it will not be exercisable until demand, which in his *j* submission meant 'proper demand', was made. I do not feel able to read the clause in this way. The reference to 'demand' certainly makes it clear that the mortgagors will not actually be in default until demand is made. In my judgment, however, it does not suffice to show that the mortgagee bank has deprived itself by contract of the right to immediate possession, which it enjoys by virtue of the statutory equivalent of a legal term of years conferred on it by the mortgage.

The last comment applies equally to cl 6 of the mortgage, which was referred
a to in argument. In my judgment, this clause on its true construction simply gives
the bank powers additional to its ordinary right to take possession as legal chargee.
It enables it, for example, to enter the property and do repairs without taking
possession. It does not, however, implicitly as a matter of contract restrict the
ordinary right of the bank to take possession in its capacity as legal mortgagee.

If then the mortgage does not itself restrict the bank's right to take immediate
b possession of the property as legal mortgagee, the defendants have to submit and
do submit that these rights have been abrogated by virtue of the events alleged in
the disputed paragraphs of their pleading. One formidable obstacle in the way of
such submission is the line of authority which clearly establishes the principle
that the existence of a cross-claim, even if it exceeds the amount of a mortgage
c debt, will not by itself defeat a right to possession enjoyed by a legal chargee.
I refer in particular to the decision of Nourse J in *Mobil Oil Co Ltd v Rawlinson*
(1981) 43 P & CR 221, the unreported decision of this court in *Barclays Bank plc v
Tennet* [1984] CA Transcript 242 and the decision of Mervyn Davies J in *Citibank
Trust Ltd v Ayivor* [1987] 3 All ER 241, [1987] 1 WLR 1157.

The principle in my view has much to commend it, since it could lead to abuse
d if a mortgagee were to be kept out of his undoubted prima facie right to possession
by allegations of some connected cross-claim which might prove wholly without
foundation: see and compare the observations of Russell LJ in *Samuel Keller
(Holdings) Ltd v Martins Bank Ltd* [1970] 3 All ER 950 at 953, [1971] 1 WLR 43 at
51. I will refer to the principle established by this line of cases as 'the *Mobil Oil*
principle'. Mr Brock, however, has submitted that the principle is not applicable
e to the present case essentially on two alternative grounds. First, he submitted,
that it is not applicable in a case where the cross-claims are not mere cross-claims
but claims which would give the mortgagor rights by way of an equitable set-off.

I say nothing about the case where a mortgagor establishes that he has a claim
to a quantified sum by way of equitable set-off. Possibly such a claim might have
f the effect of actually discharging the mortgage debt. In my judgment, however,
the *Mobil Oil* principle is applicable both where the cross-claim is a mere
counterclaim and where it is a cross-claim for unliquidated damages which, if
established, would give rise to a right by way of equitable set-off. In none of the
decisions mentioned has any distinction been drawn between the two. In the
Mobil Oil case (1981) 43 P & CR 221 at 261 Nourse J referred in terms to the
g possibility of a counterclaim or set-off. Though there was no claim for possession
in the *Samuel Keller* case the court did not find it necessary to advert explicitly to
the possibility that the claim to damages on the relevant counterclaim might give
rise to a claim by equitable set-off, as opposed to a bare cross-claim. Russell LJ said
([1970] 3 All ER 950 at 952, [1971] 1 WLR 43 at 50):

h
'It was argued that if the outcome of the Birmingham action was that
damages were awarded on the counterclaim exceeding the amount due under
the mortgage debt it would prove that [the mortgagee] would not have been
justified in obtaining the money from the bank and treating it as their own
to meet their mortgage debt. It was submitted that by reason of the
j counterclaim the mortgage debt no longer existed, but that, to my mind, is
plainly not so and I so hold.'

I cannot accept the submission that the *Mobil Oil* principle is not applicable
where the mortgagor has a claim to unliquidated damages by way of equitable
set-off, and in my judgment it makes no difference that such a claim may in the
event prove to exceed the amount of the mortgage debt.

The other ground upon which Mr Brock submitted that the *Mobil Oil* principle is not applicable was that special considerations apply where the mortgage is *a* merely one by way of guarantee intended to afford security for the debts of a third party. In this context he relied strongly on a passage in 20 *Halsbury's Laws* (4th edn) para 190, which was not referred to by the judge and states the rights of creditor and surety in these terms:

'On being sued by the creditor for payment of the debt guaranteed, a *b* surety may avail himself of any right to set off or counterclaim which the principal debtor possesses against the creditor, and any division of the High Court can give effect to it or to any equitable defence raised.'

Correspondingly, Mr Brock submitted, in the present case, on being sued by the creditor bank for possession, the defendant sureties are entitled to avail themselves of the assumed right of set-off which the company in liquidation possesses against *c* the bank.

Rowlatt on Principal and Surety (4th edn, 1982) p 103 contains a statement similar to that cited from *Halsbury*, in the following terms:

'Where the principal is entitled to a set-off against the creditor's demand arising out of the same transaction as the debt guaranteed, and in fact *d* reducing that debt, the surety is entitled to plead it in an action by the creditor against the surety alone.'

Mr Mann challenged the correctness of both these statements of law, and in support of this submission referred us to the judgment of Isaacs J in the Supreme Court of New South Wales in *Cellulose Products Pty Ltd v Truda* (1970) 92 WN *e* (NSW) 561. In that case Isaacs J subjected the passage in *Halsbury* (see 18 *Halsbury's Laws* (3rd edn) 466–467, para 860) and an equivalent passage in an earlier edition of *Rowlatt* (3rd edn, 1936, p 137) to very searching criticism. His conclusion was that the cases cited in the notes to *Halsbury* did not bear out the statement in the text. He expressed his ultimate conclusion as follows (at 588): *f*

'This review of the cases lends no support to the submission that a surety when sued is entitled to set up in equity or at law as an equitable plea any cross action for unliquidated damages which the debtor may have against the creditor in respect of the transaction, the performance of which the guarantor had entered upon his guarantee; that is, in the absence of the debtor being *g* before the court in the proceedings so as to be bound by verdict and judgments. This of course does not mean that the guarantor is without remedy; when he is sued he has a right immediately to join the debtor as a third party and claim complete indemnity from him. The debtor has then a right to join the plaintiff as a fourth party, claiming damages for breach of warranty and so obtain indemnity either in whole or in part. All the actions *h* would be heard together, the rights of all persons determined and appropriate set-offs made after verdict, and if there be any surplus of damages over and above that which is required to meet the guarantee, the debtor will have recovered that from the creditor who, in the result, will get no more than that to which he would be justly entitled.' *j*

The decision in the *Cellulose Products* case was followed by Australian courts in two subsequent decisions, namely *Covino v Bandag Manufacturing Pty Ltd* [1983] 1 NSWLR 237 and *Indrisie v General Credits Ltd* [1985] VR 251.

The reasoning of Isaacs J is, with respect to him, impressive, but for my part I would not think it right, on this striking-out application, to decide that there is any general rule that a guarantor cannot avail himself of the remedies which

otherwise may be open to the principal debtor as against the creditor or, if there
a is such a general rule, that it necessarily applies in the present case. First, Isaacs J
himself expressly recognised (at 585) that exceptions to his general rule might
arise in cases such as the present where a debtor is insolvent so that, instead of
having a full right of exoneration by the principal debtor, the surety can only
prove in the liquidation of the principal debtor for a dividend. Secondly, the
Court of Appeal in *Hyundai Shipbuilding and Heavy Industries Co Ltd v Pournaras*
b [1978] 2 Lloyd's Rep 502 expressly accepted the correctness of the passage in 20
Halsbury's Laws (4th edn) para 190, though regarding it as inapplicable on the
particular facts of that case because of the form of guarantee which had been
employed.

However, even accepting for present purposes the correctness of the general
c principle stated in *Halsbury*, that statement is expressed to apply in cases where
the surety is being sued by the creditor for payment. We have been referred to
no decisions establishing that it applies in cases in which a mortgagor surety is
being sued by a mortgagee creditor for possession of the mortgaged premises, and
I am not satisfied that it necessarily does apply. Secondly, and I regard this as the
conclusive point in the present case, any rights which a surety would ordinarily
d enjoy at common law against the creditor by virtue of the *Halsbury* principle
would in any event be capable of being excluded by agreement between himself
and the creditor. The decision in the *Hyundai Shipbuilding* case itself shows that
this is so.

In the present case cl 11 of the mortgage, so far as material, provided:

e   '. . . as between the Mortgagor and the Bank this Mortgage is to be deemed
          to be a primary security and the Mortgaged Property is to be deemed to stand
          charged with the moneys or liabilities hereby secured as if they were
          primarily due from the Mortgagor.'

In my judgment, as Mr Mann submitted, this provision makes it clear that, in
f any dispute between the bank and the mortgagors, their obligations as mortgagors,
including their obligations to deliver up possession when called upon to do so, are
to be no less extensive than they would be if the debts in question were due from
them as primary debtors rather than as mere guarantors. In particular this
provision, in my view, makes it clear that in any dispute between the bank and
the mortgagors it is not to be open to the mortgagors to rely upon any right of
g cross-claim or set-off to which the principal debtor, the company, may be entitled
as against the creditor bank.

In my judgment, therefore, paras 7 to 12 of the defence, even if accepted as
factually true, would not exclude the right of possession which is enjoyed by the
bank as legal chargee under the *Mobil Oil* principle whether or not the defendants
are in default. I therefore agree with the decision of the learned judge that these
h paragraphs afford no reasonable ground of defence, and that they should be struck
out from the pleading. Subject to s 36 of the Administration of Justice Act 1970,
I can accordingly see no reason why the judge can be said to have erred in
exercising the powers given by Ord 13, r 5 in proceeding to give judgment for
possession in favour of the bank. For no other defence to the claim was raised.

I cannot accept Mr Brock's submission that the presence of a counterclaim seeking
j an order for redemption by itself made any difference. Nor in my view did it
make any difference that the company's claim for unliquidated damages had, in
Mr Brock's words 'crystalised' by virtue of the company's liquidation.

As his last-ditch line of defence, however, Mr Brock relied on s 36 of the 1970
Act, which confers on the court a limited power to grant adjournments on
applications for possession by mortgagees. So far as material, it provides as
follows:

'(1) Where the mortgagee under a mortgage of land which consists of or includes a dwelling-house brings an action in which he claims possession of *a* the mortgaged property, not being an action for foreclosure in which a claim for possession of the mortgaged property is also made, the court may exercise any of the powers conferred on it by subsection (2) below if it appears to the court that in the event of its exercising the power the mortgagor is likely to be able within a reasonable period to pay any sums due under the mortgage or to remedy a default consisting of a breach of any other obligation arising *b* under or by virtue of the mortgage.

(2) The court—(*a*) may adjourn the proceedings, or (*b*) on giving judgment, or making an order, for delivery of possession of the mortgaged property, or at any time before the execution of such judgment or order, may—(i) stay or suspend execution of the judgment or order, or (ii) postpone the date for *c* delivery of possession, for such period or periods as the court thinks reasonable.

(3) Any such adjournment, stay, suspension or postponement as is referred to in subsection (2) above may be made subject to such conditions with regard to payment by the mortgagor of any sum secured by the mortgage or the remedying of any default as the court thinks fit . . .'   *d*

However, as the words of sub-s (1) make clear, the court in the present case could have exercised the powers conferred on it by sub-s (2) only if it appeared to it that '. . . in the event of its exercising the power the mortgagor is likely to be able within a reasonable period to pay any sums due under the mortgage . . .'

The decision of this court in *Royal Trust Co of Canada v Markham* [1975] 3 All *e* ER 433, [1975] 1 WLR 1416 shows that any order made under s 36(2) must fix a period ending with some specified or ascertainable date. Furthermore, as Sir John Pennycuick said ([1975] 3 All ER 433 at 438, [1975] 1 WLR 1416 at 1422): '"Likelihood" is a question of fact, to be determined by the judge on evidence before him.'

In the present case, so far as appears from the judge's judgment and from any *f* information which we have been given, no reliance was placed at the hearing before the learned judge on s 36 by counsel for the defendants. Mr Brock submitted that the judge ought nevertheless to have taken into account his powers under the subsection, even if his attention was not specifically directed to it. He submitted that he should have granted an adjournment. However, even if reliance had been placed specifically on the subsection, I do not see how it could *g* have justified him in withholding an immediate order for possession from the bank, since there was no evidence before him as to the likelihood of the defendants being able to pay the debts in question within a reasonable period: see and compare *Citibank Trust Ltd v Ayivor* [1987] 3 All ER 241 at 246, [1987] 1 WLR 1157 at 1164 per Mervyn Davies J. I therefore see no grounds upon which the *h* defendants could properly have been granted any relief under s 36 by the learned judge or could now be granted any relief by this court on the evidence before it.

However, as Mr Mann pointed out, even if this appeal is dismissed, and the order for possession made by the learned judge accordingly stands, it will still be open to the defendants at any time before the execution of that order to apply to the judge under s 36(2)(*b*) for an order staying or suspending execution, on proper *j* evidence that they are likely to be able within a reasonable time to pay the mortgage debts claimed by the bank. On behalf of the bank Mr Mann offered an undertaking not to seek to enforce the order for possession for a period of 28 days following the date of our judgment so as to give the defendants an opportunity to make such an application if so advised. I would for my part accept such an undertaking.

Though I have concluded that the order for possession made in favour of the
a bank must stand, this conclusion will not, of course, preclude the defendants
from pursuing such personal rights as they may have either against the company
in liquidation, for which purpose they would presumably have to obtain the leave
of the court, or against the bank. It may be that, as Mr Brock submitted, they will
be in a position to pursue the company's supposed claim against the bank by way
of subrogation. Alternatively, it may be that they could only pursue it by the
b indirect route suggested by Isaacs J in the passage from the judgment in the
Cellulose Products case which I have already cited. I express no view as to whether
either course is open to them. What is clear, however, in my view is that the
defendants could not expect the court to determine the final state of account
between the company and the bank without at least giving the company in
c liquidation the opportunity to be joined as a party to the proceedings: see *Wilson
v Mitchell* [1939] 2 All ER 869, [1939] 2 KB 869.

Finally, I would make these comments. If it were eventually to transpire that
the company's cross-claims were well founded, the defendants might perhaps be
forgiven for thinking that our law had treated them somewhat harshly. I doubt
whether they would have appreciated that, as soon as they had executed this
d mortgage, the bank would have had the right, if it chose, to take possession of
their home, even though there had as yet been no default on their part. But I
doubt whether the majority of other persons who execute legal mortgages in this
country would appreciate that they are exposed to a similar risk, a risk which
stems from long-standing principles of our law of real property.

For the reasons which I have given, I think that there are no grounds upon
e which we can properly interfere with the exercise of the discretion given to the
learned judge by Ord 13, r 5. Subject to the bank giving the undertaking offered,
I would for my part dismiss this appeal.

ANTHONY LINCOLN J. I agree with the whole of Slade LJ's judgment, and
f only wish to add these brief observations.

(1) Whether a question involving lengthy legal argument should be placed
before a court on an application to strike out will vary from case to case and may,
in some cases, be a matter of finely balanced judgment. If there is a risk that
procedural arguments will become entangled with the substantive legal
arguments, that risk can easily be averted by the formulation of a preliminary
g issue. In this case it was perfectly proper to bring the matter before the court on
an application to strike out.

(2) The authorities disclose the danger guarantors are running when they enter
into a mortgage by guarantee. They are vulnerable before the ink is dry to a claim
for possession. The right to possession may be excluded by statute or contract.
Statute offers very limited protection: see the Administration of Justice Act 1970,
h s 36. Protection by contract will only be afforded by clear terms ether expressly
formulated or to be implied. In this case there are no words or circumstances that
I can find, particularly in cl 1 of the legal mortgage, that could properly be said to
give rise to any implication excluding such dangers.

I accordingly agree that the appeal should be dismissed.

Appeal dismissed.

Celia Fox   Barrister.

Ashley Guarantee plc v Zacaria and another   *a*

COURT OF APPEAL, CIVIL DIVISION
NOURSE, RALPH GIBSON AND WOOLF LJJ
19, 20 SEPTEMBER 1991

Mortgage – Order for possession of mortgaged property – Counterclaim – Mortgagee *b*
bringing action for possession against mortgagor – Mortgagor guaranteeing debts of
principal debtor – Guarantor counterclaiming that principal debtor having cross-claims
against mortgagee giving rise to equitable set-off for unliquidated sum – Whether existence
of cross-claims for unliquidated sum defeating order for possession – Whether position of
guarantor different from position of principal debtor – Whether mortgagee entitled to
possession.   *c*

The plaintiff lent moneys to a company which were repayable on demand. By a
legal charge made between the plaintiff, the company and the defendant
mortgagors, the defendants charged their family home as security for the liabilities
of the company. Clause 1(a) of the charge provided that the plaintiff could enforce
its rights against the mortgaged property 'in the event that the Company makes   *d*
default in any of its obligations to the Lender'. The plaintiff subsequently
demanded payment of the amount owing from both the company and the
defendants but no payment was made. The plaintiff then brought an action
against the defendants claiming some £151,000, or in default possession of the
mortgaged property. The defendants contended, inter alia, that the company had
cross-claims against the plaintiff which gave it a right of equitable set-off for an   *e*
unliquidated sum exceeding the figure owed. The district judge held that the
defendants were entitled to have their claim to an equitable set-off tried before
any possession order was made. On the plaintiff's application to vary or rescind
the district judge's order for trial of the cross-claims before the application for
possession was heard, the judge dealt with the plaintiff's application as an appeal   *f*
and granted the plaintiff a possession order. The defendants appealed, contending
that, since the company had cross-claims against the plaintiff which gave it a right
of equitable set-off for a sum which they claimed exceeded the amount owed by
it to the plaintiff, nothing was in fact owed to the plaintiff and it followed that
the company was not in default of its obligations within cl 1(a) of the charge. The
defendants further contended that, since in any event the defendants were only   *g*
guarantors rather than the principal debtor of the plaintiff mortgagee, the
defendants were entitled to resist the plaintiff's action for possession.

Held – The general rule that subject to contractual or statutory limitations a
mortgagor could not defeat a legal mortgagee's right to possession by claiming an   *h*
equitable set-off for an unliquidated sum exceeding the amount of the mortgage
arrears applied irrespective of whether the mortgagor was the principal debtor of
the mortgagee or was only a guarantor, since in each case the mortgagee had, as
an incident of his estate in the land, a right to possession of the mortgaged
property and in each case the cross-claims could not be unilaterally appropriated
in discharge of the mortgage debt. The mere fact that a guarantor was not   *j*
primarily liable for payment of the debt was immaterial because when he came
to be made liable his position vis-à-vis the appropriation of cross-claims was at best
no different from, and certainly could not be better than, that of a mortgagor
who was a primary debtor. Furthermore, since it was clear that the aggregate
value of the company's cross-claims did not in fact exceed the sums owed to the

plaintiff, the company was in default of its obligations to the plaintiff within
a cl 1(a) of the mortgage agreement. It followed that the plaintiff was entitled to
enforce its rights and remedies over the mortgaged property (see p 257 *j*, p 259 *g*,
p 260 *c* to *e*, p 261 *c d* and p 262 *d*, post).

Mobil Oil Co Ltd v Rawlinson (1981) 43 P & CR 221 and *National Westminster
Bank plc v Skelton* [1993] 1 All ER 242 applied.

Per Ralph Gibson and Woolf LJJ. Where a guarantor is required to give
b possession of his home despite the existence of unliquidated claims, a stay on
terms pending trial of the claim to the set-off might be appropriate under s 36 of
the Administration of Justice Act 1970 (which empowers the court to grant relief
to a defaulting mortgagor of a dwelling house where he is likely to be able within
a reasonable period to pay the sums due or to remedy the default) if the existence
and prospects of success of the claims can be regarded as enabling the sums due to
c be paid within a reasonable time (see p 262 *d e*, post).

Notes

For right to possession of mortgaged property, see 32 *Halsbury's Laws* (4th edn)
paras 672–707, and for cases on the subject, see 35 *Digest* (Reissue) 245–261, 2036–
d 2148.

For the Administration of Justice Act 1970, s 36, see 37 *Halsbury's Statutes* (4th
edn) 397.

Cases referred to in judgments

e *Barclays Bank plc v Tennet* [1984] CA Transcript 242.
BICC plc v Burndy Corp [1985] 1 All ER 417, [1985] Ch 232, [1985] 2 WLR 132,
   CA.
Birmingham Citizens Permanent Building Society v Caunt [1962] 1 All ER 163, [1962]
   Ch 883, [1962] 2 WLR 323.
Citibank Trust Ltd v Ayivor [1987] 3 All ER 241, [1987] 1 WLR 1157.
f *Fourmaids Ltd v Dudley Marshall (Properties) Ltd* [1957] 2 All ER 35, [1957] Ch
   317, [1957] 2 WLR 931.
Hanak v Green [1958] 2 All ER 141, [1958] 2 QB 9, [1958] 2 WLR 755, CA.
Hyundai Shipbuilding and Heavy Industries Co Ltd v Pournaras [1978] 2 Lloyd's Rep
   502, CA.
Keller (Samuel) (Holdings) Ltd v Martins Bank Ltd [1970] 3 All ER 950, [1971] 1 WLR
g 43, CA.
Mobil Oil Co Ltd v Rawlinson (1981) 43 P & CR 221.
National Westminster Bank plc v Skelton [1993] 1 All ER 242, CA.
Quennell v Maltby [1979] 1 All ER 568, [1979] 1 WLR 318, CA.
Western Bank Ltd v Schindler [1976] 2 All ER 393, [1977] Ch 1, [1976] 3 WLR 341,
   CA.
h

Cases also cited or referred to in skeleton arguments

Barclays Bank Ltd v Bird [1954] 1 All ER 449, [1954] Ch 274.
British Anzani (Felixstowe) Ltd v International Marine Management (UK) Ltd [1979] 2
   All ER 1063, [1980] QB 137.
j *Federal Commerce and Navigation Ltd v Molena Alpha Inc, The Nanfri, The Benfri, The
   Lorfri* [1978] 3 All ER 1066, [1978] QB 927, CA; *affd in part* [1979] 1 All ER
   307, [1979] AC 757, HL.
First National Securities Ltd v Jones [1978] 2 All ER 221, [1978] Ch 109, CA.
Gilbert-Ash (Northern) Ltd v Modern Engineering (Bristol) Ltd [1973] 3 All ER 195,
   [1974] AC 689, HL.

Hongkong and Shanghai Banking Corp v Kloeckner & Co AG [1989] 3 All ER 513,
   [1990] 2 QB 514.
Norman Holding Co Ltd, Re [1990] 3 All ER 757, [1991] 1 WLR 10.
Parker v Housefield (1834) 2 My & K 419, 39 ER 1004.
TCB Ltd v Gray [1986] 1 All ER 587, [1986] Ch 621; *affd on other grounds* [1988]
   1 All ER 108, [1987] Ch 458, CA.

Appeal

The defendants, Sheref Zacaria and Beverley Bersch, appealed from the order of
Judge Butter QC made on 18 April 1991 whereby he allowed the appeal of the
plaintiff, Ashley Guarantee plc, against the order of District Judge Platt directing
trial of the defendants' claim to an equitable set-off before any possession order
was made in favour of the plaintiff in respect of the defendants' home at
48 Monkhams Drive, Woodford Green, Essex and made an order for possession
against the defendants' home. The facts are set out in the judgment of Nourse LJ.

Mark Warwick (instructed by *Wedlake Bell*) for the defendants.
Michael Tennet (instructed by *Heald Nickinson*) for the plaintiff.

NOURSE LJ. In *National Westminster Bank plc v Skelton* [1993] 1 All ER 242 this
court decided that the mortgagor cannot usually resist a legal mortgagee's action
for possession by claiming an equitable set-off for an unliquidated sum exceeding
the amount of the mortgage arrears. Now we have to decide whether any
distinction is to be made where the mortgagor is not the principal debtor of the
mortgagee but only a guarantor.

By cl 2 of a legal charge dated 28 November 1986 and made between the
defendants (the mortgagor) of the first part, the plaintiff, now called Ashley
Guarantee plc (the lender) of the second part, and Medeast Gulf Exports Ltd, now
called London Pride Confectionery Ltd (the company) of the third part, the
defendants charged by way of legal mortgage the residential freehold property
known as 48 Monkhams Drive, Woodford Green, Essex 'with the payment or
discharge of all money and liabilities hereby covenanted to be paid or discharged
by the Company'. Clause 1(a) and the first part of cl 1(b) of the legal charge were
in these terms:

> '1.(a) The Lender has advanced monies to the Company and the Mortgagor
> has agreed with the Lender to advance monies to the Company upon its
> security of the mortgaged property (as hereinafter defined) to the intent and
> as is hereby agreed that the Lender shall be entitled to enforce its rights and
> remedies contained referred or implied herein over and in respect of the
> mortgaged property in the event that the Company makes default in any of
> its obligations to the Lender
>   1.(b) The Mortgagor hereby covenants with the Lender that the Mortgagor
> will on demand in writing made to the Company pay or discharge to the
> Lender all moneys and liabilities which shall for the time being (and whether
> on or at any time after such demand) be due owing or incurred to the Lender
> by the Company . . .'

It is common ground that the plaintiff lent moneys to the company, that those
moneys were repayable on demand, that demands for payment were made both
on the company and on the defendants and that no payment has been made. The
plaintiff's particulars of claim issued in the Bow County Court on 1 May 1990
allege that the amount then remaining due and owing was £151,193·64. They

contain a prayer for payment of that sum, together with accrued interest, or in
a default possession of the mortgaged property. The defendants do not contest the
figure of £151,000-odd. Shortly stated, their defence is that the company has
cross-claims against the plaintiff which give it a right of equitable set-off for an
unliquidated sum exceeding that figure or indeed any other figure at which the
company's indebtedness to the plaintiff may stand. They also counterclaim for
rectification of the legal charge so as to limit the defendants' liability thereunder
b to £50,000 plus interest and costs.

The matter first came before District Judge Platt. The plaintiff asked for an
order for possession with a view to exercising its statutory power of sale out of
court. In a careful written judgment delivered on 17 January 1991 the district
judge decided that the defendants were entitled to have their claims to equitable
set-off and rectification tried before any possession order was made. He also
c ordered the action to be transferred to the Chancery Division after the time for
appealing against his order had expired.

The plaintiff applied for the district judge's order to be varied or rescinded, but
when the matter came before Judge Butter QC he dealt with it as an appeal. By
his order made on 18 April 1991 the learned judge allowed the plaintiff's appeal
d with costs, holding that it had established that it was entitled to possession and
that there was no answer to that claim. Since the mortgaged property consisted
of a dwelling house, the judge adjourned the matter for further consideration
under s 36 of the Administration of Justice Act 1970. He reserved the matter to
himself. He gave the defendants leave to appeal, although it is not clear to me
that leave was needed.

e The judge thought that the matter was concluded in favour of the plaintiff by
National Westminster Bank plc v Skelton, which he described as being of the utmost
degree of importance in the case and which had not been cited to the district
judge, no doubt because it had not then been reported. There the defendants had
charged their house by way of legal mortgage as a continuing security to the bank
for the discharge on demand by the bank on them of all present, future, actual
f and/or contingent liabilities of a named company to the bank. In other words
that, like the present, was a case where the company was the principal debtor and
the mortgagors were in the position of guarantors. They too claimed that the
company was entitled to recover unliquidated damages against the bank which
could be set off against the sums owing by the company to the bank and which
would more than extinguish the company's debt. This court was prepared to
g assume that the mortgagors would succeed in that claim, but they held that it
could not be a defence to the bank's claim to immediate possession of the property.

In explaining his reasons for that view Slade LJ, who gave the leading judgment,
referred to *Fourmaids Ltd v Dudley Marshall (Properties) Ltd* [1957] 2 All ER 35,
[1957] Ch 317, *Birmingham Citizens Permanent Building Society v Caunt* [1962] 1 All
h ER 163, [1962] Ch 883, *Samuel Keller (Holdings) Ltd v Martins Bank Ltd* [1970] 3 All
ER 950, [1971] 1 WLR 43, *Western Bank Ltd v Schindler* [1976] 2 All ER 393,
[1977] Ch 1, *Mobil Oil Co Ltd v Rawlinson* (1981) 43 P & CR 221, *Barclays Bank plc v
Tennet* [1984] CA Transcript 242 and *Citibank Trust Ltd v Ayivor* [1987] 3 All ER
241, [1987] 1 WLR 1157. He referred with approval to a principle established by
those authorities, in essence a synthesis of those deducible from *Birmingham
j Citizens Permanent Building Society v Caunt* and *Samuel Keller (Holdings) Ltd v Martins
Bank Ltd*. The principle, which Slade LJ called 'the *Mobil Oil* principle', can be
stated thus. Contract and statute apart, a legal mortgagee's right to possession of
the mortgaged property cannot be defeated by a cross-claim on the part of the
mortgagor, even if it is both liquidated and admitted and even if it exceeds the
amount of the mortgage arrears.

Slade LJ then considered a submission by counsel for the mortgagors that the
Mobil Oil principle was not applicable in a case where the cross-claims were not
mere cross-claims but claims which would give the mortgagors rights by way of
equitable set-off. As to that submission, he said ([1993] 1 All ER 242 at 249):

> 'I say nothing about the case where a mortgagor establishes that he has a
> claim to a quantified sum by way of equitable set-off. Possibly such a claim
> might have the effect of actually discharging the mortgage debt. In my
> judgment, however, the *Mobil Oil* principle is applicable both where the cross-
> claim is a mere counterclaim and where it is a cross-claim for unliquidated
> damages which, if established, would give rise to a right by way of equitable
> set-off. In none of the decisions mentioned has any distinction been drawn
> between the two.'

After referring to observations in the *Mobil Oil* and *Samuel Keller* cases, he
continued (at 249):

> 'I cannot accept the submission that the *Mobil Oil* principle is not applicable
> where the mortgagor has a claim to unliquidated damages by way of
> equitable set-off, and in my judgment it makes no difference that such a
> claim may in the event prove to exceed the amount of the mortgage debt.'

Anthony Lincoln J gave a brief concurring judgment.

It is to be noted that Slade LJ expressed no view as to the effect of a cross-claim
for a liquidated sum giving rise to a right of equitable set-off. That is not a
question for decision here. However, Mr Warwick, who appears for the plaintiff
and to whose conscientious argument the court is indebted, accepts that *National
Westminster Bank plc v Skelton* is authority, binding on this court, for the view that
the *Mobil Oil* principle applies where the mortgagor's cross-claim is one for
unliquidated damages which, if established, would give him a right of equitable
set-off. He maintains that that decision can be distinguished on a ground which
can best be understood by starting with a further reference to that case, in which
counsel for the mortgagors had gone on to submit that the *Mobil Oil* principle was
not in any event applicable because special considerations applied where the
mortgage was merely one by way of guarantee intended to afford security for the
debts of a third party. Reliance had been placed on passages in 20 *Halsbury's Laws*
(4th edn) para 190 and *Rowlatt on Principal and Surety* (4th edn, 1982) p 103, the
former of which is in these terms:

> 'On being sued by the creditor for payment of the debt guaranteed, a
> surety may avail himself of any right to set off or counterclaim which the
> principal debtor possesses against the creditor, and any division of the High
> Court can give effect to it or to any equitable defence raised.'

Counsel had submitted that on being sued by the bank for possession the
mortgagors were entitled, as sureties, to avail themselves of the assumed right of
set-off which the company possessed against the bank.

Having considered a challenge by counsel for the bank to the correctness of the
statements in *Halsbury* and *Rowlatt*, Slade LJ continued (at 251):

> 'However, even accepting for present purposes the correctness of the
> general principle stated in *Halsbury*, that statement is expressed to apply in
> cases where the surety is being sued by the creditor for payment. We have
> been referred to no decisions establishing that it applies in cases in which a
> mortgagor surety is being sued by a mortgagee creditor for possession of the
> mortgaged premises, and I am not satisfied that it necessarily does apply.

a   Secondly, and I regard this as the conclusive point in the present case, any rights which a surety would ordinarily enjoy at common law against the creditor by virtue of the *Halsbury* principle would in any event be capable of being excluded by agreement between himself and the creditor. The decision in [*Hyundai Shipbuilding and Heavy Industries Co Ltd v Pournaras* [1978] 2 Lloyd's Rep 502] itself shows that this is so.'

b   Slade LJ went on to hold that those rights had indeed been excluded by a not unfamiliar clause in the mortgage, which provided that as between the bank and the mortgagors the mortgage was deemed to be a primary security and the mortgaged property to stand charged with the moneys or liabilities thereby secured as if they were primarily due from the mortgagor.

c   Although the legal charge in the present case contains no primary security clause nor any provision to the same effect, Mr Warwick relies on those observations of Slade LJ as giving countenance to, or at any rate as not dissenting from, an argument which runs thus. Clause 1(a) of the legal charge contains an agreement that the plaintiff shall be entitled to enforce its rights and remedies over the mortgaged property in the event, and necessarily only in the event, 'that the Company makes default in any of its obligations to the Lender'. If the *d*   company has cross-claims against the plaintiff which give it a right of equitable set-off for a sum, albeit unliquidated, which exceeds the amount owed by it to the plaintiff, nothing is owed and nothing ever has been owed by the company to the plaintiff. It follows that the company has not made default in any of its obligations to the plaintiff within cl 1(a), so that the plaintiff is not entitled to enforce its right to possession of the mortgaged property. Mr Warwick emphasises that the *e*   company did not itself secure its indebtedness under the legal charge, so that the rule against unilateral appropriation of cross-claims against the mortgage debt does not apply as between the company and the plaintiff.

f   Although we have not seen a copy of any overdraft facility letter or other document governing the relationship between the plaintiff and the company, I am prepared to assume that any right of equitable set-off which the company would otherwise have against the plaintiff is not excluded. On that footing I think that so far Mr Warwick's argument is correct. I am also prepared to assume that under cases such as *Hanak v Green* [1958] 2 All ER 141, [1958] 2 QB 9 and *BICC plc v Burndy Corp* [1985] 1 All ER 417, [1985] Ch 232 each of the company's cross-claims would give rise to a right of equitable set-off, although I make it clear *g*   that I am far from certain that that is the case. However, even on those assumptions there remains an insuperable objection. Mr Warwick has been unable to satisfy me that the aggregate value of the cross-claims comes anywhere near the amount of the company's indebtedness to the plaintiff. In other words, the company *has* made default in its obligations to the plaintiff within cl 1(a) of the legal charge.

h   The company's four cross-claims are made in an action in the Chancery Division commenced by it against the plaintiff before the institution of the plaintiff's action in the county court. I need not describe them, except to say that the fourth is a claim that the plaintiff has passed off a business of the company or its subsidiary as the business of the plaintiff. The company has sought to ascribe *j*   monetary values to its other three claims, but no such attempt has been made in the case of the passing-off claim. On the basis of figures into which I need not go Mr Warwick accepts, for the purposes of this appeal, that that claim must be valued at about £25,000 if the aggregate value of all the claims is to exceed the amount of the company's indebtedness to the plaintiff. As to the passing-off claim, the only evidence of its value is to be found in the second affidavit of the first defendant, who is also a director of the company. In para 4 he says:

'The company was established in about 1978. It exported various products
to the Middle East. After about four years it developed a specialisation,   *a*
namely the export of confectionery and sweets. This business became
successful. The company developed its own brand name (Ivan Confectionery)
and its own distinctive packaging.'

In para 27, after describing the alleged passing-off, he says:

'I further verily believe that the company has lost substantial business as a   *b*
result of the Plaintiff's activities, for which the Plaintiff is liable.'

While accepting that a passing-off claim is inherently difficult to value, I cannot
treat that evidence as showing that the value here comes anywhere near the
£25,000 which Mr Warwick must demonstrate. In the circumstances, his
argument based on cl 1(a) of the legal charge is bound to fail. The plaintiff is   *c*
entitled to enforce its rights and remedies over the mortgaged property within
the terms of that sub-clause.

Is there then any further ground for holding that the *Mobil Oil* principle does
not apply in this case? In my judgment that question must be answered in the
negative. I can see no distinction in principle between a case where the mortgagor   *d*
is the principal debtor of the mortgagee and one where he is only a guarantor. In
each case the mortgagee has, as an incident of his estate in the land, a right to
possession of the mortgaged property. In each case the cross-claims cannot be
unilaterally appropriated in discharge of the mortgage debt. The fact that in the
latter case the mortgagor is not primarily liable for payment of the debt is
immaterial. When he comes to be made liable his position vis-à-vis the   *e*
appropriation of the cross-claims is at best no different from, and certainly cannot
be better than, that of a mortgagor who is the primary debtor.

I should add that Mr Tennet, for the plaintiff, has raised a further argument in
answer to Mr Warwick's argument based on cl 1(a) of the legal charge. He relies
on the fact that under a mortgage of other property made by the company the
plaintiff is a secured creditor of the company in respect of precisely the same   *f*
indebtedness as that secured by the defendants' legal charge. Accordingly, says
Mr Tennet, by virtue of the company's own mortgage it can have no equitable
right of set-off against that indebtedness. He then points to cl 1(b) of the legal
charge, which provides that the defendants will on demand in writing made to
the company pay or discharge to the plaintiff all moneys and liabilities which
shall for the time being 'be due owing or incurred to the Lender by the Company'.   *g*
In the circumstances, runs the argument, there having been an unsatisfied
demand by the plaintiff on the company, the defendants are liable for its
indebtedness and the *Mobil Oil* principle can be raised against them. Since it is
unnecessary to express an opinion on Mr Tennet's argument I prefer not to do so.
It has only sprung to life during the hearing in this court and it is based on a   *h*
mortgage by the company which we have not seen. I record it out of deference to
its ingenuity and the conciseness of its presentation.

Two further points must be briefly mentioned. First, on the basis partly of
evidence which was before the judge and partly on fresh evidence which was
admitted in this court without objection from the plaintiff, Mr Warwick submits
that the plaintiff was seeking to obtain possession of the mortgaged property not   *j*
for the purpose of protecting or enforcing its security but, at least in part, for an
ulterior or improper purpose: see *Quennell v Maltby* [1979] 1 All ER 568, [1979] 1
WLR 318. But as Judge Butter observed, the facts there were completely different
from those of the present case and I agree with him that there is no realistic

possibility that the defendants would be able to defeat the claim for possession by
a that route.

Secondly, Mr Warwick sought to contend for the first time in this court that
the legal charge had not been sealed and therefore had not been duly executed. If
that had in fact been the case, the plaintiff would not have acquired the legal
estate on which its right to possession depends. However, from everything which
I have seen and heard it seems extremely unlikely that that point could ever have
b succeeded. In the event, we did not have to consider it. Being a point on which
evidence proving due execution could have been adduced below, it was manifestly
not one which we could allow to be taken for the first time in this court.

For these reasons I have come to the conclusion that there is no defence to the
plaintiff's claim for possession and that the decision of Judge Butter should be
affirmed. I would therefore dismiss this appeal and remit the matter to him for
c further consideration under s 36 of the 1970 Act.

RALPH GIBSON LJ. I agree that this appeal should be dismissed.

If the appellants were held to be right on each of their other points, the fact
remains that there is not alleged in total by way of equitable set-off such a sum as
would extinguish, or come close to extinguishing, the sum due from the company
d to the plaintiff, payment of which the defendants have guaranteed. I say that for
the reasons which Nourse LJ has explained.

For my part, I am glad that this clear basis of decision is available to the court.

The passage from the judgment of Megarry J in *Samuel Keller (Holdings) Ltd v
Martins Bank Ltd* [1970] 3 All ER 950 at 953, [1971] 1 WLR 43 at 51, which
e Russell LJ expressly approved in this court in that case, with the agreement of
Edmund Davies and Cross LJJ, was cited in the plaintiff's argument before us and
contained the words:

> 'Even where there is a claim which is both liquidated and admitted, and it
> exceeds the mortgage debt in amount, it may be to the interest of one party
f > or the other, or both, that the mortgage and the mortgage debt should
> continue in existence.'

Megarry J held that the mortgagor had no unilateral power to discharge the
mortgage debt by appropriation without payment, that being a case where the
dispute between the mortgagor and second mortgagee was not as to the right of
possession of the property charged or the right to sell it, but as to the receipt of
g the net proceeds of sale made by the first mortgagee after satisfaction of the sum
due on the first mortgage. The mortgagor wanted the net proceeds paid into
court pending trial of his unliquidated demands against the second mortgagee.

In *National Westminster Bank plc v Skelton* [1993] 1 All ER 242, which was a
claim to possession by a mortgagee, Slade LJ, following the *Samuel Keller* case, held
h that, on the assumption that the principal debtor was entitled to a claim for
unliquidated damages by way of set-off against the plaintiff bank in an amount
which exceeded the debts secured by the mortgage, the alleged set-off afforded no
defence to the claim to immediate possession. That claim, as Slade LJ stressed,
was for possession and not payment, and the established rule was that the
mortgagee was entitled to such possession at any time after the mortgage is
j executed, except in so far as his rights are limited by contract or statute.

Respectfully, I do not doubt the basis in law upon which Slade LJ proceeded in
that case. However, it is to me an arresting concept that a mortgagor who is a
guarantor of the debt of the principal debtor (for example, and not infrequently,
the mortgagor's trading company) could be required to give possession of his

home despite the existence of unliquidated claims which are admitted or shown
to be likely to succeed, in an amount which would either exceed the sum due *a*
from the principal debtor or be such as, when established, to enable the principal
debtor or the mortgagor to pay in full. It might possibly, in a particular case, be
that an implied term could be held to have arisen which would exclude the
immediate right to possession, but it is obvious that there are difficulties against
such an implication in most ordinary cases. No such term was alleged in this case,
and I do not suggest that it could usefully have been alleged. Further, in such a *b*
case, in the case of a dwelling house, a stay on terms pending trial of the claims to
the set-off might be appropriate under s 36 of the Administration of Justice Act
1970 if the existence and prospects of success of the claims could, in all the
circumstances, be regarded as enabling the sums due to be paid within a reasonable
time.

I mention these matters because it seems to me that the danger facing the *c*
guarantor in such circumstances is plainly a matter for consideration by those
advising guarantors who are required to give a charge over property in support of
the guarantee.

I agree that the appeal should be dismissed for the reasons given by Nourse LJ.

d

WOOLF LJ. I also agree that this appeal has to be dismissed for the reasons given
by Nourse LJ. I recognise the importance to those who advise guarantors of their
having in mind the danger referred to by Ralph Gibson LJ. It may well be that,
in the case of a mortgage given in relation to a dwelling house, s 36 of the
Administration of Justice Act 1970 provides a way of mitigating the consequences
which would otherwise flow from the decision of this court in *National Westminster* *e*
Bank plc v Skelton [1993] 1 All ER 242, to which reference has already been made.

Because the question of what order is appropriate under s 36 of the 1970 Act
has been adjourned by the judge to be dealt with hereafter, I would add two
points.

First of all, in this case the defendant has a counterclaim for rectification which
would, if successful, limit his liability in any event to £50,000. That claim for *f*
rectification is not relevant with regard to the merits of the appeal because, having
regard to the terms of the mortgage, what this court was concerned with was the
state of indebtedness between the company and the plaintiff. However, when the
judge has to consider the effect of s 36 of the 1970 Act, he may well regard the
claim for rectification which has not been adjudicated upon as being a matter of *g*
materiality.

In addition, the judgment given by Nourse LJ indicates that, on the facts which
are before this court, the company's counterclaim and set-off can be taken into
account in considering whether there is any liability on the defendants in respect
of the claim for possession of their home. The set-off of the company, as against
the claim of the plaintiff, is relevant in considering the sum for which the *h*
defendants would be liable under a mortgage which is drawn in the terms referred
to in the judgment of Nourse LJ. In other words, the situation here would be one
where, if there had been a set-off available to the company for a sum which could
have been shown to have been approximately £25,000 greater than was in fact
the case, on the approach which has been adopted by this court the plaintiff would
not have been entitled to possession. *j*

Appeal dismissed.

Dilys Tausz   Barrister.

a

Practice Direction
(No 2 of 1992)

SUPREME COURT TAXING OFFICE

b *Costs – Taxation – Practice – Bill of costs – Matters to be included – Chargeable items – Excluded items – Accounts to accompany bill – Travelling expenses – Postage, couriers, telephone calls etc – Copying of documents – Charges between principal solicitor and solicitor agent – Objections – Papers to be lodged with bill – Signing of bill – Compromise offer made before hearing – Appointments and adjournments – Abatement of taxing fees – Identification of matters in issue – Removal of papers – Review of taxation – Wasted*
c *costs orders – Delay – Legal aid taxations – Supreme Court Act 1981, s 51(6) – RSC Ord 32, Ord 42, rr 4, 5, Ord 58, Ord 62, rr 10(1), 26, 27(3), 28(1)(2)(4), 29(7)(b)(c)(ii)(iii)(d), 30(1), App 2, Pt I, para 1(2), Pt II, items 1, 2, 3, 4, 5 – Supreme Court Fees Order 1980, Sch, section 5 – Civil Legal Aid (General) Regulations 1989, regs 106(1)(2), 118, 119.*

d *Legal aid – Taxation of costs – Procedure – Assisted person having financial interest in taxation – Notice to assisted person – Certificate – Legal aid summary – Certification of castings of bill of costs – Civil Legal Aid (General) Regulations 1989, regs 106(1)(2), 118, 119.*

Introduction

e This Practice Direction is issued with the concurrence of the Lord Chief Justice. In so far as it is relevant to proceedings in the Family Division, this Practice Direction is made with the concurrence of the Senior District Judge of the Family Division. Paragraphs 1.20, 2.1, 2.2 and 2.6 do not apply to the Family Division.

This Direction will apply to all taxation proceedings in the Supreme Court
f Taxing Office under RSC Ord 62 with effect from 1 December 1992. It introduces a system of identifying before taxation the items in dispute.

The Practice Notes are designed to enable complex bills to be taxed expeditiously and without loss of fairness, and have been compiled in the light of the experience of the taxing masters and taxing officers since RSC Ord 62 was comprehensively amended in 1986.

g
Direction 1: Taxation practice

1.1 Items which are properly part of a solicitor's normal overhead costs, and as such provided for in his expense rate, are wholly to be excluded. Each chargeable item is the subject of a discretionary allowance which should be shown in two
h parts, the first representing the direct cost of the work, properly itemised, and the second the appropriate allowance for care and conduct.

1.2 The allowance for care and conduct is intended to reflect all the relevant circumstances of the case and in particular the matters set out in para 1(2) of Pt I of App 2 to Ord 62. It also intended to reflect those imponderable factors, for example general supervision of subordinate staff, for which no direct time charge
j can be substantiated, and the element of commercial profit. Accordingly the allowances to be made for different items may, in the discretion of the taxing officer, be allowed at different rates. In particular it is anticipated that, save in unusual circumstances, the rate appropriate to items 1, 2, 3 and 5 in Pt II of App 2 for care and conduct will be less than the rate appropriate to item 4 for general care and conduct.

1.3 The bill should commence with a short and succinct narrative indicating the issues, the relevant circumstances, when instructions were received and when *a* the matter ended. The assessment of allowances which depend partly on arithmetical computation and partly on judgments of value is not assisted by prolixity. This narrative should be followed by a statement showing the status of the fee-earners concerned and the expense rates claimed for each.

1.4 The bill should then set out in chronological order, with dates, all the relevant events, whether or not any such event constitutes a chargeable item. *b* Where the event in question is one which does constitute a chargeable item the allowance claimed should be shown against it. Where any event, whether a chargeable item or not, has occasioned a disbursement, the amount claimed for that disbursement should be inserted alongside that event. Item 4, which comprises the general work of preparation, is to be placed after all the other items *c* save only item 5, which is to be the last item. Attention is particularly drawn to r 29(7)(c)(iii), which requires that every bill which is lodged for taxation shall be signed by the solicitor whose bill it is or, if costs are due to a firm, by a partner of that firm.

1.5 Items 1, 2 and 3 should show separately the time engaged and the allowances claimed for care and conduct and for the time engaged in travelling *d* and waiting. In the case of an interlocutory hearing, a note should be made of any order for costs made thereon and any certificate for counsel granted. If an order is drawn up a copy should be among the papers lodged in its appropriate chronological order.

1.6 Item 4. This item should be divided into three parts.

e

Part A In this part the work done and the amount claimed for it should be set out in separate sections as indicated in App 2, Pt II, para 4. If necessary (as for example where in sub-para (ii) there is more than one witness) these sections should be subdivided. Each section or subsection should contain a breakdown of the work comprised in it and should have its own separate subtotal. At the foot of the last of these sections there should be shown a total Pt A figure. Where a *f* charge is included in item 4, Pt A for correspondence and telephone attendances with counsel or his clerk, the work should only relate to such communications as are proper to be made by a fee-earner. Instructions by letter must be charged for under 'Preparation of documents'. Telephone discussions should be charged as conferences under item 2. Communications which may be included in item 4 are those which are properly fee-earner's work and deal with such matters as *g* agreeing a brief fee, or arranging conferences, or reserving counsel for a trial or hearing.

Part B The amount claimed for general care and conduct on the basis of the guidance given in para 3 of these notes should be claimed as a separate monetary amount which should also be expressed as a percentage of the total Pt A figure. *h* This part should include a statement identifying those factors in para 1(2) of Pt I of App 2 to Ord 62 which are relied on in relation to the assessment of the claim for general care and conduct.

Part C In this part an amount should be claimed for time engaged in travelling and waiting without uplift in connection with the work comprised in Pt A only. Details should be given showing to which part of that work the claim *j* or claims relate.

The section subtotals and the totals of Pts A, B and C figures referred to above should be shown in the narrative column of the bill. The aggregate of those figures should be shown in the profit costs column.

1.7 Travelling time will be allowed in respect of each item at the full amount
a of the appropriate expense rate. Waiting time will be similarly allowed but
neither travelling nor waiting time will attract any allowance for care and
conduct.

1.8 Letters and telephone calls will in general be allowed on a unit basis of six
minutes each, the charge being calculated by reference to the appropriate expense
rate. The unit charge for letters will include perusing and considering the relevant
b letters in and no separate charge should be made for incoming letters. The taxing
officer may allow an actual time charge for letters of substance and for telephone
calls which properly amount to an attendance, providing details of the work done
are provided and the time taken has been recorded.

1.9 If it is proper for service of process to be effected by a fee-earner in the
c employment of the solicitor a relevant chargeable item should be shown in sub-
para (xiii) of item 4. If service is effected by an inquiry agent or solicitor agent the
agent's charges should there be shown as a disbursement. This paragraph does not
relate to subpoenas, which are dealt with in para 1.10.

1.10 Conduct money paid to witnesses who attend a trial or hearing should be
shown as part of the expenses claimed at the trial or hearing and not included in
d the bill at the date of the service of a subpoena. Where the witness does not attend
the trial or hearing conduct money paid and (despite reasonable efforts) not
recovered should be shown at the date of service of subpoena. Work properly
done by a fee-earner in connection with the issue of a subpoena should be shown
in sub-para (ii) of item 4.

1.11 Properly kept and detailed time records are helpful in support of a bill
e provided they explain the nature of the work as well as recording the time
involved. The absence of such records may result in the disallowance or
diminution of the charges claimed. They cannot be accepted as conclusive
evidence that the time recorded either has been spent or, if spent, is 'reasonably'
chargeable.

f 1.12 Accounts must accompany the bill for all payments claimed (other than
court fees or minor out-of-pocket disbursements) whether or not these payments
have later to be vouched. In the case of substantial witness expenses and
professional fees including counsel's fees (but not those of medical experts) the
account should be accompanied by details showing the work done, the time spent,
by whom and when, and the computation of the charge. Copies of those details
g should be annexed to the copy bill served on the paying party. The importance of
this rule of practice is stressed: failure to comply with it invariably delays the
taxation and may result in a reduction in or the disallowance of item 5. Counsel's
fees should continue to be charged for each separate piece of work undertaken. A
'composite fee' must be broken down into its component parts.

1.13 Where travelling expenses are claimed they should be shown as a
h disbursement and details supplied. Local travelling expenses will not be allowed.
The definition of 'local' is a matter for the discretion of the taxing officer. While
no absolute rule can be laid down, as a matter of guidance in cases proceeding in
the High Court in London 'local' will, in general, be taken to mean within a
radius of ten miles from the Royal Courts of Justice.

1.14 The cost of postage, couriers, outgoing telephone calls, fax and telex
j messages is in general part of the solicitor's normal overhead expense, but the
taxing officer may in his discretion allow such a disbursement in unusual
circumstances or where the cost is unusually heavy, if the solicitor could not
reasonably be supposed to have taken it into account when estimating his normal
overheads for the purpose of calculating his expense rate.

1.15 The making of copies of documents is part of the solicitor's normal overhead expense. The taxing officer may in his discretion make an allowance for *a* copying in unusual circumstances or when the documents copied are unusually numerous in relation to the nature of the case: for example, they may be allowed in proceedings in the Court of Appeal. Where this discretion is invoked the number of copies made, their purpose and the charge claimed must be set out in the bill. If copies have been made out of the office the cost should be shown as a *b* disbursement. If made in the office, a charge equivalent to the commercial cost should be claimed. A charge based on the time expended by a member of the solicitor's staff will not be allowed.

1.16 Charges as between a principal solicitor and a solicitor agent will continue to be dealt with on the established principle that such charges, where appropriate, form part of the principal solicitor's charges. Where these charges relate to the *c* items 1, 2 and 3 they should be included in their chronological order. Where they relate to work done under item 4 they may either be included in the principal solicitor's item or be shown as a separate item properly detailed following afterwards. Solicitors are reminded that agency charges for advising the principal how to proceed are not recoverable.

1.17 No details of the work done need be provided for item 5(a) but on *d* taxation the party entitled to the costs must justify the amount claimed. In general the drawing of a bill of costs is not fee-earner's work and, save in exceptional circumstance, no charge should be sought for such work. Charges paid to an agent will not be allowed.

1.18 Details of the work done should be provided for any charge claimed under item 5(b). When objections are lodged they should be set out under the *e* following column headings: number of objection; page of bill; description of item; amount claimed; amount allowed; grounds for objection.

The grounds for objection should refer to any reasons given by the taxing officer for the reduction or disallowance and state why the objector disagrees. The grounds should include authorities and references relied on.

1.19 When bills are lodged for taxation they should be supported by the *f* relevant papers arranged as specified in r 29(7)(d). Failure to observe this requirement substantially increases the time and expense of the taxation process and may result in the bill being refused or the allowance for taxation reduced or disallowed.

1.20 *Statement of parties* (a) Inaccurate completion of this form, from which *g* the Supreme Court Taxing Office derives its information about the identity of the parties, causes considerable delays. The statement must include the name and address, document exchange number, reference, telephone and fax number for each solicitor or litigant in person on the record. The Supreme Court Taxing Office will communicate with the principals unless a specific written request is made for correspondence to be sent to London agents. All communications will *h* be sent to the solicitors on the record and not to costs draftsmen. (b) If the costs are payable out of a trust fund, the names and addresses of the residuary or other beneficiaries who will ultimately bear the costs should be given (with the proportion of their interest in the fund). If appropriate, directions can then be given pursuant to RSC Ord 62, r 26 to enable them to make representations on the taxation. (c) References for taxation will not be given if the statement of *j* parties is illegible or does not comply with the r 29(7)(b).

1.21 *Signing of bills* RSC Ord 62, r 29(7)(c)(iii) requires that every bill be signed in his own name by a partner in the firm of solicitors whose bill it is. This signature implies that the solicitor personally vouches for the accuracy of the bill, that it is complete and that the signatory is responsible for the factual accuracy of *a* the bill. The name of the solicitor signing the bill must also be shown in block letters. When there has been a change of solicitor in a non-legally-aided case each solicitor may sign the part of the bill relating to his firm's costs. In a legally-aided case every solicitor must sign the appropriate part of the bill.

1.22   *Papers lodged in support of the bill*   It is the responsibility of the solicitor *b* to ensure that everything necessary to justify the bill is readily accessible. Much time has been wasted in the past because papers lodged are incomplete or in disarray. Solicitors are asked to have particular regard to the following points. (a) Only one set of papers should be supplied. All duplicate and irrelevant papers should be removed from the files before papers are lodged. (b) The various items in the bill should be readily correlated with supporting papers (eg instructions *c* and briefs to counsel should be in bill order and clearly identified by a consecutive number or letter on the item and in the bill). (c) A note should be made on the bill if a supporting document is missing. (d) Originals of documents (especially instructions and briefs to counsel, drafts of documents settled by counsel and experts' reports) should be lodged. Any which are not available should be noted on the bill. (e) In legal aid cases a separate bundle in date order containing the *d* certificate, amendments and authorities should be lodged together with the relevant correspondence with the Legal Aid Board seeking such amendments and authorities and copies of any consent required from the assisted person. (f) A distinction should be made between time properly recorded and time estimated. It is helpful if the relevant part of item 4 (preparation for trial) in the bill shows the date and duration of each attendance of substance. Where the time claimed *e* on documents is substantial the receiving party should, when serving the bill, provide the paying party with a schedule of the total time claimed under item 4 (preparation), Pt A(ix) (documents) showing: (i) the date when the work was done; (ii) a description of the work; (iii) the status of the fee-earner who did the work; (iv) how long the work took. The schedule of times spent on documents *f* should be supplied with the bill on lodging the bill and papers at the Supreme Court Taxing Office, but the schedule will not be required if either the information is already contained in the bill or the documents item is agreed.

1.23   *Calderbank offers*   A party liable to pay costs to a party other than an assisted person may make a 'Calderbank offer' (see *Calderbank v Calderbank* [1975] 3 All ER 333, [1976] Fam 93) under the provisions of Ord 62, r 27(3). Subject to *g* r 27 if the offer is accepted the party whose bill it is may apply for the bill to be withdrawn and for the taxing fee to be abated in whole or in part. The existence of a *Calderbank* offer must not be made known personally to the taxing officer to whom the taxation has been referred.

The attention of the profession is drawn to the judgment in *Platt v GKN Kwikform Ltd* [1992] 1 WLR 465.

h

Direction 2: Ancillary matters

2.1   *Appointments and adjournments*   RSC Ord 62, r 30(1) requires that not less than 14 days' notice of a taxation be given. Any appointment which becomes ineffective within that time cannot therefore be allocated to another case. If an appointment given is inconvenient or a case is settled, notice should be given to *j* the Supreme Court Taxing Office immediately, preferably by fax. The interests of other litigants awaiting an appointment must be borne in mind. Applications for adjournments made within 14 days of the appointment will therefore be granted only in the most exceptional circumstances. A very strong case will have to be made for any later application, opposed or unopposed, to succeed. This

direction only applies to adjournments, not to cases where appointments are
vacated because a settlement has been reached.   *a*

2.2 *Abatement of taxing fees*   The Supreme Court Fees Order 1980, SI 1980/
821, Sch, section 5 provides for the payment of such fee as may be reasonable
having regard to the work done in the court office. As a general guide, where a
bill is withdrawn more than 21 days prior to the taxation the taxing fee will be
not less than 50%. Where the bill is withdrawn within 7 days of taxation the fee
will be not less than 75%. The taxing officer has a discretion to impose a different   *b*
fee where the circumstances require it.

2.3 *Identification of matters in issue*   In an effort to save time the paying party is
required to identify areas of disagreement and to notify the receiving party
thereof well in advance of the taxation to enable those issues to be identified and
clarified in advance. The paying party should outline the reason for disputing an   *c*
item and where a reduction is sought should suggest the reduced figure. The
taxing officer should be given this information and any response at least seven
days before the taxation.

2.4 *Removal of papers*   All papers must be removed immediately after the
taxation. Any papers not removed will be treated as abandoned and sent for
destruction without notice. No responsibility whatsoever will be accepted for   *d*
papers left after taxation, or after a proposed taxation has been settled.

2.5 *Summons to review taxations—papers for use of the court*   Applicants for
reviews of taxation are required to lodge with the Chief Clerk three bundles of
documents for the use of the judge and assessors.

Upon receipt of the summons to review the Chief Clerk will send notice to the
applicant requesting that the bundles be lodged, which should consist of copies of   *e*
the following documents: the summons to review; order/judgment or other
instrument providing for the taxation; bill of costs; objections; respondent's
answers (if any); master's answers and certificate; affidavits filed during the course
of the taxation; the legal aid certificate, any relevant amendments thereto and
authority to apply for review where applicable; any correspondence or other
documents to which reference is intended to be made at the hearing of the review.   *f*

Bundles must be clearly paginated with an index at the front of the bundle
listing all the documents and giving a page reference for each one. The bundles
must be bound together. Loose documents will not be accepted.

The bundles must be lodged within 21 days from the receipt of notice from
the Chief Clerk or such other time as the Chief Clerk may direct.   *g*

2.6 *Masters' Secretariat*   Any questions or application relating to any taxation
referred to a master should be referred to the Masters' Secretariat, which is situated
in room 2.14 (telephone number 071-936 6605/6505, fax number 071-936 6344),
who will seek the master's directions. The sitting master whose name is printed
in the Daily Cause List is available to deal with practice queries and urgent
appointments.   *h*

Direction 3: Wasted costs orders and delay

3.1 *Applications under RSC Ord 62, r 28: allegations of misconduct, neglect, delay
or wasted costs*

(i) Any party wishing to make an application under r 28 of Ord 62 must do so   *j*
on summons in accordance with RSC Ord 32. The summons may be issued at
any time after commencement of proceedings for taxation.

(ii) The summons should be so drawn as to give the other parties adequate
notice of the case to be met and thus to minimise the risk of applications for
adjournments.

(iii) The summons should indicate whether the party intends to rely upon (a) r 28(1) and r 10(1) (misconduct or neglect in the conduct of any proceedings), (b) r 28(2) and s 51(6) of the Supreme Court Act 1981 (personal liability of legal representative for costs) or (c) r 28(4) (failure to commence or conduct taxation proceedings in accordance with Ord 62 or delay in lodging a bill for taxation).

(iv) A summons under r 28(1) or (2) should give brief particulars of the facts complained of and the relief sought.

(v) A summons under r 28(4) should identify any failure or delay relied upon, the facts complained of and the relief sought.

(vi) The party making the application must indicate the time required for the application or, if it be preferable, request a short directions hearing. If possible a date and time of hearing will be given immediately; if that is not possible the applicant will be notified of the time and place as soon as possible. Once an order has been made Ord 42, r 4 will apply. The order must normally be drawn up and it is the responsibility of the applicant to do so (Ord 42, r 5). In Chancery Division proceedings it will be the responsibility of the parties to draw up the order unless the master directs otherwise. Three copies of the order must be prepared, one for sealing at the Supreme Court Taxing Office and return, one for filing at the Supreme Court Taxing Office and one for filing in room 81 (Queen's Bench Division) or the Chancery Registry as the case may be.

(vii) The party having carriage of the order must serve a copy of the order upon any opposing party.

(viii) In the event of either party being dissatisfied with the taxing officer's decision under RSC Ord 62, r 28, an appeal lies to the judge in chambers in accordance with RSC Ord 58. This must not be confused with the procedure for carrying in of objections and summons for review before the judge, which continue to be governed by RSC Ord 62, Pt VI, rr 33–35.

(ix) Any enforcement proceedings will be in the Queen's Bench Division or Chancery Division as the case may be.

Direction 4: Legal aid

Assessment of costs

4.1 Regulation 106(1) and (2) of the Civil Legal Aid (General) Regulations 1989, SI 1989/339, provides:

'(1) Where, in proceedings to which an assisted person (or a former assisted person) has been a party and which have been brought to an end by a judgment, decree or final order, there has been an agreement as to the costs to be paid by any other party to the assisted person (or former assisted person) which that person's solicitor and counsel (if any) is willing to accept in full satisfaction of the work done, the amount of those costs shall be assessed by the Area Director.

(2) Where costs are to be assessed in the circumstances specified in paragraph (1), the Area Director may, if he thinks fit, request the taxing officer of the court in which the proceedings were conducted to assess the costs on the standard basis without a taxation.'

If such request is made by the Area Director to the Supreme Court Taxing Officer or Admiralty Registrar the appropriate taxing officer will: (i) in the normal course, assess the costs without requiring the attendance of the solicitor; (ii) issue a certificate of assessment of the costs.

4.2 *Interest of the assisted person*

(i) The attention of solicitors is drawn to regs 118 and 119 of the Civil Legal *a* Aid (General) Regulations 1989, which deal with the position applying when the assisted person (a) has no interest or has an adverse interest in a taxation (reg 118) or (b) has a financial interest in the taxation (reg 119).

(ii) Whenever an assisted person has a financial interest in the taxation (which includes any case in which he has been awarded costs), the solicitors must before lodging their bill for taxation: (a) send the assisted person a copy of the bill; *b* (b) explain the extent of his interest in the taxation, which should cover in particular the power of the taxing officer to order payment out of the legal aid fund (hence by the assisted person personally) of any relevant part of the costs claimed inter partes, and the steps which can be taken to safeguard that interest; and (c) inform him/her that he/she has a right to appear on the taxation if he/she *c* so wishes.

(iii) The bill of costs must be indorsed with a certificate in Form A in the schedule hereto. If the assisted person has expressed a wish to attend the taxation his address and telephone number must be included in the statement of parties.

(iv) Regulation 119(b) provides that an assisted person shall not be required to make any contribution to the fund in respect of the costs of taxation proceedings *d* when he has a financial interest in a taxation. To enable these costs to be ascertained by the Legal Aid Board they will be separately certified in the taxing master's certificate. The legal aid summary to be completed by solicitors on each bill must show the costs of taxation separately and should be in the Form B in the schedule hereto.

4.3 The arithmetical accuracy of the summary on every taxed bill is the *e* responsibility of the solicitor whose bill it is. Every bill, whether or not it includes costs payable out of the legal aid fund, lodged for the issue of a taxing master's certificate must contain a certificate that the castings are correct in Form C in the schedule which must be signed by a partner in the firm.

Direction 5: Directions withdrawn

5.1. The following Practice Directions are hereby withdrawn:

1. Practice Direction No 1 of 1986, 9 April 1986 (*Supreme Court Practice 1993* vol 1, para 62/A5/6);
2. Practice Direction No 3 of 1986, 10 June 1986 (*Supreme Court Practice 1993* *g* vol 1, para 62/A5/7);
3. Practice Direction No 4 of 1986, 27 June 1986 ([1986] 3 All ER 724, [1986] 1 WLR 1054, *Supreme Court Practice 1993* vol 1, para 62/A5/8);
4. Practice Direction No 5 of 1986, 16 July 1986 ([1986] 3 All ER 725, [1986] 1 WLR 1053, *Supreme Court Practice 1993* vol 1, para 62/A5/9);
5. Practice Direction No 1 of 1989, 18 May 1989;   *h*
6. Practice Direction No 2 of 1989, 18 May 1989 ([1989] 2 All ER 480, [1989] 1 WLR 688, *Supreme Court Practice 1993* vol 1, para 62/A5/12);
7. Practice Direction No 4 of 1989, 1 December 1989 ([1989] 3 All ER 960, [1989] 1 WLR 1399, *Supreme Court Practice 1993* vol 1, para 62/A5/13);
8. Practice Direction No 1 of 1990, 26 June 1990 ([1990] 3 All ER 24, [1990] 1 WLR 1089, *Supreme Court Practice 1993* vol 1, para 62/A5/14);   *j*
9. Practice Direction No 2 of 1990, 20 August 1990 ([1990] 3 All ER 458, [1990] 1 WLR 1486, *Supreme Court Practice 1993* vol 1, para 62/A5/15);
10. Practice Direction No 1 of 1991, 31 January 1991 ([1991] 1 All ER 703, [1991] 1 WLR 177, *Supreme Court Practice 1993* vol 1, para 62/A5/17).

P T HURST

11 November 1992   Chief Taxing Master.

SCHEDULE

a

Form A (para 4.2)

Certificate pursuant to regulation 119

I certify that a copy of this bill has been sent to the assisted person pursuant to regulation 119 of the Civil Legal Aid (General) Regulations 1989, with an explanation of his/her interest in the taxation and the steps which can be taken to

b safeguard that interest in the taxation. He/she has/has not requested that the taxing officer be informed of his/her interest and has/has not requested that notice of the taxation appointment be sent to him/her.

Signed

c Partner in the firm of

Form B (para 4.2)

Legal aid summary to be indorsed on any bill of costs payable out of the legal aid fund

*Profit costs		£
	VAT	£
Counsel's fees		£
	VAT	£
*Other disbursements		£
	VAT	£
Costs of taxation allowed inter partes		£
	VAT	£
Costs of taxation allowed against the legal aid fund		£
	VAT	£
		£

d

e

f

* Profit costs and disbursements do *not* include the costs of taxation

Form C (para 4.3)

Certificate to be indorsed on all bills

g

I certify that the castings of this bill are correct.

Signed

Partner in the firm of

h Dated

Re A and another (minors) (abduction: acquiescence) (No 2)

COURT OF APPEAL, CIVIL DIVISION
SIR STEPHEN BROWN P, STAUGHTON AND SCOTT LJJ
11 MAY 1992

Minor – Custody – Rights of custody – Foreign custody rights – Wrongful removal or retention – Return of child – Welfare of child – Mother wrongfully removing children from Australia – Father acquiescing in removal of children to or their retention in England – Father applying for return of children to Australia – Whether appropriate for court to consider welfare interests of children – Whether court restricted to considering degree of acquiescence by father – Whether if acquiescence by father established court free to consider welfare interests of children – Child Abduction and Custody Act 1985, Sch 1, art 13(a)(b).

The parents, who were both British nationals, emigrated to Australia and were married there in 1983 and subsequently became Australian citizens. They had two boys aged six and five years. In February 1988 the mother returned to England for a holiday with the children and informed the father that she intended to remain in England permanently. After a brief reconciliation in England the parties subsequently returned to Australia but finally parted in 1990. The father formed an association with another woman and the mother decided to return to England as soon as possible. In 1991 the parties jointly applied for a divorce in Australia and it was agreed that the mother should have custody of the boys and the father should have regular access. On 18 September 1991, a few days after the decree absolute, the mother wrongfully removed the children from Australia to England. In proceedings brought by the father in England for the return of the children to Australia pursuant to the Convention on the Civil Aspects of International Child Abduction (which had the force of law in the United Kingdom by virtue of s 1(2) of the Child Abduction and Custody Act 1985 and was set out in Sch 1 thereto) the mother conceded that the removal of the children was wrongful under art 3 of the convention but sought to rely on the exceptions under art 13(a) and (b)[a] of the convention on the ground that the father had acquiesced in the removal of the children and that the return of the children would expose them to a grave risk of physical and psychological harm and place them in an intolerable situation. The judge decided that the mother had not established her case and ordered that the children be returned to Australia but on appeal the Court of Appeal held that there was evidence to establish that the father had acquiesced in the removal of the children to or their retention in England and remitted the case to the High Court for consideration of the exercise of its discretion under art 13 as to whether an order should be made for the children's return to Australia. On the remission of the case the judge held that, acquiescence in the removal on the part of the father having been established, the court had a general discretion to determine the question of the children's return according to their welfare and best interests and the mother was not required to show that the return of the children would expose them to a grave risk of physical and psychological harm and place them in an intolerable situation pursuant to art 13(b). The judge found that there had been a change of circumstances in Australia, in that the matrimonial home had been sold, the father was unemployed and was unable to pay maintenance and the mother would have to rent accommodation

---

a   Article 13, so far as material, is set out at p 275 e f, post

and would be dependent on state benefits in Australia, and concluded that the
a children's interests would be best served in their remaining in England pending
a decision of the High Court in wardship proceedings as to their future.
Accordingly, the judge dismissed the father's application. The father appealed,
contending that the consideration of the welfare of the children in the context of
the judicial discretion under art 13(a) of the convention could only be taken into
account if the court had established that the return of the children would expose
b them to a grave risk of physical and psychological harm and place them in an
intolerable situation within art 13(b).

Held – Once the court had established pursuant to art 13(a) of the convention
that the father had acquiesced in the removal of the children to or their retention
c in England, it was appropriate for the court to consider matters relating to the
interests of the children in deciding whether to order the return of the children
and it would not be appropriate for the court to restrict its discretion to a
consideration of the degree of acquiescence on the part of the father. Accordingly,
the judge had been entitled to consider the welfare interests of the children and
in all the circumstances had properly exercised her discretion by deciding that it
d would be wrong to order that the children be returned to Australia with the
possibility of yet a further move back to England if the Australian court were to
grant an application by the mother to remove the children to England
permanently. The father's appeal would therefore be dismissed (see p 278 f h,
p 280 c to j, p 281 g h and p 282 b, post).

Re A and anor (minors) (abduction: acquiescence) [1992] 1 All ER 929 considered.
e   Per Scott LJ. Paragraphs (a) and (b) of art 13 of the convention are alternative
and not cumulative and either paragraph, if satisfied, suffices to open the door to
the exercise of the discretion whether to order the return of a child to the
jurisdiction from which it has been wrongfully removed. In exercising that
discretion the court, while bearing in mind that the object of the convention is to
f discourage and prevent the abduction of children, should always take into account
the interests of the child, which although not necessarily the paramount
consideration, will always be important (see p 281 e j f and p 282 b, post).

Notes
For the return of children wrongfully removed, see Supplement to 8 *Halsbury's*
g *Laws* (4th edn) para 525A.
For the Child Adbuction and Custody Act 1985, s 1, Sch 1, arts 3, 13, see 6
Halsbury's Statutes (4th edn) (1992 reissue) 295, 310, 313.

Case referred to in judgments
A and anor (minors) (abduction: acquiescence), Re [1992] 1 All ER 929, [1992] Fam
h   106, [1992] 2 WLR 536, CA.
H and anor (minors) (abduction: custody rights), Re, Re S and anor (minors) (abduction:
custody rights) [1991] 3 All ER 230, [1991] 2 AC 476, [1991] 3 WLR 68, HL.

Case also cited
F (minor: abduction: jurisdiction), Re [1990] 3 All ER 97, [1991] Fam 25, CA.
j

Appeal
The father of two children appealed from the order of Booth J made in chambers
on 3 April 1992 dismissing his originating summons under Sch 1 to the Child
Abduction and Custody Act 1985 and declining to order the return of the children
to Australia from where they had been wrongfully removed by their mother.
The facts are set out in the judgment of Sir Stephen Brown P.

Nicholas Wall QC and *Mark Everall* (instructed by *Collyer-Bristow*) for the appellant.
Ian Karsten QC and *Lord Meston* (instructed by *Reynolds Porter Chamberlain*) for the   *a*
respondent.

SIR STEPHEN BROWN P. This is an appeal from a decision of Booth J of
3 April 1992. She then dismissed an originating summons under the Child   *b*
Abduction and Custody Act 1985, Sch 1 (which sets out the Convention on the
Civil Aspects of Child Abduction (The Hague, 25 October 1980; TS 66 (1986);
Cm 33) (the Hague Convention)), declining to order that two children, who had
been wrongfully removed from Australia to this country by their mother, should
be returned to the jurisdiction of the State of Victoria in Australia. The case has a   *c*
somewhat unusual history, for this is the second hearing in this court concerning
this case. The two children are boys, P and L, who were living with their parents
in Australia until September 1991.

The mother was born in England, but subsequently acquired Australian
citizenship. The father was born in Northern Ireland, and he also has now
acquired Australian citizenship. After the parents met they eventually emigrated   *d*
to Australia, and were married there in 1983. P was born on 2 September 1985
and L on 28 February 1987. They are therefore now aged six years and five years
respectively.

In February 1988 the mother came to England for a holiday with the children.
She informed the father after she had reached England that she wished to remain
in England with the children permanently. The husband came to England to   *e*
seek to persuade her to return, but did not then succeed. Although she
subsequently indicated that she intended to institute divorce proceedings, the
mother subsequently returned to Australia after the husband had paid a second
visit to England. In fact they returned together in September 1989. They then
acquired a matrimonial home with a mortgage, but finally separated in July 1990.
The father meanwhile commenced an association with another woman, and the   *f*
mother formed the intention of leaving Australia to return to England when it
should be possible.

In July 1991 the mother and father made a joint application for divorce in
Australia. In her petition the mother stated that she considered Australia to be
her permanent home. A decree nisi of divorce was pronounced in the Family   *g*
Court of Australia in August 1991, and the decree was made absolute on 13
September 1991. By agreement between the parties the mother had the care of
the boys. That was not a matter of dispute. The father exercised regular access,
and on the weekend before the mother left Australia he had the normal access to
the children.

On 18 September 1991 the mother wrongfully removed the children from   *h*
Australia and brought them to England. It was never in dispute that her action
in removing them from Australia was unlawful in the context of art 3 of the
convention. On 23 September 1991 the husband wrote a letter to the mother. In
February 1992 the Court of Appeal held that the terms of this letter constituted
'acquiescence' by the father within the meaning of art 13 of the Hague Convention
(see *Re A and anor (minors) (abduction: acquiescence)* [1992] 1 All ER 929, [1992]   *j*
Fam 106). Subsequently, and very shortly after having written that letter, the
father sought legal advice in Australia and then took the steps which eventually
led to the issue of this originating summons. The Attorney General's Department
in Australia (the central authority of that country) submitted a request for the
return of the children to the central authority of the United Kingdom, and the

originating summons was duly issued on 5 December 1991. By the originating
a summons the father sought the immediate return of the children to Australia.
Before the originating summons was served upon the mother the father had not
made her aware of his intention to 'go back' upon his letter of 23 September in
which he had said that he did not intend to seek to have the children returned
Australia. In the meanwhile she took steps to settle in this country and the
children were sent to school here.
b   The matter came before Thorpe J on 20 December. The father sought the
return of the children to the jurisdiction of Australia under the provisions of the
Hague Convention. It was conceded that their removal by the mother was
wrongful within the terms of art 3 and accordingly the court had to consider the
terms of art 12, which provides:

c   'Where a child has been wrongfully removed or retained in terms of
    Article 3 and, at the date of the commencement of the proceedings before
    the judicial or administrative authority of the Contracting State where the
    child is, a period of less than one year has elapsed from the date of the
    wrongful removal or retention, the authority concerned shall order the
    return of the child forthwith . . .'
d
The mother sought to rely upon the 'exception' which is contained within art
13. Article 13 provides:

    'Notwithstanding the provisions of the preceding Article, the judicial or
    administrative authority of the requested State is not bound to order the
e   return of the child if the person, institution or other body which opposes its
    return establishes that—(a) the person, institution or other body having the
    care of the person of the child was not actually exercising the custody rights
    at the time of removal or retention, or had consented to or subsequently
    acquiesced in the removal or retention; or (b) there is a grave risk that his or
    her return would expose the child to physical or psychological harm or
f   otherwise place the child in an intolerable situation . . .'

The mother sought to establish that the father had 'subsequently acquiesced' in
the removal of the children by her to England and their retention in England.
She relied upon the terms of his letter of 23 September 1991. I need not recite the
terms of that letter, which is set out in full in the judgment of Balcombe LJ at the
g previous hearing of this case in the Court of Appeal (see [1992] 1 All ER 929 at
932–933, [1992] Fam 106 at 111–112).
    The learned judge also had to consider a submission made by the mother that
the return of the children (if ordered) would expose them to a 'grave risk of
physical or psychological harm or place them in an intolerable situation' within
the terms of art 13(b). Thorpe J decided that the mother had not established that
h the father had acquiesced in the removal or retention of the children. He further
decided that she had not established a grave risk that the return of the children
would expose them to physical or psychological harm or otherwise place them in
an intolerable situation, and he ordered their return to Australia pursuant to the
provisions of art 12 of the Hague Convention.
    The mother appealed to the Court of Appeal, submitting that the learned judge
j was in error in having found that the father had not subsequently acquiesced in
the removal or subsequent retention of the children within the meaning of art
13(a) of the Hague Convention. She sought also to argue that he was in error in
failing to decide that she had established a grave risk that they would be exposed
to physical or psychological harm or otherwise placed in an intolerable situation
if their return were to be ordered.

The Court of Appeal by a majority (Balcombe LJ dissenting) held that the evidence established that the father had subsequently acquiesced in the wrongful *a* removal or retention of the children in this country by the mother, and ordered that the case should be remitted to a judge of the High Court for consideration of the exercise of the discretion which accordingly arose under art 13 as to whether he should decline to order that they be returned to the jurisdiction of the Australian court.

It was in these circumstances that the matter came before Booth J on 3 April *b* 1992. In a reserved judgment Booth J decided in the exercise of her discretion that she would decline to order the return of the children to Australia. She said:

> 'In my judgment the interests of the children are now to be taken into account and to be considered in relation to all the circumstances of the case including in relation to the general desirability that children wrongfully *c* removed from their place of habitual residence should be returned. It is clearly for the mother in this case to establish to the court that the interests of the children lie in their remaining in England, and that their future can appropriately be determined here so that it would be proper to allow those matters to prevail over the purpose and philosophy of the convention. But I do not accept the submission of Mr Everall [who appeared for the father] that *d* she should go so far as to establish that by their return they would be exposed to a grave risk of harm to bring them within the ambit of art 13(*b*). Once the discretion arises it is for the court to conduct the necessary balancing exercise between what would otherwise be required by the convention and the interests of the children, but only where it can clearly be shown that the *e* interests of the children require it should the court refuse to order their return. In all the circumstances of this case I have come to the conclusion that on balance the children's interests are better served by their being allowed to remain in England pending a determination by the High Court, in the exercise of its wardship jurisdiction, as to their future and whether it be in England or Australia. I therefore dismiss the father's application.' *f*

It is against that decision that the father now appeals.

In his notice of appeal he contends that the learned judge was wrong in law to reject the submission made on his behalf that any consideration of the welfare of the children in the context of the exercise of a judicial discretion under art 13(*a*) of the convention was only relevant as a material factor if it meant placing the *g* children in an intolerable situation under art 13(*b*). He further contends by ground 2 of his notice of appeal that the failure of the learned judge to perceive the limitations imposed on her discretion in the context of the convention led her to reject the proposition that the elements necessary to the exercise of that discretion have to exist within the framework laid down by the convention itself. Thus her conclusion that 'Once the discretion arises it is for the court to conduct *h* the necessary balancing exercise between what would otherwise be required by the convention and the interests of the children' is wrong in law and fatal to a proper exercise of a discretion under the convention because it predicates that matters relating to the welfare of children falling outside the ambit of the criteria laid down by the convention itself are relevant to the exercise of the discretion. Accordingly the learned judge should have limited considerations of welfare to *j* the criteria for 'welfare' laid down by the convention itself.

In his well-argued submissions Mr Wall QC submitted that the discretion conferred on the court of art 13(*a*) of the convention is a discretion to be exercised (a) within the context of the purpose and principles laid down by the convention and (b) by applying the criteria contained within the convention itself, and that it

is accordingly not a discretion to exercise the inherent jurisdiction of the court in
a wardship or under the Children Act 1989 so as to act in what the court perceives
to be the best interests of the child. He argued that the exercise of the discretion
must be considered in relation to, and in the context of, the scope and purpose of
the convention, which is set out in art 1 of the convention. He referred to the
citation of art 1 by Lord Brandon of Oakbrook in his speech in *Re H and anor
(minors) (abduction: custody rights), Re S and anor (minors) (abduction: custody rights)*
b [1991] 3 All ER 230 at 235, [1991] 2 AC 476 at 494:

> 'The objects of the present Convention are—(a) to secure the prompt
> return of children wrongfully removed to or retained in any Contracting
> State; and (b) to ensure that rights of custody and of access under the law of
> one Contracting State are effectively respected in the other Contracting
c States.'

He argued that the exercise of the discretion which arises as a result of the finding
of 'acquiescence' made by the Court of Appeal is limited to considering the nature
and quality of the acquiescence itself and would not entitle the court to take into
account 'welfare' considerations relating specifically to the children unless the
d court were able to find that there had been established a grave risk that the return
of the children would expose them to an intolerable situation under art 13(b). Mr
Wall submitted that the learned judge was therefore wrong to take into account
circumstances appertaining to the 'welfare' of the children. The interests of the
children in the welfare context, he said, were irrelevant to the consideration of
the exercise of discretion by the learned judge. He emphasised the purpose of the
e convention as cited by Lord Brandon of Oakbrook. He submits that the court is
simply not entitled to do what Booth J did—that is to say to consider the interests
of the children in relation to all the circumstances of the case.

He referred to a passage in the judgment of Lord Donaldson MR in the earlier
appeal where he said ([1992] 2 All ER 929 at 942, [1992] Fam 106 at 122–123):

f
> 'In the comparatively rare case in which such a judicial discretion falls to
> be exercised, there will be two distinct and wholly different issues confronting
> the court. (1) In all the circumstances is it more appropriate that a court of
> the country to which the child has been wrongfully removed or in which it
> is being wrongfully retained (country B) [in this case one can say England]
g > should reach decisions and make orders with a view to its welfare or is it
> more appropriate that this should be done by a court of the country from
> which it was removed or to which its return has been wrongfully prevented
> (country A) [Australia]? (2) If, but only if, the answer to the first question is
> that the court of country B [England] is the more appropriate court, should
> that court give any consideration whatsoever to what further orders should
h > be made other than for the immediate return of the child to country A
> [Australia] and for ensuring its welfare pending the resumption or assumption
> of jurisdiction by the courts of that country? In considering the first issue,
> the court of country B [England] should approach the matter by giving the
> fullest force to the policy which clearly underlies the convention and the Act,
> namely that wrongful removal or retention shall not confer any benefit or
j > advantage on the person (usually a parent) who has committed the wrongful
> act. It is only if the interests of the child render it appropriate that the courts
> of country B [England] rather than country A [Australia] shall determine its
> future that there can be any exception to an order for its return. This is
> something quite different from a consideration of whether the best interests
> of the child will be served by its living in country B [England] rather than

country A [Australia]. That is not the issue unless para (b) of art 13 applies.
The issue is whether decisions in the best interests of the child shall be taken *a*
by one court rather than another. If, as usually should be the case, the courts
of country B [England] decide to return the child to the jurisdiction of the
courts of country A [Australia], the latter courts will be in no way inhibited
from giving permission for the child to return to country B [England] or
indeed becoming settled there and so subject to the jurisdiction of the courts
of that country. But that will be a matter for the courts of country A *b*
[Australia].'

Mr Wall prays in aid that passage in the judgment of Lord Donaldson MR in
support of his submission that it is only in the event of the court in this country
finding that art 13(b) is applicable to the case that it can properly consider the
'welfare interests' of the child in deciding whether to decline to order the return *c*
of the child to Australia. This court has been told that unfortunately there had
been no argument about that particular matter in the course of the hearing of the
appeal before Lord Donaldson MR. Mr Karsten QC submits that on the face of it
that passage in the judgment of Lord Donaldson MR should be considered as
obiter, but in any event he submits that it does not bear the meaning contended *d*
for by Mr Wall.

Mr Karsten submits that once the mandatory effect of art 12 has been relaxed
by a finding under art 13, either under para (a) or under para (b), this gives rise to
the exercise of a discretion by the court. The court is then entitled to take into
consideration all relevant matters. He submits that whilst it is relevant that the
overall purpose and philosophy of the convention should be borne in mind, *e*
nevertheless it is appropriate for the court to consider matters relating to the
interests of the children. Once acquiescence has been established, it is not
appropriate to restrict the court's discretion to consideration of the degree of the
acquiescence. Once the door has been 'unlocked', he submits the court should be
obliged to consider whether it is appropriate in all the circumstances to decline to
order the return of the children to the country from which they have been *f*
wrongfully removed.

In this case I am satisfied that Booth J did have a discretion to take into account
the interests of the children. Support for that view is to be found in the final
paragraph of art 13:

'In considering the circumstances referred to in this Article, the judicial *g*
and administrative authorities shall take into account the information
relating to the social background of the child provided by the Central
Authority or other competent authority and the child's habitual residence.'

That paragraph suggests that it is appropriate for the court to consider the welfare
interests of the child or children. In this case Booth J considered the circumstances *h*
which followed the receipt of the letter of 23 September 1991 from the father,
which the Court of Appeal held constituted acquiescence by him in the removal
or retention of the children. She said:

'Since the judgment of Thorpe J the former matrimonial home in Victoria
has been sold, leaving the parents with a financial shortfall. The mother
would have to rent a property for herself and the boys if she were not to *j*
accept the offer of rent-free accommodation for a month with a friend of the
father. Nor is the father, who is currently unemployed, able to offer any
maintenance or other form of support, so that she and the boys would be
dependent upon state benefits. While in the long term the mother may well
be able to obtain employment in Australia, as she has done in the past,

a understandably it would not be her wish or intention to do so in the short term . . . I accept [counsel's] submission that it is relevant for this court to have regard to the fact that in Australia there is no longer any home or any financial support for the mother and for the boys, a situation for which the mother bears no greater responsibility than the father. I turn to consider which court would be the most appropriate to make long-term decisions as to the future of the children. In the event that the children were to return,

b the issue before the Family Court in Australia would arise upon the mother's application for leave to remove them permanently from the State of Victoria to bring them back to live with her in this country. The same issue would be before the English court. It is not the father's wish or intention to seek the care of the children provided that they live with the mother in Australia. He

c seeks to restore the status quo as it was between July 1990 and September 1991 and as it was confirmed by the Australian court in the divorce proceedings. The father does not challenge the mother's parenting abilities or impugn her capacity as a good mother. But he wishes the children, both of whom were born in Australia, to be brought up in that country, where he will be content with access to them. It is their long-term removal to England

d to which he objects. As to the ability to determine that issue between the parents, it appears to me that there is little to choose between the Family Court in England and that in Australia. There is no contentious issue between the parties as to the suitability of the mother to look after the children or as to the suitability of the father to have contact with them. There is also no suggestion in any of the evidence that the mother would forgo her

e responsibilities as a mother and would be prepared to leave the children in Australia and come to England without them. It is simply her case that they would be better off with her in England rather than with her in Australia. The circumstances in England as to housing and education can be made known to the Australian court as can those circumstances in Australia be made known to the English court without the necessity in either case of

f calling oral evidence. In either case welfare reports could be made available through the international service. In Australia the mother would be entitled to legal aid, as in England the father would be so entitled. It appears that the mother would be eligible for financial assistance in returning with the children to Australia, whereas the father and the lady with whom he now

g lives would have to fund their own travel arrangements to England and to that extent the father would be disadvantaged. Difficult though it would undoubtedly be for him I do not understand it to be said on his behalf that it would be impossible. I am satisfied, therefore, that the issue which arises for determination, that is whether it is in the children's interests that the mother should be permitted to live with them in England or whether they should be

h brought up in Australia where they could have more frequent contact with their father, may properly be determined in either court. If this matter rested solely upon the question of the best interests of the children I should have no doubt whatever that their welfare would be better served by their remaining in England in order that their future be determined by the High Court here. They have already had many changes of home in their comparatively short

j lives and it would unquestionably confuse and disturb them to leave England now only to return again in a matter of months should the Australian Family Court consider it right that they should make their home here. The uncertainty brought about by further litigation in Australia would now be compounded by the fact that they no longer have any home there to which to return. But in exercising discretion under art 13(a) of the convention, I

have to balance my findings as to the interests of the children and the
detriment which I am satisfied would befall them were I to order their return   *a*
against the fundamental purpose of the convention, which is to ensure as far
as possible that children wrongfully removed from the place of their habitual
residence are returned there as soon as possible ... In my judgment the
interests of the children are now to be taken into account and to be considered
in relation to all the circumstances of the case including in relation to the
general desirability that children wrongfully removed from their place of   *b*
habitual residence should be returned. It is clearly for the mother in this case
to establish to the court that the interests of the children lie in their remaining
in England, and that their future can appropriately be determined here so
that it would be proper to allow those matters to prevail over the purpose
and philosophy of the convention.'
                                                                          c
In my judgment the learned judge was fully entitled to take into account the
matters which she there expressed. She carried out the balancing exercise. She
took into account the overall purpose and philosophy of the convention. In my
judgment she was entitled to consider the welfare interests of the children after
the court had found there had been acquiescence on the part of the father within
the meaning of art 13(*a*). I do not believe that Mr Walls's submission that the   *d*
welfare of the children could only be taken into account if the terms of art 13(*b*)
had been established is a correct analysis of the position. In this case the finding
that the father had acquiesced in the removal and/or retention of the children in
England made it appropriate for the court to consider whether to decline to order
the return of the children. In my judgment it was appropriate for the learned   *e*
judge to take into account the interests of the children. I believe that on the
evidence before her she came to a conclusion which was well within her discretion.
I do not consider that it has been shown that she exercised her discretion
inappropriately or wrongly.
   Accordingly I would dismiss this appeal.
                                                                          f
STAUGHTON LJ. I agree that the discretion under art 13(*a*) of the Convention
on the Civil Aspects of Child Abduction (The Hague, 25 October 1980; TS 66
(1986); Cm 33), which is set out in Sch 1 to the Child Abduction and Custody Act
1985, is not limited in the way that Mr Wall QC submits. If there had been no
question of acquiescence in this case, these children would have been returned to
Australia pursuant to the order of Thorpe J shortly after it was made on 20   *g*
December 1991. Because there was acquiescence, they are still here today on 11
May 1992. They have, no doubt, been adapting themselves to their new home, to
a different country and to their new school. These children, aged six and five,
have already had four major moves in their lives, first from Australia to England,
then from England to Australia, then from the matrimonial home in Frankston
to the mothers' unit in Mornington, and finally from there back to England   *h*
again.
   The judge was entitled to conclude, as she did, that it would be wrong for the
court to order that they should be moved once more to Australia with the
possibility of yet a further move back again. That, as it seems to me, was an
important feature in the judge's judgment; and I think that she was right to   *j*
attach importance to it.
   I would dismiss this appeal.

SCOTT LJ. I too agree. This appeal turns on a short point of principle arising
under the Convention on the Civil Aspects of Child Abduction (The Hague, 25

October 1980, TS 66 (1986); Cm 33), the terms of which are set out in Sch 1 to
a the Child Abduction and Custody Act 1985. It is common ground that the
mother's removal of the two boys from Australia to England on 18 September
1991 was a wrongful removal for the purposes of art 3 of the convention. It has
been established by the judgment of this court given on 12 February 1992 that
by a letter to the mother, dated 23 September 1991, the father expressed his
acquiescence in the removal (see Re A and anor (minors) (abduction: acquiescence)
b [1992] 1 All ER 929, [1992] Fam 106).

Article 12 of the convention requires, prima facie, the mandatory return
forthwith of a child who has been wrongfully removed, but art 13, by reason of
the Court of Appeal decision to which I have referred, also applies in this case. So
it is common ground that the question whether or not the boys should be
c returned to Australia depends upon the discretion of the court. Their return is
not mandatory.

The discretion was exercised by Booth J. She took into account various matters
relating to the interests of the boys and concluded that she should not order their
return to Australia. The father appeals. He contends, by Mr Wall QC, that
Booth J, in taking into account various matters regarding the boys' welfare,
d misdirected herself. He submits that matters regarding their welfare can only be
taken into account on the exercise of discretion under art 13 if they establish the
criterion to be found in art 13(b), ie that there is a grave risk that their return
would expose them to physical or psychological harm or otherwise place them in
an intolerable situation.

In my judgment this submission cannot be accepted. Paragraphs (a) and (b) of
e art 13 are alternative, not cumulative. Either paragraph, if satisfied, suffices to
open the door to an exercise of discretion as to whether or not to order the return
of the child in question. In exercising the discretion contemplated by art 13, and
contemplated by the convention itself, it is right, in my opinion, for the judge to
bear in mind that the object of the convention is to discourage and prevent the
abduction of children. In the present case Booth J did take that into account. But
f she placed in the balance also the interests of the children. She said:

> '... in exercising discretion under art 13(a) of the convention, I have to
> balance my findings as to the interests of the children and the detriment
> which I am satisfied would befall them were I to order their return, against
> the fundamental purpose of the convention, which is to ensure as far as
g > possible that children wrongfully removed from the place of their habitual
> residence are returned there as soon as possible, and the fact that the
> Australian court has already been seised with their welfare in the context of
> the divorce proceedings.'

She found that, in the case before her, the balance came down against ordering
h the return of the children to Australia. I need not cite the passage that contains
that finding because Sir Stephen Brown P has already cited it. But the above
passage constitutes, in my judgment, an approach to the exercise of discretion
which cannot be faulted. The question for the court in any case where the
discretion falls to be exercised, one or other of the gateways provided by art 13
having been opened, is whether or not the child or children should be returned
j to the jurisdiction from which they have been wrongfully removed. It is
impossible, in my judgment, in answering that question, whether the gateway is
para (a) or whether it is para (b), to exclude consideration of the interests of the
children. The final paragraph of art 13 shows conclusively, in my judgment, that
that is so. It requires to be taken into account 'information relating to the social
background of the child'.

The taking into account of the interests of the children need not, for art 13 purposes, treat their interests or welfare as the paramount consideration, as would *a* be necessary under s 1 of the Children Act 1989. But to contend, as does Mr Wall, that the consideration of their interests cannot be taken into account at all unless the criterion to be found in art 13(*b*) is satisfied is, in my judgment, unwarranted by anything in the language of the convention and unwarranted in principle. The interests of the children, although not necessarily the paramount considera- tion, must, in my opinion, always be taken into account and will always be *b* important. The learned judge's approach was, in my judgment, correct in law.

So I would dismiss this appeal.

Appeal dismissed. Leave to appeal to the House of Lords refused.

12 October. *The Appeal Committee of the House of Lords (Lord Templeman, Lord Lowry* *c* *and Lord Slynn of Hadley) refused leave to appeal.*

Bebe Chua   Barrister.

d

Omar Parks Ltd v Elkington
Ron Grundy (Melbourne) Ltd v Boneheyo

COURT OF APPEAL, CIVIL DIVISION   *e*
NOURSE, STOCKER AND BELDAM LJJ
17, 18 JUNE, 8 JULY 1992

Mobile home – Agreement to occupy mobile home – Termination of agreement – Termination for non-occupation of mobile home – Occupation of mobile home – Whether occupation to be determined on date application made to court by site owner or on date *f* *application heard – Mobile Homes Act 1983, Sch 1, Pt I, para 5.*

On the true construction of the term implied by para 5[a] of Pt I of Sch 1 to the Mobile Homes Act 1983 in any agreement to which the Act applies that 'The owner shall be entitled to terminate the agreement forthwith if, on the application of the owner, the court is satisfied that the occupier is not occupying the mobile *g* home as his only or main residence' the relevant date for determining whether the occupier is or is not occupying the mobile home as his only or main residence is the date on which the application to terminate is heard and not the date when the site owner applies to the court for the termination of the agreement (see p 284 *h j*, p 285 *g* and p 288 *h j*, post).

h

Notes
For rights of site owners to terminate agreements for non-occupation of mobile homes, see 27 *Halsbury's Laws* (4th edn) paras 864–865.

For the Mobile Homes Act 1983, Sch 1, Pt I, para 5, see 32 *Halsbury's Statutes* (4th edn) 519.

j

Cases referred to in judgments
Benninga (Mitcham) Ltd v Bijstra [1945] 2 All ER 433, [1946] KB 58, CA.
Betty's Cafés Ltd v Phillips Furnishings Stores Ltd [1958] 1 All ER 607, [1959] AC 20, [1958] 2 WLR 513, HL.

---

a Paragraph 5 is set out at p 283 *j*, post

Jessop v Hanwell [1988] CA Transcript 906.

a   *Lewis v Allenby (1909) Ltd v Pegge* [1914] 1 Ch 782.

Wilson v Fynn [1948] 2 All ER 40.

Cases also cited or referred to in skeleton arguments

A-G v Hanover (Prince) [1957] 1 All ER 49, [1957] AC 436, HL.

Ajit v Sammy [1967] 1 AC 255, PC.

b   *Alexander v Mohammedzadeh* [1985] 2 EGLR 161, CA.

Lovelock v Margo [1963] 2 All ER 13, [1963] 2 QB 786, CA.

Peabody Donation Fund (Governors) v Higgins [1983] 3 All ER 122, [1983] 1 WLR 1091, CA.

R v Leicester Justices, ex p Workman [1964] 2 All ER 346, [1964] 1 WLR 707, DC.

c   *R v Tonbridge Overseers* (1884) 13 QBD 339, CA.

Scott v Bamforth (1923) 13 LJCCR 4.

Taylor v Calvert [1978] 2 All ER 630, [1978] 1 WLR 899, CA.

Appeals

Omar Parks Ltd v Elkington

d   The respondent, Victor Elkington, appealed from the judgment of Judge Eric Stockdale in the Hemel Hempstead County Court sitting at Watford dated 22 November 1991 whereby he ordered that the applicant site owner, Omar Parks Ltd, was entitled to terminate the agreement under which the respondent was permitted to station his mobile home on the pitch and surround known as 8 Beech Park, Chesham Road, Wigginton, near Tring, Hertfordshire, and that the

e   respondent give possession of the mobile home pitch to the applicant. The facts are set out in the judgment of Nourse LJ.

Ron Grundy (Melbourne) Ltd v Valerie Boneheyo
Ron Grundy (Melbourne) Ltd v Clive Boneheyo

f   The applicant site owner, Ron Grundy (Melbourne) Ltd, appealed from the judgment of Mr Recorder Rees sitting in the Northwich County Court sitting at Knutsford on 8 November 1991 whereby he dismissed the applicant's claim for possession of 22 West Site, Woodlands Park, Wash Lane, Allstock, against the respondents, Valerie Boneheyo and Clive Boneheyo. The facts are set out in the judgment of Nourse LJ.

g   The three appeals were heard together.

Andrew Arden QC and *Julian Lynch* (instructed by *Lance Kent & Co*, Berkhamsted) for Mr Elkington.

Richard Quenby (instructed by *Gregory Rowcliffe & Milners*, agents for *Dixons*, Northwich) for Miss and Mr Boneheyo.

h   *Timothy Howard* (instructed by *Tozers*, Exeter) for Omar Parks Ltd and Ron Grundy (Melbourne) Ltd.

Cur adv vult

j   8 July 1992. The following judgments were delivered.

NOURSE LJ. By the Mobile Homes Act 1983, Sch 1, Pt I, para 5, the following term is implied in any agreement to which the Act applies:

'The owner shall be entitled to terminate the agreement forthwith if, on the application of the owner, the court is satisfied that the occupier is not occupying the mobile home as his only or main residence.'

The principal question arising on these appeals is whether that term requires the occupation of the home to be judged as at the date on which the site owner applies *a* to the court or the date on which the application is heard and determined. Opposite decisions have been given in the courts below. So now we must resolve the conflict.

This is the only question arising on the appeal in *Omar Parks Ltd v Elkington*. It is therefore convenient to consider that case first. Omar Parks Ltd (Omar Parks) is the owner of Beech Park, Chesham Road, Wiggington, near Tring, Hertfordshire, *b* which is a protected site for the purposes of the 1983 Act. Mr Victor Elkington is the owner of the mobile home stationed on pitch 8 on that site. He purchased it for £21,500 on 10 September 1988. He also became the assignee of an agreement between the previous owners of the home and the predecessors in title of Omar Parks, under which he was entitled to station it on that pitch subject to the terms *c* of the agreement and the payment of the pitch fee. It is agreed that that was an agreement to which the 1983 Act applied (see s 1(1)) and that by virtue of s 2(1) there was implied in it, amongst others, the term set out in para 5 of Pt I of Sch 1 (the implied term). The home was some 14 years old and required repairs. Mr Elkington agreed to carry them out within 12 months. However, for reasons which need not be explored, it took him the best part of three years to complete *d* the bulk of them at a cost of about £12,500.

On 25 July 1991 Omar Parks issued an application in the Hemel Hempstead County Court seeking possession of pitch 8 on the ground that Mr Elkington was not occupying the home as his only or main residence. The application was heard and determined by Judge Eric Stockdale on 22 November 1991. The judge found that Mr Elkington was not occupying the home either as his only residence or as *e* his main residence before 1 September 1991, but that he had been occupying it as his only residence from and after that date, in other words that the occupation required by the implied term did not exist at the date of the application to the court but did exist at the date on which it was heard and determined. No appeal has been brought against that finding. However, the judge was of the view that *f* it was the date of the application to the court at which the required occupation had to exist. He made an order for possession accordingly. Mr Elkington now appeals against that order, which has been stayed by agreement in the meantime.

The outcome of the question depends on the true construction of the implied term read with the other provisions of the 1983 Act. Part I of Sch 1 sets out four implied terms entitling the occupier or the site owner, as the case may be, to *g* terminate the agreement, the others being set out in para 3, 4 and 6. The term set out in para 3 entitles the occupier to terminate the agreement by not less than four weeks' notice in writing. Those set out in paras 4 and 6 entitle the site owner to terminate the agreement, in the former case 'forthwith' and in the latter at the end of 'a relevant period', if, 'on the application of the owner, the court is satisfied' etc.   *h*

The critical words in the implied term are 'the court is satisfied that the occupier is not occupying'. If those were the only words on which the question depended, it could not be doubted that the occupation must be judged as at the date on which the application is heard and determined. Such would be the plain and ordinary meaning assigned to the words by the double use of the present tense. The court cannot be presently satisfied of the present existence of a given *j* state of facts before an application is heard. But it is argued that the words 'on the application of the owner', coupled with the absurdities flowing from the contrary view, displaced this plain and ordinary meaning. That argument was accepted by Judge Stockdale, the essence of whose decision was expressed thus:

a   'Mr Blohm says it must relate to the date of the application, otherwise all the site owner can do is come to the court and say: "I've no idea if I will succeed on the day of the hearing, but will the court please fix a date". No one will know until the evidence is given on the day of the hearing whether the respondent is occupying or not. It doesn't matter if he moved in on the day of the hearing. There would be chaos. I find this interpretation offensive—it is a strange way for the court to proceed. It would be strange if

b   the court had to deal with tentative applications—"Fix a date; we will then see if we have a case or not". Generally speaking, the courts determine disputes in existence on the day proceedings are commenced.'

In my judgment these considerations are not sufficient to displace the plain and ordinary meaning of the critical words. In contrast with the occupier's

c   entitlement under para 3 to terminate the agreement by notice, the site owner's entitlement under para 5 does not arise unless and until the court is satisfied in the terms of that paragraph, a satisfaction which can only be declared if and when an application is made to it. Since the site owner will be the party who wants the declaration to be made, it is natural to assume that the application will be made

d   by him. In my view the words 'on the application of the owner' do no more than recognise that state of affairs.

It is perfectly true, as was pointed out by Mr Howard on behalf of Omar Parks (he also appeared for the site owner in the other appeals), that if that is the only function of the words 'on the application of the owner', they could just as well have been omitted. If a long experience of legislative drafting had brought with

e   it a conviction that an Act of Parliament never included words of surplusage, that would no doubt have been a persuasive point. But that is not our experience and I for one do not complain of it. An emphasis of the obvious, unnecessary to a judge who has had the benefit of argument, may yet be welcome to a busy practitioner who has not. Moreover, as was pointed out by Mr Arden QC, on behalf of Mr Elkington, there are other provisions of the 1983 Act of a like

f   character, not only in paras 4 and 6. Thus s 1(5) provides for the occupier to apply to the court if the site owner fails to comply with that section. More significantly, sub-ss (2) and (3) of s 2 each provide for the court to make an order 'on the application of either party'. I think that the wording of paras 4, 5 and 6 was intended to achieve consistency with these other provisions. I doubt whether the

g   words 'on the application of the owner' were intended to have any temporal significance. If they were, they can only refer to the time when the application is heard and determined. It is impossible to give them the much greater temporal significance of requiring that the occupation of the home be judged as at the date on which the application is made.

I am also unconvinced that any absurdity flows from giving the critical words

h   their plain and ordinary meaning. Indeed, as Mr Arden observed, if the contrary view were correct, a site owner, simply by issuing an application and without prior notice, could seemingly establish his entitlement to terminate an agreement against an occupier who, in circumstances such as those experienced by Mr Elkington, had been unable to move into his home and was still living elsewhere. Such a provision would be most unusual and in stark contrast with para 4, which

j   requires notice to remedy to be given to the occupier before an application to terminate the agreement can be brought on the ground of a breach of one of its terms. If you were looking for an absurdity flowing from an Act whose purpose is to protect the occupation of residential premises, you would hardly need to look further than that. Moreover, there have long been similar provisions in other legislation, for example in the Rent Acts, where the date on which it had to be determined whether the landlord reasonably required the premises for his *a* own occupation was the date of the hearing: see *Benninga (Mitcham) Ltd v Bijstra* [1945] 2 All ER 433, [1946] KB 58. A similar rule applies to the date on which a landlord must establish his intention to demolish or reconstruct the premises, or to occupy them for the purposes of a business to be carried on by him, within s 30(1)(*f*) or (*g*) respectively of the Landlord and Tenant Act 1954: see *Betty's Cafés Ltd v Phillips Furnishing Stores Ltd* [1958] 1 All ER 607, [1959] AC 20. I *b* therefore see no reason why Parliament should not have intended a similar rule to apply to the implied term under the 1983 Act.

We were referred to only one authority under the 1983 Act, the decision of this court in *Jessop v Hanwell* [1988] CA Transcript 906, where Fox LJ said:

> '. . .the court has no alternative but to remit the issue of whether the *c* mobile home was the main residence of the respondent at the date of the originating application to the county court.'

The making of an order in that form would appear to give strong support to the contention of Omar Parks. However, it is clear, both from the judgments and from information given to us by Omar Parks' solicitors, who acted for the site *d* owner in that case also, that the date at which the occupation had to be judged was not there in issue. No argument was heard on that point. So that decision does not bind us to arrive at a conclusion contrary to that which, after hearing full argument, I believe to be correct. In *Omar Parks Ltd v Elkington* I would therefore allow the appeal and discharge the order for possession.

I now turn to *Ron Grundy (Melbourne) Ltd v Boneheyo*, in which the material facts *e* are these. Ron Grundy (Melbourne) Ltd (Ron Grundy) is the owner of Woodlands Park, Wash Lane, Allstock, Cheshire, which is also a protected site for the purposes of the 1983 Act. On 22 December 1985 Mr Clive Boneheyo became the owner of the mobile home stationed on the pitch known as 22 West Site. He acquired it by way of gift from his father, who had stationed first one and then another mobile *f* home on that pitch since 1976. Mr Boneheyo also became the assignee of an agreement (the 1976 agreement) dated 1 January 1976 and made between his father and the predecessors in title of Ron Grundy, under which he was entitled to station a mobile home on 22 West Site, subject to the terms of the agreement and the payment of the pitch fee. Again it is agreed that that was an agreement to which the 1983 Act applied and that the implied term was implied in it. The *g* nature of Mr Boneheyo's occupancy of the home between December 1985 and March 1990 is unclear. What is clear is that in the latter month he ceased to occupy it at all and that between then and August 1990 it was unoccupied. On 4 April 1990 the site was acquired by Ron Grundy. In August 1990, without the knowledge or approval of Ron Grundy, Mr Boneheyo's daughter, Miss Valerie *h* Boneheyo, moved into the home. She has since occupied it as her only residence.

On 3 December 1990 Ron Grundy commenced proceedings in the Northwich County Court against Miss Boneheyo seeking possession of 22 West Site on the ground that she had wrongfully occupied it and was therefore a trespasser. It is agreed that at that stage Ron Grundy's contention was correct. Although Miss Boneheyo had taken occupation of the home with the knowledge and approval of *j* Mr Boneheyo, there had been no assignment to her of the 1976 agreement.

No further step was taken in the proceedings against Miss Boneheyo at that stage. No doubt it was realised that the 1976 agreement could only be terminated in proceedings against Mr Boneheyo. In any event, on 14 January 1991 Ron Grundy's solicitors wrote to the Boneheyos' solicitors stating that they were commencing proceedings against Mr Boneheyo for leave to terminate the 1976

agreement under the 1983 Act. On 15 January the Boneheyos' solicitors wrote to
a Ron Grundy's solicitors as follows:

> '... we hereby give you formal notice on behalf of our clients of their
> request that your client consent to an assignment of the Agreement dated 1st
> January 1976, to which the Mobile Homes Act 1983 applies, to Miss Valerie
> Bonheyo. If we do not hear from you within the next seven days we shall
> b   assume that such consent is withheld.'

That letter was received by Ron Grundy's solicitors on the following day, 16
January. No reply having been received, on 24 January Mr Bonheyo gave Miss
Bonheyo the mobile home and assigned to her by deed the benefit of the 1976
agreement. On the following day, 25 January, Ron Grundy's solicitors wrote to
c the Boneheyos' solicitors as follows:

> '... our client does not consent to an assignment of the Agreement dated
> the 1st January 1976 to Miss V Bonheyo. It is clearly inappropriate for such
> consent to be given, or indeed sought, in view of the two actions that have
> been started, quite apart from the other factors such as Miss Bonheyo's
> d   behaviour since she started living on the Park and the fact that a section has
> been built onto the front of the Mobile Home so as to make it non-mobile.'

Meanwhile, on 17 January 1991 Ron Grundy had issued an application in the
Northwich County Court against Mr Bonheyo seeking a declaration that it be at
liberty to terminate the 1976 agreement and an order for possesion of 22 West
Site, on the ground that he was not occupying the home as his only or main
e residence. Both sets of proceedings were heard and determined by Mr Recorder
Rees on 7 and 8 November 1991. He dismissed them with costs and made a
declaration that the 1976 agreement enured for the benefit of Miss Bonheyo.
Ron Grundy now appeals in both cases.

As I have said, it is agreed that Miss Bonheyo was not entitled to the protection
f of the 1983 Act when proceedings were commenced against her on 3 December
1990. At that stage the 1976 agreement had not been assigned to her. It did not
therefore enure for her benefit under s 3(2): see below. Her case is that the 1976
agreement was lawfully assigned to her on 24 January 1991, from which date she
was, by virtue of her occupation of the home as her only residence, within the
protection of the implied term. So the first question which the learned recorder
g had to decide was the same as that which arose in *Omar Parks Ltd v Elkington*. He
decided it in favour of Miss Bonheyo, holding that the occupation of the home
had to be judged as at the date on which the application was heard and determined.
For the reasons already given, his decision on that question was correct.

The second question which the recorder had to decide was whether the
assignment of 24 January 1991 was effective, so that the 1976 agreement did
h indeed enure for the benefit of Miss Bonheyo at the date of the hearing and
determination of the application in November 1991. In order that that question
may be considered, reference must be made to two further provisions of the 1983
Act. Section 3(2) provides:

> 'Where an agreement to which this Act applies is lawfully assigned to any
> j   person, the agreement shall enure for the benefit of and be binding on that
> person.'

Paragraph 9 of Pt I of Sch 1 sets out another implied term:

> 'The occupier shall be entitled to give the mobile home, and to assign the
> agreement, to a member of his family approved by the owner, whose
> approval shall not be unreasonably withheld.'

As to those provisions, it is clear, first, that Miss Boneheyo was a member of Mr Boneheyo's family for the purposes of para 9: see s 5(3). Secondly, it was accepted *a* by Mr Howard on behalf of Ron Grundy that the 1976 agreement was 'lawfully' assigned to Miss Boneheyo within s 3(2) if Ron Grundy's approval was both sought and unreasonably refused before the assignment was executed. There can be no doubt that approval was sought by the Boneheyos' solicitors' letter of 15 January 1991 and Ron Grundy does not impugn the recorder's finding that, if it was refused, it was refused unreasonably. There having been no express refusal *b* until 25 January, the single issue which remains in dispute is whether approval was impliedly refused before 24 January when the assignment was executed. If it was not, then, notwithstanding the subsequent express refusal, the 1976 agreement was not 'lawfully' assigned and Ron Grundy is entitled to succeed on its appeal.

c
Although the recorder's decision necessarily imported a holding that Ron Grundy's approval had been impliedly refused, he did not discuss that point. He rather assumed the refusal and concentrated on its unreasonableness. However, both sides are agreed that the question whether there was an implied refusal or not depends on whether Ron Grundy was or was not given a reasonable time to consider the matter and to give or withhold its consent: see *Wilson v Fynn* [1948] *d* 2 All ER 40 at 42 per Denning J.

The question is agreed to depend on the inferences which should be drawn from the contemporaneous correspondence between the parties and the surrounding circumstances of the case. The Boneheyos' solicitors' letter of 15 January requesting approval was received by Ron Grundy's solicitors on 16 January. Two days earlier the latter had written to the former stating that they *e* were commencing proceedings against Mr Boneheyo. Those proceedings were not commenced until 17 January and it may be assumed that the instructions to commence them could still have been countermanded on 16 January. The letter of 15 January stated that if nothing was heard from Ron Grundy's solicitors within the next seven days it would be assumed that consent was withheld. The *f* instructions to commence proceedings were not countermanded and nothing further was heard from Ron Grundy's solicitors within seven days from 16 January, ie before the close of business on 23 January. In all the circumstances and bearing in mind the hostile state of play between the parties at that time, I think that those seven days were a reasonable period for Ron Grundy to consider the matter and to give or refuse its approval. The facts of the case are broadly *g* comparable with those of *Lewis & Allenby (1909) Ltd v Pegge* [1914] 1 Ch 782, on which Mr Quenby, for the Boneheyos, relied.

For these reasons I am of the opinion that Ron Grundy's approval was impliedly refused. The 1976 agreement was lawfully assigned to Miss Boneheyo by the assignment of 24 January 1991. In *Ron Grundy (Melbourne) Ltd v Boneheyo* I would therefore dismiss the appeal.
h

STOCKER LJ. I agree.

BELDAM LJ. I also agree.

Appeal in Omar Parks Ltd v Elkington allowed. Appeals in Ron Grundy (Melbourne) Ltd *j* *v Valerie Boneheyo and Ron Grundy (Melbourne) Ltd v Clive Boneheyo dismissed. Leave to appeal to the House of Lords refused.*

Raina Levy   Barrister.

a South Yorkshire Transport Ltd and another v Monopolies and Mergers Commission and another

HOUSE OF LORDS

b LORD TEMPLEMAN, LORD GOFF OF CHIEVELEY, LORD LOWRY, LORD MUSTILL AND LORD SLYNN OF HADLEY

23 NOVEMBER, 16 DECEMBER 1992

Monopolies and mergers – Reference to Monopolies and Mergers Commission – Merger affecting substantial part of United Kingdom – Substantial part of United Kingdom –
c *Merger of local bus undertakings – Reference area being 1·65% of United Kingdom and containing 3·2% population – Whether reference area 'a substantial part of the United Kingdom' – Whether commission having jurisdiction to hear reference – Fair Trading Act 1973, s 64(1)(a)(3).*

d The first respondent, a public transport company providing local passenger bus services in and around the South Yorkshire area, acquired, with the authority of the second respondent, the local transport authority, certain other bus undertakings which operated local services in the same area. The Secretary of State for Trade and Industry referred the acquisitions to the Monopolies and Mergers Commission under s 64(1)(a)ᵃ of the Fair Trading Act 1973, which empowered the Secretary of
e State to make a reference to the commission where it appeared to him that two or more enterprises had ceased to be distinct enterprises and that as a result, inter alia, the supply of over 25% of services of any description 'in a substantial part of the United Kingdom' would be carried on by one person within s 64(3). The reference area was 1·65% of the total area of the United Kingdom and contained 3·2% of the population of the United Kingdom as a whole. The commission
f concluded that the reference area was a substantial part of the United Kingdom and reported that a merger situation qualifying for investigation had been created by the acquisitions and that the merger could be expected to operate against the public interest. The Secretary of State accepted the commission's conclusions and recommendations. The respondents applied for judicial review of the commission's decision and the Secretary of State's acceptance of it. The judge granted the
g applications and quashed the decision, declaring that the commission had acted without jurisdiction because it had misdirected itself by interpreting 'substantial' as meaning 'more than de minimis' whereas it should have drawn a comparison between the United Kingdom as a whole and the reference area as to surface extent, population and the relevant economic activity. The Court of Appeal
h affirmed the decision and the commission and the Secretary of State appealed to the House of Lords.

Held – In the context of s 64(3) of the 1973 Act the reference to 'a substantial part of the United Kingdom' was enabling and not restrictive, its purpose being simply to entitle the Secretary of State to refer to the commission mergers whose effect
j was not nationwide and to ensure that the expensive, laborious and time-consuming mechanism of a merger reference was not set in motion if the effort was not worth while. Accordingly, although the commission should take into account, inter alia, the relative proportion of the area in question by comparison with the United Kingdom as a whole as regards surface area, population and

---

a Section 64, so far as material, is set out at p 292 *c* to *g*, post

economic activities, the appropriate criterion when reaching a conclusion on
jurisdiction was whether the reference area was of such a size, character and *a*
importance as to make it worthy of consideration for the purposes of the 1973
Act. Since the commission's conclusion was within the permissible field of
judgment the appeal would be allowed and it's decision upheld (see p 291 *a* to *c*,
p 295 *c d* and p 296 *d h* to p 297 *a f* to p 298 *a f g*, post).

Per curiam. When interpreting an enabling provision designed to confer on
the Monopolies and Mergers Commission the power to investigate mergers *b*
believed to be against the public interest the court should lean against an
interpretation which would give the commission jurisdiction over references
with respect to the provision of services locally in only a small minority of cases,
particularly in the context of local bus services, where the provision of adequate
services is a matter of importance to the public (see p 291 *a* to *c*, p 297 *d e* and *c*
p 298 *g*, post).

Decision of the Court of Appeal sub nom *R v Monopolies and Mergers Commission,
ex p South Yorkshire Transport Ltd* [1992] 1 All ER 257 reversed.

Notes

For merger references, see 47 *Halsbury's Laws* (4th edn) para 89. *d*
 For the Fair Trading Act 1973, s 64, see 47 *Halsbury's Statutes* (4th edn) 177.

Cases referred to in opinions

Edwards (Inspector of Taxes) v Bairstow [1955] 3 All ER 48, [1956] AC 14, [1955] 3
 WLR 410, HL.
Palser v Grinling, Property Holding Co Ltd v Mischeff [1948] 1 All ER 1, [1948] AC *e*
 291, HL.

Appeal

The Monopolies and Mergers Commission and the Secretary of State for Trade
and Industry appealed with the leave of the Appeal Committee of the House of *f*
Lords given on 2 March 1992 from the decision of the Court of Appeal (Lord
Donaldson MR and Butler-Sloss LJ (Nourse LJ dissenting)) ([1992] 1 All ER 257,
[1992] 1 WLR 291) on 28 November 1991 dismissing the appellants' appeal from
the judgment and order of Otton J hearing the Crown Office list on 22 March
1991 whereby he (i) granted the application of the respondents, South Yorkshire
Transport Ltd and the South Yorkshire Passenger Transport Authority, for judicial *g*
review of the commission's decision dated 3 July 1990 published in its report
dated 1 August 1990 (Cm 1166) that in respect of bus services in the county of
Yorkshire, the districts of Bolsover, Chesterfield, Derbyshire Dales, High Peak
and North-East Derbyshire in the county of Derbyshire and in the district of
Bassetlaw in the county of Nottingham merger situations qualifying for
investigation pursuant to s 64(1)(a) and (3) of the Fair Trading Act 1973 had been *h*
created between the first respondent and Sheffield and District Transport Co Ltd,
Michael Groves, Sheafline (PSV) Ltd and SUT Ltd, (ii) quashed the commission's
decision and (iii) declared that the decision and the acceptance of it by the
Secretary of State were unlawful and of no effect. The facts are set out in the
opinion of Lord Mustill.
 j

Michael Beloff QC and *A W H Charles* (instructed by the *Treasury Solicitor*) for the
 appellants.
David Pannick QC and *Mark Shaw* (instructed by *Simpson Curtis*, Leeds) for the
 respondents.

Their Lordships took time for consideration.

a 16 December 1992. The following opinions were delivered.

LORD TEMPLEMAN. My Lords, I have had the advantage of reading in draft the speech of my noble and learned friend Lord Mustill. I agree with it and, for the reasons given by him, I, too, would allow the appeal.

b **LORD GOFF OF CHIEVELEY.** My Lords, I have had the advantage of reading in draft the speech prepared by my noble and learned friend Lord Mustill. I agree with it and, for the reasons given by my noble and learned friend, I, too, would allow this appeal.

c **LORD LOWRY.** My Lords, I have had the advantage of reading in draft the speech of my noble and learned friend Lord Mustill. I agree with it and, for the reasons given by my noble and learned friend, I, too, would allow this appeal.

LORD MUSTILL. My Lords, on 22 March 1990 the Secretary of State for Trade *d* and Industry referred to the Monopolies and Mergers Commission for investigation and report the acquisition by the present respondents, South Yorkshire Transport Co Ltd, of certain companies operating local bus services in South Yorkshire and in parts of Derbyshire and Nottinghamshire. Upon the reference the commission had two distinct tasks. First, to decide whether the 'merger situation', as it is known, was one which satisfied the criteria for *e* investigation established by s 64(3) of the Fair Trading Act 1973. If it did not, the commission had no jurisdiction to proceed. The commission decided that the criteria were satisfied, and went on to investigate the merger. On 1 August 1990 the commission published its report, to the effect that the merger might be expected to operate against the public interest, and that the most effective means to restore competition would be to require the respondents to divest themselves *f* of the assets and businesses acquired. On the same day the Secretary of State announced that he had accepted the conclusions and recommendation of the report.

The respondents disagreed with the commission on both issues, but recognised that the conclusions and recommendations on the question of public interest were not open to effective challenge in the courts. They did, however, contest by *g* judicial review the finding of the commission, crucial to its jurisdiction, that the geographical area by reference to which the existence of a merger situation had to be ascertained (the reference area) was a 'substantial part' of the United Kingdom, within the meaning of s 64(3) of the 1973 Act. The application for judicial review was heard by Otton J, who in a valuable and comprehensive judgment held that *h* the respondents' challenge was well founded, that the commission had acted without jurisdiction and that accordingly the conclusions and recommendations in the report, and the decision of the Secretary of State to accept them, were unlawful and of no effect. The commission appealed to the Court of Appeal, which by a majority (Lord Donaldson MR and Butler-Sloss LJ (Nourse LJ dissenting)) dismissed the appeal (see [1992] 1 All ER 257, [1992] 1 WLR 291). *j* The commission appeals to your Lordships' House.

I must now set out the relevant parts of the legislation, and describe the reference area to which the legislation must be applied.

First, the legislation. The crucial sections of the 1973 Act are as follows:

'**9.** *Monopoly situation limited to part of United Kingdom:*—(1) For the purposes of a monopoly reference, other than a reference relating to exports of goods from the United Kingdom, the person or persons making the reference may, if it appears to him or them to be appropriate in the circumstances to do so, determine that consideration shall be limited to a part of the United Kingdom.

(2) Where such a determination is made, then for the purposes of that monopoly reference the provisions of sections 6 and 7 of this Act, or such of those provisions as are applicable for those purposes, shall have effect as if, wherever those provisions refer to the United Kingdom, they referred to that part of the United Kingdom to which, in accordance with that determination, consideration is to be limited.

(3) The preceding provisions of this section shall have effect subject to subsection (4) of section 50 of this Act in cases to which that subsection applies.

64. *Merger situation qualifying for investigation.*—(1) A merger reference may be made to the commission by the Secretary of State where it appears to him that it is or may be the fact that two or more enterprises (in this section referred to as "the relevant enterprises"), of which one at least was carried on in the United Kingdom or by or under the control of a body corporate incorporated in the United Kingdom, have, at a time or in circumstances falling within subsection (4) of this section, ceased to be distinct enterprises, and that either—(a) as a result, the condition specified in subsection (2) or in subsection (3) of this section prevails, or does so to a greater extent, with respect to the supply of goods or services of any description, or (b) the value of the assets taken over exceeds £30 million.

(2) The condition referred to in subsection (1)(a) of this section, in relation to the supply of goods of any description, is that at least one-quarter of all the goods of that description which are supplied in the United Kingdom, or in a substantial part of the United Kingdom, either—(a) are supplied by one and the same person or are supplied to one and the same person, or (b) are supplied by the persons by whom the relevant enterprises (so far as they continue to be carried on) are carried on, or are supplied to those persons.

(3) The condition referred to in subsection (1)(a) of this section, in relation to the supply of services of any description, is that the supply of services of that description in the United Kingdom, or in a substantial part of the United Kingdom, is, to the extent of at least one-quarter, either—(a) supply by one and the same person, or supply for one and the same person, or (b) supply by the persons by whom the relevant enterprises (so far as they continue to be carried on) are carried on, or supply for those persons . . .'

Next, there is the reference area. This was delineated by the Secretary of State, when he referred the matter to the commission, as:

'The county of South Yorkshire, the districts of Bolsover, Chesterfield, Derbyshire Dales, High Peak and North East Derbyshire in the county of Derby and the district of Bassetlaw in the county of Nottingham.'

This description in terms of local government boundaries lacks colour. It is easier to visualise the reference area as lying roughly between the Leeds/Bradford conurbation to the north, Lincolnshire to the east, Derby/Nottingham to the south and Greater Manchester to the north-west. More exactly, the spine of the area, some 45 miles long at its greatest extent, runs from just north of Derby through Matlock, and then continues through Chesterfield, Sheffield and Barnsley to a point a few miles south of the line joining Huddersfield, Wakefield and Pontefract. To the west the area encompasses the Derbyshire Dales and the Peak

District. On the eastern side of the spine there are found at the northern end the
a industrial areas of Doncaster and Rotherham. Further south a space of more open
country extends to within about ten miles of Lincoln. The total surface area is
rather more than 1,500 square miles. About 1·8m people live there. These figures
represent 1·65% and 3·2% of the totals for the United Kingdom as a whole.

I now turn to the decision under review. This was not the first occasion on
which the commission had occasion to consider the meaning of s 64(3) of the
b 1973 Act. In March 1989 the commission published its report (Cm 595 (1989)) in
another reference concerning local bus services, where a similar challenge to the
jurisdiction was made. The company concerned was Badgerline Holdings Ltd.
Since the reasoning which led the commission to reject the challenge was adopted
by the differently constituted group responsible for the report in the present case,
it is necessary to see how the commission arrived at its conclusion. The discussion
c in Ch 2 of the Badgerline report is too long to set out in full, but in summary it
was as follows. First, the commission correctly stated that the words 'a substantial
part of the United Kingdom' had to be considered in their statutory context, and
continued:

d '2.2 We had therefore to consider whether a merger situation qualifying
for investigation had been created. This involved deciding whether there
was a supply of the reference services (local bus services) in the United
Kingdom or a substantial part of the United Kingdom.

2.3 The relevant area for the supply of bus services in what is described in
the reference as the "specified area" (shown in the maps at Appendix 2.1), is
e defined as "the County of Avon together with all parts of the Counties of
Somerset and Wiltshire and of the County of Gloucester east of the River
Severn which lie within 15 miles of the County of Avon". If this area
constitutes a "substantial part of the United Kingdom" for the purposes of
the Act we are required to consider whether the market share test, as
described in paragraph 2.1 is in other respects fulfilled.'

f The commission went on to describe the various quantitative and qualitative
features of the area in question which it considered relevant and concluded:

'2.9 Thus although the specified area's population and land area represent
relatively small proportions of the figures for the United Kingdom, in a
number of respects the area plays an important part in the economic
g development and growth, and cultural life of the country. Taking all these
factors into consideration, we found that the specified area played a significant
part in the overall life of the United Kingdom and could not be regarded as
not substantial. We therefore concluded that the area was of sufficient
importance to the United Kingdom (considered as a geographical and
h economic unit) to be properly and correctly described as "a substantial part of
the United Kingdom" for the purpose of section 64(3) of the Act.'

A similar approach was adopted by the commission when, 17 months later, it
published the report now under review (Cm 1166 (1990)). The following are the
material paragraphs of Ch 2:

j '2.5 We further consider that the phrase additionally involves both a
quantitative and a qualitative assessment. In considering what quantitative
and qualitative elements should be taken into account for this purpose, we
had regard to the size of the reference area, its population; its social, political,
economic, financial and geographic significance; and whether it had any

particular characteristics that might render the area special or significant. These featured too in the previous reports and no additional relevant elements *a* have occurred to us.

2.6 As to the quantitative elements relating to the reference area, it is roughly 1·65 per cent of the total area, and has a population of some 1·8 million, or 3·2 per cent of the total population of the United Kingdom.

2.7 In considering the elements that give the reference area its particular characteristics, we noted that the area includes Sheffield, the third largest *b* metropolitan district in England on the basis of population, one of the great cities of the United Kingdom, and the towns of Barnsley, Doncaster, Rotherham and Chesterfield. As well as traditional industries based on mining and steel, the area also had a range of other manufacturing and service activities, significant academic and sports facilities, and parts of the *c* Peak District favoured for recreation.

2.8 Having taken into consideration the various factors, general and specific, mentioned previously and having done so in the context of the United Kingdom as a whole, we conclude that the area may be properly and correctly described as "a substantial part of the United Kingdom", for the purpose of section 64(3) of the Act.' *d*

In the High Court Otton J reached a different conclusion. After an extensive review of the authorities, in which he clearly demonstrated that the word 'substantial' is (as he aptly put it) like a chameleon, taking its colour from its environment, he concluded that 'substantial' in this context was not to be equated with something greater than merely nominal, and that the right approach was to *e* draw a contrast between the United Kingdom as a whole and the reference area, as regards the surface extent, the population and the relevant economic activity, here measured in terms of kilometres travelled by passenger buses. Inspecting the reasons given by the commission for assuming jurisdiction the learned judge found that it had misdirected itself by adopting the interpretation of substantial as meaning 'more than de minimis', which he had himself rejected. He went on *f* to hold that if the commission had applied the approach which he considered right the answer would inevitably have been that the reference area was not a substantial part of the United Kingdom.

In the Court of Appeal the majority of the court adopted a standpoint which, although rather differently expressed, was broadly the same as that of Otton J. By contrast, Nourse LJ held that the amount necessary to satisfy the test of *g* substantiality depends on the purpose of the Act in which the word is found; it is a variable, whose meaning expands or contracts so far as to give effect to that purpose. Nourse LJ saw no a priori reason for interpreting 'a substantial part' in s 64(3) as meaning a big or large part of the United Kingdom; it means 'a considerable part, that is a part of such dimensions as to make it worthy of consideration for the purpose of the Act' (see [1992] 1 All ER 257 at 265, [1992] *h* 1 WLR 291 at 301). The percentages might not for other purposes be regarded as being substantial but in his opinion it was worthy of consideration for the purposes of the 1973 Act.

Arriving now at the present appeal I believe that the interpretation of s 64(3) must proceed by two stages. First, a general appreciation of what 'substantial' *j* means in its present context. Second, a consideration of the elements to be taken into account when deciding whether the requirements of the word, so understood, are satisfied in the individual case.

Approaching the first stage as a matter of common language no recourse need be made to dictionaries to establish that 'substantial' accommodates a wide range

of meanings. At one extreme there is 'not trifling'. At the other, there is 'nearly
a complete', as where someone says that he is in substantial agreement with what
has just been said. In between, there exist many shades of meaning, drawing
colour from their context. That the protean nature of the word has been reflected
in the decided cases is, I believe, made quite clear by the judgment of Otton J, in
which the authorities are so thoroughly discussed as to make it unnecessary to go
through them again. It is sufficient to say that although I do not accept that
b 'substantial' can never mean 'more than de minimis', or that in *Palser v Grinling,
Property Holding Co Ltd v Mischeff* [1948] 1 All ER 1 at 11, [1948] AC 291 at 317
Viscount Simon was saying more than that in the particular statutory context it
did not have this meaning, I am satisfied that in s 64(3) the word does indeed lie
further up the spectrum than that. To say how far up is another matter. The
c courts have repeatedly warned against the dangers of taking an inherently
imprecise word, and by redefining it thrusting on it a spurious degree of precision.
I will try to avoid such an error. Nevertheless I am glad to adopt, as a means of
giving a general indication of where the meaning of the word in s 64(3) lies
within the range of possible meanings, the expression of Nourse LJ ([1992] 1 All
ER 257 at 265, [1992] 1 WLR 291 at 301): 'worthy of consideration for the
d purpose of the Act.' I will later return to another aspect of the definition suggested
by Nourse LJ.

Thus far, therefore, I accept the respondents' submission that if the commission
proceeded when examining its jurisdiction on the basis that it was enough for the
reference area to be more than trifling this was a radical misconception. At first
sight it appears that this gives them a powerful case, for we find in the report that
e the commission calls up the idea of 'something more than merely nominal'. If
this expression truly reflects the basis of the decision there is reason for the court
to interfere. Whilst acknowledging the force of this argument, I have come to
the conclusion that it gives too little weight to the reasoning of the commission
as a whole, and to the examination of the facts which the commission deemed
necessary in both the instant reference and in the Badgerline case.
f
I begin with the latter, since the report in Badgerline was the point at which
the commission started to analyse its jurisdiction in the present case. It is
interesting to note that the commission in Badgerline adopted a turn of phrase
not to be found in the report on the present reference, namely (in para 2.9) 'could
not be regarded as not substantial'. If the respondents are right, this expression
g would have been the symptom of an even more explicit misdirection than in the
present case. Yet when we look at the discussion of jurisdiction as a whole it can
be seen that the perspective is much wider. I will quote the paragraph again:

> '2.9. Thus although the specified area's population and land area represent
> relatively small proportions of the figures for the United Kingdom, in a
h > number of respects the area plays an important part in the economic
> development and growth, and cultural life of the country. Taking all these
> factors into consideration, we found that the specified area played a significant
> part in the overall life of the United Kingdom and could not be regarded as
> not substantial. We therefore concluded that the area was of sufficient
> importance to the United Kingdom (considered as a geographical and
j > economic unit) to be properly and correctly described as "a substantial part of
> the United Kingdom" for the purpose of section 64(3) of the Act.'

As I read it this passage embodies an analysis much wider than the consideration
simply of whether the reference area was larger than de minimis; and the
discussion in the remainder of Ch 2 bears this out, for it would have been quite

redundant if the commission had been applying the de minimus test and nothing else, for this could have yielded only one answer. Then, when one comes to study *a* the reasons given in the present case, which plainly intended to proceed on the same basis as in Badgerline, we find the commission equating 'substantial' with 'something real or important'; and although this is linked to the expression 'something merely nominal' by the expression 'as distinct from', I believe that this is employed as meaning 'that is to say not . . .' and does not indicate that the two turns of phrase are the opposite sides of the same coin.   *b*

Beyond this, linguistic analysis is of little help. I prefer to look at what else the commission has to say. In para 2.4 the report adopts the respondents' contention that the area is 'important and substantive in relation to a larger whole'. In para 2.5 it is said that the phrase involves both a quantitative and qualitative element. The commission then continues by marshalling the facts which it considers relevant, including the 'social, political, economic, financial and geographic *c* significance' of the reference area. I cannot see why the commission should have taken all this trouble to examine the area's characteristics if it had thought that the simple test, admitting of only one answer, was whether the area was trivial.

Accordingly, although I appreciate the reasons why in the courts below it was held that the commission had entirely misunderstood the content of the words 'a *d* substantial part', I have come to the conclusion that the report does not disclose this fundamental mistake. There remains however the question whether, even if the commission had placed the test in broadly the right part of the spectrum of possible meanings it nevertheless failed to apply the test correctly. Here, the contest is between three methods of approach: (1) an arithmetical proportion should be struck between the reference area of the United Kingdom as a whole, *e* as regards surface area, population and volume of the economic activity with which the reference is concerned. If the proportion(s) are too low, the area does not qualify; (2) an assessment in absolute terms of the size and importance of the area, independent of proportions; (3) a mixture of the two kinds of criteria.

The respondents contend for the first, proportionate, approach. At one stage of the passage of this case through the courts they placed the weight of their *f* arguments on the collocation of 'a substantial part' with 'of the United Kingdom'. On this view, one should look at the United Kingdom as a geographical feature of the map, and see how much of the map is occupied by the reference area. At other stages more significance was attached to the proportion which the economic activity in question (here, the operation of local bus services) in the reference area *g* bore to the United Kingdom as a whole. Throughout, however, the respondents relied on the fact that whatever comparison one chose to make the proportion was too low.

My Lords, although I agree that the relationship of the part to the whole is not to be ignored, I am unable to accept that proportionality is the beginning and end of the matter. As regards geographical extent the reference to a substantial part *h* of the United Kingdom is enabling, not restrictive. Its purpose is simply to entitle the Secretary of State to refer to the commission mergers whose effect is not nationwide. Like the asset-value criterion of s 64(1)(b), the epithet 'substantial' is there to ensure that the expensive, laborious and time-consuming mechanism of a merger reference is not set in motion if the effort is not worthwhile. The reference area is thus enabled to be something less than the whole. But I cannot *j* see why its relationship to the whole is the only measure of the commission's jurisdiction. Nor does the contrast with s 9, which omits the word 'substantial', yield any other result. As Nourse LJ pointed out, the introduction of this new jurisdiction for monopoly references in 1973 cannot have been intended to alter

the meaning of an expression which had been in use since 1948. It may be that
a ss 9 and 64 involve different tests. The question is not for decision here. What
does seem to me clear is that there is no cut-off point fixed by reference to
geography and arithmetic alone.

I have reached the same conclusion as regards the argument which came to the
forefront of the respondents' case in this House, namely that the decisive factor
consists of a comparison between the number of bus-miles run by the services
b under investigation and those in the country as a whole. I find this interpretation
very hard to square with the words 'part of the United Kingdom' which are surely
intended to relate to the area itself, and not (at any rate primarily) to the market
share of the area. Furthermore, the suggested criterion would produce odd
practical results, for a sparsely populated area of great extent would automatically
fail the test if poorly served by buses. Whereas, by contrast, a tiny area such as
c Inner London which would fail the respondents' test of geographical proportionality would easily qualify if bus mileage were the criterion. Moreover, as was
pointed out in argument, since local bus services are by their nature both limited
in their field of operation and in total mileage run, it is hard to see how on an
uncritical application of an arithmetical test they could ever qualify for
d investigation under the 1973 Act. It seems to me that where the task is to
interpret an enabling provision, designed to confer on the commission the power
to investigate mergers believed to be against the public interest the court should
lean against an interpretation which would give the commission jurisdiction over
references of the present kind in only a small minority of cases. This is the more
so in the particular context of local bus services, since the provision of adequate
e services is a matter of importance to the public, as witness the need felt by
Parliament to make special provision for them in the Transport Act 1985.

Accordingly, although I readily accept that the commission can, and indeed
should, take into account the relative proportions of the area by comparison with
the United Kingdom as a whole, as regards surface area, population, economic
activities and (it may be) in some cases other factors as well, when reaching a
f conclusion on jurisdiction, neither each of them on its own, nor all of them
together, can lead directly to the answer. The parties could reasonably expect that
since the test for which the respondents contend has been rejected another would
be proposed in its place. I am reluctant to go far in this direction because it would
substitute non-statutory words for the words of the Act which the commission is
obliged to apply, and partly because it is impossible to frame a definition which
g would not unduly fetter the judgment of the commission in some future situation
not now foreseen. Nevertheless I believe that, subject to one qualification, it will
be helpful to indorse the formulation of Nourse LJ already mentioned, as a general
guide: namely that the reference area must be of such dimensions as to make it
worthy of consideration for the purposes of the 1973 Act. The qualification is
h that the word 'dimensions' might be thought to limit the inquiry to matters of
geography. Accordingly I would prefer to state that the part must be 'of such size,
character and importance as to make it worth consideration for the purposes of
the Act'. To this question an inquiry into proportionality will often be material
but it will not lead directly to a conclusion.

Applying this test to the present case one will ask first whether any misdirection
j is established, and, secondly, whether the decision can be overturned on the facts.
As to the first, it is quite clear that the approach of the commission was in general
accord with what I would propose. It is true that matters such as academic and
sports activities, mentioned by the commission, are of marginal importance at
the most, but I do not regard their inclusion in the list of features to which the

commission paid regard as vitiating an appreciation of 'substantive' which was broadly correct. On the second question the parties are at odds as to the proper *a* function of the courts. The respondents say that the two stages of the commission's inquiry involved wholly different tasks. Once the commission reached the stage of deciding on public interest and remedies it was exercising a broad judgment whose outcome could be overturned only on the ground of irrationality. The question of jurisdiction, by contrast, is a hard-edged question. There is no room for legitimate disagreement. Either the commission had jurisdiction or it had *b* not. The fact that it is quite hard to discover the meaning of s 64(3) makes no difference. It does have a correct meaning, and one meaning alone; and once this is ascertained a correct application of it to the facts of the case will always yield the same answer. If the commission has reached a different answer it is wrong, and the court can and must intervene. *c*

I agree with this argument in part, but only in part. Once the criterion for a judgment has been properly understood, the fact that it was formerly part of a range of possible criteria from which it was difficult to choose and on which opinions might legitimately differ becomes a matter of history. The judgment now proceeds unequivocally on the basis of the criterion as ascertained. So far, no room for controversy. But this clear-cut approach cannot be applied to every case, *d* for the criterion so established may itself be so imprecise that different decision-makers, each acting rationally, might reach differing conclusions when applying it to the facts of a given case. In such a case the court is entitled to substitute its own opinion for that of the person to whom the decision has been entrusted only if the decision is so aberrant that it cannot be classed as rational: *Edwards (Inspector of Taxes) v Bairstow* [1955] 3 All ER 48, [1956] AC 14. The present is such a case. *e* Even after eliminating inappropriate senses of 'substantial' one is still left with a meaning broad enough to call for the exercise of judgment rather than an exact quantitative measurement. Approaching the matter in this light I am quite satisfied that there is no ground for interference by the court, since the conclusion at which the commission arrived was well within the permissible field of judgment. Indeed I would go further, and say that in my opinion it was right. *f*

I would accordingly allow the appeal, and restore the decision of the commissioners and the Secretary of State.

LORD SLYNN OF HADLEY. My Lords, I have had the advantage of reading in draft the speech prepared by my noble and learned friend Lord Mustill. I agree *g* that, for the reasons he gives, the appeal should be allowed.

Appeal allowed.

Mary Rose Plummer   Barrister.

a # Warwickshire County Council v Johnson

HOUSE OF LORDS

LORD GRIFFITHS, LORD EMSLIE, LORD ROSKILL, LORD ACKNER AND LORD LOWRY

9 NOVEMBER, 10 DECEMBER 1992

b *Consumer protection – Misleading price indication – Indication given by person 'in the course of any business of his' – Any business of his – Branch manager of retail electrical goods shop displaying notice outside shop offering to beat price of any television, hi-fi and video offered for sale elsewhere in area by £20 on the spot – Manager later refusing to sell television set to customer at reduced price – Whether notice misleading as to price – Whether failure to honour offer rendering notice misleading – Whether manager acting*
c *'in the course of any business of his' – Whether manager liable for offence of giving customer misleading indication as to price – Consumer Protection Act 1987, s 20(1)(2)(a).*

The appellant was employed as the branch manager of a retail electrical goods shop. With the authority of the owners he placed a free-standing notice outside the shop stating 'We will beat any TV HiFi and Video price by £20 on the spot'.
d While the notice was displayed a customer saw a television set offered for sale elsewhere in the area at a price of £159·95. He took the appellant to see the set and then sought to purchase an identical set at the appellant's shop for £139·95 but although the appellant had one in stock he refused to sell it at the reduced price. The customer reported the matter to the respondent council's trading
e standards department, which preferred an information against the appellant under s 20(1)[a] of the Consumer Protection Act 1987 alleging that the appellant had 'in the course of a business of his' given to the customer a misleading indication by means of the notice as to the price at which the television set was offered, in that it was not £20 less than the price at which it was offered by another shop in the area. The justices held that the appellant was acting 'in the
f course of a business of his' within s 20(2)(a) of the 1987 Act in displaying the notice outside the shop but dismissed the information on the ground that it was not misleading. The council appealed to the Divisional Court, which allowed the appeal on the ground that the notice was misleading because the appellant had refused to honour its terms and that in doing so he was acting 'in the course of a business of his' since his business was to manage the branch irrespective of the
g fact that he had no business of his own. The appellant appealed to the House of Lords, where the issues were (i) whether a notice which was not misleading on its face could subsequently become misleading by a refusal to honour its terms and (ii) whether for the purposes of s 20(2)(a) the words 'in the course of a business of his' could include an employee.

h **Held** – (1) The notice was a continuing offer and therefore whether it was misleading or not could only be tested by somebody taking up the offer. Accordingly, since the appellant had refused to honour the terms of the notice by beating 'any TV HiFi, Video price by £20 on the spot' the notice was a misleading indication as to the price at which the goods were offered, contrary to s 20(1) of
j the 1987 Act (see p 300 j to p 301 a, p 302 g to j and p 306 c d, post).

    (2) However, the words 'in the course of any business of his' in s 20(2)(a) of the 1987 Act meant any business of which the defendant was either the owner or in which he had a controlling interest, since the 1987 Act was directed against

---

a   Section 20, so far as material, is set out at p 303 *c d*, post

employers, i e the corporate body standing behind the misleading price indication, rather than the individual employees. Accordingly, since the appellant was only *a* the manager of the shop he was not guilty of the offence charged and the appeal would therefore be allowed (see p 300 *j* to p 301 *a*, p 304 *h j* and p 305 *j* to p 306 *d*, post).

Notes

b

For the offence of giving a misleading price indication, see 48 *Halsbury's Laws* (4th edn) para 301.

For the Consumer Protection Act 1987, s 20, see 39 *Halsbury's Statutes* (4th edn) 214.

c

Case referred to in opinions

Pepper (Inspector of Taxes) v Hart [1993] 1 All ER 42, [1992] 3 WLR 1032, HL.

Appeal

d

Neil Kirk Johnson appealed with leave of the Appeal Committee of the House of Lords given on 13 July 1992 from the decision of the Divisional Court of the Queen's Bench Division (Stuart-Smith LJ and Popplewell J) (156 JP 577) on 2 April 1992 allowing the appeal of the respondents, Warwickshire County Council, by way of case stated by justices for the county of Warwickshire in respect of their adjudication as a magistrates' court sitting at Stratford-upon-Avon on 27 April *e* 1990 whereby they dismissed an information preferred by an assistant county standards officer of the county trading standards department acting for and on behalf of the council against the appellant that he on 29 May 1989 at 30 High Street, Stratford-upon-Avon gave, in the course of a business of his, to Graham Rodney Thomas an indication by means of a notice stating 'We will beat any TV, *f* Hi-Fi and Video price by £20 on the spot' which was misleading as to the price at which a JVC remote control television was offered in that the price was not £20 less than the price at which it was offered by another person in Stratford-upon-Avon, contrary to 20(1) of the Consumer Protection Act 1987. The Divisional Court certified pursuant to s 1(2) of the Administration of Justice Act 1960 that two points of law of general public importance (set out at p 301 *j* to p 302 *b*, post) *g* were involved in the decision to allow the appeal but refused leave to appeal to the House of Lords. The facts are set in the opinion of Lord Roskill.

Frederick Philpott and *Claire Andrews* (instructed by *Edge & Ellison*, Birmingham) for the appellant.
Maurice Kay QC and *David Sanderson* (instructed by *D G Carter*, Warwick) for the *h* respondents.

Their Lordships took time for consideration.

10 December 1992. The following judgments were delivered. *j*

LORD GRIFFITHS. My Lords, I have had the advantage of reading in draft the speech of my noble and learned friend Lord Roskill. I agree with him and for the reasons which he gives I would allow the appeal and make the order which he proposes.

LORD EMSLIE. My Lords, I have had the advantage of reading in draft the
a speech of my noble and learned friend Lord Roskill. I agree with him and for the
reasons which he gives I would allow the appeal and make the order which he
proposes.

LORD ROSKILL. My Lords, on 24 November 1989 Warwickshire County
b Council (the respondents) as the prosecuting authority laid an information against
the appellant in respect of an offence allegedly committed against s 20(1) of the
Consumer Protection Act 1987 on 29 May 1989. The appellant was on that date
the manager of the Stratford-upon-Avon branch of Dixons Stores Group Ltd
(Dixons). The wording of the information is of some importance and I set it out
in full, emphasising the most crucial words:

c   'Neil Kirk Johnson gave, *in the course of a business of his,* to Graham Rodney
Thomas an indication by means of a notice stating "We will beat any TV HiFi
and Video price by £20 on the spot" which was misleading as to the price at
which a JVC remote control television was offered in that the price was not
£20 less than the price at which it was offered by another person in Stratford-
d upon-Avon contrary to Section 20(1) of the Consumer Protection Act, 1987.'

The essential facts are not in dispute. The appellant with the authority of
Dixons had placed outside the shop a notice in the terms set out in the information.
On 29 May while the notice was still displayed Mr Thomas saw a TV set of the
particular kind in question offered for sale elsewhere in Stratford-upon-Avon at a
price of £159·95. Mr Thomas then went to Dixons and was told that Dixons had
e an identical set in stock. Mr Thomas thereupon took the appellant to see the set
on sale elsewhere for £159·95. But when Mr Thomas sought to purchase the set
at Dixons for £139·95 the appellant refused to sell it, apparently asserting that he
was within his rights in refusing to sell the set at the reduced price. Mr Thomas
reported the matter to the respondents' trading standards department. Later,
f when he was interviewed by an officer of that department, the appellant frankly
agreed that he had been wrong but said he had acted in the heat of the moment
when he was under pressure. These proceedings then followed.

The information came before the justices at Stratford-upon-Avon on 27 April
1990. They dismissed the information. They reached the conclusion that the
notice was not misleading but they also held that the appellant 'was . . . acting in
g the course of a business of his'. The respondents understandably applied to the
justices for a case to be stated. After considerable delay the case was signed on 23
November 1990. The appeal came on for hearing in the Divisional Court on
2 April 1992. That court (Stuart-Smith LJ and Popplewell J) allowed the appeal
for the reasons given in the judgment of Popplewell J (see 156 JP 577). They held
that the notice was misleading because the appellant refused to honour the terms
h of the notice in that he refused to 'beat any TV HiFi or Video price by £20 on the
spot'. They also held, contrary to the appellant's submission on the second issue,
that in failing to honour the notice the appellant was acting 'in the course of any
business of his', interpreting that phrase as meaning 'in the course of his business,
trade or profession'. The Divisional Court dealt with the question of sentence by
j granting the appellant an absolute discharge upon payment by him of the costs
of the appeal to the Divisional Court.

The appellant invited the Divisional Court to certify two points of law of
general public importance. The Divisional Court certified these two questions:

     '1. Whether for the purposes of section 20(1) of the Consumer Protection
Act 1987 a statement, which in itself is not misleading on the face of it, can

be rendered misleading by virtue of the fact that, even in the absence of
evidence to show a general practice or intention to dishonour the offer *a*
contained therein, on one occasion the person making the statement declined
to enter into a contract within the terms of the statement.

2. Whether for the purpose of section 20(2)(*a*) of the Consumer Protection
Act 1987 an employed branch manager who fails to comply with a price
indication so that the same is to be regarded as misleading does so "in the *b*
course of any business of his".'

In addition to the two issues so certified the appellant in his printed case raised
a third issue not raised—it could not be so raised—in the Divisional Court. Before
the hearing of this appeal, your Lordships' House had heard the further
submissions in *Pepper (Inspector of Taxes) v Hart* [1993] 1 All ER 42, [1992] 3 *c*
WLR 1032 but had not at that time given judgment. The appellant invited your
Lordships in seeking to resolve the second issue to look at what was said in your
Lordships' House on 12 March 1987 (485 HL Official Report (5th Series) col
1140ff) by the minister concerned, Lord Beaverbrook, at the report stage of the
then Consumer Protection Bill when replying to an amendment moved by Lord
Morton of Shuna. Lord Morton was supported on this occasion by Lord Denning. *d*
It was said that, if your Lordships when considering the second issue found the
language of s 20(1) and (2)(*a*) ambiguous, the ambiguity should be resolved in
favour of the appellant by reason of what was then said by the minister as to the
clear intention of these subsections.

My Lords, your Lordships' House has now given judgment in *Pepper (Inspector
of Taxes) v Hart*. It has thus become proper in the strictly limited circumstances *e*
defined by Lord Browne-Wilkinson in his speech, with which the majority of
their Lordships who heard that appeal agreed, to have regard to what was said in
Parliament in the course of the passage of the Bill. I should mention for the sake
of completeness that your Lordships were assured that when the Bill was passed
through the later stages in your Lordships' House and also when it reached *f*
another place there was no further reference at any stage to this issue. But before
considering this matter further I shall first consider the two questions of
construction.

As to the first question, it was strenuously argued that because the notice was
not misleading on its face it could not subsequently become misleading by a
refusal to honour its terms. It was said that it never ceased to be a genuine offer. *g*
Overcharging could not of itself convert that notice, itself not misleading, into a
notice which was misleading. Counsel for the appellant frankly admitted that
Mr Thomas was misled. I ask: by what was Mr Thomas misled? There can only
be one answer. Mr Thomas was misled by the notice. I find myself in complete
agreement with the reasoning of the Divisional Court on this issue (156 JP 577 at
580): *h*

> 'The notice is a continuing offer and whether it is misleading or not can
> only be tested by somebody taking up the offer. It was misleading because
> [the appellant] did not in accordance with the terms of the notice beat any
> t.v., hi-fi, video price by £20 on the spot.' *j*

To hold otherwise would be seriously to restrict the efficacy of this part of the
consumer protection legislation. Seemingly innocent notices could be put up and
then when such notices were followed by a refusal to honour them by a person
acting in the course of his business no offence would be committed. I would
therefore answer the first certified question Yes.

The second certified question is more difficult. At first sight the answer given
a by the Divisional Court has the appeal of simplicity and common sense. The
appellant's business was to manage Dixons branch at Stratford-upon-Avon. His
refusal arose in the course of that business. Hence he is guilty of the offence
charged. It does not matter that he had no business of his own.

The Divisional Court was referred to a number of cases, some in the last
century, all decisions upon the construction of other statutes and upon very
b different facts. The second certified question must be answered by reference to
this statute (the Consumer Protection Act 1987) and to what can be deduced from
its language in the various relevant sections. For ease of reference I shall set out
the relevant parts of those sections to which your Lordships were referred:

c
'**20.**—(1) Subject to the following provisions of this Part, a person shall be
guilty of an offence if, in the course of any business of his, he gives (by any
means whatever) to any consumers an indication which is misleading as to
the price at which any goods, services, accommodation or facilities are
available (whether generally or from particular persons).

(2) Subject as aforesaid, a person shall be guilty of an offence if—(*a*) in the
d course of any business of his, he has given an indication to any consumers
which, after it was given, has become misleading as mentioned in subsection
(1) above . . .

39.—(1) Subject to the following provisions of this section, in proceedings
against any person for an offence to which this section applies it shall be a
defence for that person to show that he took all reasonable steps and exercised
e all due diligence to avoid committing the offence . . .

(5) This section shall apply to an offence under section . . . 20(1) above.

40.—(1) Where the commission by any person of an offence to which
section 39 above applies is due to an act or default committed by some other
person in the course of any business of his, the other person shall be guilty of
the offence and may be proceeded against and punished by virtue of this
f subsection whether or not proceedings are taken against the first-mentioned
person . . .

45.—(1) In this Act, except in so far as the context otherwise requires . . .
"business" includes a trade or profession and the activities of a professional or
trade association or of a local authority or other public authority . . .'

g
During the argument it was suggested that some support for the respondents'
construction of s 20(1) might be found in s 40(1). It was suggested that the words
'in the course of any business of his' might be read not as referring to the
immediately preceding words 'some other person' but to the earlier phrase,
namely the person who has committed 'an offence to which section 39 above
h applies'. But there are a number of difficulties in the way of this suggested
construction. First, it involves construing these words otherwise than in the order
in which they appear in the subsection. Secondly, the somewhat opaque drafting
of s 40(1) involves the incorporation via s 39(5) of the language of s 20(1) into the
opening words of the subsection. This involves treating the phrase 'in the course
of any business of his' as also appearing in the opening words of s 40(1). This
j seems to me to make it impossible to relate those same words when they appear
later in the subsection as applying to the 'person' mentioned in the opening
words. Thirdly and apart from these difficulties, as my noble and learned friend
Lord Ackner pointed out during the argument, the appellant was charged with
an offence against s 20(1) and not with an offence against s 40(1).

The obscurity of this language has puzzled commentators, to whom it has

seemed odd that when a misleading notice or advertisement is published the
person responsible for refusing to honour the advertisement, if an employee and
not the owner of the business in question, is not guilty of an offence against
s 20(1). In commenting upon the decision of the Divisional Court in the present
case Professor J C Smith wrote in discussing the phase 'any business of his' ([1992]
Crim LR 644 at 464–647):

> 'The inconvenience of holding that the offence can be committed only by
> the owner of the business is obvious but what did the draftsman mean by
> this emphatic and inelegant phrase if he did not mean any business belonging
> to the defendant? Perhaps the answer to the difficulty is to be found in
> section 40(1) [he then set out the text of s 40(1) and continued:] There is an
> ambiguity here. Does "any business of his" refer to a business of "any person"
> or of "some other person"? If the latter, we are no farther forward; but, if the
> former, there is no difficulty about convicting the employee. This assumes
> that the employer is guilty of the offence as well—*i.e.* that the offence is one
> imposing strict and vicarious liability.'

Professor Smith thus highlights the problem of construction but does not
resolve it. I have already indicated the impossibility of construing these words
out of their natural order and the effect of the incorporation of s 20(1) into s 40(1).

Counsel also drew attention to the commentary in O'Keefe *Law Relating to
Trade Descriptions* Div 2, para 3081. After setting out the differences between the
position under s 23 of the Trade Descriptions Act 1968 and this legislation, the
author suggests that the latter legislation is more restrictive than the former and
continues:

> 'The main difference between the Trade Descriptions Act 1968, s 23 and
> the 1987 Act, s 40(1) is that the latter contains a pre-requisite to any
> prosecution. This is that the commission of the [misleading price offence
> under s 20(1)] offence must have been committed by the other person "in the
> course of any business of his". Section 45 defines "business" as including "a
> trade or profession . . ." It is therefore submitted that an employee whose act
> or default results in the commission by his or her employer of an offence
> contemplated by s 39 *cannot be* prosecuted as the actual offender under s 40(1),
> though this proposition remains to be tested by a court of record. If this
> conclusion is a correct interpretation of s 40(1) it is quite a startling conclusion
> compared with previous practice under the now repealed price offences
> contained in the 1968 Act.' (O'Keefe's emphasis.)

It clearly appeared strange to these learned commentators, as indeed it appeared
to some of your Lordships during the argument, that the person actually
responsible for what happened, as the appellant clearly was, should be immune
from conviction. But study of these various sections and the changes between the
Trade Descriptions Act 1968 and this legislation has led me to conclude that the
words 'in the course of any business of his' must mean any business of which the
defendant is either the owner or in which he has a controlling interest. Not
without some reluctance I find myself unable to share the view taken by the
Divisional Court. I would therefore answer the second certified question No.

I have, in respectful agreement with Professor Smith, criticised the drafting of
these sections and I share his particular criticism of the drafting of s 40(1). As
already stated it is now, within the limitations already mentioned, permissible to
have regard to statements by a minister in Parliament in order to ascertain the
true intention of ambiguous legislation the interpretation of which has become a
matter of controversy.

As already stated at the report stage of the Bill which became the Consumer

a Protection Act 1987, Lord Morton of Shuna moved an amendment to cl 20(1) of the Bill, as it then was, to delete the words 'of his'. He said (485 HL Official Report (5th series) col 1140):

'The words "of his" appear to be quite unnecessary and unnecessarily restrictive. What is to be the position of somebody who is giving a misleading

b price indication in the course of his employer's business, possibly unauthorised by his employer? Is that employee who is acting against instructions to be safe from prosecution? That is the way it reads. There does not appear to be a necessity for the words "of his". The sense would remain if it is just "in the course of any business", which would restrict the subsection to a business use,

c so to speak, but allow the prosecution of somebody who might say, Well, it was not my business. I was acting for somebody else when I gave the misleading price.'

Lord Denning added: 'The words "of his" are not only unnecessary but misleading.'

In reply the minister, Lord Beaverbrook, said (cols 1142–1143):

d

'On the main point of this amendment as set out by the noble Lord, Lord Morton, it is a general principle of law that employers are largely responsible for the actions of their employees. I believe that it is especially right that this principle should apply in the case of misleading price indications. Policy on price indications in an individual store is rarely in the hands of individual

e employees, but it is more often a matter of centrally determined company policy. It is for the employer to ensure that his procedures and staff training are adequate and appropriate to prevent misleading price indications being given to consumers. I therefore think it is right so to draft the Bill that proceedings are directed against employers—that is the corporate body standing behind the misleading price indication—rather than individual

f employees. Accordingly we have included the words "of his" in the Bill to ensure that individual employees will not be prosecuted. It is of course for employers to institute systems and staff training to ensure that their employees do not give misleading price indications. If, in spite of all these precautions, a rogue employee nevertheless gives a misleading price

g indication, then the defence of due diligence, as set out in Clause 39, is likely to be available to his employer. But I have to say that I see little point in prosecuting individual employees in these circumstances.'

At the end of the short debate the minister said (col 1143):

h '. . . I think that we would like to look at this again carefully to see whether something has been missed and whether it can be looked at further.'

Lord Morton of Shuna then withdrew his amendment. As already stated the matter was never raised again.

In my view the answers given by the minister are consistent with the construction I have felt obliged to put upon this legislation. Although the minister

j said that the government would look into the matter again there are no further references to this issue at any later stage of the progress of the Bill through Parliament. The adoption of the contrary construction would be to reach a conclusion contrary to the plain intention of Parliament simply because the draftsman has used language which on one view has failed to give effect to that intention. On the second certified question I must therefore respectfully differ

from the Divisional Court. I would answer it No. It follows that the appeal must
be allowed and the conviction set aside.

a

As to costs, the respondents were well justifed in prosecuting the appellant for
without doubt it was he who was solely responsible for that which occurred and
which made the notice misleading. Moreover, the issue on which the appellant
has succeeded is one of general importance both to prosecuting authorities and to
questions of consumer protection. If your Lordships agree I would order the costs
of both the appellant and the respondents to be defrayed from central funds.

b

LORD ACKNER. My Lords, I have had the advantage of reading in draft the
speech of my noble and learned friend Lord Roskill. I agree with it and for the
reasons which he has given I too would allow the appeal and make the order
which he proposes.

c

LORD LOWRY. My Lords, I have had the advantage of reading in draft the
speech of my noble and learned friend Lord Roskill.

I agree with it and for the reasons which he has given I too would allow the
appeal and make the order which he proposes.

d

Appeal allowed.

Mary Rose Plummer   Barrister.

London and Blenheim Estates Ltd v Ladbroke Retail Parks Ltd

CHANCERY DIVISION

JUDGE PAUL BAKER QC SITTING AS A JUDGE OF THE HIGH COURT

5, 6 MARCH, 10 APRIL 1992

Easement – Creation – Dominant and servient tenements – Need for both dominant and servient tenement to exist in separate ownership before easement can exist – Grant of future easement – Future servient tenement transferred before dominant tenement acquired – Whether dominant owner could exercise right of grant of easement against successors in title to servient tenement.

Easement – Right to park cars – Whether capable of being an easement.

On 27 August 1987 the then registered owner (the transferor) with title absolute of a parcel of land transferred part of the land to the plaintiff for £915,200 together with a right of way over, and the right to park cars on, that part of the land retained by the transferor which had been set aside as a car park for the benefit of customers, clients or employees of retail shops and businesses on the retained land. Under cl 11 of the transfer 'the transferred land' included other land which was capable of benefiting from the rights granted provided notice was given to the transferor within five years that such land was to be included in the transferred land and that at the date of the notice the plaintiff or a subsidiary or associated company of it was still the owner of the transferred land. On 18 December 1987 the plaintiff contracted to purchase two parcels of leasehold land adjoining the retained land. The contract was completed on 10 February 1989 but in the meantime on 2 February 1988 the transferor transferred the registered ownership of the retained land to a third party, which some months later transferred the retained land to the defendants. On 1 March 1988 the plaintiff gave notice under cl 11 requiring the adjoining leasehold land which it had contracted to purchase to be included in the transferred land so that the leasehold land could have the benefit of the easements contained in the transfer of 27 August 1987. The defendant stated that the rights did not amount to interests in land and were not binding on successors in title to the transferor. The plaintiff sought a declaration that that land could have the benefit of the easements contained in the transfer of 27 August 1987, and the defendant counterclaimed for a declaration that no right to park on the retained land existed in favour of the additional land. The issues arose (i) whether a right to park could exist as a valid easement, (ii) whether the owner of the servient tenement could terminate or modify the rights under an easement by changing the use of the land, (iii) whether the rights contained in cl 11 of the transfer of 27 August 1987 could be exercised in relation to leasehold land as well as freehold land and (iv) whether the power under cl 11 to add land to benefit from the rights under the transfer could be exercised so as to bind successors in title to the transferor.

Held – Clause 11 of the transfer of 27 August 1987 was not a contract or an option but was in terms a grant of a power which did not create any interest in land unless and until it was exercised. In particular, it did not create an immediate interest in the retained land. Furthermore, an easement could not exist unless and until there was both a dominant and a servient tenement in separate ownership, and since the potential servient tenement had been transferred before

the dominant tenement had been acquired no easement could be created, with
the result that the power under cl 11 to add land to benefit from the rights under *a*
the transfer could not be exercised so as to bind successors in title to the transferor.
It followed that the plaintiff's claim failed and would be dismissed (see p 311 *j*,
p 312 *f g* and p 313 *j* to p 314 *a*, post).

Per curiam. (1) Rights contained in the grant of an easement can be exercised
in relation to leasehold land as well as freehold land (see p 314 *b c*, post).

(2) A right to park cars can amount to an easement. Furthermore, it would not *b*
be a valid objection to the existence of such an easement that charges are made,
whether for the parking itself or the general upkeep of the park (see p 316 *g h* and
p 317 *b c*, post).

(3) A servient owner can terminate or modify the rights under an easement by
changing the use of the servient land (see p 316 *j*, post). *c*

Notes

For the creation, conveyance and extinction of easements, see 14 *Halsbury's Laws*
(4th edn) paras 45–130, and for cases on the subject, see 19 *Digest* (Reissue) 26–
110, 184–743.

d

Cases referred to in judgment

A-G of Southern Nigeria v John Holt & Co (Liverpool) Ltd [1915] AC 599, [1914–15]
All ER Rep 444, PC.
Bilkus v Redbridge London Borough (1968) 207 EG 803.
Copeland v Greenhalf [1952] 1 All ER 809, [1952] Ch 488.
Cable v Bryant [1908] 1 Ch 259, [1904–7] All ER Rep 937. *e*
Dunn v Blackdown Properties Ltd [1961] 2 All ER 62, [1961] Ch 433, [1961] 2 WLR
618.
Dyce v Lady Hay (1852) 1 Macq 305, HL.
Gas and Fuel Corp of Victoria v Barba [1976] VR 755, Vict SC.
Johnstone v Holdway [1963] 1 All ER 432, [1963] 1 QB 601, [1963] 2 WLR 147,
CA. *f*
Keefe v Amor [1964] 2 All ER 517, [1965] 1 QB 334, [1964] 3 WLR 183, CA.
Le Strange v Pettefar (1939) 161 LT 300.
Newman v Jones (22 March 1982, unreported), Ch D.
Penn v Wilkins [1966] CA Transcript 36.
Prichard v Briggs [1980] 1 All ER 294, [1980] Ch 338, [1979] 3 WLR 147, CA.
Shannon Ltd v Venner Ltd [1965] 1 All ER 590, [1965] Ch 682, [1965] 2 WLR 718, *g*
CA.
Thomas v Rose [1968] 3 All ER 765, [1968] 1 WLR 1797.
Thorpe v Brumfitt (1873) LR 8 Ch App 650, LJJ.
Turley v Mackay [1943] 2 All ER 1, [1944] Ch 37.
Wright v Macadam [1949] 2 All ER 565, [1949] 2 KB 744, CA. *h*

Cases also cited

Haslemere Estates Ltd v Baker [1982] 3 All ER 525, [1982] 1 WLR 1109.
London and South Western Rly Co v Gomm (1882) 20 Ch D 562, Ch D and CA.

Action and counterclaim *j*

By a writ dated 23 July 1990 and statement of claim served on 1 August 1990 the
plaintiff, London and Blenheim Estates Ltd, sought a declaration that they and
their successors in title as proprietors of certain leasehold properties in Leicester
were entitled to the benefit of the rights specified in the first schedule to a transfer
dated 27 August 1987 made between Leicestershire Co-operative Society Ltd and

the plaintiffs (then known as G Harris Developments Ltd) over land described
a therein as 'the retained land'. The defendant, Ladbroke Retail Parks Ltd,
counterclaimed for declarations (1) that there existed no right to park on the
retained land in favour of certain land known as 'the additional land' or (2)
alternatively, that if any right to park affected the retained land the same was
exercisable only upon such part thereof as was from time to time set aside as a car
park for the benefit of customers, clients or employees of any retail shop or other
b business conducted on the retained land or for the benefit of members of the
public. The facts are set out in the judgement.

Sir William Goodhart QC and *Catherine O'Riordan* (instructed by *Marron Dodds &
Waite*, Leicester) for the plaintiff.
c *Gavin Lightman QC* and *Michael Briggs* (instructed by *Titmuss Sainer & Webb*) for
the defendant.

Cur adv vult

d 10 April 1992. The following judgment was delivered.

JUDGE PAUL BAKER QC. In this action the plaintiff seeks a declaration that
it and its successors in title as proprietors of some leasehold land in Leicester are
entitled to the benefit of easements and other rights specified in the first schedule
to a transfer of 27 August 1987 between the Leicestershire Co-operative Society
Ltd and the plaintiff, then known as G Harris Developments Ltd. The facts are
e brief and not in dispute, but they have given rise to questions of construction and
law of some difficulty and novelty.

Before 27 August 1987 the Leicestershire Co-operative Society Ltd was the
registered proprietor with title absolute of a substantial piece of land alongside
the railway in Leicester. On that date the society transferred somewhere between
f a third and a half of it to the plaintiff. The material parts of the transfer are as
follows. The first clause is the normal transfer clause, which I should read:

'1. In consideration of £915,200 the receipt whereof is hereby acknowledged Leicestershire Co-operative Society Limited . . . transfers to G. Harris
Developments Limited . . . the land shown edged red on the accompanying
plan ("the Transferred land") being part of the land comprised in the title
g above referred to together with the easements and other rights specified in
the First Schedule hereto but except and reserving the easements and other
rights specified in the Second Schedule hereto.'

I am only concerned in this case with the first schedule, which contains the rights
granted to the transferee. It is a long schedule of some 11 paragraphs, but I think
h I only need read four of them. The first one is:

'A right of way (in common with the transferor and all other persons who
may have a like right) for the Transferee its servants or agents and all other
persons authorised by it with or without vehicles at all times and for all
purposes in connection with the use of the transferred land over a roadway
j and adjacent footway intended to be constructed on the part of the land
comprised in the title above referred to retained by the Transferor ("the
retained land") [then it specifies where it is to go from and to and concludes:]
and prior to the construction of the abovementioned roadway and footway a
right of way with or without vehicles for all purposes in connection with the
use of the transferred land over [a particular part of the retained land].'

I think I can go from there to para 7. The intervening paragraphs deal with matters such as drainage and rights of entry in regard to those matters. Paragraph *a* 7 reads:

'When the Transferor's development has been completed or otherwise as may be agreed by the Transferor a right for customers clients or employees of any retail shop or other business conducted on the transferred land to park (if space is available) on any part of the retained land set aside as a car park for *b* the benefit of customers clients or employees of any retail shop or other business conducted on the retained land or for the benefit of members of the public on the like terms (as to charges and conditions of use) as are imposed upon such last-mentioned customers clients or employees but subject to the Transferee paying a reasonable share of the costs of maintaining such car park and any adjoining landscaped areas.' *c*

Then I go to para 10:

'(a) The rights of entry granted by paragraphs 2 and 4 above shall be exercisable only for the period of twenty years from the date hereof

(b) The rights granted by paragraphs 1, 3, 5, 6 and 7 above shall apply only to roadways footways and car parks constructed within twenty years *d* from the date hereto [then it deals with drains, sewers and similar constructions].'

That of course was a clause inserted to ensure compliance with the rule against perpetuities. I should perhaps conclude with para 10(c):

e

'The perpetuity period applicable to this Schedule shall be the period of twenty-one years from the date hereof.'

Now I come to what is perhaps the most important paragraph in this schedule:

'11. In this Schedule the expression "the transferred land" shall include any other land if (a) such land is capable of being benefited by the rights *f* hereby granted (b) notice is given to the Transferor within five years from the date hereof that such land is to be included in the transferred land for the purposes of this Schedule (c) at the date of such notice the original Transferee (or some other company which is a subsidiary holding or associated company of the Transferee) is the registered proprietor of or has contracted to purchase such land.' *g*

As I have mentioned paras 7 and 11 are the most important for the purposes of this case. Paragraph 7 has given rise to two of the issues before me, whether a right to park can exist as a valid easement, and whether the servient owner can terminate or modify the right by changing the use of the retained land.

On 18 December 1987 the plaintiffs contracted to purchase two adjoining *h* parcels of registered leasehold land bordering on the retained land and which it is admitted are capable of being benefited by the rights granted by the transfer. A third issue is whether the right conferred by para 11 can be exercised in relation to leasehold as opposed to freehold land.

On 2 February 1988 Wortley Developments Ltd became the registered proprietor of the retained land in succession to the co-operative society. On 1 *j* March 1988 the plaintiffs gave notice under para 11(b) requiring the leasehold land which they had contracted to purchase to be included in the transferred land and to enjoy the rights set out in the first schedule to the transfer of 27 August 1987. Later in that year, 1988, Wortley Developments Ltd transferred the retained land to the defendants.

On 10 February 1989 the contract for the sale of the leasehold land to the
plaintiffs was completed. The title was later registered at HM Land Registry. By
October 1990 a substantial car park had been laid out on the retained land.

The fourth and final issue is whether the power given by para 11 to add land to
benefit from the scheduled rights can be exercised so as to bind successors in title
of the retained land. This is by far the most difficult issue in the case. I shall take
it first. I shall then deal with the issue whether the rights can in any event be
annexed to leasehold as opposed to freehold land and then come to consider
whether a right to park can exist as an easement and if so whether it exists only so
long as the servient land can be used as a car park.

I accordingly start with para 11. It is common ground that para 11 did not
amount to an immediate grant of easements for the benefit of the newly acquired
leaseholds. For such easements to exist and bind the successors in title of the
retained land there has to be a dominant tenement, which would not occur until
all three conditions listed in the clause had been satisfied. By the time they were
satisfied the potential servient tenement had already been transferred to and
registered in the name of a third party. Accordingly, says Mr Lightman QC for
the defendants, at the time of the transfer to Wortley there was no interest in land
which could be enforced against them.

The submission of Sir William Goodhart QC for the plaintiffs, in support of the
claim that the rights became annexed to the newly acquired land, is that even
though para 11 does not create an immediate equitable easement, it creates a
registrable estate contract. If that were wrong, then, he says, as soon as the
plaintiffs contracted to purchase the leasehold land, which occurred before the
transfer to Wortley, para 11 had the effect of creating a simple option to aquire an
easement on giving notice under sub-para (b) of it. In support of this I was taken
through *Pritchard v Briggs* [1980] 1 All ER 294, [1980] Ch 338, where the nature
of rights of pre-emption and options is considered. The former, that is rights of
pre-emption, do not create an interest in land, at least until activated by the
potential vendor placing the land on the market; the latter create an immediate
interest inasmuch as the potential vendor has committed himself to conveying
the land at the will of the option holder. In so far as that is relevant, I would agree
that para 11 has the characteristic of an option rather than a right of first refusal.
The servient owner retained no control over the operation of para 11. I would
also agree that any such right has been sufficiently registered: see the Land
Registration Act 1925, s 52.

I was further referred to *Turley v Mackay* [1943] 2 All ER 1, [1944] Ch 37 and
Thomas v Rose [1968] 3 All ER 765, [1968] 1 WLR 1797, both cases of contracts
relating to land which contained terms upon which discussion arose whether they
were estate contracts for the purposes of the Land Charges Act 1925 (now the
Land Charges Act 1972). In other words, were they contracts to convey or create
a legal estate or were they contracts relating to land in other ways?

My difficulty with the submission on behalf of the plaintiff is a much more
fundamental one than trying to classify what type of contract para 11 amounts
to. In my judgment para 11 is not a contract at all. It is a term in a grant. A
conveyance or transfer of land is a grant by the vendor, normally though not
necessarily in performance of a pre-existing contract. It is not in itself a contract.
Being under seal it could not be revoked by the grantor though it could be
rejected by the grantee. Further, it may, as the transfer in this case does, contain
in addition covenants or other contractual terms.

By cl 1 of the transfer of 27 August 1987 the transferor transfers certain land
together with the easements and other rights specified in the first schedule. If the
conditions are satisfied, nothing further remains to be done. There is no

completion as occurs when an option is exercised. The real question as I see it is whether para 11 created an immediate interest in the retained land, albeit it was both future and contingent, or was it merely a power not creating any interest in land unless and until exercised? The resolution of this question requires a closer look at both the term in the grant and the nature of an interest in land.

The term in the grant (para 11) is expressed very elliptically. It purports to extend the definition of the transferred land in the schedule though not in cl 1 of the transfer, where the transferred land is defined as the specific parcel of land actually being transferred. The newly acquired land does not and cannot become part of the original transferred land for all purposes. Any set of easements applicable to it will be separate from the easements applicable to the original transferred land. To spell out the new grant in full would require some formulation such as:

> 'The transferor hereby also grants to the transferee owners and occupiers of land capable of benefiting from the rights specified in the First Schedule which the grantee shall hereafter acquire and in respect of which notice requiring this grant to apply shall have been served the easements and other rights specified in the First Schedule.'

Such a grant would in time ripen into a present grant of easements upon fulfilment of the conditions. That would be clear enough if the grantor still retained the land over which the easements were to be exercised. But what if, as in the present case, he had disposed of it before the conditions were satisfied? For this one has to look more closely at the nature of an interest in land.

The problem, as I see it, is that that broad concept 'interest in land' embraces two quite separate concepts. The first is that an easement is itself an interest in land. In the older terminology it was an incorporeal hereditament, separate from but, as it were, parasitic upon the land itself. Secondly, the expression 'interest in land' can refer to the estate in the hereditament whether corporeal or incorporeal conferred on the grantee. An easement cannot exist as an incorporeal hereditament unless and until there is both a dominant and a servient tenement in separate ownership. That never occurred in this case. Before the dominant tenement had been acquired as a dominant tenement the servient tenement had been disposed of. That, as it seems to me, is fatal to the creation of the easement.

I was referred to a number of authorities by counsel for the defendants. None covers the precise point arising here. Some of them deal with the question of identifying the dominant tenement where it is not clearly indicated in the grant. Prominent among these is *Johnstone v Holdway* [1963] 1 All ER 432, [1963] 1 QB 601 and the Australian case of *Gas and Fuel Corp of Victoria v Barba* [1976] VR 755. In the latter case Crockett J in the Supreme Court of Victoria stated the position (at 764):

> 'Next, it was argued that failure to specify the dominant tenement in the instrument is not necessarily fatal as extrinsic evidence is admissible to identify the tenement so as to establish appurtenancy. Reliance is placed upon two comparatively recent decisions of the Court of Appeal—*Johnstone v. Holdway* ([1963] 1 All ER 432, [1963] 1 QB 601) and *The Shannon Ltd. v. Venner Ltd.* ([1965] 1 All ER 590, [1965] Ch 682). In *Johnstone's Case* the conveyance contained a reservation of a right of way in favour of the plaintiff's predecessor in title. But the reservation did not specify the dominant tenement for the benefit of which the right of way was given. Upjohn, L.J. in giving the Court's judgment said ([1963] 1 All ER 432 at

435–436, [1963] 1 QB 601 at 612), "In our judgment it is a question of the construction of the deed creating a right of way as to what is the dominant tenement for the benefit of which the right of way is granted and to which the right of way is appurtenant. In construing the deed the court is entitled to have evidence of all material facts at the time of the execution of the deed, so as to place the court in the situation of the parties." That evidence allowed the court to say that it was intended that there was land for the benefit of which the easement was reserved and what that land was. In *The Shannon Ltd. v. Venner Ltd.*, the Court not only agreed that extrinsic evidence was admissible to prove both the intention that there should be, and the identity of, a dominant tenement but also held that the easement may, when the dominant tenement is not specified in the grant, be appurtenant to other land besides that conveyed by the deed. In both of these cases the court reached the conclusions it did by purporting to apply *Thorpe v. Brumfitt* ((1873) LR 8 Ch App 650).

In this case the grant expressly states that the dominant tenement is not identified until it has been acquired by the grantee and notice given. Extrinsic evidence would be needed to establish that the land so designated was capable of benefiting from the rights granted, but that is not in issue here. Extrinsic evidence could not be admitted merely to identify potential as opposed to actual dominant tenements.

The question whether there can be a future easement is one which may arise after but not before the dominant and servient tenements have been identified as being in the separate ownership of the grantee and grantor respectively. In *Cable v Bryant* [1908] 1 Ch 259, [1904–7] All ER Rep 937 an owner of a yard and a stable conveyed the stable to the plaintiff. The stable had a ventilator opening onto the yard. The yard was held under lease. The lessee subsequently acquired the freehold of the yard and erected a hoarding blocking the ventilator. In response to the plaintiff's action for infringement of the right to air over the yard it was objected that there could be no grant of an easement in reversion. The case was resolved on the point that the defendant, the former lessee, as successor in title to the former lessor could not derogate from the grant. A more obvious case of a future easement would be where developments have to take place on the servient tenement before the easement can be enjoyed. Such a case is exemplified by *Dunn v Blackdown Properties Ltd* [1961] 2 All ER 62, [1961] Ch 433, where a conveyance of land included a right to use the sewers and drains 'hereafter to pass' under a private road adjoining the land conveyed and which belonged to the vendor. It was held that such a grant was a grant of an easement to arise at a future date not limited to take effect within the perpetuity period and was therefore void. Since the Perpetuities and Accumulations Act 1964 it is seldom that grants to take effect in the future will fail on that ground, and even before the Act the rule could be complied with by careful drafting. For myself I would not see any impossibility in a grant to the owner of a dominant tenement to acquire an easement over the servient tenement at some future date. There are examples in this case: for that reason I read para 1 of the schedule. But there must be at the date of the grant what are described as the essentials of an easement, albeit that the estate in the easement is a future estate or interest. In the old terminology, if it did not follow on some prior estate or interest, it would be a springing use. In other cases the estate might be purely reversionary, as where a freehold owner of land subject to a lease grants an easement to take effect on the falling in of the lease. However that may be, in the case before me there was no

dominant tenement at the date of the grant or at the date of the disposal of the
potentially servient land. An estate or interest cannot subsist in a non-existent   *a*
hereditament. That, in my judgment, as I said, is fatal to the plaintiff's case.

On the subsidiary issue, whether the rights could have been annexed to
leasehold land, I would have accepted the submissions on the part of the plaintiff.
I have already indicated that 'the transferred land' in para 11 cannot be equated
with the land transferred by the transfer, so that it does not seem necessarily to
take its character from that land, as the defendants submit. What is required is   *b*
that at the date of the notice the original transferee 'is the registered proprietor of
or has contracted to purchase such land'. Easements can be annexed to leasehold
land; leases of at least 21 years can be registered. It seems to me a fair construction
that the land in this context should include substantial leasehold interests as well
as freehold interests, but exclude short transitory lettings.

My judgment on the first issue is sufficient to dispose of the case, but I should   *c*
go on to consider the remaining issues which have been extensively argued before
me and which relates specifically to the right to use the car park. These are
whether the right to park conferred by para 7 of the first schedule can exist as a
valid easement, and whether the servient owner can terminate or modify the
right by changing the use of the servient land. Sir William Goodhart, arguing for   *d*
the validity of para 7 as an easement, began by taking me through a number of
cases in which a right to park vehicles had been considered. He started, however,
by referring to the well-known dictum of Lord Shaw of Dunfermline, delivering
the advice of the Privy Council in *A-G of Southern Nigeria v John Holt & Co
(Liverpool) Ltd* [1915] AC 599 at 617, [1914–15] All ER Rep 444 at 453 in relation
to a claim to store goods on another's land. Lord Shaw said: *e*

> 'Their Lordships see no reason why upon the first point a right of easement
> should be exclusive of the storage claim. The law must adapt itself to the
> conditions of modern society and trade, and there is nothing in the purposes
> for which the easement is claimed inconsistent in principle with a right of
> easement as such. This principle is of general application, and was so treated   *f*
> in the House of Lords in *Dyce* v. *Hay* ((1852) 1 Macq 305 at 312) by Lord St.
> Leonards L.C., who observed: "The category of servitudes and easements
> must alter and expand with the changes that take place in the circumstances
> of mankind."'

In the event in that case it was held that the defendants were entitled to an   *g*
irrevocable licence to use the land for storage as what was done by them 'was done
by them as in their opinion upon their own lands' and not in the exercise of an
easement. Further, on the point of novelty, there is nothing novel about parking:
carriages and carts have been used for centuries, but the volume of traffic has
immeasurably increased with the coming of motor traffic.

Another case not specifically dealing with parking is the decision of the Court   *h*
of Appeal in *Wright v Macadam* [1949] 2 All ER 565, [1949] 2 KB 744, CA. This
concerned the right of a tenant of an upper flat in a house to use a coal shed in the
garden of the house. The main issue in the case concerned the application of the
Law of Property Act 1925, s 62, but Jenkins LJ said ([1949] 2 All ER 565 at 571–
572, [1949] 2 KB 744 at 752):   *j*

> 'Next, the right was, as I understand it, a right to use the coal-shed in
> question for the purpose of storing such coal as might be required for the
> domestic purposes of the flat. In my judgment, that is a right or easement
> which the law will clearly recognise, and it is a right or easement of a kind

a which could readily be included in a lease or conveyance by the insertion of appropriate words in the parcels.'

This shows that a valid easement can subsist which involves the exclusive occupation of a shed or other piece of the servient tenement.

Wright v Macadam was not cited in *Copeland v Greenhalf* [1952] 1 All ER 809, [1952] Ch 488, which directly concerned the parking of vehicles. The alleged
b servient tenement was a strip of land about 150 feet long running from the road with a width varying between 15 feet and 35 feet. It was wholly occupied with vehicles and agricultural implements save for a gangway allowing access from the road to the land beyond. The defendant was a wheelwright whose premises were on the other side of the road. The vehicles were his or his customers awaiting repair or collection. The plaintiff owned the strip and the land beyond. Upjohn J
c said ([1952] 1 All ER 809 at 812, [1952] Ch 488 at 498):

> '... in my judgment the right claimed here goes wholly outside any normal idea of an easement, that is, a right of the occupier of a dominant tenement over a servient tenement. This claim really amounts to a claim to a joint user of the land by the defendant. Practically he is claiming the whole
> d beneficial user of the strip of land on the south-east side of the track so that he can leave there as many or as few lorries as he likes for any time that he likes and enter on it by himself, his servants and agents, to do repair work. In my judgment, that is not a claim which can be established as an easement.'

It is unfortunate that *Wright v Macadam* was not cited, but it probably would
e not have made any difference. The matter must be one of degree. A small coal shed in a large property is one thing. The exclusive use of a large part of the alleged servient tenement is another. Hence I do not accept the submission that *Copeland v Greenhalf* was wrongly decided.

The next case is *Le Strange v Pettefar* (1939) 161 LT 300. The defendant was the lessee of a seaside bungalow on an estate owned by the plaintiff. The estate
f contained a roadway which passed the bungalow and allowed access to the shore. The defendant was in the habit of parking his car on the roadway, as did a number of other members of the public visiting the foreshore. The defendant's claim that he left his car on the road by virtue of his occupancy of the bungalow was rejected by Luxmoore LJ, sitting as a judge of the Chancery Division. He said (at 301):

> g 'I find it impossible to hold on the evidence before me that any such right as is claimed by the defendant either appertained or was reputed to appertain to his bungalow. The defendant left his car on the metalled surface without any objection by the owner of the soil, not because he was the occupier of a bungalow, but because the owner of the soil did not object to anyone, whether a bungalow owner or a member of the public, so doing.'

h So that claim failed on the facts. It was not that a right to park could never be an easement, but in the particular case the parking was not in right of the occupancy of land.

I now look at two unreported decisions of which I have been shown transcripts. First *Penn v Wilkins* [1966] CA Transcript 36. The plaintiff was the lessee of one of
j a row of cottages. She claimed the right to use a passageway, and a right for those having the right to use the passageway (herself and the occupiers of other cottages) to station their vehicles on a piece of land at the rear of the cottages. She failed to establish any title to the claimed right, whether by express or implied grant or under the Law of Property Act 1925, s 62. The validity as an easement of a right to park was not in issue.

The other unreported case is *Newman v Jones* (22 March 1982), a decision of Megarry V-C. One of the issues was whether the lessees of the flats in a block of 14 flats were entitled to park their cars in the grounds of the block. I need not go further into the facts. The importance of the case for present circumstances resides in the following dicta of Megarry V-C where he said:

'In view of *Wright v Macadam* [1949] 2 All ER 565, [1949] 2 KB 744 (which was not cited in *Copeland v Greenhalf* [1952] 1 All ER 809, [1952] Ch 488) . . . I feel no hesitation in holding that a right for a landowner to park a car anywhere in a defined area nearby is capable of existing as an easement. . . . An easement may take effect subject to the right of others with a like right, without any guarantee that there will be no competition. In any case, I cannot see why the mere risk of there being not enough space for all to park simultaneously should be a reason for denying that any rights at all exist, though doubtless the limited space available confines the right to one car per flat [of course, referring to the particular flats in that case].'

Finally, in this line of authority, I come to *Bilkus v Redbridge London Borough* (1968) 207 EG 803. It is a decision of Buckley J. The plaintiffs, owners of shops and land, sold part of their land to the defendant under the threat of compulsory purchase for development. In the conveyance there was a covenant by the corporation to allow the freeholders their successors, owners and lessees and occupiers of the shops—

'to have general car-parking facilities for the vehicles of persons using the brown land and any building from time to time created thereon upon the land owned by the corporation at the rear of the land coloured green.'

It was objected that the covenant was not framed as an easement and did not take effect as an easement. Buckley J disagreed. He is reported to have said (at 805):

'He [Buckley J] thought that the words "general car-parking facilities" in their context meant unrestricted car-parking facilities which were not to be interfered with by other persons and which were to be available for any kind of vehicles for any length of time, for any kind of purpose on any part of the white land, either at ground level or basement level. Both those levels were parts of the white land. The effect of clause 4 was to confer upon the plaintiffs an easement of that nature. The corporation by the covenant bound themselves for an indefinite period to permit the plaintiffs and their successors in title to have such facilities as had been outlined, and that amounted to the grant of all those facilities as an easement over the white land.'

So that is a clear authority that in some circumstances the right to park cars can amount to an easement.

The grant in the present case is more elaborate. It presupposes that there are and will continue to be retail shops and businesses conducted on the retained or servient land whose customers, clients and employees are provided with parking facilities. If that ceased to be so, either because the shops ceased to exist as such or because their parking facilities were closed down or transferred elsewhere, the right to park annexed to the shops and businesses on the transferred land would also cease to exist. That circumstance indicates to my mind that the right claimed is dependent upon the continued existence of car parking facilities on the servient land. It would be open to the owner of that land to remove the car parking facilities of the shops and businesses on the retained land and thereupon the facilities provided for the transferred land would also cease. The passage in *Keefe v Amor* [1964] 2 All ER 517 at 521, [1965] 1 QB 334 at 347 to which I was

referred, deals with a different point, that the grantee of a right of way cannot
a complain of obstructions in some part of the way so long as his right is not
substantially interfered with. In the present case the right on its true construction
is dependent upon the continued existence of car parking facilities for other
persons. That leaves the main point under this head, whether the right to park
cars can exist at all as an easement. I would not regard it as a valid objection that
charges are made, whether for the parking itself or the general upkeep of the
b park. The essential question is one of degree. If the right granted in relation to
the area over which it is to be exercisable is such that it would leave the servient
owner without any reasonable use of his land whether for parking or anything
else, it could not be an easement, though it might be some larger or different
grant. The rights sought in the present case do not appear to approach anywhere
near that degree of invasion of the servient land. If that is so—and I emphasise
c that I have not gone into the facts—I would regard the right claimed as a valid
easement. However, for the reasons given earlier, the plaintiff's claim fails. I shall
make the declaration sought in para 1 of the counterclaim.

Order accordingly.

d

Hazel Hartman   Barrister.

e # Dale v British Coal Corp

COURT OF APPEAL, CIVIL DIVISION
DILLON, STUART-SMITH AND STEYN LJJ
17 JUNE 1992

f *Court of Appeal – Leave to appeal – Requirement of leave – Interlocutory or final order
or judgment – Order disapplying limitation period – Whether interlocutory or final order
– Whether leave required to appeal from order disapplying limitation period – RSC Ord
59, r 1A(3)(4)(6).*

The plaintiff, an employee of the defendants, suffered an accident at work in 1972
g but no writ was issued against the defendants until 1988. The statement of claim
dated 21 July 1989 specifically sought a direction pursuant to s 33 of the
Limitation Act 1980 that the time limit provisions in s 11 of the 1980 Act should
not apply. On 20 July 1989 the defendants issued a summons to set aside the writ
on the grounds that the action was statute-barred. The district registrar referred
the summons to a High Court judge, who gave leave to proceed and made the
h direction sought that s 11 should not apply. The defendants appealed without
leave on the footing that the judge's order was a final order (for which leave was
not required) within RSC Ord 59, r 1A(3)ᵃ which provided that a judgment or
order 'shall be treated as final if the entire cause or matter would . . . have been
finally determined whichever way the court below had decided the issues before
it'. Under r 1A(4), where the final hearing of a cause was divided into parts a
j judgment or order made at the end of any part was for the purposes of r 1A(3) to
be treated as if it had been made at the end of the complete hearing or trial. The
plaintiff contended that the defendant's appeal was in fact an interlocutory appeal
within Ord 59, r 1A(6) for which leave to appeal was required.

___

a Rule 1A, so far as material, is set out at p 320 *b* to *e h*, post

Held – A judgment or order determining an issue as to the limitation of an action either by giving or refusing a direction disapplying s 11 of the 1980 Act was a *a* final order for the purposes of RSC Ord 59, r 1A(3), regardless of the form of the interlocutory procedure by which the matter was brought before the court since, whatever the form of that procedure, there was a determination of an issue as to the limitation of action which was part of a final judgment or order within r 1A(3) because of the application of r 1A(4). It followed that leave to appeal from such a determination was not required (see p 320 *j* to p 321 *c h*, post). *b*

Notes

For final and interlocutory judgments, see 26 *Halsbury's Laws* (4th edn) paras 504–507, and for cases on the subject, see 30 *Digest* (2nd reissue) 234–249, 2707–2885.

For the Limitation Act 1980, ss 11, 33, see 24 *Halsbury's Statutes* (4th edn) (1989 *c* reissue) 657, 686.

Cases referred to in judgments

Conry v Simpson [1983] 2 All ER 369, CA.
Ladd v Marshall [1954] 3 All ER 745, [1954] 1 WLR 1489, CA.
White v Brunton [1984] 2 All ER 606, [1984] QB 570, [1984] 3 WLR 105, CA. *d*

Cases also cited

Hattan v National Coal Board (1978) Times, 28 October, CA.
Pickles v National Coal Board (intended action) [1968] 2 All ER 598, [1968] 1 WL 997, CA.
Steinway & Sons v Broadhurst-Clegg (1983) Times, 25 February, CA. *e*
Thompson v Brown Construction (Ebbw Vale) Ltd [1981] 2 All ER 296, [1981] 1 WLR 744, HL.

Preliminary issue

By a writ issued on 7 July 1988 and served on 3 July 1989 the plaintiff, Donald Dale, brought an action against the defendant, British Coal Corp, for damages for *f* negligence arising out of an accident suffered by him on 25 June 1972. By his statement of claim the plaintiff sought a direction pursuant to s 33 of the Limitation Act 1980 that the provisions of s 11 of that Act should not apply. The defendants applied to set aside the writ on the grounds of limitation and on 12 September 1989 the district registrar in the Dewsbury district registry made an order transferring the case to the High Court. By an order dated 29 November *g* 1990 Blofeld J exercised his discretionary power under s 33 of the 1980 Act to disapply the primary period of three years' limitation imposed on actions for damages for personal injuries by s 11 of that Act and allowed the plaintiff to proceed with his action against the defendant. The defendants appealed without leave by notice to appeal issued on 14 January 1991. Subsequent to the decision *h* of Blofeld J the plaintiff died and by order dated 13 March 1992 his widow, Colleen Dale, was granted an order to carry on the proceedings. The question whether the defendants required leave to appeal was determined as a preliminary issue. The facts are set out in the judgment of Dillon LJ.

Christopher Holland QC and *Howard Elgot* (instructed by *Whitfield Hallam Goodall*, *j* Dewsbury) for the plaintiff.
Simon Hawkesworth QC and *Robert J Moore* (instructed by *Nabarro Nathanson*, Doncaster) for British Coal.

DILLON LJ. The court now has to decide a preliminary issue which is raised in
a relation to what is presented to the court as a final appeal. The issue is that it is
said for the respondent/plaintiff that the appeal is in truth interlocutory and that
the appellant needs, but has not obtained, leave to appeal. The issue is preliminary
to a further application to be made on behalf of the respondent/plaintiff seeking
to adduce further evidence in relation to the appeal. The question which will
there arise is whether the circumstances fall within the rule in *Ladd v Marshall*
b [1954] 3 All ER 745, [1954] 1 WLR 1489. The nature of the issue is that the
appeal is brought against a decision by Blofeld J of 29 November 1990, whereby
he disapplied s 33 of the Limitation Act 1980 in respect of the plaintiff's claim.
He said that there will be a direction that s 11 of the 1980 Act shall not apply to
the plaintiff's action.
c The action arises out of an accident which the plaintiff suffered at Lofthouse
Colliery near Wakefield in West Yorkshire on 25 June 1972. The writ was not
issued until 7 July 1988. By the statement of claim, though not by the writ, the
plaintiff specifically claimed, ahead of his claim for damages, a direction pursuant
to s 33 of the 1980 Act that the provisions of s 11 should not apply. That was
served on 21 July 1989. On 20 July the defendants, British Coal Corp, issued a
d summons to set aside the writ on the grounds of limitation. That summons came
before the district registrar on 12 September 1989. He made an order, after
hearing the solicitors for the plaintiff and counsel for the defendants, which we
are told was not a consent order, which provided:

> 'This case be referred to and [determined] by a Judge of the High Court as
e to:—(a) Whether the Writ of Summons was issued within the limitation
> period set out in section 11(4)(b) Limitation Act 1980, that is the date of
> knowledge of the person injured. (b) If it be found that the Writ of Summons
> was not issued within the limitation period set out in that subsection, whether
> the Plaintiff should be entitled to an Order under section 33 of the Limitation
> Act 1980, that it would be equitable to allow the action to proceed
f notwithstanding the failure to issue proceedings within the limitation
> period.'

The district registrar gave directions as to the filing of evidence and directed also
that the issues set out be listed for hearing before a judge upon receipt of
certificates of readiness from both parties, incorporating time estimates.
g That then came before Blofeld J and he made the order which I have indicated.
There was then an application by the defendant to the judge for leave to appeal.
There was some discussion about that which seems to have petered out without
leave having been in terms granted or refused. There was no application to this
court for leave to appeal, but the notice of appeal was issued on 14 January 1991,
on the footing that the order of the judge was a final order within RSC Ord 59,
h r 1A. The point is taken for the respondent/plaintiff that that is not so. Reference
was made to a decision of this court in *Conry v Simpson* [1983] 3 All ER 369, where
it appears that, under the old procedure as to leave to appeal, an appeal against the
exercise of powers under s 33 of the 1980 Act to disapply the limitation period
under s 11 had been treated as an interlocutory appeal and leave to appeal had
been duly applied for and granted.
j The matter now turns on RSC Ord 59, r 1A, which was not in the rules at the
time of the decision in *Conry v Simpson*. That was intended to remove the
difficulties which were felt over the problem whether a particular order was final
or interlocutory. These had been troubling the courts on many occasions, as

appears from the decision of this court in *White v Brunton* [1984] 2 All ER 606 and
the various authorities there referred to. RSC Ord 59, r 1A provides by para (1):　　*a*

'For all purposes connected with appeals to the Court of Appeal, a judgment
or order shall be treated as final or interlocutory in accordance with the
following provisions of this rule.'

That is plain and straightforward. Paragraph (2) I can pass over. Paragraph (3)
provides:　　*b*

'A judgment or order shall be treated as final if the entire cause or matter
would (subject only to any possible appeal) have been finally determined
whichever way the court below had decided the issues before it.'

That is plainly intended to reflect what had been referred to as the application
approach as opposed to the order approach in the judgment of Donaldson MR in　　*c*
White v Brunton [1984] 2 All ER 606. It is expanded in para (4) of Ord 59, r 1A:

'For the purposes of paragraph (3), where the final hearing or the trial of a
cause or matter is divided into parts a judgment or order made at the end of
any part shall be treated as if made at the end of the complete hearing or
trial.'　　*d*

Then there is provision that, notwithstanding anything in para (3), certain orders
are to be treated as final, but none of those is relevant for present purposes. In
para (6) the draftsmen of the rules and the Rule Committee have sought to set out
clearly all the most common forms of order which are to be treated as
interlocutory. The paragraph begins by stating:　　*e*

'Notwithstanding anything in paragraph (3), but without prejudice to
paragraph (5), the following judgments and orders shall be treated as
interlocutory . . .'

One then gets very many of them. One, which is a convenient example, is in sub-
para (c):　　*f*

'an order for or relating to the validity, service (including service out of the
jurisdiction) or renewal of a writ or other originating process.'

There can be no question that such an order is indeed interlocutory. The difficulty,
so far as limitation is concerned, is that the relevant sub-paragraph in para (6),
dealing with limitation, refers back to para (3), notwithstanding that the opening　　*g*
words of para (6) say 'Notwithstanding anything in paragraph (3)'. One thus has a
form of circular drafting which is difficult to follow. The relevant sub-paragraph
is (*ff*):

'an order directing or otherwise determining an issue as to limitation of
actions other than as part of a final judgment or order within the meaning of　　*h*
paragraph (3).'

That refers one back to para (3) and necessarily imports para (4) because para (4) is
to apply for the purposes of para (3). By virtue of para (4):

'For the purposes of paragraph (3), where the final hearing or the trial of a　　*j*
cause or matter is divided into parts, a judgment or order made at the end of
any part shall be treated as if made at the end of the complete hearing or
trial.'

That must mean that a judgment which is to be treated as if made at the end of
the complete hearing or trial is part of a final judgment or order within the
meaning of para (3). The effect of the determination on limitation by the judge

in the present case is to determine finally any question of limitation in these
a proceedings. It would have so determined any question of limitation, in fact,
whichever way the judge had decided the issues before him, because if he had
held that the 1980 Act was not to be disapplied under s 33 then the claim would
inevitably have failed.

I cannot see that it makes any distinction whether the determination of the
issue as to limitation of action is made in advance of the trial on the plea in the
b statement of claim for a direction that the provisions of s 11 shall not apply, on an
application by the defendants to strike out or on a direction by way of preliminary
issues, such as the district registrar, taking account of those pleas, has directed in
the present case. In each case there is a determination of an issue as to limitation
of actions which is part of a final judgment or order within the meaning of para
(3) because of para (4). Therefore, it is not to be treated as interlocutory under
c para (6) but is to be treated as final under para (3). It follows that leave to appeal
was not required.

Our attention has been drawn to the note in *The Supreme Court Practice 1991*
vol 1, para 59/1A/19, which is headed 'Limitation'. It is said:

> 'If an issue relating to limitation (including an application to disapply the
d > limitation period) is litigated at some procedural stage antecedent to the final
> trial (*e.g.* on an application to strike out, or an application to amend the
> pleadings, or an application to join a party) the order will be interlocutory
> (r. 1A(6)(*ff*)). If, however, the limitation issue is determined at the final trial
> any order made on the limitation issue will itself be final, by virtue of the
> concluding words of sub-rule (6)(*ff*). The same will be so, even if the
e > limitation point is tried as a preliminary issue or by way of a sub-trial, because
> an order made at the conclusion of any part of a split trial is final within the
> meaning of r. 1A(3) by virtue of r. 1A(4).

I agree with the two final sentences of that note but I have difficulty about the
first sentence, in particular in so far as it refers to an application to strike out. If
f the effect is that an issue is finally determined for the purposes of the action, then
the determination would, it would seem, count as a final judgment or order by
virtue of paras (3) and (4), whatever the procedural basis on which it is brought
before the court. It may be otherwise if the question of limitation is considered,
and the order that is made is an order refusing leave to amend or add a party and
not an order which has anything to do with limitation. I am not sure. But where,
g as here, there is a direction disapplying the 1980 Act, then it must, in my
judgment, rank as final, as equally would an order refusing to disapply the Act,
whatever the form of interlocutory procedure by which the matter had been
brought before the court. I would rule, accordingly, that leave to appeal was not
required.

h **STUART-SMITH LJ.** I agree.

STEYN LJ. I also agree.

Application dismissed.

j On 19 June 1992 the court allowed the defendant's substantive appeal, dismissed
the action and refused leave to appeal to the House of Lords (see *Dale v British Coal
Corp (No 2)* (1992) Times, 2 July). On 9 December 1992 the Appeal Committee
of the House of Lords (Lord Keith of Kinkel, Lord Jauncey of Tullichettle and
Lord Mustill) refused leave to appeal.

Carolyn Toulmin   Barrister.

Stubbings v Webb and another

HOUSE OF LORDS

LORD TEMPLEMAN, LORD BRIDGE OF HARWICH, LORD GRIFFITHS, LORD ACKNER AND LORD SLYNN OF HADLEY

12, 13 OCTOBER, 16 DECEMBER 1992

Limitation of action – Trespass to the person – Period of limitation – Extension – Person under disability – Action alleging indecent assault and rape during childhood – Plaintiff claiming damages for mental illness and psychological disturbance – Plaintiff bringing action more than six years after reaching majority but within three years of knowledge of psychological injury – Whether personal injury claim – Whether claim an action for breach of duty – Whether breach of duty including deliberate assault – Whether claim subject to six-year limitation period – Whether claim statute-barred – Limitation Act 1980, ss 2, 11, 14, 28.

The respondent issued a writ on 18 August 1987, when she was over 30 years old, claiming damages against the appellants, her stepfather and stepbrother, for mental illness and psychological disturbance allegedly caused by the former's sexual and physical abuse of her as a child between the ages of 2 and 14 and rape by the latter when she was aged 12. The respondent's case was that although she knew that she had been raped and persistently sexually abused by the appellants she did not realise she had suffered sufficiently serious injury to justify starting proceedings for damages until September 1984, when she realised that there might be a causal link between her psychiatric problems in adult life and her sexual abuse as a child. Under s 28[a] of the Limitation Act 1980 the primary limitation period of three years prescribed by s 11[b] of that Act in respect of any personal injuries action which could have been brought by the respondent was extended to January 1978, ie three years after the date on which she attained her majority, but then expired. However, the respondent contended, inter alia, that under s 11(4)(b) the primary limitation period did not begin to run until she had the requisite knowledge as defined in s 14[c] of the 1980 Act, which was less than three years before the issue of the writ. The appellants pleaded that the claim was statute-barred under the primary limitation period even as extended under s 28, and applied to have the action dismissed. The master dismissed the action but on appeal by the respondent the judge held that the respondent was entitled to pursue her action as of right under s 14 since she had sued within three years of the date of acquiring knowledge that her injury was attributable to acts of the appellants which were alleged to constitute a breach of duty. The Court of Appeal dismissed an appeal by the appellants who appealed to the House of Lords, contending in particular that s 11 of the 1980 Act did not apply to the respondent's action because it was not an 'action for damages for negligence, nuisance and breach of duty . . . where the damages claimed . . . consist of or include damages in respect of personal injuries' but was an action for tort, namely trespass to the

---

a   Section 28, so far as material, provides:

   '(1) . . . if on the date when any right of action accrued for which a period of limitation is prescribed by this Act, the person to whom it accrued was under a disability, the action may be brought at any time before the expiration of six years from the date when he ceased to be under a disability . . . notwithstanding that the period of limitation has expired . . .

   (6) If the action is one to which section 11 . . . of this Act applies, subsection (1) above shall have effect as if for the words "six years" there were substituted the words "three years" . . .'

b   Section 11, so far as material, is set out at p 327 *d e*, post

c   Section 14, so far as material, is set out at p 327 *g* to *j*, post *a*   person, for which s 2[d] of the 1980 Act prescribed a limitation period of six years from the date on which the cause of action accrued or, by virtue of s 28 in the case of a person under a disability, six years from the date when the disability ceased and that the provisions for the extension or non-application of the primary limitation period in personal injury actions did not apply to claims for damages for intentional trespass to the person.

b   **Held** – The three-year limitation period from the date of the requisite knowledge prescribed by s 11(1) and (4) of the 1980 Act for actions for negligence, nuisance and breach of duty where the damages claimed consisted of or included damages in respect of personal injuries did not apply to a cause of action based on rape or indecent assault because the juxtaposition of 'breach of duty' with 'negligence' and 'nuisance' in s 11(1) carried with it the implication that the breach of duty
c   referred to was a breach of a duty of care not to cause personal injury, rather than breach of an obligation not to infringe any legal right of another person. Accordingly, the respondent's cause of action against the appellants was subject to the six-year limitation period prescribed by s 2 of the 1980 Act for torts rather than the three years prescribed by s 11 and there being no provision in the Act
d   for extending that period the limitation period had expired before the respondent issued her writ. Accordingly, the respondent's action was time-barred and the appeals would therefore be allowed (see p 324 *b c g*, p 328 *d e* and p 329 *h* to p 330 *d*, post).

Decision of the Court of Appeal [1991] 3 All ER 949 reversed.

e   **Notes**

For the time limits for actions in tort, see 28 *Halsbury's Laws* (4th edn) paras 679–692, and for cases on the subject, see 32 *Digest* (Reissue) 485–486, 3728–3736.

For the Limitation Act 1980, ss 2, 11, 14, 28, see 24 *Halsbury's Statutes* (4th edn) (1989 reissue) 650, 657, 661, 677.

f   **Cases referred to in opinions**

Cartledge v E Jopling & Sons Ltd [1963] 1 All ER 341, [1963] AC 758, [1963] 2 WLR 210, HL.

Letang v Cooper [1964] 2 All ER 929, [1965] 1 QB 232, [1964] 3 WLR 573, CA; rvsg [1964] 1 All ER 669, [1964] 2 QB 53, [1964] 2 WLR 642.

g   *Long v Hepworth* [1968] 3 All ER 248, [1968] 1 WLR 1299.

Conjoined appeals

James Francis Webb and Stephen Webb appealed with the leave of the Appeal Committee of the House of Lords given on 20 January and 19 March 1992 respectively from the decision of the Court of Appeal (Sir Nicolas Browne-
h   Wilkinson V-C, Bingham and Nolan LJJ) ([1991] 3 All ER 949, [1992] 1 QB 197) on 27 March 1991 dismissing their appeals from the decision of Potter J given in chambers on 23 February 1990 allowing an appeal by the respondent, Lesley Jacqueline Stubbings, from the order of Master Topley dated 14 December 1989 striking out her action for damages for personal injuries arising out of sexual and physical abuse of the respondent by the appellants between December 1959 and
j   January 1971. The facts are set out in the opinion of Lord Griffiths.

Richard Mawrey QC and *Lawrence West* (instructed by *Sharpe Pritchard*, agents for *Birkett Westhorp & Long*, Colchester) for the first appellant.

---

d   Section 2 provides: 'An action founded on tort shall not be brought after the expiration of six years from the date when the cause of action accrued.'

Kieran Coonan QC and *Roy Warne* (instructed by *Greenwood Page & Ward*,
Colchester) for the second appellant.   *a*
Maurice Kay QC and *Robert Grey* (instructed by *Fisher Jones*, Colchester) for the
respondent.

Their Lordships took time for consideration.

16 December 1992. The following opinions were delivered.   *b*

LORD TEMPLEMAN. My Lords, I have had the advantage of reading in draft
the speech prepared by my noble and learned friend Lord Griffiths. I agree with
it, and for the reasons given, I would allow these appeals.

c

LORD BRIDGE OF HARWICH. My Lords, I have had the advantage of
reading in draft the speech of my noble and learned friend Lord Griffiths. I agree
with it and, for the reasons he gives, I would allow the appeals.

LORD GRIFFITHS. My Lords, the respondent will be 36 years of age on
29 January 1993. The question before your Lordships is whether the law permits   *d*
her to pursue a claim for damages against her adoptive father and stepbrother
based upon allegations that she was sexually abused by the adoptive father
between the ages of 2 and 14 and raped by her stepbrother when she was 12 and
he was 17. It should be made clear that these allegations are denied by both the
father and stepbrother who are the appellants before your Lordships. It would   *e*
obviously be a matter of grave difficulty for any court to determine where truth
lies if this action was to proceed, for it would be investigating events that are
alleged to have occurred in a period starting over 30 years ago and ending over 20
years ago. It is also to be observed that neither the stepfather nor the stepbrother
would appear to have the means to satisfy any significant award of damages.
   A summary of the respondent's allegations and the history of this litigation are   *f*
contained in the judgment of Bingham LJ (see [1991] 3 All ER 949, [1992] 1 QB
197) and the trial judge Potter J. I will not repeat them as a preface to my speech
because I have come to the conclusion that this action became statute-barred in
January 1981 six years after the respondent reached her majority on 29 January
1975 and cannot therefore be allowed to proceed. My conclusion depends upon
the construction of ss 2, 11 and 28 of the Limitation Act 1980, but before turning   *g*
to those sections it is I think helpful to consider the development of the law on
limitation of liability since 1939.
   The Limitation Act 1939 provided by s 2 that actions founded on simple
contract or tort should not be brought after the expiration of six years from the
date on which the cause of action accrued; but by s 21 of that Act it continued the   *h*
special protection afforded to public authorities introduced by the Public
Authorities Protection Act 1893 which provided a 12-month limitation period in
respect of actions brought against public authorities.
   The vast majority of actions against public authorities were actions for personal
injuries arising out of accidents and it was seen as unfair that plaintiffs injured by
a public authority should have a far shorter time in which to commence a claim   *j*
than if they had been injured by someone in the private sector. In January 1948
the Lord Chancellor appointed a committee chaired by Tucker LJ to inquire into
this question with the following terms of reference:

   '(1) whether the Public Authorities Protection Act, 1893, as amended in
   its application to England and Wales by section 21 of the Limitation Act,
   1939, and in its application to Scotland by section 48 of the Crown

a Proceedings Act, 1947, should be further amended or repealed; (2) whether the three-year limit prescribed by section 49 of the Coal Industry Nationalisation Act, 1946, section 11 of the Transport Act, 1947, and section 12 of the Electricity Act, 1947, for the bringing of certain actions against the authorities therein mentioned is satisfactory; (3) whether any alteration should be made in the time limits prescribed by the Fatal Accidents Act, 1846, and by sections 2 and 3 of the Limitation Act, 1939, for the bringing
b of certain actions in England and Wales . . .'

The Tucker Committee presented their report to Parliament on 30 June 1949 (see *Report of the Committee on the Limitation of Actions* (Cmd 7740)). In their report they made it clear that the evidence they had heard related almost entirely to actions for personal injuries. In so far as actions for personal injuries were
c concerned they made the following recommendations:

'(1) The Public Authorities Protection Act, 1893, as amended, should be wholly repealed (paras. 6–24, 31, 32). (2) The period of limitation for actions in respect of personal injuries should be two years from the accrual of the cause of action, but the court should have a discretion to grant leave to bring
d an action after the expiration of that period, but not later than six years from the accrual of the cause of action (paras. 22 and 23). (3) The period of limitation for actions founded upon contract or tort (other than actions for personal injuries) should remain at its present period of six years (paras. 19–21). (4) The periods of limitation in respect of actions brought against the Crown and the public corporations set up by the Nationalisation and similar
e Acts should be the same as the periods applicable to other public authorities and to private individuals (paras. 25 and 26) . . .'

It is I think obvious when reading the report that the committee was confining its recommendations in respect of actions for personal injury to accident cases. They said (para 23):
f
'We consider that the period of limitation we have recommended should apply to all actions for personal injuries, whether the defendant is a public authority or not. We do not think it is necessary for us to define "personal injuries", although this may possibly be necessary if legislative effect is given to our recommendations. We wish, however, to make it clear that we do not
g include in that category actions for trespass to the person, false imprisonment, malicious prosecution, or defamation of character, but we do include such actions as claims for negligence against doctors.'

I do not think it can be open to doubt that the respondent's complaints of sexual abuse and rape fall within the category of an action for trespass to the person referred to in the above paragraph. The committee were therefore
h recommending that such actions should continue to be governed by the six-year period of limitation.

The Tucker Committee recommendations, with one amendment, were given effect to by the Law Reform (Limitation of Actions &c) Act 1954, which was introduced as a private member's Bill with government support. The one
j amendment to the Tucker proposals was that instead of providing a limitation period for personal injury actions of two years with the possibility of a judicial extension to six years it was decided to introduce a slightly longer period of three years with no option to extend it. Thus s 2(1) of the 1954 Act provided:

'At the end of subsection (1) of section two of the Limitation Act, 1939 (which subsection provides, amongst other things, that there shall be a limitation period of six years for actions founded on simple contract or on tort) the following proviso shall be inserted—"Provided that, in the case of actions for damages for negligence, nuisance or breach of duty (whether the duty exists by virtue of a contract or of provision made by or under a statute or independently of any contract or any such provision) where the damages claimed by the plaintiff for the negligence, nuisance or breach of duty consist of or include damages in respect of personal injuries to any person, this subsection shall have effect as if for the reference to six years there were substituted a reference to three years."'

In *Letang v Cooper* [1964] 2 All ER 929, [1965] 1 QB 232 an attempt was made to escape from this new three-year limitation period. The plaintiff had been sunbathing on the grass in the car park of an hotel when the defendant drove his car over her legs. The accident happened on 10 July 1957 but the plaintiff did not issue her writ claiming damages for personal injuries until 2 February 1961, which was outside the three-year limitation period provided by the 1954 Act. This accident was obviously one to which the three-year limitation period was intended to apply but in an attempt to escape the consequences of failing to issue a writ within the three-year time limit the plaintiff's legal advisers claimed in both negligence and trespass to the person. This manoeuvre succeeded before the trial judge, who held that the defendant had been negligent but went on to hold that the phrase 'negligence, nuisance or breach of duty' in s 2(1) of 1954 Act did not include an action for trespass to the person so that the plaintiff had six years in which to bring her claim (see [1964] 1 All ER 669, [1964] 2 QB 53). If this decision was correct it would have nullified the effect of s 2(1) of the 1954 Act for all claims for personal injuries could henceforth be framed in trespass and thus be subject to a six-year limitation period. It is not therefore surprising that the Court of Appeal reversed the decision of the judge and held that s 2(1) applied to the plaintiff's claim which was thereby statute-barred.

Lord Denning MR solved the problem by holding that the only cause of action lay in negligence and was thus statute-barred. He said ([1964] 2 All ER 929 at 932, [1965] 1 QB 232 at 240):

'. . . when the injury is not inflicted intentionally, but negligently, I would say that the only cause of action is negligence and not trespass.'

However he also went on to hold that if he was wrong and the plaintiff had a cause of action for trespass to the person he would hold that the phrase 'breach of duty' covered a breach of any duty under the law of tort. Danckwerts LJ agreed with both Lord Denning MR's reasons for allowing the appeal. Diplock LJ held that on the facts pleaded the cause of action was one in negligence within the meaning of s 2 and that the period of limitation was therefore three years. But he also held that the words 'breach of duty' should be construed as applying to any cause of action which gives rise to a claim for damages for personal injury. Leave to appeal to the House of Lords was refused and there the matter has rested until the present case.

The next significant development in the law of limitation in personal injury cases arose out of the discovery that plaintiffs might suffer injury to their lungs in the course of their employment as a result of inhaling noxious dusts long before they realised that their health was affected and the decision of the House of Lords in *Cartledge v E Jopling & Sons Ltd* [1963] 1 All ER 341, [1963] AC 758 that time ran for the purposes of limitation from the moment that the plaintiff had suffered injury irrespective of whether or not he was aware of it. This was a great hardship, for it meant that many men who had suffered injuries as a result of their employer's negligence or breach of statutory duty were unable to recover damages because by the time they sought medical advice their claims were already statute-barred. Parliament moved swiftly to remedy this injustice by enacting the Limitation Act 1963 which enabled the court to extend the three-year limitation period in cases such as *Cartledge v E Jopling & Sons Ltd*. As rightly stated by the editors of *Clerk and Lindsell on Torts* (16th edn, 1989) para 9–46, p 406: 'Unfortunately, the provisions of the Limitation Act 1963 were over-complicated and worked extremely badly.'

The 1963 Act was therefore repealed and replaced by the Limitation Act 1975, the provisions of which now form part of the Limitation Act 1980 and provide a more satisfactory basis upon which to exercise a judicial discretion to extend the three-year limitation period. This discretion is however limited to those personal injury actions which fall within the meaning of s 11(1) of the Limitation Act 1980 which is in identical language to s 2(1) of the Law Reform (Limitation of Actions &c) Act 1954. The relevant parts of s 11 provide:

'(1) This section applies to any action for damages for negligence, nuisance or breach of duty (whether the duty exists by virtue of a contract or of provision made by or under a statute or independently of any contract or any such provision) where the damages claimed by the plaintiff for the negligence, nuisance or breach of duty consist of or include damages in respect of personal injuries to the plaintiff or any other person.

(2) None of the time limits given in the preceding provisions of this Act shall apply to an action to which this section applies.

(3) An action to which this section applies shall not be brought after the expiration of the period applicable in accordance with subsection (4) or (5) below.

(4) Except were subsection (5) below applies, the period applicable is three years from—(*a*) the date on which the cause of action accrued; or (*b*) the date of knowledge (if later) of the person injured . . .'

Subsection (5) deals with actions on behalf of the estate of a deceased person and is not relevant to this appeal.

The date of knowledge of the person injured is defined in s 14:

'(1) . . . in sections 11 and 12 of this Act references to a person's date of knowledge are references to the date on which he first had knowledge of the following facts—(*a*) that the injury in question was significant; and (*b*) that the injury was attributable in whole or in part to the act or omission which is alleged to constitute negligence, nuisance or breach of duty; and (*c*) the identity of the defendant; and (*d*) if it is alleged that the act or omission was that of a person other than the defendant, the identity of that person and the additional facts supporting the bringing of an action against the defendant; and knowledge that any acts or omissions did or did not, as a matter of law, involve negligence, nuisance or breach of duty is irrelevant . . .

(2) For the purposes of this section an injury is significant if the person whose date of knowledge is in question would reasonably have considered it sufficiently serious to justify his instituting proceedings for damages against a defendant who did not dispute liability and was able to satisfy a judgment.

(3) For the purposes of this section a person's knowledge includes knowledge which he might reasonably have been expected to acquire—(*a*) from facts observable or ascertainable by him; or (*b*) from facts ascertainable by him with the help of medical or other appropriate expert advice which it is reasonable for him to seek; but a person shall not be fixed under this subsection with knowledge of a fact ascertainable only with the help of expert advice so long as he has taken all reasonable steps to obtain (and, where appropriate, to act on) that advice.'

In the present case the principal argument in the Court of Appeal focused upon whether or not the respondent knew she had suffered significant injury over *a* three years before she commenced her action on 18 August 1987. The respondent's case was that although she knew she had been raped by one appellant and had been persistently sexually abused by the other she did not realise she had suffered sufficiently serious injury to justify starting proceedings for damages until she realised that there might be a causal link between psychiatric problems she had suffered in adult life and her sexual abuse as a child. The Court of Appeal after *b* considerable hesitation accepted this argument on behalf of the respondent. If it was necessary to decide the point I should not have found it easy to agree with the Court of Appeal. Personal injury is defined in s 38 as including 'any impairment of a person's physical or mental condition' and I have the greatest difficulty in accepting that a woman who knows that she has been raped does not know that *c* she has suffered a significant injury. The Criminal Injuries Compensation Board ever since its inception almost 30 years ago has been making substantial awards to the victims of rape varying between about £6,000 and £20,000, and since the enlargement of the scheme in 1979 this has included victims within the family setting. Sexual abuse that goes no further than indecent fondling of a child raises a more difficult question, but some of the respondent's allegations are so serious *d* that I should have had difficulty in regarding them as other than significant. However I do not find it necessary to resolve this difficult issue as I accept the first submission made on behalf of the appellants, which is that s 11(1) does not apply to a cause of action based on indecent assault or rape for which the limitation period is six years and which is not subject to extension under s 11(4)(*b*).

The Court of Appeal dealt very shortly with this argument because *e* understandably it considered itself to be bound by *Letang v Cooper*. Bingham LJ said ([1991] 3 All ER 949 at 953–954, [1992] 1 QB 197 at 204–205):

> 'In *Letang v Cooper* [1964] 2 All ER 929, [1965] 1 QB 232 the Court of Appeal (Lord Denning MR, Danckwerts and Diplock LJJ) construed the language here in question as embracing a claim based on unintentional and *f* intentional trespass to the person. Cooke J so understood the judgments in *Long v Hepworth* [1968] 3 All ER 248, [1968] 1 WLR 1299, and I consider the Court of Appeal's ruling to be binding upon us as he held it binding upon him. The Limitation Acts 1975 and 1980 were enacted in the same terms against the background of this authority, which they must be taken to have indorsed. Even in the absence of authority I would, like Cooke J, reach that *g* conclusion on construction of the statutory language alone, unless I could see some reason why Parliament should have intended to draw the suggested distinction, and I can see none. I am satisfied that this is an action falling within s 11(1) of the 1980 Act.'

Upon this passage I would make two comments. I do not think it is right to *h* assume that the enactment of the Limitation Acts 1975 and 1980 were in any way related to or intended to indorse *Letang v Cooper*. The Limitation Act 1963 was enacted to meet the problem of the insidious onset of industrial disease encountered in *Cartledge v E Jopling & Sons Ltd* [1963] 1 All ER 341, [1963] AC 758 and the 1975 Act was enacted to cure the imperfections of the 1963 Act. The 1980 Act merely re-enacts the 1975 Act. In my view no light is thrown on the *j* true construction of s 11(1) by this sequence of Acts which were passed to deal with a very different problem to that with which your Lordships are now faced. My second comment is that we now have an advantage denied to Bingham LJ because we are now permitted to look at Hansard and when we do so it becomes clear that Parliament had enacted s 2(1) of the 1954 Act with the deliberate

intention of giving effect to the Tucker Committee's advice that the three-year
a period should apply to what I will broadly describe as accident cases and should
not include causes of actions such as rape or indecent assault.

I accept that *Letang v Cooper* was correctly decided in so far as it held that
negligent driving is a cause of action falling within s 2(1) of the 1954 Act. But I
cannot agree that the words 'breach of duty' have the effect of including within
the scope of the section all actions in which damages for personal injuries are
b claimed which is the other ground upon which the Court of Appeal decided
Letang v Cooper. If that had been the intention of the draftsman it would have
been easy enough to say so in the section. On the contrary the draftsman has used
words of limitation; he has limited the section to actions for negligence, nuisance
and breach of duty and the reason he did so was to give effect to the
c recommendation of the Tucker Committee that the three-year period should not
apply to a number of causes of action in which damages for personal injury might
be claimed, namely damages for trespass to the person, false imprisonment,
malicious prosecution or defamation. There can be no doubt that rape and
indecent assault fell within the category of trespass to the person.

Lord Denning MR in *Letang v Cooper* was not prepared to assume that
d Parliament did intend to give effect to the Tucker Committee's recommendations,
but we can now look at Hansard and can see that it was the express intention of
Parliament to do so. The proposer of the Bill, Mr John Peyton MP, in moving the
second reading said (521 HC Official Report (5th series) col 1544):

> *e* 'In its main provisions the Bill follows precisely the recommendations of
> the committee which sat under the chairmanship of the then Lord Justice
> Tucker. There is only one comparatively minor point upon which the
> provisions vary from the recommendations of the Tucker committee.'

The minor point I have already identified: it was to substitute a fixed period of
three years for a two-year period which might be extended to six years. This point
f was accepted by Lord Tucker: when commenting upon it in the second reading
in the House of Lords he said (187 HL Official Report (5th series) col 825):

> 'With regard to the period, I do not think I am revealing any secrets when
> I tell your Lordships that on the Committee, once they came to the conclusion
> that the proper course was to limit the period in regard to personal accident
> cases, there was a difference of opinion about whether that period should be
> *g* two years or three years. I think the acceptance of two years with discretionary
> power to the Judge in Chambers, represented a compromise between the two
> views but for which we should not have had a unanimous Report from the
> Committee—and it is always valuable to have a unanimous Report. I have
> no strong views on this subject, but I incline to favour some fixed period.'

h   Even without reference to Hansard I should not myself have construed 'breach
of duty' as including a deliberate assault. The phrase lying in juxtaposition with
'negligence' and 'nuisance' carries with it the implication of a breach of duty of
care not to cause personal injury, rather than an obligation not to infringe any
legal right of another person. If I invite a lady to my house one would naturally
think of a duty to take care that the house is safe but would one really be thinking
j of a duty not to rape her. But, however this may be, the terms in which this Bill
was introduced to my mind make it clear beyond peradventure that the intention
was to give effect to the Tucker recommendation that the limitation period in
respect of trespass to the person was not to be reduced to three years but should
remain at six years. The language of s 2(1) of the 1954 Act is in my view apt to
give effect to that intention, and cases of deliberate assault such as we are concerned

with in this case are not actions for breach of duty within the meaning of s 11(1) of the 1980 Act.

The language of s 2(1) of the 1954 Act was carried without alteration into the 1975 Act and then into s 11(1) of the 1980 Act where it must bear the same meaning as it had in the 1954 Act.

It thus follows that the respondent's causes of action against both appellants were subject to a six-year limitation period. This period was suspended during her infancy but commenced to run when she attained her majority: see s 28 of the 1980 Act. This period expired many years before she issued her writ in these proceedings. There are no provisions for extending this period and her actions are therefore statute-barred and cannot proceed. For these reasons I would allow these appeals.

LORD ACKNER. My Lords, I have had the advantage of reading in draft the speech prepared by my noble and learned friend Lord Griffiths. I agree with it, and for the reasons given, I too would allow these appeals.

LORD SLYNN OF HADLEY. My Lords, I have had the advantage of reading in draft the speech prepared by my noble and learned friend Lord Griffiths. I agree that for the reasons he gives, these appeals should be allowed.

Appeals allowed.

Mary Rose Plummer   Barrister.

Norwich and Peterborough Building Society v Steed (No 2)

COURT OF APPEAL, CIVIL DIVISION
PURCHAS, BUTLER-SLOSS AND SCOTT LJJ
4, 5, 6 FEBRUARY, 5 MARCH 1992

Document – Non est factum – Power of attorney – Donee unaware of power of attorney – Donee tricked into signing transfer of house – Whether plea of non est factum established – Whether transfer of house ultra vires power of attorney.

Land registration – Rectification of register – Circumstances justifying rectification – Registered owner executing power of attorney – Donee of power of attorney tricked into signing transfer of property – Building society granting mortgage on property – Whether court having power to order rectification of register by removal of building society's charge – Land Registration Act 1925, s 82(1).

The appellant, the freehold owner of a house which was subject to a local authority mortgage, permitted his mother, his sister and her husband to live in the house while he was living in the United States. His sister and her husband persuaded the appellant to execute a power of attorney in favour of his mother, and then either tricked the mother into executing a transfer of the house in their favour under the power of attorney or forged her signature on the transfer, although she subsequently denied that the signature on the transfer was hers or that she knew anything about the power of attorney. On the same day the sister and her *a*   husband borrowed £15,000 from the respondent building society on the security of the property, supposedly to enable them to purchase it for £24,500 from the appellant. In fact they paid off the local authority charge, amounting to £1,800, and kept the balance. The building society was registered as the holder of a charge on the property. The sister and her husband defaulted on the mortgage repayments and the building society obtained a possession order, which, on appeal by the the appellant, who had applied to be joined as a party in the proceedings

b   and sought a stay of the order, was set aside by the Court of Appeal on the ground that, on the assumption that the transfer to the sister and her husband was a forgery, the court had power under s 82(1)ᵃ of the Land Registration Act 1925 to rectify the register not only as against the sister and her husband but also as against the building society. The Court of Appeal ordered a new trial to determine

c   the facts regarding the execution of the transfer. The building society then brought an action for possession of the property and the appellant counterclaimed for rectification of the proprietorship register by substituting himself as owner for his sister and her husband and rectification of the charges register by removal of the building society's charge. Before the trial a handwriting expert concluded that there was a high probability that the mother had signed the transfer and

d   accordingly the forgery allegation was abandoned. However, the appellant claimed that he was entitled to rely (i) on a plea of non est factum on the ground that the mother did not know that she had been appointed attorney and did not know that she was signing a transfer of the property and (ii) on a plea that the transaction fell outside the authority conferred on the mother under the power of attorney. The judge rejected those pleas but concluded that the transfer was

e   not void but merely voidable, by reason of the fraud perpetrated by the sister and her husband, and ordered that the proprietorship register be rectified by the removal of their names and the substitution of the appellant's name but he refused to order rectification of the charges register by the removal of the building society's charge. The appellant appealed to the Court of Appeal.

f   **Held** – (1) The plea of non est factum which would render the transfer void against the innocent building society had not been established notwithstanding the fact that the mother had been tricked into signing the transfer since either the mother, as donee of the power of attorney, had possessed sufficient general understanding and capability and had failed to inform herself of the purport and

g   effect of the transfer before signing it or, if she had lacked ordinary competence and capacity, the appellant as donor of the power of attorney was not entitled to repudiate the transfer on the ground of the mother's lack of understanding. Furthermore, the appellant's failure to inform his mother of her appointment showed such a want of care as to preclude him from relying on her ignorance of the power in support of his plea of non est factum (see p 339 *d* to *h* and p 348 *e f*,

h   post).

(2) The execution of a transfer on completion of sale fell within the power conferred by the power of attorney. As between the appellant and his sister and her husband, therefore, the transfer was not a nullity but merely voidable and therefore could not be against the building society (see p 340 *e* to *g* and p 348 *e f*, post).

j   (3) On the true construction of s 82 of the 1925 Act the court's power to order rectification of the register was limited to the grounds specified in paras (*a*) to (*h*) of sub-s (1) and the court had no general discretion to grant rectification merely because it might be thought just to do so. Since the appellant's case for rectification could not be brought under any of the grounds specified in s 82(1) and since his

---

a   Section 82(1) is set out at p 341 *d* to *g*, post

plea of non est factum had failed the court had no power to order rectification
against the building society. The appeal would therefore be dismissed (see p 343   *a*
c, p 345 *c*, p 347 *j* and p 348 *b* to *g*, post); *Argyle Building Society v Hammond* (1984)
49 P & CR 148 considered.

Notes

For the plea of non est factum, see 9 *Halsbury's Laws* (4th edn) para 284 and 12
Halsbury's Laws (4th edn) paras 1365–1369, and for cases on the subject, see 17   *b*
Digest (Reissue) 284–285, 511–517.

   For rectification of the land register, see 26 *Halsbury's Laws* (4th edn) paras 1054–
1058, and for cases on the subject, see 39(1) *Digest* (Reissue) 155–157, 1629–1641.

   For the Land Registration Act 1925, s 82, see 37 *Halsbury's Statutes* (4th edn)
588.
                                                                                         c

Cases referred to in judgments

Argyle Building Society v Hammond (1984) 49 P & CR 148, CA.
Calgary and Edmonton Land Co Ltd v Discount Bank (Overseas) Ltd [1971] 1 All ER
   551, [1971] 1 WLR 81.
Chowood Ltd v Lyall (No 2) [1930] 2 Ch 156, [1930] All ER Rep 402, CA.   *d*
Foster v Mackinnon (1869) LR 4 CP 704.
Hunter v Walters, Curling v Walters, Darnell v Hunter (1871) LR 7 Ch App 75.
King v Smith [1900] 2 Ch 425.
Leighton's Conveyance, Re [1936] 1 All ER 667; *rvsd* [1936] 3 All ER 1033, CA.
National Provincial Bank of England v Jackson (1886) 33 Ch D 1, CA.
Saunders v Anglia Building Society [1970] 3 All ER 961, [1971] AC 1004, [1970] 3   *e*
   WLR 1078, HL.

Cases also cited or referred to in skeleton arguments

Burchell v Thompson [1920] 2 KB 80, CA.
Doyle v East [1972] 2 All ER 1013, [1972] 1 WLR 1080.
London and Cheshire Insurance Co Ltd v Laplagrene Property Co Ltd [1971] 1 All ER   *f*
   766, [1971] Ch 499.
Midland Bank Trust Co Ltd v Green [1981] 1 All ER 153, [1981] AC 513, HL.

Appeal

Michael Derek Steed appealed from the decision of Knox J given on 15 December   *g*
1989 whereby, inter alia, he granted a declaration that the interest of the
respondent, Norwich and Peterborough Building Society, formerly Argyle
Building Society, under the its first legal charge dated 4 September 1979 took
priority to any interest of the appellant in the property, 2 Arlow Road, Winchmore
Hill, London N21. The facts are set out in the judgment of Scott LJ.
                                                                                         h

Timothy Lloyd QC and *Stephen Acton* (instructed by *Chambers Rutland & Crauford*)
   for the appellant.
J Rayner James QC and *C H Jones* (instructed by *Warrens Boyes & Archer,*
   Huntingdon) for the respondent.

5 March 1992. The following judgments were delivered.   *j*

SCOTT LJ (giving the first judgment at the invitation of Purchas LJ). This is an
appeal from the judgment of Knox J given on 15 December 1989. The appeal
concerns a freehold property, 2 Arlow Road, Winchmore Hill, London. Title to
the property is and has at all material times been registered at HM Land Registry.

In October 1964 the appellant, Mr Michael Derek Steed, purchased the property
a for the sum of £3,300. He did so with the aid of a loan from the local authority.
The loan was secured by a mortgage of the property. Mr Steed was duly registered
at HM Land Registry as the proprietor of the property. The local authority's
mortgage was duly registered in the charges register.

After the purchase the property became the home of Mr Steed and his family.
Various members of his family have resided there from time to time. The
b important ones, for the purpose of these proceedings, are his mother, his sister,
Mrs Claire Hammond, and her husband, David Hammond.

In 1976 Mr Steed emigrated to California. While he was in California his
mother, Mrs Steed, and his sister and brother-in-law, Mr and Mrs Hammond,
continued to live in the property. Under an informal family arrangement they
c paid the mortgage instalments falling due under the local authority mortgage.

On 14 April 1979 Mr Steed executed in California a power of attorney naming
his mother, Mrs Steed, as his attorney. The document had been prepared in
England by a solicitor, Mr Lawrence, of Messrs W H Hopkins & Co, acting on the
instructions of Mrs Hammond. Mrs Hammond had taken the document out to
California for Mr Steed to execute. When he had done so she brought it back to
d England.

The power of attorney gave Mrs Steed power—

> '(1) To buy, sell or exchange lands of any tenure whether by private
> contract or by public auction for such consideration and subject to such
> covenants, conditions and restrictions as the Attorney shall think fit . . .
e > (3) Generally to execute any deed or sign any document which may be
> required and to do any other act matter or thing which the Attorney shall
> consider necessary or expedient for carrying out any of the purposes or acts
> hereby authorised . . .'

It is accepted that this power of attorney was valid and effective to vest in
f Mrs Steed power on Mr Steed's behalf to sell the property and to execute a transfer
for that purpose.

There was no evidence that Mrs Steed was ever informed either by Mr Steed or
by Mrs Hammond of this power of attorney or of her power to sell the property.
There was some evidence that she was in complete ignorance of the power of
attorney and of her power of sale.

g In August or September 1979 a transfer of the property bearing, or appearing
to bear, Mrs Steed's signature came into existence. The transfer was in the usual
Land Registry form and bears the date 4 September 1979. It provided as follows:

> 'In consideration of TWENTY-FOUR THOUSAND FIVE HUNDRED pounds (£24,500)
> the receipt whereof is hereby acknowledged I MICHAEL DEREK STEED of 2 Arlow
h > Road Winchmore Hill London N21 by his Attorney MARY STEED of 2 Arlow
> Road aforesaid as beneficial owner hereby transfer to: DAVID HAMMOND and
> CLAIRE MADELEINE HAMMOND his wife both of 2 Arlow Road Winchmore Hill
> London N21, the land comprised in the title above mentioned . . .'

In the testatum the transfer was expressed to be—

j > 'Signed, sealed and delivered by the said MARY STEED as the Attorney of
> MICHAEL DEREK STEED and on behalf of the above named MICHAEL DEREK STEED.'

A signature purporting to be that of Mrs Steed appears opposite.

During the summer of 1979 Mr and Mrs Hammond had made arrangements
with Argyle Building Society, now known as Norwich and Peterborough Building
Society and the respondent on this appeal, to borrow £15,000 on the security of

the property in order to enable them to purchase the property for £24,500 from
Mr Steed. The usual conveyancing arrangements were made between the building   *a*
society's solicitors, Messrs Warrens, and the Hammonds' solicitors, W H Hopkins
& Co. These arrangements led in due course to the building society sending the
£15,000, less a sum in respect of its conveyancing costs, to W H Hopkins & Co,
pending completion of the purchase and mortgage. The Hammonds executed a
legal charge of the property in what was, presumably, the building society's usual
form of charge. This document, too, bears the date 4 September 1979. The   *b*
executed legal charge was sent to Warrens to be held, in escrow, pending
completion.

Following completion W H Hopkins & Co released to the Hammonds the
balance of the £15,000, after deduction of £1,800-odd needed to discharge the
local authority's registered charge and of a sum in respect of their own costs, and   *c*
on 17 September 1979 sent to Warrens the transfer, apparently executed by
Mrs Steed as attorney for Mr Steed, together with the discharge of the local
authority's charge and various other conveyancing documents.

On 9 October 1979 the building society submitted the transfer, the legal charge
and the discharge to the Land Registry for registration. Registration was
completed on 17 December 1979. The Hammonds' names were entered in the   *d*
proprietorship register as owners of the property in place of Mr Steed. The legal
charge in favour of the building society was entered in the charges register. The
entry in the charges register relating to the local authority's charge was deleted.

It subsequently transpired that the conveyancing arrangements I have described
were part of a fraudulent scheme of the Hammonds to obtain money for
themselves using the property as security. Mr Steed knew nothing of the sale. He   *e*
received no part of the purported consideration of £24,500 nor any benefit there
from save that £1,800 or thereabouts had been expended in discharging his
liability under the local authority mortgage.

Mrs Steed, too, insisted that she knew nothing of the sale. She died before the
case came to trial but a written statement signed by her on 16 December 1985   *f*
was received into evidence under the Civil Evidence Act 1968. In this statement
she denied that the signature on the transfer was hers. She said: '. . . I did not sign
the Transfer which has been shown to me. The signature on this document is not
my signature.' She denied that she knew anything about the power of attorney.
She said: 'Claire did not show me the power of attorney . . . nor did she tell me
that I had been made Michael's Attorney.' It is implicit from her statement that,   *g*
according to her, Mr Steed, too, had not told her that he had appointed her to be
his attorney.

The building society was, of course, an innocent third party. It had lent money
on mortgage for the purpose of an apparently genuine sale. The transfer to its
mortgagors, the Hammonds, and its own legal charge had been registered at HM
Land Registry. Everything appeared to be in order.   *h*

In addition to borrowing money from the building society on the security of
the property, the Hammonds raised money from other sources on the same
security. We have not seen the details but it appears that provident Mutual Life
Assurance Association, Barclays Bank plc and Lloyds Bank plc obtained registered
charges. They were made parties to these proceedings but, since the debt owing
to the building society now exceeds the value of the property and since they can   *j*
be in no better position than the building society, they have taken no part in the
proceedings.

For the sake of completeness I would add that the Hammonds have been
convicted of offences of dishonesty arising out of their financial arrangements

a with the building society and that a bankruptcy order has been made against Mr Hammond.

Following the completion of the transaction with the building society, Mrs Steed, Mrs Hammond and Mr Hammond continued to live in the property. But the Hammonds fell into arrears in payment of the mortgage instalments due to the building society. So the building society commenced possession proceedings.

b This was in February 1982, ten years ago. The Hammonds, of course, had no defence and the building society obtained a possession order against them. But at about this time Mr Steed returned from the United States of America and resumed residence in the property. He applied to be joined in the proceedings as a defendant and for a stay of the possession order. He contended, among other things, that his mother's signature on the transfer of 4 September 1979 was a

c forgery. He claimed to be entitled to rectification of the register both as against the Hammonds and as against the building society. The county court judge before whom the action came concluded that the building society was entitled to possession as against Mr Steed even if the transfer to the Hammonds were a forgery. So he confirmed the order for possession. Mr Steed appealed. The judgment of the Court of Appeal is reported: see *Argyle Building Society v Hammond*

d (1984) 49 P & CR 148. The judgment of the court was given by Slade LJ. He held that, on the assumption that the transfer to the Hammonds was a forgery, the court would have power under s 82(1) of the Land Registration Act 1925 to rectify the register not only as against the Hammonds but also as against the building society. He also expressed the opinion, obiter, that the court would have the like power if the transfer were merely voidable, as opposed to void. So the appeal was

e allowed, the order for possession was set aside as against Mr Steed and the case was transferred to the Chancery Division for a new trial at which the facts regarding the execution or non-execution of the transfer and Mr Steed's entitlement to rectification of the register would be determined.

On 12 December 1985 the building society commenced in the High Court the

f action that in due course came before Knox J. It sued only Mr Steed as defendant and claimed possession of the property. Mr Steed's defence served on 16 April 1987 pleaded that the transfer was forged. He counterclaimed, joining the other chargees whom I have mentioned as well as Mr Hammond's trustees in bankruptcy and Mrs Hammond as defendants to the counterclaim, for rectification of the proprietorship register, by the removal of the Hammonds' names and the

g insertion of his own name, and of the charges register, by the deletion of the entries relating to the building society's charge and the charges of the other chargees. The counterclaim, like the defence, was based on the allegation that the transfer was forged. There was no other relevant allegation. Forgery of the transfer had constituted the 'assumed facts' on the basis of which the Court of Appeal had found in Mr Steed's favour.

h   Mrs Steed died not long after she signed her statement on 16 December 1985. She had, it will be recalled, expressly denied that the signature on the transfer was hers. A handwriting expert was instructed. The expert's report dated 26 April 1989 concluded that there was a high probability that Mrs Steed did sign the transfer. The trial had been fixed to commence on 5 May 1989. The expert's report was somewhat of a bombshell and an adjournment was granted to enable

j Mr Steed to consider his position.

The upshot of this was that the forgery allegation was abandoned and wholly new lines of defence were added by amendment to Mr Steed's counterclaim for rectification. The new pleading, so far as relevant to the claim against the building society, constituted (i) a plea of non est factum based on the proposition that

Mrs Steed did not know she had been appointed attorney and did not know she was signing a transfer of the property and (ii) a plea that the transaction effected by the transfer was not a sale and was not within the power conferred by the power of attorney.

These two pleas took the place of the forgery plea as justifying the conclusion that the building society's charge was 'void' and that Mr Steed was 'entitled to an order for rectification'.

Knox J found against Mr Steed, both on the non est factum issue and also on the ultra vires issue. He concluded that the transfer was not void but was, by reason of the fraud perpetrated by the Hammonds, voidable. He, therefore, ordered that the proprietorship register be rectified by the removal of their names and the substitution of Mr Steed's name. It would seem from the pleadings to which I have referred that that should have been the end of the case. But the contention was put forward on Mr Steed's behalf that, even if the transfer were only voidable and notwithstanding that the building society was not implicated in and had had no notice of the Hammonds' fraud, none the less the court had a discretionary power under s 82 of the Land Registration Act 1925 to order that the building society's charge be deleted from the register, leaving Mr Steed with an unencumbered title and the building society to claim an indemnity under s 83. It was contended that in the circumstances of the case the discretion should be exercised in Mr Steed's favour and the charges register rectified accordingly.

I have some doubt whether these contentions were open to Mr Steed on the pleadings. But no pleading point was taken and the learned judge entertained them. He accepted that the court did, under s 82, have the wide discretionary power of rectification contended for. Indeed the contrary does not seem to have been argued. Certain dicta of Slade LJ in *Argyle Building Society v Hammond* (1984) 49 P & CR 148 were taken as establishing the point. But the learned judge, as a matter of discretion, declined to order the rectification sought.

So the upshot of the trial was that Mr Steed was restored to the position of registered proprietor but had failed to upset the building society's charge. He has appealed. There are three issues to be decided. The first issue is whether, it being accepted that the signature on the transfer is that of Mrs Steed, the appellant can repudiate the transfer under the doctrine of non est factum. If he can, then the transfer is void, no better than if Mrs Steed's signature had been forged. The second issue is whether, assuming he fails on non est factum, the appellant can repudiate the transfer as being ultra vires the power of attorney. This is put forward as an alternative basis on which the transfer should be held to be void. If the appellant succeeds on either of these issues, there would, strictly, be an issue as to whether or not an order for rectification of the register, as against the building society, ought to be made. But, for reasons which I will later mention, it seemed to us that there would be no serious answer to the appellant's rectification claim and Mr Rayner James QC for the building society did not contend otherwise. The third issue, which arises if the appellant fails to establish that the transfer was void, is, first, whether the court has power under s 82 to order rectification as against the building society and, second, if it does, whether the power should be exercised.

Non est factum

Taken literally, the doctrine of non est factum applies when the person sought to be held liable has not, in fact, signed the document (see Lord Reid in *Saunders v Anglia Building Society* [1970] 3 All ER 961 at 963, [1971] AC 1004 at 1015). But it also covers cases in which a person who has signed a document is none the less

allowed to repudiate the document. The authorities all concern cases of the latter
a sort.

We have been referred to *Hunter v Walters, Curling v Walters, Darnell v Hunter*
(1871) LR 7 Ch App 75, *National Provincial Bank of England v Jackson* (1886) 33
Ch D 1, *King v Smith* [1900] 2 Ch 425 and *Saunders v Anglia Building Society* [1970]
3 All ER 961, [1971] AC 1004. In each of these cases the victim of a fraud had
signed a document not understanding what he or she was doing. In each case an
b innocent third party had for value acquired rights under the document. In each
of these cases the existence of the doctrine of non est factum was affirmed, in each
the acceptable limits of the plea was discussed, in none was the plea allowed to
prevail. It is easy to understand why the plea is likely to be unsuccessful. A person
who signs a document at the request of another puts into circulation a document
c on which, depending on its contents, others may rely. Where a fraudster has
tricked, first, the signer of the document, in order to induce the signature, and
then some third party, who is induced to rely on the signed document, which of
the two victims is the law to prefer? The authorities indicate that the answer is,
almost invariably, the latter. The signer of the document has, by signing, enabled
the fraud to be carried out, enabled the false document to go into circulation.

d In *Saunders v Anglia Building Society* [1970] 3 All ER 961 at 963, [1971] AC 1004
at 1015–1016 Lord Reid said that the doctrine of non est factum—

> '... must be kept within narrow limits if it is not to shake the confidence
> of those who habitually and rightly rely on signatures when there is no
> obvious reason to doubt their validity ... there must be a heavy burden of
e > proof on the person who seeks to invoke this remedy'.

In the same case Lord Wilberforce said ([1970] 3 All ER 961 at 973, [1971] AC
1004 at 1027):

> '... a person who signs a document, and parts with it so that it may come
> into other hands, has a responsibility, that of the normal man of prudence, to
f > take care what he signs, which, if neglected, prevents him from denying his
> liability under the document according to its tenor.'

In each of the authorities to which were referred, and in particular in *Saunders
v Anglia Building Society*, the doctrine of non est factum is explained in different
words by different judges, but with a striking uniformity of concept and of
g emphasis. Knox J in his judgment cited a passage from the speech of
Lord Wilberforce (see [1970] 3 All ER 961 at 971, [1971] AC 1004 at 1025).
I would add the passage immediately following, where Lord Wilberforce said
([1970] 3 All ER 961 at 972, [1971] AC 1004 at 1026):

> 'How, then, ought the principle, on which a plea of non est factum is
h > admissible, to be stated? In my opinion, a document should be held to be
> void (as opposed to voidable) only when the element of consent to it is totally
> lacking, ie more concretely, when the transaction which the document
> purports to effect is essentially different in substance or in kind from the
> transaction intended. Many other expressions, or adjectives, could be used—
> "basically" or "radically" or "fundamentally" ... To this general test it is
j > necessary to add certain amplifications. First, there is the case of fraud. The
> law as to this is best stated in the words of the judgment in *Foster v Mackinnon*
> (1869) LR 4 CP 704 at 711 where it is said that a signature obtained by fraud:
> "... is invalid not merely on the ground of fraud, where fraud exists, but on
> the ground that the mind of the signer did not accompany the signature; in
> other words, that he never intended to sign, and therefore in contemplation

of law never did sign, the contract to which his name is appended." In other
words, it is the lack of consent that matters, not the means by which this   *a*
result was brought about. Fraud by itself may do no more than make the
contract voidable. Secondly, a man cannot escape from the consequences, as
regards innocent third parties, of signing a document if, being a man of
ordinary education and competence, he chooses to sign it without informing
himself of its purport and effect. This principle is sometimes found expressed
in the language that "he is doing something with his estate" . . . but it really   *b*
reflects a rule of common sense on the exigency of busy lives. Thirdly, there
is the case where the signer has been careless, in not taking ordinary
precautions against being deceived.'

There then followed the passage which I have already cited in which
Lord Wilberforce stressed the responsibility lying on persons who sign documents.   *c*
He went on to add ([1970] 3 All ER 961 at 973, [1971] AC 1004 at 1027):

'As to persons who are illiterate, or blind, or lacking in understanding, the
law is in a dilemma. On the one hand, the law is traditionally, and rightly,
ready to relieve them against hardship and imposition. On the other hand,
regard has to be paid to the position of innocent third parties who cannot be   *d*
expected, and often would have no means, to know the condition or status of
the signer. I do not think that a defined solution can be provided for all cases.
The law ought, in my opinion, to give relief if satisfied that consent was truly
lacking but will require of signers even in this class that they act responsibly
and carefully according to their circumstances in putting their signature to
legal documents.'   *e*

In my judgment these passages from Lord Wilberforce's speech express the
approach and the principles that must be applied to a non est factum plea.

In the present case there was a glaring absence of any reliable evidence as to
exactly what happened on the occasion on which Mrs Steed had placed her
signature on the transfer. Mrs Hammond gave evidence about the occasion but   *f*
the judge rejected her evidence. Mrs Steed's statement, too, dealt with her lack of
any recollection of the occasion or knowledge that she had been asked to sign a
transfer of the property. But the reliability of Mrs Steed's statement was seriously
undermined by the circumstance that she had denied ever having seen the
transfer and had denied that the signature was hers. Both these denials had been   *g*
shown to be false. It is clearly established that the onus lies on the party
repudiating the signed document to establish the necessary ingredients of non est
factum and it would, in my opinion, have been open to the learned judge simply
to have said that there was no evidence before him sufficient to establish
Mrs Steed's lack of understanding of what she had signed.

The judge did not, however, take that easy course but, instead, accepted at its   *h*
face value Mrs Steed's statement that she had not known what she was signing.
This part of Mrs Steed's statement had the merit of being believable. Neither
Mr Lawrence of W H Hopkins & Co, nor anyone else from that firm had ever
communicated with her regarding the sale of the property to the Hammonds.
The form of the transfer had been prepared by W H Hopkins & Co, acting for the
Hammonds, and submitted to Warrens, the building society's solicitors, for   *j*
approval. W H Hopkins & Co sent Warrens an authority to inspect the register.
It has not been explained how they were able to do so without taking any
instructions from Mrs Steed, but it has not been suggested that Mrs Steed
authorised them to do so. The Hammonds, intent on fraud, certainly would not
have explained the proposed sale transaction to Mrs Steed. So it is believable that,

up to the moment when the time came for her to sign the transfer, she knew
a nothing of it. She was, it may be inferred, tricked into signing without reading
the document.

Mrs Steed's evidence was not, however, that she had thought she was signing a
document of some different character from that which in fact she had signed. It
was not that she had signed under some induced misapprehension as to the nature
or character of what she was signing. Her evidence was that she had not known
b what she was signing and that, trusting her daughter, Claire, as she did, she would
have signed anything her daughter had put before her. Knox J held that: '. . .
Mrs Steed was tricked into signing what her daughter put before her because she
trusted her . . .' That, he held, was not sufficient to enable the plea of non est
factum to succeed.

Mr Lloyd QC for the appellant has attacked this part of the judgment by
c relying heavily on the proposition that Mrs Steed did not know anything about
the power of attorney and her status thereunder. In that state of ignorance she
could not, when she signed the transfer, have known she was dealing with her
son's property. She must have supposed she was dealing, in some way, with her
own affairs. So, it was argued, she was mistaken as to the essential character of the
d document she signed and of the transaction which it effected.

Submissions on these lines, as Butler-Sloss LJ pointed out during argument,
placed Mr Steed on a species of Morton's fork. Let it be supposed that Mrs Steed
was a lady of sufficient general understanding and capability to be a suitable
donee of the power of appointment. Why then did she not inform herself of the
purport and effect of the transfer before signing it? Her failure to do so brings the
e case within the second of Lord Wilberforce's amplifications. On the other hand,
let it be supposed that she lacked ordinary competence and capacity. Lord
Wilberforce referred to persons 'illiterate, or blind, or lacking in understanding'.
If Mrs Steed falls into this category, what was Mr Steed about when he appointed
her his attorney? The donor of a power of attorney who appoints as his attorney
a person incapable of understanding the import of a simple transfer can hardly be
f allowed, if the donee signs a transfer without any understanding of what he or
she is doing, to repudiate the transfer on the ground of a lack of understanding
on the part of the donee.

As to Mrs Steed's ignorance of the power of attorney, if she was ignorant of it,
the ignorance was attributable to Mr Steed's incomprehensible failure to tell her
either that he was about to or that he had made the appointment. It is known
g that he and she spoke on the telephone at about the time the power of attorney
was executed. If it was really the case that he did not mention the power of
attorney when speaking to her on that occasion and left her in ignorance of her
responsibilities and status, his failure shows, in my opinion, such a want of care as
to preclude him from relying, in support of his non est factum plea, on her
h ignorance of the power. As between an innocent third party purchaser such as
the building society on the one hand and Mr Steed on the other hand, his failure
to take the ordinary precautionary and prudent step of informing his mother of
her appointment as his attorney requires, in my judgment, that the building
society be preferred. In my judgment, and for substantially the same reasons as
those given by the learned judge, the non est factum plea fails.
j

Ultra vires

The submission that the transfer fell outside the authority conferred on
Mrs Steed under the power of attorney must be approached on the footing that,
the non est factum plea having failed, the transfer was validly executed by
Mrs Steed. The transfer purported to transfer the property in consideration of the

payment of the sum of £24,500. A transfer of property for a price is a sale.
Mr Lloyd's submission was that the reference to the price was a sham. No price   *a*
was in fact paid or ever intended to be paid. The £1,800-odd paid on discharge of
the local authority mortgage may be ignored for the purposes of the argument.
The transaction effected by the transfer was, whatever the transfer may have said,
a transfer for no, or if the £1,800 is taken into account a derisory, consideration
and was not a sale.

The building society in its defence to counterclaim pleaded estoppel by deed.   *b*
But, submitted Mr Lloyd, the Hammonds, the other parties to the transfer, could
not, by reason of their own fraud, raise an estoppel by deed. That being so, the
building society, which claimed through the Hammonds could not rely on
estoppel by deed. Mr Lloyd may be right in his answer to the estoppel by deed
point. If estoppel was to be relied on, it ought, I think, to have been estoppel by
representation. The transfer records a transaction of sale. If, in reliance on the   *c*
transfer, the building society accepted the legal charge executed by the Hammonds
and parted with the £15,000, an estoppel by representation would, as it seems to
me, bar Mr Steed from denying that the transaction completed by the transfer
was a sale. I think Mr Lloyd accepted, in principle, that that would be so. But he
pointed out that estoppel by representation was not pleaded, and that no evidence   *d*
had been led to establish that the building society in advancing the £15,000 had
relied in any relevant sense on the contents of the transfer.

I am, for two reasons, unable to accept Mr Lloyd's submissions on this ultra
vires point.

First, the transfer purports to be executed in completion of a sale. The execution
of a transfer on completion of sale is unquestionably within the power conferred   *e*
by the power of attorney. The transfer was executed by the donee of the power of
attorney. Prima facie, therefore, the transfer was, in my opinion, valid and
effective according to its tenor. No question of ultra vires arises. True the £24,500
was never paid (bar the £1,800-odd) but, despite the receipt clause, Mr Steed
would have been entitled to sue for the outstanding sum. The Hammonds would
have had no defence to an action for the price. As between Mr Steed and the   *f*
Hammonds, therefore, the transfer was not a nullity. It was merely voidable. If
it was merely voidable vis-à-vis the Hammonds, it cannot have been void as
against the building society. As a matter of principle, if a deed has been executed
by a donee of a power of attorney apparently acting within the terms of the
power, a purchaser does not, in my judgment, have to inquire further into the   *g*
substance of the transaction.

But, secondly, it seems to me plain as a pikestaff that the building society, in
parting with its money, relied on the transfer. The £15,000 was advanced in
order to enable the Hammonds to complete a purchase from Mr Steed at a price
of £24,500. The form of the proposed transfer had been approved by the building
society. The £15,000 was held by W H Hopkins & Co pending completion of the   *h*
sale. Not until the transfer in the form approved by the building society had been
executed by Mrs Steed was W H Hopkins & Co free to release the £15,000. To
say that there was no evidence that the building society relied on the transfer
being, as it purported to be, a transfer on sale, flies in the face of reality. It is true
that estoppel by representation was not pleaded, but estoppel by deed was pleaded
and the evidence was sufficient to support the former plea. If it had been necessary   *j*
I would have unhesitatingly given leave for an amendment to be made.

The learned judge dealt very shortly with the ultra vires point. He said:

'... the transfer on its face was a perfectly regular sale and as against third
parties taking a legal estate for value and in good faith it was within the

a   ostensible authority of Mrs Steed and cannot now be repudiated against such third parties. Nothing short of non est factum rendering the transfer void, or forgery which has the same legal effect but is not now alleged, will suffice to defeat the building society's innocent reliance upon the transfer.'

Save that I would not describe Mrs Steed's authority to execute the transfer as 'ostensible' authority, I am in complete and respectful agreement with the judge.

b
Rectification of the register
    The transfer of 4 September 1979 was induced by the fraud of Mr and Mrs Hammond. It was voidable but not void. The building society advanced £15,000 to the Hammonds on the security of the charge which they executed and which was subsequently registered. The question is whether the court has
c   power under s 82 of the Land Registration Act 1925 to order the register to be rectified by deletion of the entry of the building society's registered charge in the charges register. The question is primarily one of construction of the statutory language used in s 82.
    Section 82, as amended, provides as follows:

d   '(1) The register may be rectified pursuant to an order of the court or by the registrar, subject to appeal to the court, in any of the following cases, but subject to the following provisions of this section:—(*a*) Subject to any express provisions of this Act to the contrary, where a court of competent jurisdiction has decided that any person is entitled to any estate right or interest in or to any registered land or charge, and as a consequence of such decision such
e   court is of opinion that a rectification of the register is required, and makes an order to that effect; (*b*) Subject to any express provision of this Act to the contrary, where the court, on the application in the prescribed manner of any person who is aggrieved by any entry made in, or by the omission of any entry from, the register, or by any default being made, or unnecessary delay taking place, in the making of any entry in the register, makes an order for
f   the rectification of the register; (*c*) In any case and at any time with the consent of all persons interested; (*d*) Where the court or the registrar is satisfied that any entry in the register has been obtained by fraud; (*e*) Where two or more persons are, by mistake, registered as proprietors of the same registered estate or of the same charge; (*f*) Where a mortgagee has been
g   registered as proprietor of the land instead of as proprietor of a charge and a right of redemption is subsisting; (*g*) Where a legal estate has been registered in the name of a person who if the land had not been registered would not have been the estate owner; and (*h*) In any other case where, by reason of any error or omission in the register, or by reason of any entry made under a mistake, it may be deemed just to rectify the register.
h   (2) The register may be rectified under this section, notwithstanding that the rectification may affect any estates, rights, charges, or interests acquired or protected by registration, or by any entry on the register, or otherwise.
        (3) The register shall not be rectified, except for the purpose of giving effect to an overriding interest or an order of the court, so as to affect the title of the proprietor who is in possession—(*a*) unless the proprietor has caused or
j   substantially contributed to the error or omission by fraud or lack of proper care; or (*c*) unless for any other reason, in any particular case, it is considered that it would be unjust not to rectify the register against him . . .
        (5) The registrar shall obey the order of any competent court in relation to any registered land on being served with the order or an official copy thereof . . .'

It is convenient to refer at this point to s 83 of the 1925 Act, which makes provision for an indemnity to be given to those suffering loss by reason of the rectification of the register and, in certain circumstances, to those suffering loss where rectification is refused. Section 83, as amended, provides so far as relevant, as follows:

'(1) Subject to the provisions of this Act to the contrary, any person suffering loss by reason of any rectification of the register under this Act shall be entitled to be indemnified.

(2) Where an error or omission has occurred in the register, but the register is not rectified, any person suffering loss by reason of such error or omission, shall, subject to the provisions of this Act, be entitled to be indemnified . . .

(4) Subject as hereinafter provided, a proprietor of any registered land or charge claiming in good faith under a forged disposition shall, where the register is rectified, be deemed to have suffered loss by reason of such rectification and shall be entitled to be indemnified under this Act.

(5) No indemnity shall be payable under this Act in any of the following cases:—(a) Where the applicant or a person from whom he derives title (otherwise than under a disposition for valuable consideration which is registered or protected on the register) has caused or substantially contributed to the loss by fraud or lack of proper care . . .

(6) Where an indemnity is paid in respect of the loss of an estate or interest in or charge on land the amount so paid shall not exceed—(a) Where the register is not rectified, the value of the estate, interest or charge at the time when the error or omission which caused the loss was made; (b) Where the register is rectified, the value (if there had been no rectification) of the estate, interest or charge, immediately before the time of rectification . . .'

If an order of rectification is to be made the case must be brought within at least one of paras (a) to (h) of s 82(1). The dispute in the present case is as to the breadth of the power conferred by paras (a) and (b) and, to a lesser extent, paras (d) and (h). There is no doubt but that, if Mrs Steed's signature had been forged or if the non est factum plea had been made good, the case would have fallen squarely within para (g). In neither case, if the land had been unregistered, would the Hammonds or the building society have obtained a legal estate. I cannot see any reasonable basis on which an order of rectification could have been withheld. If, however, as is the case, the transfer is only voidable, para (g) does not apply. It is plain that, if title to the property had been unregistered, Mr Steed would have had no remedy against the building society. He would have recovered the property from the Hammonds but the property would have remained subject to the charge. It is submitted, however, that para (a), (b), (d) or (h) can, since title is registered, be prayed in aid. This submission is made on the footing that, under one or more of these paragraphs, the court is given a general discretion to order rectification in any case in which it may be thought just to do so. If the submission is right, then s 82, or its statutory predecessors, achieved a remarkable and unnoticed change in the substantive law. If the discretion can be exercised where there has been a fraudulent misrepresentation, as in the present case, it must be exercisable also where a merely innocent misrepresentation has been made. It would, as Mr Lloyd conceded, be exercisable also in a case where no misrepresentation inducing the transaction could be pointed to but where a registered proprietor had entered into a transaction under a misapprehension for which the other party to the transaction was not responsible, a misapprehension as to the value of the property, for example. Mr Lloyd said that in such a case the

discretion to order rectification against a bona fide purchaser, such as the building
a society in the present case, would be very unlikely ever to be exercised. But the
proposition that the discretionary power contended for can be spelt out of the
statutory language is, to me, so startling as to require the premise of the
proposition to be very carefully examined.

There is a sense in which the power to rectify under s 82 is undoubtedly
discretionary. The words in sub-s (1) are 'may be rectified'. Section 83(2) shows
b that rectification is not automatic. The power to rectify may, in a particular case,
be present but, none the less, there is a general discretion to refuse rectification. It
does not follow, however, that there is, in every case, a general discretion to grant
rectification. The power to grant rectification is limited in sub-s (1) to 'any of the
following cases'. The power to order rectification must, therefore, be found
within one or other of the sub-s (1) paragraphs and cannot be spelt out of the
c words 'may be rectified'.

Paragraphs (*a*) and (*b*) provide a power to rectify that can only be exercised by
the court. The power conferred by the other paragraphs can be exercised either
by the registrar or by the court. Paragraph (*a*) enables an order of rectification to
be made where the court 'has decided that any person is entitled to any estate
d right or interest in or to any registered land or charge . . .' This, in my judgment,
is a clear reference to an entitlement under the substantive law. An example
would be a case, such as Mr Steed's case against the Hammonds, for the setting
aside of a transaction on the ground of misrepresentation or some other sufficient
cause. Another example would be the successful assertion of a possessory title. A
third example might be the assertion of a right by a beneficiary under a trust who
e had become absolutely entitled to the land. In each of these cases, once the
entitlement had been established, the court would have power under para (*a*) to
order the register to be rectified so as to reflect the entitlement. But para (*a*) does
not, in my judgment, give any substantive cause of action where none before
existed. It does not enable a voidable transaction to be set aside as against a bona
fide purchaser who has acquired by registration a legal estate. And, if no
f entitlement as against such a purchaser can be established, para (*a*) does not, in
my judgment, enable the register to be rectified as against such a purchaser.
Paragraph (*a*) does not assist Mr Steed in his rectification claim against the building
society. Paragraph (*b*) is the paragraph on which Mr Lloyd pinned his main hopes.
It applies, he submitted, whenever any person is 'aggrieved' by an entry on the
g register. Paragraph (*b*) is something of a puzzle, not least because the form of the
'application' is not 'prescribed' by any rules made under the 1925 Act. The same
language was used in s 96 of the Land Transfer Act 1875, but there, too, no form
of application was 'prescribed'. The legislative intention underlying para (*b*) and
its statutory predecessor is difficult to identify with clarity. The reference to 'the
application in the prescribed manner' makes me believe that it was contemplated
h that some form of summary process would be prescribed in order to enable relief
to be given in clear cases. Be that as it may, the real question at issue is whether
the provision was intended simply to provide a remedy in respect of proprietary
rights that either entitled the proprietor to have some entry made on the register
or entitled the proprietor to have some entry removed from the register or
whether the provision should be construed as creating a new cause of action
j entitling the court to make rectification orders as it might in its discretion think
fit in favour of persons who would not under substantive law (apart from para (*b*))
have any proprietary rights which they could assert against the registered
proprietor or chargee. In my judgment, the question has only to be put for the
answer to be apparent. Parliament could not have intended para (*b*) to produce
new substantive rights in respect of registered land, enabling registered dispositions

to be set aside and removed from the register in circumstances where, if the land had not been registered, no cause of action would have existed. In my judgment, para (*b*), like para (*a*), provides a remedy but does not create any new substantive rights or causes of action. The scope of para (*c*) is self evident and not relevant in the present case.

Paragraph (*d*) too was relied on by Mr Lloyd. He contended that, since the transfer had been induced by the Hammonds' fraud, both the registration of the Hammonds as proprietors and the registration of the building society's legal charge could be described as having been 'obtained by fraud'. In my judgment, this is a misreading of the paragraph. The paragraph is directed, in my opinion, to fraud practised upon the Land Registry in order to obtain the entry in question. No fraud was used to obtain the entry on the charges register of the building society's legal charge.

This construction of para (*d*) derives support from the language used in s 174(1)(*c*) of the Law of Property Act 1922, the statutory predecessor of para (*d*). Section 174(1)(*c*) enabled the register to be rectified—

'Where the court or the registrar is satisfied that the registration of . . . a charge, mortgage, or other entry in the register . . . has been obtained by fraud, by annulling the registration, notice or other entry . . .'

This provision was reduced to its present succinct form in the Law of Property (Amendment) Act 1924 (see s 8 and Sch 8, para 16). It is the *registration* that must be obtained by fraud.

The registration of a forged transfer could, in my opinion, at least if the application for registration had been made by the forger, be annulled under para (*d*). The entry would have been obtained by fraud in the presenting of a forged transfer for registration. But, if a voidable disposition were registered before being avoided, I would doubt whether the register could be rectified under para (*d*), even if the disposition were voidable on account of fraud. In such a case the entry on the register would not, it seems to me, have been obtained by fraud. Rectification could, of course, in such a case be obtained under para (*a*) or para (*b*). Whether or not that is right, and it need not be decided in this case, a registered disposition made by the fraudster to a bona fide purchaser cannot in my judgment be removed from the register under para (*d*). The registration would not have been obtained by fraud. So para (*d*) cannot in my judgment assist Mr Steed as against the building society.

Paragraphs (*e*) and (*f*) are self explanatory and are of no relevance to this case.

Paragraph (*g*) does not, in the event that the transfer is voidable, assist Mr Steed as against the building society. It is, however, an important paragraph so far as an understanding of the scheme of s 82(1) is concerned.

In my opinion the scheme is reasonably clear. Paragraphs (*a*) and (*b*) give power to the court to make orders of rectification in order to give effect to property rights which have been established in an action or which are clear. Paragraph (*c*) enables orders to be made by consent. The remaining paragraphs, paras (*d*) to (*h*), are intended to enable errors to be corrected. Paragraphs (*d*), (*e*), (*f*) and (*g*) each deal with an error of a particular character. But, since these paragraphs might not cover comprehensively all errors, para (*h*) was added as a catch-all provision to cover any other errors. The breadth of the catch-all provision was, I imagine, the reason why it was thought appropriate to make the power exercisable 'where . . . it may be deemed just to rectify the register'. There are no comparable words in any of the other paragraphs.

Paragraph (*h*) is relied on by Mr Lloyd. But in order for the paragraph to be

applicable some 'error or omission in the register' or some 'entry made under a
mistake' must be shown. The entry in the charges register of the building society's
legal charge was not an error and was not made under a mistake. The legal charge
was executed by the Hammonds, who were at the time transferees under a
transfer executed by Mrs Steed as attorney for the registered proprietor. The
voidable transfer had not been set aside. The registration of the Hammonds as
proprietors took place at the same time as the registration of the legal charge.
Neither registration was an error. Neither entry was made under a mistake. So
the case for rectification cannot be brought under para (h).

As a matter of principle, if, as I think, the appellant's case for rectification as
against the building society cannot be brought under any of the paragraphs of
s 82(1), I would conclude that that must be an end to the rectification claim.
Mr Lloyd, however, has relied strongly on passages in the judgment of Slade LJ
in *Argyle Building Society v Hammond* (1984) 49 P & CR 148.

Before I come to those passages, it is convenient to refer to such earlier authority
as there is.

Chowood Ltd v Lyall (No 2) [1930] 2 Ch 156, [1930] All ER Rep 402 concerned a
strip of land which had, on first registration, been included in a registered title
notwithstanding that it was in the possession of an adjoining owner. The register
was rectified under para (h) on an application made by the adjoining owner, the
defendant. In the Court of Appeal Lawrence LJ said ([1930] 2 Ch 156 at 168–169,
[1930] All ER Rep 402 at 406):

> 'I see no reason to limit the word "mistake" in that section to any particular
> kind of mistake . . . I further agree . . . that . . . the rectification might also be
> made under clauses (a) and (g) of sub-s. 1. Moreover I am not satisfied that
> the defendant's application for rectification would not come under cl. (b) as
> being made by a person who is aggrieved by an entry in the register.
> Mr. Armitage [junior counsel for the plaintiff] suggested that cl. (b) applies
> only to a mistake made by the officials in the Registry and not to a mistake
> made or induced by one or other of the parties. I prefer not to express any
> concluded opinion on this point . . .'

Underlying this passage, as it seems to me, is Lawrence LJ's acceptance of the
importance of bringing the rectification case within one or other of the paragraphs
of s 82(1).

Calgary and Edmonton Land Co Ltd v Discount Bank (Overseas) Ltd [1971] 1 All ER
551, [1971] 1 WLR 81 concerned cautions which had been entered on the register
in order to protect interests claimed in a pending action. The action had been
struck out at first instance, an appeal to the Court of Appeal had failed but a
petition for leave to appeal to the House of Lords was still pending. On an
interlocutory notice of motion Brightman J ordered that the register be rectified
by vacating the cautions. He held that he had power to make the order either
under para (a) or under para (b) and that '. . . it matters not whether the order is
expressly made under para (a) or para (b)' (see [1971] 1 All ER 551 at 553, [1971]
1 WLR 81 at 85). I would respectfully accept that the order was justified under
para (a) but would regard the case as a classic example of the sort of case for which
para (b) was designed.

In *Re Leighton's Conveyance* [1936] 1 All ER 667 a non est factum case was raised.
The plaintiff sought rectification, first, against her daughter, who had fraudulently
induced the plaintiff to sign a transfer leading to the daughter's registration as
proprietor, and, secondly, against chargees who, without any notice of the
daughter's fraud, had advanced money to the daughter on the security of
registered charges. The case was, therefore, very similar to the present case.

Luxmoore J ordered rectification as against the daughter but, having concluded
that the non est factum plea failed, he dismissed the rectification claim against   *a*
the chargees. He said (at 673):

> 'I am satisfied that there are no grounds on which I can say that these
> charges are bad, but with regard to the equity of redemption I am satisfied
> on the evidence that what Mrs. Wardman did was at the request of and in
> reliance on her daughter, and under her influence ... It follows that the   *b*
> conveyance to Mrs. Bergin can have no effect as against Mrs. Wardman, and
> she is still entitled to the equity of redemption in the property ... With
> regard to the charges register, there is no ground for interfering with it and
> directing any rectification. They are good charges and remain enforceable
> against the property.'

c

It was not stated in the judgment which paragraph or paragraphs of s 82(1)
Luxmoore J regarded as applicable, but the report of the argument of counsel and
an editorial note suggest that the judge was invited to act under para (*d*) (at 667).
It appears also from the report of argument that rectification as against the
daughter was conceded and that the only issue in the case against the chargees
was the non est factum issue. In my opinion, para (*a*), rather than para (*d*),   *d*
provided the power to rectify as against the daughter. If the non est factum case
had succeeded, para (*g*) also would have been in point, both against the daughter
and against the chargees. It was not suggested by counsel for the mother that, if
the non est factum plea failed, she might none the less be entitled to rectification
against the chargees. And there is nothing in the judgment of Luxmoore J to
indicate that, having rejected the non est factum plea, he thought that he had any   *e*
discretionary power to order rectification of the charges register.

I now come to the judgment of Slade LJ in *Argyle Building Society v Hammond*
(1984) 49 P & CR 148. For the purposes of his judgment Slade LJ assumed that
the allegation of forgery would succeed. He assumed nothing else. References to
the 'assumed facts' are references to the facts regarding the forgery. Having set   *f*
out the text of s 82(1), he said (at 157):

> 'First, registers of title made pursuant to the 1925 Act consist of three parts,
> namely the property register, the proprietorship register and the charges
> register. The jurisdiction to rectify under the subsection plainly extends to
> all or any of these parts. Secondly, on the assumed facts in the present case,
> the court would, in our judgment, have clear jurisdiction to rectify the   *g*
> proprietorship register of the house by substituting the name of the appellant
> for that of Mr. and Mrs. Hammond, since the case would fall within all or
> any of sub-paragraphs (*a*), (*b*), (*d*), (*g*) and (*h*) of section 82(1). The present
> argument relates to the possibility or otherwise of rectification of the charges
> register.'

h

He made clear the opinion of the court that, on the assumed facts, the court
would have power to rectify the charges register against the mortgagees as well as
the proprietorship register against the Hammonds (at 158). I would respectfully
agree, save that, for the reasons I have given, I do not think the case would come
within para (*d*). It would come, in my opinion, within paras (*a*), (*b*), (*g*) and,   *j*
perhaps, (*h*).

Slade LJ then referred to *Re Leighton's Conveyance*, cited the passage from the
judgment of Luxmoore J that I have cited and continued (at 160):

> 'Reverting to the decision at first instance in the *Leighton* case, the report of
> the argument shows that the provisions of section 82(1) and (2) of the 1925

Act were drawn to the attention of Luxmoore J. We feel no doubt that he
would have appreciated that, even in the absence of a successful plea of
forgery or *non est factum*, the section would in terms have conferred a
discretion on the court to rectify the charges register, even as against the
innocent chargees. Nevertheless, it is readily intelligible that Luxmoore J.
should have considered that, when the discretion fell to be exercised, the
equities were all on one side—that is to say in favour of the chargees, who
had acted on the faith of a document of transfer which the mother had
herself executed after having failed to make inquiries which would have
revealed that the document related to the property. If the title to the land
had not been registered, the title of the daughter would, at worst, have been
voidable, not void; and under general principles of equity, mortgagees from
the daughter in good faith and for value, without notice of the facts giving
rise to the voidability, would have acquired a good title to their mortgages.
We can see no reason why the court in the *Leighton* case should have regarded
the equities as being any different, as between the mother and the chargees,
merely because the land happened to be registered land.'

In my respectful opinion, this analysis of *Re Leighton's Conveyance* is not justified
by Luxmoore J's judgment. There is nothing in the judgment or in the report of
counsel's argument to suggest that the possibility of rectification against the
chargees, in the absence of a successful plea of forgery or non est factum, was ever
considered. Slade LJ commented (at 162):

'... in a case where one or more of the conditions of section 82(1) are
fulfilled, the court has at least theoretical discretion to rectify any part of the
register, even as against innocent third parties ...'

I would respectfully agree with this comment, based as it is on the premise that
the case can be brought within one or other of the paragraphs of s 82(1). But Slade
LJ then went on to distinguish the case of a party 'deprived of his title as a result
of a forged document which he did not execute' from the case where the party
'has been deprived as a result of a document which he himself executed, albeit
under a mistake induced by fraud' and commented that 'when the court comes
to exercise its discretion, different considerations may well apply'. The paragraph
of s 82(1) under which the latter case could be brought was not identified. On the
true construction of s 82(1) there is not, in my opinion, any paragraph under
which the latter case could be brought.

Mr Lloyd's argument that the court has a general discretionary power to order
rectification of the register was based on the passages from Slade LJ's judgment to
which I have referred. The passages were not part of the ratio of the decision, by
which we are bound and with which I respectfully agree. A voidable transfer was
not part of the 'assumed facts' on which the ratio was based. In my judgment, the
obiter passages, regarding voidable transfers and innocent third parties claiming
thereunder, were based on an incorrect construction of s 82(1) and should not be
followed.

In my opinion, if the appellant's non est factum case is rejected, the court has
no power under s 82(1) to order rectification as against the building society. It is
strictly unnecessary for me to deal with the issue of discretion, which only arises
if the court has power to rectify. Knox J refused rectification as a matter of
discretion. He held that as between the appellant and the building society 'all the
equities are on the building society's side'. This would certainly be so if the land
were unregistered. But under s 83(1) the building society, if rectification were
ordered, would have what seems to me to be an unimpeachable statutory right to

an indemnity against the loss it would thereby suffer. On the other hand, if rectification were refused, the appellant would not be able to claim an indemnity *a* under s 83(2). Mr Lloyd accepted, rightly, that, since the registration of the building society's charge was not an 'error or omission', the case would not come within s 83(2). The financial consequences to the parties of ordering or refusing rectification make it difficult to weigh the 'equities'. If rectification were ordered, the loss would fall not upon the building society but upon the public purse. If rectification were refused, the public purse would be saved the burden of paying *b* an indemnity. I mention these matters not in order to indicate any disagreement with Knox J's conclusions on discretion but because the indemnity provisions in s 83 seem to me to underline that the legislature did not contemplate the power of rectification being exercisable under s 82 except in cases either where an error or omission had occurred in the register (ie paras (*d*) to (*h*)) or where a substantive cause of action against the registered proprietor required the register to be rectified *c* (ie paras (*a*) and (*b*)).

In 'error or omission' cases, ie in cases coming within paras (*d*) to (*h*), an indemnity would, if rectification were refused, be available under s 83(2) (subject always to s 83(5)(*a*)). In cases within paras (*a*) and (*b*) but not within any of paras (*d*) to (*h*), eg cases in which voidable transactions are set aside and, as a *d* consequence, rectification of the register is required, it is difficult to construct any scenario in which rectification could be withheld. The construction of s 82(1) that I have suggested seems to me to mesh with and to explain the scheme of indemnity contained in s 83. The 'general discretion' approach to s 82(1) does not.

For the reasons I have given I would dismiss this appeal.   *e*

BUTLER-SLOSS LJ. I agree.

PURCHAS LJ. I also agree that for the reasons given in the judgment of Scott LJ this appeal should be dismissed. I wish only to add that in my judgment I *f* have, after some hesitation, come to the conclusion that it is impossible to extract a general discretion to rectify the register from s 82(1)(*h*) of the Land Registration Act 1925 beyond that necessary to cover some unusual error which did not fall under paras (*d*) to (*g*). It is under paras (*a*) and (*b*) that rectification depending upon the prior determination of disputed rights by the court should be effected. With some diffidence, I find myself in agreement with Scott LJ in coming to the *g* conclusion that the analysis of the judgment of Luxmoore J in *Re Leighton's Conveyance* [1936] 1 All ER 667 in the judgment of the court delivered by Slade LJ in the passage from the judgment already cited by Scott LJ is not justified on a general reading of that case. At the time when the present case was first before this court sub nom *Argyle Building Society v Hammond* (1984) 49 P & CR 148 the plaintiff's case was based on the alleged forgery of Mrs Steed's signature upon the *h* transfer. This would have rendered the transfer void. The case would then fall squarely within s 82(1)(*g*) and therefore the conclusion (at 162) referred to by Scott LJ was perfectly correct in the context. I am, I regret, unable to agree that the judgment of the court beyond this or that, in so far as it was obiter in the context in which it was delivered, can be supported or that it binds this court.

Appeal dismissed.

Celia Fox Barrister.

Dixons Stores Group Ltd v Thames Television plc

QUEEN'S BENCH DIVISION
DRAKE J
15 JULY 1992

Evidence – Without prejudice correspondence – Correspondence not forming part of negotiations – Privilege from admission in evidence – Letters written after termination of bona fide negotiations – Letters from defendant to plaintiff suggesting parties negotiate compromise – Letters not marked without prejudice – Whether letters admissible in defendant's cross-examination of plaintiff's witness.

On 3 July 1991 the plaintiffs' solicitor wrote a letter before action to the defendants alleging that a television programme broadcast by the defendants was defamatory of the plaintiffs. A writ was issued on 11 July. Between 5 February and 10 June 1992 there was without prejudice correspondence between the parties with a view to settling the action but that was inconclusive. On 1 and 9 July 1992 the defendants' solicitors wrote to the plaintiffs' solicitors almost identical letters stating that the defendants wished to negotiate a compromise and suggesting that the defendant make an apology and statement in open court. The first letter was not headed, and made no reference to its being, without prejudice, while the second was headed 'open letter', and both were clearly intended to be referred to by the defendants at trial. The offer was not accepted by the plaintiffs and the matter came to trial, in the course of which counsel for the defendants sought to refer to the letters in cross-examination of one of the plaintiffs' witnesses. The plaintiffs' counsel objected to the letters being admitted in evidence on the ground that they were clearly written without prejudice as an offer to negotiate a settlement and were therefore subject to privilege and were inadmissible without the consent of both parties.

Held – A party to an action could write a letter containing an offer to settle the action without ipso facto attracting to that letter any privilege which could be claimed by the opposing party, provided the letter was not part of continuing negotiations. However, if the letter was a reply to a letter written without prejudice or was part of a continuing sequence of negotiations, whether by correspondence or orally, then it would be privileged and could not be admitted in evidence without the consent of both parties. It followed that since the letters were written after the negotiations and without prejudice correspondence had finished and come to nothing, they were not subject to privilege and could be used by the defendants in the course of the action without the consent of the plaintiffs (see p 351 *g h* and p 352 *d f g*, post).

Notes
For communications written without prejudice, see 17 *Halsbury's Laws* (4th edn) paras 212–213, and for cases on the subject, see 22(2) Digest (2nd reissue) 99–104, 6770–6815.

Cases referred to in judgment
Rush & Tomkins Ltd v Greater London Council [1988] 3 All ER 737, [1989] AC 1280, [1988] 3 WLR 939, HL.

Application

The defendants, Thames Television plc, applied in the course of the trial of a libel *a* action brought against them by the plaintiffs, Dixons Stores Group Ltd, claiming damages for defamation, to put in evidence two letters written by their solicitors to the plaintiffs' solicitors offering to settle the plaintiffs' claim on terms set out in the letters. The facts are set out in the judgment.

Richard Rampton QC and *Thomas Shields* (instructed by *Barlow Lyde & Gilbert*) for *b* the plaintiffs.
Michael Corkery QC and *Heather Rogers* (instructed by *D J Freeman*) for the defendants.

DRAKE J. I am asked to rule on the admissibility of two letters, both from the *c* defendants' solicitors to the plaintiffs' solicitors, one dated 1 July 1992 and the other, in almost, although not quite, identical terms, dated 9 July 1992.

The first of those letters, dated 1 July 1992, had no heading 'without prejudice', nor was there any reference in the body of the letter to it being written without prejudice. The second one, in almost identical terms, dated 9 July 1992 was *d* headed 'open letter'. Both of these letters, it is clear, were written by the defendants' solicitors with the intention that they should be referred to at the trial of the action.

The relevant history, so far as dates are concerned, is as follows. The broadcast of a programme by the defendants which gives rise to this action for libel was on 27 June 1991. On 3 July 1991 the plaintiffs' solicitors wrote a letter before action, *e* complaining of the alleged defamation in the course of that programme and calling upon the defendants to make an apology in a stated form, to make a payment to a charity to be nominated and to pay the plaintiffs' costs. There being no immediate response, the writ was issued on 11 July. On 16 July the defendants' solicitors responded to the plaintiffs' solicitors' letter of 1 July and to the fact that the writ had been issued. In that letter the defendants' solicitors stated their wish *f* to negotiate a settlement of the action. They wrote:

'However, our clients have no quarrel with yours and wish, if possible, to resolve this matter amicably. To that end, the programme editor . . . is prepared to broadcast a further Cityfile item. We enclose for your consideration a draft, which we would be happy to discuss with you.' *g*

The draft proposed broadcast was not acceptable to the plaintiffs and the action proceeded. Then I am told that on 5 February 1992, and continuing until 10 June 1992, there was correspondence between the parties without prejudice, and clearly marked as such, with a view to a settlement of the action. It came to nothing. Then on 1 July 1992 the defendants' solicitors wrote to the plaintiffs' *h* solicitors stating, in what was intended to be an open letter, but not marked as such, that they wished to negotiate a compromise of the action and suggested that an apology and a statement in open court should be made. A draft apology was included with the letter.

I understand that some query arose at that stage as to whether or not that letter was covered by 'without prejudice' privilege and accordingly on 9 July 1992 the *j* defendants' solicitors repeated the letter in very nearly identical terms, but headed it 'open letter'. They now wish to put the terms of that letter to one or more witnesses to be called for the plaintiffs, and Mr Rampton QC for the plaintiff has objected on the grounds that the letter is privileged as being without prejudice.

It is quite clear and is trite law that, where an offer of compromise is made
a without prejudice, it is subject to privilege and cannot be referred to in evidence
without the consent of both parties. I take it, although I do not think I was told
this expressly, that the letter of 16 July 1991, made in response to the letter before
action and following the issue of writ, which did expressly offer to negotiate a
settlement of the action, was the subject of an agreement for waiver of privilege,
since all that Mr Rampton claims as attracting privilege to the present letters of
b July 1992 would apply with equal force to that letter of 16 July 1991. Be that as it
may, the policy of the law is clearly to encourage settlements of actions and I
think it is quite clear that the modern tendency has been to enlarge the cloak
under which negotiations may be conducted without prejudice. I take that from
a consideration of the modern cases in which without prejudice privilege has
been considered, and it is in fact stated in those terms in *Cross On Evidence* (7th
c edn, 1990) p 452.

The mere fact of heading a letter 'without prejudice' is not in the least decisive
as to whether or not the letter is in fact privileged. The privilege exists in order to
encourage bona fide attempts to negotiate a settlement of an action and if the
letter is not written to initiate or continue such a bona fide attempt to effect a
d settlement it will not be protected by privilege. But, conversely, if it is written in
the course of such a bona fide attempt, it will be covered by privilege, and the
absence of any heading or reference in the letter to show it is written without
prejudice will not be fatal.

I have merely stated some general principles. But in the present case the
position is somewhat different. The letter itself contains no reference to a claim
e that it is written without prejudice; on the contrary, the second of the two letters
is headed 'open letter', and the defendants, whose letter it is, written by their
solicitors, expressly do not claim privilege, they want to refer to the letter in cross-
examination of the plaintiffs' witness. Mr Rampton says they cannot do so. It is
the plaintiffs who claim privilege for the defendants' letter, and Mr Rampton
submits that the very fact that it is clearly written with an offer to negotiate a
f settlement of the action means that the defendants cannot refer to it without the
plaintiffs' consent, which in the instant case is not given.

In my judgment, a party may write a letter containing an offer to settle an
action without ipso facto attracting to that letter a privilege which the opposing
party may then claim. If the letter is in reply to a letter written without prejudice
g or is part of a continuing sequence of negotiations, whether by correspondence or
orally, then it will be privileged and cannot be given in evidence without the
consent of both parties. But in the present case I am dealing with a letter which
was not part of continuing without prejudice negotiations. It was written after
certain negotiations and correspondence without prejudice had finished and come
to nothing. In my judgment, a letter containing an offer to settle an action may
h be written, and written as an open letter, and used by the party writing it in the
course of the action, provided it has relevance to the issues in the action and, as I
have already made clear, is not part of continuing negotiations.

In an action for defamation it is clear that such a letter may be highly relevant.
The damages are likely to be very much affected by the willingness or refusal of
the defendant to make an apology. True there is nothing to stop a defendant
j making an apology without first obtaining the agreement of the plaintiff, but
equally I see nothing to prevent a defendant making an offer openly to publish an
apology on terms and then referring to the letter at the trial. If, as in this case, the
offer is not accepted, it is then open to the plaintiff to say why it was not accepted;
it is open to the plaintiffs to invite the jury to take into account that the offered

apology was only made upon terms, and therefore was conditional; and it is open
to the plaintiffs to point out that, the terms not having been accepted, the *a*
defendants did not see fit to go and broadcast or publish the apology without the
conditions that they had asked for being met.

But, if the defendants are not permitted to refer to what they wish to treat as
an open letter, it seems to me that the jury will have to assess damages, if they
find for the plaintiffs on libel, on an entirely false basis. The plaintiffs' case was
opened on the basis that, following the letter before action on 3 July 1991 and the *b*
issue of the writ, the defendants replied with their offer to settle the action,
including the proposal that they should broadcast or publish an apology of a sort,
or a statement, in terms which Mr Rampton described to the jury as 'very mean'
terms. The terms were read to the jury and they were told that no apology has
been made since. I think that, as the defendants have now in July offered an
apology, it would be right for the jury to know the nature of the apology offered, *c*
together of course with the terms upon which they offered to make it.

It seems to me that this whole subject of without prejudice letters is clearly a
form of privilege which may be waived by the party claiming the privilege but,
where negotiations take place, it cannot be waived without both parties consenting
to the publication of the terms of the negotiations which have gone on. But in *d*
this case, where one party writes an open letter, I can see nothing at all to justify
privilege being attached.

I have considered particularly the speech of Lord Griffiths in *Rush & Tompkins
Ltd v Greater London Council* [1988] 3 All ER 737 at 740–744, [1989] AC 1280 at
1300–1305, to which my attention was drawn. But I do not find anything in that
speech which leads me to take the view that where one party alone makes an open *e*
statement it is open to the other party to claim privilege merely on the grounds
that the letter contains an offer to negotiate a settlement or, as in this case, to
make an apology. It seems to me, although Mr Rampton has indicated he is not
going to find fault with the distinction between the two letters, that the first letter
is in exactly the same position as the second letter, that is the letter of 1 July. It
was not part of the continuing correspondence or of the negotiations and the *f*
mere fact that it lacks the words 'open letter' does not make it privileged any
more than the mere fact that the letter of 9 July is headed 'open' makes that
unprivileged. It is the substance and context of the letters which, in my judgment,
govern their admissibility. Therefore I rule that it is open to the defendants to
put to the plaintiffs' witnesses the terms of either or both of those letters.

g

Order accordingly.

K Mydeen Esq   Barrister.

Wilson v Best Travel Ltd

QUEEN'S BENCH DIVISION
PHILLIPS J
16, 17, 18, 19 APRIL 1991

Contract – Implied term – Contract of service – Duty to carry out service with reasonable care and skill – Holiday brochure – Plaintiff injured by falling through glass doors of Greek hotel while on holiday – Holiday booked through defendant tour operator – Glass doors complying with Greek but not British safety standards – Plaintiff suing defendants for breach of duty of care to provide services with reasonable care and skill – Nature of duty of care owed by tour operator to customers – Whether defendants discharging duty of care owed to plaintiff – Supply of Goods and Services Act 1982, s 13.

The plaintiff, while staying in a hotel in Greece on a holiday booked through the defendant tour operator, sustained serious injuries after tripping and falling through glass patio doors at the hotel. The hotel was featured in the defendants' brochure, which stated that the defendants were not always able to exercise day-to-day control over holiday arrangements and that they would not accept liability for loss, damage or inconvenience unless caused by negligence on the part of their own employees but that they did 'keep an eye on' accommodation referred to in the brochure. The glass doors were fitted with ordinary 5-mm glass which complied with Greek but not British safety standards, which would have required the use of safety glass in such doors. The plaintiff claimed damages against the defendants, contending that the characteristics of the glass fitted to the patio doors were such that the hotel was not reasonably safe for use by the defendants' customers and that the defendants were in breach of the duty of care arising out of the term implied by s 13[a] of the Supply of Goods and Services Act 1982 that in a contract for the supply of services the supplier of services would carry out the service with reasonable care and skill.

Held – The duty of care owed by a tour operator to its customers in accordance with s 13 of the 1982 Act was a duty to exercise reasonable care to exclude from the accommodation offered any hotel the characteristics of which were such that guests could not spend a holiday there in reasonable safety. The duty to ensure reasonable safety was discharged if the tour operator checked that local safety regulations had been complied with and the duty did not extend to excluding a hotel whose characteristics, so far as safety was concerned, failed to satisfy the current standards applying in England, provided always that the absence of the relevant safety feature was not such that a reasonable holiday-maker might decline to take a holiday at the hotel in question, eg if a hotel included in a brochure had no fire precautions at all. Accordingly, since the defendants had inspected the accommodation offered in their brochure as part of their services, since the patio doors complied with Greek safety regulations and since the degree of danger posed by the absence of safety glass in the patio doors was not such that the plaintiff would have declined to stay at the hotel, the defendants had discharged the duty of care owed to the plaintiff, whose claim therefore failed (see p 356 *a g h* and p 358 *c* to *e g*, post).

Notes

For implied terms in a contract, see 9 *Halsbury's Laws* (4th edn) paras 351–362, and for cases on the subject, see 12(1) *Digest* (2nd reissue) 403–454, 3282–3546.

---

[a] Section 13 is set out at p 356 *c*, post

For the Supply of Goods and Services Act 1982, s 13, see 39 *Halsbury's Statutes* (4th edn) 172.

Cases referred to in judgment

Shirlaw v Southern Foundries (1926) Ltd and Federated Foundries Ltd [1939] 2 All ER 113, [1939] 2 KB 206, CA; affd [1940] 2 All ER 445, [1940] AC 701, HL.

Wall v Silver Wings Surface Arrangements Ltd (18 November 1981, unreported), QBD.

Action

The plaintiff, Richard Bernard Wilson, brought an action against the defendant, Best Travel Ltd, claiming damages for injuries suffered by him at the Vanninarchis Beach Hotel on the island of Kos in Greece when he tripped and fell through a glass patio door of the hotel on 14 August 1986. The facts are set out in the judgment.

Paul Norris (instructed by *G L Hockfield & Co*) for the plaintiff.
Frank Burton (instructed by *Hextall Erskine & Co*) for the defendants.

PHILLIPS J. In 1986 Mrs Cheryl Bromley made a booking on behalf of a party of five with the defendants for a two-week holiday at the Vanninarchis Beach Hotel on the island of Kos. The defendants' brochure, from which Mrs Bromley selected the holiday, described the hotel as follows:

> 'C Class. This friendly family-run hotel is located right on the sea shore. The informal Vanninarchis Beach is close to several shops and tavernas and a short walk from the Kardomina Harbour. It has a reception/rustic style lounge with adjoining snack bar opening on to a terrace and a souvenir shop. All rooms have private bath/WC or shower/WC and balcony. Bed and breakfast.'

Mrs Bromley's party, in addition to herself, consisted of a gentleman friend, her 14-year-old daughter Cheryl, her elder daughter Yvonne, and Yvonne's fiancé, the plaintiff. Four of the party had never been out of England before and looked forward to the holiday with keen excitement.

The party flew to Kos on 13 August 1986 and arrived at the hotel in the evening. Yvonne and the plaintiff were allocated a room on the ground floor of the hotel and the other three members of the party were given the room next door. This room had a sliding glass door that led on to a patio. At about 10.30 am on 14 August, after exploring the beach, breakfast, and a short presentation by the defendants' local representative, the plaintiff and Yvonne joined the other three members of the party in the latter's bedroom. There, in circumstances to which I shall return, the plaintiff tripped and fell against the glass patio door. The door shattered and the plaintiff fell through it, sustaining lacerations from the broken glass to the right shoulder, elbow, hand and, in particular, multiple lacerations of the right leg. The plaintiff now claims from the defendants damages in respect of the consequences of this accident. Before dealing with the issue of liability, I propose to describe those consequences.

The Injuries

[His Lordship then considered the nature of the plaintiff's injuries and his consequential loss and concluded that if liability were to be established the plaintiff would be entitled to general damages of £12,500 for pain, suffering and loss of amenity and £30,000 for future loss of earnings. His Lordship continued:]

Liability

a   How did the accident occur? The accident happened quickly with a devastating shock to the plaintiff and the other members of the party in the room at the time and it is not surprising that the picture painted by their evidence is not entirely clear. The essence of the story is not, however, in doubt. The plaintiff had just closed the sliding door on to the patio and was standing with his back to it. A heavy pair of curtains was drawn open, flanking the door, but the curtain behind
b   and to the right of the plaintiff as he faced into the room had become detached in part from the curtain rail and was trailing a little on the ground. In order to allow Cheryl Bromley access to a table close to which he was standing, the plaintiff took one or two steps back. His right foot caught in the sagging curtain and caused him to trip backwards. I think he must have fallen against the glass with his full weight, albeit not from a great distance, in order to cause the glass to break. Mr
c   Burton, counsel for the defendants, urged me to reject this account of the accident, with which all the eye-witnesses concurred. He submitted that it is more probable that the accident resulted from the plaintiff falling against the window with greater momentum as a result of some high-spirited horseplay. The evidence provides no foundation for this submission, and I reject it. I do not find that the
d   plaintiff was in any way responsible for his own misfortune. The immediate cause of his falling was the obstruction which resulted from the sagging curtain. The gravity of the consequences was attributable to the fact that the glass fractured into fragments of razor-edged sharpness.

The plaintiff's case

e   Mr Norris, counsel for the plaintiff, advanced his case in two alternative ways. The fundamental premise underlying each was that the characteristics of the glass fitted to the doors of the Vanninarchis Beach Hotel were such that the hotel was not reasonably safe for use by the defendants' customers. This constituted a breach of contract on the part of the defendants for two reasons. First, it was an implied term of the defendants' contract with the plaintiff that the structure of the hotel
f   would be reasonably safe. Second, the defendants owed the plaintiff a duty to exercise reasonable skill and care to ensure that the hotel was reasonably safe. This duty required that the hotel should have been regularly and competently inspected. Such inspections should have disclosed the nature of the glass fitted in the sliding doors of the hotel and thus the fact that the hotel was not reasonably
g   safe.

Implied warranty

In support of his first submission Mr Norris was able to point to no particular feature of the plaintiff's contract that gave rise to the implication of the term. Rather he contended that such a term fell to be implied in every contract for a
h   package holiday of the kind with which this case is concerned. He submitted that if any bystander were to ask the parties whether it was an implied term of their contract that the hotel would be reasonably safe, they would both answer, 'Of course' (see *Shirlaw v Southern Foundries (1926) Ltd and Federated Foundries Ltd* [1939] 2 All ER 113 at 124, [1939] 2 KB 206 at 227). I do not agree. The defendants would not have considered it either obvious or reasonable that they
j   should give a warranty of this kind. Mr Burton referred me to the transcript of a decision of Hodgson J in *Wall v Silver Wings Surface Arrangements Ltd* (18 November 1981, unreported), in which, in a case of very different facts, the plaintiff sought to establish a similar implied term in a contract for a package holiday. After a careful analysis of the relevant law, the judge rejected the term alleged on the ground that the implication of such a term was neither necessary

nor obvious nor reasonable. I share both his reasoning and his conclusion. Hodgson J observed:

a

'I think quite clearly that situations could arise in which the tour operator would be liable in negligence to his customers. If, for instance, a hotel included in a brochure had no fire precautions at all or was known to fail to reach the standards required by the law of the country, then the tour operator would, I apprehend, be in breach of duty.'

b

This observation is germane to the alternative way in which Mr Norris advanced his case.

Duty of care
Section 13 of the Supply of Goods and Services Act 1982 provides:

c

'In a contract for the supply of a service where the supplier is acting in the course of a business, there is an implied term that the supplier will carry out the service with reasonable care and skill.'

The nature of the services provided by a travel agent when arranging a holiday can vary enormously, depending on the nature of the holiday. I am satisfied, having read their brochure, that the service provided by the defendants included the inspection of the properties offered in their brochure. Such service is implicit from a number of passages in their brochure, including, under the heading 'Important Information':

d

'Brochure descriptions
Every effort has been made to ensure the accuracy of descriptions and information contained in this brochure. However, we are not always able to exercise day-to-day control over all the component parts of the holiday arrangements and it is always possible that an advertised amenity may be withdrawn or changed due to various reasons, for the purpose of energy or water conservation, lack of demand or for maintenance, renovation etc. We will advise you if we become aware of a major change but we cannot accept liability for the loss of an advertised amenity in such circumstances. Similarly we cannot accept liability for loss, damage or inconvenience unless caused by negligence on the part of our own employees. We would add that we do keep an eye on the accommodation.'

e

f

In my judgment, one of the characteristics of accommodation that the defendants owed a duty to consider when inspecting properties included in their brochure was safety. The defendants owe their customers, including the plaintiff, a duty to exercise reasonable care to exclude from the accommodation offered any hotel whose characteristics were such that guests could not spend a holiday there in reasonable safety. I believe that this case is about the standard to be applied in assessing reasonable safety. It is necessary at this stage to turn to the evidence in relation to the glass fitted in the doors of the Vanninarchis Beach Hotel.

g

h

Glass
Mr Vanninarchis, the manager and, with other members of his family, the owner of the Vanninarchis Beach Hotel, came to England from Kos to give evidence. He told me that the construction of his hotel was completed in 1980. The hotel had to comply with two sets of regulations, those imposed by the building authority and those imposed by the Greek tourist organisation, EOT. These regulations covered the specifications of the building, including the glass to be fitted to doors and windows. The glass for the doors of the hotel was

j

required to be 5 mm thick. The glass was also slightly tinted. At the time there
a was no one on the island of Kos who manufactured or supplied glass of that
thickness so the aluminium frames for the doors had to be sent to Athens where
a contractor made and fitted 5 mm thick glass. The doors were in due course
inspected on behalf of the authorities and approved. Licences were duly issued
and renewed by EOT, proving that the regulations were satisfied. Mr Vanninarchis
brought three of the licences with him. Mr Norris for the plaintiff suggested to
b Mr Vanninarchis that the doors of his hotel should have been fitted with safety
glass, which would fragment into innocuous small pieces if broken. Mr
Vanninarchis's reaction to this was surprise and bewilderment which impressed
me as genuine. He said that he was aware of such glass being fitted to motor cars
but in Greece it was not the practice to fit it in hotels. The regulations did not
require it and such glass was not used in building hotels. He did not accept that it
c was dangerous to fit ordinary glass in his hotel, observing that they had not had
an accident such as that which befell the plaintiff either before or after his casualty.

Expert evidence

Mr Geoffrey Tibbs, a chemist with long experience of the glass industry, was
d called to give expert evidence for the plaintiff. He told me of a number of
different types of glass. For present purposes, two are relevant. The first is
annealed glass. This is the glass that is normally used for glazing. It is generally
used in panes of 4 mm thickness, with 5 mm or 6 mm being used for larger
panes and where increased strength is required. Annealed glass breaks into sharp
and jagged pieces. The second type is toughened glass, sometimes known as
e tempered glass. Individual pieces of glass, already cut to size, are heated in a
furnace and then cooled by jets of air so that the outside surface cools before the
inside, resulting in a high compression in the surface of the glass and tension in
the centre. A greater force is required to break toughened glass compared with
ordinary annealed glass of the same thickness. Once it is broken it will
f immediately break into a very large number of small pieces which are relatively
harmless. Toughened glass is used in many car windscreens. If broken by a flying
stone it is usually necessary to push the glass out with a hand to restore visability.
The characteristic small broken pieces will have been seen at the site of many road
accidents. It cannot be cut to size after toughening, so that each piece has to be
ordered specially. It is a true safety glass.

g Mr Tibbs told me that there has been a growing awareness over recent years of
the dangers of glass, particularly in respect of large panes of glass in doors. The
present situation in this country with respect to the type of door through which
the plaintiff fell, particularly in a hotel or similar public place, is that safety glass,
either toughened or laminated, would always be used. Mr Tibbs referred me to
the relevant British Standards. In 1963 a supplement to BS 973 recommended:
h
'Glazing generally
All glass so situated that there is a reasonably foreseeable risk of injury due
to accidental breakage should be toughened glass unless otherwise required
by fire regulations.

j Doors
All glazing for doors, other than for small observation panels, should be
toughened glass except where the fire regulations apply.'

Subsequent revisions to the relevant standards emphasise the desirability of fitting
toughened glass wherever there is a risk of injury due to accidental breakage. In
1982 BS 6262 was introduced requiring the use of safety glass in doors and side

panels where there is a large single pane. Despite these standards, the fitting of
safety glass to doors has not yet been made a mandatory requirement under the *a*
building regulations. It is nonetheless the practice in England to comply with the
relevant standards.

It is apparent from this evidence that the standards currently applied in England
in the interests of safety have yet to be adopted in Greece. It is at least arguable
that, if the plaintiff's accident had occurred in England, the hotelier would be
held to be in breach of the common duty of care imposed by s 2(2) of the *b*
Occupiers, Liability Act 1957.

What is the duty of a tour operator in a situation such as this? Must he refrain
from sending holidaymakers to any hotel whose characteristics, in so far as safety
is concerned, fail to satisfy the standards which apply in this country? I do not
believe that his obligations in respect of the safety of his clients can extend this
far. Save where uniform international regulations apply, there are bound to be *c*
differences in the safety standards applied in respect of the many hazards of
modern life between one country and another. All civilised countries attempt to
cater for these hazards by imposing mandatory regulations. The duty of care of a
tour operator is likely to extend to checking that local safety regulations are
complied with. Provided that they are, I do not consider that the tour operator *d*
owes a duty to boycott a hotel because of the absence of some safety feature which
would be found in an English hotel unless the absence of such a feature might
lead a reasonable holidaymaker to decline to take a holiday at the hotel in question.
On the facts of this case I do not consider that the degree of danger posed by the
absence of safety glass in the doors of the Vanninarchis Beach Hotel called for any
action on the part of the defendants pursuant to their duty to exercise reasonable *e*
care to ensure the safety of their clients.

It is perhaps significant that Mr Norris did not expand on what action the
defendants should have taken. It was not suggested that they had a duty to warn
clients of this characteristic or that such a warning would have prevented the
accident in this case. What was, I think, implicit in the plaintiff's case was that
the defendants should not have permitted the Vanninarchis Beach Hotel to *f*
feature in their brochure. If that contention were valid, it would, on the evidence
of Mr Vanninarchis, apply to many, if not the majority, of the other hotels,
pensions and villas featured in the defendants' brochure and no doubt the
brochures of the other tour operators who send their clients to Greece.

I have the greatest sympathy for the plaintiff for the horrifying accident he has
suffered and its unhappy consequences but, for the reasons that I have given, it *g*
was an accident which involved no breach of contract or duty on the part of the
defendants.

Judgment for the defendants.

K Mydeen Esq   Barrister.

a

Practice Direction
(Chancery 5/92)

CHANCERY DIVISION

b

Practice – Summary judgment – Chancery Division – Application including claim for injunction – Summons – Return date – Adjournment where hearing likely to be more than 30 minutes – RSC Ord 14.

c *Specific performance – Summary procedure – Summons – Summons normally returnable before master – RSC Ord 86.*

d

1. Applications for summary judgment under RSC Ord 14 are made to the master save in cases where the relief sought includes an injunction which cannot be granted by the master. In those cases the application is made by summons directly to the judge in chambers. At present the return date for such summonses is chosen by the plaintiff's solicitor. This practice is disrupting the efficient functioning of the court lists. These summonses often take many hours or even days to hear, the return date has no regard to existing listing commitments and estimates of the likely length of the hearing given on behalf of the plaintiff before the defendant's evidence has been seen frequently prove to be wildly wrong.

e

2. In future the return date to be inserted in judges' summonses under Ord 14 will be a Monday. On the return date the judge will normally adjourn the effective hearing of the summons to a date to be fixed if the hearing, whether opposed or unopposed, is likely to take longer than 30 minutes. The date will be fixed in the usual way through the Clerk of the Lists, and a certificate of counsel *f* as to the estimated length of the hearing should be lodged with him.

3. In future the master may himself deal with all applications for summary judgment under Ord 86. Accordingly such summonses should normally be returnable before the master in the usual way.

4. To give effect to these changes, the following amendments are made to the Chancery Division Practice Directions.

g (1) Chancery Practice Direction (12)(x)(ii), set out in *The Supreme Court Practice 1993* vol 2, p 210, para 852, is amended by substituting a new para (ii):

h

'Where an application under Order 14 includes an application for an injunction, it usually has to be adjourned to a judge because in most cases the master cannot grant an injunction save in terms agreed by the parties. In such cases the summons should be made returnable before the judge in chambers instead of the master. The return date to be inserted in the summonses will be a Monday which is at least 10 clear days (rule 2(3)) after the summons will be served. The summons should be issued in the Listing Office (room 812), when there must be lodged two copies of the summons, and the affidavits in support with the exhibits. On the return date the *j* summons will normally be adjourned to a date to be fixed if the hearing, whether opposed or unopposed, is likely to take longer than 30 minutes. The adjourned date will be fixed in the usual way through the Clerk of the Lists, and a certificate signed by counsel as to the estimated length of the hearing must be lodged with him.'

(2) Sub-paragraph (*a*) of para (A)(i) under the heading 'B. Jurisdiction' in Chancery Practice Direction (13) relating to masters (see *The Supreme Court Practice 1993* vol 2, p 210, para 854) shall be amended to read as follows:

'(*a*) making orders for specific performance which involve an injunction (such as specific performance of repairing covenants).'

5. The listing arrangements mentioned above do not affect applications for summary judgment under Ord 14 made to the master.

By direction of the Vice-Chancellor.

J M Dyson
7 December 1992   Chief Chancery Master.

Practice Direction
(Chancery 6/92)

CHANCERY DIVISION

Practice – Chancery Division – Masters – Business before Chancery masters – Abolition of distinction between term time and vacation business – Hearings in Companies Court and before judges unaffected – RSC Ord 64, r 3.

1. As from 11 January 1993 (the first day of the Hilary Term) there will no longer be any distinction between term time and vacation so far as business before the Chancery masters is concerned. The list in *The Supreme Court Practice 1993* vol 1, para 64/3/4, setting out the classes of application treated by the Chancery masters as vacation business, is hereby cancelled.

The masters will deal with all types of business throughout the year, and when a master is on holiday his list will normally be taken by a deputy master.

2. This direction has no application to the Companies Court, or to hearings before the Chancery judges, which continue to be governed by RSC Ord 64, r 3.

By direction of the Vice-Chancellor.

J M Dyson
7 December 1992   Chief Chancery Master.

a   # Re International Bulk Commodities Ltd

CHANCERY DIVISION
MUMMERY J
23, 24 MARCH, 15 APRIL 1992

b   *Company – Receiver – Administrative receiver – Unregistered company – Receivers appointed by debenture holder – Whether receivers of unregistered company appointed by debenture holder administrative receivers – Whether powers of receivers limited to powers under debenture – Companies Act 1985, s 735(1)(4) – Insolvency Act 1986, ss 29(2), 251.*

c   A company which was incorporated in 1988 outside the United Kingdom for the purpose of worldwide trading in commodities was neither incorporated nor registered under the Companies Acts. Its sales operations in the United Kingdom were conducted by one director, and the other three directors were resident abroad. On 28 April 1989 the company granted a debenture to a bank giving the bank a first fixed charge over the company's property and book debts and a first *d*   floating charge over all its assets past and future. The debenture gave the bank power to appoint a receiver and manager in the event of failure by the company to make payment on demand. The debenture provided that the receiver so appointed was to have various specified powers in addition to those conferred by s 109 of the Law of Property Act 1925 and if he was an administrative receiver within s 29^a of the Insolvency Act 1986 his powers under Sch 1 to that Act were *e*   not limited by the specified powers. On 15 May 1990 the bank issued a facility letter up to a maximum of £2m. The company ceased trading on 26 October 1991 and on 4 February 1992 the bank terminated the facility and demanded payment of £879,026·73. No payment was made and on 7 February the bank appointed receivers. The company disputed the right of the bank to appoint *f*   receivers. The receivers applied for the determination of the court whether, in view of the fact that the company was a foreign company which was not incorporated or registered under the Companies Acts, they could act as administrative receivers under the 1986 Act or whether they were merely contractual receivers whose powers were limited to those specified in the debenture.

g

Held – Although under s 29(2) of the 1986 Act an administrative receiver was defined as the receiver or manager of a company's property appointed by the debenture holder, the term 'company' was not defined for the purposes of s 29(2) and therefore by s 251^b that term was to be construed in accordance with the definition of 'company' in s 735(1)^c of the Companies Act 1985, viz 'a company *h*   formed and registered under [the 1985] Act'. However, by s 735(4)^d that definition was subject to no contrary intention being apparent in the legislation and, having regard to the provisions of the 1986 Act relating to administrative receivers generally, there was a contrary intention that those provisions applied both to companies formed and registered under the Companies Acts and to unregistered *j*   companies (including foreign companies conducting business in England) liable to be wound up under Pt V of the 1986 Act, since the general purpose and the nature of the statutory scheme relating to the qualifications, functions, powers

---

a   Section 29, so far as material, is set out at p 365 *j* to p 366 *a*, post
b   Section 251, so far as material, is set out at p 366 *b*, post
c   Section 735(1), so far as material, is set out at p 366 *c*, post
d   Section 735(4), so far as material, is set out at p 366 *e*, post

and duties of administrative receivers were as appropriate to unregistered
companies as to registered companies and it made no sense for the purpose and a
scheme of administrative receivership to be confined to appointments of receivers
made over the property of registered companies. It followed that the applicants
were administrative receivers within s 29(2) of the Insolvency Act 1986 (see p 366
a to e h to p 367 e h to p 368 d, post).

Notes b

For administrative receivers, see 7(2) *Halsbury's Laws* (4th edn reissue) paras 1386–
1428.

For unregistered companies, see ibid paras 2363–2378, and for cases on the
subject, see 10(2) *Digest* (2nd reissue) 475–484, *12892–12951*.

For the Law of Property Act 1925, s 109, see 37 *Halsbury's Statutes* (4th edn) c
234.

For the Companies Act 1985, s 735, see 8 *Halsbury's Statutes* (4th edn) (1991
reissue) 597.

For the Insolvency Act 1986, s 29, Pt V (ss 220–229), s 251, Sch 1, see 4
Halsbury's Statutes (4th edn) (1987 reissue) 753, 874, 896, 1054.

d

Cases referred to in judgment

Anchor Line (Henderson Bros) Ltd, Re [1937] 2 All ER 823, [1937] Ch 483.
Atlantic Computer Systems plc, Re [1992] 1 All ER 476, [1992] Ch 505, [1992] 2
   WLR 367, CA.
Felixstowe Dock and Rly Co v US Lines Inc [1988] 2 All ER 77, [1989] QB 360, [1989] e
   2 WLR 109.
Law Society v United Service Bureau Ltd [1934] 1 KB 343, DC.

Cases also cited

Barrow Borough Transport Ltd, Re [1990] Ch 227.
International Westminster Bank plc v Okeanos Maritime Corp [1987] 3 All ER 137, f
   sub nom *Re a company (No 00359 of 1987)* [1988] Ch 210.

Application

By application dated 26 February 1992 Philip Sykes and John Hill of Messrs
Binder Hamlyn, the receivers of International Bulk Commodities Ltd (IBC)
appointed by Swiss Bank Corp pursuant to a facility letter dated 15 May 1990 and g
a debenture dated 28 April 1989, sought the determination of the court on the
question whether they were administrative receivers within the meaning of
s 29(2) of the Insolvency Act 1986 or receivers whose powers were limited to
those conferred by the debenture. The facts are set out in the judgment.

h
Gabriel Moss QC and *Susan Prevezer* (instructed by *Simpson Curtis*, Leeds) for the
   applicants.
Patrick Eccles QC (instructed by *Colin Bomer & Co*, Newbury) for IBC.

Cur adv vult

j
15 April 1992. The following judgment was delivered.

MUMMERY J. This application poses a difficult question of general importance
on the scope of the provisions in the Insolvency Act 1986 concerned with
administrative receivers. Do those provisions apply in the case of a foreign
company? More precisely, do they apply to a receiver of the whole, or substantially
the whole, of the property of a foreign company appointed by or on behalf of the

holders of debentures of the company secured by a charge which, as created, was
a a floating charge?

The question has arisen in the following way. The respondent company,
International Bulk Commodities Ltd (IBC), was not formed or registered under
the Companies Acts. It was incorporated in 1988 in Liberia. Its registered office
is in Monrovia. IBC trades worldwide buying and selling basic commodities such
as timber, coal and cement. In the United Kingdom IBC's sales operations were
b based in Newbury and were controlled by one of the directors, Mr Stuart
Thornhill. The other three directors of IBC are resident abroad.

On 26 October 1991 IBC ceased trading in the United Kingdom. Its business,
assets and liabilities in the United Kingdom were transferred to the Portland
Cement Co Ltd. While it was still trading in the United Kingdom IBC granted a
debenture (dated 28 April 1989) to the Swiss Bank Corp (the bank). By way of
c continuing security for the payment and discharge of all moneys and liabilities
owing by IBC to the bank, IBC granted a first fixed charge over its freehold and
leasehold property and book debts, and a first floating charge over all its assets,
undertaking and property, past and future. The debenture was in a form familiar
to English lawyers, bankers and businessmen. It included a common form power
d in cl 12 to appoint a receiver and manager of the property charged in the event of
failure to make payment of sums secured in accordance with the demand of the
bank. The clause provided that the receiver so appointed should have various
powers—

> 'in addition to the powers conferred by section 109 of the Law of Property
e Act 1925, and in the case of a receiver who is an administrative receiver
> within the meaning of section 29 of the Insolvency Act 1986, without
> limiting the powers in Schedule 1 of that Act.'

On 15 May 1990 a facility letter was issued by the bank to IBC up to a
maximum sum of £2m. On 4 February 1992 the bank terminated the facility
and demanded payment of the sum of £879,026·73. No payment was made. On
f 7 February 1992 the bank purported to appoint Mr Philip Sykes and Mr John Hill
of Messrs Binder Hamlyn as receivers pursuant to the debenture. IBC disputes
the bank's right to appoint receivers, but no step has been taken to challenge the
validity of their appointment. Both parties have invited this court to proceed on
the basis that the validity of the appointment is not and cannot be disputed or
decided on this application.
g The dispute on this application is whether the receivers, who are the applicants,
are 'administrative receivers' within the meaning of the Insolvency Act 1986, or
are simply contractual receivers appointed out of court with powers limited to
those contractually conferred by the terms of the debenture. The applicants wish
to know the nature and extent of their receivership powers as a matter of practical
h importance and pressing nature, because they have been unable so far to obtain
any assistance from the directors of IBC as to the location of books and records of
IBC, or as to the provision of information about its assets. The applicants
contemplate use of the procedures in ss 234 to 236 of the 1986 Act for the purpose
of obtaining information, but those powers are only available to the applicants if
they are 'office holders', a term defined as including administrative receivers: see
j s 234(1) of the 1986 Act.

On 26 February 1992 an application was issued for the determination of that
question. Paragraph 1 of the application seeks the following declaration, a
declaration—

> 'as to whether the applicants appointed pursuant to a facility letter dated
> 15th May 1990 and a debenture dated 28th April 1989 made between the
> respondent and the Swiss Bank Corporation are administrative receivers

within the meaning of section 29(2) of the Insolvency Act 1986, or are receivers whose powers are limited to those conferred by the said debenture.' a

I should mention other relevant matters before I refer to the statutory provisions.

(1) It is not argued that under English company law, or under the English law of mortgage, a foreign company, that is a company not formed and registered under the Companies Acts, lacks the requisite legal capacity to enter into a b debenture secured by a floating charge on property both in England and abroad and conferring a power to appoint a receiver and manager over the whole, or substantially the whole, of its property. There is no evidence that the law of the place of incorporation of IBC, Liberia, impinges on these points so as to incapacitate IBC in any relevant way.

(2) It is not disputed that the debenture, and the fixed and floating charge c created by it, are to be construed according to English law which draws no distinction, in the case of an English company at least, between property located within the property located outside the United Kingdom: see *Re Anchor Line (Henderson Bros) Ltd* [1937] 2 All ER 823 at 825–826, [1937] Ch 483 at 487–488. It is not argued that any system of law other than English law applies to determine the legal status of the receivers appointed by the bank pursuant to the debenture. d

(3) As an 'unregistered company', IBC is amenable to the jurisdiction of the English court to wind up unregistered companies under Pt V of the 1986 Act, though it may not be wound up voluntarily under that Act: see s 221(4). In this judgment I shall use the expression 'unregistered company' to mean any company which is liable to be wound up under Pt V of the 1986 Act. e

(4) The question for decision is one of construction of the 1986 Act and is not covered by any previous authority.

Before I refer to the particular provisions dealing with administrative receivers, I should also say something about the statutory background to the provisions and the evident purpose of the innovation of the concept of an administrative receiver.

In *Re Atlantic Computer Systems plc* [1992] 1 All ER 476 at 485, [1992] Ch 505 at f 524 the Court of Appeal summarised the background to the provisions of the 1986 Act relating to receivers:

'Typically, when lending money to a company, a bank will take as security a charge over all or most of the assets of the company, present and future, the charge being a fixed charge on land and certain other assets, and a floating g charge over the remaining assets. The deed authorises the bank to appoint a receiver and manager of the company's undertaking, with power to carry on the company's business. Such a receiver is referred to in the 1986 Act as an "administrative receiver".'

Subject of course to the wording of the particular statutory provisions, those h general observations are as pertinent to the case of a security granted to a bank by an unregistered company as to a security granted by a company formed and registered under the Companies Acts.

It is also noted by the Court of Appeal in *Re Atlantic Computer Systems plc* [1992] 1 All ER 476 at 486–487, [1992] Ch 505 at 525 that the report of the Review Committee on Insolvency Law and Practice ((1982) Cmnd 8558) made in June j under the chairmanship of Sir Kenneth Cork considered that the power, contained in any well-drawn floating charge, to appoint a receiver and manager of the property and undertaking of a company had been of outstanding public benefit. A significant number of companies had been forced into liquidation, and potentially viable businesses capable of being rescued had been closed down, for want of such a floating charge.

The 1986 Act built on the foundations of the typical debenture by providing
a in Pt III for administrative receivers and in Pt II machinery for the making of
administration orders intended to be used as a statutory alternative to an
administrative receiver by filling 'a lacuna perceived to exist in the case of
insolvent companies where either there is no floating charge or the holder of the
floating charge does not appoint an administrative receiver' (see [1992] 1 All ER
476 at 487, [1992] Ch 505 at 525). Once appointed an administrative receiver has
b 'all the powers normally conferred upon a receiver and manager appointed under
a floating charge' (see [1992] 1 All ER 476 at 487, [1992] Ch 505 at 525), though,
as was recognised in that case, there are features distinguishing administration
from administrative receivership.

It appears from these general observations, and from the detailed provisions of
c the 1986 Act, that Parliament intended to promote two purposes relevant to
receivers appointed by debenture holders. First, Parliament gave statutory
recognition and reinforcement to the existing regime of contractual receivers
appointed by debenture holders which had operated for the public benefit. It
conferred the statutory status of administrative receiver in those cases where the
receiver had been appointed by or on behalf of the debenture holder over the
d whole, or substantially the whole, of the company's property. The 1986 Act
contains provisions relating to many different aspects of receivership, all designed
to improve the efficacy of the contractual machinery and to protect the interests
of those affected by the receivership. There are provisions relating to qualification
for office, and to appointment and vacation of office; and to many express powers,
duties, rights and liabilities additional to those expressed in the debenture. There
e are additional administrative functions, such as the submission of a statement of
affairs and the making of reports on specified matters.

Reference was made in particular to ss 42 to 49 and 230 to 237, and to the
powers of an administrator or administrative receiver as set out in Sch 1 to the
1986 Act.

f Secondly, Parliament has provided for the situation where the power to appoint
a receiver does not exist, or where the power does exist but has not been exercised,
or where the power has been exercised, but the person by whom or on whose
behalf the receiver has been appointed consents to an order being made. There is
jurisdiction to make an order in the terms of an administration order, available as
an alternative to administrative receivership, and also available as an alternative
g to liquidation; see the provisions of ss 9, 10 and 11 of the 1986 Act.

Administrative receivership has to be viewed in the context of the whole range
of remedies now available in situations where a company is, or is likely to become,
unable to pay its debts. The changes made by the 1986 Act provide both greater
flexibility and increased protection for those affected by actual or potential
insolvency situations.

h Against that general background I now consider the detailed statutory
provisions relating to administrative receivers. Section 251 is a definition section.
It provides:

'In this Group of Parts, except in so far as the context otherwise requires—
"administrative receiver" means—(a) an administrative receiver as defined
j by section 29(2) in Chapter I of Part III . . . '

Section 29(2) is another definition in these terms:

'In this Chapter [which concerns receivers and managers in England and
Wales] "administrative receiver" means—(a) a receiver or manager of the
whole (or substantially the whole) of a company's property appointed by or
on behalf of the holders of any debentures of the company secured by a

charge which, as created, was a floating charge, or by such a charge and one
or more other securities . . .'   *a*

The crucial question is: what is a 'company' for the purposes of s 29(2)? There
is no definition of a company for this purpose either in s 29 or in s 251. It is
necessary to look at the words which appear at the foot of the defined expressions
in s 251. Those words read:

> '. . . and any expression for whose interpretation provision is made by Part   *b*
> XXVI of the Companies Act, other than an expression defined above in this
> section, is to be construed in accordance with that provision.'

I turn to Pt XXVI of the Companies Act 1985. In s 735(1) the following
definition appears: *c*

> 'In this Act—(a) "company" means a company formed and registered
> under this Act, or an existing company . . .'

The section defines an 'existing company' as meaning a company formed and
registered under the former Companies Acts.

If that were the end of the matter, as IBC submits it is, the solution to the   *d*
problem would be simple. IBC is not a company within that definition. The
applicant receivers are not, therefore, administrative receivers within the meaning
of s 29(2) of the 1986 Act and they do not have the powers of office holders which
they wish to use. The matter does not, however, stop there because s 735 of the
1985 Act provides in sub-s (4): 'The definitions in this section apply unless the
contrary intention appears.'   *e*

An intention to displace the prime facie or primary meaning of the defined
statutory term may appear in a number of ways. The intention may appear from
an express definition in different terms made for the purpose of a particular
section or group of sections: see, for example, the definition of a company in
s 388(4) of the 1986 Act to which I shall return. There is no different express
definition of 'company' for the purposes of administrative receivership provisions   *f*
generally.

A contrary intention may also appear from the subject matter and manifest
purpose of the relevant provisions when construed in the context of both the
immediately relevant provisions and of the Act as a whole: see, for example, *Law
Society v United Service Bureau Ltd* [1934] 1 KB 343 at 347–348.
                                                                                             g
The relevant question is therefore: is there any indication in the subject matter
and statutory purpose of the provisions concerning administrative receivers
generally, or in the 1986 Act considered as a whole, from which it appears that
Parliament intended that the word 'company' in the context of s 29(2)(a) should
not be confined to its prima facie meaning of a company formed and registered
under the Companies Acts, but should also embrace unregistered companies   *h*
liable to be wound up under Pt V of the 1986 Act.

In my judgment, there are indications that the provisions relating to
administrative receivers generally apply both to companies formed and registered
under the Companies Acts and to unregistered companies liable to be wound up
under Pt V. The starting point is that the legislative concept of administrative
receiver, and the statutory scheme of the provisions relating to his qualifications,   *j*
functions, powers and duties, all rest on a contractual base, namely a receiver
appointed by or on behalf of debenture holders under a debenture secured by a
floating charge. Every administrative receiver is born in this way. As already
noted, the underlying contractual regime is applicable both in the case of a

debenture granted by a company formed and registered under the Companies

a Acts, and in the case of a debenture granted by an unregistered company. The general purpose and scheme of the statutory superstructure is to strengthen and build on the continuing contractual foundation for the greater benefit of all affected—the company, the contributories, the creditors, both secured and unsecured, and the preferential creditors, as well as the public generally. The attainment of that general purpose and the nature of the scheme are prima facie

b as appropriate to the case of an unregistered company as they are to the case of a registered company.

Why should the range of companies affected by the statutory scheme of administrative receivers not be coextensive with the range of companies affected by the underlying contractual receivership regime? Why should a receiver

c appointed over the property of a registered company and a receiver appointed over the property of an unregistered company under the same form of debenture and by the same debenture holder not both fall within the definition of an administrative receiver? It makes no sense to confine the purpose and scheme of administrative receivership to appointments of receivers made over the property of registered companies.

d The foreign element is of no particular relevance where the company in question has granted a debenture secured by a floating charge in the English form. Both registered and unregistered companies may engage in activities both in England and abroad. Both may conduct business in England and abroad. Both may have creditors in England and abroad. Both may have assets located in England and abroad. Both may have directors resident in England and abroad.

e Both are liable to be wound up by the English court.

Why, for example, should the contributories and creditors of an unregistered company be denied the protection, enjoyed in the case of a registered company, of those provisions which require a receiver to be a licensed insolvency practitioner? In fact, Parliament recognised this particular problem and expressly dealt with it in s 388 of the 1986 Act in the definition of the expression 'acting as

f an insolvency practitioner' in relation to the need for qualifications and the consequences of acting without those qualifications.

Section 230(2) of the 1986 Act provides that, where an administrative receiver of a company is appointed, he must be a person who is qualified to act as an insolvency practitioner in relation to that company.

g Section 388(1) then provides:

> 'A person acts as an insolvency practitioner in relation to a company by acting—(*a*) as its liquidator, provisional liquidator, administrator or administrative receiver . . .'

Subsection (4) then provides:

h
> 'In this section . . . "company" means a company within the meaning given by section 735(1) of the Companies Act or a company which may be wound up under Part V of this Act (unregistered companies) . . .'

In my view, that provision lends support to the view that a receiver appointed over the property of an unregistered company may be regarded as an administrative

j receiver within the meaning of the 1986 Act. In that capacity he would be acting as an insolvency practitioner and must be qualified so to act.

In my judgment, the court should construe the relevant provisions, where the wording so permits, to promote and not to frustrate the evident legislative purpose, in this case reinforcing the position of contractual receivers. The express statutory definition of 'company' is only its prima facie meaning, since it is expressly provided in s 735(4) of the Companies Act 1985 that the defined *a* meaning may be displaced where a contrary intention appears. For the reasons I have stated above, a contrary intention does appear from the subject and the purpose of the provisions. The court should favour a construction which is consistent with and contributes to the smooth and efficient working of the contractual machinery recognised and reinforced by the legislation.

The position would, of course, have been plainer if Parliament had provided an *b* expanded express definition of 'company' for the purposes of the group of sections which relate to administrative receivers, such as was done in the case of s 388(4), and was also done, for example, in s 22(2)(*b*) of the Company Directors Disqualification Act 1986, where company is defined as including 'any company which may be wound up under Part V of the Insolvency Act'.

The absence of a different express definition of 'company' in Pt III of the 1986 *c* Act does not, in my view, prevent the definition in s 735(1) of the Companies Act from yielding to a contrary intention. I rest my decision on this broad approach.

Mr Moss QC, for the applicants, went through all the provisions of the Insolvency Act 1986 relating to administrative receivers. He also referred to provisions in the Company Directors Disqualification Act 1986 relating to *d* administrative receivers, and to many other provisions in the Insolvency Act 1986 and in the Companies Act 1985 which might conceivably have some bearing on this question. I do not think that it is necessary to refer to all those provisions because they really do not take the matter any further. It all comes back to the question of what meaning is to be given to the definition of 'company' in the context in which it is used? *e*

I will refer briefly to two particular aspects of his submissions. Extensive reference was made to the provisions in the Insolvency Act 1986 concerning administration orders and to the question whether they apply to the case of unregistered companies. Under s 8 of the 1986 Act the court has power to make an administration order in relation to a company if the court (a) is satisfied that *f* the company is, or is likely to become, unable to pay its debts (within the meaning given to that expression by s 123 of the 1986 Act), and (b) considers that the making of an order under the section would be likely to achieve one or more of the specified purposes. An administration order is defined in s 8(2) as:

'. . . an order directing that, during the period for which the order is in force, the affairs, business and property of the company shall be managed by *g* a person ("the administrator") appointed for the purpose by the court.'

Is 'company' in that context confined to a company formed and registered under the Companies Acts? Or does it extend to an unregistered company? If the court has power to make an administration order in relation to an unregistered company, that might strengthen the case for arguing that the provisions relating *h* to administrative receivers should also apply to unregistered companies. Notice of a petition for an administration order must be served on any person who has appointed, or is or may be entitled to appoint, an administrative receiver of the company: see s 9(2)(*a*) of the 1986 Act. Where the court is satisfied that there is an administrative receiver of the company, the court shall dismiss the petition unless it is also satisfied as to certain other matters which are referred to in s 9(3) *j* of the 1986 Act.

The position regarding administration orders over unregistered companies has not been finally settled by judicial decision. I was referred to the judgment of Hirst J in *Felixstowe Dock and Rly Co v US Lines Inc* [1988] 2 All ER 77 at 91, [1989] QB 360 at 376, where the judge stated:

'It is not in dispute that . . . (ii) Pt II of the Insolvency Act 1986 does not give the English court jurisdiction to make an administration order in respect of a foreign company.'

I also note that Picarda *Law Relating to Receivers, Managers and Administrators* (2nd edn, 1990) p 501 expresses the editor's opinion as follows:

'An administrator is a creature of statute and is appointed over the affairs, business and property of a company falling within the definition of company in section 735 of the Companies Act 1985. This means that the company in question must be formed and registered under the Companies Act 1985 or under the former Companies Acts . . . What this means, in effect, therefore, in the context of private international law is that an administrator cannot be appointed over the affairs, business or property of an overseas company.'

On the facts of this case it is not necessary for me to decide whether that view is right or wrong, and I should not decide it; the point should be left open for full argument in a case where it is necessary to the decision. I am unable to derive any assistance from the provisions relating to administrators on the question of administrative receivership. My only comment is that, if the position is that the court's power to appoint an administrator is in fact confined to companies formed and registered under the Companies Acts, it does not necessarily follow that an administrative receiver is similarly confined.

It is clear that not all the insolvency procedures are applicable to unregistered companies. As already noted, voluntary liquidation is not: see s 221(4) of the 1986 Act. Further, the two remedies of administrative receiver and administrators are different in nature, though they may be similar in purpose. As already noted, the administrative receiver starts his life as a contractual appointee, though he occupies the position recognised and reinforced by statute and may not be removed save by order of the court, s 45(1) of the 1986 Act.

Administrators, on the other hand, are entirely the creatures of statute and it is quite possible that different considerations apply to administrators than apply to administrative receivers on the question of unregistered companies.

The second point on which there was considerable discussion concerns the provisions of the Company Directors Disqualification Act 1986. That makes use in a number of sections of the concept of administrative receiver, eg in the definition of when a company becomes insolvent for the purposes of disqualification of unfit directors of insolvent companies: see s 6(2)(b); and the application of the reporting provisions affecting administrative receivers as office holders in s 7(3)(d) and (4).

The definition of 'company' in s 22(2)(b) of that Act includes any company which may be wound up under Pt V of the Insolvency Act. Those companies are unregistered companies. That definition differs from that contained in s 735 of the Companies Act 1985, as applied to the provisions of the Insolvency Act 1986.

My only comment on the relevance of the Company Directors Disqualification Act 1986 is that a decision that a receiver appointed over the property of an unregistered company is an administrative receiver for the purposes of the 1986 Act is consistent with, and does not create any particular difficulties in the operation of, the provisions of the Company Directors Disqualification Act 1986.

Mr Eccles QC, for IBC, in addition to his emphasis on the definition in s 735(1) of the 1985 Act, referred me to other specific provisions in the Insolvency Act 1986 in support of his submission that 'company' should be given its prima facie and primary meaning in relation to the provisions governing administrative receivers. I single out three sections for special mention. He referred me to s 70(1) which is the interpretation provision for a group of sections concerning receivers in Scotland. The definition of 'company' for the purpose of those provisions is 'an *a* incorporated company (whether or not a company within the meaning of the Companies Act) which the Court of Session has jurisdiction to wind up'.

Mr Eccles sought to contrast the presence of that definition in that group of sections with the absence of any such definition in relation to the administrative receivership group of sections in Pt III of that Act.

He also referred me to s 229(2) of the Insolvency Act 1986 in the group of *b* sections concerned with the winding up of unregistered companies. That reads:

'However, an unregistered company is not, except in the event of its being wound up, deemed to be a company under the Companies Act, and then only to the extent provided by this Part of this Act.'

The third section of the Insolvency Act 1986 to which he referred me was *c* s 441(2), which reads:

'Subject as above, [and sub-s (1) deals with the fact that certain provisions extend to Northern Ireland] and to any provision expressly relating to companies incorporated elsewhere than in Great Britain, nothing in this Act extends to Northern Ireland or applies to or in relation to companies registered *d* or incorporated in Northern Ireland.'

I am unconvinced that these provisions, taken singly or cumulatively, show that there is a legislative intention to confine the status of an administrative receiver to a receiver appointed by debenture holders over property of a company formed and registered under the Companies Acts. *e*

I conclude that I should grant a declaration as in the terms of para 1 of the application, that is that the applicants appointed pursuant to a facility letter dated 15 May 1990 and a debenture dated 28 April 1989 made between the respondent and the Swiss Bank Corp are administrative receivers within the meaning of s 29(2) of the Insolvency Act 1986.

I have already, before delivering this judgment, heard argument about the *f* precise form of the order. I have dealt with questions of costs and appeal and stay of the effect of the order pending appeal.

Order accordingly. Leave to appeal to the Court of Appeal granted.

Hazel Hartman   Barrister.

a # Republic of Somalia v Woodhouse Drake & Carey (Suisse) SA and others
The Mary

QUEEN'S BENCH DIVISION (COMMERCIAL COURT)
b HOBHOUSE J
26 FEBRUARY, 9, 13 MARCH 1992

Practice – Funds in court – Payment out – Funds belonging to foreign state – Application for payment out by person claiming to represent government of foreign state – Application opposed by former diplomatic representative of legitimate government overthrown in civil
c *war – Whether former diplomatic representative having locus standi to be joined as party to proceedings.*

Practice – Funds in court – Payment out – Funds belonging to foreign state – Application by solicitors representing person claiming to represent government of foreign state – Duty
d *of solicitors to obtain properly constituted authority to receive money – Court requiring confirmation that solicitors on record had properly constituted authority to receive money and that government instructing them was in fact government of foreign state.*

Conflict of laws – Foreign government – Recognition – Locus standi to sue and be sued in English court – Interim government of Republic of Somalia – Money in court belonging to
e *Republic of Somalia – Interim government appointed after international conference to resolve civil war in Somalia following overthrow of legitimate government – Interim government not having constitutional authority or stable administrative control over territory of Somalia – Interim government not recognised by British government – Whether interim government having locus standi to claim money in court belonging to republic.*
f

In January 1991 the Republic of Somalia bought and paid for a cargo of rice which was shipped on board a vessel chartered by the defendants to be discharged at the capital of the republic, Mogadishu. By the time the vessel arrived at Mogadishu the ruling president of the republic had been overthrown following an uprising and the country was in a state of civil war between various factions of tribal
g groups with no group gaining overall control of the country or Mogadishu. The ship's captain refused to enter the port of Mogadishu as he considered it unsafe because of the fighting between rival forces there. Disputes arose as to the disposal of the cargo, as a result of which on an originating summons issued by the shipowners against the charterers the Commercial Court ordered on 12 March
h 1991 that the cargo be sold and the proceeds deposited in court and that the bills of lading be placed at the disposal of the court. The bills of lading for the cargo were held by B, an ambassador of Somalia accredited to the United Nations Organisations in Geneva, but her status became uncertain after the fall of the former president. Following the sale of the cargo there was some $2·5m in court, of which $500,000 would be sufficient to satisfy the claims of the shipowners, the
j charterers and other commercial parties. In July 1991, following an international conference held in Djibouti to resolve the civil war, M, the leader of one of the warring factions in Somalia, was nominated as the provisional president and he appointed Q, the leader of another faction, as the prime minister to lead an 'interim government'. However, the interim government was unable to function in Mogadishu because the faction in control of the capital was not a party to the

international agreement. In January 1992 Q, describing himself as the 'prime minister' of the republic, appointed a firm of London solicitors to act for the 'interim government' of Somalia and to apply for the release of the money from the court to the interim government. On 7 February the Commercial Court judge ordered that, unless any party showed cause on or before 19 February why $2m should not be paid out of the fund in court, that sum would be paid to the solicitors for the interim government. B applied to be joined as a party to the proceedings and opposed any payment being made to the solicitors pursuant to the February order on the ground that there was no government in Somalia. There was evidence before the court from the Foreign and Commonwealth Office (i) that the British government's policy was not to accord recognition to governments but only to states, (ii) that where a regime came to power in a foreign state by unconstitutional means the British government would assess whether that regime could exercise effective control of the state and that it was to be inferred from the nature of the British government's dealings with the new regime whether it qualified to be treated as a government and whether the British government was dealing with it on a government to government basis and (iii) that in relation to Somalia the British government did not consider that there was any effective government of Somalia because of the continuing civil war. It was argued on behalf of the interim government that the February order for payment of the money was conclusive, that B had no locus standi to intervene and that the interim government was the only legal government, because it had international recognition from those countries and bodies which had attended the Djibouti conference.

Held – (1) Since B had no personal interest in the money in court and had no locus standi to represent the Republic of Somalia before the court, as she had received no accreditation or authority from any current government in that country and in fact claimed that there was currently no government in Somalia, and since she had no diplomatic status in the United Kingdom and no recognition from the British government as representative of the Republic of Somalia, her application to be joined as a party to the proceedings would be refused (see p 377 d to f, post).

(2) Where the issue before the court was whether money in court which was the property of a foreign state should be paid to a firm of solicitors whose authority to act on behalf of that state was in question, the court had to be satisfied that the solicitors on the record had properly constituted authority to receive the money and that the government instructing them was in fact the government of the foreign state and if the court was for any reason satisfied that the solicitors did not have the requisite authority it would, of its own motion if necessary, require the solicitors to obtain that authority and would ensure that in the meantime the money remained under the control of the court (see p 378 b to d, post).

(3) The factors to be taken into account in deciding whether a government existed as the government of a state were (i) whether it was the constitutional government of the state, (ii) the degree, nature and stability of administrative control, if any, which it exercised over the territory of the state, (iii) whether the British government had any dealings with that government and, if so, the nature of those dealings and (iv) in marginal cases the extent of international recognition that it had as the government of that state. On the evidence before it the court was not satisfied that the interim government had any constitutional authority or stable administrative control over the territory of Somalia or that it was recognised by the British government. Furthermore, the argument based on the Djibouti conference or the recognition by foreign states and international bodies did not

assist the interim government, which was a regime of one faction seeking to
a achieve a position of de jure government displacing a former government without
having effective administrative control over all people of that country. It followed
that the application on behalf of the interim government for payment out of the
money in court would be refused (see p 381 *h* and p 384 *d* to *g*, post).

Per curiam. Although loss of control by a constitutional government may not
immediately deprive it of its status, an insurgent regime will require to establish
b control before it can exist as a government (see p 383 *c*, post).

Notes

For the recognition of states and governments generally, see 18 *Halsbury's Laws*
(4th edn) paras 1425–1435.
c   For payment out of funds in court, see 37 *Halsbury's Laws* (4th edn) para 627,
and for a case on the subject, see 37(3) *Digest* (Reissue) 139, 3670.

Cases referred to in judgment

Adams v Adams (A-G intervening) [1970] 3 All ER 572, [1971] P 188, [1970] 3 WLR
d   934, DC.
Arantzazu Mendi, The [1939] 1 All ER 719, [1939] AC 256, HL.
Carl-Zeiss-Stiftung v Rayner & Keeler Ltd (No 2) [1966] 2 All ER 536, [1967] 1 AC
853, [1966] 3 WLR 125, HL.
Ford-Hunt v Raghbir Singh [1973] 2 All ER 700, [1973] 1 WLR 738.
GUR Corp v Trust Bank of Africa Ltd (Government of the Republic of Ciskei, third party)
e   [1986] 3 All ER 449, [1987] QB 599, [1986] 3 WLR 583, QBD and CA.

Application

By an originating summons issued on 12 March 1991 Woodhouse Drake & Carey
(Suisse) SA, the owners of the vessel Mary, sought and on the same day were
f granted by Hirst J an order for the sale of a cargo of rice on board the Mary and
the proceeds thereof to be deposited in court. The vessel's charterers, Aleko
Maritime Co Ltd, were named as the defendants to the summons. Legal
representatives for the government of the Republic of Somalia and Madame Bihi,
a diplomat of the former legitimate government of Somalia which had been
overthrown, also appeared before Hirst J on that day, when Hirst J further ordered
g that Madame Bihi, the holder of the original bills of lading, place the bills of
lading at the disposal of the court to enable his order to be carried out. By a
summons issued on 16 January 1992 solicitors claiming to act for the Republic of
Somalia applied for the republic and the buyers of the rice, Madigan Associates
SA, to be joined as parties to the action and for directions for the future conduct
of the action concerning the claim over the money in court. On 7 February 1992
h Saville J made an order joining the republic as the plaintiff in substitution for the
shipowners and added the shipowners and the buyers as the first and third
defendants respectively to the action. Saville J further ordered that unless any
party appeared before the court on or before 19 March and showed cause why the
sum of $US2m should not be paid out of the fund in court to the solicitors acting
for the republic that sum should be paid to the solicitors acting for the republic
j on 20 February. The order also included liberty to all parties to apply. Madame
Bihi then aplied to the court for leave to be joined as a party to the action to resist
the payment of the money to the interim government and requested the court to
invite the Attorney General to appoint an amicus curiae. The application was
heard in chambers but judgment was given by Hobhouse J in open court. The
facts are set out in the judgment.

Geraldine Andrews (instructed by *Crossman Block*) for the Republic of Somalia.
Gavin Kealey (instructed by *More Fisher Brown*) for Madame Bihi.
Stephen Richards (instructed by the *Treasury Solicitor*) as amicus curiae.

Cur adv vult

13 March 1992. The following judgment was delivered.

HOBHOUSE J. In January 1991 the Republic of Somalia bought and paid for a
cargo of rice, which was shipped on the Mary to be discharged at Mogadishu.
When the Mary arrived off Mogadishu the master refused to enter the port
because he considered it unsafe on account of the fighting that was going on
there. The bills of lading covering the cargo were in the hands of a Madame Bihi,
who was the accredited ambassador of the Republic of Somalia to the United
Nations Organisations in Geneva. Disputes arose as to what should be done with
the cargo and the shipowners issued an originating summons on 12 March 1991
in this court naming as the defendants the charterers of the vessel. On the same
day Hirst J ordered that the cargo be sold and that the net proceeds of sale be paid
into court. He ordered that the proceeds of sale be treated as if they were the
cargo for all purposes. He ordered Madame Bihi, through her solicitors, Messrs
More Fisher Brown, to place the original bills of lading at the disposal of the court
in order to facilitate the carrying out of the order. The order recited that the court
had heard 'Counsel for the plaintiffs and for the defendants and . . . Messrs More
Fisher Brown and Lloyd & Co for the competing interests in the cargo'.

The background to the situation which I have described is that in December
1990 and January 1991 there had been an uprising in Somalia in the course of
which the President, Siad Barre, had been overthrown. Somalia consists of a
number of areas each of which is dominated by a different tribal group or clan.
Following the uprising and the overthrow of the legitimate government, whatever
common interest that had been between these groups ceased and they began to
fight each other. The central government ceased to exist. Various groups put
themselves forward as entitled to control or govern either parts or the whole of
Somalia. In the north west the Somali National Movement (SNM) attempted to
set up a separate state. The north east was under the control of the Somali
Salvation Democratic Front (SSDF). The area around and to the north of the
capital, Mogadishu, was controlled by the United Somali Congress (USC) group;
but this soon split into two factions, one led by General Aidid and the other by
Mr Ali Mahdi Mohammed. Some of the bitterest fighting during the last nine
months has been taking place between these two factions in and around
Mogadishu, particularly since November 1991, with neither yet gaining control.
Further south, different areas were under the control of the Somali Democratic
Movement (SDM) and Somali Patriotic Movement (SPM) and the followers of
Siad Barre. No one group has established control over the country. The capital
has remained an area of open fighting between armed bands under the control of
no one faction. The USC remains split.

Madame Bihi was a long-standing diplomatic representative, who had been
appointed by the government of President Barre. Initially she was supportive of
the continuing claim to office of President Barre whose overthrow she did not at
that stage recognise. More recently, it appears, she has accepted that his
government has ceased to exist but she remains deeply hostile to the USC, and in
particular Mr Mahdi, who are equally hostile to her, and contends that there is at
present no government of the Republic of Somalia.

a Messrs Lloyd & Co had received their instructions from a member of Mr Mahdi's group who apparently described himself as the 'foreign minister' of the Somali Republic. In about February 1991 Mr Mahdi had been proclaimed President of Somalia by the USC. It was not clear upon what basis such an assumption of office could be made and it was not accepted by the other clans. It appears that he appointed as his prime minister, Mr Omer Arteh Qalib. In July

b 1991 after a continuous period of widespread fighting between the various groups including the two USC factions, a conference was called at Djibouti under the chairmanship of the President of the Republic of Djibouti. It was attended by the Presidents of Kenya and Uganda and representatives of the governments of Germany, the United States of America, France, Italy, Saudi Arabia, Egypt, Libya, Yemen, Nigeria, Ethiopia, Sudan, Oman, the Union of Soviet Socialist Republics,

c and China and of the Arab League, the Organisation of African Unity and the European Economic Community. From within Somalia six of the groupings were represented. The SNM declined to attend and it seems that General Aidid did not do so either. After a number of days the conference was able to reach an agreement, which was set out in a communiqué dated 21 July 1991. It included:

d 'Organisation of the State   (A) The Conference had decided to adopt the 1960 constitution for a period of not more than two years from the date of signature of the present Agreement, the formation of the Government shall be agreed between the various movements. (B) The Conference had decided to set up a National Assembly composed of 123 members based on the number of constituencies existing before 1969 with a Speaker and two

e Deputy Speakers. (C) The Conference had agreed to introduce regional autonomy in the country which entails an amendment to the constitution . . . (E) The Conference nominates his Excellency, Ali Mahdi Mohammed, as provisional President of the Somali Republic for a period of two years from the day on which he takes the oath. (F) Two Vice Presidents of the Republic shall be nominated, the first put forward by the SDM and the second by the

f SSDF and SPF. [The SDM, SSDF and SPF were three of the groupings.] (G) The Prime Minister shall be a native of the North West of the Country . . . (J) The provisional Government is charged with preparing a draft electoral law for the organisation of [a] free and democratic election of the president of the National Assembly, with forwarding a policy of respect for human rights and public liberties on the basis of the universal declaration of human

g rights and to introduce into the country an organisation based on regional autonomy . . .'

The agreement was signed by representatives of the six groups attending who also undertook to carry out the resolutions of the conference.

Accordingly, under the Djibouti Agreement Mr Mahdi became the interim

h president and on 6 August he appointed Mr Qalib as his prime minister (apparently, in the absence of a nomination by the SNM). Mr Qalib then appointed ministers to serve under him. I will refer to these persons as the 'interim government'. It appears that in practice the interim government has been unable to operate in Mogadishu and Mr Qalib has based himself in a hotel in Riyadh in Saudi Arabia.

j Prior to the Djibouti Agreement, on 12 May 1991 Mr Qalib, describing himself as the 'Prime Minister of the Somali Republic' and writing from Riyadh, instructed Messrs Crossman Block to act on behalf of 'the Interim Government of the Somali Republic'. By a further letter, also sent from Riyadh, dated 14 January 1992, Mr Qalib reconfirmed his earlier instructions on behalf of 'my Government' and gave his written consent, pursuant to RSC Ord 15, r 6(4), for 'the Interim Government of the Republic of Somalia' to be joined as the plaintiff in these a proceedings. Crossman Block have wholly taken over from Lloyd & Co and are now the sole solicitors instructed by the interim government.

Following the sale of the cargo and the payment of the net proceeds, $US2,353,991·95, into court, nothing further was done in the action until 16 January 1992, when Crossman Block issued a summons as 'solicitors for the Republic of Somalia' applying that the Republic of Somalia be joined as a party to b the action, that the buyers of the cargo be also joined (presumably so that they could be bound by any decision of the court), and that:

'Directions be given in respect of the future proceedings of this action particularly concerning the trial of the claims of all concerned parties to the monies paid into Court pursuant to the Order herein of Mr Justice Hirst c dated 13th March 1991.'

Notice of this summons was given by Crossman Block to More Fisher Brown, who, seeing that they were content that directions should be given and, perhaps surprisingly, did not wish to oppose the joinder of the additional parties, did not consider it necessary to attend the hearing, which took place before Saville J on d Friday, 7 February 1992. Mr Clements, a partner in Crossman Block, swore two affidavits, dated respectively 16 January and 6 February, which set out the case of their clients.

The summons was heard as an ordinary Friday summons in the Commercial Court and occupied about 20 minutes. Crossman Block were represented by counsel, Miss Andrews, and solicitors appeared on behalf of the shipowners, the e charterers and the buyers of the cargo. Saville J ordered the joinder of the Republic of Somalia as plaintiffs in substitution for the shipowners, who together with the buyers of the cargo were joined as additional defendants. He further ordered:

'3. Unless any party appears before this Court on or before Wednesday 19th February 1992 and shows cause why the sum of US$2,000,000 should f not be paid out of the fund which was paid into Court pursuant to the Order of Mr Justice Hirst herein dated 13th March 1991 ("the fund") to the solicitors for the Republic of Somalia (Messrs Crossman Block), the said sum shall be paid out of the fund to Messrs Crossman Block on 20th February 1992 or forthwith thereafter.'

The reason for selecting the figure of $US2m was that by the end of January 1992 g the sum in court together with accrued interest had grown to $US2·5m and $US0·5m would be fully sufficient to satisfy any claims of the shipowners, charterers and other commercial parties. He gave directions for the resolution of any dispute as to how the balance of the fund should be dealt with. He reserved the costs and gave liberty to apply. He also took an undertaking from 'the h Republic of Somalia by their counsel . . . to give notice of this order to all the existing and intending parties to this action and to Messrs More Fisher Brown the former representatives of Madame Fatuma Isak Bihi'.

More Fisher Brown, on the instructions of Madame Bihi, took advantage of the liberty to apply. They swore affidavits and put further material before the court. Their application eventually came on before the court on the afternoon of 26 j February. The initial application was: (i) that Madame Bihi be joined as a party to these proceedings as a representative of the Democratic Republic of Somalia; (ii) that para 3 of the order of Saville J should not be brought into effect; (iii) that the court should direct letters to be written to the Foreign and Commonwealth Office asking what state in Somalia is recognised by Her Majesty's government as a

foreign sovereign state and with what entity, if any, therein Her Majesty's
a government has any dealings of a governmental nature; and (iv) that the court
should request the Attorney General to appoint an amicus curiae. In a further
affidavit they put her case more clearly in the following terms:

> '. . . Mrs Bihi and the party that she represents do not call for payment out
> to them of the sum presently in court. They say that the Court should
b > appoint or direct the appointment of an amicus curiae to assist the Court
> when—as here—there is a serious problem of locus standi in view of the
> confusions that exist in their native Somalia. They also say that, until the
> Court is able to determine what, if any, is the government of Somalia with
> which HM Government has appropriate dealings of a governmental nature,
> the money in court should remain there.'

c I have not acceded to the application of Madame Bihi to be joined as a
representative or other party in this action but I have acceded to her application
that I should invite the Attorney General to appoint an amicus curiae and Mr
Richards has appeared instructed by the Treasury Solicitor. The court is grateful
for his assistance.

d Madame Bihi claims no personal interest in the money in court and accordingly
the only locus standi that she can have is as a person who is entitled to represent
the Republic of Somalia in this court. It is not suggested that the money belongs
to the former regime of Siad Barre, nor that it is the property of a government or
governmental agency rather than state property belonging to the republic. It is
clear from the evidence that both More Fisher Brown and Crossman Block have
e placed before the court that Madame Bihi has no right to represent the republic
in this court. Her evidence is that there is currently no government of Somalia.
The former government of President Siad Barre has ceased to exist and she has
received no accreditation or authority from any other government. It is not clear
that she currently has any diplomatic status although there is some evidence that
the United Nations may still for some purposes recognise her ambassadorship.
f But it is clear that she has no diplomatic status in the United Kingdom and has no
recognition from Her Majesty's government as a representative of the Republic
of Somalia in this country. Accordingly I refuse her application to be joined as a
party to this action.

The essential matter which has been argued before me is whether or not the
g order for payment out to Crossman Block should now be confirmed. At one stage
I felt some doubt whether it was open to the court to make any further order
which would postpone the payment out of the $US2m. Indeed, Miss Andrews
argued that that matter was concluded by the order of Saville J and there was no
party properly before the court on whose application the court could make any
different order. Madame Bihi had no locus standi and the Attorney General had
h not sought to intervene: cf *Adams v Adams (A-G intervening)* [1970] 3 All ER 572,
[1971] P 188.

However, having heard argument, I am satisfied that the order of Saville J was
provisional only and was subject to any further order that might be made on
further material being placed before the court. The summons upon which he
made the order was merely a summons which asked for directions and the form
j in which his order was couched was that of an order nisi, which, subject to the
time limits laid down in the order, gave an unqualified liberty to apply. His order
was not seeking to determine the rights of those represented by Crossman Block
should there be any challenge to them. Further, it is always open to a court, upon
proof of new facts, to make an order supplemental to an original order: see *Ford-
Hunt v Raghbir Singh* [1973] 2 All ER 700 at 702, [1973] 1 WLR 738 at 740 per

Brightman J. The affidavit evidence before Saville J gave him an incomplete picture of the actual situation in Somalia and the current attitude of Her Majesty's *a* government; there is now additional relevant evidence before the court. It is said that assumptions upon which he was apparently prepared to proceed have now been shown to be unsound.

In a case involving a sum of money the property of a foreign state and whether it is proper that it should be paid to a firm of solicitors whose authority to act on behalf of that state is in question, the court should, with the assistance of an *b* amicus if necessary, decline to make an order for the payment out of a sum in court to a firm of solicitors without being satisfied of the authority of that firm of solicitors. This is not a case of competing claims to the $US2m; there is no dispute that it is the property of the republic. The question is one of confirming that the legal agent on the record has a properly constituted authority to receive the sum *c* on behalf of the republic. A solicitor is an officer of the court and under the control of the court. If the court comes to the conclusion for any reason that the solicitor does not have the requisite authority it should, of its own motion if necessary, require the solicitor to obtain that authority and ensure that the relevant fund remains under the control of the court meanwhile. That is the position here if I come to the conclusion that those presently instructing Crossman *d* Block are not entitled to act as the government of the republic. Miss Andrews did not invite me to order that the sum should be paid out to Crossman Block on terms that they should not part with it without a further order of the court; in such an event she accepted that it would be better that the sum should remain in court. No criticism whatsoever of Crossman Block is involved. Their authority is contained in the letter of 14 January 1992 which is expressly the consent of the *e* interim government to being joined as plaintiffs. It can be questioned whether this consent is sufficient to comply with RSC Ord 15, r 6(4).

The case of the interim government has been succinctly summarised in one of the affidavits sworn by Mr Clements:

> 'The Republic can only pursue legal action through its duly appointed *f* executive, namely the Interim Government which instructs me . . . The fund in Court represents assets belonging to the Republic of Somalia. Somalia is for the time being represented by its Interim Government. That Government is the only institution now in a position to take possession of the funds and employ the money as it sees fit for the best interest of the State. The money is urgently required to combat the effects of famine in the country.' *g*

The question therefore is whether the interim government is the government of the Republic of Somalia. If it is not then Crossman Block do not have the authority to act on behalf of the republic: see the similar question of the authority of a solicitor in *Carl-Zeiss-Stiftung v Rayner & Keeler Ltd (No 2)* [1966] 2 All ER 536, [1967] 1 AC 853. *h*

Mr Richards supports the argument of counsel for Madame Bihi on this question. He has submitted that the money in court should not be paid out unless the court is satisfied that the interim government is indeed the government of Somalia and that, as the court should not be satisfied that this is the case, the money should meanwhile be left in court.

The policy of the United Kingdom is now not to confer recognition upon *j* governments as opposed to upon states. The new policy of Her Majesty's government was stated in two parliamentary answers in April and May 1980:

> '. . . we have conducted a re-examination of British policy and practice concerning the recognition of Governments. This has included a comparison

with the practice of our partners and allies. On the basis of this review we have decided that we shall no longer accord recognition to Governments. The British Government recognise States in accordance with common international doctrine. Where an unconstitutional change of regime takes place in a recognised State, Governments of other States must necessarily consider what dealings, if any, they should have with the new regime, and whether and to what extent it qualifies to be treated as the Government of the State concerned. Many of our partners and allies take the position that they do not recognise Governments and that therefore no question of recognition arises in such cases. By contrast, the policy of successive British Governments has been that we should make and announce a decision formally "recognising" the new Government. This practice has sometimes been misunderstood, and, despite explanations to the contrary, our "recognition" interpreted as implying approval. For example, in circumstances where there may be legitimate public concern about the violation of human rights by the new regime, or the manner in which it achieved power, it has not sufficed to say that an announcement of "recognition" is simply a neutral formality. We have therefore concluded that there are practical advantages in following the policy of many other countries in not according recognition to Governments. Like them, we shall continue to decide the nature of our dealings with regimes which come to power unconstitutionally in the light of our assessment of whether they are able of themselves to exercise effective control of the territory of the State concerned, and seem likely to continue to do so.' (See 983 HC Official Report (5th series) written answers cols 278–279.)

'In future cases where a new régime comes to power unconstitutionally our attitude on the question whether it qualifies to be treated as a Government will be left to be inferred from the nature of the dealings, if any, which we may have with it, and in particular on whether we are dealing with it on a normal Government to Government basis.' (See 985 HC Official Report (5th series) written answers col 385.)

The position in English law before 1980 is conveniently set out in 18 *Halsbury's Laws* (4th edn) para 1431:

'A foreign government which has not been recognised by the United Kingdom government as either de jure or de facto government has no locus standi in the English courts. Thus it cannot institute an action in the courts ... The English courts will not give effect to the acts of an unrecognised government ...'

Thus, recognition by Her Majesty's government was the decisive matter and the courts had no role save to inquire of the executive whether or not it had recognised the government in question.

Some writers appear still to feel that the criterion remains one of recognition by the government of this country, the difference being that, whereas before 1980 the government would say expressly whether it recognised the foreign government, now it is to be left to be ascertained as a matter of inference: see Crawford 'Decisions of British courts during 1985–86 involving questions of public or private international law' (1986) 57 BYIL 405 and the continuing references in Brownlie *Principles of Public International Law* (4th edn, 1990) and in 'Recognition in theory and practice' (1982) 53 BYIL 197 at 209 to the recognition of governments. Mr Richards did not seek to support that view and it is clearly contrary to or not adopted in other writings: see e g Mann *Foreign Affairs in English Courts* (1986) and Warbrick 'The new British policy on recognition of Governments' (1981) 30 ICLQ 568; and indeed the general tenor of Professor Brownlie's work itself. The impracticality of the 'inferred recognition' theory as a legal concept for forensic use is obvious and it cannot be thought that that was the intention of Her Majesty's government in giving the Parliamentary answers. The use of the phrase 'left to be inferred' is designed to fulfil a need for information in an international or political, not a judicial, context.

If recognition by Her Majesty's government is no longer the criterion of the locus standi of a foreign 'government' in the English courts and the possession of a legal persona in English law, what criteria is the court to apply? The answers do confirm one applicable criterion, namely whether the relevant regime is able of itself to 'exercise effective control of the territory of the State concerned' and is 'likely to continue to do so'; and the statement as to what is to be the evidence of the attitude of Her Majesty's government provides another—to be inferred from the nature of the dealings, if any, that Her Majesty's government has with it and whether they are on a normal government to government basis. The non-existence of such dealings cannot however be conclusive because their absence may be explained by some extraneous consideration—for example lack of occasion, the attitude of the regime to human rights, its relationship to another state. As the answers themselves acknowledge, the conduct of governments' in their relations with each other may be affected by considerations of policy as well as by considerations of legal characterisation. The courts of this country are now only concerned with the latter consideration. How much weight in this connection the courts should give to the attitude of Her Majesty's government was one of the issues before me.

In relation to Somalia and the present litigation, the Foreign and Commonwealth Office has on three occasions responded to inquiries by solicitors and Mr Richards has also conveyed to the court a further communication. In the first letter, dated 4 March 1991, reference was made to the fluid and confused situation that had followed upon the successful coup:

'Now that opposition forces have overthrown Siad Barre, the single objective which united them has gone. Each movement has its own clan objectives to champion. The United Somali Congress (USC), drawn from the Hawiye Clan and its sub clans, was responsible for the fighting in Mogadishu. It is they who have appointed a new Caretaker President and a Government which they claim are interim measures. A separate USC faction under General Mohammed Farrah Hassan "Aidid", who have the support of the Somali National Movement (SNM), do not recognise the new President or Government. Neither do the Somali Patriotic Movement (SPM) or SNM. They argue that the appointments run counter to the USC, SNM and SPM Agreement of 2nd October 1990. But the faction now in control in Mogadishu was not a party to that Agreement.'

They also referred to the different factions in control in different parts of the country and said: 'The general situation in Somalia continues to be insecure and confused'.

On 5 August 1991 the Foreign and Commonwealth Office wrote to Crossman Block confirming that the practice of Her Majesty's government was to recognise states not governments and accordingly 'the question of whether to recognise the purported Interim Government in Mogadishu thus does not arise for us'. They also confirmed that the purported secession of the north western part of the

country had not been recognised. They commented that 'the Interim Government
a does not command nationwide acceptance. We support efforts to establish one
that does'. They concluded: 'In these circumstances, it is very difficult to judge,
for the purposes of your case, who is the Government of Somalia.' This letter was
written after the Djibouti Conference and notwithstanding the communique that
had been issued at the conclusion of that conference. It is clear that the writer of
that letter did not consider that the conference had changed the situation or that
b any legitimate or other recognisable government had come into existence as a
result. This letter was the only letter which was before Saville J.

On 20 February 1992 the Foreign and Commonwealth Office wrote again to
More Fisher Brown. It reconfirmed that Her Majesty's government was not
concerned with the recognition of governments and had not recognised the
c purported secession. It continued:

> 'The comment in [the letter of 5 August 1991] has been somewhat
> overtaken by subsequent events, in particular fighting between rival elements
> of the United Somali Congress which broke out in November 1991 and in
> which thousands of people have been killed and injured. On 23 January the
> United Nations Security Council adopted Resolution 733 requesting the
> *d* Secretary-General to increase UN humanitarian assistance to Somalia and to
> co-operate with regional organisations (OAU and Arab League named; OIC
> later co-opted) in seeking the Mogadishu factions' agreement to a ceasefire,
> the distribution of humanitarian aid and the promotion of a political
> settlement. The UN and regional organisations met representatives of the
> Somali factions in New York on 14 February. A cessation of hostilities was
> *e* agreed in principle. A further round of talks is due in Mogadishu later in
> February to conclude the ceasefire, and to discuss the means to achieve
> national reconciliation. All factions have been invited. However, fighting in
> Mogadishu has continued since the New York meeting. The United Kingdom
> maintains informal contact with all the factions involved, but there have
> *f* been no dealings on a government to government basis.'

It is clear from this letter that Her Majesty's government does not consider that
there is at present any effective government in Somalia. It refers to 'factions' and
treats the interim, government as merely one among a number of factions.

The further letter, dated 9 March 1992, adds little to that of 20 February. It
g confirms that the attitude of Her Majesty's government has not changed and that
there is still no single body exercising administrative authority in Somalia.

Accordingly, if the question before the court is to be decided upon the basis of
the attitude adopted by Her Majesty's government, an order cannot be made in
favour of the interim government or Crossman Block. The basis for its attitude is
clearly not any disapproval of an established regime but rather that there is no
h regime which has control, let alone any administrative control which has the
requisite element of stable continuity.

Mr Richards submitted that particular weight should be given to these
communications. I have difficulty in accepting that submission without some
qualification. Once the question for the court becomes one of making its own
assessment of the evidence, making findings of fact on all the relevant evidence
j placed before it and drawing the appropriate legal conclusion, and is no longer a
question of simply reflecting government policy, letters from the Foreign and
Commonwealth Office become merely part of the evidence in the case. In the
present case no problem of admissibility of evidence arises. In so far as the letters
make statements about what is happening in the territory of some foreign state,

such letters may not be the best evidence; but as regards the question whether Her Majesty's government has dealings with the foreign government it will *a* almost certainly be the best and only conclusive evidence of that fact. Where Her Majesty's government is dealing with the foreign government on a normal government to government basis as the government of the relevant foreign state, it is unlikely in the extreme that the inference that the foreign government is the government of that state will be capable of being rebutted and questions of public policy and considerations of the interrelationship of the judicial and executive *b* arms of Government may be paramount: see *The Arantzazu Mendi* [1939] 1 All ER 719 at 722, [1939] AC 256 at 264 and *GUR Corp v Trust Bank of Africa Ltd (Government of the Republic of Ciskei, third party)* [1986] 3 All ER 449 at 466, [1987] QB 599 at 625. But now that the question has ceased to be one of recognition, the theoretical possibility of rebuttal must exist.

There is no decided English authority upon the effect of the 1980 answers. *c* *GUR Corp v Trust Bank of Africa Ltd* was concerned with a question of the recognition of a state and the competence of a subordinate body within the recognised territory of that state under the laws of that state. The 1980 answers were referred to but were not the basis of the decision. Here no question of the recognition of a state is involved. Nor does this case involve any accredited *d* representative of a foreign state in this country. Different considerations would arise if it did, since it would be contrary to public policy for the court not to recognise as a qualified representative of the head of state of the foreign state the diplomatic representative recognised by Her Majesty's government. There is no recognised diplomatic representative of the Republic of Somalia to the United Kingdom. *e*

The statements of fact in the letters from the Foreign and Commonwealth Office are confirmed by the other evidence that is before the court concerning the actual situation in Somalia. The interim government is not governing that country and does not exercise administrative or any control over its territory and population. In Situation Report No 7 of the Agency for International Development in Washington the position as at 30 January 1992 and previously was said to be: *f*

> 'At present, there is no functioning government in Somalia and the political future of the Country remains uncertain. Although various clan-based rebel groups collaborated in the effort to oust Siad Barre, they have since been unable to agree upon a national leadership. There is still tremendous distrust and infighting between and even among clans, with *g* each claiming hold over a particular region of the country ... Heavy intra-clan fighting erupted in Mogadishu on Nov. 17 between two rival factions of the USC and control of the city is still being contested.'

This report, like the letter from the Foreign and Commonwealth Office, refers to the various 'factions'. *h*

The criteria of effective control referred to in the Parliamentary answers are clearly not satisfied. In *The Arantzazu Mendi* [1939] 1 All ER 719 at 722, [1939] AC 256 at 264–265 Lord Atkin said:

> 'By "exercising *de facto* administrative control" or "exercising effective administrative control," I understand exercising all the functions of a *j* sovereign government, in maintaining law and order, instituting and maintaining courts of justice and adopting or imposing laws regulating the relations of the inhabitants of the territory with one another and with the government.'

The interim government clearly does not satisfy these criteria; the republic
a currently has no government.

However there are two other aspects upon which counsel for the interim
government has relied. These are the recognition of the interim government by
some other states and international bodies, and the fact that the interim
government was set up by the Djibouti Agreement, which resulted from an
international conference attended by many international states and bodies.

b In evaluating these arguments it is relevant to distinguish between regimes
that have been the constitutional and established government of a state and a
regime which is seeking to achieve that position either displacing a former
government or to fill a vacuum. Since the question is now whether a government
exists, there is no room for more than one government at a time nor for separate
de jure and de facto governments in respect of the same state. But a loss of control
c by a constitutional government may not immediately deprive it of its status,
whereas an insurgent regime will require to establish control before it can exist as
a government.

The argument based on the Djibouti Agreement does not assist the interim
government. The Djibouti Agreement was not constitutional. It did not create a
d de jure status for the interim government in Somalia. The interim government
was not and did not become the constitutional successor of the government of
President Siad Barre. Accordingly, if the interim government is to be treated as
the government of Somalia, it must be able to show that it is exercising
administrative control over the territory of the republic. That it is not able to do.
Accordingly that argument must fail.

e As regards the argument of international recognition and recognition by the
United Nations, although this does not as such involve control of territory or a
population, it does correspond to one aspect of statehood. A classic definition of a
state is that contained in art 1 of the Inter-American Convention on the Rights
and Duties of States (Montevideo, 26 December 1933; 137 BFSP 282) as having—
f '(*a*) a permanent population; (*b*) a defined territory; (*c*) Government; and (*d*)
capacity to enter into relations with other States.' Whilst illustrating that it is
difficult to separate the recognition of a state from the recognition of a government
of that state, this definition also shows that part of the function of a government
of a state is to have relations with other states. This is also implicit in the reference
in the 1980 parliamentary answers to dealings on a government to government
g basis.

Accordingly I consider that the degree of international recognition of an alleged
government is a relevant factor in assessing whether it exists as the government
of a state. But where, as here, the regime exercises virtually no administrative
control at all in the territory of the state, international recognition of an
unconstitutional regime should not suffice and would, indeed, have to be
h accounted for by policy considerations rather than legal characterisation; and it is,
of course, possible for states to have relations with bodies which are not states or
governments of states.

There is evidence from which it appears that the United Nations Organisation
considers that there are persons whom it may treat as the representatives of the
Republic of Somalia. Resolution 733 started with the words: 'Considering the
j request by Somalia for the Security Council to consider the situation in Somalia'.
It appears that this request was contained in a letter from Mr Qalib dated 15
December 1991 addressed to the Secretary General to the United Nations and the
President of the Security Council. Mr Qalib signed himself as the 'Prime Minister
of Somalia'. That letter was forwarded to the President of the Security Council by

Mr Fattoun Mohammed Hassan 'Chargé d'affaire ai.' Mr Hassan's letter included
the sentence: *a*

'As you know Mr Arteh [Qalib] was appointed as the interim Prime
Minister for Somalia within the context of arrangements agreed upon by all
the Somali political parties that participated in the Somali National
Reconciliation Conference held at Djibouti in July 1991.'

The text of Resolution 733 was apparently communicated to Mr Mahdi by the   *b*
Secretary General of the United Nations describing Mr Mahdi as 'His Excellency
Mr Ali Mahdi Interim President of Somalia'.

This evidence is not wholly satisfactory. The attitude of the United Nations to
the interim government could be established in a more direct fashion and more
authoritatively. The letter of Mr Hassan suggests something less than a fully   *c*
recognised status. In any event, membership of an international organisation does
not amount to recognition nor does a vote on credentials and representation
issues: see Warbrick 'The new British policy on recognition of governments'
(1981) 30 ICLQ 568 at 583, citing the Secretary General's memorandum 1950 UN
Doc S/1466. But any apparent acceptance of the interim government by the
United Nations and other international organisations and states does not suffice   *d*
in the present case to demonstrate that the interim government is the government
of the Republic of Somalia. The evidence the other way is too strong.

Accordingly, the factors to be taken into account in deciding whether a
government exists as the government of a state are: (a) whether it is the
constitutional government of the state; (b) the degree, nature and stability of
administrative control, if any, that it of itself exercises over the territory of the   *e*
state; (c) whether Her Majesty's government has any dealings with it and if so
what is the nature of those dealings; and (d) in marginal cases, the extent of
international recognition that it has as the government of the state.

On the evidence before the court the interim government certainly does not
qualify having regard to any of the three important factors. Accordingly the   *f*
court must conclude that Crossman Block does not at present have the authority
of the Republic of Somalia to receive and deal with the property of the republic.
The instructions and authority they have received from the interim government
are not instructions and authority from the government of the Republic. I direct
that no part of the sum in court should be paid out to Crossman Block without a
further order of the court.   *g*

I will consider in chambers what consequential and other directions and orders
I should make.

Order accordingly.

K Mydeen Esq   Barrister.

a # Lord Napier and Ettrick and another v Hunter and others

Lord Napier and Ettrick v R F Kershaw Ltd and others

b
HOUSE OF LORDS

LORD TEMPLEMAN, LORD GOFF OF CHIEVELEY, LORD JAUNCEY OF TULLICHETTLE, LORD BROWNE-WILKINSON AND LORD SLYNN OF HADLEY

2–5 NOVEMBER, 10 DECEMBER 1992

c *Insurance – Subrogation – Stop-loss insurance – Assured insured by stop-loss insurers against underwriting losses – Assured sustaining losses through negligence of underwriter's agent – Stop-loss insurers paying assured under policies – Assured bringing action against agent in respect of losses and recovering damages in settlement of claim – Whether stop-loss insurers having equitable proprietary right in settlement moneys – Policy providing excess to be borne by assured – Whether assured entitled to deduct from settlement moneys*
d *loss occurring below excess before reimbursing insurers by way of subrogation – Whether stop-loss insurers entitled to injunction restraining payment of settlement moneys to assured before stop-loss insurers reimbursed.*

The first plaintiff was the representative of the assureds, who were 246 Lloyd's names who were members of the same syndicate (the O syndicate) and who had
e insured themselves under personal stop-loss policies with 12 Lloyd's syndicates (the stop-loss insurers), represented by the fifth to fourteenth defendants, against losses incurred as members of the O syndicate. The stop-loss policies provided indemnity to the names for losses in excess of a stated amount up to a specified limit. As a result of the negligence of the O syndicate's managing agents, who
f wrote large numbers of policies on behalf of the names without adequate reinsurance cover, the names incurred losses as members of the O syndicate in 1982 and made claims under their stop-loss policies in respect of those losses. Those claims were met by the stop-loss insurers. Subsequently, members of the O syndicate, including the names, brought proceedings against the managing agents and more than 80 other members' agents claiming damages for negligence
g and breach of duty in respect of, inter alia, the 1982 year of account. Those proceedings were settled on payment of £116m (the settlement moneys) to the second plaintiffs, the solicitors acting for the plaintiffs in the action, to be held on behalf of, inter alios, the names. The stop-loss insurers claimed that under the principle of subrogation they had an equitable proprietary interest in the names' share of the settlement moneys to the extent of the claims they had met. In
h proceedings brought by the plaintiffs the issues arose (1) whether the stop-loss insurers had an equitable proprietary interest in any of the settlement moneys and/or whether any of the settlement moneys were impressed with a trust in their favour, and (2) whether, in any event, when determining the amount which the stop-loss insurers were entitled to claim in respect of the settlement moneys, the stop-loss insurers were entitled to be reimbursed any indemnity paid by them
j to a name before that name was fully indemnified by applying his share of the settlement moneys to a loss occurring below the excess in that name's policy. The judge determined both issues against the stop-loss insurers, who appealed to the Court of Appeal, which dismissed their appeal on the first issue but allowed it on the second issue. The stop-loss insurers appealed to the House of Lords on the first issue and the names cross-appealed on the second issue.

Held – (1) Where an insured person was paid out by an insurer for an insured
loss in respect of which he also recovered damages from a wrongdoer the insured   *a*
person was guilty of unconscionable conduct if he did not procure and direct that
the sum due to the insurers by way of subrogation be paid out of those damages,
and in order to protect the rights of the insurer under the doctrine of subrogation
the damages recovered by the insured from the wrongdoer in respect of the
insured loss were subject to an enforceable equitable proprietary lien or charge in
favour of the insurer. Accordingly, since the damages of £116m were in an   *b*
identifiable separate fund so that an equitable proprietary lien or charge in favour
of the stop-loss insurers could be enforced, the stop-loss insurers were entitled to
injunctions restraining the second plaintiff from paying and each assured from
receiving any part of the settlement moneys without providing or paying out of
the damages payable to the names the amounts which had been or should be
found due from the names to the stop-loss insurers by way of subrogation. The   *c*
stop-loss insurers' appeal would therefore be allowed (see p 391 *f* to *j*, p 396 *f* to *h*,
p 397 *a* to p 398 *a d* to *h*, p 399 *a*, p 400 *c* to *e*, p 401 *g*, p 402 *j* to p 403 *b f g*, p 406
e, p 407 *c d*, p 409 *e* to *h* and p 410 *c d*, post); *White v Dobinson* (1845) 5 LTOS 233
and *Re Miller Gibb & Co Ltd* [1957] 2 All ER 266 applied; *Yorkshire Insurance Co
Ltd v Nisbet Shipping Co Ltd* [1961] 2 All ER 487 and *Hobbs v Marlowe* [1977] 2 All   *d*
ER 241 considered.

(2) Since the names had agreed to pay the losses represented by the excesses on
their policies they were not entitled to any of the settlement moneys in respect of
those losses before the stop-loss insurers had been fully indemnified pursuant to
their right of subrogation. On the basis that the names were in effect their own
insurers for initial losses up to the stated amount and for losses in excess of the   *e*
specified limit, the settlement moneys were to be applied in subrogation
successively to insurers of the losses commencing with the losses in excess of the
specified limit, and therefore, although the names were entitled to be fully
reimbursed in respect of the losses in excess of the specified limit before the stop-
loss insurers were entitled to be indemnified, the stop-loss insurers were likewise
entitled to be fully reimbursed in respect of the amounts paid out under the stop-   *f*
loss policies before any of the settlement moneys could be paid out in respect of
the names' initial losses up to the stated amount. The names' cross-appeal would
therefore be dismissed (see p 390 *a* to *f*, p 391 *d e*, p 403 *f g*, p 405 *h* to p 406 *e* and
p 410 *c d*, post).

Quaere. Whether the equitable proprietary interest of the insurer attaches only   *g*
to the fund consisting of sums which come into the hands of the assured in
reduction of the loss paid by the insurer or whether it also attaches to a right of
action vested in the assured against the third party which, if enforced, would yield
such a fund (see p 395 *e* to p 396 *a*, p 398 *h j*, p 403 *b* to *g*, p 406 *e*, p 409 *j* to p 410
d, post); *Castellain v Preston* [1881–5] All ER Rep 493 considered.

h

Notes
For the doctrine of subrogation and its application in insurance cases, see 16
Halsbury's Laws (4th edn reissue) paras 888–889 and 25 *Halsbury's Laws* (4th edn)
paras 330–334, 523–533, and for cases on the subject, see 29 *Digest* (Reissue) 81–
83, 500–501, 755–767, 4273–4281.   *j*

Cases referred to in opinions
Blaauwpot v Da Costa (1758) 1 Eden 130, 28 ER 633.

Brooks v MacDonnell (1835) 1 Y & C Ex 500, 160 ER 204.

a   *Burnand v Rodocanachi Sons & Co* (1882) 7 App Cas 333, HL.

Castellain v Preston (1883) 11 QBD 380, [1881–5] All ER Rep 493, CA.

Commercial Union Assurance Co v Lister (1874) LR 9 Ch App 483, LJJ; *affg* LR 9 Ch App 848 n, MR.

Hobbs v Marlowe [1977] 2 All ER 241, [1978] AC 16, [1977] 2 WLR 777, HL.

King v Victoria Insurance Co Ltd [1896] AC 250, PC.

b   *London Assurance Co v Sainsbury* (1783) 3 Doug 245, 99 ER 636.

Mason v Sainsbury (1782) 3 Doug 61, 99 ER 538.

Miller Gibb & Co Ltd, Re [1957] 2 All ER 266, [1957] 1 WLR 703.

Morley v Moore [1936] 2 All ER 79, [1936] 2 KB 359, CA.

Randal v Cockran (1748) 1 Ves Sen 98, 27 ER 916, LC.

Simpson & Co v Thomson (1877) 3 App Cas 279, HL.

c   *Stearns v Village Main Reef Gold Mining Co Ltd* (1905) 10 Com Cas 89, CA.

White v Dobinson (1845) 5 LTOS 233, LC; *affg* (1844) 14 Sim 273, 60 ER 363.

Yates v White (1838) 1 Arn 85, sub nom *Yates v Whyte* 4 Bing NC 272, 132 ER 793.

Yorkshire Insurance Co Ltd v Nisbet Shipping Co Ltd [1961] 2 All ER 487, [1962] 2 QB 330, [1961] 2 WLR 1043.

d

Consolidated appeals and cross-appeal

The appellants, the fifth to fourteenth defendants, Charles Hunter, Colin Mackinnon, William Deem, Michael Seaby, Mark Swinbank, Jeremy Guy Nelson, Ron Cleverly, David McElhiney, David Holman and Derek Walker, represented the members of 12 syndicates at Lloyd's (the stop-loss insurers), each of which

e   wrote a substantial number of personal stop-loss policies issued to Lloyd's names, including 246 members of the Outhwaite Syndicate 317/661 for the 1982 year of account (the assureds) who were represented by the first respondent plaintiff, the Rt Hon Francis Nigel Baron Napier and Ettrick. Each of the policies provided for an excess to be borne by the assured with a layer of cover above that excess. The assureds made claims under the policies in respect of their underwriting losses,

f   the majority of which arose as a result of losses on the underwriting of the Outhwaite Syndicate and such claims were met. In 1989 proceedings were commenced by 987 members of the Outhwaite Syndicate (the names), including the assureds, against the syndicate's managing agents and over 80 other members' agents at Lloyd's claiming damages for negligence and breach of duty occasioning the losses of the Outhwaite Syndicate. The proceedings were settled in February

g   and March 1992 by payment to the second respondent plaintiff, Richards Butler (a firm), solicitors to the names, on behalf of, inter alios, the assured of almost £116m (the settlement moneys), including moneys attributable to the losses in respect of which the assureds had received payment from the stop-loss insurers. Shortly before the settlement moneys were due to be distributed by the second

h   plaintiff in accordance with the arrangements announced to the names, Lloyd's asserted that the settlement moneys could not be distributed because they were subject to the premium trust deeds executed by each name. Accordingly, on 10 April 1992 the plaintiffs issued an originating summons (the Lloyd's proceedings) againt the first to fourth defendants, R F Kershaw Ltd, Lloyd's, Simon Gillilan Weber-Brown and Christopher James Hodgson, seeking, inter alia, determination

j   of the respective rights to and interests in the settlement moneys in the light of Lloyd's contention. By an order of Saville J dated 12 May 1992 Bruce Cameron Douglas-Hamilton was substituted for Mr Hodgson as fourth defendant. On 14 May 1992 Saville J decided the question raised by Lloyd's adversely to those four defendants, including Lloyd's and there was no appeal therefrom. Following

the commencement of the Lloyd's proceedings the stop-loss insurers claimed an
equitable proprietary interest in that part of the settlement moneys attributable   *a*
to losses insured and paid by them and raising contentions as to the manner in
which the settlement moneys should be applied as between themselves and their
assureds. By consent the Lloyd's proceedings were amended and the stop-loss
insurers were added as defendants by an order of Saville J dated 14 May 1992 for
the purpose of having determined, inter alia, the following issues; (1) whether
the stop-loss insurers had an equitable proprietary interest in any settlement   *b*
moneys and/or whether any of the settlement moneys were impressed with a
trust in their favour; and (2) whether, in any event, in determining the amount
which the stop-loss insurers were entitled to claim in respect of the settlement
moneys, the stop-loss insurers were entitled to be reimbursed any indemnity paid
by them to an assured before that assured was fully indemnified by applying his
share of the settlement moneys to a loss occurring below the excess in that   *c*
assured's policy. On 12 June 1992 Saville J decided against the stop-loss insurers
on both issues and they appealed. On 9 July 1992 the Court of Appeal (Dillon,
Staughton and Nolan LJJ) (see (1992) Times, 17 July) allowed the appeal in part
by deciding against the stop-loss insurers on the first issue and in their favour on
the second issue. The stop-loss insurers appealed on the first issue and the assured's   *d*
cross-appealed on the second issue with the leave of the Appeal Committee of the
House of Lords given provisionally on 22 July 1992. If the stop-loss insurers were
successful in their appeal on the first issue, it was in issue whether an ancillary
order should be made ordering the second plaintiff to pay the relevant moneys to
the stop-loss insurers and/or restraining the second plaintiff from paying those
moneys to the assureds. The facts are set out in the opinion of Lord Templeman.   *e*

David Donaldson QC and *Michael Swainston* (instructed by *Clyde & Co*) for the fifth
    to thirteenth defendants and (instructed by *Waltons & Morse*) for the fourteenth
    defendants.
Anthony Boswood QC and *Stephen Moriarty* (instructed by *Richards Butler*) for the   *f*
    assureds.

Their Lordships took time for consideration.

10 December. The following opinions were delivered.

LORD TEMPLEMAN. My Lords, when an insured person suffers a loss he   *g*
will be entitled to the insurance money and may also be entitled to sue for
damages anyone responsible for the loss. For example, if a house is insured for
£100,000 against fire and is damaged by fire to an extent exceeding £100,000,
the insurance company will pay £100,000. If the fire has been caused by a
negligent builder or some other contractual or tortious wrongdoer, the insured   *h*
person will sue the wrongdoer for damages. If the house has been damaged to the
extent of £160,000, the insured person will receive damages from the wrongdoer
of £160,000. At that stage the insured person will have made a profit since he
will have only suffered a loss of £160,000 but will have collected a total of
£260,000 from the insurance company and the wrongdoer. A policy of insurance
is however a contract of indemnity and by the doctrine of subrogation the insured   *j*
person must pay back to the insurer the sum of £100,000. The insured person
will then have made neither a loss nor a profit. This appeal requires consideration
of the principles and application of the doctrine of subrogation.
    The persons insured are 246 members of the Outhwaite Syndicate 317/661 of

Lloyd's (the names). The wrongdoer was the managing agent of the syndicate

a (Outhwaite), who negligently wrote large numbers of policies on behalf of the names in respect of asbestosis claims without adequate reinsurance cover. The insurers are the appellants (the stop-loss insurers).

As members of the Outhwaite Syndicate the names were entitled to share the net premiums and personally liable to pay claims received under policies issued by Outhwaite on their behalf in the year of account 1982. The names were

b desirous of insuring themselves against part of any loss they might incur as members of the syndicate. Each name therefore paid a premium to stop-loss insurers for a policy whereby the stop-loss insurers agreed to—

'indemnify the Assured for the amount by which the Assured's overall ascertained net underwriting loss as hereinafter defined for the Underwriting

c Year(s) of Account shown in the schedule exceeds the amount stated as "Excess" in the schedule.'

The policy contained a definition of 'net underwriting loss' in the following terms:

'The Underwriters liability hereunder shall not exceed the amount stated

d as "Limit" in the Schedule. The "Limit" and "Excess" shall apply separately to each Underwriting Year of Account covered hereunder. The term "overall ascertained net underwriting loss" shall mean:—(a) such sums with which the Assured shall be debited by any of his/her Underwriting Agents in respect of his/her Underwriting results being the disclosed loss as per the Underwriting Accounts as at the end of the 36th month of each separate

e Underwriting Year of Account: less (b) such sums as the Assured shall be credited from any of his/her Underwriting results as shown in the account as at the end of the 36th month of each separate Underwriting Year of Account . . .'

One of the underwriting years of account was 1982. The limit and the excess

f varied from policy to policy.

For purposes of illustration, the arguments in the courts below and in this House assume that for the 1982 year of account a particular hypothetical name suffered a net underwriting loss of £160,000, that the excess was £25,000, and that the limit was £100,000. On these figures the stop-loss insurers paid to the name £100,000 being the fixed amount of the limit (£100,000) which exceeded

g the excess (£25,000). The names together with other names sued Outhwaite for damages for negligence and breach of duty in respect of, inter alia, the 1982 year of account. Those proceedings were compromised on payment by Outhwaite of £116m to the respondents Messrs Richards Butler as solicitors for the plaintiffs in the action. For the purposes of the illustration it is assumed that included in the

h sum of £116m Richards Butler hold £130,000 attributable to the overall ascertained net loss of £160,000 suffered by the hypothetical name for the 1982 year of account.

On these assumptions two problems arise. First, how much is payable to the stop-loss insurers by way of subrogation? Secondly, are the stop-loss insurers entitled to be paid the amounts found due to them by way of subrogation out of

j the damages now held by Richards Butler?

At first instance Saville J decided that the hypothetical name would be entitled to be fully indemnified for his loss of £160,000. He received £100,000 from the stop-loss insurers. He will receive £130,000 from Outhwaite. He will keep £60,000 and pay £70,000 to the stop-loss insurers. In the result the name will have fully recouped his loss of £160,000. This analysis however ignores the fact that the name agreed to bear the first £25,000 excess of any loss.

The problem must, in my opinion, be solved by assuming that the name insured the first £25,000 of any loss and also insured the excess over £125,000 as well as insuring the £100,000 payable under his policy with the stop-loss insurers. There would then be three insurance policies as follows: (1) a policy for the payment of the first £25,000 of any loss; (2) a policy for payment of the next £100,000 of any loss; (3) a policy for payment of any loss in excess of £125,000.

When the name suffered a loss of £160,000 the name received £25,000 under the first policy, £100,000 under the second policy and £35,000 under the third policy. The damages payable by Outhwaite were £130,000. The third insurer is entitled to be the first to be subrogated because he only agreed to pay if the first two insurances did not cover the total loss; accordingly the third insurer must be paid £35,000. The second insurer is entitled to be the second to be subrogated because he only agreed to pay if the first insurance cover proved insufficient; accordingly, the second insurer must be paid £95,000. The sum of £35,000 payable by way of subrogation to the third insurer and the sum of £95,000 payable by way of subrogation to the second insurer exhausts the damages of £130,000 received by the name from Outhwaite. There is nothing left to recoup to the second insurer the balance of £5,000 out of the £100,000 he paid under his policy. There is nothing left by way of subrogation for the first insurer in respect of the first £25,000 which he agreed to bear.

Under the stop-loss insurance the name agreed to bear the first £25,000 loss and any loss in excess of £125,000. In my opinion the name is not entitled to be in a better position than he would have been if he had taken out the three insurances I have mentioned. The name in fact acts as his own insurer for the first £25,000 loss and acts as his own insurer for any loss in excess of £125,000. So the name must pay £95,000 to the stop-loss insurers just as he would have been liable to pay £95,000 to the second insurer if he had taken out three policies. In the result, out of the loss of £160,000, the name will have borne the first £25,000 because he agreed with the stop-loss insurers that he would bear that loss. The stop-loss insurers having paid £100,000 under the policy will receive back £95,000 by way of subrogation.

Saville J reached a different conclusion. He found that the name was entitled to retain from the damages he received the whole of the loss he had sustained before recouping the stop-loss insurers. Accordingly, the name who suffered a loss of £160,000 and received £100,000 under the policy with the stop-loss insurers and a further £130,000 from Outhwaite was entitled to retain £60,000 and to recoup to the stop-loss insurers the sum of £70,000 and no more. Thus the name covered all his loss notwithstanding that he had agreed to bear the first £25,000 of the loss. For his conclusion Saville J relied on the following passage from the judgment of Brett LJ in *Castellain v Preston* (1883) 11 QBD 380 at 386, [1881–5] All ER Rep 493 at 495:

'The very foundation, in my opinion, of every rule which has been applied to insurance law is this, namely, that the contract of insurance contained in a marine or fire policy is a contract of indemnity, and of indemnity only, and that this contract means that the assured, in case of a loss against which the policy has been made, shall be fully indemnified, but shall never be more than fully indemnified. That is the fundamental principle of insurance, and if ever a proposition is brought forward which is at variance with it, that is to say, which either will prevent the assured from obtaining a full indemnity, or which will give to the assured more than a full indemnity, that proposition must certainly be wrong.'

Saville J therefore concluded that the name would be entitled to indemnify himself against the first £25,000 loss even though he had expressly contracted with the stop-loss insurers that he would bear that loss. I do not consider that *Castellain v Preston* is helpful in deciding whether a name who promised the stop-loss insurers to bear the first £25,000 loss is entitled to be put in the same position as an insured person who makes no such promise. When Brett LJ delivered his judgment upon which Saville J relied, he was not concerned with competing claims to subrogation or with any problem arising from underinsurance or partial insurance or layers of insurance. In *Castellain v Preston* a vendor, after insuring his property against fire, contracted to sell the property for £3,100. A fire then occurred and the insurance company paid the vendor £330 in respect of the damage caused by the fire. The purchaser paid the full £3,100 purchase price without deducting anything for the damage caused by the fire. The Court of Appeal held that the insurance company was entitled to be subrogated to the extent of £330 and to receive that sum from the vendor because, as Brett LJ said (11 QBD 380 at 386, [1881–5] All ER Rep 493 at 496): '. . . the assured have recovered, notwithstanding the loss, from the purchasers, the very sum of money which they were to obtain whether this building was burnt or not.' In my opinion an insured is not entitled to be indemnified against a loss which he has agreed to bear. I agree therefore with the Court of Appeal that the name must bear the loss to the extent of the excess, namely £25,000.

The second question is whether the stop-loss insurers have an interest in the moneys held by Richards Butler. For this purpose it may be assumed by way of example that the moneys held by Richards Butler include £130,000 paid by Outhwaite as damages for negligence which inflicted a loss of £160,000 on a name in respect of the 1982 year of account; can the stop-loss insurers assert an interest in that sum of £130,000 to the extent of the £95,000 which, as I have indicated, is due to them by way of subrogation?

When the hypothetical name suffered a loss of £160,000 as a result of the negligence of Outhwaite, the stop-loss insurers were bound to pay and did pay £100,000 under the policy. The stop-loss insurers immediately became entitled to be subrogated to the right of the name to sue and recover damages in an action against Outhwaite, albeit that the amount payable to the stop-loss insurers by way of subrogation could not be quantified until the action had been concluded and the damages paid. Nevertheless in my opinion the stop-loss insurers had an interest in the right of action possessed by the name against Outhwaite. That action, if brought by the name, would be an action for the benefit of the name and for the benefit of the stop-loss insurers. Where an insurer has paid on the policy, the courts have recognised the interests of the insurer in any right of action possessed by the insured person which will enable the insurer to claim back the whole or part of the sum which he has paid under the policy. The courts recognise the interests of the insurer by allowing him to sue in the name of the insured person against the wrongdoer if the insured person refuses to pursue the action.

In *Randal v Cockran* (1748) 1 Ves Sen 99, 27 ER 916 a vessel was insured against loss and the insurance company paid the amount of the insurance when the vessel was captured by the Spaniards. The owner of the vessel became entitled to share in the prize money from the sale of captured Spanish vessels in accordance with a royal proclamation. The commission for the distribution of the prize money refused to entertain a claim from the insurer. Lord Hardwicke LC—

'was of opinion, that the plaintiffs had the plainest equity that could be.
The person originally sustaining the loss was the owner; but after satisfaction *a*
made to him, the insurer. No doubt, but from that time, as to the goods
themselves, if restored in *specie*, or compensation made for them, the assured
stands as a trustee for the insurer, in proportion for what he paid . . .'

In *Blaauwpot v Da Costa* (1758) 1 Eden 130, 28 ER 633 a ship insured for £1,636
was seized by the Spaniards and the insurance company paid the sum insured. *b*
Subsequently prize money amounting to £2,050 18s 6d was paid to the executors
of one of the former owners of the vessel. The executors were ordered to pay the
sum £1,636 7s 3d to the insurers in accordance with the following judgment of
Sir Robert Henley LK (1 Eden 130 at 131, 28 ER 633 at 634):

'I am of opinion that upon the policy, and the peril happening, and the *c*
payment of the money by the underwriters, the whole rights of the assured
vested in them. The assured had this right of restitution vested in them
against the Spanish captors, which was afterwards prosecuted by the crown
by reprisals. Satisfaction having been made in consequence of that capture, I
think the plaintiffs are entitled to that benefit; and that it was received by the
executors . . . in trust for them.'
                                                                            d

In *Mason v Sainsbury* (1782) 3 Doug 61, 99 ER 538 a house had been insured
against damage and the insurance company paid under the policy when damage
was caused by the riots of 1780. The insurance company brought an action under
the Riot Act (1714) against the local authority. The insurance company sued in
the plaintiff's name and with his consent and for the benefit of the insurance *e*
company. Lord Mansfield CJ said that the contract of insurance was an indemnity
and that 'Every day the insurer is put in the place of the insured' (see 3 Doug 61
at 64, 99 ER 538 at 549).
In *Yates v White* (1838) 1 Arn 85 the owner of a vessel sued the defendant for
damaging his ship by collision. The defendant claimed to deduct from the *f*
amount of damages the sum which the plaintiff had received from his insurers in
respect of such damage. The claim was rejected.
In *White v Dobinson* (1844) 14 Sim 273 the ship Diana was insured against
damage. After a collision the insurers paid £205 in respect of the damage. The
owner of the vessel, Hicks, was awarded damages of £817 against a defendant
who was held liable for the collision. Shadwell V-C granted an injunction *g*
restraining the insured person Hicks from receiving and the wrongdoer Dobinson
from paying the sum of £817 in respect of damages without first paying or
providing for the sum £205 in respect of which the insurers were entitled to be
subrogated. On appeal Lord Lyndhurst LC said (5 LTOS 233):

'What is an insurance but a contract of indemnity? Then Hicks having *h*
received a full satisfaction under the award, what right has he to retain
money received from the insurance office as an indemnity for damage? . . .
If Hicks had received an indemnity before the payment of the money by the
company, it would clearly have been contrary to equity that he should retain
that money. Parke on Marine Assurances [Park *A System of the Law of Marine
Insurances* (8th edn, 1842)] says, that a contract to insure is one of indemnity *j*
only, and that the insured shall not receive double compensations for a loss;
but in case the loss has been paid, and the insured afterwards recovers the
amount of damages from another source, the insurer shall stand in his place
to the extent of the sum they have paid.'

Hicks then argued that the plaintiff had no remedy in equity and that his only
a course was an action in a court of law for money had and received. This argument
was rejected and the Lord Chancellor said:

> 'Here the company have paid for a loss, for which the insured afterwards
> obtains full satisfaction, and it is contrary to equity that he should retain the
> money. The underwriters have a claim upon the fund awarded, and they are
b entitled in some shape or other to recover back the money they have paid.'

The injunctions were accordingly upheld.

This is authority for the proposition that, if application is made to the court
before the wrongdoer has paid damages in respect of which an insurer is entitled
to subrogation, the court will not allow the damages to be paid over without
c satisfying the claims of the insurer.

In *Commercial Union Insurance Co v Lister* (1874) LR 9 Ch App 483 the owner of
a building insured it for £33,000 against fire but not for the full value. The
building was burnt by what was said to be the negligence of the servants of a
municipal corporation and suffered damage estimated at £56,000. The owner
brought an action for damages against the corporation. It was held by the Court
d of Appeal, upholding the Master of the Rolls, that the owner undertaking to sue
for the whole amount of damage would be allowed to conduct the action without
interference from the insurers, but would be liable for anything done by him in
violation of any equitable duty towards the insurers. In the course of his judgment
Jessel MR had said (at 484n):

> 'The total amount of the loss is admitted to exceed very largely the total
> amount of the insurances. It is alleged that the fire was caused . . . by the act
> of the corporation of *Halifax* . . . whose carelessness is alleged to have been
> the cause of the fire, and that the carelessness was of such a kind as to render
> the corporation liable for the whole of the loss. In that state of things the
> insurance company or companies is or are willing to pay the amount of the
f insurance, and they say that, having paid that amount (they pay of course by
> way of indemnity), if the assured obtains from the corporation of *Halifax* a
> sum larger than the difference between the amount of the insurance and the
> amount of the loss, he is a trustee for that excess for the insurance company
> or companies—a proposition which I take to be indisputable.'

g   In *Castellain v Preston* (1883) 11 QBD 380 at 388, [1881–5] All ER Rep 493 at
496 Brett LJ said:

> 'In order to apply the doctrine of subrogation, it seems to me that the full
> and absolute meaning of the word must be used, that is to say, the insurer
> must be placed in the position of the assured. Now it seems to me that in
h order to carry out the fundamental rule of insurance law, this doctrine of
> subrogation must be carried to the extent to which I am now about to
> endeavour to express, namely, that as between the underwriter and the
> assured the underwriter is entitled to the advantage of every right of the
> assured, whether such right consists in contract, fulfilled or unfulfilled, or in
> remedy for tort capable of being insisted on or already insisted on, or in any
j other right, whether by way of condition or otherwise, legal or equitable,
> which can be, or has been exercised or had accrued, and whether such right
> could or could not be enforced by the insurer in the name of the assured by
> the exercise or acquiring of which right or condition the loss against which
> the assured is insured, can be, or has been diminished.'

Clearly Brett LJ considered that an insurer was subrogated to any right of action subsisting when the insurer paid under the policy.

In *Re Miller Gibb & Co Ltd* [1957] 2 All ER 266, [1957] 1 WLR 703 the Export Credits Guarantee Department of the Board of Trade issued to a company a policy of insurance for 90% of the amount of any loss sustained in respect of goods sold to Brazil in the event of local regulations preventing payment or a transfer of payment from the buyer to the company. The buyer paid in Brazil into a bank for the account of Martins Bank, who were acting for the company. Transfer of this payment was prevented by Brazilian currency exchange regulations and the department accordingly paid 90% under the terms of the indemnity policy. The company was ordered to be wound up. The department gave notice to Martins Bank of their claim to be subrogated to the rights of the company with respect to the payment from Brazil when received. In January 1956 the bank received the full purchase price from Brazil and the Board of Trade claimed 90%. Wynn-Parry J ordered the liquidator of the company to execute all such documents and do all such things necessary to enable the department to obtain from Martins Bank 90% of the sum which had been received by the bank. This case is indistinguishable from the present.

In *Yorkshire Insurance Co Ltd v Nisbet Shipping Co Ltd* [1961] 2 All ER 487, [1962] 2 QB 330 a vessel was insured for £72,000 and became an actual total loss. The insurers paid £72,000. The assured brought proceedings in Canada for the loss of the vessel and the defendants paid to the assured in Canada $Can336,000-odd, then worth £75,000-odd. The pound was devalued and when the damages were transmitted to London they were worth £127,000. Diplock J held that the doctrine of subrogation only entitled the insurers to recoupment of the £72,000 which they had paid. Diplock J referred to the doctrine of subrogation in these terms ([1961] 2 All ER 487 at 490–491, [1962] 2 QB 330 at 339–341):

'The doctrine of subrogation is not restricted to the law of insurance. Although often referred to as an "equity" it is not an exclusively equitable doctrine. It was applied by the common law courts in insurance cases long before the fusion of law and equity, although the powers of the common law courts might in some cases require to be supplemented by those of the court of equity in order to give full effect to the doctrine; for example, by compelling an assured to allow his name to be used by the insurer for the purpose of enforcing the assured's remedies against third parties in respect of the subject-matter of the loss . . . The expression "subrogation" in relation to a contract of marine insurance is thus no more than a convenient way of referring to those terms which are to be implied in the contract between the assured and the insurer to give business efficacy to an agreement whereby the assured in the case of a loss against which the policy has been made shall be fully indemnified, and never more than fully indemnified . . . In my view the doctrine of subrogation in insurance law requires one to imply in contracts of marine insurance only such terms as are necessary to ensure that notwithstanding that the insurer has made a payment under the policy the assured shall not be entitled to retain, as against the insurer, a greater sum than what is ultimately shown to be his actual loss . . . Thus, if after payment by the insurer of a loss that loss, as a result of an act of a third party, is reduced, the insurer can recover from the assured the amount of the reduction because that is the amount which he, the insurer, has overpaid under the contract of insurance. This sum he can recover at common law, without recourse to equity, as money had and received . . . the duty of the assured to take proceedings to reduce his loss and the correlative right of the insurer to require him to do so was a contractual duty. The remedy for its breach, by compelling the assured to allow an action to be brought in his name, was an equitable remedy in aid of rights at common law, and was alternative to the common law remedy of recovering damages for the breach of the duty . . .'

In *Hobbs v Marlowe* [1977] 2 All ER 241 at 254–255, [1978] AC 16 at 39 Lord Diplock said:

'For my own part I prefer to regard the doctrine of subrogation in relation to contracts of insurance as having its origin at common law in the implied terms of the contract and calling for the aid of a court of equity only where its auxiliary jurisdiction was needed to compel the assured to lend his name to his insurer for the enforcement of rights and remedies to which his insurer was subrogated: see *Yorkshire Insurance Co Ltd v Nisbet Shipping Co Ltd* [1961] 2 All ER 487, [1962] 2 QB 330. But the practical effects of the doctrine of subrogation on the rights and remedies of insurer and assured are similar in many respects to the effect of an equitable assignment of a chose in action . . .'

Thus Lord Diplock, far from deciding that a court of equity could not lend its aid to compel the assured to direct that the insurer be recouped under the doctrine of subrogation out of the damages recovered from the wrongdoer, equated the right of the insurer to that of the assignee of an equitable interest, a right which equity will of course enforce.

It may be that the common law invented and implied in contracts of insurance a promise by the insured person to take proceedings to reduce his loss, a promise by the insured person to account to the insurer for moneys recovered from a third party in respect of the insured loss and a promise by the insured person to allow the insurer to exercise in the name of the insured person rights of action vested in the insured person against third parties for the recovery of the insured loss if the insured person refuses or neglects to enforce those rights of action. There must also be implied a promise by the insured person that in exercising his rights of action against third parties he will act in good faith for the benefit of the insured person so far as he has borne the loss and for the benefit of the insurer so far as he has indemnified the insured person against the insured loss. My Lords, contractual promises may create equitable interests. An express promise by a vendor to convey land on payment of the purchase price confers on the purchaser an equitable interest in the land. In my opinion promises implied in a contract of insurance with regard to rights of action vested in the insured person for the recovery of an insured loss from a third party responsible for the loss confer on the insurer an equitable interest in those rights of action to the extent necessary to recoup the insurer who has indemnified the insured person against the insured loss.

In the hypothetical case under consideration, the intervention of equity is required to ensure that the insured person exercises his right of action against the wrongdoer in good faith and that the insurer is recouped out of the damages recovered from the wrongdoer. The stop-loss insurer is out of pocket to the amount of £100,000 from the time that he pays, as he must pay, £100,000 to the name immediately the loss has been suffered. The stop-loss insurer is entitled to be recouped £95,000 as soon as the damages of £130,000 are available from the wrongdoer. The name cannot delay or frustrate recoupment without inflicting harm on the insurer who remains out of pocket to the extent of £100,000 until he is recouped. The name cannot make use of the damages payable by the wrongdoer and available for recoupment of the stop-loss insurers without the

name receiving a benefit or advantage to which he is not entitled. When I asked
why the names were defending these present proceedings, your Lordships were *a*
blandly informed that the names wished to benefit their 'cash flow' by making
use of all the damages payable by Outhwaite and deferring recoupment until
each stop-loss insurer was able to obtain a judgment against each name for money
had and received. The stop-loss insurers were not in a position to sue the name to
whom they had paid £100,000 until the action against Outhwaite resulted in
judgment or compromise which included £130,000 for the insured loss and the *b*
damages of £130,000 had been paid to the name; they were even then not in a
position to sue the name until the amount which the stop-loss insurers were
entitled to recoup under the doctrine of subrogation had been ascertained and
calculated. There are 246 names, some of whom are resident in the United States
of America and elsewhere abroad. In order to succeed in an action for money had
and received stop-loss insurers might be obliged to pursue litigation at considerable *c*
expense and subject to considerable delay in a country which knows nothing of
an action for money had and received or does not recognise the doctrine of
subrogation or confines its civil litigation to the tender mercies of juries who are
unsympathetic towards insurers. By the time that the stop-loss insurers ascertain
that they are entitled to be repaid the sum of £95,000 and no more and no less *d*
under the doctrine of subrogation and bring and succeed in a claim against the
hypothetical name to be paid £95,000, whether judgment for that sum be
obtained at home or abroad, the name, having had and received £100,000 from
the stop-loss insurers, may not be in a position to pay back £95,000. We were
informed and accept that the respondent and representative name Lord Napier
and Ettrick is a man of honour and substance and will fulfill his obligations *e*
although he is not apparently willing to fulfill them until a writ is issued and
judgment is obtained against him for money had and received[1]. But no one can
answer for the other 245 names.

If the stop-loss insurers have no equitable remedy in connection with their
rights and if a name becomes bankrupt then subrogation is a mockery. Suppose,
for example, that a name receives £100,000 from an insurer under a policy, *f*
recovers judgment for £130,000 damages from the wrongdoer and the name
goes bankrupt before he receives the damages owing £1m and possessing no
assets other than assets representing the £100,000 he has received from the
insurer and the asset of £130,000 payable by the wrongdoer. In that case, if the
argument on behalf of the names is correct, the unsecured creditors of the insured
name will benefit by double payment. The stop-loss insurers will be in a worse *g*
position than an unsecured creditor because the insurers could resist payment
under the policy whereas an unsecured creditor may choose whether to advance
moneys or not. In the case of the bankruptcy of the name, the right of the insurer
to subrogation will be useless unless equity protects that right.

Saville J and the Court of Appeal held that the stop-loss insurers were confined *h*
to their remedy for money had and received. The damages must first be
distributed to the names. The stop-loss insurers must then agree or determine by
application to the court the amount due to them respectively and must then
bring proceedings for money had and received against each of the names. All the
authorities which indicated that an insurer who pays on the policy and is entitled
to recoupment by way of subrogation has an equitable interest in the right of *j*
action of the insured person against a wrongdoer and an equitable interest in the
damages payable by the wrongdoer were said not to be binding on the courts.
Those authorities which I have cited, and there are others, included *Randal v
Cockran* 1 Ves Sen 98, 27 ER 916 decided in 1748, *White v Dobinson* 14 Sim 273,

---

1   See addendum at p 410 *f*, post

60 ER 363; *affd* 5 LTOS 233 decided in 1844, *Commercial Union v Lister* LR 9 Ch
a App 483 decided in 1874 and *Re Miller Gibb & Co Ltd* [1957] 2 All ER 266, [1957]
1 WLR 703 decided in 1957. I am not prepared to treat authorities which span
over two centuries in a cavalier fashion. The principles which dictated the
decisions of our ancestors and inspired their references to the equitable obligations
of an insured person towards an insurer entitled to subrogation are discernible
and immutable. They establish that such an insurer has an enforceable equitable
b interest in the damages payable by the wrongdoer. The insured person is guilty
of unconscionable conduct if he does not provide for the insurer to be recouped
out of the damages awarded against the wrongdoer. Equity will not allow the
insured person to insist on his legal rights to all the damages awarded against the
wrongdoer and will restrain the insured person from receiving or dealing with
those damages so far as they are required to recoup the insurer under the doctrine
c of subrogation.

Where the insured person has been paid policy moneys by the insurer for a loss
in respect of which the insured person recovers damages from a wrongdoer the
insured person is guilty of unconscionable conduct if he does not procure and
direct that the sum due to the insurer shall by way of subrogation be paid out of
d the damages.

It is next necessary to consider how equity copes with such unconscionable
conduct. Saville J and the Court of Appeal appear to have thought that equity can
only interfere by creating a trust fund held in trust by trustees for different
beneficiaries in different shares, the trustees being burdened with administrative
and investment duties, the trustees being liable for all the duties imposed on
e trustees but being free from liability if the trust fund is lost without negligence.
I agree that if this were the only method of protecting the rights of an insurer the
practical disadvantages would be fearsome. Fortunately, equity is not so inflexible
or powerless. In order to protect the rights of the insurer under the doctrine of
subrogation equity considers that the damages payable by the wrongdoer to the
insured person are subject to an equitable lien or charge in favour of the insurer.
f The charge is imposed by equity because the insurer, once he has paid under the
policy, has an interest in the right of action against the wrongdoer and an interest
in the establishment, quantification, recovery and distribution of the damages
awarded against the wrongdoer. It would be unconscionable for the insured
person, who has received £100,000 from the insurer, to put damages of £130,000
into his own pocket without providing for the recoupment of the insurer who
g only contracted to indemnify the insured person.

The insurer can give notice to the wrongdoer of his equitable charge. When
the wrongdoer is ordered or agrees to pay £130,000 and has notice of the rights
of the insurer to subrogation, the wrongdoer can either pay the damages into
court or decline to pay without the consent of both the insured person and the
h insurer. It would be the duty of the insured person to direct the wrongdoer to
pay £95,000 of the damages to the insurer in recoupment and to pay the balance
of £35,000 to himself. The equitable charge in favour of the insurer is enforceable
against the damages ordered to be paid; that charge can be enforced so long as the
damages form an identifiable separate fund. If, in the present case, Richards
Butler had distributed the damages to the names before the stop-loss insurers
j issued proceedings or notified Richards Butler of their equitable charge, the stop-
loss insurers would have been reduced to exercising their rights to sue the names
for money had and received.

In the present case damages of £116m are in a separate fund held by Richards
Butler on behalf of the names albeit that the damages in the fund also include
moneys held on behalf of other names and other insurers. For the reasons I have
indicated it would be unconscionable for the names to take their shares of the

damages without providing for the sums due to the stop-loss insurers to be paid out of those damages. The equitable charge still affects the damages and affects *a* Richards Butler, who hold the damages with notice of the charge.

It is true that it may not be possible to distribute the damages between the stop-loss insurers and the names at once because the amounts due to the names as opposed to other names may still be uncertain and because the amounts due to the stop-loss insurers in any particular case by way of subrogation may still be uncertain. These uncertainties are due to the fact that losses of Lloyd's underwriters *b* surface and are quantified in some cases many years after the relevant year of account. The calculations are also complicated by the fact that the damages of £116m are in compensation of claims extending over different years of account with different names and insurers and with insurance policies containing different provisions. Delay in distributing the damages cannot be blamed on the stop-loss insurers. Delay is as much a disadvantage to the stop-loss insurers as it is to the *c* names. It is in the interests of everybody that the damages shall be distributed as soon as possible. Interim distributions can be made in favour of those names and stop-loss insurers whose rights and liabilities have been or are now capable of being calculated with certainty. If necessary the court will decide how much can now be distributed. Any reserves for uncertain events can be invested in joint *d* names for the benefit of the name and the stop-loss insurers concerned.

In the result I would allow the appeal by the stop-loss insurers against the refusal of Saville J and the Court of Appeal to grant any relief in equity against the names and Richards Butler. In my opinion the stop-loss insurers are entitled to injunctions restraining Richards Butler from paying and each name from receiving any part of the damages of £116m now held by Richards Butler without *e* first providing or paying out of the damages payable to the name the amounts which have been or shall be found to be due from that name to the stop-loss insurers by way of subrogation.

I would dismiss the cross-appeal by the names against the declaration made by the Court of Appeal in these terms: *f*

'That, when determining the amount which stop loss insurers are entitled to claim in respect of the Settlement monies, the stop loss insurers are entitled to be reimbursed any indemnity paid by them to an assured before that assured is fully indemnified by applying his share of the Settlement monies to a loss occurring below the excess in that assured's policy.'

g

Since drafting this speech I have read in draft the speech to be delivered by my noble and learned friend Lord Goff of Chieveley. He agrees that the doctrine of subrogation confers on the insurer an equitable proprietary lien or charge on the moneys recovered by the insured person from a third party in respect of the insured loss. I agree that in the circumstances it is not now necessary to decide *h* whether the equitable lien or charge attaches also to the rights of action vested in the insured person to recover from a third party. I have expressed the view that the doctrine of subrogation does apply in those circumstances but in any future case, if the point becomes material, that view may require reconsideration in the light of further research. Subject to this observation I agree with the views expressed by Lord Goff and I also agree with the speeches to be delivered by my *j* noble and learned friends Lord Jauncey of Tullichettle and Lord Browne-Wilkinson.

The names must pay the costs of the stop-loss insurers before this House and in the courts below.

LORD GOFF OF CHIEVELEY. My Lords, I, too, have reached the conclusion
a that the appeal should be allowed. I start with the common law. In *Yorkshire
Insurance Co Ltd v Nisbet Shipping Co Ltd* [1961] 2 All ER 487, [1962] 2 QB 330, a
case concerned with marine insurance, Diplock J analysed the principle of
subrogation in purely contractual terms. He said ([1961] 2 All ER 487 at 490,
[1962] 2 QB 330 at 339–340):

b   'The expression "subrogation" in relation to a contract of marine insurance
    is thus no more than a convenient way of referring to those terms which are
    to be implied in the contract between the assured and the insurer to give
    business efficacy to an agreement whereby the assured in the case of a loss
    against which the policy has been made shall be fully indemnified, and never
    more than fully indemnified.'

c   He went on to say that subrogation is concerned solely with the mutual rights
and liabilities of the parties to the contract of insurance. The remedies of the
insurer were, he said, essentially common law remedies; in particular, if the
assured has, after payment of the loss by the insurer, received a sum from a third
party in reduction of the loss, the insurer can recover the amount of the reduction
d as money had and received (for which Diplock J referred to *Bullen and Leake's
Precedents of Pleadings* (3rd edn, 1868) p 187). The only role which Diplock J
assigned to equity was to come to the aid of the common law by compelling the
assured to allow his name to be used in proceedings against the third party: see
also his judgment, as Lord Diplock, in *Hobbs v Marlowe* [1977] 2 All ER 241 at
254–255, [1978] AC 16 at 39.
e   Now there is no reason why, subject to the one matter to which Lord Diplock
refers, the principle of subrogation in the field of insurance should not have
developed as a purely common law principle. But as a matter of history it did not
do so. It is true that our law of marine insurance was very largely established by
Lord Mansfield, in a remarkable series of decisions during his tenure of office as
Chief Justice at the Court of King's Bench, so much so that Park J dedicated the
f first edition of his treatise on the law of marine insurance (Park *A System of the
Law of Marine Insurances* (1786)) to Lord Mansfield, describing the subject in the
dedication as one which 'must be admitted to be the exclusive property of your
Lordship'. But in the early editions of the book there is little trace of the principle
of subrogation, though there is much learning on the subject of abandonment.
g Lord Mansfield CJ's decision in the leading case of *Mason v Sainsbury* (1782) 3
Doug 61, 99 ER 538 established that payment of a claim by an insurer did not
preclude him from thereafter proceeding in the name of the assured against the
wrongdoer who had caused the relevant damage, and recovering damages in full
from him. The payment of the loss by the insurer to the assured did not affect
the liability of the wrongdoer; the action against him was to be considered 'as if
h the insurers had not paid a farthing' (see 3 Doug 61 at 64, 99 ER 538 at 540).
However the insured could not proceed against the third party in his own name;
he had to proceed in the name of the assured (see *London Assurance Co v Sainsbury*
(1783) 3 Doug 245, 99 ER 636).
    It is of some interest that in *Mason v Sainsbury* the action against the wrongdoer
was brought in the name of the assured with his consent, for the benefit of the
j insurer. Here we can see an early example of the fact that the insurer, upon
payment to the assured of his loss, receives from him as a matter of course not
merely a receipt for the money, but also what has for many years been called a
letter of subrogation signed by the assured which authorises the insurer to proceed
in this way, and indeed nowadays may assign the relevant rights of action to the

insurer. It is very difficult to imagine an insurer paying a claim without taking this elementary precaution, especially as the assured can have little or no incentive to refuse to sign such a document. I strongly suspect that letters of subrogation have been a commonplace of insurance claims for a very long time, and that it is their regular use which explains what appears to be a dearth of authority on such matters as proceedings to compel the assured to allow the insurer to commence proceedings in his name, and actions for money had and received by insurers against assured, because third parties would have settled direct with the insurer as expressly authorised by the assured (hence, pace Lord Diplock, the absence of any reference to such an action in *Bullen and Leake's Precedents of Pleading* (3rd edn). On the other hand, there is a substantial body of case law on the subject of the respective rights of insurer and assured in the institution, control and settlement of proceedings against wrongdoers who have caused the relevant loss (as to which see *MacGillivray and Parkington on Insurance Law* (8th edn, 1988) paras 1191ff).

At all events, what appears to have happened is not simply that equity came to the aid of the common law by compelling an assured whose loss has been paid to allow the insurer to proceed in his name against a third party wrongdoer responsible for the loss, but that a principle of subrogation was the subject of separate development by courts of equity in a line of authority dating from *Randal v Cockran* (1748) 1 Ves Sen 99, 27 ER 916, which was decided before Lord Mansfield was appointed Chief Justice of the Court of King's Bench. This line of authority is traced in the speech of my noble and learned friend Lord Templeman, and I am therefore spared the burden of setting it out in this opinion. Spasmodic but consistent, the cases assert that recoveries by the assured which reduce the loss paid by the insurer are held in trust for the insurer, so much so that by 1881 Jessel MR regarded this proposition as indisputable (see *Commercial Union Insurance Co v Lister* (1874) LR 9 Ch App 848n). This principle was moreover recognised not only in courts of equity, but also in courts of common law (see the decision of the Court of Common Pleas in *Yates v White* (1838) 1 Arn 85, 4 Bing NC 272, 132 ER 793, subsequently approved by this House in *Simpson & Co v Thomson* (1877) 3 App Cas 279, in which Lord Cairns LC (at 285–286) cited in extenso passages from the judgment in *Yates v Whyte* 4 Bing NC 272 at 282–283, 132 ER 793 at 797 in which reliance was placed on *Randal v Cockran*, and Lord Blackburn (at 293) relied on *Randal v Cockran* itself in a passage to which I shall refer later in this opinion. It is perhaps also relevant that in 1783 Lord Mansfield CJ had justified his conclusion that the insurer could not proceed in his own name but must proceed in the name of the assured on the ground that 'Trustee and cestui que trust cannot both have a right of action': see *London Assurance Co v Sainsbury* (1783) 3 Doug 245 at 253, 99 ER 636 at 640.

I agree with my noble and learned friend Lord Browne-Wilkinson that the decisive case in the line of equity cases is *White v Dobinson* (1844) 14 Sim 273, 60 ER 363; *affd* (1845) 5 LTOS 233. The case was concerned with a collision at sea. The owner of one of the ships, after payment by his underwriter of £205, was awarded £600 damages in arbitration proceedings against the other shipowner. Shadwell V-C, relying upon *Randal v Cockran* and *Blaauwpot v da Costa* (1758) 1 Eden 130, 28 ER 633, granted an interlocutory injunction which had the effect of retaining the fund, and not letting it pass into the hands of the assured. The injunction appears to have restrained both the assured from receiving, and the other shipowner from paying, the money without first paying or providing for the sum of £205 paid by the insurer (see 5 LTOS 233). Lord Lyndhurst LC discharged the injunction as against the other shipowner, but otherwise maintained it in force. The case is important for a number of reasons. First, the

insurer's case was advanced on the basis that he had a lien on the sum awarded,
a and was resisted on the ground that the insurer's right, if it existed at all, was a
right to proceed at law in an action for money had and received, and was not an
equitable right. That argument was rejected. Second, the Lord Chancellor also
rejected a claim by a bank as assignee from the assured, on the ground that the
bank's security was taken subject to all the equities which would have affected the
money received in the hands of the assured himself. Third, the Lord Chancellor
b held that the insurers had a claim upon the fund awarded, and were 'entitled in
some shape or other to recover back the money they have paid'.

Now it is true that the case was concerned with an interlocutory injunction, a
point which evidently concerned the Lord Chancellor himself. But he nevertheless
upheld the injunction on the basis of the authority cited to him, in which, as he
c said (5 LTOS 233):

> '. . . we have the clearly expressed opinions of Lord Hardwicke [in *Randal
> v Cockran* (1748) 1 Ves Sen 98, 27 ER 916] and Lord Northington [in
> *Blaauwpot v da Costa* (1758) 1 Eden 130, 28 ER 633], recognized by Mr. Baron
> Parke, and more recently by Lord Abinger [in *Brooks v MacDonnell* (1835) 1 Y
> & C Ex 500, 160 ER 204], who at that time possessed considerable experience
d > of the practice in equity, from having presided for several years on the equity
> side of the Court of Exchequer . . .'

Subsequent authorities to the same effect are *King v Victoria Insurance Co* [1896]
AC 250 at 255–256 per Lord Hobhouse, who (in a passage in which he appears to
have placed no reliance upon the existence of an assignment by the assured of its
e rights and causes of action against the third party) expressed the opinion that the
assured would have held any damages recovered from the third party as trustee
for the insurer, and *Re Miller Gibb & Co Ltd* [1957] 2 All ER 266, [1957] 1 WLR
703. The only case in equity which appears at first sight to be inconsistent with
this line of authority is *Stearns v Village Main Reef Gold Mining Co Ltd* (1905) 10
Com Cas 89. However, as my noble and learned friend Lord Browne-Wilkinson
f has pointed out, that case was concerned with the recovery of an overpayment;
indeed, it was upon that basis that it was distinguished by Wynn-Parry J in *Re
Miller Gibb & Co Ltd* [1957] 2 All ER 266 at 272, [1957] 1 WLR 703 at 710–711.

Despite Saville J's reservations on this point, I can discern no inconsistency
between the equitable proprietary right recognised by courts of equity in these
cases and the personal rights and obligations embodied in the contract of insurance
g itself. No doubt our task nowadays is to see the two strands of authority, at law
and in equity, moulded into a coherent whole; but for my part I cannot see why
this amalgamation should lead to the rejection of the equitable proprietary right
recognised in the line of cases to which I have referred. Of course, it is proper to
start with the contract of insurance, and to see how the common law courts have
h worked out the mutual rights and obligations of the parties in contractual terms
with recourse to implied terms where appropriate. But, with all respect, I am
unable to agree with Diplock J that subrogation is in this context concerned *solely*
with the mutal rights and obligations of the parties under the contract. In this
connection, I observe from the report of *Yorkshire Insurance Co Ltd v Nisbet Shipping
Co Ltd* [1961] 2 All ER 487, [1962] 2 QB 330 that the important case of *White v
j Dobinson* (1844) 14 Sim 273, 60 ER 363; *affd* 116 LTOS 233 was not cited in
argument, and indeed the existence of an equitable proprietary right was not in
issue in that case. In these circumstances I cannot derive from Diplock J's
judgment any justification for sweeping the line of equity cases under the carpet
as though it did not exist. In my opinion, this line of authority must be recognised,

and appropriate weight should be given to the views expressed in the cases by the distinguished judges who decided them. I wish to add that I do not read s 79 of *a* the Marine Insurance Act 1906 (concerned with the right of subrogation) as in any way detracting from this conclusion.

Even so, an important feature of these cases is that the principle of subrogation in the law of insurance arises in a contractual context. It is true that in some cases at common law it has been described as arising as a matter of equity. Thus in *Burnand v Rodocanachi Sons & Co* (1882) 7 App Cas 333 at 339 Lord Blackburn *b* described it simply as 'an equity'. Furthermore, it has not been usual to express the principle of subrogation as arising from an implied term in the contract. Even so it has been regarded, both at law and in equity, as giving effect to the underlying nature of a contract of insurance, which is that it is intended to provide an indemnity but no more than an indemnity. Not only does this principle inform the judgments of the Court of Appeal in the leading case of *c* *Castellain v Preston* (1883) 11 QBD 380, [1881–5] All ER Rep 493, but it underlies Lord Lyndhurst LC's judgment in *White v Dobinson* (1845) 5 LTOS 233. In so far as the principle requires the payment of money, it could no doubt be formulated as an implied term, to which effect could have been given by the old action for money had and received. But I do not see why the mere fact that the purpose of *d* subrogation in this context is to give effect to the principle of indemnity embodied in the contract should preclude recognition of the equitable proprietary right, if justice so requires. If I search for a parallel, the closest analogy is perhaps to be found in the law of agency, in which, although the relationship between principal and agent is governed by a contract, nevertheless the agent may be held in certain circumstances to hold money, which he has received from a third party in his *e* capacity as agent, as trustee for his principal. It is by no means easy to ascertain the circumstances in which a trusteeship exists; but, in a valuable discussion in *Bowstead on Agency* (15th edn, 1985) pp 162–163, Professor Francis Reynolds suggests that it is right to inquire—

'whether the trust relationship is appropriate to the commercial relationship *f* in which the parties find themselves; whether it was appropriate that money or property should be, and whether it was, held separately, or whether it was contemplated that the agent should use the money, property or proceeds of the property as part of his normal cash flow in such a way that the relationship of debtor and creditor is more appropriate.'

He also suggests that— *g*

'a central question, perhaps too often overlooked (because not directly in issue), is whether the rights of the principal are sufficiently strong, and differentiable from other claims, for him to be entitled to a prior position in respect of them on the agent's bankruptcy.'

h

I have little doubt that the distinguished judges who decided the cases in the line of equity authority to which I have referred must have considered that money received by an assured from a third party in reduction of a loss paid by an insurer should not be treated as available for the assured's normal cash flow, and further that the rights of the insurer to such money were sufficiently strong to entitle the insurer to priority in the event of the assured's bankruptcy, as was indeed held by *j* Wynn-Parry J in *Re Miller Gibb & Co* [1957] 2 All ER 266, [1957] 1 WLR 703. I for my part can see no good reason to depart from this line of authority. However, since the constitution of the assured as trustee of such money may impose upon him obligations of too onerous a character (a point which troubled Saville J in the present case), I am very content that the equitable proprietary right of the insurer

should be classified as a lien, as proposed by my noble and learned friend Lord
a Templeman, and indeed as claimed by the insurer in *White v Dobinson* (1844) 14
Sim 237, 60 ER 363 itself. Indeed a lien is the more appropriate form of
proprietary right in circumstances where, as here, its function is to protect the
interest of the insurer in an asset only to the extent that its retention by the
assured will have the effect that he is more than indemnified under the policy of
insurance.
b   There is one particular problem to which I wish to refer, although, as I
understand it, it does not fall to be decided in the present case. Does the equitable
proprietary interest of the insurer attach only to a fund consisting of sums which
come into the hands of the assured in reduction of the loss paid by the insurer?
Or does it attach also to a right of action vested in the assured which, if enforced,
would yield such a fund? The point is not altogether easy. I can see no reason in
c principle why such an interest should not be capable of attaching to property in
the nature of a chose in action. Moreover that it should do so in the present
context appears to have been the opinion of Lord Blackburn in *Simpson v Thomson*
(1877) 3 App Cas 279 at 292–293. On the other hand, cases such as *Morley v Moore*
[1936] 2 All ER 79, [1936] 2 KB 359 appear to point in the opposite direction, as
d perhaps does the decision of Lord Lyndhurst LC in *White v Dobinson* (1845) 5
LTOS 233 to discharge the injunction as against the owner of the ship at fault in
that case. However, since the point was not directly addressed in the argument
before your Lordships, I am reluctant to reach any conclusion upon it without a
full examination of the authorities relating to the respective rights and obligations
of insurer and assured, especially with regard to the conduct and disposal of
e litigation relating to causes of action of the relevant kind. I therefore wish to
reserve my opinion upon this question, the answer to which I do not regard as
necessary for the resolution of the issue which has arisen in the present case.
    For these reasons, I would allow the appeal. For the reasons given by my noble
and learned friends Lord Templeman and Lord Jauncey of Tullichettle, I would
dismiss the cross-appeal.
f

LORD JAUNCEY OF TULLICHETTLE. My Lords, I have had the
advantage of reading in draft the speeches of my noble and learned friends Lord
Templeman, Lord Goff of Chieveley and Lord Browne-Wilkinson. I agree that
for the reasons which they have given the appeal of the stop-loss insurers should
be allowed and I cannot usefully add anything to what they have said. I also agree
g that the cross-appeal by the names should be refused and wish only to add a few
words of my own thereanent.
    The cross-appeal raises the question of how moneys recovered (the recoveries)
by the names in the Outhwaite actions are to be applied as between the names
and the stop-loss insurers. A typical policy granted by the stop-loss insurers
h undertook to—

> 'indemnify the Assured for the amount by which the Assured's overall
> ascertained net underwriting loss as hereinafter defined for the Underwriting
> Year(s) of Account shown in the schedule exceeds the amount stated as
> "Excess" in the schedule.'

j The policy further provided that the insurers liability should not exceed a specified
limit. The names contended that the recoveries should be applied first towards
their losses above the specified limit, second towards their losses up to the excess
and thereafter to the stop-loss insurers. The latter accepted that the recoveries
should be applied in the first instance towards the names' losses above the specified
limit but contended that they should then be applied for their benefit. The

competing arguments may perhaps be best illustrated by a hypothetical example
which was relied upon in the Court of Appeal and before this House. A name   *a*
having a policy with an excess of £25,000 and insurers' liability limited to
£100,000 suffers a total loss of £160,000, but receives £100,000 under his policy
and later recovers £130,000 in the action. The names argued that the £130,000
fell to be applied as to £35,000 to meet the uninsured top slice of the loss, as to
£25,000 to meet the initial excess and as to the remaining £70,000 for the benefit
of the stop-loss insurers. There was no dispute as to the application of £35,000   *b*
but the stop-loss insurers maintained that the remaining £95,000 should be
applied for their benefit leaving them with a liability to the insured of only
£5,000. In short the question was whether the names were entitled to recoup
themselves out of the recoveries for their initial uninsured £25,000 loss in priority
to the stop-loss insurers. Saville J held that the names were so entitled but the
Court of Appeal held that they were not. Your Lordships were informed that a   *c*
sum of about £6m was affected by this issue.

The basis of the stop-loss insurers' right to receive any part of the recoveries is
the doctrine of subrogation. In *Castellain v Preston* (1883) 11 QBD 380 at 386,
[1881–5] All ER Rep 493 at 495 Brett LJ said:

> 'The very foundation, in my opinion, of every rule which has been applied   *d*
> to insurance law is this, namely, that the contract of insurance contained in a
> marine or fire policy is a contract of indemnity, and of indemnity only, and
> that this contract means that the assured, in case of a loss against which the
> policy has been made, shall be fully indemnified, but shall never be more
> than fully indemnified.'   *e*

He later went on to give an enlarged definition of subrogation pointing out that
'the insurer must be placed in the position of the assured' (see 11 QBD 380 at 388,
[1881–5] All ER Rep 493 at 496). He pointed out that although an insurer who
had not yet fully indemnified an insured could not, in relation to prior recoveries,
be subrogated to any right of action nevertheless it would be contrary to the   *f*
doctrine of subrogation if the insured's loss were not diminished vis-à-vis the
insurer (see 11 QBD 380 at 389–390, cf [1881–5] All ER Rep 493 at 496). Brett LJ
was thus equiparating the effect of recoveries made before indemnification by the
insurer with those made afterwards. In the case of recoveries made towards a loss
which was indemnifiable but had not yet been indemnified the matter could
equally well be approached by saying that the loss which the insurer had   *g*
undertaken to meet was the initial loss diminished by all relevant recoveries prior
to payment by the insurer. This appears to have been the approach of Cotton LJ
in *Castellain v Preston* 11 QBD 380 at 393, [1881–5] All ER Rep 493 at 498, where
after referring to the loss insured against he said:

> 'In order to ascertain what that loss is, everything must be taken into   *h*
> account which is received by and comes to the hand of the assured, and
> which diminishes that loss. It is only the amount of the loss, when it is
> considered as a contract of indemnity, which is to be paid after taking into
> account and estimating those benefits or sums of money which the assured
> may have received in diminution of the loss.'
>   *j*

He said (11 QBD 380 at 395, [1881–5] All ER Rep 493 at 498):

> 'The principle which I have enunciated goes further, and if there is a
> money or any other benefit received which ought to be taken into account in
> diminishing the loss or in ascertaining what the real loss is against which the

a   contract of indemnity is given, the indemnifier ought to be allowed to take advantage of it in order to calculate what the real loss is . . .'

A similar approach was adopted by Lord Blackburn in *Burnand v Rodocanachi Sons & Co* (1882) 7 App Cas 333 at 339 in these words:

b   'The general rule of law (and it is obvious justice) is that where there is a contract of indemnity (it matters not whether it is a marine policy, or a policy against fire on land, or any other contract of indemnity) and a loss happens, anything which reduces or diminishes that loss reduces or diminishes the amount which the indemnifier is bound to pay; and if the indemnifier has already paid it, then, if anything which diminishes the loss comes into the hands of the person to whom he has paid it, it becomes an equity that the person who has already paid the full indemnity is entitled to be recouped by having that amount back.'

c

What is, in my view, particularly significant about the foregoing dicta is the emphasis which they place upon the fact that in the context of recoveries subrogation is concerned only with the loss against which the assured is insured rather than any general loss. If an assured has suffered an insured loss and an *d*   uninsured loss full indemnification of the former subrogates the insurers irrespective of the fact that the assured has not yet recovered the uninsured loss.

Saville J in rejecting the argument of the stop-loss insurers said that it 'involves the proposition that they can take account of the recovery before the assured has been reimbursed for his loss'. He concluded his judgment by saying:

e   'The question to be asked . . . is whether the recovery together with the indemnity will more than compensate the assured for the loss. If it will, then, if this arises before payment, the amount of the indemnity will be reduced so as to avoid overcompensation, while, if it occurs after payment, the assured will have to repay the amount of overcompensation to his indemnifiers. I can only repeat that any approach which does not achieve *f*   this result but instead leaves the assured over- or under-compensated must be wrong, since it offends the very reason why subrogation exists in our law.'

With respect to the learned judge it seems to me that he was there confusing the whole loss suffered by the assured with the loss against which the insurer had agreed to indemnify him. When the indemnity extends to the total loss sustained *g*   the two will be coincident but in the present case they were not. In my view Staughton LJ was correct in stating that—

'It is [the loss against which the policy has been made] which the insured must have been reimbursed for, if the insurer is to claim any benefit by way of subrogation.'

h

In this case the stop-loss insurers undertook to indemnify the assured for the amount by which their overall ascertained underwriting loss exceeded a specified excess but did not exceed a stated limit. In the given example they undertook to meet losses neither below £25,000 nor above £125,000. When they paid over the £100,000 to the names the latter were fully indemnified against the insured *j*   loss although they themselves had further uninsured losses of £60,000 and the stop-loss insurers were subrogated to any recoveries which reduced the insured loss. If in the given example recovery of £130,000 had been achieved before the stop-loss insurers were called upon to pay what would have been the loss which the names had at that stage sustained? The insurers would answer '£30,000' upon the view that a recovery of £130,000 had reduced an initial loss of £160,000 to that figure. The names however would answer, 'We have sustained a loss of £30,000 lying within a band between £25,000 and £55,000 for which loss we are entitled to indemnity from the insurers'. My Lords, not only does the names' answer defy common sense but it also involves their accepting that they have sustained no loss in respect of the initial excess, a loss whose existence is a prerequisite to any liability on the part of the stop-loss insurers. To put the matter another way, the names' answer involves treating the 'loss against which the policy has been made' not as provided for in that policy but as the first £100,000 without excess, an exercise for which there is, in my view, no warrant whatsoever. Suppose that instead of carrying the first £25,000 themselves the names had insured that sum with another insurer. Could they on receipt of the £130,000 of recoveries have paid £25,000 to that insurer at the expense of the stop-loss insurers? The answer can only be No. The fact that they have chosen to carry their own insurance for that sum cannot in my view place them in a better position vis-à-vis the other insurers than would have been an insurer of that sum. When an insured loss is diminished by a recovery from a third party, whether before or after any indemnification has been made, the ultimate loss is simply the initial loss minus the recovery and it is that sum to which the provisions of the policy of assurance apply including any provision as to an excess.

My Lords, for the foregoing reasons and for those given by my noble and learned friend Lord Templeman I consider that the Court of Appeal reached a correct conclusion on this matter and that the cross-appeal should be dismissed.

LORD BROWNE-WILKINSON. My Lords, I agree with the speeches of my noble and learned friends Lord Templeman and Lord Jauncey of Tullichettle. I add some words of my own on the question whether the stop-loss insurers have a proprietary interest in the damages recovered by the names from Outhwaite because we are differing from the Court of Appeal on that point.

Dillon LJ (with whom Staughton and Nolan LJJ agreed on this point) based his conclusion that the doctrine of subrogation does not give rise to any proprietary interest primarily on the statement of the law by Diplock J in *Yorkshire Insurance Co Ltd v Nisbet Shipping Co Ltd* [1961] 2 All ER 487 at 490, [1962] 2 QB 330 at 339–340 and, as Lord Diplock, in *Hobbs v Marlowe* [1977] 2 All ER 241 at 254–255, [1978] AC 16 at 39. Lord Diplock said, in effect, that in relation to insurance the right of subrogation was a common law doctrine based on the implied terms of the contract of insurance, the role of equity being limited to aiding the common law right of recovery by forcing the assured to permit the insurers to sue third parties in the name of the assured. It was the view of the Court of Appeal that, as a common law doctrine, the right of subrogation enjoyed by insurers was unlikely to give rise to a trust or other equitable or proprietary right.

However, the researches of counsel in the present case have failed to disclose any reported decision before the fusion of law and equity in which an insurer successfully sued the assured at law for money had and received, being moneys recovered by the assured from a third party wrongdoer in reduction of the insured loss. Nor has any case been found in which a court of equity was asked to make an order directing the assured to permit the insurers to sue in the name of the assured. Nor can I find in *Bullen and Leake's Precedents of Pleadings* (3rd edn, 1868) p 187 (on which Diplock J relied in the *Yorkshire Insurance* case [1961] 2 All ER 487 at 491, [1962] 2 QB 330 at 341) any precedent for a common law action for money had and received brought by the insurer against the insured.

On the other side, the authorities cited by Lord Templeman show a series of decisions from 1748 onwards in which courts of equity were themselves enforcing

rights of subrogation against the assured and in which both equity and common
a law courts referred to the assured as holding benefits received from a third party
as 'trustee' for the insurers or subject to a lien in favour of the insurers.

In my judgment therefore Lord Diplock's dicta are not well founded if they
suggest that subrogation in insurance cases was purely a common law doctrine
and that equity only intervened for the purpose of enabling the insurer to sue in
the name of the assured. Equity itself enforced rights of subrogation against the
b assured. Despite the lack of reported cases, it may well be that before 1875 the
common law also recognised the right of insurers to sue the assured for money
had and received. The probability is that in the majority of cases there was a letter
of subrogation obtained from the assured when the insurance moneys were paid.
Such a letter would regulate the rights of the insurers to sue and the destination
of the moneys recovered.
c
What, then, was the basis on which equity enforced rights of subrogation? Was
it merely a personal obligation of the assured to account to the insurers for benefits
received from third party wrongdoers in diminution of the insured loss, or was it
a proprietary right of the insurers in the damages recovered from third parties?
In my judgment, the authorities show that it was a proprietary right in the
d damages recovered.

First, the question arose whether, in an action at law by the assured against the
third party wrongdoer, the damages recoverable had to be reduced by the amount
of the insurance moneys received by the assured. It was argued that, unless such
reduction were made, the assured would be obtaining double compensation. In
Yates v White (1838) 1 Arn 85 such an argument was rejected by the Court of
e Common Pleas on the ground that the assured was not making a double recovery
since he would be a trustee for the insurers of the moneys recovered from the
third party wrongdoer. Tindal CJ said (at 91):

> 'The principle that the insured stands as trustee for the insurer, after the
> latter has paid, is established by the case of *Randal* v. *Cockran* ((1748) 1 Ves
> *f* Sen 98, 27 ER 916): whatever money therefore the plaintiff may recover in
> the present action, equity will undoubtedly compel him to pay over to the
> underwriters.'

Park J followed the decision in *Mason v Sainsbury* (1782) 3 Doug 64, 99 ER 538,
holding that there would be no double recovery by the assured since he would
hold the damages recovered as trustee for the insurer. Both *Mason v Sainsbury* and
g *Yates v White* were approved by this House in *Simpson & Co v Thomson* (1877) 3
App Cas 279.

Next, the question arose whether an insurer entitled by way of subrogation
could at law sue a third party wrongdoer in his own name or only in the name of
the assured. It was held that he could only sue in the name of the assured: see
h *London Assurance Co v Sainsbury* (1783) 3 Doug 245, 99 ER 638. Lord Mansfield
CJ said (3 Doug 245 at 253, 99 ER 638 at 640):

> 'If the insurer could sue in his own name, no release by the insured would
> bar, nor would a verdict by him be a bar. It is impossible that the insured
> should transfer, and yet retain his right of action. Trustee and cestui que
> *j* trust cannot both have a right of action.'

However, in my judgment the decisive case is *White v Dobinson* (1844) 14 Sim
273, 60 ER 363; *affd* (1845) 5 LTOS 233. In that case Hicks had insured the ship
Diana with the plaintiff. Diana was in collision with Xenophon owned by
Dobinson. The plaintiff paid the full sum due under the insurance to Hicks.
Hicks then brought an action against Dobinson as owner of the Xenophon and

was awarded £600 damages. Hicks had assigned to a bank whatever he recovered from the owner of the Xenophon. The plaintiff sought, and Shadwell V-C granted, an interlocutory injunction restraining Hicks from receiving and Dobinson from paying the £600 damages without first recouping to the plaintiff the amount of the insurance he had paid, on the ground that by way of subrogation the plaintiff had a lien in equity on the fund. Lord Lyndhurst LC upheld the Vice-Chancellor's decision, but discharged the injunction against Dobinson. First, the Lord Chancellor disregarded the rights of the bank as assignee from Hicks since the bank's rights were 'subject to all the equities which would have affected the money recovered'. Second, he held that 'the underwriters have a claim upon the fund awarded, and are entitled in some shape or other to recover back the money they have paid'.

Although this was only an interlocutory decision, it was argued for two days and decided by a distinguished Lord Chancellor. It is clear that it recognised that the insurer enjoyed a proprietary right in the damages (not merely a personal right of recovery from Hicks) both because the injunction froze the damages in specie and because the assignment of the damages to the bank was disregarded as being subject to the plaintiff's equities in the fund. This is therefore a clear decision before the fusion of law and equity that equity treated an insurer entitled to be subrogated as having a proprietary interest in damages recovered from a third party wrongdoer.

However, it should be noted that Lord Lyndhurst LC did not continue the injunction against the third party wrongdoer, Dobinson. The case therefore established only that there is a proprietary right in the damages once recovered by the assured.

In *Re Miller Gibb & Co Ltd* [1957] 2 All ER 266, [1957] 1 WLR 703 the insurer was held to have a proprietary interest in the damages recovered from the third party wrongdoer. In my judgment, that case was rightly decided.

With one possible exception we were not referred to any decided case pointing in the other direction. The Court of Appeal in the present case treated the decision in *Stearns v Village Main Reef Gold Mining Co* (1905) 10 Com Cas 89 as being to the contrary effect. In that case, gold belonging to the defendants had been insured by the plaintiffs. The Transvaal government, shortly before the outbreak of the Boer War, commandeered the defendants' gold to the value of £21,880. In 1899 the plaintiffs were paid £7,239-odd by the Transvaal government, which payment the court decided had to be treated as a reduction in the defendants' loss. On 2 August 1900 the plaintiffs, in ignorance of the payment by the Transvaal government, accepted liability for the full £21,880 and paid the sum into the joint names of the plaintiffs and the defendants to await the outcome of certain other litigation. On 19 November 1902 the £21,880 together with the amount earned on it was paid out to the defendants. When the plaintiffs subsequently learnt of the payment by the Transvaal government, they sued to recover the £7,239 plus interest. The trial judge held that the plaintiffs were entitled to recover the £7,239 plus interest from 2 August 1900 (the date of its investment in the joint names) until 19 November 1902 (the date of its payment out to the defendants). The defendants appealed and the plaintiffs cross-appealed, claiming interest down to the date of trial on the ground that the defendants were trustees. Only Stirling LJ dealt in his judgment with the cross-appeal. He rejected the claim for interest, holding that the relationship was one of debtor and creditor not that of trustee and cestui que trust.

That case is difficult to understand. So far as trusteeship was concerned, there was no fund capable of being the subject matter of a trust since the moneys were recovered by the assured from the third party (the Transvaal government) before

the plaintiff insurers settled the insurance claim. It was a case of overpayment by
a the insurers under a mistake, not subsequent recovery by the assured from a third
party of a fund for which the assured was accountable to the insurer. The only
possible form of equitable relief in that case would be to have imposed on the
assured some form of constructive trusteeship not of specified funds but as a
general equitable liability.

Although the principles underlying subrogation as stated in *Castellain v Preston*
b (1883) 11 QBD 380, [1881–5] All ER Rep 493 apply to sums recovered from a
third party whether such recovery takes place before or after the insurers have
paid under the policy, the proper legal analysis of the parties' rights does depend
on the order of receipts. If the assured recovers from the third party (thereby
reducing the insured loss) before the insurers have paid under the policy, there is
an overpayment of the insurance money: there is no fund of money which can
c be the subject matter of a trust or charge. If, on the other hand, the assured does
not recover from the third party until after payment of the insurance moneys the
moneys recovered from the third party constitute a defined fund which can be
impressed with a lien or trust.

The decision of Stirling LJ in that case goes no further than the facts of that case
d demanded, namely to hold that an overpaid assured is not accountable as a
constructive trustee for the amount of the overpayment, there being no defined
trust fund. He was not considering a case where there was a defined fund arising
from a subsequent recovery by the insured which the insured was still holding.

In my judgment, therefore, an insurer who has paid over the insurance moneys
does have a proprietary interest in moneys subsequently recovered by an assured
e from a third party wrongdoer. Although many of the authorities refer to that
right as arising under a trust, in my judgment the imposition of a trust is neither
necessary nor desirable: to impose fiduciary liabilities on the assured is
commercially undesirable and unnecessary to protect the insurers' interests. In
my judgment, the correct analysis is as follows. The contract of insurance contains
an implied term that the assured will pay to the insurer out of the moneys
f received in reduction of the loss the amount to which the insurer is entitled by
way of subrogation. That contractual obligation is specifically enforceable in
equity against the defined fund (ie the damages) in just the same way as are other
contracts to assign or charge specific property, eg equitable assignments and
equitable charges. Since equity regards as done that which ought to be done
under a contract, this specifically enforceable right gives rise to an immediate
g proprietary interest in the moneys recovered from the third party. In my
judgment, this proprietary interest is adequately satisfied in the circumstances of
subrogation under an insurance contract by granting the insurers a lien over the
moneys recovered by the assured from the third party. This lien will be
enforceable against the fund so long as it is traceable and has not been acquired
h by a bona fide purchaser for value without notice. In addition to the equitable
lien, the insurer will have a personal right of action at law to recover the amount
received by the assured as moneys had and received to the use of the insurer.

As to the question whether the insurers have a proprietary interest in the
assured's cause of action against the third party (as contrasted with the damages
actually recovered) I prefer to express no concluded view. I do not think that the
j proprietary interest in the damages necessarily postulates a pre-existing proprietary
interest in the cause of action. The contrary view could be reached by an argument
along the following lines. Any equitable proprietary right must be based on the
contract between the insurers and the assured. The implied terms of such contract
are established by the decided authorities. Some of those implied terms may be
inconsistent with the insurers having any right of property in the cause of action

as opposed to the damages recovered. Thus, the third party can compromise the
claim with the assured alone, without requiring the concurrence of the insurers.   *a*
Again, the third party will obtain a good discharge for a judgment only if he pays
the assured as opposed to the insurers. If the insurers have a proprietary interest
in the cause of action it could be argued that the assured alone could neither effect
a valid compromise nor give a good discharge: the insurers also would have to be
parties. Accordingly, it could be said that the implied terms of the contract
between the insurers and the assured are such that equity would not be specifically   *b*
enforcing the parties' bargain if it treated the insurers as having proprietary rights
in the cause of action inconsistent with the rights of the assured and that
accordingly the rights of the insurers are purely personal rights to require the
assured either to pursue the cause of action against the third party or to permit
the insurers to do so in his name. But there are plainly factors pointing the other
way and since the question was not fully argued I prefer to express no view on the   *c*
point.

For these reasons, in addition to those given by my noble and learned friends
Lord Templeman and Lord Jauncey of Tullichettle, I would allow the appeal and
dismiss the cross-appeal.

d

LORD SLYNN OF HADLEY. My Lords, I have had the advantage of reading
in draft the speech of my noble and learned friend Lord Templeman. I agree that,
for the reasons he gives, the appeal should be allowed and the cross-appeal
dismissed.

17 December. The House of Lords let it be known that the following addendum   *e*
should be added to the speeches.

LORD TEMPLEMAN. Their Lordships are now given to understand that,
although joined to the action as a representative name, Lord Napier and Ettrick
was not in fact insured by any of the stop-loss insurers and that there was therefore
no question of him personally delaying any payment to the stop-loss insurers.   *f*

*Appeal allowed against first respondent. Stop-loss insurers granted injunction in terms
set out in speech of Lord Templeman. Cross-appeal dismissed.*

Mary Rose Plummer   Barrister.
g

a   # R v Hendon Justices and others, ex parte Director of Public Prosecutions

QUEEN'S BENCH DIVISION
MANN LJ, FRENCH AND AULD JJ
8, 9 JUNE, 8 JULY 1992

b

Magistrates – Proceedings – Control by judicial review – Non-appearance of prosecution – Justices dismissing charge without giving prosecution opportunity to present case – Prosecutor applying for certiorari to quash dismissal – Whether justices acting unreasonably – Whether certiorari can issue to quash acquittal arising from dismissal of
c   *information which was a nullity – Magistrates' Courts Act 1980, s 15.*

On 10 April 1991 the two accused were arrested and charged with the attempted burglary of a dwelling house. When they appeared before the justices they elected summary trial and pleaded not guilty. The hearing of the charges was then adjourned to 1 May for summary trial. On 30 April the Crown Prosecution
d   Service received a computer-prepared list of the magistrates' court's hearings for 1 May which contained no reference to the accuseds' case and when the Crown Prosecution Service made inquiries of the court they were mistakenly informed that the court which was in fact due to hear the accuseds' case was not sitting the next morning. The Crown Prosecution Service accordingly failed to arrange an appearance by a prosecutor and when the next morning it became clear that the
e   Crown Prosecution Service had been misinformed a senior lawyer on the Crown Prosecution Service staff telephoned the court to say that he was on his way and then set out for the court, which was some eight miles away. When he arrived at 11.45 am he found that the justices had exercised their power under s 15[a] of the Magistrates' Courts Act 1980 to dismiss the informations for want of prosecution 15 minutes earlier. The Crown Prosecution Service applied for judicial review of
f   the justices' decision to dismiss the informations against the accused.

Held – It was unreasonable for justices to exercise the power conferred by s 15 of the 1980 Act to dismiss an information as a means of punishing the Crown Prosecution Service for what they perceived to be inefficiency and therefore the
g   justices had acted unreasonably in exercising their power under s 15 to dismiss the informations because the prosecution had failed to appear when they were aware that the prosecutor was on his way to court and the case was otherwise ready to be presented. Furthermore, certiorari could issue to quash an acquittal arising from the dismissal of an information which was a nullity arising out of the justices wrongly declining jurisdiction although mandamus would usually be
h   the more appropriate remedy where the prosecution wished to proceed upon the information. Since the justices' decision to dismiss the informations was unreasonable, in the sense that no reasonable bench could have come to that decision, the decision was a nullity and mandamus would issue requiring the justices to hear the informations according to law (see p 415 h to p 416 b and p 419 e g to p 420 a, post).
j   *Associated Provincial Picture Houses Ltd v Wednesbury Corp* [1947] 2 All ER 680 applied.

Dictum of Lord Roskill in Harrington v Roots [1984] 2 All ER 474 at 479 explained.

---

a   Section 15, so far as material, is set out at p 414 j, post

R v Simpson [1914] 1 KB 66, *R v Middlesex Justices, ex p DPP* [1952] 2 All ER 312 and *Harrington v Roots* [1984] 2 All ER 474 considered.

Dictum of Mann LJ in *R v Sutton Justices, ex p DPP* [1992] 2 All ER 129 at 133 not followed.

Notes

For control of justices' proceedings by judicial review, see 29 *Halsbury's Laws* (4th edn) para 474, and for cases on the subject, see 16 *Digest* (Reissue) 429, 4719–4724 and 33 *Digest* (Reissue) 176–179, 1368–1387.

For the Magistrates' Courts Act 1980, s 15, see 27 *Halsbury's Statutes* (4th edn) (1992 reissue) 171.

Cases referred to in judgment

Anisminic Ltd v Foreign Compensation Commission [1969] 1 All ER 208, [1969] 2 AC 147, [1969] 2 WLR 163, HL.

Associated Provincial Picture Houses Ltd v Wednesbury Corp [1947] 2 All ER 680, [1948] 1 KB 223, CA.

Dimes v Grand Junction Canal Proprietors (1852) 3 HL Cas 759, 10 ER 301.

DPP v Nasralla [1967] 2 All ER 161, [1967] 2 AC 238, [1967] 3 WLR 13, PC.

Harrington v Roots [1984] 2 All ER 474, [1984] AC 473, [1984] 3 WLR 142, HL; rvsg sub nom *R v Dorking Justices, ex p Harrington* [1983] 3 All ER 29, [1983] QB 1076, [1983] 3 WLR 370, DC.

Hoffmann-La Roche (F) & Co AG v Secretary of State for Trade and Industry [1974] 2 All ER 1128, [1975] AC 295, [1974] 3 WLR 104, HL.

London and Clydeside Estates Ltd v Aberdeen DC [1979] 3 All ER 876, [1980] 1 WLR 182, HL.

O'Reilly v Mackman [1982] 3 All ER 1124, [1983] 2 AC 237, [1982] 3 WLR 1096, HL.

R (Giant's Causeway &c Tramway Co) v Antrim Justices [1895] 2 IR 653, Ir QB.

R v Birmingham Justices, ex p Lamb [1983] 3 All ER 23, [1983] 1 WLR 339, DC.

R v Brown (1857) 7 E & B 757, 119 ER 1427.

R v Clerkenwell Metropolitan Stipendiary Magistrates, ex p DPP [1984] 2 All ER 193, [1984] QB 821, [1984] 2 WLR 244, DC.

R v Duncan (1881) 7 QBD 198, DC.

R (Hastings) v Galway Justices [1906] 2 IR 499, Ir KB.

R v Greater Manchester Coroner, ex p Tal [1984] 3 All ER 240, [1985] QB 67, [1984] 3 WLR 643, DC.

R v Middlesex Justices, ex p DPP [1952] 2 All ER 312, [1952] 2 QB 758, DC.

R v Neal [1949] 2 All ER 438, [1949] 2 KB 590, CCA.

R v Simpson [1914] 1 KB 66, DC.

R v Sutton Justices, ex p DPP [1992] 2 All ER 129, DC.

R v Swansea Justices, ex p DPP (1990) 154 JP 709, DC.

R v West [1962] 2 All ER 624, [1964] 1 QB 15, [1962] 3 WLR 218, CCA.

Ridge v Baldwin [1963] 2 All ER 66, [1964] AC 40, [1963] 2 WLR 935, HL.

Smith v East Elloe RDC [1956] 1 All ER 855, [1956] AC 736, [1956] 2 WLR 888, HL.

Cases also cited or referred to in skeleton arguments

Connelly v DPP [1964] 2 All ER 401, [1964] AC 1254, HL.

Crane v DPP [1921] 2 AC 299, [1921] All ER Rep 19, HL.

Haynes v Davis [1915] 1 KB 332, DC.

R v Bennett (1908) 24 TLR, DC.

a   *R v Cardiff Magistrates' Court, ex p Cardiff City Council* (1987) Times, 24 February, DC.

R v Crown Court at Wolverhampton, ex p Crofts [1982] 3 All ER 702, [1983] 1 WLR 204, DC.

R v Griffiths (1980) 72 Cr App R 307, CA.

R v Thames Magistrates' Court, ex p Polemis [1974] 2 All ER 1219, [1974] 1 WLR 1371, DC.

b   *R v Uxbridge Justices, ex p Smith* [1977] RTR 93, DC.

R (Drohan) v Waterford Justices [1901] 2 IR 548, Ir QB.

R v Watford Justices, ex p DPP [1990] RTR 374, DC.

Vaux's Case (1591) 4 Co Rep 44a, 76 ER 992.

Weight v MacKay [1984] 2 All ER 673, [1984] 1 WLR 980, HL.

c   *Williams v DPP* [1991] 3 All ER 651, [1991] 1 WLR 1160, DC.

Application for judicial review

The Director of Public Prosecutions applied, with the leave of Otton J given on 26 July 1991, for judicial review by way of an order of certiorari to quash the decision of the first respondents, the justices sitting at the Hendon Magistrates'
d   Court, on 1 May 1991 dismissing two informations charging the second and third respondents, Thomas Peter Harty and Patrick Cash, with attempted burglary. The facts are set out in the judgment of the court.

Tom Kark (instructed by the *Crown Prosecution Service,* Wood Green) for the Director of Public Prosecutions.
e   *Clare Montgomery* (instructed by the *Treasury Solicitor*) as amicus curiae.

The respondents did not appear.

Cur adv vult

f   8 July 1992. The following judgment of the court was delivered.

MANN LJ. There is before the court an application for judicial review for which leave to move was given by Otton J on 26 July 1991. The applicant is the Crown Prosecution Service, and the decision impugned is a decision of justices for the
g   petty sessional area of Barnet when sitting at the Hendon Magistrates' Court on 1 May 1991. By that decision the justices dismissed two informations which had been laid by the applicant against Thomas Peter Harty and Patrick Cash. The respondents to the application are the justices, Mr Harty and Mr Cash. The respondents neither appeared nor were represented but Mr John Clark, who is the clerk to the Barnet justices, filed an affidavit. The relief which is claimed is an
h   order of certiorari to quash the decision.

The matter arises as follows. On 10 April 1991 Mr Harty and Mr Cash were arrested and charged with the attempted burglary of a dwelling house on that day. They appeared before the Hendon Magistrates' Court on 12 April and were remanded until 18 April. There was then a further remand until 25 April, when the justices determined mode of trial and accepted jurisdiction. The defendants
j   were put to their election, elected summary trial and pleaded not guilty. The case was remanded until 1 May for summary trial at the Hendon Magistrates' Court. On 30 April the applicant received the computer prepared list of the Hendon Magistrates' Court for 1 May. It contained no reference to Mr Harty and Mr Cash but this did not of itself surprise the applicant because its officers knew the computer was often not updated with remands of a week or less. However, and

importantly, the list did not show any cases listed in court 2 for the morning session but showed cases listed in court 1 for that session. The applicant's officer *a* made inquiries at the list office and was informed that court 2 was not sitting on the next morning. The clerk to the justices has deposed that he is unable to find any member of his staff who passed on such wrong information. It was wrong because, despite its absence from the list, court 2 was to sit at 10 o'clock to hear the case of Mr Harty and Mr Cash. However, in the light of the list and of the wrong information, the applicant cancelled the attendance of the prosecutor who *b* had been booked for the morning session in court 2 and gave the papers in the case of Mr Harty and Mr Cash to the advocate prosecuting in court 1. Next morning it became clear to the applicant that it had been misinformed. The morning list showed the cases of Mr Harty and Mr Cash listed in court 2 at 10 am and the two defendants were produced from custody for that time. Their advocate *c* was present, as were all of the prosecution witnesses, who had been duly warned for 1 May. Mr Richard Blake, a senior lawyer on the applicant's staff, was informed of the position. Mr Blake, who was eight miles away at the applicant's office in Wood Green, made inquiries as to the whereabouts of the papers in the case and then set out for Hendon in order to retrieve the papers from court 1 and to prosecute in court 2. Before setting out Mr Blake had telephoned the gaoler's *d* office at the court and asked that the court be informed he was on his way. The custody officer has deposed that the court 'was informed that . . . Mr. Richard Blake was on his way to court to conduct the case'. However, when Mr Blake arrived at 11.45 am he discovered that the two informations had been dismissed for want of prosecution 15 minutes earlier. It is the decision to dismiss which is now impugned. *e*

Mr Tom Kark who appeared for the applicant submitted that the decision was void and that an order of certiorari should issue to quash it, thereby depriving the decision of any effect it may have had. Mr Clark in his affidavit submitted that the justices were entitled to conclude by 11.30 am that the prosecution had had sufficient opportunity to prosecute the charges and accordingly rightly dismissed *f* the informations. He states that the clerk in court had, on a telephone inquiry, been informed by the applicant that a prosecutor would be sent 'as soon as conveniently possible'.

The powers and duties of justices are derived from statute, and in particular from the Magistrates' Courts Act 1980. Amongst the provisions of that Act which deal with the summary trial of an information are ss 9, 10(1) and 15(1), which *g* (re-enacting earlier provisions) provide as follows:

'**9.**—(1) On the summary trial of an information, the court shall, if the accused appears, state to him the substance of the information and ask him whether he pleads guilty or not guilty.

(2) The court, after hearing the evidence and the parties, shall convict the *h* accused or dismiss the information.

(3) If the accused pleads guilty, the court may convict him without hearing evidence.

10.—(1) A magistrates' court may at any time, whether before or after beginning to try an information, adjourn the trial, and may do so, notwithstanding anything in this Act, when composed of a single justice . . . *j*

15.—(1) Where at the time and place appointed for the trial or adjourned trial of an information the accused appears or is brought before the court and the prosecutor does not appear, the court may dismiss the information or, if evidence has been received on a previous occasion, proceed in the absence of the prosecutor . . .'

It was in the exercise or purported exercise of the power conferred by s 15(1) that
a the respondent justices acted in dismissing the informations against Messrs Harty
and Cash. We observe that, when regard is had to the published list, there may
be room for argument as to whether 10 am in court 2 was the time and place
appointed for the trial. We do not enter that room. The main thrust of Mr Kark's
submission was, in effect, that the decision was in the circumstances so
unreasonable that no reasonable bench could have come to it (cf *Associated*
b *Provincial Picture Houses Ltd v Wednesbury Corp* [1947] 2 All ER 680 at 683, [1948]
1 KB 223 at 230 by Lord Greene MR). He submits that the proper course in the
circumstances would have been for the justices to exercise their power under
s 10(1) and to adjourn the trial in order that the prosecution could have an
opportunity to present the evidence which was available to be called (as to the
c exercise of the power, see *R v Swansea Justices, ex p DPP* (1990) 154 JP 709).
This court, in the exercise of its supervisory jurisdiction over magistrates'
courts, will ordinarily treat as a nullity a decision of such a court if it is so
unreasonable that no reasonable bench in like circumstances could have come to
it. In so doing, the court is not acting in an appellate capacity but is acting so as to
ensure that the inferior court is acting within the limits of the powers which have
d been granted to it by Parliament. It is implicit in the enactment that a conferred
power is not to be exercised unreasonably (cf *Ridge v Baldwin* [1963] 2 All ER 66,
[1964] AC 40 and *Anisminic Ltd v Foreign Compensation Commission* [1969] 1 All ER
208 at 245, [1969] 2 AC 147 at 209 by Lord Wilberforce). If it is, then the exercise
is outwith the conferred power and can be characterised as 'illegal', 'void' or a
'nullity', although until so characterised it may be capable of having its ostensible
e effect (cf *London and Clydeside Estates Ltd v Aberdeen DC* [1979] 3 All ER 876 at
883, [1980] 1 WLR 182 at 189 by Lord Hailsham of St Marylebone and also *F*
Hoffmann-La Roche & Co AG v Secretary of State for Trade and Industry [1974] 2 All
ER 1128 at 1154, [1975] AC 295 at 366 by Lord Diplock). The capacity of
decisions which are to be characterised as nullities to have an ostensible effect
f until so characterised has on occasions caused them to be described as 'voidable'.
The contrast is presumably with decisions which have no ostensible effect because
(to adapt Lord Radcliffe's phrase) they bear the brand of invalidity upon their
foreheads (see *Smith v East Elloe RDC* [1956] 1 All ER 855 at 871, [1956] AC 736 at
769–770). However, Lord Wilberforce has observed that the distinction between
void and voidable is a difficult one and he has not wished to be taken as recognising
g that it exists (see *Anisminic Ltd v Foreign Compensation Commission* [1969] 1 All ER
208 at 244, [1969] 2 AC 147 at 208). There is no recent authority which suggests
that it does in the area of law with which we are concerned, and we think that
nowadays the void and voidable distinction is ordinarily no more than a
convenient nomenclature to distinguish decisions all of which are outwith the
conferred power, but some of which will and some of which will not have an
h ostensible effect until their character is judicially decided.
We regret to say that in our judgment the decision of the respondent justices
in the present case was so unreasonable that no reasonable bench in like
circumstances could have come to it. We express our judgment with regret
because we are sure the lapse was uncharacteristic of justices who were doing
their best and because we are fully appreciative of the pressures upon a busy court
j such as is Hendon. However, the duty of the court is to hear informations which
are properly before it. The prosecution has a right to be heard and there is a public
interest that, save in exceptional circumstances, it should be heard. A court's
irritation at the absence of a prosecutor at the appointed time is understandable.
That said, it can seldom be reasonable to exercise the power under s 15 of the
1980 Act (as opposed to that under s 10(1)) where the justices know that a

prosecutor is on the way to their court and the case is otherwise ready to be presented. In this case, according to the custody officer, the justices knew that Mr *a* Blake was on his way and in any event a further telephone call would have established the position precisely. The exercise was not reasonable in this case as it was not in *R v Sutton Justices, ex p DPP* [1992] 2 All ER 129. We entertain the strongest suspicion that the justices were here acting so as to punish what they saw as the inefficiency of the Crown Prosecution Service. We think any inefficiency was merely apparent and liable to be dispelled on inquiry. We also *b* think that the power conferred by s 15 is not one conferred for punitive purposes.

The decision being unreasonable in the *Wednesbury* sense, the question arises as to whether the order of certiorari which is sought is an available remedy. Upon this question we had the assistance of oral and written argument from Miss Clare Montgomery, who was appointed by the Attorney General to act as amicus curiae. *c* We are indebted to her for those arguments.

The question arising may seem a surprising one because certiorari is usually thought to lie in respect of any order of an inferior tribunal, whilst mandamus clearly lies to require the hearing of an information which has been dismissed as a result of a jurisdiction having been wrongly declined (see for example *R v Clerkenwell Metropolitan Stipendiary Magistrates, ex p DPP* [1984] 2 All ER 193, *d* [1984] QB 821). However, in *R v Simpson* [1914] 1 KB 66 at 75 Scrutton J said 'there never has been a case in which an acquittal by a Court of summary jurisdiction has been quashed by certiorari', and we have not been referred to any fully reported case since that time in which an 'acquittal' (as opposed to a conviction) has been quashed by certiorari. If there is a principle by reference to which the remedy is not granted in respect of an 'acquittal', then the position of *e* the court will be different upon a judicial review from its position upon an appeal by case stated, when, by statute, it has power to direct a conviction after dismissal by justices (see the 1980 Act, ss 111 and 112).

In *R v Simpson* this court had before it an application for certiorari to quash an order dismissing an information on the ground that the magistrates' court had had an improper constitution. The application was refused. Ridley J thought that *f* the case was one to which the maxim 'nemo debet bis vexari' applied. He said (at 71–72):

> 'It is true that the charge in the present case was not one of a very serious character, but the principle involved is one of great importance, and if it were once assailed by the introduction of exceptions, they might in course of *g* time be applied to very different cases. If, therefore, I find that these defendants have once stood in danger and have been acquitted, then in my opinion this Court ought not to grant a certiorari to quash the acquittal. The question, therefore is, have the defendants, in the words of Lord Coleridge C.J. in *Reg. v. Duncan* ((1881) 7 QBD 198 at 199), stood in danger of *h* imprisonment?'

Ridley J then referred to the Irish cases of *R (Giant's Causeway &c Tramway Co) v Antrim Justices* [1895] 2 IR 653 and *R (Hastings) v Galway Justices* [1906] 2 IR 499 and quoted from that part of the judgment of Lord O'Brien LCJ in the latter case where he said (at 502–503):

> 'There is no instance in the history of our law of an acquittal under such *j* circumstances being brought up on *certiorari*. What is the principle? That a man cannot be put in peril twice for the same offence. Was this man put in peril before the tribunal that is alleged to be biassed? I am of opinion that he was, and for this reason, that the order of a biassed tribunal is voidable only,

a   and not void. That such an order is voidable only, and not void, clearly follows from the case of *Dimes* v. *The Grand Junction Canal Co.* ((1852) 3 HL Cas 759, 10 ER 301)—a familiar case, and one of the highest authority. Now, if the order is voidable only, and not void, the accused was in peril when he stood before the tribunal. Though in this case he was acquitted, he might have been convicted. He was certainly in peril, because he might have been arrested and imprisoned on a voidable order, and a very considerable time

b   might elapse before a voidable order could be avoided by proceedings by way of *certiorari*. Until avoided, a voidable order justifies both arrest and imprisonment.'

Ridley J held that the distinction pointed out was one on which the court should take its stand and accordingly that the improper constitution of the court rendered
c   its decision 'voidable' so that the defendants had once stood in peril. Bailhache J also quoted from Lord O'Brien LCJ and his judgment was to the like effect as that of Ridley J (see [1914] 1 KB 66 at 76). Scrutton J concluded that the application should be refused but his ground was different from that of the other two members of the court. He said (at 75):

d   'I am inclined to think, though in my view it is not necessary for us to decide that point, that where a person acts as a member of a Court when he is under a statutory disqualification the Court cannot be said to be a Court of competent jurisdiction. If that be so, a defendant tried by that Court would never have been in peril, for the proceedings would be a mere nullity. But I

e   do not propose to decide that point for the following reason. If we were to quash this acquittal, and fresh proceedings were to be subsequently instituted against the defendants in respect of the same alleged offence, the defendants would not be able to plead autrefois acquit, for the acquittal having been quashed there would be no acquittal in existence. If, however, in any subsequent proceedings the defendants should raise the plea of autrefois

f   acquit it will be open to the Court to decide whether the previous hearing was before a Court of competent jurisdiction. That is the ground, a somewhat narrow one, on which I am prepared to decide this case.'

The ability of a court of trial to determine whether a prior 'acquittal' is a 'nullity' was later to be established by the Court of Criminal Appeal in *R v West*
g   [1962] 2 All ER 624, [1964] 1 QB 15.

R v Simpson was amongst the authorities which were before a Divisional Court of five judges presided over by Lord Goddard CJ in *R v Middlesex Justices, ex p DPP* [1952] 2 All ER 312, [1952] 2 QB 758. The case related to a trial on indictment during which the conduct of the chairman of sessions was such as subsequently to earn the severest disapprobation of this court. The defendant was
h   acquitted by the jury and the Director of Public Prosecutions applied for an order of certiorari. However, despite the disapprobation this court concluded that the relief sought could not be granted for there had not been 'anything in the nature of a mistrial'. Lord Goddard CJ said ([1952] 2 All ER 312 at 314, [1952] 2 QB 758 at 769):

j   'To constitute a mistrial the proceedings must have been abortive from beginning to end so that, had the record been drawn up, the error would have been apparent: *R. v. Neal* ([1949] 2 All ER 438, [1949] 2 KB 590). Here the defendant was properly arraigned and the jury sworn to try him, so technically he was in peril, and as they returned a verdict of Not Guilty, however improperly that verdict may have been obtained, this court cannot, as it seems to us, direct a new trial. In *R. v. Simpson*, ([1914] 1 KB 66 at 75) SCRUTTON, J., said: ". . . there never has been a case in which an acquittal by a *a* court of summary jursidiction has been quashed by certiorari, and, although in some cases judges have acted proprio vigore in making precedents, I do not myself feel disposed to do so in this case." Nor do we. An acquittal by a jury seems to be a fortiori.'

In *R v Dorking Justices, ex p Harrington* [1983] 3 All ER 29, [1983] QB 1076 this *b* court (Robert Goff LJ and Glidewell J) applied the principle it derived from the *Middlesex Justices* case to the dismissal of an information by justices after proceedings which it had not been argued were a 'nullity'. The circumstances of the case were these. The defendant pleaded not guilty to two charges and the prosecution applied for an adjournment as one of its witnesses was not available. The justices announced an adjournment to a date which excited protest from the *c* defendant as he was to be on holiday on that date. The justices thereupon dismissed the informations without giving the prosecutor the opportunity to proceed immediately with the witnesses whom he did have available and which opportunity he would have wished to have taken. On those circumstances the House of Lords reversed the decision of this court and it was held that the proceedings were a 'nullity' (see *Harrington v Roots* [1984] 2 All ER 474, [1984] *d* AC 473). Lord Roskill, who delivered the leading speech, said that, having decided to refuse the adjournment, it was, by reason of s 9(2) of the 1980 Act, the duty of the justices to invite the prosecutor to proceed (see [1984] 2 All ER 474 at 478, [1984] AC 743 at 751). The breach of duty caused the dismissal of the information to be a nullity. Lord Roskill said ([1984] 2 All ER 474 at 479, [1984] AC 743 at *e* 753):

> 'My Lords, I am clearly of the view that what happened in the instant case was, to adapt Lord Sumner's phrase, no trial at all. The dismissal of these informations was without jurisdiction and was a nullity. To borrow the phrase of Coleridge J in *Brown's* case (1857) 7 E & B 757 at 761, 119 ER 1427 *f* at 1429, the duty of adjudging was declined. Both on principle and authority I see no reason why, had the prosecution sought to take the matter further, mandamus should not have issued to the justices directing them to hear and determine these informations according to law. Since in my view their orders were a nullity I do not think that it would have been right to order certiorari to issue as well.' *g*

Lord Roskill referred to both *R v Simpson* and the *Middlesex Justices* case. The latter he regarded as being a case where the chairman had been 'acting within his jurisdiction' and inferentially so also did he regard *R v Simpson* (see [1984] 2 All ER 474 at 480, 479, [1984] AC 743 at 753, 752). He observed ([1984] 2 All ER 474 at 479, [1984] AC 743 at 752): *h*

> 'No doubt in some cases the distinction between actions by justices which are without jurisdiction and thus a nullity and actions which are an erroneous exercise of jurisdiction may be fine.'

Nowhere in Lord Roskill's speech is any countenance given to the distinction *j* between void and voidable decisions. His own distinction between actions without jurisdiction and actions which are an erroneous exercise of jurisdiction must, we respectfully believe, have been intended to be read in the light of the *Anisminic* decision [1969] 1 All ER 208 esp at 213–214, [1969] 2 AC 147 esp at 171 where Lord Reid said:

'It has sometimes been said that it is only where a tribunal acts without

a jurisdiction that its decision is a nullity. But in such cases the word "jurisdiction" has been used in a very wide sense, and I have come to the conclusion that it is better not to use the term except in the narrow and original sense of the tribunal being entitled to enter on the enquiry in question. But there are many cases where, although the tribunal had jurisdiction to enter on the enquiry, it has done or failed to do something in

b the course of the enquiry which is of such a nature that its decision is a nullity. It may have given its decision in bad faith. It may have made a decision which it had no power to make. It may have failed in the course of the enquiry to comply with the requirements of natural justice. It may in perfect good faith have misconstrued the provisions giving it power to act so

c that it failed to deal with the question remitted to it and decided some question which was not remitted to it. It may have refused to take into account something which it was required to take into account. Or it may have based its decision on some matter which, under the provisions setting it up, it had no right to take into account. I do not intend this list to be exhaustive. But if it decides a question remitted to it for decision without

d committing any of these errors it is as much entitled to decide that question wrongly as it is to decide it rightly.'

Lord Diplock has included inferior courts within the bodies to which this statement of principle applies (O'Reilly v Mackman [1982] 3 All ER 1124 at 1129, [1983] 2 AC 237 at 278) and this court has so applied it (R v Greater Manchester

e Coroner, ex p Tal [1984] 3 All ER 240 at 249, [1985] QB 67 at 82 to 83). We have already stated that in our judgment the respondent justices' decision to dismiss the information was outwith their statutory power. It was thus a nullity and could not have sustained a plea of autrefois because there had not been a lawful acquittal (see [1984] 2 All ER 474 at 479, [1984] AC at 752 by Lord Roskill referring to DPP v Nasralla [1967] 2 All ER 161 at 166, [1967] 2 AC 238 at 249–

f 250 by Lord Devlin). Whether the decision is to be described as void or voidable is, with respect to Ridley and Bailhache JJ and the Irish judges whom they followed, a question of nomenclature which we do not find it helpful to answer. As to the actual decision in R v Simpson, there is plainly now much to be said for the then contemporary view of Scrutton J that the justices' decision was a nullity.

In our judgment, certiorari can go to quash a decision which is a nullity and

g which by hypothesis is accordingly not an acquittal. We recognise the defiance of logic in stating that the order can go, but in practice decisions which are nullities are quashed as a convenient way of preventing the continuance of an ostensible effect. However, it will usually be more appropriate to issue mandamus where the prosecution wishes to proceed upon the information (see Lord Roskill above).

h Mandamus is, like certiorari, a discretionary remedy. In exercising discretion the court will take into account a variety of factors. Amongst them will be the time since the alleged offence was committed, for the court should be slow to issue mandamus where the case is dependent on recollection which may have dimmed. In R v Birmingham Justices, ex p Lamb [1983] 3 All ER 23 at 28, [1983] 1 WLR 339 at 344 McNeill J had regard to the fact that the defendants 'might properly feel

j that they have been acquitted and it would be wrong to allow them to feel, however erroneously, that they would be put in jeopardy for a second time'. An important factor the other way is that properly presented prosecutions for a serious offence should be heard. In this case, the offence alleged against Messrs Harty and Cash was a serious one, the date of commission is not remote and the defendants can have no reasonable belief that the dismissal of the charges was

other than a fortuity. In our judgment, mandamus should issue requiring the
justices to hear the informations according to law.

We add this. Our decision as to the availability of a remedy is inconsistent with
the decision of this court in *R v Sutton Justices, ex p DPP* [1992] 2 All ER 129 at
133, where it was said, without discussion, that certiorari would not go to quash
an acquittal. The question was not argued on that occasion. In the light of the
full argument which we have now had, we are convinced that the decision was
wrong on this point (see *Ex p Tal* [1984] 3 All ER 240 at 248, [1985] QB 67 at 81),
although whether mandamus would have been granted on the facts of that case
may be doubted.

Application allowed. Order of mandamus granted.

Dilys Tausz   Barrister.

R v International Stock Exchange of the United Kingdom and the Republic of Ireland Ltd, ex parte Else (1982) Ltd and another
R v International Stock Exchange of the United Kingdom and the Republic of Ireland Ltd, ex parte Roberts

COURT OF APPEAL, CIVIL DIVISION
SIR THOMAS BINGHAM MR, McCOWAN AND LEGGATT LJJ
12, 13, 14, 16 OCTOBER 1992

*Company – Shares – Listing of shares by stock exchange – Quotations committee of stock
exchange cancelling company's listing – Company not challenging cancellation – Whether
shareholders entitled to be notified of and given opportunity to make representations about
committee's impending decision to cancel listing – Whether shareholders having right to
challenge cancellation of listing by judicial review – Council Directive (EEC) 79/279,
art 15.*

*Judicial review – Leave to apply for judicial review – Sufficient interest – Application to
challenge decision to cancel listing of shares by stock exchange – Applicant overcoming
restrictions on tardy applications – Whether application should fail on ground that
applicant lacked sufficient interest in decision challenged – Supreme Court Act 1981,
s 31(3)(6).*

In June 1989 the Stock Exchange suspended the listing of a company's shares
following the arrest of its chairman on suspicion of insider-dealing offences.
Although he was subsequently acquitted of the charges the suspension of the
shares was continued and in November 1990 the quotations panel of the Stock
Exchange decided that the company's listing should be cancelled. The company
appealed to the quotations committee, which upheld the decision. Thereafter the
company itself did not challenge the decisions of the committee or the panel but
the applicants, who were shareholders in the company, applied for judicial review
of the committee's decision to cancel the listing. During the hearing of their

applications the questions arose whether the applicants had locus standi to
a challenge the committee's decision to cancel the listing and whether as shareholders
they were entitled under art 15*ᵃ* of Council Directive (EEC) 79/279 to be notified
of, and given the opportunity to make representations about, the committee's
impending decision whether the company's listing should be cancelled. Article
15 was promulgated with the purpose of co-ordinating the conditions of the
admission of securities to official listing in member states and provided that the
b refusal of admission of a security to official listing or the discontinuing of such a
listing should be subject to the right to apply to the courts against such a decision.
It was common ground that the council of the Stock Exchange had been
designated as the competent authority for listing in the United Kingdom and that
the quotations committee was empowered to act on its behalf. The judge directed
c that a reference be made to the Court of Justice of the European Communities
under art 177 of the EEC Treaty on the interpretation of art 15. The Stock
Exchange appealed against the judge's direction for a reference to the Court of
Justice.

Held – Although Council Directive (EEC) 79/279 expressly recognised the
d responsibility of competent listing authorities to protect the interests of investors,
which was always to be the overriding concern of a competent authority when
exercising its powers in dealing with conditions imposed and obligations
undertaken by companies whose securities were admitted to listing, the primary
purpose of the directive was to co-ordinate the listing practice of competent
authorities in member states with a view to establishing a common market in
e securities and not in any direct way to provide additional protection for investors.
The directive was concerned with relations between competent authorities and
companies and issuers, and the right to apply to the courts under art 15 was
conferred on a company or issuer alone. Accordingly, although investors such as
the applicants were liable to suffer prejudice if the public listing of a company
was cancelled and although they could not effectively resist a potentially damaging
f cancellation unless they were given notice of an impending decision and the
grounds of cancellation and an opportunity to make representations, the directive
did not confer any enforceable rights on investors to have recourse to the courts.
Furthermore, since the rights claimed by the applicants, particularly those claimed
before a cancellation decision was made, subverted the directive's intention that
g regulatory authorities should be able to take quick and decisive action when
necessary, since there was no provision in the directive for circularising
shareholders and giving them information, since the directive did not address
problems arising from the principles that a company was a legal entity separate
and distinct from its shareholders and that a shareholder could not as such act on
behalf of or enforce the rights of the company, and since the directive did not
h define 'investors' so that it could not properly be given direct effect, art 15 plainly
did not entitle the applicants to be notified of or given the opportunity to make
representations about the committee's impending decision that the company's
listing should be cancelled or to challenge its decision in the courts. Recourse to
the Court of Justice for a ruling on the construction of art 15 was therefore
unnecessary. Accordingly, the appeal would be allowed and the order for reference
j quashed (see p 427 *c*, p 430 *a b e* to p 431 *f*, p 432 *d* to *g*, p 433 *c* and p 434 *d* to *g*,
post).

Per curiam. If a shareholder seeking leave to apply for judicial review of the
cancellation of the listing of a company's shares is, exceptionally, able to overcome

---

a Article 15 is set out at p 428 *h j*, post

the restriction on tardy applications in s 31(6)[b] of the Supreme Court Act 1981, it is questionable whether his claim to relief ought to fail for lack of sufficient   *a* interest within s 31(3) and RSC Ord 53, r 3(7)[c] (see p 432 c d, post).

Notes

For the official listing of securities, see 7(1) *Halsbury's Laws* (4th edn reissue) para 284 and 45 *Halsbury's Laws* (4th edn) para 5.

For the requirement of sufficient interest to apply for judicial review and the   *b* effect of delay in applying for relief, see 1(1) *Halsbury's Laws* (4th edn reissue) paras 63, 169–170, and for a case on the subject, see 37(3) *Digest* (Reissue) 138, 3666.

For the Supreme Court Act 1981, s 31, see 11 *Halsbury's Statutes* (4th edn) (1991 reissue) 991.

For the EEC Treaty, art 177, see 50 *Halsbury's Statutes* (4th edn) 325.   *c*

Cases referred to in judgments

Bulmer (H P) Ltd v J Bollinger SA [1974] 2 All ER 1226, [1974] Ch 401, [1973] 3 WLR 202, CA.

R v Pharmaceutical Society of GB, ex p Association of Pharmaceutical Importers [1987]   *d* 3 CMLR 951, CA; *on reference* Joined cases 266 and 267/87 [1989] 2 All ER 758, [1990] 1 QB 534, [1989] ECR 1295, CJEC.

Srl CILFIT v Ministry of Health Case 283/81 [1982] ECR 3415.

Cases also cited or referred to in skeleton arguments

Amministrazione delle Finanze dello Stato v Simmenthal SpA Case 106/77 [1978] ECR   *e* 629.

Associated Provincial Picture Houses Ltd v Wednesbury Corp [1947] 2 All ER 680, [1948] 1 KB 223, CA.

Brind v Secretary of State for the Home Dept [1991] 1 All ER 720, [1991] 1 AC 696, HL.

Calvin v Carr [1979] 2 All ER 440, [1980] AC 574, PC.   *f*

Customs and Excise Comrs v ApS Samex (Hanil Synthetic Fiber Industrial Co Ltd, third party) [1983] 1 All ER 1042.

Foss v Harbottle (1843) 2 Hare 461, 67 ER 189.

Freight Transport Association Ltd v London Boroughs Transport Committee [1991] 3 All ER 915, [1991] 1 WLR 308, HL.

Garland v British Rail Engineering Ltd [1982] 2 All ER 402, [1983] 2 AC 751, CJEC   *g* and HL.

Hadmor Productions Ltd v Hamilton [1982] 1 All ER 1042, [1983] 1 AC 191, HL.

Hoffmann-La Roche (F) & Co AG v Secretary of State for Trade and Industry [1974] 2 All ER 1128, [1975] AC 295, HL.

  h

---

b   Section 31, so far as material, provides:

'... (3) No application for judicial review shall be made unless the leave of the High Court has been obtained in accordance with rules of court; and the court shall not grant leave to make such an application unless it considers that the applicant has a sufficient interest in the matter to which the application relates ...

(6) Where the High Court considers that there has been undue delay in making an application   *j* for judicial review, the court may refuse to grant—(a) leave for the making of the application; or (b) any relief on the application if it considers that the granting of the relief sought would be likely to cause substantial hardship to, or substantially prejudice the rights of, any person or would be detrimental to good administration ...'

c   Rule 3(7) provides: 'The Court shall not grant leave unless it considers the applicant has a sufficient interest in the matter to which the application relates.'

IRC v National Federation of Self-Employed and Small Businesses Ltd [1981] 2 All ER
a   93, [1982] AC 617, HL.
Marleasing SA v Comercial Internacional de Alimentación SA Case C-106/89 [1990]
     ECR I-4135.
Oberkreisdirektor des Kreises Borken v Handelsonderneming Moormann BV Case 190/87
     [1988] ECR 4689.
Practice Direction [1982] 3 All ER 800, [1982] 1 WLR 1375.
b   Practice Note [1990] 1 All ER 128.
Prudential Assurance Co Ltd v Newman Industries Ltd [1982] 1 All ER 354, [1982]
     Ch 204, CA.
R v IRC, ex p Commerzbank AG [1991] STC 271, DC.
R v Life Assurance and Unit Trust Regulatory Organisation Ltd, ex p Ross [1992] 1 All
c   ER 422, [1993] QB 17, DC; affd [1993] QB 17, CA.
R v Monopolies and Mergers Commission, ex p Argyll Group plc [1986] 2 All ER 257,
     [1986] 1 WLR 763, CA.
R v Panel on Take-overs and Mergers, ex p Datafin plc (Norton Opax plc intervening)
     [1987] 1 All ER 564, [1987] QB 815, CA.
R v Secretary of State for Health, ex p US Tobacco International Inc [1992] 1 All ER
d   212, [1992] QB 353, DC.
R v Secretary of State for Transport, ex p Factortame Ltd Case C-213/89 [1991] 1 All
     ER 70, [1991] 1 AC 603, CJEC and HL.
R v Thames Magistrates' Court, ex p Greenbaum (1957) 55 LGR 129, CA.
Roudolff, Criminal proceedings against Case 803/79 [1980] ECR 2015.
Salomon v A Salomon & Co Ltd [1897] AC 22, [1895–9] All ER Rep 33, HL.
e   Shaw (John) & Sons (Salford) Ltd v Shaw [1935] 2 KB 113, [1935] All ER Rep 456,
     CA.
Sindesmos Melon tis Eleftheras Evangelikis Ekklisias v Greece Case C-381/89 OJ 1992
     C 103, p 5, CJEC.
Töpfer (August) & Co GmbH v EC Commission Case 112/77 [1978] ECR 1019.

f ## Appeals, cross–appeal and applications

R v International Stock Exchange of the UK and the Republic of Ireland,
ex p Else (1982) Ltd and anor

By notice dated 7 March 1991 the applicants, Else (1982) Ltd and Leonard Brealey
as trustee of Vale Private Pension Trust, applied for leave to apply for judicial
g review of (1) the decision of the Quotations Panel of the International Stock
Exchange of the United Kingdom and the Republic of Ireland Ltd (the Stock
Exchange) on 29 June 1989 to suspend dealings in the shares of the company
known as Titaghur plc, formerly known as the Titaghur Jute Factory plc, in
which the applicants held shares, (2) the decision of the panel taken on 23
November 1990 to delist the shares of Titaghur plc and (3) the decision of the
h Committee on Quotations of the Stock Exchange on 7 December 1990 to uphold
the decision of the panel to delist the shares of the company. On 7 June 1991
Auld J, hearing the Crown Office list, granted the applicants leave to move for
judicial review in respect of the committee's decision but refused them leave to
challenge the panel's decisions. On 23 July 1992 Popplewell J hearing the
substantive application refused the applicants leave to amend their notice of
j motion to challenge the panel's decision but, on 24 July 1992, in order to enable
him to give judgment, directed that two questions on the interpretation and
effect of art 15 of Council Directive (EEC) 79/279 be referred to the Court of
Justice of the European Communities for a preliminary ruling under art 177 of
the EEC Treaty, namely (1) whether art 15 of the directive was to be interpreted
as giving to a registered shareholder in an officially listed company, the listing of

which the competent authorities had decided to discontinue, the right to apply to
the relevant national court in relation to such decision and (2) whether, where the   *a*
competent authorities of a member state were considering whether to discontinue
the official listing of a company, art 15 conferred a right on a registered
shareholder in the company to be heard by the competent authorities in relation
to such decision. The Stock Exchange appealed from the order for reference. By
their amended respondent's notice the applicants cross-appealed from, inter alia,
that part of Popplewell J's judgment whereby by implication he concluded that   *b*
the committee's decision of 7 December 1990 was a lawful decision, his refusal of
leave to reamend the notice of motion for judicial review, his decision to refer the
second of the two questions referred to the Court of Justice and his failure to refer
a further question on the interpretation of the directive as to the obligation of the
Stock Exchange to notify shareholders in advance of any decision being taken to   *c*
cancel the listing of the company and the possible reasons for such decision. The
applicants also applied (1) to renew their application made before Auld J on 7 June
1991 for leave to move for judicial review of the panel's decision made on 23
November 1990, (2) for leave to appeal from the order of Popplewell J refusing
them leave to reamend their notice of motion for judicial review of the panel's
decision on 23 November 1990 and (3) for leave to amend their respondent's   *d*
cross-notice of appeal. The facts are set out in the judgment of Sir Thomas
Bingham MR.

R v International Stock Exchange of the UK and the Republic of Ireland Ltd,
ex p Thomas

By notice of motion dated 6 June 1991 the applicant, Gerard Patrick Thomas, a   *e*
shareholder in Titaghur plc, applied for leave to move for judicial review of the
decision of the Committee on Quotations of the International Stock Exchange of
the United Kingdom and the Republic of Ireland Ltd (the Stock Exchange) on 7
December 1990 to cancel the listing of the company's shares. On 7 June 1991
Auld J granted leave and directed that his application be heard at the same time   *f*
as the applications of Else (1982) Ltd and Leonard Brealey. On 24 July 1992
Popplewell J made the same order for reference to the Court of Justice of the
European Communities as in *R v International Stock Exchange of the UK and the*
Republic of Ireland, ex p Else (1982) Ltd and anor. The Stock Exchange appealed. By
his respondent's notice the applicant sought an order that Popplewell J's order for
reference be varied so that two further questions on the interpretation of art 15   *g*
of Council Directive (EEC) 79/279 be referred at the same time. The facts are set
out in the judgment of Sir Thomas Bingham MR.

Roger Henderson QC, Adrian Brunner and *John Cone* (instructed by *Peter Gerrard*)
for the Stock Exchange.
Monique Allan and *Marc Rowlands* (instructed by *Arnold Deacon Greene & Co,*   *h*
Sleaford) for the applicants Else (1982) Ltd and Mr Brealey.
Mr Thomas appeared in person.

Cur adv vult

16 October 1992. The following judgments were delivered.   *j*

SIR THOMAS BINGHAM MR. This appeal concerns a company named
Titaghur plc. The company (as I shall call it) was incorporated in Scotland in 1883.
It runs a substantial jute business in India, where it has some 18,000 employees.
The shares of the company were first listed by the Stock Exchange in London in
1912 and continued to be so listed until 1988.

a In May 1988 the International Stock Exchange of the United Kingdom and the Republic of Ireland (which I shall for brevity call 'the Stock Exchange') suspended the listing of the company's shares because annual listing charges had not been paid. This omission was rectified and the listing was restored after one month's intermission.

b On 28 June 1989 the listing of the company's shares was again suspended by the Stock Exchange. The immediate cause of this suspension was the arrest of the chairman of the company on suspicion of insider-dealing offences. (He was later prosecuted on a number of counts and, after the events giving rise to this appeal, acquitted.) The suspension of the listing continued, partly because of uncertainty concerning the chairman's position, partly because the Stock Exchange was concerned about possible failures to notify dealings in the company's shares and c partly because the Stock Exchange was concerned about the adequacy of the financial information provided by the company and about its accounts. There were meetings between representatives of the company and the Stock Exchange concerning these matters, which were also raised in correspondence. It was made clear that the company wished the suspension to be ended, but it appears that in November 1990 the company's broker was told that the quotations department d of the Stock Exchange had decided to take the matter of the listing of the company to the panel of the quotations committee with a recommendation that the listing be cancelled. The broker indicated that he would probably not attend the quotations panel but might appeal against any cancellation decision to the quotations committee. The case was duly referred to the panel, which on 23 November 1990 concluded that the listing should be cancelled.

e The company (by its broker) was informed of this decision and exercised its right to appeal to the committee. The committee met on 7 December 1990 to hear the appeal. A director and two representatives of its brokers attended on behalf of the company. The committee decided to uphold the decision of the panel and accordingly directed that the company's listing should be cancelled in f view of the inadequacy of the financial information currently available concerning the company.

The company itself has taken no formal step at any time to challenge the decisions of the panel or the committee. It is not a party to these proceedings and has played no part in them.

The proceedings arise out of applications for judicial review made by three g applicants. All of the applicants are shareholders in the company, having bought shares off-market during the period when the listing was suspended and before it was cancelled. Two of the applicants (Else (1982) Ltd and Leonard Brealey as a trustee of a private pension trust) sought leave to challenge the panel's decisions to suspend the company's listing in June 1989 and to cancel the listing in November 1990 and the committee's decision to cancel the listing in December h 1990. They were granted leave to challenge the committee's decision, but refused leave to challenge the panel's decisions. Following this refusal, no renewed application for leave to challenge the panel's decisions was made until, during the hearing of this appeal, application was made to this court for leave to move to challenge the panel's cancellation decision. We refused that application. The third applicant, Gerard Patrick Thomas, is a Scots solicitor. He sought and obtained j leave to move to challenge the committee's cancellation decision. He has not sought to challenge either of the panel's decisions.

Following an order for expedition, the hearing of these substantive applications took place before Popplewell J in June 1992. At that hearing the applicants attacked the committee's decision as irrational, disproportionate and tainted by bias or the appearance of bias. The judge rejected these criticisms.

Before the judge an issue of European Community law arose on which the judge held it necessary to seek a ruling from the Court of Justice of the European *a* Communities under art 177 of the EEC Treaty to enable him to give judgment. Although the applicants in the court below contended that the issue should be decided in their favour, they did not resist the course adopted by the judge if he was left in doubt on the issue, subject to settling appropriate questions. The Stock Exchange, on the other hand, contended below that the issue should be decided in their favour and opposed a reference. The judge having decided to refer, they *b* appeal against his decision to do so. They continue to argue that the Community law issue should be resolved in their favour. As an authority responsible for regulating an important international market, they have further urged the practical importance of knowing where they stand as quickly as possible. The apparent cogency of that consideration has caused the hearing of this appeal, on the Community law issue, to be expedited. It has proved convenient also to *c* consider an issue of domestic law closely related to the Community law issue. For the avoidance of doubt I should make clear that by 'domestic law' I mean, for present purposes, the law of England not including that part of it which derives directly from the law of the Community.

d

The issues

The central issues on this appeal are these. 1. Were the applicants as shareholders entitled to be notified of and given the opportunity to make representations (which should have been duly considered) about the committee's impending decision whether the company's listing should be cancelled (a) in Community law? (b) in domestic law? 2. Are the applicants as shareholders entitled to *e* challenge the committee's decision to cancel the company's listing (a) in Community law? (b) in domestic law?

In relation to questions such as 1(a) and 2(a), I understand the correct approach in principle of a national court (other than a final court of appeal) to be quite clear: if the facts have been found and the Community law issue is critical to the court's final decision, the appropriate course is ordinarily to refer the issue to the *f* Court of Justice unless the national court can with complete confidence resolve the issue itself. In considering whether it can with complete confidence resolve the issue itself the national court must be fully mindful of the differences between national and Community legislation, of the pitfalls which face a national court venturing into what may be an unfamiliar field, of the need for uniform *g* interpretation throughout the Community and of the great advantages enjoyed by the Court of Justice in construing Community instruments. If the national court has any real doubt, it should ordinarily refer. I am not here attempting to summarise comprehensively the effect of such leading cases as *H P Bulmer Ltd v J Bollinger SA* [1974] 2 All ER 1226, [1974] Ch 401, *Srl CILFIT v Ministry of Health* Case 283/81 [1982] ECR 3415 and *R v Pharmaceutical Society of GB, ex p Association* *h* *of Pharmaceutical Importers* [1987] 3 CMLR 951, but I hope I am fairly expressing their essential point.

It is convenient, with that point in mind, to turn to the Community law issue. This arises, and arises only, from Council Directive (EEC) 79/279 of 5 March 1979, the admission directive. I shall refer to it as 'the directive'. Since its correct construction lies at the heart of this appeal, the directive must be analysed in a *j* little detail.

The directive

The directive was made under the EEC Treaty and in particular arts 54(3)(*g*)

and 100 thereof. Article 54(3)(g) required the Council and the Commission to
a carry out their duties under the Treaty in particular—

> 'by co-ordinating to the necessary extent the safeguards which, for the
> protection of the interests of members and others, are required by Member
> States of companies or firms within the meaning of the second paragraph of
> Article 58 with a view to making such safeguards equivalent throughout the
b Community.'

The second paragraph of art 58 contained a stipulative definition of 'companies or
firms'. Article 100 required the Council to issue directives for the approximation
of such provisions laid down by law, regulation or administrative action in
member states as directly affect the establishment or functioning of the common
market.
c The directive was intended, as its long title makes plain, to co-ordinate the
conditions for the admission of securities to official stock exchange listing. This
was a step towards establishment of a common market in securities. In other
member states, as here, conditions (imposed for the protection of investors) had
to be met before a security was admitted to listing. There could be no truly
d common market so long as different conditions were imposed by the various
members states. Still less could there be a truly common market if it was open to
national authorities, under the guise of protecting investors, to make the
admission of local securities to listing easier than that of foreign securities. The
policy objectives to be achieved by co-ordinating the listing conditions in the
various member states were outlined in the fifth recital to the directive: to provide
e equivalent protection for investors at Community level, because of the more
uniform guarantees offered to investors in the various member states; to facilitate
Community-wide listing of member state securities; and to enable member states
to penetrate each other's securities markets so as to contribute to establishment of
a European capital market. The directive applied to entities not covered by the
second paragraph of art 58 of the Treaty and was acknowledged to go beyond
f art 54(3)(g), but was seen as directly affecting the establishment and functioning
of the Common Market within the meaning of art 100.
The seventh recital to the directive is of such significance to this appeal as to
justify verbatim quotation:

> 'Whereas there should be the possibility of a right to apply to the courts
g against decisions by the competent national authorities in respect of the
> application of this Directive, although such right to apply must not be
> allowed to restrict the discretion of these authorities.'

Co-ordination was in the first instance to be limited to establishing minimum
conditions for the admission of securities to official stock exchange lists in
h member states, but issuers were to have no right to listing.
Section I of the directive contains general provisions. These prescribe minimum
conditions to be satisfied by securities admitted to official listing in member states
and minimum obligations to which issuers shall be subject. While member states
may impose conditions and obligations more stringent than the minimum, they
may not (generally speaking) discriminate in doing so. Member states may in
j accordance with applicable national rules require issuers of securities admitted to
official listing to inform the public on a regular basis of their financial position
and the general course of their business.
Section II of the directive concerns the authorities competent to admit securities
to official listing and contains the provisions most central to this appeal. Member

states are required to designate such competent authorities. It is common ground
in this case that the Council of the Stock Exchange is so designated and that the
committee on quotations is empowered to act on its behalf. Member states are to
ensure that the competent authorities have such powers as may be necessary for
the exercise of their duties and, by para 3 of art 9:

'Without prejudice to the other powers conferred upon them, the
competent authorities may reject an application for the admission of a
security to official listing if, in their opinion, the issuer's situation is such that
admission would be detrimental to investors' interests.'

This is supplemented by art 10:

'By way of derogation from Article 5, Member States may, solely in the
interests of protecting the investors, give the competent authorities power to
make the admission of a security to official listing subject to any special
condition which the competent authorities consider appropriate and of which
they have explicitly informed the applicant.'

Article 12 authorises competent authorities (in addition to any other sanction)
to publicise the fact that an issuer is failing to comply with its obligations. Article
13 requires an issuer whose securities are admitted to official listing to provide
the competent authorities with all the information they consider appropriate 'to
protect investors or ensure the smooth operation of the market' and, by para 2 of
this article:

'Where protection of investors or the smooth operation of the market so
requires, an issuer may be required by the competent authorities to publish
such information in such a form and within such time limits as they consider
appropriate. Should the issuer fail to comply with such requirement, the
competent authorities may themselves publish such information after having
heard the issuer.'

This section of the directive ends with arts 14, 15 and 16, which I quote in full:

'*Article 14*

1. The competent authorities may decide to suspend the listing of a security
where the smooth operation of the market is, or may be, temporarily
jeopardized or where protection of investors so requires.

2. The competent authorities may decide that the listing of the security be
discontinued where they are satisfied that, owing to special circumstances,
normal regular dealings in a security are no longer possible.

Article 15

1. Member States shall ensure decisions of the competent authorities
refusing the admission of a security to official listing or discontinuing such a
listing shall be subject to the right to apply to the courts.

2. An applicant shall be notified of a decision regarding his application for
admission to official listing within six months of receipt of the application
or, should the competent authority require any further information within
that period, within six months of the applicant's supplying such information.

3. Failure to give a decision within the time limit specified in paragraph 2
shall be deemed a rejection of the application. Such rejection shall give rise
to the right to apply to the courts provided for in paragraph 1.

Article 16

Where an application for admission to official listing relates to certificates
representing shares, the application shall be considered only if the competent
authorities are of the opinion that the issuer of the certificates is offering
adequate safeguards for the protection of investors.'

Section III of the directive covers the publication of information to be made available to the public. Section IV covers co-operation between member states. Our attention was drawn to art 18, which requires member states to co-operate and communicate with each other. Article 19 imposes a duty of professional secrecy but provides that communication between the competent authorities of member states shall not be a breach of it. Section V made provision for a contact committee composed of representatives of member states and the Commission to discuss implementation of the directive and practical problems arising from it and to advise the Commission.

At its request the court was referred to the proposal from the Commission, the opinion of the European Parliament and the opinion of the economic and social committee to which reference is made in the second, third and fourth recitals of the directive. These show, as one would expect, that the original draft of the directive was modified before its final adoption, but they throw no definitive light on the issue between the parties in this court. It is, however, of interest that the proposed directive contained no precursor of the seventh recital in the directive, although it did provide in art 10(2) that each member state should provide for a right of appeal to the courts against a decision to refuse an application for listing. The economic and social committee criticised that proposal, suggesting that a right of appeal should be provided against any decision of the competent authorities and not just against a decision to refuse an application for listing. The Parliament also felt that there should be greater rights of appeal against the decisions of the national authorities responsible for the admission of securities to quotation. It advised that there should be a right of administrative appeal against decisions to refuse listing, against decisions that information should be published, against decisions that listing be discontinued and against decisions by the competent authorities of their own motion to list a security (a power not in the event conferred by the directive itself). There was no suggestion that the right of appeal should be conferred on additional parties.

The parties to this appeal agree that the directive takes direct effect. We were told that the researches of counsel had unearthed no relevant authority on its construction.

The applicants' argument on the directive

On behalf of the applicants, a long and detailed argument was advanced. I understood the essential steps in the argument to be these. (1) The directive is a measure intended to protect investors, including shareholders such as the applicants. (2) Shareholders such as the applicants are likely to suffer loss or prejudice if the public listing of the company in which they hold shares is cancelled. (3) Shareholders such as the applicants cannot effectively resist a potentially damaging cancellation unless they are notified of an impending decision, unless they are informed of the grounds on which the decision may be taken, unless they have the opportunity to make representations and unless the competent authority is bound to consider these representations before making a decision. (4) The seventh recital of the directive and art 15 impose no restriction upon the parties granted a right to apply to the courts. (5) In the light of (1) to (4) above the intention of art 15 is, or at any rate may be, to confer rights on shareholders such as the applicants to be notified of an impending decision whether a listing should be cancelled, to be informed of the grounds relied on and to be given an opportunity to make representations and, after the decision has been made, to challenge it. (6) The English court should accordingly seek a ruling from the Court of Justice on the correct construction of the directive, and the judge was right to refer.

Each of these steps calls for careful consideration.

The conditions which national authorities impose on admission to listing are imposed for the protection of investors. The body of investors includes existing shareholders. It also includes, very particularly in this context, potential future investors. In dealing with conditions imposed and obligations undertaken by companies whose securities are admitted to listing, the directive expressly recognises the responsibility of the competent authorities to protect the interests of investors, which must always be their overriding concern when exercising their powers. But the primary purpose of the directive is to co-ordinate the listing practice of competent authorities in the various member states with a view to establishing a common market in securities and not, in any direct way, to provide additional protection for investors.

I accept without question that shareholders such as the applicants are liable to suffer loss or prejudice if the public listing of a company in which they hold shares is cancelled. But so they may if the listing is suspended or, in a less obvious way, if an application for listing is refused. The applicants accept that the directive does not, in either of these situations, confer upon shareholders any right of recourse to the court.

I accept that in the ordinary way step (3) in the applicants' argument is likely to be factually correct.

I accept that the seventh recital of the directive and art 15 do not in express terms define the parties upon whom a right to apply to the courts is conferred. But several considerations compel me to what I regard as an inevitable conclusion that the right is conferred on a company or an issuer alone. (i) In the proposed directive the right provided for was one of appeal. While the Economic and Social Committee and the Parliament favoured a wider right of appeal, there is no suggestion that they or anyone envisaged any right other than a right of appeal. In any ordinary situation, a right of appeal is accorded to the party who has been the subject of an adverse decision. There is nothing to suggest that any party other than a company or issuer was seen as potentially the subject of any adverse decision or as having any right of appeal. (ii) The directive is concerned with relations between competent authorities (who are responsible for protecting the interests of investors) and companies or issuers. Nothing in the directive suggests that competent authorities may have direct relations with investors. (iii) Once it is accepted, as it must be, that the directive gives investors no right of recourse to the courts in respect of suspension and refusal of listing, it cannot rationally be construed as conferring such a right on investors in respect of cancellation.

I cannot accept the soundness of step (5). In addition to reasons already given, I see powerful further objections, particularly to the rights the applicants claim before a cancellation decision is made. (i) Such rights would in my view gravely restrict the discretion of the competent authorities, which the seventh recital indicates must not be allowed. The applicants do not, I think, deny that the procedure for which they contend could substantially postpone the date at which a cancellation might become effective, but they suggest that only suspension need take place urgently; thereafter the rights of a company and investors are frozen and a delay in cancellation (they say) carries no risk. Often this may be so, but I do not accept it is necessarily so. Article 14 lays down different tests for suspension and cancellation. It is for the competent authority to decide in the exercise of its informed judgment which of these courses, if either, is appropriate on given facts. Recent history in more than one field emphasises the need for regulatory authorities to take quick and decisive action where the situation requires it. The directive, in my view, recognises that need and gives effect to it. The applicants' argument subverts that intention. (ii) It is obvious that with a company of any

size the task of circularising all shareholders and giving them the information
a they need to make a decision is a substantial and expensive task. If the directive
envisaged such a procedure it could scarcely avoid all reference to the questions:
who is to carry out this task? and who is to pay? Spare though the style of
Community draftsmanship may be, it would be surprising to find a lacuna as
gross as this. (iii) There are deeply-rooted principles of company law that a
company is a legal entity separate and distinct from its shareholders and that a
b shareholder may not as such act on behalf of or enforce the rights of the company.
On the applicants' argument, difficult questions would be bound to arise where,
as here, a cancellation decision is accepted by a company but challenged by some
(although only a small minority) of shareholders. It would arise even more acutely
in the common case where cancellation is requested by a company, if resisted by
a small minority of shareholders. These are, again, obvious problems posed by
c the applicants' argument which the directive fails to address. This would be very
surprising if that argument were right. If it is wrong, the directive does not give
rise to these problems and they are rightly ignored. (iv) The directive does not
define 'investors'. This is understandable if, as I hold, the directive confers no
enforceable rights on investors. But on the applicants' argument, in an instrument
having direct effect, it would be very important to know who the class of
d 'investors' included. A number of possible categories have been suggested, in
addition to shareholders. But it is hard to suppose that potential buyers of
securities, a class of much concern to the competent authorities, could enjoy the
rights the applicants claim, and this lack of definition weighs powerfully against
the applicants' argument, because an instrument of such uncertain scope cannot
e properly be given direct effect. In the result, I feel able with complete confidence
to reject the applicants' argument based on the directive. For reasons which I have
tried to give, I do not share the doubts felt by the learned judge about the effect
to be given to it. If I did, I would of course respect his exercise of discretion to
refer, which would in any event have been the proper course. But taking the
view I do, I do not find it necessary to seek a ruling on this question from the
f Court of Justice to enable me to give judgment. It follows that I would allow the
appeal of the Stock Exchange on this point and quash the order made under
art 177 of the Treaty.

Domestic law

g It was not suggested that the law of England, independently of Community
law, permitted an affirmative answer to the question posed at 1(b) above. Nor, I
think, was it argued that domestic law, independently of Community law,
conferred a right on shareholders as envisaged by question 2(b). But the applicants
argued (and the Stock Exchange broadly denied) that as shareholders they had a
sufficient interest in the cancellation decision within the meaning of s 31(3) of
h the Supreme Court Act 1981 and RSC Ord 53, r 3(7) to enable a grant of leave to
move for judicial review to be properly made, subject of course to the applicants
meeting the other qualifying conditions.
On the facts here, no application for leave to move was made before the
cancellation decision. I decline to speculate what the position would have been
had the applicants been in a position to apply, and had they done so, at that stage.
j When the applicants applied for leave to move Auld J was tentatively of opinion
that they could show a sufficient interest. He was no doubt mindful that they
were not busybodies but claimed, as shareholders, to have a direct financial
interest in the company which the cancellation decision affected. At the
substantive hearing Popplewell J took a different view, ruling that the applicants

had no sufficient interest. The applicants appeal against that decision. In the
event, however, the judge did investigate and rule upon the various grounds   a
relied upon to challenge the committee's cancellation decision (with the exception
of additional grounds which he did not, quite rightly, allow the applicants to
pursue). He rejected that challenge. It follows that whether the applicants had a
sufficient interest to mount a retrospective challenge to the cancellation decision
is strictly academic unless or until this court is persuaded that the judge was
wrong to reject that challenge. The applicants do not appeal on that aspect. It is   b
therefore undesirable to express a concluded view. I would simply observe that
the problems facing any shareholder seeking to mount such a challenge are
formidable in the extreme. In a highly sensitive and potentially fluid financial
market, the factors listed in s 31(6) of the 1981 Act have a special significance.
And the courts will not second-guess the informed judgment of responsible
regulators steeped in knowledge of their particular market. But if, exceptionally,   c
a shareholder were able to overcome these formidable problems, I question
whether his claim to relief should fail for lack of sufficient interest.

The order resulting from this hearing is not entirely straightforward. I would
be grateful if counsel could prepare draft minutes of order, which should be
copied to Mr Thomas and, if agreed by all parties, submitted to the associate.   d

McCOWAN LJ. I agree with Sir Thomas Bingham MR's judgment and would
add only a few words of my own.

Miss Allan for the applicants in the first appeal conceded before this court that
only the company in question, as the applicant for listing, has the right to apply
to the courts in respect of a refusal of admission to listing. But, she argued,   e
art 15(1) only provides, as she put it, 'a broad scenario', which is cut down in
respect of a refusal of admission to listing by paras (2) and (3), but not in respect
of discontinuance of listing, as to which the article is silent.

To my mind, however, it would be very odd if art 15 contemplated that a
wider class of persons than the company should have the right to apply to the
courts in respect of discontinuance of listing than in respect of admission to listing   f
but neglected to say so. Moreover, Miss Allan has been unable to point to anything
in art 15 to suggest that an application to the courts in respect of discontinuance
can be made by a different body or class of persons than that which the article
clearly says can make the application in respect of listing, namely the company.

In my judgment, therefore, the terms of art 15 itself are plainly against her
submissions.   g

LEGGATT LJ. It is the policy of the EEC Treaty to abolish restrictions on
freedom of establishment. One way of furthering this policy is to co-ordinate
safeguards for the protection of individuals by rendering the safeguards 'equivalent'
throughout the Community. A series of directives has applied this principle to   h
companies. But that does not detract from the distinction which English law
recognises between a company and its members. The court cannot interfere with
the internal management of a company acting within its powers. Although the
court will interfere to prevent fraud on a minority of shareholders, it will not
ordinarily recognise any independent right of action by an individual shareholder
based on an allegation of damage to the value of his shareholding, whether caused   j
by the directors or by third parties. Nothing in Community law departs from
that principle unless the applicants' submission in the present case is correct that
Council Directive (EEC) 79/279 accords to individual shareholders the right to
apply to the court for the purpose of objecting to the discontinuance of the listing
of the company of which they are members.

a   Community legislation about stock exchanges is mainly concerned with the listing of securities. Directive 79/279 has been followed by directives dealing with requirements for furnishing particulars of securities for which listing has been applied, and with information which must be published regularly by companies with listed shares. These directives are intended to protect investors as well as to facilitate access to the markets of the member states. By force of the Stock Exchange (Listing) Regulations 1984, SI 1984/716, these directives apply to

b   the United Kingdom.

The scheme of the relevant Community legislation, and Directive 79/279 in particular, is to provide for the co-ordination of conditions for admission to listing by designating a competent authority in each member state to police the process. Ancillary provision is made for the suspension of listing and for discontinuance of listing. But although one of the main aims of controlling admission to listing

c   is the protection of investors, the directive is concerned with the means of control by the competent authority rather than with conferring rights on investors so that they may look out for themselves.

The function of Directive 79/279, known as 'the admission directive', is 'coordinating the conditions for the admission of securities to official stock

d   exchange listing'. The recitals show that this process is likely to provide protection for investors by rendering more uniform the practices in the member states. The general approach is prescribed by art 3, which says:

e   'Member States shall ensure that: —securities may not be admitted to official listing on any stock exchange situated or operating within their territory unless the conditions laid down by this Directive are satisfied, and that —issuers of securities admitted to such official listing, whether admission takes place before or after the date on which this Directive is implemented, are subject to the obligations provided for by this Directive.'

Article 4 provides that the admission of securities to official listing is subject to the conditions set out in Schs A and B relating to shares and debt securities, and

f   that the issuers of listed securities must fulfil the obligations in the corresponding Schs C and D. Schedule A therefore contains conditions for the admission of shares, and Sch C deals with the obligations of companies whose shares are admitted. Paragraph 2 of Sch C is concerned with treatment of shareholders. By sub-para (*b*)—

g   'The company must ensure, at least in each Member State in which its shares are listed, that all the necessary facilities and information are available to enable shareholders to exercise their rights . . .'

This includes information about shareholders' meetings and notices about dividends and new shares.

h   Section II of the directive is headed: 'Authorities competent to admit securities to official listing.' In that section art 9 by para 1 requires member states to designate the competent authority 'to decide on the admission of securities to official listing'. Paragraph 3 provides:

j   'Without prejudice to the other powers conferred upon them, the competent authorities may reject an application for the admission of a security to official listing if, in their opinion, the issuer's situation is such that admission would be detrimental to investors' interests.'

Article 10 applies to any special condition to which the competent authority may make the admission of a security subject, and of which they have informed the applicant, that is, the person applying for the admission. Article 11 refers to a

refusal to admit. Articles 12 and 13 apply to failure by the issuer to comply with
obligations and to publish information. Article 14 is concerned with suspension
and discontinuance of the listing. Finally, art 15 (2) relates to notification to an
applicant of a decision regarding his application for admission, and para 3 provides
that a deemed rejection of the application 'shall give rise to the right to apply to
the courts provided for in paragraph 1'. The would-be issuer is both the applicant
for admission and the person with the right to apply to the courts. Paragraph 1
itself says:

> 'Member States shall ensure decisions of the competent authorities refusing
> the admission of a security to official listing or discontinuing such a listing
> shall be subject to the right to apply to the courts.'

'Decisions' are made under art 9(1); 'decisions refusing' may be made under
art 9(3) or under art 11; and 'decisions discontinuing' may be made under
art 14(2).

In my judgment as a matter of construction the fact that the decisions have to
be 'subject to the right to apply to the courts' means that as with a deemed
rejection under art 15(3), it is the giving to the applicant of an adverse decision by
the competent authority that also gives to the applicant a right to apply to the
courts. There is no other person to whom that right is given: it is given solely to
the applicant. Miss Allan argues that because the directive is for the protection of
investors it is they who must have a right to apply to the court. That is a non
sequitur. Nothing in the language of the directive accords such a right to
investors, actual or potential. I am fortified in this conclusion by the fact that, if
the law were otherwise, the consequences of extending to persons other than the
company the right to apply to the court would be commercially intolerable. If
the number of shareholders was large, the process of identifying and
communicating with them might be onerous, protracted and expensive. As
Mr Henderson QC has pointed out, it might jeopardise confidentiality. It might
even allow the will of a majority to be thwarted, if not overborne, by the
protestation of an individual shareholder. I therefore conclude that the correct
application of Community law in this case is so obvious as to leave no scope for
any reasonable doubt, that recourse to the Court of Justice of the European
Communities is unnecessary and that the appeal should be allowed and the cross-
appeal dismissed.

*Appeals allowed; cross-appeal in first appeal dismissed; first two applications of
respondents in first appeal dismissed and third application allowed. Leave to appeal to
the House of Lords refused.*

Mary Rose Plummer   Barrister.

a # R v Doncaster Magistrates' Court, ex parte Goulding

QUEEN'S BENCH DIVISION

NEILL LJ AND McCULLOUGH J

b 15, 24 OCTOBER 1991

Magistrates – Committal for sentence – Offence triable summarily or on indictment – Discontinuance of summary trial and committal to Crown Court – Circumstances of offence – Character and antecedents of accused – Accused charged with offences triable either way – Justices agreeing to try case summarily – Whether stipendiary magistrate having power to commit accused to Crown Court for sentence – Whether circumstances
c of offence part of accused's character and antecedents – Whether decision of one bench to try case summarily precluding subsequent committal to Crown Court for sentence by another bench – Principles to be applied when committing for sentence – Magistrates' Courts Act 1980, ss 19(1), 38.

d The applicant was charged with three offences of possession of controlled drugs. When he was brought before the bench of lay justices they decided under s 19[a] of the Magistrates' Courts Act 1980 that although the offences were triable either way they were suitable for summary trial. The applicant then pleaded guilty to possession but not guilty to possession with intent to supply. The justices adjourned the case for trial but when the applicant appeared before a stipendiary
e magistrate for trial and sentence the trial was unable to proceed and the magistrate expressed surprise that the justices had thought the case suitable for summary trial and stated that on the next occasion they ought to reconsider the matter, discontinue the summary trial and proceed as examining magistrates. When the applicant next appeared before the stipendiary magistrate he changed his plea on
f the outstanding charge to guilty and the magistrate committed him to the Crown Court for sentence because of his previous convictions (none of which had involved drugs or had resulted in a custodial sentence) and because he considered that the justices had been wrong to proceed with summary trial. The applicant applied for judicial review of the magistrate's decision, contending that there was no jurisdiction to commit him to the Crown Court for sentence having regard to
g the justices' earlier decision that the offences were suitable for summary trial.

Held – Once a magistrates' court had decided under s 19(1) of the 1980 Act to proceed summarily on an offence triable either way because the 'circumstances of the offence' indicated that summary trial was more appropriate the court nevertheless had power under s 38[b] of that Act to commit the defendant to the
h Crown Court for sentence after conviction if his 'character and antecedents', which included anything that reflected on the defendant's character and anything about the circumstances of the offence which subsequently came to the court's attention after deciding to try the offence summarily, were such that a greater punishment should be imposed than the magistrates' court had power to impose. For the purposes of s 38 the defendant's 'character and antecedents' meant
j anything that reflected on his character, even if it was a circumstance of the offence, and any such matter could be taken into account in deciding whether to commit him for sentence provided it was not known to the justices when they

---

a   Section 19, so far as material, is set out at p 437 *d* to *f*
b   Section 38, so far as material, is set out at p 437 *g h*

took their decision to try the case summarily and the new matter was more than
the filling in of detail, which would be a matter of degree, and it did not matter *a*
whether the justices' ignorance of that matter resulted from their failure to make
any or any proper inquiry or from the failure of the prosecution to inform them
of it or from any other cause. It followed that the stipendiary magistrate had had
jurisdiction under s 38 to commit the applicant to the Crown Court for sentence
and that the application for judicial review would therefore be dismissed (see
p 442 *b c g* to *j*, p 445 *c d* and p 446 *b* to *d*, post).   *b*

R v Vallett [1951] 1 All ER 231, R v King's Lynn Justices, ex p Carter [1968] 3 All
ER 858 and R v Lymm Justices, ex p Brown [1973] 1 All ER 716 applied.

Notes
For power of justices to commit for sentence for an offence triable either way, see *c*
11(2) Halsbury's Laws (4th edn reissue) para 821.

For the Magistrates' Courts Act 1980, ss 19, 38, see 27 Halsbury's Statutes (4th
edn) (1992 reissue) 173, 191.

Cases referred to in judgment   *d*
R v Broadcasting Complaints Commission, ex p Owen [1985] 2 All ER 522, [1985] QB
   1153, [1985] 2 WLR 1025, DC.
R v Cardiff Stipendiary Magistrate, ex p Morgan [1989] Crim LR 503, DC.
R v Derby and South Derbyshire Magistrates, ex p McCarthy (1980) 2 Cr App R (S)
   140, DC.
R v Guildhall Justices, ex p Cooper (1983) Times, 6 May, DC.   *e*
R v Harlow Justices, ex p Galway [1975] Crim LR 288, DC.
R v Hartlepool Justices, ex p King [1973] Crim LR 637, DC.
R v King's Lynn Justices, ex p Carter [1968] 3 All ER 858, [1969] 1 QB 488, [1968]
   3 WLR 1210, DC.
R v Lymm Justices, ex p Brown [1973] 1 All ER 716, [1973] 1 WLR 1039, DC.
R v Tower Bridge Magistrate, ex p Osman [1971] 2 All ER 1018, [1971] 1 WLR   *f*
   1109, DC.
R v Vallett [1951] 1 All ER 231, 34 Cr App R 251, CCA.
R v Warrington Justices, ex p Mooney (1980) 2 Cr App R (S) 40, DC.

Application for judicial review   *g*
Mark Anthony Goulding applied, with the leave of Brooke J given on 23 May
1991, for judicial review by way of an order of, inter alia, (i) certiorari to quash
the decision of Mr J E Barry, a stipendiary magistrate sitting at the Doncaster
Magistrates' Court on 25 February 1991, committing the applicant to the Crown
Court for sentence under s 38 of the Magistrates' Courts Act 1980, (ii) an order of *h*
mandamus requiring the Doncaster Magistrates' Court to hear and determine the
charges against the applicant according to law and (iii) an order of prohibition
directed to the Crown Court at Doncaster restraining the court from adjudicating
on the charges in respect of which the applicant was committed by the magistrate
for sentence. The facts are set out in the judgment of McCullough J.
                                                                                                       j
Richard Gordon (instructed by Attey Bower & Jones, Doncaster) for the applicant.
Jeremy R Baker (instructed by the Crown Prosecution Service, Doncaster) for the
   Director of Public Prosecutions, as an interested party.
The stipendiary magistrate did not appear.

Cur adv vult

24 October 1991. The following judgments were delivered.

a

McCULLOUGH J (delivering the first judgment at the invitation of Neill LJ). Mr Mark Anthony Goulding applies by way of judicial review to quash the decision of the Doncaster stipendiary magistrate, Mr J E Barry, on 25 February 1991 to commit him to the Crown Court at Doncaster under s 38 of the Magistrates' Courts Act 1980 to be sentenced for three offences of possession of
b controlled drugs, contrary to the Misuse of Drugs Act 1971, to which he had earlier pleaded guilty. All were triable either summarily or on indictment.

The question for this court is the familiar one of whether there was jurisdiction to commit for sentence having regard to an earlier decision that the offences were suitable for summary trial and to the factual basis on which that earlier decision was taken. It is submitted on behalf of the applicant that the grounds put forward
c by the stipendiary magistrate to justify his decision were insufficient in law to entitle him to commit the applicant to the Crown Court for sentence.

The legislation

Where a person appears before a magistrates' court charged with an offence
d which is triable either summarily or on indictment s 19(1) of the Magistrates' Courts Act 1980 requires the court to—

> 'consider whether, having regard to the matters mentioned in subsection (3) below and any representations made by the prosecutor or the accused, the offence appears to the court more suitable for summary trial or for trial on indictment.'

e

Subsection (3) provides:

> 'The matters to which the court is to have regard under subsection (1) above are the nature of the case; whether the circumstances make the offence one of serious character; whether the punishment which a magistrates' court
f would have power to inflict for it would be adequate; and any other circumstances which appear to the court to make it more suitable for the offence to be tried in one way rather than the other.'

The law recognises, however, that there may be cases where the initial view that punishment which the magistrates' court would have power to inflict would be adequate calls for revision in the light of fresh information which becomes
g available after conviction. Accordingly s 38 provides:

> 'Where on the summary trial of an offence triable either way . . . a person . . . is convicted of the offence, then, if on obtaining information about his *character and antecedents* the court is of the opinion that *they* are such that greater punishment should be inflicted for the offence than the court has
h power to inflict, the court may . . . commit him . . . to the Crown Court for sentence . . .'

The power to commit for sentence first appeared in s 29(1) of the Criminal Justice Act 1948. This was replaced by s 29 of the Magistrates' Courts Act 1952 which was in turn replaced by s 38 of the 1980 Act. In each of these sections the
j operative words have been the same.

The criteria now found in ss 19(3) and 38 of the 1980 Act are different. None is mentioned in both sections. Looking at the sections on their own, one might have concluded that 'the circumstances of the offence' and the 'character and antecedents' were mutually exclusive concepts. On their face they are different. Either an offence is serious or it is not; the character and antecedents of the defendant cannot affect this. It is, of course, true to say that the circumstances of an offence that a man has committed reflect on his character and they are antecedent to the court proceedings, but ss 19(3) and 38 are worded consistently with the assumptions (i) that all the circumstances which make the offence of a serious character are to be mentioned when the mode of trial is being considered and (ii) that those aspects of the defendant's character and antecedents which make it appear that the court's powers of punishment are inadequate will appear after conviction. When the mode of trial is under consideration neither previous convictions nor any other discreditable feature in the defendant's history can properly be mentioned by the prosecution. If the defending advocate volunteers them, it will be to make the point that, while his client's record is not unblemished, the blemish is slight, so that the powers of the justices to inflict punishment will more likely be adequate. The same will apply to other offences which the defendant intends to ask to be taken into consideration. These cannot properly be mentioned by the prosecution at this first stage unless the defendant agrees. All this is catered for in the words 'any other circumstances which appear to the court to make it more suitable for the offence to be tried in one way rather than the other'. It is obviously convenient, and it is not unjust, to commit for sentence a defendant who pleads guilty if it should later transpire that the decision to try him summarily was for some reason mistaken, but had this been the intention of Parliament a suitable addition to the words of s 38 could have made express provision for this.

Despite these considerations, the cases which here turned on the interpretation of the power to commit for sentence show that the words 'character and antecedents' have in the context of the power to commit for sentence been interpreted as embracing such circumstances of the offence as bear on the defendant's character.

Some of the cases concerned offences triable either summarily or on indictment. Others concerned the summary trial of indictable offences. The provisions governing the procedure to be adopted by the magistrates in each type of offence differ slightly: see s 24(1) of the Criminal Justice Act 1925 (as amended by the 1948 Act) and s 28 of the 1948 Act, which were replaced, without significant alteration, by ss 18 and 19 of the Magistrates' Courts Act 1952. In 1977, when a number of hitherto indictable offences were made triable either summarily or on indictment, the procedure enabling indictable offences alleged against those aged 17 and over to be tried summarily was abolished and the scheme now found in the 1980 Act was introduced: see ss 16 and 20 of the Criminal Law Act 1977.

Of these earlier provisions it is necessary to mention the terms of only s 24(1) of the Criminal Justice Act 1925. This read:

> 'Where a person ... is charged before a court of summary jurisdiction with an indictable offence, being one of the offences specified in the Second Schedule to this Act, the court, if it thinks it expedient so to do, having regard to ... [the character and antecedents of the accused,] the nature of the offence, the absence of circumstances which would render the offence one of a grave or serious character and all the other circumstances of the case (including the adequacy of the punishment which a court of summary jurisdiction has power to inflict), and if the accused ... consents to be dealt with summarily, may ... deal summarily with the offence ...'

By s 79 of and Sch 9 to the Criminal Justice Act 1948 the words in square brackets ceased to have effect. Both the presence of the words 'character and antecedents' in the original s 24(1) and their removal contemporaneously with the enactment of s 29 of the 1948 Act might have been thought to indicate that 'character and antecedents' did not embrace the circumstances of the offence.

The authorities

a   In all of the decided cases, after summary trial had been decided upon, the defendant pleaded guilty and was later committed to the Crown Court (or Quarter Sessions) for sentence, and the lawfulness of the committal was later challenged.

The question for decision in those cases, as in this, can be formulated as follows: Did the magistrates' court, having earlier decided to try the case summarily, have power to commit the convicted person for sentence on obtaining information as
b   to his character and antecedents which made the court consider that his character and antecedents were such that greater punishment should be inflicted in respect of the offence than the court had power to inflict? The crucial words are 'character and antecedents'.

The earliest case is *R v Vallett* [1951] 1 All ER 231, 34 Cr App R 251, a decision of the Court of Criminal Appeal. Vallett was charged with four offences of larceny
c   as a servant. She was a supervisor at a laundry and knew the arrangements made by her employers to combat thefts. She made use of this knowledge to carry out thefts over a long period. After summary trial had been decided (presumably under s 24(1) of the Criminal Justice Act 1925 as amended) she pleaded guilty and asked for a further 96 offences to be taken into consideration; she had no previous
d   convictions. She was committed for sentence to Quarter Sessions under s 29(1) of the Criminal Justice Act 1948 and sentenced to two years' imprisonment. On appeal it was submitted that there was no power to commit her for sentence because she had never previously been convicted and she bore a good reputation. Her appeal was dismissed.

In giving the judgment of the court Lord Goddard CJ said (at 231–232):
e
'... "character" ... certainly relates, in my opinion, to something more than the fact that a person has been previously convicted, and the word "antecedents" is as wide as can be conceived ... The character and antecedents of the appellant show that she has been a shameless thief for a long period of time ...'

f   The report does not give the dates of the offences nor does it reveal how many of the facts were known to the justices when they decided to try her summarily and how many emerged later. The report of counsel's argument (see 34 Cr App R 251) would suggest that he did not submit that this was relevant.

R v King's Lynn Justices, ex p Carter [1968] 3 All ER 858, [1969] 1 QB 488 concerned three defendants, C, S and W, who were jointly charged that between
g   October 1967 and January 1968, being servants to Jaegar & Co Ltd, they stole 489 ladies' garments of a total value of just under £3,500. At the outset and without hearing the circumstances of the charge the justices agreed to try the case summarily in accordance with s 29 of the 1952 Act. The three then pleaded guilty. Thereafter the bench was told the following. S and W who were cleaners
h   employed by the company had confessed to a long series of thefts between the dates in the charge. C was superior to S and W and in a position of trust. He had approached the other two and had requested them to take the garments out of the premises in rubbish bags and then transfer them to the boot of C's car, of which they had been given the key. Although C had only admitted being involved during the last week of the thefts, the court thought it right to take
j   against him what S and W had said; so he too was regarded as having been involved throughout. The applications were all dismissed. The report reveals that the court certified the following point of general public importance but refused leave to appeal to the House of Lords: what matters could be taken into consideration as going to character and antecedents within s 29 of the 1952 Act? (See [1968] 3 All ER 858 at 862, [1969] 1 QB 488 at 497–498.)

Lord Parker CJ said ([1968] 3 All ER 858 at 862, [1969] 1 QB 488 at 497):

'As I see it, speaking for myself, the expression "character and antecedents" being as wide as it possibly can be, justices are entitled to take into consideration in deciding whether or not to commit, not merely previous convictions, not merely offences which they are asked to take into consideration, but matters revealed in the course of the case connected with the offence charged which reflects in any way on the accused's character. Of course, in the ordinary way where justices do their duty under s. 19(2) of the Act of 1952, the circumstances of the offence which reflect on character and antecedents will already have emerged, and if, notwithstanding that, the justices decide to deal with the case summarily, they cannot take those matters into consideration again when they are considering committal under s. 29; there must be something more than has been revealed at the stage when they decided to deal with the case summarily. On the other hand where, as in the present case, they have either been persuaded to deal with the case summarily, or have embarked on the summary trial without making any proper inquiry, or without conducting their inquiry as examining magistrates far enough to understand the nature of the case, then, as it seems to me, they are fully entitled to take into consideration those matters relating to the offence which had been revealed at the trial and which do reflect on the character and antecedents.'

It may be asked how this principle applied to the facts of the case, i e what new circumstances emerged after it was decided to try the case summarily. The charge itself showed that there were three defendants, that all were servants and that the value of the goods stolen between 1 October 1967 and 10 January 1968 was nearly £3,500. The fact that C was superior to S and W and had corrupted them was new. But what emerged which made the parts played by the other two worse than was apparent from the charge itself? In *R v Tower Bridge Magistrate, ex p Osman* [1971] 2 All ER 1018 at 1020, [1971] 1 WLR 1109 at 1111 Lord Parker CJ described the *King's Lynn Justices* case as 'very special' and added:

'. . . the gravity of the case was not revealed until the prosecution case was opened, when it was found that these thefts had been going on over a very long period.'

It must, I think, be presumed that the court assumed that the lay justices would not have realised from the span of three and a half months in the dates of the charge that there had been a series of thefts, rather than one, at some time during that period when all 489 garments had been taken.

It was the absence of new facts which led to the committal for sentence being quashed in *R v Tower Bridge Magistrate, ex p Osman* [1971] 2 All ER 1018, [1971] 1 WLR 1109. Osman had been charged with three offences of theft of goods of small value from the Bricklayers' Arms goods depot of British Railways covering the period 1 January 1970 to 23 November 1970. The only thing that emerged after the stipendiary magistrate had decided on summary trial under s 19 of the 1952 Act and Osman had pleaded guilty was that he was himself employed by British Railways.

Lord Parker CJ said ([1971] 2 All ER 1018 at 1020, [1971] 1 WLR 1109 at 111):

'. . . it was perfectly patent to anybody who read the charges, and in particular this magistrate, who had had this trouble with this depot in the past, and particularly when the thefts were alleged to have occurred over

such a long period, that this was a typical case of pilfering by an employee of
the railways . . . it is not a question of something more being revealed in the
prosecution case which enhanced the gravity of the offences. Here the gravity
of the offences was undoubtedly to this magistrate patent on the very face of
them . . .'

In *R v Lymm Justices, ex p Brown* [1973] 1 All ER 716, [1973] 1 WLR 1039 the
defendant was charged with two offences of theft; the first alleged theft of a lady's
twin set on 29 June 1971; fewer particulars of the second are given in the report,
and all one knows is that it charged him on divers dates over a period of months
with the theft of a great list of articles on perhaps 20 or some such number of
occasions (see [1973] 1 All ER 716 at 718–720, [1973] 1 WLR 1039 at 1041–
1043). After the justices had agreed to try the case summarily under s 19 of the
1952 Act and the defendant had pleaded guilty they were told that he had
committed the thefts while on duty as a police officer at the airport where the
thefts had taken place. He asked for one further offence, of which no details are
given, to be taken into consideration. The application to quash the committal was
dismissed because the justices discovered after they had agreed to try the case
summarily and after the conviction that the applicant was a police officer and had
committed the offence when on duty.

Lord Widgery CJ, having cited the judgment of Lord Parker CJ in the *King's
Lynn Justices* case, said ([1973] 1 All ER 716 at 719, [1973] 1 WLR 1039 at 1042):

'Lord Parker CJ was saying in the clearest terms that although it is right
and desirable for justices to make as full an enquiry as possible before
committing themselves to a decision to try the case summarily, yet if they do
not do that, either because they have been over-persuaded by the prosecution,
or for any other reason, they can have regard to facts subsequently emerging
in deciding whether or not to apply s 29, and that in my judgment is exactly
what the justices did in this case. They discovered after they had agreed to
try the case summarily and after the conviction that the applicant was a
policeman and had committed these offences when on duty. Those were
matters of antecedents for the purpose of s 29, as is not disputed . . .'

Last before the changes made by the Criminal Law Act 1977 come two cases
noted briefly in the Criminal Law Review. The Crown Office does not have a
transcript of the judgment in either. In *R v Hartlepool Justices, ex p King* [1973]
Crim LR 637 the decision to commit was quashed because after it had been
decided to try the case summarily and the defendant, who had no previous
conviction, had pleaded guilty the only new factor to emerge was that the facts of
the offence (an assault occasioning actual bodily harm) were more serious than
the justices had imagined. He had not been previously convicted.

In *R v Harlow Justices, ex p Galway* [1975] Crim LR 288 the justices had
embarked on a summary trial of eight offences concerning forged income tax
forms without further inquiry, and after the defendant had pleaded guilty it
became apparent that he had systematically defrauded the revenue of £5,000 and
was asking for 19 further offences to be considered. It was held that the justices
were entitled to commit for sentence even though they had failed to make proper
inquiry at the earlier stage.

We know only four cases on this topic which have been decided since the
coming into force of the 1977 Act, viz *R v Warrington Justices, ex p Mooney* (1980)
2 Cr App R (S) 40, *R v Derby and South Derbyshire Magistrates, ex p McCarthy* (1980)
2 Cr App R (S) 140, *R v Guildhall Justices, ex p Cooper* (1983) Times, 6 May (the

court has seen a transcript of the judgments) and *R v Cardiff Stipendiary Magistrate, ex p Morgan* [1989] Crim LR 503. In each the committal for sentence was quashed *a* because after the decision to try the case summarily was taken nothing more than the filling in of detail emerged.

There is no post-1977 equivalent of *R v Vallett* [1951] 1 All ER 231, *R v King's Lynn Justices, ex p Carter* [1968] 3 All ER 858, [1969] 1 QB 488 and *R v Lymm Justices, ex p Brown* [1973] 1 All ER 716, [1973] 1 WLR 1039—the three decisions which established the proposition that 'character and antecedents' mean anything *b* that reflects on the defendant's character, even if it is the circumstances of the offence.

Even so, these earlier cases must, in my judgment, be taken by this court to have decided the meaning of 'character and antecedents' in s 38 of the 1980 Act. I say so for the following reasons.

(a) The operative words of s 38 are identical with those in s 29 of the 1948 Act. *c*

(b) The criteria in s 19(3) of the 1980 Act do not differ significantly from those in the corresponding earlier provisions.

(c) Although there has been no post-1977 case where a committal was upheld on the basis that circumstances relating to the offence, which emerged after the mode of trial had been decided, fell within the words 'character and antecedents', *d* it is implicit in the judgments in all of the cases since 1977 that had there been more than the filling in of detail the committals would not have been quashed, even although those details related to the offence.

(d) In his judgment in *R v Warrington Justices, ex p Mooney* Bridge LJ noted that the 1977 Act had changed the law, reviewed the earlier cases and said that it was not altogether easy to reconcile them. Yet he said nothing to suggest that the *e* words 'character and antecedents' should be construed more restrictively than hitherto. Nor is there a hint of this in the other three cases.

(e) Parliament must be taken to have known the construction that had been put on this phrase to 1977, and in re-enacting the earlier provision for committal for sentence in the same words, must be taken to have intended them to be used in the same sense. *f*

The principles derived from the cases

In my judgment, the principles to be applied to the interpretation of s 38 of the 1980 Act are, therefore, as follows: (1) 'character and antecedents' mean anything that reflect on the defendant's character, even if it is a circumstance of the offence; (2) any such thing may be taken into account in deciding whether to *g* commit for sentence, provided (a) that it was not known to the justices when they took their decision to try the case summarily, and (b) that the new matter is more than the filling in of detail; (3) it does not matter whether the justices' ignorance of that thing resulted from their failure to make any or any proper inquiry or from the failure of the prosecution to inform them of it or from any other cause. *h*

To these principles I would respectfully add two comments. (a) Whether or not new facts are more than the mere filling in of detail must be a matter of degree. (b) It would seem to follow from (1) that many circumstances of an offence will qualify, since many bear on the character of the person who commits it. It is only right to observe that neither counsel made any submission to the effect that these were not the principles to be applied. *j*

The application of the principles for the present case

The offences committed by the applicant were all committed on 20 December 1990 at his home address. One alleged simple possession of a quantity of cannabis

resin; the second alleged simple possession of LSD tables (lysergide); the third also
a alleged possession of LSD tablets (lysergide), but with intent to supply them to
another. LSD is a class A controlled drug; cannabis resin is in class B. The first
two offences were contrary to s 5(2) of the Misuse of Drugs Act 1971 and the third
contrary to s 5(3).

On 4 January 1991 the bench, which then consisted of lay justices, considered
whether the offences appeared more suitable for summary trial or for trial on
b indictment.

The prosecuting solicitor gave the following information to the bench. On 20
December 1990 police officers searched the applicant's house. They found two
plastic bags hidden in the loft opening; one contained cannabis; the other
contained 44 individual silver foil wraps of LSD. On a work surface in the kitchen
were a pair of scales and a tin containing £70. The applicant admitted that the
c drugs were his. He said that he believed they were cannabis and LSD. He refused
to answer questions about the scales or the £70. It was suspected that he intended
to supply the drugs to his girlfriend, with whom he shared the house, but he
made no admission that he intended to supply them to anyone. She was in full-
time employment. There was no evidence that the £70 was his rather than hers.
d There was no further evidence of intent to supply.

The prosecuting solicitor told the bench that she considered the case a difficult
one and that they might think that their powers of sentencing were not adequate.
The defending solicitor submitted that the summary trial would be appropriate.
He said that the LSD was less than usually strong. The prosecutor told the bench
that he had no evidence to confirm its strength.

e The bench decided on summary trial. The applicant pleaded guilty to the two
charges of possession and not guilty to the charge of possession with intent to
supply. The matter was thereafter adjourned for trial.

The applicant next appeared before the court on 17 January 1991. On this
occasion Mr Barry, the stipendiary magistrate, was sitting. The trial of the most
serious of the offences was then to have taken place, but, as the sole prosecution
f witness was unable to attend, it had to be adjourned again.

During the hearing on 17 January 1991 Mr Barry expressed surprise that the
justices had thought the case more suitable for summary trial and said that they
would on the next occasion be able to reconsider the matter, discontinue the
summary trial and proceed with inquiries into the case as examining justices. In
saying so it was clear that he had expected the applicant to maintain his plea of
g not guilty and that he had in mind the provisions of s 29 of the 1980 Act.

On 25 January 1991 the applicant appeared again. He then changed his plea on
the outstanding charge to guilty, and the case was further adjourned, doubtless
for the preparation of a social inquiry report.

Finally one comes to 25 February 1991, when the decision under challenge was
h taken. Mr Barry was again sitting. He was provided with details of the applicant's
previous convictions and findings of guilt and with a social inquiry report dated
15 February 1991. It hardly needs to be said that none of this was before the
bench on 4 January 1991. He also heard mitigation from counsel for the applicant,
Mr Hennis.

The applicant was born on 1 November 1967. He had been before the courts
j on seven previous occasions. His convictions and findings of guilt included:
handling a stolen skirt in 1985 for which he was fined £35; burglary of an
unoccupied shop and theft of a refrigerator worth £10 in 1987 and, at the same
appearance, handling stolen cash from a gas meter, for both of which he was
conditionally discharged; theft later in 1987 for which he was fined £60;

fraudulent use of a vehicle excise licence for which he was fined £30 in 1989;
a variety of motoring offences for which he was conditionally discharged on *a*
3 December 1990 and, on the same date, driving whilst disqualified for which he
was placed on probation for 12 months and disqualified for 12 months. This last
appearance was 17 days before he was found in possession of cannabis and LSD.
He had not previously been convicted of any offence involving drugs or served
any custodial sentence.

The following passages appeared in the social inquiry report: *b*

'12. Mr. Goulding tells me he has used cannabis on occasion since leaving
home at the age of seventeen years. He states he had not experienced L.S.D.
until the summer of last year when the drug became widely available and
was associated with "Acid House Parties". 13. Mr. Goulding tells me he
purchased an ounce of cannabis for his own and his girlfriend's personal use. *c*
With regard to the L.S.D. he tells me he was offered the drug in a fairly large
quantity i.e. forty-five tablets for a discount price. He states he bought the
drug from people whom he did not know from, he thinks, the London area.
He states he has not previously purchased that amount but assures me the
tablets were for his and his girlfriend's use. 14. The charge of intent to supply
arises from the purchase of the drugs with intent to share them with his   *d*
girlfriend and was not in any way, he assures me, for profit.'

The report also recorded that the applicant had told the probation officer that
he had bought the drugs with money he had saved to repaint his car, that the £70
was the remainder of his savings, that he used the scales to weigh his cannabis and
that he had now finished with drugs. The view was expressed that it was unlikely *e*
that he had been addicted to them in any way. The applicant had said that he had
taken steps to find employment and was hopeful of a place on an employment
training scheme in the near future. He had spent five weeks in custody and it was
suggested that if a sentence of imprisonment was imposed it should be suspended.

In his address in mitigation Mr Hennis said that there was no evidence that the *f*
applicant had supplied anyone with drugs, nor could it be inferred that he had
arranged to do so. He repeated his assertion that the LSD was less than usually
strong and therefore, he suggested, much less damaging. Mr Barry, who had not
heard such an assertion made in any previous case, rejected this submission. Mr
Hennis also said that the applicant had intended to supply only his girlfriend. Mr
Barry found this incredible in view of the amount of LSD. He committed the *g*
applicant to the Crown Court for sentence.

In his affidavit he set out his reasons for doing so. I would summarise them
like this:

(1) The justices on 4 January 1991 would have assumed that the applicant had
an unblemished record. He had seen his record which included 'convictions for
burglary, handling stolen goods, fraudulent use of a vehicle excise licence and *h*
driving whilst disqualified: his past conduct had been serious enough to justify
probation orders'. (In fact there had been only one such order, but no point was
taken about this.) (2) The social inquiry report, prepared since 4 January 1991,
showed 'a practice of using unlawful drugs since he was 17 years old and Class A
drugs since the summer of 1990'. (3) The justices on 4 January 1991 would have
been entitled to proceed on the basis that the LSD was, as Mr Hennis represented, *j*
under strength, as the prosecution had not made any representation to the
contrary. He, on the other hand, had rejected that submission. He therefore
supposed that the offence was more serious than the magistrate had been led to
believe.

a The fact that the applicant's assertion that he only intended to supply his girlfriend was false was not a factor in his decision to commit for sentence.

Had he not been given the information set out in (1) and (2) above he would not have committed for sentence.

Mr Barry also says in his affidavit that he thought that the prosecution had been wrong in not asking the justices to commit for trial and had consciously looked for a lawful way in which he could commit the applicant for sentence.

b Before us Mr Richard Gordon, counsel for the applicant, submitted that the learned magistrate prejudged the question of whether or not he should commit the applicant for sentence. He allowed himself to be influenced by his view that the prosecution had been wrong not to ask for committal for trial and thereafter looked for a way to commit for sentence. This attitude coloured his approach and flawed his judgment. His decision was therefore unlawful.

c I cannot accept this submission. The learned stipendiary cannot be criticised for forming the view he did about the prosecution's failure to ask for a committal for trial or the justices' decision to try the case summarily. There can be few in his position who would have thought otherwise. True it is, as he volunteered, that he looked for a way in which he could commit, but he was only looking for *d* a lawful way in which to do so. There is no reason to think that he would have contemplated adopting any other. It is a common experience for a judge who has formed an overall view of what the justice of a case requires to see whether the law permits him or precludes him from reaching that result.

Next Mr Gordon submitted that Mr Barry was wrong to infer from the social inquiry report 'a practice of using unlawful drugs since he was 17 years old and *e* Class A drugs since the summer of 1990'. Thus he took into account an immaterial consideration.

It is difficult to say more than I do not accept this; such an inference could reasonably be drawn from the material before him.

Mr Gordon also submitted that the learned stipendiary was in error in assuming that the justices had accepted jurisdiction on the basis that the LSD was of low *f* strength and wrong to use his own belief that this could not be so, since he had not previously heard this said of LSD.

Again I cannot accept this. When there is an issue of fact in the criminal case the version more favourable to the defendant must be accepted unless it is so manifestly wrong that it can be dismissed or unless the contrary is proved beyond reasonable doubt. I do not think it unreasonable for Mr Barry to have assumed *g* that lay justices would proceed on this basis, even although he, with his greater professional experience, felt able to reject the applicant's assertion. Mr Barry has been both the stipendiary magistrate for South Yorkshire and a recorder of the Crown Court since 1985 and had practised at the Bar on the North Eastern Circuit for over 20 years before that.

h But, even if my view were wrong and if Mr Barry were in error, either in his own dismissal of the applicant's assertion or in his assumption that the justices assumed it to be good, this would not enable the applicant to succeed in this application. Here the words of May LJ in *R v Broadcasting Complaints Commission, ex p Owen* [1985] 2 All ER 522 at 533, [1985] QB 1153 at 1177 are pertinent:

j 'Where the reasons given by a statutory body for taking or not taking a particular course of action are not mixed and can clearly be disentangled, but where the court is quite satisfied that even though one reason may be bad in law, nevertheless the statutory body would have reached precisely the same decision on the other valid reasons, then this court will not interfere by way of judicial review. In such a case, looked at realistically and with justice, such a decision of such a body ought not to be disturbed.'

I believe that to be the position here. Mr Barry's affidavit makes clear that, although his rejection of the applicant's submission about the strength of the LSD and his assumption that the justices had accepted it were things he took into account, the operative factors without which he would not have committed were the applicant's criminal record and the fact that the social inquiry report demonstrated that the applicant's involvement with dangerous drugs on 20 December 1990 was not his first. Though implicit, it is clear that he would have committed on the basis of the applicant's previous criminal record and the contents of the social inquiry report alone—plainly matters of 'character and antecedents'; a committal on that basis would have been lawful.

I would dismiss this application.

NEILL LJ. I have had the advantage of considering in draft the judgment which has been delivered by McCullough J. I agree with it. For the reasons which are set out in that judgment I too would dismiss this application.

Application dismissed.

Dilys Tausz   Barrister.

a
R v Tower Hamlets London Borough Council, ex parte Begum
R v Tower Hamlets London Borough Council, ex parte Rahman
b
COURT OF APPEAL, CIVIL DIVISION

LORD DONALDSON OF LYMINGTON MR, BUTLER-SLOSS AND STAUGHTON LJJ

15, 20, 30 JULY 1992

Housing – Homeless person – Duty of housing authority to provide accommodation –
c Application for priority need accommodation – Application by person suffering mental
incapacity – Application made by another person on behalf of person suffering mental
incapacity – Housing authority rejecting application – Whether application for priority
need housing may be made on behalf of person unable to complete application form –
National Assistance Act 1948, s 21(1) – Housing Act 1985, ss 59(1)(c), 62.

d In two separate appeals concerning applications by homeless people for priority
need housing under s 62[a] of the Housing Act 1985 the question arose whether
the application could be made by a person acting on behalf of a potential applicant
who was unable, through lack of capacity, either to make or to consent to the
making of the application. In the first case the applicant, who was 24, had arrived
from Bangladesh with his family in 1991. He was moderately to severely mentally
e handicapped and was believed to have a mental age of between 10 and 13. At first
the family lived with relatives, but subsequently the applicant, assisted by an
organisation which assisted people with mental handicap living in the community,
applied to the local authority for accommodation under s 62 of the 1985 Act on
the basis that he fell within s 59(1)(c)[b] of that Act, which provided that a person
f who was vulnerable as a result of, inter alia, 'mental illness or handicap or physical
disability' was to be treated as a having a priority need for housing. However, the
local authority concluded that, given his mental condition and assessed mental
age, the applicant was not capable of making an application under s 62, nor could
he have acquiesced in any application and he was therefore to be treated as not
having made the application. The applicant applied for leave to move for judicial
g review but the judge refused the application. The applicant appealed and was
granted leave by the Court of Appeal, which then heard the substantive
application. In the second case, the appellant, who was 24, deaf and had limited
speech, had arrived from Bangladesh with her family in 1989. In July 1990 the
appellant and her father attended the homeless persons unit of the local authority
and she signed an application under s 62 for priority housing in accordance with
h s 59(1)(c). However, the local authority concluded that she lacked the necessary
capacity to make the application. The appellant applied for judicial review but
the judge dismissed the application on the basis that, for the purposes of an
application under s 62, prima facie there had to be knowledge on the part of the
applicant that an application was being made. The appellant appealed. In both
j cases the local authority contended that the structure of the 1985 Act presupposed
an applicant of sufficient comprehension to be able to make an application or to
consent to an application being made on his behalf and that persons under such
disability as not to understand that an application was being made were excluded

---

a   Section 62, so far as material, is set out at p 451 *g h*, post

b   Section 59(1) is set out at p 451 *e f*, post

from the mechanism of the 1985 Act and their needs, including the need to be accommodated, had to be met by social services departments under the National *a* Assistance Act 1948, s 21(1)ᶜ of which authorised local authorities to provide residential accommodation for persons aged 18 or over who 'by reason of . . . infirmity or any other circumstances are in need of care and attention which is not otherwise available to them'.

Held – An application for priority housing under s 62 of the 1985 Act could be *b* made by a person with capacity to make it, by another person with the consent of the applicant or by someone acting on behalf of a person who was entitled to make an application but who was unable through mental incapacity to make or consent to the making of an application, provided the writer or maker of the application on behalf of that person could demonstrate reasonable grounds for making the application and that he was acting bona fide in the best interests of *c* the applicant, since on its true construction s 62 was procedural and provided no barrier of mental capacity to the acceptance of an application. Furthermore, the purpose of the legislation was to include within its framework those with mental illness or handicap without reference to a definable cut-off point of mental capacity and s 59(1)(c) of the 1985 Act clearly contemplated that applications *d* could be made by those under a disability or who were vulnerable. Moreover, although the 1985 and 1948 Acts overlapped, they fulfilled different needs: the 1985 Act presupposed homelessness or the threat of it, whereas the 1948 Act catered for those who were in need of care, albeit that they might be adequately housed. It followed that the applicant and the appellant were clearly within the ambit of the 1985 Act and had made valid applications for priority housing on *e* which the local authority was bound to act. Accordingly the decision of the local authority in each case would be set aside (see p 454 *a* to *g*, p 455 *e f h* and p 456 *b c*, post).

Notes

For accommodation for homeless persons and priority need for accommodation, *f* see 22 *Halsbury's Laws* (4th edn) paras 509–510, and for cases on the subject, see 26 *Digest* (Reissue) 797–801, 5325–5338.

For the National Assistance Act 1948, s 21, see 40 *Halsbury's Statutes* (4th edn) 23.

For the Housing Act 1985, ss 59, 62, see 21 *Halsbury's Statutes* (4th edn) (1990 *g* reissue) 98, 101.

Cases referred to in judgments

Associated Provincial Picture Houses Ltd v Wednesbury Corp [1947] 2 All ER 680, [1948] 1 KB 223, CA.

Khawaja v Secretary of State for the Home Dept [1983] 1 All ER 765, [1984] 1 AC 74, *h* [1983] 2 WLR 321, HL.

R v Oldham Metropolitan B C, ex p G (1992) Times, 20 April.

Cases also cited or referred to in skeleton arguments

Cocks v Thanet DC [1982] 3 All ER 1135, [1983] 2 AC 286, HL.

F v West Berkshire Health Authority (Mental Health Act Commission intervening) [1989] *j* 2 All ER 545, [1900] 2 AC 1, HL.

Lewis v North Devon DC [1981] 1 All ER 27, [1981] 1 WLR 328.

R v Bath City Council, ex p Sangermano (1984) 17 HLR 94.

R v Brent London BC, ex p Omar (1991) 23 HLR 446.

---

c Section 21(1), so far as material, is set out at p 453 *g*, post

R v Chiltern DC, ex p Roberts (1990) 23 HLR 387.

a *R v Eastleigh BC, ex p Beattie* (1984) 17 HLR 168.

R v Fulham Hammersmith and Kensington Rent Tribunal, ex p Zerek [1951] 1 All ER 482, [1951] 2 KB 1, DC.

R v Lambeth London BC, ex p Ly (1986) 19 HLR 51.

Roberts v Dorset CC (1976) 75 LGR 462.

Zamir v Secretary of State for the Home Dept [1980] 2 All ER 768, [1980] AC 930,
b HL.

Application for judicial review and appeal

R v Tower Hamlets London BC, ex p Begum

Ferdous Begum appealed from the order of Rose J made on 28 November 1991
c whereby he dismissed her motion for judicial review, brought with the leave of
Popplewell J given on 2 September 1991, of the decision of the respondent, Tower
Hamlets London Borough Council, communicated to the appellant's father by
letter dated 11 July 1991 that the appellant had not made an application to the
council pursuant to Pt III of the Housing Act 1985 as a homeless person and
therefore the council was under no obligation to make inquiries into the
d appellant's homelessness pursuant to s 62 of that Act. The facts are set out in the
judgment of Butler-Sloss LJ.

R v Tower Hamlets London BC, ex p Rahman

Lutfur Rahman applied by way of renewed application, with the leave of the
Court of Appeal (Lord Donaldson MR, Stocker and Butler-Sloss LJJ) given on 23
e March 1992, for judicial review of the decision of the respondent, Tower Hamlets
London Borough Council, given on 18 February 1992 that the applicant had not
on 28 January 1992 made an application to the council pursuant to Pt III of the
Housing Act 1985, the original application for such leave having been refused by
Macpherson J on 13 March 1992. The court ordered that the substantive
f application be retained for hearing by the Court of Appeal. The relief sought was
an order of certiorari to quash the council's decision, an order of mandamus
requiring the council to consider and determine the application and a declaration
that on 28 January 1992 the applicant had made a valid application to the council
pursuant to Pt III of the 1985 Act. The facts are set out in the judgment of Butler-
Sloss LJ.

g
Robert Carnwath QC and Terence Gallivan (instructed by T V Edwards) for the
applicant Rahman.

David Watkinson and Leslie Thomas (instructed by Hereward & Foster) for the
appellant Begum.

Ashley Underwood and Lisa Giovannetti (instructed by J E Marlowe) for the council.
h council.

Cur adv vult

j 30 July 1992. The following judgments were delivered.

BUTLER-SLOSS LJ (giving the first judgment at the invitation of Lord
Donaldson MR). The two matters before this court, one an appeal from the
dismissal of judicial review and the second the retention by this court of a
substantive application for judicial review after the granting of leave, raise the
same issue under the Housing Act 1985 as to the right of people suffering from

mental illness or mental handicap to apply for priority housing. The relevant facts of each appeal are as follows.

Lutfur Rahman

The applicant is 24. He and his family came to England from Bangladesh in 1991. His family consists of his mother and two sisters aged 16 and 11. They lived at first with relatives in Tower Hamlets and then approached the homeless persons unit. They have been housed in temporary accommodation pending inquiries. The housing authority decided that the mother was homeless, in priority need, and was intentionally homeless and that accommodation would not be provided beyond 3 February 1992. There has been no challenge to that decision.

The applicant came to the attention of the Community Team for People with Learning Difficulties (CTLD), which is part of the Royal London Trust and which assists people with mental handicap living in the community. The applicant was assessed by the same psychologist as Ferdous Begum (see post), who concluded that he had both moderate and in some respects severe mental handicap, that he had hearing difficulties and that he is functioning at a mental age of between 10 and 13.

The applicant, assisted by the CTLD, applied to the housing authority for accommodation under the provisions of s 59(1)(c) of the 1985 Act. A representative of the housing authority interviewed the family and the applicant and concluded that the applicant was not capable of making an application under s 62, and on 19 February 1992 another representative of the housing authority wrote to the applicant's mother setting out the applicant's mental condition and assessed mental age, and continued:

'I must therefore conclude that [Lutfur] is dependant on you. In all of these circumstances I conclude that he cannot have acquiesced in any application for housing and is not capable of making an application for rehousing. It follows that I must treat him as not having made an application and I therefore conclude that the purported application was merely a device by which you sought to get round the unchallenged finding of your intentional homelessness.'

On 13 March 1992 Macpherson J refused leave to move for judicial review, but leave was granted by a division of this court on 23 March 1992 and the hearing of the substantive application was retained to be heard by this court.

Ferdous Begum

The appellant is 24. She and her family arrived in England from Bangladesh on 17 December 1989. She has a father, mother, either two or three sisters and a brother. On arrival, after a night with relatives her father approached the homeless persons unit of the respondent housing authority, who housed the family in temporary accommodation pending inquiries. The housing authority found the father to be intentionally homeless and indicated that they would not provide accommodation for the family beyond 18 July 1990. The father took no steps to set aside that decision.

The appellant is profoundly deaf and has very limited speech. She communicates with her family by means of signs and words understood only by them. She has been assessed to a limited extent by a psychologist, who considered that she was functioning far below her potential level but did not come to a conclusion as to her mental age. Additional evidence has been accepted by this court which shows that she has an ability to function quite successfully within the family.

The appellant and her father attended the homeless persons unit on 17 July
a 1990 and she signed an application for priority housing in accordance with the
provisions of s 59(1)(c) of the 1985 Act. By letter dated 11 July 1991 a
representative of the housing authority notified the appellant's father that they
considered that she had not made an application. After setting out her disabilities
the letter concluded:

b   'Her only means of communication with us has been through you. In all
of those circumstances I conclude not only that she could not have acquiesced
in any act or omission by you rendering her homeless, I find that she cannot
have acquiesced in any application for housing. It follows that I must treat
her as not having made an application and I therefore conclude that the
purported application was merely a device by which you sought to get
c   around the unchallenged finding of your intentional homelessness.'

The appellant was granted leave to move for judicial review by Popplewell J on
2 September 1991, but the application was dismissed by Rose J on 28 November
1991.

The 1985 Act provides a framework in Pt III within which local housing
d authorities try to cope with the problems of homelessness within their local areas.
It consolidates earlier legislation dealing with the same problem. Section 58
defines homelessness and threatened homelessness. Section 59(1) sets out the
categories of priority need for accommodation, and para (c) is relied upon in both
cases before this court:

e   'The following have a priority need for accommodation—(a) a pregnant
woman or a person with whom a pregnant woman resides or might
reasonably be expected to reside; (b) a person with whom dependent children
reside or might reasonably be expected to reside; (c) a person who is vulnerable
as a result of old age, mental illness or handicap or physical disability or other
special reason, or with whom such a person resides or might reasonably be
f   expected to reside; (d) a person who is homeless or threatened with
homelessness as a result of an emergency such as flood, fire or other disaster.'

Section 60 defines intentional homelessness. Section 62 deals with the inquiry
into cases of possible homelessness or threatened homelessness and provides in
general terms for the application to be made:

g   '(1) If a person (an "applicant") applies to a local housing authority for
accommodation, or for assistance in obtaining accommodation, and the
authority have reason to believe that he may be homeless or threatened with
homelessness, they shall make such inquiries as are necessary to satisfy
themselves as to whether he is homeless or threatened with homelessness.
(2) If they are so satisfied, they shall make any further inquiries necessary
h to satisfy themselves as to—(a) whether he has a priority need, and (b) whether
he became homeless or threatened with homelessness intentionally . . .'

Pending inquiries the housing authority have an interim duty under s 63 to
make accommodation available to the applicant. Notification of the decision and
the reasons for it is covered by s 64. Once a housing authority are—

j   'satisfied that he has a priority need and are not satisfied that he became
homeless intentionally, they shall . . . secure that accommodation becomes
available for his occupation.' (See s 65(2).)

Sections 65 and 69 also lay other duties upon the housing authority to provide
accommodation for a limited period and to offer advice and assistance.

A local housing authority may refer an applicant to another housing authority and house him in the meantime (ss 67 and 68). False statements, withholding *a* information and failure to disclose change of circumstances are dealt with in s 74.

Section 75 states:

'For the purposes of this Part accommodation shall be regarded as available for a person's occupation only if it is available for occupation both by him and by any other person who might reasonably be expected to reside with *b* him . . .'

In discharge of their duties local housing authorities are assisted by the *Code of Guidance for Local Authorities on Homelessness.* The Secretary of State is empowered to issue such guidance by virtue of s 71(2) and a local housing authority is required to have regard to it. Paragraph 3.2 in ch 3 deals with 'What is an application?' and continues: *c*

'Under s. 62 of the Act an authority is required to take action whenever someone approaches it for help in obtaining housing and the authority has reason to believe that s/he may be homeless or threatened with homelessness. This duty exists regardless of which department of the local authority the applicant approaches or of the way in which the application is made. *d* Authorities should be aware of the need to recognise people who should be treated as homeless even if there is no formal application and they should monitor all applications.'

In paras 6.10 and 6.11 of ch 6 the code of guidance deals specifically with the groups within the community falling within s 59(1)(c) and in para 6.10 they are *e* advised in cases of vulnerability to have regard to medical advice and where appropriate to seek social services advice. Paragraph 6.11 refers in particular to liaison between the health authority and the housing authority. Section 72 of the Act sets out the duty of co-operation between local housing authorities and also by social service authorities when called on to render assistance to a local housing authority. *f*

The Act however does not state nor does the code of guidance assist as to the application itself—who may make it and in particular whether it can be made by someone acting on behalf of a potential applicant unable himself through lack of comprehension either to make or consent to the making of such an application for priority housing. This point has not previously been the subject of judicial *g* scrutiny and is by no means without difficulty.

The case for both the applicant and the appellant is that the Act provides a comprehensive set of rules for homelessness. Section 62, which alone deals with the threshold of the application, lays down no criteria nor rules for the making of the application. Section 59(1)(c) expressly recognises that the more vulnerable sections of society will be applicants and among them those who are old, with *h* mental illness or mental handicap. There is in the Act no restriction or limitation as to the degree of mental illness or mental handicap of a potential applicant any diminution in which will obviously reduce the cognitive ability of a person and in some cases may extinguish it. Indeed, the code of guidance recognises that an application may be informal, and local housing authorities are advised to have regard to medical advice and advice from social services. *j*

The primary argument of Mr Carnwath QC for the applicant and of Mr Watkinson for the appellant is that there is no line to be drawn between those with sufficient understanding to make their own applications or to consent to their applications being made by others on their behalf, and those with no comprehension whatsoever who none the less are homeless or threatened with

homelessness and whose plight ought to be considered and redressed within the
a framework of Pt III of the Act.

The secondary argument of both the applicant and the appellant is they have
in fact sufficient understanding of the concept of homelessness and the need to
seek help to come within the meaning of an applicant who knew he was making
an application or consented to an application being made on his behalf. In
considering this argument, the letter of the housing officer in each case clearly
b demonstrates that he fell into error. For entirely understandable reasons, since in
each case the parent had been declared intentionally homeless, the application
under s 59(1)(*c*) was seen as a device to get round the refusal of housing on the
previous application of the family. This approach, that it was a device, was
subsequently abandoned by the housing authority. But it undoubtedly had an
c effect on the thought processes of the housing officer and casts doubt on each
decision. However, it is unnecessary to pursue this issue any further since Mr
Underwood for the housing authority, with the advantage of further evidence as
to the abilities of each of these young people, accepted that the housing authority
would in any event have to reconsider their cases.

Mr Carnwath argued that the question 'Who is an applicant?' is not a matter
d for the decision of the local housing authority to be challenged on the ground of
Wednesbury unreasonableness (see *Associated Provincial Picture Houses Ltd v
Wednesbury Corp* [1947] 2 All ER 680, [1948] 1 KB 223) but is a jurisdictional fact
as to the point at which the duties laid upon the housing authority come into
existence. Consequently, if the housing authority can be shown to have come to
the wrong decision, this court may, if appropriate, substitute its own decision for
e that of the housing authority.

Mr Underwood for the respondent local authority argued that the structure of
the Act presupposes an applicant of sufficient comprehension to be able to make
an application or consent to an application being made on his behalf. In these two
cases the housing authority themselves involved a psychologist to assist in the
assessment of each of them. A line has to be drawn which excludes those under
f such a disability as not to understand that an application is being made. There is
nothing in the Act to show that a person with no mental ability can none the less
be treated as an applicant without his knowledge. He pointed to the sections of
the Act which require notification by the applicant of change of circumstances
and the provisions in respect of false statements. He invited our attention to
g s 21(1) of the National Assistance Act 1948 part of which remains in force (with
amendments) and authorises a local authority to make arrangements to provide—

> '(*a*) residential accommodation for persons aged eighteen or over who by
> reason of age, infirmity or any other circumstances are in need of care and
> attention which is not otherwise available to them.'

h
Section 21(1)(*a*) of the 1948 Act is however administered by the social services
department and not the housing authority. The framework of the legislation
therefore is that those incapable of understanding what they are doing or of
making an application themselves do not come within the 1985 Act but their
needs, including the need to be accommodated, are met by social services within
j the structure of the 1948 Act.

Rose J asked himself the question in regard to Ferdous Begum: does the mind
go with the application? and answered it on the basis that—

> 'the word "application" prima facie involves knowledge on the part of the
> applicant that an application is being made.'

Although I see the force of the argument, in the context of the 1985 Act I do not believe that it is correct. There is nothing in the Act to demonstrate that s 62 *a* is substantive rather than procedural and provides hurdles of mental capacity to surmount before an application can be accepted. On the contrary, s 59(1)(*c*) contemplates that applications will be made by those under a disability or who are vulnerable. Such legislation is in accord with the expressed policy of government departments to accept within the community those who might in former days have been shut away in long-stay institutions. I cannot construe from *b* the statute any indication that a line has to be drawn among those targeted by s 59(1)(*c*) according to degrees of mental capacity less than the normal capacity to make an application. The purpose of the framework of the overall legislation is to include those with mental illness or handicap without reference to a definable cut-off point of mental capacity. The argument that applicants are required to inform the housing authority of changes of circumstances would, in the context *c* of someone under a disability, be the obligation of the person who made or assisted in the making of the application. The offence of making a false statement is not restricted to the applicant alone.

In my view an application may be made under s 59(1)(*c*) by a person with capacity to make it, or by another with the consent of the applicant, or by *d* someone on behalf of a person who is entitled to make an application but is unable through mental incapacity to make or consent to the making of an application. In the latter case the writer or maker of the application on behalf of another must demonstrate reasonable grounds for making the application and for acting on behalf of the actual applicant and that he is acting bona fide in the interests of the person unable to act without such help. An application by a well- *e* meaning busybody would not be an acceptable application under s 62.

The 1985 Act and the 1948 Act undoubtedly overlap, and those administering each Act may from time to time have to consider the needs of the same person. There would be nothing surprising in that position since the wording of s 72(*b*) of the 1985 Act and of the code of guidance both contemplate the involvement of both services in housing the vulnerable homeless. However, the two Acts fulfil *f* different roles and meet different needs. The 1948 Act caters for those in need of care and attention who may none the less be adequately housed, with no question of homelessness or threat of homelessness. But their inability to manage their own affairs may require them nevertheless to be accommodated in sheltered housing and to leave their own homes. Part III of the 1985 Act presupposes either homelessness or threat of homelessness; otherwise the application would not be *g* made. Further, there is an important practical difference. Social services run residential accommodation for the person in need under the provisions of s 21(1) of the 1948 Act. They do not have a stock of housing as such and, without recourse to the local housing authority, would not be in a position to house the family of the person in need. The 1985 Act on the other hand specifically *h* recognises in s 75 an obligation to house not only the applicant with priority need but some at least of his family, if he lives with one or more of them. Section 75 does not however cast a duty upon the local housing authority to house all members of a large extended family but only those who come within the definition of 'any other person who might reasonably be expected to reside with *j* him'.

In problems which may arise both within the ambit of the 1985 Act and the 1948 Act the people involved will inevitably be within the most vulnerable group contemplated by the legislation and it is especially important that their needs are recognised and their problems addressed without passing them from one department to another.

The question whether a person is an applicant within the ambit of s 62 of the
1985 Act is not in my judgment a matter for the discretion of the local housing
authority to be reviewed upon *Wednesbury* principles. It is a question whether the
person comes within those contemplated by Pt III of the 1985 Act as applicants
for priority housing, the receipt of whose applications will be the threshold for
the assumption by the local housing authority of their various duties under the
Act. Henry J in *R v Oldham Metropolitan BC, ex p G* (1992) Times, 20 April decided
that dependent children could not be applicants in their own right under the
provisions of Pt III of the 1985 Act. I do not wish to comment upon the issue
raised in that decision, but the judge made general observations about applicants
under s 62 which included the proposition that a person can only be considered
as an applicant if he can establish a priority need. I do not agree. In my view the
housing authority has to accept genuine applications and consider, on the facts
revealed in the application and after any necessary inquiries, whether a duty arises
under Pt III of the 1985 Act. The housing authority has to establish the precedent
fact, as it was described by Lord Fraser in *Khawaja v Secretary of State for the Home
Dept* [1983] 1 All ER 765 at 771, [1984] 1 AC 74 at 97, that an application for
housing, in however informal terms, has been made. The question whether an
application has been made and whether the housing authority have erred in their
approach to this issue is a collateral question preceding the main decision-making
process. Consequently I agree with Mr Carnwath that, if he can demonstrate that
the housing authority wrongly excluded an application, this court has the
jurisdiction to substitute its own decision. For the reasons which I have set out
earlier I consider that both the appellant and the applicant made applications
which the housing authority was bound to receive and to act upon and
consequently they were not justified in rejecting them. It would seem to me
unlikely that the housing authority would be able to reject applications made in
similar circumstances although, of course, in carrying out their duties they may
have a variety of options in responding to the applications.

In each case I would set aside the decision of the local housing authority.

STAUGHTON LJ. I agree with the orders proposed by Butler-Sloss LJ and Lord
Donaldson MR for the reasons which they have given. In particular, I agree that
a decision whether a person has made an application under s 62(1) of the Housing
Act 1985 is not one which Parliament has entrusted to the local housing authority.
If the authority has concluded that no application was made, it will be for the
courts to decide whether the authority was right. But I prefer to express no
opinion on the other requirement in s 62(1), that 'the authority have reason to
believe that he may be homeless or threatened with homelessness . . .' That was
not in issue in these cases.

LORD DONALDSON OF LYMINGTON MR. I too would set aside the
decisions of the local housing authority for the reasons given by Butler-Sloss LJ.

This appeal and application are concerned with a human problem affecting the
least advantaged citizens. I appreciate that what may be compendiously described
as 'social services' and 'housing' are often, as a matter of administrative
convenience, dealt with by separate departments in a single local authority and
may, where there is multi-tiered local government, be dealt with by different
authorities. This should be of no concern to the person who is homeless or
threatened with homelessness (the 'homeless person'). Whether he applies to the
right or the wrong department or authority should not matter. That department
or authority should either itself deal with the application or pass it on to what it
considers to be the correct department or authority *and* should tell the homeless

person what it has done. It should not tell that person to apply elsewhere. The game of 'pass the parcel' has no place in this field. And, if disputes arise between departments or authorities as to whether this is a 'social services' or a 'housing' problem, that should be sorted out between them and should not directly involve the homeless person.

I agree that reading s 59(1)(c) with s 62 makes it clear that no 'application' in the ordinary sense of the word is required of a homeless person as otherwise it would be quite impossible for some people who are 'vulnerable as a result of old age, mental illness or handicap' to attract the protection which it is the clearly intended duty of housing authorities to provide under Pt III of the 1985 Act. Accordingly s 62 must be construed as contemplating only that the homeless person and his circumstances will be brought to the attention of the housing authority by an application by him, by someone else on his behalf and with his authority or by someone else on his behalf and in his interests, such person having a bona fide concern with those interests.

In my judgment s 62(1) of the 1985 Act contains a double-barrelled threshold or precedent question of fact which has to be answered in the affirmative if the local housing authority's duties under Pt III of the Act are to come into force. The first part of this question is whether a person has applied to it for accommodation in the sense which I have indicated. The second part is whether the authority has reason to believe that he *may* be homeless or threatened with homelessness. This is to be distinguished from the Pt III duty which follows immediately afterwards in the same sentence, namely, to make such inquiries as are necessary to satisfy itself as to whether he *is* homeless or threatened with homelessness. I cannot believe that Parliament intended that whether or not a local housing authority became subject to the duties set out in Pt III of the Act should depend upon whether it happened to be credulous or incredulous, myopic or far-sighted. The intention must have been that an objective test should be applied. The authority's decision on both aspects of this threshold question therefore falls to be reviewed not on *Wednesbury* (see *Associated Provincial Picture Houses Ltd v Wednesbury Corp* [1947] 2 All ER 680, [1948] 1 KB 223) but on *Khawaja* principles—does the evidence justify the conclusion (see *Khawaja v Secretary of State for the Home Dept* [1983] 1 All ER 765 at 777, [1984] AC 74 at 105 per Lord Wilberforce).

We have not had to consider whether an application can be made under s 62 by or on behalf or in the interests of a child. This was considered by Henry J in *R v Oldham Metropolitan BC, ex p G* (1992) Times, 20 April. I express no view on the basis of that decision, save to say that children who do not come within s 59(1)(c) or (d) are not within the priority need category. Although 'dependent children' feature in para (b) they do so as a qualification of a different applicant, namely one with whom they reside or might reasonably be expected to reside. They do not feature in that paragraph in their own right.

Application granted and appeal allowed. Leave to appeal to the House of Lords refused.

18 January 1993. The Appeal Committee of the House of Lords gave leave to appeal.

Frances Rustin Barrister.

McClory and others v Post Office

CHANCERY DIVISION
DAVID NEUBERGER QC SITTING AS A DEPUTY JUDGE OF THE HIGH COURT
11, 12, 13, 14, 20 FEBRUARY 1992

b *Employment – Suspension – Obligation on employer when suspending or dismissing*
employee – Contract of service – Implied terms – Employee suspended on full pay –
Suspension depriving employee of opportunity to work overtime – Express term of
contract requiring employee to work overtime if required – Express term of contract
giving employer discretionary power of suspension – Whether rules of natural justice
applying to contracts of employment – Whether employer owing implied duty to act
c *reasonably in exercising power of suspension – Whether employer under implied duty to*
provide overtime.

The three plaintiffs were employed by the Post Office as postmen under contracts
of employment which provided by cl 3 that it was a condition of their employment
that they were liable to work overtime if required and by cl 7 that they could be
d suspended either with or without pay if there was a need for inquiries to be made
into alleged misconduct by them. On 25 September 1987 the plaintiffs were
involved in a fight with other Post Office workers at a public house which resulted
in their being arrested and charged with assault. On 7 October the Post Office
suspended the plaintiffs on full pay pending its own inquiry into the incident.
e On 13 November the plaintiffs appeared before justices and pleaded not guilty to
all charges and were committed to the Crown Court for trial. The Post Office
then commenced its own internal inquiry and after Post Office staff involved in
the incident and the plaintiffs themselves had been interviewed the suspension
was lifted on 5 April 1988 and the plaintiffs returned to work. The plaintiffs were
subsequently acquitted of all charges after their trial in the Crown Court. The
f plaintiffs brought an action for damages against the Post Office claiming
compensation for loss of overtime payments during the period of suspension,
contending that the Post Office was in breach of implied terms in the plaintiffs'
contracts of employment to the effect, inter alia, (i) that the plaintiffs had a right
to be provided with the opportunity to undertake overtime and (ii) that in
exercising its right of suspension under cl 7 the Post Office was under a duty to
g act reasonably, to observe the rules of natural justice and to act fairly. The Post
Office contended that there was no general obligation on an employer to act
reasonably, to observe the rules of natural justice or to act fairly when dismissing
or suspending an employee for misconduct.

h **Held** – (1) The rules of natural justice could not be imported into the purely
contractual relationship of employer and employee and therefore an employer
was entitled to make a decision affecting an employee without first informing the
employee that the decision was about to be made. Likewise the employer was not
required to act fairly in the sense of balancing his own interests against the
employee's interests when deciding to suspend an employee since the fairness or
j otherwise of the decision was a matter for the employer, not the court.
Furthermore, it was not necessary to imply a term into the contract of employment
that the employer had to give the employee the reasons for his suspension before
suspending him, but in any event the plaintiffs must have been aware of the
reason for their suspension (see p 462 *h j*, p 463 *a* to *g* and p 464 *a b*, post); dictum
of Lord Wilberforce in *Malloch v Aberdeen Corp* [1971] 2 All ER 1278 at 1294
applied.

(2) However, on the true construction of cl 7 of the plaintiffs' contracts of
employment, there was an implied term that the Post Office would act reasonably *a*
in exercising its right to suspend an employee and would only continue that
suspension for as long as there were reasonable grounds for doing so, since the
fact that cl 7 empowered the Post Office to suspend an employee without pay for
an indefinite period implied that the suspension had to be reasonable. Nevertheless,
in deciding that an employer's contractual discretionary right to suspend an
employee was subject to an implied term that it would only be exercised *b*
reasonably, the court would not step into the arena of the employer/employee
relationship and substitute its own judgment for that of the employer. On the
facts, the Post Office had not been in breach of the implied term that it act
reasonably when suspending an employee because it had had reasonable grounds
for effecting the suspension and reasonable grounds for continuing it. Accordingly, *c*
the plaintiffs' claim failed, but, even if they had succeeded on liability, they could
not have obtained damages because on the true construction of cl 3 of their
contracts of employment there was no implied term giving them a right to
overtime since cl 3, while expressly imposing on the employee an obligation to
work overtime if the employer so required, contained no concomitant obligation
on the employer actually to provide overtime (see p 464 *h* to p 465 *a f* to p 466 *c*, *d*
p 467 *b h*, p 468 *d* and p 469 *a* to *j*, post).

Notes

For implied terms in contracts of employment, see 16 *Halsbury's Laws* (4th edn
reissue) para 54.

For implied contractual terms generally, see 9 *Halsbury's Laws* (4th edn) paras *e*
351–362, and for cases on the subject, see 12(1) *Digest* (2nd reissue) 403–454,
3282–3546.

Cases referred to in judgment

Bauman v Hulton Press Ltd [1952] 2 All ER 1121.
British Home Stores Ltd v Burchell [1980] ICR 303, EAT.   *f*
Chaplin v Hicks [1911] 2 KB 786, [1911–13] All ER Rep 224, CA.
Dakri (A) & Co Ltd v Tiffen [1981] ICR 256, EAT.
Devonald v Rosser & Sons [1906] 2 KB 728, [1904–7] All ER Rep 988, CA.
Gunton v Richmond upon Thames London Borough [1980] 3 All ER 577, [1981] Ch
   448, [1980] 3 WLR 714, CA.
Johnstone v Bloomsbury Health Authority [1991] 2 All ER 293, [1992] QB 333, [1991] *g*
   2 WLR 1362, CA.
Langston v Amalgamated Union of Engineering Workers [1974] 1 All ER 980, [1974]
   1 WLR 185, CA.
Langston v Amalgamated Union of Engineering Workers (No 2) [1974] ICR 510, NIRC.
Lavarack v Woods of Colchester Ltd [1966] 3 All ER 683, [1967] 1 QB 278, [1966] 3 *h*
   WLR 706, CA.
Liverpool City Council v Irwin [1976] 2 All ER 39, [1977] AC 239, [1976] 2 WLR
   562, HL.
MacRae (Kenneth) & Co Ltd v Dawson [1984] IRLR 5, EAT.
Malloch v Aberdeen Corp [1971] 2 All ER 1278, [1971] 1 WLR 1578, HL.
Ridge v Baldwin [1963] 2 All ER 66, [1964] AC 40, [1963] 2 WLR 935, HL.   *j*
United Bank Ltd v Akhtar [1989] IRLR 507, EAT.
Western Excavating (ECC) Ltd v Sharp [1978] 1 All ER 713, [1978] QB 761, [1978]
   2 WLR 344, CA.
White v Reflecting Roadstuds Ltd [1991] IRLR 331, EAT.
Woods v WM Car Services (Peterborough) Ltd [1981] ICR 666, EAT; affd [1982] ICR
   693, CA.

Cases also cited

a *Alexander v Standard Telephones and Cables Ltd (No 2)* [1991] IRLR 286.
   Bird v British Celanese Ltd [1945] 1 All ER 488, [1945] KB 336, CA.
   Carr v Alexander Russell Ltd [1979] ICR 469, Ct of Sess.
   City and Hackney Health Authority v National Union of Public Employees [1985] IRLR
     252, CA.
   Collier v Sunday Referee Publishing Co Ltd [1940] 4 All ER 234, [1940] 2 KB 647.
b *Council of Civil Service Unions v Minister for the Civil Service* [1984] 3 All ER 935,
     [1985] AC 374, HL.
   Hanley v Pease & Partners Ltd [1915] 1 KB 698, [1914–15] All ER Rep 984, DC.
   Harris (Ipswich) Ltd v Harrison [1978] ICR 1256, EAT.
   Lister v Romford Ice and Cold Storage Co Ltd [1957] 1 All ER 125, [1957] AC 555,
     HL.
c *Post Office v Roberts* [1980] IRLR 347, EAT.
   R v East Berkshire Health Authority, ex p Walsh [1984] 3 All ER 425, [1985] QB 152,
     CA.
   Shirlaw v Southern Foundries (1926) Ltd and Federated Foundries Ltd [1939] 2 All ER
     113, [1939] 2 KB 206, CA.
d *Spafax Ltd v Harrison* [1980] IRLR 442, CA.
   Spencer v Marchington [1988] IRLR 392.
   Trollope & Colls Ltd v North West Metropolitan Regional Hospital Board [1973] 2 All
     ER 260, [1973] 1 WLR 601, HL.
   Turner v Sawdon & Co [1901] 2 KB 653, CA.
   West Midlands Co-op Society Ltd v Tipton [1986] 1 All ER 513, [1986] AC 536, HL.
e

Action

The plaintiffs, James Gordon McClory, Andrew Perez and Stephen Keith Shipman,
brought an action against the defendant, the Post Office, claiming damages and a
declaration that the manner of the plaintiffs' suspensions from their employment
f by the defendant and/or the length of time of the suspension were in breach of
the plaintiffs' contracts of employment in that they were unfair and/or in breach
of the rules of natural justice. The facts are set out in the judgment.

Robert Reid QC and *Anne Wakefield* (instructed by *Simpson Millar*, Leeds) for the
   plaintiffs.
g *Jeffrey Burke QC* and *David Griffith-Jones* (instructed by *Hammond Suddards*) for the
   defendant.

Cur adv vult

h

20 February 1992. The following judgment was delivered.

DAVID NEUBERGER QC. This is a claim by three former employees of the
j defendant, the Post Office, for damages to compensate them for the loss of income
which they would have received by way of overtime payments during the period
that they were suspended on full pay by the defendant.

   The three plaintiffs were employed by the defendant as postmen higher grade
under effectively identical forms of contract entered into in each case in 1984.
Clause 2 of that contract provided for a fixed rate of weekly pay. Clause 3
provided for a 43-hour week and then stated as follows:

'The Post Office have the responsibility of providing a public service. This puts a special obligation on all employees to play their part in maintaining *a* the kind of service which the public has a right to expect. For this reason it is a condition of employment that you are liable to work overtime and to attend at such varying times on weekdays and Sundays as the needs of the service demand. You may also be required to work elsewhere than at your initial place of employment. These obligations are implemented in accordance with Post Office rules.' *b*

Clause 6 referred to termination, providing for a period of notice dependent on length of service, except in case of misconduct. Clause 7 provided:

'In the event of misconduct or where there is a need for enquiries to be *c* made into alleged misconduct you may be suspended from your employment, either with or without pay.'

The plaintiffs all worked at the sorting and post office at Mount Pleasant, Islington, where over 3,000 people were and are employed by the defendant.

On 25 September 1987 the plaintiffs went to the Wilmington Arms public *d* house in Rosebery Avenue. There was another group of employees of the defendant at that public house at the same time, albeit that they were not employed at Mount Pleasant, but at another of the defendant's offices, Calthorpe House. At some point during the evening there appears to have been something of a fight. A number of people were injured, most significantly two of the Calthorpe House employees, Mr Silk, who was knocked out, and Mr Sheddon, *e* who fractured his ankle.

The police formed the view that there was sufficient evidence to justify bringing prosecutions against all three plaintiffs on the following counts, namely assault occasioning grievous bodily harm, assault occasioning actual bodily harm and violent disorder.

The plaintiffs were arrested and charged on 7 October 1987, when they were *f* released on police bail. The defendant immediately suspended them on full pay. The suspension was effected orally, and was not formally communicated to them in writing until they each received letters from the defendant on 5 November 1987. Those letters referred to the alleged offences, the suspension and the fact that the plaintiffs had appeared in the magistrates' court on 16 October, when they were remanded on bail to appear again on 13 November. The letters stated *g* that the defendant was carrying out its own inquiries 'in order to assess what action, if any, it needs to take'. The letters went on to say that it was likely that the defendant would wish to interview the plaintiffs in due course.

The person responsible for carrying out the internal inquiries was Mr Curtis, the personnel and industrial relations manager at Mount Pleasant. He decided to *h* wait until 13 November to see whether the plaintiffs would plead guilty or not. In fact they pleaded not guilty and were sent for trial in the Crown Court. Accordingly, Mr Curtis started his inquiries. He fixed appointments for 16 and 17 November in order to interview the various Calthorpe House employees who had been present at the Wilmington Arms on 25 September. However, on that occasion he was only able to speak to four of those employees, none of whom had *j* been directly involved in the incident. He prepared a brief summary of what they told him, and also provided an aide-mémoire summarising the effect of their evidence, which he considered to be fairly inconclusive so far as the guilt of the three plaintiffs was concerned.

Subsequently, on 4 December, he interviewed two more of the Calthorpe

House employees, who had been on leave at the time of the earlier interviews.
a One of these was Mr Silk. Mr Curtis again prepared a summary of their evidence
and an aide-mémoire to its effect. He formed the view that the evidence was still
inconclusive, and that Mr Sheddon was a centrally important witness whom he
had to interview. Immediately after this, Mr Curtis wrote and asked Mr Sheddon
to come and see him about the incident. In fact, Mr Sheddon was difficult to
contact, as he was on temporary leave attending a course at the North London
b Polytechnic. Mr Curtis wrote to Mr Sheddon at the polytechnic and at his home
address. He also contacted Mr Meadows, who was apparently responsible for
personnel at Calthorpe House, and to the principal at the Polytechnic, with a view
to seeing Mr Sheddon.

Eventually, when Mr Curtis had more or less given up hope of interviewing
c him, Mr Sheddon came to see him on 24 February 1988. As Mr Curtis's note of
that meeting shows, Mr Sheddon's recollection of what happened at the
Wilmington Arms was so unclear as to be useless.

Meanwhile, Mr Curtis had reached the position where he considered it
appropriate to interview the plaintiffs themselves, and he wrote to each of them
on 12 February inviting them to come and see him 12 days later. The solicitors
d acting for the plaintiffs in the criminal proceedings replied on their behalf,
indicating that they considered it inappropriate for their clients to discuss the
incident, bearing in mind that they were facing criminal proceedings in
connection with it. Accordingly, they asked Mr Curtis to postpone the interview
until after the court hearing. Having discussed the matter fully with the Post
Office solicitors, Mr Curtis replied to the plaintiffs' solicitors on 23 March
e reiterating his intention to have a meeting with each of the plaintiffs, and those
meetings took place on 28 March.

The attitude of each of the plaintiffs was that they were not prepared to discuss
the incident in view of the advice they had received from their solicitors.
Mr Curtis asked two of the plaintiffs for assurances that there would be no
violence if they returned to work, and a similar assurance was sought from the
f remaining plaintiff on the next day. In each case the assurance was given.

In these circumstances the suspension on each of the plaintiffs was lifted, and
they returned to work at Mount Pleasant on 5 April. In due course, in July, the
criminal proceedings against the plaintiffs came on for trial in the Crown Court
at Southwark and, after a six-day hearing, they were all acquitted by the jury of
g all charges.

Arising from these facts, the plaintiffs have brought proceedings against the
defendant, alleging that the imposition of the suspension from 7 October 1987 to
5 April 1988 and/or the length of those suspensions constitute a breach of contract
by the defendant, and that as a result of this breach the plaintiffs have suffered
loss and damage, namely the loss of the opportunity to earn overtime payments.
h In this connection, the parties have very sensibly agreed, for the purpose of these
proceedings only, the net earnings which the plaintiffs would in practice have
received during the period of suspension had they been allowed to work overtime
in the same manner that they had actually been working overtime before the
suspension.

In order to succeed, the plaintiffs accept that they have to rely upon the breach
j by the defendant of one or more terms which the plaintiffs claim to have been
implied into their respective contracts of employment. These implied terms are
set out in the amended statement of claim and are as follows:

'(a) The employee is entitled to be provided during the period of his
employment with work to do and with the opportunities to undertake such

overtime and rest-day working and to earn such bonuses as is usual or the norm for the particular employee or for an employee in his position;

(b) Any suspension of an employee should be only following full information to the employee by the employer of the reasons for the suspension;

(c) Following a suspension, the employee should within a reasonable time be given an opportunity by the employer to answer any matters put forward by the employer as reasons for the suspension;

(d) Any suspension of the employee by the employer should be for such period only as was reasonable in all the circumstances;

(e) In exercising any contractual right to suspend the Plaintiffs or any of them the Defendants would observe the rules of natural justice and act fairly in the circumstances.'

I shall refer to these alleged implied terms as 'term (a)', 'term (b)' etc.

So far as liability is concerned, it seems to me that term (a) takes matters no further. If the suspensions were lawful under cl 7 of the contract, and were not in breach of any other implied term, then, so far as term (a) is concerned, it must yield to the express right of the defendant to suspend under cl 7. If authority is required for the proposition that an implied term must yield, at least so far as it is necessary to give proper effect to an express term, to that express term, I would refer to *Johnstone v Bloomsbury Health Authority* [1991] 2 All ER 293, [1992] QB 333.

Before turning to the other four implied terms, it is right to consider briefly the law relating to implied terms more generally. There are two categories of implied term: one is a term implied into a relationship because it creates a particular status; the other category is where a term is implied into a contract, which apparently forms the complete bargain between the parties. This case has been argued before me on the footing that the terms sought to be implied fall only into the second category. It is clear that terms can be implied into a contract of employment, just as into any other contract. However, in cases falling into the second category, it is equally clear that a term will only be implied if it is necessary to give efficacy to the contract or (which is often a different way of saying the same thing) it is so obvious a term that it goes without saying. Thus, in relation to a contract of employment, an employer cannot exercise a power contained in his favour in the contract in such a way as to put the employee into a position which requires him to do something which is, in practical terms, impossible: see for instance *United Bank Ltd v Akhtar* [1989] IRLR 507 esp at 511. However, as the decision of the House of Lords in *Liverpool City Council v Irwin* [1976] 2 All ER 39, [1977] AC 239 emphasises, one does not imply a term into a contract merely because it is reasonable to do so. Indeed, in the field of employment contracts, it seems clear from the decision in *Western Excavating (ECC) Ltd v Sharp* [1978] 1 All ER 713, [1978] QB 761 that there is, at least in general, no term to be implied into a contract of employment that the employer will behave reasonably.

Furthermore, it seems clear beyond doubt that, as a matter of contract, an employer is not obliged to act reasonably in deciding to dismiss an employee and is not obliged to give reasons or to act in accordance with the rules of natural justice in connection with such dismissal (see *Ridge v Baldwin* [1963] 2 All ER 66 at 71–72, [1964] AC 40 at 64–66 per Lord Reid and *Malloch v Aberdeen Corp* [1971] 2 All ER 1278 at 1281–1282, 1286, 1292, 1294, 1297–1298, [1971] 1 WLR 1578 at 1581, 1586, 1593, 1595–1596, 1599 per Lord Reid, Lord Morris of Borth-y-Gest, Lord Guest, Lord Wilberforce and Lord Simon of Glaisdale).

I turn now to term (b). I do not consider that it is right to imply such a term.

a It is neither necessary to imply such a term for the contract of employment to function, nor is it obvious that the parties would have envisaged such a term. Indeed, one can easily conceive of cases where it would be inappropriate to put to the employee the matters the subject of the investigation which gave rise to the suspension. I have in mind cases where the employee may have been alleged to have victimised or threatened other employees, who may have gone in confidence

b to the employer to complain, or cases where information has been given to the employer by the police on a strictly confidential basis, because the employee should not be told that the police are carrying out investigations.

In any event, it seems to me that term (b) is getting close to alleging that the rules of natural justice should apply between employer and employee to the extent that the employer should not be entitled to make a decision which may

c substantially affect the employee without first informing the employee that the decision is about to be made. I do not consider it right to import the rules of natural justice, which are connected with judicial decisions and some administrative decisions, into the purely contractual relationship of employer and employee. There is no precedent for it, and indeed the argument that any such rules should

d be applied appears to me to be inconsistent with the observations in the House of Lords in the two cases to which I have referred. I have in mind particularly the reasoning of Lord Wilberforce in *Malloch v Aberdeen Corp* in the passage to which I have made reference.

Quite apart from this, it seems to me wholly unrealistic to contend that the plaintiffs were unaware of the reason for their suspension. They were suspended

e on the very day that they were charged, and they were suspended by the employee of the defendant who, as I understand it, actually collected them from the police station. If they had had any doubts about the reasons for their suspensions, I cannot but believe that they would have taken the matter up with the defendant, either through their solicitors or through their trade union. Furthermore, it seems to me that, on a fair reading, the letters of 5 November 1987, which they

f each received, informed them of the reason. In any event, I find it very hard to see what damage the plaintiffs can say they suffered from any breach of the implied term, if, contrary to my view, there was such an implied term and there was a breach of it.

I turn then to term (c). I decline to imply this term effectively for the same reason as I decline to imply term (b).

g Even if term (c) is to be implied, I am by no means satisfied that the plaintiffs were not given the opportunity to make representations within a reasonable time. For reasons which I shall develop a little more fully later in this judgment, it does not seem to me that the defendant was unreasonable in waiting until all the Calthorpe House employees had been interviewed about the incident before

h interviewing the plaintiffs.

Quite apart from this, even if there was a breach of term (c), I do not consider that the plaintiffs have established any damage as a result. It will be recalled that, when they were eventually interviewed in March 1988, they refused to say anything about the incident. On the balance of probabilities, it seems to me that, if they had been interviewed immediately after they pleaded not guilty in the

j magistrates' court in November 1987, they would have adopted exactly the same position: they had retained the same solicitors who were acting for them in March 1988, and who had advised them then to say nothing. Even if the plaintiffs had adopted a different attitude in November 1987 and given their version of what happened at the Wilmington Arms, I do not think that the defendant would have taken a different view from that which it did, namely not to lift the suspension until it had interviewed all the relevant Calthorpe House employees and had considered the effect of their evidence.

I turn then to terms (d) and (e). Bearing in mind the authorities to which I have referred, there is some apparent force in the contention that there should be no implied term that the right of suspension in cl 7 of the contract will be exercised reasonably. However, I do not think that the authorities are by any means conclusive of the issue.

The mere fact that there is no general obligation on an employer to act reasonably seems to me, in the end, not to take matters much further. One is here concerned with the proper construction of cl 7, and whether there is an implied term that the defendant will exercise its power thereunder reasonably, and not with a general principle. Equally, the fact that an employer does not have to act reasonably when exercising his express or implied right to determine a contract of employment does not seem to me to lead to the conclusion that the right to suspend in cl 7 of this contract, on its true construction, can be exercised unreasonably. Quite apart from this general point, it is worth bearing in mind that the employer/employee relationship continues during (and quite probably after) the period of suspension, whereas dismissal determines it forever.

I was referred to *White v Reflecting Roadstuds Ltd* [1991] IRLR 331. I have to say that I find it a difficult case. As in *United Bank Ltd v Akhtar* [1989] IRLR 507 the Employment Appeal Tribunal was there concerned with an employer exercising his purported right under a mobility clause in an employment contract. The judgment of the Employment Appeal Tribunal in *White v Reflecting Roadstuds Ltd*, which was given by Wood J, states, in terms, that the decision in *United Bank Ltd v Akhtar* did not decide that it was an implied term that the mobility clause would be implemented reasonably by an employer, and indeed it was said (at 335) that any such finding would have been contrary to the approach of the Court of Appeal in *Western Excavating (ECC) Ltd v Sharp* [1978] 1 All ER 713, [1978] QB 761. That is an observation upon which the defendant justifiably relies in the present case. However, Wood J went on to say that such a clause could not be implemented capriciously or if 'there were no reasonable or sufficient grounds for the view that [the employee] required to be moved' (at 335).

I have some difficulty in fully comprehending the distinction between implying a term that the exercise of a discretion should be effected reasonably, on the one hand, and, on the other hand, implying a term that the exercise of a discretion must only be on reasonable grounds. So far as there is a distinction, it seems to me that the judgment in *White v Reflecting Roadstuds Ltd* assists the plaintiffs' argument as to the implication of a term that the right to suspend under cl 7 in the instant case must only be exercised on reasonable grounds, just as much as it may be said that it assists the defendant's contention that there is no general implication of reasonableness into cl 7 (at 335).

I have come to the conclusion that the plaintiffs' argument on reasonableness is correct, at least to the extent that there is to be implied into cl 7 a term that the defendant's right to suspend will not be exercised on unreasonable grounds. (That is not precisely how terms (d) or (e) are pleaded, but I do not think anything hangs on that.)

In the first place, it appears to me significant that cl 7 entitles the defendant to suspend not only on full pay (as happened in the instant case), but on no pay. In my judgment, the fact that the defendant could suspend without pay for an indeterminate period does support the plaintiffs' contention that some sort of

reasonableness implication is appropriate. Secondly, I think the plaintiffs derive
a some support for their contention that the power to suspend should be subject to
some sort of reasonableness implication from observations of the Employment
Appeal Tribunal in *A Dakri & Co Ltd v Tiffen* [1981] ICR 256 esp at 260. The
defendant urges on me that I should prefer the approach of the Scottish
Employment Appeal Tribunal in *Kenneth MacRae & Co Ltd v Dawson* [1984]
IRLR 5, where it was held that there was no implied term in the contract there
b under consideration that any suspension would be for a reasonable period.
However, doing the best I can with that report, it appears to me that the
suspension clause in that case was quite clear in its terms, to the effect that the
suspension could be for whatever period the employer wanted. Thirdly, it seems
to me that the conclusion I have reached is consistent with the approach of the
c Employment Appeal Tribunal in *White v Reflecting Roadstuds Ltd* [1991] IRLR 331
at 335.

The defendant argues in the instant case that there is no need to imply a
reasonableness term, because the employee can always rely upon the term implied
into all contracts of employment that the employer will not act so as to render the
performance of the contract by the employee intolerable: see eg per Browne-
d Wilkinson J in *Woods v WM Car Services (Peterborough) Ltd* [1981] ICR 666 at 670.
In my judgment, there is very little difference between a provision such as cl 7
being subject to an 'intolerability implied term' and being subject to a
'reasonableness implied term'. It is also said on behalf of the defendant that by
implying any sort of reasonableness term, the court would be stepping into the
arena of the employer/employee relationship. However, in my view, in holding
e that an employer's contractual discretionary right is subject to an implied term
that it will only be exercised on reasonable grounds, the court is not putting itself
in a position where it will substitute its own judgment for that of the employer.
The court is merely holding that the employer cannot exercise his power under
the relevant contractual provision on unreasonable grounds. The band of
reasonableness may be wide, and it is only if the employer goes outside that band
f that the court can interfere.

Accordingly, in so far as terms (d) and (e) are based on reasonableness, the
plaintiffs succeed to the extent that I judge it right to imply a term that the
defendant will only exercise its right to suspend under cl 7 on reasonable grounds
and will only continue that suspension so long as there are reasonable grounds for
g doing so. However, I do not think that the plaintiffs succeed any further than this
on terms (d) and (e). In the first place, to go any wider on reasonableness would, I
think, be to fall foul of the approach of the Court of Appeal in *Western Excavating
(ECC) Ltd v Sharp*, as explained by Wood J in *White v Reflecting Roadstuds Ltd*
[1991] IRLR 331 at 335. So far as the obligation to act in accordance with the
principles of natural justice is concerned, I do not consider the plaintiffs can
h succeed. I have already rejected an application of those principles to the contractual
right to suspend so far as terms (a) and (b) are concerned, and my observations
apply to terms (d) and (e).

So far as fairness is concerned, if that involves balancing the interests of the
employer and employee, I can see no warrant for implying such an obligation on
the defendant in the exercise of its powers under cl 7. It is getting close to alleging
j an obligation to act in accordance with natural justice. In any event, it seems to
me that any obligation to act fairly runs into two further problems. First, it falls
foul of the general principles upon which terms are implied into contracts: I do
not see it as necessary or obvious that such a term be implied. Secondly, it involves

a severe risk of the court having to descend into the decision-making process and
involving itself more closely than is appropriate in the adminstrative and
organisational decisions of the defendant as employer.

However, having decided that there is an implied term upon which the
plaintiffs can rely in principle, I have reached the conclusion that the defendant
was not in breach of it. In other words, I do not consider that it can be fairly said
that the suspensions or their continuance were effected by the defendant on other
than reasonable grounds. Further, if there is an implied term that the defendant
would only exercise its power to suspend reasonably, I consider that such an
implied term was satisfied in the instant case. It is true that the suspensions were
for a substantial time, namely six months, and anyone must have sympathy with
the plaintiffs in this connection. However, I have to ask myself whether the
defendant had reasonable grounds for effecting the suspension in the first place,
and whether there were reasonable grounds for continuing it for the six-month
period. So far as the initial decision to suspend is concerned, it seems to me that it
was made on reasonable grounds. The alleged offences against the three plaintiffs
were serious; the very fact that the police had charged them with the offences
suggested that there was definite evidence that they might have been guilty. It
was certainly not unreasonable for the defendant to be concerned about the
suitability of the plaintiffs to continue working in close proximity with many
other employees at Mount Pleasant, bearing in mind the nature of the allegations
made against them. The fact that the victims were other Post Office workers, and
that the plaintiffs had been wholly or partially dressed in Post Office uniforms in
a public place at the time of the alleged offences were also factors which could
perfectly properly have been taken into account by the defendant when deciding
to suspend the plaintiffs.

So far as the length of suspension is concerned, counsel for the defendant was
clearly right to point out that one should look at events as they occurred, and not
with the wisdom of hindsight. The six-month period looks a long time in
retrospect, but that is not, in my judgment, how one should judge the length of
the suspension. The first five or six weeks' delay was due to Mr Curtis waiting to
see whether the plaintiffs pleaded guilty or not, on the basis that if they pleaded
guilty it would be unnecessary to carry out investigations. That seems to me to
be wholly justifiable. Thereafter, he very promptly initiated the first interviews.
The next three-week delay was caused by assimilating the inconclusive nature of
the evidence gathered from the first four Calthorpe House employees and
awaiting the return from leave of the two Calthorpe Houses employees
interviewed in early December. There then followed a delay of some twelve
weeks, owing to the difficulty which Mr Curtis had in finding Mr Sheddon, who
he believed to be a very important witness. Bearing in mind Mr Curtis's
understandable, indeed correct, assessment of the evidence he had obtained by
early December 1987, it was a perfectly rational opinion for him to form that
Mr Sheddon was an essential witness. Whilst the counsel of perfection, particularly
with wisdom of hindsight, might suggest that Mr Curtis could have found
Mr Sheddon earlier, it does not seem to me that the steps that he took in tracking
down Mr Sheddon justify adverse criticism. Certainly, the fact that Mr Sheddon's
evidence provided completely unhelpful is not something which Mr Curtis could
reasonably have foreseen.

In my opinion, having gathered the evidence together, Mr Curtis was clearly
justified in forming the view that, having done his best to collate all the evidence
from sources other than the plaintiffs, there was insufficient evidence to conclude
that the plaintiffs were responsible for the violence which occurred at the

Wilmington Arms. The delay which followed the interview with Mr Sheddon
a was not long, and was partially caused by the plaintiffs' solicitors writing to
Mr Curtis and explaining that they had advised the plaintiffs not to talk to the
defendant about the incident, which led Mr Curtis seeking the advice of the Post
Office solicitors. Thereafter, having interviewed the plaintiffs and obtained
assurances about their future conduct, he reinstated them.

b In my view, that was not an unreasonable course for the defendant to take. To
put it more accurately, the defendant, as it seems to me, had reasonable grounds
for continuing suspension from 7 October to 5 April. On the face of it, the point
made by counsel for the plaintiffs that nothing had really changed between the
date upon which the plaintiffs were suspended and the date upon which they
were reinstated is a good one: on both dates they stood charged with serious
c offences, and on both dates the defendant had no clear idea whether they were
guilty or not. Accordingly, it is argued on behalf of the plaintiffs, it cannot have
been reasonable for the defendant to suspend the plaintiffs initially and continue
the suspension for six months. Although initially attracted by that argument, I
have come to the clear conclusion that it should be rejected. Mr Curtis was quite
rightly embarking on an exercise which it is appropriate for an employer to
d undertake when considering whether or not to dismiss an employee who is
suspected of an offence: see the decision of the Employment Appeal Tribunal in
British Home Stores Ltd v Burchell [1980] ICR 303. He was aware that before he
could take any disciplinary action with regard to the plaintiffs, he had to be
satisfied in his own mind that they were more likely than not guilty of the
offences of which they stood charged. He carried out as thorough an investigation
e as reasonably could have been expected of him, at the end of which he was by no
means satisfied on the evidence he had got that the plaintiffs were in fact
responsible for the offences of which they stood charged. Accordingly, he decided
that the right course to take was to reinstate them and await the outcome of the
criminal proceedings.

f I am fortified in the conclusion I have reached by another point made by
counsel for the defendant. He contended that it would have been perfectly proper
for the defendant simply to suspend the plaintiffs on the date they were charged,
with a view to awaiting the outcome of the criminal proceedings. While he may
have put the point a little high, there is some force in his additional point that
that is what the plaintiffs' solicitors themselves were inviting the defendant to do
g in their letter of 19 February 1988. However, in this connection it seems to me
that the essential point is that it would have been difficult to say that the defendant
had exercised its power of suspension under cl 7 on unreasonable grounds or in
an unreasonable way if it had suspended the plaintiffs from the moment that they
were charged until their acquittal without making inquiries, on the basis that the
investigations envisaged by cl 7 were, as it were, being carried out by the Crown
h in the criminal proceedings.

Accordingly, I am of the view that the plaintiffs' claim fails on liability.

In case this matter goes further, and because I have heard full argument on the
point, I turn to the plaintiffs' claim for damages, should they have succeeded on
liability. It involves consideration of a point of principle, which I do not find
entirely easy. It is the defendant's contention that, even if the plaintiffs succeed
j on liability, they cannot succeed in damages, because, as they were suspended on
full pay, the plaintiffs' only loss arises from their inability to work overtime, and
they had no right to work overtime.

In my judgment, unless the plaintiffs can establish a right to work overtime,
and therefore to receive overtime payments, they could not succeed in recovering

any damages in this action even if they succeeded on liability. On the face of it, the decision of the Court of Appeal in *Chaplin v Hicks* [1911] 2 KB 786, [1911–13] *a* All ER Rep 224 might suggest that damages based on the loss of a chance can be awarded even if the chance is to recover a sum to which the plaintiff is not strictly entitled. However, I think that, as explained in *Lavarack v Woods of Colchester Ltd* [1966] 3 All ER 683 at 691, [1967] 1 QB 278 at 295 per Diplock LJ, the decision in *Chaplin v Hicks*, as properly analysed, does depend upon the fact that the plaintiff had a legal right to the sum which, as a result of the defendant's breach of contract, *b* she lost the prospect of obtaining. It also seems to me that the decisions of the Court of Appeal in *Lavarack v Woods of Colchester Ltd* itself and in *Gunton v Richmond upon Thames London Borough* [1980] 3 All ER 577, [1981] Ch 448 are consistent with this view.

In those circumstances, can the plaintiffs establish a right, as opposed to an obligation, to work overtime? I have already referred to cl 3 of the plaintiffs' *c* contract, which refers to an obligation, and does not refer to a right on the employee to work overtime. Accordingly, in order to succeed on damages, the plaintiffs have to rely on an implied term, and it is in this connection that term (a) comes into focus. In the absence of authority, I would find it difficult to imply a term that the plaintiffs had a right to work overtime. *d*

Having said that, the plaintiffs' contention on this aspect does receive a degree of assistance from authority. Counsel for the plaintiffs cited *Devonald v Rosser & Sons* [1906] 2 KB 728, [1904–7] All ER Rep 988, but I think that case is fairly easily distinguishable, on the basis that the employee was entitled to be paid only in respect of work actually done; given that he had to make himself available for the employer full time, if the employer required it, it is easy to understand how *e* the court was prepared to imply an obligation on the employer to provide work. A case of more assistance on this point to the plaintiffs is *Bauman v Hulton Press Ltd* [1952] 2 All ER 1121. There, the plaintiff was to receive a fixed sum and also a payment in respect of specific items of work done for the defendant. Streatfeild J held that there was an implied obligation to provide that plaintiff with work. I think that case is distinguishable from the instant case, principally for three *f* reasons. First, it does appear that the fixed rate of pay received by the plaintiff was a much lower proportion of the total receipts he can reasonably have expected from commissions. In other words, the fixed rate of pay was little more than a retainer. Secondly, the case appears to have turned essentially on the juridical nature of the relationship between the plaintiff and the defendant rather than what the implied rights and obligations of the parties were once the nature of the *g* relationship had been established (at 1122). Thirdly, the terms of the contract between the parties were very different from the terms in the instant case (at 1122). Accordingly, I do not think that that case can be decisive of the issue in the instant case.

The third, and perhaps the most formidable, authority cited on behalf of the *h* plaintiffs on this aspect is the decision in *Langston v Amalgamated Union of Engineering Workers* [1974] 1 All ER 980, [1974] 1 WLR 185. In the first round of this case it seems to me that the furthest one can go is to say that the Court of Appeal held that, on the facts of the case, it was arguable that it was a breach of contract for the employer to suspend the employee on full pay, because he was obliged to provide the employee with work. However, when the matter was sent *j* back to the National Industrial Relations Court (see *Langston v Amalgamated Union of Engineering Workers (No 2)* [1974] ICR 510), it seems to me that part of the ratio is, on the face of it, of considerable assistance to the plaintiffs in the instant case; and the observations of the court do support the proposition that, because of the

fact that he would thereby earn overtime, the plaintiff did have an implied right
a to be provided with work, and in particular with overtime, by the employer (see
esp at 522 per Sir John Donaldson P).

In light of that decision, it is with some diffidence that I have reached the
conclusion that, even if they had succeeded on liability, the plaintiffs would
nonetheless have failed to establish any claim to damages. In seeking to establish
terms (b) to (e), counsel for the plaintiffs quite rightly emphasised that one should
b be careful of having too much regard to previous instance where the court had
implied terms or declined to imply terms, on the basis that each contract must be
construed in light of its own particular provisions. It seems to me that that must
apply to term (a) as well. None of the reports of the decisions at the various stages
in *Langston's* case indicate what the terms of the contract in that case were. Nor
c do any of the reports indicate whether the employee in that case had been
employed by the employer and provided with overtime by him prior to entering
into the contract of employment which was being considered.

In the instant case, I have to construe the particular contract of employment
which the parties have signed. I think there are a number of reasons to support
the contention that there is no implied provision to the effect of term (a). First,
d the contact specifically deals with overtime in cl 3, and imposes an obligation on
the employee to work overtime if the employer requires it, but signally omits
any concomitant obligation on the employer to provide overtime work on any
basis whatever to the employee. Secondly, it does not provide for the employee
to work at any particular place, and indeed provides that the employee may be
required to work somewhere other than the initial place of employment. The
e parties must have appreciated that different amounts of overtime might be
available at different places, and I think this provision is more consistent with the
defendant's contention that there is no obligation to provide overtime. Thirdly,
the nature of the plaintiffs' case on term (a) effectively involves an implied
obligation on the defendant to act fairly or equitably between the various
employees in apportioning overtime. I have already indicated that I consider that
f the court should be slow to imply an obligation on an employer to act fairly or in
accordance with the rules of natural justice in carrying out a discretionary power
under a contract of employment. Fourthly, there is no suggestion that the
plaintiffs had been employed by the defendant prior to 1984, so it cannot be
suggested on behalf of the plaintiffs that there was some sort of course of dealing
g prior to the contract which would have given rise to the argument that both
parties were aware that overtime at Mount Pleasant was allocated by the defendant
between employees on an equitable basis in practice (as I understand has remained
the case at all times since before 1984). Fifthly, cl 2 of the contract provides what
the plaintiff is entitled to by way of pay, and it seems to me that to accede to the
plaintiffs' case on this issue would not merely be adding an implied employer's
h obligation in respect of overtime to an express employee's obligation in respect of
overtime in cl 3, but it would also be adding an implied obligation on the
employer to make payments to the employee to an express obligation in cl 2 of
the contract so far as basic pay is concerned. Sixthly, it seems to me that a
provision such as term (a) is neither necessary nor obvious.

In these circumstances, I must dismiss the claims of all three plaintiffs.

j

Action dismissed.

Hazel Hartman   Barrister.

Re Hartlebury Printers Ltd (in liq) and others   *a*

CHANCERY DIVISION

MORRITT J

13, 16, 20 MARCH 1992

Redundancy – Employer's duty to consult appropriate trade union – Employer 'proposing *b*
to dismiss [employees] as redundant' – Proposing – Consultation with union required to
take place 'at the earliest opportunity' – Company – Winding-up order – All employees
automatically made redundant without union consultation when company wound up by
court – Whether administrators under duty to consult union before making application to
court which resulted in winding up – Whether administrators 'proposing to dismiss
[employees] as redundant' – Whether administration order a 'special circumstance' *c*
relieving corporate employer from duty to consult union on proposed redundancies –
Employment Protection Act 1975, ss 99, 100, 101 – Insolvency Act 1986, s 130 –
Council Directive (EEC) 75/129.

Between January 1989 and April 1990 the defendant company suffered trading
losses in excess of £15m and it became apparent to the directors that without *d*
fundamental reorganisation the business would cease to be viable by the end of
May 1990. The company accordingly entered into negotiations with a prospective
purchaser in an attempt to secure its long-term future but was advised to seek an
administration order to protect it from creditors during the period of the
negotiations. Accordingly, on 31 May 1990 an administration order was made in *e*
respect of the company and administrators were appointed. The viability of the
administration depended, inter alia, on the company maintaining its orders from
customers. Prior to the commencement of the administration the directors
considered mitigating the costs of the administration by reducing manning but
that was judged inappropriate given the need to maintain a viable operation.
Subsequently it became apparent that the conditions for the viability of the *f*
administration were not being met because of lost orders. On 25 June the
prospective purchaser of the company indicated that its new business structure
would involve the dismissal of some employees. The employee's union was
informed of that fact by the administrators and on 29 June it approved 28
proposed redundancies. However, as a result of the failure to arrange further
funding for the administration, the administrators applied to the court for *g*
directions recommending that the administration continue for the time being in
the hope that the company could be rescued. The application was heard on 3 July,
when the judge directed that the company be compulsorily wound up. The effect
of the winding-up order was to make all 136 employees redundant. The union
applied to an industrial tribunal for a protective award under s 101[a] of the *h*
Employment Protection Act 1975 and applied to the court for leave under
s 130(2)[b] of the Insolvency Act 1986 to commence and/or pursue those proceedings.
The union contended that for the purposes of ss 99[c] and 100[d] of the 1975 Act the
company was 'an employer proposing to dismiss as redundant' the company's
employees when the administration order was applied for or that the

 j

---

a   Section 101, so far as material, is set out at p 474 *c* to *f*, post
b   Section 130(2), so far as material, provides: 'When a winding-up order has been made . . . no action
     or proceedings shall be proceeded with or commenced against the company . . . except by leave of
     the court . . .'
c   Section 99, so far as material, is set out at p 473 *b* to *g*, post
d   Section 100, so far as material, is set out at p 473 *j* to p 474 *b*, post

administrators were likewise 'proposing to dismiss as redundant' the company's
a employees when the winding-up order was made and that in both cases there had
been a failure to consult 'from the earliest opportunity' as required by s 99(3) of
that Act. The union further contended that, construing ss 99 and 100 of the 1975
Act in accordance with Council Directive (EEC) 75/129[e], which envisaged that
the duty to consult arose when an employer was 'contemplating' redundancies,
the administrators must have contemplated when they decided to apply to the
b court for directions that the discharge of the administration order and the winding
up of the company would result in the redundancies. The administrators
contended, inter alia, that, where a company was in administration, that in itself
was a 'special circumstance' within s 99(8) of the 1975 Act exempting them from
the consultation requirements in s 99(3) and that the proposal for the winding up
was made by the administrators not as agents for the company but as officers of
c the court.

Held – (1) On the true construction of ss 99 and 100 of the 1975 Act an employer
'proposing to dismiss [employees] as redundant' did not include an employer who
was merely thinking about the possibility of redundancies since 'contemplating'
d in Council Directive (EEC) 75/129 was to be equated with 'proposing' and an
employer who was merely thinking about the possibility of redundancies could
not be said to be 'proposing to dismiss as redundant' any employees. Accordingly,
the fact that the administrators recognised the possibility of redundancies if the
court did not accept their suggestion that the administration should continue but
instead wound up the company was not sufficient to give rise to an obligation to
e consult. It followed that there was no prima facie breach of duty (see p 478 *d* to *f*,
post).

(2) An administration order was not in itself a 'special circumstance' within
s 99(8) of the 1975 Act thereby relieving a company employer from the duty to
consult the appropriate trade union on proposed redundancies. Whether a
f company in administration was relieved from that requirement depended on the
circumstances of the case when considered in the light of the duties and
responsibilities of the administrator, and a combination of those circumstances
together with the existence of an administration order might give rise to special
circumstances within s 99(8) when neither would when taken in isolation. On
the facts, however, since the company when in administration had not proposed
g to dismiss as redundant all its employees, the questions of whether there were
special circumstances and whether there were any reasonably practicable steps
open to the administrators did not arise. The union's application would therefore
be dismissed (see p 480 *a* to *g*, post); *Clarks of Hove Ltd v Bakers' Union* [1979] 1 All
ER 152 considered.

h **Notes**
For the effect of a winding-up order, see 7(2) *Halsbury's Laws* (4th edn reissue) para
1489.

For an employer's duty to consult trade unions about proposed redundancies,
see 16 *Halsbury's Laws* (4th edn reissue) para 381, and for cases on the subject, see
20 *Digest* (reissue) 446–448, 3674–3680.
j For the Employment Protection Act 1975, ss 99, 100, 101, see 16 *Halsbury's
Statutes* (4th edn) (1990 reissue) 180, 182, 183.

For the Insolvency Act 1986, s 130, see 4 *Halsbury's Statutes* (4th edn) (1987
reissue) 811.

---

e Council Directive (EEC) 75/129, so far as material, is set out at p 477 *h* to p 478 *a*, post

Cases referred to in judgment

Atlantic Computer Systems plc, Re [1990] BCLC 729; *rvsd in part* [1992] 1 All ER a
476, [1992] Ch 505, CA.
Capita Finance Group Ltd v Rothwells Ltd (1989) 15 ACLR 348, NSW SC.
Clarks of Hove Ltd v Bakers' Union [1979] 1 All ER 152, [1978] 1 WLR 1207, CA.

Cases also cited

Association of Patternmakers and Allied Craftsman v Kirvin Ltd [1978] IRLR 318, b
EAT.
Barrow Borough Transport Ltd, Re [1990] Ch 227.
Bristol Airport plc v Powdrill [1990] 2 All ER 493, [1990] Ch 744, CA.
Charnley Davies Ltd, Re (No 2) [1990] BCLC 760.
Currie v Consolidated Kent Collieries Corp Ltd [1906] 1 KB 134, CA.   c
Francovich v Italy Joined cases C-6/90 and C-9/90 [1992] IRLR 84, CJEC.
Hamish Armour v Association of Scientific Technical and Managerial Staffs [1979] IRLR
24, EAT.
Marleasing SA v Comercial Internacional de Alimentación SA Case C-106/89 [1990]
ECR I-4135.
Sovereign Distribution Services Ltd v Transport and General Worker' Union [1990] ICR d
31, EAT.
Spiller-French (Holdings) Ltd v Union of Shop Distributive and Allied Workers [1980] 1
All ER 231, EAT.
Union of Shop Distributive and Allied Works v Leancut Bacon Ltd (in liq) [1981] IRLR
295, EAT.
e

Summons

By summonses dated 8 January 1991 addressed to Ian Napier Carruthers and
David Robert Wilton of Messrs Cork Gully, the joint liquidators of Hartlebury
Printers Ltd, Hartlebury Reprographics Ltd and Optoscan Ltd, the applicant, the
Graphical Paper and Media Union, applied pursuant to s 130(2) of the Insolvency f
Act 1986 for an order that the union be at liberty to commence and/or continue
proceedings against each of the respondent companies before an industrial
tribunal in relation to complaints made to the tribunal by the National Graphical
Association (1982) and the West Midlands Graphical Society for a declaration and
protective award pursuant to s 10 of the Employment Protective Act 1975 in
relation to the companies' alleged breaches of s 99 of that Act. The facts are set g
out in the judgment.

Ingrid Simler (instructed by *Kershaws*) for the applicant.
Mark Phillips (instructed by *Wragge & Co*, Birmingham) for the liquidators.

h
Cur adv vult

20 March 1992. The following judgment was delivered.

MORRITT J. By these three summonses the Graphical Paper and Media Union
seeks leave pursuant to s 130(2) of the Insolvency Act 1986 to commence and/or j
continue proceedings against Hartlebury Printers Ltd, Hartlebury Reprographics
Ltd and Optoscan Ltd, each of which was compulsorily wound up on 3 July 1990.
On 14 September 1990 the union applied to an industrial tribunal for a declaration
and protective award pursuant to s 101 of the Employment Protection Act 1975

on the ground that each of the three companies had dismissed all its respective
a employees as redundant without complying with its duty to consult the union as
imposed by s 99 of the 1975 Act. Those are the proceedings which the union
wishes to continue or, if necessary, to commence.

The relevant provisions of s 99 are as follows:

b
'(1) An employer proposing to dismiss as redundant an employee of a
description in respect of which an independent trade union is recognised by
him shall consult representatives of that trade union about the dismissal in
accordance with the following provisions of this section . . .

(3) The consultation required by this section shall begin at the earliest
opportunity, and shall in any event begin—(a) where the employer is
proposing to dismiss as redundant 100 or more employees at one establishment
c within a period of 90 days or less, at least 90 days before the first of those
dismissals takes effect; or (b) where the employer is proposing to dismiss as
redundant 10 or more employees at one establishment within a period of 30
days or less, at least 30 days before the first of those dismissals takes effect . . .

(5) For the purposes of the consultation required by this section the
employer shall disclose in writing to trade union representatives—(a) the
d reasons for his proposals; (b) the numbers and descriptions of employees
whom it is proposed to dismiss as redundant; (c) the total number of
employees of any such description employed by the employer at the
establishment in question; (d) the proposed method of selecting the
employees who may be dismissed; and (e) the proposed method of carrying
e out the dismissals, with due regard to any agreed procedure, including the
period over which the dismissals are to take effect . . .

(7) In the course of the consultation required by this section the employer
shall—(a) consider any representations made by the trade union representatives; and (b) reply to those representations and, if he rejects any of those
representations, state his reasons.

f (8) If in any case there are special circumstances which render it not
reasonably practicable for the employer to comply with any of the
requirements of subsections (3), (5) or (7) above, the employer shall take all
such steps towards compliance with that requirement as are reasonably
practicable in those circumstances.

(9) This section shall not be construed as conferring any rights on a trade
g union or an employee except as provided by sections 101 to 103 below.'

Section 126(1) incorporates the definition of 'employer' contained in s 30(1)
Trade Union and Labour Relations Act 1974 which, so far as relevant, provides:

'"employer" . . . (a) where the reference is to an employer in relation to an
h employee means the person by whom the employee is (or in a case where the
employment has ceased, was) employed and (b) in any other case means a
person regarded in that person's capacity as one for whom one or more
workers work or have worked or normally work or seek to work . . .'

Section 100 of the 1975 Act provides:

j '(1) An employer proposing to dismiss as redundant—(a) 100 or more
employees at one establishment within a period of 90 days or less; or (b) 10
or more employees at one establishment within a period of 30 days or less,
shall notify the Secretary of State, in writing, of his proposal—(i) in a case
falling within paragraph (a) above, at least 90 days before the first of those

dismissals takes effect; and (ii) in a case falling within paragraph (b) above, at least 30 days before the first of those dismissals takes effect, and where the notice relates to employees of any description in respect of which an independent trade union is recognised by him, he shall give a copy of the notice to representatives of that union . . .

(6) If in any case there are special circumstances rendering it not reasonably practicable for the employer to comply with any of the requirements of subsections (1) to (5) above, he shall take all such steps towards compliance with that requirement as are reasonably practicable in those circumstances.'

Section 105(1) renders an employer who fails to comply with s 100 liable to a fine.

Section 101, so far as relevant, provides:

'(1) An appropriate trade union may present a complaint to an industrial tribunal on the ground that an employer has dismissed as redundant or is proposing to dismiss as redundant one or more employees and has not complied with any of the requirements of section 99 above.

(2) If on a complaint under this section a question arises as to the matters referred to in section 99(8) above, it shall be for the employer to show— (a) that there were special circumstances which rendered it not reasonably practicable for him to comply with any requirement of section 99 above; and (b) that he took all such steps towards compliance with that requirement as were reasonably practicable in those circumstances.

(3) Where the tribunal finds a complaint under subsection (1) above well-founded it shall make a declaration to that effect and may also make a protective award in accordance with subsection (4) below.

(4) A protective award is an award that in respect of such descriptions of employees as may be specified in the award, being employees who have been dismissed, or whom it is proposed to dismiss, as redundant, and in respect of whose dismissal or proposed dismissal the employer has failed to comply with any requirement of section 99 above, the employer shall pay remuneration for a protected period . . .'

The amount of any such award is dealt with in s 101(5) and payment thereof may be enforced by an employee pursuant to s 103 by a complaint to an industrial tribunal. If the employer is insolvent the employee is entitled to recover the amount due to him from the redundancy fund and the Secretary of State is subrogated to the employee's rights against the employer (see ss 122 and 125 of the Employment Protection (Consolidation) Act 1978).

The three companies in question formed part of the Hartlebury Group. There is no relevant factual distinction between them and I shall refer to each of them as 'the company'. The group carried on business as printers. Between January 1989 and April 1990 it sustained trading losses in excess of £15m and had lost one of its major customers. The position by mid-April 1990 was that it was evident to the directors that without a fundamental reorganisation of the group's debt structure the business was not viable and the group would founder by the end of May 1990 through distress proceedings threatened by its landlord. At this stage any operational changes in manning levels or methods of working would not have affected the group's ability to pay its debts and any associated cost savings would not have been sufficient to avoid the substantial loss caused principally through the interest charges on the group's burgeoning level of debt.

The directors were negotiating with two prospective purchasers, one of which

was Times Publishing of Singapore. On 11 May 1990 the group approached
a Messrs Cork Gully for advice. By a report dated 31 May Cork Gully advised the
directors to seek an administration order 'to provide the protection from creditors
needed to allow time for an agreement to be concluded with a third party which
would ensure the survival of the business'. On the same day Vinelott J made an
administration order in respect of the company for the purposes prescribed by
s 8(3)(*a*), (*c*) and (*d*) of the Insolvency Act 1986, namely survival of the company,
b or the whole or part of its undertaking as a going concern, a voluntary
arrangement and the more advantageous realisation of its assets. At about the
same time Times Publishing provided a letter of intent to acquire the group's
business which envisaged that six to eight weeks would be required to complete
the negotiations. Three factors were fundamental to the success of the negotiations,
namely acceptance by unsecured creditors of a voluntary arrangement that would
c substantially reduce the group's immediate burden of debt, that the leasing
company should accept a substantial write-off of the capital element of the lease
liability and hence corresponding reduction in lease payments, and that the
landlord should accept revisions to the terms of the tenancy agreement for the
Hartlebury premises and in doing so forgo any increase at the next rent review in
d September 1990.

The viability of the administration depended on the company maintaining its
orders and being under no liability to make payments to the lessors for the
printing equipment as part of the costs of the administration. In addition, the
administrators obtained an indemnity for £250,000 from Schroeder Ventures
Ltd to cover the costs of the administration and thought that the group had
e £500,000-worth of assets subject to floating charges which, by virtue of s 19(4) of
the 1986 Act, would be available to pay the expenses of the administration.

Immediately prior to the commencement of the administration consideration
was given to mitigating the costs of the administration by reducing manning.
After a detailed review, this was judged to be inappropriate because it would have
had no significant effect on the trading losses and because there was limited scope
f for reduced manning if a viable operation was to be retained. In addition, it could
have restricted the options available to Times Publishing and the costs of the
redundancy settlements would have exceeded the anticipated savings under the
period of the negotiations.

On 1 June 1990 at meetings of the company's employees the administrators
g explained the reasons for and implications of the administration order. On
14 June, at further meetings of the company's employees the administrators
advised them that trading had progressed as expected and that representatives of
Times Publishing would be visiting the following week. Each employee was
given a letter making it plain that they continued to be employed by the company
and that the administrators had not adopted their contracts of employment. On
h 20 June the administrators explained to a representative of the union the objects
of the administration, but by the end of the third week of the administration,
namely 20 June, it was apparent that the conditions for the viability of the
administration were not being met. First, a number of customers cancelled their
orders. Second, it was discovered that the value of the assets of the group, subject
to floating charges, was only £100,000. Third, the judgment of Ferris J in *Re*
j *Atlantic Computer Systems plc* [1990] BCLC 729 suggested that leasing charges
would be payable as expenses of the administration. By the week commencing
25 June 1990 expenditure was exceeding income at the rate of £200,000 per
week. The indemnity cover from Schroeder Ventures Ltd, which had been
increased to £350,000, would be exhausted by 1 July.

On 25 June Times Publishing gave the first indication that the structure of the business it was interested in acquiring would involve dismissing some of the employees. The union was so informed and on 27 June one of the administrators met a representative of the union to advise him of the terms proposed by Times Publishing which would involve 28 redundancies in the group. The proposals and redundancies were approved by the union on 29 June.

On 27 June the administrators wrote to Schroeder Ventures Ltd setting out the financial situation in the administration and stating that unless arrangements for further funding were concluded by 9 am, Friday 29 June, the administrators would have to apply to the court for directions. No such arrangements were made.

On 2 July Mr Carruthers, one of the administrators, swore an affidavit setting out the history of the administration. In paras 24, 25 and 26 he stated:

'24. Based on progress to date I believe that the opportunity still remains for the purposes laid down in section 8(3)(a), (b) and (d) of the Act to be achieved. The principal difference between the present position in the administration and that envisaged at the time the administration petitions were presented is that the cushion provided by floating charge assets to meet any unexpected deterioration in the group's position is almost non-existent. Had this position been known at the time the petitions were presented it is unlikely that I would have recommended the appointment of administrators.

25. In summary, achievements to date include (i) progress made in the negotiations with Times Publishing (ii) constructive discussions with creditors and leasing companies, and (iii) the financial support already provided by Schroeders and the indication which they have given that further support will be provided.

26. The administrators are concerned that the insufficiency of floating charge assets leaves little scope for unforeseen circumstances to be dealt with. Nevertheless it is our view that the administration should be allowed to continue at least for the time being in the hope that the purposes for which the orders were made might be achieved.'

The application came before Scott J on 3 July. The order he made directed the administrators to present a petition for the winding up of the company and dispensed with its advertisement. Scott J ordered that upon presentation of the petition the administration order should be discharged, the administrators be released, the company be wound up and the administrators be appointed liquidators of the company. The effect of the winding-up order was to discharge all the company's employees. In respect of the respective companies there were 48, 47 and 41 employees.

In the complaint to the industrial tribual Mr Lowe, the union's representative, states:

'I contend that there has been a failure to consult in accordance with statutory provisions and claim a protective award. [Subsequently, after setting out some of the facts to which I have referred, he continued:] I contend that (a) previously agreed redundancies could have been imple-mented to rationalise the Company, (b) there was time to consult and discuss and possibly agree further redundancy measures to maintain a going concern, (c) discussions with the third party were still progressing, eventually a third party did purchase part of the assets of Hartlebury Group establishing a new trading company, (d) we had been led to believe that the approval of revised a terms and conditions along with redundancies would secure the ongoing business.'

It is common ground that, given the numbers of the company's employees made redundant by the winding-up order the minimum period of consultation required was at least 30 days before the first of the dismissals took effect: see s 99(3)(b) of the 1975 Act. But the union contends that that subsection requires
b consultation to begin at the earliest opportunity. The case for the union is that prior to the administration order the directors must have contemplated or seriously considered the possibility of redundancies but did not then make any attempt to consult the union. The union does not suggest that there was any failure to consult with regard to the proposals to make 28 employees redundant because those proposals were not implemented, but the union does contend that
c when the administrators decided to apply to the court they must then have contemplated the redundancies which resulted from the discharge of the administration order and the winding up of the company.

The administrators dispute both these contentions. They contend that at neither stage did the company propose to dismiss any of its employees as redundant. They claim that the powers and duties imposed on them by Pt II of
d the 1986 Act necessarily excludes s 99 of the 1975 Act. They claim that an administration order in relation to an employer is always a 'special circumstance' within s 99(8) of the 1975 Act and that there were no steps towards compliance which in the circumstances were reasonably practicable.

The claims of the union and any derivative rights of the employees are only
e justiciable before the industrial tribunal. Thus this is not a case where the rights sought to be enforced can be determined in the liquidation. In those circumstances I should grant leave if I am satisfied that the claim the union wishes to advance has some prima facie merit and prospect of success. As Rogers CJ Comm D said in *Capita Finance Group Ltd v Rothwells Ltd* (1989) 15 ACLR 348 at 349 in relation to a provision of the Companies (New South Wales) Code 1981 in identical terms
f to s 130(2) of the Insolvency Act 1986:

> 'It is necessary to understand the rationale which buttresses the requirement for showing the existence of a prima facie case. The provisional liquidators and liquidator respectively are entitled to be protected from involvement in court proceedings which may be perhaps only of a nuisance nature or which
> g may be thought to be totally devoid of any substance. The resources of the company in liquidation should not be frittered away in defending baseless claims.'

The first point to consider is when, in accordance with s 99 of the 1975 Act, the duty to consult arises. Part IV of the Act was enacted to comply with the Council
h Directive (EEC) 75/129. Article 2(1) provides:

> 'Where an employer is contemplating collective redundancies, he shall begin consultations with the workers' respresentatives with a view to reaching an agreement.'

Article 3(1) corresponds with s 100 of the 1975 Act and provides:

j
> 'Employers shall notify the competent public authority in writing of any projected collective redundancies. This notification shall contain all relevant information concerning the projected collective redundancies and the consultations with workers' representatives provided for in Article 2, and particularly the reasons for the redundancies, the number of workers to be

made redundant, the number of workers normally employed and the period over which the redundancies are to be effected.'

Thus the directive distinguishes between redundancies which are contemplated and those which are projected. Sections 99 and 100 of the 1975 Act apply to 'an employer proposing to dismiss as redundant'.

The union contends that both those sections should be construed to give effect to the directive so that the duty under s 99 arises when an employer has redundancies in contemplation. That it is the duty of the court, if possible, to construe United Kingdom legislation so as to comply with the United Kingdom's obligations under an EEC directive is not in doubt. But that must be achieved, if at all, by proper processes of construction, not so far as the court is concerned by the equivalent of legislation.

Dealing first with the directive, it seems to me that the word 'projected' in art 3 is used in the sense of 'then intended' after the processes of consultation with the union have been completed. Thus the contemplation referred to in art 2(1) is something less than intention. Nevertheless, the range of mental states included within the word is wide. It would extend from merely 'thinking about' to 'having in view or expecting'. In the latter sense, but not the former, the word would equate with the verb 'to propose'.

Approaching that problem from the wording of s 99 I think it is clear, not least from sub-s (5), that the phrase 'an employer proposing to dismiss as redundant' cannot include one who is merely thinking about the possibility of redundancies. Thus I cannot construe the word 'proposing' to embrace the full range of possible meanings of the word 'contemplating' but I can construe 'contemplating' in a sense equivalent to 'proposing'. Article 2(1) of the directive has not, so far as I know, been construed by the Court of Justice of the European Communities. Thus, I assume, because it is for the Court of Justice and not for me to decide, that s 99 does comply with the United Kingdom's obligations.

As the union accepts, the onus is on them to establish a prima facie breach of duty. There is no evidence before me and no allegation of fact in the complaint to suggest that prior to the making of the administration order the company was proposing to dismiss as redundant any employee. In those circumstances I do not give leave in respect of that part of the union's case.

The administrators, as responsible insolvency practitioners, are greatly concerned at the suggestion that the duty imposed on the employer by ss 99 and 100 of the 1975 Act must be observed by them given their status, functions and responsibilities under Pt II of the 1986 Act. An administrator is an officer of the court. He has the powers conferred by Sch 1, which include the power to dismiss the company's employees. In exercising his powers he is deemed to act as the company's agent: see s 14(1) and (5). By s 17 he is required to manage the affairs of the company in accordance with the directions of the court or, where his proposals have been approved by the creditors, in accordance with those proposals. Section 18 requires him to apply to the court for the discharge of the administration order if he considers that the purposes for which it was made cannot be achieved, or if the creditors require him to do so. He may pay the remuneration of the company's employees out of assets subject to a floating charge but such remuneration is not charged on those assets unless the contract of employment was adopted by him (see s 19(4) and (5)). If the company is subsequently wound up remuneration, within prescribed limits, due at the date of the administration order ranks as a preferential debt but remuneration earned during the period of the administration, though provable, is not preferential: see s 387(3)(a) of the 1986 Act.

It is accepted that the company is the employer, but it is submitted that the
a proposal is that of the administrators not as agents for the company but as officers
of the court. It is contended that the duty imposed by s 99 of the 1975 Act on the
company and the duties imposed on the administrators by the 1986 Act are so
mutually repugnant that they cannot exist side by side. If the duty imposed by
s 99 was absolute and the administrators were bound to adopt the suggestions of
the union then there would be much more force in this submission. But the
b provisions of s 99(7) and (8) show that the duty is not absolute and that the
administrators may, for stated reasons, and after proper consideration, reject the
union's views. If, in exercise of his statutory powers the administrator dismisses
an employee he does so as agent for the company. The administrators contend
that such agency only arises on the exercise of the power. But the exercise of the
power must include the necessary preliminaries to its exercise. If administrators
c propose to dismiss an employee it seems to me that their proposal must be the
proposal of the company and therefore of the employer.

I cannot construe either the 1986 Act or the 1975 Act to reach the conclusion
the administrators seek. Nor do I see any justification for a strained construction
which I was invited to adopt, given the provisions of s 99(7) and (8). In the last
d resort I was invited to conclude that the 1986 Act impliedly repealed or amended
s 99 of the 1975 Act so as to exclude an employer which is a company in
administration. This seems to me to be wholly unjustified. Not only is it not
necessary because of s 99(7) and (8) but it would be quite inconsistent with the
principle that if possible United Kingdom legislation should be construed so as to
conform with the obligations of the United Kingdom. It is true that art 1(2)(*d*) of
e Council Directive (EEC) 75/129 excludes workers affected by the termination of
an establishment's activities where that is the result of a judicial decision, but this
cannot exclude any company in administration. Thus the implied repeal for
which the administrators contend would give rise to a breach of the United
Kingdom's obligations. Accordingly, in my judgment, 'an employer proposing
to dismiss as redundant' does include cases where the employer is a company in
f administration and the administrator proposes the dismissals.

The administrators then contended that if a company employer is in
administration that per se is a special circumstance within s 99(8). A similar point
arose in *Clarks of Hove Ltd v Bakers' Union* [1979] 1 All ER 152, [1978] 1 WLR
1207. In that case the company dismissed all its employees and called in a receiver
on the same day. The industrial tribunal considered that insolvency did not
g constitute special circumstances. Appeals to the Employment Appeal Tribunal
and the Court of Appeal were in each case allowed. In the Court of Appeal
Geoffrey Lane LJ, in reference to the decision of the industrial tribunal, said
([1979] 1 All ER 152 at 159, [1978] 1 WLR 1207 at 1215):

> *h* 'What they said, in effect, was this, that insolvency is, on its own, neither
> here nor there. It may be a special circumstance, it may not be a special
> circumstance. It will depend entirely on the cause of the insolvency whether
> the circumstances can be described as special or not. If, for example, sudden
> disaster strikes a company, making it necessary to close the concern, then
> plainly that would be a matter which was capable of being a special
> circumstance; and that is so whether the disaster is physical or financial. If
> *j* the insolvency, however, was merely due to a gradual run-down of the
> company, as it was in this case, then those are facts on which the industrial
> tribunal can come to the conclusion that the circumstances were not special.
> In other words, to be special the event must be something out of the ordinary,
> something uncommon; and that is the meaning of the word "special" in the
> context of this Act.'

Thus the circumstances must be special in the sense of being out of the ordinary. Moreover, as s 99(8) makes plain, they must be such as to render it not reasonably practicable for the employer to comply with any of the requirements of sub-s (3), (5) or (7).

In my judgment it is plain that an administration order does not per se render it impracticable for the company employer to comply with those requirements. It may or may not, depending on the other circumstances of the case. Those circumstances would have to be considered in the light of the duties and responsibilities of the administrator. A combination of those circumstances and the existence of an administration order may well give rise to special circumstances within s 99(8) when neither would when taken in isolation. Thus I do not accept any of the submissions of the administrators which seek to put a company in administration in a different position to any other employer. But the questions remain whether the company in administration ever did propose to dismiss as redundant all its employees; if it did, whether the circumstances were special; and, if they were, whether there were any steps towards compliance with the requirements of s 99 which were reasonably practicable in the circumstances. I have already quoted the relevant paragraphs from the affidavit of the administrators in support of the application to Scott J on 3 July. In my judgment, para 26 shows quite clearly that the administrators were not proposing the redundancies that resulted from the winding up of the company. Their proposal was indeed the exact opposite. The redundancies occurred because of the decision of the court. They did not stem from any proposal of the administrators. The union does not challenge the honesty of the deponent but they contend that I should give leave so that in the industrial tribunal they may cross-examine the administrator as to his real state of mind. But in my judgment this will not do. The affidavit is accepted as truthful. It did not contain proposals for redundancy. The fact, if it be one, that the administrators recognised the possibility of redundancies if the court did not accept their suggestion that the administration should continue but wound up the company is not, in my judgment, sufficient to give rise to an obligation to consult. Thus, in my judgment, the questions of whether there were special circumstances and whether there were any reasonably practicable steps open to the administrators do not arise.

In all these circumstances I do not think that the proceedings the union wishes to pursue in the industrial tribunal have any legal merit and I dismiss this application.

Application dismissed.

Hazel Hartman   Barrister.

a   Stoke-on-Trent City Council and another v B & Q plc

(Case C-169/91)

COURT OF JUSTICE OF THE EUROPEAN COMMUNITIES

b   JUDGES DUE (PRESIDENT), KAKOURIS, RODRÍGUEZ IGLESIAS, MURRAY (PRESIDENTS OF CHAMBERS), MANCINI, JOLIET, DÍEZ DE VELASCO, KAPTEYN AND EDWARD
ADVOCATE GENERAL VAN GERVEN
2 JUNE, 8 JULY, 16 DECEMBER 1992

European Economic Community – Imports – Reduction in volume of imports – Quantitative
c   *restriction on imports from another member state – Measures having equivalent effect – Prohibition on Sunday trading – Opening of do-it-yourself store on Sundays – Substantial proportion of goods sold in store imported from other member states – Prohibition affecting sale of domestic and imported products – Prohibition on Sunday trading having effect of reducing imports from other member states – Whether prohibition proportionate to objective of statute – Whether restriction according with national or regional socio-*
d   *cultural characteristics – Whether prohibition contravening Community law – Shops Act 1950, s 47 – EEC Treaty, art 30.*

The appellant regularly traded at its do-it-yourself stores and garden centres in the United Kingdom on Sundays in the respondent councils' areas selling items which were not exempted from the prohibition on Sunday trading contained in s 47[a] of
e   and Sch 5 to the Shops Act 1947. A proportion of the goods sold were imported from member states of the European Economic Community (the EEC). The appellant lost 23% of its turnover when its stores were closed on Sundays and the Sunday trading restrictions also affected trade between the United Kingdom and the rest of the EEC generally. The respondent councils sought injunctions to
f   restrain the appellant from opening its stores on Sundays in contravention of the 1947 Act. The appellant contended that s 47 was unenforceable because by preventing it from selling on Sunday goods imported from other member states s 47 infringed art 30[b] of the EEC Treaty, which prohibited quantitative restrictions on imports between member states and all measures having equivalent effect, and that the restriction on Sunday trading contained in s 47 was contrary to
g   Community law because it was disproportionate to the object of ensuring that working and non-working hours were so arranged as to accord with national or regional socio-cultural characteristics. The judge held that s 47 did not infringe art 30 of the EEC Treaty and that the councils were entitled to the injunctions sought. The appellant appealed directly to the House of Lords, which referred to
h   the Court of Justice of the European Communities for a preliminary ruling under art 177 of the EEC Treaty a number of questions on the interpretation of art 30 and the effect of a recent ruling of the court thereon.

Held – Since national rules restricting the opening of shops on Sundays pursued an aim which was justified under Community law, namely to ensure that
j   working and non-working hours were so arranged as to accord with particular national or regional socio-cultural characteristics, it was for member states to

---

a   Section 47 is set out at p 497 d e, post
b   Article 30 provides: 'Quantitative restrictions on imports and all measures having equivalent effect shall, without prejudice to the following provisions, be prohibited between Member States.'

make choices relating to the particular national or regional socio-cultural
characteristics in compliance with the requirements of Community law, in   a
particular the principle of proportionality. Moreover, since the restrictive effects
on trade of national rules prohibiting shops from opening on Sundays affected
the sale of both domestic and imported products and therefore did not make the
marketing of products from other member states more difficult than the
marketing of national products and since the restrictive effects were not excessive
when the national interest in attaining the aim of the legislation was weighed   b
against the Community interest in ensuring the free movement of goods, the
prohibition on quantitative restrictions on imports and all measures having
equivalent effect laid down in art 30 of the EEC Treaty did not apply to such
legislation. Accordingly, art 30 of the EEC Treaty was to be interpreted as
meaning that the prohibition that it laid down did not apply to s 47 of the 1950   c
Act (see p 518 f to h and p 519 b to d g, post).

Torfaen BC v B & Q plc Case 145/88 [1990] 1 All ER 129, Union départementale
des syndicats CGT de l'Aisne v SIDEF Conforama Case C-312/89 [1991] ECR I-997
and Criminal proceedings against Marchandise Case C-332/89 [1991] ECR I-1027
applied.

d

Notes

For general restrictions on Sunday trading, see 47 Halsbury's Laws (4th edn) paras
632–644, and for cases on the subject, see 47(1) Digest (Reissue) 564–568, 2994–
3017.

For the free movement of goods in the European Economic Community and
justifications for restrictions between member states, see 52 Halsbury's Laws (4th   e
edn) paras 12·55–12·111.

For the Shops Act 1950, s 47, Sch 5, see 19 Halsbury's Statutes (4th edn) (1990
reissue) 424, 447.

For the EEC Treaty, arts 30, 177, see 50 Halsbury's Statutes (4th edn) 276, 325.

f

Cases cited

Aragonesa de Publicidad Exterior SA v Departmento de Sanidad y Seguridad Social de
    la Generalitat de Cataluña Joined cases C-1/90 and C-176/90 OJ 1991 C220, p 8,
    CJEC.
Blesgen v Belgium Case 75/81 [1982] ECR 1211.
Bond van Adverteerders v Netherlands Case 352/85 [1988] ECR 2085.   g
Bonfait BV v Ministère Public Case C-269/89 [1990] ECR I-4169.
Buet v Ministère public Case 382/87 [1989] ECR 1235.
Cinéthèque SA v Fédération nationale des cinémas français Joined cases 60 and 61/84
    [1985] ECR 2605.
Debus v Ministère Public Joined cases C-13/91 and C-113/91 OJ 1992 C167, p 5,
    CJEC.   h
Delattre, Criminal proceedings against Case C-369/88 [1991] ECR I-1487.
Denkavit Futtermittel GmbH v Land Baden-Württemberg Case C-39/90 [1991] ECR
    I-3069.
Direction générale des impôts v Forest Case 148/85 [1986] ECR 3449.
Drei Glocken GmbH v USL Centro-Sud Case 407/85 [1988] ECR 4233.
EC Commission v Belgium Case C-249/88 [1991] ECR I-1275.   j
EC Commission v Belgium Case C-287/89 [1991] ECR I-2233.
EC Commission v Belgium Case C-1/90 [1991] ECR I-2023.
EC Commission v France Case 269/83 [1985] ECR 837.
EC Commission v Italy Case 103/84 [1986] ECR 1759.
EC Commission v Italy Case 63/86 [1988] ECR 29.

Union départementale des syndicats CGT de l'Aisne v SIDEF Conforama Case C-312/89
     [1991] ECR I-997.   *a*
Union Laitière Normande v French Dairy Farmers Ltd Case 244/78 [1979] ECR 2663.
van der Haar and Kaveka de Meern BV, Criminal proceedings against Joined cases 177
     and 178/82 [1984] ECR 1797.
Webb, Criminal proceedings against Case 279/80 [1981] ECR 3305.
Wurmser, Criminal proceedings against Case 25/88 [1989] ECR 1105.
                                                                                                b

Reference
By order dated 20 May 1991 the House of Lords referred to the Court of Justice
of the European Communities for a preliminary ruling under art 177 of the EEC
Treaty three questions (set out at p 517 *j* to p 518 *c*, post) on the interpretation of
art 30 of the EEC Treaty which concerned the applicability of art 30 to s 47 of the   *c*
Shops Act 1950. The questions were raised in the course of two appeals pending
before the House of Lords brought by B & Q plc in which Stoke-on-Trent City
Council and Norwich City Council were respondents from the decision of
Hoffmann J ([1991] 4 All ER 221, [1991] Ch 48) on 18 July 1990 whereby he
granted the respondents injunctions restraining B & Q plc from opening or
causing to be opened on Sundays its do-it-yourself shops for the serving of   *d*
customers in contravention of s 47 of the Shops Act 1950. Stoke-on-Trent City
Council, Norwich City Council, B & Q plc, the United Kingdom and the
Commission of the European Communities submitted written observations to
the court. Oral argument was presented to the court by Stuart Isaacs QC and Neil
Calver (instructed by *Sharpe Pritchard*, agents for *S W Titchener*, Stoke-on-Trent
and *R M Auton*, Norwich) on behalf of the two councils, by David Vaughan QC,   *e*
Gerald Barling QC, Nicholas Davidson and David Anderson (instructed by *Hepherd
Winstanley & Pugh*, Southampton) for B & Q plc, by the Attorney General (Rt Hon
Sir Nicholas Lyell QC) and Nicholas Paines (instructed by the *Treasury Solicitor*)
for the United Kingdom, and by R Wainwright, legal adviser, and A Ridout, a
national civil servant seconded to the commission's legal department, on behalf   *f*
of the commission. The language of the case was English. The facts are set out in
the report for the hearing presented by the Judge Rapporteur.

The Judge Rapporteur (M Díez de Velasco) presented the following report
for the hearing.
                                                                                                g
I—FACTS AND PROCEDURE
     1. The House of Lords is seised of two consolidated appeals between Stoke-on-
Trent City Council and B & Q plc, and between Norwich City Council and B & Q
plc, concerning the applicability of art 30 of the EEC Treaty to s 47 of the Shops
Act 1950.
     2. Section 47 of the 1950 Act provides: *h*

     'Every shop shall, save as otherwise provided by this Part of this Act, be
     closed for the serving of customers on Sunday: Provided that a shop may be
     open for the serving of customers on Sunday for the purposes of any
     transaction mentioned in the Fifth Schedule to this Act.'

Schedule 5 to the Act contains a list of items which may be sold in shops on   *j*
Sundays, such as intoxicating liquors, certain foodstuffs, tobacco, newspapers and
other products of everyday consumption.
     3. After the judgment of the court in *Torfaen BC v B & Q plc* Case C-145/88
[1990] 1 All ER 129 at 156–157, [1990] 2 QB 19 at 53, in which the court held
that—

a
'art 30 of the Treaty must be interpreted as meaning that the prohibition which it lays down does not apply to national rules prohibiting retailers from opening their premises on Sunday where the restrictive effects on Community trade which may result therefrom do not exceed the effects intrinsic to rules of that kind',

b
the respondent local authorities each issued proceedings against the appellant (B & Q) for a final injunction to enforce compliance with s 47 of the 1950 Act in B & Q's Stoke-on-Trent and Norwich stores. On 18 July 1990 the High Court held (in the judgment appealed against before the House of Lords) that the local authorities were entitled to final injunctions (see [1991] 4 All ER 221, [1991] Ch 48).

c
4. B & Q was granted leave to appeal directly to the House of Lords pursuant to Pt II of the Administration of Justice Act 1969, on the ground that a point of law of general public importance was involved.

5. The *factual and expert evidence adduced by B & Q* included the following matters. (a) B & Q operates the largest chain of do-it-yourself (DIY) stores and garden centres in the United Kingdom, with more than 250 stores in England,

d
Wales and Scotland selling a wide range of DIY and gardening items; the majority of goods sold in B & Q's stores are not listed in Sch 5 to the 1950 Act. (b) B & Q's stores are 'mixed' shops within the meaning of s 50 of the 1950 Act and are therefore entitled to be open on Sundays for the serving of customers with items included in Sch 5. Many of B & Q's shops have in the past regularly opened on Sundays for the sale of both Sch 5 goods and non-Sch 5 goods. (c) During B & Q's

e
financial year 1988–89 total purchases from all sources was £490m at manufacturers' prices. Of this £59m was spent on purchasing goods from other member states of the EEC. (d) The average loss of sales when B & Q stores were closed for trading on Sundays is about 23%. This loss of turnover is across the whole range of B & Q's goods to a greater or lesser extent and, save to a very small degree, is not recovered over the remaining six days. (e) Comparisons of the sales

f
turnover of shops that were closed on Sundays with that of shops open on Sundays during the same period showed that the total sales per square foot of shops that opened on Sundays were significantly greater than the total sales per square foot of those shops that were closed on Sundays. (f) Losses caused by Sunday closure do not just affect imports by individual businesses, but have an effect on the United Kingdom's trade. The reduction of imports into the United Kingdom

g
from other EEC member states resulting from enforcement of the Sunday trading restrictions currently in force in England and Wales would, as at 1990, be likely to be in the order of £670m across all ranges of retail goods. The equivalent figure for the DIY and garden sector alone is about £150m per annum.

6. For their part, the *local authorities accepted* in the High Court that Sunday

h
trading restrictions do have a restrictive effect upon trade between the United Kingdom and the rest of the EEC sufficient to satisfy the criteria laid down by the Court of Justice in *Procureur du Roi v Dassonville* Case 8/74 [1974] ECR 837. In that connection the local authorities' own expert witness confirmed that a once-and-for-all increase in retail sales of 1% to 2% would be a possible assumption if the Sunday trading restrictions were lifted. He also noted, however, that even a

j
2% increase in consumer spending on retail goods would only increase imports from the rest of the Community by 0·5% to 0·8%, namely less than 1%.

7. After delivery of the judgment appealed against in the national proceedings, the court in two judgments of 28 February 1991 held that art 30 of the Treaty must be interpreted as meaning that the prohibition which it lays down does not apply to national legislation prohibiting the employment of staff on Sundays

(*Union départementale des syndicats CGT de l'Aisne v SIDEF Conforama* Case C-312/89 [1991] ECR I-997) or on Sundays after 12 noon (*Criminal proceedings against* **a** *Marchandise* Case C-332/89 [1991] ECR I-1027).

8. Before the House of Lords it became apparent that the parties are at issue on two specific points, namely: (a) the interpretation and effect of the judgment of the Court of Justice in the *Torfaen* case and in particular the nature of the task reserved to the national court in determining whether the effects of national rules remain within the limits of the effects intrinsic to trading rules; and (b) the **b** possible application of the principles laid down in the *Conforama* and *Marchandise* judgments, cited above, to the United Kingdom legislative situation.

9. In the light of the foregoing considerations, the House of Lords requested the court to give a preliminary ruling on the following questions:

'1. Whether the effect of the Court of Justice's rulings in Case C-312/89 **c** *Conforama* and C-332/89 *Marchandise* is to determine that the prohibition contained in Article 30 of the EEC Treaty does not apply to national rules, such as those in issue in Case 145/88, *Torfaen Borough Council v. B & Q plc*, which prohibit retailers from opening their premises on Sunday for the serving of customers with certain goods;

2. If not whether it is nevertheless immediately apparent, whether or not **d** evidence is adduced, that the restrictive effects on intra-Community trade which may result from national rules such as those in Question 1 above do not exceed "the effects intrinsic to rules of that kind", as that phrase is used in the ruling of the Court of Justice in Case 145/88;

3. If not, on what criteria and by reference to what, if any, factual or other **e** evidence the national court must determine the question whether or not the restrictive effects on intra-Community trade which may result from national rules such as those in Question 1 above exceed "the effects intrinsic to rules of that kind" within the meaning of that phrase as used in the ruling of the Court of Justice in Case 145/88.'

10. The order for reference was registered at the court registry on 1 July 1991. **f**

11. In accordance with art 20 of the Protocol on the Statute of the Court of Justice written observations were submitted by B & Q plc, represented by David Vaughan QC, Gerald Barling QC, Nicholas Davidson, Barrister, David Anderson, Barrister, and Anthony Askham, Solicitor, by Stoke-on-Trent City Council and Norwich City Council, represented by Stuart Isaacs QC and Neil Calver, Barrister, by the United Kingdom, represented by Lucinda Hudson, acting as agent, and **g** Nicholas Paines, Barrister, and by the Commission of the European Communities, represented by its legal adviser, R Wainwright, and by A Ridout, acting as agents.

12. Upon hearing the report of the Judge Rapporteur and the views of the Advocate General, the court decided to open the oral procedure without any preparatory inquiry. **h**

II—WRITTEN OBSERVATIONS SUBMITTED TO THE COURT

1. With regard to the *first and second questions,* B & Q plc, the appellant in the national proceedings, asserts at the outset that the approach of the Court of Justice in *Torfaen*'s case, cited above, was correct, since Sunday trading rules such as those contained in the 1950 Act are, in the light of available evidence, measures having **j** equivalent effect to quantitative restrictions on trade within the meaning of art 30 and, pursuant to the division of competence underlying art 177 of the EEC Treaty, the Court of Justice correctly entrusted the national court with the task of determining the proportionality or otherwise of the national provisions at issue,

the current objective of the national Sunday trading rules and whether that
a objective falls within the permissible range of objectives including that defined
by the court as being 'to ensure that working and non-working hours are so
arranged as to accord with national or regional socio-cultural characteristics' (see
[1990] 1 All ER 129 at 156, [1990] 2 QB 19 at 53 (para 14)).

According to B & Q plc, since the ascertainment of the objective of the Sunday
trading rules in the 1950 Act is a matter of national law which the Court of Justice
b does not have jurisdiction to determine, particularly where the current objective
of the national measure is genuinely in doubt, or is disputed, it should be
concluded that the United Kingdom courts are in the best position to decide both
what the current objective of the 1950 Act is, and whether or not that objective
fits within the range approved by the Court of Justice.

Moreover, to invite the Court of Justice to determine the *issue of proportionality*
c
would be not only to seek artificially to create some uniformity of law, despite
the dramatic variation in laws as between the member states and within the
member states, but also to vest the Court of Justice with power to harmonise
national laws, which is a function to be performed by the Council of Ministers.

In B & Q's submission, it is perfectly possible for an identical law to be
d proportionate in some member states and disproportionate in others. From that
standpoint, a decision by the court in the *Torfaen* case that the 1950 Act satisfied
the principle of proportionality (in so far as such a decision would have been
possible in art 177 proceedings) might have resolved doubts on this one specific
issue, at least in the United Kingdom, and at least until circumstances there had
changed sufficiently for another court to make a further preliminary reference.
e It would however have left the courts in all member states no wiser as to the
proportionality of many other national measures, each of which could potentially
form the subject of a further preliminary reference under art 177.

Yet a series of isolated decisions on proportionality by the Court of Justice,
reached on principles which are less than clear, would tend to produce uncertainty
and speculative litigation. It would discourage the active application of
f Community law principles by the national courts themselves, and would increase
the number of references to an already overburdened court.

B & Q further considers that the task allotted to the United Kingdom courts in
the *Torfaen* judgment was not affected by the judgments in the *Conforama* and
Marchandise cases, since there is nothing in those two judgments to suggest that
g the court wished to depart from the judgment of the Sixth Chamber in the
Torfaen case. On the contrary, the judgment in that case appears to be expressly
approved on each of the four occasions on which it is mentioned in each judgment
(see, for example, the *Marchandise* judgment [1991] ECR I-1027 at 1040, 1042
(paras 10–12, 19)); the only hint of a difference in approach appears in the
judgments in *Conforama* [1991] ECR I-997 at 1025 (para 12) and *Marchandise*
h [1991] ECR I-1027 at 1041 (para 13), where the court states that the restrictive
effects on trade 'which *may* stem [from the French/Belgian rules] do not *seem*
disproportionate to the aim pursued' (my emphasis).

Yet that difference is more apparent than real. The use of the word 'seem' in
the *Conforama* and *Marchandise* judgments indicates, consistently with paras 6 and
7 respectively of the judgments (see *Conforama* [1991] ECR I-997 at 1024;
j *Marchandise* [1991] ECR I-1027 at 1039) (where the court emphasises its lack of
jurisdiction to rule on the compatibility of national law with the Treaty) and with
the very nature of art 177 proceedings, that the Court of Justice is not itself
deciding the proportionality issue and that this remains a question of fact for the
national court, as stated in the *Torfaen* case.

In fact, the difference in emphasis between the judgment in *Torfaen* and those in *Conforama* and *Marchandise* can be explained by the different national laws, the different types of evidence which were in issue and the differing approach of the parties.

As far as *differences in legislation* are concerned, B & Q maintains that: (a) the French and Belgian laws at issue in the *Conforama* and *Marchandise* cases were entirely *general* employee protection measures, not restricted to shopworkers, let alone to the performance of particular functions by shopworkers, as is the 1950 Act; (b) whereas the French and Belgian laws only prevent *employees* from working in shops on Sundays, they have no effect on the smaller owner-run shops which can in both countries remain open all day on Sundays; (c) though exceptions may be made to the general Sunday closing rule in both France and Belgium, those exceptions do not give rise to the bizarre and anomalous results reached by the application of Sch 5 to the 1950 Act. The anomalous nature of the exceptions to s 47 of the 1950 Act, and indeed the existence of the exceptions themselves, are relevant to the proportionality of the Sunday trading rules as a whole; (d) whereas French and Belgian laws apply across the whole territory of those states, albeit with a limited scope (at least in France) for local authorities to permit regional derogations, the strict rule in force in England and Wales has no counterpart in Scotland, where Sunday trading remains wholly deregulated.

As regards the *differences in factual evidence* B & Q emphasises that both Mr Advocate General Van Gerven and the court in the *Conforama* and *Marchandise* cases indicated that on the basis of the evidence in those cases only a potential effect on trade between member states was shown. In the *Torfaen* case, on the other hand, even before the evidence of the effect on trade had been fully developed (which did not occur until after the court's judgment) the national court had found as a fact that there was an absolute reduction in imports as a result of the enforcement of the 1950 Act. In this connection and as the Advocate General remarked, the questions themselves asked the Court of Justice to assume that there was an actual effect on the volume of goods imported from other member states. These differences are highly significant. Had the court in the *Conforama* and *Marchandise* cases been faced with the type of evidence available to it in the *Torfaen* case, then, even allowing for the differences in the national laws, it must be considered unlikely that it would have expressed the preliminary views which it did.

As regards the *difference in approach* of the parties, B & Q points out that in the *Torfaen* case it was envisaged by both sides that the Court of Justice would decide the main issue of whether art 30 of the EEC Treaty had any application to the 1950 Act and that, if it so held, any remaining issues of fact could be dealt with by the national court by means of further evidence. Indeed, in the *Torfaen* case the local authority expressly reserved for a later stage the right to adduce in the national court evidence relating to issues such as proportionality. Thus, for example, there was no attempt at the stage of the art 177 reference in the *Torfaen* case to quantify the *overall* effect of the 1950 Act on trade between the United Kingdom and the rest of the Community. On the other hand, in the *Conforama* and *Marchandise* cases, all parties, including the Commission, expressly requested the court to express its views on the issue of proportionality. In that situation the court would have been entitled to assume that it had been put in possession of *all* facts and matters relevant to proportionality. In those circumstances it is hardly surprising that the court felt able to express a view (although it manifestly did *not* determine the issue).

Nevertheless, if, notwithstanding all the foregoing, the Court of Justice wished to depart from the line taken in the *Torfaen* case and form a view as to the *a* objective of the provisions of the 1950 Act, on the basis of the available evidence, and as to the application to those provisions of the principle of proportionality, it should express the view that those provisions seem incompatible with art 30 of the EEC Treaty.

According to B & Q, irrespective of the fact that there are strong arguments for saying that no discernible objective can be attributed to the Sunday trading restrictions in question, those rules are disproportionate since the 'objective' of *b* s 47 of the 1950 Act cannot possibly have sufficient importance to outweigh a reduction in intra-Community trade of around 1bn ECU per annum.

B & Q considers that the importance of the objective may be regarded as less where the restriction is subject to many exceptions. Thus, the exceptions to s 47 of the 1950 Act have the effect that many shops, such as B & Q, are permitted to open on Sunday for the sale of much of their stock. Similarly, the fact that the *c* whole of Scotland is exempt from the restriction is a further indication of the degree of importance attached to the objective (whatever it may be) of s 47. In the same way, the total absence of any analogous restriction for workers in all industrial and commercial sectors other than retailing has a bearing on the importance of the aim.

d In any event, it would be difficult to find a measure whose enforcement is given lower priority than s 47. A significant number of local authorities do not enforce it at all; none enforces it fully; those authorities which do attempt to enforce the restrictions do so only against a few, usually the largest traders in the area. The vast majority of retail establishments are left to decide whether to open on Sunday or not.

e In B & Q's view, it is also relevant to take into account other negative effects of the law in addition to the restrictions on inter-state trade, such as the loss of employment, particularly part-time employment opportunities, which enforcement of s 47 would entail; and indeed the fact that Sunday has become the most important trading day for non-essential, leisure items, such as garden and DIY products. Other days of the week could not compensate for the loss of such *f* revenue.

B & Q concludes its observations on the first and second questions by pointing out that, contrary to the situation in 1950, a very large proportion of shop workers employed on Sundays are now part-time workers. Although part-time workers need to be protected, the measures designed to protect full-time workers (particularly in the context of weekend working) are not appropriate for part-*g* time workers, given that it is at the weekend in particular that part-time jobs are available in the retail sector.

Even if (which is not the case) the objective of the Sunday trading rules were held to extend beyond the protection of shopworkers (for example to the protection of what some regard as the 'traditional' English and Welsh Sunday), all *h* the available evidence suggests that none of the alternative measures, or even the introduction of total deregulation as in Scotland, would adversely affect the present level of achievement to any perceptible degree. This is because, on the one hand, the existence of 'mixed' shops, such as the stores of B & Q, means that even under the existing law many shops are entitled to open on Sunday for the sale of *some* of their goods and, on the other hand, the Scottish experience shows *j* that even with total deregulation, in the ordinary event, only 15% to 20% of shops choose to open on Sunday.

Since the *third question* asked by the House of Lords is, in B & Q's view, no more than a shortened version of the second question referred to the court in *Reading BC v Payless DIY Ltd* Case C-304/90 it refers to its written observations in that case.

In the light of the foregoing, B & Q proposes that the court should answer the questions put by the House of Lords as follows: *First question*: No; *Second question*: No; *Third question*: B & Q refers to its answers to questions 1, 2 and 4 raised by the court making the reference in the *Reading* case Case C-304/90.

2. *Stoke-on-Trent City Council and Norwich City Council* (the councils), the respondents in the national proceedings, after reviewing the relevant provisions of the 1950 Act and their origin, begin by recalling the difficulties caused by the *Torfaen* judgment to legal writers who, very correctly in their view, pointed out the ambiguities of the court's approach in that case.

That approach is unsatisfactory because it is difficult to see what was the distinction between the national legislation in issue in the *Torfaen* case and that in issue in *Quietlynn Ltd v Southend-on-Sea BC* Case C-23/89 [1990] 3 All ER 207, [1991] 1 QB 454. In the latter case, the court ruled that national provisions prohibiting the sale of lawful pornographic items from unlicensed pornographic establishments could in no way be assimilated to a measure having an effect equivalent to a quantitative restriction on imports, though it was apparent from the first question submitted to the court in that case that, just as in the *Torfaen* case, the court was asked to proceed on the basis that the effect of the national rules was to have restricted the retailer from selling goods imported from other member states and so to have resulted in less imported goods from member states being sold than would otherwise have been the case.

However, in the councils' submission, those difficulties and ambiguities have been resolved by the court's rulings in the *Conforama* and *Marchandise* cases, cited above. In connection with the reply to be given to the first question the councils point out that, in both cases, the court: (a) found that national rules prohibiting Sunday employment in the retail sector were not designed to control trade between member states; (b) stated that rules of that type applied to domestic and imported products alike, and that, as it had already said in the *Torfaen* case, the marketing of products imported from other member states was not therefore made more difficult than the marketing of domestic products; (c) summarised the *Torfaen* ruling, staging that the national rules in issue there were similar to those in issue in the instant cases; (d) concluded first that, in those circumstances, rules such as those at issue, like those in the *Torfaen* case, pursued an aim which was justified with regard to Community law; (e) concluded, secondly, that the restrictive effects which such measures might have on trade did not seem disproportionate to the aim pursued.

In the councils' submission, since national rules such as s 47 of the 1950 Act are materially indistinguishable from the legislation at issue in the *Conforama* and *Marchandise* cases, it is clear that the court's rulings in those cases are determinative in their favour of the first question referred to the court by the House of Lords.

As to the *second and third questions* raised by the House of Lords, the councils point out that they both involve a consideration of the phrase 'the effects intrinsic to rules of that kind', used in the *Torfaen* judgment [1990] 1 All ER 129 at 156, [1990] 2 QB 19 at 53 (para 17) and reflected in paras 15 and 16 thereof. That phrase appears to have its origin in art 3 of Commission Directive (EEC) 70/50 of 22 December 1969, which provides that national measures governing the marketing of products come within the prohibition of art 30 where the restrictive effects exceed the effects intrinsic to trade rules, which is the case, in particular, where the restrictive effects on the free movement of goods are out of proportion to their purpose (the so-called 'balancing test') or when the same objective can be attained by other means which are less of a hindrance to trade (the so-called 'necessity test').

The councils submit that, since the court in the *Torfaen* case correctly recognised that a trade rule may have some restrictive effect on the free movement of goods

which is within limits permitted by Community law, sense can be made of the
phrase only if the 'intrinsic' effects of a trading rule are taken to mean those effects
which are regarded by Community law as proportionate.

They submit in that connection that Community law offers no single approach
to the question of proportionality. In fact, both the court's case law, where the
necessity test has been used as the sole test in the application of the proportionality
principle in many art 30 cases, and the Treaty itself (for example, arts 109, 115
and 226) afford examples where the balancing test is not taken into consideration
in the application of the proportionality principle.

As regards specifically the rules at issue, the councils submit that the test laid
down in paras 15 and 16 of the *Torfaen* ruling only requires that national rules
such as s 47 satisfy the necessity test. That follows from the fact that the first
sentence of para 15 of the *Torfaen* ruling expressly refers only to the necessity test,
and from the fact that paras 15 to 17 of that ruling, read as a whole, must be
interpreted as meaning that the question whether the restrictive effect of such
measures on the free movement of goods exceed the effects intrinsic to trade rules
is to be determined by reference only to the necessity test.

Moreover, the necessity test is the only one applicable to the particular measure
in issue in the present case; there is no economic meaning to a general test of
proportionality or disproportionality in the context of the aim of s 47 measured
against the effects on intra-Community trade. In fact, though some intangible
things may be capable of valuation, quantities can only be meaningfully compared
if it is possible to measure them in the same units.

On the second question, which seeks to ascertain whether it is immediately
apparent, whether or not evidence is adduced, that the restrictive effects on intra-
Community trade which may result from national rules such as those in issue do
not exceed 'the effects intrinsic to rules of that kind', the councils submit that the
proportionality of national rules such as s 47 is immediately apparent and that,
for that reason, evidence in relation thereto is unnecessary.

They observe that in the *Conforama* and *Marchandise* cases the court, according
to them, was conscious of the ambiguities in the language of the *Torfaen* judgment
and significantly omitted from its rulings the words '. . . where the restrictive
effects on Community trade which may result therefrom do not exceed the effects
intrinsic to rules of that kind'. The reason why the court did so was precisely that
it was immediately apparent, and did not require evidence to establish, that the
restrictive effects of national rules such as s 47 do not exceed the effects intrinsic
to rules of that kind. In other words, it would be odd and illogical for the approach
taken by the court towards national rules such as s 47 to be different from that
which it took in the *Conforama* and *Marchandise* cases towards national rules of
the kind in issue in those cases.

As to the argument based on the use by the court in the *Conforama* and
Marchandise cases of the word 'seem' in the phrase 'the restrictive effects on trade
which may stem from such rules do not seem disproportionate to the aim
pursued' (the *Conforama* judgment [1991] ECR I-997 at 1025 (para 12) and the
Marchandise judgment [1991] ECR I-1027 at 1041 (para 13)), an argument
according to which the court left it to the national court to rule on the question
of proportionality, the councils submit that such an argument would not be
seriously sustainable. In particular, any such argument (1) seeks to read too much
into the single word 'seem', (2) would be contrary to the whole tenor of the
rulings, (3) would mean that the court had rejected the Commission's argument,
which the Advocate General in para 7 of his opinion supported (see [1991] ECR
997 at 1012), that the assessment of the need for and proportionality of specific
legislation cannot be left to the national courts, and (4) completely ignores the

actual answers given by the court in the *Conforama* case [1991] ECR I-997 at 1025 (para 13) and in the *Marchandise* case [1991] ECR I-1027 at 1041 (para 14).   *a*

In any event, on the evidence summarised by the first instance court, s 47 must be deemed to be proportionate, since the restrictive effect of that provision on Community trade was minimal.

As regards the third question as to what *criteria* and by reference to what, if any, *factual* or other *evidence*, the *national court must determine* the question whether or not the *restrictive effects* on intra-Community trade which may result from   *b* national rules such as those in issue exceed 'the effects intrinsic to rules of that kind', the councils submit, first, that it is well established that it is for the national law of a member state to determine the procedural conditions which govern actions in the national courts in order to enforce a right conferred by Community law and, secondly, that under Community law there is no requirement for the determination of the substantive question to be made by reference to evidence of   *c* any nature.

In that connection, the councils submit that the reference in para 16 of the *Torfaen* ruling to a '*question of fact*' cannot mean that the court was imposing on the national court a requirement to adduce factual evidence in circumstances where the national court, in accordance with its own rules of procedure and   *d* evidence, would not require the adduction of such evidence in order to resolve the question of the proportionality of the national rules in question. Moreover, the *Conforama* and *Marchandise* rulings make no reference to any question of fact.

In the above circumstances, the councils invite the court to rule, as follows:

> 'The effect of the Court of Justice's rulings in the *Conforama* case Case   *e* C-312/89 and the *Marchandise* case Case C-332/89 is to determine that the prohibition contained in art 30 of the EEC Treaty does not apply to national rules, such as those in issue in *Torfaen BC v B & Q plc* Case 145/88, which prohibit retailers from opening their premises on Sunday for the serving of customers with certain goods.'

In the event that, contrary to the councils' submission, the court answers   *f* question 1 in the negative, the councils invite the court to rule on question 2 as follows:

> 'The restrictive effects on intra-Community trade which may result from national rules such as those in question 1 above do not exceed the effects intrinsic to rules of that kind.'   *g*

If, contrary to the councils' submissions, the court answers question 2 in the negative, the councils invite the court to rule on question 3 as follows:

> 'The question whether or not the restrictive effects on intra-Community trade which may result from national rules such as those in question 1 above exceed the effects intrinsic to rules of that kind must be determined by the   *h* national court (1) by reference to the sole criterion whether the objective of the national rules can be attained by other means which are less of a hindrance to trade and (2) in accordance with its own rules of procedure and evidence.'

3. The *United Kingdom* begins its observations by referring to the unsatisfactory state of affairs existing in the United Kingdom as a result of differing   *j* interpretations of the *Torfaen* decision, with the result that different United Kingdom courts have reached different conclusions about a matter as fundamental as the validity of an Act of Parliament and the effect of a provision of the EEC Treaty. It considers in that regard that although it is true that to some extent that

a   situation has arisen as a result of the impression received by national courts that there *must be a doubt* to be resolved as to the compatibility of the United Kingdom legislation with the EEC Treaty, it is nevertheless the case that that view was not shared by Mr Advocate General Van Gerven in his opinion in the *Conforama* and *Marchandise* cases or by the court in its judgments in those cases.

b   Similarly it stresses that in spite of important differences of detail as between the Belgian and French legislation highlighted by the *Conforama* and *Marchandise* cases in their written observations in the cases concerning them, and the many derogations therein from the general principle, the *decision* adopted by the court *in those cases* could not have been clearer, inasmuch as art 30 of the Treaty does not apply to national legislation prohibiting the employment of staff on Sundays.

c   In his opinion concerning those cases, Mr Advocate General Van Gerven referred extensively to the court's judgment in the *Torfaen* case and made it clear that he regarded the United Kingdom legislation as being, from the point of view of art 30, indistinguishable from the French and Belgian legislation. Referring to the *Torfaen* judgment, he stated ([1991] ECR I-997 at 1009 (para 5)):

d   'Whereas Case C-145/88 was concerned with a general prohibition on Sunday trading, these cases are concerned with a prohibition on employing workers on Sundays. In my view that distinction is not of great importance: as regards the application of Article 30 of the Treaty the effects on intra-Community trade resulting from the two types of legislation are very similar.'

He also considered that—

e   'legislation of the kind at issue in these cases, which is not designed to govern patterns of trade between Member States or to partition the market, can easily be regarded as remaining within the limits of what is necessary.' (See [1991] ECR I-997 at 1016 (para 13).)

f   In the United Kingdom's view, the *reasoning* underlying the *Conforama* and *Marchandise* judgments, in which the court followed the Advocate General's opinion, is perfectly applicable to national legislation of the kind in issue.

It stresses that in the judgments cited the court held that national rules governing the opening hours of retail premises reflect certain political and economic choices in so far as their purpose is to ensure that working and non-working hours are so arranged as to accord with national or regional socio-cultural *g*   characteristics, which in the present state of Community law is a matter for the member states; and the lawfulness of such rules, it says, remains subject to the requirement that the obstacles to intra-Community trade do not exceed what is necessary in order to ensure the attainment of the objective in view.

In its view, the latter criteria would, for example, prohibit rules which placed imported products at a disadvantage compared to domestic goods, or contained *h*   some restriction totally foreign to the objective pursued. In the United Kingdom's submission, that is also what the court had in mind in the *Torfaen* judgment when it referred to the effects exceeding those intrinsic to rules of this kind. However, the United Kingdom legislation does not place imported products at any disadvantage compared to domestic goods, nor does it contain any provisions foreign to the objective which it is pursuing. There are therefore no grounds *j*   upon which it could be said that the law goes beyond what is necessary to ensure the objective in view.

In any event, the court did not take up what had already been held in the *Torfaen* judgment whereby it is for the national courts to determine whether national legislation such as that at issue remains within the limits laid down, and expressly stated that the restrictive effects on trade which may stem from such rules do not seem disproportionate to the aim pursued.

    The United Kingdom is of the view that the only arguments raised in support of the proposition that the legislation has effects exceeding those intrinsic to trading rules fall into two categories. First, it is sometimes argued that it is not permissible for member states to make Sunday a non-working or non-trading day. The second type of argument accepts that member states are entitled to make Sunday a non-working or non-trading day, but asserts that member states ought to have created more exceptions to the prohibition. Apart from the fact that such arguments are of little relevance since they are all inconsistent with the discretionary power reserved to member states in the matter, the United Kingdom considers that to accept the second type of argument would involve accepting that the objective of the United Kingdom legislation is at least in part 'illegitimate'. In such a situation a court would be forming its own view of what 'accords with national or regional socio-cultural characteristics' in the United Kingdom, contrary to the reasoning in both the *Torfaen* case and in the *Conforama* and *Marchandise* cases.

    As to the factual or other *evidence* on the basis of which the national court must determine whether the effects of the national rules at issue in the present case exceed the effects intrinsic to rules of that kind, the United Kingdom is of the opinion that the relevant criteria are those which relate to the question whether the legislation places imported products at a disadvantage compared to domestic goods or has restrictive effects upon imports which are totally foreign to the objective pursued. But those criteria are not relevant if they are invoked in support of an argument that a member state has misjudged or wrongly evaluated its objectives or that a lesser degree of restriction upon Sunday trading would be sufficient for social or cultural purposes.

    In particular it considers that, since the function of the courts is to review the acts of the legislature but not to substitute their own policies or values, it is not appropriate to speak of what may have been the 'true' intention of the United Kingdom Parliament in adopting the legislation at issue, or of the wisdom of the result achieved by it. Since the court has left it to the member states to make the evaluation of national and regional socio-cultural characteristics relevant to the arrangement of working hours, and to set working hours which accord with those characteristics, it maintains that the legislation at issue is merely the expression of a power of evaluation left to member states in the pursuit of an aim held by the court to be justified under Community law. On the other hand, if the legislation had discriminated against imports or contained restrictions foreign to that objective, it would not have passed the judge's test.

    As regards balancing the *estimated additional sales* of imported goods against the objectives of the legislation, the United Kingdom doubts the utility of estimates of the effect of the legislation upon imports which would take place in the absence of the legislation.

    First, it is extremely difficult, if not impossible, to make a reliable estimate: B & Q's calculations were drawn from a time when their shops were open on Sundays whilst many of their competitors were closed.

    Secondly, those estimates appear not to take into account the fact that the extra money which would be spent on the additional Sunday purchases would be unavailable for spending on other imported goods or services, such as foreign holidays. It is not clear how to compensate for that factor.

    Thirdly, even if a reliable figure could be produced, it is impossible to make a meaningful comparison between the social interests protected by the legislation

and a figure for the value of imports. It could not sensibly be said, for example,
a that the law would be disproportionate if its abolition could increase spending on
imported goods by, say, £10 per person or 1%, but acceptable if its abolition
would only increase such spending by £5 per person or 0·5%.

4. *The Commission*, taking together the three questions asked by the national
court, begins by emphasising that it is true that national rules pursuing economic
and social policies, which have a direct effect on the sale of goods, are likely to
b affect the sale of imported goods and therefore the import of such goods.
Nevertheless, rules of that kind prohibiting retailers from opening their premises
on Sundays constitute measures which are equally applicable to imported and
domestic products since they have the same effect on all goods whatever their
origin and, consequently, the marketing of products imported from other
c member states is not rendered more difficult than the marketing of domestic
products.

It recalls that in the *Torfaen* judgment, already cited, the court held that in such
a case it was necessary to consider first of all whether rules such as those at issue
pursue an aim which is justified with regard to Community law and, secondly,
whether the restrictive effects of such rules exceed what is necessary to achieve
d the aim in view (the proportionality rule).

With regard to the first aspect, the Commission points out that the court has
already held that national rules governing the hours of work, delivery and sale in
the bread and confectionery industry constitute a legitimate choice of social and
economic policy, consistent with the objectives of public interest pursued by the
Treaty (see *Summary proceedings against Oebel* Case 155/80 [1981] ECR 1993) and
e that national rules prohibiting the employment of workers on Sunday also
pursued an aim which was justified in Community law (see the *Conforama* and
Marchandise cases, cited above). Furthermore, in the *Torfaen* judgment [1990] 1
All ER 129 at 156, [1990] 2 QB 19 at 53 (para 14), the court also held:

'The same consideration [as in the *Oebel* case] must apply as regards national
f   rules governing the opening hours of retail premises. Such rules reflect
certain political and economic choices in so far as their purpose is to ensure
that working and non-working hours are so arranged as to accord with
national or regional socio-cultural characteristics, and that, in the present
state of Community law, is a matter for the member states.'

g It may therefore be concluded that s 47 of the 1950 Act pursues an objective
which is justified with reference to Community law.

As regards the question of *proportionately*, the Commission states that, on the
basis of art 3 of Commission Directive (EEC) 70/50 of 22 December 1969,
pursuant to which the prohibition laid down in art 30 covers national measures
governing the marketing of products where the restrictive effect of such measures
h on the free movement of goods exceeds the effects intrinsic to trade rules, the
court held in its *Torfaen* judgment [1990] 1 All ER 129 at 156, [1990] 2 QB 19 at
53 (para 16): 'The question whether the effects of specific national rules do in fact
remain within that limit is a question of fact to be determined by the national
court.'

That being so, it considers that in the present case such a question *cannot be left
j* *to be determined by the national court*, since, if the national courts were left to
determine such questions, they might reach different conclusions on cases which
were similar, not to say identical, in the absence of a unified interpretation by a
single court at Community level. On the contrary, the examination of a particular
national law must allow it to be concluded whether or not it is contrary to

Community law and must give to the national judge such elements on the question of interpretation which allow him to decide the case before him. That *a* was what the court did in the *Oebel, Conforama* and *Marchandise* cases already cited.

With specific regard to the legislation at issue, the Commission asserts that the restrictive effects on the free movement of goods of a prohibition on Sunday trading, with exceptions for objects of everyday consumption, would not appear to be excessive having regard to the purpose in view. The restrictive effects are in fact quite limited. In the present case the House of Lords has found that there are *b* respectable grounds for thinking that the complete abolition of restrictions on Sunday trading could lead to a once-and-for-all increase of about 1% to 2% in the retail sector. Thus the maximum potential increase in the sales of goods imported from other member states is of the order of 2% and likely to be less.

In its view, the absence of a common approach to Sunday trading in member states does not in itself diminish trade within the Community. Differences *c* between days and hours of the opening of shops may on the contrary increase trade between member states having a common frontier: it is quite conceivable that in frontier areas consumers cross the frontier to buy goods which they cannot buy in their own country on that day.

In its view, the foregoing considerations lead to the conclusion that the *d* prohibition on Sunday trading does not have disproportionate effects on the free movement of goods in relation to its legitimate aim. Moreover, in the light in particular of the exceptions which are provided for the sale of products of everyday consumption, it does not appear that the same objective could be achieved by means which are less of a hindrance to trade. On the other hand the existence of those exceptions cannot, in itself, affect the legality under Community *e* law of the general ban, since, as was observed by Mr Advocate General Van Gerven in his opinion in the *Torfaen* case [1990] 1 All ER 129 at 153, [1990] 2 QB 19 at 49 (para 32), the effectiveness of a national rule is not relevant for the purposes of art 30 of the EEC Treaty, except in so far as it may be a means of arbitrary discrimination or disguised restriction against goods from other member states, which is not so in the present case. *f*

It points out that those arguments have now effectively been indorsed by the court in its judgments in the *Conforama* and *Marchandise* cases, which are fully applicable to the 1950 Act. Although the French and Belgian legislation at issue in those cases concerned national rules prohibiting the employment of workers on a Sunday rather than national rules prohibiting the serving of customers, the *g* principles laid down by the court in those cases are applicable also in the present case. Furthermore, there is nothing to suggest that the proportionality of the rules in question with regard to their objective, which is justified under Community law, should be analysed in any different manner from that applied with regard to rules prohibiting the employment of workers on Sunday.

Having regard to the foregoing, the Commission proposes that the following *h* reply should be given to the questions referred to the court:

'Article 30 of the EEC Treaty must be interpreted as meaning that the prohibition which it lays down does not apply to national rules prohibiting the opening of shops on Sunday.'

8 July 1992. **The Advocate General (Walter Van Gerven)** delivered the *j* following opinion[1] in *Rochdale BC v Anders* Case C-306/88[2], *Reading BC v Payless*

1 Translated from the Dutch
2 See *Rochdale BC v Anders* Case C-306/88 [1993] 1 All ER 520n

DIY Ltd Case C-304/90[3] and *Stoke-on-Trent City Council v B & Q plc* Case C-169/91.

a   Mr President, Members of the Court,

1. These cases once again concern the compatibility with the EEC Treaty provisions on the free movement of goods of the prohibition in England and Wales on the operation of a shop on Sundays (hereinafter referred to as the Sunday trading ban or the United Kingdom Sunday trading provisions). Three sets of proceedings are pending before English courts against persons charged with

b   infringements of the Sunday trading ban.

The court addressed these issues for the first time in the *Torfaen* judgment (see *Torfaen BC v B & Q plc* Case C-145/88 [1990] 1 All ER 129, [1990] 2 QB 19). The judgments of the court in *Union départementale des syndicats CGT de l'Aisne v SIDEF Conforama* Case C-312/89 [1991] ECR I-997 (the *Conforama* case) and *Criminal proceedings against Marchandise* Case C-332/89 [1991] ECR I-1027 (the *Marchandise*

c   case), concerning French and Belgian labour legislation prohibiting the employment of workers on Sundays or on Sundays after 12 noon respectively, are closely related.

Legal and factual background

d   2. Section 47 of the Shops Act 1950 lays down the following prohibition:

'Every shop shall, save as otherwise provided by this Part of this Act, be closed for the serving of customers on Sunday: Provided that a shop may be open for the serving of customers on Sunday for the purposes of any transaction mentioned in the Fifth Schedule to this Act.'

e   Schedule 5 contains a list of items which may be sold in shops on Sundays, such as intoxicating liquors, tobacco, newspapers, certain foodstuffs and other products of everyday consumption. Offences against this prohibition are punishable under s 59 of the 1950 Act, which provides:

'In the case of any contravention of any of the foregoing provisions of this

f   Part of this Act, the occupier of the shop shall be liable to a fine not exceeding level 4 on the standard scale.'

It appears that the maximum amount of the fine for a contravention is £1,000[4]. The Sunday trading ban does not apply in Scotland.

3. The Sunday trading ban as imposed by the 1950 Act is a matter of controversy in Great Britain. As the House of Lords observes in its order for

g   reference in *Stoke-on-Trent City Council v B & Q plc, Norwich City Council v B & Q plc* Case C-169/91 (the *B & Q* case), it is an issue on which feelings run very high. British public opinion is very divided on it: one-third of the population appears to be in favour of retention of the law, and two-thirds are in favour of abolition or amendment, though without any agreement as to the form which such

h   amendment should take. Since 1936 the United Kingdom Sunday trading

---

3   In paras 10 and 11 of its judgment given on 16 December 1992 in *Reading BC v Payless DIY Ltd* Case C-304/90 the Court of Justice of the European Communities said that the answer to be given to the first question referred to the court in that case was the same as that given in *Stoke-on-Trent*

i   *City Council v B & Q plc* Case C-169/91 [1993] 1 All ER 481 and that it was therefore unnecessary to give a ruling on the other questions submitted. The judgment of the Court of Justice in the *Reading BC* case accordingly does not call for a report.

4   As from 1 October 1992 the amount of fine for level 4 on the standard scale was increased to £2,500: see the Criminal Justice Act 1982, s 37(2), as substituted by the Criminal Justice Act 1991, s 17(1)

provisions have withstood many attempts by private members Bills in Parliament, and in one case even by the government, to secure their abolition or amendment. It should be added that for some time the law has to a considerable extent been disregarded, and that contraventions are not systematically prosecuted.

The judgment in the *Torfaen* case seems to have given rise to divergent interpretations by national courts. Both in Great Britain (with regard to the Sunday trading ban) and in France (with regard to the legislation at issue in the *Conforama* judgment) this has led to acquittal in some cases and conviction in others. Even after the judgments in the *Marchandise* and *Conforama* cases, great uncertainty continues to prevail at least in Great Britain with regard to the compatibility of the 1950 Act with Community law. This has recently led the High Court of Justice to stay proceedings brought by local authorities for contravention of the Act, since it is of the opinion that in order to resolve those cases the situation under Community law must first be clarified. For the same reasons the United Kingdom has pressed the court to give a ruling in the *B & Q* case as a matter of priority.

4. The earliest of the three cases, *Rochdale BC v Anders* C-306/88, concerns proceedings brought by Rochdale Borough Council against Stewart John Anders. Mr Anders is charged with opening his shop at Dale Mill on Sundays for transactions other than those mentioned in Sch 5 to the 1950 Act. Rochdale Borough Council has applied to the High Court of Justice, Queen's Bench Division, for an injunction restraining Mr Anders himself and his servants or agents from opening the shop on Sundays for the serving of customers, save for the transactions listed in Sch 5 to the 1950 Act (see [1988] 3 All ER 490). Mr Anders admits the contravention of the Sunday trading ban, but contends that the ban conflicts with Community law since it constitutes a measure having equivalent effect prohibited under art 30 of the Treaty and is not justified under any of the exemptions contained in art 36 or on any other basis.

The High Court referred to the court four questions for a preliminary ruling (see [1988] 3 All ER 490 at 494). After being made aware of the judgments in the *Torfaen, Conforama* and *Marchandise* cases it decided to maintain only the fourth question. It is worded as follows:

'If the prohibition referred to in Question 1 [the Sunday trading ban] contravenes Article 30 and is not justified under Article 36, is it totally unenforceable against a trader in the Member State or only unenforceable to the extent that it prohibits transactions involving goods manufactured in or imported from other Member States?'

5. *Reading BC v Payless DIY Ltd* Case C-304/90 involves 20 informations laid by Reading Borough Council against five defendants in the national proceedings (Payless DIY Ltd, Wickes Building Supplies Ltd, Great Mills (South) Ltd, Homebase Ltd, on the one hand, and B & Q plc on the other); all are alleged to have opened their shop premises on Sundays for transactions other than those listed in Sch 5 to the 1950 Act. (The observations submitted by Payless DIY Ltd are supported by Wickes Building Supplies Ltd, Great Mills (South) Ltd and Homebase Ltd.) Whilst the parties are agreed that the Sunday trading ban constitutes a measure having equivalent effect, opinions differ as to whether it is justified. Reading and Sonning Magistrates' Court has asked the Court of Justice to give a preliminary ruling on the following questions, which to a large extent concern the scope of the *Torfaen* judgment:

'1. Where the legislation of a Member State prohibits retail premises from opening on Sundays for the personal serving of customers with the objective of ensuring so far as possible that shopworkers do not have to work on Sundays, with a view to maintaining what many regard as the traditional English Sunday, is such an objective one that is justified with regard to Community law within the meaning of paragraphs 12 to 14 of the judgment in Case 145/88 *Torfaen Borough Council v B & Q plc* ([1990] 1 All ER 129 at 156, [1990] 2 QB 19 at 52–53)?

2. When applying the test laid down by the Court of Justice in paragraph 15 of the judgment in *Torfaen* (the proportionality test) to such legislation: (a) Is the national court required to apply the criteria set out in Article 3 of Directive 70/50? (b) If so, does the national measure have to satisfy each of the criteria identified in the indents in the second paragraph of Article 3? (c) Is it the function of the national court to examine the facts (as proved by evidence) and come to its own conclusion regarding the applicability of those criteria, or is the function of the national court limited to deciding whether or not a national legislature acting reasonably could have adopted the legislative measure in question having regard to those criteria? (d) When assessing the restrictive effects of the national legislation on the free movement of goods, and also when comparing the restrictive effect on trade (if any) of the various different means that might be used to achieve the objective of the legislation, must the national court look only at the extent to which the effects on imported goods exceed the effects on domestic goods or can it look at the totality of the restrictive effects on intra-Community imports? (e) Is the relevant restrictive effect on trade to be examined in relation to: the overall effect on intra-Community trade in goods and/or services; or the effect on the sectors in which the undertaking in question operates; or the effect on that undertaking? (f) How is a national court to compare the restrictive effects on the free movement of goods arising from the national legislation with the objective of that legislation?

3. Has Article 36 of the EEC Treaty any and if so what application to a national measure such as that in question?

4. Is the answer to any of the above questions affected by the existence of exceptions to the legislative prohibition on Sunday trading?'

6. In the most recent case, the *B & Q* case, the House of Lords asks a number of questions intended to clarify the relationship between the judgments in the *Conforama* and *Marchandise* cases and the *Torfaen* judgment. The defendant in the main proceedings is once again (as in the *Torfaen* case and now in the *Payless* case) B & Q plc, one of the largest operators of do-it-yourself shops and garden centres in the United Kingdom. The majority of the garden and do-it-yourself items sold in its shops are not mentioned in Sch 5 to the 1950 Act. Following the court's judgment in the *Torfaen* case, Stoke-on-Trent City Council and Norwich City Council brought proceedings against B & Q for a final injunction to enforce compliance with the Sunday trading ban. On 18 July 1990 the High Court held that the local authorities were entitled to that injunction, but did not order it since B & Q gave appropriate undertakings (see [1991] 4 All ER 221, [1991] Ch 48). B & Q nevertheless appealed to the House of Lords on the basis that a point of law of general public impotance was involved, namely the function of the national courts in assessing the Sunday trading ban in relation to the principle of proportionality.

Before the House of Lords it became apparent that there are two main points at issue between the parties: the interpretation and effect of the *Torfaen* judgment—in particular the nature of the task reserved to the national court in determining 'the effects intrinsic to trading rules'—and the application of the

Conforama and *Marchandise* judgments to the United Kingdom legislative
situation.   *a*

The House of Lords requested the court to give a preliminary ruling on the
following three questions:

'1. Whether the effect of the Court of Justice's rulings in Case C-312/89
Conforama and C-332/89 *Marchandise* is to determine that the prohibition
contained in Article 30 of the EEC Treaty does not apply to national rules,   *b*
such as those in issue in Case 145/88 *Torfaen Borough Council v. B & Q plc*,
which prohibit retailers from opening their premises on Sunday for the
serving of cutomers with certain goods;
2. If not, whether it is nevertheless immediately apparent, whether or not
evidence is adduced, that the restrictive effects on intra-Community trade
which may result from national rules such as those in Question 1 above do   *c*
not exceed "the effects intrinsic to rules of that kind", as that phrase is used in
the ruling of the Court of Justice in Case 145/88;
3. If not, on what criteria and by reference to what, if any, factual or other
evidence the national court must determine the question whether or not the
restrictive effects on intra-Community trade which may result from national   *d*
rules such as those in Question 1 above exceed "the effects intrinsic to rules
of that kind" within the meaning of that phrase as used in the ruling of the
Court of Justice in Case 145/88.'

7. In my remarks I shall rearrange the questions referred to the court in the
following manner. First of all I shall deal with the first question submitted by the   *e*
House of Lords on the significance of the *Conforama* and *Marchandise* judgments
for the United Kingdom Sunday trading provisions. In doing so I shall begin by
examining the points of difference between the *Torfaen* judgment and the
Conforama and *Marchandise* judgments and then place these three judgments in
the context of the court's recent case law on the applicability in principle of art 30
(paras 8 to 17, post). Before embarking on the questions relating to the assessment   *f*
of justification and proportionality, I shall first examine who is to carry out that
assessment, the Court of Justice or the national court (paras 18 to 20, post). I shall
then deal with the first question from the magistrates' court on the justification
under Communiy law of the Sunday trading ban (paras 21 to 25, post). The
question of proportionality then arises, in relation to which I shall deal with the
second and third questions raised by the House of Lords, and the numerous sub-   *g*
questions contained in the second question submitted by the magistrates' court
(paras 26 to 32, post). Finally, I shall deal, in so far as may be necessary, with the
magistrates' court's remaining questions, together with the sole question still
before the court in *Rochdale BC v Anders* Case C-306/88 (paras 33 and 34, post).

                                                                                     h

Comparison of the Torfaen judgment and the Conforama and Marchandise judgments
8. Both Payless DIY (Case C-304/90) and B & Q (Case C-169/91) argue that a
distinction must be drawn between the French and Belgian labour provisions at
issue in the *Conforama* and *Marchandise* cases respectively and the United Kingdom
Sunday trading provisions at issue in the *Torfaen* case (and in these cases). The
former provisions are said to be of a very general nature, aimed at the protection   *j*
of employees, so that the general rule is that workers may not be employed on
Sundays. In England and Wales, on the other hand, the population is free to
choose whether or not to work on Sundays, with the exception of the staff of
retailers. The French and Belgian laws prevent workers from being employed in
shops on Sundays, and thus have no effect on small owner-run shops, which can

in both France and Belgium remain open all day on Sundays. Though the French
a and Belgian provisions contain exceptions, these do not give rise to such
inconsistent results as the exceptions to the United Kingdom Sunday trading ban.
Finally, the French and Belgian laws apply across the whole territory of those
states, albeit with a limited possibility in France for local authorities to permit
regional derogations. However, s 47 of the 1950 Act does not apply in Scotland.

    9. As I stated in my opinion in the *Conforama* and *Marchandise* cases, I do not
b consider the above-mentioned points of difference between the national provisions
in question to be decisive in regard to the application of art 30 of the Treaty.
What is important is the effect of the provisions in both cases on intra-Community
trade, and that is very similar (see [1991] ECR 1-997 at 1009 (para 5)). In both
cases specific legislation, relating either to labour law or to trade regulation, results
c in a large number of trading outlets within the territory in which the legislation
concerned is applicable being closed on Sundays. Notwithstanding the differences
in scope and conditions between the provisions in question, it follows from their
general tenor that they have a definite (and pro rata) impact on sales of both
national and imported products.

    In view of the importance of this point I should like to add the following
d observation. A comparative examination of the situation in the other member
states leads to the conclusion that the closing of shops on Sundays is general
within the Community (for a comparative law review, see amongst others, Askam
Burke and Ramsden *EC Sunday Trading Rules* (1990). See also EC Commission
Measures taken in the field of commerce by the Member States of the European Communities
(1985)). Such a review reveals numerous differences in geographical and temporal
e scope (in certain member states shops must already shut on Saturday afternoon,
in others only on Sunday afternoon), detailed rules of application (including
derogations from the primary rule) and legal basis (statutory provision relating to
trade regulation or to labour law, administrative decree, collective labour
agreement, decision of a trade association, or even custom). In every member
state the sale of national and imported products is therefore impeded to a greater
f or lesser extent as a result of the closure of shops on Sunday. It seems to me a
hopeless task to differentiate between the national or even regional provisions or
customs in the matter in the member states in order to determine whether or not
one situation or another falls under the prohibition contained in art 30 of the
Treaty. A certain degree of generalisation in the assessment of these rules and
g practices therefore seems to me, in the context of the free movement of goods, to
be entirely justified.

    10. B & Q also seeks to demonstrate that these judgments must be distinguished
on account of *differences between the facts* underlying them. It argues that if in the
Conforama and *Marchandise* cases the court had had before it the evidence which
was available in the *Torfaen* case, even having regard to the differences between
h the national provisions concerned, it would most probably have come to a
different conclusion.

    On this point I can be brief. In my opinion in the *Conforama* and *Marchandise*
cases I stated that the facts of the *Conforama* case, as expressly stated by the national
court, were analogous to those of the *Torfaen* case: both cases involved
undertakings operating in a sector which deals to a large extent in products
j imported from other member states and in which a considerable proportion of
sales is made on Sundays, so that closure on Sundays has the effect of reducing the
volume of sales and thus the volume of imports from other member states (see
para 5 of my opinion ([1991] ECR I-997 at 1009–1010)). I therefore see no reason
to distinguish the *Torfaen* case from the *Conforama* and *Marchandise* cases on
account of factual differences either.

The applicability in principle of art 30 of the EEC Treaty and the court's
recent case law   a

11. The first question raised by the House of Lords seeks to obtain a definite
answer with regard to the consequences of the court's judgments in the *Conforama*
and *Marchandise* cases for the United Kingdom Sunday trading rules. In those
judgments the court concluded that—

> 'it must therefore be held that the prohibition contained in Article 30 of   b
> the Treaty, properly construed, does not apply to national legislation
> prohibiting the employment of staff on Sundays [after 12 noon].' (See the
> *Conforama* judgment [1991] ECR I-997 at 1025 (para 13); the *Marchandise*
> judgment [1991] ECR I-1027 at 1041 (para 14), with the added phrase in
> square brackets.)

This judgment caused confusion in Great Britain inasmuch as it departed from   c
the formula used in the *Torfaen* case. In that judgment the court stated ([1990] 1
All ER 129 at 156, [1990] 2 QB 19 at 53 (para 17)):

> '. . . art 30 of the Treaty must be interpreted as meaning that the
> prohibition which it lays down does not apply to national rules prohibiting
> retailers from opening their premises on Sunday where the restrictive effects   d
> on Community trade which may result therefrom do not exceed the effects
> intrinsic to rules of that kind.'

In addition the court stated ([1990] 1 All ER 129 at 156, [1990] 2 QB 19 at 53
(para 16)):

> 'The question whether the effects of specific national rules do in fact   e
> remain within that limit is a question of fact to be determined by the national
> court.'

12. According to B & Q, it follows from those judgments, as was rightly
emphasised in the *Torfaen* case, that the prohibition contained in art 30 of the
EEC Treaty is in principle applicable: the Sunday trading ban contained in the   f
1950 Act does amount to a measure having equivalent effect within the meaning
of art 30. The court was therefore right to leave it to the national court to assess
the proportionality of the rules, the actual objective pursued by them and their
justification under Community law.

On the other hand, the city councils of Stoke-on-Trent and Norwich and the   g
United Kingdom submit that it follows from the *Conforama* and *Marchandise* cases
that the prohibition contained in art 30 is not applicable to national rules which,
as in the *Torfaen* case, prohibit retailers from opening their shops on Sundays for
the sale of certain goods to customers. The city councils argue that as regards the
reply to that question the United Kingdom Sunday trading rules cannot be
distinguished from the provisions at issue in the *Conforama* and *Marchandise* cases.   h
The ruling in those cases is thus fully applicable to the United Kingdom Sunday
trading rules. The United Kingdom goes on to take the view that the
proportionality test applied by the court in those cases is equally applicable to the
United Kingdom Sunday trading rules at issue in the *Torfaen* case.

The Commission also considers that the prohibition contained in art 30, in
accordance with the judgments in the *Conforama* and *Marchandise* cases, is not   j
applicable to the United Kingdom Sunday trading rules.

13. It seems to me that the *Conforama* and *Marchandise* judgments and the
Torfaen judgment are not in conflict as regards the applicability in principle of
art 30 to provisions such as the United Kingdom Sunday trading ban. The

different formulation of the court's judgment results merely from the fact that in

a the first-mentioned cases the court itself assessed the issue of proportionality (see the *Conforama* judgment [1991] ECR I-997 at 1025 (para 12), the *Marchandise* judgment [1991] ECR I-1027 at 1041 (para 13)), whilst in the *Torfaen* case it referred that question to the national court. If the court had been of the view in the *Conforama* and *Marchandise* cases that the French and Belgian labour provisions did not fall within the scope of art 30 at all, it could have said so straight away. As

b I have stated, there is a difference between the various judgments in regard to the application of the proportionality test. In this connection it is necessary to provide the referring courts with terms of reference concerning the criteria to be applied and by whom they are to be applied. Only then can the consistency of the court's case law on the free movement of goods be safeguarded. It is not acceptable that

c with regard to the same legislation attracting criminal sanctions for infringements national courts should decide in one case that it is valid under Community law (resulting normally in conviction of the person who has infringed the law) and in another that the law is invalid (normally leading to acquittal).

14. A study of the court's recent case law on the free movement of goods reveals, in my view, the following *guiding principles.*

d   In the first place, it is clearly established that the court's broad *Dassonville* (*Procureur du Roi v Dassonville* Case 8/74 [1974] ECR 837) and *Cassis de Dijon* (*Rewe-Zentral AG v Bundesmonopolverwaltung für Branntwein* Case 120/78 [1979] ECR 649) formula continues to apply with undiminished scope. The starting point for the court's analysis continues to be the finding that 'all trading rules . . . which are capable of hindering, directly or indirectly, actually or potentially,

e intra-Community trade' are to be regarded as measures having equivalent effect prohibited by art 30 (see the judgment in *Procureur du Roi v Dassonville* Case 8/74 [1974] ECR 837 at 852 (para 5). For recent applications of this formula see, inter alia, the judgments in *SCP Boscher Studer et Fromentin v SA British Motors Wright* Case C-239/90 [1991] ECR I-2023 (para 13), *EC Commission v Belgium* Case C-287/89 [1991] ECR I-2233 (para 16) and *Aragonesa de Publicidad Exterior SA v*

f *Departmento de Sanidad y Seguridad Social de la Generalitat de Cataluña* Joined cases C-1/90 and C-176/90 (OJ 1991 C220, p 8) (para 9) 'even though the hindrance is slight and even though it is possible for imported products to be marketed in other ways' (see judgments in *Criminal proceedings against van de Haar and Kaveka de Meern BV* Joined cases 177 and 178/82 [1984] ECR 1797 at 1812–1813 (para

g 13), *EC Commission v France* Case 269/83 [1985] ECR 837 at 846 (para 10) and *EC Commission v Italy* Case 103/84 [1986] ECR 1759 at 1773 (para 18)). The only qualification of that rule remains, as a matter of principle, the *Cassis de Dijon* 'rule of reason': in the absence of common rules (relating to the manufacture of the products in question, or to their marketing) obstacles to free movement within the Community resulting from disparities between national laws must be

h accepted in so far as those provisions may be recognised as being necessary in order to satisfy mandatory requirements (see the judgment in *Rewe-Zentral AG v Bundesmonopolverwaltung für Branntwein* Case 120/78 [1979] ECR 649 at 662 (para 8); see most recently, inter alia, the judgments in *GB-INNO-BM v Confédération du Commerce Luxembourgeois* Case C-362/88 [1990] ECR I-667 at 686 (para 10), *SARPP v Chambre Syndical des Raffineurs et Conditionneurs de Sucre de France* Case

j C-241/89 [1990] ECR I-4695 at 4723–4724 (para 31) and *Pall Corp v P J Dahlhausen & Co* Case C-238/89 [1990] ECR I-4827 at 4848 (para 12)); moreover, the laws must be necessary and proportionate to the objective pursued, and if a member state has the choice of several different means of attaining the same objective it is under an obligation to use that which is least restrictive of intra-Community trade (cf more recently, inter alia, the judgment in *Drei Glocken GmbH v USL Centro-Sud* Case 407/85 [1988] ECR 4233 at 4278 (para 10); judgments in *Buet v* *a* *Ministère public* Case 382/87 [1989] ECR 1235 at 1252 (para 13); *Bonfait v Ministère Public* Case C-269/89 [1990] ECR I-4169 at 4180 (para 11); *SARPP* judgment Case C-241/89 [1990] ECR I-4695 at 4723–4724 (para 31); *Pall* judgment Case C-238/89 [1990] ECR I-4827 at 4848 (para 12)). Furthermore, the court's judgment in *Criminal proceedings against Oosthoek's Uitgeversmaatschappij BV* Case 286/81 [1982] ECR 4575, in which the *Cassis de Dijon* formula was applied to legislation relating *b* to the manner in which a product is marketed (in addition to rules on the composition, labelling and presentation of the product itself), has recently been repeatedly reaffirmed; thus art 30 applies to legislation which restricts intra-Community trade because, by restricting or prohibiting certain forms of advertising and certain means of sales promotion, it may adversely affect marketing opportunities for imported products (see the judgment in *Criminal* *c* *proceedings against Oosthoek's Uitgeversmaatschappij BV* Case 286/81 [1982] ECR 4575 at 4587–4588 (para 15); that rule was recently reaffirmed in *Buet v Ministère Public* Case 382/87 [1989] ECR 1235 at 1251 (paras 7 to 8), *GB-INNO-BM v Confédération du Commerce Luxembourgeois* Case C-362/88 [1990] ECR I-667 at 686 (para 7), the *SARPP* case Case C-241/89 [1990] ECR I-4695 at 4723 (para 29), *SCP* *d* *Boscher Studer et Fromentin v SA British Motors Wright* Case C-239/90 [1991] ECR I-2023 at 2038 (para 14) and the *Aragonesa* case Joined cases C-1/90 and C-176/90 (OJ 1991 C220, p 8) (para 10); see also the judgments in *Criminal proceedings against Delattre* Case C-369/88 [1991] ECR I-1487 at 1539 (para 50) and *Criminal proceedings against Monteil and Samanni* Case C-60/89 [1991] ECR I-1547 at 1570 (para 37)).   *e*

15. Moreover, the court's recent case law shows that, in examining whether national legislation pursues an *objective justified* under Community law, the court is sympathetic to legislation which reflects lawful socio-economic or socio-cultural policy choices which are consistent with the public interest objectives pursued in the Treaty. Illustrations of this may be found in the *Oebel* and *Cinéthèque* judgments. *Summary proceedings against Oebel* concerned national legislation *f* which sought to improve working conditions (protection of workers in small and medium-sized bakeries against permanent night work which might damage their health) and the protection of small family businesses against ruinous competition from larger industrial undertakings (see the judgment in *Summary proceedings against Oebel* Case 155/80 [1981] ECR 1993 at 2006 (para 4), and the facts of the judgment (at 1998), where the German government explains this second *g* objective). In *Cinéthèque SA v Fédération nationale des cinémas français* Joined cases 60 and 61/84 [1985] ECR 2605 at 2626 (para 23) the court held that national legislation providing for a temporary ban on the distribution of films in video-cassette form, in order to encourage the production of films—irrespective of their origin—and thus to protect the film industry, was pursuing an objective justified *h* under Community law.

This approach may also be found in the court's case law with regard to the *provision of services*: I am thinking here particularly of the judgments in *Société Générale Alsacienne de Banque SA v Koestler* Case 15/78 [1978] ECR 1971 at 1981 (para 5) (where the court deemed acceptable legislation barring the legal recovery of gaming debts for 'reasons founded on the social order', that is to say reasons of *j* an ethical and political nature), *Procureur du Roi v Debauve* Case 52/79 [1980] ECR 833 at 857 (para 16) (in which a prohibition on cable television advertising was held to be acceptable in order to guarantee pluralism in the media), *Bond van Adverteerders v Netherlands* Case 352/85 [1988] ECR 2085 at 2136 (para 38) and

Criminal proceedings against Webb Case 279/80 [1981] ECR 3305 at 3325 (paras 18
a and 19) (where the court held a licence requirement for the provision of
manpower in the territory of a member state to be justified in the interests of
'good relations on the labour market' and the protection of the 'lawful interests
of the workforce concerned').

16. Finally, with regard more specifically to the *proportionality test*, it seems
that the court regards that test as satisfied where national legislation clearly has no
b connection, or merely a very indirect or uncertain one, with imports from other
member states or the national legislation in question does not impede imports
and exports. (There are various illustrations of this: see the judgment in *Criminal
proceedings against Oebel*, cited above; the judgments in *Blesgen v Belgium* Case 75/
81 [1982] ECR 1211; *Direction générale des impôts v Forest* Case 148/85 [1986] ECR
c 3449; *H Krantz GmbH & Co v Ontvanger der Directe Belastingen* Case C-69/88 [1990]
ECR I-583; *Quietlynn v Southend-on-Sea BC* Case C-23/89 [1990] 3 All ER 207,
[1991] 1 QB 454; and *Sheptonhurst v Newham BC* Case C-350/89 [1991] ECR I-2387.
In connection with the freedom to provide services there was recently a hint of
this idea in *Society for the Protection of Unborn Children Ireland Ltd v Grogan* Case
C-159/90 [1991] 3 CMLR 849 at 872 (para 24): the link between the provision of
d information in one member state on the clinical termination of pregnancies in
another member state and the pregnancy termination service itself (carried out
by a provider of services completely independent of the providers of the
information, themselves established in the first member state) was held by the
court to be too tenuous for a constitutional prohibition applicable in the first
member state on the provision of information to be regarded as a restriction on
e the freedom to provide services within the meaning of art 59 of the Treaty.

There is not likely to be any such sufficient link with the restrictions on imports
mentioned in art 30, so it may be inferred from *Cinéthèque* Joined cases 60 and 61/
84 [1985] ECR 2605 at 2627 (para 21), *Krantz* Case C-69/88 [1990] ECR I-583 at
597 (para 10) and *Quietlynn* Case C-23/89 [1990] 3 All ER 207 at 221, [1991] 1 QB
454 at 470 (para 11), if the legislation in question is clearly not intended to
f regulate trade between member states. Thus legislation whose application is
restricted to the marketing of products in the local retail trade or in shop premises
(regulation of delivery times of bread to individual customers and retailers in
Summary proceedings against Oebel, prohibition on the sale 'for consumption on the
premises' of beverages of a high alcohol content in *Blesgen v Belgium* Case 75/81
[1982] ECR 1211; prohibition on the sale of sex articles without a licence in
g *Quietlynn Ltd v Southend-on-Sea BC*) may not be deemed to be a measure having
equivalent effect because it clearly cannot obstruct intra-Community trade.

Moreover, it is clear from those and other judgments that the court will apply
the proportionality test *itself* where, having regard to the information provided
by the referring court, there is no possible dispute in that respect. (See, inter alia,
h the recent judgments in *Buet, GB-INNO-BM, Boscher* and *Aragonesa*, already referred
to; cf also the judgments in *SARPP* Case C-241/89 [1990] ECR I-4695 at 4721
(para 21); *Freistaat Bayern v Eurim-Pharm GmbH* Case C-347/89 [1991] ECR I-1747
at 1770–1772 (paras 27 to 35); *Denkavit* Case C-39/90 [1991] ECR I-3069 at 3108
(para 24); *Debus v Ministère Public* Joined cases C-13 and C-113/91 (OJ 1992 C167,
p 3) (paras 24 and 25). Illustrations can also be found in other areas of Community
j law: see, for example, with regard to the provision of services, the recent judgment
in *Stichting Collectieve Antennevoorziening Gouda v Commissariaat voor de Media* Case
C-288/89 (OJ 1991 C224, p 3) (paras 23 and 24).)

17. The *Torfaen, Conforama* and *Marchandise* judgments must be seen in the
context of this recent case law. All three judgments implicitly but clearly assume

that the rules in question are to be regarded as trading rules under the *Dassonville*
formula. Furthermore, in each of those cases the court states that the rules in *a*
question are not intended to govern the flow of trade between member states (see
the *Torfaen* judgment Case C-145/88 [1990] 1 All ER 129 at 156, [1990] 2 QB 19
at 53 (para 14 in fine), the *Conforama* judgment Case C-312/89 [1991] ECR I-997
at 1024 (para 8) and the *Marchandise* judgment Case C-332/89 [1991] ECR I-1027
at 1040 (para 9)), that they apply to imported and domestic products without
distinction and that the marketing of products imported from other member *b*
states is not made more difficult than the marketing of domestic products (see the
Torfaen judgment (para 11), the *Conforama* judgment (para 9) and the *Marchandise*
judgment (para 10)). In addition, it is expressly stated in the three judgments that
the compatibility of the rules in question with art 30 depends on whether the
obstacles to trade caused by the rules exceed what is necessary in order to attain *c*
the objective in view (proportionality test) and whether that objective is justified
under Community law (justification test) (see the *Torfaen* judgment (para 12), the
Conforama judgment (para 10) and the *Marchandise* judgment (para 11)).

Finally, the court discusses both these tests. With regard to the justification
test, the court accepts in all three cases that the provisions in issue pursue an
objective which is justified under Community law; they reflect certain political *d*
and economic choices, inasmuch as they seek to ensure that working and non-
working hours are so arranged as to accord with national or regional socio-cultural
characteristics, the assessment of which, in the present state of Community law,
is a matter for the member states (see the *Torfaen* judgment (para 14), the
Conforama judgment (para 11) and the *Marchandise* judgment (para 12)). As
regards the proportionality test, however, a considerable difference is to be *e*
observed between the three judgments, as I have already stated (see para 13
above): unlike its approach in the *Torfaen* judgment (see the quotation in para 11
above), the court itself applied the proportionality test in *Conforama* (para 12) and
Marchandise (para 13) as follows:

> 'It must further be stated that the restrictive effects on trade which may *f*
> stem from such rules do not seem disproportionate to the aim pursued.'

It appears from the foregoing that the court itself replies to the question
whether the objective pursued by national legislation is *justified* under Community
law and that in the *Torfaen* case it gave an affirmative reply in relation to the
United Kingdom Sunday trading rules (see para 22, post). On the other hand, the *g*
court has not yet given a clear ruling on the question who is to apply the
proportionality test.

Who is to apply the justification and proportionality tests under Community law?
18. This question of principle is not as such submitted by the national courts.
Nevertheless it is of decisive importance. As may be seen in particular in the *h*
preliminary question formulated in *Reading BC v Payless DIY Ltd* Case C-304/90,
the English courts have inferred from the *Torfaen* judgment that at least the
assessment of the proportionality of the United Kingdom Sunday trading rules is
a matter for them. B & Q goes still further in its interpretation of the *Torfaen*
case: besides the proportionality test, the determination of the actual objective of
the legislation and the examination of the question whether that objective falls *j*
within the objectives held to be justified under Community law by the court are,
it says, matters for the national courts. Those, it argues, are questions of national
law which fall outside the jurisdiction of the Court of Justice, in particular where
the objective of the legislation is open to doubt or is disputed.

Reading Borough Council, Stoke-on-Trent City Council, Norwich City Council,
a the United Kingdom and the Commission, on the other hand, consider that the
justification and proportionality under Community law of a national measure
cannot be left to the national courts. If it were, the uniform application of
Community law would be placed at risk.

19. It is clear that, in the context of a reference for a preliminary ruling, it is
the joint task of the court and the national courts to determine whether a national
b measure is compatible with Community law. The court's view as a matter of
principle on this point is abundantly clear, and is reiterated at the beginning of
the judgments in *Conforama* [1991] ECR I-997 at 1024 (para 6) and *Marchandise*
[1991] ECR I-1027 at 1039 (para 7):

c 'It must be observed *in limine* that although the Court has no jurisdiction,
in preliminary reference proceedings, to rule on the compatibility of a
national provision with the Treaty, it is nevertheless empowered to provide
the national court with all the criteria for the interpretation of Community
law which will enable the latter to assess that compatibility for the purpose
of giving judgment in the case before it.'

d In my view, the collaboration between the court and the national courts may
be stated as follows. First, the national court must, in the formulation of its
question, provide the court with all the necessary factual information and the
national legal framework, so that the court is afforded the possibility of making a
ruling with full knowledge of the facts. (The court has repeatedly emphasised
that the need to arrive at a useful interpretation of Community law makes it
e essential to define the legal context within which the interpretation requested
must be placed: see the judgments in *Union Laitière Normande v French Dairy
Farmers Ltd* Case 244/78 [1979] ECR 2663 at 2681 (para 5) and *Irish Creamery Milk
Suppliers Association v Ireland* Joined cases 36 and 71/80 [1981] ECR 735 at 748
(para 6).) The court cannot, however, rule on the correctness of that information
or legal framework. (That is settled case law: see, inter alia, the judgments in
f *Oehlschläger v Hauptzollamt Emmerich* Case 104/77 [1978] ECR 791 at 797 (para 4)
and *Hauptzollamt Bremen-Freihafen v Drünert* Case 167/84 [1985] ECR 2235 at
2246 (para 12).) The court must then provide the national court with all relevant
information with regard to Community law, including the criteria to be used in
assessing the issues of justification and proportionality. Finally, it is for the
g national court, on the basis of the reply given to it by the court, to assess the
compatibility or incompatibility of national legislation with Community law and
to determine the necessary consequences under national law.

20. With regard specifically to the assessment of justification and proportionality under Community law, the collaboration outlined above in general terms
takes the following form.
h As regards the *assessment of justification*, it is for the national court, with the
assistance of the parties, to identify as clearly as possible the policy objectives
pursued by national legislation and to bring them to the court's knowledge. (On
the question whether it is desirable for there to be contact between the court and
national courts where certain elements are missing from the preliminary
reference, I would refer to T Koopmans 'The technique of the preliminary
j question—a view from the Court of Justice' in Schermers et al (eds) *Article 177
EEC: Experiences and Problems* (1987) p 327 at p 333: 'It would be a great help if
the Court of Justice could make contact with the referring court if it should
discover that some elements of information are missing. Rules of procedure
applicable to the national courts make it impossible, however, for most of them

to reopen the case after having suspended it when they put their questions to the
Court of Justice. In particular, national rules on litigation before civil and criminal *a*
courts—as opposed to administrative courts or tribunals—are normally too strict
to permit an exchange of information after the order for a reference has been
made.') On the other hand, it is for the court to decide finally whether the
objectives thus identified are consistent with an objective pursued by Community
law or—where they fall within areas which in the current state of Community
law are within the competence of the member states—whether Community law *b*
is in any way opposed to the objectives pursued by the national measure.

With regard to the *assessment of proportionality*, it is in my view for the court,
and for the court alone, clearly and imperatively to indicate in its case law the
criteria to be used in that assessment (see paras 28 to 31, post). It is then the joint
task of the court and the national court to apply those criteria drawn from existing *c*
case law to the concrete legal and factual context. In that connection the national
court, in its order for reference, must give the fullest possible description of the
legislation in issue (legal basis, scope, detailed rules and practice governing its
application) and its restrictive effect on intra-Community trade. If it appears from
the findings of the national court and the arguments submitted to the court that
there is no room for any doubt, the court itself—as I have already stated (see *d*
para 16 above)—will state the results of the assessment under Community law.
That indeed is what was done in the *Conforama* and *Marchandise* cases. If the court
has not itself made an assessment on the basis of the information provided to it (it
may be inferred from judgments such as those recently delivered in *Schäfer Shop
BV v Minister van Economische Zaken* Case 12/88 [1989] ECR 2937 at 2962–2963
(para 23) and *Ministre des Finances v Richardt* Case C-367/89 [1992] 1 CMLR 61 at *e*
81 (para 25) that the court does refer the assessment of proportionality more
frequently to the national court), then the national court, where necessary after
further examination of the legislative and factual context, and in the light of the
court's reply to the preliminary question, must arrive at its own decision regarding
the application of the proportionality requirement. *f*

The requirement of an objective which is justified under Community law
21. In its first question Reading and Sonning Magistrates' Court seeks to
determine whether the objective underlying the United Kingdom Sunday trading
provisions is justified under Community law within the meaning of paras 12 to *g*
14 of the *Torfaen* judgment Case C-145/88 [1990] 1 All ER 129 at 156, [1990] 2
QB 19 at 52–53. The magistrates' court considers that that objective is to ensure
'so far as possible that shopworkers do not have to work on Sundays, with a view
to maintaining what many regard as the traditional English Sunday'.

According to Reading Borough Council and the United Kingdom, that question
was answered in para 13 of the *Torfaen* judgment, and it is sufficient that one of *h*
the objectives of the Sunday trading provisions should be justified under
Community law for those provisions to be compatible as a whole with Community
law. The Commission, too, considers that the court in the *Torfaen* case, as in the
Conforama and *Marchandise* cases, gave an affirmative reply to the question
whether the legislation in question pursued an objective justified under
Community law. *j*

B & Q, on the other hand, contends that the question put by the magistrates'
court is based on a false premise. The objective of s 47 of the 1950 Act is limited
to protecting full-time shop workers. If the question were whether that objective
is justified under Community law, the answer would be in the affirmative,
provided that the legislation in practice attains that objective and satisfies the

a proportionality requirement. Payless DIY adds that, in so far as the Sunday trading ban reflects 'certain political and economic choices' made by the United Kingdom Parliament, s 47 is certainly no longer in accord with 'national or regional socio-cultural characteristics' in England and Wales. As a result of the increase in part-time working in the retail sector there is little need for legislative protection of part-time workers by means of the Sunday trading ban, since in their case there can be no suggestion of overworking or exploitation by the employer.

b 22. Like Reading Borough Council, the United Kingdom and the Commission, I am of the opinion that the question raised by the magistrates' court has already been answered in the *Torfaen* case itself. It is sufficient in that connection to read the relevant grounds of the judgment (paras 13 and 14). In so far as there might still have been some doubt after the *Torfaen* case with regard to the justification under Community law of that objective, it was entirely removed by the

c judgments in the *Conforama* and *Marchandise* cases. There the court expressly stated that—

> 'legislation such as the legislation at issue pursues an aim which is justified with regard to Community law. The Court has already held, in its judgment of 23 November 1989 in the *Torfaen* case, that national rules governing the

d opening hours of retail premises reflect certain political and economic choices in so far as their purpose is to ensure that working and non-working hours are so arranged as to accord with national or regional socio-cultural characteristics, and that, in the present state of Community law, is a matter for the Member States.' (See the *Conforama* judgment [1991] ECR I-997 at

e 1025 (para 11) and the *Marchandise* judgment [1991] ECR I-1027 at 1040– 1041 (para 12).)

It follows unambiguously from those judgments that the United Kingdom Sunday trading provisions pursue an objective justified under Community law, regard being had to the policy choices underlying those provisions. There the

f matter could rest, were it not for the fact that in judicial pronouncements and academic writing in the various member states doubts have been expressed concerning the import of these judgments in relation to the grounds of justification recognised by the Treaty or by the court. I should therefore like to make a few general obervations.

23. The question arises whether, in addition to the grounds of justification

g exhaustively enumerated in art 36 of the EEC Treaty and the specific 'mandatory requirements' under art 30 of the EEC Treaty which have hitherto been recognised in the court's case law (effectiveness of fiscal controls, fairness of commercial transactions, consumer protection, environmental protection), the court also recognises a general, less specific category of grounds of justification, that is to say, in the terms of the *Torfaen, Conforama* and *Marchandise* cases, those 'which reflect

h certain political and economic choices . . . [in accordance] with national or regional socio-cultural characteristics, [the assessment of which,] in the present state of Community law, is a matter for the Member States'. (With regard to the freedom to provide services the court has for some considerable time recognised the protection of workers as an 'imperative public interest requirement' justifying a restriction on intra-Community trade: that occurred for the first time in *Criminal*

j *proceedings against Webb* Case 279/80 [1981] ECR 3305 at 3325 (para 19); cf most recently the judgments in *Gouda's* case Case C-288/89 (OJ 1991 C224, p 3) (para 14), and in *EC Commission v Netherlands* Case C-353/89 (OJ 1991 C224, p 3) (para 18).)

Before answering that question I should make the following remark. It seems to me that certain further *special* mandatory requirements may be added to the list of mandatory requirements inherent in art 30 of the EEC Treaty (which may *a* be relied upon solely in order to justify non-discriminatory national provisions). I have in mind requirements which are consistent with specific objectives or interests which may be derived from other provisions of the Community Treaties—particularly after the amendments made by the Single European Act— relating more specifically to economic and social policy (for example, the improvement of working conditions), economic and social cohesion, research and technical development and the protection and enhancement of the environment. *b* (In some cases the court does not await recognition of an objective in a Treaty provision in order to regard it as an imperative requirement. For example, the court regarded environmental protection as an essential Community objective well before the entry into force of the Single European Act: see the judgment in *Procureur de la République v Association de défence des brûleurs d'huiles usagées* Case *c* 240/83 [1985] ECR 531 at 549 (para 13). In the *Webb* judgment Case 279/80 [1981] ECR 3305, too, the protection of workers was also recognised, this time in connection with the freedom to provide services, as an 'imperative public interest requirement', some considerable time before the entry into force of the Single European Act.)

The question, then, is whether there is also a place for a *general* ground of *d* justification for national provisions which reflect political and economic choices in keeping with national or regional socio-cultural characteristics. As the court's case law now stands an affirmative answer cannot as such be inferred from the judgments concerning such provisions. In *Summary proceedings against Oebel* Case 155/80 [1981] ECR 1993 at 2008 (para 12), in which the court regarded the national provisions in question as 'a legitimate element of economic and social *e* policy', the court immediately added: 'consistent with the objectives of public interest pursued by the Treaty', and pointed out that the intention of the legislation was 'to improve working conditions in a manifestly sensitive [production] industry'. In the *Torfaen* case [1990] 1 All ER 129 at 156, [1990] 2 QB 19 at 52–53 (paras 13 and 14) the court expressly recognised, referring to *f* *Summary proceedings against Oebel*, that national measures relating to the opening hours of shops are also consistent with the objectives of public interest pursued by the Treaty. Subsequently, it was confirmed in the *Marchandise* case [1991] ECR I-1027 at 1042 (para 19) that in these measures the 'objective is worker protection'. In other words, in those judgments the court is consciously making a connection with specific mandatory requirements already recognised in the case *g* law.

24. It is not my intention in these remarks to preclude the possibility that there may well be a place for a ground of justification generally concerning 'national rules which reflect certain political and economic choices in keeping with national or regional socio-cultural characteristics'. I am thinking of provisions adopted in policy areas which in the current state of Community law (still *h* predominantly economically orientated) lie *outside* the competence of the Community and are thus not *consistent* with an essential Treaty objective, but are not contrary to one either. Examples are national provisions concerning questions of a purely political, moral or religious nature or the protection of the cultural and linguistic identity of a people, whose assessment is undoubtedly, to take the words of the Sunday trading judgments, 'in the present state of Community law *j* ... a matter for the Member States'. (With regard to the relationship between a policy for promoting a national language as an expression of national identity and culture and freedom of movement for workers, see the judgment in *Groener v Minister of Education* Case C-379/87 [1989] ECR 3967.) Nevertheless, here too, in

order to prevent an undesirable proliferation of grounds of justification, I consider
a that as close a connection as possible must be sought with the grounds provided
for in art 36 of the EEC Treaty (indeed, it is far from hypothetical that such
provisions may be able to rely on the grounds mentioned in that provision of
'public morality, public policy or public security [or] the protection of national
treasures possessing artistic . . . value'), the objectives of Community law
recognised in the European treaties and the fundamental rights which form part
b of the Community legal order, in the light of which those grounds and objectives
must be construed. (See, in relation to the freedom to provide services (arts 66
and 56 of the EEC Treaty), the judgment in *Elliniki Radiophonia Tiléorassi-Anonimi
Etairia v Dimotiki Etairia Pliroforissis* Case C-260/89 [1991] ECR I-2925 at 2964
(para 45). With regard to the freedom to provide services the court has held,
c moreover, in the recent judgments on the Netherlands 'Mediawet' that a national
cultural policy, connected, through the operation of a pluralistic broadcasting
system, with the protection of freedom of expression, may constitute an
imperative public interest requirement justifying a restriction on the freedom to
provide services: see the *Gouda* judgment Case C-288/89 (OJ 1991 C224, p 3)
(para 23); *EC Commission v Netherlands* C-353/89 (OJ 1991 C224, p 3) (para 30).)
d   However that may be, it must in any event be correct that (i) it is in the final
analysis for the court—desirable though it may be for the national court to make
its own view known to the court—to determine whether the objective is justified,
and (ii) that a national measure whose objective is justified under Community
law must still be assessed against the principle of proportionality. This assessment
serves to ensure that a measure which is justified in itself does not nevertheless
e conflict with the principle of the free movement of goods.
   25. The foregoing general observations permit me to share the view formed
by the court in the Sunday trading cases with regard to the justification under
Community law of Sunday trading rules. Whatever may be the reasons for the
enactment and retention of the United Kingdom Sunday trading ban, it seems to
be clear, as was confirmed by the United Kingdom at the hearing, that those
f provisions are intended to ensure that shopworkers should not (or as little as
possible) have to work on Sundays. That gives them, inter alia, the possibility of
devoting that day to family or friends in non-occupational activities. In so far as
such an objective is aimed at social protection, as the court has held, it is consistent
with one of the objectives of Community law, that is to say the improvement of
g working conditions and the protection, by means of regular rest periods, of the
health of shopworkers. The fact that a specific day, Sunday, is chosen for that
purpose reflects a choice in keeping with a national or regional socio-cultural
preference in a policy area outside the sphere of competence of the Community;
subject to application of the proportionality test, I cannot see why it should be
contrary to Community law.
h
The Community proportionality requirement
   26. In its second question the House of Lords seeks to determine whether it is
immediately apparent, whether or not evidence is adduced, that a measure such
as the Sunday trading ban is proportionate to the objective pursued which is
justified under Community law. In the event that the reply to that question
j should be in the negative, the House of Lords seeks in its third question to
ascertain on what criteria and by reference to what evidence the national court
must determine whether the restrictive effects of the legislation under examination
exceed the effects intrinsic to rules of that kind. The first three sub-questions and
the sixth sub-question of the second question submitted by the Reading and

Sonning Magistrates' Court are along the same lines. The first sub-questions once
again concern the criteria to be applied by national courts; more specifically they *a*
concern the question whether and to what extent the criteria mentioned in art 3
of Commission Directive (EEC) 70/50 are applicable. The third sub-question
seeks to ascertain to what extent the national court, in its assessment of the
proportionality requirement, must abide by the conclusion of the national
legislature. In the sixth sub-question the national court asks how a national court
is to compare the restrictive effects of the legislation with the objective pursued *b*
by that legislation.

27. As I have already stated (see para 20 above), it is ultimately for the national
court to assess the proportionality of the national measure in question. I do not
think there are any measures in respect of which it is prima facie clear, that is to
say without any evidence being adduced, that they satisfy the proportionality test. *c*
However, as I have observed, the information provided to the court by the
national court in its reference for a preliminary ruling may be so clear and
uncontested with regard to the absence or near absence of any restrictive effect of
the legislation on intra-Community trade that the result of the proportionality
test is obvious and can be stated by the court itself.

The reply to the third sub-question raised by the Reading and Sonning *d*
Magistrates' Court follows from that. In my view the national court may not
automatically accept the view of the national legislature or limit itself to deciding
whether the national legislature, in the light of the proportionality requirement,
could reasonably have adopted the legislative provisions in question. (That
approach appears to have been taken in the judgment of the High Court of Justice,
Chancery Division, in *Stoke-on-Trent City Council v B & Q plc* [1991] 4 All ER 221, *e*
[1991] Ch 48.) I think that is clear from the court's case law, in particular the
judgment in *Criminal proceedings against Miro BV* Case 182/84 [1985] ECR 3731.
In that judgment the court expressly rejected an argument put forward by the
German government to the effect that it was for the national legislature to assess
the need for a prohibition on the use of the name 'Jenever', and that the national
courts were bound to follow that assessment (at 3744 (para 14)): *f*

'As regards the latter argument, it must be stated that neither Article 30 of
the Treaty nor indeed Article 36 reserves certain matters to the exclusive
jurisdiction of the Member States. When in order to satisfy mandatory
requirements recognized by Community law national legislation creates *g*
obstacles to the fundamental principle of the free movement of goods, it
must observe the limits laid down by Community law. It is for the Court,
which interprets Community law in the final instance, and for the national
courts, which reach their decisions on the basis of that interpretation, to
ensure that those limits are observed. In the final analysis the German
Government's argument amounts to a repudiation of review by the Court *h*
and therefore runs counter to the uniformity and effectiveness of Community
law. It must therefore be rejected.'

28. That brings me to the questions on the *criteria* to be applied by the national
courts, and where appropriate by the Court of Justice, in assessing proportionality.
I shall begin by dealing with the questions on the significance of art 3 of *j*
Commission Directive 70/50 in the application of the proportionality test. The
starting point is para 15 of the *Torfaen* judgment, in which express reference was
made to that directive. For the sake of clarity I shall reproduce the text of the
relevant provision of the directive:

a   'This directive also covers measures governing the marketing of products which deal, in particular, with shape, size, weight, composition, presentation, identification or putting up and which are equally applicable to domestic and imported products, where the restrictive effect of such measures on the free movement of goods exceeds the effects intrinsic to trade rules.

b   This is the case, in particular, where:—the restrictive effects on the free movement of goods are out of proportion to their purpose;—the same objective can be attained by other means which are less of a hindrance to trade.'

29. The magistrates' court asks first of all whether the national court is required to apply the criteria set out in art 3 of Commission Directive 70/50. According to Reading Borough Council that is certainly so. By expressly referring in the *Torfaen* *c* case to the above-mentioned provision and by adopting its wording, the court, it argues, indicated that art 3 of Commission Directive 70/50 accurately reflects the scope of art 30. In my opinion that interpretation goes too far. Since the expiry of the transitional period (that is to say since 1 January 1970) Commission Directive 70/50 has played a modest role: the prohibition imposed by art 30 of *d* the EEC Treaty has since then had direct effect and thus 'its implementation does not require any subsequent intervention of the Member States or Community institutions' (see the judgment in *Iannelli & Volpi SpA v Meroni* Case 74/76 [1977] ECR 557 at 575 (para 13). In any event the directive was regarded by the Commission mainly as a set of guidelines. A Mattera *Le Marché Unique Européen. Ses règles, son fonctionnement* (2nd edn, 1990) p 42 confirms that 'the objective of *e* the Commission was to lay down an "authoritative point of reference" based on its experience acquired in investigating numerous cases of "measures having equivalent effect", in order to enable Member States to be better acquainted with the extent of their obligations in the matter'). In its case law the court thus refers to Commission Directive 70/50—in particular to the list of categories of measures having equivalent effect contained in art 2(3)—only where the wording of the *f* directive tallies with its settled case law. (I think that is clearly to be seen in the judgments in *EC Commission v Italy* Case 56/87 [1988] ECR 2919 at 2928 (para 7) and *EC Commission v Belgium* Case C-249/88 [1991] ECR I-1275 (para 7 in fine), where it is stated: 'This interpretation of Article 30 [that is to say that provided for in art 2(3)(c) to (e) of Directive 70/50] is confirmed by the Court's settled case *g* law'.) To a certain extent that may be compared with the court's reference to the general programmes adopted by the Council on the right of establishment and the freedom to provide services, to which it sometimes has regard, since they 'provide useful guidance with a view to the implementation of the provisions of the Treaty' (see, inter alia, the recent judgment in *EC Commission v Italy* Case 63/ 86 [1988] ECR 29 at 52 (para 14)).

h   The criteria for the assessment of proportionality under Community law must therefore be found in the court's case law. That, I think, also provides the answer to the next question raised by the magistrates' court, namely whether a national measure must satisfy *each* of the criteria mentioned in art 3(2) of Directive 70/50; here again it is the court's case law that is decisive, and not that provision of the directive.

j   30. What, then, are the criteria for applying the proportionality requirements at Community law, as they may be deduced from the court's case law? As was emphasised twice in the *Torfaen* judgment [1990] 1 All ER 129 at 156, [1990] 2 QB 19 at 52–53 (paras 12, 15), the starting point is that the restrictive effects of national legislation on intra-Community trade may not exceed what is necessary in order to ensure the attainment of the objective justified under Community law. There are two aspects to that, which may be summarised as follows.

First of all, it must be determined whether the national measure in question is *objectively necessary* in order to further the attainment of the objective pursued by it. That means that the measure must be *relevant* (effective), that is to say of such a nature as to afford effective protection of the public interest involved (cf the wording adopted by the court in *Criminal proceedings against Wurmser* Case 25/88 [1989] ECR 1105 at 1128 (para 13)), and must be *essential* in order to attain the objective, which implies that the competent legislator does not have an equally effective alternative available to it which would have a *less restrictive* effect on the free movement of goods. (The criterion set out in the last indent of the second sub-paragraph of art 3 of Commission Directive 70/50 is to the same effect as this latter aspect of the necessity test.) Secondly, even if the national measure is effective and essential with regard to the objective pursued, it must be determined whether the restriction caused thereby to intra-Community trade is *in relation*, that is to say *proportionate*, to that objective. (In other words this is an application of the test mentioned in the first indent of the second sub-paragraph of art 3 of Commission Directive 70/50.) It may be seen from the foregoing that the proportionality test in the broad understanding of the term essentially contains both a dual necessity criterion (relevance and indispensability of the measure) and a proportionality criterion in the strict sense.

31. That brings me to the last sub-question (f) of the second question submitted by the magistrates' court. In it the national court seeks additional information on the *manner* in which the restrictive effects on the free movement of goods arising from national legislation must be *compared* with the objective pursued by that legislation.

That request for clarification is also implicit in the third question submitted by the House of Lords. Here we are concerned with the crux of the proportionality test. It may be seen from the analysis of the proportionality requirement set out above that that assessment comprises various comparisons: first, it must be examined whether the means provided for in the legislation are relevant, that is to say have a causal connection with the objective pursued. Then it must be examined whether the measure in question is essential, that is to say the objective could not equally well be attained by means of other measures less restrictive of the free movement of goods. That entails comparing two possible measures in the light of the objective pursued. Finally, it must be determined whether the restriction on trade caused by the measure in question is not disproportionate to its objective, which implies the comparison of a specific restriction on trade with the objective pursued.

Each of these comparisons entails the balancing of points of comparison which are not, or not fully, quantifiable. That is particularly true of the last-mentioned comparison, in which two conflicting values are weighed against each other, namely the greatest possible freedom of intra-Community trade and the objective pursued by the national legislation in question. Such a comparison naturally implies an assessment which cannot be made solely on the basis of quantifiable data, but that does not mean that the assessment is impossible. More specifically, in the present cases I think it is clear that the obstacles to intra-Community trade caused by the United Kingdom Sunday trading provisions go no further than is necessary and are not excessive, regard being had to the objective pursued by the legislation. The fact that the legislation, as is expressly confirmed by the magistrates' court in its reference for a preliminary ruling, affects domestic and imported products without distinction and pro rata and does not seriously hamper

sales through the same channels on the week as a whole (which is confirmed by
a the forecast mentioned by the magistrates' court to the effect that the removal of
the ban would have only a limited effect on total imports from other member
states, that is to say about 0·8%) can only support my conclusion, as has already
been acknowledged by the court in the *Conforama* and *Marchandise* cases: this is
legislation which is not discriminatory, is not intended to regulate trade and
whose effects on intra-Community trade are not such as to lead to partitioning of
b the market.

32. Again in relation to the application of the proportionality test, the Reading
and Sonning Magistrates' Court referred to the court two supplementary sub-
questions (points (d) and (e) of the second question). In the first place the court is
asked whether the national court, in assessing the effects of the legislation in
c question, may take account of the totality of the restrictive effects on intra-
Community imports or only of the restrictive effects on imported goods compared
to domestic goods. The answer to that is that in its case law the court does not
restrict itself to the *discriminatory* effect of national legislation on imported goods,
but takes account in its assessment of *all restrictions* on intra-Community trade
caused by the legislation. Even in cases where it is clear that a national measure is
d applicable without distinction to domestic and imported products and the court
finds that there is no question of any intention to partition markets or manipulate
trade flows, it takes as the criterion for the purposes of the proportionality test the
totality of the restrictions caused to intra-Community trade (in particular in the
Cinéthèque judgment Joined cases 60 and 61/84 [1985] ECR 2605 at 2626 (para 22)
and the *Torfaen* judgment Case 145/88 [1990] 1 All ER 129 at 156, [1990] 2 QB
e 19 at 52 (para 12).

These authorities also seem to me to provide an answer to the other question
submitted by the magistrates' court, that is to say the *market* to be taken into
consideration in assessing the restrictive impact of the measure in question.
Should this be all intra-Community trade in goods or services, the sector in which
f the undertaking in question operates or even the undertaking itself? The final
decision must, I think, be based on as complete as possible a set of uncontested
empirical data on the *actual effects* of a specific measure on the totality of intra-
Community trade. It seems to me to be an impossible task to define the 'relevant
market' in a given sector, (series of) products or undertaking. To decide otherwise
would entail the risk that a measure could be considered disproportionate, and
g therefore contrary to Community law, in respect of one specific industrial sector,
product or group of products, or undertaking, but not of others.

Remaining questions

I do not need to go into the third question submitted by the Reading and
Sonning Magistrates' Court, that is to say whether the United Kingdom Sunday
h trading rules fall within the sphere of application of art 36 of the Treaty: the
legislation at issue constitutes a non-discriminatory measure covered by the 'rule
of reason' inherent in art 30 of the Treaty. Even if it is considered that the United
Kingdom Sunday trading provisions in part pursue a public health objective
inasmuch as they envisage rest periods for a significant section of the population
(see para 25 above) (cf my opinion in the *Torfaen* case [1990] 1 All ER 129 at 153,
j [1990] 2 QB 19 at 48 (para 30)), in relation to non-discriminatory national
measures that ground of justification performs the same function as the mandatory
requirements inherent in art 30 of the EEC Treaty (see the *Aragonesa* judgment
Joined cases C-1/90 and C-176/90 (OJ 1991 C220, p 8) (para 13), and my opinion
in that case (para 14). Moreover, the assessment of proportionality in the context

of art 36 of the EEC Treaty is conducted in the same manner as described above
in relation to art 30 of the EEC Treaty.   *a*

I have already, on a previous occasion, replied as follows to the fourth and final
question submitted by the magistrates' court, that is to say the importance to be
attached to the fact that the United Kingdom Sunday trading rules provide for
exceptions (see my opinion in the *Torfaen* case Case C-145/88 [1990] 1 All ER 129
at 153–154, [1990] 2 QB 19 at 49–50 (para 32); it was already clear in the *Torfaen*
case that there were significant doubts as to the effectiveness of the United *b*
Kingdom Sunday trading rules: see [1990] 1 All ER 129 at 154, [1990] 2 QB 19 at
49 (para 32)). Although I accept that the question of the justification at
Community law of a national measure must be decided in the light of the
intrinsic characteristics of the measures and their actual application, objections
based on the allegedly uneven or inconsistent application of the legislation within
the same member state may well afford a cause of action under national law but, *c*
as long as there is no question of deliberate discrimination or disguised restrictions
on trade *between member states,* not under Community law.

34. I thus come to the last question, namely the sole remaining question
submitted by the High Court in *Rochdale BC v Anders* Case C-306/88. It is asked
in the event (which has not arisen) that the national measure in question should *d*
be found to contravene art 30 of the Treaty. In such a case, does the prohibition
imposed by Community law extend to the application of the legislation to
domestic products? According to Rochdale Borough Council, the answer to that
must be in the negative: were the court to declare the Sunday trading provisions
to be incompatible with art 30 of the EEC Treaty and not justified under art 36,
the provisions would become inapplicable only to products imported from other *e*
member states. This approach seems to me to be quite impractical. In the case of
simple products the distinction is already difficult to draw (how does one prove
for example that a specific kind of fruit which is also grown in Great Britain is or
is not imported?), and in the case of composite products, for example machines,
cars etc, this method of proceeding is entirely unrealistic. Nevertheless, it must
be accepted that Community law is not applicable to a purely domestic situation. *f*
(This has been repeatedly affirmed by the court, in particular with regard to
freedom of movement for workers (see, most recently, the judgment in *Steen v
Deutsche Bundespost* Case C-332/90 [1992] 2 CMLR 406), freedom of establishment
(see, inter alia, the judgment in *Criminal proceedings against Nino* Joined cases C-54/
88, C-91/88 and C-14/89 [1990] ECR I-3537) and freedom to provide services (see
the recent judgment in *Portugal v Morais* Case C-60/91 [1992] 2 CMLR 533).) The *g*
extent to which partial incompatibility of the measure in question with
Community law affects the overall validity of the measure within a member state
is a question of national law.

Conclusion   *h*

35. On the basis of the foregoing considerations I propose that the court should
reply to the questions referred to it in the present cases as follows.

In *Rochdale BC v Anders* Case C-306/88: The prohibition contained in art 30 of
the EEC Treaty is not applicable to a purely domestic situation in a member state.
It is for national law to determine the effect of a finding that a measure is
incompatible with art 30 of the EEC Treaty on the application of that measure to *j*
domestic products.

In *Reading BC v Payless DIY Ltd* Case C-304/90: Legislation of a member state
which prohibits shops from opening on Sundays pursues an objective which is
justified under Community law.

In *Reading BC v Payless DIY Ltd* Case C-304/90 and *Stoke-on-Trent City Council v*
a *B & Q plc* Case C-169/91: (1) As a matter of principle it is for the national court,
on the basis of the criteria laid down in the case law of the Court of Justice and
the reply given to it by the court following a reference for a preliminary ruling,
to determine the proportionality of a national measure under Community law.
In that connection it must in particular investigate whether the measure, regard
being had to its intrinsic characteristics and actual application, is objectively
b necessary in order to facilitate the realisation of its objective, that is to say it
contributes to the attainment of the objective and the legislature has no equally
effective alternative at its disposal which would have less restrictive effects on
intra-Community trade. In addition, the national court must, on the basis of as
complete as possible a set of undisputed empirical data, investigate whether the
restrictions on intra-Community trade as a whole occasioned by the measure are
c in proportion to the objective pursued which is justified under Community law.
(2) In so far as the information on the relevant legislation and the facts provided
to the Court of Justice by the national court in the preliminary reference
procedure is sufficient—and thus not in the absence of evidence—the court may
itself apply the proportionality test, in which case it is for the national court,
d where the measure is held to be disproportionate, to declare it to be incompatible
with Community law and determine the consequences under national law of that
declaration.

16 December 1992. **THE COURT OF JUSTICE** delivered the following
e judgment.

1. By order of 20 May 1991, which was received at the court on 1 July 1991,
the House of Lords referred to the court for a preliminary ruling under art 177 of
the EEC Treaty a number of questions on the interpretation of art 30 of the
Treaty.
f   2. The questions were raised in two sets of proceedings brought by Stoke-on-
Trent City Council and Norwich City Council against B & Q plc (B & Q).
3. In those proceedings, the two prosecuting authorities accuse B & Q of
contravening ss 47 and 59 of the Shops Act 1950 by opening their shops on
Sundays for commercial transactions other than those listed in Sch 5 to that Act.
4. Schedule 5 to the 1950 Act contains a list of items which, by way of
g exception, may be sold in shops on Sundays. They include, in particular,
intoxicating liquors, certain foodstuffs, tobacco, newspapers and other products
of everyday consumption.
5. In the proceedings before the House of Lords, before which the cases are
pending at last instance, it became apparent that the parties differed as to the
interpretation to be given to the court's judgments in, on the one hand, *Torfaen*
h *BC v B & Q plc* Case C-145/88 [1990] 1 All ER 129, [1990] 2 QB 19 and, on the
other, *Union départementale des syndicats CGT de l'Aisne v SIDEF Conforama* Case
C-312/89 [1991] ECR I-997 (*Conforama*) and *Criminal proceedings against
Marchandise* Case C-332/89 [1991] ECR I-1027 (*Marchandise*).
6. In view of the dispute as to the proper interpretation of the above-mentioned
j judgments, the House of Lords stayed the proceedings and referred the following
questions to the Court of Justice for a preliminary ruling:

'1. Whether the effect of the Court of Justice's rulings in Case-312/89
Conforama and C-332/89 *Marchandise* is to determine that the prohibition
contained in Article 30 of the EEC Treaty does not apply to national rules,

such as those in issue in Case 145/88 *Torfaen Borough Council v. B & Q plc*,
which prohibit retailers from opening their premises on Sunday for the   *a*
serving of customers with certain goods;

2. If not, whether it is nevertheless immediately apparent, whether or not
evidence is adduced, that the restrictive effects on intra-Community trade
which may result from national rules such as those in Question 1 above do
not exceed "the effects intrinsic to rules of that kind", as that phrase is used in
the ruling of the Court of Justice in Case 145/88;   *b*

3. If not, on what criteria and by reference to what, if any, factual or other
evidence the national court must determine the question whether or not the
restrictive effects on intra-Community trade which may result from national
rules such as those in Question 1 above exceed "the effects intrinsic to rules
of that kind" within the meaning of that phrase as used in the ruling of the   *c*
Court of Justice in Case 145/88.'

7. Reference is made to the report for the hearing for a fuller account of the
facts of the cases pending before the national court, the relevant legislation, the
procedure and the written observations submitted to the court, which are
mentioned or discussed hereinafter only in so far as is necessary for the reasoning
of the court.   *d*

The first question

8. The national court's first question seeks to determine whether it follows
from the court's judgments in the *Conforama* and *Marchandise* cases that the
prohibition laid down in art 30 of the Treaty does not apply to national legislation   *e*
such as that in question. That same legislation was also the subject of the court's
judgment in the *Torfaen* case, cited above.

9. In those three judgments the court found that the various bodies of national
legislation concerning the closing of shops on Sundays were not intended to
regulate the flow of goods.

10. It is also apparent from those judgments that such legislation may indeed   *f*
have adverse repercussions on the volume of sales of certain shops, but that it
affects the sale of both domestic and imported products. The marketing of
products from other member states is not therefore made more difficult than the
marketing of national products.

11. Furthermore, in the above-mentioned judgments the court recognised that
the legislation at issue pursued an aim which was justified under Community   *g*
law. National rules restricting the opening of shops on Sundays reflected certain
choices relating to particular national or regional socio-cultural characteristics. It
was for the member states to make those choices in compliance with the
requirements of Community law, in particular the principle of proportionality.

12. As far as that principle is concerned, the court stated in its judgment in the   *h*
Torfaen case that such rules were not prohibited by art 30 of the Treaty where the
restrictive effects on Community trade which might result from them did not
exceed the effects intrinsic to such rules and that the question whether the effects
of those rules actually remained within that limit was a question of fact to be
determined by the national court.

13. In its judgments in the *Conforama* and *Marchandise* cases, however, the   *j*
court found it necessary to make clear, with regard to similar rules, that the
restrictive effects on trade which might result from them did not appear to be
excessive in relation to the aim pursued.

14. The court considered that it had all the information necessary for it to rule

on the question of the proportionality of such rules and that it had to do so in
a order to enable national courts to assess their compatibility with Community law
in a uniform manner since such an assessment cannot be allowed to vary according
to the findings of fact made by individual courts in particular cases.

15. Appraising the proportionality of national rules which pursue a legitimate
aim under Community law involves weighing the national interest in attaining
that aim against the Community interest in ensuring the free movement of
b goods. In that regard, in order to verify that the restrictive effects on intra-
Community trade of the rules at issue do not exceed what is necessary to achieve
the aim in view, it must be considered whether those effects are direct, indirect
or purely speculative and whether those effects do not impede the marketing of
imported products more than the marketing of national products.

c 16. It was on the basis of those considerations that in its judgments in the
Conforama and *Marchandise* cases the court ruled that the restrictive effects on
trade of national rules prohibiting the employment of workers on Sundays in
certain retailing activities were not excessive in relation to the aim pursued. For
the same reasons, the court must make the same finding with regard to national
rules prohibiting shops from opening on Sundays.

d 17. It must therefore be stated in reply to the first question that art 30 of the
Treaty is to be interpreted as meaning that the prohibition which it lays down
does not apply to national legislation prohibiting retailers from opening their
premises on Sundays.

The second and third questions
e 18. In view of the answer given to the first question, it is unnecessary to give a
ruling on the second and third questions.

Costs
19. The costs incurred by the United Kingdom and the Commission of the
f European Communities, which have submitted observations to the court, are not
recoverable. Since these proceedings are, so far as the parties to the main
proceedings are concerned, in the nature of a step in the proceedings before the
national court, the decision on costs is a matter for that court.

On those grounds, the court, in reply to the questions referred to it by the
g House of Lords by order of 20 May 1991, hereby rules that art 30 of the Treaty is
to be interpreted as meaning that the prohibition which it lays down does not
apply to national legislation prohibiting retailers from opening their premises on
Sundays.

Mary Rose Plummer   Barrister.

Note
Rochdale Borough Council v Anders
(Case C-306/88)

COURT OF JUSTICE OF THE EUROPEAN COMMUNITIES
JUDGES DUE (PRESIDENT), KAKOURIS, RODRÍGUEZ IGLESIAS, MURRAY (PRESIDENTS OF
CHAMBERS), MANCINI, JOLIET, DÍEZ DE VELASCO, KAPTEYN AND EDWARD
ADVOCATE GENERAL VAN GERVEN
2 JUNE, 8 JULY, 16 DECEMBER 1992

After judgment was given by Caulfield J sitting in the Queen's Bench Division at
Manchester on 23 May 1988 in *Rochdale BC v Anders* [1988] 3 All ER 490 four
questions were referred by that court to the Court of Justice of the European
Communities for a preliminary ruling pursuant to art 177 of the EEC Treaty (see
[1988] 3 All ER 490 at 494). On 16 December 1992 the Court of Justice, having
heard the opinion of the Advocate General at the sitting on 8 July 1992 and after
having given its judgment in *Stoke-on-Trent City Council v B & Q plc* Case C-169/91
[1993] 1 All ER 481, gave its judgment in the *Rochdale BC* case, in which it stated
that it had been informed by the Queen's Bench Division that in view of the
judgment of the Court of Justice in *Torfaen BC v B & Q plc* Case 145/88 [1990] 1
All ER 129, [1990] 2 QB 19 the first three questions had become devoid of
purpose but that a decision on the fourth question was still required. The Court
of Justice pointed to its answer in the *Stoke-on-Trent City Council* case, which was
concerned with rules substantially similar to those in question in the *Rochdale BC*
case, and said that it followed that it was likewise unnecessary to reply to the
fourth question. The decision of the Court of Justice in the *Rochdale BC* case
accordingly does not call for a fuller report.

                                        Mary Rose Plummer   Barrister.

a ## K and another v P and others (J, third party)

CHANCERY DIVISION
FERRIS J
1, 5 MAY, 22, 23 JUNE 1992

b *Practice – Third party proceedings – Defence – Illegality – Action by plaintiff against defendant based on conspiracy and fraud – Defendant issuing third party notice against plaintiff's accountant alleging negligence and breach of contract and claiming contribution in respect of damages if payable – Third party applying to have notice struck out – Whether illegality a valid defence to claim for contribution – Civil Liability (Contribution) Act 1978, ss 1(1), 2(1)(2), 6(1).*

c In the course of an action brought by the plaintiffs against six defendants claiming damages for fraud and conspiracy to defraud arising out of various property transactions, the third defendant, who had been the plaintiffs' financial adviser, issued a third party notice against the third party, who was the plaintiffs' accountant, under s 1(1)[a] of the Civil Liability (Contribution) Act 1978, which d provided that 'any person liable in respect of any damage ... may recover contribution from any other person liable in respect of the same damage'. The notice claimed an indemnity from the third party against any damages payable by the third defendant to the plaintiffs on the basis that the accountant had acted in breach of contract or negligently in failing to advise the plaintiffs properly or at all in regard to the transactions. The master dismissed the third party's e application to have the notice struck out. The third party appealed, contending that a party who was held merely to have been negligent could not be required to contribute to damages payable by a party who had been guilty of fraud. The question arose whether the common law maxim ex turpi causa non oritur actio afforded a defence to a claim under the 1978 Act.

f **Held** – The common law maxim ex turpi causa non oritur actio was not available as a defence to a claim for contribution to damages under the 1978 Act since the specific purpose of that Act was to enable claims for contribution to be made as between parties who had no claim to contribution under the general law and the only necessary ingredients of the statutory cause of action under the Act were that g a person or persons, viz the plaintiffs, had a cause of action against a third party in respect of the same damage as gave rise to the plaintiffs' cause of action against the defendant. It was clear that to permit the ex turpi causa defence to be relied on as an answer to such a claim would narrow to a substantial extent the deliberately wide wording of s 6(1)[b] of the 19878 Act, which made a person liable in respect of any damage if the person who suffered the damage was entitled to recover h compensation from him in respect of that damage 'whatever the legal basis of his liability, whether tort, breach of contract ... or otherwise'. Accordingly, it was irrelevant that the plaintiffs' cause of action against the defendants arose from conspiracy or fraud while their cause of action against the third party arose from breach of a contractual or tortious duty of care. Moreover, under s 2(1) and (2)[c] of j the 1978 Act all the factors which, in relation to common law claims, were relevant to the ex turpi causa defence could be taken into account when assessing the amount of the contribution, even to the extent of assessing a nil contribution.

---

a   Section 1(1) is set out at p 526 e, post
b   Section 6(1) is set out at p 526 f, post
c   Section 2, so far as material, is set out at p 526 g, post

Since it was impossible to say, with the degree of certainty necessary to make a
striking-out order, that the third party would inevitably be exempted from *a*
making contribution under s 2(2) of the 1978 Act, it followed that the third party
notice could not be struck out and the appeal would therefore be dismissed (see
p 528 *c d j* to p 529 *b* and p 530 *a* to *e*, post).

Notes

For third party proceedings, see 37 *Halsbury's Laws* (4th edn) paras 254–260, and *b*
for cases on the subject, see 37(2) *Digest* (Reissue) 404–413, 2481–2532.

For the maxim ex turpi causa non oritur actio, see 12 *Halsbury's Laws* (4th edn)
para 1136, and for cases on the subject, see 1(1) *Digest* (2nd reissue) 57–58, 469–
475.

For the Civil Liability (Contribution) Act 1978, ss 1, 2, 6, see 13 *Halsbury's* *c*
Statutes (4th edn) (1991 reissue) 578, 580, 583.

Cases referred to in judgment

Chettiar v Chettiar [1962] 1 All ER 494, [1962] AC 294, [1962] 2 WLR 548, PC.
Euro-Diam Ltd v Bathurst [1988] 2 All ER 23, [1990] 1 QB 1, [1988] 2 WLR 517,
　CA. *d*
Saunders v Edwards [1987] 2 All ER 651, [1987] 1 WLR 1116, CA.
Thackwell v Barclays Bank plc [1986] 1 All ER 676.
Tinsley v Milligan [1992] 2 All ER 391, [1992] Ch 310, [1992] 2 WLR 508, CA.
Weld-Blundell v Stephens [1920] AC 956, [1920] All ER Rep 32, HL.

e

Summons

J, the third party in an action brought by the plaintiffs against the defendants
claiming damages for conspiracy to defraud in respect of a number of property
transactions carried out by the defendants on the plaintiffs' behalf, appealed from
the order of Master Munrow dated 3 Octoberr 1991 dismissing his application by
summons dated 6 June 1991 for an order that the third party notice claiming an *f*
indemnity or alternatively a contribution from J in respect of J's alleged failure
properly to advise the plaintiffs in relation to the transactions, be struck out. The
appeal was heard and judgment was given in chambers. The case is reported,
with an edited version of the judgment, by permission of Ferris J. The facts are
set out in the judgment.

g

Peter Roth (instructed by *Warner Cranston*) for the third party.
Steven Whitaker (instructed by *Lester Maddrell & Co*, Cheltenham) for the third
　defendant.
The plaintiff and the other defendants did not appear.

h

Cur adv vult

23 June 1992. The following judgment was delivered.

FERRIS J. This is an appeal by the third party, an accountant, from an order of *j*
Master Munrow made on 3 October 1991 dismissing his application that a third
party notice served upon him by the third defendant in the main action should
be struck out.

In order to understand the nature of the application it is necessary first to
consider the plaintiffs' claim against the third defendant. This is not as
straightforward as it ought to be because the statement of claim is long and
complex and in some respects obscure. There are six defendants altogether,

including the third defendant, and separate claims are made against three groups
of defendants.

The first plaintiff is a distinguished musician. The second plaintiff is his
brother. In about 1971 the first plaintiff established a music school (the centre).
For about the first twelve years of its existence the centre was carried on as an
unincorporated organisation. The second plaintiff became its administrator in
1980. It seems that the centre flourished and that by the early 1980s it had over
300 pupils and 31 part-time teachers. It outgrew its premises and in 1982 the
plaintiffs decided to acquire and convert other premises (the bakery) to become
the new premises of the centre.

The third defendant appears to have come on to the scene in about 1982 as a
financial adviser in connection with the proposal to acquire and develop the
bakery for the purposes of the centre. It is said that he advised that the centre
should be incorporated and a company (CMC) was duly formed on 29 April 1983.
Presumably CMC took over the running of the centre soon after that. The third
defendant became the managing director of CMC at or soon after its incorporation.
It is said that, at the third defendant's instance, it was proposed to raise finance for
CMC from a lender (BMT) and that the third defendant became managing
director because BMT would prefer to deal with a man having a proven business
record than with a musician.

In para 5 of the statement of claim the plaintiffs allege that various defendants,
including the third defendant—

'conspired amongst themselves and others to defraud the Plaintiffs, and
with intent to injure the Plaintiffs, by a scheme for extracting moneys from
the Plaintiffs by way of inflated valuations and percentage fees and
commission payments based upon such inflated valuations and by otherwise
exposing the Plaintiffs to liabilities, and calculated to make a profit for
themselves . . . and/or companies in which the same were interested . . . by
false representations, including forged and/or fraudulently altered and/or
concealed loan application documentation by [the third defendant].'

The overt acts of the alleged conspiracy are said to be set out in the statement
of claim. So far as the third defendant is concerned they can, I think, be
summarised as follows. (1) The third defendant fraudulently altered in a number
of material respects an application which had been signed on behalf of CMC by
the first plaintiff for a loan on the security of the bakery. (2) The third defendant
concealed from the plaintiffs the true impact of arrangements made between
CMC and two companies which I will describe simply as Crescent and Highdene
in which, unknown to the plaintiffs, the third defendant was personally interested.
(3) In May 1983 BMT, to which the application signed by the first plaintiff and
altered by the third defendant had been submitted, offered CMC a loan of
£185,500 on the security of the bakery. This was £80,000 in excess of the loan
asked for in the application in its unaltered form. The plaintiffs say that they
accepted this loan on behalf of CMC on the advice of the third defendant. (4) The
third defendant concealed from the plaintiffs what is said to have been a false and
fraudulent overvaluation of the bakery made in June 1983 by another of the
alleged conspirators in order to support an even higher level of loan by BMT.
(5) On 24 June 1983 BMT offered to lend CMC £420,000 on the security of the
bakery in substitution for its previous offer to lend £185,500. On 27 June 1983
this offer was purportedly accepted by CMC, the acceptance being signed by the
third defendant and, on the face of it, by the plaintiffs. It is said that neither of
the plaintiffs actually signed this acceptance, their apparent signatures being
forgeries made by a person or persons unknown on behalf of the conspirators or
their connected companies. (6) In August 1983 the third defendant claimed from
CMC a commission of £16,000 for himself and £8,000 for Highdene in respect

of certain commercial arrangements, not involving the bakery, negotiated
between CMC and BMT. It is said that this claim led the other directors of CMC *a*
to investigate the third defendant's activities and to dismiss him as a director of
CMC. (7) Between May and July 1983 the third defendant caused the first plaintiff
to sign in blank some cheques drawn on CMC's bank account by fraudulently
representing that these cheques would be used to pay small and urgent bills of
CMC. It is said that in fact the third defendant used six of these cheques to pay to
himself and certain other parties sums amounting to about £30,000, allegedly in *b*
connection with the financing of the centre.

Although these allegations, if made good, clearly amount to wrongdoing on
the part of the third defendant in relation to a number of individual matters, they
do not convey to my mind a particularly comprehensible account of a conspiracy
or of systematically fraudulent conduct. The rest of the statement of claim does
not make matters much clearer. It contains allegations which do not directly *c*
involve the third defendant. These include allegations against various solicitors of
negligence in connection with the execution by CMC and the plaintiffs of a legal
charge in favour of BMT to secure a loan of £420,000, the giving of personal
guarantees by the plaintiffs in respect of this indebtedness and subsequent
proceedings brought by BMT in which a possession order was made in respect of *d*
the bakery and a money judgment was given against the plaintiffs as guarantors
for a sum of nearly £375,000. It seems, although the statement of claim does not
set out the matter in any systematic way, that CMC drew down the full loan of
£420,000 and subsequently defaulted in its payments to BMT. It does not appear
precisely how the £420,000 was expended by CMC. After obtaining the possession
order in respect of the bakery, BMT sold it for about £183,000. Bankruptcy *e*
proceedings appear to have been taken against the plaintiffs by BMT. Receiving
orders were made against them in the county court but, on appeal, these orders
were, it is said, rescinded on terms which are not stated but which are said to have
been fulfilled.

The plaintiffs' underlying complaint seems to be that CMC borrowed more
than it needed and spent more of the borrowed money than it could afford to *f*
spend, with the result that there was a loss for which the plaintiffs have been held
personally liable as guarantors. But how this complaint lines up with the alleged
conspiracy and fraudulent conduct is not clear to me. I have not, of course, had
the advantage of having the plaintiffs' claim explained to me by their own counsel.

The plaintiffs claim damages from a number of defendants, including the third
defendant, under the following heads: (1) general damages for conspiracy; (2) *g*
exemplary damages on the basis that the acts complained of were calculated to
make a profit for the conspirators or their companies and constituted a cynical
disregard for the plaintiffs' rights; (3) damages for deceit as an alternative to
damages for conspiracy.

The general damages for conspiracy and the alternative damages for deceit are *h*
claimed to include the following: (a) moneys 'expended upon the CMC' by the
plaintiffs after the commencement of the company; (b) legal costs in fighting
BMT; (c) the stain and stigma of bankruptcy; (d) loss of earnings by the plaintiffs;
(e) the effect upon the health of the first plaintiff; (f) loss of reputation of the first
plaintiff; (g) distress and suffering; (h) loss of opportunity to develop the centre;
(i) other consequential loss. The want of grammatical sense in this summary *j*
reflects, I fear, a similar defect in the statement of claim itself.

The prayer for relief so far as the third defendant is concerned seeks damages
for conspiracy to defraud, exemplary damages, an indemnity in respect of any
liabilities to BMT under what is described as 'the said deed', which presumably

means the legal charge or other instrument containing the personal guarantee
a given by the plaintiffs, damages for deceit and interest.

From this analysis of the statement of claim it is clear that all the plaintiffs'
claims against the third defendant are based upon allegations of fraud of one kind
or another and that no relief is claimed on any basis which does not involve fraud.

The third party notice with which I am concerned is dated 9 November 1990.
After referring to the action it continues as follows:

b

> 'The Third Defendant denies the Plaintiffs' claim against him but if
> contrary to his contentions he is held liable to the Plaintiffs, he claims against
> you to be indemnified against the Plaintiffs' claims and the costs of this
> action, alternatively contribution to such extent of the Plaintiffs' claims as the
> Court may think fit, on the grounds that (1) At all material times, you were
c
> the accountants retained by and advising the Plaintiffs and each of them in
> respect of the proposed transaction (and in particular the financial aspects
> thereof) in relation to which the said alleged liability of the Plaintiffs and
> each of them to [BMT] was incurred; (2) In about the period from January to
> September 1983, you acted in breach of contract and negligently towards the
> Plaintiffs and each of them in that you failed to advise them properly or at all
d
> with regard to the said proposed transaction and the financial aspects thereof
> and in particular failed to explain the full nature and extent thereof to the
> Plaintiffs and each of them and/or failed to advise the Plaintiffs as to the
> commercial prudence of the same and/or the risks inherent in proceeding
> with the same and/or failed to warn them not to enter into the same. (3) That
> insofar as any financial information was or may have been communicated by
e
> The Third Defendant he did so in reliance upon information supplied by
> you.'

No third party directions have been sought, so that there is no order that the
notice shall stand as a statement of claim in the third party proceedings.
Nevertheless the third party and his advisers seem to have acted as if such a
f direction had been given, for a document expressed to be a defence and
counterclaim of the third party has been served. I do not need to refer to this.

On 6 June 1991 there was issued on behalf of the third party a summons
seeking an order that the third party notice be struck out pursuant to RSC Ord 18,
r 19 and the inherent jurisdiction of the court. It was this summons which was
g dismissed by the master, from whose decision this appeal is brought.

I say at once that, as Mr Roth accepted on behalf of the third party, Ord 18, r 19
appears to be inapplicable because a third party notice is not a pleading. But there
is no doubt that the court has an inherent jurisdiction to strike out any proceeding
which is an abuse of its process; and it is such an abuse to commence and maintain
a proceeding which has no prospect whatever of success. The test is, of course, a
h strict one. If there is any doubt about the ultimate outcome, the proceeding must
be left on foot.

Before the master the attack on the third party notice was, I understand, based
on somewhat technical issues, such as the want of particularity in the allegations
made against the third party, the fact that there is no assertion that he was part of
the conspiracy in which the third defendant is said to have joined and an argument
j that the third defendant and the third party are not on any view liable to the
plaintiffs in respect of the same damage, so that the case is not within s 1(1) of the
Civil Liability (Contribution) Act 1978, which I shall mention in some detail
later. It was not, I think, surprising that the master rejected these arguments.
Any complaint of want of particularity could and should be dealt with by

appropriate directions in the third party proceedings. Moreover it is difficult, if not impossible, to determine whether the third defendant and the third party are *a* liable in respect of the same damage until there has been a trial in order to determine what, if any, damage they are each liable for.

On this appeal Mr Roth, on behalf of the third party, advanced arguments of a more fundamental nature than those advanced before the master. He contended that, as the plaintiffs' claim against the third defendant is based exclusively on conspiracy and fraud, the third defendant will only be held liable to the plaintiffs *b* if he is found guilt of serious dishonesty. In contrast, it is not said by the third defendant or by anyone else that the third party was guilty of any form of dishonesty. If he is liable to the plaintiffs at all it can only be on the basis of professional negligence. Mr Roth contended that it is inconceivable that a party who has been held to be merely negligent should be required to contribute to the *c* damages payable by a party who has been found guilty of fraud. It is rather as if a burglar, when sued for the recovery of the stolen property or its value, sought contribution from a security guard who, by falling asleep while on duty, had made the burglary possible. It was said, with obvious force, that no such claim could ever succeed. The maxim ex turpi causa non oritur actio and its related rules would be applicable. *d*

It is evident that the third defendant and the third party are not, on any view of the case, joint contractors or joint tortfeasors or in a relationship where contribution is available under equitable principles. The sole basis of the third defendant's claim for contribution is the 1978 Act, of which the material provisions for present purposes are s 1(1), which needs to be read in conjunction with s 6(1), and s 2(1) and (2). Section 1(1) provides: *e*

> 'Subject to the following provisions of this section, any person liable in respect of any damage suffered by another person may recover contribution from any other person liable in respect of the same damage (whether jointly with him or otherwise).'

Section 6(1) provides: *f*

> 'A person is liable in respect of any damage for the purposes of this Act if the person who suffered it (or anyone representing his estate or dependants) is entitled to recover compensation from him in respect of that damage (whatever the legal basis of his liability, whether tort, breach of contract, breach of trust or otherwise).' *g*

Section 2, so far as material, provides:

> '(1) Subject to subsection (3) below, in any proceedings for contribution under section 1 above the amount of the contribution recoverable from any person shall be such as may be found by the court to be just and equitable having regard to the extent of that person's responsibility for the damage in *h* question.
>
> (2) Subject to subsection (3) below, the court shall have power in any such proceedings to exempt any person from liability to make contribution, or to direct that the contribution to be recovered from any person shall amount to a complete indemnity . . .' *j*

Section 2(3) is not material for present purposes.

It appears to me that the arguments which I have heard involve the consideration of three separate questions, namely: (1) does the ex turpi causa maxim and its related rules (which I will refer to as 'the ex turpi causa defence') afford a defence to a claim for contribution under the 1978 Act? (2) if the ex turpi causa defence is capable of so applying, can it be said, with the degree of certainty

necessary for a striking-out order to be made, that the defence will exclude any
a contribution from the third party in the circumstances of this case? (3) leaving
aside the ex turpi causa defence, can it be said with the necessary degree of
certainty that the court will, under s 2(1) and (2) of the 1978 Act, exempt the
third party from liability to make contribution even if he has been negligent in
the performance of some duty of care owed to the plaintiffs?

b (1) *Is the ex turpi causa defence available as an answer to a claim to
contribution under the 1978 Act?*
    The defence is, of course, one which is part of the common law, not statute,
being founded upon public policy. For an application of the defence in a case
where a claimant, in order to make good his claim, was obliged to assert his own
fraudulent purpose, I was referred to *Chettiar v Chettiar* [1962] 1 All ER 494,
c [1962] AC 294. The defence has been considered in a number of recent cases in
which it has been held that it is to be applied in a flexible and pragmatic way.
There were cited to me *Thackwell v Barclays Bank plc* [1986] 1 All ER 676, *Saunders
v Edwards* [1987] 2 All ER 651, [1987] 1 WLR 116, *Euro-Diam Ltd v Bathurst*
[1988] 2 All ER 23, [1990] 1 QB 1 and, by means of a note from counsel after the
d conclusion of argument, *Tinsley v Milligan* [1992] 2 All ER 391, [1992] Ch 310. In
the *Euro-Diam* case ([1988] 2 All ER 23 at 28–29, [1990] 1 QB 1 at 35) Kerr LJ
summarised the relevant principles. I quote the following from that summary,
but for the sake of brevity I omit some of the references to authority and the
elaboration of point (3) and the whole of point (4), which seem to me not to assist
in the present case:

e
    '(1) The ex turpi causa defence ultimately rests on a principle of public
    policy that the courts will not assist a plaintiff who has been guilty of illegal
    (or immoral) conduct of which the courts should take notice. It applies if, in
    all the circumstances, it would be an affront to the public conscience to grant
    the plaintiff the relief which he seeks because the court would thereby appear
    to assist or encourage the plaintiff in his illegal conduct or to encourage others
f in similar acts: see para (2)(iii) below. The problem is not only to apply this
    principle, but also to respect its limits, in relation to the facts of particular
    cases in the light of the authorities. (2) The authorities show that in a number
    of situations the ex turpi causa defence will prima facie succeed. The main
    ones are as follows. (i) Where the plaintiff seeks to, or is forced to, found his
g claim on an illegal contract or to plead its illegality in order to support his
    claim ... For that purpose it makes no difference whether the illegality is
    raised in the plaintiff's claim or by way of reply to a ground of defence ...
    (ii) Where the grant of relief to the plaintiff would enable him to benefit
    from his criminal conduct ... (iii) Where, even though neither (i) nor (ii) is
    applicable to the plaintiff's claim, the situation is nevertheless residually
h covered by the general principle summarised in (i) above. This is most
    recently illustrated by the judgment of Hutchison J in *Thackwell v Barclays
    Bank plc* [1986] 1 All ER 676 at 687, 689, as approved by this court in *Saunders
    v Edwards* [1987] 2 All ER 651 at 660, 666, [1987] 1 WLR 1116 at 1127,
    1134, and in particular per Nicholls LJ (see [1987] 2 All ER 651 at 664, [1987]
j 1 WLR 1116 at 1132). (3) However, the ex turpi causa defence must be
    approached pragmatically and with caution, depending on the circumstances:
    see eg per Bingham LJ in *Saunders v Edwards* [1987] 2 All ER 651 at 666,
    [1987] 1 WLR 1116 at 1134.'

    On behalf of the third party, Mr Roth contended that this is a clear case. The
fact that the claim is made in third party proceedings in the context of a denial by
the third defendant that he has conspired against the plaintiffs or defrauded them

must not be allowed to conceal the fact that the claim for contribution from the third party necessarily asserts the contrary, albeit on a contingent basis. The *a* position is equivalent to that which would exist if the third defendant were claiming contribution by means of a separate action after being held liable to the plaintiffs. In such an action the third defendant would have to plead that he had inflicted loss on the plaintiffs by conspiracy or fraud and had been required to compensate the plaintiffs for such loss. He would then have to plead that the loss was attributable to the third party's professional negligence in failing to draw the *b* attention of the plaintiffs to what the third defendant and others were doing. It would not, however, be possible for the third defendant to suggest that the third party was in any way guilty of any illegal conduct. A claim formulated in this way would, it was said, be a clear case for the application of the ex turpi causa defence, falling squarely within point (2)(i) of Kerr LJ's summary.

In opposition to this, Mr Whitaker, on behalf of the third defendant, pointed *c* out that this is not a case where the third defendant is himself asserting against the third party a cause of action in contract or tort. What the third defendant is asserting is a statutory cause of action under the 1978 Act, the only necessary ingredients of which are that a person or persons, namely the plaintiffs, have against the third party a cause of action in respect of the same damage as gives rise *d* to that person or person's cause of action against the third defendant. It does not matter that the plaintiffs' cause of action against the third defendant arises from conspiracy or fraud whereas their cause of action against the third party arises from breach of a contractual or tortious duty of care.

Mr Whitaker relied upon the wording of s 6(1) of the 1978 Act, which says that a party is liable in respect of any damage, and so potentially in the position of *e* being able to claim or having to make contribution, 'whatever the legal basis of his liability, whether tort, breach of contract, breach of trust or otherwise'. He pointed out that the 1978 Act replaced s 6 of the Law Reform (Married Women and Tortfeasors) Act 1935, which created a right of contribution between joint tortfeasors 'where damage is suffered by any person as a result of a tort (whether a crime or not)'. The concluding words show that a claim to contribution might *f* arise under the 1935 Act out of tortious conduct committed by two or more persons even though one or both of them may have committed a crime in the course of such conduct. In relation to such a claim the ex turpi causa defence could have had no application. The 1978 Act extends the potential for contribution beyond joint tortfeasors to joint contractors, joint trustees and others who are *g* liable in respect of the same damage. Although there is no reference to crime in the 1978 Act which corresponds to the reference in s 6 of the 1935 Act, it is hardly to be supposed that Parliament, while creating a considerable extension of the right of contribution in cases other than cases of tort, nevertheless intended to narrow the right to contribution previously given to tortfeasors by the 1935 Act. Apart from other considerations, it is manifest that the words of s 6(1) of the 1978 *h* Act are intended to be interpreted widely, hence the use of the words 'whatever the basis of his liability' and the emphasis added by the word 'otherwise' at the end of the enumerated causes of action.

Mr Whitaker also referred me to some passages in the speeches of Viscount Finlay and Lord Dunedin in *Weld-Blundell v Stephens* [1920] AC 956 at 966–968, 976, [1920] All ER Rep 32 at 37–38, 42. These passages contain observations *j* about the absence of a right of contribution between tortfeasors, but they relate to the law as it stood before 1935. While they provide a context in which to appraise the changes made by the 1935 Act, which was I think the purpose for which Mr Whitaker cited them, I did not find them of direct assistance.

I do, however, accept the other parts of Mr Whitaker's argument. In my

judgment the ex turpi causa defence is not available as an answer to a claim for
a contribution under the 1978 Act. The specific purpose of that Act, as of the 1935
Act before it, was to enable claims for contribution to be made as between parties
who had no claim to contribution under the general law. To permit the ex turpi
causa defence to be relied upon as an answer to such a claim would, in my view,
narrow to a substantial extent the deliberately wide wording of s 6(1) of the 1978
Act and would, in effect, make a claim for contribution subject to a condition
b precedent which is not to be found in the Act. Moreover, s 2(1) and (2) give the
court ample power to fix the amount of the contribution at a level, including a
zero level, which takes account of all the factors which, in relation to common
law claims, are relevant to the ex turpi causa defence.

c (2) *If it were available in respect of a claim under the 1978 Act, would the
ex turpi causa defence clearly exclude a claim to contribution by the third
defendant in this case?*

In view of the answer that I have given to the first question this second question
does not arise and it would be unwise for me to attempt to answer it on a
hypothetical basis. However, I would say that, on a striking-out application, I
d would find it difficult to hold with certainty that the ex turpi causa defence,
assuming it to be available, would exclude a claim to contribution under the 1978
Act unless I were also satisfied, with the same degree of certainty, that there must
be exemption from contribution under s 2(2). Whether I am so satisfied is the
third question, to which I now turn.

e (3) *Can it be said with certainty that the court will, under s 2(2), exempt
the third party from liability to make a contribution?*

The question for the consideration of the court at the stage when the amount
of contribution has to be assessed is how much, if anything, ought to be
recoverable by the third defendant from the third party 'having regard to the
extent of [the third party's] responsibility for the damage in question' (see s 2(1)
f of the 1978 Act). In considering whether at this stage it is possible to say that the
answer to this question must be 'nothing' I must assume that the third defendant
will be found guilty of conspiracy or fraud as alleged by the plaintiffs and also
that the third party will be found to be negligent as regards the plaintiffs in the
respects mentioned in the third party notice.

In so far as the plaintiffs are seeking to recover from the third defendant money
g which he has obtained for his own benefit or for the benefit of companies which
are, in effect, his alter ego, I can see that the third party would have an
overwhelming argument that it cannot be just and equitable to require him to
contribute to whatever the third defendant is ordered to pay to the plaintiffs.
Contribution, if ordered, would enable the third defendant or his fellow
h conspirators to retain part of the proceeds of their conspiracy or fraud. Similar
considerations would, it appears to me, be applicable to any claim that the third
party should contribute to any exemplary damages which the third defendant
may be ordered to pay to the plaintiffs, for exemplary damages would never be
recoverable by the plaintiffs direct from the third party. Indeed, it may well be
that a claim for contribution in respect of exemplary damages is not within s 1(1)
j on the facts of this case, so that one never gets to s 2 in relation to such a claim.

However, as I understand it, the plaintiffs' claim against the third defendant
goes well beyond a claim to recover the benefits actually obtained by conspiracy
or fraud. It extends, it seems, to a claim for compensation in respect of all the loss
which the plaintiffs say that they have suffered as a result of the transaction
concerning CMC and the bakery, including the amounts which the plaintiffs

have had to pay as guarantors and compensation for loss of earnings, loss of reputation and mental anguish. If, as I must assume for present purposes, the plaintiffs have a good cause of action in professional negligence against the third party, then it must be at least possible, if not indeed likely, that the damages recoverable by the plaintiffs from the third party would include damages under at least some of these heads. I can see that the third party would have a cogent argument that even if he were liable to compensate the plaintiffs in respect of these matters it would not be just and equitable to require him to make a contribution to the third defendant's liability. But what the court has to consider is the third party's responsibility for the damages in question. Once it is assumed that the third party would be liable to the plaintiffs for damages of a particular kind, it must follow that he has *some* responsibility for those damages. In order to carry out the exercise required by s 2(1) it would be essential, in my judgment, to evaluate the relative responsibilities of the third defendant and the third party. I do not see how this can be done without a trial of both the action and the claim to contribution. Certainly I feel unable at this stage to say, with the degree of certainty necessary to make a striking-out order, that the third party will inevitably be exempted from making contribution under s 2(2).

(4) Conclusion

In the result, although I have considerable sympathy with the third party in the position in which he finds himself and I think it may well be the case that the third defendant will fail to obtain contribution from him, I do not consider that this will inevitably be so. Accordingly it would not be right to strike out the third party notice on the ground that the claim to contribution is doomed to failure. I therefore dismiss this appeal.

Appeal dismissed.

Jacqueline Metcalfe   Barrister.

R v Birmingham City Council, ex parte Ferrero Ltd

COURT OF APPEAL, CIVIL DIVISION
FOX, RUSSELL AND TAYLOR LJJ
30 APRIL, 1, 23 MAY 1991

Judicial review – Availability of remedy – Alternative remedy available – Alternative remedy by way of appeal – Consumer protection – Local authority issuing suspension notice in respect of unsafe product – Manufacturer having statutory right of appeal – Manufacturer applying for judicial review of notice – Whether judicial review appropriate when alternative statutory remedy available – Consumer Protection Act 1987, ss 14, 15.

Consumer protection – Consumer safety – Suspension notice – Suspected contravention of safety provisions – Consultation with trader – Whether enforcement authority under duty to consult trader before serving suspension notice – Consumer Protection Act 1987, s 14.

The respondents manufactured chocolate eggs, each of which contained a plastic capsule which itself contained a kit which could be assembled to make a small toy a representing well-known cartoon characters, one of which was known as the 'Pink Panther'. In October 1989 a little girl accidentally swallowed part of a 'Pink Panther' toy and died from asphyxiation as a result. The appellant local authority, through its trading standards officer, issued a suspension notice under s 14^a of the Consumer Protection Act 1987 prohibiting the supply of eggs containing the 'Pink Panther' toy for a period of six months. Despite attempts by the respondents to persuade it to do so, coupled with offers of undertakings, the local authority

b declined to withdraw the notice. The respondents applied for judicial review by way of an order of certiorari quashing the local authority's decisions to issue the notice and to refuse to withdraw it, contending, inter alia, that the council had acted unfairly in failing to consult them before issuing the suspension notice. The judge granted the relief sought. The local authority appealed, contending, inter alia, (i) that the judge had erred in entertaining the respondents' application and

c granting relief when they had a statutory right of appeal under s 15^b of the 1987 Act, which provided that a person having an interest in any goods in respect of which a suspension notice was in force could apply to a magistrates' court for an order setting aside the notice, and (ii) that the local authority had not acted unfairly in failing to consult the respondents before issuing the notice.

d **Held** – Where there was an alternative remedy and especially where Parliament had provided a statutory appeal procedure it was only exceptionally that judicial review would be granted. In determining whether an exception should be made and judicial review granted it was necessary for the court to look carefully at the suitability of the statutory appeal in the context of the particular case and to ask

e itself what, in the context of the statutory provisions, was the real issue to be determined and whether the statutory appeal procedure was suitable to determine it. Given that the statutory emphasis under the 1987 Act was on consumer safety, that the Act aimed at withholding goods from the public if there was reasonable suspicion that they were unsafe and that the suspension prohibiting supply was to remain in force until the goods were cleared of danger even if the process by

f which the enforcement authority reached its decision was flawed, and given that the appeal to the magistrates' court under s 15 was at least as expeditious, if not more so, than judicial review and was more suited than judicial review to the resolution of issues of fact and that if the goods were shown not to contravene the safety provisions not only would the notice be set aside but the enforcement authority would be required to pay compensation to any person having an interest

g in the goods even if the enforcement authority had reasonable grounds for its suspicion, an appeal under s 15 was geared exactly to deciding the real issue to be determined, which was whether the goods contravened a safety provision. The fact that the respondents could not have expressed their complaint about the reasonableness of the local authority's decision on a s 15 appeal was not sufficient

h reason for granting judicial review. Instead, the respondents should have been left to pursue their appeal under s 15. The local authority's appeal would therefore be allowed and the judge's decision to grant judicial review reversed (see p 537 c d g, p 538 a b j to p 539 a c to e g, p 540 d e and p 544 g h, post).

Dicta of Donaldson MR in *R v Epping and Harlow General Comrs, ex p Goldstraw* [1983] 3 All ER 257 at 262 and of Donaldson MR, May and Glidewell LJJ in *R v*

j *Chief Constable of the Merseyside Police, ex p Calveley* [1986] 1 All ER 257 at 261–262, 263–264, 267 applied.

Per curiam. A local authority is under no duty to consult a trader either before or after the service of a suspension notice since such a duty cannot be implied at

---

a   Section 14, so far as material, is set out at p 534 f to p 535 b, post
b   Section 15, so far as material, is set out at p 535 c to f, post

common law because to do so would frustrate the statutory purpose of achieving
consumer safety and enabling the immediate withdrawal from sale of unsafe or *a*
dangerous goods; the statutory scheme with its provisions for appeal and
compensation is sufficient to achieve justice (see p 543 *d e* and p 544 *h*, post);
dictum of Lord Reid in *Wiseman v Borneman* [1969] 3 All ER 275 at 277 applied.

Notes *b*
For the discretion to refuse judicial review where an alternative remedy is
available, see 1(1) *Halsbury's Laws* (4th edn reissue) para 61.

For suspension orders in respect of goods suspected of contravening safety
provisions, see Supplement to 41 *Halsbury's Laws* (4th edn) para 664A.

For the Consumer Protection Act 1987, ss 14, 15, see 39 *Halsbury's Statutes* (4th *c*
edn) 208, 209.

Cases referred to in judgments
Associated Provincial Picture Houses Ltd v Wednesbury Corp [1947] 2 All ER 680, *d*
   [1948] 1 KB 223, CA.
Birss v Secretary for Justice [1984] 1 NZLR 513, NZ CA.
Cooper v Wandsworth District Board of Works (1863) 14 CBNS 180, 143 ER 414.
Dixon v Commonwealth (1981) 55 FLR 34, Aust Fed Ct.
Hadmor Productions Ltd v Hamilton [1982] 1 All ER 1042, [1983] 1 AC 191, [1982]
   2 WLR 322, HL. *e*
John v Rees, Martin v Davis, Rees v John [1969] 2 All ER 274, [1970] Ch 345, [1969]
   2 WLR 1294.
Preston v IRC [1985] 2 All ER 327, [1985] AC 835, [1985] 2 WLR 836, HL.
R v Chief Constable of the Merseyside Police, ex p Calveley [1986] 1 All ER 257, [1986]
   QB 424, [1986] 2 WLR 144, CA.
R v Epping and Harlow General Comrs, ex p Goldstraw [1983] 3 All ER 257, CA. *f*
R v Hallstrom, ex p W [1985] 3 All ER 775, sub nom *Ex p Waldron* [1986] QB 824,
   [1985] 3 WLR 1090, CA.
R v Hillingdon London Borough, ex p Royco Homes Ltd [1974] 2 All ER 643, [1974]
   QB 720, [1974] 2 WLR 805, DC.
R v Paddington Valuation Officer, ex p Peachey Property Corp Ltd [1965] 2 All ER
   836, [1966] 1 QB 380, [1965] 3 WLR 426, CA. *g*
R v Secretary of State for Health, ex p US Tobacco International Inc [1992] 1 All ER
   212, [1992] QB 353, [1991] 3 WLR 529, DC.
Wiseman v Borneman [1969] 3 All ER 275, [1971] AC 297, [1969] 3 WLR 706, HL.

h

Appeal
Birmingham City Council appealed from the order dated 7 March 1990 of
Hutchison J hearing the Crown Office list on 22 February 1990 whereby on the
application of Ferrero Ltd (Ferrero) he granted judicial review by way of an order
of certiorari quashing the council's decision set out in a notice dated 8 November
1989 prohibiting Ferrero for a period of six months from that date from *j*
supplying, offering to supply, agreeing to supply or exposing for supply 'Kinder
Surprise' products comprising milk chocolate egg shells containing a 'Pink
Panther' toy, or, in the alternative, the council's decision to continue the
prohibition. The court gave leave for the Secretary of State for Trade and Industry
to intervene in the appeal. The facts are set out in the judgment of Taylor LJ.

Anthony Scrivener QC and *Ian Croxford* (instructed by *Sharpe Pritchard*, agents for
S Dobson, Birmingham) for the council.
Michael Beloff QC and *Richard Spearman* (instructed by *Taylor Joynson Garrett*) for
Ferrero.
John Laws (instructed by the *Treasury Solicitor*) for the Secretary of State.

Cur adv vult

23 May 1991. The following judgments were delivered.

TAYLOR LJ (giving the first judgment at the invitation of Fox LJ). Ferrero Ltd
(Ferrero) make chocolate eggs called 'Kinder Surprise'. Each egg contains a plastic
capsule containing in its turn a kit from which a small toy can be made. The
object is to enhance the attractiveness of the eggs to children. Ferrero have used a
variety of different toys in their eggs, many of which represent well-known
cartoon characters. In October 1989 a new toy, depicting the 'Pink Panther', was
introduced. Tragically, a month later, on 5 November 1989, a little girl, just over
three years old, swallowed one of the 'Pink Panther' feet which had come loose
from a toy. It lodged in her throat causing her death, from asphyxiation. Three
days later the appellants, Birmingham City Council, through their trading
standards office, issued a suspension notice under s 14 of the Consumer Protection
Act 1987. The notice prohibited Ferrero for a period of six months from that date
from supplying 'Kinder Surprise' eggs containing the 'Pink Panther' toy. Despite
attempts by Ferrero to persuade them coupled with offers of undertakings, the
council declined to withdraw the notice.

Ferrero decided to apply for judicial review. They were granted leave, and the
matter came before Hutchison J. On 7 March 1990 he granted to Ferrero an order
of certiorari and quashed both the decision of the council to issue the notice and
their refusal to withdraw it. The council now appeal against those decisions.

Statutory provisions

It is convenient, first, to set out the relevant statutory provisions contained in
Pt II of the Consumer Protection Act 1987. Section 10(1) makes it an offence,
inter alia, to supply any consumer goods which fail to comply with the general
safety requirement. Section 10(2) defines the general safety requirement in the
following terms so far as is relevant:

'For the purposes of this section consumer goods fail to comply with the
general safety requirement if they are not reasonably safe having regard to
all the circumstances, including—(*a*) the manner in which, and purposes for
which, the goods are being . . . marketed, the get-up of the goods . . . and any
instructions or warnings which are given . . . with respect to the keeping, use
or consumption of the goods; (*b*) any standards of safety published by any
person either for goods of a description which applies to the goods in question
or for matters relating to goods of that description . . .'

Subsection (3) provides:

'For the purposes of this section consumer goods shall not be regarded as
failing to comply with the general safety requirement in respect of—(*a*)
anything which is shown to be attributable to compliance with any
requirement imposed by or under any enactment or with any Community
obligation; (*b*) any failure to do more in relation to any matter than is
required by—(i) any safety regulations imposing requirements with respect

to that matter; (ii) any standards of safety approved for the purposes of this subsection by or under any such regulations and imposing requirements *a* with respect to that matter; (iii) any provision of any enactment or subordinate legislation imposing such requirements with respect to that matter as are designated for the purposes of this subsection by any such regulations.'

Section 11 empowers the Secretary of State to make regulations for the purposes of s 10(3) and other specified safety purposes. *b*

Section 13 deals with prohibition notices and notices to warn and provides as follows, so far as is relevant:

'(1) The Secretary of State may—(*a*) serve on any person a notice ("a prohibition notice") prohibiting that person, except with the consent of the Secretary of State, from supplying, or from offering to supply, agreeing to *c* supply, exposing for supply or possessing for supply, any relevant goods which the Secretary of State considers are unsafe and which are described in the notice; (*b*) serve on any person a notice ("a notice to warn") requiring that person at his own expense to publish, in a form and manner and on occasions specified in the notice, a warning about any relevant goods which the Secretary of State considers are unsafe, which that person supplies or has *d* supplied and which are described in the notice. (2) Schedule 2 to this Act shall have effect with respect to prohibition notices and notices to warn; and the Secretary of State may by regulations make provision specifying the manner in which information is to be given to any person under that Schedule . . .'

e

It will be necessary later in this judgment to refer to the terms of Sch 2, which, inter alia, prescribe requirements of consultation in regard to prohibition notices and notices to warn.

The crucial sections for the purposes of this case are ss 14 and 15. Section 14 provides as follows, so far as is relevant:

f

'(1) Where an enforcement authority has reasonable grounds for suspecting that any safety provision has been contravened in relation to any goods, the authority may serve a notice ("a suspension notice") prohibiting the person on whom it is served, for such period ending not more than six months after the date of the notice as is specified therein, from doing any of the following things without the consent of the authority, that is to say, supplying the *g* goods, offering to supply them, agreeing to supply them or exposing them for supply. (2) A suspension notice served by an enforcement authority in respect of any goods shall—(*a*) describe the goods in a manner sufficient to identify them; (*b*) set out the grounds on which the authority suspects that a safety provision has been contravened in relation to the goods; and (*c*) state that, *h* and the manner in which, the person on whom the notice is served may appeal against the notice under section 15 below . . . (4) Where a suspension notice has been served on any person in respect of any goods, no further such notice shall be served on that person in respect of the same goods unless—(*a*) proceedings against that person for an offence in *j* respect of a contravention in relation to the goods of a safety provision (not being an offence under this section); or (*b*) proceedings for the forfeiture of the goods under section 16 or 17 below, are pending at the end of the period specified in the first-mentioned notice . . . (6) Any person who contravenes a suspension notice shall be guilty of an offence and liable on summary conviction to imprisonment for a term not exceeding six months or to a fine not exceeding level 5 on the standard scale or to both.

(7) Where an enforcement authority serves a suspension notice in respect of any goods, the authority shall be liable to pay compensation to any person having an interest in the goods in respect of any loss or damage caused by reason of the service of the notice if—(a) there has been no contravention in relation to the goods of any safety provision; and (b) the exercise of the power is not attributable to any neglect or default by that person . . .'

Section 15 deals with appeals to magistrates' courts and provides as follows, so far as is relevant:

'(1) Any person having an interest in any goods in respect of which a suspension notice is for the time being in force may apply for an order setting aside the notice.

(2) An application under this section may be made—(a) to any magistrates' court in which proceedings have been brought in England and Wales or Northern Ireland—(i) for an offence in respect of a contravention in relation to the goods of any safety provision; (ii) for the forfeiture of the goods under section 16 below; (b) where no such proceedings have been so brought, by way of complaint to a magistrates' court . . .

(3) On an application under this section to a magistrates' court in England and Wales or Northern Ireland the court shall make an order setting aside the suspension notice only if the court is satisfied that there has been no contravention in relation to the goods of any safety provision . . .

(5) Any person aggrieved by an order made under this section by a magistrates' court in England and Wales or Northern Ireland, or by a decision of such a court not to make such an order, may appeal against that order or decision—(a) in England and Wales, to the Crown Court . . . and an order so made may contain such provision as appears to the court to be appropriate for delaying the coming into force of the order pending the making and determination of any appeal . . .'

Section 16 provides for forfeiture and empowers an enforcement authority in England and Wales or Northern Ireland to apply for an order for the forfeiture of any goods on the grounds that there has been a contravention in relation to the goods of a safety provision, such application being required to be made to a magistrates' court.

Ferrero's complaints

Ferrero's case for judicial review was based on several grounds. It was said that the council had failed to consider a British Standard (BS 5665) regarding safety of toys which they had an express duty to consider under s 10(2)(b) of the 1987 Act. Conversely, they had regard to the Toys (Safety) Regulations 1989, SI 1989/1275, made under s 11 of the 1987 Act, which were an irrelevant consideration since they did not come into force until 1 January 1990. Moreover, it was claimed that the council had, in any event, wrongly applied the three provisions in those regulations said to have been breached. It was further contended that the council acted unfairly in failing to consult Ferrero before issuing the notice. Finally, the council were said to have acted irrationally in failing to accede to Ferrero's request to lift the suspension notice and accept an undertaking instead.

The learned judge found in favour of Ferrero on each of these issues. He dealt finally with the issue which has been in the forefront of the council's case in this court. That was whether this was an appropriate case for judicial review at all. Again, the learned judge found for Ferrero, and it is to that issue that I now turn.

Judicial review or appeal?

Should Ferrero have been granted judicial review, or ought they to have *a*
pursued their statutory right of appeal under s 15 of the 1987 Act? There is much
authority on the approach of this court to judicial review where a statutory appeal
procedure has not been exhausted. The learned judge rightly declined Mr Beloff
QC's invitation to adopt the critical view of recent judicial decisions expressed in
Wade *Administrative Law* (6th edn, 1988) pp 712–716, and accepted that he should
follow the decisions of this court and the reasoning behind them.   *b*

In *R v Epping and Harlow General Comrs, ex p Goldstraw* [1983] 3 All ER 257 at
262 Donaldson MR said:

> 'But it is a cardinal principle that, save in the most exceptional
> circumstances, that jurisdiction will not be exercised where other remedies
> were available and have not been used.'   *c*

In *R v Chief Constable of the Merseyside Police, ex p Calveley* [1986] 1 All ER 257 at
261–262, [1986] QB 424 at 433 Donaldson MR, after citing that passage, said:

> 'This, like other judicial pronouncement on the interrelationship between
> remedies by way of judicial review on the one hand and appeal procedures
> on the other, is not to be regarded or construed as a statute. It does not   *d*
> support the proposition that judicial review is not available where there is an
> alternative remedy by way of appeal. It asserts simply that the court, in the
> exercise of its discretion, will very rarely make this remedy available in these
> circumstances. In other cases courts have asserted the existence of this
> discretion, albeit with varying emphasis on the reluctance to grant judicial *e*
> review, Thus in *R v Paddington Valuation Officer, ex p Peachey Property Corp
> Ltd* [1965] 2 All ER 836 at 840, [1966] 1 QB 380 at 400, Lord Denning MR,
> with the agreement of Danckwerts and Salmon LJJ, held that certiorari and
> mandamus were available where the alternative statutory remedy was
> "nowhere near so convenient, beneficial and effectual". In *R v Hillingdon
> London Borough, ex p Royco Homes Ltd* [1974] 2 All ER 643 at 648, [1974] QB *f*
> 720 at 728 Widgery CJ said: ". . . it has always been a principle that certiorari
> will go only where there is no other equally effective and convenient
> remedy". In *R v Hallstrom, ex p W* [1985] 3 All ER 775 at 789–790, [1986]
> QB 824 at 852 Glidewell LJ, after referring to this passage, said: "Whether
> the alternative statutory remedy will resolve the question at issue fully and
> directly, whether the statutory procedure would be quicker, or slower, than *g*
> procedure by way of judicial review, whether the matter depends on some
> particular or technical knowledge which is more readily available to the
> alternative appellate body, these are amongst the matters which a court
> should take into account when deciding whether to grant relief by way of
> judicial review when an alternative remedy is available."'
>
h

May LJ said ([1986] 1 All ER 257 at 263–264, [1986] QB 424 at 435):

> 'I respectfully agree with the Divisional Court that the normal rule in cases
> such as this is that an applicant for judicial review should first exhaust
> whatever other rights he has by way of appeal. In *Preston v IRC* [1985] 2 All
> ER 327 at 330, [1985] AC 835 at 852 Lord Scarman said: "My fourth   *j*
> proposition is that a remedy by way of judicial review is not to be made
> available where an alternative remedy exists. This is a proposition of great
> importance. Judicial review is a collateral challenge; it is not an appeal.
> Where Parliament has provided by statute appeal procedures, as in the taxing
> statutes, it will only be very rarely that the courts will allow the collateral

a   process of judicial review to be used to attack an appealable decision." In the same case Lord Templeman, with whose speech all the other Law Lords agreed, said ([1985] 2 All ER 327 at 337, [1985] AC 835 at 862): "Judicial review should not be granted where an alternative remedy is available."'

Glidewell LJ said ([1986] 1 All ER 257 at 267, [1986] QB 424 at 440):

b   '. . . I also agree that, where application is made for judicial review but an alternative remedy is available, an applicant should normally be left to pursue that remedy. Judicial review in such a case should only be granted in exceptional circumstances.'

These are very strong dicta, both in this court and in the House of Lords as cited, emphasising that where there is an alternative remedy and especially where Parliament has provided a statutory appeal procedure it is only exceptionally that judicial review should be granted. It is therefore necessary, where the exception is invoked, to look carefully at the suitability of the statutory appeal in the context of the particular case. In the present context the statutory provisions are all contained in Pt II of the 1987 Act, and are thus concerned with consumer safety. Section 14 is clearly aimed at providing enforcement authorities with a means of *d*   swift, short-term action to prevent goods which have come to their notice from endangering the public. Section 14 is the only provision which enables action to be taken by a local authority against a trader, other than through the courts. The action does not require proof that the goods contravene a safety provision, but merely that the authority has reasonable grounds for suspecting they do. The notice is effective only for six months. It is intended to be an emergency holding *e*   operation. The suspension notice has to inform the recipient of his appeal rights (s 14(2)(c)), and the very next section, s 15, sets them out. They provide for application to a magistrates' court, which can set aside the notice only if satisfied that there has been no contravention of a safety provision. If the goods are not shown to be safe, the notice will remain in place. Conversely, if the goods are shown not to contravene the safety provision, the notice is set aside. Moreover, in *f*   that event, even if the enforcement authority had reasonable grounds for their suspicion, they are required to pay compensation to any person having an interest in the goods (s 14(7)).

As one would expect, therefore, the statutory emphasis is on the safety of the consumer. The provisions aim at withholding goods from the public if there is *g*   reasonable suspicion that they are unsafe. Unless they are then cleared of the danger, it is right that the suspension should remain, even if the process by which the enforcement authority reached its decision was flawed. It cannot be right that dangerous goods should continue to be marketed simply because of some procedural impropriety by the enforcement authority in the process of deciding to issue a suspension notice. Common sense dictates that protection of the public *h*   must take precedence over fairness to the trader. So, if goods are in fact dangerous, it would be nothing to the point to show that, in deciding to issue a suspension notice, the local authority took into account an irrelevant matter or failed to take account of one which was relevant. Parliament has recognised this by making the sole issue, on a s 15 appeal, whether there has in fact been a contravention of the safety provision. Protection is given to the trader by providing for compensation *j*   if there has been no contravention.

An appeal under s 15 does not require leave, as judicial review does. It should therefore be capable of being brought on more quickly, which is an important consideration since the notice is only effective for six months. An appeal comes before justices, who can try, as a contested issue of fact on oral evidence, whether

the goods are in contravention of a safety provision, whereas judicial review
normally proceeds on affidavit evidence. A further appeal on the merits can be   *a*
made by an aggrieved party to the Crown Court.

Accordingly, in the present case, there was available an appeal specifically
provided by Parliament to enable a party aggrieved by a suspension notice to
challenge it. The appeal was at least as expeditious, if not more so, than judicial
review. It was more suited than judicial review to the resolution of issues of fact.
The statutory scheme leant in favour of upholding the notice unless the goods   *b*
were shown to be safe; but, should they turn out on appeal or otherwise to be
safe, any aggrieved party was entitled to compensation.

In these circumstances, what prompted the learned judge to decide that this
was an exceptional case in which judicial review should be granted, notwithstanding the alternative remedy? He gave his reasons as follows:
                                                                                  c
'Mr Mitting QC [for the council] submits that the present is a case in which
the applicants ought to have pursued their s 15 remedy. So far from regarding
as a difficulty the fact relied on by Mr Beloff that the magistrates can deal
with the simple question whether there were grounds for making the order,
Mr Mitting submits that this is the crucial factual question, which can most
conveniently and simply be determined by that tribunal of fact. Implicit in   *d*
this argument, however, is his recognition of the problem that a conclusion
adverse to the applicants will leave the order in place. It is simply not within
the magistrates' power to determine the issues of whether the order should
have been lifted or fairness, or irrationality. Mr Beloff points out that, since
Mr Mitting invites me to regard myself as precluded from entertaining this   *e*
application merely because there is a limited right of appeal to the magistrates,
his approach involves that even if the council had been actuated by malice I
could not grant relief. This, Mr Beloff submits, is to elevate the ends above
the means. It is plain, on any view, that this is a question of discretion, in
which I must reach a judgment as to whether the s 15 remedy is a remedy
which in the circumstances the applicants ought to have pursued in preference   *f*
to their present application. I unhesitatingly conclude that it is not. It is true,
and I take into account, that if the magistrates were to determine the issue of
safety in favour of the applicants, the suspension notice would fall. If however
they were to conclude that it had not been established that there had been no
contravention in relation to the goods of any safety provision, then the notice
would have to remain in place and none of the substantial matters on which   *g*
I have reached conclusions favourable to the applicants could have been aired.
The applicants' real complaints here are not so much on the issue of breach
of or compliance with the general safety requirement; they have to do with
the other public law issues which I have considered in this already over-long
judgment. Everything points to the exercise of my discretion in favour of   *h*
the granting of the relief sought.'

With respect to the learned judge, he did not, in my view, ask himself the right
questions. He asked whether, on a s 15 appeal, Ferrero could have aired their
various complaints about the *Wednesbury* reasonableness of the council's decision,
lack of consultation and refusal to accept an undertaking in lieu of the notice (see
Associated Provincial Picture Houses Ltd v Wednesbury Corp [1947] 2 All ER 680,   *j*
[1948] 1 KB 223). Having concluded they could not, he held they were entitled
to proceed by judicial review. He should have asked himself what, in the context
of the statutory provisions, was the real issue to be determined and whether a s 15
appeal was suitable to determine it. The real issue was whether the goods

contravened a safety provision and the s 15 appeal was geared exactly to deciding
a that issue. If the goods did contravene the safety provision and were dangerous to
children then, surely, procedural impropriety or unfairness in the decision-
making process should not persuade a court to quash the order. The determining
factors are the paramount need to safeguard consumers and the emergency nature
of the s 14 powers. Suppose that judicial review of a s 14 notice were entertained
where the enforcement authority suspected certain goods to be poisonous.
b Suppose further the affidavit evidence raised a strong presumption that the goods
were poisonous, but it was clear the authority had taken into consideration
irrelevant factors or had omitted to consider relevant ones. The court would
clearly decline to quash the notice. Even supposing the affidavit evidence showed
a head-on conflict between experts as to whether the goods were poisonous or not,
the court would hardly quash the notice with possibly fatal results, simply because
c of the defect in the decision-making process. In such a situation it would be
desirable to reach a conclusion on the facts, and that could only be done by
hearing the experts and having them cross-examined, an exercise to which a s 15
appeal would be well suited.

To test the suitability of a s 15 appeal in all situations, the question was raised
d in argument and mentioned in the passage cited from the learned judge's
judgment, as to the availability of judicial review were malice to be alleged.
Clearly, as the authorities cited make clear, there is no absolute rule excluding
judicial review in all cases where an alternative remedy exists. The factors to be
taken into account will vary. It may be that, in the context of these statutory
provisions, if an arguable case of malice were to be raised it might be appropriate
e to grant judicial review rather than leave the applicant to his s 15 remedy.
I should observe, however, that if the goods truly contravened a safety provision,
it would seem unlikely that malice would be established, and even if it were, the
notice might nevertheless need to remain in place.

We were referred to *R v Secretary of State for Health, ex p US Tobacco International
f Inc* [1992] 1 All ER 212, [1992] QB 353. There it is true that regulations under
s 11 of the 1987 Act, prohibiting goods said to be injurious to the public, were
quashed because of unfairness in the decision-making process. But there no appeal
procedure was provided; the regulations were permanent not temporary; there
was a statutory duty to consult and the goods (oral snuff), although said to be
injurious over a long period, were not suspected (as here) of being capable of
inflicting instant death, so that the same emergency did not apply.
g I am of the opinion that so far from being an exception to the general rule, the
present case was one in which Ferrero should have been left to pursue their appeal
under s 15. The decision was a matter of judicial discretion, and it is well
established that this court should be slow to reverse the discretion of a learned
trial judge. The principles were set out in *Hadmor Productions Ltd v Hamilton*
h [1982] 1 All ER 1042 at 1046, [1983] 1 AC 191 at 220 by Lord Diplock. He was
dealing with interlocutory appeals, but his observations have been applied
generally to appeals against discretionary decisions. He said:

'On an appeal from the judge's grant or refusal of an interlocutory
injunction the function of an appellate court, whether it be the Court of
j Appeal or your Lordships' House, is not to exercise an independent discretion
of its own. It must defer to the judge's exercise of his discretion and must not
interfere with it merely upon the ground that the members of the appellate
court would have exercised the discretion differently. The function of the
appellate court is initially one of review only. It may set aside the judge's

exercise of his discretion on the ground that it was based on a misunderstanding of the law or of the evidence before him or on an inference *a* that particular facts existed or did not exist, which, although it was one that might legitimately have been drawn on the evidence that was before the judge, can be demonstrated to be wrong by further evidence that has become available by the time of the appeal; or on the ground that there has been a change of circumstances after the judge made his order that would have justified his acceding to an application to vary it. Since reasons given by *b* judges for granting or refusing interlocutory injunctions may sometimes be sketchy, there may also be occasional cases where even though no erroneous assumption of law or fact can be identified the judge's decision to grant or refuse the injunction is so aberrant that it must be set aside on the ground that no reasonable judge regardful of his duty to act judicially could have reached it. It is only if and after the appellate court has reached the conclusion *c* that the judge's exercise of his discretion must be set aside for one or other of these reasons that it becomes entitled to exercise an original discretion of its own.'

For the reasons already given, I am of opinion that the learned judge's decision to exercise his discretion in favour of granting judicial review was based upon a *d* misunderstanding or error of law. It is therefore open to this court to reverse the learned judge's discretionary decision, and in my view we should do so. Ferrero should have been left to pursue their statutory appeal. They had in fact lodged an appeal pursuant to s 15, which they withdrew after their success on judicial review. The matter is now academic since the six-month life of the suspension notice terminated long ago, but I would allow the council's appeal on this ground *e* alone.

That being so, it is strictly unnecessary to consider other issues raised on the appeal. However, two of those issues raised points of general importance and in addition to the arguments for the council and Ferrero, we gave leave to Mr Laws to intervene and address us on those issues on behalf of the Secretary of State. We *f* are grateful to all three counsel for their cogent submissions, and although our conclusions on these issues must be obiter, I hope they may be helpful for the guidance of enforcement authorities who, we are told, are presently in a state of some uncertainty.

The two issues are (1) whether an enforcement authority has a duty to consult the proposed recipient of a s 14 notice before the decision to issue it and (2) *g* whether the authority is under any duty, or whether it is appropriate, to accept an equivalent undertaking from a person served and lift the notice.

Duty to consult?

The additional facts bearing on this issue were as follows. Although the 'Pink *h* Panther' toy was introduced only in October 1989, Ferrero had been marketing 'Kinder Surprise' eggs with other toy kits since 1974. They had sold some 216m such eggs in the United Kingdom, and 460m worldwide. Prior to the death of Jennifer Ashton there had been one previous fatal accident in Northern Ireland in May 1985 when a toy broke, the pieces were not cleared away, and a three-year-old child choked on one of them. The Department of Trade and Industry, after *j* correspondence with Ferrero, suggested stronger warning should be printed on the wrappers, but took no further actions. In 1988 Hertfordshire County Council expressed concern as to whether there might be breaches of the Toys (Safety) Regulations 1974, SI 1974/1367, but after counsel had been consulted took the view that no breach could be established. Both Ferrero and Birmingham City

Council learnt of Jennifer Ashton's death on 6 November 1989, the day after it
a had occurred. Ferrero instructed their distributors not to dispatch further 'Pink
Panther' products to the trade. On 7 November Mr Galland of the council's
trading standards office spoke to Miss Wooll at Ferrero. She informed him of the
action which had been taken. A meeting was arranged for 9 November. There
was an issue as to whether Mr Galland told Miss Wooll that the council were
going to issue a suspension notice, but the case has proceeded below and in this
b court on the basis that he did. Mr Galland had meanwhile gleaned information
from a number of sources, including the local authority in Northern Ireland
concerned with the previous fatality there, Hertfordshire County Council, the
coroner's office, to discover the cause of Jennifer Ashton's death, and the
Department of Trade and Industry. Tests were done on a 'Pink Panther' toy, and
Mr Galland discussed the case with a lawyer in the council's common law
c department. However, apart from the telephone call with Miss Wooll, he did not
consult Ferrero.

Ferrero submitted, and the learned judge accepted, that the council had a duty
to consult them before deciding whether to issue the notice. Mr Beloff submitted
fairness required it. Whilst the 1987 Act does not provide for such consultation,
d he relied upon the principle laid down in *Cooper v Wandsworth District Board of
Works* (1863) 14 CBNS 180, 143 ER 414, in particular in the judgments of Willes
and Byles JJ. Willes J said (14 CBNS 180 at 190, 143 ER 414 at 418):

> 'I apprehend that a tribunal which is by law invested with power to affect
> the property of one of Her Majesty's subjects, is bound to give such subject
> an opportunity of being heard before it proceeds: and that the rule is of
e > universal application, and founded upon the plainest principles of justice.'

Byles J said (14 CBNS 180 at 194, 143 ER 414 at 420):

> '. . . a long course of decisions . . . establish that, although there are no
> positive words in a statute requiring that a party shall be heard, yet the justice
f > of the common law will supply the omission of the legislature.'

However, it is important to note the context in which those observations were
made. That appears in the judgment of Erle CJ, who said (14 CBNS 180 at 188–
189, 143 ER 414 at 417):

> 'I think the board ought to have given notice to the plaintiff, and to have
g > allowed him to be heard. The default in sending notice to the board of the
> intention to build, is a default which may be explained. There may be a great
> many excuses for the apparent default. The party may have intended to
> conform to the law. He may have actually conformed . . . though by accident
> his notice may have miscarried . . . I cannot conceive any harm that could
> happen to the district board from hearing the party before they subjected
h > him to a loss so serious as the demolition of his house; but I can conceive a
> great many advantages which might arise in the way of public order, in the
> way of doing substantial justice, and in the way of fulfilling the purposes of
> the statute, by the restriction which we put upon them, that they should hear
> the party before they inflict upon him such a heavy loss.'

j   Thus, emphasis was laid on 'fulfilling the purposes of the statute'. That factor
was also emphasised by Lord Reid in his statement of the principle in *Wiseman v
Borneman* [1969] 3 All ER 275 at 277, [1971] AC 297 at 308 where he said:

> 'For a long time the courts have, without objection from Parliament,
> supplemented procedure laid down in legislation where they have found that

to be necessary for this purpose. But before this unusual kind of power is
exercised it must be clear that the statutory procedure is insufficient to *a*
achieve justice and that to require additional steps would not frustrate the
apparent purpose of the legislation.'

Mr Beloff sought to rely upon certain employment cases involving dismissal or
suspension where the employee did not have an opportunity to make
representations—*John v Rees, Martin v Davis, Rees v John* [1969] 2 All ER 274 at *b*
305, [1970] Ch 345 at 397, *Birss v Secretary for Justice* [1984] 1 NZLR 513 and
Dixon v Commonwealth (1981) 55 FLR 34—but these cases did not involve a
statutory purpose or statutory procedure as contemplated by Lord Reid. The
present case does. It is therefore important to consider the two preconditions
mentioned by Lord Reid as being necessary before the common law will imply a
duty to consult. I do so in reverse order. *c*

Would a duty to consult frustrate the purpose of the 1987 Act?
    As already observed, the purpose of Pt II of the 1987 Act is to achieve consumer
safety, and s 14 is an emergency measure to protect consumers against goods the
enforcement authority reasonably suspects are in contravention of the safety
provision. Likewise, s 13 empowers the Secretary of State to issue a prohibition *d*
notice if he considers goods unsafe.
    It is submitted on behalf of the council and of the Secretary of State that in this
statutory context the common law will not supplement the procedure prescribed
in the 1987 Act by requiring consultation with the trader, because to do so would
frustrate the statutory purpose. If a local authority which suspected goods were *e*
dangerous, or if the Secretary of State who considered them so, had to consult the
trader, receive his representations and then consider them before acting under
s 14 or s 13, time would pass to the possible danger of the public. Clearly that
could defeat the object of the legislation.
    Facing this problem realistically, Mr Beloff conceded that in cases of urgency
no duty to consult would be implied. He says, however—and this is common *f*
ground—that there was not such a degree of urgency in the present case. It was
therefore not necessary to serve a s 14 notice on 8 November, rather than wait for
the arranged meeting with Ferrero on 9 November and consider the matter
thereafter.
    But if the supposed duty to consult were to depend upon the facts and urgency
of each case, enforcement authorities would be faced with a serious dilemma. *g*
What amounts to urgency is incapable of precise definition, and would be open
in many cases to honest and reasonable differences of opinion. There would be a
danger that although the authority reasonably suspected goods were dangerous
they would feel bound to delay serving a notice until they consulted the trader,
whereas, without a duty to consult, they would have served forthwith. Valuable *h*
time would be lost and danger could result.

Is the statutory procedure insufficient to achieve justice?
    It should first be noted that the statutory scheme does lay down very specific
requirements for consultation where Parliament thought them appropriate.
Thus, the Secretary of State must consult 'organisations . . . representative of *j*
interests substantially affected by the proposal' before making regulations under
s 11. Schedule 2 to the 1987 Act provides for consultation where the Secretary of
State serves a prohibition notice or a notice to warn. Where a prohibition notice
has been served, Pt I of Sch 2 provides for a trader to make representations to be

considered. There is thus express provision for consultation after service of the
a notice, but not before. Part II of Sch 2 provides that if the Secretary of State
proposes to serve a notice to warn on a person in respect of goods, he shall give an
opportunity to that person to make representations before the notice is served.

By contrast, there is no provision under s 14 for representations to be made and
considered, either before or after service of a suspension notice. However, as
already observed, there are provisions for appeal under s 15 and for compensation
b under s 14(7). Thus, the scheme of the 1987 Act makes no provision for
consultation before the service either of a s 13 prohibition notice or a s 14
suspension notice. The rationale of that is to avoid danger to the public by delay.
But, in the case of the s 13 notice, representations can be made to revoke the
notice and they must be considered. In the case of a s 14 notice, there is an appeal,
and, if no contravention has occurred, compensation.
c

Conclusions on consultation
In these circumstances, although there is no statutory duty to consult, the
question is whether, bearing in mind the necessary conditions stated by Lord Reid,
the common law should imply a duty to consult. In my opinion the answer is
d No. To imply such a duty would tend to frustrate the statutory purpose.
Moreover, ample safeguards for the trader are built into the statutory scheme. No
doubt an enforcement authority, mindful of the entitlement to compensation
should no contravention have occurred, will seek in each case to obtain the fullest
information it can, commensurate with the perceived risk to the public of
delaying service of the notice. They may, if time permits, think it right to consult
e the trader. It may be that in the present case the council would have been wiser
to have waited until after meeting Ferrero on 9 November before deciding to
serve their notice. But, for the reasons already given, I do not think they were
under a duty to do so. They served the notice at their peril.

Undertaking in lieu of suspension notice
f Following the service of the notice on 8 November Ferrero sought, at the
meeting of 9 November and on subsequent occasions, to persuade the council to
accept an undertaking instead. The undertaking they were prepared to offer
would have imposed the same restriction on Ferrero as was imposed by the notice.
Mr Beloff stresses moreover that, in terms of duration, it would have offered a
g more lasting protection to the public. The notice was effective only for six months
whereas the undertaking was without limit of time. The advantage to Ferrero of
this proposal would have been the removal of the stigma attaching to a suspension
notice. Such stigma would not, it is said, have attached to an undertaking, and
the existence of the notice was damaging Ferrero's business in other countries
because it was seen as a penal measure applied by the authorities and wrongly
h thought to affect all Ferrero's products.
The council declined to accede to Ferrero's proposal. It was argued, and the
learned judge accepted, that the council had acted irrationally in refusing to lift
the notice. No one doubted Ferrero's probity; their undertaking could therefore
be relied upon, and since it would have achieved the same result as the notice but
for a longer period, it should have been accepted. Here, again, this court has had
j the advantage, which the learned trial judge did not, of fuller argument on behalf
of the council and of Mr Laws's argument on behalf of the Secretary of State.
Mr Beloff is right in asserting that s 14 gives the enforcement authority a
discretionary power to issue a suspension notice. They are not bound to do so.
However, should they do so, Mr Beloff's submission amounts to this: that if the

trader is reputable and offers an undertaking with similar effect to the notice, it is
irrational for the enforcement authority not to accept the undertaking and *a*
withdraw the notice. This argument, if correct, would logically apply also to a
prohibition notice issued by the Secretary of State.

The counter-arguments are based on four distinct submissions. It is first
submitted that it cannot be right to impose the burden on the enforcement
authority of deciding whether the trader in question can be relied upon to honour
his undertaking. There will be instances, such as the present case, where the *b*
authority believes the trader's assertion that he will not market the goods. But, in
many cases, the trader's reliability may be unknown. He may be dishonest; he
may turn out to be weak-willed or change his mind. In doubtful cases an
enforcement authority would again be placed in a dilemma.

Secondly, once the authority has withdrawn the notice, it would have no power *c*
to issue a fresh notice in relation to the same goods, should the undertaking be
breached. Section 14(4) forbids it.

Thirdly, the sanction specifically provided by s 14 itself would no longer bite if
an undertaking were accepted instead. Section 14(6) provides that a person
contravening the notice commits a criminal offence punishable by imprisonment
or a fine, or both. Were an undertaking to be substituted, there would be no *d*
immediate penalty or sanction at all. The most that the authority could do, and it
may not be free from legal difficulty, would be to apply for an injunction upon a
breach of the undertaking. Only if the injunction were obtained and were then
further disobeyed would the court be able to punish the wrongdoers. Thus, the
purpose and scheme of the 1987 Act providing for a notice and a criminal sanction
if it be not obeyed would be frustrated. *e*

Finally, Mr Laws drew attention to the existence of 128 local authority trading
standards departments in Great Britain. If a suspension notice were lifted in one
local authority area by reason of an undertaking, there might well be problems of
enforcement in other areas.

In my judgment these are powerful and convincing arguments. I do not think *f*
the appellants' refusal to accept an undertaking in lieu of the statutory suspension
notice can properly be described as irrational. Nor can I accept the proposition
that, absent any slur on the trader's reputation, an offer of an undertaking in lieu
of a suspension notice should be accepted by the enforcement authority.

Accordingly, I would find in favour of the council on both of the issues which
we were expressly invited to consider. But, as indicated earlier, I would allow the *g*
appeal on the first ground raised by the council.

RUSSELL LJ. I agree.

FOX LJ. I also agree. *h*

Appeal allowed. Leave to appeal to the House of Lords refused.

25 July. *The Appeal Committee of the House of Lords (Lord Bridge of Harwich,
Lord Ackner and Lord Jauncey of Tullichettle) refused leave to appeal.*

Sophie Craven   Barrister. *j*

a R v Life Assurance and Unit Trust Regulatory Organisation Ltd, ex parte Ross

COURT OF APPEAL, CIVIL DIVISION
GLIDEWELL, STOCKER AND McCOWAN LJJ
13, 14, 15 APRIL, 11 JUNE 1992

b

Investment business – Self-regulating organisation – Lautro – Intervention in member's business – Duty to hear representations before making decision to intervene – Whether regulatory body under duty to invite or hear representations before making decision to intervene in member's business and if so from whom.

c

Investment business – Self-regulating organisation – Lautro – Intervention in member's business – Intervention affecting appointed representative of member – Right of appeal – Whether appointed representative having right of appeal to Lautro's appeal tribunal – Financial Services Act 1986, s 8 – Lautro Rules 1988, rr 2.12(1), 7.3(11), 7.23.

d The applicant was a director and shareholder of a company, WG, which was an appointed representative of a life insurance society. Following investigations by Lautro, the recognised self-regulating organisation for life assurance and unit trust business under s 8[a] of the Financial Services Act 1986, into the connection between WG and various persons who had been charged with fraud, Lautro decided on 30 October 1990 to exercise its intervention powers so as to prohibit *e* the life insurance society and three associated companies from accepting any new investment business from WG or from soliciting investment business from the public through WG or any of its representatives. Lautro's grounds for intervening were that there was evidence that there had been serious breaches of Lautro's rules in respect of the business conducted on behalf of the life insurance society by WG and that the imposition of the restrictions was necessary in the interests of *f* investors since there was evidence highlighting serious deficiencies in the life insurance society's internal systems for monitoring the performance of WG and in particular ensuring that WG complied with Lautro's code of conduct. An intervention notice to that effect was served on the life insurance society and a copy was sent to WG. The life insurance society then terminated its agency *g* agreement with WG, which, since it no longer had any status as an authorised representative of the life insurance society, could not thereafter conduct investment business. The applicant applied on behalf of WG for judicial review of Lautro's decision on the grounds that WG, as a person or body directly affected by the decision, had not been given an opportunity to make representations before the decision was made and the notice issued, and further, that WG had a right of *h* appeal under Lautro's rules which it had not been afforded the opportunity of exercising. The Divisional Court dismissed the application. The applicant appealed to the Court of Appeal, contending (i) that the failure by Lautro to give WG an opportunity to make representations before the service of the intervention notice was unfair and rendered the notice invalid, and (ii) that WG was subject to Lautro's rules by virtue of r 2.12(1)[b] of those rules and therefore was a member of *j* Lautro under s 8(2) of the 1986 Act, which provided that the members of a self-regulating organisation such as Lautro were 'the persons who, whether or not members of the organisation, are subject to its rules in carrying on . . . business'

---

a   Section 8, so far as material, is set out at p 549 *a* to *c*, post
b   Rule 2.12(1), so far as material, is set out at p 550 *g*, post

and as such, or by virtue of r 7.3(11)[c] of Lautro's rules, W G had a right of appeal to the appeal tribunal constituted under Lautro's rules.

Held – (1) The effect of r 2.12(1) of Lautro's rules was to provide that the life insurance society had to have rules which would ensure that appointed representatives such as WG complied with Lautro's rules under a regime in which appointed representatives were subject to the life insurance society and not directly to Lautro. Accordingly, WG was not a member of Lautro either by reason of actual membership or under s 8(2) of the 1986 Act. Moreover, although r 7.23[d] of Lautro's rules stated that 'a person' had a right of appeal to the appeal tribunal, that did not enlarge the category of appellants against an intervention notice beyond the recipients of the notice. It followed that WG did not have a right of appeal to the appeal tribunal (see p 555 g j to p 556 b and p 561 j, post).

(2) A decision-making body such as Lautro was required to exercise its powers fairly and although that duty was not owed to every person who might be affected, however remotely, by its decision it was owed to the members, and also to persons who although not members or under the direct control of the decision-making body were in a relationship with a person or firm who was under such direct control if it was apparent that a decision arising out of the relationship would be likely to affect the second person adversely. That duty might well, in appropriate circumstances, include a duty to allow the affected person to make representations before the decision was reached, particularly when his livelihood or ability to earn was likely to be adversely affected. However, since a self-regulating organisation such as Lautro might have to act with urgency in intervening in the business of a member in order to protect investors and it would be incompatible with that object to require the organisation to hear representations from a member or other person affected by its decision before it acted, fairness did not require that an affected person be given an opportunity to make representations before the intervention notice was served. Nevertheless, if a decision-making body did exercise its intervention powers without giving an affected person the opportunity to make representations beforehand its procedures ought to provide that those who might otherwise have expected to have been allowed to make representations should be allowed to make immediate application to set aside the decision or to appeal against it. Accordingly, Lautro had not acted unfairly in failing to give WG an opportunity to make representations before the intervention notice was served but in so far as Lautro's rules did not give WG the right to make representations after the notice was served the rules were unfair. However, since WG had limited its challenge to the intervention notice to Lautro's failure to allow the making of representations before service of the notice, which did not of itself invalidate the notice, the appeal would be dismissed (see p 557 b c, p 559 b c g to j, p 560 f g and p 561 a b e to j, post); dictum of Lord Diplock in *Cheall v Association of Professional Executive Clerical and Computer Staff* [1983] 1 All ER 1130 at 1136 applied; dictum of Lord Denning MR in *Re Liverpool Taxi Owners' Association* [1977] 2 All ER 589 at 594 not followed.

Decision of the Divisional Court of the Queen's Bench Division [1992] 1 All ER 422 affirmed.

Notes

For the rules of natural justice, see 1(1) *Halsbury's Laws* (4th edn reissue) paras 84–100, and for cases on the subject, see 1(1) *Digest* (2nd reissue) 160–184, 1046–1136.

c   Rule 7.3(11) is set out at p 551 c d, post
d   Rule 7.23, so far as material, is set out at p 555 j, post

a For self-regulating organisations under the Financial Services Act 1986, see Supplement to 32 *Halsbury's Laws* (4th edn) para 330.

For the Financial Services Act 1986, s 8, see 30 *Halsbury's Statutes* (4th edn) (1991 reissue) 175.

Cases referred to in judgments

b *Cheall v Association of Professional Executive Clerical and Computer Staff* [1983] 1 All ER 1130, [1983] 2 AC 180, [1983] 2 WLR 679, HL.

Cooper v Wandsworth Board of Works (1863) 14 CBNS 180, 143 ER 414.

Liverpool Taxi Owners' Association, Re [1972] 2 All ER 589, [1972] 2 QB 299, [1972] 2 WLR 1262, CA.

Lloyd v McMahon [1987] 1 All ER 1118, [1987] AC 625, [1987] 2 WLR 821, HL.

c *R v Birmingham City Council, ex p Ferrero Ltd* [1993] 1 All ER 330, CA.

R v Cambridge University (Dr Bentley's Case) (1723) Fortes Rep 202, 92 ER 818.

R v Panel on Take-overs and Mergers, ex p Datafin plc (Norton Opax plc intervening) [1987] 1 All ER 564, [1987] QB 815, [1987] 2 WLR 699, CA.

Ridge v Baldwin [1963] 2 All ER 66, [1964] AC 40, [1963] 2 WLR 935, HL.

Wiseman v Borneman [1969] 3 All ER 275, [1971] AC 297, [1969] 3 WLR 706, HL.

d *Wood v Woad* (1874) LR 9 Exch 190, [1874–80] All ER Rep 408.

Cases also cited or referred to in skeleton arguments

A-G of Hong Kong v Ng Yuen Shiu [1983] 2 All ER 346, [1983] 2 AC 629, PC.

Albert v Belgium (1983) 5 EHRR 533, E Ct HR.

Benthem v Netherlands (1986) 8 EHRR 1, E Ct HR.

e *Bodén v Sweden* (1988) 10 EHRR 367, E Ct HR.

Brind v Secretary of State for the Home Dept [1991] 1 All ER 720, [1991] 1 AC 696, HL.

Cinnamond v British Airports Authority [1980] 2 All ER 368, [1980] 1 WLR 582, CA.

f *Council of Civil Service Unions v Minister for the Civil Service* [1984] 3 All ER 935, [1985] AC 374, HL.

DPP v Schildkamp [1969] 3 All ER 1640, [1971] AC 1, HL.

Durayappah v Fernando [1967] 2 All ER 152, [1967] 2 AC 337, PC.

Enderby Town Football Club Ltd v Football Association Ltd [1971] 1 All ER 215, [1971] Ch 591, CA.

g *Furnell v Whangarei High Schools Board* [1973] 1 All ER 400, [1973] AC 660, PC.

Kaplan v UK (1980) 4 EHRR 64, E Comm HR.

König v Federal Republic of Germany (1979) 2 EHRR 170, E Ct HR.

Lewis v Heffer [1978] 3 All ER 354, [1978] 1 WLR 1061, CA.

R v British Pharmaceutical Industry Association Code of Practice Committee, ex p Professional Counselling Aids Ltd (1990) Independent, 1 November.

h *R v Chief Constable of the Thames Valley Police, ex p Cotton* [1990] IRLR 344, CA.

R v Secretary of State for Transport, ex p Pegasus Holidays (London) Ltd [1989] 2 All ER 481, [1988] 1 WLR 990.

R v Wear Valley DC, ex p Binks [1985] 2 All ER 699.

Transocean Marine Paint Association v EC Commission Case 17/74 [1974] ECR 1063.

j *Waddington v Miah* [1974] 2 All ER 377, [1974] 1 WLR 683, HL.

Appeal

David Hugh Ross, the finance director and a shareholder of Winchester Group plc, appealed from the decision of the Divisional Court of the Queen's Bench Division (Mann LJ and Hidden J) ([1992] 1 All ER 422) given on 5 July 1991 dismissing his application made, with the leave of Otton J given on 15 January

1991, for (1) judicial review by way of an order of certiorari to quash the notice of exercise of intervention powers by the board of the Life Assurance and Unit Trust *a* Regulatory Association Ltd (Lautro) dated 30 October 1990 issued to Norwich Union Life Insurance Society, Norwich Union Asset Management Ltd, Norwich Union Pensions Management Ltd and Norwich Union Trust Managers Ltd, prohibiting the Norwich Union companies from accepting investment business from Winchester Group plc and (2) judicial review by way of an order of mandamus of the refusal of the board of Lautro to permit an appeal to the appeal *b* tribunal constituted under Lautro's rules against the notice. The facts are set out in the judgment of Glidewell LJ.

Andrew Collins QC and *Cherie Booth* (instructed by *Manches & Co*) for Mr Ross.
Michael Beloff QC and *Richard Gordon* (instructed by *Slaughter & May*) for Lautro. *c*

Cur adv vult

11 June 1992. The following judgments were delivered.

GLIDEWELL LJ. This is an appeal against a decision of the Divisional Court *d* (Mann LJ and Hidden J) which, in a judgment given on 5 July 1991 (see [1992] 1 All ER 422), refused Mr Ross relief on his application for judicial review. The appellant, Mr David Hugh Ross, is the finance director of, and a shareholder in, Winchester Group plc (Winchester). The respondent body is the Life Assurance and Unit Trust Regulatory Organisation Ltd (Lautro).

In these proceedings Mr Ross seeks to challenge a notice of exercise of *e* intervention powers issued by the board of Lautro to Norwich Union Life Insurance Society (Norwich Union), and three associated or subsidiary companies, dated 30 October 1990. I shall call this 'the intervention notice'. Mr Ross also challenges the refusal by the board of Lautro to permit him, or Winchester, to appeal against the intervention notice to the appeal tribunal constituted under Lautro's rules. *f*

The relief claimed against Lautro was originally an order of certiorari to quash the intervention notice, and a declaration that the notice was unlawful. By leave of the Divisional Court, Mr Ross was permitted to argue two further issues: firstly, whether Winchester was a member of Lautro and, secondly, whether Winchester, either as a member or as a non-member of Lautro, had any right of appeal against *g* the intervention notice of 30 October 1990.

Self-regulation under the Financial Services Act 1986
The Financial Services Act 1986 introduced a regime for the control of persons and bodies carrying on various kinds of financial business, or offering financial services, by what has come to be known as self-regulation. *h*

It is necessary to start by considering the structure of the 1986 Act, so far as is relevant. Section 3 of that Act provides:

'No person shall carry on ... investment business in the United Kingdom unless he is an authorised person under Chapter III or an exempted person under Chapter IV of this Part of this Act.' *j*

Section 4 makes it an offence to carry on investment business in contravention of s 3.

By section 7(1):

'... a member of a recognised self-regulating organisation is an authorised person by virtue of his membership of that organisation.'

Section 8 provides:

> *a*   '(1) In this Act a "self-regulating organisation" means a body (whether a body corporate or an unincorporated association) which regulates the carrying on of investment business of any kind by enforcing rules which are binding on persons carrying on business of that kind either because they are members of that body or because they are otherwise subject to its control.
>
> *b*   (2) In this Act references to the members of a self-regulating organisation are references to the persons who, whether or not members of the organisation, are subject to its rules in carrying on the business in question.
>
> (3) In this Act references to the rules of a self-regulating organisation are references to the rules (whether or not laid down by the organisation itself) which the organisation has power to enforce in relation to the carrying on of
>
> *c*   the business in question or which relate to the admission and explusion of members of the organisation or otherwise to its constitution . . .'

By s 114 of the 1986 Act the Secretary of State for Trade and Industry is empowered to transfer many of his functions under this Act to a body corporate which is able and willing to discharge those functions. In the exercise of that

d power, the Secretary of State has transferred many such functions to the Securities and Investments Board Ltd (the SIB). Where I refer to sections of the 1986 Act which confer powers upon the Secretary of State which are now exercised by the SIB, I shall refer to that body.

By ss 9 and 10 of the 1986 Act a self-regulating organisation may apply to the SIB for an order declaring it to be a recognised self-regulating organisation for the

e purposes of that Act. In order to secure recognition, a self-regulating organisation must have rules which comply with the requirements of Sch 2 to the 1986 Act. For present purposes, the relevant requirements in that schedule are:

> '1.—(1) The rules and practices of the organisation must be such as to secure that its members are fit and proper persons to carry on investment
>
> *f*   business of the kind with which the organisation is concerned . . .
>
> 2. The rules and practices of the organisation relating to—(a) the admission and explusion of members; and (b) the discipline it exercises over its members, must be fair and reasonable and include adequate provision for appeals . . .'

g There is a special regime for insurance companies which are authorised to conduct business under s 3 or s 4 of the Insurance Companies Act 1982. By s 22 of the 1986 Act an insurance company authorised under those sections of the 1982 Act to carry on insurance business which is investment business within the meaning of the 1986 Act is an authorised person by virtue of the authorisation under the 1982 Act, and not by virtue of membership of a self-regulating

h organisation. However, s 129 of and Sch 10 to the 1986 Act have the effect of making an insurance company which is a member of a recognised self-regulating organisation subject to the rules of that self-regulating organisation in the conduct of investment business.

By s 44(1) an appointed representative, as defined in s 44(2), is an 'exempted person'. By s 44(2):

j

> 'For the purposes of this Act an appointed representative is a person— (a) who is employed by an authorised person (his "principal") under a contract for services which—(i) requires or permits him to carry on investment business to which this section applies; and (ii) complies with subsections (4) and (5) below; and (b) for whose activities in carrying on the whole or part of that investment business his principal has accepted responsibility in writing;

and the investment business carried on by an appointed representative as
such is the investment business for which his principal has accepted *a*
responsibility.'

The remainder of s 44 governs the relationship between an appointed
representative and his or its principal. The relationship between them is essentially
one of contract, and s 44 contains a number of requirements as to the contents of
such a contract. The effect of the section is to make the principal responsible to *b*
investors for the business carried on by the appointed representative.

Thus, under the self-regulatory structure created by the 1986 Act, the SIB may
accord recognition to a self-regulating organisation, and may in appropriate
circumstances revoke that recognition. A recognised self-regulating organisation
controls those authorised persons who are members of it by requiring them to
comply with the rules of the organisation. The authorised person as principal *c*
controls its appointed representatives who are exempted persons within s 3 by
virtue of them being representatives whose authorisation may be terminated.

In the present case Lautro is a recognised self-regulating organisation. Norwich
Union is an authorised person by virtue of s 22 of the 1986 Act, but is a member
of and is subject to control under the rules of Lautro. Winchester was, at the
material time, an appointed representative of Norwich Union, and therefore an *d*
exempted person. It is common ground that the business carried on by Winchester
as an appointed representative of Norwich Union was investment business within
the meaning of the 1986 Act.

As I have said, it is claimed on Winchester's behalf that, in addition to being an
exempted person, it was also a member of Lautro itself, and thus in addition an *e*
appointed person. I shall return later to this argument, which is in issue.

Lautro's rules at the relevant time

Lautro's rules were revised in February 1992. One of the revisions relates to a
matter which arises in this appeal, and I shall refer to it later. However, on
30 October 1990, when the intervention notice was issued, Lautro's then current *f*
rules (1988) included the following provisions which are relevant to the present
appeal:

'... 2.12 (1) A Member shall—(a) establish and maintain rules and
procedures ... by reference to which each officer, employee, company
representative and appointed representative of the Member can ensure *g*
that he complies with these Rules and the Principles in his dealings with
investors ...

3.4 (1) The Member shall ensure that a person is not appointed as a
company representative of that Member except on terms which impose on
him a duty to act in the performance of his functions as a company
representative in such a way as to comply with the Code of Conduct ... *h*

3.5A (1) A body corporate or an unincorporated association shall not be
appointed as, or be permitted to continue as, a Member's appointed
representative unless the Member is satisfied that the controllers, directors
and senior management of that body or association are of good character and
are competent and otherwise suitable to manage the marketing of investment
contracts on the Member's behalf ...' *j*

Rule 7.3 covers the intervention powers of Lautro. Paragraph (2) provides:

'The Board may prohibit a Member in the course of the Member's relevant
investment business from—(a) entering into transactions of any specified
kind either at all or to any specified extent or in specified circumstances;

(b) soliciting business or business of a specified kind from, or except from, persons of a specified kind or in, or except in, specified circumstances; (c) carrying on business in, or except in, a specified manner.'

It was under this provision that the intervention notice was issued. Paragraphs (9) to (12) provide:

'(9) The powers conferred on the Board by this Rule shall be exercisable by notice given to the Member concerned; and the notice shall state the date on which it is to take effect.

(10) The Board may, on their own motion or on the application of the Member concerned, by notice rescind or vary the notice given under paragraph (9) above; and if the Board refuse such an application by the Member they shall give the Member notice of the refusal. A notice under this paragraph shall state the date on which it is to take effect.

(11) A Member to whom a notice under this Rule is given may appeal against that notice to the Appeal Tribunal in accordance with Chapter VIII of this Part and the notice shall state that that right exists and the time within which it may be exercised; and (a) a notice under paragraph (9) above shall state the reasons why it appears to the Board to be desirable for the protection of investors for them to exercise their powers in the manner and in relation to the Member in question; and (b) a notice under paragraph (10) above shall state why the notice under paragraph (9) is being rescinded or varied.

(12) Where the reasons stated in a notice under this Rule relate specifically to matters which (a) refer to a person identified in the notice other than the Member in question; and (b) are in the opinion of the Board prejudicial to that person in any office or employment, the Board shall, unless they consider it impracticable to do so, serve a copy of the notice on that person.'

Chapter VIII of the rules provides for the setting up of and the procedure of an appeal tribunal to which a member on whom an intervention notice is served may appeal.

It will be seen that where Lautro is advised to serve or is considering the service of an intervention notice on a member, the rules do not place any obligation on it to give that member any advance warning of the intended action, or to give him any opportunity to make representations before the intervention notice is served. However, under r 7.3(10) the member may, once the notice is served, apply to the board to rescind it, and under r 7.3(11) may appeal against the notice to the appeal tribunal. Thus a member of Lautro upon whom an intervention notice is served is in much the same position as a defendant to an action at law against whom an ex parte injunction is obtained. He may apply immediately it is served to set it aside and, also or instead of making such application, he may appeal against the imposition of the injunction.

It will be seen, however, that although the rules required that if the notice related to and was prejudicial to a person other than a member a copy of the notice must be served upon him, such a person not only did not have any prior opportunity of making representations why the notice should not be issued, but was not given, under the rules, the right to apply to set it aside, or any right to appeal against the notice. It is this lack in the rules of Lautro of any such rights for persons affected which forms the general basis of Mr Ross's complaint in these proceedings.

The facts

Many affidavits were filed in these proceedings, but for our purposes it has not been necessary to refer to them in any detail, because the facts are carefully summarised in the judgment of Mann LJ in the Divisional Court, and indeed the *a* parties themselves have helpfully agreed a statement of facts. The summary which follows is drawn from those two sources.

Winchester Group Ltd was incorporated on 24 August 1989. The directors then were Mr V A Tee, Mr P A Medland and Mr R L Kissane. All were at that time employed in the Winchester office of the Royal Life Insurance Co Ltd. The company did not trade at that time. *b*

On 11 January 1990 all three of the then directors resigned, and Mr Ross was appointed as the sole director, with Miss Susan Bird as secretary. Only two shares were issued to Mr Ross and Miss Bird, which they held as nominees.

In an affidavit sworn on 17 December 1990 Mr Tee deposes: 'I am 51% shareholder in The Winchester Group Plc . . .' Presumably one of the two issued *c* shares was held by the shareholder as nominee for Mr Tee. Mr Kissane played no part in the company after his resignation.

By a letter dated 9 March 1990 Mr White, national sales manager of the Norwich Union, wrote to Mr Ross, saying in principle he was—

> 'willing to appoint the Winchester Group as Appointed Representatives of *d* the Norwich Union on the basis of the two directors Susan Lesley Bird and David Hugh Ross as shown on the application form dated 9 February 1990 . . . The appointment of the Winchester Group is on the basis that Mr Victor Tee is no longer a Director, a Shareholder or an employee and we will inform you as soon as we have received a response to our request to the Royal [Life] for a reference. Until the outcome of these enquiries Mr Tee must not be *e* associated in any way with the Winchester Group.'

On 13 March 1990 Winchester was formally appointed as appointed representative of Norwich Union by a letter of that date. The letter did not contain any reference to Mr Tee.

It is right to say that Mr Ross asserts that since that time Mr Tee has not been *f* associated with the running of Winchester's business, although of course on his own evidence he was the majority shareholder in that company.

It seems that Norwich Union did not obtain a satisfactory reference for Mr Tee from the Royal Life Insurance Ltd. Moreover, as the Divisional Court put it ([1992] 1 All ER 422 at 428):

> '. . . Mr Tee was not the only person who had, or had had, an apparent *g* connection with Winchester and whose activities excited attention. In September 1990 Mr Kissane was arrested and charged with fraud arising out of activities when he was employed by Royal Life.'

This fact and the alleged connection between Mr Kissane and Mr Tee and *h* Winchester came to the attention of Lautro. Moreover, in October 1990 a Mr Randhir Singh was arrested on fraud charges arising out of his employment by Abbey Life, and the SIB informed Lautro that there was some apparent connection between Randhir Singh and Winchester.

As a result (and I am here quoting from the judgment) ([1992] 1 All ER 422 at 428): *j*

> 'On 15 October the chief executive of Lautro notified Norwich of Lautro's intention to conduct a full investigation into the business carried on by Winchester. The investigation was conducted by Mr Ian Wells, a senior enforcement officer of Lautro. On 22 October documents were removed

a   from Winchester's offices by Mr Wells, in company with the compliance officer of Norwich, and the documents were examined by Mr Wells over the next few days. After a short while Mr Wells felt able to tell the chief executive officer of Lautro that "in his opinion there was evidence to show that there had been serious breaches of the Lautro Rules 1988 in respect of the business conducted on behalf of Norwich Union by" Winchester. On 29 October representatives of Norwich were informed at a meeting of Mr Well's opinion

b   and grounds for it and that the board of Lautro would meet on the following day to consider a written report by Mr Wells upon the business undertaken by Winchester. The board did so meet and resolved to exercise its powers of intervention under r 7.3(2) of the Lautro Rules 1988. The board also approved a press release, which summarised, but in some detail, the terms of the notice. The notice was, as is required by r 7.3(9) of the Lautro Rules 1988, served

c   upon Norwich and the three associated companies.'

And copies of it were also served on Winchester by fax on 31 October 1990.

The press release, which was dated 31 October 1990, summarised the effect of the intervention notice, and contained the following passage:

d   'The Board took the view that the reports called into question whether certain of the controllers, directors and senior managers of the Winchester Group were fit and proper, competent and otherwise suitable to manage the marketing of investment contracts on behalf of Norwich Union.'

On 1 November 1990 Norwich Union wrote to Mr Ross telling him the effect
e   of the intervention notice, and saying:

       'We have, therefore, suspended The Winchester Group as an Appointed Representative of the Norwich Union to take effect immediately and to continue until such time as they hear further from us to the contrary.'

f   Winchester at once sought a meeting with Lautro. This meeting took place on 6 November 1990, and was attended also by representatives of Norwich Union. Winchester complained that they had had no opportunity to make any representations, and that they lacked particulars of the allegations made against them, to which there was no direct response from Lautro. However, Winchester did make attempts to rebut some of the allegations contained in the notice itself.

g   Winchester's position is, and always has been, that the allegations in the intervention notice were unfounded and that some at least of the factual material on which the allegations were based was inaccurate. Lautro later accepted that some of the facts alleged were not correct and that some of the allegations must be qualified. As a result of this acceptance that some of the facts were incorrect,

h   the board of Lautro, on 26 March 1991, reconsidered the question whether intervention remained justified, but decided that it remained necessary and desirable in the interests of investors. In the meantime, Norwich had made it clear that they were not exercising their right to appeal under the rules of Lautro. They notified Mr Ross of their decision not to appeal by letter dated 23 November 1990.

j   On 11 January 1991 Norwich Union gave three months' notice of the termination of their agency agreement of 13 March 1990 with Winchester. That notice therefore expired on 11 April 1991.

Winchester were only entitled to conduct their investment business lawfully by reason of being an authorised representative of Norwich. Once its position as such authorised representative was first suspended, and then terminated,

Winchester was unable to conduct any investment business. As the Divisional
Court commented ([1992] 1 All ER 422 at 430–431):   *a*

> 'The inhibition placed upon Norwich has unquestionably had, as Lautro
> must have known it would have, a seriously damaging effect upon that
> investment business and hence upon Winchester, their shareholders, staff,
> employees and investors. Mr Beloff [for Lautro] was not disposed to challenge
> this proposition although he said there might be room for dispute as to *b*
> whether some of the damage which has in fact been suffered was caused by
> Norwich's termination of the agency agreement. Accepting that qualification,
> I regard it as plain that the effect of an intervention notice cast in the terms
> which were here employed and which were reflected in an accompanying
> press release, must be most damaging to the authorised representative with
> whom further business is inhibited until (if ever) the notice is withdrawn.' *c*

The issues

In this appeal the following issues arise, or could have arisen. I will set them
out in the order in which I propose to deal with them. (i) Does Mr Ross have a
sufficient interest within RSC Ord 53, r 3(7) to entitle him to apply for judicial *d*
review? (ii) Is the exercise by Lautro of its power to serve an intervention notice
subject to judicial review? (iii) Is, or was, Winchester a member of Lautro?
(iv) Whether or not Winchester was a member of Lautro, did it have a right to
appeal under Lautro's rules to the appeal tribunal? (v) Did the failure by Lautro
to give Winchester an opportunity to make representations before the service of
the intervention notice invalidate that notice so that it should be quashed? This *e*
is the major issue.

Conclusion on issues (i) and (ii)

At a hearing before Otton J on 15 January 1991, when he gave leave to move,
counsel for Lautro raised the question whether Mr Ross had a sufficient interest *f*
to entitle him to make the application. The matter was not further pursued, and
was not raised before us by Mr Beloff QC. My own view is that the proper
applicant was probably Winchester rather than Mr Ross personally, but I regard
this as a technicality. The parties quite rightly treated Mr Ross as Winchester's
representative for this purpose. This point therefore disappears.

Mr Beloff concedes that the decision of this court in *R v Panel on Take-overs and* *g*
Mergers, ex p Datafin plc (Norton Opax plc intervening) [1987] 1 All ER 564, [1987]
QB 815 establishes that the decisions of a body with the functions and constitution
of Lautro render those decisions susceptible to judicial review. Whether he will
adhere to this concession if this matter proceeds any further, I do not know.

I turn to consider the respective submissions on the other three issues.   *h*

(iii) Is, or was, Winchester a member of Lautro?

Mr Collins QC for Mr Ross bases his submission that Winchester was a member
of Lautro firstly upon the wording of s 8(2) of the 1986 Act. To repeat, that
subsection provides:

> 'In this Act references to the members of a self-regulating organisation are *j*
> references to the persons who, whether or not members of the organisation,
> are subject to its rules in carrying on the business in question.'

Mr Collins then points out that by r 2.12(1) Lautro requires its members to
establish and maintain procedures by reference to which appointed representatives
can ensure that they comply with Lautro's rules. Thus, he submits, Winchester

was subject to the rules of Lautro, and therefore it follows a member within the
a statutory meaning of that word.

Mr Collins accepts that this involves a person or body being simultaneously an
authorised person and an exempted person under s 3. However, he points out
that another provision of the 1986 Act, namely s 64(4)(*b*), seems to envisage this.
Section 64 of the 1986 Act is the first section of Ch VI, which deals with the
powers of intervention exercisable directly by the SIB in cases where there is no
b recognised self-regulating organisation with powers of intervention. Section 64(4)
provides that Ch VI is not to apply where there is a recognised self-regulating
organisation, and that the chapter shall not apply to:

> '. . . (*b*) an appointed representative whose principal . . . is a member of [a
> recognised self-regulating organisation] and is subject to the rules of such an
c > organisation . . . in carrying on the investment business in respect of which
> his principal or each of his principals has accepted responsibility for his
> activities . . .'

Mr Collins submits that this wording implies that there may be appointed
representatives who are subject to the rules of recognised self-regulating
d organisations.

Mr Beloff in reply submits that the dichotomy between authorised persons and
exempted persons is a major feature of the whole structure of the 1986 Act. It is
thus most unlikely that the legislature intended that one person or body should
be capable of being in both categories. He submits that, though the wording of
s 8(2) is at first sight difficult, there can be persons, for example, who have
e voluntarily agreed to abide by the rules of a recognised self-regulating organisation
and who would thus fall within the statutory definition of membership of that
organisation. For an example of this, he refers us to a code of practice of the
Association of the British Pharmaceutical Industry, with which some firms who
are not members of the association nevertheless voluntarily agree to comply.

Mr Collins's reference to s 64(4)(*b*), Mr Beloff submits, is based upon a
f misreading of that provision. The phrase 'is subject to the rules of such an
organisation' qualify the principal in that case, not the appointed representative.
As for r 2.12(1), Mr Beloff submits that this supports his submission, not that of
Mr Collins, since what it does is to provide that Norwich Union must have rules
which will ensure that appointed representatives such as Winchester comply with
the Lautro rules. Just as a sub-lessee may be required by his sublease to comply
g with some of the covenants in the headlease, and is answerable to his sub-lessor if
he should breach those covenants, so r 2.12(1) provides a regime in which
appointed representatives will be subject to Norwich Union, not directly to
Lautro.

With these arguments advanced by Mr Beloff, I, for my part, agree. I think it
h is clear that, despite the obscure wording of s 8(2), Winchester and firms in its
position are not, and were not, members of Lautro either by reason of actual
membership or by reason of the statutory definition.

(iv) Did Winchester have a right of appeal apart from membership?

The argument here is based upon the wording of r 7.23, which starts: '(1) A
j person may appeal to the Appeal Tribunal . . .' This contrasts with r 7.3(11),
which starts: 'A Member to whom a notice under this Rule is given may appeal
. . .' In his judgment on this aspect of the matter Mann LJ said ([1992] 2 All ER
422 at 436):

> 'Mr Collins said that "a person" includes any person whether a member or
> not, and in particular is apt to include a person, such as was Winchester, who

is referred to in a prohibition notice. I cannot accept this suggestion. I regard
r 7.23 as restating, by way of convenient compilation, rights of appeal which   *a*
are given elsewhere in the rules. At least one of those rights is given to a
person who is not a member, that is to say to the disappointed applicant for
membership (see rr 7.23(2) and 7.23(1)(b)(i)). I regard it as impossible to use
the words "any person" to enlarge the category of appellants against a
prohibition notice beyond recipients of the notice.'
                                                                              b
I agree with this, and therefore reject Mr Collins's argument under this head.
   This brings me to the main issue.

(v) Was the intervention notice invalid because the procedure was unfair to Winchester?
   The submissions made by Mr Collins for Winchester on this issue can be
summarised as follows: (i) in exercising its functions as a recognised self-regulating   *c*
organisation, Lautro was under a duty to act in accordance with the rules of
natural justice—to act fairly in the circumstances; (ii) that duty was owed not
merely to Lautro's member, Norwich Union, but to persons or bodies who would
be prejudicially affected by its decisions, in particular to those whose earnings or
profits would be affected; (iii) fairness required that a body in the position of
Winchester should be notified that Lautro was considering issuing an intervention   *d*
notice, and be given the opportunity to make representations before the decision
to issue the intervention notice.
   Mr Collins refers us to several well-known authorities in support of his
propositions. The earliest, the classic origin of the principle for which he contends,
is *Cooper v Wandsworth Board of Works* (1863) 14 CBNS 180, 143 ER 414. This   *e*
decision contained two well-known dicta, the first of which is from Willes J (14
CBNS 180 at 190, 143 ER 414 at 418):

   'I apprehend that a tribunal which is by law invested with power to affect
   the property of one of Her Majesty's subjects, is bound to give such subject
   an opportunity of being heard before it proceeds: and that that rule is of
   universal application, and founded upon the plainest principles of justice.'   *f*

The second passage is in the judgment of Byles J (14 CBNS 180 at 194, 143 ER
414 at 420):

   '... a long course of decisions, beginning with *Dr. Bentley's* Case [*R v
   Cambridge University* (1723) Fortes Rep 202, 92 ER 818], and ending with   *g*
   some very recent cases, establish, that, although there are no positive words
   in a statute requiring that the party shall be heard, yet the justice of the
   common law will supply the omission of the legislature.'

   Mr Collins also refers us to *Wood v Woad* (1874) LR 9 Exch 190, [1874–80] All
ER Rep 408 and the decisions of the House of Lords in *Ridge v Baldwin* [1963] 2   *h*
All ER 66, [1964] AC 40 and *Wiseman v Borneman* [1969] 3 All ER 275, [1971] AC
297.
   To these I would add a passage from the speech of Lord Bridge of Harwich in
Lloyd v McMahon [1987] 1 All ER 1118 at 1161, [1987] AC 625 at 702–703 in
which he said:

   'My Lords, the so-called rules of natural justice are not engraved on tablets   *j*
   of stone. To use the phrase which better expresses the underlying concept,
   what the requirements of fairness demand when any body, domestic,
   administrative or judicial, has to make a decision which will affect the rights
   of individuals depends on the character of the decision-making body, the
   kind of decision it has to make and the statutory or other framework in

a which it operates. In particular, it is well established that when a statute has conferred on any body the power to make decisions affecting individuals, the courts will not only require the procedure prescribed by the statute to be followed, but will readily imply so much and no more to be introduced by way of additional procedural safeguards as will ensure the attainment of fairness.'

b As to the first of Mr Collins's propositions, I have no doubt that Lautro was and is obliged to exercise its powers fairly. Indeed, para 2 of Sch 2 to the 1986 Act (which I have already quoted) requires that Lautro's rules relating to the admission and expulsion of members and the discipline it exercises over its members must be fair and reasonable and include adequate provision for appeals. Thus Lautro is under a duty not merely at common law but by statute to be fair in these respects *c* towards its members.

I find much more difficulty with the second proposition advanced by Mr Collins. In effect this raises the question: to whom is the duty of fairness owed? Is it owed to persons and bodies who are not members of Lautro? None of the authorities to which I have so far referred dealt with a situation in which a decision was made which directly affected one party, A, and at the same time *d* indirectly affected a second party, B, so as to raise the question: is there any duty in the decision-making authority to be fair towards B?

In support of his proposition, Mr Collins quotes a short passage from the judgment of Lord Denning MR in *Re Liverpool Taxi Owners' Association* [1972] 2 All ER 589, [1972] 2 QB 299, a decision of this court. In that case Liverpool *e* Corporation was considering increasing the maximum number of licensed taxis in its area. The association objected. During the course of discussion the chairman of the relevant committee publicly undertook that the number of licensed taxis would not be increased until a private Bill which contained relevant provisions had been enacted and come into force. Despite that undertaking, before the legislation was enacted, the committee and the corporation decided to increase *f* the number of licensed taxis.

On a renewed application for leave to move for what would now be called judicial review, this court granted the application. All three members of the court took the view that the corporation was bound by its undertaking and could not resile from it without at least giving the association an opportunity to make representations. This was therefore the reason for the decision.

g However, in the course of his judgment Lord Denning MR said ([1972] 2 All ER 589 at 594, [1972] 2 QB 299 at 307):

'... when the corporation considers applications for licences under the Town Police Clauses Act 1847 they are under a duty to act fairly. This means that they should be ready to hear not only the particular applicant, but also *h* any other persons or bodies whose interests are affected.'

Mr Collins argues that this applies in the circumstances of the present case. However, the question whether, apart from the undertaking, the association had a right to make representations was not in issue in that case. Indeed, it was a question about which Roskill LJ expressed doubts (see [1972] 2 All ER 589 at 596, *j* [1972] 2 QB 299 at 311). I cannot therefore regard the two sentences from the judgment of Lord Denning MR which I have quoted as being an authority on the question which we have to consider.

The issue arises because of the self-regulatory structure which has been created under the 1986 Act. As I have said, a recognised self-regulating organisation controls those authorised persons who are members of it. The authorised persons, as principals, control their appointed representatives, who are thus exempted persons. Thus the line of control in the present case is for Lautro to control the *a* operations of Norwich Union, and Norwich Union in turn, by virtue of its contractual relationship, to control Winchester. However, there is no doubt that decisions made by Lautro, particularly in relation to the issue of intervention notices, will frequently have a very considerable affect upon the appointed representatives, such as Winchester. I agree with Mr Beloff that there seems to be no direct authority on the question whether, and to what extent, the controlling *b* authority owes a duty of fairness to the appointed representative thus indirectly affected by its decisions.

Mr Beloff submits that the first question we have to answer is: is there any known rule of natural justice that a person who is not the subject of an administrative decision should nevertheless have the right to make representations *c* before the decision is made?

In his judgment in the Divisional Court Mann LJ said ([1992] 1 All ER 422 at 433):

> 'In my judgment, Mr Collins's contention runs counter to an important policy consideration. It is this: if the law is to imply an obligation to hear *d* representations, then it must also specify with precision to whom that obligation is owed. If persons beyond the subject of the decision are included, then specificity becomes impossible. In *Cheall v Association of Professional Executive Clerical and Computer Staff* [1983] 1 All ER 1130 at 1135, [1983] 2 AC 180 at 190 Lord Diplock said: "Decisions that resolve disputes between the parties to them, whether by litigation or some other adversarial dispute- *e* resolving process, often have consequences which affect persons who are not parties to the dispute; but the legal concept of natural justice has never been extended to give such persons as well as the parties themselves rights to be heard by the decision-making tribunal before the decision is reached." These remarks were made in a different context to this, but I regard them as *f* apposite. I think it important that a regulatory body should know with precision from whom (if anyone) they have to invite or receive representations without first having to form an impugnable judgment as to who those persons are.'

Mr Cheall was the secretary of the local branch of a trade union. Disenchantment *g* with the policy of that union led him to resign from it and to join another union, APEX. The decision by APEX to admit him as a member breached what was known as the Bridlington agreement, which governed the relationships between trades unions. The TUC disputes committee, on a complaint by the other union, found that APEX had acted in breach of the Bridlington agreement. During the course of its consideration the disputes committee did not invite, or receive, any *h* representations from Mr Cheall. On receipt of the disputes committee's decision, APEX purported to terminate Mr Cheall's membership. He then sought a declaration that APEX was not entitled to do this.

Bingham J dismissed Mr Cheall's action; the Court of Appeal (by a majority) allowed his appeal, but the House of Lords, in turn, allowed an appeal against this court's decision and upheld Bingham J. One of the issues before the House was *j* whether Mr Cheall had been entitled to be heard by the disputes committee of the TUC before it made its decision. Their Lordships held that there was no principle of natural justice requiring the TUC to hear him. It was in that context that Lord Diplock expressed the opinion which I set out above.

However, I note that towards the conclusion of his speech Lord Diplock said ([1983] 1 All ER 1130 at 1136, [1983] 2 AC 180 at 191):

'Different considerations might apply if the effect of Cheall's expulsion from APEX were to have put his job in jeopardy, either because of the existence of a closed shop or for some other reason. But this is not the case.'

I accept that very frequently a decision made which directly affects one person or body will also affect, indirectly, a number of other persons or bodies, and that the law does not require the decision-making body to give an opportunity to every person who may be affected however remotely by its decision to make representations before the decision is reached. Such a principle would be unworkable in practice. On the other hand, it is my opinion that, when a decision-making body is called upon to reach a decision which arises out of the relationship between two persons or firms only one of whom is directly under the control of the decision-making body, and it is apparent that the decision will be likely to affect the second person adversely, then as a general proposition the decision-making body does owe some duty of fairness to that second person, which, in appropriate circumstances, may well include a duty to allow him to make representations before reaching the decision. This will particularly be the case when the adverse effect is upon the livelihood or the ability to earn of the second person or body.

In the present case I do not agree with Mann LJ, with all respect to him, that there is any great difficulty in defining the persons from whom, applying the principle to which I have just referred, the decision-making authority might be required to seek representations. Indeed, r 7.3(12) of Lautro's rules required Lautro to serve a copy of the intervention notice on Winchester, since that notice referred to Winchester and was, in the opinion of Lautro, prejudicial to Winchester in its position as the appointed representative of Norwich Union.

Mr Beloff submits that the requirement of notice to bodies such as Winchester was necessary to ensure that they did not breach the intervention notice, but in my view the limitation of the category of those entitled to be given notice to persons who will be prejudicially affected can only mean that it is the prejudice which brings with it the necessity to serve. Thus in my view this Lautro rule has already defined, with some clarity, the persons who shall be served, and to whom in my opinion in appropriate circumstances Lautro owes a general duty to act fairly.

This brings me to Mr Collins's third point: did fairness require that Winchester should be notified before the decision to serve the intervention notice was reached? I notice that Lautro's rules at the time did not require Lautro to give its members, such as Norwich Union, the opportunity to make representations before serving an intervention notice. The reason for this is, in my view, made clear in r 7.3(1) of Lautro's rules, which I have not so far quoted. That rule, which is the first of the rules dealing with Lautro's intervention powers, authorises the board '. . . in any case where it appears to them that it is desirable in the interests of investors . . .' to exercise their powers of intervention. Thus an intervention notice is appropriate when the board conclude, on the material before them, that the interests of investors require the practice about which the board are concerned to cease immediately pending further investigation of the allegations.

The decision whether or not to exercise this power, and to serve a notice before hearing the persons to whom it is directed or whom it will affect, must be one which the board must balance against what they regard as the interests of investors. The board in this sense will be moved by similar considerations to those which affect a court in deciding whether to grant an injunction ex parte.

On this issue, Mann LJ said in his judgment ([1992] 1 All ER 422 at 434):

'The purpose of an exercise of intervention powers under the Lautro Rules 1988, or an exercise under Pt I of the 1986 Act, is the protection of investors.

The achievement of that purpose must on occasion require action which has
urgently to be taken, and the entertainment of representations may not be *a*
compatible with the urgency. Mr Collins recognised that this could be so,
but said that at least there must be a duty to consider whether time admits of
the receipt of representations and in this case there was no such consideration
by Lautro. In my judgment, once it is recognised, as inevitably it must be,
that a self-regulating organisation may have to act with urgency in order to
achieve its purpose, then it would be undesirable to encumber it with the *b*
necessity to make a judgment as to whether time admits of an opportunity
to make representations. That was the approach of the Court of Appeal in *R
v Birmingham City Council, ex p Ferrero Ltd* [1993] 1 All ER 530. That case
concerned the exercise of powers under Pt II of the Consumer Protection Act
1987. Under those powers an enforcement authority can by notice prohibit *c*
a person from supplying goods which the authority suspects of contravening
a safety provision. There is an appeal against a notice to a magistrates' court,
but there is no express provision for representations prior to service of the
notice. The court held that such a provision should not be implied. Taylor
LJ, with whom Fox and Russell LJJ agreed, said (at 542): "But if the supposed
duty to consult were to depend upon the facts and urgency of each case, *d*
enforcement authorities would be faced with a serious dilemma. What
amounts to urgency is incapable of precise definition, and would be open in
many cases to honest and reasonable differences of opinion. There would be
a danger that although the authority reasonably suspected goods were
dangerous they would feel bound to delay serving a notice until they
consulted the trader, whereas, without a duty to consult, they would have *e*
served forthwith. Valuable time would be lost and danger could result." I
regard these observations as applicable to the position of a self-regulating
organisation. It appears to me that the omission from the Lautro Rules 1988
reflects an omission from the 1986 Act, and in my judgment the omission
was made with a deliberation in each case which makes an implication *f*
impossible.'

I agree with these observations, but with a qualification. This is that, in my
view, if a decision-making body is to exercise powers such as those of serving an
intervention notice without giving anybody the opportunity to make representations beforehand, its procedures should provide that those who might otherwise
expect to have been allowed to make representations should at least be allowed to *g*
make immediate application to set the decision aside and to appeal against it. In
this respect the situation is very similar to that which obtains when a court grants
an ex parte injunction.

In *Wiseman v Borneman* [1969] 3 All ER 275 at 286, [1971] AC 297 at 318 Lord
Wilberforce said: *h*

'Thirdly, it is true, as the judgments in the Court of Appeal point out, that
ex parte applications are frequently made to the courts and granted without
hearing the party affected, but merely to say this, overlooks that procedure
invariably exists, and is where necessary invoked, for enabling the party
affected rapidly to seek annulment or amendment of the order made against *j*
him.'

At the relevant time r 7.3(1) of Lautro's rules gave a member on whom an
intervention notice was served the right to apply (immediately) for the board to
rescind the notice, and r 7.3(11) gave a right to the member to appeal against the
notice and against any decision not to rescind it. At that time the rules gave no
such rights to other persons served with the notice, such as Winchester.

In February 1992, however, Lautro's rules were amended so as to give other
a persons served with an intervention notice the right to appeal against it—see new
rr 7.28 and 7.3(12). In my view, when the intervention notice was served on
31 October 1990 Lautro's rules were defective in not giving such a right of appeal
to a person or body in the position of Winchester, and in not giving such a person
the right to seek to have the decision to serve the notice rescinded. In other words,
whilst the power to decide to serve an intervention notice without first hearing
b representations from persons affected was not in itself so unfair as to invalidate
the notice, a lack of any means by which the person could immediately thereafter
challenge the notice was in my opinion a breach of the requirements of fairness
which the law should imply.

Rule 7.3(12) of Lautro's rules requires service of a copy of an intervention
c notice upon a person or firm in the position of Winchester because the notice
relates specifically to matters prejudicial to that person or firm. If, in accordance
with the view I have just expressed, such a person or firm were given the right to
apply immediately the notice was served for it to be rescinded, this remedy might
well be of no effect if a press notice was issued at the time of service of the
intervention notice, as was done in this case. If it transpired that the intervention
d notice was not justified, and Lautro rescinded it, a press notice might already have
caused substantial damage to the person affected. Although this is not a matter in
respect of which we are asked to grant any relief, I believe that Lautro should
reconsider its practice in this respect, and consider deferring the issue of a press
notice until after the person affected has had the opportunity to apply for the
notice to be rescinded and to make representations to that effect, and Lautro's
e board have ruled in the application.

For the reasons I have given, I conclude that if (but only if) Lautro did not
afford to a person or firm served with an intervention notice in accordance with
r 7.3(12) the opportunity to apply to the board to rescind the notice, and/or to
appeal against it, then the lack of such remedies would be unfair and the procedure
f unlawful.

However, Mr Collins (if I have understood him correctly) has expressly limited
his challenge to Lautro's failure to allow the making of representations before the
service of the intervention notice. As I have said, I do not consider that this of
itself invalidated the notice. If Mr Collins had sought to base an argument on the
omission from the rules which I have characterised as unfair, we should have had
g to consider whether the opportunity given to Winchester on 6 November 1990
to make representations to Lautro's board rectified this defect. We were not,
however, asked to consider this. I am therefore not prepared to quash the
intervention notice.

Although I consider that at the relevant time Lautro's rules, and thus its
procedure, were defective in the respects I have outlined, for the reasons I have
h given I conclude that Lautro was not required by law to afford to Winchester the
opportunity to make representations as to why an intervention notice should not
be served before deciding whether or not to serve such a notice.

I would therefore dismiss this appeal.

j **STOCKER LJ.** I agree.

McCOWAN LJ. I also agree.

Appeal dismissed. Leave to appeal to the House of Lords refused.

L I Zysman Esq   Barrister.

Harris v Director of Public Prosecutions
Fehmi v Director of Public Prosecutions

QUEEN'S BENCH DIVISION

McCOWAN LJ AND POPPLEWELL J

21 JULY 1992

Criminal law – Offensive weapons – Article with blade or point – Lock-knife with blade less than three inches in length – Whether knife a 'folding pocketknife' – Whether carrying such a lock-knife in a public place an offence – Criminal Justice Act 1988, s 139.

A lock-knife having a pointed blade less than three inches in length and which is capable of being secured in an open position by means of a locking device which requires a trigger mechanism to be activated before the blade can be folded back into the handle is an article the carrying of which in a public place is an offence under s 139[a] of the Criminal Justice Act 1988. Such a knife is not a 'folding pocketknife' the carrying of which in a public place is not an offence by virtue of s 139(3), since a folding pocketknife is a knife which is readily and immediately foldable at all times simply by the folding process and the presence of a locking mechanism which requires a further process, namely activating a trigger mechanism, to fold the blade back into the handle takes the knife outside the definition of 'folding pocketknife' (see p 565 b c, post).

Notes

For the offence of having an article with a blade or point in a public place, see 11(1) *Halsbury's Laws* (4th edn reissue) para 168.

For the Criminal Justice Act 1988, s 139, see 12 *Halsbury's Statutes* (4th edn) (1989 reissue) 1211.

Cases stated

Harris v DPP

John Harris appealed by way of a case stated by Mr Alan C Baldwin, metropolitan stipendiary magistrate for the petty sessional division of North Westminster, sitting at Wells Street Magistrates' Court on 15 February 1991 in respect of his decision to convict the appellant of the offence of having with him without good reason or lawful authority an article which had a blade or was sharply pointed, namely a lock-knife, contrary to s 139(1) of the Criminal Justice Act 1988. The question for the opinion of the High Court is set out at p 563 e f, post. The facts are set out in the judgment of McCowan LJ.

Fehmi v DPP

Ahmet Fehmi appealed by way of a case stated by the magistrates for the Thames Division in respect of their adjudication on 3 October 1991 whereby they convicted the appellant of the offence of having with him in a public place without good reason or lawful authority an article with a blade or point, namely a blade, contrary to s 139(1) of the Criminal Justice Act 1988. The question for the opinion of the High Court is set out at p 564 a, post. The facts are set out in the judgment of McCowan LJ.

---

a Section 139, so far as material, is set out at p 564 b c, post

Bryan McGuire (instructed by *Rance & Co*) for the appellant Harris.
a *Laurence Giovene* (instructed by *R Voss & Son*) for the appellant Fehmi.
John McGuinness (instructed by the *Crown Prosecution Service*, Harrow) for the
Director of Public Prosecutions.

McCOWAN LJ. These are two appeals by way of cases stated which have been
heard together because they raise a single point. The first is an appeal by John
b Harris. In his case an information was preferred by the Director of Public
Prosecutions against him that on 3 November 1990 at Prebend Street, Islington,
he had with him, without good reason or lawful authority, an article which had a
blade or was sharply pointed, namely a lock-knife, contrary to s 139(1) of the
Criminal Justice Act 1988. At the conclusion of the respondent's case, the
c appellant submitted that there was no case to answer on the basis that the knife
was a folding pocketknife and that the cutting edge of its blade was less than three
inches in length, so that the knife did not fall within the provisions of s 139 of
the 1988 Act.

The case was heard by Mr Alan C Baldwin, a metropolitan stipendiary
magistrate sitting at Wells Street on 15 February 1991. In the case stated he says
d he was—

'of the opinion that it could not be said that this lockknife was a folding
pocket knife. Accordingly I rejected the submission advanced on behalf of
the Appellant. The Appellant called no evidence, and I convicted him in
relation to the information.'

e The question for the opinion of the High Court is:

'Whether I was right in law to find that a folding knife carried in the
pocket having a pointed blade of less than 3″ in length and capable of being
secured in an open position by a locking device was not a folding pocket
knife within the meaning of Section 139 Criminal Justice Act 1988.'

f
The other appellant is Mr Ahmet Fehmi. In his case an information was laid
against him that on 14 September 1990 at Bethnal Green Road, London E2, he
had with him in a public place, without good reason or lawful authority, an
article with a blade or sharp point, namely a blade, contrary to s 139 of the 1988
Act.

g The case is stated by justices for the Thames Division who tried the case on
3 October 1991. They were asked as a preliminary issue to examine the knife the
subject of the charge, and to rule whether they considered it an article the carrying
of which in a public place was prohibited by s 139. They did examine it and they
found these facts:

h 'a) that the article was a knife with a blade the cutting edge of which was
less than three inches. b) that the blade was capable of being folded. c) that
when the blade was fully opened it automatically locked in that
position. d) that to fold the blade back into the handle it was necessary to
activate a button triggered mechanism . . .'

j It appears that it was contended by the respondent that the mechanism which
locked the blade in the open position was such as to render the knife not one
which the provisions of the section permitted to be carried lawfully in a public
place. The justices found that the knife was one the carrying of which in a public
place was an offence under s 139, and they state that the question for the opinion
of the High Court—

'is whether in finding as we did that the knife was one the carrying of which in a public place is an offence was a correct determination or decision *a*
in law.'

We were shown one of the knives in question, there being no difference between the two. What we observed was that when you first open it manually you cannot then fold it back. You have first to press a button on it in order to fold it back, so that when fully opened the result is that it requires to be unlocked. *b*

I look next at s 139 and read it in so far as it is relevant:

'(1) Subject to subsections (4) and (5) below, any person who has an article to which this section applies with him in a public place shall be guilty of an offence.

(2) Subject to subsection (3) below, this section applies to any article which *c*
has a blade or is sharply pointed except a folding pocketknife.

(3) This section applies to a folding pocketknife if the cutting edge of its blade exceeds 3 inches . . .'

Appearing for Mr Harris, Mr McGuire said that the only question in the case is whether the presence of the locking mechanism is sufficient to prevent it being a folding pocket knife. He points out that this is a penal statute and, accordingly, *d*
he submits, clear words are required. They are not, he says. There is nothing in the section which says that the presence or absence of a locking device affects the matter. The court asked him how far he took the argument. What, for example, of a knife which required a screwdriver to undo a screw before it could be unlocked and then folded back into the closed position? His answer was that it *e*
would be still a folding knife because it could be, albeit by a somewhat lengthy process, folded away. Again, the court asked him what he submitted was the thinking behind the statute. He accepted in this context that it does make a difference if the knife can be folded readily away. He accepted that it is obviously a more effective stabbing weapon if it is locked, for the very plain reason that without a lock there is a dangerous tendency, dangerous, that is to say, from the *f*
point of view of the wielder, to fold onto the wielder's hand.

Mr Giovene appeared for the other appellant, Mr Fehmi. His arguments were somewhat different. He stressed the other side of the coin. He submits that it is not more dangerous for being locked. He says that from the point of view of the user, it is much safer because it will not come back upon his hand. Mr Giovene went so far as to describe it as a safety device. Again, he would not agree with Mr *g*
McGuire about the screw to which I referred a little while ago, because Mr Giovene says that the section covers manual folding and, if it is necessary to use a screwdriver in order to undo the locking device, then, this is mechanical folding and not manual folding. There was some discussion about what is called a switch blade. As I understand it, that means that by pressing a button the blade will *h*
automatically fold outwards and, again, by pressing a button, it will automatically fold in again. Since this is a pivotal device and Mr Giovene was stressing the element of pivoting, I asked him why that would not cover the switch blade. His answer is that it does not cover the switch blade because the section is concerned to cover manual folding and not mechanical folding.

For my part, I cannot accept his argument in this respect, because that would *j*
certainly involve importing a number of additional words into the section. His basic argument, as I have already indicated, is that to fold the blade it has to have a pivot. If it is pivoted, he asked rhetorically, how can it be said that because it has a locking device it is no longer a folding pocketknife? Two hands, he stresses, are required to open this type of knife. That sharply differentiates it from a flick

knife. The locking device, he submits, cannot change the nature of the animal.

a The question is whether it folds open and folds shut.

For the respondent in each case, Mr McGuinness answers the question from the court as to the thinking behind the statute by saying this. When the knife is locked it becomes in effect a fixed-blade knife and the intention of the statute is to prevent the carrying of such a knife. I accept that point.

In my judgment, the right approach to the matter is this. To be a folding
b pocketknife the knife has to be readily and indeed immediately foldable at all times, simply by the folding process. A knife of the type with which these appeals are concerned is not in this category because, in the first place, there is a stage, namely when it has been opened, when it is not immediately foldable simply by the folding process and, secondly, it requires that further process, namely the
c pressing of the button.

For these reasons, I would give the answer to the questions in each case, that the tribunals were right to find as they did, and I would dismiss the appeals.

POPPLEWELL J. I agree.

d *Appeals dismissed.*

Dilys Tausz   Barrister.

e # Hopkins v Norcross plc

QUEEN'S BENCH DIVISION
DAVID LATHAM QC SITTING AS A DEPUTY JUDGE OF THE HIGH COURT
31 MARCH, 1, 9 APRIL 1992

f *Contract – Damages for breach – Wrongful dismissal – Loss of earnings – Set-off of retirement pension received on dismissal – Employers terminating employment of employee in breach of contract – Employee receiving retirement pension equalling total loss of salary up to normal retirement date – Employee bringing action for wrongful dismissal – Whether retirement benefits received by way of pension deductible from damages for wrongful dismissal.*

g

The plaintiff was employed by the defendant company for 27 years and was the chairman of one of its divisions when he was wrongfully dismissed on 12 September 1989 at the age of 58. The plaintiff was a member of the company's pension scheme, not having opted out when employees became entitled in 1986
h to make provision for their pensions in schemes other than those run by their employers. Under the terms of the scheme the plaintiff was entitled on leaving employment for whatever reason over the age of 50 and before the age of 60 to an immediate pension calculated as a proportion of the pension that he would have been entitled to had he retired on his 60th birthday. There were no provisions in the scheme modifying the plaintiff's absolute entitlement to the
j pension and since he was unable to find any alternative employment the benefits he received by way of pension were equivalent to the loss of his salary for the period between the date of his dismissal and the date of his 60th birthday. In an action by the plaintiff for wrongful dismissal the defendants admitted liability and damages were assessed as being the loss of salary for the period between the date of dismissal and the date of normal retirement. The question arose whether

the pension arising out of the termination of employment should be set off against the damages to which the plaintiff was entitled for wrongful dismissal. *a* The defendants contended that, since it was a basic principle in the assessment of damages for breach of contract that the plaintiff was to be placed in the same position as if the contract had been performed, failure to take into account the pension money would provide the plaintiff with double the amount to which he was entitled under his contract of employment because if he had not been dismissed he would have continued to earn his salary up to 1 October 1991 and *b* since he had received precisely the same sum by way of pension, which would not have been payable but for the termination, he had lost nothing.

Held – In a claim for damages for wrongful dismissal pension benefits received by a plaintiff as a result of that dismissal were not, in the absence of any term in the contract of employment or pension rules expressly prohibiting payment in *c* such circumstances, to be set off against the damages to which the plaintiff was entitled, because there was no relevant distinction between damages for lost earnings arising out of a claim in contract for wrongful dismissal and damages arising out of a claim in tort for lost earning capacity as a result of injury, where it was established law that money payable under a pension, be it a disability or *d* retirement pension, was not deductible, and it would not be satisfactory if the answer to the question whether a pension was to be deducted depended on the way in which the claim was formulated. Furthermore, since the plaintiff could have opted out of the company pension in 1986 but chose not to, and since it was accepted that any pension that he would have received as a result would not have been deductible, it would be unjust for there to be a different result merely *e* because the pension was provided by the employer. It followed that the pension payments received by the plaintiff were not deductible from the figure which had been agreed as the damages for wrongful dismissal (see p 571 *e*, p 572 *b* to p 573 *b*, post).

Parry v Cleaver [1969] 1 All ER 555 and *Smoker v London Fire and Civil Defence Authority, Wood v British Coal Corp* [1991] 2 All ER 449 applied. *f*

Notes
For deduction for benefits received or receivable from damages, see 12 *Halsbury's Laws* (4th edn) para 1152 and 34 *Halsbury's Laws* (4th edn) para 83, and for cases on the subject, see 17 *Digest* (Reissue) 117–118, 195–200 and 36(1) *Digest* (2nd *g* reissue) 489–491, 4199–4203.

Cases referred to in judgment
British Transport Commission v Gourley [1955] 3 All ER 796, [1956] AC 185, [1955] 2 WLR 41, HL.
Guy v Northern Ireland Police Authority (14 April 1989, unreported), NI QBD. *h*
Livingstone v Rawyards Coal Co (1880) 5 App Cas 25, HL.
Parry v Cleaver [1969] 1 All ER 555, [1970] AC 1, [1969] 2 WLR 821, HL.
Robinson v Harman (1848) 1 Exch 850, [1843–60] All ER Rep 383, 154 ER 363.
Smoker v London Fire and Civil Defence Authority, Wood v British Coal Corp [1991] 2 All ER 449, [1991] 2 AC 502, [1991] 2 WLR 1052, HL.

j

Action
By writ and statement of claim the plaintiff, John Edward Hopkins, brought an action against the defendants, Norcross plc, claiming damages for wrongful dismissal. On 14 June 1991 Master Miller granted the plaintiff's summons under RSC Ord 14 for leave to enter judgment for damages to be assessed. On 10

December 1991 Master Miller ordered for assessment of damages to be tried
a before a judge. The facts are set out in the judgment.

Stephen Auld (instructed by *Clifford Chance*) for the plaintiff.
Philip Naughton QC and *Adrian Lynch* (instructed by *Slaughter & May*) for the
   defendants.

b   *Cur adv vult*

9 April 1992. The following judgment was delivered.

DAVID LATHAM QC. Mr Hopkins commenced employment with a
c company within the Norcross Group of companies on 16 July 1962 as a production
engineer, and remained in employment with one or other members of the group
for the next 27 years. In January 1981 he was appointed managing director of
Norcross plc (the defendants) responsible for all of its UK based activities, and in
May 1988 he became chairman of the defendants' ceramics division. On 11
September 1989 the defendants' chief executive, Michael Doherty, called
d Mr Hopkins into his office, informed him that he was relieving him of the
chairmanship of the ceramics division, instructed him to clear his desk, go home
and remain there until 15 September 1989, when he would be seen again. On 15
September 1989 Mr Hopkins met Mr Doherty and the defendants' secretary and
group legal adviser, David Hamilton. Mr Hopkins was dismissed, handed a form
P45 dated 12 September 1989, and a cheque in respect of his salary for the first 12
e days of September 1989. He has not worked for the defendants since then, nor
has he been able to find any alternative employment. He was, at the time,
employed under a contract of employment entitling him to remain so employed
(subject to immaterial exceptions) until his normal retirement date, as defined in
the rules of a pension scheme operated by the defendants (which I shall refer to in
more detail later), which was his 60th birthday, that is 1 October 1991.
f   Mr Hopkins commenced these proceedings claiming damages for wrongful
dismissal. A defence was served; but Mr Hopkins issued a summons under RSC
Ord 14, which was heard by Master Miller, who ordered on 14 June 1991 that
Mr Hopkins be at liberty to enter judgment against the defendants for damages
and interest to be assessed, which judgment was entered on 25 June 1991. By
g further order of 10 December 1991 Master Miller ordered that the assessment of
damages be tried before a judge (without a jury), which is how the matter comes
before me. The parties have in fact resolved most of the issues; and there is a
written agreement which deals with all matters save for one issue of law. It has
been agreed that Mr Hopkins's claim for damages against the defendants for
wrongful dismissal is to be assessed as £99,604 (after tax) plus interest pursuant
h to s 35A of the Supreme Court Act 1981 at such rate and for such period as the
court shall determine, and that the amount in fact received by Mr Hopkins from
the pension scheme which I have already referred to over the period from his
dismissal to 1 October 1991 was £99,604. The issue of law is whether or not this
latter sum is to be deducted from the damages for wrongful dismissal either in
whole or in part.
j   Before I consider the issue of law, it is necessary to set out certain terms of the
contract on which he was employed at the relevant time, and the provisions of
the pension scheme. The contract of employment, referred to before me as the
'service agreement', provided as follows: (a) Mr Hopkins's employment was
conditional upon his being a member of the pension scheme operated by the
defendants known as 'the Norcross Security Plan' (the plan); (b) his contributions

to the plan in accordance with the rules of the plan in force from time to time would be deducted from his salary on a monthly basis and, if required to do so, Mr Hopkins would sign an appropriate form authorising the making of such deductions; (c) the service agreement superseded any subsisting agreement between the defendants and Mr Hopkins relating to his employment.

By s 15(1) of the Social Security Act 1986, which came into force on 6 April 1988, the term set out in (a) above was rendered void; the policy of the 1986 Act was to entitle employees if they so wished to make provision for their pensions in schemes other than those run by their employers. However, Mr Hopkins did not avail himself of that right, and remained a member of the plan, subject to changes I will refer to later, until the date of his dismissal.

Originally the plan provided Mr Hopkins with his basic pension entitlement, and was at the relevant time administered by a trustee upon trusts and subject to the powers and provisions contained in rules all which have been referred to as 'the plan rules'. Mr Hopkins became a member of the plan on 1 April 1975, and thereafter contributed 5% of his pensionable salary, which was deducted by the defendants and paid to the trustee on his behalf. The defendants in their turn made such contributions to the plan as the plan's actuary calculated to be required to provide the appropriate benefits.

In addition, the defendants set up a further scheme which operated originally by way of topping up the benefits available to employees such as the plaintiff, called 'the Norcross Supplementary Pension Scheme' (the scheme), which was established on 29 March 1979 and was administered by the defendants. The relevant rules setting out the trusts and powers were referred to before me as 'the scheme rules'. The scheme was non-contributory. Mr Hopkins became a member on 1 April 1979.

On 1 November 1986 changes were made to the plan and scheme. The name of the scheme was changed to 'the Norcross Senior Executive Pension Scheme' and the assets representing all the scheme members' rights in the plan were transferred to the scheme; thereafter the contributions which had previously been paid to the plan were paid to the scheme. The effect was that his pension entitlement was now entirely governed by the scheme rules. By further change on 14 October 1988 it was proposed that the scheme should be merged with the plan; and Mr Hopkins signed the appropriate form of authority authorising a transfer of all the assets representing the interests of the members of the scheme back to the plan and to deduct from his salary his contributions to the plan. With effect from 1 December 1988, when the assets were transferred, the scheme was terminated; but the trustee of the plan undertook that the plan would provide precisely the same benefits to former members of the scheme as they were entitled to under the scheme, and subject to the scheme rules. The formal documentation completing this change had not been executed by the time that Mr Hopkins was dismissed. But there is no dispute that Mr Hopkins was, after 1 December 1988, entitled to all the benefits that he had previously been entitled to under the scheme, and subject to the scheme rules.

The scheme rules amongst other things entitled him, on leaving employment for whatever reason before the age of 60, but over the age of 50, to an immediate pension calculated in accordance with a formula, expressed as a fraction of the pension that he would have been entitled to had he retired at the age of 60, and determined by reference to his actual and potential pensionable service, not upon the amount of his contributions. This entitlement was one he could exercise, and did exercise, as of right. There was no relevant discretion in either the defendants or the trustee of the scheme to reduce or delay payment of that pension. The only provision in the scheme rules affecting the absolute entitlement of a person in

Mr Hopkins's position to the pension is in cl 15.3, which makes payment of the
a pension a loan in circumstances where the pensioner will be entitled, for whatever
reason, to claim an amount equivalent to the pension from third parties. It has
no direct relevance to the issue before me, save to indicate that provision can be
made either in the rules of a pension scheme or the terms of employment of an
employee entitled to a pension to modify the entitlement of the pensioner to his
pension.
b The question raised by the issue of law is whether or not moneys received by
way of pension arising out of a termination of employment are to be set off
against the damages to which the former employee is entitled where the
termination of the contract of employment was wrongful. The defendants say
that as a matter of first principle such sums must be deductible. Had Mr Hopkins
c not been dismissed, he would have continued to earn his salary up to 1 October
1991. His only contractual entitlement was to that sum of money. Since he
received precisely the same sum of money by way of pension which would not
have been payable but for the termination, he has lost nothing. The only relevance
that his pension entitlement has to the computation of damages is the possible
shortfall, if that on the figures were to be the case, between the pension to which
d he would have been entitled had he continued to work his full contract period
and the pension that he is in fact receiving as a result of the reduced service. I have
been referred to the judgment of Parke B in *Robinson v Harman* (1848) 1 Exch 850
at 855, [1843–60] All ER Rep 383 at 385, where he sets out clearly the basic rule
for the assessment of damages for breach of contract:

e 'The rule of the common law is, that where a party sustains a loss by reason
of a breach of contract, he is, so far as money can do it, to be placed in the
same situation, with respect to damages, as if the contract had been
performed.'

This principle has been reiterated time and time again both in order to establish
f a claim for damages, and to restrict or constrain an award of damages so as to
ensure that a plaintiff only obtains that to which he is strictly entitled. And, at
first sight, the application of this principle should produce a simple and
straightforward answer to the question, which is that to fail to take into account
the pension would provide Mr Hopkins with substantially greater compensation
in money terms than that to which he was entitled under the contract.
g Surprisingly, there does not appear to have been any reported case in which
this issue has been determined by the courts in any claim for damages for
wrongful dismissal. There is, however, substantial and clear authority on the
question of deductibility of a disability pension from damages for lost earning
capacity in personal injury actions. In *Parry v Cleaver* [1969] 1 All ER 555, [1970]
AC 1 the House of Lords held that a disability pension payable to a policeman on
h being discharged from the police force by reason of disability resulting from the
accident for which the tortfeasor was to blame was to be ignored in assessing his
financial loss by way of lost earning capacity. It was considered to be analogous to
a payment made under an insurance policy. Lord Reid analysed the nature of the
pension as follows ([1969] 1 All ER 555 at 559–560, [1970] AC 1 at 16):

j 'It is generally recognised that pensionable employment is more valuable
to a man than the mere amount of his weekly wage. It is more valuable
because by reason of the terms of his employment money is being regularly
set aside to swell his ultimate pension rights whether on retirement or on
disablement. His earnings are greater than his weekly wage. His employer is
willing to pay £24 per week to obtain his services, and it seems to me that he

ought to be regarded as having earned that sum per week. The products of
the sums paid into the pension fund are in fact delayed remuneration for his *a*
current work. That is why pensions are regarded as earned income. But the
man does not get back in the end the accumulated sums paid into the fund
on his behalf. This is a form of insurance. Like every other kind of insurance
what he gets back depends on how things turn out. He may never be off
duty and may die before retiring age leaving no dependants. Then he gets
nothing back. Or he may by getting a retirement or disablement pension get *b*
much more back than has been paid in on his behalf. I can see no relevant
difference between this and any other form of insurance. So, if insurance
benefits are not deductible in assessing damages and remoteness is out of the
way, why should his pension be deductible . . . a pension is the fruit, through
insurance, of all the money which was set aside in the past in respect of his
past work.' *c*

Lord Pearce stated ([1969] 1 All ER 555 at 577, [1970] AC 1 at 37):

'These [pensions], whether contributory or non-contributory, flow from
the work which a man has done. They are part of what the employer is
prepared to pay for his services. The fact that they flow from past work *d*
equates them to rights which flow from an insurance privately effected by
him. He has simply paid for them by weekly work instead of weekly
premiums.'

Lord Wilberforce stated ([1969] 1 All ER 555 at 582, [1970] AC 1 at 42):

'On the two related grounds, each of which would separately justify the *e*
conclusion, namely (a) that the police pension is payable in any event and is
not dependent on loss of earning capacity and (b) that the pension is to be
regarded as the reward or earning of pre-injury service and therefore not
entering into the computation of lost post-injury wages, I would reach the
conclusion that it should not be deducted against damages recoverable from
a third person for approved loss of earning capacity.' *f*

This case attracted criticism on the basis that it resulted in practice in what
appeared to be double recovery. It was considered that the result was particularly
unfair when the tortfeasor was the employer himself who had made a substantial
proportion of the contributions to the pension which was ultimately received. In
Smoker v London Fire and Civil Defence Authority, Wood v British Coal Corp [1991] 2 *g*
All ER 449, [1991] 2 AC 502 an attempt was made on behalf of employers who
had in each case been the tortfeasor, to argue that *Parry v Cleaver* was wrongly
decided, alternatively that it did not apply to cases where the employer was the
tortfeasor.

Both arguments were decisively rejected by the House of Lords. As far as the *h*
latter argument was concerned, Lord Templeman said ([1991] 2 All ER 449 at
457, [1991] 2 AC 502 at 543–544):

'In the present case counsel for the appellants sought to distinguish the
decision of this House in *Parry v Cleaver* [1969] 1 All ER 555, [1970] AC 1 on
the ground that the appellants are in the triple position of employers,
tortfeasors and insurers. In my opinion this makes no difference to the *j*
principle that the plaintiff has bought his pension, which is, in the words of
Lord Reid, "the fruit, through insurance, of all the money which was set
aside in the past in respect of his past work". The fruit cannot be appropriated
by the tortfeasor.'

Lord Templeman was therefore saying that it was the nature of the payment
a which mattered and not its source, which echoed Lord Reid in *Parry v Cleaver*
[1969] 1 All ER 555 at 559, [1970] AC 1 at 15, where he said:

> 'Surely the distinction between receipts which must be brought into
> account and those which must not must depend not on their source but on
> their intrinsic nature.'

b   Returning to *Smoker's* case, Lord Templeman considered that double recovery
was not involved, unlike those cases involving payments corresponding to wages,
such as those payments which are state payments intended to replace earnings
and sick pay received from employers during the continuation of employment.
Lord Lowry ([1991] 2 All ER 449 at 459–460, [1991] 2 AC 502 at 546) cited a
c judgment of MacDermott LJ in *Guy v Northern Ireland Police Authority* (14 April
1989, unreported) in the context of this argument:

> 'It is easy to stigmatise such a result as unjust, unreasonable or contrary to
> public policy. But in my judgment it is the legal result that flows from *Parry
> v Cleaver*. I also consider it to be a fair result for it arises from the plaintiff's
> own providence in participating albeit compulsorily in an "insurance" scheme
d which aimed to give him protection on all kinds of "rainy days".'

As a matter of policy, therefore, their Lordships declined to overrule *Parry v
Cleaver*.

As can be seen from the passages which I have cited, no distinction is drawn
between a disability pension on the one hand and a retirement pension on the
e other. Indeed, quite the opposite is the case. It is the nature of the payment which
is consistently referred to, and not the event upon which it becomes payable. It
follows that, at least in actions for damages for personal injuries, there is no
relevant distinction between a disability pension and a retirement pension.

Is there then a relevant distinction between damages for lost earnings arising
out of a claim for wrongful dismissal, and damages arising out of a claim for lost
f earning capacity as a result of injury? It was put to me by the defendants on the
basis that there was a relevant distinction to be drawn between damages for
breach of contract on the one hand and damages in tort on the other. It is true
that the scope of damages in contract and tort can be different. For example, in
the present case the only earnings which Mr Hopkins could claim to have lost in
contract are those to which he was contractually entitled; in other words he is not
g entitled to any assessment of the probability, however assessed, of his having, but
for the unlawful decision to dismiss him, worked beyond the age of 60. On the
other hand, had he been injured, his damages could have included an assessment
of the probability of that happening. But once the scope of the damages has been
determined, to what extent is there a difference in determining how to provide
h the appropriate compensation?

I have already cited the principle which is generally applicable in contract cases.
In cases in which there is a claim for damages arising from injury, Earl Jowitt
stated in *British Transport Commission v Gourley* [1955] 3 All ER 796 at 799, [1956]
AC 185 at 197:

j

> 'The broad general principle which should govern the assessment of
> damages in cases such as this is that the tribunal should award the injured
> party such a sum of money as will put him in the same position as he would
> have been in if he had not sustained the injuries (see per Lord Blackburn in
> *Livingstone v. Rawyards Coal Co.* ((1880) 5 App Cas 25 at 39) . . .'

This was described by Lord Pearson in *Parry v Cleaver* [1969] 1 All ER 555 at
585, [1970] AC 1 at 46 as 'the dominant principle'. It is almost precisely the same   *a*
formulation as that of Parke B in *Robinson v Harman* (1848) 1 Exch 850 at 855,
[1843–60] All ER Rep 383 at 385 with the substitution of the phrase 'if he had
not sustained the injuries' for the phrase 'as if the contract had been performed'.
Both formulae are clearly aimed at ensuring that damages provide proper
compensation and no more for the injury be it by way of breach of contract or
tort. It seems to me that there is no room in those circumstances for a different   *b*
approach to the question of deductibility of a pension dependent upon whether
the claim is in contract or in tort. It has to be remembered that in *Smoker's* case,
the claim for damages for personal injuries was one which could have been made
either in tort or in contract. It would not be particularly satisfactory if the answer
to the question of whether or not a pension was to be deducted depended upon
the way in which the claim was formulated.   *c*

There does, however, appear to me to be one respect in which the fact that the
claim can be made in contract is relevant. There is no reason why provision
should not be made either in the terms of employment, or in the rules of any
pension scheme, to provide that pensions should not be payable in the event of a
claim being made against the employer as a result of an event which in itself gives   *d*
rise to the entitlement to the pension. To that extent, the cases where the
defendant is the provider of the pension could be in a different category from
those where the defendant is a third party. The defendants in the present case
seek to say that on their true construction, the service agreement and the scheme
rules produce that result. It is said that, by necessary implication, the retirement
pension is to be treated as part payment towards, or in lieu of, any entitlement of   *e*
Mr Hopkins to his full period of employment or notice. I cannot see how
anything can be implied into the scheme rules to produce that result when
Mr Hopkins's entitlement to the retirement pension is expressed to be absolute.
Nor do I see any basis upon which a term to such effect could be implied into the
service agreement. There is no more justification for implying such a term into
Mr Hopkins's contractual arrangements than there would have been in the case   *f*
of Mr Smoker and Mr Wood.

Finally the defendants sought to say that by asserting his right to the pension
Mr Hopkins was no longer entitled to damages for wrongful dismissal because he
was unable to show that he was ready, willing and able to comply with his
obligations under the contract of employment. But, once the defendants had   *g*
made it plain that they no longer had any use for him, what was he to do? The
logic of the defendants' argument would result in his being deprived of any
entitlement to damages, however small the pension, once he asserted his right to
it. Was he supposed to wait, without money, for the dispute with the defendants
to be resolved? The answer must be No. The situation is no different from any
other where a party to a contract wrongfully prevents the other party from being   *h*
able to carry out his obligations and earn his reward. Provided at the time that
the breach occurs the innocent party is ready, willing and able, but for the other
party's wrongful action, to perform the contract, as Mr Hopkins undoubtedly
was, he must be entitled to his damages, subject to the duty to mitigate his loss.

I am therefore satisfied that as a matter of law the pension payments received
by Mr Hopkins are not deductible from the figure which has been agreed as the   *j*
damages for wrongful dismissal. Despite the fact that this gives the appearance,
as I have already indicated, of double recovery, it follows necessarily from the
character of pension arrangements. It also has the virtue of ensuring that
Mr Hopkins is in the same position as he would have been in had he made his
own separate provision for pension. For there is no dispute that if he had made

independent arrangements, as he was entitled to after the Social Security Act 1986
a came into force, any pension that he received as a result of those arrangements
would not have been deductible. In the absence of any express terms in an
occupational pension provided by employers or in the contract of employment, it
would seem to me to be illogical and unjust for there to be a different result
merely because the pension is provided by the employer.

b *Judgment for plaintiff.*

K Mydeen Esq Barrister.

c # Practice Direction

HOUSE OF LORDS

House of Lords – Leave to appeal – Petition for leave to appeal – Lodging of petition –
d *Supporting documents – Supporting documents to be accepted only in exceptional*
circumstances – House of Lords Practice Directions and Standing Orders applicable to
Civil Appeals (1992), para 3.1.

House of Lords – Leave to appeal – Criminal cause or matter – Petition for leave to
appeal – Lodging of petition – Supporting documents – Supporting documents to be
e *accepted only in exceptional circumstances – House of Lords Practice Directions applicable*
to Criminal Appeals (1992), para 5.1.

The following addition to the *Practice Directions and Standing Orders applicable to*
Civil Appeals (the Blue Book, January 1992) of the House of Lords has been made.

f *Practice Direction 3*
    At the end of para 3.1 insert:

        'Supporting documents, including extracts from *Hansard*, will only be
        accepted in exceptional circumstances.'

g The following addition to the *Practice Directions applicable to Criminal Appeals* (the
Red Book, June 1992) of the House of Lords has been made.

Practice Direction 5
    At the end of para 5.1 insert:

h   'Supporting documents, including extracts from *Hansard*, will only be
        accepted in exceptional circumstances.'

JAMES VALLANCE WHITE
Principal Clerk and
Fourth Clerk at the Table.

1 February 1993

Wynne v Secretary of State for the Home Department

HOUSE OF LORDS

LORD TEMPLEMAN, LORD GOFF OF CHIEVELEY, LORD JAUNCEY OF TULLICHETTLE, LORD MUSTILL AND LORD SLYNN OF HADLEY

28, 29 OCTOBER 1992, 21 JANUARY 1993

Prison – Expenses – Removal from prison for judicial purposes – Production of prisoner in court for purposes of civil litigation – Expenses of producing prisoner in court in interests of justice – Expense of conveying prisoner from prison to court – Prisoner granted leave to apply for judicial review of decisions of prison governor and Secretary of State – Prisoner refused legal aid to bring judicial review proceedings and wishing to attend court to argue case in person – Secretary of State requiring prisoner to make formal application to be taken to court and to pay costs of production in court – Whether prisoner required to meet costs of his production in court – Procedure for arranging for prisoner to be produced in court or to give evidence by other means – Criminal Justice Act 1961, s 29(1).

In 1982 the appellant was sentenced to life imprisonment for manslaughter committed a year after his release on licence after serving a sentence of life imprisonment for murder imposed in 1964. He was detained as a category A prisoner in prison in the north of England. In 1990 he was granted leave to apply for judicial review of decisions made by the prison governor that he was guilty of a disciplinary offence and by the Secretary of State to continue to his category A status. Initially the appellant was granted legal aid in respect of both proceedings but the legal aid certificates were later discharged, with the result that his solicitors ceased to act for him. The appellant wished to proceed in person and was informed by the prison authorities that if he wished to be produced in court for that purpose he would have to complete the relevant form of request to the prison governor to be taken to court and undertake to pay the costs of his production. On receipt of the form the appellant tore it up. He then wrote to the Crown Office claiming that he ought to be produced either free of charge to himself or at a charge related to his ability to pay no more than the cost of his own journey by public transport. Had he completed the form it was likely that his request would have been granted but that he would have been required to pay £419 towards the costs of transporting him under escort to the High Court in London. The appellant sought judicial review of the decision that he should pay the expenses of his production in court and the requirement that he should make formal application to be produced in court. The Divisional Court dismissed his application. The appellant appealed, contending that the Secretary of State's decision to refuse to exercise his powers of removal of a prisoner from one place to another under s 29(1)[a] of the Criminal Justice Act 1961 in order to produce the applicant in court for the judicial review proceedings except on terms of payment was unlawful and unreasonable since it hindered or impeded the appellant's constitutional right of access to the court. The Court of Appeal dismissed his appeal on the ground that, since the appellant was rightly required to make

---

a   Section 29(1), so far as material, provides: 'If the responsible Minister is satisfied, in the case of a person detained in any part of the United Kingdom in a prison . . . that the attendance of that person at any place in that or any other part of the United Kingdom . . . is desirable in the interests of justice . . . the responsible Minister may direct that person to be taken to that place.'

formal application for his production in court and had not done so, it was
a inappropriate for the court to grant him any form of relief. However, the court
was divided on the substantive issue of whether the Secretary of State's decision
not to exercise his discretion under s 29(1) unless the prisoner paid the cost of
transporting him under escort was unlawful and gave leave to the appellant to
appeal to the House of Lords.

b **Held** – A prisoner wishing to appear in court to argue his case in person in civil
litigation was required to make formal application to the governor of the prison
for a direction to be made under s 29 of the 1961 Act for his production in court.
Since the appellant had not made such an application, there was no relevant
decision of the Secretary of State which could be the subject of judicial review.
The appeal would therefore be dismissed (see p 576 *d e*, p 577 *j* to p 578 *b* and
c p 582 *e* to *g*, post).

Per curiam. Where there is a conflict between the interest of a prisoner involved
in civil proceedings in appearing in court and the public interest that he should
be kept secure during his term of imprisonment, either by remaining in prison
or, where appropriate, by travelling to court in secure conditions, that conflict
should where possible be resolved by practical means, with a view to ensuring
d that both interests are protected. In the event of problems arising, e g if the Home
Office are unable to assess the merit's of the prisoner's case or if his case is against
the Home Office and there would be the possible appearance of bias if the Home
Office were to assess the merits of the application or if the prisoner is regarded as
such a high security risk that the Home Office is reluctant to allow him out of
e prison at all, the matter should if possible be drawn to the judge's attention to
seek his guidance on the question whether the attendance of the prisoner is
required or whether it is possible to devise some practical solution for hearing the
prisoner's evidence or receiving his submissions orally or in writing without his
attendance at court (see p 576 *d e*, p 580 *g*, p 581 *d* to *h* and p 582 *e* to *g*, post).

Decision of the Court of Appeal sub nom *R v Secretary of State for the Home Dept,*
f *ex p Wynne* [1992] 2 All ER 301 affirmed.

Notes
For facilities in connection with litigation and production and presence in court,
see 37 *Halsbury's Laws* (4th edn) paras 1179–1180, and for cases on the subject, see
37(3) Digest (Reissue) 409–410, 5363–5368.
g   For the Criminal Justice Act 1961, s 29, see 34 *Halsbury's Statutes* (4th edn) 677.

Cases referred to in opinions
Becker v Home Office [1972] 2 All ER 676, [1972] 2 QB 407, [1972] 2 WLR 1193,
CA.
Golder v UK (1975) 1 EHRR 524, E Ct HR.
h *R v Norwich Magistrates' Court, ex p Roberts* (14 June 1991, unreported), DC.
Raymond v Honey [1982] 1 All ER 756, [1983] 1 AC 1, [1982] 2 WLR 465, HL.
Walsh v Governor of Brixton Prison [1984] 2 All ER 609, [1985] AC 154, [1984] 3
WLR 205, HL.

Appeal
j Edward Thomas Wynne appealed with the leave of the Court of Appeal from the
decision of that court (Lord Donaldson MR, Staughton and McCowan LJJ) (sub
nom *R v Secretary of State for the Home Dept, ex p Wynne* [1992] 2 All ER 301,
[1992] 1 QB 406) on 19 December 1991 dismissing his appeal from the order of
the Divisional Court of the Queen's Bench Division (Mann, Nolan LJJ and Judge J)
dated 23 July 1991 dismissing his application for judicial review by way of (1) a

declaration that the decision of the Secretary of State for the Home Department
referred to in the letter from the Treasury Solicitor to the Crown Office dated 12   *a*
June 1991 that the appellant, a prisoner detained at HM Prison Frankland, was
required, in accordance with Home Office policy, to meet the costs of his
production in court, for the purpose of pursuing his applications for judicial
review of a finding of guilt on a disciplinary charge and the allocation to him of
category A status, and to make formal application to be produced in court, was
unlawful and unreasonable, (2) certiorari quashing the decision and (3) mandamus   *b*
requiring the Secretary of State to produce the appellant at court as and when
required for the hearing of the applications for judicial review. The facts are set
out in the opinion of Lord Goff.

James Munby QC (instructed by the *Official Solicitor*) for the appellant.
Michael Beloff QC, Nigel Pleming QC and *Clive Lewis* (instructed by the *Treasury*   *c*
    Solicitor) for the Secretary of State.

Their Lordships took time for consideration.

21 January 1993. The following opinions were delivered.   *d*

LORD TEMPLEMAN. My Lords, I have had advantage of reading in draft the
speech of my noble and learned friend Lord Goff of Chieveley. I agree with it
and, for the reasons given by my noble and learned friend, I would dismiss the
appeal.
     e

LORD GOFF OF CHIEVELEY. My Lords, the appellant, Edward Thomas
Wynne, is a prisoner in Frankland Prison, Durham, where he is a category A
inmate. He is currently serving his second life sentence. He was sentenced to life
imprisonment for murder in 1964, and was released in 1980. In 1982 he was
sentenced to life imprisonment for manslaughter, the offence having been   *f*
committed a little over a year after his release from prison in 1980.
    The appellant has brought two sets of proceedings for judicial review. In the
first, dated 25 October 1989, he has complained of a decision by the deputy
governor of Gartree Prison (where the appellant was then imprisoned) whereby
he found that the appellant was guilty of recklessly endangering another person,
and ordered that a caution be entered on his prison record. In the second, dated   *g*
19 February 1990, he has complained that the Secretary of State decided on 22
January 1990 to allocate category A status to him, and failed or refused to give
reasons for his decision. In March 1990 Kennedy J granted leave to apply for
judicial review in respect of both complaints. The appellant was granted legal aid
in respect of these proceedings, but in October 1990 the legal aid certificates were
discharged, and as a consequence his solicitors ceased to act for him.   *h*
    In the result the appellant has found himself in the position where he has
launched proceedings for judicial review for which he has been granted leave to
apply, but he has no lawyers acting for him who can appear on his behalf.
Furthermore, he himself, being in prison, cannot appear in person unless he is
produced in court for that purpose. The prison authorities at Frankland Prison
made it clear to him that, if he wished to be produced in court to represent   *j*
himself on the date fixed for the hearing of his applications (20 June 1991), he
would have to complete the relevant request/complaint form and undertake to
pay the costs of his production. On receipt of a letter informing him of the
position, the appellant tore it up, and made no request. He then wrote to the
Crown Office, informing the office of his attitude, which appears to have been

that he must be produced either free of charge to himself or at a charge related to
a an ability to pay only the cost of his own journey by public transport.

It appears that there has been an increase in the number of applications for
judicial review by persons serving prison sentences. Where leave is given to apply,
or an application for leave is renewed after an initial refusal, there is then a
hearing; and a problem arises in those cases where the applicant, like the present
appellant, is not represented by counsel. The court has no power to compel his
b attendance, which under the relevant statutory provision (s 29(1) of the Criminal
Justice Act 1961) is a matter for the discretion of the Home Secretary. The manner
in which this power should be exercised has been the subject of a booklet, issued
by the Home Office, called the *Productions Manual*. Under the guidelines set out
in this booklet, which deal with a wide range of circumstances, it is stated that it
c is generally not the prison service's function to bear the costs arising from the
production of an inmate to a court for the purpose of civil proceedings. It follows
that in such cases, if a prisoner is unable or unwilling to pay the costs of his
production, he will not be produced to conduct his proceedings in person.

The problem which arises in such circumstances surfaced recently in *R v
Norwich Magistrates' Court, ex p Roberts* (14 June 1991, unreported). On that
d occasion the Divisional Court, having heard that the present appellant's applications
for judicial review were due to be heard the following week, proposed that his
applications should be treated as a test case; this was agreed to by counsel
representing the Home Office. The Official Solicitor was invited to intervene as
amicus curiae. He accepted the invitation, but later agreed to act on behalf of the
appellant; and an application was made on 12 July 1991 for judicial review of the
e Home Secretary's decision that the appellant should be expected in accordance
with Home Office policy to meet the costs of his production in court for the
purpose of pursuing his two applications for judicial review, and that the appellant
was required to make formal application to be produced in court. The relief
sought was a declaration that the decision was unlawful, an order of certiorari to
f quash the decision, and an order of mandamus requiring the Secretary of State to
produce the appellant at the hearing of his applications for judicial review.

A Divisional Court (Mann, Nolan LJJ and Judge J) held that the court had no
power to order the production of a prisoner so that he might argue his own case,
and that a prisoner can appear to argue his own case only if the Secretary of State
exercises his power under s 29(1) of the 1961 Act to make a production order.
g The court further held, having regard in particular to the decision of the Court of
Appeal in *Becker v Home Office* [1972] 2 All ER 676, [1972] 2 QB 407 (by which it
was bound), that a requirement to pay travel costs, escort costs, or both, as a
condition of a production order may be a lawful requirement, and the Secretary
of State was entitled to have a practice whereby he normally requires such
payment to be made. Accordingly, the court dismissed the application. The
h appellant then appealed to the Court of Appeal, which dismissed the appeal. The
appellant now appeals to your Lordships' House by leave of the Court of Appeal.

I turn first to the decision of the Court of Appeal. The ground upon which the
appeal was dismissed was very simple. It was expressed by Lord Donaldson MR
as follows ([1992] 2 All ER 301 at 312, [1992] 1 QB 406 at 424):

j   'I would dismiss this appeal because in my judgment [the appellant] was
       rightly required to make formal application for his production in court, he
       did not do so and in those circumstances it is inappropriate to grant any form
       of relief in respect of a hypothetical decision which would only have been
       reached, if at all, had [the appellant] made such an application.'

This is plainly right. There was, in the circumstances, no relevant decision of

the Home Secretary, which was the assumed basis of the appellant's application
for judicial review. That there was no such decision was also recognised by *a*
Staughton and McCowan LJJ (see [1992] 2 All ER 301 at 317, 319, [1992] 1 QB
406 at 429, 432). Even so, all members of the Court of Appeal considered in their
judgments the substantive argument on the appeal, and on this there was a
division of opinion between Staughton and McCowan LJJ on the one hand and
Lord Donaldson MR on the other. As a result of this division of opinion, leave
was given to the appellant to appeal to your Lordships' House. *b*

I feel driven to say that, in those circumstances, the Court of Appeal should not
have given leave to appeal. It was inevitable from the outset that this House would
have to dismiss the appeal, for there was no basis upon which the Court of
Appeal's decision could be disturbed. In truth, the Court of Appeal were giving
leave to appeal because of a difference of opinion among the members of the
court expressed in what were in law no more than prolonged obiter dicta. At the *c*
outset of the argument before the Appellate Committee, it was drawn to the
attention of counsel for the appellant, Mr Munby QC, that the substantive
argument on the appeal raised what was in truth a hypothetical question; and
this was not disputed. Nevertheless, the arguments having been prepared at
considerable public expense, in litigation which was intended as a test case, *d*
counsel were allowed to develop their arguments before the Appellate Committee.
Now however this House has to decide how to dispose of the matter.

It is well established that this House does not decide hypothetical questions. If
the House were to do so, any conclusion, and the accompanying reasons, could in
their turn constitute no more than obiter dicta, expressed without the assistance
of a concrete factual situation, and would not constitute a binding precedent for *e*
the future. Furthermore, if in the present case the appellant had made a formal
application for production which had been pursued to the stage of decision, it is
not at all clear that other factors might not then have emerged. In particular, if it
had then transpired that (as may be the case) the appellant lacked the means to
pay the expenses required of him, and if an indication had then been made by the
court that the appellant was required to attend the hearing of his applications to *f*
enable them to proceed, it is possible that further steps might have been taken
with a view to obtaining legal aid for the appellant, or even that, by analogy to
para 57 of the *Production Manual*, the requirement to recover full production costs
might have been waived by the Home Secretary.

In the circumstances, your Lordships' House is placed in a position of *g*
considerable embarrassment. I am very conscious that the present case was
selected as a test case to resolve the legal and practical problems which arise when
a prisoner wishes to appear in court as a litigant in person. It has unfortunately
proved to be unsuitable as a test case to resolve the legal problems; and your
Lordships' House is not equipped to resolve the practical problems. Even so, I am
minded to draw attention to certain practical considerations which may be of *h*
assistance in future to the authorities concerned. If this approach finds favour
with the remainder of your Lordships, and there is agreement about the
observations so made, then at least it may be felt that the time and expense
devoted to this appeal have not been entirely wasted.

Before I proceed to the practical considerations to which I wish to draw
attention, I propose first to set out the approach at present adopted by the Home *j*
Office in cases of this kind, as evidenced in an affidavit sworn in the present case
by Miss Norma Williams, a senior executive officer and deputy head of that
section of the prison service which is responsible for category A prisoners. In her
affidavit she described how, if the appellant had completed the request/complaint
form, his request for production would have been dealt with. She stated:

a 'Had [the appellant] completed the form however, this would have been referred to me whereupon I would have considered it on its merits, balancing such factors as the security implications of moving a category A prisoner with whether or not the interests of justice did or did not require him to be produced. I should say that even if an inmate does have the funds to meet the costs of his production, the application might nevertheless be refused if, prima facie, the interests of justice would not be served or the security risks
b involved would be too great.'

I pause to comment that I infer from this paragraph that an assessment may be made of the prospects of success of the applicant in proceedings commenced by him and that, if his application is judged to be without merit, it may be concluded that the interests of justice will not be served by the applicant's production. In the
c next paragraph Miss Williams turned to the question of expenses. She stated:

'It is the usual practice, in cases where the production of an inmate for civil proceedings is authorised, to require the payment of production costs, in order that the burden does not fall solely on the taxpayer. In [the appellant's] case, the costs of producing him in the High Court for the hearing of his two
d applications have been calculated at £419. Although he is a Category A prisoner and would therefore travel in a secure prison vehicle, with an escort of one Principal or Senior Officer and two other officers and would be lodged overnight in a London prison, he would be charged the same costs as a Category B prisoner travelling by taxi.'

e In the following paragraph, she explained that the expenses so charged would consist, apart from the 'taxi fare', of subsistence for the officers (but not their wages) over the relevant period. Paragraphs 7 and 8 read as follows:

'7. Had [the appellant] applied to be produced and agreed to meet his production costs, it is probable that I would have authorised his production,
f provided, taking account of his history of violent behaviour, I was satisfied regarding the security arrangements.

8. There is provision for production costs to be waived but it is unlikely that I would have agreed to waive them in [the appellant's] case, particularly as his legal aid had been withdrawn. This indicates to me that the legal aid authorities did not consider that there was sufficient merit in his case to
g warrant legal representation for [the appellant] at public expense or alternatively, that [the appellant] had sufficient funds to instruct a Solicitor and/or Counsel.'

Next, I propose briefly to refer to the approach adopted in the courts below. The exercise of the power under s 29 had previously been considered by the Court
h of Appeal in *Becker v Home Office* [1972] 2 All ER 676, [1972] 2 QB 407. In that case the only question at issue was whether the Secretary of State had power to require, as a condition of the exercise of his discretion to produce a prisoner, that the costs of production should be borne by the prisoner. It was held by the Court of Appeal that the Secretary of State had such a power. However, in the present case it has been submitted by Mr Munby, on behalf of the appellant, that the
j Secretary of State must exercise his discretion in such a manner as to ensure (1) that he does not impede the prisoner's constitutional right of access to the court in person, and further so as to ensure (2) that there is no breach of this country's treaty obligations under art 6 of the European Convention for the Protection of Human Rights and Fundamental Freedoms (Rome, 4 November 1950; TS 71 (1953); Cmd 8969) or (3) that there is no breach of chapter 40 of Magna Carta

(1215). In support of the first of these submissions, Mr Munby invoked in particular the decision of this House in *Raymond v Honey* [1981] 1 All ER 756, *a* [1983] 1 AC 1, and in support of the second he relied in particular on the decision of the European Court of Human Rights in *Golder v UK* (1975) 1 EHRR 524. These submissions were rejected both by the Divisional Court and by the majority of the Court of Appeal. The Divisional Court distinguished *Raymond v Honey* as being concerned only with a prisoner's right of access to the courts by a written communication, referring to the statement by Lord Fraser of Tullybelton in *b* *Walsh v Governor of Brixton Prison* [1984] 2 All ER 609 at 612, [1985] AC 154 at 163 that the argument that a prisoner has a right to be produced in court by the governor raised quite different issues from those raised in *Raymond v Honey*. They further considered that the Secretary of State was under no obligation to exercise his discretion so as to conform with art 6; and they did not attach any separate *c* importance to Magna Carta. As I have stated earlier, their broad conclusion was that a prisoner can only appear to argue his own case if the Secretary of State exercises his power to make a production order; and that (applying *Becker v Home Office*) a requirement to pay travel costs, escort costs, or both, as a condition of such an order may be a lawful requirement. The majority of the Court of Appeal reached a similar conclusion. Lord Donaldson MR, however, adopted a rather *d* different position. In particular, he considered that a prisoner has a 'basic human right' to attend court on an occasion upon which the court is adjudicating upon his rights; and he further considered that it was wrong in principle that a prisoner's ability to attend court should depend upon his ability to pay the expenses of his production in court. In addition, he considered that major problems arose if the Home Office (or indeed other government departments or *e* prison staff) were party to the proceedings, in that the decision-taker, in forming an opinion of whether the prisoner's attendance in court was necessary, might at least appear to be acting as a judge in his own cause in assessing the prisoner's prospects of success in the relevant litigation—a point upon which Staughton LJ, too, expressed concern, although he hoped that some practical means could be *f* evolved for escaping from that difficulty.

For reasons which I have already expressed, questions such as these must be regarded as hypothetical for the purposes of this appeal, and cannot properly be decided by your Lordships' House on this occasion. Even so, I must confess that I have been struck by the fact that such problems may be susceptible of practical solution, as to which I wish to make the following observations. *g*

There is a sense in which the problems which have been discussed in the present case reveal a possible conflict between two interests. The first is the interest of prisoners who, if involved in litigation while they are in prison, may require to appear in court. In the present case the relevant litigation is an application by the prisoner for judicial review; and I will take that case as my example. In many such cases, the problem of appearance in court may be solved *h* by a grant of legal aid to finance the prisoner's legal representation; for, on the hearing of an application for judicial review, the evidence is on affidavit, and the hearing will take the form of rival submissions by counsel. Only if the prisoner has no means and legal aid is refused is a problem likely to arise. The present case is surely exceptional in that, although leave was granted to the appellant to apply for judicial review, nevertheless his legal aid certificates have been discharged. It *j* is not of course known to your Lordships why this should have occurred; it may have been for reasons which have no connection with the merits of the appellant's case. Nor is it known whether consideration was given to an appeal by the appellant against the discharge of his certificates. It is however this combination of circumstances which has created a problem in the present case.

As against the interest of the prisoner in appearing in court, there is however a
a countervailing public interest. This is the public interest that the prisoner should
be kept secure during his term of imprisonment, either by his remaining in
prison, or (where appropriate) by his travelling to court in secure conditions, for
example, in a secure vehicle, accompanied by an adequate escort. The latter is,
however, expensive, and if the production of prisoners in court for the conduct of
civil litigation should become a frequent occurrence, not only would a considerable
b expense fall upon the prison service, but it would suffer a loss of manpower at a
time when the service is already under severe pressure. Furthermore, if such a
facility was readily available to prisoners, free of charge, it could well become the
subject of abuse by inmates who might be tempted to exploit the system. In these
circumstances, it is scarcely surprising to find that the Home Office has established
c guidelines under which prisoners will not normally be produced in court for the
purpose of civil proceedings unless they pay the expenses of their production,
though limited to the 'taxi' fare and subsistence of the prison escort. It is not to be
forgotten that, in ordinary life, litigants have to convey themselves to court at
their own expense; and in certain circumstances (for example, where the litigant
is suffering from a severe disability) this could entail substantial expense.

d   Faced with this conflict of interests, it is I think desirable that where it occurs it
should, where possible, be resolved by practical means, with a view to ensuring
that both interests are protected. I feel fortified in this view by the fact that in
Golder v UK (1975) 1 EHRR 524 the European Court of Human Rights expressed
the opinion not only that the right of access to the courts is not absolute but also
that it is not the function of the court to elaborate a general theory of limitations
e to the right admissible in the case of convicted prisoners. This approach appears
to provide support for the view that a search for practical solutions may be
desirable.

If I take the present case as my example, it seems to me that the Home Office is
faced with two particular problems. The first relates to the assessment of the
f merits of the appellant's application where, on the one hand, the judge has given
him leave to apply for judicial review, but on the other hand his legal aid
certificates have subsequently been discharged; the second relates to the
embarrassment, and the possible appearance of bias, if the Home Office makes
such an assessment in a case where it is itself the other party to the proceedings.
Faced with a situation of this kind, the natural reaction must be that the matter
g should if possible be brought before the court for guidance, if necessary on a
mention. Such guidance cannot of course be binding on the Home Secretary, in
whom alone the relevant discretion is vested under the statute; but as para 57 of
the *Productions Manual* shows, a practice may be established under which such
guidance will be followed. Furthermore, if circumstances arise in which legal aid
is not available to the prisoner, and (as may be the position in the present case) he
h is unable to meet the expenses, so that he can neither appear nor be represented
in court, then once again the matter could be drawn to the attention of the judge,
to seek his guidance on the question whether the attendance of a prisoner is
required. Paragraph 57 of the *Productions Manual*, to which I have already referred,
is concerned with such circumstances and indicates that, in exceptional
circumstances, the requirement that the costs of production be met by the
j prisoner may be waived. The example there given is of a case where strong
compassionate grounds exist, and the court has indicated that the prisoner (who
has not been granted legal aid and lacks the mean to pay the full production costs)
is required to attend the hearing; in such circumstances it is regarded as
appropriate to waive, in whole or in part, payment of the production costs. It is
possible, moreover, that other problems could arise, for example where the

prisoner is regarded as such a high security risk that the Home Office is reluctant
to allow him out of prison at all. Once again, a mention of the matter in court
could lead to an authoritative and independent assessment of the necessity for his
production, and if necessary the devising of some practical solution for hearing
his evidence or receiving his submissions, orally or in writing.

I recognise that none of these suggestions can be regarded as having any binding
effect; further, their implementation may involve practical problems of which I
am unaware. But, feeling as I do that the problems raised on the present appeal
may be of relatively rare occurrence and, on the occasions where they do arise,
may be capable of a practical solution by seeking the guidance of the court, I was
concerned to draw these possibilities to the attention of those charged with
responsibility in matters of this kind, especially as among the documents before
your Lordships was a letter from the assistant Treasury Solicitor to the chief clerk
of the Crown Office, in which he stated that he was instructed that the Home
Office was most anxious to co-operate with the court in finding a solution to the
problem. If these suggestions bear fruit, it is possible that problems of this kind
may be susceptible of solution; but even if they are not, any case of this kind
which comes forward for a decision on the merits in the future will more likely
be set against a factual situation in which every attempt to deal with the particular
matter on a practical basis will have been explored.

LORD JAUNCEY OF TULLICHETTLE. My Lords, I have had the
advantage of reading in draft the speech of my noble and learned friend Lord
Goff of Chieveley. I agree with it and, for the reasons given by my noble and
learned friend, I too would dismiss the appeal.

LORD MUSTILL. My Lords, I have had the advantage of reading in draft the
speech prepared by my noble and learned friend Lord Goff of Chieveley. I agree
with it and for the reasons given by my noble and learned friend, I too would
dismiss the appeal.

LORD SLYNN OF HADLEY. My Lords, I have had the advantage of reading
in draft the speech of my noble and learned friend Lord Goff of Chieveley. I agree
that, for the reasons he gives, the appeal should be dismissed.

I also support the suggestions he makes for dealing with these cases in the
future. Although I do not consider, whether by analogy to the provisions of the
European Convention for the Protection of Human Rights and Fundamental
Freedoms (Rome, 4 November 1950; TS 71 (1953); Cmd 8969) or otherwise, that
there is any absolute right for a litigant to be present at any hearing of his case (as
opposed to a right of access to the court to have a claim ventilated), it seems likely
that, if a judge to whom the prisoner's application to be present is mentioned
considers that it is desirable for a prisoner to be brought to a hearing at public
expense, the Secretary of State would give that expression of opinion full weight.
That opinion is, of course, subject always to overriding considerations of security.

Equally if the judge indicates that in his view the point is a substantial one
which requires the presence of counsel (particularly if the applicant cannot afford
to pay to be present or if a serious question of law is raised) then no doubt the
legal aid committee would take his opinion into account in deciding whether to
give or to continue legal aid.

Appeal dismissed.

Mary Rose Plummer   Barrister.

R v Roberts

a

COURT OF APPEAL, CRIMINAL DIVISION
LORD TAYLOR OF GOSFORTH CJ, HUTCHISON AND HOLLAND JJ
6, 19 OCTOBER 1992

b *Criminal law – Murder – Concerted action – Joint unlawful enterprise – Remoteness of risk of co-accused killing victim or causing serious bodily injury – Victim dying after attack by two defendants – Each alleging other struck fatal blow – Whether jury should have been directed as to remoteness of risk of co-accused killing or causing serious bodily injury.*

c The appellant and another man, G, went to the house of a 69-year-old recluse with the intention of robbing him. While they were at the house there was a struggle in the course of which the victim was killed by blows to the face with a blunt instrument, which could have been an axe or a spade, and a major injury to the back of the head, which was more likely to have been caused by an axe than a spade. The appellant and G were arrested and charged with murder and robbery.
d When interviewed by the police each blamed the other. The appellant's account was that there had been a struggle between the victim and G during which the appellant had pulled the victim off G and had seen G hit the victim repeatedly with an axe. The appellant denied that he had ever struck the victim but admitted that he had taken the victim's wallet, which had fallen to the floor in the course
e of the struggle with G. G's account was that the appellant went into the victim's house first, that the victim made a grab for G, who fell to the ground, that, as he was trying to fend the victim off, he saw the appellant hit the victim on the back of the head with a shovel and then on the front of the head knocking him to the ground and that by the time he got up the appellant had gone. The judge directed the jury that, although the prosecution case was that the two accused had been
f present together in an agreed enterprise to rob the victim, agreeing expressly or tacitly that he should be killed or that really serious bodily injury should be inflicted upon him intentionally if it became necessary to do so, all that the prosecution had to prove against the accused who did not inflict the blows was that the other accused had inflicted blows with the intention of killing or causing the victim really serious bodily injury and that the former had lent himself to the
g joint criminal enterprise of stealing from the victim and that he foresaw or realised that the latter might kill the victim or intentionally inflict really serious bodily injury on him in the course of the offence. The appellant was convicted of murder and robbery. He appealed against his conviction for murder on the ground that the judge had failed to direct the jury that it was for them to decide
h whether the risk of G killing the victim or causing him serious bodily injury was so remote as not to make the appellant guilty of murder.

Held – The principle that a person involved in a joint unlawful enterprise could be guilty of murder if he realised (without agreeing to such conduct being used) that the other party involved might kill or intentionally inflict serious injury but
j nevertheless continued to participate with the other party in the venture and the other party, with the requisite intent, killed in the course of the venture, was of general application. It applied whether weapons were carried or not and whether the object of the enterprise was to cause physical injury or to commit some other unlawful act such as burglary or robbery. Only rarely would it be necessary to direct the jury that they must distinguish between a fleeting but rejected

consideration of a risk and a continuing realisation of a real risk since to realise
something might happen was to contemplate it as a real and not fanciful *a*
possibility. A person who fleetingly thought of the risk of his co-accused using
violence with murderous intent in the course of a joint enterprise only to dismiss
it from his mind had banished the risk from his mind and could not be said to
have foreseen or realised that his co-accused might commit murder. Since the
trial judge had given the clearest possible directions of law to the jury on the real
issue, which was not whether the appellant realised force might be used but *b*
whether he realised only that some physical harm might be done or that really
serious injury might be inflicted, the appeal would be dismissed (see p 590 *c* to *h*
and p 591 *a*, post).

Dictum of Lord Lane CJ in *R v Hyde* [1990] 3 All ER 892 at 895–896 applied.

Chan Wing-siu v R [1984] 3 All ER 877 considered.   *c*

Notes
For criminal liability in joint enterprise, see 11(1) *Halsbury's Laws* (4th edn reissue)
paras 43–50, 435, and for cases on the subject, see 14(1) *Digest* (2nd reissue) 108–
114, 857–898.
                                                                        d

Cases referred to in judgment
Chan Wing-siu v R [1984] 3 All ER 877, [1985] AC 168, [1984] 3 WLR 677, PC.
Hui Chi-ming v R [1991] 3 All ER 897, [1992] 1 AC 34, [1991] 3 WLR 495, PC.
R v Hyde [1990] 3 All ER 892, [1991] 1 QB 134, [1990] 3 WLR 1115, CA.
R v Slack [1989] 3 All ER 90, [1989] QB 775, [1989] 3 WLR 513, CA.   *e*
R v Wakely [1990] Crim LR 119, CA.

Appeal
Kelvin James Roberts appealed with the leave of the single judge against his
conviction on 16 March 1991 in the Crown Court at Cardiff before Waterhouse J *f*
and a jury of murder, by a majority of 11 to 1, for which he was sentenced to life
imprisonment. He had on 27 February 1991 on the same indictment and before
the same court pleaded guilty to robbery, for which on 16 March 1991 he was
sentenced to eight years' imprisonment concurrent with the life sentence. A
co-accused, Anthony Gray, was convicted unanimously of the same offences and
was sentenced to life imprisonment and 12 years' imprisonment concurrent. The *g*
grounds of appeal were (1) that the judge should have directed the jury that for
the appellant to have been guilty of murder he must have (a) at least tacitly agreed
that serious harm should be done to the victim, (b) lent himself to the infliction
of such harm, (c) recognised that there was a real and substantial risk that the co-
defendant, Gray, would kill or seriously injure the victim and (d) participated in
the joint enterprise with such foresight and (2) when the jury asked for further *h*
directions the judge was wrong to direct them only in the terms of *R v Hyde*
[1990] 3 All ER 892, [1991] 1 QB 134 and failed (a) to answer the jury's question,
(b) having regard to the verdicts already returned on the co-defendant, Gray, to
direct the jury that they had to be satisfied that the appellant was still participating
in the joint enterprise to rob at the time that the fatal blows were struck and (c) to
direct the jury in the terms of ground (1) above. The facts are set out in the *j*
judgment of the court.

Diana Cotton QC (who did not appear below) (assigned by the *Registrar of Criminal
Appeals*) for the appellant.

Gerard Elias QC and *David Aubrey* (instructed by the *Crown Prosecution Service,*
a   Cardiff) for the Crown.

Cur adv vult

19 October 1992. The following judgment of the court was delivered.

b   **LORD TAYLOR OF GOSFORTH CJ.** On 27 February 1991 in the Crown
Court at Cardiff the appellant pleaded guilty to robbery. On 16 March 1991 at
the same court he was convicted of murder by a majority of eleven to one. He
was sentenced to life imprisonment and eight years' imprisonment concurrent
for the robbery.

c   He had been jointly charged with a co-accused, Anthony Gray. Gray was
convicted unanimously by the jury at the same trial of the same offences and was
sentenced to life imprisonment for murder and 12 years' imprisonment for
robbery.

The appellant now appeals against his conviction for murder with leave of the
single judge.

d   On 4 August 1990 John Davies, a 69-year-old recluse, was robbed and beaten to
death at his home near Merthyr Tydfil. The case for the Crown was that the
appellant and Gray were jointly responsible for his murder. For their part the
appellant and Gray blamed one another.

John Davies lived mainly on his pension, but he had some £300 left from a
Criminal Injuries Compensation Board award, which he kept in a building
e   society. As a result of the attack upon him which gave rise to that award, he kept
an axe by his chair for self-protection.

The appellant was 5 ft 2 ins, weighed only 8 stone 5 lb and was 39 at the time
of the killing. The co-accused, Gray, was 49 and a much bigger man. The accused
knew one another, but were not friends. Gray knew the victim slightly, but the
appellant did not.

f   Gray spent the day of the murder drinking. The appellant, who lived in
Swansea, had left his wife the day before the killing and had hitchhiked to
Merthyr Tydfil. He had lost all his money in a betting shop and bumped into
Gray by chance in the street on 4 August. They went for a drink at a Rugby club
and from there set off for the victim's home. Each suggested in evidence that it
g   was the other's idea. The appellant admitted he knew they were going to rob an
old man.

Gray's account was that the appellant went into the victim's house first to
collect some money which the victim gave to him. Gray thought this was
consensual but, as the two men were walking out, the victim made a grab for
Gray, who fell to the ground. As he was trying to fend the victim off, he claimed
h   to have seen the appellant hit the victim on the back of the head with a shovel.
The appellant then, according to Gray, struck the victim again with the shovel on
the front of the head knocking him to the ground. By the time Gray got up the
appellant had gone.

The police interviewed the appellant three times and he gave evidence at the
trial. By contrast to Gray's account, in his first interview the appellant initially
j   said that he had followed Gray into the house. Gray had demanded money in a
menacing way. The victim had picked up an axe, there was a struggle between
Gray and the victim and the appellant ran away. Eventually he admitted that he
had returned and there had been a struggle between the victim and Gray in the
yard during which he, the appellant, had pulled the victim off Gray and had seen

Gray hit the victim repeatedly with an axe. The appellant denied that he had ever struck the victim.   *a*

In his second interview the appellant admitted taking the victim's wallet, which had fallen to the floor in the course of the struggle with Gray. This formed the basis of the appellant's plea of guilty to robbery. He also admitted that he was prepared to contemplate the use of violence when he and Gray went to the house, although not to the extent of killing the victim. In both the second and third interviews the appellant reiterated that only Gray had used violence and his own   *b* role had been confined to pulling the victim off Gray.

In evidence the appellant gave substantially the same account, repeating that only Gray had struck the victim. He admitted that he had contemplated there might be some violence when they went to the victim's house. He gave inconsistent answers as to the degree of violence he foresaw, but twice said that   *c* he foresaw the risk of really serious injury.

Following the killing Gray went to a public house. He gave himself up to the police on 7 August and blamed the appellant for the killing. Meanwhile the appellant had gone to a different public house on leaving the victim. Witnesses described him as looking shaky and upset. He was arrested in a lodging house on 8 August and blamed Gray for the murder.   *d*

The deceased's body was discovered in the yard of his cottage the day after the murder. The medical evidence was that death had been caused by blows to the face with a blunt instrument. There was also a major injury to the back of the head and a number of defence injuries to the hands and arms. The injuries to the face could have been inflicted by an axe or a spade, but not a fist. The evidence was neutral as to whether the attack involved more than one assailant. The injury   *e* to the back of the head was more likely to have been caused by an axe than a spade. There was no trace of blood-staining on the appellant's clothes.

The learned judge in summing up the case gave the jury a number of directions of law. He then summarised the case for each defendant and went on to review the evidence in detail. Finally, he summarised the arguments for the Crown and   *f* for the defence.

The jury returned verdicts of guilty against the co-accused, Gray, before reaching a verdict on the charge of murder in respect of the appellant. They sought the learned judge's further directions on the distinction between murder and manslaughter before retiring again and thereafter convicted the appellant.

The grounds of appeal are based solely on criticisms of the learned judge's   *g* directions to the jury on joint enterprise. He gave directions on this matter twice—the first time in the course of his general directions on law, the second in response to the question from the jury after they had convicted Gray.

The essential part of the first passage was as follows:

'[The prosecution case] is that these two men were both present at the time   *h* when the fatal blows were inflicted taking part in an agreed robbery, that it was agreed expressly or at least tacitly understood between them that John Davies should be killed, for example to avoid identification of either of them or that at least really serious bodily injury should be inflicted upon the deceased if it became necessary to do so in the course of achieving the purpose of robbing him and avoiding the risk of being caught for that offence. So   *j* that is the nature of the case, members of the jury, that these two men were there present together in an agreed enterprise to rob John Davies, involving the use of force to him and it being expressly or tacitly agreed between them that he should be killed or that really serious bodily injury should be inflicted upon him intentionally if it became necessary to do so in the course of achieving the purpose of robbing and avoiding the risk of being caught for that offence . . . But I must further direct you that the prosecution do not in fact have to go as far as that in relation to proof against the man who did not inflict the blows, whom I will call 'man B'. Assuming that man A inflicted the blows with the intention of killing or causing John Davies really serious bodily injury, if you are sure that that was done by A, all that the prosecution has to prove against the other man so that he will be guilty of murder is that he lent himself to the joint criminal enterprise of stealing from John Davies and that he foresaw or realised that the other man A might kill him or inflict intentional really serious bodily injury on John Davies in the course of carrying out that offence. In other words, that the man who did not, he must have realised that the man who did in fact do the killing might intentionally kill or intentionally inflict really serious bodily injury on John Davies. That means of course that he continued in the joint venture of theft, assisting and encouraging A in the carrying out of the enterprise, whilst realising that it might involve murder. If you are sure, members of the jury, that that was the position with the person who did not inflict the blows, then that other person is guilty of murder as well as the person who actually inflicted the blows.'

The learned judge then went on to direct the jury that, by contrast, if they found that B had—

'lent himself to the criminal enterprise without agreeing that really serious injury might be intentionally inflicted on John Davies if necessary, and merely realising that some lesser physical injury might be inflicted upon him, falling short of intentional serious bodily injury, then your verdict in respect of B should be not guilty of murder but guilty of manslaughter even though A is guilty of murder. The reason for that is that it would be clear in your view that A had intentionally committed murder in the sense that he would have unlawfully killed John Davies with the intention of causing him really serious bodily injury, but that in doing so he had gone beyond the limits of anything agreed or foreseen by B as part of what might be done, because B would on that finding only have contemplated the possibility that some physical injury falling short of serious bodily injury might be inflicted upon the deceased man.'

The jury's question prompting the learned judge's second direction on joint enterprise was: 'Can you please clarify as unambiguously as possible the differences between manslaughter and murder?'

The learned judge sought the views of both counsel for the Crown and counsel for the appellant (not Miss Cotton QC who has appeared for him on this appeal). With both counsel's agreement he then read to the jury a passage from the judgment of this court given by Lord Lane CJ in *R v Hyde* [1990] 3 All ER 892 at 896, [1991] 1 QB 134 at 139 as follows:

'If B realises (without agreeing to such conduct being used) that A may kill or intentionally inflict serious injury, but nevertheless continues to participate with A in the venture, that will amount to a sufficient mental element for B to be guilty of murder if A, with the requisite intent, kills in the course of the venture. As Professor Smith points out, B has in those circumstances lent himself to the enterprise and by so doing he has given assistance and encouragement to A in carrying out an enterprise which B realises may involve murder.'

After repeating that passage the learned judge went on as follows:

'That is the position as far as realisation is concerned. Of course, if there was an agreement, an actual agreement, either express or implied, that A should kill or intentionally inflict serious injury, that would be murder. But, as I understand it, the prosecution do not put the case quite as high as that in this case, they are saying that you must be sure that B realised that A might kill with the requisite intent in the course of the venture. That is the position so far as murder is concerned. If you are not satisfied that he realised that A might kill with the requisite intent in the course of the venture, you should nevertheless be sure that he realised that in the course of the venture A might inflict some harm on B, or indeed whether A or B might inflict some harm on B falling short of really serious bodily harm, then the proper verdict would be guilty of manslaughter but not guilty of murder. So it is the realisation that goes to the core of the matter or the realisation I have explained to you in relation to an intent to kill or cause really serious bodily injury, or whether the prosecution failed to establish that. If they have failed to establish that, are you sure that this defendant must have realised it in the course of the joint venture that some injury might be inflicted on the victim John Davies, some physical injury?'

Miss Cotton submits that, in the circumstances of the present case, the learned judge's directions were incorrect, or at least insufficient. This was not a case in which the object of the joint venture was to assault the victim; nor was it a case in which lethal weapons or indeed any weapons were being carried. In those circumstances Miss Cotton argues that it was wrong or insufficient for the judge to identify the degree of foresight required to be proved against the appellant as merely that Gray 'may' or 'might' intentionally kill or inflict really serious injury. She submits he should have emphasised that the requisite foresight to be proved against the appellant must be that such an intentional killing or infliction of really serious injury by Gray was a 'real' or 'substantial' or 'serious' possibility.

This submission is based upon a passage in the advice of the Privy Council delivered by Sir Robin Cooke in *Chan Wing-siu v R* [1984] 3 All ER 877, [1985] AC 168. In that case the three appellants broke into a flat carrying knives. Two stabbed the occupier while the third held his wife. She too was slashed as the three left the flat. The husband died. It was held that a secondary party was criminally liable for acts of the primary offender if the crime was foreseen by him as a possible incident of the criminal unlawful enterprise and that it was proved beyond reasonable doubt that that was so. Sir Robin Cooke said ([1984] 3 All ER 877 at 880–881, [1985] AC 168 at 175):

'The case must depend rather on the wider principle whereby a secondary party is criminally liable for acts by the primary offender of a type which the former foresees but does not necessarily intend. That there is such a principle is not in doubt. It turns on contemplation or, putting the same idea in other words, authorisation, which may be express but is more usually implied. It meets the case of a crime foreseen as a possible incident of the common unlawful enterprise. The criminal culpability lies in participating in the venture with that foresight.'

However, reliance is placed upon a passage as follows ([1984] 3 All ER 877 at 883, [1985] AC 168 at 179):

'Where there is an evidential foundation for a remoteness issue, it may be necessary for the judge to give the jury more help. Although a risk of a *a* killing or serious bodily harm has crossed the mind of a party to an unlawful enterprise, it is right to allow for a class of case in which the risk was so remote as not to make that party guilty of a murder or intentional causing of grievous bodily harm committed by a co-adventurer in the circumstances that in the event confronted the latter. But if the party accused knew that lethal weapons, such as a knife or a loaded gun, were to be carried on a criminal expedition, the defence should succeed only very rarely. In cases

b where an issue of remoteness does arise it is for the jury (or other tribunal of fact) to decide whether the risk *as recognised by the accused* was sufficient to make him a party to the crime committed by the principal. Various formulae have been suggested, including a substantial risk, a real risk, a risk that something might well happen. No one formula is exclusively preferable; indeed it may be advantageous in a summing up to use more than one. For

c the question is not one of semantics. What has to be brought home to the jury is that occasionally a risk may have occurred to an accused's mind, fleetingly or even causing him some deliberation, but may genuinely have been dismissed by him as altogether negligible. If they think there is a reasonable possibility that the case is in that class, taking the risk should not

d make that accused a party to such a crime of intention as murder or wounding with intent to cause grievous bodily harm.' (Sir Robin Cooke's emphasis.)

Miss Cotton submits that in the present case remoteness did arise and, accordingly, the word 'might' used by the learned judge was insufficient. He should have gone further along the lines suggested in *Chan Wing-siu v R*.

e Reference was made to that case in *R v Slack* [1989] 3 All ER 90, [1989] QB 775. There the appellant and B burgled a house. B stabbed the elderly householder with a knife carried and handed to him by the appellant. The trial judge posed the question to the jury concerning the appellant:

f 'Did [he] contemplate and foresee that Buick *might* kill or cause grievous bodily harm to Mrs Crowder as part of their joint enterprise and did she die as a result of such conduct by Buick? If so it is open to you to find that he so intended and that he is guilty of murder.' (The judge's emphasis.)

That direction was approved by this court. In *R v Hyde* [1990] 3 All ER 892, [1991] 1 QB 134 the three appellants were convicted of murder. They had not carried weapons, but they had jointly set out to attack the victim, who died from

g injuries inflicted by kicking. In dismissing the appeals Lord Lane CJ said ([1990] 3 All ER 892 at 895, [1991] 1 QB 134 at 138):

'There are, broadly speaking, two main types of joint enterprise cases where death results to the victim. The first is where the primary object of the participants is to do some kind of physical injury to the victim. The

h second is where the primary object is not to cause physical injury to any victim but, for example, to commit burglary. The victim is assaulted and killed as a (possibly unwelcome) incident of the burglary. The latter type of case may pose more complicated questions than the former, but the principle in each is the same.'

j After referring to *Chan Wing-siu v R, R v Slack, R v Wakely* [1990] Crim LR 119 and observations by Professor Smith on the latter two cases, Lord Lane CJ went on to state the law in the passage read and repeated to the jury by the trial judge in the present case and quoted above.

In *Hui Chi-ming v R* [1991] 3 All ER 897, [1992] 1 AC 34, another case from Hong Kong concerning joint enterprise, Lord Lowry giving the advice of the

Privy Council, quoted with approval an extensive part of Lord Lane CJ's judgment in *R v Hyde*, culminating with the passage cited by the trial judge in the present *a* case. Lord Lowry went on ([1991] 3 All ER 897 at 909, [1992] 1 AC 34 at 51):

> 'That passage from the judgment in *R v Hyde* [1990] 3 All ER 892 at 895–896, [1991] 1 QB 134 at 138–139 correctly states, in their Lordships' opinion, the law applicable to a joint enterprise of the kind described, which results in the commission of murder by the principal as an incident of the joint *b* enterprise.'

In our judgment the principle stated by Lord Lane CJ in *R v Hyde* is of general application, whether weapons are carried or not and (as Lord Lane CJ expressly said) whether the object of the enterprise be to cause physical injury or to do some other unlawful act, eg burglary or robbery. True, it will be easier for the Crown *c* to prove that B participated in the venture realising that A might wound with murderous intent if weapons are carried or if the object is to attack the victim or both. But that is purely an evidential difference, not a difference in principle.

With regard to the passage relied upon in *Chan Wing-siu v R* we are doubtful whether the defendant B, who fleetingly thinks of the risk of A using violence with murderous intent in the course of a joint enterprise only to dismiss it from *d* his mind and go on to lend himself to the venture, can truly be said, at the time when he so lends himself, to 'foresee' or 'realise' that A might commit murder. In such a case B can hardly have such foresight or realisation at the time he lends himself to the venture because he has banished the risk from his mind. The words 'realise' and 'realisation' used by Lord Lane CJ and by the trial judge here aptly described the test, because to realise something may happen is surely to *e* contemplate it as a real not fanciful possibility. Accordingly, we are inclined to the view that seeking to distinguish between a fleeting but rejected consideration of a risk and a continuing realisation of a real risk will, in most cases, be unnecessary. It would also over-complicate directions to juries and possibly lead to confusion.

However, even accepting that it may be necessary or desirable in some cases, *f* due to possible remoteness of the risk, for the judge to give the jury more help, we do not think the present case fell into that category. This was not, to take an extreme example, a case of burglars entering in the erroneous belief that the householder was on holiday and one of them encountering and killing the householder. Here, the appellant knew the plan was to rob an old man in his *g* cottage. He consistently conceded in evidence that he knew the victim was unlikely to yield up his money or goods without resistance. The nub of the case was therefore not whether the appellant realised force might be used but whether he realised only that some physical harm might be done or that really serious injury might be inflicted. As to that, the learned judge gave the clearest possible directions of law to the jury both at the beginning of his summing up and after *h* their question.

Miss Cotton further argued that the learned judge ought to have isolated and drawn to the jury's attention the facts and evidence bearing on this appellant's state of mind. Specifically, she submits, he ought to have pointed out that no weapons were being carried and that the object of the venture was robbery, not assault. *j*

In our judgment the learned judge's review of the evidence was full and fair. It could have left the jury in no doubt about the object of the enterprise and the absence of weapons. Moreover, the learned judge towards the end of his summing up reminded the jury clearly of the arguments put forward on behalf of the appellant.

a In our judgment the learned judge fully discharged his duty, both in his directions of law and his summary of the evidence and the issues. Accordingly, this appeal must be dismissed.

Appeal dismissed.

b   N P Metcalfe Esq   Barrister.

Canterbury City Council v Colley and another

HOUSE OF LORDS

c LORD TEMPLEMAN, LORD ACKNER, LORD OLIVER OF AYLMERTON, LORD MUSTILL AND LORD WOOLF

30 NOVEMBER 1992, 21 JANUARY 1993

Town and country planning – Permission for development – Revocation – Compensation
d *– Depreciation of value of interest in land – Statutory assumption that planning*
permission would be granted for development – Permission granted for demolition of
house and erection of new dwelling – House demolished but no new dwelling erected –
Permission for erection of new dwelling revoked – Compensation sought for revocation of
planning permission – Whether planning permission assumed to be still subsisting was
same as revoked permission – Whether assumption must be made that planning permission
e *would be granted even though permission incapable of being implemented – Town and*
Country Planning Act 1971, s 164(4).

In 1961 outline planning permission was granted for the demolition of a house and the erection of a new dwelling on the same site. In 1963 the house was demolished but no new dwelling was ever erected. In 1986 the appellants
f purchased the site for £14,500 and thereafter a lengthy dispute ensued between the appellants and the respondents, the local planning authority, relating to the continuing validity of the 1961 planning permission. In the meantime the appellants made a new application for the erection of a house within the same curtilage as the original house. That application was refused but in June 1987 the council notified the appellants that the original permission was regarded as valid
g and it would consider proposals for implementing it. However, in November 1987 the council made an order revoking the 1961 permission and following a public inquiry, that order was confirmed in August 1989. A claim by the appellants under s 164[a] of the Town and Country Planning Act 1971 was referred to the Lands Tribunal to determine the amount of compensation payable to them
h following the revocation of planning permission for the erection of the house. Under s 164 the appellants were entitled to compensation for expenditure incurred and any loss sustained which was directly attributable to the revocation of planning permission, but under s 164(4) the amount of any loss or damage consisting of depreciation of the value of an interest in the land was to be calculated on the assumption that 'planning permission would be granted for
j development of the land of any class specified in [Sch 8 to the Act, which included rebuilding buildings in existence on 1 January 1948 or coming into existence thereafter]'. The tribunal made an interim award consisting of, inter alia, £106,750 depreciation in the value of the land, being the difference between the

---

a Section 164, so far as material, is set out at p 593 *h*, post

value of the land with the benefit of the 1961 permission (£115,000) and its value
without planning permission (£8,250). In arriving at that figure the tribunal *a*
disregarded the statutory assumption in s 164(4) that planning permission would
be granted for rebuilding the house, on the grounds that if the assumption in
s 164(4) was applied the planning permission which was assumed to be still
subsisting was the same permission which had been revoked and was incapable
of being implemented. The tribunal further found that, if the post-revocation
value of the land was calculated on the statutory assumption that permission *b*
would be granted, its value would be £70,000, reflecting the difference in value
between the land with the original planning permission and the land with the
assumed permission, thus reducing the compensation to £45,000. The council
appealed, contending that s 164(4), in its plain and natural meaning, required the
calculation of depreciation to be made on the assumption that planning permission
would be granted for the rebuilding of the house. The Court of Appeal allowed *c*
the appeal. The appellants appealed to the House of Lords, contending that a
purposive construction to s 164(4) and Sch 8 should be adopted by which the
assumption of planning permission should not be made where the permission
revoked was or amounted in substance to the permission assumed under the
section. *d*

Held – Having regard to the legislative history of s 164(4) of the 1971 Act, the
clear purpose of the Act was to limit the amount of compensation payable for
depreciation due to a revocation of planning permission by fixing a base value for
the land in all cases on the footing that planning permission for any class of Sch 8
development would be granted, including development of the class which was *e*
the subject matter of the revoked permission. Accordingly, even though the 1961
planning permission was incapable of implementation, the assumption required
to be made under s 164(4) for the purposes of assessing any loss or damage
consisting of depreciation in the value of the land resulting from the revocation
of the 1961 planning permission was that planning permission would be granted *f*
for the rebuilding of the house. The appeal would therefore be dismissed (see
p 593 *d*, p 595 *e f* and p 598 *c* to *h*, post).

Notes
For compensation for refusal of planning permission, see 46 *Halsbury's Laws* (4th
edn) paras 192–194, 198–200, and for cases on the subject, see 47(1) *Digest* *g*
(Reissue) 151, 546–547.
    Section 164(4) of and Sch 8 to the Town and Country Planning Act 1971 were
replaced by s 107(4) of and Sch 3 to the Town and Country Planning Act 1990.
For s 107 of and Sch 3 to the 1990 Act, see 46 *Halsbury's Statutes* (4th edn) (1991
reissue) 641, 915. *h*

Cases referred to in opinions
Central Control Board (Liquor Traffic) v Cannon Brewery Co Ltd [1919] AC 744, HL.
Stock v Frank Jones (Tipton) Ltd [1978] 1 All ER 948, [1978] 1 WLR 231, HL.

Appeal *j*
The claimants, Mark John Colley and Janine Elaine Colley, appealed with the
leave of the Court of Appeal from the decision of that court (Sir Donald Nicholls
V-C, Taylor and Farquharson LJJ) (90 LGR 321) on 20 March 1992 allowing the
appeal of the respondents, Canterbury City Council, by way of case stated by the
Lands Tribunal (J C Hill Esq) on 7 May 1991 in respect of its interim decision
dated 27 March 1991 on a reference by the appellants in respect of the

a compensation payable by the respondents, as the local planning authority, on the revocation of planning permission for the erection of a house on a site formerly known as Marley House, Pean Hill, Whitstable, Kent. The question raised by the case stated related solely to the interpretation and application of s 164(4) of the Town and Country Planning Act 1971 on the calculation of the loss or damage sustained by the appellants attributable to the revocation of planning permission.

b The facts are set out in the opinion of Lord Oliver.

David Keene QC and *Barry Payton* (instructed by *Hempsons*) for the appellants.
Roger Henderson QC and *Edward Cousins* (instructed *Sharpe Pritchard*, agents for *P Wilson-Sharp*, Canterbury) for the respondents.

c Their Lordships took time for consideration.

21 January 1993. The following opinions were delivered.

LORD TEMPLEMAN. My Lords, for the reasons to be given by my noble and learned friend Lord Oliver of Aylmerton I would dismiss this appeal.

d **LORD ACKNER.** My Lords, I have had the advantage of reading in draft the speech of my noble and learned friend Lord Oliver of Aylmerton. I agree with it and for the reasons he gives I too would dismiss this appeal.

LORD OLIVER OF AYLMERTON. My Lords, s 45 of the Town and
e Country Planning Act 1971 (re-enacting provisions which first appeared in s 21 of the Town and Country Planning Act 1947) empowers a local planning authority, subject to certain conditions and subject, in the absence of consent from persons affected, to confirmation by the Secretary of State, to order the revocation or modification of a planning permission which has been granted.
f Where such an order (other than one made with the consent of the person affected) has been made and confirmed, a person interested in the land who has incurred expenditure rendered abortive by the order or who has otherwise sustained loss directly attributable to the revocation or modification is entitled, under s 164 of the 1971 Act, to claim and receive compensation for the expenditure or loss so incurred or sustained. Section 164(4), however, contains a
g provision limiting the amount of any loss capable of being claimed for depreciation of the value of an interest in the land affected by the revocation or modification. It is in these terms:

> 'In calculating, for the purposes of this section, the amount of any loss or damage consisting of depreciation of the value of an interest in land, it shall
h be assumed that planning permission would be granted for development of the land of any class specified in Schedule 8 to this Act.'

Schedule 8 (which is headed 'Development not Constituting New Development') is primarily related to the provisions of s 169 of the 1971 Act, which applies not to a revocation of an existing planning permission but to the refusal by the Secretary of State, either on an appeal or on a reference, of an application for
j planning permission. If the application is for development of a class specified in Pt II of Sch 8, that section confers a right to compensation. Part I of the schedule relates to development not ranking under s 169 for compensation for a refusal for planning permission and it embraces, for relevant purposes, the rebuilding of buildings in existence on 1 January 1948 or coming into existence thereafter so long as the cubic content of the original building is not exceeded by certain defined limits.

The present appeal, which is brought with the leave of the Court of Appeal, relates to a property at Whitstable known as Marley House for which, subject to conditions and detailed approval, an outline planning permission had been granted on 15 November 1961 by the Kent County Council, then the local planning authority, for 'the demolition of house and erection of new dwelling'. Following that permission, the house originally standing on the property was demolished in September 1963 but no new dwelling was ever in fact erected. On 31 January 1986 the appellants purchased the site at a price of £14,500 and there thereafter ensued a lengthy dispute between the appellants and the respondents, now the planning authority for the area, relating to the continuing validity of the 1961 planning permission. That dispute was finally resolved in the appellants' favour. In the interim the appellants had made a new application for the erection of a house within the same curtilage as the original Marley House although not in precisely the same position. That application was refused but in June 1987 the respondents told the appellants that the original permission was regarded as valid and that they would consider proposals for implementing it. The appellants sought to follow this up and expended moneys in abortive design expenditure. That sum is not now in dispute. On 12 November 1987, however, the respondents notified the appellants that they had made an order revoking the 1961 permission and had submitted it to the Secretary of State for confirmation. Following a public inquiry the order was confirmed on 17 August 1989. The appellants then made a claim for compensation under s 164 which was referred to the Lands Tribunal. On 27 March 1991 the tribunal made an interim award of £108,626·84 consisting of £106,750 depreciation in value of the land and £1,876·84 abortive design expenditure. The only question currently in issue is the correctness of the tribunal member's assessment of the depreciation in value of the land at the sum of £106,750, which was arrived at by, in effect, disregarding the assumption required to be made by s 164(4). The member valued the land with the benefit of the 1961 permission at £115,000. Without that permission, and disregarding the statutory assumption, the valuation was £8,250. On the basis of making the statutory assumption, however, the member found that the post-revocation value of the land was £70,000, thus reducing the compensation on this footing to £45,000.

In reaching the conclusion that he did in apparent defiance of the express requirement of s 164(4) the member was much influenced by the fact that the development to which the revoked permission related was, in substance at least, the very permission which the subsection required to be assumed to be still subsisting. As it happened, the evidence satisfied him that the 1961 permission would have enabled the appellants to build a considerably larger house than the original Marley House, with the result that the actual value of the site with the 1961 permission was greater than that which resulted from the simple application of the statutory assumption. The statutory assumption would, however, result, on any analysis, in the appellants being deprived of a substantial part of their real loss by the attribution of a notional planning permission which was in fact incapable of implementation. Indeed, as Mr Keene QC has forcefully argued, if one supposes a planning permission covering merely the erection of a building of the same size and on the same site as the building demolished, the effect of the statutory assumption is to eliminate any compensation at all for the undoubted depreciation of the land value occasioned by the revocation. The tribunal member's view was that this could not possibly have been the intention of Parliament in enacting a provision designed to provide compensation. He said:

'It seems to me that in revocation order cases section 164 will only operate
as Parliament intended it to operate if the development resulting from the
Schedule 8 assumption, although a hypothetical one, is not that which also
corresponds with the subject of the associated revocation order. This could
be achieved by notionally adding to at the end of sub-section (4) of section
164 words such as "unless such planning permission is the subject of
revocation order proceedings".'

From this decision the respondents appealed by way of case stated to the Court of
Appeal, which, on 20 March 1992, allowed the appeal but granted leave to the
appellants to appeal to your Lordships' House (see 90 LGR 321).

My Lords, that the results of the application of s 164(4) can, in appropriate
circumstances, be anomalous is beyond doubt. The respondents' argument
involves, as Sir Donald Nicholls V-C pointed out in his judgment in the Court of
Appeal (90 LGR 321 at 334):

'. . . as a necessary corollary, the proposition that in assessing compensation
for the revocation of permission to demolish and rebuild a house, the valuer
must assume that permission to rebuild the house would be granted. On its
face the proposition seems bizarre.'

Indeed the result of the statutory assumption, where the holder of a permission
to demolish and rebuild has actually carried out the demolition at the date when
the permission is revoked, is to leave him without a house and with a site upon
which he can neither rebuild nor, effectively, claim any compensation for its
depreciation in value.

Nevertheless, the provisions of s 164(4) are, in terms, mandatory and I cannot,
for my part, see any escape from the proposition that they require to be applied
even in the case postulated of the notional permission to be assumed being the
very permission that has in fact been revoked. It has been suggested that
something turns on the use by the legislature of the word 'assumed' and it is
argued that you cannot 'assume' that which, because it cannot in fact be
implemented, is incapable of being rationally assumed. That, however, I find
myself quite unable to accept. The section is, in terms, postulating an artificial
assumption and dealing with a situation where no planning permission is in fact
in existence or likely to be in existence.

More convincing, perhaps, is the appeal to the well-known canon enunciated
by Lord Atkinson in *Central Control Board (Liquor Traffic) v Cannon Brewery Co Ltd*
[1919] AC 744 at 752 that an intention to take away the property of a subject
without giving him a legal right to compensation for the loss of it is not to be
imputed to the legislature unless that intention is expressed in unequivocal terms.
But the difficulty here is that, even assuming that there is room for the application
of this principle in a section whose express purpose is to provide and, at the same
time, to limit compensation, the terms of the section are indeed entirely
unequivocal.

Then it is said that the provision, if applied strictly in accordance with its terms,
leads to an absurdity. It is pointed out that in the case of a refusal of planning
permission for development specified in Pt II of the Sch 8 there is, in s 169,
specific provision for compensation to be assessed on the full difference in the
value of the land with the permission and the value of the land without it. It is, it
is argued, absurd that where permission has been granted and is then revoked
there should be a harsher rule and one which can, in certain circumstances, result

in the subject receiving no compensation at all. Reliance is placed on the speech
of Lord Simon of Glaisdale in *Stock v Frank Jones (Tipton) Ltd* [1978] 1 All ER 948, *a*
[1978] 1 WLR 231. But that reference is, as it seems to me, fatal to the submission.
What Lord Simon said was ([1978] 1 All ER 948 at 954, [1978] 1 WLR 231 at
237):

> '. . . a court would only be justified in departing from the plain words of
> the statute were it satisfied that: (1) there is clear and gross balance of *b*
> anomaly; (2) Parliament, the legislative promoters and the draftsman could
> not have envisaged such anomaly and could not have been prepared to accept
> it in the interests of a supervening legislative objective; (3) the anomaly can
> be obviated without detriment to such legislative objective; (4) the language
> of the statute is susceptible of the modification required to obviate the
> anomaly.'   *c*

Even assuming that the anomaly, which arises only in very limited
circumstances, is such as to satisfy the second of these conditions, it is really
impossible, as Mr Keene was, I think, constrained to admit, to suggest any way in
which the statutory language could be modified save by the addition, for which
there is no context, of some such words as those used by the member of the Lands *d*
Tribunal. That involves more than a mere purposive construction. It involves
substantially rewriting the section on the supposition that the legislature, had it
thought about the particular case, would have expressed itself in substantially
different terms from those which it in fact chose to use. Accepting, as I do, that
the appellants have suffered hardship in being deprived of a substantial part of
the value represented by the revoked permission, I cannot, for my part, regard *e*
this as a legitimate approach to construction of the statute.

In a clear and most helpful address, Mr Keene's final appeal was to a
consideration of the legislative history in order to support a submission that a
purposive construction of s 164 leads to the conclusion that sub-s (4) cannot be
applied in accordance with its literal terms where this would result in compensation
being denied. The origins of the section and of Sch 8 and their subsequent *f*
amendment and incorporation into a succession of consolidating statutes has been
fully and carefully analysed and described in the judgment of Sir Donald Nicholls
V-C (see 90 LGR 321 at 335–339), which, in the ordinary way, I would be content
simply to adopt in full without repetition. In deference to Mr Keene's very careful
and detailed submission, however, I will endeavour to describe the history in
summary form. There was nothing revolutionary or novel about the provisions *g*
of ss 45 and 164 or those of Sch 8. Substantially similar provisions were first
enacted in the Town and Country Planning Act 1947 in ss 21 and 22 and Sch 3.
In particular, the assumption in s 164(4) formed an essential part of the
compensation calculation and was provided for in s 22(7) of the 1947 Act. Whilst,
however, in that Act it served the purpose of providing a valuation base from *h*
which depreciation of land value for compensation purposes was to be calculated,
the rationale of that valuation base was quite different. The philosophy behind
the 1947 Act was not only that development, whether it consisted of building
operations or change of user, should be controlled but that the development value
of land, over and above the value attributable to an artificially defined 'existing
use' of the land, should be taken into public ownership. Thus, when the 1947 Act *j*
came into force on the appointed day (1 July 1948) a landowner became entitled
to develop his land in a way not classified as an existing use only upon payment
to the public purse, in the shape of a Central Land Board, of a development charge
under s 69 of that Act which was to be calculated, in effect, by reference to the
amount by which the value of the land was enhanced by permission for the

proposed development. The existing use for the purposes of these provisions was
a defined by Sch 3 to the 1947 Act, Pts I and II of which were in substantially the
same terms as Pts I and II of Sch 8 to the 1971 Act, save that they were headed
respectively 'Development Included in Existing use for purposes other than
Compensation under s. 20' and 'Development Included in Existing use for all
Purposes'. The signficance of this distinction was that it was provided in s 20 (the
forerunner of s 169 of the 1971 Act) that, where, on an application for permission
b to carry out development of a class specified in Pt II, that application, either on
appeal or on a reference, was refused by the Secretary of State or was granted
subject only to conditions, compensation could be claimed from the local planning
authority for the difference between the value which the land would have had
had the permission been granted or granted unconditionally and its value without
the permission or with only the conditional permission. No provision, however,
c was made for compensation for refusal of permission to carry out development of
a class specified in Pt I of the schedule and although this may seem arbitrary it
could not, as Sir Donald Nicholls V-C remarked in the course of his judgment (at
338), have been accidental. The existing use provisions of Sch 3 had a further
relevance. Under Pt VI of the 1947 Act there was established a compensation
d fund of an arbitrary sum of £300m to meet claims by landowners for loss of
development value as a result of the Act, that is to say the difference between the
unrestricted value of land immediately prior to 1 July 1948 and its value subject
to the restrictions imposed by the 1947 Act. Since development charges were to
be levied only on development other than that comprised in the existing use
provisions in Sch 3, s 61 provided that the restricted value of the land for the
e purposes of this compensation was to be calculated on the assumption that
planning permission would be granted for development of any class specified in
this schedule.

It is against this scheme that ss 21 and 22 of the 1947 Act fall to be considered.
Section 21 was, for material purposes, in substantially the same terms as s 45 of
f the 1971 Act, but the compensation provisions in s 22, albeit substantially in the
same terms as those of s 164, contained a crucial difference in the form of a
proviso that no compensation should be paid for depreciation in value unless (for
relevant purposes) a development charge had been paid in respect of the revoked
permission. Subsection (7) provided for the assessment of compensation in
accordance with the Acquisition of Land (Assessment of Compensation) Act 1919
g and required it to be assumed (using words identical with those of s 164(4) of the
1971 Act) that planning permission would be granted for any class of development
specified in Sch 3. In the context of the scheme of the Act this was perfectly
logical. Since, by definition, the development charge which formed the essential
condition for payment of compensation became payable only on a development
which was not within the existing use, it was both rational and necessary to
h provide in the calculation of the amount of depreciation a base value which
assumed the existence of a permission for existing use development.

So far so good. The difficulty arises in the next stage in the legislative history.
The planning legislation was substantially amended in 1953 and 1954 when
development charges were abolished. The Town and Country Planning Act 1954
contained, in s 38, provision for compensation for revocation of a planning
j permission similar to that contained in s 21 of the 1947 Act. It did this, however,
not by enacting a new compensation permission but by incorporating and
applying s 22 of the 1947 Act but deleting the proviso which excluded
compensation for depreciation in value when no development charge had been
paid. The formula for the calculation of the amount of depreciation which was
provided in s 22(7) was thus not only retained but was expressly incorporated by

reference. This may be said to have been arbitrary and illogical because, with the abolition of the development charge, the reason for the statutory assumption in fixing a base value for calculation might be thought to have gone, so that it would have been logical simply to repeal that part of s 22(7) which included the statutory assumption. But this was not done and I cannot, for my part, regard the omission as having been accidental. Where a statute contains a provision in words substantially identical with those used in a previous Act it may be possible to argue that the words of the later Act take on, from their context, a meaning different from that which they bore in the previous enactment. But, where the later statute expressly incorporates and applies a section from an existing statute, it is, as it seems to me, quite impossible to attribute to it in its new application a meaning different from that which it bore in the statute from which it is taken. The section had a perfectly clear meaning in the context of the 1947 Act and clearly applied equally to the case where the permission revoked was one for a development specified in Sch 3. When it was incorporated referentially in the 1954 Act and repeated in terms, as it subsequently was in the 1962 and 1971 consolidating Acts, it cannot have changed its meaning. Thus the legislative history, far from providing support for the purposive construction which Mr Keene seeks to urge upon your Lordships, seems to me to underline the impossibility of escaping the conclusion that the clear purpose of the legislature was to limit the amount of compensation payable for depreciation due to a revocation of planning permission by fixing a base value for the land in all cases on the footing that planning permission for any class of Sch 8 development would be granted. That must include, however arbitrary it may seem, even development of that very class which was the subject matter of the revoked permission.

The conclusion is not one which I embrace with any enthusiasm and it may well be that the particular circumstance of the revoked permission being the very permission comprehended in the statutory assumption was not one which the legislature foresaw as ever likely to occur. But, whilst this provides a sound reason for the hope expressed by Sir Donald Nicholls V-C that Parliament may look again at what he described as 'an anachronistic relic' (at 340), it cannot provide an avenue for escape from the clear and express words of the section. I would dismiss the appeal.

LORD MUSTILL. My Lords, I have had the advantage of reading in draft the speech prepared by my noble and learned friend Lord Oliver of Aylmerton. I agree with him and, for the reasons which he has given, I, too, would dismiss this appeal.

LORD WOOLF. My Lords, having had the advantage of reading in draft the speech of my noble and learned friend Lord Oliver of Aylmerton, I would also dismiss this appeal for the reasons he gives.

Appeal dismissed.

Mary Rose Plummer　Barrister.

Deposit Protection Board v Dalia and another

CHANCERY DIVISION
SIR DONALD NICHOLLS V-C
12, 15 JUNE, 3 JULY 1992

Bank – Deposit protection scheme – Deposit protection fund – Insolvent bank – Assignment of part of deposit after petition presented to wind up insolvent bank but before winding-up order made – Whether assignee of part of deposit entitled to compensation from deposit protection fund – Banking Act 1987, ss 58(1), 59, 60.

Under ss 58[a] and 60[b] of the Banking Act 1987 the Deposit Protection Board was required to pay out of the deposit protection fund to each depositor who had a protected deposit with a recognised bank or licensed institution which became insolvent an amount equal to three-quarters of his protected deposit, but limited to a maximum deposit of £20,000. Under s 59(1)(a)[c] of the 1987 Act a company wound up by the court became insolvent on the making of a winding-up order. On 5 July 1991 the Bank of England presented a petition to the court for an order that an authorised institution under the 1987 Act (BCCI) be wound up on the ground that it was insolvent. The petition was due to be heard on 30 July. Certain depositors with BCCI took steps to maximise the amount of the payments they could claim from the deposit protection fund by assigning sums of £20,000 to family members or close friends who could then each look to the fund for payment of £15,000 in respect of the £20,000 share of the deposit assigned to him. On 30 July the Banking Act 1987 (Meaning of Deposit) Order 1991 was made providing that in future the definition of 'deposit' in the 1987 Act excluded a sum to which a person became entitled, otherwise than by operation of law, after presentation of a winding-up petition. BCCI was wound up on 14 January 1992. The question arose whether the assignees of deposits made before 30 July 1991 were entitled to payment out of the deposit protection fund pursuant to s 58(1) of the 1987 Act.

Held – Since the essential purpose of s 58 was to pay compensation to those entitled to deposits in an insolvent bank it would be inconsistent with that purpose to confine 'depositor' in all circumstances to the person who made the deposit. Accordingly, if the original depositor had assigned his interest to an assignee, so that the assignee became entitled to look to the bank for repayment, the assignee was the person entitled to compensation. Accordingly, a declaration would be granted that for the purpose of the deposit protection scheme under the 1987 Act an assignee under an assignment made before 30 July 1991 of part of a deposit was to be treated as entitled to the assigned part of the deposit and as having made a deposit of an amount equal to that part (see p 605 *e f*, p 606 *d e*, p 607 *d e* and p 608 *h j*, post).

Notes

For compensation payments to depositors, see 3(1) *Halsbury's Laws* (4th edn reissue) paras 115–117.

For the Banking Act 1987, ss 58, 59, 60, see 4 *Halsbury's Statutes* (4th edn) (1987 reissue) 589, 591, 592.

---

a   Section 58, so far as material, is set out at p 602 *g*, post
b   Section 60, so far as material, is set out at p 603 *a* to *c*, post
c   Section 59(1), so far as material, provides: 'For the purposes of this Part of this Act a body corporate ... becomes insolvent—(*a*) on the making of a winding-up order against it ...'

Cases referred to in judgment

Brice v Bannister (1878) 3 QBD 569, CA.
Britt v Buckinghamshire CC [1963] 2 All ER 175, [1964] 1 QB 77, [1963] 2 WLR 722, CA.
Hanlon v Law Society [1980] 2 All ER 199, [1981] AC 124, [1980] 2 WLR 756, HL.
Jones v Farrell (1857) 1 De G & J 208, 44 ER 703, LC and LJJ.
Kirkness (Inspector of Taxes) v John Hudson & Co Ltd [1955] 2 All ER 345, [1955] AC 696, [1955] 2 WLR 1135, HL.
Weddell v J A Pearce & Major (a firm) [1987] 3 All ER 624, [1988] Ch 26, [1987] 3 WLR 592.

Cases also cited

A-G v Prince Ernest Augustus of Hanover [1957] 1 All ER 49, [1957] AC 436, HL.
Black-Clawson International Ltd v Papierwerke Waldhof-Aschaffenberg AG [1975] 1 All ER 810, [1975] AC 591, HL.
Courtauld v Legh (1869) LR 4 Exch 126.
Lennon v Gibson & Howes Ltd [1919] AC 709, PC.
McGreavy, Re, ex p McGreavey v Benfleet UDC [1950] 1 All ER 442, CA.
MacManaway, Re [1951] AC 161, PC.
Steel Wing Co Ltd, Re [1921] 1 Ch 349, [1920] All ER Rep 292.
Stephens v Cuckfield RDC [1960] 2 All ER 716, [1960] 2 QB 373, CA.

Originating summons

The plaintiff, the Deposit Protection Board (a body corporate established pursuant to the Banking Acts 1979 and 1987), issued an originating summons dated 15 April 1992 seeking the court's determination on the question whether a person entitled by reason of assignment of part of a deposit as defined by s 5(1) of the 1987 Act was a depositor holding a protected deposit entitled to a compensation payment from the plaintiff pursuant to s 58(1) of the 1987 Act. The respondents to the summons were the first defendant, Varsha Dalia, an assignee of a protected deposit joined in the proceedings to represent all such assignees, and the second defendant, Barclays Bank plc, joined in the proceedings to represent contributory institutions within the meaning of s 52(1) of the 1987 Act. The facts are set out in the judgment.

John Jarvis QC and *Jonathan Nash* (instructed by *Clifford Chance*) for the board.
Lord Irvine of Lairg QC and *Philip Sales* (instructed by *Ashurst Morris Crisp*) for the first defendant.
Michael Brindle QC and *Bankim Thanki* (instructed by *Lovell White Durrant*) for the second defendant.

Cur adv vult

3 July 1992. The following judgment was delivered.

SIR DONALD NICHOLLS V-C. To alleviate hardship when a bank becomes insolvent the Banking Act 1979 set up the deposit protection fund. Money from the fund was payable to depositors on the insolvency of a recognised bank or licensed institution. A depositor was to be paid three-quarters of the amount of his deposit, but limited to a maximum deposit of £10,000. The fund was continued under the Banking Act 1987. The maximum amount for a protected deposit was increased to £20,000. So a depositor owed £20,000 by an authorised institution which has failed can look to the Deposit Protection Board for £15,000.

a A depositor owed £100,000 or £50,000 or any other amount over £20,000 can likewise look to the board, but his claim also is limited to the same top figure of £15,000.

The Bank of Credit and Commerce International SA, usually known simply as BCCI, was an authorised institution under the 1987 Act. On 5 July 1991 the Bank of England presented a petition to the court for an order that BCCI be wound up. One of the grounds relied on was that the company was insolvent. Provisional

b liquidators were appointed and BCCI ceased trading in England. Depositors ceased to be able to withdraw their money. Fearing the worst, some depositors took steps to maximise the amount of the payments from the deposit protection fund. An enterprising firm of accountants, having taken expert legal advice, wrote around to BCCI depositors telling them of a scheme the accountants had

c prepared. The scheme was that a depositor should formally transfer and assign part of his or her deposit to family members or close friends 'who can be trusted'. For instance, a depositor with a deposit of £100,000 would transfer £20,000 to each of five relations or friends. Instead of the compensation payable to him being limited to £15,000 as the maximum amount of compensation payable to any one depositor, each of his five assignees could look to the fund for payment of £15,000

d in respect of the £20,000 share of the deposit assigned to him. By this means the total compensation payable by the fund would be increased to £75,000. Depositors were urged to hurry, 'for you only have until Monday evening 29th July'. This was because the winding-up petition was due to come before the court again on 30 July.

Some fifty or so depositors, possibly more, signed transfers in July 1991 in

e respect of sums totalling several million pounds. There were over 200 assignees. One depositor alone, whose deposits exceeded half a million pounds, executed 26 assignments of £20,000 each.

The scheme was quickly stopped in its tracks. Parliament never intended that the limit on the amount of compensation payable to individual depositors could be side-stepped by dispositions made after formal steps had been taken to initiate

f the winding-up process. On 30 July 1991 the Banking Act 1987 (Meaning of Deposit) Order 1991, SI 1991/1776 was made. It provided that in future the definition of 'deposit' in the 1987 Act excluded a sum to which a person became entitled, otherwise than by operation of law, after presentation of a winding-up petition. In the case of BCCI, where a winding-up petition had already been presented, the changed definition took effect from 31 July. So the loophole, if

g such it was, was closed although subsequently some months elapsed before a winding-up order was eventually made on 14 January 1992.

The question before me is whether these assignments did have their intended effect for compensation purposes. The first defendant is an assignee joined in the proceedings to represent all assignees. At the outset I should emphasise that in

h the proceedings the only question raised is one of law, to be answered on the assumption that the assignments were genuine and valid transactions and that there was no arrangement or understanding that an assignee would hold for the assignor any compensation received by him from the fund. The board, which administers the fund, has reserved the right to pursue such matters if this should become necessary. I must also emphasise that the answer I give to the question

j before me will be of general application. Its effect will not be confined to assignments made in circumstances similar to those which existed regarding BCCI in July 1991. The 1991 order has dealt with how similar assignments will operate in future. I have to look at the matter more broadly, and consider also the effect of a valid assignment made before winding up became an imminent prospect.

The deeds of assignment

The assignments were on a printed form of deed. The document recited the *a*
'vendor's' deposit in a specified account with BCCI. The operative part provided
that in consideration of £1 'the vendor by this deed sells, assigns and transfers the
sum of [£20,000] of the deposit to the purchaser'. The depositor also signed a
letter addressed to BCCI, whereby BCCI was given notice of the 'absolute'
assignment in question. The bank was instructed that the sum of £20,000 from
the deposit account was now held by the assignee, who was described as 'the *b*
purchaser', and that he should now be identified by the bank 'as a depositor'. The
letter added:

> 'If, for administrative reasons, you are unable to arrange for the completion
> of formalities to designate a separate deposit account in the name of the
> purchaser, I/we confirm that I/we hold the abovementioned sum on trust for *c*
> the purchaser.'

Before me it was common ground that the assignments were not statutory
assignments in conformity with s 136 of the Law of Property Act 1925, but that
they were effective as equitable assignments.

d

The legislation

The deposit protection scheme is now regulated by Pt II of the 1987 Act.
Institutions authorised by the Bank of England to carry on a deposit-taking
business in this country are required to make contributions to the deposit *e*
protection fund as levied from time to time by the board. The amount of the
contribution of each institution varies according to the size of its deposit base. At
present there are over 500 contributing institutions, of which the second
defendant is one. The overall sum required to meet the payments due under the
scheme to BCCI depositors is in the region of £78m. The sum in issue on this
summons is about £3·7m. *f*

Sections 58 to 62 are concerned with payments out of the fund. Section 58 is
the section which makes provision for the payment of compensation to depositors.
Subsection (1), so far as material, provides:

> 'Subject to the provisions of this section, if at any time an institution
> becomes insolvent and at that time—(*a*) it is an authorised institution . . . the
> Board shall as soon as practicable pay out of the Fund to each depositor who *g*
> has a protected deposit with that institution an amount equal to three-
> quarters of his protected deposit.'

Subsection (2) contains a comparable provision applicable when an administration order is made under the Insolvency Act 1986. I pause to make an initial
observation. The 1987 Act contains no definition of 'depositor'. In this context *h*
that word would, I believe, naturally be read as meaning the person who made
the deposit in question. To qualify for compensation the deposit made by him
must be a protected deposit.

Section 59 defines when a company becomes insolvent for the purposes of s 58.
It was this provision that gave rise to the loophole sought to be exploited by BCCI *j*
depositors. Under s 59(1)(*a*) the relevant event in the case of a winding up by the
court is the making of the winding-up order, not the presentation of the winding-
up petition.

Section 60 defines the expression 'protected deposit'. I must quote the first two
subsections:

a
'(1) . . . in relation to an institution in respect of which a payment falls to be made under section 58(1) above any reference in this Act to a depositor's protected deposit is a reference to the total liability of the institution to him immediately before the time when it becomes insolvent, limited to a maximum of £20,000, in respect of the principal amounts of and accrued interest on sterling deposits made with United Kingdom offices of the institution.

b
(2) . . . in relation to an institution in respect of which a payment falls to be made under section 58(2) above any reference in this Act to depositor's protected deposit is a reference to the liability of the institution to him in respect of—(a) the principal amount of each sterling deposit which was made by him with a United Kingdom office of the institution before the making of the administration order and which under the terms on which it was made

c
is or becomes due or payable while the order is in force; and (b) accrued interest on any such deposit up to the time when it is or becomes due and payable as aforesaid; but so that the total liability of the institution to him in respect of such deposits does not exceed £20,000.'

d
Subsection (2), concerned with payments when administration orders are in force, provides clear support for the view that the draftsman had in mind what I have described as the natural meaning of the word depositor in this context. Subsection (2)(a) refers to the principal amount of each sterling deposit 'made by him'. This assumes that a depositor is the person who will have made the deposit in question. It assumes that the person to whom the institution has a liability

e
('the liability of the institution to him') is one and the same person as the person who made the deposit ('. . . in respect of . . . each sterling deposit which was made by him'). Subsection (1) is consistent with this.

The same assumption appears in sub-s (6). This subsection excluded certain deposits for compensation purposes. It reads:

f
'In determining the total liability of an institution to a depositor for the purposes of subsection (1) above, or the liability or total liability of an institution to a depositor for the purposes of subsection (2) above, no account shall be taken of any liability in respect of a deposit if . . . (c) the institution is a former authorised institution and the deposit was made after it ceased to be an authorised institution or a recognised bank or licensed institution under

g
the Banking Act 1979 unless, *at the time the deposit was made*, the depositor did not know and could not reasonably be expected to have known that it had ceased to be an authorised institution, recognised bank or licensed institution.'

The words I have emphasised assume that the depositor who made the deposit will be the same person as the depositor to whom a compensation payment is to

h
be made under s 58. When an institution has ceased to be an authorised institution, liability of the institution to him for compensation purposes depends upon his state of mind 'at the time the deposit was made'.

Trusts

Thus far one might think that, in applying the £20,000 limit on which the

j
three-quarters compensation is to be paid, attention is to be focused simply on all the outstanding United Kingdom sterling deposits made by a particular depositor. They are to be aggregated because the £20,000 limit is on 'the total liability of the institution to him' in respect of such deposits. However, to look only at the persons who were the actual depositors would not be satisfactory. Some special provision has to be made for depositors who are nominees or trustees. Section 61

addresses this problem, by modifying ss 58 and 60 in certain cases. Section 61(2) provides that persons who are entitled to a deposit as trustees shall be treated as 'a single and continuing body of persons distinct from the persons who may from time to time be the trustees'. Further, if the same persons are entitled as trustees 'to different deposits' under different trusts, they are treated as a separate and distinct body with respect to each trust.

Section 61(3) deals with one particular type of trust, bare trusts:

> 'Where a deposit is held for any person or for two or more persons jointly by a bare trustee, that person or, as the case may be, those persons jointly shall be treated as entitled to the deposit without the intervention of any trust.'

'Bare trustee' means in short a person who holds the deposit on trust for another person who has the exclusive right to direct how it shall be dealt with (s 106).

This subsection covers two situations. It covers the simple case where A holds a deposit as nominee for B. In this type of case the scheme of the legislation is that one ignores the trust and has regard exclusively to the identity of the beneficiary. B is to be 'treated as entitled to the deposit without the intervention of any trust'. In my view this provision makes sense only if the twofold consequence to which it leads is that, by reason of being so treated, B is to be regarded as the depositor (1) for the purpose of receiving compensation under s 58 and also (2) for the purpose of the definition of protected interest in s 60. That is the consequence which is intended to flow from the provision that, although not the depositor, B is to be treated as entitled to the deposit.

Section 61(3) also covers the case where A holds a deposit on trust for B and C jointly. They are to be treated as jointly entitled to the deposit without the intervention of a trust. Cases of jointly entitled depositors are covered by sub-s (6):

> '. . . where two or more persons are jointly entitled to a deposit . . . each of them shall be treated as having a separate deposit of an amount produced by dividing the amount of the deposit to which they are jointly entitled by the number of persons who are so entitled.'

The wording here ('is treated as having a separate deposit') is different from sub-s (3) ('treated as entitled to the deposit'), but in my view the intended effect is clear and is the same in both cases.

Subsection (7) deals with cases where a deposit has been made out of a clients' account or the like. The subsection echoes the language of sub-s (3) by providing that the clients shall be treated 'as entitled to' the appropriate proportion of the deposit. Subsection (8) deals with the special case where an authorised institution is itself a trustee and holds sums which, but for the exclusion in s 5(3)(a), would be a deposit. The subsection negatives the s 5 provision by directing that each of those who made deposits with the institution are to be 'treated as having made a deposit'.

Two important points are discernible in these compressed provisions. First, one thread running through them is that where A is the person who made the deposit but B is the person beneficially entitled to the deposit, B is the material person for the purposes of the protection scheme. The draftsman employed several different forms of words to achieve this result. One form is that B is to 'be treated as entitled to the deposit' made by A, as in sub-s (3). The draftsman used words to the like effect in sub-s (7). Secondly, the section is concerned with the beneficial interests existing when a payment falls to be made. This is as one would

expect. If A deposits money with a bank, and sometime later makes a declaration
a of trust in respect of the whole of the sum deposited in favour of his child B
absolutely, sub-s (3) will apply if the bank subsequently becomes insolvent. I can
see nothing in s 61 to suggest that these trust provisions apply only if the trust
existed at the time the deposit was made.

b ### Statutory assignments

Against this background I turn to the question of assignments. I start by noting
that the relationship between banker and customer is one of debtor and creditor
and is based on contract. The credit balance in a customer's bank account is a
chose in action. It can be the subject of an assignment. Assignment of the right
to payment of the sum of money in a bank account is to be distinguished from
c the more usual means by which a customer transfers money to someone else.
Normally he will write a cheque, or withdraw the money and hand it over.
Exceptionally he may not do so. Money may be deposited on terms that make
early withdrawal disadvantageous. Then it may be in the parties' interests to leave
the money in the account but transfer the benefit of the account to the third party
by some other means, for instance by the depositor constituting himself a trustee
d of the account for the benefit of the third party, or by him assigning the money
in his account to the third party.

I shall consider first the simple case where A makes an out-and-out assignment
to B of the whole of his interest in a deposit or deposits. He does so in writing,
and he gives written notice to the bank as required by s 136 of the Law of
Property Act 1925. In my view in the case of such a statutory assignment the
e person to whom compensation is payable under s 58 of the 1987 Act is B. He is
the person who has become entitled to the deposit in place of A. The expression
'depositor' in that section is apt to embrace him as the assignee of A, and the
'protected deposit' referred to is the liability of the bank to him in respect of the
United Kingdom sterling deposit or deposits to which he is entitled.

f The factor which has weighed most with me in reaching this conclusion is the
scheme of the 1987 Act as shown by its treatment of trusts. To confine 'depositor'
in all circumstances to the person who made the deposit would be inconsistent
with the object s 61 seeks to achieve. Thus the natural meaning of the word
'depositor' must give way to the extent necessary to enable the underlying purpose
of the 1987 Act to be achieved.

g Under the 1987 Act if A holds a deposit on trust for B absolutely, B becomes
the material person. He is to be 'treated as entitled to the deposit without the
intervention of any trust' (see s 61(3)). As already noted, the twofold consequence
is that B is regarded as the depositor for the purpose of receiving compensation
and also for the purpose of the definition of protected deposit in s 60. In my view
it is inconceivable that Parliament intended that an assignee of the whole of a
h deposit under a statutory assignment should be in a worse position, for the
purposes of the deposit protection scheme, than the beneficiary under a declaration
of trust. Parliament cannot have intended that the right to compensation should
turn on fine legal distinctions between an assignee's rights to a deposit under an
absolute assignment and a beneficiary's rights under a declaration of trust. In each
case the entire beneficial interest in the deposit belongs to B to the exclusion of A
j who made the deposit.

Indeed, the assignee ought, if anything, to be in a better position. As a statutory
assignee the legal right to the money in the account passes to him, he is entitled
to all legal remedies to recover the money and he can give a good discharge to the
bank without the concurrence of the assignor. The bank must pay him and not

the assignor. A beneficiary under a declaration of trust is not so well placed: the
bank will continue to deal with the trustee, and in the ordinary course the deposit
will be repaid by the bank to the trustee, not the beneficiary.

I recognise that the draftsman may not have had assignments in mind at all.
That would be understandable. Assignments of money in a bank account, except
by way of charge, are not everyday transactions. The absence of express provison
in the section means that the court, treading circumspectly, must look at the
underlying purpose of the legislation and construe the draftsman's language with
that purpose in mind. Here the essential purpose is to pay compensation to those
entitled to deposits in an insolvent bank. If the original depositor has assigned his
interest to an assignee, so that the assignee has become entitled to look to the bank
for repayment, achievement of the legislative purpose requires the assignee to be
the person entitled to compensation. That is necessarily implicit in the legislative
scheme, and s 58 must be so read and understood. The correctness of this approach
is confirmed by the treatment afforded to trusts.

Equitable assignments

I turn next to consider the position where part only of a deposit has been
assigned. It was common ground before me that such an assignment cannot be a
statutory assignment but is equitable only, even when written notice has been
given to the debtor bank. In my view, for compensation purposes the position of
an assignee in such a case is the same as discussed above regarding a statutory
assignee. There is no reason in principle why, for the purposes of the deposit
protection scheme, an assignee of part of a deposit should be treated any differently
from an assignee of the whole of a deposit. Indeed it would be absurd if the
following two cases were not treated the same: (1) A has two deposits each of
£10,000, and he assigns one deposit to B and the other to C; and (2) A has one
deposit of £20,000, and he assigns one-half to B and the other half to C.

I have in mind that in certain respects statutory assignments and equitable
assignments have different legal consequences. These differences are not material
for present purposes. An equitable assignee is entitled to look to the bank for
payment. If the bank pays the assignor after receiving notice of the assignment
he must pay again: *Jones v Farrell* (1857) 1 De G & J 208, 44 ER 703 and *Brice v
Bannister* (1878) 3 QBD 569. The assignee may have to join the assignor in a
proceedings he brings against the bank, but this is a pragmatic procedur
requirement and does not affect the assignee's substantive right to the assign
part of the debt. On this the authorities are conveniently summarised by Scott J
in *Weddell v J A Pearce & Major (a firm)* [1987] 3 All ER 624 at 633–637, [1988]
Ch 26 at 38–43.

I mention one further point. The trust provisions in s 61 draw no distinction
of consequence between a declaration of trust relating to the whole deposit and
one relating to a defined part of a deposit. That is not surprising. In the present
case the assignors declared themselves to be trustees of the assigned parts of the
deposits if BCCI was unable to designate separate deposit accounts in the assignees'
names. I am unable to see why equitable assignments, with this fall-back
declaration of trust, ought to be treated in any way differently for compensation
purposes than if in place of assignments there had been simple declarations of
trust. Had there been, there could have been no room for doubt.

The 1991 order

I am confirmed in my conclusions by the terms of the 1991 order. Paragraph
2(1) of the order reads:

a 'For the purposes of sections 60, 61 and 62 of the Banking Act 1987 the definition of deposit in section 5 of that Act shall be treated as excluding any sum to which a person becomes entitled (otherwise than by operation of law), or comes to be treated as entitled for the purposes of sections 58 and 60 of that Act, after a petition is presented for the winding up of the institution, or, in the case of an institution in respect of which such a petition has been presented before the date on which this Order comes into force, 30th July b 1991.'

The effect of para 3 is to make comparable provision for voluntary winding up.

This order was the legislative response to the accountants' scheme for BCCI depositors. If assignees do not qualify to be treated as depositors for compensation purposes, the order was unnecessary. Clearly the order was prepared in some c haste, but it cannot be brushed aside as having been made out of an excess of caution. That appraisal of the order might have more force if the order had provided simply that from 31 July any sum to which a person became entitled other than by operation of law would not qualify as a deposit. That course was not adopted. The order excluded an entitlement arising, otherwise by operation d of law, after presentation of a winding-up petition. Markedly, and deliberately, the order left untouched a deposit 'to which a person becomes entitled (otherwise than by operation of law)' pre-presentation of a winding-up petition. An assignment of a deposit, in whole or in part, made while a bank is trading normally was not struck down. This difference in treatment between pre- and post-petition assignments is so stark that the inevitable conclusion is that pre- e petition assignments were not intended to be outlawed. The order proceeded on the basis that 'depositor' does embrace a person who did not make the deposit but subsequently became entitled to it, by operation of law or otherwise. The order was content that pre-petition assignees should still qualify for compensation under the scheme.

A further feature is to be noted. As one would expect, and consistently with f what I have said regarding the purpose and scheme of the 1987 Act, the order treated assignments and trusts on the same footing. The order applied both to interests arising under assignments ('any sum to which a person becomes entitled') and to interests arising under trusts ('or comes to be treated as entitled'). The latter phrase harks back to the bare trust provision in s 61(3). Interests arising, whether under assignments or trusts, were struck down if the entitlement arose g after presentation of a winding-up petition. In both cases they were left untouched for compensation purposes if the entitlement arose pre-petition.

I must mention why this order is a legitimate aid to construction of the statute. It is an unusual order. It was not made in exercise of a power to prescribe rules or procedures to be followed in carrying out the 1987 Act. The order was made in h exercise of a power conferred on the Treasury by s 7 of the 1987 Act. The Treasury has power, after consultation with the Bank of England, to amend the meaning of deposit for the purposes of all or any of the provisions of the 1987 Act. Thus the effect of the order was to amend one of the statutory provisions. In such a case the subordinate legislation may be used in order to construe the parent Act: see *Hanlon v Law Society* [1980] 2 All ER 199 at 218, [1981] AC 124 at 193 per Lord j Lowry. In the same case Lord Scarman ([1980] 2 All ER 199 at 213, [1981] AC 124 at 186) referred approvingly to observations of Harman LJ in *Britt v Buckinghamshire CC* [1963] 2 All ER 175 at 180, [1964] 1 QB 77 at 88:

'A power is given to the minister by the Act itself to modify another section of the Act so that, when the minister does produce that modification

... that regulation becomes in fact part of the Act. It is like an amending section of the Act; so that, in my judgment, reference can be made to that *a* regulation because it is embodied in the Act itself and, having a quasi-parliamentary validity, is a good indication of the wishes of the legislature, just as much as if it were enacted in the Act itself.'

Thus, insofar as the provisions of the 1987 Act are ambiguous, guidance can be sought from the 1991 order in the same way as guidance can be sought from a *b* later enactment for the construction of an earlier one: *Kirkness (Inspector of Taxes) v John Hudson & Co Ltd* [1955] 2 All ER 345, [1955] AC 696.

Other provisions in the 1987 Act

How, then, do provisions such as sub-ss (2) and (6) of s 60 work? I recognise that all the pieces of this statutory jigsaw do not fit neatly together. This, however, *c* does not assist on the point now under consideration. Whatever answer is given on the assignment point, there will be some untidiness within the statute. Section 60(2), for example, has to be made to work in a case where the person entitled to be paid compensation is a beneficiary under a bare trust and not the person who made the deposit. How s 60(2) is to be construed and applied in such a case, or in the equivalent case of an assignment, is a question that need not be decided in the *d* instant case. That question can be left for a future occasion when it gives rise to a live issue.

Not customers

I was pressed with an argument that the assignees were not customers of BCCI. *e* The purpose of the 1987 Act was to provide some protection for persons who had chosen to become customers of the bank and who were accepted by the bank as customers. The 1987 Act was not intended to protect non-customers. I do not think this presentation advances the arguments. To substitute 'customer' for 'depositor' does not provide an answer on the matters mentioned above.

f

The legislative history

The parties made submissions based on the legislative antecedents of the Act currently in force. In particular, s 27 of the Protection of Depositors Act 1963 defined 'depositor' as 'a person entitled, or prospectively entitled, to repayment of a deposit, whether made by him or not'. This definition was not carried forward into the later Acts, although both the 1979 Act and the current Act did reproduce *g* some of the provisions regarding depositors which were contained in the 1963 Act.

I shall not pursue these points. They provide little assistance compared with the guidance given by the scheme of the 1987 Act itself.

h

Conclusion

For these reasons I shall make a declaration to the effect that for the purposes of Pt II of the 1987 Act, an assignee of part of a deposit as defined in s 5 is to be treated as entitled to the assigned part of the deposit and as having made a deposit of an amount equal to that part.

Order accordingly.

Celia Fox   Barrister.

a # AB and others v South West Water Services Ltd

COURT OF APPEAL, CIVIL DIVISION
SIR THOMAS BINGHAM MR, STUART-SMITH AND SIMON BROWN LJJ
2, 3, 16 NOVEMBER 1992
b

Damages – Exemplary damages – Nuisance – Claim in public nuisance against public
authority – Statutory water undertaker supplying contaminated drinking water to
customers – Water undertaker knowing water to be contaminated – Water undertaker
wilfully and deliberately misleading customers by asserting water safe to use and drink –
c *Water undertaker knowing statement to be unfounded – Plaintiffs bringing claim for*
damages for breach of duty – Whether aggravated or exemplary damages available in
claim for nuisance.

The plaintiffs suffered ill effects as the result of drinking contaminated water
from the defendant water undertaker's drinking water system which had been
d polluted when 20 tonnes of aluminium sulphate were accidently introduced into
the system at a water treatment works. The defendants were subsequently
prosecuted and convicted for contamination of the water supply for which they,
as a statutory water undertaker, were responsible. The plaintiffs brought actions
against the defendants claiming damages for, inter alia, breach of statutory duty,
for failing to take reasonable care to supply wholesome water, for strict liability
e for the escape of a dangerous thing, for breach of contract, in nuisance and in
negligence. In addition the plaintiffs claimed exemplary and or aggravated
damages in respect of the conduct of the defendants, their servants or agents after
the date of the pollution, alleging that the defendants, by their servants or agents,
who were employees of a statutory body and public servants, had acted in an
f arrogant and high-handed manner in ignoring the complaints made by their
customers, and instead had wilfully and deliberately misled them by sending a
circular letter to all customers asserting that the water from the treatment works
was of the right alkalinity and was safe to use and drink when that statement was
known to be unfounded as no adequate toxicity tests had been carried out. The
plaintiffs further alleged that the defendants withheld any accurate or consistent
g information as to what had happened and as to the state of the water, failed to
give any proper information to public health authorities, hospitals, doctors and
pharmacists or their own customers as to any precautions that should be taken to
minimise the effects of the consumption of contaminated water, failed to close
down the water treatment works or provide clean water from an alternative
source and instead continued to supply contaminated drinking water with the
h result that the plaintiffs consumed contaminated water for a longer period and in
greater quantities than they would otherwise have done, with a proportionately
greater impact on their health. The defendants, who admitted liability for
compensatory damages, applied to strike out the claim for exemplary and/or
aggravated damages as disclosing no reasonable cause of action, contending that a
claim for exemplary damages in the context of an action for damages for personal
j injuries arising out of breach of common law or statutory duty was not
maintainable as a matter of law. The judge refused to strike out the claim for
exemplary damages, on the ground that it was arguable that the plaintiffs could
recover exemplary and/or aggravated damages for the tort of nuisance. The
defendants appealed to the Court of Appeal.

Held – (1) Since it had been laid down by the House of Lords in 1964 that awards
of exemplary damages should be restricted to torts which were recognised at that　*a*
time as grounding a claim for exemplary damages and, since public nuisance was
not such a tort, exemplary damages could not be recovered by a plaintiff for
particular damage resulting from public nuisance (see p 620 *g*, p 621 *d* to *f*, p 625
d, p 627 *c* to *f* and p 629 *d g*, post); *Rookes v Barnard* [1964] 1 All ER 367 and
Cassell & Co Ltd v Broome [1972] 1 All ER 801 applied.

(2) In any event the plaintiffs could not recover exemplary damages on the　*b*
facts, since the defendants had not been exercising executive power derived from
local or central government when the contaminated water was supplied but had
instead been carrying out a commercial operation and there was no evidence that
the defendants had knowingly continued the nuisance for the purpose of gaining
a pecuniary or other advantage and therefore the case did not fall into either of　*c*
the two categories for which exemplary damages could be awarded. Moreover,
the large number of plaintiffs made the claim unsuitable for the award of
exemplary damages. Where a public nuisance affected hundreds or even thousands
of plaintiffs the court would be unable to assess the amount of exemplary damages
to be awarded to any one of them without knowing at the outset the total award
of exemplary damages to punish or deter the defendant, the number of successful　*d*
plaintiffs and the extent to which they were individually affected by the
defendant's behaviour. Accordingly, the claim for exemplary damages would be
struck out (see p 622 *h* to p 623 *b g* to p 624 *f*, p 625 *d*, p 627 *h j*, p 628 *d e* and
p 629 *d g*, post); *Rookes v Barnard* [1964] 1 All ER 367 applied.

(3) Furthermore, the plaintiffs could not claim aggravated damages for their
anger and indignation at the defendants' high-handed conduct because the　*e*
plaintiffs could only claim compensatory damages, and anger and indignation
were not proper subjects for compensatory damages. Accordingly, the claim for
aggravated damages would also be struck out (see p 624 *h j*, p 625 *d* and p 629 *a*
to *d g*, post); dictum of Woolf J in *Kralj v McGrath* [1986] 1 All ER 54 at 61
applied.　*f*

Decision of Wright J [1992] 4 All ER 574 reversed.

Notes

For aggravated and exemplary damages, see 12 *Halsbury's Laws* (4th edn)
paras 1189–1190, and for cases on the subject, see 17 *Digest* (Reissue) 80–82, *11–*　*g*
17.

Cases referred to in judgments

Alexander v Home Office [1988] 2 All ER 118, [1988] 1 WLR 968, CA.
Ashby v White (1703) 2 Ld Raym 938, 92 ER 126; *rvsd on other grounds* (1704) 1　*h*
　　Bro Parl Cas 62, 1 ER 417, HL.
Bell v Midland Rly Co (1861) 10 CBNS 287, 142 ER 462.
Benson v Frederick (1766) 3 Burr 1845, 97 ER 1130.
Bradford Metropolitan City Council v Arora [1991] 3 All ER 545, [1991] 2 QB 507,
　　[1991] 2 WLR 1377, CA; *rvsg* [1989] ICR 719, EAT.
Cassell & Co Ltd v Broome [1972] 1 All ER 801, [1972] AC 1027, [1972] 2 WLR　*j*
　　645, HL.
Catnic Components Ltd v Hill & Smith Ltd [1983] FSR 512.
Crouch v Great Northern Rly Co (1856) 11 Exch 742, 156 ER 1031.
Drane v Evangelou [1978] 2 All ER 437, [1978] 1 WLR 455, CA.
Emblen v Myers (1860) 6 H & N 54, 158 ER 23.

a   *Guppys (Bridport) Ltd v Brookling, Guppys (Bridport) Ltd v James* (1983) 14 HLR 1, CA.

Huckle v Money (1763) 2 Wils 205, 95 ER 768.

Kralj v McGrath [1986] 1 All ER 54.

Lonrho plc v Fayed [1991] 3 All ER 303, [1992] 1 AC 448, [1991] 3 WLR 188, HL.

Lonrho plc v Tebbit [1991] 4 All ER 973; *affd* [1992] 4 All ER 280, CA.

Mafo v Adams [1969] 3 All ER 1404, [1970] 1 QB 548, [1970] 2 WLR 72, CA.

b   *Munro v Ministry of Defence* (21 November 1984, unreported), QBD.

Riches v News Group Newspapers Ltd [1985] 2 All ER 845, [1986] QB 256, [1985] 3 WLR 432, CA.

Rookes v Barnard [1964] 1 All ER 367, [1964] AC 1129, [1964] 3 WLR 269, HL.

Rylands v Fletcher (1868) LR 3 HL 330, [1861–73] All ER Rep 1.

c   *Wileman v Minilec Engineering Ltd* [1988] ICR 318, EAT.

Wilkes v Wood (1763) Lofft 1, 98 ER 489.

Williams v Currie (1845) 1 CB 841, 135 ER 774.

d   **Cases also cited or referred to in skeleton arguments**

Alcock v Chief Constable of the South Yorkshire Police [1991] 4 All ER 907, [1992] 1 AC 310, HL.

Amministrazione delle Finanze dello Stato v Simmenthal SpA Case 106/77 [1978] ECR 629.

Amministrazione delle Finanze dello Stato v SpA San Giorgio Case 199/82 [1983] ECR

e   3595.

Archer v Brown [1984] 2 All ER 267, [1985] QB 401.

Barrs v Bethell [1982] 1 All ER 106, [1982] Ch 294.

Bourgoin SA v Ministry of Agriculture Fisheries and Food [1985] 3 All ER 585, [1986] QB 716, QBD and CA.

f   *Clark v Urquhart, Stracey v Urquhart* [1930] AC 28, HL.

Comet BV v Produktschap voor Siergewassen Case 45/76 [1976] ECR 2043.

Cruise v Terrell [1922] 1 KB 664, [1922] All ER Rep 130, CA.

Davis v Bromley UDC (1903) 67 JP 275, CA.

Devonshire v Jenkins [1978] CA Transcript 283.

Doyle v Olby (Ironmongers) Ltd [1969] 2 All ER 119, [1969] 2 QB 158, CA.

g   *Duke v GEC Reliance Ltd* [1988] 1 All ER 626, [1988] AC 618, HL.

EC Commission v Greece Case 68/88 [1989] ECR 2965.

Emmott v Minister for Social Welfare Case C-208/90 [1991] IRLR 387, CJEC.

Esso Petroleum Co Ltd v Southport Corp [1954] 2 All ER 561, [1954] 2 QB 182, CA; *rvsd in part* [1955] 3 All ER 864, [1956] AC 218, HL.

Factortame Ltd v Secretary of State for Transport (No 2) Case C-213/89 [1991] 1 All

h   ER 70, [1991] 1 AC 603, CJEC and HL.

Flli Costanzo SpA v Comune di Milano Case 103/88 [1989] ECR 1839.

Foster v British Gas plc Case C-188/89 [1990] 3 All ER 897, [1991] 1 QB 405, CJEC; *ruling applied* [1991] 2 All ER 705, [1991] 2 AC 306, HL.

Garden Cottage Foods Ltd v Milk Marketing Board [1983] 2 All ER 770, [1984] AC 130, HL.

j   *H v Ministry of Defence* [1991] 2 All ER 834, [1991] 2 QB 103, CA.

Halsey v Esso Petroleum Co Ltd [1961] 2 All ER 145, [1961] 1 WLR 683.

Hicks v Chief Constable of the South Yorkshire Police [1992] 2 All ER 65, HL.

Holden v Chief Constable of Lancashire [1986] 3 All ER 836, [1987] QB 380, CA.

Joyce v Sengupta (1992) Times, 18 September, CA.

Kenny v Preen [1962] 3 All ER 814, [1963] 1 QB 499, CA.

Lavender v Betts [1942] 2 All ER 72.

Litster v Forth Dry Dock and Engineering Co Ltd [1989] 1 All ER 1134, [1990] 1 AC 546, HL.

McCarey v Associated Newspapers Ltd [1964] 3 All ER 947, [1965] 2 QB 86, CA.

McMillan v Singh (1984) 17 HLR 120, CA.

Manson v Associated Newspapers Ltd [1965] 2 All ER 954, [1965] 1 WLR 1038.

Marleasing SA v Comercial Internacional de Alimentación SA Case C-106/89 [1990] ECR I- 4135.

Marshall v Southampton and South West Hampshire Area Health Authority (Teaching) Case 152/84 [1986] 2 All ER 584, [1986] QB 401, CJEC.

Messenger Newspapers Group Ltd v National Graphical Association (1982) [1984] IRLR 397; *affd* [1984] 1 All ER 293, CA.

Metall und Rohstoff AG v ACLI Metals (London) Ltd [1984] 1 Lloyd's Rep 598, CA.

Miles v Cain (25 November 1988, unreported), QBD at Chelmsford; *rvsd* (1989) Times, 15 December, CA.

Millington v Duffy (1984) 17 HLR 232, CA.

National Enterprises Ltd v Racal Communications Ltd [1974] 3 All ER 1010, [1975] Ch 397, CA.

Perera v Vandiyar [1953] 1 All ER 1109, [1953] 1 WLR 672, CA.

R v Reading Justices, ex p South West Meat Ltd (1991) Times, 18 November, DC.

R v Royal Pharmaceutical Society of GB, ex p Association of Pharmaceutical Importers, R v Secretary of State for Social Services, ex p Association of Pharmaceutical Importers Joined cases 266 and 267/87 [1989] 2 All ER 758, [1990] 1 QB 534, CJEC.

Read v Croydon Corp [1938] 4 All ER 631.

Rewe-Zentralfinanz eG v Landwirtschaftskammer für das Saarland Case 33/76 [1976] ECR 1989.

Robitaille v Vancouver Hockey Club Ltd (1981) 124 DLR (3d) 228, BC CA.

Rook v Fairrie [1941] 1 All ER 297, [1941] 1 KB 507, CA.

Sedleigh-Denfield v O'Callaghan [1940] 3 All ER 349, [1940] AC 880, HL.

Sutcliffe v Pressdram Ltd [1990] 1 All ER 269, [1991] 1 QB 153, CA.

Vorvis v Insurance Corp of British Columbia (1989) 58 DLR (4th) 193, Can SC.

W v Meah, D v Meah [1986] 1 All ER 935.

Whitham v Kershaw (1885) 16 QBD 613, [1886–90] All ER Rep 295, CA.

Appeal

By a master statement of claim served on 11 December 1991 following directions made by Wright J on 6 December 1991 that their actions begun by writs should proceed in the form of a group action, some 182 plaintiffs claimed against the defendants, South West Water Services Ltd, a water undertaker within Sch 3 to the Water Act 1945, damages for breach of common law or statutory duty, for strict liability under *Rylands v Fletcher* (1868) LR 3 HL 330, [1861–73] All ER Rep 1, for breach of contract, in nuisance and in negligence in respect of personal injury suffered by the plaintiffs as the result of drinking water which had been contaminated at the defendants' water treatment works at Lowermoor, Camelford in Cornwall when some 20 tonnes of aluminium sulphate were introduced into the drinking water system. By paras 18 to 27 of the statement of claim the plaintiffs claimed aggravated and as exemplary damages, alleging that the defendants, their servants or agents, as servants of the public, had acted arrogantly and in a high-handed manner in ignoring complaints made by their customers, and instead had wilfully and deliberately misled them as to the true state of affairs by sending a circular letter to all customers on or about 14 July 1988 asserting

that the water from the Lowermoor treatment works was of the right alkalinity
a and was safe to use and drink when that statement was unfounded and known to
be unfounded by the persons making it, as no adequate toxicity tests had in fact
been carried out; that until about the middle of August 1988 the defendants
withheld any accurate or consistent information as to what had happened and as
to the state of the water and failed to give any proper information to public health
authorities, hospitals, doctors and pharmacists or their own customers as to any
b precautions that should be taken to minimise the effects of the consumption of
contaminated water; that the defendants failed to close down the water treatment
works and provide clean water from an alternative source, and continued to
supply drinking water through pipes which had themselves been contaminated
by the chemical with the result that the plaintiffs consumed contaminated water
c for a longer period and in greater quantities than they would have done had they
been properly informed what had happened with a proportionately greater
impact on their health; and that when the plaintiffs found out the truth in the
middle of August 1988 their feelings of indignation were justifiably aroused by
the high-handed manner in which the defendants had dealt with the incident.
The defendants applied by summons to strike out paras 18 to 27 of the statement
d of claim containing allegations relating to the claim for aggravated and exemplary
damages. The plaintiffs applied by summonses to amend their writs and to add a
cause of action for deceit. On 20 March 1992 Wright J ([1992] 4 All ER 574)
refused the defendants' application to strike out paras 18 to 27 of the statement of
claim. The defendants appealed with the leave of the judge. The facts are set out
in the judgment of Stuart-Smith LJ.
e

Christopher Symons QC and *Jonathan Nash* (instructed by *Herbert Smith*) for the
    defendants.
J Melville Williams QC and *Charles Pugh* (instructed by *Pannone Napier*, Sheffield,
    John Whiting & Co, Camelford and *Sproulls*, Bodmin) for the plaintiffs.
f

Cur adv vult

16 November 1992. The following judgments were delivered.

g **STUART-SMITH LJ** (giving the first judgment at the invitation of Sir Thomas
Bingham MR). On 6 July 1988 about 20 tonnes of aluminium sulphate was
accidentally introduced into the defendants' drinking water system at their
treatment works at Lowermoor, Camelford in Cornwall. The plaintiffs, of whom
there are some 180, drank the contaminated water and claim to have suffered a
variety of ill effects as a result. Individual writs and the master statement of claim
h in the group action allege a number of different causes of action based on these
facts. It is said that the water supplied was a defective product for which the
defendants are liable under s 2(1) of the Consumer Protection Act 1987, that there
was a public nuisance for which the defendants were prosecuted and convicted in
the Crown Court at Exeter on 8 January 1991 and that the plaintiffs have suffered
particular damage. It is alleged that the defendants were in breach of their
j statutory duty to take all reasonable care to provide a supply of wholesome water,
contrary to s 31 of and Sch 3 to the Water Act 1945; they are also said to be liable
in negligence, under the rule in *Rylands v Fletcher* (1868) LR 3 HL 330, [1861–73]
All ER Rep 1, for breach of contract and finally, for good measure, for breach of
Council Directive (EEC) 80/778.

The defendants have admitted that they are liable for breach of statutory duty in failing to supply wholesome water and admit their liability to pay compensatory damages. But the plaintiffs are not content with that. They allege that they are entitled to exemplary and/or aggravated damages in addition. These claims are made in paras 18 to 27 of the statement of claim and are based on facts alleged to have occurred after the initial contamination on 6 July 1988. The complaints can be summarised as follows: the servants or agents of the defendants as employees of a statutory body acted in an arrogant and high-handed manner in ignoring complaints made by their customers; they wilfully and deliberately misled them as to the true state of affairs by sending a circular letter to all customers on 14 July 1988 asserting that the water from Lowermoor treatment works was of the right alkalinity and was safe to use and drink. The plaintiffs assert that that statement was unfounded and known to be so by the persons making it, as no toxicity tests had in fact been carried out. Thereafter it is alleged that the defendants withheld any accurate or consistent information as to what had happened and as to the state of the water; and they failed to give any proper information to the public health authorities, hospitals, doctors, pharmacists and their own customers as to any precautions that should be taken to minimise the ill effects of drinking the water; they failed to close down the plant and supply fresh water by means of bowsers. In the result the plaintiffs continued to consume the water for longer than they would otherwise have done with proportionately greater damage to their health. Finally, it is said that when they found out the truth of the matter in mid-August their feelings of indignation were justifiably aroused by the high-handed manner in which the defendants dealt with the incident.

The defendants applied pursuant to RSC Ord 18, r 19 to strike out those allegations contained in paras 18 to 27 of the statement of claim in which those claims for exemplary and aggravated damages are made. Wright J refused to strike them out (see [1992] 4 All ER 574). He did so on the basis that in his opinion it was arguable that the plaintiffs could recover exemplary and/or aggravated damages for the tort of nuisance. He did not accept that any other tort would entitle them to make such a claim. He also gave a very clear warning to the plaintiffs that the mere fact that he did not strike out the claim should not encourage them to think that they were likely to win. He pointed out that they might face very considerable difficulty in establishing the facts said to give rise to such a claim and he drew attention to the fact that the defendants had already been convicted and fined in the lower court, so that on that score the trial court might well think it was not a case for exemplary damages. Mr Symons QC accepted before the judge, as he did before us, that the fact of this conviction and punishment was not of itself an absolute bar to the claim, on the basis that the facts adduced in the Crown Court and upon which sentence was based bore no relation to the plaintiffs' allegations in paras 18 to 27 of the statement of claim, which of course are strenuously denied by the defendants. I say no more about this concession; without hearing further argument I must not be taken as accepting that it was rightly made. The defendants now appeal that decision.

Before considering the grounds of appeal it is necessary to bear in mind the proper approach of a court in an application to strike out. The pleaded facts must be assumed to be true. It is only in a clear and obvious case, or one that is 'doomed to fail', to use the words of Lord Bridge of Harwich in *Lonrho plc v Fayed* [1991] 3 All ER 303 at 314, [1992] 1 AC 448 at 470, that the court should take this draconian step. Moreover in a developing field of law the court may be reluctant to determine a difficult point of law on the scanty facts pleaded in the statement of claim: see *Lonrho plc v Tebbit* [1991] 4 All ER 973 per Browne-Wilkinson V-C (whose decision was upheld on appeal: see [1992] 4 All ER 280).

But in my judgment this is not a developing field of the law. The law has been
a authoritatively stated in two decisions of the House of Lords, namely *Rookes v
Barnard* [1964] 1 All ER 367, [1964] AC 1129 and *Cassell & Co Ltd v Broome* [1972]
1 All ER 801, [1972] AC 1027. Moreover, even if a point of law is difficult, the
court should not shrink from deciding it if it will decide the issues between the
parties. I have no doubt that in this case it will be of great benefit to the parties to
have the point of law decided one way or the other. If it is decided in favour of
b the defendants, then the plaintiffs' cases can be settled on ordinary compensatory
principles. If it is decided in favour of the plaintiffs, then the parties will have to
proceed to what will be extensive discovery and together with the court decide
how the factual issues are to be tried, which will be no easy matter with so many
plaintiffs, each seeking exemplary damages.

c In relation to the claim for exemplary damages Mr Symons for the defendants
advances three main arguments: (1) that nuisance is not a cause of action that can
found a claim for exemplary damages; (2) if that submission is wrong, the
allegations in this case do not bring the case into either of the categories laid down
by Lord Devlin in *Rookes v Barnard*; (3) that in any event this is not an appropriate
case for exemplary damages: it is a claim for damages for personal injuries and
d bears no resemblance to any case in which exemplary damages have been awarded.

Can a cause of action in nuisance found a claim for exemplary damages?
Although this was the only basis on which Wright J held the plaintiffs' claim was
arguable, by a respondent's notice Mr Melville Williams QC contends that an
award can be made on a claim based on negligence or breach of statutory duty.
The defendants' submission was based on the proposition that the combined effect
e of *Rookes v Barnard* and *Cassell & Co Ltd v Broome* is that such a claim must pass
two tests. First, it must be in respect of a cause of action for which prior to 1964
such an award had been made and, secondly, that it must fall within one of the
two categories identified by Lord Devlin in *Rookes v Barnard*. If that proposition
is correct Mr Symons submits that there is no case prior to 1964 where exemplary
damages were awarded for nuisance. The contrary argument is that there is no
f limitation of exemplary damages to specific torts where they had been awarded
prior to 1964 and if there is, then nuisance is such a case.

It is necessary to start with a consideration of Lord Devlin's speech in *Rookes v
Barnard*, with which all the other members of the House agreed. He explained
the nature of exemplary and aggravated damages as follows ([1964] 1 All ER 367
g at 407, [1964] AC 1129 at 1221):

'Exemplary damages are essentially different from ordinary damages. The
object of damages in the usual sense of the term is to compensate. The object
of exemplary damages is to punish and deter. It may well be thought that
h this confuses the civil and criminal functions of the law; and indeed, so far as
I know, the idea of exemplary damages is peculiar to English law. There is
not any decision of this House approving an award of exemplary damages
and your Lordships therefore have to consider whether it is open to the
House to remove an anomaly from the law of England. It must be
remembered that in many cases of tort damages are at large, that is to say,
j the award is not limited to the pecuniary loss that can be specifically proved.
In the present case, for example, and leaving aside any question of exemplary
or aggravated damages, the appellant's damages would not necessarily be
confined to those which he would obtain in an action for wrongful dismissal.
He can invite the jury to look at all the circumstances, the inconveniences
caused to him by the change of job and the unhappiness maybe by a change

of livelihood. In such a case as this, it is quite proper without any departure
from the compensatory principle to award a round sum based on the *a*
pecuniary loss proved. Moreover, it is very well established that in cases
where the damages are at large the jury (or the judge if the award is left to
him) can take into account the motives and conduct of the defendant where
they aggravate the injury done to the plaintiff. There may be malevolence or
spite or the manner of committing the wrong may be such as to injure the
plaintiff's proper feelings of dignity and pride. These are matters which the *b*
jury can take into account in assessing the appropriate compensation. Indeed,
when one examines the cases in which large damages have been awarded for
conduct of this sort, it is not at all easy to say whether the idea of compensation
or the idea of punishment has prevailed.'

He then reviewed *Wilkes v Wood* (1763) Lofft 1, 98 ER 489, *Huckle v Money* (1763) *c*
2 Wils 205, 95 ER 768 and *Benson v Frederick* (1766) 3 Burr 1845, 97 ER 1130. He
described them as the type of case where an award of exemplary damages 'serves
a valuable purpose in restraining the arbitrary and outrageous use of executive
power' (see [1964] 1 All ER 367 at 408, [1964] AC 1129 at 1223). They are cases
of trespass to property or the person or false imprisonment. He then reviewed a
number of other authorities which did not fall into this category. He said ([1964] *d*
1 All ER 367 at 410–411, [1964] AC 1129 at 1225–1227):

'These authorities convince me of two things. First, that your Lordships
could not without a complete disregard of precedent, and indeed of statute,
now arrive at a determination that refused altogether to recognise the
exemplary principle. Secondly, that there are certain categories of cases in *e*
which an award of exemplary damages can serve a useful purpose in
vindicating the strength of the law, and thus affording a practical justification
for admitting into the civil law, a principle which ought logically to belong
to the criminal. I propose to state what these two categories are; and I propose
also to state three general considerations which, in my opinion, should always *f*
be borne in mind when awards of exemplary damages are being made. I am
well aware that what I am about to say will, if accepted, impose limits not
hitherto expressed on such awards and that there is powerful, though not
compelling, authority for allowing them a wider range. I shall not therefore
conclude what I have to say on the general principles of law without returning
to the authorities and making it clear to what extent I have rejected the *g*
guidance they may be said to afford. The first category is oppressive, arbitrary
or unconstitutional action by the servants of the government. I should not
extend this category,—I say this with particular reference to the facts of this
case,—to oppressive action by private corporations or individuals. Where
one man is more powerful than another, it is inevitable that he will try to use
his power to gain his ends; and if his power is much greater than the other's, *h*
he might perhaps be said to be using it oppressively. If he uses his power
illegally, he must of course pay for his illegality in the ordinary way; but he
is not to be punished simply because he is the more powerful. In the case of
the government it is different, for the servants of the government are also the
servants of the people and the use of their power must always be subordinate
to their duty of service. It is true that there is something repugnant about a *j*
big man bullying a small man and very likely the bullying will be a source
of humiliation that makes the case one for aggravated damages, but it is not
in my opinion punishable by damages. Cases in the second category are those
in which the defendant's conduct has been calculated by him to make a profit

for himself which may well exceed the compensation payable to the plaintiff.
a I have quoted the dictum of ERLE, C.J., in *Bell* v. *Midland Ry. Co.* ((1861) 10
CBNS 287 at 304, 142 ER 462 at 469). MAULE, J., in *Williams* v. *Currie* ((1845)
1 CB 841 at 848, 135 ER 774 at 776–777) suggests the same thing; and so
does MARTIN, B., in an obiter dictum in *Crouch* v. *Great Northern Ry. Co.*
((1856) 11 Exch 742 at 759, 156 ER 1031 at 1038). It is a factor also that is
taken into account in damages for libel; one man should not be allowed to
b sell another man's reputation for profit. Where a defendant with a cynical
disregard for a plaintiff's rights has calculated that the money to be made out
of his wrongdoing will probably exceed the damages at risk, it is necessary
for the law to show that it cannot be broken with impunity. This category is
not confined to moneymaking in the strict sense. It extends to cases in which
c the defendant is seeking to gain at the expense of the plaintiff some object,—
perhaps some property which he covets,—which either he could not obtain
at all or not obtain except at a price greater than he wants to put down.
Exemplary damages can properly be awarded whenever it is necessary to
teach a wrongdoer that tort does not pay. To these two categories, which are
established as part of the common law, there must of course be added any
d category in which exemplary damages are expressly authorised by statute.
I wish now to express three considerations which I think should always be
borne in mind when awards of exemplary damages are being considered.
First, the plaintiff cannot recover exemplary damages unless he is the victim
of the punishable behaviour. The anomaly inherent in exemplary damages
would become an absurdity if a plaintiff totally unaffected by some oppressive
e conduct which the jury wished to punish obtained a windfall in consequence.'

It is not in the speech of Lord Devlin that one finds the limitation for which
Mr Symons contends, but in the speeches of four of their Lordships in *Cassell &
Co Ltd v Broome* [1972] 1 All ER 801, [1972] AC 1027, namely Lord Hailsham of
St Marylebone LC, Lord Diplock, Lord Wilberforce and Lord Kilbrandon, and
f perhaps also Lord Reid. The Appellate Committee consisted of seven Lords of
Appeal, so four constituted a majority. Under the heading 'Did *Rookes v Barnard*
extend exemplary damages to fresh torts?' Lord Hailsham LC said ([1972] 1 All
ER 801 at 828, [1972] AC 1027 at 1076):

'Having rejected the theory that Lord Devlin's speech can be pushed aside
g as having been delivered per incuriam, I hope I may now equally dispose of
another misconception. I do not think that he was under the impression
either that he had completely rationalised the law of exemplary damages, nor
by listing the "categories" was he intending, I would think, to add to the
number of torts for which exemplary damages can be awarded. Thus I
disagree with the dictum of Widgery LJ in *Mafo v Adams* [1969] 3 All ER
h 1404 at 1410, [1970] 1 QB 548 at 558 (which, for this purpose, can be treated
as an action for deceit) when he said: "As I understand LORD DEVLIN's speech,
the circumstances in which exemplary damages may be obtained have been
drastically reduced, but the range of offences in respect of which they may be
granted has been increased, and I see no reason since *Rookes* v. *Barnard* why,
when considering a claim for exemplary damages, one should regard the
j nature of the tort as excluding the claim." This would be a perfectly logical
inference if Lord Devlin imagined that he was substituting a completely
rational code by enumerating the categories and stating the considerations.
It is true, of course, that actions for deceit could well come within the
purview of the second category. But I can see no reason for thinking that

Lord Devlin intended to extend the category to deceit, and counsel on both
sides before us were constrained to say that, though it may be paradoxical, *a*
they were unable to find a single case where either exemplary or aggravated
damages had been awarded for deceit, despite the fact that contumelious,
outrageous, oppressive, or dishonest conduct on the part of the defendant is
almost inherently associated with it. The explanation may lie in the close
connection that the action has always had with breach of contract (see the
discussion in Mayne and MacGregor [*Damages* (12th edn, 1961) ch 41, esp at *b*
para 968]).'

It is plain, in my judgment, that Lord Hailsham LC answers the question posed
at the beginning of this section in the negative.

Lord Wilberforce, save on points which he had expressly dealt with, agreed
with Lord Hailsham LC (see [1972] 1 All ER 801 at 866, [1972] AC 1027 at 1121). *c*
He did not expressly deal with the matter. His reference to 'the range of torts for
which punitive damages may be given (trespass to person or property, false
imprisonment and defamation, being the commonest)' also suggests that he
would confine the award to certain specific torts (see [1972] 1 All ER 801 at 860,
[1972] AC 1027 at 1114).

Lord Diplock put the matter beyond doubt. He said ([1972] 1 All ER 801 at *d*
874, [1972] AC 1027 at 1130–1131):

   'Finally on this aspect of the case I would express my agreement with the
   view that *Rookes v Barnard* was not intended to extend the power to award
   exemplary or aggravated damages to particular torts for which they had not
   previously been awarded, such as negligence and deceit. Its express purpose *e*
   was to restrict, not to expand, the anomaly of exemplary damages.'

Lord Kilbrandon agreed, inter alia, with the speech of Lord Hailsham LC. He
delivered an opinion of his own on certain matters but it does not touch upon
this point.

Lord Reid, after referring to *Rookes v Barnard*, said ([1972] 1 All ER 801 at 837, *f*
[1972] AC 1027 at 1086):

   'Theoretically we might have held that as purely punitive damages had
   never been sanctioned by any decision of this House (as to which I shall say
   more later) there was no right under English law to award them. But that
   would have been going beyond the proper function of this House. There are *g*
   many well established doctrines of the law which have not been the subject
   of any decision by this House. We thought we had to recognise that it had
   become an established custom in certain classes of case to permit awards of
   damages which could not be justified as compensatory, and that that must
   remain the law. But we thought and I still think it well within the province
   of this House to say that that undesirable anomaly should not be permitted *h*
   in any class of case where its use was not covered by authority.'

It is not altogether clear from that passage whether Lord Reid is referring to
specific causes of action or torts when he refers to classes of cases, or whether
possibly he had in mind Lord Devlin's two categories. I am inclined to think it is
the former since he later refers to the categories as such. Moreover he said ([1972] *j*
1 All ER 801 at 837, [1972] AC 1027 at 1087):

   'Critics [of Lord Devlin's speech] appear to have thought that he was
   inventing something new. This was not my understanding. We were
   confronted with an undesirable anomaly. We could not abolish it. We had
   to choose between confining it strictly to classes of cases where it was firmly

a   established, although that produced an illogical result, or permitting it to be extended so as to produce a logical result. In my view it is better in such cases to be content with an illogical result than to allow any extension.'

This seems to me to support the view that Lord Reid would confine it to those torts where authority had previously recognised that exemplary damages could be awarded, since if the claim merely had to fall into one of the two categories *b*   this would be a logical extension of the classes of cases in which they could be awarded.

I can find nothing in the speeches of the other members of the House which shows a contrary view. The dicta of the House on this point were obiter; but they are clearly of the highest authority and Mr Melville Williams did not seriously argue that we should not follow them.

c   In *Catnic Components Ltd v Hill & Smith Ltd* [1983] FSR 512 at 541 Falconer J held that the plaintiff could not recover exemplary damages for infringement of patent since there was no authority to this effect prior to *Rookes v Barnard*. It also appears to have been the view of Michael Wright QC (as Wright J then was) sitting as a deputy judge of the High Court in *Munro v Ministry of Defence* (21 November 1984, unreported).

d   But in the present case the judge was impressed by a group of cases, two of them decisions of this court, in the field of race and sex discrimination. In *Alexander v Home Office* [1988] 2 All ER 118 at 123, [1988] 1 WLR 968 at 976 May LJ, in a judgment with which Ewbank J agreed, said:

e   'In so far as exemplary damages are concerned, counsel for the plaintiff submitted that in some racial discrimination cases it would be appropriate to award these as well as compensation including aggravated damages. In the instant case, however, exemplary damages were not asked for in the court below and counsel did not ask for an award of such damages from us. Nevertheless, provided that the facts of a given case fall within the principles applicable, in essence those laid down in the two well-known decisions of the *f*   House of Lords in *Rookes v Barnard* and *Cassell & Co Ltd v Broome* to which I have referred, I see no reason why an award of exemplary damages could not be made in a racial discrimination case.'

This passage is plainly obiter and the point was never argued that such a claim *g*   would not lie for a post-1964 tort.

In *Wileman v Minilec Engineering Ltd* [1988] ICR 318 at 328 Popplewell J said that there might be exceptional cases of sex discrimination where exemplary damages might be awarded; but no award was made in that case. Again this dictum is obiter and the point does not appear to have been argued.

In *Bradford Metropolitan City Council v Arora* [1991] 3 All ER 545, [1991] 2 QB *h*   507 it was alleged that the council by their officers had discriminated against the claimant both on grounds of sex and race. The industrial tribunal had awarded exemplary damages of £1,000. On appeal to the Employment Appeal Tribunal this award was set aside on the ground that selection of individuals for employment by a local authority did not constitute an exercise of public powers in respect of which exemplary damages could be awarded (see [1989] ICR 719). In other words *j*   the case did not come within Lord Devlin's first category. The Court of Appeal allowed an appeal from this decision and restored the award of exemplary damages. It is important to notice however that the only issue before the court was whether the officers were acting in a private or public capacity: see the argument of Mr Sedley QC ([1991] 2 QB 507 at 509) and per Neill LJ ([1991] 3 All ER 545 at 549–550, 552, [1991] 2 QB 507 at 515, 518). The case therefore proceeded on the assumption that exemplary damages could be awarded for a statutory tort created after 1964; the point formed no part of the ratio of the case *a* and it is not binding upon us.

Mr Symons also pointed out that relevant sections of the Sex Discrimination Act 1975 (namely ss 63, 65(1)(*b*), (2) and (3) and s 66(4)) and the Race Relations Act 1976 (ss 54, 56 and 57, which are in similar terms to the 1975 Act) appear to authorise the award only of compensatory damages. This point does not seem to have been argued in any of the three cases to which I have referred. *b*

Wright J was also influenced by the decision of this court in *Guppys (Bridport) Ltd v Brookling, Guppys (Bridport) Ltd v James* (1983) 14 HLR 1. That was a case where the landlords attempted to reconstruct flats. The course of reconstruction caused serious disruption to two tenants, Mr Brookling and Mr James, who occupied two separate rooms and, in breach of an undertaking to the court, *c* washing and sanitary facilities were disconnected and discontinued and the electricity cut off. The county court judge awarded the defendants damages for trespass including £1,000 exemplary damages. The Court of Appeal upheld the award. Stephenson LJ (with whose judgment Sir David Cairns agreed) held that the evidence of trespass was thin, as there was little evidence of direct interference with the rooms occupied by the defendants; but the tort of nuisance had been *d* committed. He said (at 32):

'*Drane* v *Evangelou* ([1978] 2 All ER 437, [1978] 1 WLR 455) shows that exemplary damages are available to a tenant who is treated monstrously by a landlord where the case can be, and is, put in trespass. I would hold that it can also be available to a tenant where he can only, if that is his case, put his *e* case in nuisance. So I would allow the court to consider nuisance as a ground of the plaintiffs' liability, and accordingly to go on to consider whether the case is one for exemplary damages, as the learned judge thought.'

Once again the point was not argued that it was not open to the court to award exemplary damages for nuisance because there was no case of such an award before *Rookes v Barnard*. It seems to have been assumed that such an award could *f* be made because the circumstances were very akin to trespass and the case clearly fell within Lord Devlin's second category.

Accordingly, in my judgment there is no binding authority of this court which compels us to disregard the dicta of the House of Lords in *Cassell & Co Ltd v Broome* to which I have referred. And accordingly I would hold that before an *g* award of exemplary damages can be made by any court or tribunal the tort must be one in respect of which such an award was made prior to 1964.

Before I consider specifically whether nuisance was such a tort, I propose to deal shortly with the respondent's notice in which it is contended that exemplary damages can be awarded for negligence and breach of statutory duty created post-1964. The only case of negligence on which Mr Melville Williams relied was *h* *Emblen v Myers* (1860) 6 H & N 54, 158 ER 23. It does not assist the plaintiffs; it was regarded as a case of trespass by Lord Devlin for which aggravated and not exemplary damages were awarded: see *Rookes v Barnard* [1964] 1 All ER 367 at 408, 412, [1964] AC 1129 at 1223, 1229. The statutory duty relied upon in this case is created by the Consumer Protection Act 1987 and the Water Act 1945; in the former case there could not have been, and in the latter case there was not, an *j* award of exemplary damages before 1964.

Nuisance, unlike negligence and deceit, was not a tort specifically referred to by their Lordships in *Cassell & Co Ltd v Broome*. The question therefore whether or not exemplary damages were awarded for nuisance prior to 1964 depends on a proper view of *Bell v Midland Rly Co* (1861) 10 CBNS 287, 142 ER 462. The

a plaintiff had a statutory right to connect up railway tracks from his wharf to the defendants' line and to run waggons from his wharf on those lines. The defendants had built their own wharf and had blocked the plaintiff's access to the lines so that his tenants could not get their goods out and had in consequence left and gone to the defendants' wharf. The blockage occurred on the defendants' land. The plaintiff therefore had a statutory right of access which was akin to an

b easement or right of way. In breach of their statutory duty to allow access the defendants had blocked it. Wrongful interference with a right of way is a nuisance; and I think *Bell's* case may properly be regarded as a case of nuisance; but I do not find it necessary to decide the point, because I am quite satisfied that, if exemplary damages are to be awarded for nuisance, such awards should be

c confined to those cases of private nuisance where there is deliberate and wilful interference with the plaintiff's rights of enjoyment of land where the defendant has calculated that the profit or benefit for him will exceed the damages he may have to pay. The *Guppys (Bridport) Ltd* case is an excellent example of this. Where there has been a public nuisance, a plaintiff who can show particular damage can sue in tort. But it is an entirely different class of case; there is no conduct

d deliberately and wilfully aimed at the plaintiffs as individuals. There is no case prior to 1964 of exemplary damages being awarded to a plaintiff who proved particular damage resulting from a public nuisance; and I would not extend the remedy to such a case. The essence of public nuisance is that the defendant's conduct is unlawful and a crime in that his act or omission endangers the life, health, property, morals or comfort of the public or obstructs the public in the

e exercise or enjoyment of a right common to all Her Majesty's subjects; the public includes a class of the public. It is only actionable as a civil wrong when a private individual has suffered particular damage other than and beyond the general inconvenience and injury suffered by the public. In private nuisance, on the other hand, the conduct of the defendant which results in the nuisance is of itself not

f necessarily or usually unlawful. A private nuisance—

> 'may be and usually is caused by a person doing on his own land something which he is lawfully entitled to do. His conduct only becomes a nuisance when the consequences of his acts are not confined to his own land but extend to the land of his neighbour by (1) causing an encroachment on his neighbour's land, when it closely resembles trespass, (2) causing physical
>
> *g* damage to his neighbour's land or building or works or vegetation upon it, or (3) unduly interfering with his neighbour in the comfortable and convenient enjoyment of his land.' (See *Clerk and Lindsell on Torts* (16th edn, 1989) p 1356, para 24–03.)

If I am wrong in concluding that exemplary damages cannot be awarded where

h the claim is based on particular damage flowing from public nuisance, does the case fall within either of Lord Devlin's two categories? It is not clear from the judge's judgment into which of the two categories he thought this case fell or whether he thought it fell into both, since he does not expressly deal with the point. By implication he must have held that it was in one or other or both.

The first category is 'oppressive, arbitrary or unconstitutional action by the

j servants of the government'. It is common ground that this category of persons is not limited to the servants of central government, but includes servants of local government and the police.

In *Cassell & Co Ltd v Broome* [1972] 1 All ER 801 at 829–830, [1972] AC 1027 at 1077–1078 Lord Hailsham LC said:

'. . . I would be surprised if it included only servants of the government in the strict sense of the word. It would, in my view, obviously apply to the *a* police . . . and almost as certainly to local and other officials exercising improperly rights of search or arrest without warrant, and it may be that in the future it will be held to include other abuses of power without warrant by persons purporting to exercise legal authority.'

Lord Reid said ([1972] 1 All ER 801 at 838, [1972] AC 1027 at 1087–1088):   *b*

'With regard to the first I think that the context shows that the category was never intended to be limited to Crown servants. The contrast is between "the government" and private individuals. Local government is as much government as national government, and the police and many other persons are exercising governmental functions. It was unnecessary in *Rookes v Barnard* *c* to define the exact limits of the category. I should certainly read it as extending to all those who by common law or statute are exercising functions of a governmental character.'

Lord Wilberforce said ([1972] 1 All ER 801 at 865, [1972] AC 1027 at 1120):

'There is not perhaps much difficulty about category 1; it is well based on *d* the cases and on a principle stated in 1703—"if *public officers* will infringe men's rights, they ought to pay greater damages than other men to deter and hinder others from the like offences" (*Ashby v White* (1703) 2 Ld Raym 938 at 956, 92 ER 126 at 137 per Holt CJ). Excessive and insolent use of power is certainly something against which citizens require as much protection today; a wide interpretation of "government" which I understand your Lordships *e* to endorse would correspond with Holt CJ's "public officers" and would partly correspond with modern needs.' (Lord Wilberforce's emphasis.)

Lord Diplock said of the first category ([1972] 1 All ER 801 at 873, [1972] AC 1027 at 1130):
                                                                                f
'It would embrace all persons purporting to exercise powers of government, central or local, conferred on them by statute or at common law by virtue of the official status or employment which they held.'

In the court below Mr Symons had conceded that the defendants' servants might be within the first category. However before us he sought and was granted *g* leave to withdraw the concession. At the time of these events the defendants were a nationalised body set up under statute for a commercial purpose, namely the supply of water. They have since been privatised, but carry on essentially the same functions. Although it is conceivable that governmental functions could be delegated or entrusted to a nationalised industry with appropriate powers to carry out such functions, perhaps for example with powers of entry and search, I do not *h* think it can possibly be argued that the defendants' servants or agents were performing such a function in this case. A serious mishap had occurred in the course of the defendants' commercial operations, their reaction to it was open to serious criticism if the allegations in the statement of claim are true, as they must be assumed to be for the purpose of this case. But their conduct was not an exercise of executive power derived from government, central or local, and no *j* amount of rhetoric describing it as arbitrary, oppressive, unconstitutional, arrogant or high-handed makes it so. It would have been no different if the defendants had already been privatised and their servants were answerable to a board of directors and the shareholders rather than a board set up under statute.

a Mr Melville Williams sought to argue that, since the defendants could properly be regarded as an 'emanation of the state' for the purpose of direct enforcement of EEC Directives, it followed that the defendants' servants were exercising executive power as government servants when performing their function of supplying water, the subject matter of Council Directive (EEC) 80/778.

b I hope I do no injustice to the argument, which I found difficult to follow. There seems to me to be no logical nexus between the premise and the conclusion. I cannot see that it is arguable that the case falls within the first category.

c Lord Devlin's second category includes those cases in which the defendant's conduct has been calculated by him to make a profit for himself which may well exceed the compensation payable to the plaintiff. This category is not confined to money-making in the strict sense. It extends to cases in which the defendant is seeking to gain some object at the expense of the plaintiff which either he could not properly or lawfully gain at all or which he could only get at a price in excess of what he is prepared to pay. The cases of harassment of tenants in order to obtain possession of premises are a good example of this.

The relevant allegation in the statement of claim on which this claim is based is para 26, which is in these terms:

d
> 'The plaintiffs will, in the alternative, seek exemplary damages under the second limb of *Rookes v Barnard*, namely that the defendants conduct after 6th July 1988 was calculated by them to make a profit for themselves which may well exceed that payable to the plaintiffs. As to the particulars hereunder the plaintiffs aver that such a motive can properly be inferred from the *e* matters hereinbefore set out in paragraphs 19–24 inclusive.'

In my judgment this paragraph is totally lacking in particularity and is little more than an incantation of Lord Devlin's second category.

In argument Mr Melville Williams submitted that the following propositions could be derived from the matters pleaded in paras 19 to 24 which I have earlier *f* summarised: (1) that there was a deliberate decision to continue the nuisance by supplying impure water; (2) a recognition that that decision might involve the defendants in the payment of damages; (3) an inference that the defendants made a judgment that it would pay in a wide sense to commit the tort and pay damages.

He submitted that it was sufficient that there was some economic advantage *g* and he suggested that what he described as the preservation of economic or managerial reputation in the view of impending privatisation might be enough. I can see that steps (1) and (2) may be arguable. But I have great difficulty with step (3). The essence of the second category is that the tort is knowingly committed for the purpose of gaining some pecuniary or other advantage. The award is to show that tort does not pay. It cannot possibly be said that the *h* defendants continued the nuisance for this purpose. In my judgment what the allegation amounts to is an attempt by the defendants to cover up the fact that they had committed a tort. That may be reprehensible but not uncommon conduct. The object of such conduct may well be to limit the amount of damages payable to the victim, but that is an entirely different concept from that involved in the second category. In my judgment the case does not fall within either of the *j* two categories for which exemplary damages are awarded.

Finally, Mr Symons submitted that, even if the claim survived the first two arguments, which in my view it does not, this is not a case in which exemplary damages can be awarded, it being essentially an action for damages for personal injuries caused by breach of statutory duty and negligence. For my part I doubt

whether this submission really adds very much. If the case does not get through
the first two hoops, it plainly is not a case for exemplary damages.   *a*

There is however one aspect of the case which in my view makes it peculiarly
unsuitable for an award of exemplary damages, even if the first two hoops are
negotiated, and that is the number of plaintiffs. Unless all their claims are
quantified by the court at the same time, how is the court to fix and apportion
the punitive element of the damages? Should the court fix a global sum of £x
and divide it by 180, equally among the plaintiffs? Or should it be divided   *b*
according to the gravity of the personal injury suffered? Some plaintiffs may have '
been affected by the alleged oppressive, arbitrary, arrogant and high-handed
behaviour, others not. If the assessment is made separately at different times for
different plaintiffs, how is the court to know that the overall punishment is
appropriate? The point was touched on in *Riches v News Group Newspapers Ltd*
[1985] 2 All ER 845 at 856, [1986] QB 256 at 277 in the judgment of Stephenson   *c*
LJ. That was a libel case with ten plaintiffs where a very large sum had been
awarded as exemplary damages; the judge had not directed the jury how they
were to deal with the problem of a number of plaintiffs. Stephenson LJ
commented that the problem 'furnishes yet another complication engendered by
the survival of the right to exemplary damages and another argument in favour   *d*
of abolishing the right'.

In the present case there is the further complication to which I have already
referred of the conviction and fine of the defendants. These problems persuade
me that there would be a serious risk of injustice to the defendants in this case if
an award of exemplary damages were to be made against them. There is no
injustice to the plaintiffs in refusing to permit such an award; they are not   *e*
foregoing compensation to which they are entitled, but an additional windfall
based solely on the defendants' alleged improper conduct.

For all these reasons therefore I would strike out the claim to exemplary
damages.

I turn to the claim for aggravated damages. This is made in para 27 of the
statement of claim and is as follows: *f*

'Further, the plaintiffs will seek aggravated damages on the basis that their
feelings of indignation were justifiably aroused by the highhanded manner
in which the defendants dealt with the incident, as set out in paragraphs 19–
24 inclusive and, further, they continued to drink the water for longer than
would have been the case had the defendants reacted promptly, frankly and   *g*
efficiently.'

I have already cited the passage from the speech of Lord Devlin where he
explains what aggravated damages are. In my judgment if the plaintiffs
experienced greater or more prolonged pain and suffering because the nuisance
continued for longer than it should have done or they drank more contaminated   *h*
water with ill effect that is a matter for which they are entitled to be compensated
by way of general damages.

Likewise, if uncertainty as to the true position caused by the defendants' lack
of frankness following the initial incident led to real anxiety and distress, that is
an element for which they are entitled to compensation under general damages
for suffering. But anger and indignation is not a proper subject for compensation;   *j*
it is neither pain nor suffering. *Kralj v McGrath* [1986] 1 All ER 54 was a claim
for damages for personal injury resulting from medical negligence. There was a
claim for aggravated damages on the basis that the plaintiff had been subject to
outrageous treatment at the defendant's hands in the course of childbirth. Woolf
J said (at 61):

a 'It is my view that it would be wholly inappropriate to introduce into claims of this sort, for breach of contract and negligence, the concept of aggravated damages. If it were to apply in this situation of a doctor not treating a patient in accordance with his duty, whether under contract or in tort, then I would consider that it must apply in other situations where a person is under a duty to exercise care. It would be difficult to see why it could not even extend to cases where [actions for] damages are brought for

b personal injuries in respect of driving. If the principle is right, a higher award of damages would be appropriate in a case of reckless driving which caused injury than would be appropriate in cases where careless driving caused identical injuries. Such a result seems to me to be wholly inconsistent with the general approach to damages in this area, which is to compensate the

c plaintiff for the loss that she has actually suffered, so far as it is possible to do so, by the award of monetary compensation and not to treat those damages as being a matter which reflects the degree of negligence or breach of duty of the defendant.'

I agree. Accordingly, I would strike out para 27 of the statement of claim.

d

SIMON BROWN LJ. I agree.

SIR THOMAS BINGHAM MR. A defendant accused of crime may ordinarily

e be ordered (if convicted) to pay a financial penalty. In such a case he will enjoy the constitutional safeguards afforded to defendants in criminal cases, which may include trial by jury, and the sum he is ordered to pay is received by the state, not (even in the case of a private prosecution) by the prosecutor. In a civil case, arising out of a civil wrong (whether or not it is also a crime), the defendant may be ordered to pay damages. In the ordinary way, damages bear no resemblance to a

f criminal penalty. The damages awarded to a plaintiff will be such as will compensate him for the loss he has suffered as a result of the wrong, so far as money can. The court looks to the extent of the plaintiff's loss, not to the quality of the defendant's conduct. Since the damages are awarded to compensate the plaintiff they are of course paid to him.

g Exemplary (or, as they were once revealingly called, punitive) damages cut across this simple distinction. They are awarded in civil cases, so that the defendant does not enjoy the safeguards afforded to defendants in criminal cases including, save in a small minority of cases, trial by jury. They are paid to the plaintiff, not the state. But they are not paid to compensate the plaintiff, who will be fully compensated by the ordinary measure of damages. They are paid to

h punish or deter the defendant, to mark the disapproval which his conduct has provoked. For the plaintiff such damages represent a bonus, an addition to the sum needed to compensate him fully for the loss he has suffered as a result of the wrong done to him.

In his leading speech on this topic in *Rookes v Barnard* [1964] 1 All ER 367,

j [1964] AC 1129 Lord Devlin recognised the law on exemplary damages as anomalous. But he (and the other members of the House, all of whom agreed with him) did not think it open to them to refuse to recognise the exemplary principle and in any event held that there were certain classes of case in which it served a valuable purpose. So the House ruled that awards of exemplary damages should not be abolished but should be curtailed or restricted. The view which the House of Lords adopted was not an inevitable one. It has been the subject of

academic criticism and judicial reservation in this country, and courts in the
Commonwealth and the United States have taken a more expansive view. But the a
conclusion of the House did not lack a compelling rationale, and that the House
did intend to curtail or restrict awards of exemplary damages is not in my opinion
open to doubt. It is the extent of that curtailment or restriction which raises the
first, and major, issue in this appeal.

In his speech Lord Devlin was not, as I understand him, concerned to identify
certain causes of action which could and others which could not properly ground b
claims for exemplary damages. His focus was not on causes of action at all.
Rather, his concern was to identify those elements which had been present in
claims which had led to awards of exemplary damages in the past and which
served to justify retention of the principle. Statute apart, he identified two such
elements giving rise to two categories or classes of case.

In the first category there had been what he variously described as an 'arbitrary
and outrageous use of executive power' and 'oppressive, arbitrary or unconstitutional action by the servants of the government' (see [1964] 1 All ER 367 at 408,
410, [1964] AC 1129 at 1223, 1226). Minute textual analysis of these expressions
is inappropriate. This was a judgment, not a statute. But there can be no doubt
what Lord Devlin was speaking about. It was gross misuse of power, involving d
tortious conduct, by agents of government. According to the traditional
classification of the law of tort, such misuse of power could give rise to any one of
a number of causes of action, which Lord Devlin was not at pains to identify.

The second category covered cases in which the defendant had acted tortiously
on a calculation that the economic benefits to him of his unlawful conduct would
outweigh any compensation he might be liable to pay the injured party. The e
rationale underlying this category was clearly stated ([1964] 1 All ER 367 at 411,
[1964] AC 1129 at 1227): 'Exemplary damages can properly be awarded whenever
it is necessary to teach a wrongdoer that tort does not pay.' This again suggests
that it was the quality of the conduct complained of rather than the cause of
action pleaded which governed the right to claim exemplary damages.

Lord Devlin's speech in *Rookes v Barnard* was the subject of detailed exegesis by f
an enlarged Appellate Committee of the House of Lords in *Cassell & Co Ltd v
Broome* [1972] 1 All ER 801, [1972] AC 1027.

It appears to me that Lord Hailsham LC in his speech held or at least assumed
that it was not enough for a claim in tort to fall within one or other of
Lord Devlin's categories unless it was also founded on a cause of action recognised g
as grounding a claim for exemplary damages before *Rookes v Barnard*. This
assumption must, I think, underlie his view that Lord Devlin did not intend his
second category to extend to claims in deceit, although 'actions for deceit could
well come within the purview of the second category'. I think it must also
underlie his views that 'the second category was ample to cover any form of
injury committed within the scope of those torts for which ... exemplary h
damages may be awarded' and that exemplary damages might have been awarded
in *Mafo v Adams* [1969] 3 All ER 1404, [1970] 1 QB 548 if it had been shown that
the defendant was actuated by hope of gain 'and if the action had been one of
trespass' (see [1972] 1 All ER 801 at 828, 831, [1972] AC 1027 at 1076, 1079–
1080).

Lord Reid may have had the same idea in mind when holding it undesirable j
that the anomaly of exemplary damages should be permitted 'in any class of case
where its use was not covered by authority' (see [1972] 1 All ER 801 at 837, [1972]
AC 1027 at 1086).

The principle that exemplary damages may be awarded for some torts (falling
into the two classes) but not others is, I think, explicit in the speech of

a Lord Wilberforce when he referred to 'the range of torts for which punitive damages may be given (trespass to person or property, false imprisonment and defamation, being the commonest)' (see [1972] 1 All ER 801 at 860, [1972] AC 1027 at 1114). He also expressed general agreement with Lord Hailsham LC.

Lord Diplock dealt with this aspect as follows ([1972] 1 All ER 801 at 874, [1972] AC 1027 at 1130–1131):

b 'Finally, on this aspect of the case I would express my agreement with the view that *Rookes v Barnard* was not intended to extend the power to award exemplary . . . damages to particular torts for which they had not previously been awarded, such as negligence and deceit. Its express purpose was to restrict, not to expand, the anomaly of exemplary damages.'

c Lord Kilbrandon agreed with the speeches of Lord Hailsham LC and Lord Reid.

I cannot pretend to find the answer at all clear, but I incline to think that a majority of the House regarded an award of exemplary damages as permissible only where (a) a case fell within one or other of Lord Devlin's categories and (b) was founded on a tort for which exemplary damages had been awarded before *d* *Rookes v Barnard*. This may involve a misreading of their Lordships' speeches in *Cassell & Co Ltd v Broome*, but I think it is the basis upon which the Court of Appeal should, until corrected, proceed.

If it is correct to import a cause of action test, this court is bound to hold that the plaintiffs' claims in negligence cannot found a claim for exemplary damages even if they fall within one or other of Lord Devlin's categories. Our attention *e* has been drawn to no negligence claim leading to such an award before 1964 (or, I think, since). By contrast, I understand *Bell v Midland Rly Co* (1861) 10 CBNS 287, 142 ER 462, in which damages described as exemplary were awarded, to have been founded in private nuisance, possibly in addition to other causes of action. More recently, in *Guppys (Bridport) Ltd v Brookling, Guppys (Bridport) Ltd v James* (1983) 14 HLR 1 the Court of Appeal upheld an award of damages for *f* private nuisance, although the present issue was not raised or addressed.

It does not, however, appear that there has ever, before *Rookes v Barnard* or since, been an award of exemplary damages for public nuisance. In one sense, public nuisance is private nuisance writ large. But there are significant differences. First, the causing of a public nuisance in a number of its forms is a crime (and a crime for which, in this case, the defendants were prosecuted) which a private *g* nuisance will rarely, if ever, be. I describe this difference as significant because Lord Devlin in *Rookes v Barnard* [1964] 1 All ER 367 at 412, [1964] AC 1129 at 1230 regarded conduct falling within his two categories as not ordinarily falling within the criminal law. He would plainly have regarded the award of exemplary damages as even more anomalous in cases where the conduct in question already *h* attracted the sanctions of the criminal law. Secondly, a public nuisance may lead to numerous complainants, which a private nuisance will not. I describe this difference as significant because it highlights an obvious and intractable difficulty: in the case of a public nuisance affecting hundreds or even thousands of plaintiffs, how can the court assess the sum of exemplary damages to be awarded to any one of them to punish or deter the defendant without knowing at the outset the *j* number of successful plaintiffs and the approximate size of the total bill for exemplary damages which the defendant must meet? If, as I think, a claim in public nuisance falls foul of the cause of action test, assuming there is one, these seem to me good reasons for holding that it will not support an award of exemplary damages.

It is, however, necessary to consider whether the plaintiffs' claims for exemplary damages, if otherwise good on the facts as pleaded, fall within one or other or both of Lord Devlin's two categories.   *a*

In contending that the facts pleaded bring the case within the first category (abuse of power), the plaintiffs naturally relied on Lord Hailsham LC's broad approach in considering what bodies might count as 'emanations of government' for purposes of this principle (see *Cassell & Co Ltd v Broome* [1972] 1 All ER 801 at 829, [1972] AC 1027 at 1077). The defendants were at first prepared to accept, as they did before the judge, that they were a body falling within the category   *b* although, at the prompting of the court, they qualified that concession. I do not for my part find it helpful, in considering whether they fall within the rule or not, to inquire whether they are a body whose decisions are judicially reviewable in public law, or whether they are a body through which the United Kingdom performs its obligations in Community law. We are here concerned with a judge-   *c* made principle of domestic private law, devised to address a particular problem, and other rules arising in different contexts seem to me to have little bearing. If the defendants' conduct was as pleaded, as we must for present purposes assume, it was highly reprehensible, but the conduct complained of was quite unlike the abuses of power which Lord Devlin had in mind and I cannot regard the defendants, for any purposes relevant to these claims, as wielding executive or   *d* governmental power. They were a publicly owned utility acting as monopoly supplier of a necessary commodity, enjoying certain statutory powers and subject to certain obligations, but they were not acting as an instrument or agent of government. I regard this case as falling well outside the first category.

The plaintiffs have not in my opinion pleaded a claim arguably falling within the second category either. It is true that the defendants' conduct is said, in   *e* para 26 of the master statement of claim, to have been 'calculated by them to make a profit for themselves which may well exceed that payable to the plaintiffs'. This is plainly directed towards establishing a second category claim. But it is, as it stands, bare assertion, and for particulars of the facts from which the necessary motive can be inferred reference is made to paras 19 to 24. Paragraph 19 pleads that the defendants misunderstood the gravity of the contamination. It is thus   *f* inconsistent with the calculation inherent in second category cases. Paragraphs 20, 21 and 23, suggesting that the public and the health authorities were denied information and given misinformation, give no particulars of how, or why, or by whom on their behalf, the defendants judged these tortious acts to be economically advantageous. Paragraphs 22 and 23 allege that the defendants deliberately   *g* allowed the public to consume water which the defendants knew to be contaminated, with a proportionately greater and more widespread injury to health, but again give no particulars of how, or why, or by whom on their behalf, the defendants judged these tortious acts to be economically advantageous. The paragraphs referred to do not in my opinion contain facts from which the necessary inference could be drawn. The plaintiffs say that when they obtain   *h* discovery they will either obtain material to support the allegation or they will drop it. That is not in my view a correct approach. Unless the plaintiffs already have enough material to plead a plausible (even if incomplete) case, the pleading should not be allowed to stand. It is not permissible to plead a bare assertion in the hope that material to support it will turn up on discovery.

I turn, lastly, to the claim in para 27 of the master statement of claim for   *j* aggravated damages. The plaintiffs are of course entitled to be fully compensated for all they suffered as a direct result of the defendants' admitted breach of duty. The ordinary measure of compensatory damages will cover all they have suffered as a result of that breach, physically, psychologically and mentally. Full account will be taken of the distress and anxiety which such an event necessarily causes.

To the extent that any of these effects was magnified or exacerbated by the
a defendants' conduct, the ordinary measure of damages will compensate. The
question is whether, in addition to that full compensatory measure, the plaintiffs
have pleaded a sustainable claim for additional compensation by way of aggravated
damages. This is claimed in para 27 on the basis that the plaintiffs' feelings of
indignation were aroused by the defendants' high-handed way of dealing with
the incident. I know of no precedent for awarding damages for indignation
b aroused by a defendant's conduct. Defamation cases in which a plaintiff's damages
are increased by the defendant's conduct of the litigation (as by aggressive cross-
examination of the plaintiff or persistence in a groundless plea of justification) are
not in my view a true exception, since injury to the plaintiff's feelings and self-
esteem is an important part of the damage for which compensation is awarded.
c In very many other tort actions (and, for that matter, actions in contract, boundary
disputes, partnership actions and other disputes) the plaintiff is indignant at the
conduct of the defendant (or his insurers). An award of damages does not follow;
nor, in my judgment should it, since this is not damage directly caused by the
defendant's tortious conduct and this is not damage which the law has ever
recognised.

d   Despite the learned judge's thoughtful and thorough judgment, I have in the
end reached a different view and concluded that paras 18 to 27 of the master
statement of claim should be struck out. But I agree with his conclusion that in
the special circumstances of this case it is appropriate to decide the issues of law
raised by these paragraphs at this early stage. Ordinarily, I would prefer to wait
until the facts had been investigated. The issues of law might not then arise. If
e they did, they could be decided on the reality of established facts and not the
hypothesis of assumed facts. I am persuaded that here the legal decision should
not await investigation of the facts, for three reasons. (1) The defendants having
admitted liability, the parties wish to settle but cannot do so while they continue
to differ on the appropriate measure of damage. It is desirable that they should be
guided on the appropriate measure to facilitate the negotiation of early settlements.
f (2) Discovery relevant to these issues is likely to be a laborious, costly and time-
consuming process. If the issues do not arise, it is undesirable that the process be
embarked upon. (3) The full trial of even one test case (with the attendant appeals)
would be costly and would delay resolution of all the other claims. Both cost and
delay are better avoided.

g   I therefore conclude that this court would be failing in its duty if it did not
grasp the nettle and give its answer to these legal problems.

For these reasons, as well as those which Stuart-Smith LJ has given, I would
allow the defendants' appeal.

Appeal allowed. Leave to appeal to the House of Lords refused.

Frances Rustin   Barrister.

Re Jokai Tea Holdings Ltd

a

COURT OF APPEAL, CIVIL DIVISION

SIR NICOLAS BROWNE-WILKINSON V-C, PARKER LJ AND SIR JOHN MEGAW

30, 31 JANUARY, 1, 15 FEBRUARY 1989

Practice – Order – 'Unless' orders and other peremptory orders – Non-compliance with *b*
'unless' order – Consequences – Non-compliance with order striking out claim or defence
unless act done within specified time – Whether pleading should be struck out if failure to
comply with 'unless' order not contumacious.

Where the court has to decide what consequences should follow from non-
compliance with an order that a pleading be struck out unless further and better *c*
particulars are served within a specified time, the relevant question is whether
such failure to comply with the 'unless' order is intentional and contumacious.
The court should not be astute to find excuses for such failure since obedience to·
peremptory orders of the court is the foundation of its authority, but, if the non-
complying party can clearly demonstrate that there was no intention to ignore or *d*
flout the order and that the failure to obey was due to extraneous circumstances,
the failure ought not to be treated as contumacious and ought not to disentitle
him to rights which he would otherwise have enjoyed (see p 636 *f*, p 637 *d*, p 639
j and p 641 *b c e h*, post).

Janov v Morris [1981] 3 All ER 780 considered.

e

Notes

For 'unless' orders, see 37 *Halsbury's Laws* (4th edn) para 32, and for cases on the
subject, see 37(2) *Digest* (Reissue) 200–202, *1319–1336*.

Cases referred to in judgments

Allen v Sir Alfred McAlpine & Sons Ltd [1968] 1 All ER 543, [1968] 2 QB 229, *f*
[1968] 2 WLR 366, CA.

Birkett v James [1977] 2 All ER 801, [1978] AC 297, [1977] 3 WLR 38, CA and
HL.

Janov v Morris [1981] 3 All ER 780, [1981] 1 WLR 1389, CA.

Samuels v Linzi Dresses Ltd [1980] 1 All ER 803, [1981] QB 115, [1980] 2 WLR
836, CA.

g

Tolley v Morris [1979] 2 All ER 561, [1979] 1 WLR 592, HL.

Cases also cited

Husband's of Marchwood Ltd v Drummond Walker Developments Ltd [1975] 2 All ER
30, [1975] 1 WLR 603, CA.

h

Snell v Unity Finance Co Ltd [1963] 3 All ER 50, [1964] 2 QB 203, CA.

Interlocutory appeal

The defendants, Jokai Tea Holdings Ltd (Jokai) and Frendial Ltd, appealed from
the decision of Mervyn Davies J given on 4 February 1988 whereby he gave
judgment for the plaintiffs, Punjab National Bank (the bank), where principal *j*
place of business was in New Delhi, India in its action seeking rectification of the
register of members of Jokai by striking out Frendial as the holder of 999 ordinary
shares of 1p each and 1,484,251 deferred ordinary shares of 70p each in Jokai and
substituting the name of the bank as the holder of the shares, and ordered
rectification of the register as sought, on the grounds that the defendants had

failed to comply with an order made by Mr Registrar Scott on 9 November 1987
a ordering the defendants to serve further and better particulars of their defence
within 56 days in default of which the points of defence should be struck out and
the bank should be at liberty to apply for judgment. The facts are set out in the
judgment of Sir Nicolas Browne-Wilkinson V-C.

b Allan Heyman QC and Daniel Serota (instructed by D J Freeman & Co) for the
defendants.
J M Chadwick QC and Mark Phillips (instructed by Slaughter & May) for the bank.

Cur adv vult

c 15 February 1989. The following judgments were delivered.

SIR NICOLAS BROWNE-WILKINSON V-C. In this case Punjab National
Bank (the bank) seek an order against Jokai Tea Holdings Ltd (Jokai) and Frendial
Ltd (Frendial) for the rectification of the register of members of Jokai by striking
out Frendial as the holder of 999 ordinary shares of 1p each and 1,484,251
d deferred ordinary shares of 70p each in Jokai and by inserting the name of the
bank as the holder of the shares.
    Although the questions for our decision are procedural, to understand them it
is necessary to refer in outline to the complicated background facts. Esal
(Commodities) Ltd (Esal) is a United Kingdom company. The moving spirits
e behind Esal were two brothers, Rajendra and Ranjit Sethia. Esal went into
liquidation on 7 November 1984 with an estimated deficiency of some £200m.
The joint liquidators of Esal are Mr Weiss and Mr Jordan, both of whom are
partners in Messrs Cork Gully.
    Before the liquidation of Esal, the bank acted as one of its bankers. Most of the
dealings were between Esal and the London office of the bank. The bank has
f lodged proofs for debt in the liquidation of Esal at a figure of approximately
£92m. There is substantial evidence that Rajendra Sethia was guilty of fraud.
One employee of the bank has been convicted of falsification of documents
relating to Esal. The former manager of the London office of the bank has been
charged in India with offences relating to Esal's accounts but not, so we
understand, offences relating to the particular transactions in question in this case.
g There is substantial evidence that the bank's documents at the London office are
suspect and that information relating to the affairs of Esal was suppressed by the
London office of the bank in its dealings with the head office of the bank in India.
    The particular transactions in question in these proceedings are as follows. Esal
had a subsidiary, Shadereed Ltd (Shadereed). On 20 May 1981 Shadereed acquired
h all the shares in Frendial for £3·65m. Frendial had a subsidiary, Jokai. Jokai in
turn had a subsidiary, Jokai India Ltd, which owned and conducted a tea
plantation in India, the present value of which is estimated at between $US30 and
$US35m. The purchase of the shares in Frendial was financed by Esal, who for
that purpose borrowed $US6·241m from the bank. The method by which that
borrowing took place was complex, possibly deliberately. On 16 September 1981
j Frendial (the company whose shares had been bought in May of that year) entered
into a guarantee securing to the bank the repayment of $US6·25m loaned to Esal.
That guarantee was secured by a charge granted by Frendial on the shares in Jokai
(the 1981 charge). By a further charge carrying the date 27 January 1984 Frendial
granted a further charge over the same shares in favour of the bank to secure
further lending to Esal (the 1984 charge).

By these proceedings, the bank, as mortgagee, seeks to secure its registration as the holder of the shares. In the past, there has been much confusion as to whether *a* Shadereed held the shares in Frendial beneficially or (as the Sethia brothers alleged) as nominees for them personally. Though little is clear in this confused case, it does now seem that it is accepted that Shadereed holds the shares in Frendial beneficially and that accordingly, indirectly, the Indian tea plantation is one of the few valuable assets available to the liquidators of Esal, subject to the claim of the bank as mortgagee of the shares in Jokai. The issue in this case, therefore, is *b* between the bank, as alleged secured creditor and chargee of the shares in Frendial, and the liquidators of Esal.

Originally the board of Frendial comprised two nominees of Esal and two nominees of Ranjit Sethia (Mr Kini and Mr Sen). The Esal nominees resigned in February 1984, with the result that when the joint liquidators of Esal were *c* appointed in January 1985 the only directors of Frendial were two nominees of Ranjit Sethia. On 22 April 1985 two members of Cork Gully, Mr London and Mr Rishi, were appointed directors of Frendial to represent the interests of the joint liquidators of Esal. But it appears that the conduct of these proceedings was left to Mr Kini and Mr Sen, who were giving instructions to Frendial's then solicitors, Messrs Zaiwalla & Co. There was a manifest deadlock on the board of Frendial *d* since Mr London and Mr Rishi were looking after the interests of Esal whereas Mr Kini and Mr Sen were looking after the interests of Ranjit Sethia, who claimed to be a beneficial owner of the shares in Frendial. This deadlock and conflict was not resolved until Shadereed was put into liquidation and Mr Hughes and Mr Copp were appointed joint liquidators; on 12 October 1987 they then appointed themselves to the board of Frendial. Therefore from 12 October 1987 onwards *e* there was a majority on the board of Frendial representing the interests of the joint liquidators of Esal.

There is one further background matter which I must mention. In the summer of 1986 the bank entered into direct negotiations with Ranjit Sethia. These negotiations led to an agreement dated 16 June 1986 (the confidential agreement). *f* Under that agreement Ranjit was released from all his personal obligations to the bank under various guarantees and agreements. In return he agreed to use his best endeavours to secure the bank's registration as holder of the shares in Jokai. It was a term of the agreement that it should remain confidential to the parties: it was unknown to the liquidators of Esal and to the members of the board of Frendial until, I believe, January 1988. The position therefore was that the two *g* nominees of Ranjit Sethia on the board of Frendial were ostensibly resisting the claim of the bank to registration at the same time as Ranjit Sethia himself was under an obligation to use his best endeavours to secure the bank's registration as holder of the shares.

Against that background I can turn to the procedural history of the case. On 30 April 1985 the bank issued its originating motion for rectification of the register. *h* Substantial evidence was sworn on both sides. The case at that stage being made on behalf of the respondents to the motion, Frendial and Jokai (the defendants), was that the Frendial shares belonged beneficially not to Shadereed but to the Sethia brothers and that accordingly the 1981 and 1984 charges were invalid. On 20 November 1985 Hoffmann J ordered the matter to proceed on pleadings. Points of claim were served on 11 December 1985 and points of defence on 2 *j* January 1986. The defence served put forward two grounds of defence, viz (1) that the Sethia brothers were the beneficial owners and therefore the charges were not entered into bona fide for the benefit of Frendial and (2) that the 1984 charge was granted on 30 January 1984 (not 27 January 1984 as it was dated) after the

granting of a Mareva injunction restraining the disposal of assets. On 28 January
1986 points of reply were served. Thereafter no further steps were taken in the
proceedings by the bank for nearly a year.

On 23 January 1986 the bank served a request for further and better particulars
of the defence. Although the requests were copious, none of them related to the
defence alleging the invalidity of the 1984 charge by reason of the Mareva
injunction. The request for particulars was not answered. On 10 August 1987 the
bank issued a summons asking for an order for the particulars. On 14 October
the time was extended by consent until 6 November 1987. Particulars not having
been given by 6 November, the summons was restored and came before Mr
Registrar Scott on 9 November 1987. He ordered the further and better particulars
to be served within 56 days and ordered that in default the points of defence
should be struck out and the bank should be at liberty to apply for the relief
claimed in the originating notice of motion. I will call this order 'the unless
order'.

The defendants' solicitors, still Zaiwalla & Co, wrote to Mr London to tell him
of the making of the unless order; most unfortunately that letter specified that
the time limit expired on 15 January 1988, whereas in truth the 56 days expired
on 5 January 1988. That error was not corrected until 30 December 1987. In the
meantime it had been arranged that there should be a meeting of the board of
Frendial on 4 January 1988 to consider the matter.

On 4 January 1988 (ie one day before the expiry of the 56 days) the defendants
issued a summons to extend the time for complying with the request for further
and better particulars, for a stay of the unless order and for leave to amend their
defence 'due to further documents now being made available to the liquidators'.
Although the amended points of defence were said to be annexed to the summons,
they were not so annexed. On 5 January 1988 the bank restored its originating
notice of motion for judgment. On 12 and 13 January 1988 further and better
particulars of the existing points of defence were served. The matters came before
Mervyn Davies J effectively on 27 January 1988. On that morning the defendants'
proposed amendments to the points of defence were for the first time produced
to the bank.

The proposed amended points of defence abandoned the whole of the existing
defence, with the exception of the allegation that the 1984 charge was void as
being in breach of the Mareva injunction. In its place there was substituted a new
defence. Shortly stated, the defence was that the 1981 and 1984 charges were
unlawful as being in breach of s 54 of the Companies Act 1948 and its statutory
successor, ie that by granting the charges Frendial was giving financial assistance
for the purchase of its own shares in that it was giving security for the repayment
of the loan made by the bank to Esal for the purchase of the Frendial shares by
Shadereed. The possibility of such a defence being raised had been ventilated a
considerable time before. However it will be appreciated that until 12 October
1987 the liquidators of Esal were not in control of the affairs of the defendants to
the bank's application, ie Frendial and Jokai.

On 4 February 1988 Mervyn Davies J gave judgment for the bank and ordered
rectification of the register. The defendants, Frendial and Jokai, appeal against
that decision.

The judge was faced with a difficult question. On the one side, the defendants
were in plain breach of the unless order. As a result, by operation of the unless
order itself, the existing defence of the defendants had been struck out and, in the
absence of any defence, the bank was plainly entitled to be registered as the holder
of the shares. On the other hand, the defendants had made an application for

leave to amend their defence by abandoning all those paragraphs of which
particulars had been ordered and which they had singularly failed to give, and   *a*
raising a different defence. Before the judge, they did not ask to be allowed to
serve the further particulars out of time since it was pointless for them to do so.
In the circumstances the judge formulated the question for his decision in the
following way:

> 'The question for the court is whether or not the bank is entitled to   *b*
> judgment by reason of the [defendants'] breach of the 56-day order; if not,
> whether the [defendants] should have leave to amend the defence in the way
> proposed. So I proceed to consider whether or not the bank is entitled to
> judgment by reason of the breach.'

The judge then directed himself by reference to the judgment of Roskill LJ in   *c*
Samuels v Linzi Dresses Ltd [1980] 1 All ER 803 at 812, [1981] QB 115 at 126:

> 'In my judgment, therefore, the law today is that a court has power to
> extend the time where an "unless" order has been made but not been
> complied with; but that it is a power which should be exercised cautiously
> and with due regard to the necessity for maintaining the principle that orders   *d*
> are made to be complied with and not to be ignored. Primarily, it is a
> question for the discretion of the master or the judge in chambers whether
> the necessary relief should be granted or not.'

The judge then said that it was 'plain that in this case the bank is entitled to
judgment by reason of the breach of the 56-day order if one considers the matter   *e*
simply on the basis put forward by the bank'. He pointed out that there was a
breach, that particulars had been sought since 23 January 1987, that extensions of
time had been given and that the unless order had been made on 9 November
and had not been complied with.

Having reached the conclusion that the bank was plainly entitled to judgment
'on the basis put forward by the bank', he continued: *f*

> 'However, that plain position is complicated by the fact that [the
> defendants] now wish to substitute a new defence. It is difficult to see why
> [the defendants], having ignored a court order during a time when they
> could have come to the court and asked for leave to amend, should now have
> the indulgence of not only being excused their breach of the order but also   *g*
> being allowed to amend so late and in so radical a fashion. Be that as it may,
> I think the right course for me to take is to consider the proposed defence on
> the footing that, if it shows, albeit late, that there is perhaps a truly arguable
> case for [the defendants], it may be right not to give judgment for the bank
> but instead to allow the new defence out of time on some such term as that
> [the defendants] pay the costs to date.'   *h*

The judge then proceeded to consider whether on the evidence before him a
truly arguable case had been shown. He said:

> 'All I can do is to consider whether or not [the defendants'] assertions have
> some reasonable prospect of acceptance at trial, bearing in mind that the   *j*
> assertions must be proved with some particularity in light of the fact that the
> activity mentioned in s 54 involves the commission of a criminal offence.'

He then considered the material before him and expressed his conclusion as
follows:

'Weighing the considerations put forward for [the defendants] against those put forward for the bank, I am driven to the conclusion that the chances of [the defendants] placing a s 54 taint on the bank's charges are slight. That, however, is not to say that [the defendants'] case is unarguable. With oral evidence and accountancy explanations of the records available, it may be possible to show matters in another light. However, again, that possibility does not, I think, in itself justify allowing the new defence in the circumstances of this case, that is to say where there has been a breach of an unless order.'

He then turned 'in this doubtful frame of mind' to certain other considerations.

The first of those other considerations was the deadlock on the board of Frendial. He pointed out that, since 12 October 1987, that deadlock had been at an end and that the three professional directors who were in the majority on the board ought to have been well aware of the making of the unless order and ought to have appreciated its importance. He relied on the fact that, within the 56-day period limited by the unless order, the board of Frendial had taken no steps to explain their position to the court. He also noted that the defendants' counsel had relied for their submission respecting s 54 far more heavily on documents which had been available to them at all times than on documents that only became available to them on 13 January 1988 in the circumstances I will mention later. He said that there was some basis for the bank's submission that the internal difficulties of Frendial ought not to operate to the prejudice of the bank. He further took into account the fact that Frendial was without assets apart from the Jokai shares, which meant that if the bank were to succeed at trial its costs would have to come out of the Jokai shares. Finally he dealt with the submission that the action should be allowed to proceed on the terms that the defendants should be ordered to pay some of the costs already incurred by the bank and noted that, although a suggestion of some guarantee for immediate payment had been made both by counsel for the defendants and by the judge himself, no concrete proposal had been forthcoming.

The judge concluded by saying that he had taken those considerations into account as well as the many other observations made by counsel. In the result he reached the conclusion that 'my discretion should be exercised in favour of the bank'.

It is common ground that the judge was right in treating the matter as being within his discretion. As Mr Chadwick QC, for the bank, has rightly stressed, it follows that this court has no right to intervene and substitute its own decision unless in some way the judge misdirected himself with regard to the principles to be applied or, in exercising his discretion, has taken into account matters which he ought not to have done or has failed to take into account matters which he ought to have done, or if the decision of the judge is plainly wrong. Therefore the first, and basic, question is whether the judge erred in one or other of those ways in exercising his discretion.

The judge started by asking himself whether the bank was entitled to judgment 'by reason of' the defendants' default in complying with the unless order; on his formulation of the question, in his view the question whether the defendants should have leave to amend only arose if the bank was not so entitled. The judge never in fact decided whether leave to amend should be given, though he considered the virtues of amendment in the course of deciding the first question. Having reached the prima facie view that the bank was entitled to judgment, the judge then went on to consider whether the application for leave to amend and the other factors mentioned at the end of his judgment rebutted that prima facie

conclusion. On this approach, the judge only considered the excuses put forward
for failure to comply with the unless order as one of the extra factors taken into *a*
account by him at the end of his judgment.

In my view, the questions the judge posed for himself were wrong in law.
Even if the bank were entitled to judgment, on no footing would that be 'by
reason of' the failure to comply with the unless order: the bank's entitlement
would be by reason of having proved its claim in the absence of a defence. The
judge's second question (should there be leave to amend the defence?) is prefaced *b*
by the words 'if not': ie the question of leave to amend only arose if the bank
were not entitled to judgment. At first sight these are purely semantic objections,
since the judge did go on to consider the factors relevant to leave to amend. But
in my judgment, by posing the questions in this way, the judge was led to an
erroneous approach in substance. He did in fact reach a prima facie view that the *c*
bank was entitled to judgment, the reasons given by him all relating to the
defendants' failure to comply with the unless order and not the strength of the
bank's case. Having reached that prima facie view he proceeded to consider the
other factors.

On the evidence before him, the bank was manifestly entitled to judgment on
its claim as mortgagee if there were no defence impugning the validity of the *d*
charges. Therefore the essential question was whether the defendants should have
leave to amend so as to raise such a defence. The failure to comply with the unless
order was a relevant factor in considering the question of leave to amend (not the
bank's entitlement to judgment in the absence of a defence) and it was impossible
to consider the bank's right to judgment and form a prima facie view on that
issue without deciding whether leave to amend should be given. On that analysis *e*
the judge was bound to consider whether leave to amend should be given before,
or at least concurrently with, the question whether the bank was entitled to
judgment.

Two differing principles of law are applicable in this case, viz: (1) that a litigant
is not to be deprived of a trial of his real case by the refusal of leave to amend *f*
unless such amendment will give rise to uncompensatable damage to the other
party; (2) that a litigant who fails to comply with a peremptory order of the court
will not normally be permitted to continue to litigate either that or any other
action based on the same claim or defence. The judge did not in terms refer to
the first of those principles, nor does his approach suggest that he had it in mind.
The question is how those two principles are to be reconciled in the present case. *g*

In *Samuels v Linzi Dresses Ltd* [1980] 1 All ER 803, [1981] QB 115 the court did
not give any direct guidance as to the approach to the exercise of the court's
discretion in cases where a claim or defence has been struck out by reason of a
failure to comply with an unless order beyond saying that such a discretion should
be exercised 'cautiously'. However, Roskill LJ referred to the analogous case
where the question is whether a plaintiff's claim should be struck out for want of *h*
prosecution, to which the principles laid down in *Birkett v James* [1977] 2 All ER
801, [1978] AC 297 apply. The first class of case considered in *Birkett v James* is
where the plaintiff has been guilty of 'intentional and contumelious conduct'.
Disobedience to a peremptory order is 'generally' to be treated as contumelious
conduct: see *Tolley v Morris* [1979] 2 All ER 561 at 571, [1979] 1 WLR 592 at 603
per Lord Diplock. Where there has been such contumelious disobedience not *j*
only the plaintiff's original action but also any subsequent action brought by him
based on the same cause of action will be struck out: see *Janov v Morris* [1981] 3
All ER 780, [1981] 1 WLR 1389. The basis of the principle is that orders of the
court must be obeyed and that a litigant who deliberately and without proper

excuse disobeys such an order is not allowed to proceed. The rationale of such

a penalty being that it is contumelious to flout the order of the court, if a party can explain convincingly that outside circumstances account for the failure to obey the peremptory order and that there was no deliberate flouting of the court's order, his conduct is not contumelious and therefore the consequences of contumely do not flow.

b In *Janov v Morris* a plaintiff whose first action had been struck out for failure to comply with an unless order brought a second action based on the same cause of action. The basis of the decision was that the failure to comply with the peremptory order was contumacious: see per Watkins LJ ([1981] 3 All ER 780 at 785, [1981] 1 WLR 1389 at 1395). It is clear that the court, in reaching the conclusion that the conduct was contumacious, placed much reliance on the fact that no explanation or excuse had been given by the plaintiff for his disobedience

c to the order.

In my judgment, in cases in which the court has to decide what are the consequences of a failure to comply with an unless order, the relevant question is whether such failure is intentional and contumelious. The court should not be astute to find excuses for such failure since obedience to orders of the court is the

d foundation on which its authority is founded. But, if a party can clearly demonstrate that there was no intention to ignore or flout the order and that the failure to obey was due to extraneous circumstances, such failure to obey is not to be treated as contumelious and therefore does not disentitle the litigant to rights which he would otherwise have enjoyed.

The questions therefore which arise in the present case are whether, apart from

e the defendants' conduct in failing to comply with the unless order, leave to amend the defence should be given and, if so, whether such failure to comply was contumelious. The judge did not approach the case in that way and, in my judgment, erred in principle. We must therefore exercise the discretion ourselves.

As to the first of those questions, the action has proceeded to close of pleadings, but discovery has not taken place. This is not, as the judge suggested, a very late

f application for leave to amend, fundamental though the proposed amendments are. On normal principles, leave to amend would be given provided that such leave did not cause the bank uncompensatable damage and the proposed amendment raises an arguable defence.

Mr Chadwick for the bank relies on three points showing uncompensatable

g damage. First, it is said that all the costs of the proceedings to date would be thrown away and, even if an order for payment of such costs is imposed as a condition of leave, it will be enforceable only against Frendial (which has no assets apart from the Jokai shares claimed by the bank) or against Jokai itself. Mr Heyman QC met this objection by agreeing that a condition of leave should be that the costs thrown away should be paid forthwith and the leave should be

h conditional on £50,000 being paid into court within 28 days as security for the payment of such costs. In my judgment, this offer meets the first point.

Next, Mr Chadwick urges that the need for the bank to continue litigation against these defendants and thereby incur further irrecoverable costs in the future gives rise to uncompensatable damage. But this consequence flows from the bank being forced to bring proceedings against these defendants at all and

j does not flow from the giving of leave to amend.

Thirdly, Mr Chadwick submits that by reason of the delay caused by the opening up of the new s 54 defence the bank, if ultimately successful, will have been kept out of its money for a further period whilst having to borrow like sums at interest from other parties. The 1981 and 1984 charges secure 'all moneys' due

from Esal to the bank and the amount of the debt far exceeds the value of the
Jokai shares. Therefore, it is said, the delay will lead to further loss. This point **a**
was not taken below, is not the subject of a respondent's notice and gives rise to a
number of factual issues which have not been dealt with on the evidence. In my
judgment, it is not right to allow the bank to raise this issue at this stage.

Is the s 54 defence sought to be raised by the amended defence arguable? The
judge held that there was an arguable case that the 1981 charge was given as
security for the repayment of moneys borrowed by Esal for the purchase of **b**
Frendial. The bank does not dispute this. At the hearing, we investigated at some
length the documentary evidence bearing on the issue to see if the judge was
right in saying that the chances of the defence succeeding were slight. In my
judgment, in the circumstances of this case, it is impossible to form any concluded
view on the matter given the limited material before the court and the **c**
background of possible fraud and falsification of the records of the London office
of the bank. Nor, on the view I take of the case, is it appropriate for the court on
an application for leave to amend to do more than satisfy itself that the case
sought to be raised is fairly arguable.

The position as to the 1984 charge is different. The judge took the view that if,
at the trial, the 1981 charge was found to be unlawful under s 54 the same would **d**
probably apply to the 1984 charge. At present I find some difficulty in seeing
how this result would follow, since the 1984 charge appears to have nothing to
do with the money borrowed to buy the Frendial shares. Mr Chadwick sought to
reopen the question whether there was an arguable case as to the invalidity of the
1984 charge. If the 1984 charge is valid, that is sufficient to entitle the bank, as
mortgagee, to be registered as holder of Jokai shares, even if the 1981 charge is **e**
invalid. Again, the bank has not served a respondent's notice that the judge's
finding on this point was to be challenged. Mr Chadwick's submissions gave rise
to further arguments by Mr Heyman that the 1984 charge was invalid for quite
other reasons, namely misrepresentation. In my judgment, it is not right, in the
absence of a respondent's notice, to permit the bank to challenge this finding of **f**
the judge since it opens up new areas of investigation. Moreover, the defence
based on the allegation that the 1984 charge was granted in breach of the Mareva
injunction has at all times been pleaded in the defence and cannot be decided
without a full investigation of surrounding circumstances.

The remaining question is whether the defendants' failure to comply with the
unless order is contumelious and that, in consequence, in the exercise of our **g**
discretion we should debar them from putting forward an amended defence. In
my judgment, there is no question of the conduct being contumelious down to
12 October 1987. At all relevant times down to that date the board of Frendial
was deadlocked and the de facto control of the litigation appears to have been in
the hands of Ranjit's nominee, Mr Rani. The bank had chosen to enter into the
confidential agreement with Ranjit which required him to support the bank's **h**
claim and not to resist it. Mr Chadwick did not seek to rely on the defendants'
conduct before 12 October 1987 as a reason for refusing them leave to amend.

What of the position after 12 October 1987? The unless order was made on
9 November 1987 but the directors of Frendial were misled by the letter from
their solicitors giving the date of expiry of the 56-day period as being 15 January
instead of 5 January. The necessary board meeting to consider the raising of the **j**
new defence had been called for 4 January 1988. As soon as the true position was
brought to the attention of the board, the defendants' summons for a stay and for
leave to amend was issued. That was on 4 January, that is to say one day before
the unless order expired and the original defence was struck out.

It may be thought that the defendants were in any event rather lax in not
a taking earlier steps either to comply with the unless order or to apply for leave to
amend. But there is another factor which affected the position. The present
proceedings are only one of the disputes between the bank and the joint liquidators
of Esal. As a result of the examination in the liquidation of Esal of Mr Golani (the
present manager of the London office of the bank) the liquidators of Esal had
been provided by the bank with over 30,000 documents. The use which could be
b made of such documents by the liquidators was limited by agreement between
the parties and by order of the court. The bank were concerned that the
documents so obtained should not be disclosed to third parties or used for
improper purposes. The liquidators of Esal desired to disclose certain of those
documents to the directors of Frendial, taking the view that the documents would
assist Frendial in defending these proceedings by raising the s 54 defence. On 26
c November 1987 the joint liquidators sought the bank's consent to make such
disclosure. On 30 November the bank's solicitors replied asking for particulars of
the documents to be disclosed and stating that if this were not done the liquidators
would have to apply to the court. Despite reminders on 9 December 1987 and on
5 January 1988 the liquidators of Esal neither gave the particulars of the
d documents nor applied to the court. On 11 January 1988 the liquidators of Esal
did apply to the court and on 13 January 1988 Mervyn Davies J ordered the
disclosure of the documents to Frendial.

The relevance of this dispute as to the documents is that before Frendial could
prepare the proposed amended defence they wished to see the additional
documents which they knew the liquidators of Esal regarded as relevant. This
e seems to me to be a wholly reasonable attitude for them to adopt. It is nothing to
the point that in the event the defendants relied primarily on documents which
they already held rather than on the documents disclosed after 13 January 1988.
They did in fact rely on certain of the latter documents and, in any event until
the documents were seen it was impossible for anyone to know what was in them.
f I am left with the impression that the bank were being deliberately obstructive
in withholding the documents.

In these circumstances, I consider that the defendants have given an explanation
of their failure within the 56-days limited by the unless order either to serve the
particulars ordered or obtain leave to amend the defence. Although the defendants
should have acted with greater diligence, the failure to comply with the unless
g order is primarily due to the mistake as to the date of the expiry of the order and
the obstructive conduct of the bank in relation to the documents. The defendants'
explanation shows that they were not defying or ignoring the court order and in
the result it is, in my judgment, impossible to characterise their conduct as
contumelious. Accordingly, the failure to comply with the unless order does not,
in my judgment, provide sufficient reason for refusing to exercise the discretion
h of the court in giving leave to the defendants to amend their defence and thereby
have a trial of the dispute on the merits.

I would therefore allow the appeal. If within 28 days the defendants pay into
court £50,000 as security for costs, they should have leave to amend their points
of defence. The bank's application for judgment should be dismissed. The bank's
costs of the originating motion down to 27 January 1988 should be taxed and
j paid forthwith by the defendants. If the £50,000 is not paid in within the 28
days, the appeal will be dismissed.

PARKER LJ. I agree. As we are differing from the learned judge I shall,
however, add a contribution of my own.

The order of 9 November provided that, if the particulars were not delivered within 56 days, the whole defence, not merely the parts of it to which the *a* particulars related, should be struck out. It did not, however, as some penal orders do, go on to provide, in addition, that the bank should be at liberty to enter final judgment for the relief claimed in the writ. It merely gave the bank liberty to apply for the relief claimed.

The defendants having not complied with the order, the defence was then struck out by force of the order and the bank applied for the relief claimed. *b* Although, however, the defendants had failed to comply with the order, they had on the day before time expired issued a summons seeking an extension of time, a stay of the order of 9 November and leave to make an unspecified amendment. Furthermore, on 12 and 13 January they delivered further and better particulars of the defence, albeit it had by then been struck out by virtue of the order of 9 November. One further event occurred before, on 27 January, the bank's *c* application and the defendants' summons came on before the judge, namely that the defendants had drafted the amendment which they desired to make.

With the exception of what I may call the 'breach of Mareva' defence, it is accepted that the original defence must go but it is sought to raise the new defence under s 54. *d*

The effective position as it came before the judge was, therefore, that the bank was seeking judgment and the defendants were seeking leave to resist, not on the basis of the original defence of which particulars had been ordered, but on the basis of a separate defence of which particulars had not been ordered and an entirely new defence.

Leaving aside for the moment the effect of the defendants' failure to comply *e* with the penal order, the first issue, and one of paramount importance, was whether the new defence was arguable. If, as the bank contended, it was not, clearly the defendants could not be allowed to pursue it further. On this issue, however, the bank failed. The judge held that the defence was arguable. He therefore had to consider whether the defendants should be allowed to raise it. There were, as it seems to me, two possible reasons why they should not be so *f* allowed: (a) if they were so allowed it would cause prejudice to the bank which could not be compensated in costs; (b) if the defendants' conduct had been so heinous that it was a proper exercise of the judge's discretion to prevent them from (i) pursuing that part of the original defence of which particulars had not been ordered and (ii) from presenting a new and arguable defence to the court. It *g* is to be stressed that the defendants were not seeking to be allowed to pursue those parts of the original defence of which particulars had been ordered. Save as to the 'breach of Mareva' defence they were thus accepting the effect of the order.

As to the prejudice point, it could, and in my view should, have been dealt with by the imposition of the condition proposed by Sir Nicolas Browne-Wilkinson V-C, with which I entirely agree. As to the second point, I have used *h* the expression 'so heinous' because it appears to me that there must be degrees of appropriate consequences even where the conduct of someone who has failed to comply with a penal order can properly be described as contumacious or contumelious or in deliberate disregard of the order, just as there are degrees of appropriate punishments for a contempt of court by breach of an undertaking or injunction. Albeit deliberate, one deliberate breach may in the circumstances *j* warrant no more than a fine, whilst another may in the circumstances warrant imprisonment. In each case all the circumstances must be taken into account, including the nature of the relief which is sought by the party in default. It is one thing for a plaintiff who has been struck out for want of prosecution to issue a

writ claiming precisely the same relief the next day. It is quite another for a
a defendant to raise an arguable defence not previously before the court and thus
in no way associated with the penal order.

It is plain on the authorities that, albeit with caution, a defendant whose
defence has been struck out for failure to comply with a penal order can, in
appropriate circumstances, be permitted to continue the very same defence of
which particulars were ordered. It is, in my view, clear that, albeit there must
b still be caution, the position of a defendant who seeks only to rely on a defence
which was not the subject of the penal order for particulars and to raise an
arguable defence not previously raised is stronger. To shut out the new arguable
defence would require more heinous conduct than would be required to justify a
refusal to reinstate the very defence of which particulars had been ordered. In
c essence, the question in each case must be whether the punishment fits the crime.

In the present case I have no doubt that the defendants' conduct was not
sufficient to warrant the punishment inflicted. Indeed, assuming that the
particulars delivered on 12 and 13 January were sufficient or even arguably
sufficient, I should have been very doubtful indeed whether it would have been a
proper exercise of discretion to refuse them leave to pursue the original defence.
d They had issued their summons in time, they had delivered the particulars late
no doubt, which the penal order was designed to force them to produce and there
was an explanation for the failure.

In my judgment, the learned judge erred in the specific matters stated by Sir
Nicolas Browne-Wilkinson V-C, but even if it had not been possible to pinpoint
errors in approach, I would have allowed the appeal, subject, of course, to the
e condition, on the simple ground that in all the circumstances the learned judge
was plainly wrong.

SIR JOHN MEGAW. I agree.

The noun 'contumely', as defined in the *Shorter Oxford English Dictionary*,
f reflecting, I believe, the sense in which it would ordinarily be understood, is
'Insolent reproach or abuse'. The conduct of the defendants, having regard to all
the circumstances, could not be described as 'contumelious'. With all respect, it
seems to me that the word 'contumacious' would be more apt than 'contumelious'
in the passages in Lord Diplock's discussion of the effect of failure to comply with
a peremptory order in *Allen v Sir Alfred McAlpine & Sons Ltd* [1968] 1 All ER 543
g at 556, [1968] 2 QB 229 at 259 and in *Birkett v James* [1977] 2 All ER 801 at 807,
[1978] AC 297 at 321. 'Contumacy' means 'Perverse and obstinate resistance to
authority'. Surely it is that characteristic, not 'insolent reproach or abuse', which
is a frequent hallmark of a litigant's failure to comply with a peremptory order?
But, even if 'contumacious' should be substituted for 'contumelious' in Lord
Diplock's formula, the result in this case would still be the same. To the question:
h was the defendants' failure to comply with the peremptory order properly to be
described as showing perverse and obstinate resistance of authority? the answer,
as I see it, must again be No.

In my view, in that respect the learned judge did not apply the right criterion.

Appeal allowed.

Celia Fox   Barrister.

Grand Metropolitan Nominee (No 2) Co Ltd v Evans

a

COURT OF APPEAL, CIVIL DIVISION
PURCHAS AND MANN LJJ
11, 12 MARCH, 8 MAY 1992

b

Practice – Order – 'Unless' orders and other peremptory orders – Non-compliance with 'unless' order – Consequences – Non-compliance with order striking out claim or defence unless act done within specified time – Whether pleading should be struck out if failure to comply with 'unless' order not contumelious.

c

Where the court makes an order that unless the party to whom the order is directed serves further and better particulars of a pleading within a specified time the pleading will be struck out and judgment entered for the other party, the court will only strike out the pleading for failure to comply with that order if the conduct of the party whose pleading is to be struck out is contumelious (see p 649 *d* to *f* and p 650 *e*, post).

d

Re Jokai Tea Holdings Ltd (1989) [1993] 1 All ER 630 applied.

Notes

For 'unless' orders, see 37 *Halsbury's Laws* (4th edn) para 32, and for cases on the subject, see 37(2) *Digest* (Reissue) 200–202, *1319–1336.*

e

Case referred to in judgments

Jokai Tea Holdings Ltd, Re (1989) [1993] 1 All ER 630, [1992] 1 WLR 1196, CA.

Interlocutory appeal

The defendant, John Austin Evans, trading as 'The Fish Factory', appealed from the decision of Leonard J given on 19 November 1991 whereby he declared that the defendant had failed to comply with the order of Master Turner dated 8 October 1991 requiring service of further and better particulars of the defence by 4 pm on 30 October on the ground that the particulars which were served were inadequate and gave judgment for the plaintiff, Grand Metropolitan Nominee (No 2) Co Ltd, formerly Compass Contract Services (UK) Ltd, in its action claiming the sum of £47,832·85 plus interest due under an agreement dated 11 April 1984 for the provision of services to the defendant's restaurant premises at 25–27 High Street, Wrexham. The facts are set out in the judgment of Purchas LJ.

f

g

David Kemp QC and *Charles Williams* (instructed by *Gwilym Hughes & Partners,* Wrexham) for the defendant.
Simon Browne-Wilkinson (instructed by *Lovell White Durrant*) for the plaintiff.

h

Cur adv vult

j

8 May 1992. The following judgments were delivered.

PURCHAS LJ. This is an appeal by John Austin Evans, trading as 'The Fish Factory', from an order of Leonard J dated 19 November 1991, which was made on the summons of Grand Metropolitan Nominee (No 2) Co Ltd, formerly Compass Contract Services (UK) Ltd (Compass), and also on Compass's notice of

appeal from the order of Master Turner dated 8 October 1991 granting to the
a appellant leave to serve an amended defence and counterclaim.

By his order Leonard J provided:

> '1. As to the plaintiff's summons dated 6th November 1991: 1.1 there be
> a declaration that the defendant has failed to comply with the order of Master
> Turner dated 8th October 1991 requiring a service of further and better
> *b* particulars by 4.00 p.m. on 30th October 1991 by reason of the fact that the
> particulars which were served were inadequate. 1.2 Judgment be entered for
> the plaintiff with costs to be taxed if not agreed, such costs to include the
> costs of this summons.
>
> 2. As to the plaintiff's notice of appeal dated 21st October 1991, without
> prejudice to the order set out at paragraph 1 above, it is ordered that: 2.1 The
> *c* appeal be allowed with costs . . .
>
> 3. As to the defendant's summons dated 12th November 1991 (leave to
> re-amend the replies to the request dated 29th July 1988 for further and
> better particulars of the defence and counterclaim) there be no order.
>
> 4. Leave to appeal.'

d The appellant appealed from paras 1 and 2 of this order.

[His Lordship then set out the relevant parts of the statement of claim and the
defence and counterclaim and continued:] On receipt of the defence and
counterclaim the solicitors then acting for Compass wrote on 19 January 1987
stating that before they could settle a defence to the counterclaim they would
require details of loss and damage referred to in paras 34, 35, 36 and 42 before
e they would be able to instruct counsel, and asked for an open-ended extension of
time. This was granted. The remainder of the year 1987 appears mainly to have
been spent by the appellant's solicitors in obtaining the necessary architects' and
other experts' evidence without any objection by Compass about the delay.
During these months there was a regular interchange of correspondence between
the respective solicitors, those for Compass seeking specific documents referred to
f in the pleadings and pressing for the further and better particulars of the damage
claimed in the paras 34, 35, 36 and 42. The appellant's solicitors appear to have
been doing their best to provide some of the documents and repeating that they
were still investigating the matter and referring to counsel. Finally, after further
delay, particulars (the voluntary particulars) were delivered under cover of a letter
of 16 March 1988. These particulars were restricted to the four paragraphs listed
g in the third paragraph of Compass's solicitors' letter of 19 January 1987. They
contained much narrative and great detail of the manner in which it was alleged
that Compass and/or the architects, SBA Associates, and/or the builders involved
had failed properly to carry out the works. In summary, the particulars of para
34 ran to 12 pages, of paras 35 and 36 to 7 pages, and of para 42 to 8 pages. There
h has been a substantial issue as to whether these pleadings were properly delivered
as further particulars or whether they raised fresh claims, which should have been
separately pleaded by amending the defence and counterclaim. The objection,
however, was not taken for nearly four months, when the solicitors now acting
for Compass had taken over the conduct of these matters. Compass's initial
reaction was to seek a general extension of time in which to serve this reply and
j defence to counterclaim. This was granted by the appellant.

The first challenge to the voluntary particulars came in a letter from Compass's
solicitors dated 21 July 1988, asserting that the voluntary particulars did not
comply with RSC Ord 18, r 12, and giving formal notice of objection that they—

> 'are extremely lengthy and appear on a number of issues to contain the
> substance of your client's case. In our view there are two alternatives open to

you, you may either apply for leave to rely on these particulars in which case
we shall resist such an application or you should apply to serve an amended *a*
defence and counterclaim so that you may include the particulars. We reserve
our position as to whether or not we would object to that application, much
does depend upon the way the amended defence and counterclaim is pleaded.'

Under cover of the same letter Compass served the reply and defence to
counterclaim. For the purposes of this judgment it is not necessary to analyse in *b*
detail the matters alleged in the defence and counterclaim which were admitted
and those which were disputed. I would, however, comment that it is skillfully
and precisely drawn and would have formed the basis, if necessary, of the
identification of questions of law which could be the subject of a trial of
preliminary issues. I should mention, however, that in relation to paragraphs
which formed the area of dispute in this appeal, the following issues were raised *c*
in the reply and defence and counterclaim.

[His Lordship then set out those issues and continued:] On 29 July 1988
solicitors for Compass served a formal request for further and better particulars
of the defence and counterclaim. This was also a lengthy document (21 pages).
Again, for the purposes of this judgment, it is not necessary to refer to the details
of this request. It related to most of the paragraphs between para 4 and para 43 *d*
inclusive of the defence and counterclaim. I need only refer to the request under
paras 34, 35, 38 and 43. I shall return to consider these when I come to the
particulars supplied by the appellant.

The appellant's solicitors disputed that the voluntary particulars were
objectionable except as being in technical breach of Ord 18, r 12, since they were *e*
not served with the consent of the plaintiff. Regrettably they also seem to have
overlooked the letter from Compass's solicitors of 12 January 1987. By their letter
of 17 August 1988 they made a suggestion that the matter should be raised on
the summons for directions. However, the formal request for further particulars
of most of the remaining paragraphs of the defence and counterclaim besides the
paragraphs covered by the voluntary particulars remained unanswered until 12 *f*
April 1988. The issue of the validity of the voluntary particulars seems to have
become lost in other matters being canvassed in correspondence between the
parties arising out of the impending summons for directions and the obtaining
of reports from experts such as surveyors, catering consultants etc—see the letter
from Compass's solicitors dated 31 January 1989.

In their letter of 4 April 1989 Compass's solicitors reasserted their objection to *g*
the voluntary particulars. However, on 12 April 1989 the replies to Compass's
request for further and better particulars were served by the appellant. Therefore
at the stage when these further and better particulars were served there was still
an issue between the parties as to whether the voluntary particulars were
appropriate or not.

[His Lordship then set out details of the request for further and better *h*
particulars and the replies served by the appellant and continued:] On 29 January
1989 Compass applied to the master for a declaration that the voluntary
particulars—

'did not form part of the pleading in this action, and that the defendant *j*
was not entitled to refer to the contents thereof at the trial; alternatively, that
this document should be struck out under R.S.C. Order 18, rule 19(*b*) or,
alternatively, under the inherent jurisdiction of the court.'

An order was further sought that within 14 days the defendant should provide
the particulars requested under paras 34, 35, 38 and 43 of the defence and

counterclaim in a request dated 28 July 1988 and an order, pursuant to RSC Ord
a 18, r 19, that the replies already delivered should be struck out. This application
was supported by an affidavit from Barbara Anne Morris, a solicitor in Compass's
present solicitors' firm. Paragraph 6 of this affidavit stated:

> 'It is the plaintiff's case that the way in which the defendant has sought to
> plead his case is seriously defective in that, contrary to the rules, (a) he has
b > sought to plead substantive parts of his case by way of voluntary particulars
> thus depriving the plaintiff of pleading to those parts of his case in reply. (b)
> failed to properly particularise other substantial parts of his case thus
> depriving the plaintiff of the opportunity of knowing the case it has to meet.
> In short because of the unorthodox procedure that the defendant has adopted
> without the leave of the court the pleadings in this action are in a wholly
c > unsatisfactory state, which is causing the plaintiff real prejudice. On a
> number of occasions my firm has drawn to the attention of the defendant's
> solicitor the passage in Volume 1 of the White Book at 18/12/47 which states
> as to voluntary particulars: ". . . if no objection is taken by the opposite party
> to the service of such particulars, they will presumably stand as part of the
> pleadings in the action: but if objection is taken, the party concerned must
d > apply for leave to serve the particulars under an order of the court. Clearly
> the device of 'voluntary particulars' must not be used unilaterally to amend
> or add to particulars or vary the case of a party, in a way which the court
> would not sanction".'

In swearing this affidavit the deponent appears to have overlooked the fact that
e the voluntary particulars were delivered at the request of Compass's then solicitors.
Master Turner, after hearing the summons and reading the affidavit of Barbara
Anne Morris, made the order for the declaration in relation to the voluntary
particulars as sought. He further ordered that the defendant should serve an
amended defence and counterclaim, and should provide the particulars which
f were requested under paras 35 and 43 in the request of 28 July 1988. It is not
clear whether anything further was said about the provenance of the voluntary
particulars originating in the specific request made by Compass on receipt of the
defence and counterclaim. We were, however, told by counsel that a draft
proposed amended defence and counterclaim was not placed before the master
and that the leave to serve a proposed pleading was not leave itself to serve the
g pleading. The master ordered that a draft should first be submitted in order to
give Compass an opportunity to consider the proposed amended defence and
counterclaim and to decide whether or not to oppose the subsequent application
for leave to serve it.

It is not clear whether Master Turner gave any detailed consideration to the
contents of the voluntary particulars to determine whether, apart from the
h apparent breach of RSC Ord 18, r 12, they were objectionable as raising new issues
which ought to have been pleaded by way of amendment of the defence and
counterclaim. All the indications are that he did not. He did, however, apparently
consider the further and better particulars of paras 33, 34, 35 and 42 on 11 April
1989 because he distinguished the answers given to those of paras 33 and 34,
which seem to have been adequate, from those given for paras 35 and 42, which
j were not. The particulars supplied under paras 34 and 35 were, of course, in
relation to the appointment etc of the architects or design consultants on the one
hand and of the builders on the other. The particulars provided under each
referred partly to the voluntary particulars, partly to a general allegation
concerning the failure to exercise skill etc and partly to reports to be prepared in
the future which would presumably become subject to an order for an exchange

of experts' reports. In these circumstances, it is quite understandable that the
master might have considered that, having made the order depriving the appellant *a*
of the right to refer to the voluntary particulars, allowed his more general
particulars to stand and also retained what was in effect an offer by him to
exchange experts' reports at the appropriate time, justice would be done between
the parties. I see nothing of greater significance in the exclusion of these two
paragraphs. So far as para 38 was concerned there were extensive particulars
already pleaded. For some reason the master seems to be less than satisfied with *b*
the particulars supplied under para 38, and I must return to this matter shortly.
So far as the particulars provided under para 43 are concerned Mr Kemp QC, who
has presented the appeal, concedes that the reply under para 43 was, to adopt his
words, 'stupid and one that could not be sustained'. As I have already commented,
all that was required under para 43 was a plea of set off, which finds itself
elsewhere in the pleadings in any event. It did not further the appellant's case in *c*
any material respect. As Mr Kemp now concedes that this paragraph should be
struck out, I do not find it necessary to comment upon it further. The master was
entitled to consider that the particulars provided under this paragraph were
inadequate.

In pursuance of Master Turner's orders the appellant submitted a draft amended *d*
defence and counterclaim under cover of a letter dated 8 January 1990. This
pleading had four schedules which were to be delivered separately. In order to
bring the matter wholly up to date, these schedules, which contained considerable
detail of the technical defects and damage resulting, were withheld for the
purpose of bringing the position up to date. In this way it was intended that the
pleading as finally delivered would not require further amendment. This was *e*
acceptable to Compass's solicitors, who granted the appellant's solicitors the
necessary extension.

[His Lordship then considered paras 34, 35, 38 and 43 of the draft amended
defence and counterclaim and continued:] By letter of 24 April 1990 the
appellant's solicitors gave notice that they would seek directions that the claims
under paras 39 and 40 of the defence and counterclaim should be tried as *f*
preliminary issues. This led to a further exchange of letters. These two paragraphs
of the defence and counterclaim in fact open the whole ambit of the breach of
warranty and agreement in relation to the consultancy contract and the proposal
document. The appellant served amended further and better particulars on 15
May 1990 which, for the purposes of this appeal, do not seem to have made any
material alteration or met the complaints being made by Compass. On 22 January *g*
1991 there was an appointment for directions before the master. On this
appointment solicitors acting for Compass gave notice that they intended to apply
for an order that, unless the appellant provided the further and better particulars
of paras 38 and 43 of the defence and counterclaim in compliance with Master
Turner's order of 4 December 1989 within 14 days, they would seek an order that *h*
the defence and counterclaim should be struck out and judgment entered for the
plaintiff with costs. The debate on the appeal has centred around the understanding
of Master Turner's order of 4 December 1989 which led to the further summons
seeking a peremptory 'unless' order. The court has had placed before it two
affidavits, one from Mr Jones, the solicitor responsible for the conduct of the
appellant's case throughout, and a second affidavit from Barbara Anne Morris. *j*

Mr Jones, in para 2(g) of his affidavit of 3 January 1992, gave his understanding
of the order made by Master Turner, namely that the voluntary particulars could
not stand and that the defendant should serve a proposed amended defence and
counterclaim on Compass within 35 days. He could not recall any substantial

discussion on the issue of the further particulars allegedly outstanding on paras
a 34, 35, 38 and 43 under the request dated 29 July 1988. Mr Jones had the firm
impression that the reason for the order in respect of paras 38 and 43 was not that
the contents of the particulars were inadequate or inadmissible but that they were
delivered by reference to the voluntary particulars which by now had been made
subject to the order disqualifying them. In her affidavit sworn on 6 March 1992
Miss Morris accepted that Mr Jones believed genuinely in what he had said in his
b affidavit but expressed her view, namely that she had no doubt that Mr Jones was
wrong, firstly, because of her clear recollection in relation to the substance of
argument put forward about the request in para 43 and, secondly, because she
could not see any reason, if the order was based on formal matters only, that there
should have been a difference made between two of the four paragraphs. Looking
c at this generally, I think that Mr Browne-Wilkinson's submissions are correct that
it is Miss Morris's version of affairs that should be accepted subject to the fact that
Mr Jones genuinely thought that it was merely a matter of form. This is of
considerable significance in this appeal.

In the meanwhile the appellant was pressing for a summons for directions.
There was an exchange of letters in July and August 1990 in which solicitors for
d Compass said that they did not wish to add anything to the draft summons for
directions. It was not possible to get a hearing for the summons until 22 January
1991, so accordingly the appellant served a summons on Compass on 28 August
1990, with 22 January 1991 as the return date. On this summons the appellant
sought leave to serve the proposed amended defence and counterclaim and also
an order for the trial of the preliminary issue as discussed in the earlier
e correspondence. Compass's solicitors on the hearing of this summons, having
given notice that they would seek an 'unless' order for the further and better
particulars of paras 38 and 43, were unsuccessful in persuading Master Hodgson
to accede to this as they had not served a proper summons. At the same time the
master refused leave to the appellant to serve his amended defence and
counterclaim because it was not in proper form, and declined to make an order
f for the trial of a preliminary issue. Shortly after this a summons was issued on
behalf of Compass returnable on 14 May 1991. This sought the following orders:

> '1. Unless the defendant do serve the further and better particulars of the
> defence and counterclaim ordered by Master Turner on 14th December 1990
> within 14 days from the date hereof the defendant's defence and counterclaim
g > be struck out and judgment entered for the plaintiff with costs to be taxed if
> not agreed.'

By letter dated 11 April 1991 a further amended defence and counterclaim was
served upon Compass's solicitors. It is necessary only to refer in summary to paras
34, 35 and 36 by saying that the main alteration between this document and the
h proposed amended defence and counterclaim, which did not find favour with
Master Hodgson, is that the detailed particulars previously annexed to the
pleading by way of schedule have now been brought into the body of the pleading
itself. Paragraphs 38 and 43 remain unamended from the original pleadings.
However, the particulars of damage in relation to paras 34 and 42 still remain
appended in two schedules.
j The appointment fixed for 14 May 1991 went off owing to a misunderstanding
between counsel for the appellant, who thought that he was attending to deal
with a summons for directions, and the solicitor and counsel for Compass, who
were seeking their 'unless' order for the further particulars. By agreement the
matter was stood over and a new appointment obtained on 8 October 1991, when

the various matters came before Master Turner. This is the order which is the basis of this appeal. On this occasion the master made two orders. The first order granted leave to the appellant to serve its amended defence and counterclaim, and ordered that Compass should serve any amended reply or any amended defence to counterclaim within three months. Further directions were given about inspection etc and the balance of directions adjourned until 6 February 1992. The second order read as follows:

'1. Unless the defendant do serve the further and better particulars of the defence and counterclaim ordered by Master Turner on 4th December 1989 by 4.00 pm on 30th October 1991 the defendant's defence and counterclaim be struck out and judgment entered for the plaintiffs with costs to be taxed [if] not agreed.'

In compliance with the 'unless' order the appellants served further and better particulars on 28 October 1991.

By a summons dated 12 November 1991 the appellant sought leave to serve a reamended pleading of replies to the request for further and better particulars of 29 July 1988. This sought to affect substantial amendments to the particulars provided, including those under paras 38 and 43. What in effect this pleading seeks to do is to relate the answers in relation to paras 38 and 43 back to the matters pleaded in the amended defence and counterclaim, thus obviating the necessity for further and better particulars. On this summons Leonard J made no order after the hearing on 19 November 1991.

I now turn to the judgment of Leonard J. Having heard argument from Mr Browne-Wilkinson, for Compass, and Mr Denzil Davies, for the appellant, the judge accepted the description given by Mr Browne-Wilkinson that during the years since the original claim and defence under the counterclaim was served there has been a 'substantial escalation of the case'. Mr Denzil Davies had argued that from the earliest point the material was present for the plaintiff to see if one is considering the issues rather than the extent of the evidence to be led to those issues. Leonard J did not accept Mr Denzil Davies's submissions and referred to them in these terms:

'That may be so, but all that is background to the question I have to consider of whether there was indeed a failure to comply with the "unless" order. I have come to the conclusion that there was such a failure. It is not, in my judgment, a sufficient answer for the defendant to say that the plaintiffs knew what sort of allegation was being made. There was the clear order, admittedly followed by purported compliance within the period limited in the order. But it was only purported compliance, which, in my judgment, was not real and genuine. In addition to that there is the fact that there is, in my judgment, a history of delay throughout this case on the part of the defendant. I have said enough about the chronology already to indicate the nature of that delay. One would not be afraid of the mere fact of the escalation of the case providing that the proper principles of pleading have been followed and provided in particular that the orders of the master were observed. In this case I think they were not and I think it is a serious matter. Set against that background of general delay, it seems to me to provide proper material for saying that the defence and counterclaim should be struck out. That means that the plaintiffs are entitled to their judgment.'

Mr Kemp referred the court to the authorities and quotations cited in *The County Court Practice 1992* p 233 under 'Dismissal of action for disobedience to order', in particular to the judgments of the Court of Appeal in *Re Jokai Tea*

Holdings Ltd (1989) [1993] 1 All ER 630, [1992] 1 WLR 1196. This authority is
a not mentioned in *The Supreme Court Practice 1991* under the appropriate
commentary, and is not fully described even in *The County Court Practice 1992*.
The court obtained the full transcript of the judgment, which made it clear that,
with respect to Leonard J, his approach was all too arbitrary. He was not,
regrettably, referred to this authority, which for some reason appears not to have
received the publicity which it deserves.

b   Mr Browne-Wilkinson in his submissions in support of the judgment properly
told the court that Compass's attitude to the difference in the approach of Mr
Jones and Miss Morris in connection with the orders made by Master Turner for
the further and better particulars was accepted to be the result of an honest
misunderstanding on the part of Mr Jones as to the ratio of the master's order. I
c have already indicated in this judgment that I accept Miss Morris's approach to.
the order. On this basis Mr Browne-Wilkinson had originally submitted that it
was not necessary to show that the conduct of the party whose pleading is to be
struck out was contumelious but merely a serious failure to comply with the
order. As a result of being shown the transcript of *Re Jokai Tea Holdings Ltd* during
the course of his submissions to the court Mr Browne-Wilkinson properly and
d frankly accepted that he could no longer support the order to strike out the whole
of the defence and counterclaim on the basis of the concession that he had made.
After very careful review of the authorities, Sir Nicolas Browne-Wilkinson V-C
expressed this view, with which I respectfully and wholeheartedly agree ([1993]
1 All ER [1992] 1 WLR 1196 at 1203):

e   'In my judgment, in cases in which the court has to decide what are the
consequences of a failure to comply with an unless order, the relevant
question is whether such failure is intentional and contumelious. The court
should not be astute to find excuses for such failure since obedience to orders
of the court is the foundation on which its authority is founded. But if a
party can clearly demonstrate that there was no intention to ignore or flout
f   the order and that the failure to obey was due to extraneous circumstances,
such failure to obey is not to be treated as contumelious and therefore does
not disentitle the litigant to rights which he would otherwise have enjoyed.'

This court, as indeed was Leonard J, is bound by this authority. I am forced,
with regret, to hold that Leonard J's order to strike out the defence and
g counterclaim cannot be justified on any version of the facts. [His Lordship then
considered the appeal against para 2 of Leonard J's order, which he allowed, and
concluded:]

In the event of the course that this appeal has taken, it has not been necessary
to consider whether the order made by Master Turner in its 'unless' form ought
more properly to have been restricted to the paragraphs the particulars of which
h were still found to be inadequate. In a pleading containing many different issues,
it would be a truly draconian step to strike out the whole of an extensive claim
with many different facets because of the failure in respect of one or two of the
many allegations to comply with an order to give further and better particulars,
unless it was to mark the court's displeasure at the deliberate and contumelious
conduct of one of the parties. This is not the position here, as Mr Browne-
j Wilkinson has readily conceded. It might have been a far more appropriate course
to consider whether the order should have been to strike out those particular
paragraphs in toto but to leave the rest of the defence and counterclaim standing.
This matter has not been properly argued and I express no concluded view about
it. Before parting with this matter, however, I wish to return to express a view on
the adequacy of the further and better particulars supplied under para 38 of the

defence and counterclaim. If it were necessary for the resolution of this appeal, I would have been of the view that the particulars delivered thereunder in the *a* amended further and better particulars were an adequate reply and in any event should not have been a ground for a draconian order. I do not consider that they represented a failure to comply with the 'unless' order of Master Turner, in turn relating back to his order in 1989.

It is otherwise, however, in relation to the further and better particulars pleaded under para 43 to which I have referred earlier in this judgment and which Mr *b* Kemp has not attempted to support. It may be that there were grounds upon which the judge could have taken some action, notwithstanding the concession now made that the conduct of those representing the appellant was not contumelious. I would exercise the powers granted to this court to make an order that the court below could make and order that the whole of para 43 of the *c* amended defence and counterclaim be struck out. This was a course to which Mr Kemp raised no objection. I would therefore, subject to this one matter, allow this appeal and order that the action should proceed. What further directions should be given should, I consider, be more appropriately dealt with elsewhere than in this court. I would, however, recommend that serious consideration should be given to transferring the action to the official referees' court. The *d* defendant's amended notice of appeal does not mention Leonard J's making of 'no order' on their summons of 12 November 1991 (leave to reamend further and better particulars) and the matter has not been argued. This can be appropriately dealt with in due course, hopefully on a reference to the official referee.

MANN LJ. I agree. *e*

Appeal allowed.

Celia Fox   Barrister.

a # Allen v Bloomsbury Health Authority and another

QUEEN'S BENCH DIVISION
BROOKE J

b 16, 17 DECEMBER 1991, 13 JANUARY 1992

Damages – Unwanted pregnancy – Negligence – Measure of damages – Woman pregnant at time of operation for sterilisation – Hospital negligently failing to diagnose pregnancy – Health authority admitting liability – Assessment of damages for financial loss incurred in bringing up unplanned child – Cost of education – Principles by which financial cost of c *bringing up unplanned child to be measured.*

The plaintiff married in June 1971 and had her first child in 1973. From 1971 until 1975, when her second child was born, she was in full-time employment. She then stayed at home until 1979, by which time both children were at private schools. Her marriage broke down in 1979 and she took a part-time job while d looking after the two children. In 1985 the plaintiff decided to be sterilised because she wished to go back to full-time employment in order, in the absence of any maintenance from her husband, to improve the family's standard of living and because she wished to be freer to lead her own life. In June 1985 the plaintiff underwent a sterilisation operation at a hospital managed by the defendant health authority. In September 1985, when she had just accepted a full-time job, the e plaintiff discovered that at the time of the operation she had been four weeks pregnant by her then partner, whom she did not wish to marry, and that her pregnancy had survived the operation. If the pregnancy had been diagnosed at the time of the operation she would have had it terminated, but by the time it was diagnosed she felt it was too late to terminate it. The plaintiff feared that the f sterilisation operation would harm the foetus and suffered anxiety until February 1986, when she gave birth to a healthy daughter. The plaintiff brought an action for damages against the health authority claiming the cost and expense of bringing up her daughter until she was 18. The health authority admitted liability and the only issue was the quantum of damages. It was accepted that, but for the daughter's birth, the plaintiff would have been able to obtain full-time g employment and that the daughter's birth and upbringing had made a substantial difference to the plaintiff's life and had caused her emotional difficulties and financial insecurity.

Held – For the purposes of assessing the measure of damages which a plaintiff mother was entitled to recover for negligence on the part of a hospital doctor h which resulted in an unplanned birth, the mother was entitled to recover (i) general damages for the discomfort and pain associated with the continuation of her pregnancy and delivery of her child, although the benefit of not having to undergo an abortion had to be offset against that, (ii) damages for the financial loss incurred in the upkeep of the child through to adulthood and for the financial loss suffered because of loss of earnings or the incurring of expense as a result of j her obligation to the child which she would otherwise have sought to avoid, and (iii), in an appropriate case, general damages for the foreseeable additional anxiety, stress and burden involved in bringing up a handicapped child. However, a claim for damages for tiredness and wear and tear in bringing up an unplanned healthy child would not be allowed since it was offset by the benefit of bringing a healthy child into the world and seeing it grow to maturity. In measuring the future cost

of maintaining an unplanned child the defendant was liable to pay for all expenses
which might reasonably be incurred in the education and upkeep of the child, *a*
having regard to all the circumstances of the case and, in particular, having regard
to the child's condition in life and his reasonable requirements at the time the
expenditure was incurred. In all the circumstances the plaintiff was entitled to
damages totalling £96,631 (see p 657 *d* to *h*, p 658 *b* to *d*, p 662 *a h j* and p 663 *d*
to *g*, post).

Thake v Maurice [1986] 1 All ER 497 and Emeh v Kensington and Chelsea and *b*
Westminster Area Health Authority [1984] 3 All ER 1044 applied.

Udale v Bloomsbury Area Health Authority [1983] 2 All ER 522 and Salih v Enfield
Health Authority [1991] 3 All ER 400 considered.

Per curiam. If as a result of a doctor's negligence an unplanned child is born to
parents who have put all their other children through expensive private education,
a very substantial claim for the cost of private education of a healthy child of a *c*
reasonably wealthy family might have to be met from the funds of the health
authority responsible for the doctor's negligence (see p 662 *e*, post).

Notes

For the assessment of damages, see 12 *Halsbury's Laws* (4th edn) para 1200. *d*

Cases referred to in judgment

Benarr v Kettering Health Authority (1988) 138 NLJ 179.
Emeh v Kensington and Chelsea and Westminster Area Health Authority [1984] 3 All
    ER 1044, [1985] QB 1012, [1984] 2 WLR 233, CA.
Gardiner v Mounfield (1989) 5 BMLR 1. *e*
Gold v Haringey Health Authority [1987] 2 All ER 888, [1988] QB 481, [1987] 3
    WLR 649, CA.
Hedley Byrne & Co Ltd v Heller & Partners Ltd [1963] 2 All ER 575, [1964] AC 465,
    [1963] 3 WLR 101, HL.
McKay v Essex Area Health Authority [1982] 2 All ER 771, [1982] QB 1166, [1982] *f*
    2 WLR 890, CA.
Salih v Enfield Health Authority [1991] 3 All ER 400, CA.
Sherlock v Stillwater Clinic (1977) 260 NW 2d 169, Minn SC.
Thake v Maurice [1986] 1 All ER 497, [1986] QB 644, [1986] 3 WLR 337, CA; *rvsg*
    in part [1984] 2 All ER 513, [1986] QB 644, [1985] 2 WLR 215.
Udale v Bloomsbury Area Health Authority [1983] 2 All ER 522, [1983] 1 WLR 1098. *g*

Action

By a writ and statement of claim dated 24 June 1988 the plaintiff, Linda Annette
Allen, claimed damages from the first defendant, the Bloomsbury Health
Authority, and the second defendant, Dr Esther Anderton, for personal injury
and consequential loss and damage occasioned to her by the negligence of the *h*
servants or agents of the first defendant as the health authority for the Elizabeth
Garrett Anderson Hospital and/or the second defendant in their investigation and
treatment of the plaintiff as a patient from 25 June 1985. The proceedings against
the second defendant were subsequently discontinued. The facts are set out in the
judgment. *j*

Michael Brent QC and Peter Latham (instructed by Sheridan & Co, Kingston upon
    Thames) for the plaintiff.
Jon Williams (instructed by Beachcroft Stanleys) for the health authority.

Cur adv vult

13 January 1992. The following judgment was delivered.

a

BROOKE J. In this action by a writ issued on 24 June 1988 the plaintiff, Linda Annette Allen, claims damages against the Bloomsbury Health Authority for personal injury and consequential loss and damage caused by the negligence of the defendants' servants or agents during a period in the summer of 1985 when she was in their care at the Elizabeth Garrett Anderson Hospital. The background
b to the plaintiff's claim is that in June 1985 she underwent an operation at that hospital under general anaesthetic for dilatation and curettage (D & C) and sterilisation. She makes no complaint about the way in which that operation was conducted. However, when she attended a follow-up out-patients' clinic there on 12 August 1985 she told a doctor that she had not had a period since before the
c operation and that her stomach and breasts felt swollen.

I need say no more about the detail of what occurred because the defendant health authority admitted in its defence that its responsible servant was negligent in that it was not ascertained at or shortly after the appointment that the plaintiff was by now about 12 weeks pregnant. Although she and her partner had been taking contraceptive precautions she had apparently conceived about four weeks
d before she attended hospital to be sterilised and her pregnancy had survived the operations which took place.

The defendants accept that if the pregnancy had been diagnosed then the plaintiff would have had it terminated and they did not try to contend that she had acted unreasonably in deciding not to have a termination when the pregnancy was in fact diagnosed at 17 weeks. The plaintiff gave birth to a baby daughter,
e Faye, on 10 February 1986, and in this action she claims the cost and expense involved in giving up her job and in bringing up Faye until the age of 18 together with general damages for negligence. The only issue I have to decide is the amount of the damages she should recover.

Mrs Allen was born in July 1949. She married in June 1971 and until February
f 1975 she had a well-paid job as the United Kingdom representative for the French company Pierre Balmain, in charge of their duty-free shops. Her job involved, among other things, responsibility for that company's duty-free shops at Heathrow and Gatwick Airports, with a staff of two girls working under her supervision. Although her son Scott was born in October 1973 she enjoyed flexible working hours which enabled her to go out and do her job at the airport on a full-time
g basis after her husband came home from work, since the airport shops stayed open till midnight.

She gave up this job in February 1975, the month before her daughter Leigh was born. She then stayed at home looking after the children until January 1979 by which time they were both at private schools of one kind or another. She then obtained a full-time job with a company called Alder International at London
h Airport.

Unhappily her marriage broke down in May 1979, when she separated from her husband. She went to live with the two children in a three-bedroomed house in Chessington, and she had to give up full-time employment the following month when her Danish au pair returned to Denmark. Three months later she obtained a part-time job between 9 am and 1 pm each day with a firm of
j insurance brokers in Kingston where she remained until February 1986, a week before Faye was born. She has not worked since then.

Her husband, against whom she obtained a decree absolute in October 1983, has steadfastly avoided all her efforts to obtain an effective order against him that he should pay maintenance for his two children. Her mother and her mother-in-law helped her by having the children to stay during the holidays when she was at work.

Mrs Allen is an attractive and capable woman who was certainly not averse to marrying again if she encountered a suitable man, but although she had two *a* boyfriends with children of a similar age to her own she did not remarry during the years leading up to Faye's conception and birth. She found her work with the insurance brokers quite arduous. She had started there as a clerical assistant, but later she had been put in charge of a new computer system. This work was mentally taxing, and she was working at a fairly high level of pressure all the four hours she worked there each day. *b*

Early in 1985 she decided she wished to be sterilised. By that time she was associating with a man who had three children. He wished to marry her but she had no wish to marry him: she looked on him as a very good friend, and he often accompanied her on visits to the hospital.

The defendants drew my attention to a letter from her general practitioner in *c* October 1984 to the effect that she felt drained and washed out and to a note taken at the hospital in March 1985 that she often felt exhausted. Mrs Allen did not dispute the accuracy of these notes. She said, however, that at that time she had been anxious because she often felt exhausted and depressed when other mothers of her age with similar commitments seemed to cope much better and there did not seem to be any explanation for it. In the spring of 1985 she was *d* referred to a specialist at University College Hospital who carried out tests and explained to her that this was an understandable consequence of previous trouble she had had with her kidneys. She then felt much better once she knew that there was a physical cause for her occasional tiredness, and I accept her evidence.

In the summer of 1985 she underwent her sterilisation operation. She then decided to apply for a full-time job. The children were now 11 and 10 and in the *e* absence of any support from their father she wanted to improve their standard of living and also to be more free to lead her own life. She was offered a managerial job by Avon Cosmetics which she turned down because it would have taken her to a part of south-west London which she felt was a little unsafe. She then applied for and was offered a job by a company who was selling 'world time clocks' which *f* it was hoping to sell to travel agents and to companies which did business with organisations all over the world. She was to be paid £7,500 with commission, which she told me was likely to be £2,500 per year, plus the use of a company car, a remuneration package comparable to what Avon had offered her. Unhappily at the precise time she was offered this job she learnt that she was in fact 17 weeks pregnant and she decided to stay where she was until her baby was born and to *g* benefit from the entitlement to maternity allowance and maternity leave she had earned with her current employers.

The defendants contended that in view of her complaints of exhaustion she would not have been able to hold down a full-time job if Faye had not been born. They also carried out a company search which showed that her new would-be employers were struck off the Register of Companies in 1989 and that their *h* accounts in 1985 and 1986 did not evidence any ability to pay Mrs Allen the level of wages they were offering her. However that may be, I was impressed by the way she gave evidence in the witness box. I am quite satisfied on the balance of probabilities that she would have been able to obtain full-time employment on the open market in some form of supervisory capacity to which she could also bring her clerical and computer skills, at the same level of pay as both Avon and *j* her would-be new employers were willing to offer her. Although she would have been tired from time to time, as many working mothers are, there seemed to me to be no good reason why she could not have kept a full-time job.

Mrs Allen was devastated by the news that she was pregnant. She decided she wanted an abortion, and her general practitioner signed an appropriate certificate.

However, after discussing the matter with a doctor at the hospital and seeing the
a results of an ultra-sound scan she changed her mind. Thereafter she had an
uneventful pregnancy and there were no complications at Faye's birth. She was
extremely anxious and worried, however, all through the remainder of her
pregnancy that the D & C operation might have harmed the baby in some way
and that she would give birth to a handicapped child. Although all the available
tests were carried out and she was assured by her doctors and by a very close
b friend of hers who gave evidence at the trial that it was most unlikely that the
four-week-old foetus would have suffered any harm, they could not completely
exclude the possibility and this understandably preyed on her mind. Fortunately
her fears proved unfounded and Faye was born a completely healthy child.

   Originally Faye shared her mother's bedroom, but this was no longer practicable
after she was about a year old. Accordingly, Mrs Allen borrowed money from the
c building society who are the mortgagees of her house which enabled her to
convert the garage into a bedroom for her son, with a toilet attached to it, since
the only toilet in the house was upstairs and he would not have been able to reach
it without walking through the lounge.

   Mrs Allen has not gone back to work yet because she would have had to pay
d somebody to look after Faye while she was working part-time. Because she would
also have lost income support she would not have been financially better off, and
she thought it better to stay at home and look after her daughter herself. Faye
started at school in January 1991. After a good start she was unfortunately very
unsettled in the autumn term because a teacher left, which unsettled her whole
class.

e Faye has always been a stubborn child and just at the moment she is prone to
long temper tantrums if she does not get her way. Her mother understandably
gets worn down by these incidents and often finds Faye very difficult to handle
on her own. She told me that a recent holiday in Florida, where Faye and she had
been taken by a man she had agreed to marry, turned out to be a complete disaster
because of her daughter's turbulent behaviour, and her relationship with this
f man has not really recovered from that experience.

   Faye also has a slight speech defect which has led to her having regular speech
therapy since she was three years old. I was told she talks like a child much
younger than she is. Her diction is not clear and she used to be quite difficult to
understand. Now that she is at school it is believed that she has slight dyslexia.
g Subject to all these things, I was told she is a lovely child. Her mother's eyes lit up
when she said this, and both her son and her friend confirmed how attractive a
child Faye now is.

   The recent problems at school led to Faye throwing more tantrums at home,
and I was told about one vivid recent example of this when she had not wanted to
have a bath on a Saturday morning. Her mother could not cope with this at all,
h and eventually after about ninety minutes her son Scott managed to calm Faye
down.

   Mrs Allen told me that, once the trial was over and she had some financial
security so that she could think of engaging a child-minder for Faye, she would
probably go back to part-time employment for four hours a day at Easter next
year. She would need to pay for a child-minder for the weeks when her holidays
j and Faye's did not coincide. Faye's school day ends at 3.15 pm and she did not
wish to be out at work all day while Faye was at primary school. She would hope
to move to full-time employment in 1997 when Faye is 11. Once Fay is 14 she
would be too old for a child-minder but she would need to have some base on
which she could rely while her mother was out at work. All this appeared to me
to be completely reasonable.

Mrs Allen did not wish to name Faye's father. Her son Scott told me that his mother had told him who he was, and he had seen this man at the hospital after *a* Faye's birth. I am quite satisfied on the evidence I heard that, despite some suggestions to that effect in the contemporary hospital notes, Faye's father is not the man to whom I made reference earlier, although that man gave Mrs Allen and her children a great deal of support and help in the months before and after Faye's birth.

Mrs Allen told me that Faye's father was prone to being very violent. He had *b* refused to pay her anything for Faye's maintenance and if she had ever tried to get an order against him she was certain that he would then move out of the accommodation he rents and be very difficult to trace. She had failed in spite of all her efforts to obtain any maintenance from her former husband for her two older children, and it was not contended by the defendants that she ought *c* reasonably to have mitigated her damages by trying to obtain an order against Faye's father. In any event, she told me that she does not know where he is now living and she has not seen him for over six months.

Faye's birth and upbringing have made a substantial difference to Mrs Allen's life. Faye was born at a time when her two children were both nearly of secondary school age, and at the age of 35 she had good prospects of obtaining an interesting, *d* well-paid full-time job. I consider on the evidence that she would probably have remarried before she was 40 and then continued at work, combining her work, as many women now do, with her role as wife and mother to a probably expanded family, since her second husband may well have had children of the same age as her own. She was, and is, a very competent woman.

In the event she had to do the best she could to make ends meet on the income *e* support and child benefit she received. Her two older children have regularly taken holiday jobs to help with the family finances, and their mother has never been able to afford to pay them pocket money since Faye was born. They each paid for themselves from their earnings when the whole family went to Ibiza for a holiday in 1987 when Faye was 18 months old. Mrs Allen usually dresses Faye *f* in secondhand clothes passed down from older children, and she certainly cannot afford to buy much in the way of clothes for herself. She still wears most of the clothes she wore when Faye was born. She cannot afford to let Faye enjoy the extras her school contemporaries enjoy, such as dancing or drama, as she has no money to spare for clothes or tuition fees.

Both her older children still live at home. Leigh is now 16 and has just started *g* a two-year college course. Scott is 18 and has been earning about £140 a week working for building contractors, although he is temporarily laid off. He pays for all his clothes and his holidays and other expenses out of his earnings and gives his mother £30 per week for his keep.

By carefully husbanding her slender resources Mrs Allen has just managed to keep things going without running into debt. She currently receives £104 per *h* week from income support and child benefit. 90% of this goes on regular household bills and with the balance and what she receives from Scott when he is at work she pays the food bills and for miscellaneous items of family expenditure. The contrast in financial terms between her life before and after Faye's birth is very striking.

Her social life has also been very seriously affected. I accept the evidence I heard *j* that her potential male acquaintances lost serious interest in her once they found out that she had had a young child. In about April 1991 she became engaged to marry a man with whom she had had a fairly close relationship ten years before, but this engagement ended abruptly as a result of the disastrous holiday to which I have referred. Although she is now seeing this man again, she is having to take

her relationship with him very much more cautiously now because of the
a difficulties over Faye's behaviour and she really does not know how things will
turn out.

So much for the facts. I turn now to the law. Although a claim of this type has
not yet been considered by the House of Lords, the principles on which damages
are to be awarded have been considered a number of times by the Court of Appeal,
and I was referred to all the leading cases which have been decided in the last
b seven years. I derive from these cases the following principles which should guide
me when I consider Mrs Allen's claim.

(1) If a doctor fails to act towards his patient with the standard of care
reasonably to be expected of him, and as a foreseeable result of the doctor's breach
of duty a child is born whose potential for life would have been lawfully
c terminated but for the doctor's negligence, the law entitles the mother to recover
damages for the foreseeable loss and damage she suffers in consequence of the
doctor's negligence (see *Emeh v Kensington and Chelsea and Westminster Area Health
Authority* [1984] 3 All ER 1044, [1985] QB 1012).

(2) A plaintiff mother is entitled to recover general damages (and any associated
financial special damage) for the discomfort and pain associated with the
d continuation of her pregnancy and the delivery of her child, although she must
set off against this claim a sum in respect of the benefit of avoiding the pain and
suffering and associated financial loss which would have resulted from the
termination of her pregnancy under general anaesthetic, since in the events which
have happened she has not had to undergo that operation (see *Emeh's* case [1984]
3 All ER 1044 at 1056, [1985] QB 1012 at 1028 per Purchas LJ, *Thake v Maurice*
e [1986] 1 All ER 497 at 508, [1986] QB 644 at 682 per Kerr LJ, *Gardiner v Mounfield*
(1989) 5 BMLR 1 at 5–6 per Scott Baker J).

(3) She is also entitled to damages for economic loss quite unassociated with
her own physical injury which falls into two main categories: (i) the financial loss
she suffers because when the unwanted baby is born she has a growing child to
f feed, clothe, house, educate and care for until the child becomes an adult; (ii) the
financial loss she suffers because she has lost or may lose earnings or incur other
expense because of her obligations towards her child which she would have
sought to avoid (see *Emeh's* case [1984] 3 All ER 1044 at 1053, 1056, [1985] QB
1012 at 1025, 1028 per Slade and Purchas LJJ respectively; adopted and applied
by the Court of Appeal in *Thake v Maurice* [1986] 1 All ER 497, [1986] QB 644).

g (4) Although the law recognises that it is foreseeable that if an unwanted child
is born following a doctor's negligence a mother may suffer wear and tear and
tiredness in bringing up a healthy child, the claim for general damages she might
otherwise have had on this account is generally set off against and extinguished
by the benefit of bringing a healthy child into the world and seeing one's child
grow up to maturity (see *Thake v Maurice* [1986] 1 All ER 497 at 508, [1986] QB
h 644 at 682 per Kerr LJ).

(5) However, the law is willing to recognise a claim for general damages in
respect of the foreseeable additional anxiety, stress and burden involved in
bringing up a handicapped child, which is not treated as being extinguished by
any countervailing benefit, although this head of damages is different in kind
from the typical claim for anxiety and stress associated with and flowing from an
j injured plaintiff's own personal injuries (see *Emeh's* case [1984] 3 All ER 1044 at
1052, [1985] QB 1012 at 1022 per Waller LJ).

Academic writers (for example, Kennedy and Grubb *Medical Law* (1989)
pp 584–585) have observed that the courts have not yet had to identify analytically
the precise nature of the claim they have recognised as viable. In *Emeh's* case Slade
LJ could see no reason why, under public policy, the plaintiff should not recover

'such financial damage as she can prove she has sustained' by the negligence in question, whether or not the child is healthy (see [1984] 3 All ER 1044 at 1054, *a* [1985] QB 1012 at 1025); and Purchas LJ could see no reason to introduce into the 'perfectly ordinary, straightforward rules of recovery of damages', whether or not they are damages from a breach of contract or from tort, some qualification to reflect special social positions (see [1984] 3 All ER 1044 at 1056, [1985] QB 1012 at 1028).

For my purpose I am content to assume that the Court of Appeal has recognised *b* that in the unique circumstances surrounding the breach of a doctor's duty to a pregnant woman (or a woman who may become pregnant against her wishes) she should be entitled to recover damages for the two quite distinct foreseeable heads of loss which I identified when I was analysing the principles which should guide me in this case. The first, a claim for damages for personal injuries during the *c* period leading up to the delivery of the child, is a claim which is comparable to, though different from, a claim for damages for personal injuries resulting from the infliction of a traumatic injury to a plaintiff by a negligent defendant. The second, a claim for the economic loss involved in the expense of losing paid employment and the obligation of having to pay for the upkeep and care of an unwanted child, is a totally different type of claim, although it may in turn be *d* associated with a different type of claim for damages for the loss of amenity associated with bringing up a handicapped child.

I realise that if Parliament does not intervene this is likely to mean that different limitation periods may apply to the two types of claim, since it is hard to see how s 11 of the Limitation Act 1980 would apply to a claim limited to the financial costs associated with the upbringing of the unwanted child since this would be, *e* on the facts of a case like the present, a straightforward *Hedley Byrne* (see *Hedley Byrne & Co Ltd v Heller & Partners Ltd* [1963] 2 All ER 575, [1964] AC 465) type of claim for foreseeable economic loss caused by negligent advice or misstatement. However, this is not a matter I have to decide in this case.

One important issue does, however, arise for my decision. This relates to the *f* principles by which the financial cost of bringing up the unwanted child is to be measured. By definition the mother has decided in this class of case that she did not want to have another baby, and in many cases she could not afford to have another baby without considerable hardship to herself and/or the other members of her family. The baby, for its part, did not choose to be born and has no claim itself for the cost of being reared (see *McKay v Essex Area Health Authority* [1982] 2 *g* All ER 771, [1982] QB 1166).

Should the tortfeasor whose negligence has 'caused' the baby's 'wrongful birth' be compelled to pay the 'reasonable' costs of its upkeep? If so, how should those costs be measured, given that it is of the essence of the tortfeasor's negligence that the cost of upkeep is being borne by a mother who looked to him to exercise reasonable care in preventing her from incurring it? Alternatively, should the *h* tortfeasor merely have to pay what is 'necessary', whatever that word means in this context? Is it 'necessary' for a child to have extra music lessons or to go on school trips or to go away for holidays or to be able to buy books and equipment for his interests and hobbies like his school contemporaries? If the test is necessity, how does a judge measure necessity without descending to the criteria adopted *i* by the old poor law guardians or the modern curators of the social fund?

The Court of Appeal has not, so far as I am aware, answered these questions, although there is a hint of an answer in one of the leading cases. This hint, however, might be interpreted at its face value as running contrary to the views which were recently expressed by at least one very experienced judge at first instance.

In *Emeh's* case [1984] 3 All ER 1044 at 1056, [1985] QB 1012 at 1028 Purchas
a LJ expressly adopted the summary of the majority decision of the Supreme Court
of Minnesota in *Sherlock v Stillwater Clinic* (1977) 260 NW 2d 169 at 170–171.
That court had held that the parents might—

> 'recover the reasonable costs of rearing the unplanned child subject to
> offsetting the value of the child's aid, comfort and society during the parent's
b > life expectancy.'

Slade LJ referred to the mother's entitlement to recover 'such financial damage as
she . . . has sustained' and Waller LJ said that 'damages can be awarded which may
in some cases be an encouragement and help to bring up an unplanned child' (see
[1984] 3 All ER 1044 at 1054, 1051, [1985] QB 1012 at 1025, 1021), but I do not
c find any statement of principle to which more than one member of the court
adhered, presumably because it did not have to decide any issue of principle in
this context when it considered the sums which had been suggested by the trial
judge as being appropriate if he was wrong, as the court held that he was, in
dismissing the plaintiff's claim on liability.

There were six relevant decisions by judges at first instance which were brought
d to my attention or were mentioned during the hearing.

In *Udale v Bloomsbury Area Health Authority* [1983] 2 All ER 522, [1983] 1 WLR
1098 Mr and Mrs Udale lived with their four children in a nice part of Hemel
Hempstead. He was a heavy goods vehicle driver and she worked part-time as a
telephonist-operator. She claimed damages in respect of her unwanted fifth child.
Although at a trial in February 1983 Jupp J decided against her on liability on this
e point on public policy grounds (on which he was later overruled by the Court of
Appeal in *Emeh's* case) he assessed damages by reference to supplementary benefit
(£1,750 for just over 4 years) up to trial and by reference to a publication called
'The Money Book' which provided evidence which underpinned an estimate of
£4,500 as the future cost of bringing up the child until he reached the age of 16.
f Jupp J said ([1983] 2 All ER 522 and 529, [1983] 1 WLR 1098 at 1106):

> 'I take the round sum of £5,000 as the proper assessment, bearing in mind
> Mrs Udale's belief that the basic figures are rather tight and the possibility
> that income tax may begin to impinge when the older children go out into
> the world and David gets nearer to 16.'

g

In *Emeh's* case the judgments in the Court of Appeal show that Park J had
assessed the cost of maintaining the child up to the date of trial at the end of 1982
when she was five and a half at £1,736 and the future cost, after taking into
account child allowance, at £507 pa to which he applied a multiplier of eight.
h Nothing is said about the social circumstances of the plaintiff and her Nigerian
husband except that she already had three children.

In *Thake v Maurice* [1984] 2 All ER 513, [1986] QB 644 Mr and Mrs Thake had
five children before the unwanted sixth child was born. They lived in a three-
bedroomed council house. He was a guard with British Rail, and he had his
vasectomy when they were having the greatest difficulty managing on his pay.
j His wife contributed to the family income by doing domestic work when she did
not have a child under school age. They clothed their family by use of jumble
sales and a clothing club and they had not had a holiday for years. Their unplanned
daughter shared a bedroom with one of her brothers and one of her sisters. In
these circumstances Peter Pain J said ([1984] 2 All ER 513 at 527, [1986] QB 644
at 668):

'I confine myself to the costs of Samantha's birth and upkeep. The plaintiffs
have claimed for this on a moderate basis. They have made their calculations *a*
on the basis of the supplementary benefits scales. This is right. Samantha has
been born into a humble household and the defendant should not be expected
to do more than provide her with necessaries.'

The parties had agreed, subject to liability, the cost of the child's layette and
upkeep to her first birthday at £717, the cost of her upkeep in the next three *b*
years at £960, and the claim from her fourth to her seventh birthday (she was
nearly five at the time of trial) at £5,000. These figures made allowance for the
state benefits the child's mother received in respect of her child. The Court of
Appeal ([1986] 1 All ER 497, [1986] QB 644) was not concerned with this part of
Peter Pain J's judgment.

In *Benarr v Kettering Health Authority* (1988) 138 NLJ 179 Hodgson J was *c*
concerned with a quite different type of family. He said that he supposed that
once upon a time they would have been categorised as upper middle class. They
had had three children and their claim was in respect of a fourth unplanned child.
Mr Benarr was in settled and lucrative employment and had insured his life for
£300,000, and the judge found that he and his wife were deeply interested in
obtaining the best possible education for their children. The parties reached *d*
agreement on most of the heads of damage claimed (which are not reported,
although the total award was just over £60,000) but the judge had to decide
whether they were entitled to recover the cost of private education. He observed
that the assessment of damages in claims of this nature had never been subjected
to detailed jurisprudential analysis and that the best available guidance was the *e*
judgment of Peter Pain J in *Thake v Maurice*. He found that whatever the results
of the litigation, whether successful or not, the fourth child would have been
privately educated so long as financial disaster did not overtake the family. He
quoted the relevant part of Peter Pain J's judgment and continued (138 NLJ 179
at 180):

'It is clear there that Peter Pain J was taking into account the financial *f*
status of the family and directing his mind, correctly, in my view—and this,
I think is not seriously in dispute—to the sort of expenditure which would
be incurred for a child in that state of life. In other words, in my judgment
he was addressing his mind to what would be necessary to a child so
circumstanced. Perhaps an analogy could be made to the test of necessaries as *g*
applied to an infant's contract. If that be the right test, and I think it is, it
would follow that if the victim of a negligent vasectomy is a father who
would in any event have privately educated his children, he is entitled to be
compensated for what in the circumstances of that family could properly be
called a necessary. I therefore conclude that the plaintiff is entitled to be
compensated for the future expense to which he will be put in respect of *h*
Catherine's education.'

At the date of trial the child was four and a half years old. The term fees for
pre-preparatory school (ages 4 to 7) were then £315, for preparatory school (ages
8 to 12) £961 and for the local private secondary school at Wellingborough,
where the family lived (ages 13 to 17) £1,066, and Hodgson J eventually made an *j*
award, for reasons which need not concern me, of just under £20,000 under this
head, based on a multiplier of eight.

In *Salih v Enfield Health Authority* [1991] 3 All ER 400, when the relevant child
was nearly six at the date of trial, Drake J adopted in his calculations an undisputed
multiplicand of £1,050 a year, said to represent the additional basic costs of

a providing for a family of two adults and three children compared with a family of two adults and two children, but he did not have to decide anything in relation to the basis on which that sum was assessed or what was meant by basic costs. Mr Salih's income as the owner of a clothing factory is not reported and Mrs Salih's earning capacity seems to have been comparable to Mrs Allen's in the present case.

b Finally, my attention was drawn to *Gardiner v Mounfield* (1989) 5 BMLR 1. Scott Baker J's judgment reveals nothing at all about the plaintiff mother except that she was young and almost certainly unmarried and that she had lived in Lincolnshire. Her unplanned daughter was nearly five at the date of trial. The cost of maintenance was agreed at £1,200 for the first two years of the child's life. Of the next two years Scott Baker J said: 'I think the figure is broadly £750 for two years, say £1,500'. He had presumably adjusted the agreed figures for *c* inflation and, perhaps (something which does not feature in some of the earlier cases) because the child was getting older and more expensive to care for. Of the future he said (at 6):

d 'Turning to future loss, the child is nearly five. She is likely to become more expensive as she gets older. In 11 years' time she will be 16. Part of the cost of maintenance will be met by child benefit, the loss is the additional cost. I assess this at £20 per week, ie £1,040 per annum. I take a multiplier of 8 . . .'

The award for future loss under this head was, therefore, £8,320. The basis on which the judge arrived at his figures does not appear in the report of his *e* judgment.

It will be evident that there is not yet any clear guidance from the Court of Appeal about the basis on which the future cost of maintaining the unplanned child should be assessed. Both Peter Pain and Hodgson JJ referred to defendants being expected to do no more than provide necessaries. It is likely that both those *f* very experienced judges had in mind the jurisprudence underlying what is now s 3 of the Sale of Goods Act 1979 which defines 'necessaries' as 'goods suitable to the condition in life of the minor and to his actual requirements at the time of sale and delivery'. Indeed, Hodgson J expressly referred to this legislation, and a glance at some of the rather quaint examples of a bygone age which are cited in *Chitty on Contracts* (26th edn, 1989) vol 1, para 563 gives a flavour of what he *g* probably had in mind:

'1. *Necessaries.* Engagement and wedding rings, regimental uniform (for an enlisted soldier), presents for a fiancée, a racing bicycle for a youth earning (in 1898) 21s a week, the hire of horses and for work done for them, and the hire of a car to fetch luggage from a station six miles away.
h 2. *Not Necessaries.* Fancy waistcoats for a Cambridge undergraduate already sufficiently supplied with clothing . . . jewelled solitaire sleeve-links for the son of a deceased baronet, a large quantity of tobacco for an army officer, lessons in flying for a law student . . . a hunter for an impecunious cavalry officer and a collection of snuff boxes and curios.'

j Provided that the word 'necessary' is understood in this light (although the latest of these examples in a current textbook was decided in 1930 and one of them goes back to 1739) there is no inconsistency, in my judgment, between this test and the test adopted by the Supreme Court of Minnesota which was adopted and approved by Purchas LJ in *Emeh's* case.

In my judgment in this type of case defendants are liable to pay for all such expenses as may be reasonably incurred for the education and upkeep for the *a* unplanned child, having regard to all the circumstances of the case and, in particular, to his condition in life and his reasonable requirements at the time the expenditure is incurred.

Before I leave this consideration of the legal principles which I should apply when quantifying Mrs Allen's claim, I remind myself that the Court of Appeal has made it clear that I should exclude all the considerations which moral *b* philosophers or theologians might regard as relevant when I compute the figure which I consider appropriate for the cost of Faye's care.

In *Gold v Haringey Health Authority* [1987] 2 All ER 888 at 890, [1988] QB 481 at 484 Lloyd LJ said that many would agree with the surprise expressed by a judge in an earlier unreported case that the law acknowledged an entitlement in a mother to claim damages for the blessing of a healthy child. He pointed out *c* that the conflict of decisions at first instance about the relevant considerations of public policy had been resolved, so far as the Court of Appeal was concerned, by the unanimous decision of that court in *Emeh's* case.

As I have said, these issues have not yet been considered by the House of Lords and in the six years since *Emeh's* case was decided Parliament has done nothing to *d* negate or mitigate the effect of that decision even though contemporary commentators pointed out that it cleared the way for potentially heavy future awards of damages for the cost of maintaining children in this class of case.

If an unplanned child is born after a failure by a hospital doctor to exercise the standard of care reasonably to be expected of him and the child's parents have sent all their other children to expensive private boarding schools for the whole *e* of their education then it appears to me that as the law now stands a very substantial claim for the cost of private education of a healthy child of a reasonably wealthy family might have to be met from the funds of the health authority responsible for the doctor's negligence. However, if this is regarded as inappropriate on policy grounds it is, as Waller LJ pointed out in *Emeh's* case, for *f* Parliament, not the courts to determine policy questions: judges at first instance, at any rate, can do no more than try to identify and apply principles approved by the higher courts unless and until Parliament intervenes.

Having stated the legal principles which I should apply I turn finally to the itemised heads of damage which Mrs Allen claims.

[His Lordship then considered the claims for damages under the various heads *g* and continued:]

Mrs Allen's claim for pain and suffering and loss of amenity
For the period up to the birth, with the associated fear that Faye might be handicapped (there is an offset for not having an abortion and any loss of earnings associated with that) I award £1,250.   *h*

Left to myself, I would decline, however, to make any further award under this head. In a case where the future child is foreseeably born handicapped, for example, because the effects of rubella have not been explained to its pregnant mother by a negligent defendant, I can see reasons why a court is willing to award the mother an extraordinary item of general damages for the burden of bringing up a handicapped child. In this case, however, no evidence was adduced on Mrs *j* Allen's behalf of anything she told the defendants' staff at the hospital as to what might happen to her social life if in August 1985 she was allowed, through negligence, to carry to birth an unwanted child, and what I have seen recorded in the hospital notes bears no hint that her social life might be affected in the way it has been. Similarly, although the care of Faye has obviously had its anxieties, *a* which may have been exacerbated by Mrs Allen's financial plight because this case has taken so long to come to court, I do not see how, if I apply the 'perfectly ordinary, straightforward rules of recovery of damages' to which Purchas LJ referred in *Emeh*'s case, I should award additional damages against the defendants because the child when born had temper tantrums or defective speech or slight dyslexia.

b In my judgment, in the absence of any further illumination from the Court of Appeal about the principles underlying this head of damage and in the absence of any evidence tending to show that in or before August 1985 the defendants ought reasonably to have foreseen that an unborn child might present Mrs Allen with any particular problems when born, the proper course for me to adopt is to apply the guidance given by Kerr LJ in *Thake v Maurice* [1986] 1 All ER 497 at 509, *c* [1986] QB 644 at 683:

> 'The joy of parents at the birth of a healthy child, though with the consequent time and trouble which needs to be devoted to its upbringing, are both virtually impossible to assess in terms of money. It is therefore right that in law they should be treated as cancelling each other out.'

d I remind myself of the evidence that despite all her current problems Faye is a lovely child.

The defendants have, however, conceded that a total figure of £2,500 is proper, and I certainly do not wish to expose them to the risk of an appeal over so small an amount. I therefore award £2,500.

e *Award of general damages*

In these circumstances, I make the following award of general damages:

Mrs Allen's future loss of earnings till Faye is 11	£29,715·84
Child-minding costs when Faye is 11 to 14	2,850·00
Cost of maintaining Faye till she is 18	27,152·00
f Mrs Allen's claim for pain and suffering and loss of amenity	2,500·00
Interest on £2,500 at agreed rate of 5%	125·00
	£62,342·84

The award

g Subject to any further adjustment for interest, to take into account the short period between trial and judgment, the total award, therefore, is:

Special damages	£25,232·77
Interest on special damages	9,055·68
General damages (including interest)	62,342·84
h	£96,631·29.

Judgment for the plaintiff for damages of £96,631·29.

K Mydeen Esq   Barrister.

Channel Tunnel Group Ltd and another v Balfour Beatty Construction Ltd and others

HOUSE OF LORDS

LORD KEITH OF KINKEL, LORD GOFF OF CHIEVELEY, LORD JAUNCEY OF TULLICHETTLE, LORD BROWNE-WILKINSON AND LORD MUSTILL

12–15 OCTOBER 1992, 21 JANUARY 1993

Arbitration – Stay of court proceedings – Power of court to order stay – Contract providing for disputes to be settled by arbitration after initial reference to panel of experts – Court proceedings commenced without any reference being made to panel – Application for stay of court proceedings – Whether fact that reference had not been made to panel preventing court from ordering stay – Arbitration Act 1975, s 1.

Arbitration – Injunction – Interlocutory injunction – Power of court – Arbitration agreement – Seat of arbitration abroad – Building contract – Defendants threatening to suspend performance of building contract – Whether court having power to grant injunction restraining defendants from suspending performance of contract where seat of arbitration abroad – Arbitration Act 1950, s 12(6)(h) – Supreme Court Act 1981, s 37.

The appellants were the concessionaires under a concession granted by the English and French governments for the construction and operation of the Channel tunnel between England and France. They entered into a contract dated 13 August 1986 with the respondents, a joint venture of French and English companies, for the design and construction of the tunnel. The contract, which was governed by the principles common to both English and French law and in the absence of such common principles by general principles of international trade law, provided that any dispute between the parties should first be referred to a panel of experts for settlement and then be finally settled by arbitration in Brussels under the rules of the International Chamber of Commerce. The appellants were entitled under the contract to issue a variation order for, and the respondents were obliged to carry out if so ordered, 'additional work of any kind necessary for the completion of the Works'. The price of any such additional work was, in the absence of provision in the contract, to be agreed between the parties, and in the event of disagreement the appellants were to fix a price which they considered to be reasonable and proper and if that was not accepted by the respondents the dispute was to be referred to the panel of experts, the respondents being obliged to proceed in the meantime with the works so ordered. When the contract was signed it was envisaged that although a cooling system would eventually be required it was not necessary for the opening of the tunnel and therefore provision was made in the lump sum works merely for the design and not the supply of such a system. It later transpired that a cooling system would be needed for the opening of the tunnel and in 1988 the appellants issued a variation order for the provision of such a system. The parties were unable to reach agreement as to the price for the construction of the cooling system and on 3 October 1991 the respondents wrote to the appellants threatening to suspend work on the cooling system unless the appellants agreed and paid the respondents' proposed price for the construction of the cooling system by 7 October. The appellants did not agree to the respondents' demand and instead commenced an action in the High Court for an interim injunction restraining the respondents from suspending work on the cooling system. The respondents applied for a stay *a* of the proceedings under s 1*ᵃ* of the Arbitration Act 1975 on the basis that the proceedings were in respect of a dispute which the parties had agreed, under the contract, to refer to arbitration. The judge refused a stay on the ground that neither party was in a position to embark on arbitration since no reference had been made to the panel of experts and such a reference was a necessary preliminary to an arbitration. The judge further held that he had jurisdiction under s 12(6)(*h*)*ᵇ* of the Arbitration Act 1950 to grant an interim mandatory injunction against the

b respondents pending the arbitration and was prepared to do so, but in the event he made no order because the respondents gave an undertaking that they would not suspend work on the cooling system without giving the appellants 14 days' notice. The respondents appealed to the Court of Appeal, which allowed their appeal and stayed appellants' action under s 1(1) of the 1975 Act on the grounds that it was not necessary that all preliminary steps had to have been taken to

c enable an arbitration to proceed before the court's jurisdiction to stay under s 1 could be invoked. The court further held that there was no power to grant an injunction under s 12(6)(*h*) of the 1950 Act where the arbitration was to take place abroad. The appellants appealed to the House of Lords against the stay granted under s 1(1) of the 1975 Act.

d
Held – (1) The court had power pursuant to its inherent jurisdiction to grant a stay of an action brought before it in breach of an agreed method of resolving disputes by some other method. Furthermore, a stay of the appellants' action ought to be granted because the parties were large commercial enterprises negotiating at arm's length in the light of long experience of construction

e contracts who had clearly decided that the two-stage procedure, despite its potential weaknesses, had a balance of practical advantage over the alternative of bringing proceedings in the national courts and because, having agreed to take their complaints to experts and if necessary arbitrators, they should be required in the interests of the orderly regulation of international commerce to have resort to their chosen tribunal to settle their commercial differences. Moreover, since it

f could not be said on the evidence before the court that the appellants' claim was so unanswerable that there was nothing to arbitrate, there was 'a dispute' between the parties with regard to the subject matter of the action and therefore no reason to withhold a stay (see p 667 *h j*, p 668 *b*, p 670 *d e*, p 677 *e f h*, p 678 *c* to *f* and p 681 *e* to *g*, post).

g (2) Where the court made an order staying an action pending a foreign arbitration it had no power under s 12(6) of the 1950 Act to grant an interim injunction since none of the powers conferred on the court by that Act applied to arbitrations conducted abroad under a law other than English law. Accordingly, the chosen curial law of the arbitration being Belgian law the court had no power under s 12(6) to grant an interim injunction requiring the respondents to continue

h work on the cooling system pending the decision of the panel or the arbitrators (see p 667 *h j*, p 668 *b*, p 670 *g*, p 683 *a b f* to *h* and p 684 *d e*, post).

(3) The court had power to grant an interlocutory injunction under s 37*ᶜ* of the Supreme Court Act 1981 in support of a cause of action which the parties had agreed should be the subject of a foreign arbitration, notwithstanding that proceedings in England had been stayed under s 1 of the 1975 Act so that the

j agreed method of adjudication should take place, since the cause of action remained potentially justiciable before the English court despite the stay. Accordingly, although the commencement of the action was a breach of the arbitration agreement, so that the respondents were not properly before the court,

---

a   Section 1, so far as material, is set out at p 676 *b* to *e*, post

b   Section 12(6), so far as material, is set out at p 676 *f g*, *post*.

c   Section 37, so far as material, is set out at p 668 *e*, post.

the court had power under s 37 of the 1981 Act to grant an interlocutory injunction to prevent the respondents stopping work on the cooling system. *a* However, as a matter of discretion the injunction sought by the appellants would not be granted because the injunction sought was the same relief which would be claimed from the panel and the arbitrators and therefore if the court were to grant the injunction it would largely pre-empt the decision of the panel and arbitrators. The appeal would therefore be dismissed and the appellants' action stayed (see p 667 *h j*, p 668 *b*, p 669 *d* to *j*, p 670 *h*, p 687 *c d*, p 689 *f* and p 690 *e g* *b* to p 691 *a g*, post); *Siskina (cargo owners) v Distos Cia Naviera SA, The Siskina* [1977] 3 All ER 803 distinguished; *Bremer Vulkan Schiffbau Und Maschinenfabrik v South India Shipping Corp Ltd* [1981] 1 All ER 289 considered.

Per curiam. The court has power to stay an action under s 1(1) of the 1975 Act where the reference to arbitrators is to take place, if at all, only after the matter has been referred to someone else, because a stay under s 1(1) does not *c* automatically give rise to a reference to arbitration but merely requires and empowers the court to do no more than stay the action, thereby cutting off the plaintiff's preferred method of enforcing his claim. It is then up to the plaintiff to choose to set an arbitration in motion on pain of losing his claim if he chooses not to do so (see p 667 *h j*, p 668 *b* and p 679 *f j* to p 680 *a*). *d*

Per Lord Browne-Wilkinson (Lord Keith and Lord Goff concurring). It is doubtful whether the general power to grant injunctions conferred on the court by s 37 of the 1981 Act is restricted to certain exclusive categories (see p 667 *j* to p 668 *a* and p 670 *a* to *c*, post); dictum of Lord Diplock in *Siskina (cargo owners) v Distos Cia Naviera SA, The Siskina* [1977] 3 All ER 803 at 825 doubted.

Decision of the Court of Appeal [1992] 2 All ER 609 affirmed. *e*

Notes

For stay of court proceedings pending arbitration, see 2 *Halsbury's Laws* (4th edn reissue) paras 616–620, and for cases on the subject, see 3 *Digest* (Reissue) 70–76, 360–390.

For the interlocutory powers of the court to grant an interim injunction in *f* arbitration proceedings, see 2 *Halsbury's Laws* (4th edn reissue) para 677.

For the Arbitration Act 1950, s 12, see 2 *Halsbury's Statutes* (4th edn) (1992 reissue) 585.

For the Arbitration Act 1975, s 1, see ibid 644.

For the Supreme Court Act 1981, s 37, see 11 *Halsbury's Statutes* (4th edn) (1991 reissue) 1001. *g*

Cases referred to in opinions

Athenee (cargo owners) v Athenee (1922) 11 Ll L Rep 6, CA
Bremer Vulkan Schiffbau Und Maschinenfabrik v South India Shipping Corp Ltd [1981] 1 All ER 289, [1981] AC 909, [1981] 2 WLR 141, HL.
British Airways Board v Laker Airways Ltd [1984] 3 All ER 39, [1985] AC 58, [1984] *h* 3 WLR 413, HL.
Castanho v Brown & Root (UK) Ltd [1981] 1 All ER 143, [1981] AC 557, [1980] 3 WLR 991, HL.
Doleman & Sons v Ossett Corp [1912] 3 KB 257, CA.
Etri Fans Ltd v NMB (UK) Ltd [1987] 2 All ER 763, [1987] 1 WLR 1110, CA.
Fehmarn, The [1957] 2 All ER 707, [1957] 1 WLR 815; *affd* [1958] 1 All ER 333, *j* [1958] 1 WLR 159, CA.
Foster & Dicksee v Hastings Corp (1903) 87 LT 736.
Hamlyn & Co v Talisker Distillery [1894] AC 202, [1891–4] All ER Rep 849, HL.
Hayter v Nelson and Home Insurance Co [1990] 2 Lloyd's Rep 265.
Home and Overseas Insurance Co Ltd v Mentor Insurance Co (UK) Ltd (in liq) [1989] 3 All ER 74, [1990] 1 WLR 153, CA.

McCreary Tire and Rubber Co v CEAT SpA (1974) 501 F 2d 1032, US Ct of Apps
a   (3rd Cir).
Nissan (UK) Ltd v Nissan Motor Co Ltd [1991] CA Transcript 848.
Racecourse Betting Control Board v Secretary of State for Air [1944] 1 All ER 60,
    [1944] Ch 114, CA.
Siskina (cargo owners) v Distos Cia Naviera SA, The Siskina [1977] 3 All ER 803,
    [1979] AC 210, [1977] 3 WLR 818, HL.
b   *South Carolina Insurance Co v Assurantie Maatschappij 'de Zeven Provincien' NV*
    [1986] 3 All ER 487, [1987] AC 24, [1986] 3 WLR 398, HL.
Spiliada Maritime Corp v Cansulex Ltd, The Spiliada [1986] 3 All ER 843, [1987] AC
    460, [1986] 3 WLR 972, HL.

c Appeal

Channel Tunnel Group Ltd and France Manche SA, a company incorporated in
France with limited liability, appealed with the leave of the Appeal Committee of
the House of Lords given on 11 June 1992 from the decision of the Court of
Appeal (Neill, Woolf and Staughton LJJ) ([1992] 2 All ER 609, [1992] QB 656) on
22 January 1992 allowing the appeal of the respondents, Balfour Beatty
d Construction Ltd, Costain Civil Engineering Ltd, Tarmac Construction Ltd,
Taylor Woodrow Construction Holdings Ltd, Wimpey Major Projects Ltd, all of
whom had registered offices in England, and GIE Transmanche Construction,
Bouygues SA, Lyonnaise des Eaux-Dumez (formerly known as Dumez SA),
Société Auxiliaire d'Entreprises SA, Société Générale d'Entreprises SA and Spie
Batignolles SA, all of whom had registered offices in France, from the judgment
e of Evans J given on 27 November 1991 and order dated 4 December 1991
whereby he ordered (1) that the respondents' application under s 1 of the
Arbitration Act 1975 and/or the inherent jurisdiction of the court for a stay of the
proceedings brought by the appellants for an interlocutory injunction restraining
the respondents from suspending work in respect of the cooling system for the
f Channel tunnel be dismissed and (2) that, on the respondents by their counsel
undertaking that they would not suspend work in respect of the cooling system
without giving the appellants 14 days' notice, there be no order on the appellants'
application for an interlocutory injunction. The facts are set out in the opinion of
Lord Mustill.

g *Anthony Grabiner QC* and *Mark Barnes QC* (instructed by *Freshfields*) for the
appellants.
Gordon Pollock QC and *Andrew White* (instructed by *Masons*) for the respondents.

Their Lordships took time for consideration.

h 21 January 1993. The following opinions were delivered.

LORD KEITH OF KINKEL. My Lords, for the reasons given in the speech to
be delivered by my noble and learned friend Lord Mustill, which I have had the
opportunity of considering in draft and with which I agree, I would dismiss this
j appeal. I would add that I also agree with the observations contained in the speech
of my noble and learned friend Lord Browne-Wilkinson.

LORD GOFF OF CHIEVELEY. My Lords, for the reasons given by my noble
and learned friend Lord Mustill, I too would dismiss the appeal. I also wish to
express my agreement with the point raised by my noble and learned friend Lord
Browne-Wilkinson. Like him, I am concerned that the jurisdiction to grant an

injunction, which is unfettered in the statute, should be rigidly confined to exclusive categories by judicial decision.

LORD JAUNCEY OF TULLICHETTLE. My Lords, I have the advantage of reading in draft the speech prepared by my noble and learned friend Lord Mustill. I agree with him, and for the reasons which he gives, I, too, would dismiss the appeal.

LORD BROWNE-WILKINSON. My Lords, I have read and agree with the speech of my noble and learned friend Lord Mustill. For the reasons which he gives I too would dismiss the appeal.

I add a few words of my own on the submission that the decision of this House in *Siskina (cargo owners) v Distos Cia Naviera SA, The Siskina* [1977] 3 All ER 803, [1979] AC 210 would preclude the grant of any injunction under s 37(1) of the Supreme Court Act 1981, even if such injunction were otherwise appropriate. If correct that submission would have the effect of severely curtailing the powers of the English courts to act in aid, not only of foreign arbitrations, but also of foreign courts. Given the international character of much contemporary litigation and the need to promote mutual assistance between the courts of the various jurisdictions which such litigation straddles, it would be a serious matter if the English courts were unable to grant interlocutory relief in cases where the substantive trial and the ultimate decision of the case might ultimately take place in a court outside England.

Section 37(1) of the Supreme Court Act 1981 provides:

'The High Court may by order (whether interlocutory or final) grant an injunction or appoint a receiver in all cases where it appears to the court to be just and convenient to do so.'

Despite the breadth of these words, in *The Siskina* this House laid down certain limits on the powers which it confers. In that case, the plaintiffs were seeking leave to serve the defendants out of the jurisdiction. The only ground on which the plaintiffs could rely under RSC Ord 11 was the then r 1(1)(i), viz that the writ claimed an injunction against the defendants dealing with their assets within the jurisdiction. Since the contract in question contained a foreign exclusive jurisdiction clause, the only injunction capable of being granted by the English courts in the ordinary course of events would have been an interlocutory injunction. In that context, Lord Diplock said ([1977] 3 All ER 803 at 824, [1979] AC 210 at 256):

'The words used in sub-para (i) are terms of legal art. The sub-paragraph speaks of "the action" in which a particular kind of relief, "an injunction", is sought. This presupposes the existence of a cause of action on which to found "the action". A right to obtain an interlocutory injunction is not a cause of action. It cannot stand on its own. It is dependent on there being a pre-existing cause of action against the defendant arising out of an invasion, actual or threatened, by him of a legal or equitable right of the plaintiff for the enforcement of which the defendant is amenable to the jurisdiction of the court. The right to obtain an interlocutory injunction is merely ancillary and incidental to the pre-existing cause of action.'

This passage, read in isolation, suggests that there are only two limits on the general power conferred by s 37, viz (1) that the court must have personal jurisdiction over the defendants in the sense that they can be duly served either personally or under RSC Ord 11 (other than r 1(1)(i)) and (2) that the plaintiffs have a cause of action under English law.

a However, it was submitted for the respondents that two other passages in Lord Diplock's speech impose a third requirement, viz (3) that the interlocutory injunction must be ancillary to a claim for substantive relief to be granted in this country by an order of the English court.

It was said that this third limit is to be found in two other passages in Lord Diplock's speech ([1977] 3 All ER 803 at 823, 825, [1979] AC 210 at 254, 256):

b '[Section 37], speaking as it does of interlocutory orders, presupposes the existence of an action, actual or potential, claiming substantive relief which the High Court has jurisdiction to grant and to which the interlocutory orders referred to are but ancillary ... To come within [sub-para (i)] the injunction sought in the action must be part of the substantive relief to which the plaintiff's cause of action entitles him; and the thing that it is c sought to restrain the foreign defendant from doing in England must amount to an invasion of some legal or equitable right belonging to the plaintiff in this country and enforceable here by a final judgment for an injunction.'

On the basis of that alleged third requirement, the respondents contended that since the contract in the present case contains a foreign arbitration clause which d the Arbitration Act 1975 requires the action to be stayed, the court has no power to grant an interlocutory injunction. Although the respondents have been validly served (ie there is jurisdiction in the court) and there is an alleged invasion of the appellants' contractual rights (ie there is a cause of action in English law), since the final relief (if any) will be granted by the arbitrators and not by the English court, the English court, it is said, has no power to grant the interlocutory e injunction.

In my judgment that submission is not well founded. I can see nothing in the language employed by Lord Diplock (or in later cases in this House commenting on The Siskina) which suggest that a court has to be satisfied, at the time it grants interlocutory relief, that the final order, if any, will be made by an English court. The two passages I have quoted refer to the substantive relief being relief which f the English court has 'jurisdiction to grant' and the rights 'enforceable here'; see also [1977] 3 All ER 803 at 824, [1979] AC 210 at 256: '... some legal or equitable right which it has jurisdiction to enforce by final judgment'. These are words which indicate that the relevant question is whether the English court has power to grant the substantive relief, not whether it will in fact do so. Indeed, in many g cases it will be impossible, at the time interlocutory relief is sought, to say whether or not the substantive proceedings and the grant of the final relief will or will not take place before the English court. My noble and learned friend Lord Mustill has demonstrated in his speech that in the context of arbitration proceedings whether it is the court or the arbitrators which make such final determination will depend upon whether the defendant applies for a stay. The same is true of h ordinary litigation based on a contract having an exclusive jurisdiction clause: the defendant may not choose to assert his contractual right to have the matter tried elsewhere. Even more uncertain are cases where there is a real doubt whether the English court or some foreign court is the forum conveniens for the litigation: is the English court not to grant interlocutory relief against a defendant duly served and based on a good cause of action just because the English proceedings may j subsequently be stayed on the grounds of forum non coveniens?

I therefore reach the conclusion that The Siskina does not impose the third limit on the power to grant interlocutory injunctions which the respondents contend for. Even applying the test laid down by The Siskina the court has power to grant interlocutory relief based on a cause of action recognised by English law against a defendant duly served where such relief is ancillary to a final order whether to be granted by the English court or by some other court or arbitral body.

Finally I should make it clear that I have merely been considering the effect of
the decision in *The Siskina* on the assumption that it correctly states the law. The
tests it laid down in absolute terms have already received one substantial
modification: see *Castanho v Brown & Root (UK) Ltd* [1981] 1 All ER 143, [1981]
AC 557; *British Airways Board v Laker Airways Ltd* [1984] 3 All ER 39, [1985] AC
58. Moreover, in *South Carolina Insurance Co v Assurantie Maatschappij 'de Zeven
Provincien' NV* [1986] 3 All ER 487, [1987] AC 24 Lord Goff of Chieveley (with
whom Lord Mackay of Clashfern agreed) reserved the question whether the law
as laid down by *The Siskina* (as subsequently modified) was correct in restricting
the power to grant injunctions to certain exclusive categories. With respect, I
share the same doubts as are there expressed and reserve the question for
consideration when it arises.

LORD MUSTILL. My Lords, since this is a long judgment I will state at the
outset my answers to the questions posed in argument, before developing the
reasons.

1. *Should the action brought by the appellant against the respondents be stayed?*
I consider that the action can and should be stayed pursuant to the inherent
jurisdiction of the court to inhibit proceedings brought in breach of an agreed
method of resolving disputes. I thus arrive at the same conclusion as the Court of
Appeal, but by a different route. It is therefore unnecessary to decide whether, as
held by the Court of Appeal, the court would also have power to stay the action
under s 1 of the Arbitration Act 1975. I nevertheless briefly state reasons for
concluding, with some hesitation, that such a power does exist in the circumstances
of the present case.

2. *Is there in fact any dispute between the parties with regard to the subject matter
of the action?*
In common with the Court of Appeal I conclude that this question should be
answered in the affirmative.

3. *Does the court have power to grant an injunction to prevent the respondents
from ceasing work under an agreement dated 13 August 1986 (the construction
contract)?*
The Court of Appeal held that no such power is conferred by s 12(6)(*h*) of the
Arbitration Act 1950, and I agree.
The Court of Appeal also held that the court had no power to grant the
injunction under s 37(1) of the Supreme Court Act 1981. As I understand it the
Court of Appeal would in any event have declined to uphold the grant of an
injunction. For my part I consider that such a power does exist, but that it should
not be exercised in the circumstances of the present case. Again, therefore, I reach
the same conclusion as the Court of Appeal but by a different route.
In the result I would dismiss the appeal.

I. INTRODUCTION

1. *The contract*
The appellants are the concessionaires under a concession granted by Her
Majesty's government and the government of the French Republic for the
construction and operation of the Channel tunnel. The respondents are a joint
venture of (a) 'Translink', the members of which are five British construction

companies, the first to fifth respondents, who are themselves carrying on business
a in joint venture, and (b) the sixth respondents, GIE Transmanche Construction, the members of which are five French construction companies, the seventh to eleventh respondents.

Under an agreement dated 13 August 1986 (the construction contract) the appellants employed the respondents to design and commission the tunnel. The works to be carried out under the construction contract are divided into (a) target
b works, (b) lump sum works and (c) procurement items. The target works broadly comprise the boring and lining of the three tunnels. That work is more or less complete. The lump sum works essentially comprise (a) the design and construction of the terminals at each end of the tunnels and (b) the design, supply, installation and commissioning of mechanical and electrical fixed equipment in
c the tunnels and terminals (fixed equipment).

There is provision in the contract for variation of the works. Clause 51 of the conditions of contract allows the appellants to 'make any variation of the form, quality or quantity of the works or any part thereof that may, in [its] opinion, be desirable' and provides that no such variation will in any way vitiate or invalidate the contract. The clause provides that the appellants and the respondents should
d seek to agree the terms of the variation; if no agreement is reached, the appellants may confirm the order, and, subject to certain exception, the respondents must then comply.

When the contract was signed, it was envisaged that the tunnel would eventually require a cooling system, but that it would not be required at the opening. Accordingly, the lump sum works originally included provision for the
e design of such a system, but not the supply of the mechanical works forming the system itself. Later it became apparent that a cooling system would be needed, even at the opening. Accordingly, the appellants issued a variation order no 3 for the provision of such a system. The order was confirmed in April 1988. Thereupon the cooling system itself became part of the fixed equipment and the
f lump sum works.

The present dispute arose, inter alia, because the parties failed to agree the price for the variation and because of the discontinuance of an interim agreement to pay the respondents on a cost plus basis (see below). The contract contains a number of provisions for the assessment and payment of sums due under it. In particular, cl 60(2) of the conditions of contract provides for the contractor to
g submit monthly statements including (in respect of the lump sum works) an estimate of the likely value of lump sum works to be executed in that and the following month. Clause 60(3) provides for the employer to review the contractor's statement and to issue a 'certificate of advance payment' stating in relation to each of the items set out in the contractor's statement, what in the employer's opinion is the proper figure. Clause 60(3) then provides that the
h amount stated as payable in the certificate of advance payment shall be payable on the first banking day of the next month.

Clause 52 of the conditions of contract provides for the valuation of variations to the works, by reference to the rates or prices set out in the contract or in the breakdown of the lump sum price approved under the contract; if none are applicable, the rates or prices are to be agreed between the parties or, failing
j agreement, fixed by the employer at such rates or prices as in its opinion shall be reasonable and proper.

Clause 52(5) provides that if the contractor does not accept any rate or price fixed by the employer under cl 52 as reasonable and proper, the dispute shall be referred to a panel of experts for determination under cl 67.

Clause 67 provides as follows:

'Settlements of Disputes   *a*

67(1) If any dispute or difference shall arise between the Employer and the Contractor during the progress of the Works (but not after the issue of the Maintenance Certificate for the whole of the Works or the last of such certificates under Clause 62(1) or after abandonment of the Works or termination or alleged termination of the Contract), then, subject to Article   *b* 6(4) Clauses 73(5) and 74(4) and the rules of the procedure for the calling in of the Performance Bond in Schedule 25, such dispute or difference shall at the instance of either the Employer or the Contractor in the first place be referred in writing to and be settled by a Panel of three persons (acting as independent experts but not as arbitrators) who shall unless otherwise agreed by both the Employer and the Contractor within a period of 90 days after   *c* being requested in writing by either party to do so, and after such investigation as the Panel think fit, state their decision in writing and give notice of the same to the Employer and the Contractor. The Panel shall be constituted in the manner set out in Clause 67(6).

(2) The Contractor shall in every case continue to proceed with the Works with all due diligence and the Contractor and the Employer shall both give   *d* effect forthwith to every such decision of the Panel (provided that such decision shall have been made unanimously) unless and until the same shall be revised by arbitration as hereinafter provided. Such unanimous decision shall be final and binding upon the Contractor and the Employer unless the dispute or difference has been referred to arbitration as hereinafter provided.   *e*

(3) Subject to Article 6(4) of the Contract Agreement, if:—(i) either the Employer or the Contractor be dissatisfied with any unanimous decision of the Panel given under Clause 67(1), or (ii) the Panel shall fail to give a unanimous decision for a period of 90 days, or such other period as may be agreed by both the Employer and the Contractor, after being requested by either party to do so, or (iii) any unanimous decision of the Panel is not given   *f* effect in accordance with Clause 67(2) then either the Employer or the Contractor may within 90 days after receiving notice of such decision or within 90 days after the expiration of the said period of 90 days or such other period as may be agreed by the Employer and the Contractor (as the case may be) notify the other party in writing that the dispute or difference is to be referred to arbitration. If no such notice has been given by either party to the   *g* other within such periods, the Panel's decision shall remain final and binding upon the parties . . .

(4) All disputes or differences in respect of which a notice has been given under Clause 67(3) by either party that such dispute or difference is to be referred to arbitration and any other dispute or difference of any kind   *h* whatsoever which shall arise between the Employer or the Maitre d'Oeuvre and the Contractor in connection with or arising out of the Contract, or the execution of the Works or after their completion and whether before or after the termination, abandonment or breach of the Contract shall be finally settled under the Rules of Conciliation and Arbitration of the International Chamber of Commerce by three arbitrators appointed under such Rules.   *j* The Employer and the Contractor shall each nominate and appoint one arbitrator and the third arbitrator shall be appointed by the International Chamber of Commerce. The seat of such arbitration shall be Brussels. Save as provided in clause 67(3), the said arbitrator/s shall have full power to open up, revise and review any decision, opinion, direction, certificate or valuation

a of the Employer and/or the Maitre d'Oeuvre. Neither party shall be limited in the proceedings before such arbitrator/s to the evidence or arguments put before the Panel for the purpose of obtaining his said decision. No decision given by the Panel in accordance with the foregoing provisions shall disqualify a member of the Panel from being called as a witness and giving evidence before the arbitrator/s on any matter whatsoever relevant to the dispute or difference referred to the arbitrator/s as aforesaid.

b (5) The reference to arbitration may proceed notwithstanding that the Works shall not then be or be alleged to be complete, provided always that the obligations of the Employer and the Contractor shall not be altered by reason of the arbitration being conducted during the progress of the Works . . .'

c The provision just quoted refers to the Rules of Conciliation and Arbitration of the International Chamber of Commerce (the ICC). The English text of these rules (the corresponding French version is not before your Lordship's House) provides as follows.

Article 8(5):

d 'Before the file is transmitted to the arbitrator . . . the parties shall be at liberty to apply to any competent judicial authority for interim or conservatory measures, and they shall not by so doing be held to infringe the agreement to arbitrate or to affect the relevant powers reserved to the arbitrator . . .'

Article 24:

e '1. The arbital award shall be final.

2. By submitting the dispute to the International Chamber of Commerce, the parties shall be deemed to have undertaken to carry out the resulting award without delay and to have waived the right to any form of appeal insofar as such waiver can be validly made.'

f Clause 68 of the contract is to the following effect:

'The construction, validity and performance of the Contract shall in all respects be governed by and interpreted in accordance with the principles common to both English law and French law, and in the absence of such common principles by such general principles of international trade law as

g have been applied by national and international tribunals. Subject in all cases, with respect to the works to be respectively performed in the French and in the English part of the site, to the respective French or English public policy (ordre public) provisions.'

It is common ground that the first stage of the procedure—reference to the

h panel of experts under cl 67(1)—is not itself an arbitration within the Arbitration Act 1975, but that the second stage is an arbitration.

2. *The dispute*

Variation order no 3 was issued on 16 November 1987 and confirmed as an order under cl 51 on 29 April 1988, and the parties entered into discussions as to

j the price payable in respect of that variation. The extent of the work was not fully defined. In December 1989 the respondents indicated that the programme required them to order pipeline materials in the very near future, and the respondents asked that the appellants fund the committed cost of procurement on an interim basis pending final agreement of the total sales value. The appellants agreed to this expressly on the basis that it was an interim measure until a final price was settled. Prior to March 1991, the respondents therefore billed, and the appellants paid, on a cost plus basis.

The parties were unable to reach agreement regarding the price of variation order no 3. By the end of 1990 the parties' estimates (in 1985 values) were respectively £112m (the respondents) excluding the cost of additional delay and disruption, and £78m (the appellants), inclusive of delay and disruption, in each case excluding building and civil works.

Therefore, by letter dated 19 March 1991, the appellants informed the respondents that they would no longer continue with the interim arrangement and indicated that they would thenceforth issue certificates of advance payment based on its estimates of value. The appellants stated that they were willing to discuss the matter further but that in the event that agreement was not possible the appellants would have no option but to fix a rate pursuant to the contract.

From then on, the appellants issued their monthly certificates and made their monthly payments on the basis of their own estimates of value. Between the beginning of March and the end of September 1991, seven such monthly payments were made. The respondents sought payment on the basis of their own estimates of value, thereby making clear that they did not accept the appellants' valuation. Neither side referred the difference on valuation to the panel for determination by it under cl 67.

By the end of July 1991 the respondents had made a submission to the appellants claiming a right to a 'reasonable sum' in respect of the whole of the fixed equipment works.

By September 1991 the cumulative difference between the sums applied for by the respondents (excluding sums relating to delays and disruption) and those paid by the appellants amounted to about £17m (in 1985 values). The respondents claimed to have been approaching a point at which the amount certified would not even cover the costs which they were incurring, and that this point was ultimately reached in November 1991. The appellants claim that this is not correct.

By letter dated 3 October 1991, the respondents required (a) that the appellants agree to the respondents' proposed figure for the construction of the Sangatte buildings (part of the cooling system works excluded from the estimates) and (b) that the appellants pay the respondents in full in accordance with the amounts applied for in respect of all cooling works, pending the final valuation of variation order no 3.

Unless the appellants agreed to these requirements in writing at close of business on Monday, 7 October 1991 the respondents would 'be obliged to suspend all work relating to the cooling system'. The letter went on to draw the appellants' attention to 'the very serious consequences' which would ensue, and it itemised some of them. The matter was widely publicised in the French press and media on 7 and 8 October 1991.

After correspondence between the parties in the week commencing 7 October 1991, the respondents wrote on 14 October 1991 effectively confirming their position. On the same day the appellants issued the present proceedings for an injunction to restrain the respondents from carrying out that threat. The respondents did not then, and did not thereafter suspend the cooling system works.

Meanwhile the respondents had submitted a claim to the appellants to the effect that there had been such a fundamental change to the character of the works that the originally agreed lump sum price was no longer applicable, and that they were accordingly entitled to be paid a reasonable price for the fixed equipment works on a cost plus basis. This claim led to a panel reference resulting,

nearly four months after the decision of the Court of Appeal in the present action,
a in a ruling that unless the parties could reach an agreement on interim funding
the appellants should make large extra monthly payments for the fixed
equipment. Having received this favourable award the respondents intimated to
the appellants that they did not intend to suspend works on the cooling system.
However, on 23 April 1992 the appellants lodged a request for arbitration with
the ICC seeking to set aside the decision of the panel. This led to an award made
b by the arbitrators on 30 September 1992 which set aside the decision of the panel
and substituted a provision for the retention by the respondents, for the account
of the appellants, of the amounts thus far paid by the appellants pursuant to the
decision of the panel.

c
The litigation
The writ in the present action was issued by the appellants on 14 October 1991.
The relief claimed was as follows:

> '(a) an injunction restraining the Defendants and each of them, by
d themselves, their servants or agents in breach of their obligations under an
> agreement in writing dated 13th August 1986 made between the Plaintiffs
> and the Defendants ("the Contract") from suspending work relating to the
> Cooling System; (b) Costs; (c) Such further or other relief as to the Court
> seems just.'

Three days later the appellants issued an application in the Commercial Court
e for:

> '(1) an injunction restraining the Defendants and each of them, by
> themselves, their servants or agents in breach of their obligations under an
> agreement in writing dated 13th August 1986 made between the Plaintiffs
> and the Defendants ("the Contract") from suspending work relating to the
f Cooling System . . .'

On the same day the respondents issued a cross-application to stay all further
proceedings in the action pursuant to s 1 of the Arbitration Act 1975. There
followed in short order an exchange of 11 affidavits, supported by hundreds of
pages of exhibits. These prepared the ground for a hearing before Evans J at the
g conclusion of which on 27 November 1991 the learned judge read a prepared
judgment, leading to an order that: (1) upon the present respondents undertaking
not to suspend work on the cooling system without giving the appellants 14 days'
notice, no order should be made on the appellants' application for an injunction.
Without this undertaking Evans J would have granted an injunction; (2) the
application by the respondents for a stay of the action was refused.

h   There followed an appeal by the respondents, which was heard by the Court of
Appeal (Neill, Woolf and Staughton LJJ) during three days commencing on 18
December 1991. On 22 January 1992 the Court of Appeal handed down written
judgments, of which the leading judgment was that of Staughton LJ. Reversing
the judgment of Evans J the court stayed the action. It also refused an injunction
(see [1992] 2 All ER 609, [1992] QB 656).
j   I pause to draw attention to these dates. At the conclusion of his judgment
Staughton LJ paid tribute to the quality of the arguments, and the way in which
the papers had been prepared. I would like to echo this and to add my own
appreciation of the full and careful judgments delivered. As will appear, I find
that after an exchange of printed cases, full oral argument and ample time for
reflection I am led to differ from these judgments in certain respects. Nevertheless,

I respectfully suggest to your Lordships that to carry this complex and difficult
matter through from the commencement of the proceedings to the conclusion of   *a*
judgment in the Court of Appeal within the period of three months reflects the
greatest credit on all concerned.

3. *The legislative background*
     The centre of the dispute is s 1 of the 1975 Act: *b*

> '(1) If any party to an arbitration agreement to which this section applies,
> or any person claiming through or under him, commences any legal
> proceedings in any court against any other party to the agreement, or any
> person claiming through or under him, in respect of any matter agreed to be
> referred, any party to the proceedings may at any time after appearance, and
> before delivering any pleadings or taking any other steps in the proceedings, *c*
> apply to the court to stay the proceedings; and the court, unless satisfied that
> the arbitration agreement is null and void, inoperative or incapable of being
> performed or that there is not in fact any dispute between the parties with
> regard to the matter agreed to be referred, shall make an order staying the
> proceedings.
> (2) This section applies to any arbitration agreement which is not a   *d*
> domestic arbitration agreement; and neither section 4(1) of the Arbitration
> Act 1950 nor section 4 of the Arbitration Act (Northern Ireland) 1937 shall
> apply to an arbitration agreement to which this section applies . . .
> (4) In this section "domestic arbitration agreement" means an arbitration
> agreement which does not provide, expressly or by implication, for arbitration *e*
> in a State other than the United Kingdom and to which neither—(a) an
> individual who is a national of, or habitually resident in, any State other than
> the United Kingdom; nor (b) a body corporate which is incorporated in, or
> whose central management and control is exercised in, any State other than
> the United Kingdom; is a party at the time the proceedings are commenced.'

Next, there is s 12(6)(h) of the 1950 Act: *f*

> 'The High Court shall have, for the purpose of and in relation to a reference,
> the same power of making orders in respect of . . . (h) interim injunctions or
> the appointment of a receiver; as it has for the purpose of and in relation to
> an action or matter in the High Court . . .'

Reference was also made in argument to s 25 of the Civil Jurisdiction and   *g*
Judgments Act 1982:

> '(1) The High Court in England and Wales or Northern Ireland shall have
> power to grant interim relief where—(a) proceedings have been or are to be
> commenced in a Contracting State other than the United Kingdom or in a   *h*
> part of the United Kingdom other than that in which the High Court in
> question exercises jurisdiction; and (b) they are or will be proceedings whose
> subject-matter is within the scope of the 1968 Convention as determined by
> Article 1 (whether or not the Convention has effect in relation to the
> proceedings) . . .
> (3) Her Majesty may by Order in Council extend the power to grant   *j*
> interim relief conferred by subsection (1) so as to make it exercisable in
> relation to proceedings of any of the following descriptions, namely—
> (a) proceedings commenced or to be commenced otherwise than in a
> Contracting State; (b) proceedings whose subject-matter is not within the
> scope of the 1968 Convention as determined by Article 1; (c) arbitration
> proceedings . . .

a
(5) An Order in Council under subsection (3) which confers power to grant interim relief in relation to arbitration proceedings may provide for the repeal of any provision of section 12(6) of the Arbitration Act 1950 or section 21(1) of the Arbitration Act (Northern Ireland) 1937 to the extent that it is superseded by the provisions of the Order . . .

b
(7) In this section "interim relief", in relation to the High Court in England and Wales or Northern Ireland, means interim relief of any kind which that court has power to grant in proceedings relating to matters within its jurisdiction, other than—(a) a warrant for the arrest of property; or (b) provision for obtaining evidence.'

No Order in Council has yet been made under s 25(3)(c).

Finally I must refer to s 37(1) of the Supreme Court Act 1981:

c
'The High Court may by order (whether interlocutory or final) grant an injunction or appoint a receiver in all cases where it appears to the court to be just and convenient to do so.'

d
II. THE APPLICATION FOR A STAY

There are two ways in which the respondents seek to uphold the grant of a stay. First, on the ground that the dispute is between parties 'to an arbitration agreement to which this section applies', and that the dispute between them is 'in respect of any matter agreed to be referred', within the meaning of s 1 of the 1975 Act, so that the court is obliged to stay the action. Secondly, because this is an appropriate *e* case in which to exercise the inherent power of the court to stay proceedings brought before it in breach of an agreement to decide disputes in some other way. Whilst proposing both solutions Mr Pollock QC for the respondents showed little warmth for the second; no doubt because it offered his clients a remedy which was discretionary, in contrast to the mandatory stay under s 1. Nevertheless, I am *f* satisfied that this is the correct route, and that the court not only possesses a discretion to grant a stay in such cases such as the present, but also that this is a remedy which ought to be exercised in the present case.

First, as to the existence of the power to stay proceedings in a case which comes close to s 1 of the 1975 Act, and yet falls short either because of some special feature of the dispute-resolution clause, or because for some reason an agreement *g* to arbitrate cannot immediately, or effectively, be applied to the dispute in question. It is true that no reported case to this effect was cited in argument, and in the only one which has subsequently come to light, namely *Etri Fans Ltd v NMB (UK) Ltd* [1987] 2 All ER 763, [1987] 1 WLR 1110, the court whilst assuming the existence of the power did not in fact make an order. I am satisfied however that the undoubted power of the court to stay proceedings under the general *h* jurisdiction, where an action is brought in breach of agreement to submit disputes to the adjudication of a foreign court, provides a decisive analogy. Indeed until 1944 it was believed that the power to stay in such a case derived from the arbitration statutes. This notion was repudiated in *Racecourse Betting Control Board v Secretary of State for Air* [1944] 1 All ER 60, [1944] Ch 114, but the analogy was nevertheless maintained. Thus, per MacKinnon LJ ([1944] 1 All ER 60 at 65, *j* [1944] Ch 114 at 126):

'It is, I think, rather unfortunate that the power and duty of the court to stay the action [on the grounds of a foreign jurisdiction clause] was said to be under the Arbitration Act, 1889, s. 4. In truth, that power and duty arose under a wider general principle, namely, that the court makes people abide by their contracts, and, therefore, will restrain a plaintiff from bringing an action which he is doing in breach of his agreement with the defendant that any dispute between them shall be otherwise determined.'

So also, in cases before and after 1944: see *Athenee (cargo owners) v Athenee* (1922) 11 Ll L Rep 6 per Atkin LJ and *The Fehmarn* [1957] 2 All ER 707 at 709–710, [1957] 1 WLR 815 at 819 per Willmer J, approved on appeal ([1958] 1 All ER 333 at 336, [1958] 1 WLR 159 at 163). I see no reason why the analogy should not be reversed. If it is appropriate to enforce a foreign jurisdiction clause under the general powers of the court by analogy with the discretionary power under what is now s 4(1) of the 1950 Act to enforce an arbitration clause by means of a stay, it must surely be legitimate to use the same powers to enforce a dispute-resolution agreement which is nearly an immediately effective agreement to arbitrate, albeit not quite. I would therefore hold that irrespective of whether cl 67 falls within s 1 of the 1975 Act, the court has jurisdiction to stay the present action.

My Lords, I also have no doubt that this power should be exercised here. This is not the case of a jurisdiction clause, purporting to exclude an ordinary citizen from his access to a court and featuring inconspicuously in a standard printed form of contract. The parties here were large commercial enterprises, negotiating at arm's length in the light of a long experience of construction contracts, of the types of disputes which typically arise under them, and of the various means which can be adopted to resolve such disputes. It is plain that cl 67 was carefully drafted, and equally plain that all concerned must have recognised the potential weaknesses of the two-stage procedure and concluded that despite them there was a balance of practical advantage over the alternative of proceedings before the national courts of England and France. Having made this choice I believe that it is in accordance, not only with the presumption exemplified in the English cases cited above that those who make agreements for the resolution of disputes must show good reasons for departing from them, but also with the interests of the orderly regulation of international commerce, that having promised to take their complaints to the experts and if necessary to the arbitrators, that is where the appellants should go. The fact that the appellants now find their chosen method too slow to suit their purpose, is to my way of thinking quite beside the point.

Since this conclusion is sufficient to uphold the decision of the Court of Appeal to stay the action it would be possible now to pass to the next issue. Since, however, provisions in the same general shape as cl 67 are common in the construction industry, and since the meaning of s 1(1) of the 1975 Act has been the subject of elaborate argument, it is right to make some observations on the question whether (as the Court of Appeal has held) the court has, independently of any inherent power, both the right and the duty to stay the action under s 1. The subject is not easy, but limitations of space forbid a full discussion.

I first recall the words of s 1(1):

> 'If any party to an arbitration agreement . . . commences any legal proceedings . . . in respect of any matter agreed to be referred . . . the court . . . shall make an order staying the proceedings.'

Most of the argument on this subsection was confined to the words 'an arbitration agreement'. These words are not clear, and there is substantial force in the submission that cl 67 is not (in the words of s 7(1) of the 1975 Act) 'an agreement . . . to submit to arbitration present or future differences', but an agreement to submit such differences to resolution by a panel of experts, the arbitrators providing no more than a contingent form of appeal—such as the

a Commercial Court would provide in a reference falling within the Arbitration Act 1979. Whilst acknowledging the force of this argument, if the words of the section were the only source of uncertainty I would have been prepared without undue difficulty to hold that cl 67 is 'an arbitration agreement'. What has given me much more reason to hesitate is the nature of the relief which the court is empowered and bound to accord, when an action is brought which falls within s 1(1), namely 'an order staying the proceedings'. The problem can best be
b illustrated by reference to the words of the Convention on the Recognition and Enforcement of Foreign Arbitral Awards (New York, 10 July 1958; TS 20 (1976); Cmnd 6419), which was the impetus for the enactment of the English legislation. Article II(3) provides as follows;

c   'The court of a Contracting State, when seized of an action in a matter in respect of which the parties have made an agreement within the meaning of this article shall, at the request of one of the parties, refer the parties to arbitration, unlesss it finds that the said agreement is null and void, inoperative, or incapable of being performed.'

d   What springs to mind at once is that the application of this formula to cl 67 requires the court to do the impossible, namely to refer the dispute to the arbitrators, whereas it is to the panel of experts that the matter must first be sent if it is to be sent anywhere at all. If the English legislation had followed the convention, as strictly speaking it should have done, it would have been hard to
e resist the conclusion that the duty to stay does not apply to a situation where the reference to the arbitrators is to take place, if at all, only after the matter has been referred to someone else.
       In the end I have come to the conclusion that the different wording of the Act does not compel this conclusion. The convention envisages a procedure, somewhat similar to the former English practice, now largely in disuse where the order of
f the court called into being a reference to arbitration to which both parties were at once compulsorily remitted. Instead, the Act requires and empowers the court to do no more than stay the action, thereby cutting off the plaintiff's preferred method of enforcing his claim. It is then up to the plaintiff whether he sets an arbitration in motion, but if he chooses not to do so he loses his claim.
       My Lords, this a real, not simply a verbal, distinction and I have come to believe
g that it results from a deliberate choice by the legislature between the two different ways of giving effect to an arbitration agreement. The idea of a compulsory reference was mooted before the great reforms of the 1850s, but was rejected in favour of the discretionary stay embodied in s 11 of the Common Law Procedure Act 1854. This choice was perpetuated, not only in the Arbitration Act 1889 but
h also in the Arbitration Clauses (Protocol) Act 1924, the purpose of which was to give effect to the League of Nations Protocol of 24 September 1923, notwithstanding that the latter (like its successor of 1958) required the courts of the member state, not simply to stay the action, but to refer the matter to arbitration. Later, we see the same contrast between the New York Convention and the 1975 Act. In the light of the history which I have sketched I believe that
j this was not an accident of drafting, which might require the 1975 Act to be interpreted in the same sense as the underlying convention, but the outcome of a deliberate choice. If so, there is no reason to read s 1(1) as meaning anything other than what it says, and since it is perfectly possible to stay the action without referring the matter to arbitration, my principal difficulty in applying s 1(1) to cl 67 is resolved.

Thus, I would be willing to hold, in company with the Court of Appeal, that the respondents are entitled to a stay under the 1975 Act, but prefer to reach the　*a* same practical result by what seems to me the simpler and more natural route by way of the inherent jurisdiction.

I must add by way of footnote that the House was much pressed during argument by examples of various forms of claims, against which one or other conclusion was to be tested. Valuable though these were as a means of focusing attention, I shall not explore them here, partly because it could be impossible to　*b* do justice to them within a reasonable compass, but more importantly because it is inappropriate to rule on issues which are not now for decision. I will however state that I have found nothing in them which raises doubts as to the conclusion just expressed, and that all of them seem capable of a practical solution by the deployment of either the power under s 1(1), as thus understood; or the inherent　*c* power to stay; or both powers successively; or the admittedly rather delphic words '... null and void, inoperative or incapable of being performed ...' in s 1(1).

III. THE EXISTENCE OF A DISPUTE

The appellants submit that even if s 1 of the 1975 Act applies to cl 67, a stay　*d* should nevertheless be refused because 'there is not in fact any dispute between the parties with regard to the matter agreed to be referred'. In summary, they say that there is only one ground upon which the respondents could even attempt to justify their stance in threatening to stop work whilst at the same time purporting to keep the contract in existence, namely that the matter falls within the civilian doctrine of 'l'exception d'inexécution', that it is common ground that this doctrine　*e* is capable of exclusion by express provision in the contract and that such an express exclusion is to be found in the words of cl 67(2), which provide that 'the Contractor shall in every case continue to proceed with the Works with all due diligence ...' Thus, according to the appellants, the respondents really have no case at all, and since they have no case there cannot be any 'dispute between the parties with regard to the matter agreed to be referred'.　*f*

It will be recalled that this qualification on the right of the defendant to a mandatory stay had its origin in the MacKinnon committee report (Report of Committee on the Law of Arbitration (Cmd 2817 (1927)), under the chairmanship of MacKinnon J, para 43 of which read:

> 'Our attention has been called to a point that arises under the Arbitration　*g* Clauses (Protocol) Act, 1924. Section 1 of that Act in relation to a submission to which the protocol applies deprives the English Court of any discretion as regards granting the stay of an action. It is said that cases have already not infrequently arisen, where (e.g.) a writ has been issued claiming the price of goods sold and delivered. The defendant has applied to stay the action on the ground that the contract of sale contains an arbitration clause, but without　*h* being able, or condescending, to indicate any reason why he should not pay for the goods, or the existence of any dispute to be decided by arbitration. It seems absurd that in such a case the English Court must stay the action, and we suggest that the Act might at any rate provide that the Court shall stay the action if satisfied that there is a real dispute to be determined by arbitration ...'　*j*

In recent times, this exception to the mandatory stay has been regarded as the opposite side of the coin to the jurisdiction of the court under RSC Ord 14 to give summary judgment in favour of the plaintiff where the defendant has no arguable defence. If the plaintiff to an action which the defendant has applied to stay can

show that there is no defence to the claim, the court is enabled at one and the
a same time to refuse the defendant a stay and to give final judgment for the
plaintiff. This jurisdiction, unique so far as I am aware to the law of England, has
proved to be very useful in practice, especially in times when interest rates are
high, for protecting creditors with valid claims from being forced into an
unfavourable settlement by the prospect that they will have to wait until the end
of an arbitration in order to collect their money. I believe however that care
b should be taken not to confuse a situation in which the defendant disputes the
claim on grounds which the plaintiff is very likely indeed to overcome, with the
situation in which the defendant is not really raising a dispute at all. It is
unnecessary for present purposes to explore the question in depth, since in my
opinion the position on the facts of the present case is quite clear, but I would
c indorse the powerful warnings against encroachment on the parties' agreement
to have their commercial differences decided by their chosen tribunals, and on
the international policy exemplified in the English legislation that this consent
should be honoured by the courts, given by Parker LJ in *Home and Overseas
Insurance Co Ltd v Mentor Insurance Co (UK) Ltd (in liq)* [1989] 3 All ER 74 at 78,
[1990] 1 WLR 153 at 158–159 and Saville J in *Hayter v Nelson and Home Insurance
d Co* [1990] 2 Lloyd's Rep 265.

Approaching the matter in this spirit I must ask whether the only matter
embraced in the writ, namely the question whether the respondents should
return to work, is the subject of a dispute. The fact that there are numerous areas
of dispute on the events leading up to the respondents' threat to leave the site does
not of course mean in itself that there is a dispute about the central issue, namely
e whether the doctrine of 'l'exception d'inexécution' has been ousted and if so
whether the facts justified its application. That the doctrine is a part of the
international trade law which is made applicable to the contract by cl 68 is
common ground, and it is also common ground (at least for the purposes of these
proceedings) that the docrine is capable of being excluded by consent. Beyond
f this, however, the parties are sharply at odds, and so also are their experts on
foreign law. It is suggested that the court has sufficient material, in the shape of
the experts' affidavits, to decide the matter here and now for itself. I am quite
unable to agree. Whether the panel and the arbitrators will need help from expert
witnesses, or whether they will feel able to use their own knowledge and
experience to decide the point on their own, I do not know. What does seem to
g me absolutely clear on this is that an English court could not properly conclude
in the light of affidavit evidence alone that the appellants' claim is so unanswerable
that there is nothing to arbitrate. There would have to be cross-examination of
the experts, and once one reaches this point it is perfectly obvious that the
qualifying words in s 1 do not apply, and that there is no reason to withhold a
stay.   .

h

IV. INTERIM RELIEF UNDER S 12(6) OF THE 1950 ACT

Thus far, the question has been whether the appellants' claim for a final
injunction should be allowed to proceed to trial in the High Court. If it should,
the exercise of the discretion to grant an interlocutory injunction pending trial
j will be governed by well-established rules, and no questions of principle will arise.
If, however, as I believe to be the case the action should not in the absence of some
unforeseen future difficulty in the operation of cl 67 be permitted to go forward,
a difficult and important question will arise concerning the power of the court to
order the respondents back to work pending the decision of the panel or, as the
case may be, the arbitrators. The appellants base their claim for an injunction,

first, on the special powers conferred by s 12(6)(h) of the 1950 Act and, secondly, on the general power of the court to grant an injunction under s 37(1) of the *a* Supreme Court Act 1981. These different foundations for the claim raise entirely different issues, which call for separate considerations.

The main problem with the claim based on s 12(6)(h) is to decide whether this provision has any application at all to an arbitration agreement of the type contained in cl 67 of the construction contract. The respondents say that it has none, because the clause contemplates a foreign arbitration which is outside the *b* scope of this particular part of the 1950 Act. The Court of Appeal accepted this contention. If the respondents are wrong on this point it will be necessary to consider whether the discretion created by s 12(6)(h) should be exercised in a special way in relation to arbitrations conducted abroad.

It is by now firmly established that more than one national system of law may *c* bear upon an international arbitration. Thus, there is the proper law which regulates the substantive rights and duties of the parties to the contract from which the dispute has arisen. Exceptionally, this may differ from the national law governing the interpretation of the agreement to submit the dispute to arbitration. Less exceptionally it may also differ from the national law which the parties have expressly or by implication selected to govern the relationship between themselves *d* and the arbitrator in the conduct of the arbitration: the 'curial law' of the arbitration, as it is often called. The construction contract provides an example. The proper substantive law of this contract is the law, if such it can be called, chosen in cl 68. But the curial law must I believe be the law of Belgium. Certainly there may sometimes be an express choice of a curial law which is not the law of the place where the arbitration is to be held: but in the absence of an explicit *e* choice of this kind, or at least some very strong pointer in the agreement to show that such a choice was intended, the inference that the parties when contracting to arbitrate in a particular place consented to having the arbitral process governed by the law of that place is irresistible.

In all these instances one or more national laws may be relevant because they *f* are expressly or impliedly chosen by the parties to govern the various aspects of their relationships. As such, they govern the arbitral process from within. But national laws may also apply ab extra, when the jurisdiction of the national court is invoked independently of any prior consent by the parties. An obvious case exists where the claimant, in face of an arbitration agreement, brings an action before a national court which must apply its own local law to decide whether the *g* action should be stayed, or otherwise interfered with. Equally obvious is the case of the national court which becomes involved when the successful party applies to it for enforcement of the arbitrator's award. But a national court may also be invited, as in the present case, to play a secondary role, not in the direct enforcement of the contract to arbitrate, but in the taking of measures to make the work of the chosen tribunal more effective. Here, the matter is before the *h* court solely because the court happens to have under its own procedural rules the power to assert a personal jurisdiction over the parties, and to enforce protective measures against them. Any court satisfying this requirement will serve the purpose, whether or not it has any prior connection with the arbitral agreement or the arbitration process. In the present case, the English court has been drawn into this dispute only because it happens to have territorial jurisdiction over the *j* respondents, and the means to enforce its orders against them. The French court would have served just as well, and if the present application had been made in Paris we should have found the French court considering the same questions as have been canvassed on this appeal, but from a different perspective.

a   The distinction between the internal and external application of national arbitration laws is important. In my opinion, when deciding whether a statutory or other power is capable of being exercised by the English court in relation to cl 67, and if it is so capable whether it should in fact be exercised, the court should bear constantly in mind that English law, like French law, is a stranger to this Belgian arbitration, and that the respondents are not before the English court by choice. In such a situation the court should be very cautious in its approach both
b   to the existence and to the exercise of supervisory and supportive measures, lest it cut across the grain of the chosen curial law.

Thus, in the present instance I believe that we should approach s 12 of the 1950 Act by asking: can Parliament have intended that the power to grant an interim injunction should be exercised in respect of an arbitration conducted abroad
c   under a law which is not the law of England? For an answer to this question one must look to the origins of s 12, which lie in s 2 of the Arbitration Act 1889. This provided:

'A submission, unless a contrary intention is expressed therein, shall be deemed to include the provisions set forth in the First Schedule to this
d   Act . . .'

Schedule 1 comprised a list of nine statutory implied terms. Two of these (paras (a) and (b)) related to the constitution of the arbitral tribunal. Those imposed by paras (c), (d) and (e) were concerned with the time for making the award. Paragraph (f) dealt compendiously with the examination of the parties on oath, with production of documents, and with the general duty to 'do all other things
e   which during the proceedings on the reference the arbitrator or umpire may require'. Paragraph (g) empowered the arbitrators to examine on oath witnesses other than the parties. Paragraph (h) stipulated that the award was to be final and binding, and para (i) empowered the arbitrators to make orders for costs, and to tax or settle the amount of costs.

f   It seems to me absolutely plain for two reasons that Parliament cannot have intended these provisions to apply to a foreign arbitration. The first reason is that the chosen mechanism was to make these provisions into implied terms of the arbitration agreement, and such terms could not sensibly be incorporated into an agreement governed by a foreign domestic arbitration law to whose provisions they might well be antithetical: see, for example, the provisions concerning the
g   administration of oaths, discovery and orders for costs.

Secondly, s 2 of the 1889 Act, unlike s 12 of the 1950 Act, was concerned exclusively with the internal conduct of the arbitration, and not at all with any external powers of the court. I can see no reason why Parliament should have had the least concern to regulate the conduct of an arbitration carried on abroad pursuant to a foreign arbitral law. Furthermore, it was expressly stipulated in s 28
h   that the 1889 Act should not extend to Scotland or Ireland. It is absurd to suppose that Parliament should have intended that the same French arbitration should at the same time be subject to implied terms under English law but not under the law of Scotland. I do not believe that in such a situation either law was intended to apply.

j   When we turn to the Arbitration Act 1934, which introduced a miscellaneous series of amendments, we find that the list of statutory implied terms relating to the powers of the arbitrators, contained in Sch 1 to the 1889 Act, was enlarged by the addition of powers to order specific performance and make an interim award. In addition, s 8(1) provided that in relation to the matters set out in Sch 1 to the 1934 Act:

'The Court shall have, for the purpose of and in relation to a reference, the same power of making orders . . . as it has for the purpose of and in relation *a* to an action or matter in the Court.'

The powers listed in Sch 1 were the same as those now set out in s 12(6) of the 1950 Act. Quite plainly the reference to 'the Court' was to the English court, and when one looks at the items in the list (such as the ordering of discovery and interrogatories) it is easy to see that they were concerned with powers which the *b* English court would never at that time even have thought of exercising in relation to actions in a foreign court. This being so, I can see no reason why the legislature should have wished to make the powers available to the court in respect of foreign arbitrations. Indeed it appears from paras 30 and 31 of the MacKinnon committee's report that notwithstanding the width of its terms of reference the committee chose not to deal with foreign arbitrations.   *c*

In these circumstances, if the present case had arisen in 1949 the court would I believe have held without difficulty that the relevant parts of the 1889 and 1934 Acts did not apply to foreign arbitrations. The 1950 Act was a consolidating statute which merely rearranged and in some instances re-worded the existing legislation, and it cannot have had the effect of enlarging the categories of *d* arbitration to which the former legislation applied. In these circumstances I consider that none of the terms of the 1950 Act, of which the provisions cited from the 1889 and 1934 Acts were the precursors, apply to foreign arbitrations and that since these include s 12(6) the power conferred by s 12(6)(*h*) to grant an interim injunction is not available to the court in respect of foreign arbitrations such as the present.   *e*

V. AN INJUNCTION UNDER S 37 OF THE SUPREME COURT ACT 1981

I turn to the claim for an interlocutory injunction under s 37(1) of the Supreme Court Act 1981. The focus of the inquiry now shifts from the numerous types of remedy under s 12 of the 1950 Act which are specially designed for the narrow purpose of promoting the efficacy of the arbitral process, to a single remedy *f* which is not so designed and which is capable of employment in a wide variety of situations, many far removed from the present. By definition, the making of an order under s 12 cannot be inconsistent with the spirit of the arbitration agreement or with the policy of the court to enforce such agreements, although in making use of its powers under the section the court must be careful not to *g* meddle unduly in matters which properly belong to the arbitrator. Under s 37(1) by contrast the arbitration clause is not the source of the power to grant an injunction but is merely a part of the facts in the light of which the court decides whether or not to exercise a power which exists independently of it. Accordingly it does not follow that even in a situation where, if s 12(6) applied to the arbitration in question, the court would be justified in making an interim order under *h* s 12(6)(*h*), the court would be equally justified, or would even have the power, to do so under s 37(1). In the present case the respondents contend that in a situation where the interlocutory injunction claimed is ancillary to an action which the court has stayed it has no power to grant an injunction even if it considers that to do so would be in the interests of justice. Alternatively, the respondents contend that even if such a power does exist it should be exercised with great caution, and *j* that the conditions for its exercise do not exist in the present case. The Court of Appeal sustained the first of these grounds of objection, to which I now turn.

1. *The power to grant an injunction*
   (1) The respondents begin with an argument of general principle. Although

the words of s 37(1) and its forebears are very wide it is firmly established by a
a long history of judicial self-denial that they are not to be taken at their face value
and that their application is subject to severe constraints. This process has
culminated in a chain of decisions in your Lordships' House: see *Siskina (cargo
owners) v Distos Cia Naviera SA, The Siskina* [1977] 3 All ER 803, [1979] AC 210,
Castanho v Brown & Root (UK) Ltd [1981] 1 All ER 143, [1981] AC 557, *British
Airways Board v Laker Airways Ltd* [1984] 3 All ER 89, [1985] AC 58 and *South
b Carolina Insurance Co v Assurantie Maatschappij 'de Zeven Provincien' NV* [1986] 3
All ER 487, [1987] AC 24. These are too well known to need rehearsal, and it is
sufficient for present purposes to quote from the speech of Lord Brandon of
Oakbrook in the *South Carolina* case [1986] 3 All ER 487 at 495–496, [1987] AC
24 at 39–40:

c   'The first basic principle is that the power of the High Court to grant
    injunctions is a statutory power conferred on it by s 37(1) of the Supreme
    Court Act 1981, which provides: "The High Court may by order (whether
    interlocutory or final) grant an injunction . . . in all cases in which it appears
    to the court to be just and convenient to do so." That provision is similar to
d   earlier provisions of which it is the successor, namely s 45(1) of the Supreme
    Court of Judicature (Consolidation) Act 1925 and s 25(8) of the Supreme
    Court of Judicature Act 1873. The second basic principle is that, although
    the terms of s 37(1) of the 1981 Act and its predecessors are very wide, the
    power conferred by them has been circumscribed by judicial authority dating
    back many years. The nature of the limitations to which the power is subject
e   has been considered in a number of recent cases in your Lordships' House:
    Siskina (cargo owners) v Distos Cia Naviera SA, The Siskina [1977] 3 All ER 803,
    [1979] AC 210, *Castanho v Brown & Root (UK) Ltd* [1981] 1 All ER 143, [1981]
    AC 557 and *British Airways Board v Laker Airways Ltd* [1984] 3 All ER 39,
    [1985] AC 58. The effect of these authorities, so far as material to the present
    case, can be summarised by saying that the power of the High Court to grant
f   injunctions is, subject to two exceptions to which I shall refer shortly, limited
    to two situations. Situation (1) is when one party to an action can show that
    the other party has either invaded, or threatens to invade, a legal or equitable
    right of the former for the enforcement of which the latter is amenable to
    the jurisdiction of the court. Situation (2) is where one party to an action has
    behaved, or threatens to behave, in a manner which is unconscionable. The
g   third basic principle is that among the forms of injunction which the High
    Court has power to grant is an injunction granted to one party to an action to
    restrain the other party to it from beginning, or if he has begun from
    continuing, proceedings against the former in a foreign court. Such
    jurisdiction is, however, to be exercised with caution because it involves
h   indirect interference with the process of the foreign court concerned.'

In reliance on this line of authority the respondents maintain that the English
court can never grant an injunction in support of a cause of action which the
parties have agreed shall be the subject of an arbitration abroad, and a fortiori
where the court has itself halted the proceedings in England, in furtherance of its
j duty under s 1 of the 1975 Act, so that the agreed method of adjudication shall
take place. In support, the respondents call up the tentative expression of opinion
by Bingham LJ in *Nissan (UK) Ltd v Nissan Motor Co Ltd* [1991] CA Transcript 848,
to the effect that interim relief in the shape of an interlocutory injunction cannot
be granted in a case such as the present since the defendant is not properly before
the court.

My Lords, I cannot accept this argument. I prefer not to engage the question whether the law is now firmly established in terms of Lord Brandon's statement, *a* or whether it will call for further elaboration to deal with new practical situations at present unforeseen. For present purposes it is sufficient to say that the doctrine of *The Siskina*, put at its highest, is that the right to an interlocutory injunction cannot exist in isolation, but is always incidental to and dependant on the enforcement of a substantive right, which usually although not invariably takes the shape of a cause of action. If the underlying right itself is not subject to the *b* jurisdiction of the English court, then that court should never exercise its power under s 37(1) by way of interim relief. If this is a correct appreciation of the doctrine, it does not apply to the present case. Let us take the matter by stages.

First, there is the situation where a contract entirely English in all its aspects is subject to an agreement for arbitration in London. This agreement, being a *c* 'domestic' arbitration agreement, may be enforced by a discretionary stay under s 4(1) of the 1950 Act. Here, it is quite clear that the presence of the clause does not deprive the court of jurisdiction over a dispute arising under the contract. If an action is brought to enforce the contract, and either the defendant does not apply for a stay, or the court decides in its discretion not to grant one, the action proceeds in exactly the same way as if the arbitration clause did not exist. *d* Moreover even if the court does choose to grant a stay the court retains its jurisdiction over the dispute. If all goes well this jurisdiction will never be exercised, but if the arbitration breaks down the court is entitled to resume seisin of the dispute and carry it forward to judgment. (Authority for these propositions is scarcely necessary, but mention may be made of *Doleman & Sons v Ossett Corp* [1912] 3 KB 257 and *Hamlyn & Co v Talisker Distillery* [1894] AC 202, [1891–4] *e* All ER Rep 849.) It follows that the conditions for the grant of an interlocutory injunction are satisfied, since the purpose of the injunction is to support a cause of action which is justiciable before the English court.

The example may now be changed a little, so as to postulate that one of the parties is a national of a state other than the United Kingdom. The arbitration *f* agreement now ceases to be 'domestic', and the stay is no longer discretionary under the 1950 Act but mandatory under the 1975 Act. Does this make any difference? None, in my opinion, for the cause of action is still potentially justiciable by the English court, and will in fact be adjudicated upon if the defendant does not apply for a stay, or if the circumstances are such as to bring into play the exceptions in s 1 of the 1975 Act, or if something happens at a later *g* stage which demands the lifting of any stay which has been granted and the resumption of the action before the court. Here again the restrictions on the grant of an interlocutory injunction do not apply.

Let us now make a further change, and postulate an arbitration agreement which calls for arbitration abroad. This may indeed have an indirect effect on the availability of injunctive relief. Very often it happens that where there is an *h* arbitration agreement between foreign parties the English court has jurisdiction only because the agreement stipulates that the arbitration shall be held in London, thereby justifying the inference of English law as the substantive proper law of the contract, and hence giving the court jurisdiction over the cause of action under Ord 11, r 1(1)(d)(iii). If the seat of the arbitration is abroad this source of jurisdiction is cut off, and the inhibitions created by the *Siskina* authorities will *j* preclude the grant of an injunction. Nevertheless, if the facts are such that the court has jurisdiction in some way other than the one just described I can see no reason why the additional foreign element should make any difference to the residual jurisdiction of the court over the dispute, and hence to the existence of

the power to grant an injunction in support. So also in the present case. If the
a respondents had really wanted to find out as a matter of urgency whether they
were entitled to carry out their threat to stop work they might perhaps have
decided that it was better to press for a speedy trial in the Commercial Court,
rather than wind up the cumbersome method of cl 67, and hence abstained from
asking for a stay. In such a case there could be no doubt about the power of the
court to grant an injunction. Similarly, if cl 67 had for some reason broken down
b and the parties had been forced to resume the action. I am unable to see why the
fact that the action is temporarily, and it may very well be permanently, in
abeyance should adversely affect the powers of the court, although of course it
may make all the difference to the way in which those powers should be exercised.

For these reasons I consider that although the commencement of the action
c was a breach of the arbitration agreement, and that in this sense the respondents
were not 'properly' before the court, this does not bring into play the limitations
on the powers of the court established by the *Siskina* line of cases. I should add
that the same result must have followed if the appellants had done what they
promised to do, and submitted their disputes to the panel and the arbitrators,
rather than to the court. The power exists either in both cases or in neither and
d the appellants' breach of the arbitration agreement in bringing an action destined
to be stayed cannot have conferred on the court a power to grant an injunction
which it would not otherwise possess. The existence of a pending suit is thus an
irrelevance.

(2) This brings me to the respondents' next argument, that since in s 25(3) of
the 1982 Act Parliament has created the opportunity to confer powers on the
e court to grant interim relief including interlocutory injunctions in support of
arbitrations, and has not yet brought such powers into effect, the court should
never in the absence of such legislation presume to exercise whatever powers in
this respect may already be conferred by the general law. I cannot agree. We are
concerned here with powers which the court already possesses under s 37 of the
f 1981 Act. The only question is whether the court ought permanently and
unconditionally to renounce the possibility of exercising such powers in a case
like the present. I am unable to see why the fact that Parliament is contemplating
the specific grant of interim powers, not limited to interlocutory injunctions in
support of arbitrations but has not yet chosen to do so should shed any light on
the powers of the court under existing law. It may be that if and when s 25 is
g made applicable to arbitrations, the court will have to be very cautious in the
exercise of its general powers under s 37 so as not to conflict with any restraint
which the legislature may have imposed on the exercise of the new and specialised
powers. Meanwhile, however, although the existence of these new powers in
reserve may well be one of the factors which lead the court to be cautious about
granting relief in the cases of the present kind, it is another matter to hold that
h the court should cut itself altogether off from the possibility of a remedy, and I
would not be prepared to go so far.

(3) I would return a similar answer to the argument which assumes that (as I
have already suggested) s 12(6)(*h*) of the 1950 Act does not apply to foreign
arbitrations, and reasons from this to the conclusion that the general powers of
the court to grant an injunction are equally inapplicable in such a case. At the
j time many years ago when the forebears of s 12(6) were conceived the world of
international arbitration was very different from what it is today, and the
possibility that national courts of one country might have a useful albeit
subordinate role to play in an arbitration conducted in another country might
well have appeared too implausible to call for a specific provision. The fact that

the specialist powers conferred by the Arbitration Acts are not available in a case such as the present does not entail that the general powers of the court can never *a* be deployed: although, again, this is undoubtedly a powerful reason why the courts should approach their use with great caution.

(4) Next, the respondents call in aid the long-established principle indorsed by Lord Diplock in *Bremer Vulkan Schiffbau Und Maschinenfabrik v South India Shipping Corp Ltd* [1981] 1 All ER 289 at 296, [1981] AC 909 at 979 that the English court *b* has no general supervisory power over the conduct of arbitrations more extensive than the powers conferred by the powers of the Arbitration Acts. My Lords, this principle is an essential element in the balance of the partnership which exists under English law between the arbitral process and the courts, and I say nothing to shed any doubt whatever upon it. In my judgment however it does not bear upon the present appeal. *c*

In the first place, the attempt in the *Bremer Vulkan* case to enjoin the further conduct of the arbitration, on the ground of excessive delay, foundered on the absence of any legal or equitable right of the plaintiffs to be enforced or protected, and was thus another case in the *Siskina* line of authority; whereas in the present case, for the reasons already stated, the appellants do assert a cause of action under the construction contract justiciable under English courts. *d*

Secondly, the injunction claimed in the *Bremer Vulkan* case would have involved a direct interference by the court in the arbitral process, and thus an infringement of the parties' agreement that the conduct of the dispute should be entrusted to the arbitrators alone, subject only to the limited degree of judicial control implicit in the choice of English law, and hence of English statute law, as part of the curial law of the contract. The purpose of interim measures of protection, by contrast, *e* is not to encroach on the procedural powers of the arbitrators but to reinforce them, and to render more effective the decision at which the arbitrators will ultimately arrive on the substance of the dispute. Provided that this and no more is what such measures aim to do, there is nothing in them contrary to the spirit of international arbitration. *f*

For similar reasons I am unable to agree with those decisions in the United States (there has been no citation of authority on this point from any other foreign source) which form one side of a division of authority as yet unresolved by the Supreme Court. These decisions are to the effect that interim measures must necessarily be in conflict with the obligations created assumed by the subscribing nations to the New York Convention, because they 'bypass the agreed upon *g* method of settling disputes': see *McCreary Tire and Rubber Co v CEAT SpA* (1974) 501 F 2d 1032 at 1038. I prefer the view that when properly used such measures serve to reinforce the agreed method, not to bypass it.

2. *A procedural difficulty* *h*

Finally, I must refer to a problem of procedural mechanics, quite unconnected with the ideals of international arbitration. It is this. If the court stays an action brought in breach of an arbitration clause, how can it grant an injunction in an action which is no longer before it? No difficulty arises where the stay is discretionary, under s 4(1) of the 1950 Act or under the inherent powers of the *j* court, since the court can grant the injunction first before electing to impose a stay. This is what happened in *Foster & Dicksee v Hastings Corp* (1903) 87 LT 736, a case very similar to the present on the facts. This expedient seems however less defensible where the court is obliged by statute to render up its control of the dispute as soon as the defendant so requires.

Puzzling as this question undoubtedly seems at first acquaintance, I believe on
a reflection that the answer is straightforward. Once again, it is helpful to approach
the matter by stages. Let us take first the case where the English court, before
which no proceedings have been brought except for interim relief, makes an
order under s 25 of the 1982 Act in support of an action brought in the courts of
a foreign state. Here, it is obvious that the court is not making an order in an
English action. By granting the order, the court does not engage itself at all in the
b resolution of the dispute, but merely seeks to make the resolution of the dispute
by the foreign court more effective. It is a free-standing item of ancillary relief.
Next, let it be assumed that the foreign proceedings take the shape of an
arbitration, rather than litigation. Once again, if the English court grants an
interlocutory injunction by way of interim protection under s 37 of the 1981 Act
c it is not playing any part in the decision of the dispute, but is simply doing its
best to ensure that the resolution by the arbitrators is fruitful. Common sense
and logic suggest that the analysis must be the same where the application for the
interlocutory injunction is associated with the commencement of an action which
the court is obliged to stay. Common sense, because it cannot be right that by
starting the action the plaintiff automatically forfeits any right to ancillary relief
d to which he would otherwise be entitled. Logic, because the purpose of the stay
is to remove from the court the task of deciding the substantive dispute, so that it
can be entrusted to the chosen tribunal. This is what the court is bound to do, by
virtue of the New York Convention. But neither the arbitration agreement nor
the convention contemplate that by transferring to the arbitrators the substance
of the dispute, the court also divests itself of the right to use the sanctions of
e municipal law, which are not available to the arbitrators, in order to ensure that
the arbitration is carried forward to the best advantage.

I thus see no difficulty in principle in an order which combines a mandatory
stay with an interlocutory injunction by way of interim relief.

For these various reasons I consider, here differing from the Court of Appeal,
f that the court does have power in the present case to grant the injunction for
which the appellants contend, notwithstanding that their action has been stayed.
Whether this is a power which the court ought to exercise in the circumstances
of the present case is an entirely different matter.

3. *The exercise of the discretion*

g On the assumption that the court does have power to grant the appellants an
injunction, a decision on whether the power should be exercised requires the
making of certain assumptions.

The first assumption must hold good whatever course your Lordships' House
decides to follow. Since the action is now stayed, the appellants' only justification
for claiming interim relief is that it is needed to render more efficacious the cl 67
h procedures, and any decision favourable to the appellants which may emerge
from them. We must therefore assume that the appellants' next step will be to set
about at once pursuing the same remedy, or type of remedy, through the medium
of cl 67 as they sought in the action. Only one item of substantive relief was
claimed by the writ, and although this was cast in negative form it was in
substance a claim for a final mandatory injunction: or, what seems to me the
j same thing, an order for specific performance of the respondents' obligation to
work continuously on the contract. Absent any evidence of Belgian law, we must
also assume that this is an order which the panel and arbitrators would have
power to make, if minded to do so. How long the proceedings will take is
impossible to predict, apart from saying that if the appellants had gone straight to

the panel in October 1991 rather than starting an action, the cl 67 proceedings would no doubt have been comfortably finished by now. At all events, we should *a* in my opinion assume that if the panel rules in favour of the appellants the respondents will appeal to the arbitrators and that a final ruling on the claim is not likely to emerge for some considerable time.

We must also make assumptions about what will happen on the alternative hypotheses that the injunction is and is not granted. As to the latter, since the respondents have never qualified their threat to withdraw from work unless their *b* financial demands are met, we must assume that 15 months after the threat was first made, at a time when the entire tunnel project is 15 months nearer completion, the respondents will at once stop work and thereby imperil even further the financial viability of a troubled enterprise, risking an immense liability in damages if they are subsequently found to have asserted a right which they did *c* not possess. Some scepticism on this score is inevitable, but since the parties are still at odds about the availability of interim relief to prevent the respondents from carrying out their threat, I can see no choice but to assume that the threat is not just empty bluster, but is one which the respondents will carry out if free to do so.

If, on the other hand, an injunction is granted pending a final resolution of the *d* dispute the completion of the cl 67 procedures is bound to take a considerable time; during which, we must assume, the work under the construction contract will be approaching a conclusion.

Amidst all these assumptions, there is one hard fact which I believe to be conclusive, namely that the injunction claimed from the English court is the same as the injunction claimed from the panel and the arbitrators, except that the *e* former is described as interlocutory or interim. In reality its interim character is largely illusory, for as it seems to me an injunction granted in November 1991, and a fortiori an injunction granted today, would largely pre-empt the very decision of the panel and arbitrators whose support forms the raison d'être of the injunction. By the time that the award of the panel or arbitrators is ultimately made, with the respondents having continued to work meanwhile it will be of *f* very modest practical value, except as the basis for a claim in damages by the respondents: although exactly how modest, it is impossible on the present evidence to say.

In these circumstances, I do not consider that the English court would be justified in granting the very far-reaching relief which the appellants claim. It is *g* true that mandatory interlocutory relief may be granted even where it substantially overlaps the final relief claimed in the action; and I also accept that it is possible for the court at the pre-trial stage of a dispute arising under a construction contract to order the defendant to continue with a performance of the works. But the court should approach the making of such an order with the utmost caution, and should be prepared to act only when the balance of advantage plainly favours the *h* grant of relief. In the combination of circumstances which we find in the present case I would have hesitated long before proposing that such an order should be made, even if the action had been destined to remain in the High Court. These hesitations are multiplied by the presence of cl 67. There is always a tension when the court is asked to order, by way of interim relief in support of an arbitration, a *j* remedy of the same kind as will ultimately be sought from the arbitrators: between, on the one hand, the need for the court to make a tentative assessment of the merits in order to decide whether the plaintiff's claim is strong enough to merit protection, and on the other the duty of the court to respect the choice of tribunal which both parties have made, and not to take out of the hands of the arbitrators (or other decision-makers) a power of decision which the parties have

a entrusted to them alone. In the present instance I consider that the latter consideration must prevail. The court has stayed the action so that the panel and the arbitrators can decide whether to order a final mandatory injunction, there will be very little left for the arbitrators to decide.

Any doubts on this score are to my mind resolved by the choice of the English rather than the Belgian courts as the source of interim relief. Whatever exactly is

b meant by the words 'competent judicial authority' in art 8(5) of the ICC Rules, the Belgian court must surely be the natural court for the source of interim relief. If the appellants wish the English court to prefer itself to this natural forum it is for them to show the reason why, in the same way as a plaintiff who wishes to pursue a substantive claim otherwise than in a more convenient foreign court:

c see *Spiliada Maritime Corp v Cansulex Ltd, The Spiliada* [1986] 3 All ER 843 at 855, [1987] AC 460 at 476. They have not done so. Apparently no application for interim relief has been made to the court in Brussels. It is perhaps just permissible to take notice that the contemporary Belgian law of arbitration differs from the law of other European countries, but beyond this I would certainly not be willing to go since, most remarkably, no evidence of Belgian law is before the court. If

d the appellants had wished to say that the Belgian court would have been unable or unwilling to grant relief, and that the English court is the only avenue of recourse, it was for them to prove it, and they have not done so. Moreover, even if evidence to this effect had been adduced I doubt whether it would have altered my opinion. This is not a case where a party to a standard form of contract finds himself burdened with an inappropriate arbitration clause to which he had not

e previously given his attention. I have no doubt that the dispute-resolution mechanisms of cl 67 were the subject of careful thought and negotiation. The parties chose an indeterminate 'law' to govern their substantive rights; an elaborate process for ascertaining those rights; and a location for that process outside the territories of the participants. This conspicuously neutral 'anational' and extra-judicial structure may well have been the right choice for the special needs of the

f Channel tunnel venture. But whether it was right or wrong, it is the choice which the parties have made. The appellants now regret that choice. To push their claim for mandatory relief through the mechanisms of cl 67 is too slow and cumbersome to suit their purpose, and they now wish to obtain far reaching relief through the judicial means which they have been so scrupulous to exclude. Notwithstanding

g that the court can and should in the right case provide reinforcement for the arbitral process by granting interim relief, I am quite satisfied that this is not such a case, and that to order an injunction here would be to act contrary both to the general tenor of the construction contract and to the spirit of international arbitration.

h *Appeal dismissed.*

Mary Rose Plummer   Barrister.

Welsh v Chief Constable of the Merseyside Police and another

QUEEN'S BENCH DIVISION AT LIVERPOOL

28 FEBRUARY, 1, 27 MARCH 1991

TUDOR EVANS J

Negligence – Duty to take care – Existence of duty – Crown Prosecution Service – Duty owed to accused in criminal case – Administrative responsibility as prosecutor to keep court informed as to state of adjourned criminal case – Crown Prosecution Service undertaking to inform magistrates' court that plaintiff's offences had been taken into consideration by Crown Court – Crown Prosecution Service failing to inform magistrates' court – Plaintiff not appearing before magistrates to answer charges – Plaintiff arrested and kept in custody under warrant of arrest issued by magistrates – Whether Crown Prosecution Service under duty to inform magistrates' court that plaintiff's offences had been taken into consideration by Crown Court – Whether Crown Prosecution Service owing duty of care to plaintiff – Whether Crown Prosecution Service immune from proceedings – Crown Proceedings Act 1947, s 2(5).

On 24 July 1987 the plaintiff appeared before a magistrates' court charged with two offences of theft. He was remanded on bail to appear before the court on 19 August. On 7 August the plaintiff was due to appear in the Crown Court to be dealt with for numerous criminal matters. Before the case was called on in the Crown Court the plaintiff's counsel informed the police officer in charge of the case, counsel for the prosecution and a representative of the Crown Prosecution Service that the plaintiff wanted the offences of theft with which he had been charged in the magistrates' court, and to which he intended to plead guilty, to be taken into consideration when he was sentenced by the Crown Court. The police officer contacted the magistrates' court to obtain the necessary details and was assured by a police officer at the court that the offences were suitable to be taken into consideration by the Crown Court. He then spoke on the telephone to a solicitor employed by the Crown Prosecution Service responsible for prosecutions in the magistrates' court, who agreed to and approved the proposal that the offences should be taken into consideration by the Crown Court. The officer asked the solicitor to indorse the file that the offences were being taken into consideration that morning so that the magistrates' court could be informed of that fact. It was agreed between the plaintiff's legal advisers and the Crown Prosecution Service representative that the offences should be taken into consideration and that was in fact done when the plaintiff appeared before the judge in the Crown Court. On 19 August the plaintiff failed to answer to his bail at the magistrates' court, believing that the magistrates had been informed that the offences had been taken into consideration. In fact the magistrates' court was not aware of that fact and issued a warrant for his arrest not backed for bail. On 19 December the plaintiff was arrested, taken to a police station and held in custody under the warrant until he was released by the magistrates' court on 21 December 1987. The plaintiff brought an action against the police and the Crown Prosecution Service alleging that he had suffered loss, damage and distress as the result of the defendants' negligent failure to ensure that the magistrates' court was informed that the offences for which he had been bailed had subsequently been taken into consideration by the Crown Court. On the application of the Crown Prosecution Service the registrar struck out the plaintiff's claim against it

pursuant to RSC Ord 18, r 19(1)(a)[a] on the ground that the Crown Prosecution
a   Service did not owe the plaintiff any duty of care. The plaintiff appealed. The
Crown Prosecution Service claimed immunity from proceedings under s 2(5)[b] of
the Crown Proceedings Act 1947, which provided that no proceedings lay against
the Crown 'in respect of anything done or omitted to be done by any person while
discharging or purporting to discharge any responsibilities of a judicial nature
vested in him, or any responsibilities which he has in connection with the
b   execution of judicial process'. The Crown Prosecution Service contended (i) that
in assuming responsibility for informing the magistrates' court that the plaintiff's
offences had been taken into consideration by the Crown Court it was discharging
a responsibility which it had in connection with the execution of a judicial
process, (ii) that its advocate at the resumed hearing before the magistrates was
c   immune from suit and that accordingly in that respect it was protected against
the action and (iii) that the action was akin to an abuse of process in which proof
of malice was an integral part of the action and that negligent abuse of process
was not a cause of action.

Held – (1) Section 2(5) of the 1947 Act was directed to the immunity of judicial,
d   not administrative, functions and since the recording of the fact that an offence
had been taken into consideration or communicating that fact to a particular
court did not fall within the ambit of judicial functions but was instead an
administrative act the Crown Prosecution Service could not claim immunity
from the plaintiff's proceedings under that Act (see p 699 j, post).
(2) Although the Crown Prosecution Service was immune from any action
e   based on the failure of its advocate at the resumed hearing before the magistrates
to inform the bench that the plaintiff's offences had been taken into consideration
by the Crown Court, that immunity did not extend to any failure by the Crown
Prosecution Service to carry out its general administrative responsibility or
practice as prosecutor to keep the court informed as to the state of an adjourned
f   criminal case or its particular responsibility to do so in the plaintiff's case by virtue
of having undertaken to do so (see p 699 j to p 700 d, post); *Saif Ali v Sydney
Mitchell & Co (a firm)* [1978] 3 All ER 1033 and *Kirkham v Chief Constable of the
Greater Manchester Police* [1990] 3 All ER 246 applied.
(3) An action in respect of acts or omissions which preceded a court process
could be framed in negligence without proof of malice being required.
g   Accordingly, since on the assumed facts the Crown Prosecution Service had a
general administrative responsibility as prosecutor to keep a court informed as to
the state of an adjourned criminal case or had in practice assumed such a
responsibility and had done so in the plaintiff's case, the relationship between the
plaintiff and the Crown Prosecution Service was sufficiently proximate for the
Crown Prosecution Service to owe a duty of care to the plaintiff to see that the
h   magistrates' court was informed that the offences committed by the plaintiff had
already been taken into consideration by the Crown Court. Furthermore, it was
fair, just and reasonable for such a duty to exist and there were no public policy
grounds to exclude the existence of such a duty. The appeal would therefore be
allowed and the plaintiff's claim reinstated in so far as it alleged negligence on the
part of the Crown Prosecution Service prior to the resumed hearing before the
j   magistrates (see p 699 c d, p 703 b e f and p 704 h, post); *Business Computers*

---

a   Rule 19(1), so far as material provides: 'The Court may at any stage of the proceedings order to be
struck out . . . any pleading or the indorsement of any writ in the action . . . on the ground that—
(a) it discloses no reasonable cause of action . . .'
b   Section 2(5) is set out at p 699 g, post

International Ltd v Registrar of Companies [1987] 3 All ER 465 and *Al-Kandari v J R*
Brown & Co (a firm) [1988] 1 All ER 833 distinguished; dictum of Lord Denning *a*
MR in *Roy v Prior* [1969] 3 All ER 1153 at 1155, CA and *Kirkham v Chief Constable*
of the Greater Manchester Police [1990] 3 All ER 246 considered.

Notes
For the duty of care generally, see 34 *Halsbury's Laws* (4th edn) para 5, and for
cases on the subject, see 36(1) *Digest* (2nd reissue) 21–54, *132–235*. *b*
For claims against the Crown for liability in tort, see Supplement to 11
Halsbury's Laws (4th edn) para 13.
For the liability of the Crown in tort, see 45 *Halsbury's Laws* (4th edn) para
1210, and for cases on the subject, see 11 *Digest* (Reissue) 692–694, *299–312*.
For the Crown Prosecution Service, see 11(1) *Halsbury's Laws* (4th edn reissue) *c*
paras 645–651.
For the Crown Proceedings Act 1947, s 2, see 13 *Halsbury's Statutes* (4th edn)
(1991 reissue) 11.

Cases referred to in judgment
Al-Kandari v J R Brown & Co (a firm) [1988] 1 All ER 833, [1988] QB 665, [1988] 2 *d*
    WLR 671, CA.
Anns v Merton London Borough [1977] 2 All ER 492, [1978] AC 728, [1977] 2 WLR
    1024, HL.
Business Computers International Ltd v Registrar of Companies [1987] 3 All ER 465,
    [1988] Ch 229, [1987] 3 WLR 1134.
Caparo Industries plc v Dickman [1990] 1 All ER 568, [1990] 2 AC 605, [1990] 2 *e*
    WLR 358, HL.
Clarke v Bruce Lance & Co (a firm) [1988] 1 All ER 364, [1988] 1 WLR 881, CA.
Davis v Radcliffe [1990] 2 All ER 536, [1990] 1 WLR 821, PC.
Hill v Chief Constable of West Yorkshire [1987] 1 All ER 1173, [1988] QB 60, [1987]
    2 WLR 1126, CA; *affd* [1988] 2 All ER 238, [1989] AC 53, [1988] 2 WLR 1049, *f*
    HL.
Kirkham v Chief Constable of the Greater Manchester Police [1990] 3 All ER 246,
    [1990] 2 QB 283, [1990] 2 WLR 987, CA.
McNaughton (James) Papers Group Ltd v Hicks Anderson & Co (a firm) [1991] 1 All
    ER 134, [1991] 2 QB 113, [1991] 2 WLR 641, CA.
Morgan Crucible Co plc v Hill Samuel Bank Ltd [1991] 1 All ER 148, [1991] Ch 295, *g*
    [1991] 2 WLR 655, CA.
Myers v Elman [1939] 4 All ER 484, [1940] AC 282, HL.
Peabody Donation Fund (Governors) v Sir Lindsay Parkinson & Co Ltd [1984] 3 All ER
    529, [1985] AC 210, [1984] 3 WLR 953, HL.
R v Batchelor (1952) 36 Cr App R 64, CCA.
R v Hicks (1924) 18 Cr App R 11, CCA. *h*
R v McMinn (1945) 30 Cr App R 138, Assizes.
R v Nicholson (1948) 32 Cr App R 98, CCA.
Roy v Prior [1970] 2 All ER 729, [1971] AC 470, [1970] 3 WLR 272, HL; *rvsg* on
    other grounds [1969] 3 All ER 1153, [1970] 1 QB 283, [1969] 3 WLR 635, CA.
Saif Ali v Sydney Mitchell & Co (a firm) [1978] 3 All ER 1033, [1980] AC 198, [1978]
    3 WLR 849, HL. *j*
Yuen Kun-yeu v A-G of Hong Kong [1987] 2 All ER 705, [1988] AC 175, [1987] 3
    WLR 776, PC.

Appeal
The plaintiff, Anthony Welsh, appealed from the order of District Judge Bowyer,

sitting as a registrar of the High Court on 7 February 1991 whereby he struck out
a pursuant to RSC Ord 18, r 19(1)(*a*) the plaintiff's claim against the second
defendant, the Crown Prosecution Service, for damages alleging that it negligently
failed to ensure that the Ormskirk Magistrates' Court, from which the plaintiff
was on bail for two offences of theft, had been informed that the offences had
subsequently been taken into consideration in the Crown Court and that, as a
result of that failure, the magistrates' court had issued a warrant for the plaintiff's
b arrest resulting in his detention and that he thereby suffered loss, damage and
distress. The first defendant, the Chief Constable of the Merseyside Police, against
whom a similar claim had been made, was not involved in the striking-out
application. The facts are set out in the judgment.

c A T Goff (instructed by *Canter Levin & Berg*, Liverpool) for the plaintiff.
Martyn Bennett (instructed by the *Treasury Solicitor*) for the Crown Prosecution
Service.

Cur adv vult

d 27 March 1991. The following judgment was delivered.

TUDOR EVANS J. The plaintiff appeals against the order of District Judge
Bowyer, sitting as a registrar of the High Court. On 7 February 1991 he struck
out the plaintiff's claim against the second defendant, the Crown Prosecution
Service, pursuant to RSC Ord 18, r 19(1)(*a*) on the ground that the second
e defendant did not owe the plaintiff any duty in law.
The plaintiff claims damages against the first defendant (the Chief Constable of
Merseyside Police) and the second defendant alleging that they negligently failed
to ensure that a magistrates' court, from which the plaintiff was on bail for two
offences of theft, was informed that the offences had subsequently been taken
into consideration at the Crown Court. It is alleged that, as a result of the failure,
f the magistrates' court issued a warrant for the plaintiff's arrest, that he was
detained and that he thereby suffered loss, damage and distress.
There is no doubt that the warrant was lawfully issued and that the plaintiff's
arrest was lawful. It is not the plaintiff's case that the second defendant maliciously
and without reasonable cause brought about the plaintiff's arrest. His case is that
g there was a want of care by the second defendant in failing to record the relevant
information and/or to pass it on to the magistrates' court or in failing to ensure
that the advocate who appeared at the resumed hearing when the magistrates
issued the warrant was properly instructed so that he could have told the court
that the offences had been taken into consideration. The issue which I have to
decide is whether the second defendant owed the plaintiff a duty of care.
h It is the second defendant's case that on any view of the law it is immune from
these proceedings because of the provisions of s 2(5) of the Crown Proceedings
Act 1947. If not generally immune, it is submitted that the advocate at the
resumed hearing is immune from suit and that accordingly in that respect the
second defendant is protected against this action. But it is also contended that the
action is akin to an abuse of process and that malice is an integral part of such an
j action. According to counsel, any act or omission which results in a legal process
causing a plaintiff loss and damage must be proved to be malicious. It is submitted
that negligent abuse of process is a cause of action not known to the law.
Since the appeal comes before me under Ord 18, r 19, I have to decide the issue
on the assumption that the facts pleaded in the reamended particulars of claim
are true: see, for example, *Hill v Chief Constable of West Yorkshire* [1987] 1 All ER

1173 at 1176, [1988] QB 60 at 66 per Fox LJ. But Mr Bennett, counsel for the
second defendant, conceded in the course of the hearing that the facts pleaded in   *a*
para 4 of the defence of the first defendant are true. It was as the result of
allegations pleaded in that paragraph that the plaintiff joined the second defendant
in the action but the specific allegations have not been adopted in the reamended
particulars of claim. Nevertheless, Mr Goff, counsel for the plaintiff, advanced
part of his argument on the assumption that the matters pleaded in para 4 are
true and I shall therefore assume them as fact.   *b*
   The assumed facts upon which I shall decide the issue are these. (i) The second
defendant is responsible, inter alia, for the preparation and the presentation of
cases in magistrates' courts and in the Crown Court. (ii) On 24 July 1987 the
plaintiff appeared before the Ormskirk Magistrates' Court charged with two
offences of theft. He was remanded on bail to appear at the court on 19 August   *c*
1987. (iii) The plaintiff was due to appear on 7 August 1987 in the Crown Court
at Liverpool to be dealt with for numerous criminal matters the details of which
I need not repeat. They are contained in further and better particulars of the
reamended particulars of claim. (iv) On 7 August 1987 in the Crown Court but
before the case was called on, counsel then representing the plaintiff informed
Det Con Kanczes, the officer in charge of the case, as well as counsel for the   *d*
prosecution and a representative of the second defendant, that the plaintiff had
been charged with the offences of theft at the Ormskirk Magistrates' Court, that
he intended to plead guilty to them and that he wanted to have the offences taken
into consideration when he was sentenced in the Crown Court. (v) Det Con
Kanczes was asked to contact the magistrates' court to obtain the necessary details
and for permission to have the offences taken into consideration. (vi) Upon   *e*
telephoning the magistrates' court, the detective constable was told by a police
officer that the offences were suitable to be taken into consideration. (vii) He then
spoke on the telephone to a solicitor employed by the Crown Prosecution Service
(and I quote now from para 4(f) of the amended defence)—

> 'responsible for Ormskirk who agreed to and approved the proposal that   *f*
> the said offences should be taken into consideration. The solicitor told
> Detective Constable Kanczes the particulars of the offence. Detective
> Constable Kanczes told the solicitor that the matter was being taken into
> consideration that morning (that is the 7th August 1987) and he asked the
> solicitor to indorse the file accordingly.'
>   *g*

It is agreed that the reference to 'the offence' in this passage is an error. It is
common ground that two offences were to be and were in fact taken into
consideration. (viii) The detective constable typed out 'another offence' form
stating that on 20 November 1986 the plaintiff stole two purses. It is unnecessary
to refer to the details. (ix) The detective constable took several copies of the form
to the court where the plaintiff's case was to be heard. He gave copies of the form   *h*
to counsel for the prosecution, to counsel then appearing for the plaintiff and to
the representative of the Crown Prosecution Service. Further, he told counsel for
the prosecution that the Crown Prosecution Service 'at Ormskirk' had agreed to
the offences being taken into consideration on that day. (x) It was agreed between
the plaintiff's legal advisers and counsel for the second defendant that the offence
should be taken into consideration. (xi) On 7 August 1987 the plaintiff appeared   *j*
before a judge in the Crown Court at Liverpool, who took the offences into
consideration. (xii) On 19 August 1987 the plaintiff failed to answer to his bail at
the Ormskirk Magistrates' Court, believing that the magistrates had been
informed that the offences had been taken into consideration. But the court was
not aware of the fact and issued a warrant for his arrest not backed for bail.

(xiii) At about 11.30 pm on Saturday, 19 December 1987 the plaintiff was arrested
a for the theft of a cassette. He was taken to a police station, where, at about
1.05 am the next day, police officers became aware of the warrant for the
plaintiff's arrest. They arrested the plaintiff. At about 4.00 am the plaintiff was
bailed to appear at a police station for the theft of the cassette but he remained in
custody because of the warrant. He was transferred to another police station,
where he remained until he was released by the Ormskirk Magistrates' Court on
b 21 December 1987. (xiv) Throughout the arrest, the plaintiff (and his father)
protested that the warrant should not have been issued because all matters had
been dealt with in the Crown Court at Liverpool.

Fact (iv) is derived from the particulars of claim and the further and better
particulars thereunder and from para 4. They are not in conflict. Facts (v) to (ix)
c come from para 4.

There is a note in the file from the learned registrar in the course of which it is
stated that the 'plaintiff's claim is for false imprisonment'. That is not so. On the
facts as I have summarised them, it is alleged that the defendants owed the
plaintiff a duty of care of which they were in breach. False imprisonment as a
consequence of the negligence is an essential element of the claim for damages
d for loss, damage and distress: see para 5 of the reamended particulars of claim.

In so far as it relates to the second defendants, the duty of care is pleaded in
para 3 of the reamended particulars of claim in these terms:

'It was a duty of the representative of the second defendant present at the
Liverpool Crown Court on the 7th August 1987 to record and/or to cause to
e be recorded and/or to pass on and/or to cause to be passed on the information
that the plaintiff had had those offences taken into consideration when he
was sentenced by His Honour Judge Pickering on the 7th August 1987.
Further the representatives of the second defendant knew or should have
known that if the aforesaid information was not recorded and/or passed on
to the Ormskirk Magistrates' Court, the said Ormskirk Magistrates' Court
f would issue a warrant for the plaintiff's arrest when he failed to attend at the
Magistrates' Court on the 19th August 1987. Further the representatives of
the second defendant knew or should have known that following the
aforesaid matters being taken into consideration the plaintiff would have
been told that these matters had now been dealt with and that he need not
appear at the Ormskirk Magistrates' Court for sentence thereon. In the
g premise the representatives of the second defendant owed the plaintiff a duty
of care.'

In answer to a request for further and better particulars of the particulars of
claim, it is stated that the duty is not statutory: it is owed at common law and
arose from the fact that the second defendant was responsible for the preparation
h and presentation of cases as stated in fact (i) above.

The duty as pleaded is confined to the representative at Liverpool Crown Court.
But the facts in para 4 involve the passing on to the solicitor employed by the
second defendant 'for Ormskirk' of information that the plaintiff was asking for
the two offences to be taken into consideration, the solicitor's agreement to that
course and a request made to him 'to mark the file accordingly', which I shall
j interpret as meaning that he was asked to note on the file that the offences were
to be taken into consideration in order that the information would be passed on
or made available to the magistrates' court so that the magistrates would be aware
of what had happened. The question of duty therefore arises at three stages: first,
at the Crown Court on 7 August 1987, secondly, when the information was
conveyed on that date to the solicitor for Ormskirk and, thirdly, when the

advocate appearing for the prosecution failed (as it is reasonable to infer that he did) to inform the magistrates that the offences had been taken into consideration.　*a*

Mr Goff submitted that the second defendant had an administrative responsibility to record or pass on the information, alternatively, if it did not have such a responsibility, it in practice passed on such information, alternatively that it is reasonable to infer that in this particular case it undertook to do so because of the facts in (vii) above. Counsel formulated the following proposition as containing the criteria by which it is necessary to decide whether a duty of care is owed to a 　*b* particular plaintiff: first, it is necessary to consider the principle of reasonable foreseeability of loss and damage and, in so far as different factors may be involved, the question of proximity. It is then necessary to consider whether it would be fair, just and reasonable to hold such a duty to exist and finally the question has to be answered whether there is any ground of public policy for excluding a duty.　*c*

I have been referred to a large number of authorities in support of this proposition, but I need only list them since Mr Bennett accepted the proposition as I have stated it. The authorities to which I was referred are *Anns v Merton London Borough* [1977] 2 All ER 492, [1978] AC 728, *Governors of the Peabody Donation Fund v Sir Lindsay Parkinson & Co Ltd* [1984] 3 All ER 529, [1985] AC 210, *Yuen Kun-yeu v A-G of Hong Kong* [1987] 2 All ER 705, [1988] AC 175, *Davis v* 　*d* *Radcliffe* [1990] 2 All ER 536, [1990] 1 WLR 821, *Caparo Industries plc v Dickman* [1990] 1 All ER 568, [1990] 2 AC 605, *James McNaughton Papers Group Ltd v Hicks Anderson & Co (a firm)* [1991] 1 All ER 134, [1991] 2 QB 113 and *Morgan Crucible Co plc v Hill Samuel Bank Ltd* [1991] 1 All ER 148, [1991] Ch 295.

Mr Bennett submitted that the second defendant did not have any administrative responsibility to pass on information. There is an affidavit sworn by 　*e* Mr Nasser, a barrister employed by the Treasury Solicitor, in which he states:

'I ... contend that it is not part of the responsibility of the Crown Prosecution Service to record (save for its own purposes) such matters. The record of the proceedings is drawn up by an officer of the Court. Further, it is not part of the responsibility of the Crown Prosecution Service to pass on 　*f* to an inferior Court such matters. The Crown Prosecution Service does not as a matter of practice receive papers regarding offences shown on T.I.C. [taken into consideration] Forms and therefore cannot know whether such offences are the subject of proceedings or not in other courts.'

There is evidential material in the contention contained in this paragraph 　*g* which would obviously be important when considering findings of fact at trial but the accuracy of which I cannot assume or assess at this stage.

But Mr Bennett submitted that, on authority, it is the duty of the police to make a record of offences taken into consideration. He relied upon *R v Hicks* (1924) 18 Cr App R 11, where Lord Hewart CJ said:

'In this case ... it is not easy to see what other charges were taken into 　*h* account by the court below when it passed sentence. There is no note here on the indictment. The most convenient procedure is for the officer in charge of the case to make a list of the places, dates and offences alleged with which the court of trial is asked to deal, and to state also on what charges warrants have been issued. That list should be filed in the court below and in this 　*j* Court.'

On the basis of this passage, which I agree is in the nature of a practice note, Mr Bennett submitted that it is the police who have the duty to make a note of offences which have been taken into consideration and that, so noted, the

information will be passed on to any other court, superior or inferior, which has
a an interest in the case.

There is no direct evidence upon which I can decide whether the second
defendant also had the responsibility to note or to send on the information or that
they assumed it in practice. The Crown Prosecution Service was established by
the Prosecution of Offences Act 1985. Neither in that Act nor in the Code for
Crown Prosecutors, issued pursuant to s 10 of the Act, is there any indication of
b such a responsibility. The claim is put by the plaintiff as arising at common law
and not from any statute. But Mr Goff relied on the fact that the second defendant
is responsible for the preparation and prosecution of cases at the Crown Court and
magistrates' courts and was so in respect of the cases against the plaintiff in the
Crown Court at Liverpool and the Ormskirk Magistrates' Court. This suggests to
me that the second defendant had some responsibility to keep the magistrates'
c court informed, especially as it was in charge of a case which was still pending
final disposal before the magistrates. If it is wrong to assume that the prosecution
has a duty to keep the court informed as to the state of an adjourned criminal
case, the matters contained in fact (vii) seem to be explicable at this stage only on
the assumption that, at least in practice, the second defendant assumed a
d responsibility. Why else should the solicitor for Ormskirk be informed and then
be asked to indorse the file? I think that it is reasonable to assume that the solicitor
would not have been asked if it were not the practice for him to indorse the file.
If the facts do not justify the inference of a practice it seems to me to follow from
fact (vii) that on this occasion he was asked and he agreed to indorse the file. It is
not suggested that he refused to do so. On this last assumption of fact, Mr Goff
e submitted that the second defendant on this occasion assumed a responsibility to
pass on the information and that, in failing to do so, it was in breach of the duty.
Counsel relied upon the decision of the Court of Appeal in *Kirkham v Chief
Constable of the Greater Manchester Police* [1990] 3 All ER 246, [1990] 2 QB 283. In
that case the police had assumed a responsibility to inform the prison authorities
that a man in their custody and who subsequently committed suicide was suicidal
f but due to an oversight they failed to do so. They were held liable to the man's
widow.

Before I consider Mr Bennett's submissions that there was no duty of care in
law, I shall refer to his argument based on the Crown Proceedings Act 1947.
Section 2(5) of Act provides:

g   'No proceedings shall lie against the Crown by virtue of this section in
respect of anything done or omitted to be done by any person while
discharging or purporting to discharge any responsibilities of a judicial nature
vested in him, or any responsibilities which he has in connection with the
execution of judicial process.'

h Mr Bennett relied on the disjunctive part of the subsection and he contended
that, if the second defendant had an administrative responsibility or assumed it
in practice or in this particular case, it was discharging a responsibility which it
had in connection with the execution of a judicial process.

I do not accept that submission. In my opinion, the language of the subsection
shows that it is directed to the immunity of judicial and not of administrative
j functions. It is a subsection which is dealing with judicial functions. In my view,
recording that an offence has been taken into consideration or communicating
the fact does not fall within the language of the subsection.

However, Mr Bennett's submission that the second defendant is immune from
any action based upon the failure of the advocate at the resumed hearing to

inform the magistrates that the offences had been taken into consideration is well
founded. It is not necessary to go further than the decision of the House of Lords   *a*
in *Saif Ali v Sydney Mitchell & Co (a firm)* [1978] 3 All ER 1033, [1980] AC 198.
That was a case in which a solicitor, sued in negligence by his client, sought
indemnity or contribution from a barrister who was alleged to have been
negligent in advising and in settling pleadings in accordance with the negligent
advice. The House of Lords reaffirmed the immunity which a barrister has from
an action for negligence in respect of his management of a case in court. This   *b*
immunity has been recognised in the relationship between the professional and
lay client on the one hand and the barrister instructed on their behalf on the
other. Here, the relationship is between the prosecutor and the accused, parties
not on the same side, but in my view this makes no difference bearing in mind
that the immunity is based on a ground of public policy: see, for example, the   *c*
speech of Lord Wilberforce in *Saif Ali's* case [1978] 3 All ER 1033 at 1037, [1980]
AC 198 at 212. Moreover, the immunity in respect of court proceedings extends
to a solicitor acting as an advocate: see the same speech of Lord Wilberforce
([1978] 3 All ER 1033 at 1039, [1980] AC 198 at 215). If, therefore, a solicitor
acting on behalf of the second defendant failed as an advocate in court to inform
the court that the offences had been taken into consideration, the second defendant   *d*
and the solicitor would be immune from any action based on that failure.

I am therefore solely concerned with the question whether the second defendant
owed the plaintiff a duty of care apart from what happened at the resumed
hearing.

In support of his contention that this is an action for abuse of process and that
an allegation of malice is an essential part of such action, Mr Bennett relied upon   *e*
Roy v Prior [1970] 2 All ER 729, [1971] AC 470. It is necessary to consider the
history of that case. The defendant was a solicitor. He acted for a man charged
with larceny. The plaintiff was a doctor of whom the accused was a patient. It
was thought that the plaintiff could give evidence helpful to the accused at his
trial. A witness summons was issued by the defendant but not served on the   *f*
plaintiff. The plaintiff claimed that the defendant did not take the necessary steps
to inform him about the summons or to serve it. According to the plaintiff's case,
the defendant at the trial, acting maliciously and without reasonable or probable
cause, instructed counsel to apply to the judge for a warrant of arrest. The
defendant gave evidence in support of the application. The judge issued the
warrant. The plaintiff was detained. He alleged that the defendant falsely stated   *g*
on oath that the plaintiff was evading service. The defendant applied to strike out
the statement of claim as disclosing no reasonable cause of action.

The matter came before the Court of Appeal (see [1969] 3 All ER 1153, [1970]
1 QB 283) on the defendant's appeal from the refusal of a judge in chambers to
strike out the action. It is necessary to consider how the action was framed. The
plaintiff had drafted the pleading himself. Its terms are set out in the speech of   *h*
Lord Morris of Borth-y-Gest ([1970] 2 All ER 729 at 732, [1971] AC 470 at 472–
473). It was alleged in para 5 of the statement of claim that:

> 'The Defendant omitted to take necessary and sufficient steps to intimate
> [sic] the plaintiff about the issue of the said witness summons; omitted to
> take necessary and sufficient steps to serve the witness summons . . .'   *j*

It was pleaded in para 9:

> 'The Defendant conducted himself negligently in respect of the Plaintiff
> in that, having omitted to take necessary and sufficient steps to intimate [sic]
> the Plaintiff about issue of the witness summons and to take necessary and

a sufficient steps to serve the witness summons on the Plaintiff, he the Defendant, being a solicitor failed to ascertain the reasons for the non-attendance of the Plaintiff as a witness; made unfounded allegations of wilful evasion against the Plaintiff; and thus improperly caused the arrest and detention of the Plaintiff.'

b Other allegations in the statement of claim were interpreted by the Court of Appeal as amounting to an action for procuring the plaintiff's arrest and imprisonment by instituting judicial process maliciously and without reasonable cause.

The claim was unanimously struck out by the Court of Appeal on the ground that it was based on the evidence which had been given by the defendant at the criminal trial, and that, since there was an absolute immunity from suit in respect *c* of the evidence of a witness on the ground of public policy, the action must fail. In so far as the action was based upon the instructions given by the defendant to counsel to apply for a bench warrant, it was struck out because the decisive factor was not the instructions to counsel but the defendant's evidence and that the immunity of a witness was not capable of being outflanked by such a means. But the plaintiff also argued the case in negligence. This was rejected by Lord Denning *d* MR in these terms ([1969] 3 All ER 1153 at 1155, [1970] 1 QB 283 at 288):

'Next counsel for the plaintiff sought to say that an action would lie in negligence on the ground that there was a duty owed by the defendant to the plaintiff to take proper care before he made an application for a warrant. I do not go into the bounds of the duty of care, because the claim in negligence *e* too must fail for the same reasons. No matter how an action is framed, it cannot be used as a way of getting round the high principle that a witness is not liable to a civil suit for words which he says in the witness box.'

Winn LJ described the claim in negligence as 'impossible to sustain', but he did not otherwise comment upon it (see [1969] 3 All ER 1153 at 1155, [1970] 1 QB *f* 283 at 288).

Mr Bennett relied upon the passage from the judgment of Lord Denning MR for the proposition that there is no action for a negligent breach of process. It is to be noted that the Court of Appeal refused leave to appeal to the House of Lords but the Appeal Committee gave leave on terms that the pleading should be amended in order to disclose an action for malicious arrest. The House of Lords *g* allowed the plaintiff's appeal on the amended claim on the grounds that the plaintiff was not suing on the basis of the defendant's evidence at the trial. The defendant's evidence was but one step in the procuring of the plaintiff's arrest by an abuse of the process of the court. The issue of negligence was not argued before the House of Lords and it is therefore submitted by Mr Bennett that the judgment on that issue in the Court of Appeal stands and that I am bound by it.

h But the Court of Appeal rejected the claim in negligence on the ground that, however the cause of action may be framed, it could not be allowed to infringe the rule of public policy which protects evidence given by a witness. It seems to me that the Court of Appeal was considering a cause of action in negligence in relation to that principle alone. It was not considering whether an action in *j* respect of acts or omissions which precede a court process can be framed in negligence, which is the issue I have to decide. Nevertheless, in deciding that issue, I must take into account the history of the causes of action which relate to court proceedings and related matters. They are malicious prosecution, abuse of process and misfeasance in a public office. Malice is an essential element in these torts. There is no reported case in which a negligent abuse of process has been recognised.

I think it appropriate here to consider the proposition agreed between the parties as containing the test by which to decide whether a duty of care exists. *a* First, Mr Bennett accepted that it was reasonably foreseeable by the second defendant that the plaintiff would suffer loss if the magistrates' court were not informed that the offences had been taken into consideration but he qualified this concession by submitting that the plaintiff was represented by solicitors and that the second defendant would therefore contemplate that the plaintiff's solicitors would inform the court. In my view that is an argument based on causation, that *b* is that the effective cause of the damage was the failure of the plaintiff's solicitors to inform the court. Causation is not an argument available at this stage. Then Mr Bennett submitted that the parties were not proximate. He contended that they could not be neighbours bearing in mind that they were antagonists in adversarial litigation. Counsel relied on the decision of Scott J in *Business Computers* *c* *International Ltd v Registrar of Companies* [1987] 3 All ER 465, [1988] Ch 229 and *Al-Kandari v J R Brown & Co (a firm)* [1988] 1 All ER 833, [1988] QB 665. In the latter case Lord Donaldson MR said ([1988] 1 All ER 833 at 835–836, [1988] QB 665 at 672):

> 'A solicitor acting for a party who is engaged in "hostile" litigation owes a duty to his client and to the court, but he does not normally owe any duty to *d* his client's opponent (see *Business Computers International Ltd v Registrar of Companies* [1987] 3 All ER 465, [1988] Ch 229). This is not to say that, if the solicitor is guilty of professional misconduct and someone other than his client is damnified thereby, that person is without a remedy, for the court exercises a supervisory jurisdiction over solicitors as officers of the court and, *e* in an appropriate case, will order the solicitor to pay compensation (see *Myers v Elman* [1939] 4 All ER 484, [1940] AC 282). That said, it should be emphasised that in the present case there is no allegation and no suspicion of any misconduct on the part of the defendant solicitors.'

Both of these cases were concerned with civil litigation. I think that it is highly *f* arguable that the Crown Prosecution Service, responsible for the preparation and presentation of criminal charges of many types and of varying gravity is not in the same position as a solicitor acting at arm's length in adversarial civil litigation. The traditions which govern the attitude of a prosecutor in criminal cases in this country suggest otherwise. The Code for Prosecutors issued under the powers conferred by s 10 of the 1985 Act stating, for example in para 8, the factors to be *g* taken into consideration when deciding whether to prosecute in cases where a conviction might otherwise be secured is another example which emphasises the difference. There are many other instances: for example, the duty to make available to the defence witnesses who can give material evidence and whom the prosecution do not intend to call and also the obligation to inform the defence of any previous convictions of a prosecution witness. All these practices are alien to *h* civil litigation.

Apart from Mr Goff's other submissions on proximity, the question of proximity is raised by the plaintiff as arising from fact (vii), that is that the 'solicitor for Ormskirk' approved of the offences being taken into consideration and, by reasonable inference, he agreed to note the file. The plaintiff relies in this context on *Kirkham v Chief Constable of the Greater Manchester Police* [1990] 3 All *j* ER 246 at 250, [1990] 2 QB 283 at 289, where Lloyd LJ said:

> 'The question depends in each case on whether, having regard to the particular relationship between the parties, the defendant has assumed a

a
responsibility towards the plaintiff, and whether the plaintiff has relied on that assumption of responsibility.'

In my view the solicitor for Ormskirk assumed responsibility towards the plaintiff on the basis of fact (vii) or at least it is highly arguable that he did. Moreover, the assumed facts show that the plaintiff was relying on that responsibility. He did not expect to have to answer to his bail. Mr Bennett

b
contended that the plaintiff had not pleaded the case on this basis, but that is a difficult argument for the second defendant bearing in mind that the plaintiff's case on this aspect of the facts arises out of matters in para 4 of the amended defence of the first defendant conceded by Mr Bennett to be true.

Next, in my view it is fair, just and reasonable to hold that a duty of care exists on the assumed facts of this case. Mr Bennett submitted that it would be wrong

c
to look at this aspect of the question of duty within the narrow confines of this case. There may be cases, he contended, in which there are a very large number of offences taken into consideration and the burden on the second defendant would be such that it would not be fair or just or reasonable to cast a duty. I do not agree.

Finally, is there any ground of public policy for excluding a duty? To hold that

d
a duty exists does not impugn the decision of the magistrates' court. It does not infringe any of the immunities which arise from the conduct of cases or from the evidence of witnesses. In *Business Computers International Ltd v Registrar of Companies* [1987] 3 All ER 465, [1988] Ch 229 Scott J, in rejecting the existence of a duty of care in the circumstances of that case, was influenced by the existence of

e
safeguards against impropriety which are to be found in the rules and procedure that controlled the litigation. There are none such on the facts of the present case. I can find no reason for excluding a duty on the grounds of public policy.

It follows that in my view, by every one of the agreed tokens by which to test the existence of a duty, a duty is found to exist. Mr Bennett has not produced an authority which unambiguously states that proof of malice is an integral part in

f
an action which touches on a judicial process. No authority has been produced to show that a duty of care cannot exist at stages anterior to litigation or resumed litigation. In these circumstances, subject to one or two other arguments raised by Mr Bennett, I would decline to strike out this action.

In the first of these arguments, Mr Bennett submitted that the plaintiff's claim is flawed since it is based upon the misconception that, because the judge took the

g
two offences into account, it must follow that they ceased to exist. It is said that the offences did not cease to exist and that the plaintiff is still accountable for them. Counsel referred to *R v Batchelor* (1952) 36 Cr App R 64 at 67–68, in which Lord Goddard CJ, delivering the judgment of the court, considered the effect of taking offences into consideration. He said:

h
    'Everyone knows now—at least, I hope they do—what is the effect of taking offences into account. It is a convention; it is not statutory. I have often thought it would have been a good thing if the matter had been dealt with by statute in the Criminal Justice Act, 1948, but it was not. It is simply a convention under which, if a court is informed that there are outstanding charges against a prisoner who is before it for a particular offence, the court

j
    can, if the prisoner admits the offences and asks that they should be taken into account, take them into account, which means that the court can give a longer sentence than it would if it were dealing with him only on the charge mentioned in the indictment. But, technically, taking offences into account does not amount to a conviction. That was decided in this court not very

long ago where a man had been charged with an offence and found Guilty
by a jury and then had asked for another offence to be taken into consideration, *a*
which was done. Then he appealed against the conviction for what I may call
the main offence and this court set aside the conviction. Then the man was
rearrested and charged with the offence which had been taken into
consideration. In one case (McMinn ((1945) 30 Cr App R 138)) a judge on
circuit had held that the taking into consideration of an offence amounted to
a conviction on which a plea of *autrefois convict* could be based. But an appeal *b*
to this court in another case (Nicholson ((1948) 32 Cr App R 98 at 127))
showed that that decision was wrong, and that the prisoner had never been
convicted of the offence taken into consideration, and it was right that he
should be tried for it, because, although the sentence for the original offence
for which he had been tried was probably longer than it would have been *c*
had the offence not been taken into consideration, as that conviction was
quashed, he had never been punished or tried for the offence which had been
taken into consideration. Therefore, we said that it was quite proper to try
him for the second offence which had been taken into consideration but had
not been the subject of a charge.'

In this case, it is difficult to envisage circumstances in which the offences which *d*
were taken into consideration could be revived, bearing in mind that the plaintiff
pleaded guilty to the matters for which he appeared before the Crown Court at
Liverpool on 7 August (the main offence) and that since these matters could not
be revived neither could the offences which were taken into consideration. But I
must accept what the court said in *R v Batchelor* (1982) 36 Cr App R 64, whatever *e*
may be the reality in this particular case. Mr Bennett argued, on the basis of *R v
Batchelor*, that, since the plaintiff could still be convicted of the offences taken into
consideration, the negligent failure to transmit the information to the Ormskirk
court is irrelevant. In my view, that is not an argument which goes to the question
whether a duty was owed; it might go to the question whether the alleged
negligence caused the plaintiff damage. But causation is not a matter for decision *f*
at this stage.

A further argument raised by Mr Bennett was that the Crown Prosecution
Service is a single persona and that, on any view of the facts, it was seised of the
two matters which were taken into consideration. It was therefore argued, as I
understood it, that the Crown Prosecution Service was seised of the two matters
and that the question of transmitting information from one branch of the service *g*
to another cannot arise. This argument overlooks the fact that the second
defendant is responsible for the negligent acts and omissions of its servants.

I can only strike out an action under RSC Ord 18, r 19 in a plain and obvious
case. The power conferred by the rule can only be exercised where the case is clear
beyond doubt: see the authorities cited in *The Supreme Court Practice 1991* Vol 1, *h*
para 18/19/3 and see also the judgment of Balcombe LJ in *Clarke v Bruce Lance &
Co (a firm)* [1988] 1 All ER 364 at 366, [1988] 1 WLR 881 at 884, to which I was
specifically referred. This is far from being a plain and obvious case. In my
judgment the appeal must be allowed.

Appeal allowed. *j*

Mary Rose Plummer   Barrister.

Chief Adjudication Officer and another v Foster

HOUSE OF LORDS,
LORD TEMPLEMAN, LORD BRIDGE OF HARWICH, LORD ACKNER, LORD BROWNE-WILKINSON
AND LORD SLYNN OF HADLEY
6, 7, 8 OCTOBER 1992, 28 JANUARY 1993

Social security – Income support – Disability premium – Calculation of amount – Entitlement to severe disability premium – Circumstances in which persons to be treated as being severely disabled – Secretary of State having power to make regulations specifying circumstances in which persons to be treated as being severely disabled – Disabled person entitled to disability premium if no non-dependants living with him – Claimant disabled and living with parents – Secretary of State making regulations providing that parents classed as non-dependants – Claimant no longer entitled to severe disability premium – Whether regulations ultra vires – Social Security Act 1986, s 22(4) – Income Support (General) Regulations 1987, reg 17(1), Sch 2, para 13(2)(a)(ii)(iii).

Social security commissioner – Appeal to social security commissioner – Jurisdiction of commissioner – Whether commissioner having jurisdiction to determine whether social security regulations ultra vires – Social Security Act 1975, s 101(1).

The appellant was a severely disabled single woman who lived at home with her parents. She received a severe disablement allowance under the Social Security Act 1975 and also income support under the Social Security Act 1986 calculated in accordance with reg 17(1)[a] of the Income Support (General) Regulations 1987. The amount payable by way of income support included a severe disability premium because she was in receipt of attendance allowance under para 13(2)(a)(i)[b] of Sch 2 to the 1987 regulations and had no non-dependants aged 18 or over residing with her within sub-para (2)(a)(ii) thereof. However, on 8 October 1989 following an amendment of the definition of 'non-dependant' in the regulations her parents were no longer classed as non-dependants and an adjudication officer ruled that she no longer qualified for the premium. His decision was affirmed by a social security appeal tribunal. On appeal by the appellant under s 101(1)[c] of the 1975 Act, the social security commissioner allowed her appeal, holding that para 13(2)(a)(ii) and (iii) was ultra vires the Secretary of State's power to make regulations under s 22(4)[d] of the 1986 Act, which provided that regulations could be made specifying 'circumstances in which persons [were] to be treated as being or as not being severely disabled'. The commissioner held that regulations made under s 22(4) were limited to specifying circumstances directly related to the degree of physical or mental disability and could not prescribe other circumstances which might affect the extent of the disabled person's needs. The chief adjudication officer and the Secretary of State appealed. The Court of Appeal

---

a   Regulation 17(1), so far as material, provides: '. . . a claimant's weekly applicable amount shall be the aggregate of such of the following amounts which may apply in his case . . . (d) the amount of any premiums which may be applicable to him, determined in accordance with Parts III and IV of Schedule 2 (premiums) . . .'

b   Paragraph 13, so far as material, is set out at p 713 e f, post

c   Section 101(1), so far as material, provided: '. . . an appeal lies to a Commissioner from any decision of a social security appeal tribunal on the ground that the decision of the tribunal was erroneous in point of law.'

d   Section 22(4) is set out at p 713 d, post

allowed the appeal, holding that the commissioner had no jurisdiction to question the vires of a regulation made by the Secretary of State and that para 13(2)(*a*)(ii) *a* and (iii) was intra vires. The appellant appealed to the House of Lords.

Held – (1) The commissioners, in exercising their appellate functions under s 101 of the 1975 Act, had jurisdiction to determine any challenge to the vires of a provision in regulations made by the Secretary of State on the ground that it was beyond the scope of the enabling power whenever it was necessary to do so in *b* order to determine whether a decision under appeal was erroneous in point of law (see p 707 *d*, p 710 *g*, p 712 *h j* and p 718 *f g*, post).

(2) The regulation-making power conferred on the Secretary of State by s 22(4) of the 1986 Act, read in the context of the social security legislation as a whole, was not intended to be confined to defining the degree of disability which was to qualify as severe but permitted the Secretary of State in delimiting the category *c* of persons who were to be treated as severely disabled to take account of any circumstances relevant to the disabled person's needs. Accordingly, para 13(2)(*a*)(ii) and (iii) of Sch 2 to the 1987 regulations was intra vires. The appeal would therefore be dismissed (see p 707 *d*, p 714 *h* to p 715 *a f*, p 717 *e* and p 718 *e* to *g*, post). *d*

Decision of the Court of Appeal [1991] 3 All ER 846 affirmed.

Notes

For income support, see Supplement to 33 *Halsbury's Laws* (4th edn) para 856A.

As from 1 July 1992, s 101(1) of the Social Security Act 1975 was replaced by s 23(1) of the Social Security Administration Act 1992. For s 23 of the 1992 Act, *e* see 40 *Halsbury's Statutes* (4th edn) 820.

As from 1 July 1992, s 22(4) of the Social Security Act 1986 was replaced by s 135(6) of the Social Security Contributions and Benefits Act 1992. For s 135 of the 1992 Act, see ibid 673.

Cases referred to in opinions *f*

Associated Provincial Picture Houses Ltd v Wednesbury Corp [1947] 2 All ER 680, [1948] 1 KB 223, CA.

Bugg v DPP, DPP v Percy (1992) Independent, 8 September, DC.

Dunkley v Evans [1981] 3 All ER 285, [1981] 1 WLR 1522, DC.

Edinburgh City DC v Secretary of State for Scotland 1985 SC 261, 1985 SLT 551, Ct *g* of Sess (OH and IH).

Nottinghamshire CC v Secretary of State for the Environment [1986] 1 All ER 199, [1986] AC 240, [1986] 2 WLR 1, HL.

O'Reilly v Mackman [1982] 3 All ER 1124, [1983] 2 AC 237, [1982] 3 WLR 1096, HL.

Pepper (Inspector of Taxes) v Hart [1993] 1 All ER 42, [1992] 3 WLR 1032, HL. *h*

Social Security Decision R(SB) 15/89, Tribunal of Comrs.

Stubbings v Webb [1993] 1 All ER 322, [1993] 2 WLR 120, CA.

Warwickshire CC v Johnson [1993] 1 All ER 299, [1993] 2 WLR 1, HL.

Appeal

Rosaleen Foster appealed with the leave of the Appeal Committee of the House of *j* Lords given on 3 June 1991 from the decision of the Court of Appeal (Beldam and Nolan LJJ (Lord Donaldson MR dissenting)) ([1991] 3 All ER 846, [1992] QB 31) on 21 February 1991 allowing the appeal of the Chief Adjudication Officer and the Secretary of State for Social Security from the decision of the social security commissioner (Mr R A Sanders) given on 5 December 1990 whereby he allowed a the appellant's appeal from the decision of Birkenhead South Social Security Appeal Tribunal (chairman Mrs Susan Wright) given on 7 February 1990 that para 13(2)(a)(ii) and (iii) of the Income Support (General) Regulations 1987, SI 1987/1967, were not ultra vires the Secretary of State under s 22(4) of the Social Security Act 1986 and accordingly that the appellant was not entitled to a severe disability premium. The facts are set out in the opinion of Lord Bridge.

b *Richard Drabble* and *Mark Rowland* (instructed by *Hodge Jones & Allen*) for the appellant.
Michael Beloff QC and *Christopher Katkowski* (instructed by *Solicitor to the Departments of Health and Social Security*) for the respondents.

c Their Lordships took time for consideration.

28 January 1993. The following opinions were delivered.

d **LORD TEMPLEMAN.** My Lords, for the reasons given by my noble and learned friend Lord Bridge of Harwich I would dismiss the appeal.

e **LORD BRIDGE OF HARWICH.** My Lords, the appellant is a young single woman who is severely disabled and who lives at home with her parents. The extent of her disability is such that she is entitled to and does receive under the Social Security Act 1975, as amended by subsequent legislation, attendance allowance, severe disablement allowance and mobility allowance. These are non-contributory benefits which are not means-tested. Under the Social Security Act 1986 and regulations made thereunder she is also entitled to the income-related benefit known as income support. This is a form of social security payment designed to provide or supplement the income of those in need so as to ensure that it does not fall below a certain minimum level. The minimum level is f known as 'the applicable amount'. The applicable amount in relation to any individual varies according to the circumstances of that individual as provided by Pt IV of the Income Support (General) Regulations 1987, SI 1987/1967. In particular the applicable amount otherwise determined is to be enhanced by the amount of any 'premium' to which the individual is entitled under Pt III of Sch 2 g to the 1987 regulations. One of these is the severe disability premium, entitlement to which is prescribed by para 13 of Sch 2. The issue in this appeal is whether, in the relevant circumstances and in accordance with the regulations in force since 9 October 1989, the appellant is entitled to the severe disability premium as part of her income support. The adjudication officer held that she was not and the Birkenhead South Social Security Appeal Tribunal affirmed his decision. On h appeal to a social security commissioner, it was held by Mr Commissioner Sanders that so much of para 13(2)(a) as operated to defeat the appellant's claim to the severe disability premium was in excess of the Secretary of State's regulation-making power and that this was severable from the remainder of the sub-paragraph which established her entitlement. He accordingly allowed her appeal. From this decision the chief adjudication officer and the Secretary of State appealed j to the Court of Appeal. The court (Lord Donaldson MR, Beldam and Nolan LJJ) ([1991] 3 All ER 846, [1992] QB 31) held first, unanimously, that the commissioner had no jurisdiction to question the vires of a regulation made by the Secretary of State, so that the appeal fell strictly to be allowed on this ground alone. They went on to hold, however, that in the circumstances it was both possible and appropriate for the court to consider the substantive issue of the vires of the provision which

the appellant sought to impugn by the device of allowing her to invoke the
original jurisdiction of the Court of Appeal to entertain an application for judicial   *a*
review. On the issue of vires the majority (Beldam and Nolan LJJ) held the
relevant provision to be intra vires; Lord Donaldson MR held it to be ultra vires,
but further held that it was not severable from the remainder of the regulation.
In the result the appellant failed. The appellant now appeals from it by leave of
your Lordships' House.

b

The jurisdiction of the commissioners
    The issue as to the commissioners' jurisdiction is in one sense academic, since,
if your Lordships were to affirm the Court of Appeal on this issue, it would still
be necessary to go on, as the Court of Appeal did, to determine the issue of the
vires of the provision under challenge and it is only if the appellant succeeds on
this second issue that she can effectively succeed in the appeal. The jurisdiction   *c*
issue, however, has far-reaching procedural implications for the future, it has
been very fully argued and it is important that your Lordships should resolve it,
the more so, perhaps, since the Court of Appeal's decision in the instant case runs
counter to the practice of the social security commissioners established by a long
series of decisions, both by single commissioners and by tribunals of   *d*
commissioners, holding that they had jurisdiction to decide and in fact deciding
issues as to the vires of secondary legislation. Some of those decisions have been
reviewed by the courts without any previous suggestion that issues of vires were
beyond the jurisdiction of the commissioners.
    Part III of the Social Security Act 1975 is headed 'Determination of Claims and
Questions'. It has been extensively amended by subsequent legislation and any   *e*
reference in this opinion to the provisions of the Act will be to their form as in
force at the material time. The fasciculus of ss 97 to 104 is headed 'Adjudication
officers, social security appeal tribunals and Commissioners'. Section 97 provides
that in the first instance an adjudication officer is to determine any claim for
benefit and any question arising in connection with a claim for benefit except
questions required by some other provision in Pt III to be determined otherwise   *f*
than by an adjudication officer. From the adjudication officer's decision the
claimant has an appeal as of right to a social security appeal tribunal: see s 100.
From the decision of a social security appeal tribunal an appeal lies to a social
security commissioner on the ground that the decision of the tribunal was
'erroneous in point of law': see s 101. The commissioners, who are of comparable
standing to circuit judges, normally sit singly but the chief commissioner may   *g*
direct that an appeal involving a question of law of special difficulty be dealt with
by a tribunal of three commissioners. Provision for an appeal from a
commissioner's decision to the Court of Appeal is made by s 14 of the Social
Security Act 1980. An appeal lies on a point of law, but only with the leave of the
commissioner or the Court of Appeal and the parties entitled to appeal include   *h*
the Secretary of State.
    This is only the barest outline of the statutory scheme for the adjudication of
benefit claims. But it focuses immediately on the central question, which is
whether a claimant otherwise entitled to some social security benefit which has
been denied to him by the adjudication officer and the appeal tribunal in reliance
on some provision in a regulation which the Secretary of State had no power to   *j*
make is entitled to succeed on appeal to the commissioner on the ground that the
decision against him was 'erroneous in point of law' or whether, as must follow if
the Court of Appeal were right, before he invokes the statutory machinery by
which alone his claim can be enforced, he must first proceed by way of an

application for judicial review to have the offending provision quashed or declared

a invalid. It is common ground that the principle of *O'Reilly v Mackman* [1982] 3 All ER 1124, [1983] 2 AC 237 has no application, since there can be no abuse of process by a party who seeks a remedy by the very process which statute requires him to pursue. It was further rightly accepted by Mr Beloff QC before your Lordships that a decision giving effect to secondary legislation which is ultra vires is, indeed, in the ordinary meaning of the words 'erroneous in point of law'. The

b question then is whether, when that phrase is used in s 101 of the 1975 Act, there is something in the context in which it appears which requires by necessary implication that it be given a restricted meaning so as to exclude from its ambit any errors of law referable to a misuse by the Secretary of State of his regulation-making power.

c I shall seek to summarise, hoping that I do them justice, the several considerations relied on in the judgments of the Court of Appeal and in the arguments advanced for the respondents before your Lordships as giving rise to such an implied restriction and consider them in turn.

It is pointed out, rightly, that, if the commissioner can base his decision in any case on the invalidity of some provision in regulations made under the 1975 Act,

d it must follow that appeal tribunals and adjudication officers can do likewise. Adjudication officers may be, and no doubt normally are, civil servants without legal qualifications and it cannot have been intended by Parliament, it is said, that such relatively lowly officials should have power to question the validity of regulations made by the Secretary of State. Closely allied to this point is the point made that the Secretary of State is not a party to an appeal from the adjudication

e officer to the appeal tribunal and cannot, therefore, appear before it to defend the vires of any provision in regulations which is challenged or himself appeal to the commissioner from an adverse decision of an appeal tribunal. I think both these objections are theoretical rather than real. Under s 99(2) the adjudication officer to whom a claim or question is submitted may either decide it himself or refer it to an appeal tribunal and I should expect that, whenever a claimant before an

f adjudication officer sought to mount a challenge to the vires of some provision in regulations, the adjudication officer, if he thought there might be any substance in the point, would refer it to an appeal tribunal. Moreover, there is a chief adjudication officer whose duty it is under s 97(1C) to advise adjudication officers on the performance of their functions and I should expect him to give or to have given advice to this effect. Again, once such a challenge is before an appeal

g tribunal, the adjudication officer becomes a party to the proceedings and, on this or any other issue of law of whatever nature, there seems no reason why the arguments on which the department wishes to rely in opposition to the claimant should not be addressed to the appeal tribunal and, if appropriate, to the commissioner on appeal in the name of the adjudication officer; I presume this is

h what happens in practice.

Thus the reality, I believe, is that, whenever there is a serious challenge to the validity of a provision in regulations which stands in the claimant's way, the issue, unless the department accepts that the challenge is well made, will effectively be decided at the level of the commissioner and from there either the claimant or the Secretary of State may seek leave to appeal to the Court of Appeal. Certainly

j we have not been told of any case where difficulty has arisen from a decision taken at a level below that of the commissioner relating to a question of vires, although the commissioners have consistently held ever since 1976 that they have jurisdiction to entertain such questions.

Next, reliance is placed on s 96(1), which provides, so far as material:

'. . . the Secretary of State may review any decision given by him on any
question within section 93(1) above if—(*a*) new facts have been brought to
his notice; or (*b*) he is satisfied that the decision—(i) was given in ignorance
of some material fact; (ii) was based on a mistake as to some material fact; or
(iii) was erroneous in point of law.'

Questions which are to be determined by the Secretary of State under s 93(1)
include questions governed by regulations. It is said that the use of the phrase
'erroneous in point of law' in s 96 cannot possibly have been intended to give to
the Secretary of State jurisdiction to decide whether he has himself exceeded the
powers conferred upon him to make regulations. Hence it is argued that the same
phrase when used in s 101 of the same Act must be given the same restricted
meaning. With respect, I believe this point to be misconceived. Section 96 must
be construed in the context of the fasciculus of ss 93 to 96 relating to the
adjudication by the Secretary of State of the questions which he is required to
determine under s 93. Section 94, so far as material, provides:

'(1) A question of law arising in connection with the determination by the
Secretary of State of any question within section 93(1) above may, if the
Secretary of State thinks fit, be referred for decision to the High Court . . .
(3) Any person aggrieved by the decision of the Secretary of State on any
question of law within subsection (1) above which is not referred in
accordance with that subsection may appeal from that decision to the
court . . .'

The questions of law which, under this section, the Secretary of State may either
refer to the High Court or determine himself, subject to an appeal to the High
Court, must include any question which depends on the vires of a provision in
regulations. It would be absurd that the Secretary of State, confronted with such
a question, should, instead of referring it to the High Court, require the party
before him to institute separate proceedings by way of judicial review. Moreover,
the power to review a previous decision under s 96(1)(*b*)(iii) as having been
erroneous in point of law would clearly apply to a case where the Secretary of
State had made one or more decisions on the basis that a certain regulation
governed the question to be determined and in a later case the High Court, on a
reference or appeal under s 94, had held that same regulation to be ultra vires.
Accordingly, if the phrase 'erroneous in point of law' is used in the same sense in
s 101 as in s 96 it bears its ordinary unrestricted meaning.
   It is said that, if the commissioner were intended to have power to hold a
provision in a regulation to be ultra vires and to determine whether or not it was
severable, one would expect to find that he was also empowered to make a
declaration to that effect, which he is not. This, again, I find quite unconvincing.
The commissioner has no power and no authority to decide anything but the
issue which arises in the case before him, typically, as in this case, whether in
particular circumstances a claimant is or is not entitled to the benefit claimed. If
the success of the claim depends, as here, on whether a particular provision in a
regulation is both ultra vires and severable, the commissioner's decision of that
question is merely incidental to his decision as to whether the claim should be
upheld or rejected. If not appealed, his opinion on the question may be followed
by other commissioners, but it has, per se, no binding force in law. To my mind
it would be very surprising if the commissioners were empowered to make
declarations of any kind and the absence of such a power does not, in my opinion,
throw any light on the question presently in issue.

Lord Donaldson MR quoted in his judgment from the headnote to a decision
a of a tribunal of commissioners (*Social Security Decision R(SB)* 15/89), where it is
said:

> '. . . the determination of whether a right to benefit exists and the
> quantification of benefit necessarily [import] a duty for the statutory
> authorities (including the adjudication officer) to consider whether the
> *b* regulation in question has a legal existence when that existence is challenged
> [but] it was not a proper function of the statutory adjudication authorities to
> entertain arguments as to the "reasonableness" of provisions in delegated
> legislation . . .'

Lord Donaldson MR commented ([1991] 3 All ER 846 at 855, [1992] 1 QB 31 at
c 48):

> 'I fully accept that, under the further framework, if the commissioners
> have this power, so has each of the many hundreds of relatively junior
> adjudication officers. I do not, however, understand the logic of the
> distinction between questions of "existence" and questions of "reasonable-
> ness". One reason at least for setting aside subordinate legislation upon
> *d* grounds of *Wednesbury* unreasonableness (see *Associated Provincial Picture
> Houses Ltd v Wednesbury Corp* [1947] 2 All ER 680, [1948] 1 KB 223) would
> be that Parliament never intended the regulation-making power to be
> exercised in that way. That is really indistinguishable from a question of
> "existence" or "vires".'

e It is, of course, correct that, if the commissioners have jurisdiction to question
the vires of secondary legislation, the scope of that jurisdiction must, at least
theoretically, embrace a challenge on the ground of irrationality as well as
illegality. But, in the case referred to, the full judgment of the tribunal of
commissioners shows that, in distinguishing between 'legal existence' and
'reasonableness', they were not making a point peculiar to their own jurisdiction,
f but were relying on authority which they interpreted as precluding any court or
tribunal from condemning as irrational delegated legislation enacted under a
statutory power which may only be exercised subject to parliamentary control by
affirmative or negative resolution. The judgment cites a well-known passage
from the speech of Lord Scarman in *Nottinghamshire CC v Secretary of State for the
g Environment* [1986] 1 All ER 199 at 204, [1986] AC 240 at 250, and a passage from
the judgment of Lord Jauncey, as Lord Ordinary, in the Scottish case of *Edinburgh
City DC v Secretary of State for Scotland* 1985 SC 261 at 274–275 (see *Social Security
Decision R(SB)* 15/89 at pp 11–13). The latter case goes rather further than the
former. It was concerned with an order made under the Rating and Valuation
(Amendment) Scotland Act 1984. Although the order was debated in the House
h of Commons, a prayer to annul it was not moved. In an action for reduction of
the order the district council attacked it on grounds of (1) illegality, (2) irrationality
and (3) impropriety of procedure. The Secretary of State disputed that the last
two grounds could be applied to statutory instruments considered by Parliament.
The relevant part of Lord Jauncey's judgment is sufficiently summarised in the
following passage from the headnote (see 1985 SLT 551 at 552):
j

> 'The Lord Ordinary distinguished between such orders and orders
> exercisable entirely at the hand of a Minister or authority, and held that a
> statutory instrument considered by Parliament could only be held to be ultra
> vires upon the ground of illegality, in the narrower sense, where is was

patently defective in that it purported to do what it was not authorised to do
by the enabling statute, or where the procedure followed departed from the   *a*
requirements of the enabling statute.'

On appeal to the Inner House this judgment was affirmed.

This is not the occasion when it would be appropriate for your Lordships to
consider whether to go beyond the speech of Lord Scarman, unanimously agreed
to by the Appellate Committee, in the *Nottinghamshire* case, which leaves room   *b*
for possible exceptions in extreme cases from any absolute rule that the courts
may not condemn as irrational secondary legislation which has been subject to
parliamentary scrutiny. But I have no doubt that the social security commissioners
have good pragmatic reasons not to take it upon themselves to identify any such
exceptional case, but to leave that to the higher courts, who, as Lord Jauncey
pointed out, have never yet done so in any reported case.   *c*

Your Lordships were referred in argument to the hitherto unreported judgment
of the Divisional Court (Woolf LJ and Pill J) delivered by Woolf LJ in *Bugg v DPP,
DPP v Percy* (1992) Independent, 8 September. This examines comprehensively
the authorities bearing on the question how far a magistrates' court, hearing a
prosecution for an offence under byelaws, may properly entertain a challenge to   *d*
the vires of the byelaws. In brief summary, the judgment draws a distinction
between what Woolf LJ calls 'substantive invalidity' and 'procedural invalidity'
and concludes that it is within the jurisdiction of a magistrates' court to determine
the issue of substantive invalidity, where the byelaw is alleged to be bad on its
face, either as beyond the power of the enabling legislation under which it
purports to have been made or as patently unreasonable, but that where procedural   *e*
irregularity is alleged the issue can only be determined on examination of the
relevant evidence in proceedings to which the byelaw-making authority is a party
and is therefore beyond the competence of a criminal court, which should
presume that byelaws were made in accordance with the prescribed procedure
unless and until they have been set aside by the appropriate court with jurisdiction
to do so.   *f*

It seems to me neither necessary nor appropriate for your Lordships in the
instant case to consider the issue with which this judgment was concerned, or to
determine whether a comparable distinction between substantive and procedural
invalidity should be made in relation to the jurisdiction of the commissioners.
Here no question of procedural validity arises. The provision in the regulations   *g*
which is challenged is either within or without the scope of the enabling power.
Hence the issue is one of pure statutory construction unaffected by evidence. So
far as I am aware all previous issues of vires determined by the commissioners
have been of the same character. How an issue of procedural invalidity should be
determined in this field can be safely left for decision if and when it arises.

My conclusion is that the commissioners have undoubted jurisdiction to   *h*
determine any challenge to the vires of a provision in regulations made by the
Secretary of State as being beyond the scope of the enabling power whenever it is
necessary to do so in determining whether a decision under appeal was erroneous
in point of law. I am pleased to reach that conclusion for two reasons. First, it
avoids a cumbrous duplicity of proceedings which could only add to the already
overburdened list of applications for judicial review awaiting determination by   *j*
the Divisional Court. Secondly, it is, in my view, highly desirable that when the
Court of Appeal, or indeed your Lordships' House, is called upon to determine an
issue of the kind in question it should have the benefit of the views upon it of one
or more of the commissioners, who have great expertise in this somewhat esoteric
area of the law.

The issue of vires

a   Income support is one of the income-related benefits for which provision is made by Pt II of the Social Security Act 1986. The provisions of the 1986 Act which are relevant for present purposes are the following:

> '**20** . . . (3) A person in Great Britain is entitled to income support if—
> (*a*) he is of or over the age of 18 . . .

b   **21.**—(1) . . . where a person is entitled to income support—(*a*) if he has no income, the amount shall be the applicable amount; and (*b*) if he has income, the amount shall be the difference between his income and the applicable amount . . .

>   **22.**—(1) The applicable amount shall be such amount or the aggregate of such amounts as may be prescribed.

c   (2) The power to prescribe applicable amounts conferred by subsection (1) above includes power to prescribe nil as an applicable amount . . .

>   (3) In relation to income support . . . the applicable amount for a severely disabled person shall include an amount in respect of his being a severely disabled person.

d   (4) Regulations may specify circumstances in which persons are to be treated as being or as not being severely disabled . . .'

Applicable amounts are governed by the 1987 regulations and the conditions of entitlement to the various 'premiums' are those specified in paras 8 to 14 of Sch 2. Paragraph 13, headed 'Severe Disability Premium', provides so far as relevant:

e
> '(1) The condition is that the claimant is a severely disabled person.
>
> (2) For the purposes of sub-paragraph (1), a claimant shall be treated as being a severely disabled person if, and only if—(*a*) in the case of a single claimant or a lone parent—(i) he is in receipt of attendance allowance, and (ii) subject to sub-paragraph (3), he has no non-dependants aged 18 or over
f residing with him, and (iii) no-one is in receipt of an invalid care allowance under section 37 of the Social Security Act in respect of caring for him . . .'

Sub-paragraph (2)(*b*) establishes a more elaborate set of conditions which a claimant who has a 'partner' must satisfy in addition to being in receipt of attendance allowance. I need not set these out but may mention that, like the conditions in sub-para (2)(*a*)(ii) and (iii), they all relate to matters other than the degree of
g disablement of the claimant. Sub-paragraph (3), which provides that certain categories of persons are to be disregarded for the purpose of sub-para (2)(*a*)(ii), is not presently relevant.

The appellant's contention is that the only conditions of eligibility for the severe disability premium which the Secretary of State is empowered to impose
h by s 22(4) must relate directly to the claimant's disablement. If this is right, it must follow that the only valid condition imposed, in the case of single claimants, lone parents and claimants with partners alike, is that the claimant must be in receipt of attendance allowance, which, as we shall see, is payable only to those with a very severe degree of disability. If the other conditions are both ultra vires and severable, it must further follow that ever since the 1987 regulations came
j into force any person in receipt of attendance allowance has also been entitled to the severe disability premium as part of the applicable amount of his income support irrespective of his domestic circumstances and whether or not any invalid care allowance was in payment in respect of him.

The argument for the appellant points out correctly that, in contrast with the power conferred by s 22(2) to prescribe nil as an applicable amount, the Secretary

of State is obliged by s 22(3) to include in the applicable amount for a severely
disabled person *some* amount in respect of his being such a person. Hence, it is *a*
submitted, if the purpose of s 22(3) is not to be frustrated, s 22(4) must be
construed as solely referrable to the nature and degree of a person's physical or
mental disability. Thus the Secretary of State may specify circumstances directly
related to the degree of physical or mental disability but can take no account of
other circumstances which may affect the extent of the disabled person's needs.

The contrary argument for the respondents is that sub-ss (3) and (4) of s 22 *b*
must be read together. Any person qualifying as a member of the category of
severely disabled persons within sub-s (3) is certainly entitled to an addition, on
that account, to any other applicable amount for which he qualifies. But sub-s (4)
is, in effect, a deeming provision whereby the Secretary of State, in defining the
category of persons who are to be treated as being severely disabled for the
purposes of sub-s (3), may do so by reference to circumstances which either relate *c*
to their degree of physical or mental disability or affect the extent of their need
for income support arising from that disability. Reliance is placed on the striking
similarity between the language of s 22(4) and the language used to confer other
regulation-making powers for the purposes of Pt II of the 1986 Act by s 20(12),
which provides, inter alia: *d*

> 'Regulations may make provision for the purposes of this Part of this Act—
> (*a*) as to circumstances in which a person is to be treated as being or not being
> in Great Britain . . . (*d*) as to circumstances in which a person is or is not to be
> treated as—(i) engaged or normally engaged in remunerative work;
> (ii) available for employment; or (iii) actively seeking employment . . . (*f*) as *e*
> to circumstances in which a person is or is not to be treated as receiving
> relevant education; (*g*) as to circumstances in which a person is or is not to be
> treated as occupying a dwelling as his home . . . (*k*) as to circumstances in
> which persons are to be treated as being or not being members of the same
> household; (*l*) as to circumstances in which one person is to be treated as
> responsible or not responsible for another.' *f*

In all these cases, it is said, the simple questions whether a person is in Great
Britain, is engaged in remunerative work etc are questions of fact. But in giving
the Secretary of State power by regulation to make provision as to circumstances
in which a person is to be treated as being or not being in Great Britain, engaged
in remunerative work etc the Secretary of State is clearly empowered to look *g*
beyond the question of fact to the surrounding circumstances and, for example,
to provide that in certain circumstances a person who, as a matter of fact, is not
physically in Great Britain shall be treated as being in Great Britain or, conversely,
that in other circumstances a person who is physically in Great Britain shall be
treated as not being in Great Britain.

This is a very formidable argument and it seems to me that, if the only power *h*
intended to be conferred on the Secretary of State by s 22(4) were a power to
define the degree of disability which was to qualify as severe for the purposes of
sub-s (3), the language used was totally inappropriate to effect that purpose. Thus,
even without looking beyond the 1986 Act, it would be my opinion that the
regulation-making power under sub-s (4) cannot be confined as the appellant
suggests, but allows the Secretary of State in delimiting the category of persons *j*
who are to be treated as severely disabled for the purposes of sub-s (3) to take
account of any circumstances relevant to the disabled person's needs.

This opinion is powerfully reinforced if one reads the 1986 Act, as one should,
in the context of the social security legislation as a whole and compares the

subsection which your Lordships have to construe with the elaborate provisions
a in the 1975 Act which confer on disabled persons benefits which are not income-
related and are wholly dependent on their degree of disability. The most severe
degree of disability attracts an attendance allowance under s 35 of the 1975 Act.
To qualify for this a person must be so severely disabled mentally or physically
that he requires from another person either frequent attention in connection with
his bodily functions or supervison to avoid substantial danger to himself or others.
b Distinct from this, and normally payable to any person who qualifies for
attendance allowance in addition thereto, is the severe disablement allowance
provided for by s 36. The normal qualification for this, in addition to incapacity
for work, is a loss of physical or mental faculty assessed 'such that the assessed
extent of the resulting disablement amounts to not less than 80 per cent.': see
c s 36(5). The assessment is to be made in accordance with the provisions of Sch 8.
Paragraph 1 of the schedule sets out the general principles to be applied, including
the requirement in para 1(c) that the assessment should be made 'without
reference to the particular circumstances of the claimant other than age, sex, and
physical and mental condition'. Paragraph 2 enables provision to be made by
regulations for 'further defining the principles on which the extent of disablement
d is to be assessed' and in particular regulations may direct 'that a prescribed loss of
faculty shall be treated as resulting in a prescribed degree of disablement'.

Given that the social security legislation in force when the 1986 Act was passed
already contained this very precise code for determining what degree of physical
or mental disability was to qualify a person for severe disability allowance, if it
was intended in 1986 that the qualification for a severe disability premium as part
e of the applicable amount of a person's income support should be governed by a
similar code and subject to a similar restriction to that imposed by para 1(c) of
Sch 8, it is to my mind almost inconceivable that this should not have been
achieved by reference to this ready-made code, or at least by the use of similar
language. It is to my mind quite inconceivable that it was intended to be achieved
by the brief and expansive language of s 22(4) of the 1986 Act.
f These considerations were the basis of the opinion I had formed at the
conclusion of the oral arguments, which I understand all your Lordships shared,
that the appellant must fail on the vires issue. But since the oral argument on the
appeal your Lordships' House has ruled in *Pepper (Inspector of Taxes) v Hart* [1993]
1 All ER 42, [1992] 3 WLR 1032 that in certain circumstances the parliamentary
history of a provision in a Bill and references to it in Hansard may be considered
g when that provision reaches the statute book and falls to be construed. Since the
delivery of that judgment the respondents have invited your Lordships to consider
the circumstances in which s 22(3) and (4) came to be enacted and certain passages
from the debates in both Houses as satisfying the conditions of admissibility as
aids to construction laid down in *Pepper v Hart* and your Lordships have had the
h benefit of submissions in writing by both parties directed to this issue.

The Bill which became the Social Security Act 1986 did not, when first
introduced, contain any specific provision relating to income support for the
severely disabled. In your Lordships' House an amendment was moved to the
clause which became s 20 of the 1986 Act, requiring that any scheme for income
support should provide for a 'community care addition' payable to certain persons.
j I need not set out the text of the somewhat elaborate subsection which it was
proposed to introduce, but it was said by the mover of the amendment to be
intended to apply 'to a very small number of very severely disabled people' and to
be payable 'only according to the needs of the claimant's special circumstances
and the extent to which other payments or benefits under this part of the Bill fail

to meet those needs' (see 477 HL Official Report (5th series) col 13). This amendment was opposed by the government but was agreed to on a division. When the Lords' amendments were considered by the House of Commons, the Minister of Social Security moved that the House disagree with this amendment but at the same time he moved as an alternative amendment the two subsections which are now sub-ss (3) and (4) of s 22. The minister said (102 HC Official Report (6th series) cols 399–400):

'We are seeking to accept the spirit of the way in which the amendment was spoken to and passed in the other place . . . As an additional sign of our good intentions, I point out that there is no need to amend the Bill to provide for a severe disablement premium. There are ample powers within the Bill as it stands for us to have as many premiums as we wish. We have thought it right to make clear our intentions and to respond to the feelings both in this place and the other place. Nevertheless, we wished to table an amendment that specifically provides for a severe disablement premium. We are proposing a higher and additional premium for a particular group of disabled people. It will be paid on top of the other structural improvements for disabled people in the Bill, and in particular the disablement premium. As I have said, in effect it provides the two-tier disablement premium that many commentators, including the Select Committee, have urged upon us. It will be paid as an extra amount to severely disabled people who are living on their own, and who are most likely to need extra support and care. It will be paid to them direct and as of right within the income support scheme. It will also form part of the assessment of need in the housing benefit rules. In considering the issue, we have sought criteria that are consistent with other social security arrangements. Our intention is that receipt of the higher rate of attendance allowance should be the first qualifying condition. The present domestic assistance addition already has a condition that there must be no one in the household capable of carrying out normal domestic duties. The purpose behind that rule, on the need for extra support to maintain independence that cannot otherwise be provided, is a sensible one. We have recently announced a major extension of the invalid care allowance as the benefit that is paid to those caring for disabled people. Consistent with that, we intend that the extra disablement premium will be paid direct to a severely disabled person where there is no one receiving or eligible for the invalid care allowance in respect of that person's care needs. We envisage setting the rate at the same level as for invalid care allowance, currently, although shortly to rise, £23 a week. This will be paid on top of the disablement premium in relevant cases. It is nearly double the rate of the basic disablement premium for a single person that is illustrated in the technical annex.'

On a division the government amendment was carried in lieu of the Lords' amendment.

When the Bill was again before the House, the Lord President of the Council, moving that the government amendment be agreed to, said (479 HL Official Report (5th series) cols 386–387):

'The additional premium will be paid directly as of right to severely disabled people who meet certain criteria. The first is that they should be in receipt of the higher rate of attendance allowance: so it will apply to those in households where there is no one capable of carrying out normal domestic duties. We think the purpose behind that rule—the need for extra support

to maintain independence that cannot otherwise be provided—is a sound
one. We have recently announced the extension of invalid care allowance—
the benefit that is paid to those caring for disabled people. Consistent with
that, we intend that the extra disablement premium will be paid directly to
a severely disabled person where there is no one receiving or eligible for the
invalid care allowance in respect of that person's care needs. We envisage
setting the rate at the same level as for invalid care allowance—currently £23
a week. It is nearly double the rate of the disablement premium in relevant
cases.'

This time on a division the government amendment was agreed to by this House.
    This account of the circumstances in which s 22(3) and (4) came to be enacted
and the statements made by the government spokesman moving the relevant
amendment in both Houses seem to me to provide precisely the kind of material
which was considered in *Pepper v Hart* to be available as an aid to statutory
construction. Section 22(4) is undoubtedly ambiguous, as the difference of
opinion in the courts below clearly shows. But it was made perfectly clear to both
Houses that it was intended to use the regulation-making power conferred by
sub-s (4) so as to provide that a person was only to be treated as severely disabled
for the purposes of sub-s (3) if he was in receipt of attendance allowance and living
in a household with no other adult able to care for him and where no invalid care
allowance was in payment to any other person to provide for his care. This is, of
course, precisely what, in principle, para 13 of Sch 2 to the 1987 regulations sets
out to achieve. Parliament, having enacted the two subsections with full
knowledge of how the regulation-making power was proposed to be used, must
clearly have intended that it should be effective to authorise such use. Thus the
parliamentary material unequivocally indorses the conclusion I had reached as a
matter of construction independently of that material.
    The significance of this, following as it does two other cases decided by your
Lordships' House since *Pepper v Hart* (*Stubbings v Webb* [1993] 1 All ER 322, [1993]
2 WLR 120 and *Warwickshire CC v Johnson* [1993] 1 All ER 299, [1993] 2 WLR 1)
where the parliamentary material has been found decisive of a statutory
ambiguity, is to illustrate how useful the relaxation of the former exclusionary
rule may be in avoiding unnecessary litigation. Certainly in this case, if it had
been possible to take account of the parliamentary material at the outset, it would
have been clear that it refuted the appellant's contention and there would probably
never have been any appeal to the commissioner, let alone beyond him. I doubt
if any of us who were party to the decision in *Pepper v Hart* anticipated that
within so short a time after it Hansard would be found to provide the answer in
three other cases before the House. But this encourages the hope that as time
passes the effect of the new rule will be to prevent or to curtail much litigation
relating to ambiguous statutory provisions which would otherwise be fought
through the courts.

The subsidiary point
    Counsel for the appellant argued before your Lordships another point to which
the judgments in the Court of Appeal make no reference, although we were told
that the point was raised before it. The point arises in the following way.
Regulation 3(1) of the 1987 regulations defines 'non-dependant' as meaning 'any
person . . . who normally resides with the claimant' subject to the list of exceptions
in reg 3(2). As the regulation was originally drafted one of these exceptions was 'a
person who jointly occupies the claimant's dwelling'. If construed widely this
exception seems almost coextensive with the definition. Be that as it may, the

respondents do not dispute that this exception applied to the appellant's parents
so that they were not 'non-dependants' under Sch 2, para 13(2)(*a*)(ii). But by para 3 *a*
of the Income Support (General) Amendment No 3 Regulations 1989, SI 1989/
1678, which came into force on 9 October 1989, the relevant exception in reg 3(2)
of the 1987 regulations was amended by the addition of the following words:

> '. . . and either is a co-owner of that dwelling with the claimant or his
> partner (whether or not there are other co-owners) or is liable with the *b*
> claimant or his partner to make payments in respect of his occupation of the
> dwelling.'

It is common ground that the amended exception does not apply to the appellant's
parents, who are accordingly 'non-dependants' as defined. But the appellant
boldly submits that the 1989 amendment should be struck down on the ground
of irrationality. The object of the amendment was clearly to narrow the scope of *c*
the original exception, which was probably wider than had been intended. It may
perhaps not be immediately apparent what policy consideration requires that an
exception from the category of 'non-dependants' be made in favour of adults
normally residing with claimants either on the ground that they are joint
occupiers with the claimants, whatever that was intended to mean, or that they *d*
are co-owners as provided by the amended regulation. But that is a matter for the
Secretary of State and Parliament, not for the courts. It seems to me unarguable
that the amended exception in reg 3(2) should be invalidated as irrational. Even
if it were, it would not assist the appellant. There is no power to reinstate the
unamended exception.

I would dismiss the appeal.   *e*

LORD ACKNER. My Lords, I have had the advantage of reading in draft the
speech of my noble and learned friend Lord Bridge of Harwich. I agree with it
and for the reasons which he gives would also dismiss the appeal.

LORD BROWNE-WILKINSON. My Lords, I have read the speech of my *f*
noble and learned friend Lord Bridge of Harwich. I agree with it and for the
reasons which he gives would also dismiss the appeal.

LORD SLYNN OF HADLEY. My Lords, for the reasons given by my noble
and learned friend Lord Bridge of Harwich I too would dismiss this appeal.
          g

Appeal dismissed.

Mary Rose Plummer   Barrister.

a

Kent County Council v C and another

FAMILY DIVISION
EWBANK J
29, 30 JULY 1992

b   *Family proceedings – Orders in family proceedings – Care order – Order for contact between child and any named person – Whether court can order that no contact take place between parent and child – Children Act 1989, ss 31, 34(2).*

Family proceedings – Orders in family proceedings – Care order – Court granting care order in favour of local authority but adding direction for continued involvement of
c   *guardian ad litem – Whether court having power to make directions in relation to care orders – Whether direction a fetter on powers of local authority.*

The local authority applied, with the consent of the mother and guardian ad litem, to the family proceedings court under s 31[a] of the Children Act 1989 for a care order in respect of a girl aged four. At the hearing the local authority
d   proposed that a rehabilitation programme be entered into to assess the relationship between the mother and child. However, the guardian ad litem took the view that, given the history of the case, rehabilitation would be unsuccessful and would merely prolong the child's sense of impermanence, and advised instead that the child be placed with long-term foster parents. The justices were concerned about
e   the guardian ad litem's views and concluded that although they had power under s 34(2)[b] of the 1989 Act to order that there be no contact between mother and child, which would effectively prevent the local authority from carrying out the rehabilitation plan, they ought not to exercise that power in the circumstances. Instead, when making the care order they added a direction that the local authority should allow the guardian ad litem to have continued involvement
f   with the child for three months to enable him to investigate the rehabilitation process so that if appropriate he could apply on behalf of the child to have contact with the mother terminated under s 34(2). The local authority appealed. The questions arose (i) whether in an appropriate case the family proceedings court had power to order that no contact take place between a parent and child and (ii) whether the court had power to add a direction when making a care order under
g   the 1989 Act.

Held – (1) When making a care order under the 1989 Act it was open to the family proceedings court to make an order under s 34(2) that no contact take place between a parent and child, but since in most cases that would be ill-advised the preferable course would be to make no order under s 34(2) for contact (see
h   p 722 *g h*, post).
    (2) The family proceedings court had no power under the 1989 Act to make directions in relation to care orders since, once a care order had been made, then,

---

a   Section 31, so far as material, provides:
j   '(1) On the application of any local authority . . . the court may make an order—(*a*) placing the child with respect to whom the application is made in the care of a designated local authority . . .
      (2) A court may only make a care order . . . if it is satisfied—(*a*) that the child concerned is suffering, or is likely to suffer, significant harm; and (*b*) that the harm, or likelihood of harm, is attributable to—(i) the care given to the child, or likely to be given to him if the order were not made, not being what it would be reasonable to expect a parent to give to him . . .'
b   Section 34(2) is set out at p 722 *a*, post

subject to any subsequent orders as to contact under s 34, the responsibility and duties of the court ceased and responsibility for the care of the child fell on the local authority, and the addition of a direction of any sort to a care order would be a fetter on the local authority's plans, authority and responsibility. Accordingly, since the pace and success of any rehabilitation programme entered into after the care order was made was a matter which could only be decided by the local authority, the appeal would be allowed and the direction deleted from the order (see p 722 *j* to p 723 *b j*, post); *A v Liverpool City Council* [1981] 2 All ER 385 applied.

Notes
For the making of care orders on the application of the local authority, see Supplement to 24 *Halsbury's Laws* (4th edn) para 732A.

For the Children Act 1989, ss 31, 34, see 6 *Halsbury's Statutes* (4th edn) (1992 reissue) 431, 437.

Case referred to in judgment
A v Liverpool City Council [1981] 2 All ER 385, [1982] AC 363, [1981] 2 WLR 948, HL.

Appeal
Kent County Council appealed from an order made by the Margate and Ramsgate Family Proceedings Court on 3 June 1992 whereby on the application of the council it granted a care order in respect of L, a four-year-old girl, but added a direction that the guardian ad litem be allowed to have continued involvement with the child in order that he could investigate the rehabilitation process between the mother and L so that L could apply to have contact terminated if appropriate. The grounds of the appeal were, inter alia, (i) that the justices had no jurisdiction to attach a condition to the care order which had been agreed by the parties and approved by the justices and (ii) that the justices had no jurisdiction to make the direction, because, inter alia, it was a fetter on the discretion of the local authority in the exercise of its functions under the Children Act 1989. The facts are set out in the judgment.

Roger McCarthy (instructed by *D P Clephan*, Maidstone) for the local authority.
Martin O'Dwyer (instructed by *Daniel & Edwards*, Ramsgate) for the guardian ad litem.
Pierre Janusz (instructed by *Girlings*, Margate) for the mother.

EWBANK J. This is an appeal against an order made by the Margate and Ramsgate Family Proceedings Court on 3 June 1992. The family proceedings court had before it an application by the local authority for a care order with respect to a child, L, who is now nearly four years old. The child was represented by a guardian ad litem and her mother was also a party.

The local authority asserted that the threshold conditions under which a care order could be made had been met. The threshold conditions are set out in s 31 of the Children Act 1989. The mother and the guardian ad litem agreed that the conditions were met and accordingly there was no contest on the question of whether a care order should be made. However, it was the local authority's plan that there should be a period of assessment of the relationship between L and her mother and of the mother's parenting skills and her willingness to respond to counselling, and that a programme of rehabilitation should be entered into.

The guardian ad litem took a different view. In his report, having considered
_a_ all the circumstances of this sad case, he said:

> 'I would have immense concerns if consideration were given to further
> assessing the relationship between [L] and her mother and thus protract [L's]
> sense of impermanence. It is my view that there is enough evidence available
> to suggest rehabilitation would not be possible.'

_b_
The guardian ad litem recommended a care order and recommended that L
should be placed permanently with another family.

The guardian ad litem had been to a well-known and eminent consultant
psychiatrist, who described L as suffering from an 'emotional disorder characterised
by anxious, withdrawn and fearful behaviour accompanied by temper tantrums'.
_c_ He described how L was physically abused by her mother and stepfather and he
also described his concerns regarding L's parenting by her mother. In conclusion,
the consultant child psychiatrist said:

> 'The longstanding nature of the difficulties and the poor response to
> treatment of those difficulties reduces the likelihood that any treatment
_d_ > programme would be successful. On balance, therefore, despite the mother's
> co-operation and her wish for improvement, it is likely that any rehabilitation
> plan would be likely to fail.'

The justices were concerned about the views of the guardian ad litem and
considered whether they should, if they had the power, agree with a proposal that
_e_ there should be a rehabilitation. They took the view that under s 34(2) of the
1989 Act they had the power to order that there should be no contact between
the mother and the child, thus preventing the local authority from carrying out
the rehabilitation plan. Having decided they had that power they decided not to
exercise it and made no order under that section. But because of their concern
_f_ they made a direction at the same time as they made the care order. The direction
reads as follows:

> '. . . we direct to the Local Authority that the Guardian ad Litem be allowed
> to have continued involvement with [L] so that he can investigate the
> rehabilitation process so that the child could apply to have contact terminated
> if appropriate—The guardian's involvement to last up to three months after
_g_ > . . . the placement at [the mother and child unit to which it was proposed
> that the child should go].'

The local authority appeals against the order made by the family proceedings
court. The local authority says that the justices had no power to add a direction of
_h_ any sort to the care order and, in particular, they had no power to order that the
guardian ad litem be allowed to have continued involvement with L, so that
effectively he could apply if he felt that the rehabilitation process was not
succeeding.

The first question which has been considered on this appeal is whether the
justices were right in thinking that they had power in an appropriate case to order
_j_ that there should be no contact between the mother and child under s 34(2). The
general provision as to contact between a parent and a child in the event of a care
order is set out in s 34(1), which provides that the local authority shall allow
reasonable contact between the parent and the child. Section 34(2), however,
which overrides s 34(1), provides:

'On an application made by the authority or the child, the court may make such order as it considers appropriate with respect to the contact which is to *a* be allowed between the child and any named person.'

Subsection (3) provides for applications made by various other people including other people with parental responsibility. Section 34(5) enables the court to make such an order without any specific application.

The question which arises is whether the court can make an order for no *b* contact, ie whether it could properly be said to be an order which was appropriate with respect to the contact between the child and the parent.

The argument against that interpretation, which appears to be the obvious interpretation, is that under s 34(8)—

'The Secretary of State may by regulations make provision as to . . . (b) the *c* circumstances in which, and conditions subject to which, the terms of any order under this section may be departed from by agreement between the local authority and the person in relation to whom the order is made . . .'

Such regulations have been made. They are the Contact with Children Regulations 1991, SI 1991/891, and reg 3 is the relevant regulation. It is headed: *d* 'Departure from terms of court order on contact under section 34' and provides:

'The local authority may depart from the terms of any order under section 34 . . . by agreement between the local authority and the person in relation to whom the order is made . . .'

It then provides certain conditions.   *e*

It is said that it would be pointless for the court to make an order that there should be no contact when that order can be overridden and departed from by the local authority with the agreement of the parent. It is said that the most the court should do if it thinks that contact should not take place is to say that there should be no order as to contact, leaving it to the local authority and the parent by agreement to make any other provisions they wish to do so. It is said that it *f* would be wrong that the court should be put in a position of making an order on the merits of the case that there should be no contact when the next day the local authority and the parent could depart from that order.

That seems to me to be a good argument for saying that the court in the ordinary way ought not to make an order for no contact between the parent and *g* the child, but I do not think it is a satisfactory argument in the interpretation of s 34(2) and (3). I think it is open to the court to make such an order if they think it is appropriate although it would be ill-advised in most cases. It would be better in the ordinary case, where the court thinks there should be no contact, to say there is no order for contact, which, in fact, is what the family proceedings court had done in this case.   *h*

The fundamental point in the appeal, however, does not depend on that issue. The court has made a direction to the local authority that the guardian ad litem be allowed to have continuing involvement with a view to making an application in due course if thought appropriate. There is nothing in the 1989 Act which provides for the court to tack on any direction to a care order and I have to say, in my judgment, that the addition of a direction of any sort to a care order is a fetter *j* on the local authority's plans, authority and responsibility.

Under s 22(3) of the Children Act 1989 the local authority has the duty 'to safeguard and promote [the] welfare' of children in care and, in my judgment, responsibility for the care of the child is firmly with the local authority once a care order is made. The responsibility and duties of the court cease on the making

of the care order, subject to the provisions of s 34 which makes provision for
a contact orders being made by the court.

The pace and success of any rehabilitation programme, after a care order is
made, are to be decided upon by the local authority and only the local authority.
Neither the court nor the guardian ad litem has any function in the assessment of
the rehabilitation programme. It is open to various people, as set out in s 34, to
make applications for contact and the local authority, under s 34(4), can apply for
b authority to refuse contact, but unless such an application is made the court is not
involved. In *A v Liverpool City Council* [1981] 2 All ER 385 at 388–389, [1982] AC
363 at 373 Lord Wilberforce said in relation to the High Court:

> 'The court's general inherent power is always available to fill gaps or to
> supplement the powers of the local authority; what it will not do (except by
c > way of judicial review where appropriate) is to supervise the exercise of
> discretion within the field committed by statute to the local authority.'

That is still the position and the direction given by the family proceedings court
runs contrary to that principle.

The guardian ad litem takes the view that this decision is against the interests
d of the child and in some way the inconvenience of the decision ought to be got
round. He suggests, for example, that instead of making a care order an interim
care order should have been made with a view to reviewing the progress of
rehabilitation in six or nine months time. This, in my view, would be contrary
to the principle of the 1989 Act. First of all, under s 1(2) it is provided:

> '. . . the court shall have regard to the general principle that any delay in
e > determining the question is likely to prejudice the welfare of the child.'

Secondly, under s 32(1), there is specific provision for the timetabling of care
proceedings. It would be a deliberate flouting of the principles of the 1989 Act,
with a view to achieving a result which ought not to be sought, to embark on that
course.
f A second suggestion made by the guardian ad litem is that he should be
reappointed on the question of contact between the child and the mother, and
that the court should adjourn that question so that there would be a continuing
issue relating to contact and the guardian ad litem could make an application for
contact to be brought to an end if he felt that the rehabilitation process was
failing. This, too, seemed to be a manoeuvre to keep open an issue which ought
g to be closed. Moreover, having regard to reg 3 of the Contact with Children
Regulations 1991, which I have referred to, it could be overridden by the local
authority.

There has been a brief discussion as to whether in fact the guardian ad litem
has the power under s 34(2) to make an application in any event. Section 34(2)
h provides for the application to be made by the authority or the child and the
question has been raised whether the child, in that context, means the child
himself if he is of sufficient age and understanding to make the application. This
is not an issue which I have thought necessary to decide.

This case, in effect, turns on whether the family proceedings court can keep the
power of review over a care order by making directions in relation to the care
j order. The simple answer is that it cannot do so, and the appeal is accordingly
allowed and the direction in the order is deleted.

Appealed allowed. No order for costs.

Bebe Chua   Barrister.

Lillicrap and another v Nalder & Son (a firm)   *a*

COURT OF APPEAL, CIVIL DIVISION
DILLON, RUSSELL AND FARQUHARSON LJJ
29 JUNE 1992

Discovery – Legal professional privilege – Waiver – Implied waiver – Extent – Client *b*
instituting legal proceedings against solicitor – Solicitor acting for client in series of
transactions – Client bringing action against solicitor for breach of contract and negligence
in respect of one transaction – Solicitor wishing to rely on previous transactions in which
he acted for client to show client would have proceeded with transaction even if properly
advised as to risk – Client seeking delivery up of documents in previous transactions –
Whether documents relating to previous transactions covered by waiver of privilege – *c*
Whether documents relating to previous transactions relevant to issue in proceedings.

The plaintiffs, who were property developers, retained the defendant firm of
solicitors to act for them in a series of transactions. In respect of one such
transaction, the purchase of a property, the plaintiffs complained that the solicitors
had been negligent in failing to advise them of the existence of a right of way   *d*
over part of the land purchased. A writ was issued, pleadings exchanged and the
action set down for trial. Shortly before the trial the solicitors sought leave to
reamend their defence to admit negligence, but they continued to assert that the
plaintiffs would have continued with the purchase of the land even if they had
known of the existence of the right of way. In support of that assertion the   *e*
solicitors referred to six other transactions in which they had acted for the
plaintiffs where the plaintiffs had proceeded despite advice from the solicitors
that various risks were involved. On the basis that the solicitors should not be
allowed to make use of documents relating to the other transactions in which
they had acted for the plaintiffs because they were covered by solicitor/client
privilege, the plaintiffs issued a summons for the delivery up of all documents   *f*
relating to those other transactions. The judge gave the solicitors leave to reamend
their defence but refused leave to add the further particulars of the other
transactions and made the order for delivery up sought by the plaintiffs, on the
ground that the plaintiffs' waiver of legal professional privilege covering the
documents did not extend to those documents connected with the other
transactions. The solicitors appealed from the order for delivery up. The plaintiffs   *g*
contended that the other transactions were the subject of separate retainers and
not one general retainer and that therefore by instituting proceedings the plaintiffs
had waived privilege only in respect of the transaction the subject of the
proceedings.

Held – The institution of civil proceedings against a solicitor by his client   *h*
constituted an implied waiver of professional privilege in relation to all relevant
documents concerned with the suit to the extent necessary to enable the court to
adjudicate the dispute fully and fairly. However, such waiver extended only to
matters relevant to an issue in the proceedings and could not be used as a roving
search into anything else in which the solicitor may have happened to have acted   *j*
for the client. The issue between the parties was one of causation of loss, which
the plaintiffs had to establish in order to be entitled to substantial damages, and it
was a defence to that issue for the solicitors to establish, by reference to the earlier
transactions, that the plaintiffs would have gone ahead with the transaction the
subject of the proceedings irrespective of the advice they had received, and the

documents in the other transactions, although otherwise privileged, were relevant
a to the determination of that issue. Accordingly, the plaintiffs' implied waiver of
privilege extended to the documents in the other transactions. The appeal would
therefore be allowed and the order for delivery up of those documents set aside
(see p 729 *d* to *j*, p 730 *b c e* to *g* and p 731 *d g* to p 732 *a d j* to p 733 *b*, post).

Sykes v Midland Bank Executor and Trustee Co Ltd [1970] 2 All ER 471 followed.

Dictum of Nourse LJ in *Goddard v Nationwide Building Society* [1986] 3 All ER
b 264 at 271 considered.

Notes

For legal and professional privilege, see 13 *Halsbury's Laws* (4th edn) paras 71–74,
and for cases on the subject, see 18 *Digest* (*2nd reissue*) 154–169, 1379–1482.
c For waiver of privilege, see 13 *Halsbury's Law* (4th edn) para 84, and for cases
on the subject, see 18 *Digest* (*2nd reissue*) 253–254, 2256–2267.

Cases referred to in judgments

Ashburton (Lord) v Pape [1913] 2 Ch 469, [1911–13] All ER Rep 708, CA.
d *Berger v Raymond Sun Ltd* [1984] 1 WLR 625.
Carradine Properties Ltd v D J Freeman & Co (a firm) (1982) Times, 19 February,
CA.
Goddard v Nationwide Building Society [1986] 3 All ER 264, [1987] QB 670, [1986]
3 WLR 734, CA.
R v P [1991] 3 All ER 337, [1991] 2 AC 447, [1991] 3 WLR 161, HL.
e *Sykes v Midland Bank Executor and Trustee Co Ltd* [1970] 2 All ER 471, [1971] 1 QB
113, [1970] 3 WLR 273, CA.

Cases also cited

British Coal Corp v Dennis Rye Ltd (No 2) [1988] 3 All ER 816, [1988] 1 WLR 1113,
f CA.
Euroshipping Corp of Monravia v Minister of Agricultural Economics and Marketing
1979 (1) SA 673, CPD.
General Accident Fire and Life Assurance Corp Ltd v Tainter, The Zephyr [1984] 1 All
ER 35, [1984] 1 WLR 100.

g ### Application for leave to appeal and interlocutory appeal

By writ dated 5 March 1991 the plaintiffs, Bertram Alan Lillicrap and Mary
Lillian Lillicrap, brought an action against the defendants, Nalder & Son, a firm
of solicitors, claiming, inter alia, damages for breach of contract and negligence
in relation to their intended purchase of the property known as the Stable Block,
h Heligan Manor, St Ewe, Cornwall, in that the defendants, who had been retained
to act as the plaintiffs' solicitors in the purchase, had failed to advise the plaintiffs
(a) that there was a right of way over part of the land and (b) that there was no
right of way in favour of the purchasers of the property over another part of the
land. The defendants by their defence denied negligence but, after the exchange
of pleadings and discovery, sought by a summons in the action to reamend their
j defence by withdrawing the denial of negligence and admitting negligence and
by adding an averment that the plaintiffs would have proceeded with the
transaction even if they had been advised as it was alleged that they should have
been. By a further summons in the action the plaintiffs sought an order requiring
the defendants to deliver up all files, papers and documents relating to all
transactions carried out on behalf of the plaintiffs by the defendants in their

capacity as solicitors to the plaintiffs except those relating to the purchase and sale
of the Stable Block. By orders dated 17 June 1992 May J gave the defendants leave   *a*
to reamend the defence to admit liability and to plead the particulars, but refused
leave to plead further particulars referring to six other transactions in which the
defendants had acted for the plaintiffs on the plaintiffs' purchase of other
properties, and made the order for delivery up of documents sought by the
plaintiffs. The judge refused leave to appeal. The defendants applied to the Court
of Appeal for leave to appeal. The facts are set out in the judgment of Dillon LJ.   *b*

Rupert Jackson QC and *Andrew Stafford* (instructed by *Hancock & Lawrence*, Truro)
    for the defendants.
Hugh Bennett QC and *Lindsay Boswell* (instructed by *Preston Goldburn*, Falmouth)
    for the plaintiffs.
                                                                                      c

DILLON LJ. This case comes before us on an application by the defendants, a
firm of solicitors called Nalder & Son, for leave to appeal against an order made
by May J on 17 June 1992. Leave to appeal against that order was refused on that
occasion by May J. The application for leave comes before us rather than before
the single judge because of the urgency of the matter. It comes before us with a   *d*
direction that the hearing of the application should be followed by the hearing of
the appeal if leave is granted. In fact we have heard on the application the full
argument of both sides on the appeal. Accordingly, we grant leave to appeal and
I now proceed to deliver judgment on the appeal.
    The plaintiffs, husband and wife, are property developers and the defendants,
as I have said, are a firm of solicitors who practice at Truro in Cornwall. The   *e*
complaint by the plaintiffs arises from their having retained the defendants in
November 1988 in relation to the plaintiffs' then proposed purchase, subject to
contract, of a property known as the Stable Block, Heligan Manor Buildings, near
Mevagissey in Cornwall, with the intention of developing the property as a
private mews-style development of four units. On 6 February 1989 contracts
were exchanged for part of the property known as the green land and an option   *f*
was granted to the plaintiffs to purchase another part of the property called the
red land. The reasons why it was dealt with that way does not matter for present
purposes. It was a requirement of the vendors. On 27 February 1989 the plaintiffs
completed the purchase of the green land and on 2 June 1989 they exercised their
option to purchase the red land. On 5 June 1989 contracts for the purchase of the
red land were exchanged and on 7 July 1989 the purchase of the red land was   *g*
completed. The complaint of the plaintiffs is that, in acting as solicitors on that
transaction, or those purchases, the defendants acted negligently in that they
failed to advise the plaintiffs of the existence of a right of way over, I think, part
of the green land, and they also failed to advise the plaintiffs that the title did not
show that the vendors were entitled to any right of way along a particular track   *h*
shown on the plan which provided the only convenient way of obtaining access
to, and egress from, part of the property.
    The writ in the action was issued on 5 March 1991. A statement of claim was
served a few days later. A defence was served on 19 April 1991. In June 1991 the
statement of claim was amended and an amended defence was served on 26 July
1991. Discovery proceeded and the action was set down on 18 November 1991.   *j*
On 29 January 1992 it was listed for trial on 8 April 1992. On 24 March 1992 the
defendants' solicitors put forward a draft of a reamended defence. This altered
the previous defence in two major respects. Firstly, the denial of negligence,
which there had been in the former defences, was withdrawn and instead

negligence was admitted. In addition, in pursuing their denial of the allegation
a in the amended statement of claim—that 'if the Plaintiffs had been advised of the
existence of the [one] right of way and the absence of a right of way along the
[track I have mentioned] they would not have proceeded with the purchase of the
Property or any part thereof'—particulars of that denial were added in para 3;
firstly, in 3(A):

b   'The Defendant avers that the Plaintiffs would have proceeded with the
       transaction, even if they had been advised as it is alleged [that] they should
       have been'

and certain matters were set out and, in addition and as further particulars under
para 3, reference was made to six other transactions in which the defendants had
acted for the plaintiffs on the plaintiffs' purchase, or negotiations for purchase, of
c other properties in Cornwall, in each of which in substance—and it is not
necessary to go into details—at some stage the plaintiffs had elected to proceed
despite advice by the defendants of risks or of the defendants having pointed out
that the time-scale the plaintiffs were wanting to go ahead on prevented them
from making prudent inquiries. That is the general nature of it. It was sought,
d therefore, to add these further particulars in para 3(B).
The case was therefore adjourned and applications were made in respect of
these amendments. There was a summons by the defendants to reamend and a
summons by the plaintiffs who took the view that the defendants should not be
allowed to make use of documents relating to other transactions in which the
defendants had acted as solicitors for the plaintiffs. Following the general practice
e in cases where privileged documents are in the hands of persons not entitled to
hold them, a summons was issued for the plaintiffs, calling for an order that the
defendants deliver up all files, papers and documents relating to all transactions
carried out on behalf of the plaintiffs except those relating to the purchase and
sale of the particular Heligan Manor Stable Block. May J's order gave the
defendants leave to reamend the defence to admit liability and to plead the
f particulars under 3(A) but not 3(B). He refused them leave to introduce 3(B). He
gave directions, with which we are not concerned, as to further and better
particulars of the amendments, and he further ordered that the defendants—

       '(1) do forthwith deliver up to the Plaintiffs all original and copy documents
       belonging to the Plaintiffs and presently in the Defendant's possession or
g   control (2) do forthwith deliver up to the Plaintiffs any documents and copy
       documents prepared by any person on the basis of any confidential
       information belonging to the Plaintiffs and not arising under the retainer
       specifically pleaded in paragraph 2 of the Amended Statement of Claim (3)
       be restrained until after judgment in this action or until further Order in the
       meantime from publishing or making use of any confidential information
h   belonging to the Plaintiffs and not arising under the retainer specifically
       pleaded in paragraph 2 of the Amended Statement of Claim.'

The position of the plaintiffs is this, as clearly explained by Mr Bennett QC on
their behalf in this court. Each retainer of a solicitor is a separate retainer for a
particular transaction. If a property developer buys seven properties from different
i vendors on different occasions and the same solicitor acts for the developer on
each purchase, there will have been seven retainers. There is not one continuing
retainer which continues whether or not there is anything to be done for the
client at a particular time. It is not right to say, and this is no doubt common
ground, of any person at any particular time in any general sense that 'X' is his

solicitor. Therefore it is said that the institution of proceedings by the plaintiffs
against the defendants in respect of this one transaction in respect of the Stable *a*
Block merely waives the professional privilege of the plaintiffs in relation to
documents concerned with that transaction only. Reference is made to the
judgment of Nourse LJ in *Goddard v Nationwide Building Society* [1986] 3 All ER
264 at 271–272, [1987] QB 670 at 685, where he said:

> 'Thirdly, the right of the party who desires the protection to invoke the *b*
> equitable jurisdiction does not in any way depend on the conduct of the third
> party into whose possession the record of the confidential communication
> has come. Thus, several eminent judges have been of the opinion that an
> injunction can be granted against a stranger who has come innocently into
> the possession of confidential information to which he is not entitled ...
> This view seems to give effect to the general rule that equity gives relief *c*
> against all the world, including the innocent, save only a bona fide purchaser
> for value without notice. It is directly in point in the present case and our
> decision necessarily affirms it. Fourthly, once it is established that a case is
> governed by *Lord Ashburton v Pape* [1913] 2 Ch 469, [1911–13] All ER Rep
> 708, there is no discretion in the court to refuse to exercise the equitable
> jurisdiction according to its view of the materiality of the communication, *d*
> the justice of admitting or excluding it or the like. The injunction is granted
> in aid of the privilege which, unless and until it is waived, is absolute. In
> saying this, I do not intend to suggest that there may not be cases where an
> injunction can properly be refused on general principles affecting the grant
> of a discretionary remedy, for example on the ground of inordinate delay.'
> *e*

Thus the client has the right to insist on his professional legal privilege and it is
for him to choose whether or not to waive it. But it is accepted that the waiver
may be implied and that there is an implied waiver where the client brings
proceedings for professional negligence against the solicitor. Mr Bennett suggests
that the waiver is only in respect of documents and information concerned with
that particular retainer. This may in general prima facie be so, but it is not *f*
difficult to envisage scenarios where it is apparent that the waiver must have a
wider scope.

One scenario, which emerged from the mention by Mr Jackson QC of a case in
which he had appeared before this court a few months ago, is on these lines. A
firm of solicitors has been retained by a property development company to act on
the purchase of a particular property for development. The same firm of solicitors *g*
has acted for the property company on numerous other purchases of land for
development over the last five years or so. In the particular purchase, with which
the litigation is concerned, it is found that on the plan on the contract submitted
by the vendor's solicitors, which is a copy of the plan on the land certificate of the
vendor's title, the property shown is of a smaller area than the property being sold
appears to be on inspection on the site. That is in fact because one of the boundary *h*
fences on the site is not on the true boundary line but certain land belonging to
an adjoining owner appears to be within the curtilage of the property on the site.
Against that background, it was said that the solicitors were negligent in failing
to advise the clients to check carefully the contract plan against what was apparent
on the site. *j*

It is clear, for instance, from the judgment of Donaldson LJ in *Carradine
Properties Ltd v D J Freeman & Co (a firm)* (1982) Times, 19 February that the
precise scope of the solicitor's duty will depend, inter alia, upon the extent to
which the client appears to need advice. Thus an inexperienced client will need
and will be entitled to expect the solicitor to take a much broader view of the

scope of his retainer and of his duties than will be the case with an experienced
client. In the hypothetical case which I have assumed, the solicitor had indeed on
a the first occasion when he acted advised his client to check the contract plan
against the boundaries on site and, by the time of the transaction which gave rise
to the claim against the solicitor, the solicitor knew from his experience with the
client that it was the normal practice of this experienced client to check the plan
on the contract against the boundaries on the site. In those circumstances I have
b no doubt that the client would not be entitled to say that any waiver of privilege
only applied to privilege in respect of the final transaction, which was the
transaction in suit, and did not extend to waiver of what had emerged during
earlier transactions.

Mr Bennett seemed to be prepared to accept that there would be a wider waiver
in those circumstances but he said that was because the later transaction was
c linked to the advice given on the first transaction and to what the solicitor had
learnt of his client over the earlier transactions, and that that linkage justified
holding that there was a wider waiver of privilege.

For my part, I accept May J's formulation of the scope of the waiver. He said:

d 'I return to what I regard as the heart of the matter—waiver. A client who
sues his solicitor invites the court to adjudicate the dispute and thereby, in
my judgment, waives privilege and confidence to the extent that is necessary
to enable the court to do so fully and fairly in accordance with the law,
including the law of evidence. I suspect that at the fringes each case will
depend on its own facts. Normally, the waiver will extend to facts and
e documents material to the cause of action upon which the plaintiff sues and
to the defendant's proper defence to that cause of action. The bringing of a
claim for negligence in relation to a particular retainer will normally be a
waiver of privilege and confidence for facts and documents relating to that
retainer, but not without more for those relating to other discrete retainers.'

f I agree with that. The waiver can only extend to matters which are relevant to
an issue in the proceedings and, privilege apart, admissible in evidence. There is
no waiver for a roving search into anything else in which the solicitor or any
other solicitor may have happened to have acted for the clients. But the waiver
must go far enough not merely to entitle the plaintiff to establish his cause of
action but to enable the defendant to establish a defence to the cause of action if
g he has one. Thus it would extend to matters under earlier retainers, as in the
hypothetical example I have given, which established that the experience of the
client was to the knowledge of the solicitor such that the solicitor was not in
breach of duty as alleged.

The relevance in the present case is not to the establishing of negligence on the
part of the solicitors, for that is now admitted. But it goes to the question of
h causation of loss. The decision of this court in *Sykes v Midland Bank Executor and
Trustee Co Ltd* [1970] 2 All ER 471, [1971] 1 QB 113, shows that, while any
negligence on the part of the solicitor is a breach of his contract of retainer
sounding in nominal damages, then 40 shillings, it is for the plaintiff to establish
causation in order to claim substantial damages. The plaintiff has to show that, if
properly advised, he would on the balance of probabilities have acted otherwise.
j In *Sykes's* case the partner in the firm, who were the plaintiffs, candidly admitted
that he did not know whether, if he had been given the full information that he
should have been given, he would have taken a different course from that which
he did take. The case was about an onerous clause in a lease which was a trap
because it was only to be appreciated on a close reading that the clause was not
simple and straightforward. Because the onus was on the plaintiffs and the

plaintiffs' witness candidly said that he did not know whether he would have acted otherwise, Salmon LJ said ([1970] 2 All ER 471 at 479, [1971] 1 QB 113):   a

'I can see no evidence on which a court could properly hold that on a balance of probabilities the plaintiffs would not have taken the risk of entering into the underleases at the rents reserved, had they been advised of the true effect of the clauses in question.'

Thus it is a defence to the claim for substantial damages in the present case if   b
the plaintiffs fail to satisfy the court that had they been properly advised they would not have gone ahead with their purchases of the Stable Block.

The matters sought to be raised therefore by para 3(B) of the particulars in the reamended defence are matters clearly relevant to an issue in the proceedings, namely, the issue of causation. They do not merely go to questions of credibility. Privilege apart, therefore, it seems to me that the plea should have been allowed   c
and the documents should, subject to the discretion of the judge at the trial, have been referred to.

May J was led to take a different view because the solicitors, through having acted for the plaintiffs on these previous transactions, would be in a better position in resisting the claim for damages as a result of their admitted negligence in   d
relation to the transaction in suit than if other solictors had acted on the six other transactions. He said that he could see no reason which enabled the defendant solicitors to improve their evidential position relating to damages because they rather than other firms of solicitors happened to have acted on the other transactions.

But, in my judgment, these documents are within the waiver on the judge's   e
own definition in his judgment, which I have read out. They are material to the defendants' proper defence to the cause of action upon which the plaintiffs sue. It matters not that, because they happen to know of these transactions, the defendants are in a better position than if they did not know of them because other solicitors had been concerned. There is always a risk that a defendant who has had dealings with a plaintiff in respect of other matters is in a better position   f
than someone who has never had any previous dealings, because the first defendant will know more about the plaintiff's affairs. But, privilege apart, that is no ground for refusing to allow material to be used. It is not a valid plea that otherwise admissible material should not be admitted because, if the defendants had not known of it, they would not have been trying to bring it in. So far as the   g
privilege is concerned, the judge's own definition deals with the point.

The judge further intimated that, even if he had determined the privilege and confidence issues in favour of the defendants, he would still have refused them leave to include the draft para 3(B) in their reamendment of their defence. He treated this paragraph as one which would only be admissible in a case of similar fact evidence and he referred to the recent criminal case of R v P [1991] 3 All ER   h
337, [1991] 2 AC 447.

I do not regard this as a strict case of similar fact evidence. It is merely a question of trying the issue in civil proceedings of whether, on the balance of probabilities, the plaintiffs would or would not have resiled from the transaction, or taken some course other than they did, if they had been properly advised about the rights of way, the presence of one and the absence of the other. But I note that   j
in the judge's judgment he refers to a decision of Warner J in Berger v Raymond Sun Ltd [1984] 1 WLR 625. In that case Warner J was the trial judge at the trial of an action, one of the issues in which was whether the plaintiff's signature on certain share transfers had been forged by one of the defendants who was her son. Warner J allowed evidence that certain other transfers of shares, apparently signed

by other members of the family, had been forged by that defendant. He
a concluded, carrying out the balancing exercise of the prejudice each way in
accordance with the approach of a criminal court in a similar fact case, that the
prejudice to the plaintiff would be much the greater if he refused to allow certain
of these forged transfers to be proved. It is to be noted however that he was
reaching that decision as the judge at the trial, and that particular balancing
exercise is one to be exercised by the judge at the trial.

b   Accordingly, nothing that I say in this judgment is to affect the discretion of
the judge at the trial. That is not a discretion we can seek to exercise merely by
reading a page or two in the reamended defence, and identifying the other
transactions which the defendants seek to rely on. This second point does not, in
my judgment, provide any answer at the present stage to the defendants' claim to
amend their pleadings by introducing 3(B) and to retain the documents or copies
c of the documents until the trial. If the scope of waiver of privilege is as broad as
on the definition by May J I believe it to be, then that in itself is the answer to the
point founded on the citation from Nourse LJ in *Goddard v Nationwide Building
Society* [1986] 3 All ER 264 at 271, [1987] QB 670 at 685.

Accordingly, I would allow this appeal and I would set aside the order of May J
d in so far as it granted the three injunctions against the defendants, which I have
read, and I would grant the defendants leave to include para 3(B) in the
reamendment of their defence.

RUSSELL LJ. Liability is admitted in this case. Damages and their causation
are denied. There is therefore on the pleadings a live issue to be tried, namely
e whether the damage allegedly suffered by the plaintiffs was caused by the
admitted negligence of the defendants. In an attempt to defeat the plaintiffs'
claim on causation, the defendants seek to demonstrate that the plaintiffs were
prepared to engage in a measure of commercial speculation irrespective of the
advice they received from their solicitors. It is in support of that case that the
f defendants seeks to adduce in evidence the earlier transactions where both the
defendants and the plaintiffs were involved as solicitors and clients respectively.

The objection to this course is based upon the sacrosanct nature of the
relationship between client and solicitor. I recognise of course that concept of
legal professional privilege which is plainly in the public interest. However, in
my judgment, once it is conceded that there is implied waiver of privilege when
g proceedings are instituted against a solicitor, I can see no warrant for the
submission that the waiver is confined to the documents and communications
between solicitor and client within the specific retainer forming the subject
matter of the proceedings. The parameters of the retainer, to my mind, erect an
artificial barrier. In my judgment, by bringing civil proceedings against his
solicitor, a client impliedly waives privilege in respect of all matters which are
h relevant to the suit he pursues and, most particularly, where the disclosure of
privileged matters is required to enable justice to be done. This is another way of
expressing the view that May J expressed in the passage to which Dillon LJ
referred.

This brings me to the content of the proposed amendment at para 3(B) of the
reamended defence. It is trite law that a pleading is concerned with facts and not
j with evidence. Whether the earlier transactions will in the end affect the result of
this case will depend upon the evidential findings of the judge. The case however
cannot be tried on the pleadings and I, for my part, do not think that it was ever
within the discretion of May J at the interlocutory stage to shut out these
defendants from raising issues simply because May J had reservations about their
probative value. Potentially the earlier transactions, or some of them, may assist

the defendants. If the evidence is admitted the defendants will be able properly to defend themselves. In my judgment if the evidence is shut out, there is at least *a* a risk that the defendants will have been deprived of the opportunity of running a defence that would be legitimately open to them.

Towards the end of his judgment May J went on to express the view that, even if he had found in favour of the defendants on the privilege point, he would, nevertheless, in the exercise of his discretion, have declined to permit the defendants to amend in the way that they desired. He based the exercise of this *b* discretion upon his assessment of the case as one involving similar facts. For my part, with respect to the learned judge, I do not think that this is a case of similar facts properly so-called.

The admission of the evidence relating to the earlier transactions will not depend, and does not depend, upon the nature and circumstances of those earlier transactions, but rather upon the plaintiff's reaction to legal advice during the *c* course of his relationship with his solicitors in those earlier retainers. That reaction might have been demonstrated in a case wholly dissimilar to the instant case but in my view would nevertheless be admissible.

For all these reasons, as well as those appearing in the judgment of Dillon LJ, and in agreement with him, I too would allow this appeal and I would grant the *d* defendants the relief which they claim.

FARQUHARSON LJ. The facts and chronology of this case have already been set out in the judgment of Dillon LJ and I do not repeat them save to observe that the application now before us on the part of the defendant to amend the defence by the introduction of paras 3(A) and (B) was made at a very late hour. *e*

There is no dispute that the documents relating to the six additional transactions are the subject of professional privilege nor that the information contained in those documents is confidential. The question before us is whether that privilege has been impliedly waived by the launching of these proceedings. As Mr Bennett QC points out, the only act which is said to constitute such a waiver is the issue of the writ on 5 March 1991. The endorsement of the writ is restricted to a claim *f* for damages for negligence in relation to the defendants' failure to give the necessary advice to the plaintiffs on matters arising from the Heligan Manor Stable Block transaction. There is no reference in the writ to the six other transactions in which the defendants acted as solicitors for the plaintiffs and upon which the former seek to rely. Nor is it suggested that any later act on the part of the plaintiffs amounted to a waiver of the privilege attaching to the documents *g* which relate to those transactions. It is conceded by the plaintiffs that the issuing of the writ did amount to a waiver by the plaintiffs of all documents arising from the transactions sued upon. What is in dispute is the breadth of that waiver. Does it relate only to the Heligan Manor transaction, which is the subject of the claim, or does it extend to documents otherwise privileged which are relevant to the *h* determination of the issue between the parties namely whether, even if the defendants had correctly advised the plaintiffs about the existence or otherwise of the rights of way, the latter would have taken their advice.

The defendants seek to show in the particulars of the six other transactions that, even if proper advice had been tendered, the plaintiffs would have ignored it as they had done in the past; in other words, the issue was one of causation. For my *i* part I would have difficulty in holding that the defendants should, as a matter of principle, be prevented from adducing evidence which is relevant to that issue. A proper interpretation of the waiver in this case is, in my judgment, one that embraces not only the documents and advice arising from the Heligan Manor transaction, but also documents or information otherwise subject to privilege

which were relevant to the issues between the parties and which it would have
a been unfair to exclude. Whether the evidence sought to be adduced by the
defendants is relevant to the main issue is, in the last analysis, a matter for the
trial judge. We are here concerned with whether the documents should be
excluded as a matter of principle. I accordingly say nothing about the weight of
that evidence but, looking at it as a matter of principle in the circumstances of
this case, I would hold that the bringing of the present proceedings by the
b plaintiffs involved the waiver of the privilege attaching to the documents created
in the six transactions.

For those reasons I respectfully agree with the judgments that have been
delivered and with the orders proposed.

c *Appeal allowed. Leave to appeal to the House of Lords refused.*

Carolyn Toulmin   Barrister.

d # Re Manda

COURT OF APPEAL, CIVIL DIVISION
BALCOMBE, LEGGATT LJJ AND SIR JOHN MEGAW
20, 31 JULY 1992

e *Ward of court – Protection of ward – Confidential papers in wardship proceedings –*
Disclosure of documents – Application for leave to disclose documents used in wardship
proceedings – Disclosure to ward for purposes of litigation – Matters to be considered –
Ward attaining majority before hearing of appeal – Interests of minor – Public interest in
due administration of justice – Prospects of success in litigation for which disclosure sought
– Inhibition of frankness on part of witnesses in wardship proceedings – Whether court
f *should order disclosure of documents.*

In 1986 F, a 12-year-old boy who was suspected of being sexually abused, was
made a ward of court and committed to the care of the local authority. In 1990
the wardship was discharged and F was returned to his parents. The parents, who
at all times vehemently denied that F had been sexually abused, wished to
g investigate the possibility of bringing a claim in negligence and trespass to the
person on behalf of their son against the health authority whose consultant
paediatrician had examined F and who had raised the possibility of non-accidental
injury. The parents accordingly applied in the wardship proceedings for leave to
disclose to experts retained by them all relevant documents in order that counsel's
h opinion could be obtained with a view to obtaining legal aid. Since the parents
had themselves been defendants in the wardship proceedings all of the material
which they sought leave to disclose was already known to them and was in the
hands of their solicitors but leave was nevertheless required under s 12(1)(a)[a] of
the Administration of Justice Act 1960 if the disclosure was not to be a contempt
of court. The district judge granted the application and on appeal by the local
j authority his decision was upheld by the judge. The local authority appealed.

---

a Section 12(1), so far as material, provides: 'The publication of information relating to proceedings
before any court sitting in private shall not of itself be contempt of court except . . . (*a*) where the
proceedings—(i) relate to the exercise of the inherent jurisdiction of the High Court with respect
to minors . . . or (iii) otherwise relate wholly or mainly to the maintenance or upbringing of a
minor . . .'

Before the hearing of the appeal F attained the age of 18 and expressed his wish to
pursue the proposed action. The appeal proceeded on the basis that he would be *a*
the plaintiff in any proceedings against the local authority and that, as he had
himself been a defendant in the wardship proceedings, albeit represented by the
Official Solicitor as his guardian ad litem, he was properly aware of all the
documents for which leave to disclose was sought.

Held – The court would permit evidence given and documents lodged in *b*
wardship proceedings to be disclosed for use in other proceedings by the ward if
his interests, which were always the most important factor, and the public interest
in the administration of justice that all relevant information should be available
for use in those proceedings outweighed any public interest in the confidentiality
of the evidence and the documents. In the case of a minor the court would also *c*
take into account the prospects of success in the litigation for which disclosure
was sought, but in the case of a ward who had attained his majority he was to be
taken as being able to make up his own mind as to what was in his best interests
and the court merely had to satisfy itself that his proposed action was not bound
to fail. On balance, the facts that F had become an adult and was thus able to
make up his own mind as to what was in his best interests and that the proposed *d*
litigation could not be said to be bound to fail and the public interest that all
relevant information should be available in the litigation outweighed any
detriment to children's proceedings generally caused by the possibility that in
future such cases witnesses, in particular professional witnesses, would feel
inhibited from being totally frank. Accordingly, in the exercise of the court's
discretion disclosure of the wardship material by F to his advisers ought to be *e*
permitted and the appeal would therefore be dismissed (see p 743 *b* to *f*, p 744 *c*
to *g*, p 745 *g h* and p 746 *a* to *c g*, post).

Dicta of Rees J in *Re R (M J) (an infant) (proceedings transcripts: publication)* [1975]
2 All ER 749 at 756 and of Waite J in *Re X and ors (minors) (wardship: disclosure of
documents)* [1992] 2 All ER 595 at 606–607 applied. *f*

Per Leggatt LJ and Sir John Megaw. It is at least doubtful whether there would
be the same frank and ready co-operation essential for the proper functioning of
the wardship system, which depends on court welfare officers being able to obtain
frank and ready co-operation from people as diverse as doctors, school teachers,
neighbours, the child in question, the parents themselves and other close relations,
including other children in the same family, if it were to become known or *g*
suspected that a statement made in response to a request for help in wardship
proceedings was liable, without some very strong reason, to be made available for
use in legal proceedings which reopened in public litigation disputes to which the
voluntary statement was relevant, but which the giver of the statement would
sensibly have assumed would have been decided once and for all in the privacy of
the wardship proceedings (see p 746 *b c e f*, post). *h*

Notes
For the publication of information relating to wardship proceedings, see 24
Halsbury's Laws (4th edn) para 591, and for cases on the subject, see 28(3) *Digest*
(2nd reissue) 309–311, 2899–2908.

For the Administration of Justice Act 1960, s 12, see 11 *Halsbury's Statutes* (4th *j*
edn) (1991 reissue) 179.

Cases referred to in judgments
Brown v Matthews [1990] 2 All ER 155, [1990] Ch 662, [1990] 2 WLR 879, CA.
F (a minor) (publication of information), Re [1977] 1 All ER 114, [1977] Fam 58,
[1976] 3 WLR 813, CA.

F (minors) (wardship: police investigation), Re [1989] Fam 18, [1988] 3 WLR 818,
    CA.
F v Wirral Metropolitan BC [1991] 2 All ER 648, [1991] Fam 69, [1991] 2 WLR
    1132, CA.
R (M J) (an infant) (proceedings transcripts: publication), Re [1975] 2 All ER 749,
    [1975] Fam 89, [1975] 2 WLR 978.
Scott v Scott [1913] AC 417, [1911–13] All ER Rep 1, HL.
X and ors (minors) (wardship: disclosure of documents), Re [1992] 2 All ER 595, [1992]
    Fam 124, [1992] 2 WLR 784.

Cases also cited or referred to in skeleton arguments

Bellenden (formerly Satterthwaite) v Satterthwaite [1948] 1 All ER 343, CA.
Gaskin v Liverpool City Council [1980] 1 WLR 1549, CA.
Osenton (Charles) & Co v Johnston [1941] 2 All ER 245, [1942] AC 130, HL.

Appeal

Leeds City Council appealed with the leave of the judge from the order of Hollis
J made on 31 January 1992 dismissing the council's appeal from the order of
District Judge Hebbert made in wardship proceedings on 16 August 1991
granting the first and second defendants, Patrick Manda and Elizabeth Manda
(the parents), leave to disclose documents in their possession relating to the
wardship of the third defendant, their son Francis Manda, for the purpose only of
applying for legal aid and obtaining counsel's opinion in relation to proposed
proceedings against the Leeds Western Area Health Authority and Dr Christopher
Hobbs for negligence. The facts are set out in the judgment of Balcombe LJ.

Shaun Spencer QC and *James Goss* (instructed by *P Rogerson*, Leeds) for the council.
James Wadsworth QC and *Julian Picton* (instructed by *McAra & Co*, Leeds) for the
    parents.

Cur adv vult

31 July 1992. The following judgments were delivered.

BALCOMBE LJ. Francis Manda was born on 12 June 1974. He is the youngest
of six children of Patrick and Elizabeth Manda. Patrick Manda (the father) is a
native of Zambia, Elizabeth Manda (the mother) is a native of Eire. Francis was
born in Zambia, but the family came to Birmingham when he was six weeks old,
and in 1975 moved to Dublin to allow the father to study. In 1979 the family
moved back to Zambia. Francis found this transition difficult because they did
not speak English in his school. In October 1982 the family moved again, this
time to Leeds, and Francis attended Crossgates Primary School, where he was
observed to be totally passive: he would neither speak nor eat. He was seen by an
educational psychologist and a child psychiatrist and was diagnosed as being an
elective mute. In July 1983 he started to attend the day unit of the department of
child and family psychiatry at St James's Hospital, Leeds.

On a number of occasions during the remainder of 1983, during the year 1984
and in the first half of 1985 Francis was observed to be bruised. He was examined
in October 1983, June 1984 and again in June 1985 by a consultant paediatrician,
Dr Hobbs, who raised the possibility of non-accidental injury. In June 1985, after
further inquiries, a case conference was held by the social services department of
the Leeds City Council and Francis was placed on the register of child abuse. He
continued to attend the day unit and St Kevin's Middle School, both part-time.

However, his conduct at school continued to cause anxiety: in September 1985 whilst at school he did not speak, participate in class or even move unless *a* individually coaxed; he was frequently in tears. Meanwhile throughout the latter part of 1985 and in the early weeks of 1986 bruises continued to be observed.

On 20 January 1986 Francis was again examined by Dr Hobbs. He reported that he found Francis unhappy and withdrawn and noted a pattern of bruising strongly suggestive of non-accidental injury. Dr Hobbs also observed anal abnormalities which were compatible with, but not diagnostic of, sexual abuse of *b* Francis. As a result of that report the council obtained a place of safety order in relation to Francis and he went to live in a small family group home at Easedale Close, Leeds.

I should make it clear that the father and the mother have at all times vehemently denied that Francis was sexually abused, and have maintained that his admitted bruising was attributable to the ordinary rough and tumble of *c* childhood.

On 25 February 1986 the council issued an originating summons in wardship seeking care and control of Francis. Evidence was filed on behalf of the council by Jill Low, a social worker employed by the council, Dr Hobbs, by two teachers and the special needs co-ordinator at St Kevin's Middle School, and by Dr Margaret *d* Hallas, a consultant psychiatrist at St James's Hospital. The father and the mother, who were defendants to the wardship proceedings, each filed affidavits, as did a brother and two sisters of Francis, and a police surgeon who examined Francis on 1 February 1986 and found no abnormalities on a rectal examination and no injuries other than a small bruise on the right thigh. The senior housemother in charge of the Easedale Close Community Home also swore an affidavit on behalf *e* of the father and the mother deposing, inter alia, to the fact that Francis bruised easily and recording a list of the bruises noticed whilst he had been living in the home. Francis was himself joined as a defendant to the wardship proceedings: the Official Solicitor acted as his guardian ad litem and filed a full report dated 27 November 1986.

The full hearing of the wardship proceedings took place before Swinton *f* Thomas J from 3 to 8 December 1986. The following is an extract from a note of the judgment of Swinton Thomas J given on 10 December 1986 which was put in evidence before us:

'In the light of the evidence I have heard it would be impossible to make a definitive finding that Francis Manda had been physically or sexually abused *g* by the father but there is evidence that physical and sexual abuse while in the care of the parents has taken place. This caused great concern for the welfare of the child and militate[s] against his return. I am aware [that] the diagnosis [of] physical and sexual abuse could be mistaken and aware that the best interests of the child is that he should be with his brothers and sisters and family. However, regard must be had to the paramount welfare of this *h* particular child who is an elective mute and emotionally disturbed. It is accepted that he is now progressing and that a return to the home at this time would cause him to become again emotionally disturbed. The child is emotionally vulnerable. He is a damaged boy and development could be retarded by a return home.' *j*

An order was then made continuing the wardship, committing the care of Francis to the council under s 7(2) of the Family Law Reform Act 1969, and directing that access to Francis by his parents should be at the discretion of the council. Thereafter Francis continued to live at the Easedale Close Community Home and enjoyed regular and successful access with his mother and father.

On 28 February 1989 the mother and the father applied for care and control of
a Francis and on 24 November 1989 he returned home on trial. On 8 June 1990
the wardship was discharged and Francis has since lived with his parents and
other members of his family at the family home in Leeds. There were further
hearings in the wardship proceedings leading up to the events just mentioned,
and for that purpose further evidence was filed on behalf of the council by a social
worker, Michael Munnelly, by the father on behalf of himself and the mother,
b and there was a further report by the Official Solicitor and two reports by a child
psychiatrist, Dr Mary Ward.

On 15 November 1990 the father and the mother issued an application in the
wardship proceedings in the following terms:

c   '... for leave to disclose all relevant documents to the first and second
defendants [the parents] experts in respect of a potential claim by the first
and second defendants against Leeds City Council and/or Leeds Area Health
Authority and/or Dr Christopher Hobbs for damages for negligence in
connection with this wardship.'

There are a number of points to be made about this application. Firstly, there
d is no suggestion that the potential claim is to be made by the parents on behalf of
Francis: it seems clear that they were contemplating action on their own behalf.
This is confirmed by the affidavit sworn in support of the application by the
parents' solicitor on 14 March 1991, para 5 of which reads:

e   'Almost all the documents which make up the file in the wardship
proceedings are likely to be relevant to the issues to be addressed in the
proposed proceedings. Without them the assessment of whether the first and
second defendants can sustain a course [sic] of action against the proposed
defendants will be seriously hampered.'

Secondly, it is now no longer proposed to bring a claim against the council and
f Dr Hobbs: the Leeds Western Area Health Authority is now the only proposed
defendant and they have voluntarily disclosed all their records to the parents'
solicitors. Thirdly, since the parents were themselves defendants in the wardship
proceedings, all of the material which they seek leave to disclose is already known
to them and is in the hands of their solicitors; this was in no sense a 'fishing'
expedition. They required leave to disclose these documents because without
g leave such disclosure would be a contempt of court: see s 12(1)(a) of the
Administration of Justice Act 1960. Fourthly, the purpose for which they sought
leave was restricted to that of submitting it to their experts, so that counsel's
opinion might be taken and that (subject to that opinion) they might be granted
legal aid to prosecute the claim against the health authority.

District Judge Hebbert granted the parents' application on 16 August 1991 by
h an order which, so far as relevant, was in the following terms:

j   'The first and second defendants be at liberty for the purpose only of
applying for legal aid of obtaining such professional advice as is necessary to
take counsel's opinion and of obtaining in relation to proposed proceedings
against Leeds Western Area Health Authority to disclose all documents
referred to in pargraphs 3, 4 and 5 of the affidavit of Judith McAra sworn
herein on the 14 day of August 1991.'

From this order the council appealed to the judge. Their appeal came before
Hollis J on 31 January 1992, who dismissed it. Although the form of the
application had not changed, the judge appears to have accepted that any proposed
action would be brought by or on behalf of Francis since he said:

'In this case I have come to the conclusion that if Francis could successfully
sue the area health authority it might be to his advantage. I specifically offer *a*
no view as to whether he has any chance of success.'

From this order the council appeal to this court. Since the hearing before
Hollis J Francis has attained his majority, on 12 June 1992. We have seen an
affidavit sworn by Francis on 13 April 1992 in which he expressed the wish to
pursue the proposed action when he is 18, and we were told by counsel that *b*
Francis has, since his birthday, confirmed that wish to the solicitor previously
instructed by his parents. Accordingly the hearing before us proceeded on the
basis that Francis would be the plaintiff in any proceedings that may be brought
against the health authority and further that, as he was himself a defendant in the
wardship proceedings (albeit represented by the Official Solicitor as his guardian
ad litem), he was properly aware of all the documents for the disclosure of which *c*
leave is now sought.

I now turn to consider the principles upon which the court should act on an
application for leave to disclose material relating to wardship proceedings. These
principles have never been given statutory form and are to be found by a
consideration of the relevant case law.

The starting point is the speeches in the House of Lords in *Scott v Scott* [1913] *d*
AC 417, [1911–13] All ER Rep 1. Although technically obiter, since the case itself
was concerned with the hearing of a nullity suit in camera, these have long been
regarded as the classic exposition of the reasons for the privacy which attaches to
proceedings in wardship. Viscount Haldane LC said ([1913] AC 417 at 437,
[1911–13] All ER Rep 1 at 9): *e*

'... the chief object of Courts of justice must be to secure that justice is
done. In the two cases of wards of Court and of lunatics the Court is really
sitting primarily to guard the interests of the ward or the lunatic. Its
jurisdiction is in this respect parental and administrative, and the disposal of
controverted questions is an incident only in the jurisdiction. It may often *f*
be necessary, in order to attain its primary object, that the Court should
exclude the public. The broad principle which ordinarily governs it therefore
yields to the paramount duty, which is the care of the ward or the lunatic.'

Lord Shaw of Dunfermline said ([1913] AC 417 at 482–483, [1911–13] All ER
Rep 1 at 33–34): *g*

'The three exceptions which are acknowledged to the application of the
rule prescribing the publicity of Courts of justice are, first, in suits affecting
wards; secondly, in lunacy proceedings; and, thirdly, in those cases where
secrecy, as, for instance, the secrecy of a process of manufacture or discovery
or invention—trade secrets—is of the essence of the cause. The first two of
these cases, my Lords, depend upon the familiar principle that the jurisdiction *h*
over wards and lunatics is exercised by the judges as representing His Majesty
as parens patriæ. The affairs are truly private affairs; the transactions are
transactions truly intra familiam; and it has long been recognized that an
appeal for the protection of the Court in the case of such persons does not
involve the consequence of placing in the light of publicity their truly
domestic affairs ... But I desire to add this further observation with regard *j*
to all of these cases, my Lords, that, when respect has thus been paid to the
object of the suit, the rule of publicity may be resumed. I know of no
principle which would entitle a Court to compel a ward to remain silent for
life in regard to judicial proceedings which occurred during his tutelage, nor

a a person who was temporarily insane—after he had fully recovered his sanity
and his liberty—to remain perpetually silent with regard to judicial
proceedings which occurred during the period of his incapacity.'

If, as is now submitted, one of the matters which is relevant to the exercise of
the discretion to allow wardship material to be disclosed is the fact that witnesses
have given their evidence in the belief that it would remain confidential, then
b that is not consistent with the final passage cited above from the speech of Lord
Shaw of Dunfermline. If a ward who has attained his majority is to be totally free
to refer to the wardship proceedings, the confidentiality which the witnesses may
have believed they enjoyed cannot be relevant. However, the nature of wardship
has changed considerably since 1913. At that time wardship was largely confined
to protecting wealthy young women from the depredations of fortune-hunters
c and to disputes between the parents of minors over their care and control and (in
the absence of legal aid) even then only when there was money available. The
extensive use of the wardship procedure by local authorities in aid of their
statutory responsibilities was then unknown; it was in fact a phenomenon of the
two decades between 1971 and 1991.

The next case is *Re R (M J) (an infant) (proceedings transcripts: publication)* [1975]
d 2 All ER 749, [1975] Fam 89, a decision of Rees J at first instance. This was the
case of an eight-year-old ward, and the application was to release a transcript of
evidence given in the wardship and adoption proceedings relating to the child,
for use in the bankruptcy of the adoptive father of the ward, who had in the
earlier proceedings given evidence as to his financial position. Rees J granted the
application, saying in the course of his judgment ([1975] 2 All ER 749 at 755–
e 756, [1975] Fam 89 at 96–98):

'The central questions in this application are whether there are any criteria
which apply to the exercise of the court's discretion to permit publication
and, if so, what they are. It is plain in my judgment that the first and most
important consideration is the interest of the ward ... it was common
f ground among all concerned in the application, and I so hold, that no
legitimate interest of the minor would be prejudiced if the application were
granted ... It was submitted on behalf of the Official Solicitor that leave
should *only* be given in cases in which disclosure could be shown to be for the
benefit of the minor involved in the particular case or for the benefit of
minors generally in future cases. I do not accept that submission. Where it is
g plain—as here—that disclosure would not harm any legitimate interest of
the minor, that is an important factor to be taken into account in favour of
giving leave. Equally, in support of the contrary view, it is proper to take
into account that it has not been shown that it would be for the positive
benefit of this minor nor that of minors in future cases that disclosure should
h be granted ... The case against granting the application may, I hope, not
unfairly be stated thus. It is conceded that disclosure in the instant case will
not harm any legitimate interest of the minor. But harm will be done in
future cases if the application is granted because witnesses will, or may, be
deterred from giving evidence with that degree of frankness which is the
essential need in cases involving the welfare of minors. The proper approach
j to the application is to ask whether the disclosure can be justified as being
conducive to the good exercise of the wardship jurisdiction. To that question
the answer is No ... My conclusions are these. A judge dealing with such an
application has an unfettered discretion to grant or to refuse it. He will place
the interest of the minor in the forefront of his consideration. He will also

give considerable weight to the public interest in ensuring that frankness shall prevail in such proceedings by preserving confidentiality. The public interest in upholding the law of the land by providing relevant evidence for use in other legitimate proceedings must be considered together with all the other circumstances of the case. I do not believe that it would be either possible or profitable to attempt to lay down any general principles governing the exercise of this discretion beyond what I have attempted to state above.' (Rees J's emphasis.)

The next relevant case is *Re F (a minor) (publication of information)* [1977] 1 All ER 114, [1977] Fam 58, a decision of this court. The issue there was whether it was a contempt of court to publish information about wardship proceedings relating to a 16-year-old girl, when the publishers did not know that the girl was a ward of court at the time of publication, or that what they published related to wardship proceedings in private. Although the headnotes state that *Re R (M J) (an infant) (proceedings transcripts: publication)* [1975] 2 All ER 749, [1975] Fam 89 was approved, that was not in relation to the point which arises in this case. However, in the course of their judgments both Scarman and Geoffrey Lane LJJ quoted with approval the statement of Lord Shaw of Dunfermline in *Scott v Scott* [1913] AC 417 at 483, [1911–13] All ER Rep 1 at 33–34 that the cloak of secrecy which the court wraps around wardship proceedings lasts no longer than is necessary in the interests of the ward (see [1977] 1 All ER 114 at 126, 137, [1977] Fam 58 at 93, 107).

Re F (minors) (wardship: police investigation) [1989] Fam 18 was another decision of this court. That was a case where the local authority had instituted wardship proceedings in respect of 17 minors, and in the course of the hearing it was alleged that 15 adult defendants to those proceedings, parents and relatives of the children, had committed acts of gross indecency on them. The police then applied for disclosure of the judgment and evidence in the wardship proceedings, in order that they might be used in the investigation of criminal offences. Four of the defendants objected on the ground that disclosure was against the public interest as the knowledge that evidence given in private could be released for publication would inhibit frankness. Although their objections failed, this court accepted that this was a material consideration to be taken into account in the exercise of its discretion to authorise publication, and expressly approved the statement by Rees J of the relevant principles in *Re R (M J) (an infant) (proceedings transcripts: publication)* [1975] 2 All ER 749, [1975] Fam 89 (see [1989] Fam 18 at 26 per Sir Stephen Brown P). Accordingly, at least in this court, it must be accepted that the possible inhibition of frankness on the part of witnesses in wardship proceedings is a relevant factor to be taken into account on an application for leave to disclose material used in the wardship.

Brown v Matthews [1990] 2 All ER 155, [1990] Ch 662, another decision of this court, concerned the use, in other proceedings, of a confidential report given by a court welfare officer in custody proceedings consequent upon the divorce of the child's parents. The inhibition of frankness argument was again raised, but Ralph Gibson LJ said ([1990] 2 All ER 155 at 162, [1990] Ch 662 at 672):

'It seems clear to me that any person asked by a [court] welfare officer to provide information for such a report, whether a party to the proceedings, or a friend or relation of a party, or a doctor or teacher who has treated or taught the child, would know that the information which he or she gives to the welfare officer, and his or her identity as the giver of it, would be made known for the purposes of the court's inquiry, and therefore disclosed to the parties. Most such people, I think, would, if they thought about it, suppose that the information would not be used for any other purpose, but they would be neither surprised nor indignant if told that it would be used for another purpose if the court considered that it was proper, in the interests of justice, for it to be disclosed at the court's direction. For my part, therefore, I do not think that there is any reason to believe that there would be any significant effect on the willingness of the people of this country to provide information to welfare officers in preparing reports for the court if people were told that normally no use would be made of the information given save in and for the proceedings in which the report has been ordered, but that it might also be used at the order of the court if justice required that it be not limited solely to that primary use.'

Nicholls LJ took a somewhat different view ([1990] 2 All ER 155 at 169, [1990] Ch 662 at 681):

'Thus the court charged with the task of exercising its discretion will, on the confidentiality aspect, need to have regard, amongst other matters, to the contents and source of the information sought to be used, and the extent to which release of the confidentiality would be likely to be detrimental to the welfare of the child in question, or to the proper functioning of a system which depends on court welfare officers being able to obtain frank and ready co-operation from people as diverse as doctors, school teachers, neighbours, the child in question, the parents themselves and other close relations, including other children in the same family. There may be cases, at one extreme, where release would not be harmful under either of these heads, even though the particular proceedings for which the report was prepared have still not been heard. At the other extreme, there may perhaps be cases where the source and nature of the information are such that release would be detrimental even after all proceedings relating to the child are over and, indeed, even after the child has become of full age, or has died. There might, for instance, be an extreme case in which release would be inimical to the proper functioning of the court welfare officer system in that it might deter others similarly placed in future from coming forward and speaking freely to welfare officers.'

Fox LJ agreed with both judgments.

Last in this line of cases is *Re X and ors (minors) (wardship: disclosure of documents)* [1992] 2 All ER 595, [1992] Fam 124. That case, before Waite J at first instance, was an application by a newspaper for leave (1) to have access to wardship files relating to certain wards or ex-wards (although the ex-wards were still minors) and (2) to disclose documents drawn from those files for the purposes of a libel suit in which the newspaper was the defendant and two paediatricians, who had examined the children concerned, were the plaintiffs. In the course of his judgment Waite J quoted a passage from an affidavit by the senior assistant director of social services of a local authority which had been the plaintiff in some of the wardship proceedings ([1992] 2 All ER 595 at 604–605, [1992] Fam 124 at 135):

'Wardship, in my respectful view, is essentially a private matter and is entered into by Local Authorities to seek the powers of the High Court to consider the extent to which children may need the protection of the Court. Information is given and received on that basis and the proceedings can only be conducted with complete candour if that is seen as the exclusive question before the court. I am seriously concerned that once this principle is breached it will become increasingly difficult for Local Authorities to obtain, collate and present the evidence which may be necessary to secure the well-being of children within its area.'

a

The judge summarised his duty ([1992] 2 All ER 595 at 606, [1992] Fam 124 at 136):

'On the basis of the authorities mentioned at the beginning of this judgment, I interpret my duty as being to inquire how the newspaper's *b* application, judged as a whole, will affect: (1) the children; (2) the public interest in the due administration, in accordance with its parental functions, of the wardship jurisdiction; (3) the public interest in the fair and informed administration of justice in the libel action.'

In relation to the second factor he said ([1992] 2 All ER 595 at 606–607, [1992] *c* Fam 124 at 137–138):

'The impact of the application on the wardship jurisdiction (turning now to the second inquiry) needs to be assessed with that jurisdiction's precise nature in mind. It is in part adversarial, in which respect it shares the characteristics of all other litigation. It is, in part, administrative and paternal, *d* in which respect its proceedings are (in Lord Shaw's phrase in *Scott v Scott* [1913] AC 417 at 483, [1911–13] All ER Rep 1 at 33) "truly intra familiam". In that latter role it calls for help from many quarters; from parents, friends or relatives who may be required in the interests of their children to lay bare painful or embarrassing secrets; from welfare officers, who may be called upon to disclose matters relevant to a child's welfare which it would be *e* hurtful or unprofessional to announce in public; from doctors and others who are bound by constraints of professional confidence; and from social workers needing encouragement to speak openly about their views and discoveries despite the vulnerability to criticism from all quarters to which their profession makes them uniquely subject. In this context it is right to *f* examine the prospective impact of the application upon the custodial jurisdiction in wardship, not only in relation to the particular cases of the X, Y and Z children, but also for its probable effect on the future working of the jurisdiction as a whole, for under our system of law permission granted in one case is liable to be relied on as a ground of permission in others. Nor is it any answer to that broader approach to say that the days of wardship's role in *g* the field of social work intervention in child care are very nearly over because of the imminent coming into effect of the Children Act 1989. It would be rash to start writing obituaries today for a jurisdiction which has survived with protean tenacity down the centuries, and which will, in any event, survive for other purposes. When assessed from this perspective, the effect of the application upon the jurisdiction itself and its future functioning would, *h* in my view, be substantial. The relatives, reporting officers, social workers and other professional people who provided reports and evidence for these three wardship proceedings, were taking part in an exercise that must have been tense for all of them and painful for many. Their contribution was underpinned by an assurance of confidentiality. Any breach of that assurance is likely to leave them feeling let down and discouraged from exercising the *j* same openness in future and the greater the breach, the greater the discouragement. Others in analogous positions of trust and responsibility towards children are likely, on learning of it, to feel a similar inhibition. The familial character of the jurisdiction can only suffer as a result.'

Although, as the judge mentioned, since the coming into force of the Children

a Act 1989 wardships by local authorities are no longer possible—see s 100(1)—it seems to me that the same issues can and will arise when local authorities seek the intervention of the court by the exercise of its inherent jurisdiction relating to children: see s 100(3) of the 1989 Act. So the principles relevant to the disclosure of material used in proceedings relating to children are still relevant and important.

b In the present state of the authorities, and subject to anything that may be said by the House of Lords should the question come before them, I can summarise the principles applicable to the disclosure of material used in proceedings relating to children as follows. (1) The interest of the particular child concerned will always be the most important factor, since it is to protect those interests that the

c court imposes the curtain of privacy. (2) Where the child is still a minor, the court will have to decide where its interests lie, although the older the child the more relevant are its own views and wishes. (3) Where the child concerned has attained majority, he or she alone (unless mentally incompetent) is entitled to decide what are his or her interests. This is the inevitable consequence under our law of the attainment of adult status. (4) If, as is usually the case, the material is

d to be disclosed for use in other proceedings, the public interest in the administration of justice requires that all relevant information should be available for use in those proceedings. (5) If it be the case that, in particular proceedings relating to children, information has been obtained on an express assurance of confidentiality, that must also be a very relevant factor. It would, however, be most undesirable for such an express assurance to be given unless the information

e could not otherwise be obtained. (6) Where no such express assurance has been given, persons who give evidence in child proceedings may normally assume that their evidence will remain confidential. They are not entitled, however, to assume that it will remain confidential in all circumstances and I have to say that I share the view of Ralph Gibson LJ in *Brown v Matthews* [1990] 2 All ER 155 at 162,

f [1990] Ch 662 at 672 as to the attitude of persons involved in a professional capacity with children. Certainly, if social workers and others in a like position believe that the evidence they give in child proceedings will in all circumstances remain confidential, then the sooner they are disabused of that belief the better.

I now turn to consider the application of these principles to the facts of the present case. At the time the case was heard befor the district judge and Hollis J,

g Francis was still under the age of 18. It is difficult to see how his interests would have been advanced by the proposed proceedings against the health authority, whether those proceedings were brought by his parents in their own right or on his behalf. The matter of which he and they primarily complain is the years he spent away from the family home, but this was in consequence of orders of the court, first the place of safety order and then the orders made in the wardship

h proceedings. So that is not something of which any tortious act on the part of the health authority was causative within the view of the law—cf *F v Wirral Metropolitan BC* [1991] 2 All ER 648, [1991] Fam 69. I consider later other possible heads of damage which Francis may be able to claim, but these are trivial when brought into the balance against the expense and trauma of litigation and the possible harm caused to Francis by the revival of painful memories. Hollis J said

j in the course of his judgment:

> 'In this case I have come to the conclusion that if Francis could successfully sue the area health authority it might be to his advantage. I specifically offer no view as to whether he has any chance of success.'

In my judgment this was a wrong approach. I do not see how it is possible for a court to consider whether the disclosure of material is for the benefit of a minor *a* without a consideration of the prospects of success in the litigation for which disclosure is sought. If the proposed litigation is bound to fail it is difficult to see how it could ever be for the benefit of the minor to permit disclosure for the purpose of that litigation. So for this reason alone I am satisfied that the judge applied the wrong test in the exercise of his discretion. He also allowed the exercise of his discretion to be influenced by other irrelevant factors, viz: (1) that *b* the health authority had voluntarily disclosed all their records to the parents' solicitors; and (2) that the Official Solicitor (who no longer had any locus standi) was not opposing the parents' application.

In my judgment the exercise by the judge of his discretion was vitiated by reason of the matters which I have set out above. It is therefore open to this court to exercise the discretion anew. In doing so there is one overriding factor: Francis *c* is now an adult. He is therefore able to make up his own mind as to what is in his best interests and however mistaken we may consider him to be, provided that the litigation which he wishes to pursue cannot be categorised as bound to fail, this court must accept his decision. Mr Wadsworth QC, who represented the parents on this appeal and whom we treated as if he also represented Francis, *d* accepted (without actually conceding) that Francis had little or no prospect of succeeding in a claim for damages for that of which he principally complained, his separation from his family. However, he submitted that if there had been no valid consent to Dr Hobbs's examinations of Francis, and in particular to the examination of his anal region, he might have a cause of action in trespass to the person, as well as a cause of action in negligence, for which it could not be said *e* that no damage had been suffered. While I entertain very serious doubts as to the possibility of any such claim against the health authority being successfully established, I am unable to say that it must be bound to fail. If Francis wishes to advance such a claim then that is his prerogative as an adult. If one adds to that the public interest that all relevant information should be available in these proceedings, in my judgment these two factors outweigh any detriment to *f* children's proceedings generally by the possibility that in future such cases witnesses—and in particular professional witnesses—will feel inhibited from being totally frank. This last is the main ground upon which the council is pursuing this appeal. As the council's solicitor said in her affidavit of 28 October 1991 in opposition to the parents' application for disclosure: *g*

'The impact of acceding to such an application on the wardship jurisdiction and its future functioning would be substantial. The medical experts, social workers and teaching staff who provided evidence in this case, like all witnesses in any wardship proceedings, did so under the umbrella of an assurance of confidentiality. Breaches of that assurance must, objectively, be *h* disquieting and discouraging of the exercise of openness in future.'

Whether any of the witnesses referred to in this passage were given an express assurance of confidentially is not stated—it is more likely to have been implied. But, whether express or implied, the primary consideration here is the interests of Francis, who has become an adult, as perceived by him. It is for this reason that this case differs on its facts from all the other cases to which I have referred, since *j* in none of those cases was it suggested that the disclosure of the information could be for the positive benefit of the ward. Either it was accepted that the ward's interests would not be prejudiced—as in *Re R (MJ) (an infant) (proceedings transcripts: publication)* [1975] 2 All ER 749, [1975] Fam 89 and *Re X and ors (minors) (wardship: disclosure of documents)* [1992] 2 All ER 595, [1992] Fam 124—

a or it was accepted that they might be prejudiced but that this was outweighed by other relevant considerations—as in *Re F (minors) (wardship: police investigation)* [1989] Fam 18.

There is one further point. The order of the district judge was in the terms set out above. It will in any event require to be varied to substitute Francis (the third defendant) for his parents (the first and second defendants) as the person to whom

b liberty is given. This, of course, will have the consequence that the parents will remain bound for all purposes by the provisions of s 12(1)(*a*) of the Administration of Justice Act 1960. However, the order also restricts disclosure for the purposes of obtaining professional advice in order to see whether Francis has a cause of action against the health authority for which he may be granted legal aid. By his

c order Hollis J dismissed the appeal against the order of the district judge, so that that order remains unvaried. However, it seems to me to follow from the reasons I have given above that if Francis's advisers do take the view that he has a cause of action against the health authority, for which he is granted legal aid, then the disclosed documents must also be available for use in that action, and it would be an unnecessary waste of costs to require him to make a further application to the

d court for a second stage disclosure. Waite J considered a similar point in *Re X and ors (minors) (wardship: disclosure of documents)* [1992] 2 All ER 595 at 602–603, [1992] Fam 124 at 132–133, and he ruled that it was artificial to look separately at the question of inspection in isolation from the disclosure (by way of evidence in the libel action) to which it was an essential preliminary. I agree. Hollis J deliberately did not follow the procedure adopted by Waite J in *Re X and ors*

e *(minors).* He said:

'As to the public interest, I can see no harm in inspection as asked for and I specifically do not deal with the subsequent disclosure as evidence in subsequent proceedings because that may never arise. I appreciate that, according to Waite J's decision in *Re X and ors (minors)*, the two have got to be

f considered on this application but, in fact, I go no further than deal with the question of inspection.'

I do not see how, in the light of what I have said above, if Francis's advisers take the view that he has a cause of action, and he is then granted legal aid, it could be right for a judge to refuse disclosure of the material for the purposes of the action.

g If that were a serious possibility it were better to refuse leave now. Mr Spencer QC, for the council, did not seek to oppose this view.

Accordingly, while I would dismiss the substance of the appeal, I would vary the order below so as to grant leave to Francis to disclose the wardship material for the purpose in the first place of showing it to his advisers and, if as a result he is advised he has a cause of action for which legal aid is granted, for the purposes

h of that action. Of course, if the action is never commenced, all further disclosure remains prohibited.

LEGGATT LJ. The salient points in this appeal are that, Francis having attained his majority, the action is now his action, that all the documents in question have been disclosed to the parties and that initially the only further disclosure sought

j is to experts. It is common ground that Francis has no cause of action for having been parted from his parents, since that was by court order; but he may have a cause of action in negligence or trespass to the person arising out of his medical treatment. His present predicament is that according to the council's contention he cannot obtain disclosure of his medical records unless he can show that he has a cause of action, but he cannot know whether he has a cause of action without disclosure of the document at least to his own experts.

The fact that the judge paid regard to irrelevant matters does not in this case invalidate his conclusion: it merely permits us to exercise our own discretion. In my judgment the principle that the confidentiality of information about an infant should be preserved ought not to be allowed to produce the result in this case that the ward for whose benefit medical records were prepared is precluded from using them himself for the purpose of instructing experts with a view to taking proceedings in tort to which the records are relevant. That is not to detract from the caveat entered by Sir John Megaw in his judgment, which I have had the benefit of reading in draft. Subject to that, I agree that for the reasons canvassed by Balcombe LJ this appeal should be dismissed, and that the order should issue which he proposes.

SIR JOHN MEGAW. I agree with the order proposed by Balcombe LJ. I agree in substance with the reasons given by him, though in one respect, not affecting the decision of the appeal, I respectfully venture to express a view which is, I think, somewhat different from his view as to the weight which should be given to the factor of public interest in the preservation of confidentiality for the sake of what is described by Nicholls LJ in *Brown v Matthews* [1990] 2 All ER 155 at 169, [1990] Ch 662 at 681 as 'the proper functioning of [the] system'.

I believe that it would be, at least, doubtful whether there would be the same 'frank and ready co-operation', essential for that proper functioning, if it were to become known, or suspected, that a statement made in response to a request for help in wardship proceedings—sometimes bitterly contested proceedings—was liable, without some very strong reason, to be made available, perhaps years later, for use in a second round, or a replay, of legal proceedings, reopening, in public litigation, disputes to which the voluntary statement was relevant, but which the giver of the statement would sensibly have assumed would have been decided once and for all in the privacy of the wardship proceedings.

If there is such a risk to the proper functioning of the system, it does not automatically cease to have relevance as a factor in the exercise of the court's discretion because the former ward has become 18. As Geoffrey Lane LJ put it in *Re F (a minor) (publication of information)* [1977] 1 All ER 114 at 137, [1977] Fam 58 at 107: 'The embargo on publication of matters disclosed in a private hearing is not necessarily perpetual.'

However, giving the weight which I think should be given to this factor, I agree that the balance, in the exercise of our discretion in this case, still favours granting leave to disclose the wardship material.

Appeal dismissed. Order below varied. Leave to appeal to the House of Lords refused.

Celia Fox   Barrister.

Practice Note

a

COURT OF APPEAL, CRIMINAL DIVISION
LORD TAYLOR OF GOSFORTH CJ, JUDGE AND HIDDEN JJ
8 FEBRUARY 1993

b *Sentence – Life imprisonment – Discretionary life sentence – Part of sentence to be served before case referred to Parole Board – Relevant part – Practice – Judge not obliged to specify relevant part of sentence but should do so save in exceptional cases – Duty of judge when specifying relevant part – Order to be made in open court – Counsel for defendant to be permitted to address court – Judge to give reasons – Judge no longer to make written report to Secretary of State – Criminal Justice Act 1991, s 34.*

c

LORD TAYLOR OF GOSFORTH CJ gave the following direction at the sitting of the court.

1. Section 34 of the Criminal Justice Act 1991 empowers a judge when passing a sentence of life imprisonment—where such a sentence is not fixed by law—to specify by order such part of the sentence ('the relevant part') as shall be served *d* before the prisoner may require the Secretary of State to refer his case to the Parole Board.

2. Thus the discretionary life sentence falls into two parts: (a) the relevant part, which consists of the period of detention imposed for punishment and deterrence, taking into account the seriousness of the offence, and (b) the remaining part of the sentence, during which the prisoner's detention will be governed by *e* considerations of risk to the public.

3. The judge is not obliged by statute to make use of the provisions of s 34 when passing a discretionary life sentence. However the judge should do so, save in the very exceptional case where the judge considers that the offence is so serious that detention for life is justified by the seriousness of the offence alone, *f* irrespective of the risk to the public. In such a case, the judge should state this in open court when passing sentence.

4. In cases where the judge is to specify the relevant part of the sentence under s 34, the judge should permit counsel for the defendant to address the court as to the appropriate length of the relevant part. Where no relevant part is to be specified, counsel for the defendant should be permitted to address the court as to *g* the appropriateness of this course of action.

5. In specifying the relevant part of the sentence, the judge should have regard to the specific terms of s 34 and should indicate the reasons for reaching his decision as to the length of the relevant part.

6. Whether or not the court orders that s 34 should apply, the judge shall not, following the imposition of a discretioary life sentence, make a written report to *h* the Secretary of State through the Lord Chief Justice as has been the practice in recent years.

N P Metcalfe Esq   Barrister.

Bank of Crete SA v Koskotas and others (No 2)

a

CHANCERY DIVISION
MILLETT J
18 JUNE 1992

b

Discovery – Production of documents – Confidence – Order that material disclosed to be used solely for action in which production ordered – Application to vary order to permit disclosure pursuant to legal obligation in foreign jurisdiction – Whether proper to vary order to permit use of information for purpose other than that for which it was obtained – Whether court should prevent disclosure for other purposes in a foreign jurisdiction under compulsion of law.

c

The plaintiff, a Greek bank, brought proceedings in England against the defendants, its former chief executive and others, to recover some $US200m of its funds allegedly misappropriated by them. In the course of the proceedings certain banks with branches in London were ordered to disclose to the plaintiff d
bank information and documents relating to the accounts of certain customers, such information and documents to be used only for the purposes of the plaintiff bank's action against the defendants. At the same time the governor of the Bank of Greece appointed a team of special investigators to investigate the whereabouts of the misappropriated funds. The head of the Bank of Greece investigation team was obliged under Greek law to prepare reports of the results of his investigations e
and to submit them to the plaintiff bank, which was in turn obliged to submit them to the governor of the Bank of Greece and the Greek examining magistrate appointed to investigate the criminal aspects of the alleged fraud. The head of the investigation team wished to use the information and documents disclosed under the order made in the plaintiff bank's action in the preparation of his reports, and the plaintiff bank accordingly applied for leave to make the material available to f
him. The question arose whether the court should order disclosure of the material when it was for a purpose other than that for which it had been obtained.

Held – Where the court ordered disclosure of information to a plaintiff for a g
particular purpose it would only be in exceptional circumstances that the court would authorise that plaintiff voluntarily to make use of it for any other purpose. However, the court would not be astute to prevent disclosure for other purposes in a foreign jurisdiction under compulsion of law. Accordingly, the court would not place the plaintiff bank in the position of either having to infringe its h
undertakings to the court or be in breach of its duties under Greek law. The plaintiff bank would therefore be given leave to use the material for the preparation of reports on the misappropriation and to supply such reports or any material disclosed under the order to any person to whom it was obliged to supply the reports or material under the law of any other jurisdiction (see p 753 *h j*, p 754 *f* to *j* and p 755 *a c* to *e*, post).

j

Notes

For confidential use of documents disclosed, see 13 *Halsbury's Laws* (4th edn) para 66, and for cases on the subject, see 18 *Digest* (2nd reissue) 102–107, 883–895.

Cases referred to in judgment

a *A-G v Guardian Newspapers Ltd (No 2)* [1988] 3 All ER 545, [1990] 1 AC 109, [1988] 3 WLR 776, HL.

Crest Homes plc v Marks [1987] 2 All ER 1074, [1987] AC 829, [1987] 3 WLR 293, HL.

Marcel v Comr of Police of the Metropolis [1992] 1 All ER 72, [1992] Ch 225, [1992] 2 WLR 50, CA.

b *Norwich Pharmacal Co v Customs and Excise Comrs* [1973] 2 All ER 943, [1974] AC 133, [1973] 3 WLR 164, HL.

Sony Corp v Anand, Seiko Time (UK) Ltd v Domicrest (Fancy Goods) Ltd [1981] FSR 398.

Application

c The plaintiff, Bank of Crete SA (the bank), applied in an action brought by it against the defendants, George Koskotas and others, relating to the alleged misappropriation of some $US200m by Mr Koskotas, for leave to use, for the purpose of preparing audit reports for the bank, all or any of the material disclosed under an order made on 5 October 1989 by Morritt J requiring an English bank *d* and several foreign banks with branches in London (the respondent banks) to disclose to the bank information and documents relating to certain of the respondent banks' account-holders. Paragraph 5 of Morritt J's order permitted the bank to use any such information and documents disclosed only for the purpose of its action against the defendants. The facts are set out in the judgment. The application was heard in camera but judgment was given by Millett J in open *e* court.

Ian Geering QC and *Caroline Lewis* (instructed by *Denton Hall Burgin & Warrens*) for the bank.

The defendants did not appear and the respondent banks were not represented.

f **MILLETT J.** I heard this application in camera but, as the case is of some importance, I am giving judgment in open court. The application is in an action which relates to the alleged misappropriation of approximately $US200m from the Bank of Crete (the bank) by its former chief executive, George Koskotas, and others. It is alleged that they took steps to conceal the misappropriation from the bank, for example by causing computer files to be rewritten to create false records, *g* by creating false documents and false entries, and by removing documents or having them removed.

The Bank of Greece has caused investigations into the affairs of the bank to be made by special investigators, whose task has been made particularly difficult by reason of the fact that the bank's documents cannot be taken at face value. The special investigators have, therefore, had to rely to a large extent upon evidence *h* obtained from other banks in order to discover what has happened.

In order to assist the investigations into the alleged fraud, the tracing of the bank's money and the recovery of its money from those who misappropriated it, the bank has made application to this court to obtain documents and information. Such applications have been made against an English bank and several overseas banks with branches in London. On 5 October 1989 Morritt J made an order *j* requiring each of the respondent banks to disclose to the bank information and documents relating to the accounts of certain of their account-holders. Paragraph 5 of the order made by Morritt J permitted the bank to make use of all or any of the information or documents disclosed pursuant to the order only for the purpose of the action which the bank had commenced in this country against Mr Koskotas and others. That paragraph was subsequently varied by an order of

mine, made on 24 July 1990, which permitted the bank to use all or any of the
information or documents disclosed pursuant to the order of 5 October 1989 in   *a*
the conduct of or to commence any civil proceedings within or outside the
jurisdiction of this court against any person relating to any matter disclosed
pursuant to the order.

The head of the team of special investigators responsible for investigating the
foreign exchange transactions of the bank is a Mr Stefanides. His investigations
into the whereabouts of the misappropriated funds and as to the actions taken by   *b*
Mr Koskotas to dispose of them are now drawing to a close. He is under an
obligation to produce final audit reports of the results of his investigations and to
provide them to the provisional commissioner of the bank. In order to compile
full and proper audit reports, he needs to use, inter alia, the information and
documents which were disclosed under the order of 5 October 1989. He wishes
to report upon (a) how the moneys were misappropriated from the bank, (b) how   *c*
they were transferred to the United Kingdom, (c) the information obtained from
each of the respondent banks in order to identify the bank accounts into which
the bank's money was paid, how and when it was paid out of those accounts, and
the account or accounts held at any other bank to which the money paid out of
those accounts was credited, and (d) his conclusion that the money so transferred   *d*
to the United Kingdom belonged to the bank.

The matters referred to in para (a) and possibly para (d) above would not require
the use of documents or information disclosed under the order of 5 October 1989.
It appears, however, that Mr Stefanides could not cover the other matters without
referring to such documents and information, and he is of the opinion that unless
those matters are dealt with the audit reports which he is under a duty to compile   *e*
will be worthless and even misleading. He has not yet prepared any reports, even
in draft, nor has he made any use of the documents or information in question
pending the leave of this court. He would, however, wish to exhibit the
documents in question including bank statements and not merely refer to them
or extracts from them; but he would propose expunging from any exhibited
document all entries which relate exclusively to persons unconnected with the   *f*
investigation.

The main purpose of the audit reports will be for use in the bank's civil
proceedings in Greece against Mr Koskotas and others; and, to that extent, the use
of the information and documents obtained under the order of 5 October 1989 is
already permitted. The reports, including the information disclosed pursuant to   *g*
the order of 5 October 1989, are necessary to support the bank's case that Mr
Koskotas embezzled money from the bank and then laundered the money by
transferring sums to banks in England and elsewhere and then transferring them
back to Greece. It is considered to be essential for the bank to be able to use
material obtained under the order of 5 October 1989, in order to show that when
Mr Koskotas credited bank accounts belonging to himself or his wife, he was   *h*
crediting them with money representing or derived from money which he had
embezzled from the bank, and not with his own money.

The bank now applies to me for an order that it be at liberty to use all or any of
the material disclosed pursuant to the order made on 5 October 1989, or other
similar orders, for the purpose of preparing audit reports for the provisional
commissioner of the bank. Under Greek law, the provisional commissioner is   *j*
under a duty to provide copies of such reports both to the governor of the Bank
of Greece by whom he was appointed, and to the examining magistrate, an official
of the Greek judicial system appointed to investigate criminal aspects of the fraud
alleged to have been perpetrated on the bank. The examining magistrate has
already brought criminal charges against Mr Koskotas and others in relation to

the funds which he is alleged to have misappropriated from the bank. Mr
a Koskotas has now been extradited from the United States of America and is
awaiting trial in Greece.

So far as concerns the governor of the Bank of Greece, it is unlikely that the
copy of the report furnished to him would go beyond his office, but the examining
magistrate may invite any individual who is criminally implicated by the report
to make comments on the report, and for that purpose a copy of the report would
b be provided to the individual or individuals concerned. There is an obvious
danger that such a course could lead to leakage of the contents of the report, and
indeed on earlier occasions copies of similar reports or extracts therefrom have
been published in the Greek press.

The order which Morritt J made and which I extended was further extended
c by Ferris J more recently, in order to permit the use of the material obtained
under the orders of this court to be made available to the Greek criminal courts
in order to prevent an innocent party being wrongly convicted on false evidence
given by Mr Koskotas. I am now asked to extend the order still further in order
to enable the special investigators to complete the audit reports which they are
under a legal duty to complete and provide to the provisional commissioner in
d the knowledge that, if so provided, it will be the duty of the provisional
commissioner to make them available both to the governor of the Bank of Greece
and to the examining magistrate for the purpose of criminal proceedings in
Greece.

There is no doubt that I have jurisdiction to vary the terms of my previous
order and to release the bank from the undertakings which it gave previously.
e The matter lies in my discretion. The question is whether my discretion should
be exercised in favour of disclosure. Each of the respondent banks has been made
a party to the application. It is the duty of each of the banks to obtain the
instructions of its customer. None of the banks considers that it is in a position to
consent to the order sought. None of the banks objects to the making of the
order. Each of the account-holders has been notified of the application. None of
f them has responded and none of them appears to oppose it.

There is a dearth of authority on the question I have to decide. I have been
referred to a number of cases. The first is *Sony Corp v Anand, Seiko Time, (UK) Ltd
v Domicrest (Fancy Goods) Ltd* [1981] FSR 398. That case concerned a proposed
action to prevent infringement of copyright. The plaintiffs discovered that their
g name was being dishonestly applied to low quality cassette tapes, and obtained
Anton Piller orders against the importers. The action in which the Anton Piller
orders were obtained was an action for discovery only and was brought in
accordance with the doctrine established by *Norwich Pharmacal Co v Customs and
Excise Comrs* [1973] 2 All ER 943, [1974] AC 133. The plaintiffs sought the order
for the purpose of identifying the suppliers. The plaintiffs gave an undertaking
h not to use any documents or information obtained as a result of the execution of
the order save for the purpose of bringing civil proceedings in connection with
the subject matter of the dispute. They obtained information revealing the
identity of suppliers of infringing goods in Hong Kong and Taiwan. The plaintiffs
then applied to the court for leave to bring civil proceedings anywhere in the
world against the suppliers and to initiate criminal proceedings in any part of the
j world against anyone other than the defendants.

In the course of his judgment in *Sony Corp v Anand* Browne-Wilkinson J held
that the general principle that materials obtained by exercise of the court's
coercive powers are not, without the leave of the court, to be used otherwise than
for the purpose for which those powers were exercised, did not apply in the
circumstances of the case before him, so that the question of leave did not arise.

The reason he gave was that the action in which the information was obtained
was an action for information only. As he put it (at 401–402):   *a*

> 'The rule that I have just been mentioning refers to the position where
> there is an action between A and B to assert some general legal right against
> B, B gives discovery of confidential information as incidental to the pursuit
> of that main action by A against B. In those circumstances, the rule is that
> the information has only been disclosed for the purposes of the action A   *b*
> against B and cannot, without the leave of the court, be used for any other
> purpose. There is however quite a different species of action in which the
> subject-matter of the legal claim established is a right to discovery of
> information. It was recently revived by the decision of the House of Lords in
> *Norwich Pharmacal Company v. Commissioners of Customs and Excise* ([1973] 2
> All ER 943, [1974] AC 133). In such an action the only claim of A against B   *c*
> is an order that B do disclose to A certain information. It is the old Chancery
> bill for discovery. The purpose of the action is to enable A, having got that
> information from B, to pursue his claim against third parties. The *Anton
> Piller* jurisdiction is based on that principle. The defendants in the action
> have been shown to be in possession of infringing material . . .'
>   *d*

and are bound to give information to the person whose rights have been infringed.
Browne-Wilkinson J continued:

> 'It is therefore, in my judgment, established that one of the main purposes
> of the *Anton Piller* order is to enable the plaintiff to get information from the
> defendants for the very purpose of using such information not against those   *e*
> defendants but against third parties. It therefore seems to me that information
> obtained under an *Anton Piller* order . . . can be used for the purposes of
> pursuing claims against third parties implicated in the same wrongful
> handling of the same infringing goods.'

Accordingly the use of information and documents obtained under an Anton *f*
Piller order for the purpose of pursuing claims against third parties does not
infringe the general rule that documents and information obtained by the exercise
of the court's coercive powers are not to be used otherwise than for the purpose
for which those powers were exercised. Browne-Wilkinson J then gave an
alternative reason for authorising the use of the information for the purpose of
criminal proceedings. His reason was that there was evidence before him that in *g*
Hong Kong the criminal remedies against infringements of copyright and trade
mark were thought to be superior to the civil remedies.
     In that case the plaintiffs were seeking to make use of the material for the
purpose of bringing criminal proceedings themselves. The justification for giving
leave was that civil proceedings are not an end in themselves but are designed
either to secure monetary compensation or injunctive relief to prevent continuance *h*
of the acts complained of. In some jurisdictions, criminal proceedings are more
appropriate or are superior to civil proceedings; and where the plaintiffs are
seeking to achieve their end by criminal proceedings rather than civil proceedings,
it is not necessarily an abuse of the general principle to make use of the material
for this purpose.
     In *Crest Homes plc v Marks* [1987] 2 All ER 1074 at 1078, [1987] AC 829 at 853 *j*
Lord Oliver repeated the rule:

> 'The purpose of an Anton Piller order is, primarily, the preservation of
> evidence which might otherwise be removed, destroyed or concealed but it
> operates, of course, also as an order for discovery in advance of pleadings . . .'

and said that there is an implied undertaking to the court by the plaintiff not to
a use the material or allow it to be used for any purpose other than the proper
conduct of the action on behalf of the client. He made it clear that the court has
jurisdiction to release or modify the implied undertaking, that the general
principle must be that the court will do so in the exercise of its discretion but only
in special circumstances and where the release or modification would not occasion
injustice to the person giving discovery, but that each case must turn on its own
b individual facts. In that case the determinative point to Lord Oliver's mind was
that it was adventitious that there happened to be two actions and that the purpose
for which the material was sought to be used was a different action from that in
which it had been obtained. The existence of two actions had been occasioned by
purely technical considerations. The cause of action was the same in each case and
c the parties were identical, or at least similar. It was therefore a pure technicality
that the order under which the material had been obtained was made in
proceedings other than those for which it was sought to be used.

That was the basis upon which I extended Morritt J's original order to permit
the material to be used in civil proceedings brought anywhere in the world for
the recovery of the bank's misappropriated funds. Civil proceedings are not an
d end in themselves. In the present case the purpose of the English proceedings was
to obtain the restoration of funds alleged to have been misappropriated from the
bank. For that purpose it may be necessary to bring proceedings in many different
jurisdictions. The use of material obtained in the course of English proceedings
for the purpose of similar proceedings in other jurisdictions would not infringe
the general principle, and accordingly I gave leave.

e However, the English proceedings were brought by the bank for the purpose
of recovering the moneys of which it had been defrauded, not for the purpose of
enabling the bank or its provisional commissioner to compile an audit report for
use by the governor of the Bank of Greece, nor for the purpose of enabling
criminal proceedings to be brought in Greece. Those criminal proceedings are
f not being brought by the bank, nor is the recovery of the bank's money their
object. If the use of the material for such a purpose is to be justified, its justification
must lie elsewhere.

On behalf of the bank, Mr Geering QC referred me to *A-G v Guardian
Newspapers Ltd (No 2)* [1988] 3 All ER 545 at 659, [1990] 1 AC 109 at 281, where
Lord Goff set out the scope of the equitable doctrine of confidence and in
g particular the three limiting principles which apply to that doctrine. The third
limiting principle is that, although the basis of the law's protection of confidence
is that there is a public interest that confidences should be preserved and protected
by the law, nevertheless that public interest may be outweighed by some other
countervailing public interest which favours disclosure. In my judgment such
considerations are not directly in point, since the objection, if any, to the use of
h the material in the present case for the purpose of criminal proceedings in Greece
is not based on the doctrine of confidentiality but rather on the right of privacy.
The material obtained from the banks was ordered to be disclosed because it was
within the account-holders' power and was compellable from them. Material
obtained by the use of the court's coercive powers, whether from a defendant in
respect of material in his possession, or from his bank in respect of material which
j is confidential to him but which is within his power, may in general be used only
for the purpose for which it has been obtained. To use it for any other purpose
would be to invade the defendant's privacy. But I agree with Mr Geering's
submission that the right of privacy is no more unlimited than the right of
confidentiality. The doctrine of confidentiality exists to support the individual's
right of privacy.

There are, of course, wide policy considerations in the present case. There is a need for international co-operation between the courts of different jurisdictions *a* in order to deal with multinational frauds. Ferris J recognised the pressing need to prevent a foreign court from wrongly convicting an accused on the basis of allegations which the English court had material to disprove. The court granted leave for the use of the material to prevent an injustice. I have little doubt that it would have done so even if there were a clear risk that this would result not merely in the acquittal of the accused but also in the prosecution of his accuser. *b* In the present case, each of the account-holders is implicated in an alleged fraud, either as a principal or as an accessory or, at the very least, as a recipient of misappropriated funds.

I have considered what would be the position if this were an entirely domestic matter. It could not, I think, arise in quite the same form in such a case for the account-holders might have been entitled to refuse discovery by asserting the *c* privilege against self-incrimination. On the other hand, that privilege would not have availed the account-holders if the banks were served with subpoenas duces tecum. Such considerations do not arise in the present case since by virtue of s 14(1) of the Civil Evidence Act 1968 the privilege does not extend to protection against the possibility of prosecution in a foreign jurisdiction. *d*

There is, however, some assistance to be gained from the decision of the Court of Appeal in *Marcel v Comr of Police of the Metropolis* [1992] 1 All ER 72, [1992] Ch 225. In that case the Serious Fraud Office obtained, by the use of statutory powers, documents which it required for use in criminal proceedings against a person who was also a defendant in a civil action. The Serious Fraud Office then voluntarily produced that material to the plaintiff to assist him in the prosecution *e* of the civil proceedings. The Court of Appeal held that that was wrong in principle, but it refused to order the return of the material because it was plain that the court would have ordered discovery of the documents if they had been in the defendant's own possession, and there would have been no answer to a subpoena duces tecum against the Serious Fraud Office.

In my judgment, the correct approach to the present case is as follows. The *f* purpose for which the material has been obtained is the recovery by the bank of misappropriated funds. Save in exceptional circumstances, it would not be right to authorise the bank voluntarily to make use of the material for any other purpose. There were special circumstances which led Ferris J to extend the order in order to prevent a miscarriage of justice. However, *voluntary* disclosure is one *g* thing; disclosure under compulsion of law is another. By enabling the bank to obtain information which it needs for the successful prosecution of its civil remedies, the court should not place the bank in an impossible position in which it must either infringe its undertaking to this court or find itself in breach of its duties under Greek law. The fact that a party which seeks the assistance of the English court to obtain material for the purpose of an English action may find *h* itself under a legally enforceable obligation in another jurisdiction to disclose the material for some other purpose is no doubt a factor to be taken into account by the court when considering whether to give such assistance, but unless the material is of only marginal relevance to the English action it ought not normally to preclude the court from assisting the applicant to obtain the material it needs *j* for the successful prosecution of the action.

Now that the bank is in possession of the material, it is the obligation of the bank to prepare audit reports. Such reports ought to be full and proper reports and not misleading or worthless reports. Precisely how its obligation is to be performed is a matter for the bank, but this court ought not to place any obstacle in the way of the proper performance by the bank of its obligations under Greek

law. Once the report is completed, the provisional commissioner of the bank will
a be bound to notify the governor of the Bank of Greece that the audit report is
complete. It would be wrong for this court to prevent the provisional
commissioner from complying with his legal obligation under Greek law to
convey that information to the Bank of Greece. Thereafter it will be a matter for
the Bank of Greece to exercise whatever powers it has under Greek law to compel
production of the audit reports. If the governor obtains them, it will be a matter
b for Greek law to determine whether or not he should provide them to the
examining magistrate and what use if any the examining magistrate should make
of them. Such questions involve considerations of public policy, but in my
judgment they are questions of Greek public policy, and should be determined
accordingly without the restraining hand of this court. If, under Greek law, either
the governor of the Bank of Greece or the examining magistrate can compel the
c production of the audit reports, so be it. It is frequently the case that material
obtained by a party to English civil proceedings may be required to be produced
in criminal proceedings in England. By a parity of reasoning, I see no reason why
the English court should be astute to prevent a party who has obtained material
in this country by the use of the coercive powers of the English court from
d producing such material in a foreign jurisdiction if compellable to do so.

Accordingly the order which I propose to make is to add a proviso to the
existing order to the effect that nothing in the order shall prevent the plaintiff, its
servants or agents from using any information or documents disclosed pursuant
to the order for the purpose of producing, in such form as it may think
appropriate, audit reports or from supplying such audit reports or any information
e or documents disclosed pursuant to the order to any person to whom the plaintiff
is under a duty under the law of any other jurisdiction to supply such audit
reports, information or documents, or from informing any such person that such
audit reports have been prepared.

Order accordingly.

Jacqueline Metcalfe   Barrister.

R v Chief Constable of the Kent County Constabulary and another, ex parte L (a minor)

R v Director of Public Prosecutions, ex parte B (a minor)

QUEEN'S BENCH DIVISION

WATKINS LJ AND FRENCH J

11, 12, 13 FEBRUARY, 26 MARCH 1991

Judicial review – Availability of remedy – Decision to prosecute – Juvenile – Offence committed by juvenile – Discretion to continue or to discontinue criminal proceedings – Policy of cautioning juveniles – Police recommending prosecution rather than caution – Crown Prosecution Service deciding not to discontinue prosecution – Whether Crown Prosecution Service's decision amenable to judicial review – Prosecution of Offences Act 1985, s 10(1).

Criminal law – Proceedings – Prosecution of adult – Decision not to discontinue prosecution – Whether decision of Crown Prosecution Service not to discontinue prosecution of adult amenable to judicial review.

The applicant L was aged 16 when he was charged with assault occasioning actual bodily harm contrary to s 47 of the Offences against the Person Act 1861. The decision to prosecute him was taken despite the fact that the criteria for administering a caution, set out in the code issued pursuant to s 10(1)[a] of the Prosecution of Offences Act 1985 and in guidelines issued by the Home Secretary, were made out in his case, since it was felt that the circumstances of L's offence went considerably beyond the great majority of incidents alleging violence or the threat of violence in juvenile cases and was too serious for a caution to be appropriate. The applicant B, then aged 12, was charged with theft. In her case the decision to prosecute was taken because the offence was considered serious and there was no question of administering a caution because she refused to admit the offence, although had she done so a caution would have been considered appropriate. L applied for judicial review by way of orders of certiorari to quash the decision of the police to prosecute him and that of the Crown Prosecution Service not to discontinue proceedings against him pursuant to its powers under s 23[b] of the 1985 Act, and mandamus to compel the Crown Prosecution Service to discontinue the proceedings. B sought judicial review by way of orders of certiorari to quash the decisions of the police to recommend that she be charged with theft and to so charge her and of the Crown Prosecution Service not to discontinue proceedings against her, and an order of prohibition to prevent the Crown Prosecution Service from taking any further steps to prosecute her.

a   Section 10(1), so far as material, provides: 'The [Director of Public Prosecutions] shall issue a Code for Crown Prosecutors giving guidance on general principles to be applied by them—(a) in determining, in any case—(i) whether proceedings for an offence should be instituted or, where proceedings have been instituted, whether they should be discontinued . . .'

b   Section 23, so far as material, is set out at p 767 c d, post

Held – The discretion of the Crown Prosecution Service to continue or to
a discontinue criminal proceedings against a juvenile was subject to judicial review
by the High Court but only where it could be demonstrated that the decision had
been made regardless of or clearly contrary to a settled policy of the Director of
Public Prosecutions which had been formulated in the public interest, such as a
policy of cautioning juveniles. It was, however, likely that it would be only rarely
that a defendant could succeed in showing that a decision was fatally flawed in
b such a manner. Although in L's case the policy of cautioning juveniles applied, it
could not be said, in view of the seriousness of the offence, that the decision to
continue the prosecution was in any way flawed. In B's case the more general
policy that a prosecution should not occur unless required in the public interest
applied, but again it was very difficult to envisage a circumstance, fraud or
dishonesty apart, which would permit a challenge to a decision to prosecute or to
c continue proceedings unless it could be demonstrated, in the case of a juvenile,
that there had been either a total disregard of the policy or, contrary to it, a lack
of inquiry into the circumstances and background of the juvenile, previous
offences, general character etc by the prosecutor and later by the Crown
Prosecution Service and it was unlikely that the possibility that such disregard
d had happened could be shown. In B's case the evidence did not demonstrate that
the Crown Prosecution Service had fallen below the standard of care and inquiry
to be expected in the circumstances, nor could it be supposed that the CPS had
not considered the public interest and all other matters which had to be borne in
mind in deciding whether a 12-year-old girl should appear before a juvenile court.
It followed, therefore, that although decisions of the Crown Prosecution Service
e might in principle be reviewed, in practice it was rarely likely to be successfully
reviewed. In neither L's case nor that of B could there be said to have been a flaw
in the decision to continue criminal proceedings, and accordingly their applications
would be dismissed (see p 770 *d* to *j* and p 771 *d* to *g*, post).

Per curiam. If judicial review lies in relation to current criminal proceedings,
in contrast to a failure to take any action against a person suspected of a criminal
f offence, it will lie against the Crown Prosecution Service, as the body which has
the last and decisive word (see p 767 *h j* and p 771 *g*, post).

Semble. (1) Judicial review of a decision not to discontinue the prosecution of
an adult is unlikely to be available (see p 771 *a g*, post).

(2) A decision to discontinue criminal proceedings by the Crown Prosecution
Service can be equated with a decision by the police not to prosecute and is,
g therefore, open to judicial review only on the restricted basis available to a person,
assuming he has locus standi, seeking to challenge a decision by the police (see
p 768 *g* and p 771 *g*, post); *R v Metropolitan Police Comr, ex p Blackburn* [1968] 1
All ER 763 applied.

h **Notes**

For the institution of criminal proceedings generally, see 11(1) *Halsbury's Laws*
(4th edn) para 646.

For the Offences against the Person Act 1861, s 47, see 12 *Halsbury's Statutes*
(4th edn) (1989 reissue) 105.

For the Prosecution of Offences Act 1985, ss 10, 23, see ibid 941, 959.

j

Cases referred to in judgment

Gouriet v Union of Post Office Workers [1977] 3 All ER 70, [1978] AC 435, [1977] 3
WLR 300, HL.

Hallett v A-G [1989] 2 NZLR 87, NZ HC.

Hill v Chief Constable of West Yorkshire [1988] 2 All ER 238, [1989] 1 AC 53, [1988]
2 WLR 1049, HL.   *a*
Holgate-Mohammed v Duke [1984] 1 All ER 1054, [1984] AC 437, [1984] 2 WLR
660, HL.
R v Derby Crown Court, ex p Brooks (1984) 80 Cr App R 164, DC.
R v General Council of the Bar, ex p Percival [1990] 3 All ER 137, [1991] 1 QB 212,
[1990] 3 WLR 323, DC.
R v Metropolitan Police Comr, ex p Blackburn [1968] 1 All ER 763, [1968] 2 QB 118, *b*
[1968] 2 WLR 893, CA.
R v Metropolitan Police Comr, ex p Blackburn (No 3) [1973] 1 All ER 324, [1973] QB
241, [1973] 2 WLR 43, CA.
R v Panel on Take-overs and Mergers, ex p Datafin plc (Norton Opax plc intervening)
[1987] 1 All ER 564, [1987] QB 815, [1987] 2 WLR 699, CA.
R v Telford Justices, ex p Badhan [1991] 2 All ER 854, [1991] 2 QB 78, [1991] 2   *c*
WLR 866, DC.
Raymond v A-G [1982] 2 All ER 487, [1982] QB 839, [1982] 2 WLR 849, CA.
Riches v DPP [1973] 2 All ER 935, [1973] 1 WLR 1019, CA.
Turner v DPP (1978) 68 Cr App R 70.

d

Cases also cited
*Leech v Parkhurst Prison Deputy Governor, Prevot v Long Larton Prison Deputy
Governor* [1988] 1 All ER 485, [1988] AC 533, HL.
Newby v Moodie (1987) 78 ALR 603, Aust Fed Ct; *affd* 83 ALR 523, Aust Fed Ct
(Full Ct).
R v Bolton Justices, ex p Scally [1991] 2 All ER 619, [1991] 1 QB 537, DC.   *e*
R v London Residuary Body, ex p Inner London Education Authority (1987) Times,
24 July, CA.
R v Secretary of State for the Home Dept, ex p Ruddock [1987] 2 All ER 518, [1987] 1
WLR 1482.

f

Applications for judicial review
    R v Chief Constable of the Kent County Constabulary and anor, ex p L (a minor)
L, a minor, applied by his next friend and father, with the leave of Hutchison J
granted on 30 July 1990, for judicial review by way of an order of certiorari to
quash a decision of the Chief Constable of the Kent County Constabulary to   *g*
commence a prosecution against him for an offence of assault occasioning actual
bodily harm, an order of certiorari to quash a decision or decisions of the Crown
Prosecution Service not to discontinue proceedings against him for that offence
pursuant to its powers under s 23 of the Prosecution of Offences Act 1985 and an
order of mandamus to compel the Crown Prosecution Service to exercise its
powers under that section and discontinue the proceedings against him. The facts *h*
are set out in the judgment of Watkins LJ.

R v DPP, ex p B (a minor)
B, a minor, applied, with the leave of Otton J granted on 24 July 1990, for judicial
review by way of an order of certiorari to quash a decision of the Youth and *j*
Community Service to recommend charging her with theft, an order of certiorari
to quash a decision by officers of the Metropolitan Police to charge her with theft,
an order of certiorari to quash a decision of the Crown Prosecution Service not to
discontinue proceedings against her for theft, and an order of prohibition to

prevent the Crown Prosecution Service taking any further steps in the prosecution
a against her. The facts are set out in the judgment of Watkins LJ.
The two applications were heard together.

Robert Rhodes QC and *Lewis Marks* (instructed by *Berry & Berry*, Tunbridge Wells)
for L.
Roger McCarthy (instructed by *D P Clephan*, Maidstone) for the Chief Constable.
b *David Cocks QC* and *Henry Cleaver* (instructed by *Stephen Fidler & Co*) for B.
Andrew Collins QC and *Mark Dennis* (instructed by the *Crown Prosecution Service*)
for the Director of Public Prosecutions.
Victor Temple (instructed by *C S Porteous*) for the Metropolitan Police.

Cur adv vult

c

26 March 1991. The following judgment was delivered.

WATKINS LJ. There are before this court two applications which, because the
main issues arising from them are identical, were, with the consent of all
d concerned, heard together. Those issues are as follows. (1) Is the decision by either
the Commissioner of Police of the Metropolis or a chief constable to prosecute a
juvenile for an offence subject to judicial review and does it make any difference
that a caution is an available option? (2) If there is such an option is the decision
by the Crown Prosecution Service (the CPS) not to discontinue the prosecution
similarly reviewable?
e Both applicants, who are juveniles, have leave to move for relief from Hutchison
J and Otton J respectively. The juveniles concerned are L, born on 27 December
1973, who, when 16, was charged with an assault occasioning actual bodily harm,
contrary to s 47 of the Offences against the Person Act 1861, and B, born on
7 March 1978, who, when 12 years of age, was charged with theft, contrary to the
f Theft Act 1968.
L seeks an order of certiorari to quash a decision of the Chief Constable of the
Kent County Constabulary to prosecute him, a similar order to quash the decision
of the CPS not to discontinue proceedings against him, pursuant to its powers
under s 23 of the Prosecution of Offences Act 1985, and an order of mandamus
directed to the CPS to compel them to exercise those powers and to discontinue
g proceedings against him. Interim relief has already been granted to L to prohibit
the CPS from taking any further steps in the prosecution of him pending the
determination of this application. The grounds relied upon by L are that: (1) the
decision to prosecute him was one which no chief constable properly directing
himself could reasonably have made; (2) the CPS unreasonably exercised their
statutory discretion or unreasonably failed to exercise that discretion in deciding
h not to discontinue proceedings; (3) in particular both the chief constable and the
CPS failed to take account of all relevant circumstances which are: the nature of
the offence, the age of the applicant, the fact that he has no previous convictions,
he has never previously been cautioned and he is content for the matter to be
dealt with by way of caution, he admits the offence, he has apologised to the
complainant, he comes from a good home and has been disciplined by his parents,
j no serious injury was occasioned to the complainant, the recommendation to
caution of the juvenile offender liaison team (JOLT), the Guidelines on Cautioning
given in Home Office circular 14/1985 (the cautioning guidelines), the effect that
a criminal conviction might have upon him, the absence of special reasons for not
administering a caution, the absence of any public interest in the prosecution of

him, his welfare and the desirability of diverting juvenile from the courts; (4) the
chief constable and the CPS must have taken into account some matter which   *a*
should not have been considered.

B seeks an order of certiorari to quash a decision taken by the Youth and
Community Service (YACS) to recommend charging her with theft, an order of
certiorari to quash the decision of the commissioner to charge her with theft, an
order of certiorari to quash the decision of the CPS not to discontinue proceedings
against her and an order of prohibition directed to the CPS to stop them taking   *b*
any further steps in the prosecution of her. The grounds upon which she relies
are: (1) an indication having been given by the police that her case was to be
referred to the YACS, no inquiries were ever made by that or any other agency in
relation to the applicant's home or social circumstances; (2) no attempt was made
to contact the applicant or her father to discuss the case in accordance with the   *c*
spirit of the cautioning guidelines; (3) the decision to prosecute was made without
sufficient regard to the circular and without diverting the matter to the YACS for
proper inquiries, the matter not being sufficiently grave for a prosecution to take
place; (4) the CPS had not referred the matter back to the YACS for inquiries
despite representations in that behalf; (5) an indication was given to the applicant
that if she admitted the offence she would be cautioned. The inference to be   *d*
drawn from that is that if she did not admit the offence prosecution would ensue.
This indicates that other methods of disposal were not considered.

The facts, largely uncontested, leading to the charge against L are that in the
early evening of 14 November 1989 there was a brief argument and confrontation
between the victim, then 16, and a smaller, younger boy. L approached them
both and said, 'You shouldn't pick on little kids.' Then, without warning, L   *e*
punched the victim on the nose twice, knocking him to the ground, causing his
nose to bleed and fracturing the maxillary spine of his nose. As he lay on the
ground in some pain he felt a kick to his head. L admitted to the police punching
the victim twice, breaking his nose, so he thought, and kicking him, not on the
head but in the back, 'Just enough to say, "Come on, get back up" because he just   *f*
really wound me up.'

L's file was sent to the JOLT, a group comprising a probation officer, a social
worker and a police officer. On 13 February 1990 the victim's father wrote to the
JOLT expressing approval to L being dealt with by way of caution. A week later
L wrote to the victim a letter of apology, following which the JOLT recommended
that L be cautioned. Despite this acting Chief Inspector Gamble, on 25 February   *g*
1990, decided to prosecute and so informed the JOLT. On 1 April 1990 L was
charged with causing grievous bodily harm to the victim with intent.

The JOLT wrote direct to the CPS, who by then had the file from the police,
recommending that L be cautioned. In his affidavit Inspector Gamble states:

    '9. .... in every juvenile case ... the first and foremost aim should be to   *h*
    caution juveniles rather than prosecute them for the reasons dealt with in
    [the cautioning guidelines]. I would estimate that I have recommended a
    caution or [no further action] in 98 per cent of the juvenile cases I have
    considered since 1985. Despite the above considerations I must bear in mind
    the seriousness of any alleged offence and the public interest in ensuring that   *j*
    appropriate cases are recommended for prosecution.
    10. The circumstances of the incident involving [L] and his alleged actions
    go considerably beyond the great majority of juvenile incidents alleging
    violence or the threat of violence which come before me for my
    recommendation. In making the statement in the preceding sentence I draw

a on very detailed experience of the range of incidents excusable or otherwise which bring juveniles to the attention of the Police.'

Mr Jones, Senior Crown Prosecutor in the North Kent branch office of the CPS, states in his affidvit that he received L's case file and reviewed the case applying the relevant principles set out in the *Guide for Crown Prosecutors* (which I shall call 'the code') and notified the police that the charge should be reduced from an
b offence under s 18 of the 1861 Act to an offence under s 47. He telephoned Chief Inspector Powell, in charge of the administrative support unit for Tunbridge Wells, to discuss the case.

His affidavit continues:

c '6. . . . I was then informed that JOLT had recommended a caution, but that the Acting Chief Inspector had disagreed and decided to prosecute: the Chief Inspector said that he had agreed with that view. He read to me the JOLT recommendation in full. I ascertained that [L] had no previous convictions or cautions.

7. I reconsidered whether the prosecution should continue in the light of all the information I now had: see in particular paragraph 10 of [the code].
d Although the criteria for a caution were made out, I was of the opinion that a caution was inappropriate and that the prosecution should continue.

8. I reached my decision because I considered the offence to be a serious one, involving two blows to the face without any provocation or mitigating circumstances, the second of which was sufficient to knock the victim to the ground. While the victim was on the ground, [L] had kicked him in the
e head. Although the injuries were not as serious as had been feared initially, they were by no means trivial. This was in my view an incident which went far beyond an ordinary case of schoolboy bullying and a prosecution was merited, notwithstanding [L's] apparent remorse . . .

9. I referred the file to a colleague, a Senior Crown Prosecutor who specialises in cases involving juveniles. He agreed that a prosecution should
f continue.'

We were informed that L was cautioned in March 1990 for possessing a small amount of cannabis. That cannot of course, affect L's present application.

The allegation against B is that during the morning of 21 February 1990 she knocked on the door of a house and asked the householder to sponsor her for a
g run shortly to take place. Having no money in his pocket, the householder went into his kitchen to obtain money, leaving the front door open. He returned and gave B £1 and signed her form, whereupon she left. The householder saw her through the window near the dustbins of the next-door house. She was holding a grey shopping bag and was emptying the contents of that onto the ground. He went outside and asked her what she was doing. Receiving no reply he returned
h to his house, whereupon his cleaning lady said that 'her bag had gone missing'.

The householder then asked B to come back to his house and when she did so he went to the next-door neighbour's house and picked up the empty grey bag from the dustbins. When he returned again to his own house the cleaning lady identified the grey bag as hers in the presence of B. B asked the householder not
j to call the police and produced a red wallet from inside her anorak, which the cleaning lady also identified as hers. While the householder was telephoning the police B ran away.

When seen later on by police officers B admitted that she had been collecting for her school that morning and had gone to the house, she said, but had not stolen anything. That is a denial she has maintained ever since.

Her case was referred to the YACS, which is a team of police officers whose task includes liaison with schools in the area and dealing with cases referred to them *a* in accordance with para 9 of the cautioning guidelines.

The history of the work of those police officers on the case is, it was alleged by Mr Cocks QC for B, rather confusing and suggests an inadequacy of liaison and investigation into, inter alia, B's home circumstances as well as an indecisiveness at times as to what their recommendation should be.

An appropriate form was sent to the director of social services, the education *b* officer and the probation service for such comments as they wished to make, but no comments were received. Following a recommendation by the YACS that B should be charged with theft, she was so charged on 5 April 1990.

That recommendation is explained in his affidavit by Pc Allen as follows:

'5. On 15th March 1990 I visited [the school] which was attended by [B]. *c* I discussed both [B] and the case in general with the Headmaster and other members of the staff. I was subsequently informed by the school that [B] was continuing to deny the offence.

6. I considered making a visit to [B's] home even though such a visit is not the usual practice upon the first referral of a juvenile to the Youth and *d* Community Service. I decided against such a visit in the light of the apparent language difficulties with [B] and her family and [B's] continued denial of the offence.

7. As part of my review of the case I considered the guidelines on cautioning juveniles contained in the Home Office Circular 14/1985 ... A caution could not be administered as [B] was not prepared to admit the *e* offence as required in the criteria set out in the said guidelines. I reached the conclusion that it was not a suitable case in which to recommend any alternative action other than proceeding to charge.'

There seems to be no doubt that had B admitted the offence she would have been cautioned. However, on 24 May 1990 the CPS, having received her file on *f* 5 May, advised that prosecution of her should proceed despite strong representations from B's solicitors that they should order discontinuance of the prosecution.

Mr Blake, Principal Crown Prosecutor, in his affidavit explains the decision to proceed as follows:

'4. On 14th May 1990 I reviewed the case file applying the relevant *g* principles set out in the "Code for Crown Prosecutors" ...

5. I was satisfied that the evidential sufficiency criteria for the offence of theft as charged was made out.

6. In considering the public interest criteria I had regard in particular to paragraph 8(iii) [of the code] ... I reached the conclusion that the case could be properly disposed of by the administering of a caution if [B] was prepared *h* to admit the offence in accordance with the criteria set out in the guidelines on cautioning contained in Home Office Circular 14/1985 ...

7. On 16th May 1990 I informed Mr. Fidler, [B's] solicitor, that the case could not be disposed of by way of a caution unless [B] admitted the offence.

8. On 24th May 1990, being aware that [B] was still not prepared to admit the offence, I reviewed the case again. In accordance with my duties under *j* the Code for Crown Prosecutors (see particularly paragraphs 15–18 ...) I considered whether the public interest required a prosecution rather than a disposal of the case other than by way of a caution. I reached the conclusion that the case was a relatively serious one having particular regard to the

a allegation that [B] had gained entry into another's house by a trick in order to steal. I therefore advised that the prosecution should continue notwithstanding the age and character of [B].'

One of the documents which had a prominent place in submissions made to us was Home Office circular 14/1985, including the cautioning guidelines (this has since been replaced by Home Office circular 59/1990). Others were a general *b* order, an instruction manual and the code. Considerable reliance was placed upon their contents by Mr Rhodes QC for L and Mr Cocks QC for B.

The use of a caution as a means of dealing with mainly juvenile offenders is of some antiquity. It seems to have been mooted, if not in a small way introduced, in 1929. In 1932 Lord Trenchard favoured an extension of the practice, such as it then was. It has never had a statutory basis and only acquired a measure of formal *c* recognition in about 1968. It is not affected by, for example, s 5 of the Children and Young Persons Act 1969. The first Home Office circular relating to cautions was published in 1978. The circular current at all material times was circular 14/1985. In 1985 the number of offenders cautioned was 238,000, an increase of just over 100,000 in ten years.

d That circular and the guidelines were disseminated to chief officers of police under cover of a letter of commendation by the Home Secretary. The letter includes the following:

e 'This work has taken as its starting point that there is no rule in law that suspected offenders must be prosecuted. It has long been recognised in the case of juveniles that there may be positive advantages for society as well as for the individual in using prosecution as a last resort. Cautioning provides an important alternative to prosecution in the case of juvenile offending . . . The Home Secretary sees the issue of the present guidelines as a means to encourage the consistent application of policy in cautioning decisions, which will be a complementary process to the existence and growth of such special *f* schemes. However, he wishes chief officers to be aware of his view that the issue of these guidelines should also provide the opportunity for a review of local arrangements, where this has not already been done, to ensure that liaison arrangements with social services departments, the probation service and where appropriate the Education Welfare Service, are such as to encourage the participation of those agencies in decision making. This may be *g* particularly appropriate where there is doubt in the mind of the police as to whether a caution is the right course in an individual case.'

The guidelines start with the general statement:

'It is recognised both in theory and in practice that delay in the entry of a young person into the formal criminal justice system may help to prevent *h* his entry into that system altogether. The Secretary of State commends to chief officers the policy that the prosecution of a juvenile is not a step to be taken without the fullest consideration of whether the public interest (and the interests of the juvenile concerned) may be better served by a course of action which falls short of prosecution. Thus chief officers will wish to ensure that their arrangements for dealing with juveniles are such that prosecution *j* does not occur unless it is absolutely necessary. As a general principle in the case of first time juvenile offenders where the offence is not serious, it is unlikely that prosecution will be a justifiable course . . .

2. A formal caution may represent one form of entry into the criminal justice system. It will for example be cited should the offender subsequently

appear before a juvenile court. It is therefore important that the issue of a caution should be a formal procedure which takes full account of its consequences for the individual concerned and that it should take place only where strict criteria are fully met . . .

Criteria for a caution

4. Before a caution is issued to a juvenile, the following criteria must be met in full.

(a) *The evidence available must comply with the Attorney General's guidelines on criteria for prosecution* ie a conviction should be more likely than an acquittal before a court. Cautioning must not be used as a substitute for a weak prosecution case. If there is insufficient evidence to support a prosecution, it will not be right to use cautioning as an alternative.

(b) *The juvenile must admit the offence* It is not sufficient that the juvenile should merely admit all or some of the facts which constitute the offence; he must recognise his guilt. If there is no admission in circumstances where otherwise a caution would have been issued, the proper course may be to take no further action.'

The guidelines recommend obtaining consent of the parents or guardian of the juvenile to a caution being issued, consideration of the seriousness of the offence, the offender's record, consultation with other agencies and the interests of an aggrieved party.

The Chief Constable of Kent issued a general order following receipt of the guidelines. This, so far as material, states:

'1. In line with Home Circular 14/1985, force policy has been revised. The main features of the new policy are: (a) The introduction of "immediate cautions" for juvenile first offenders. (b) Wider scope for cautioning recidivist juveniles. Future policy will address the following issues and information concerning this will be published in due course: (c) The extension of cautioning to young adults and the "at risk" and elderly. (d) Cautioning of adults for drunkenness and for possession of small amounts of cannabis for personal use in certain circumstances. (e) The system to be adopted in the recording and citation of adult cautions. Meanwhile the tenets of Home Office Circular 14/1985 will be borne in mind when prosecution decisions are reached concerning adults. The changes at "a" and "b" above will necessitate some delegation of authority to issue cautions and endorse decisions on crime reports as explained hereunder. It should be noted that current force policy concerning documentation of detainees, crime reporting and recording practices and any requirement to submit statistical forms, report certain crimes, etc., in particular cases is unchanged.'

An instruction manual issued by the Metropolitan Police Commissioner, so far as material, states as follows:

'21.1 Except where it has been immediately decided that no further action is to be taken, an immediate caution has been administered, or a juvenile offender has been charged, all cases in which it has been established that an offence has been committed by a juvenile and that there is sufficient evidence to ensure the likelihood of a conviction, are to be referred to the YACS for a decision as to further action . . .

21.11 It is a rebuttable presumption in law that a child between the ages of 10 and 14 is incapable of knowing right from wrong. All officers should therefore bear in mind that, in addition to producing evidence that the accused committed the offence, evidence is also necessary to show that, at the

a time of the offence, that the child is aware that his/her act was seriously wrong i.e. went beyond childish mischievousness . . .
22.21 As a general rule the YACS will caution all first offenders.'

The Code for Crown Prosecutors is a statutory code issued by the Director of Public Prosecutions pursuant to s 10 of the 1985 Act. The code contains the following:

b '8. The factors which can properly lead to a decision not to prosecute will vary from case to case, but broadly speaking, the graver the offence, the less likelihood there will be that the public interest will allow of a disposal less than prosecution, for example, a caution. Where, however, an offence is not so serious as plainly to require prosecution, the Crown Prosecutor should always apply his mind to the public interest and should strive to ensure that

c the spirit of the Home Office Cautioning Guidelines is observed . . . (iii) *Youth* The stigma of a conviction can cause irreparable harm to the future prospects of a young adult, and careful consideration should be given to the possibility of dealing with him or her by means of a caution . . .
15. It is a long standing statutory requirement that the courts shall have

d regard to the welfare of the juvenile appearing before them, in criminal as in civil proceedings. It is accordingly necessary that in deciding whether or not the public interest requires a prosecution the welfare of the juvenile should be fully considered.
16. There may be positive advantages for the individual and for society, in using prosecution as a last resort and in general there is in the case of

e juvenile offenders a much stronger presumption in favour of methods of disposal which fall short of prosecution unless the seriousness of the offence or other exceptional circumstances dictate otherwise. The objective should be to divert juveniles from court wherever possible. Prosecution should always be regarded as a severe step.
17. The Home Office has issued guidelines to the police on cautioning

f juvenile offenders and on related decision making. Where the police are unable to make an immediate decision to caution, the guidelines suggest that there may be advantages in their seeking the advice and views of other interested agencies, such as the Social Services Department, the Probation Service and the Education Welfare Service, on whether to caution or institute

g proceedings. Where the Crown Prosecutor decides that the public interest does not require the institution or continuation of proceedings against a juvenile and it appears that there has been no prior consultation, the Crown Prosecutor should consider whether to ask the police to bring the circumstances of the individual's involvement to the attention of the appropriate agency. Crown Prosecutors should be aware of the general

h arrangements and procedures for inter-agency consultation in their areas and are encouraged to contribute their experience to the development and improvement of such arrangements. Crown Prosecutors must satisfy themselves that the spirit of the Cautioning Guidelines has been applied before continuing a prosecution instituted by the police against a juvenile. The Crown Prosecutor should, taking account of the views of all the agencies

j concerned of which he is aware and having regard to the Cautioning Guidelines, refer back to the police any case where he considers that a lesser disposal, eg a caution, would be an adequate response and, in the final analysis, will not hesitate to exercise his power to discontinue proceedings where he is satisfied that a prosecution is not required in the public interest. When considering whether or not to continue proceedings, the Crown

Prosecutor should have regard to the circumstances of any previous cautions
the juvenile may have been given by the police. Where these are such as to   *a*
indicate that a less formal disposal in respect of the present offence would
prove inadequate, a prosecution will be appropriate.'

In the case of L it can fairly and properly be said that, the question of seriousness
apart, all the criteria for cautioning had been fulfilled. He had admitted his guilt,
he had written a letter of apology to the victim, his parents had consented to the   *b*
caution, the victim's parents were agreeable to that course and L had, to some
extent at least, been disciplined by his parents in the home. The choice in his case
lay between the administration of the caution, on the one hand, and prosecution,
on the other. B's case is different. The administration of the caution was not an
option for her because she had not admitted her guilt. The stark question was,
therefore, whether to prosecute her or not. I think, as said previously, it is clear   *c*
from the evidence we have that had B admitted the offence she would undoubtedly
have been dealt with by way of caution.

Most of the submissions to us were forceful and detailed, not unexpectedly, for
these applications raise unique considerations. They were concerned with the
question, common to both, of whether the decision of the police to prosecute, as
opposed to administering a caution, and that of the CPS to refuse to discontinue   *d*
the prosecution are subject to judicial review.

Mr Collins QC for the CPS submitted that, since the CPS ultimately decides
whether a prosecution should continue, then if any decision to prosecute, or not,
is judicially reviewable it is the decision of the CPS and not any prior decision of
the police.   *e*

He pointed to s 3 of the 1985 Act, which, so far as relevant, states:

'(1) The Director shall discharge his functions under this or any other
enactment under the superintendence of the Attorney General.
(2) It shall be the duty of the Director . . . (*a*) to take over the conduct of
all criminal proceedings, other than specified proceedings, instituted on
behalf of a police force (whether by a member of that force or by any other   *f*
person) . . .'

He also pointed to para 10 of the code, which states:

'The use by the Crown Prosecutor of his power to terminate proceedings
whether by using the procedure under Section 23 of the Prosecution of
Offences Act 1985 or the continuing power to withdraw or offer no evidence,   *g*
is in many ways the most visible demonstration of the Service's fundamental
commitment towards ensuring that only fit and proper cases are taken to
trial. Unless, of course, advice has been given at a preliminary stage, the
police decision to institute proceedings should never be met with passive
acquiescence but must always be the subject of review. Furthermore, the   *h*
discretion to discontinue is a continuing one, and even when proceedings are
under way Crown Prosecutors should continue to exercise their reviewing
function. There may be occasions when time and other practical constraints
limit the depth of the initial review of the case. It is important that cases
should be kept under continuous review, not least because the emergence of
new evidence or information hitherto unknown to the Crown Prosecutor   *j*
may sometimes cast doubt on the propriety of the initial decision to proceed.
Crown Prosecutors must be resolute when made aware of evidence or
information of this nature and should not hesitate to bring proceedings to an
end in appropriate cases. Public confidence in the Service can only be

maintained if there is no doubting its commitment to taking effective action at whatever stage whenever it is right to do so. Prosecutions instituted in circumstances apparently falling outside the spirit of the Home Office Cautioning Guidelines should be queried with the police and may be discontinued where the Crown Prosecutor is satisfied that proceedings would not be in the public interest. It will be the normal practice to consult the police whenever it is proposed to discontinue proceedings instituted by them. The level of consultation will depend on the particular circumstances of the case of the accused, but the final decision will rest with the Crown Prosecutor.'

Section 23 of the 1985 Act also requires, I think, to be noted. So far as relevant, it states:

'(1) Where the Director of Public Prosecutions has the conduct of proceedings for an offence, this section applies in relation to the preliminary stages of those proceedings . . .
(3) Where, at any time during the preliminary stages of the proceedings, the Director gives notice under this section to the clerk of the court that he does not want the proceedings to continue, they shall be discontinued with effect from the giving of that notice but may be reviewed by notice given by the accused under subsection (7) below . . .'

Mr McCarthy for the chief constable supported Mr Collins's contention, saying, inter alia, that the CPS have the power and duty to correct police errors. Any challenge, he said, after the prosecution has been taken over by the CPS should be directed to them because the police will then have no control whatsoever over the prosecution.

Mr Temple for the Commissioner of Police of the Metropolis gave like support. He contended that the police in the form of the YACS are, in a sense, a form of filter, a preliminary decision-maker, whose decision is reassessed and not necessarily adopted by the CPS.

The stance adopted by both Mr Rhodes and Mr Cocks on this point appeared to be that the CPS and the police were, in principle, equally vulnerable to judicial review and the decisions of both of them were, on review, subject to identical tests.

The point has not previously arisen for determination. That probably is because the CPS are comparatively new to the prosecution process. They have unquestionably the sole power to decide whether a prosecution should proceed. They are entirely dominant in that very important respect and all the erstwhile corresponding power of the police has been stripped away. The CPS are the prosecutor and the police are the initiators of criminal proceedings which may, or may not, dependent upon the decision of the CPS, be disposed of by the courts. The power of the CPS includes that of referring a case back to the police for a caution to be substituted for the continuance of proceedings.

I have come to the conclusion that if judicial review lies in relation to current criminal proceedings, in contrast to a failure to take any action against a person suspected of a criminal offence, it lies against the body which has the last and decisive word, the CPS.

A refusal to prosecute or even possibly to caution by the police is another matter. In that event the police may be vulnerable to judicial review, but only upon a basis which, as the cases show, is rather severely circumscribed.

The extent of that basis appears in the well-known judgments of Lord Denning MR, Salmon and Edmund Davies LJJ in *R v Metropolitan Police Comr, ex p Blackburn*

[1968] 1 All ER 763, [1968] 2 QB 118. In a later case, *R v Metropolitan Police Comr, ex p Blackburn (No 3)* [1973] 1 All ER 324 at 331, [1973] QB 241 at 254, Lord   a
Denning MR, referring to a failure to enforce the law, stated: '... the police have
a discretion with which the courts will not interfere. There might, however, be
extreme cases in which he [the commissioner] was not carrying out his duty. And
then we would.'

In *R v General Council of the Bar, ex p Percival* [1990] 3 All ER 137 at 152, [1991]   b
1 QB 212 at 234, in giving the judgment of the court, I stated, having quoted
from, inter alia, *Ex p Blackburn* [1968] 1 All ER 763, [1968] 2 QB 118:

> 'Reference was also made by counsel ... to a passage in *de Smith's Judicial
> Review of Administrative Action* (4th edn, 1980) pp 549–550, to the effect that
> the discretion of a prosecuting authority though broad is not unreviewable.
> In our view such discretion is plainly reviewable but the question is whether   c
> the limits of review should be as strict as those contended for by the Bar
> Council. Much will depend, we think, on the powers of the body subject to
> review, the procedures which it is required to follow and on the way in
> which a particular proceeding has been conducted; there is potentially an
> almost infinite variety of circumstances. We do not think it right that strictly   d
> defined limits should be set to the judicial review of a body which can
> broadly be described as a prosecuting authority. Each case must be considered
> with due regard to the powers, functions and procedures of the body
> concerned and the manner in which it has dealt (or not dealt) with the
> particular complaint or application.'

That was obviously not intended to indicate a lesser limitation for judicial   e
review of the police than appears in *Ex p Blackburn*. The statement relates to other
bodies with very different responsibilities and discretions to which perhaps a less
rigorous approach to judicial review might apply.

In the present cases it is not inaction by the police which is complained of but
the positive action of charging the two applicants and thus commencing criminal   f
proceedings instead of in L's case cautioning him and in the case of B taking no
action against her whatsoever, as well, of course, as the failure of the CPS to
discontinue proceedings in both cases.

It seems to me that a decision to discontinue proceedings by the CPS can be
equated with a decision by the police not to prosecute and is, therefore, open to
judicial review only upon the restricted basis available to someone, assuming he   g
has locus standi, seeking to challenge a decision by the police. Accordingly, that
situation does not require further to be addressed in this judgment.

That which calls essentially for decision here is whether, in respect of juveniles,
the CPS are open to challenge when deciding (1) to refrain from discontinuing
proceedings in a situation where the criteria for cautioning can be said, with one
possible exception, namely the seriousness of the offence, to have been met and   h
(2) although cautioning is not an option, there has been in respect of a very young
child an insufficiency of consideration of relevant circumstances before
commencement of the proceedings by the police which is perpetuated in the
decision by the CPS to continue those proceedings.

Mr Collins submitted that there is no circumstance in which the CPS decision   j
to continue proceedings can be impugned in this court. If a decision to prosecute
is wrongfully made the criminal court has, he said, ample powers, if abuse of its
process is thereby occasioned, to refuse to deal with the proceedings. Otherwise,
he said, an acquittal or the imposition of a nominal fine may be its response to an
unmeritorious prosecution.

Mr McCarthy (though Mr Rhodes contended he appeared to be arguing
a somewhat to the contrary in his skeleton argument) submitted to us that there is
no judicial review of a decision to prosecute in an individual case. He quoted the
words of Viscount Dilhorne in *Gouriet v Union of Post Office Workers* [1977] 3 All
ER 70 at 88, [1978] AC 435 at 487:

'The Attorney-General has many powers and duties. He may stop any
b prosecution on indictment by entering a nolle prosequi. He merely has to
sign a piece of paper saying that he does not wish the prosecution to continue.
He need not give any reasons. He can direct the institution of a prosecution
and direct the Director of Public Prosecutions to take over the conduct of any
criminal proceedings and he may tell him to offer no evidence. In the
exercise of these powers he is not subject to direction by his ministerial
c colleagues or to the control and supervision of the courts.'

If a challenge of any kind can be made, Mr McCarthy further submitted, it is
severely limited and for that he relied upon, inter alia, *Ex p Blackburn* [1968] 1 All
ER 763, [1968] 2 QB 118, *Ex p Blackburn (No 3)* [1973] 1 All ER 324, [1973] QB
241, *Hill v Chief Constable of West Yorkshire* [1988] 2 All ER 238 at 240–241, [1989]
d 1 AC 53 at 59, *Raymond v A-G* [1982] 2 All ER 487 at 491, [1982] QB 839 at 847
and *R v General Council of the Bar, ex p Percival* [1990] 3 All ER 137 at 147, 152,
[1991] 1 QB 212 at 228, 234.

Mr Temple suggested that a challenge to a decision to prosecute could be
mounted but possibly only where it could be demonstrated that, for example,
Home Office guidelines had been ignored or an unreasonable policy had been
e adopted to the effect that all alleged burglars would be prosecuted or the prosecutor
had behaved fraudulently.

The arguments presented by Mr Rhodes and Mr Cocks are founded on the
following propositions.

(1) The exercise by the chief constable and the commissioner of his
administrative discretion is reviewable: see *Holgate-Mohammed v Duke* [1984] 1 All
f ER 1054 at 1057, [1984] AC 437 at 443, which is to be preferred to Lord Denning
MR's obiter comments in *Ex p Blackburn* [1968] 1 All ER 763 at 769, [1968] 2 QB
118 at 126 and *Hallett v A-G* [1989] 2 NZLR 87.

(2) Support is to be found in *Ex p Percival* and *Ex p Blackburn* for the contention
that judicial review lies against a prosecuting authority of a decision to prosecute.

g (3) Although to enable every person prosecuted to delay his trial by seeking
judicial review of the decision to prosecute could pose serious administrative
problems, such applications could be contained by the filtering process of
obtaining leave and the penalty of costs for the unsuccessful: *R v Panel on Take-
overs and Mergers, ex p Datafin plc (Norton Opax plc intervening)* [1987] 1 All ER
564 at 578, [1987] QB 815 at 840.

h (4) A lower court's power to stop the proceedings because of an abuse of process
is an inadequate remedy because it is not available in a case where a defendant
intends to plead guilty: *R v Derby Crown Court, ex p Brooks* (1984) 80 Cr App R
164.

(5) A Crown Prosecutor has to exercise executive discretion under statute in
deciding whether a prosecution which has been taken over should be discontinued.
j The code which he has to follow fairly closely resembles the Attorney General's
guidelines, *Criteria for Prosecution*[1], which were promulgated in February 1983.

(6) The executive discretion exercised by a Crown Prosecutor in continuing or

---

1   The relevant criteria are now contained in the *Guide for Crown Prosecutors* issued under s 10 of the
Prosecution of Offences Act 1985

discontinuing a prosecution is one which is reviewable by the court if exercised in bad faith or based on the wrong principle: *Raymond v A-G* [1982] 2 All ER 487, *a* [1982] QB 839, *Turner v DPP* (1978) 68 Cr App R 70 at 77, *Riches v DPP* [1973] 2 All ER 935 at 941, [1973] 1 WLR 1019 at 1026 and *R v Telford Justices, ex p Badhan* [1991] 2 All ER 854 at 863, [1991] 2 QB 78 at 90, where the statement that the decision to commence criminal proceedings is not reviewable is not a considered statement of the law and is obiter (I was a party to that judgment and I am obliged, I think, to agree with that contention).   *b*

(7) It has for many years been the policy of the Director of Public Prosecutions that he should not prosecute in every case where there was sufficient evidence but 'wherever it appears that the offence or the circumstances of its commisison is or are of such a character that a prosecution in respect thereof is required in the public interest' (see 483 HC Official Report (5th series) col 681, where Lord *c* Shawcross when Attorney General quoted from the first regulations under which the Director of Public Prosecutions worked, which quotation is set out in the guidelines issued by the Attorney General, *Criteria for Prosecution*. That statement is specially apt in the case of a juvenile.

I have come to the conclusion that, in respect of juveniles, the discretion of the CPS to continue or to discontinue criminal proceedings is reviewable by this court *d* but only where it can be demonstrated that the decision was made regardless of or clearly contrary to a settled policy of the Director of Public Prosecutions evolved in the public interest, for example the policy of cautioning juveniles, a policy which the CPS are bound to apply, where appropriate, to the exercise of their discretion to continue or discontinue criminal proceedings. But I envisage that it will be only rarely that a defendant could succeed in showing that a *e* decision was fatally flawed in such a manner as that.

The policy of cautioning, instead of prosecuting, has for some time now been well settled and plays a prominent part in the process of decision-making both by the police and by the CPS when consideration has properly to be given to whether, in any individual case, there should be (a) no action taken or (b) a caution delivered *f* or (c) a prosecution and thereafter (d) a continuance or discontinuance of criminal proceedings.

That policy applied, obviously, to the case of L. It did not apply to the case of B because cautioning was not for her an option. The policy, which can, I think, rightly be so called, which is applicable to her is another. It is that which is far more generally expressed, that is to say that a prosecution should not occur unless *g* it is required in the public interest, regard being given to the stigma of a conviction which can cause irreparable harm to the future prospects of a young person and to his previous character, parental attitude and the likelihood of the offence being repeated: see the Attorney General's 1983 guidelines.

I find it very difficult to envisage, with regard to that policy, a circumstance, fraud or dishonesty apart possibly, which would allow of a challenge to a decision *h* to prosecute or to continue proceedings unless it could be demonstrated, in the case of a juvenile, that there had been either a total disregard of the policy or, contrary to it, a lack of inquiry into the circumstances and background of that person, previous offences and general character and so on, by the prosecutor and later by the CPS. But here too I envisage the possibility of showing that such disregard had happened as unlikely. Therefore, although the CPS decision may *j* in principle be reviewed, in practice it is rarely likely to be successfully reviewed.

I have confined my views as to the availability of judicial review of a CPS decision not to discontinue a prosecution to the position of juveniles because, of course, the present cases involve only juveniles. My view as to the position of

adults, on the other hand, in this respect is that judicial review of a decision not
a to discontinue a prosecution is unlikely to be available. The danger of opening
too wide the door of review of the discretion to continue a prosecution is manifest
and such review, if it exists, must, therefore, be confined to very narrow limits.
Juveniles and the policy with regard to them are, in my view, in a special position.

The arguments of both Mr Rhodes and Mr Cocks as to the merits, on the facts,
of their applicants' cases were extensively deployed. Without, I hope, seeming to
b denigrate the force of them I believe the response to them can be brief.

I preface what follows with the observation that it is not suggested that the
procedures for inquiring into the circumstances of juveniles are inadequate in
any way.

I grant that L could be said to be the victim of what might be thought to be a
stern decision. All the criteria, save for the seriousness of the offence, are on his
c side. However, the senior police officer who dealt with him felt that the
circumstances of the offence warranted prosecution, the satisfactory criteria
notwithstanding. That was a view which the CPS, as the affidavits show, felt able
to share after a conversation with an even more senior police officer involved.

It may be that some other police officer would have taken the opposite view,
d but he who took the decision was very experienced in juvenile cases and advised
cautions in about 98% of them. I feel unable to say that, although there may be
room for two views about the seriousness of the offence with which L is charged,
the decision to continue the proceedings was in any way flawed. It was a proper
exercise of discretion.

For those reasons I would dismiss L's application.

e B's application is basically founded on, I suspect, sympathy as much as the
alleged failure by the YACS to investigate circumstances adequately and likewise
the CPS to ensure that that had been done. I do not think upon the affidavit
evidence that it has come anywhere near being demonstrated that the CPS fell
below the standard of care and inquiry to be expected in the circumstances, nor
before the matter was referred to the CPS did the police. The prosecution evidence
f continues to be challenged and it reveals, if it were true, quite a determined and
blatantly executed offence. I detect nothing to alert me to suppose that the CPS
did not consider the public interest and all other matters which had to be borne
in mind in deciding whether a 12-year-old girl should appear before the juvenile
court. I would dismiss her application too.

French J, who is not able to be here, agrees with my judgment.
g Finally I make a restriction order under s 39 of the Children and Young Persons
Act 1933. That affects of course the publication of the names of the juveniles.

Applications dismissed.

Kate O'Hanlon   Barrister.

R v Inland Revenue Commissioners, ex parte *a* Mead and another

QUEEN'S BENCH DIVISION
STUART-SMITH LJ AND POPPLEWELL J
9, 10, 11, 20 MARCH 1992

b

Judicial review – Availability of remedy – Decision to prosecute – Offence in connection with tax evasion – Commissioners' policy of selective prosecution – Commissioners deciding to prosecute applicants but not other taxpayers alleged to be guilty of similar offences – Whether decision amenable to judicial review – Whether availability of alternative remedies precluding application for judicial review – Whether decision unlawful and *c* *ultra vires.*

In November 1990, following an investigation of the tax affairs of S, who had acted as the accountant to the applicants and other taxpayers, the Commissioners of Inland Revenue, who operated a policy of selective prosecution, ordered the prosecution of the applicants for criminal offences in connection with tax evasion, *d* and in March 1991 summonses were served on them. Criminal charges were brought against S relating to the affairs of several taxpayers, including the applicants, but it was decided not to prosecute any of the other taxpayers although it was clear that they were alleged to have been knowingly involved in, and to have benefited from, significant and protracted dishonesty towards the Revenue. The applicants sought judicial review of the Revenue's decision to prosecute them. *e* Although they did not challenge the lawfulness of the Revenue's selective prosecution policy, they contended (i) that a comparison of their cases should have been made with those of the other taxpayers and only if there were distinguishing features which made the applicants' cases more serious was the decision to prosecute them justified and (ii) that, in the absence of such a *f* comparative exercise, the decision to prosecute them was unfair and involved an inconsistent treatment of taxpayers, and was accordingly unlawful and ultra vires. The Revenue contended (i) that a decision to prosecute an adult in the courts taken by the relevant prosecuting authority was not amenable to judicial review since there was adequate protection in the inherent powers of the criminal court to dismiss a prosecution for abuse of process or alternatively (ii) that if there was *g* such a jurisdiction the decision to prosecute the applicants was not reviewable.

Held – (1) (Per Stuart-Smith LJ, Popplewell J contra) As a matter of principle, a decision to prosecute an adult in the courts by a prosecuting authority was in theory susceptible to judicial review, although the circumstances in which such jurisdiction could be successfully invoked would be rare in the extreme. *h* Furthermore, the fact that there were alternative remedies in the magistrates' courts or the Crown Court in respect of some matters, ie abuse of process or inadequate evidence to justify trial or conviction, did not prevent direct access to the High Court if those remedies did not cover the whole ambit of the jurisdiction in judicial review. Accordingly, the decision by the Revenue to prosecute the applicants was amenable to judicial review (see p 782 *d e j* to p 783 *b*, post); *R v* *j* *Metropolitan Police Comr, ex p Blackburn* [1968] 1 All ER 763, *Selvarajan v Race Relations Board* [1976] 1 All ER 12, *R v General Council of the Bar, ex p Percival* [1990] 3 All ER 137 and *R v Chief Constable of the Kent County Constabulary, ex p L (a minor)* [1993] 1 All ER 756 considered.

a (2) (Per Stuart-Smith LJ, Popplewell J contra) Although it was a principle of public law that an authority charged with the duty of exercising its discretion had to do so fairly and consistently, each case had to be considered in the light of its own facts to see whether the conduct of which complaint was made was unfair or inconsistent. Although it might be inherent in the Revenue's selective prosecution policy that there might be inconsistency and unfairness between one dishonest taxpayer and another who was guilty of a very similar offence, any requirement

b that all dishonest taxpayers guilty of similar offences should be treated in like manner would be both inconsistent with the policy of selectivity and impracticable. The requirement of fairness and consistency in the light of the Revenue's policy of selective prosecution was that each case had to be considered on its merits fairly and dispassionately to see whether the criterion for prosecution was satisfied. The

c decision to prosecute had then to be taken in good faith for the purpose of fulfilling the Revenue's objective of collecting taxes and not some ulterior, extraneous or improper purpose. Since the applicants did not dispute that their cases had been so considered and since they did not challenge the lawfulness of the Revenue's selective prosecution policy, the application would (Popplewell J concurring on the ground that the court had no jurisdiction to hear the

d application) be dismissed (see p 777 *e*, p 783 *c* to *g*, p 784 *b* to *e* and p 785 *f*, post); *HTV Ltd v Price Commission* [1976] ICR 170, *IRC v National Federation of Self-Employed and Small Businesses Ltd* [1981] 2 All ER 93 and *Preston v IRC* [1985] 2 All ER 327 considered.

Notes

e For the institution of criminal proceedings generally, see 11(1) *Halsbury's Laws* (4th edn) para 646.

For proceedings for criminal offences relating to tax, see 23 *Halsbury's Laws* (4th edn reissue) paras 1735–1737.

Cases referred to in judgments

f *DPP v Humphrys* [1976] 2 All ER 497, [1977] AC 1, [1976] 2 WLR 857, HL.
Hallett v A-G [1989] 2 NZLR 87, NZ HC.
Holgate-Mohammed v Duke [1984] 1 All ER 1054, [1984] AC 437, [1984] 2 WLR 660, HL.
HTV Ltd v Price Commission [1976] ICR 170, CA.
IRC v National Federation of Self-Employed and Small Businesses Ltd [1981] 2 All ER 93, [1982] AC 617, [1981] 2 WLR 722, HL.

g *Preston v IRC* [1985] 2 All ER 327, [1985] AC 835, [1985] 2 WLR 836, HL.
R v Chief Constable of the Kent County Constabulary, ex p L (a minor) [1993] 1 All ER 756, DC.
R v Crown Court at Derby, ex p Brooks (1984) 80 Cr App R 164, DC.
R v Crown Court at Norwich, ex p Belsham [1992] 1 All ER 394, [1992] 1 WLR 54,

h DC.
R v General Council of the Bar, ex p Percival [1990] 3 All ER 137, [1991] 1 QB 212, [1990] 3 WLR 323, DC.
R v Metropolitan Police Comr, ex p Blackburn [1968] 1 All ER 763, [1968] 2 QB 118, [1968] 2 WLR 893, CA.
R v Oxford City Justices, ex p Smith (1982) 75 Cr App R 200, DC.

j *R v Panel on Take-overs and Mergers, ex p Datafin plc (Norton Opax plc intervening)* [1987] 1 All ER 564, [1987] QB 815, [1987] 2 WLR 699, CA.
R v Telford Justices, ex p Badhan [1991] 2 All ER 854, [1991] 2 QB 78, [1991] 2 WLR 866, DC.
Raymond v A-G [1982] 2 All ER 487, [1982] QB 839, [1982] 2 WLR 849, CA.

Riches v DPP [1973] 2 All ER 935, [1973] 1 WLR 1019, CA.
Selvarajan v Race Relations Board [1976] 1 All ER 12, [1975] 1 WLR 1686, CA.   *a*
Turner v DPP (1978) 68 Cr App R 70.

Cases also cited
A-G of Hong Kong v Ng Yuen Shiu [1983] 2 All ER 346, [1983] 2 AC 629, PC.
Connelly v DPP [1964] 2 All ER 401, [1964] AC 1254, HL.
Council of Civil Service Unions v Minister for the Civil Service [1984] 3 All ER 935,   *b*
    [1985] AC 374, HL.
Padfield v Minister of Agriculture Fisheries and Food [1968] 1 All ER 694, [1968] AC
    997, HL.
R v Board of Inland Revenue, ex p MFK Underwriting Agencies Ltd [1990] 1 All ER
    91, [1990] 1 WLR 1545, DC.
R v Caird (1970) 54 Cr App R 499, CA.   *c*
R v Central Criminal Court, ex p Randle [1992] 1 All ER 370, [1991] 1 WLR 1087,
    DC.
R v Civil Service Appeal Board, ex p Cunningham [1991] 4 All ER 310, CA.
R v Crown Court at Manchester, ex p Cunningham (1991) Times, 31 October, DC.
R v Gilmore [1992] Crim LR 67, CA.   *d*
R v Lancashire CC, ex p Huddleston [1986] 2 All ER 941, CA.
R v Metropolitan Police Comr, ex p Blackburn (No 3) [1973] 1 All ER 324, [1973] QB
    241, CA.
R v Secretary of State for the Home Dept, ex p Khan [1985] 1 All ER 40, [1984] 1
    WLR 1337, CA.
R v Secretary of State for the Home Dept, ex p Mowla [1992] 1 WLR 70, CA.   *e*
R v Secretary of State for the Home Dept, ex p Ruddock [1987] 2 All ER 518, [1987] 1
    WLR 1482.

Application for judicial review
Arthur Mead and Brian Cook applied, with the leave of Macpherson J given on   *f*
19 June 1991, for judicial review by way of an order of certiorari to quash the
decisions of the Commissioners of Inland Revenue in or about November 1990 to
prosecute them for alleged criminal offences and in or about March 1991 to serve
summonses against them in respect of those alleged criminal offences. The
applicants also sought a declaration that the decisions were ultra vires and
unlawful. The facts are set out in the judgment of Stuart-Smith LJ.   *g*

Michael Beloff QC, Robert Rhodes QC *and* David Pannick *(instructed by* Berwin
    Leighton) *for the applicants.*
Alan Moses QC, Jonathan Fisher *and* Rabinder Singh *(instructed by the* Solicitor of
    Inland Revenue) *for the Crown.*

          h

Cur adv vult

20 March 1992. The following judgments were delivered.

STUART-SMITH LJ.   *j*
Introduction
    This is an application for judicial review of a decision made by the
Commissioners of Inland Revenue in November 1990 to prosecute Arthur Mead
and Brian Cook (the applicants) for criminal offences in connection with tax

evasion and a consequent decision in March 1991 to serve summonses on them.
a The applicants seek an order of certiorari to quash the decisions and a declaration
that they are ultra vires and unlawful. The application is brought pursuant to
leave granted by Macpherson J on 19 June 1991.

The facts

b The charges relate to offences alleged to have been committed between 1981
and 1985 inclusive at a time when the applicants owned and controlled a company
called Protech Instruments and Systems Ltd (Protech). During this period
Geoffrey Charles Scannell, who is now retired, was the professional accountant
advising the applicants and Protech. There are five charges against Mr Mead. Two
of them are joint with Dr Cook and Mr Scannell, two are joint with Mr Scannell
alone. One is against Mr Mead alone. There are also five charges against Dr Cook;
c in addition to the joint charges with Mr Mead, he faces two charges jointly with
Mr Scannell and one in which he alone is charged. The joint charges are much
the most serious. They fall into two groups: those that allege fraudulent extraction
of funds from Protech: the Revenue case is that by means of forged invoices and
false accounting the costs of Protech were exaggerated and the sales were deflated
d thereby diminishing the apparent profits. The money was eventually paid into
an offshore account. The other group relates to the alleged fraudulent provision
of private building work charged to Protech. These charges are said to be specimen
charges. It is possible that the applicants may face a further charge of conspiracy.

According to the Revenue the tax avoided was £272,308 of which some
£158,000 is attributable to Dr Cook and the balance to Mr Mead. The individual
e charges involve in each case sums of about £750. It is very unlikely that if these
stood alone the applicants would face prosecution. Both applicants deny the
charges.

Mr Scannell was a partner in the firm of Messrs Thompson Scannell, chartered
accountants. He is charged with 17 offences, including those involving the
f applicants. They relate to the affairs of six other taxpayers who were his clients;
the offences are alleged to have been committed between 1981 and 1988 inclusive,
and again they are specimen charges. The matters arise out of a long-running
investigation of Mr Scannell's activities and involve a total of some 50 taxpayers
in all and it is still continuing.

None of the other taxpayers, or at least none of the six whose affairs are the
g subject of charges against Mr Scannell, is to be prosecuted, although it is clear that
some are alleged to have been knowingly involved in and to have benefited from
significant and protracted dishonesty towards the Revenue, although it is said
that the amounts of tax avoided is significantly less, the highest amounting to
£65,101; but it is right to say that these figures are disputed by the applicants.
Some, perhaps most, of these other taxpayers are to be called as witnesses against
h Mr Scannell. In most of the other six cases the Revenue have been content to
exact penalties instead of proceeding by way of prosecution. The amount of
penalty can be up to 100% of the tax avoided.

The Revenue's policy in relation to prosecution can conveniently be found set
out in the *Report of the Committee on Enforcement Powers of the Revenue Departments*
(Cmnd 8822) under the chairmanship of Lord Keith of Kinkel, dated March 1983
j (the Keith Report):

'*Departmental views*
22.1.4. The Inland Revenue explained and justified their prosecution
policy to us in the same terms as they had used to the Royal Commission on

Criminal Proceedings. They noted first, that the tax legislation contains (civil) money penalties for many offences, up to and including fraud. As they said: "It clearly envisages that severe money penalties will be the common punishment of the tax evader". They also fully acknowledged "the practical consideration that the burden of preparing a large number of prosecutions to the required standard and of seeing them through the courts would require many more trained and qualified staff". They stressed the importance of prosecution as a deterrent, and that there should be no categories of offence where the weapon was never deployed "because it is the possibility of prosecution which prevents the spread of tax fraud to unacceptable limits". They pointed out that "simple objective criteria such as the amount of tax evaded" might be used to set de minimis limits to exclude the smaller cases, but were unsuited to be the sole basis for decisions to prosecute. While recognising, therefore, the possible pitfalls in selectivity, the Department sought to avoid them by reserving the decision to prosecute to officials at Under Secretary or Deputy Secretary level.

Discussion and conclusions

22.1.5. We had no hesitation in rejecting the extreme alternatives of "prosecute all or none". We found no reason to disturb the settled practice of over fifty years of Inland Revenue taking civil money penalties for the overwhelming majority of detected offences of tax evasion. We regard as justified the Department's view that an ultimate sanction of prosecution is essential to protect the integrity of a tax system which is primarily dependent upon the accuracy of information passed to it by its taxpayers and others. When asked to sign a declaration on a tax return, the taxpayer is faced with the admonitory statement "false statements can result in prosecution". It follows that, if the deterrent is to retain its credibility, prosecution ought to follow in, as the Department put it, "some examples of all classes of tax fraud".'

At paras 22.1.7 and 22.1.8 the committee deal with the 'badges of heinousness' as follows:

'22.1.7. The presence of one of the "badges" of heinousness as viewed by the Department makes a case more likely to be selected for prosecution. Bearing in mind that the presence of intention to deceive is crucial we find it difficult to find anything to object to in the Department's selection as criteria of (b) evidence of collusion between the taxpayer and others; (c) evidence that documents have been forged with intent to deceive the Revenue; or (d) evidence of other irregularities which are denied on challenge. We likewise endorse the Department being more ready to initiate criminal proceedings against individuals who (category (f)) have already enjoyed the benefit of a negotiated settlement following a previous investigation or who, (category (e)) while making a show of cooperation, withhold significant information leading to a materially incomplete disclosure in a current investigation.

22.1.8. The remaining indicia of heinousness are more subjective in that they require the Board to take a view about either the status of the potential offender (category (a)) or about particular exceptional circumstances in relation to the offence itself, for example, the amount of tax at risk in absolute terms or where the nature of the fraud is particularly ingenious (category (g)). This amounts to selecting a case for prosecution for exemplary purposes, both as a warning to others who might be minded to do likewise and as a *a* reminder to the general public that the "big" offender in any sense cannot escape the public disgrace of a criminal trial.'

Mr Roberts is an under secretary in the Inland Revenue and director of the compliance and collection division of the Board of Inland Revenue. It was he who authorised the prosecution of the applicants. Before doing so he considered reports by the Revenue investigators and their group leader together with a
b covering report by a principal inspector of taxes and the assistant director of the compliance and collection division. These reports indicated that the type of offences to which I have referred were committed by the applicants, that they were well aware of the nature of the frauds and had taken an active and extensive role in the perpetration of them. He did not accept that the offences against them as individuals could properly be described as venial. In his affidavit he says:

c
'I was aware, before making the order to prosecute, that other clients of Mr Scannell who had participated in schemes of tax evasion on Mr Scannell's advice were not being recommended to me for consideration for prosecution. I took the view, however, that the fact that these other clients were not being proposed for prosecution was not a reason why I should not order that
d criminal proceedings be taken against Mr Scannell, Dr Cook and Mr Mead.'

Mr Roberts therefore makes it clear that he considered the cases of the applicants on their own merits and not in comparison with those of others.

The nature of the challenge
e The applicants do not challenge the lawfulness of the Revenue's policy of selective prosecution as set out in the Keith Report. What is complained of is the application of the policy in the case of the applicants. Mr Beloff QC for the applicants submits that Mr Roberts, or someone else in the Revenue, should have compared their cases with that of the other six taxpayers, or the other 48 or
f however many there are who were engaged in similar frauds and were clients of Mr Scannell and only if there were distinguishing features which made their cases more serious than the others is the decision to prosecute them justified. In the absence of this comparative exercise and in the light of the evidence which suggests that other clients of Mr Scannell had been engaged in similar schemes, can the decision to prosecute be lawful? He submits that the decision is unfair
g and involves inconsistent treatment of taxpayers and is unlawful and ultra vires the powers of the Revenue for that reason. He sought at one time to rely on a document called the 'Taxpayer's Charter', which is apparently a publication put out by the Revenue which contains the statement: 'You will be treated in the same way as other taxpayers in similar circumstances.'

For my part I do not think the document is concerned with the Revenue's
h policy on prosecution; but in any event Mr Beloff accepted that it added nothing to his case. Mr Beloff also submitted that the applicants had a legitimate expectation that they would be treated equally with other taxpayers, that is to say allegedly fraudulent taxpayers, and this expectation was not fulfilled unless the comparative exercise, to which I have referred, was conducted and established the
j necessary distinguishing features between their cases and that of others of Mr Scannell's clients.

The Revenue's response
Mr Moses QC for the Crown submits that a decision to prosecute an adult in the courts taken by the relevant prosecuting authority is not amenable to judicial

review; alternatively, if there is jurisdiction to entertain such an application, this decision is not reviewable.

Is the decision to prosecute an adult in the courts taken by the relevant prosecuting authority judicially reviewable?

I pose the question in that way because: (i) a decision *not* to prosecute is reviewable (see *R v Metropolitan Police Comr, ex p Blackburn* [1968] 1 All ER 763, [1968] 2 QB 118); (ii) a decision by the Crown Prosecution Service to prosecute a juvenile is reviewable (see *R v Chief Constable of the Kent County Constabulary, ex p L (a minor)* [1993] 1 All ER 756); (iii) it may be that there is a distinction between a prosecution before a domestic or professional tribunal and a prosecution in the courts.

There is no authority directly in point, though there are expressions of opinion by judges in this court in recent cases. Mr Beloff submits that as a matter of principle such a decision, being an exercise of executive or administrative discretion by a person acting pursuant to a public duty, whether empowered by statute, statutory instrument or the prerogative, is subject to the supervisory procedures of the court (see *R v Panel on Take-overs and Mergers, ex p Datafin plc (Norton Opax plc intervening)* [1987] 1 All ER 564 esp at 575–577, [1987] QB 815 esp at 836–838 per Lord Donaldson MR).

The Board of Inland Revenue is the creature of statute, its function being to collect and cause to be collected every part of inland revenue (see the Inland Revenue Regulation Act 1890, ss 1 and 13, and the Taxes Management Act 1970, s 1). There is no express statutory power to prosecute; but it is common ground that the Revenue have such power in aid of their overall function.

In *R v Metropolitan Police Comr, ex p Blackburn* [1968] 1 All ER 763, [1968] 2 QB 118 the court appears to have drawn a distinction between matters of policy in relation to prosecution, which is reviewable, and the exercise of discretion in each individual case, which is not. Lord Denning MR said ([1968] 1 All ER 763 at 769, [1968] 2 QB 118 at 136):

'Although the chief officers of police are answerable to the law, there are many fields in which they have a discretion with which the law will not interfere. For instance, it is for the Commissioner of Police, or the chief constable, as the case may be, to decide in any particular case whether enquiries should be pursued, or whether an arrest should be made, or a prosecution brought. It must be for him to decide on the disposition of his force and the concentration of his resources on any particular crime or area. No court can or should give him direction on such a matter. He can also make policy decisions and give effect to them, as, for instance, was often done when prosecutions were not brought for attempted suicide; but there are some policy decisions with which, I think, the courts in a case can, if necessary, interfere. Suppose a chief constable were to issue a directive to his men that no person should be prosecuted for stealing any goods less than £100 in value. I should have thought that the court could countermand it. He would be failing in his duty to enforce the law.'

And Salmon LJ said ([1968] 1 All ER 763 at 771, [1968] 2 QB 118 at 138–139):

'In my judgment the police owe the public a clear legal duty to enforce the law—a duty which I have no doubt they recognise and which generally they perform most conscientiously and efficiently. In the extremely unlikely event, however, of the police failing or refusing to carry out their duty, the

court would not be powerless to intervene. For example, if, as is quite
unthinkable, the chief police officer in any district were to issue an instruction
that as a matter of policy the police would take no steps to prosecute any
housebreaker, I have little doubt but that any householder in that district
would be able to obtain an order of mandamus for the instruction to be
withdrawn. Of course, the police have a wide discretion whether or not they
will prosecute in any particular case. In my judgment, however, the action
which I have postulated would be a clear breach of duty. It would be so
improper that it could not amount to an exercise of discretion.'

In *Selvarajan v Race Relations Board* [1976] 1 All ER 12, [1975] 1 WLR 1686
Lawton LJ drew an analogy between the functions of the Race Relations Board
and the Director of Public Prosecutions. He said of the director ([1976] 1 All ER
12 at 21, [1975] 1 WLR 1686 at 1697):

'He receives complaints from public bodies and members of the public; he
can start investigations; and if he is of the opinion that there is sufficient
evidence to justify a prosecution, he can initiate one; but he does not decide
guilt or innocence. As far as I know, the courts have never interfered with
the exercise of the director's discretion; but it does not follow that they could
not do so if he refused or failed to perform his public duties or acted corruptly
or unfairly . . . '

Mr Beloff relies on these last few words.

In *R v General Council of the Bar, ex p Percival* [1990] 3 All ER 137, [1991] 1 QB
212 this court held that a decision by the Bar Council in professional conduct
proceedings to prefer a less serious charge than that which the complainant
maintained should be preferred was reviewable, though the application was
dismissed on the merits. Mr Moses seeks to distinguish that case on two grounds.
First he submits that a decision to prefer a lesser rather than a more serious charge
is akin to a decision not to prosecute, and for reasons to which I shall shortly come
there is a material difference between the two. Second because that is a case of a
domestic or professional tribunal and not a prosecution in the courts. But the
court did not seem to draw any such distinction and considered the question
under the heading 'Is a prosecuting authority's decision whether or not to
prosecute reviewable at all?' (see [1990] 3 All ER 137 at 149–152, [1991] 1 QB 212
at 231–234), Watkins LJ, giving the judgment of the court after reviewing the
authorities including *Ex p Blackburn* and *Selvarajan v Race Relations Board*, said
([1990] 3 All ER 137 at 152, [1991] 1 QB 212 at 234):

'In our view such discretion is plainly reviewable but the question is
whether the limits of review should be as strict as those contended for by the
Bar Council. Much will depend, we think, on the powers of the body subject
to review, the procedures which it is required to follow and on the way in
which a particular proceeding has been conducted; there is potentially an
almost infinite variety of circumstances. We do not think it right that strictly
defined limits should be set to the judicial review of a body which can
broadly be described as a prosecuting authority. Each case must be considered
with due regard to the powers, functions and procedures of the body
concerned and the manner in which it has dealt (or not dealt) with the
particular complaint or application. This complaint should not, we think,
fail because the applicant is unable to demonstrate that it was not dealt with
at all or excluded by the adoption of an illegitimate prior policy. It falls to be
decided, in our view, on the substantive issues of irrationality and/or

procedural irregularity, with due regard to the nature of the discretion
involved.'   a

In *R v Chief Constable of the Kent County Constabulary, ex p L (a minor)* [1993] 1 All
ER 756 this court held that the discretion of the Crown Prosecution Service to
continue or discontinue a prosecution against a juvenile was reviewable but only
where it could be shown that the decision was made regardless of or clearly
contrary to a settled policy of the Director of Public Prosecutions evolved in the   b
public interest such as a policy of cautioning juveniles. The two applications in
that case failed on the merits.

Watkins LJ, after referring to the passage in his judgment in *Ex p Percival*,
which I have quoted above, said (at 788): 'The statement relates to other bodies
with very different responsibilities and discretions to which perhaps a less rigorous
approach to judicial review might apply.'   c

Contrary to Mr Beloff's submissions, I agree with Mr Moses that Watkins LJ is
here saying that it may be easier to obtain judicial review against such a body
rather than the police, who at the time of *Ex p Blackburn* were the prosecuting
authority. Be that as it may, the fact that it is difficult to review the discretion of
a body charged with the duty of prosecuting in the courts does not mean that it is
impossible.   d

In the next passage in his judgment in *Ex p L* Watkins LJ drew a distinction
between the decision not to prosecute or to discontinue a prosecution which was
reviewable on the principles laid down in *Ex p Blackburn* and a decision to
prosecute or continue a prosecution. He then dealt with a submission that is the
foundation of Mr Moses's contention in this case (at 768–769):   e

'Mr Collins [counsel for the CPS] submitted that there is no circumstance
in which the CPS decision to continue proceedings can be impugned in this
court. If a decision to prosecute is wrongfully made the criminal court has,
he said, ample powers, if abuse of its process is thereby occasioned, to refuse
to deal with the proceedings. Otherwise, he said, an acquittal or the   f
imposition of a nominal fine may be its response to an unmeritorious
prosecution.'

And later he said (at 769–770):

'The arguments presented by Mr Rhodes and Mr Cocks [counsel for the
applicants] are founded on the following propositions. (1) The exercise by   g
the chief constable and the commissioner of his administrative discretion is
reviewable: see *Holgate-Mohammed v Duke* [1984] 1 All ER 1054 at 1057,
[1984] AC 437 at 443, which is to be preferred to Lord Denning MR's obiter
comments in *Ex p Blackburn* [1968] 1 All ER 763 at 769, [1968] 2 QB 118 at
126 and *Hallett v A-G* [1989] 2 NZLR 87. (2) Support is to be found in *Ex
p Percival* and *Ex p Blackburn* for the contention that judicial review lies   h
against a prosecuting authority of a decision to prosecute. (3) Although to
enable every person prosecuted to delay his trial by seeking judicial review of
the decision to prosecute could pose serious administrative problems, such
applications could be contained by the filtering process of obtaining leave
and the penalty of costs for the unsuccessful: *R v Panel on Take-overs and
Mergers, ex p Datafin plc (Norton Opax plc intervening)* [1987] 1 All ER 564 at   j
578, [1987] QB 815 at 840. (4) A lower court's power to stop the proceedings
because of an abuse of process is an inadequate remedy because it is not
available in a case where a defendant intends to plead guilty: *R v Derby Crown
Court, ex p Brooks* (1984) 80 Cr App R 164. (5) A Crown Prosecutor has to
exercise executive discretion under statute in deciding whether a prosecution

a   which has been taken over should be discontinued. The code which he has
to follow fairly closely resembles the Attorney General's guidelines, *Criteria
for Prosecution*, which were promulgated in February 1983. (6) The executive
discretion exercised by a Crown Prosecutor in continuing or discontinuing a
prosecution is one which is reviewable by the court if exercised in bad faith
or based on the wrong principle: *Raymond v A-G* [1982] 2 All ER 487, [1982]
QB 839, *Turner v DPP* (1978) 68 Cr App R 70 at 77, *Riches v DPP* [1973] 2 All

b   ER 935 at 941, [1973] 1 WLR 1019 at 1026 and *R v Telford Justices, ex
p Badhan* [1991] 2 All ER 854 at 863, [1991] 2 QB 78 at 90, where the
statement that the decision to commence criminal proceedings is not
reviewable is not a considered statement of the law and is obiter (I was a party
to that judgment and I am obliged, I think, to agree with that contention).

c   (7) It has for many years been the policy of the Director of Public Prosecutions
that he should not prosecute in every case where there was sufficient evidence
but "wherever it appears that the offence or the circumstances of its
commission is or are of such a character that a prosecution in respect thereof
is required in the public interest" (see 483 HC Official Report (5th series) col
681, where Lord Shawcross when Attorney General quoted from the first

d   regulations under which the Director of Public Prosecutions worked, which
quotation is set out in the guidelines issued by the Attorney General, *Criteria
for Prosecution*. That statement is specially apt in the case of a juvenile. I have
come to the conclusion that, in respect of juveniles, the discretion of the CPS
to continue or to discontinue criminal proceedings is reviewable by this court
but only where it can be demonstrated that the decision was made regardless

e   of or clearly contrary to a settled policy of the Director of Public Prosecutions
evolved in the public interest, for example the policy of cautioning juveniles,
a policy which the CPS are bound to apply, where appropriate, to the exercise
of their discretion to continue or discontinue criminal proceedings. But I
envisage that it will be only rarely that a defendant could succeed in showing
that a decision was fatally flawed in such a manner as that.'

f   These are substantially the same arguments that were advanced by Mr Moses
in this case. He does not however submit that *Ex p L* was wrongly decided; he
seeks to distinguish it on the grounds that it related to juveniles and the policy of
Parliament and the prosecuting authorities to keep juveniles out of the criminal
system altogether. This policy would be frustrated once a decision to prosecute

g   was implemented by a court appearance. Watkins LJ undoubtedly considered
that there was or might be a difference between adults and juveniles. After
summarising the policy with regard to juveniles as being that—

'a prosecution should not occur unless it is required in the public interest,
regard being given to the stigma of a conviction which can cause irreparable

h   harm to the future prospects of a young person and to his previous character,
parental attitude and the likelihood of the offence being repeated',

he said (at 770–771):

'I find it very difficult to envisage, with regard to that policy, a circumstance,

j   fraud or dishonesty apart possibly, which would allow of a challenge to a
decision to prosecute or to continue proceedings unless it could be
demonstrated, in the case of a juvenile, that there had been either a total
disregard of the policy or, contrary to it, a lack of inquiry into the
circumstances and background of that person, previous offences and general
character and so on, by the prosecutor and later by the CPS. But here too I

envisage the possibility of showing that such disregard had happened as
unlikely. Therefore, although the CPS decision may in principle be reviewed, *a*
in practice it is rarely likely to be successfully reviewed. I have confined my
views as to the availability of judicial review of a CPS decision not to
discontinue a prosecution to the position of juveniles because, of course, the
present cases involve only juveniles. My view as to the position of adults, on
the other hand, in this respect is that judicial review of a decision not to
discontinue a prosecution is unlikely to be available. The danger of opening *b*
too wide the door of review of the discretion to continue a prosecution is
manifest and such review, if it exists, must, therefore, be confined to very
narrow limits. Juveniles and the policy with regard to them are, in my view,
in a special position.'

It may be that in those last words Watkins LJ had in mind the distinction *c*
Mr Moses seeks to make. And naturally he relies strongly on the expression of
opinion there set out. But in my judgment the distinction is only a reason why it
is even more unlikely in the case of an adult that a successful application for
judicial review could be made. The existence of the policy in relation to juveniles
is at least a yardstick against which a decision could be tested. There is no such *d*
policy in the case of adults. It does not in my judgment affect the principle that a
decision to prosecute by the prosecuting authority is in theory susceptible to
judicial review, albeit the circumstances in which such jurisdiction could be
successfully invoked will be rare in the extreme. Absurd examples, such as a
policy only to prosecute black men or the political opponents of an outgoing
government, which are virtually unthinkable, do however point to the theoretical *e*
existence of the jurisdiction to review. Fraud and corruption are perhaps other
examples where the jurisdiction could be invoked. Mr Moses submitted that a
person who is prosecuted has adequate protection in the inherent powers of the
court, both magistrates' courts and the Crown Court, to protect them from abuse
of process and of course to dismiss it if the evidence is insufficient to make out
the case. So far as abuse of process is concerned, the court's powers are to be *f*
exercised within well-established principles which are strictly limited (see *R v
Crown Court at Norwich, ex p Belsham* [1992] 1 All ER 394, [1992] 1 WLR 54, *R v
Telford Justices, ex p Badhan* [1991] 2 All ER 854, [1991] 2 QB 78 and *R v Crown
Court at Derby, ex p Brooks* (1984) 80 Cr App R 164). He submitted that this court
should not interfere, by permitting direct access to a litigant seeking judicial *g*
review, with the prosecutor's right of access to the courts which have power to
control abuse of process. He relied on *DPP v Humphrys* [1976] 2 All ER 497 esp at
508–510, 527–528, 533–534, [1977] AC 1 esp at 23–25, 46, 53 per Viscount
Dilhorne, Lord Salmon and Lord Edmund-Davies, as showing that a trial judge
has no power to refuse to allow a prosecution to proceed merely because he
considers that as a matter of policy it ought not to have been brought. *h*

Mr Moses also pointed to the inconvenience and delay in the criminal process
which would be occasioned by such application for review being entertained by
this court, a feature which is highlighted in this case because a passage in the
affidavit of Mr Bunker, who is the applicants' tax consultant, indicates that an
application to the magistrates' court to strike out the prosecution on grounds of
prejudice caused by delay is in contemplation. I pause only to say at this stage *j*
that, if Mr Beloff is right and judicial review will lie, then it will also lie on the
grounds of abuse of process, though as a matter of discretion, if that is the only
ground, the court will not entertain it because the litigant has an appropriate
alternative remedy in the magistrates' court or the Crown Court. It would in my
view be an abuse of process to follow these proceedings, if unsuccessful, with an

a application to strike out for abuse of process, a matter which could have been raised in this court.

I see much force in these submissions of Mr Moses. Nevertheless I cannot see why, if this court has jurisdiction to quash an executive discretion on well-recognised principles of judicial review, the fact that there is an alternative remedy in respect of some matters, ie abuse of process and inadequate evidence to justify trial or conviction, should prevent direct access to this court if those *b* remedies do not cover the whole ambit of the jurisdiction in judicial review. If there is a gap the litigant should be able to avail himself of it. The gap is very small in the case of a juvenile; it is even smaller in the case of an adult, but it is not, at least in theory, non-existent.

c *Is the decision to prosecute the applicants unlawful and ultra vires?*

Mr Beloff submits that though the gap may be narrow, the applicants are able to steer their cases through it. It is a principle of public law that an authority charged with the duty of exercising its discretion must do so fairly and consistently. The cases abound with statements to this effect. *HTV Ltd v Price Commission* [1976] ICR 170 at 185–186, 191–192 per Lord Denning MR and per Scarman LJ, *d* approved in *Preston v IRC* [1985] 2 All ER 327 at 339–341, [1985] AC 835 at 864–867 per Lord Templeman and *IRC v National Federation of Self-Employed and Small Businesses Ltd* [1981] 2 All ER 93 at 112, [1982] AC 617 at 651 per Lord Scarman are but a few examples. But all these cases have to be considered in the light of their own facts to see what was considered unfair or inconsistent conduct. The crucial factor in the present case is that the Revenue operate a selective policy of *e* prosecution. They do so for three main reasons: first their primary objective is the collection of revenue and not the punishment of offenders; second they have inadequate resources to prosecute everyone who dishonestly evades payment of taxes; and third and perhaps most importantly they consider it necessary to prosecute in some cases because of the deterrent effect that this has on the general body of taxpayers, since they know that if they behave dishonestly they may be *f* prosecuted. It is inherent in such a policy that there may be inconsistency and unfairness as between one dishonest taxpayer and another who is guilty of a very similar offence. Nevertheless while not challenging the validity of the policy Mr Beloff submits that there must be grafted onto it a requirement to treat all dishonest taxpayers guilty of similar offences in like manner: either all must be *g* prosecuted or none. I reject this submission for two reasons. First it is inconsistent with the policy and cannot be operated consistently with it: you cannot be both selective and treat every case alike. Second it seems to me to be quite impracticable. How are the Revenue to decide what cases are alike? What is to be the basis of the group of cases that has to be considered? Over what period of time are the group to be considered? Are all cases involving forgery to be in one group? Or those *h* involving forgery and false accounting? Are those who make a full disclosure to be in the same group as those who deny that they have acted dishonestly, although the Revenue consider that there is evidence that they have? These questions only have to be posed to demonstrate that it is quite impossible to answer them; and certainly in my judgment Mr Beloff was quite unable to proffer any convincing answer. What he did say was that there is an identifiable group of taxpayers here *j* who were all clients of Mr Scannell. That appears to me to be a wholly adventitious and irrelevant consideration. It does not affect the nature or gravity of the offence; it only arises because in the course of investigation of Mr Scannell's tax affairs the Revenue have uncovered alleged dishonest tax evasion on the part of a number of his clients, he is simply the common source from which the inquiry springs and the information flows.

There may be other dishonest taxpayers who have been advised by dishonest accountants and who have embarked on similar schemes; why should they not *a* be part of the group? Does the group consist only of the six other taxpayers referred to in Mr Bunker's affidavit or the much larger number who are still being investigated and may turn out to have indulged in similar practices?

In my judgment the requirement of fairness and consistency in the light of the Revenue's selective policy of prosecution is that each case is considered on its merits fairly and dispassionately to see whether the criterion for prosecution was *b* satisfied; there is no dispute that the applicants' cases was so considered. The decision to prosecute must then be taken in good faith for the purpose of fulfilling the Revenue's objectives of collecting taxes and not for some ulterior, extraneous or improper purpose, such as the pursuit of some racialist bias, political vendetta or corrupt motive. This again is not in dispute.

The principle that a public body must not frustrate a citizen's legitimate *c* expectation takes the case no further. The only legitimate expectation that a dishonest taxpayer can have is that he may be selected for prosecution in accordance with the Revenue's stated policy, and that in considering whether to do so the decision maker will act fairly in the sense that I have just defined.

Only if that policy could be attacked on grounds of irrationality could the *d* applicants succeed. They do not attempt to do so. It was a policy that was approved by the Keith Committee and it seems to me, for the three reasons that I have given earlier, not only a rational policy but very probably the only workable policy.

For these reasons, in my judgment, this application must be dismissed.

e

POPPLEWELL J. I agree that this application should be dismissed. I only add some words of my own because I have even greater doubts than Stuart-Smith LJ whether we have jurisdiction in this case.

The relevant decisions have already been referred to. For my part I can envisage no situation in practice which could give rise to a remedy by way of judicial *f* review which could not equally be treated by the courts as an abuse of its process. To my mind there is an essential difference in a situation where for instance it is decided as a matter of policy not to prosecute a white man because of his colour but as a matter of policy to prosecute a black man because of his colour. Although they may well be mirror images of the same situation the only way to challenge a failure to prosecute is by judicial review. However once the decision to prosecute *g* is taken, the criminal courts are seised with jurisdiction. All the examples which Mr Beloff QC for the applicants posed seemed to me to be examples of abuse of process.

The decisions governing this particular problem leave the matter very much at large. Stuart-Smith LJ has already referred to what Watkins LJ said in *R v Chief Constable of the Kent County Constabulary, ex p L (a minor)* [1993] 1 All ER 756 esp *h* at 769 where he qualified what was said by the court in *R v Telford Justices, ex p Badhan* [1991] 2 All ER 854, [1991] 2 QB 78. It is clear however that Watkins LJ did contemplate a distinction between the prosecution of adults and juveniles— the latter being the subject of the decision in *Ex p L*. He said (at 771): 'Juveniles and the policy with regard to them are, in my view, in a special position.'

In *Badhan*'s case a three-man Divisional Court consisting of Watkins, Mann LJJ *i* and Otton J decided that in a justices' inquiry into a rape case which was 16 years old they had power to refuse to undertake that inquiry on the ground that to do so would be an abuse. Mann LJ gave the judgment of the court and said ([1991] 2 All ER 854 at 862–863, [1991] 2 QB 78 at 90):

'We emphasise that the power which the justices have is one to prevent an
abuse of process. They have no power to refuse to embark on an inquiry
because they think that a prosecution should not have been brought because
it is, for example, mean-minded, petty or animated by personal hostility. It
is for this reason that the powers of the justices are said to be "very strictly
confined" (see *R v Oxford City Justices, ex p Smith* (1982) 75 Cr App R 200 at
204 per Lord Lane CJ). That being said, there is here a point of constitutional
importance. It is the duty of any court, be that court superior or inferior, to
protect its process from abuse. We believe that the number of cases in which
examining justices are called upon to perform that duty is, and will remain,
small. That it should remain small will be the result of a responsible exercise
by prosecuting authorities of their powers to initiate proceedings. *An exercise
of those powers is not reviewable here.*' (My emphasis.)

For my part I would have been happy to accept and adopt what Mann LJ there
said.

I would also like to add that while it is true that judicial review is a remedy
which is calculated to be adaptable and broad in its concept (see Lord Donaldson
MR in *R v Panel on Take-overs and Mergers, ex p Datafin plc (Norton Opax plc
intervening)* [1987] 1 All ER 564, [1987] QB 815) it has to be observed that attempts
to stifle prosecutions by general allegations of unfairness in one form or another
are now a growth industry. Direct access by way of judicial review is hardly
calculated to stem that flow.

As Stuart-Smith LJ has already pointed out, the suggestion that in the instant
case there should hereafter be some application to the magistrates' court on the
ground of abuse of process due to delay highlights the problems of this sort of
application in a criminal case which ought to be speedily resolved and where an
accused already has more than ample protection from the criminal courts and
from a jury against any perceived unfairness. I would for my part be prepared to
hold that we have no jurisdiction.

In the result, however, I agree with Stuart-Smith LJ that on the facts of this case
the application should be dismissed.

*Application dismissed. The court refused leave to appeal to the House of Lords but
certified, pursuant to s 1(2) of the Administration of Justice Act 1960, that the following
points of law of general public importance were involved in the decision: (1) whether a
decision by the Revenue to prosecute an adult for an alleged criminal offence is susceptible
to judicial review; and (2) if so, whether a decision to prosecute may be successfully
challenged on the ground that the prosecuting authority has not (for reasons set out in the
Divisional Court judgments) compared the position of the proposed defendant with other
alleged offenders.*

*6 July. The Appeal Committee of the House of Lords (Lord Keith of Kinkel, Lord Goff of
Chieveley and Lord Slynn of Hadley) refused leave to appeal.*

Siew Ling Choo   Barrister.

Practice Direction

a

(Chancery 1/93)

CHANCERY DIVISION

Practice – Chancery Division – Ex parte applications to master and consent orders – File to be bespoken from registry – Masters normally to deal only with cases allocated to them – Procedure in emergencies – Minutes of orders to be made by consent.

b

1. It has been the practice for many years for the Chancery masters to be available at 2.15 pm on working days for ex parte applications, to give advice about court procedure and to deal with urgent consent applications and urgent applications for stays of execution and the like.

c

2. Those intending to make such applications have been required to bespeak the file from the registry, 7th Floor, Thomas More Building (telephone: 071-936 7391 or 6146) by not later than 12 noon on the day of the application. In future the file must be bespoken by 4.30 pm on the previous day, except in cases of real emergency.

d

3. In future, and except in cases of real emergency, masters will only deal with ex parte applications relating to cases allocated to them (see Chancery Practice Direction (13)(A) in *The Supreme Court Practice 1993* vol 2, p 210, para 853).

4. Accordingly Chancery Practice Direction (5)(vi) in *The Supreme Court Practice 1993* vol 2, p 194, para 809 will now be replaced by the following:

e

'(vi) Masters are normally available to hear ex parte applications at 2.15 pm on working days. Notice should be given to the masters' clerk in room TM709 or by telephone on 071-936 6146 or 7391 by 4.30 pm on the previous day, except in cases of real emergency when notice may be given at any time.

If the allocated master (as shown in paragraph (13)(A) below) is not available on any particular day, the applicant will be informed and (except in cases of emergency) asked to come when the master is next available. Applications will only be heard by another master in cases of emergency or when the allocated master is on vacation.

f

Minutes of orders to be made by consent, signed by all relevant solicitors or parties, should, except in emergency, be left initially in room TM709 and not with the master.'

g

By direction of the Vice-Chancellor.

J M Dyson
Chief Chancery Master.

12 February 1993

a

Practice Direction

QUEEN'S BENCH DIVISION

Practice – Queen's Bench Division – Lists – Masters' lists – Short notice list – Urgent applications lasting five minutes or less – Conditions for inclusion in list – Form of
b *summons – Fee – Lodging – Indorsement of backsheet – Lodging party to hand original summons to master at hearing – RSC Ord 4, r 8(1), Ord 66.*

1. This practice direction only concerns litigation proceeding before the masters of the Queen's Bench Division.

2. Under this practice direction a new list will be introduced on an experimental
c basis entitled the 'short notice list'. This list will be available from 20 April 1993.

3. The short notice list is intended for applications which are expected to last for no more than five minutes and are fairly to be described as urgent. Applications for 'unless' orders will normally be considered as suitable for inclusion in this list.

4. The short notice list may only be used if EITHER all the following conditions
d are met: (a) all parties concerned in the summons are represented by solicitors and (b) all such solicitors have offices or agents who have been duly instructed in the London postal districts EC, WC, W1 and SW1 and (c) all such solicitors are equipped with facsimile transmission equipment (fax) and their fax numbers appear upon their printed stationery OR all parties to the summons consent to the summons being entered in the short notice list, in which case a certificate of
e such consent must be indorsed upon the backsheet of the document lodged.

5. To enter a summons in the short notice list it should be typed or printed as required by RSC Ord 66 and the appropriate fee paid. Thereafter the document upon which the receipt of the fee is marked should be lodged in room E216 at the Royal Courts of Justice. When issued in accordance with para 7 of this practice direction this document will become the original summons.

f 6. The backsheet of the document lodged in room E216 must be indorsed with the following:

> 'For entry in Short Notice List. We certify that the minimum number of clear days required by the Rules of Court to elapse between the service of this summons and the return day is   [*fill in*] days.'

g In addition the backsheet must show the fax number, the telephone number and reference number of each party to the summons and the name of the assigned master. If no master has been assigned then the backsheet must be indorsed with the words 'No assigned master'.

7. As soon as practicable after the lodging of the document in room E216 the
h Queen's Bench Masters' Secretary's listing officer shall insert upon it the date, time and place of the hearing and the name of the master in whose short notice list the summons will be heard. He shall then issue the summons by application of the court seal.

8. A copy of the original summons shall then be transmitted by the court by fax to all parties to the summons at the fax numbers shown on the backsheet.

j 9. On receipt of information through the court's fax equipment that successful transmission has been effected to all parties to the summons, the listing officer shall forthwith enter the summons for hearing in the short notice list. In the event of confirmation of successful transmission not being received through the court's fax equipment from all parties to the summons, the listing officer shall forthwith inform any party to whom a copy of the summons has been successfully transmitted that the hearing is cancelled by reason of inability to serve all parties. Such information may be communicated by telephone, fax or otherwise at the *a* court's discretion.

10. The party who lodged the document in room E216 pursuant to para 5 of this practice direction shall be responsible for retrieving the original summons from that room before the hearing and shall hand it to the master at the hearing. Any order made on the hearing of the summons will be indorsed by the master *b* on the original summons and not upon a fax copy.

11. In the event of the assigned master being on leave or for any other reason temporarily absent from the Royal Courts of Justice then the Queen's Bench Masters' Secretary's listing officer may insert upon the document to be issued the name of some other master. In this event it should be assumed that a transfer has been effected pursuant to RSC Ord 4, r 8(1). *c*

12. This practice direction is issued with the approval of the Lord Chief Justice.

KEITH TOPLEY
Senior Master,
20 January 1993 Queen's Bench Division.

d

Morris and others v Director of Serious Fraud *e* Office and others

CHANCERY DIVISION
SIR DONALD NICHOLLS V-C
14, 15, 16, 31 JULY 1992

f

Company – Investigation by Serious Fraud Office – Seizure of documents – Disclosure to third party – Disclosure to liquidator of company – Liquidators applying for production of documents acquired by Serious Fraud Office under compulsory powers – Whether Serious Fraud Office having general power to disclose to liquidators documents obtained under compulsory powers – Whether third parties whose documents are in possession of Serious Fraud Office entitled to object to disclosure to liquidators – Insolvency Act 1986, g s 236 – Criminal Justice Act 1987, ss 2(3), 3.

In the course of his investigation into the affairs of an insolvent deposit taking institution (BCCI) the Director of the Serious Fraud Office obtained a large number of documents from various sources, including the firm of chartered *h* accountants who had provided auditing and accounting services to BCCI for some years prior to its liquidation. The documents were obtained either directly by the Serious Fraud Office pursuant to s 2(3)[a] of the Criminal Justice Act 1987, which empowered the Director to give notice to any person requiring him to produce any documents which appeared to the Director relevant to an investigation being conducted by the Serious Fraud Office, or by the police under search warrants and *j* subsequently disclosed to the Serious Fraud Office. The liquidators of BCCI

_____
a Section 2(3), so far as material, provides: 'The Director may by notice in writing require the person under investigation or any other person to produce at such place as may be specified in the notice and either forthwith or at such time as may be so specified documents which appear to the Director to relate to any matter relevant to the investigation . . .'

wished to obtain access to the records in the possession of the accountants but

a they were unwilling to make voluntary disclosure because of the possibility that the liquidators might bring legal proceedings against them. The liquidators accordingly applied under s 236*ᵇ* of the Insolvency Act 1986 for an order requiring the Serious Fraud Office to produce certain documents in its possession, including documents seized from the accountants and documents seized by the police from the premises of third parties. The Serious Fraud Office supported the application,

b contending that it was at liberty to give assistance to the liquidators, and that it could in its discretion make voluntary disclosure to the liquidators of documents in its possession obtained pursuant to the exercise of its compulsory powers or by the police. The liquidators contended that on a s 236 application the court was not concerned with the position of a third party whose documents were in the

c possession of the respondent to the application but was only concerned with whether the information sought would assist the liquidators and whether the person from whose possession the documents were sought would be prejudiced. The question arose as to the extent of the Serious Fraud Office's power to make disclosure to the liquidators.

d **Held** – (1) The Serious Fraud Office's compulsory powers of investigation existed to facilitate the discharge of its primary functions of investigating serious fraud and instituting and conducting criminal proceedings relating to serious fraud and were not to be regarded as encroaching upon the rights of individuals more than was fairly and reasonably necessary to achieve the purpose for which the powers were created. Although s 3*ᶜ* of the 1987 Act authorised disclosure of information

e obtained in the exercise of those powers to certain persons, office-holders of a company such as liquidators, provisional liquidators, administrators and administrative receivers were not included among those to whom disclosure could be made. Furthermore, there was no justification for implying a general power for the Serious Fraud Office to disclose information obtained in the exercise

f of the compulsory powers conferred by the 1987 Act to persons not named in s 3. Likewise, information obtained by the police and subsequently disclosed to the Serious Fraud Office was subject to the same limitations on further disclosure as those applicable to information directly obtained by the Serious Fraud Office pursuant to an exercise of the compulsory powers contained in s 2 of the 1987 Act (see p 794 *h* to p 795 *c h* to p 796 *b*, post).

g (2) When exercising its discretion under s 236 of the 1986 Act to order the Serious Fraud Office to disclose information obtained in the exercise of its compulsory powers the court had to weigh the advantages and disadvantages of making the order sought and when the documents belonged to or related to the affairs of a third party the court had to take into account any prejudice the third party might suffer if disclosure was ordered. Further, persons from whom

h documents were seized or the true owners of the documents were in general entitled to be given an opportunity to present to the court any objections they

---

b   Section 236, so far as material, provides:
   '. . . (2) The court may, on the application of the office-holder, summon to appear before it—(*a*)

j   any officer of the company, (*b*) any person known or suspected to have in his possession any property of the company or supposed to be indebted to the company, or (*c*) any person whom the court thinks capable of giving information concerning the . . . business, dealings, affairs or property of the company.
   (3) The court may require any such person as is mentioned in subsection (2)(*a*) to (*c*) . . . to produce any books, papers or other records in his possession or under his control relating to the company or the matters mentioned in paragraph (*c*) of the subsection . . .'

c   Section 3, so far as material, is set out at p 794 *d e*, post

might have to the disclosure of the documents. Accordingly, in the ordinary way when an application was made or was proposed to be made against the Serious *a* Fraud Office for an order under s 236 requiring disclosure of documents acquired by the office under its compulsory powers, a third party who might be affected by the disclosure ought to be notified of the application and the Serious Fraud Office's attitude to disclosure, and asked whether he objected to an order being made. If his assent was not forthcoming, he should be joined as a respondent to the application. However in exceptional cases, if it was just to do so, the court *b* could make an order under s 236 in the exercise of its discretion even though the third party had not been notified. In the circumstances the court would make an order in an agreed form concerning the documents in the possession of the accountants, would leave the form of the order relating to production of certain third party documents to be agreed between the parties and would adjourn the application so far as it related to the documents of other persons not parties to the *c* application (see p 796 e to p 797 a h, 798 a e to h and p 800 d to g, post); *Marcel v Comr of Police of the Metropolis* [1992] 1 All ER 72 considered.

Notes

For the court's power to order an inquiry into a company's dealings under the *d* Insolvency Act 1986, see 7(2) *Halsbury's Laws* (4th edn reissue) paras 1677–1678, and for cases on the subject, see 10(1) *Digest* (2nd reissue) 452–458, 9458–9493.

For the Insolvency Act 1986, s 236, see 4 *Halsbury's Statutes* (4th edn) (1987 reissue) 886.

For the Criminal Justice Act 1987, s 2, 3, see 12 *Halsbury's Statutes* (4th edn) (1989 reissue) 1072, 1077. *e*

Cases referred to in judgment

British and Commonwealth Holdings plc, Re (Nos 1 and 2) [1992] 2 All ER 801, [1992] Ch 342, [1992] 2 WLR 931, CA.
Marcel v Comr of Police of the Metropolis [1992] 1 All ER 72, [1992] Ch 225, [1992] *f* 2 WLR 50, CA.
Rolls Razor Ltd, Re [1968] 3 All ER 698.

Cases also cited

Barlow Clowes Gilt Managers Ltd, Re [1991] 4 All ER 385, [1992] Ch 208.
Bishopsgate Investment Management Ltd (in prov liq) v Maxwell [1992] 2 All ER 856, *g* [1993] Ch 1, CA.
Cloverbay Ltd (joint administrators) v Bank of Credit and Commerce International SA [1991] 1 All ER 894, [1991] Ch 90, CA.
Hargreaves (Joseph) Ltd, Re [1900] 1 Ch 347, Ch D and CA.
Highgrade Traders Ltd, Re [1984] BCLC 151, CA.
London and County Securities Ltd v Nicholson [1980] 3 All ER 861, [1980] 1 WLR *h* 948.

Application

Christopher Morris, Nicholas Roger Lyle, John Parry Richards and Stephen John Akers, the joint liquidators of the Bank of Credit and Commerce International SA (BCCI), applied for an order under s 236 of the Insolvency Act 1986 that the first *j* respondent, the Director of the Serious Fraud Office, produce all books, correspondence and documents in the custody or power of the first respondent relating to BCCI as specified in a schedule to the application. Price Waterhouse (a firm of chartered accountants who had provided auditing and accounting services to BCCI prior to its liquidation) and Control Securities plc were the second and third respondents. The facts are set out in the judgment.

a   *Edward Bannister QC* and *Susan Prevezer* (instructed by *Lovell White Durrant*) for the liquidators.
A G Bompas (instructed by the *Treasury Solicitor*) for the Serious Fraud Office.
Roger Kaye QC and *Paul Girolami* (instructed by *Herbert Smith*) for Price Waterhouse.
Peter R Griffiths (instructed by *D J Freeman*) for Control Securities.

Cur adv vult

b

31 July 1992. The following judgment was delivered.

SIR DONALD NICHOLLS V-C. As everyone knows, the Bank of Credit and Commerce International SA, or BCCI for short, is in the course of being wound up. It is hopelessly insolvent. The task confronting the liquidators is gargantuan.
c   BCCI and other companies in the group carried on business through 365 branches and agencies in about 70 countries. The group's records are scattered throughout the world. In many countries the liquidators do not have unrestricted access to the group's documents. In the United Kingdom alone there are 100m documents, principally at BCCI's headquarters in the City of London and at 40 warehouse and
d   branch premises. By January 1992 some 40m documents in 26,000 boxes had been logged on computer. The process of logging and reviewing all the documents in this country will take two years.

Price Waterhouse
One of the many problems facing the liquidators is the recoverability of loans
e   shown in certain customer accounts. These are known as the problem loans. The liquidators need to establish whether each loan is recoverable and in which jurisdiction, whether any security given is valid and enforceable, whether there were any connected but unrecorded transactions regarding the loan, and whether the bank has any related claims against the customer or others.
f   Messrs Price Waterhouse, the well-known firm of chartered accountants, provided auditing and accounting services to BCCI for some years prior to its liquidation. From June 1987 Price Waterhouse co-ordinated the worldwide audits and reviewed the consolidation of the accounts of BCCI and its associated company, Bank of Credit and Commerce International (Overseas) Ltd. They produced periodic reports for the college of banking supervisers. This body was
g   established in 1988 to supervise and regulate the affairs of the group. Its members comprised the regulatory authorities of the United Kingdom, United Arab Emirates, Luxembourg, Cayman Islands and other countries. The group's majority shareholders are situated in the United Arab Emirates, BCCI was incorporated in Luxembourg and BCCI Overseas in the Cayman Islands. As a result of the 1989 audit, some partners in Price Waterhouse became members of
h   a committee set up by the Abu Dhabi government to investigate the problem loans. The committee was later reconstituted as a committee of BCCI and other companies in the group.
Not surprisingly, the liquidators turned to Price Waterhouse to help with the problem loans. It would be absurd for the liquidators to undertake afresh the identical task of investigation of the problem loans already carried out by Price
j   Waterhouse and the investigating committee. The liquidators wanted to see the documents Price Waterhouse have regarding these loans, including the audit working papers. Price Waterhouse did not wish to be unhelpful but they were not willing to produce everything sought. They considered that the all-embracing nature of the request was oppressive. They were concerned at the effect disclosure could have on proceedings the BCCI group has brought or may yet bring against them. They were not prepared to make voluntary disclosure. Their solicitors

suggested that the liquidators should make an application under s 236 of the Insolvency Act 1986. The liquidators did not adopt that suggestion. Instead they followed a different course. a

The Serious Fraud Office

There is evidence of fraud, on a massive scale, in the conduct of BCCI's business. The Director of the Serious Fraud Office (the SFO) is investigating these matters, with a view to bringing criminal proceedings. Three persons have already been b charged in England.

In the course of his investigations the Director has obtained large numbers of documents from a variety of sources here and abroad. One source comprises copies of documents produced in response to notices served by the Director under s 2(3) of the Criminal Justice Act 1987. That subsection empowers the Director to give notice to any person requiring him to produce any documents which c appear to the Director to relate to a matter relevant to an investigation being conducted by the SFO. Another source consists of documents seized by the police exercising compulsory powers. A constable can enter and search premises and seize and retain documents pursuant to a search warrant issued by a justice of the peace under s 8 of the Police and Criminal Evidence Act 1984. A constable has d similar power if duly authorised by a police inspector pursuant to s 18 of that Act. A constable who is lawfully on any premises has power to seize documents and other items under s 19. Again, a constable has power to enter and search and take possession of documents pursuant to a search warrant issued by a justice of the peace, following information laid by a member of the SFO, under s 2(4) of the 1987 Act. One circumstance in which a warrant may be issued under s 2(4) is e when a person has failed to comply with a notice served by the SFO under s 2(3).

Pursuant to notices served under s 2(3) the SFO has been supplied with many copy documents by Price Waterhouse. Further, in exercise of their powers the police have seized documents from Control Securities plc, its associated company Inarive Group (UK) Ltd, their subsidiaries and Mr Nazmudin Virani. I shall refer to these persons altogether as 'the Control group'. Mr Virani was the chairman f and chief executive of Control Securities before he was arrested. The documents seized from the Control group are voluminous. They were placed in over 200 sealed bags. Copies of about half these documents have already been supplied by the police to the SFO. The rest are still being copied, and copies will be handed over to the SFO when made. g

The police have also taken possession of documents from other sources I shall mention later.

The s 236 application against the SFO

With this background the liquidators launched against the SFO an application under s 236, seeking production of 23 categories of documents. The liquidators' h view is that production of the documents by the SFO is the most expeditious and cost-effective way of obtaining documents required for the purposes of their investigations regarding pending proceedings by or against BCCI, and regarding the problem loans and other matters. The need to obtain some of the documents is urgent as there is a risk of claims becoming statute-barred.

The vast majority of the documents sought comprises copies of documents j obtained directly by the SFO pursuant to a notice under s 2(3) of the 1987 Act or copies of documents seized by the police under search warrants. The Director's view is that these documents acquired under compulsory powers will assist the liquidators in carrying out their task, and he wishes to disclose them to the liquidators if permitted by law to do so. Production of these documents will not prejudice the SFO in the performance of its duties.

About 16 of the categories of documents sought relate to documents obtained from Price Waterhouse. For instance, category 1 comprises reports prepared for meetings of the investigating committee dated April and June 1991; category 2 comprises minutes of certain meetings of this committee; and category 3 is concerned with correspondence between Price Waterhouse, BCCI and the controlling shareholders in connection with matters under investigation by the investigating committee. I need say no more about the Price Waterhouse documents. The parties reached agreement on the form of an order regarding them, and Price Waterhouse did not oppose an order being made in that form.

Further categories of documents sought comprise copies of the documents seized by the police from the Control group. The attitude of the Control group is that they do not object to an order being made subject to certain safeguards and conditions.

The remaining categories relate to documents seized from the premises of persons who are not parties to this application: from the home addresses of Mr Abedi and Mr Naqvi, two former officers of BCCI, from a safe deposit box in the name of Mr Iqbal, also a former officer of BCCI, and from Capcom Financial Services Ltd. Capcom Financial Services is a broker through which many of the bank's treasury transactions took place. A flight log for a BCCI jet was also seized in the course of a search at Stanstead Airport.

The issues

This state of affairs has given rise to two principal issues. First, the liquidators contended that, in general, on a s 236 application the court is not concerned with the position of a third party whose documents are in the possession of the respondent to the application. The court is not concerned with any ground of objection the third party might have. The court is concerned only with whether the person from whose possession the documents are sought will be prejudiced, and with whether the information sought will assist the liquidator. The court balances these two interests if there is a conflict. Accordingly, it was submitted, there was no need for Capcom Financial Services, or Mr Abedi or the other former BCCI officers, to be joined in the proceedings or to be told of them, nor are the Control group's concerns of any materiality on this application brought by the liquidators against the SFO.

For its part the SFO is concerned lest it become an unwilling participant in future applications of this nature, diverting its staff from getting on with their investigations of serious fraud. In its submissions the SFO went further than the liquidators. It contended, and this is the second issue, that as a matter of law it is at liberty to give assistance to liquidators, and that in its discretion it may make voluntary disclosure to them of documents in the SFO's possession pursuant to an exercise of the compulsory powers mentioned above.

The Control group refuted the liquidators' submissions on the first of these issues. They contended that the second issue does not arise because a s 236 application has been made and is before the court. Price Waterhouse wished to be heard on both issues. They feared they might be prejudiced in the future by an adverse decision given in these proceedings to which they are parties. I gave them leave to argue both points. Despite their agreement to the form of the order being made against them, Price Waterhouse have an interest in these issues. They are live issues, and the SFO needs to know where it stands. In the result I heard full argument on both points.

Voluntary disclosure to office-holders

The SFO was created as a serious fraud office for England and Wales and Northern Ireland by the Criminal Justice Act 1987. The Director is appointed by the Attorney General and he discharges his functions under the superintendence of the Attorney General. His functions are set out in s 1. By s 1(3) he may *a* investigate any suspected offence which appears to him on reasonable grounds to involve serious or complex fraud. He may institute and have the conduct of, or take over the conduct of, criminal proceedings which appear to him to relate to such fraud (s 1(5)). The Attorney General may assign to him other functions in relation to fraud (s 1(6)). Section 2 confers on the Director wide powers but only for the purposes of an investigation under s 1. This power has been extended in *b* relation to the Isle of Man, Jersey and Guernsey.

Section 3 is concerned with the disclosure of information by the SFO. Subsection (1) relates to information disclosed by the Commissioners of Inland Revenue to the SFO for the purposes of a prosecution of a tax offence. Where such information is subject to an obligation of secrecy under the Taxes Management Act 1970 it may be disclosed by the SFO for defined criminal prosecution purposes *c* 'but not otherwise'. Subsection (3) contains a similar provision regarding information subject to a secrecy obligation under other statutes. Subsection (5) provides:

> 'Subject to subsections (1) and (3) above and to any provision of an agreement for the supply of information which restricts the disclosure of the *d* information supplied, information obtained by any person in his capacity as a member of the Serious Fraud Office may be disclosed ... (*a*) to any government department or Northern Ireland department or other authority or body discharging its functions on behalf of the Crown ... (*b*) to any competent authority; (*c*) for the purposes of any prosecution in England and Wales, Northern Ireland or elsewhere; and (*d*) for the purposes of assisting *e* any public or other authority for the time being designated for the purposes of this paragraph by an order made by the Secretary of State to discharge any functions which are specified in the order.'

Subsection (6) contains a list of competent authorities. It includes several classes *f* of persons appointed to carry out investigative functions under statutes, such as inspectors appointed under the Companies Act 1985, the Building Societies Act 1986 and the Financial Services Act 1986. The list includes any body having supervisory, regulatory or disciplinary functions in relation to any profession or any area of commercial activity. It also includes any person or body having, under the law of any country or territory outside the United Kingdom, functions *g* corresponding to any of the functions of any person or body mentioned in the list.

Since the SFO is the creature of statute, its powers and functions comprise, and are confined to, the powers and functions expressly or impliedly conferred or imposed upon it by the statute. The information obtained by the SFO is obtained to enable or assist it to carry out its primary functions of investigating serious *h* fraud and instituting and conducting criminal proceedings relating to serious fraud. Section 3 authorises disclosure of that information to other persons, but liquidators and provisional liquidators and administrators and administrative receivers, conveniently referred to as 'office-holders', are not included in the list of these to whom disclosure may be made.

In the absence of an express power to make disclosure to office-holders, is a *j* power to make disclosure to them to be implied? In my view it is not. Whether the list in s 3 is to be regarded as exhaustive for all purposes in respect of information obtained by the SFO from all types of sources is not a matter I need pursue on this application. Suffice to say I can see no justification for implying a general power for the SFO to disclose information, *obtained in the exercise of compulsory powers conferred by the Act*, to persons not named in s 3. That, surely, is only what one would expect. The compulsory powers of investigation exist to facilitate the discharge by the SFO of its statutory investigative functions. The powers conferred by s 2 are exercisable only for the purposes of an investigation under s 1. When information is obtained in exercise of those powers the SFO may use the information for those purposes and purposes reasonably incidental thereto and such other purposes as may be authorised by statute, but not otherwise. Compulsory powers are not to be regarded as encroaching more upon the rights of individuals than is fairly and reasonably necessary to achieve the purpose for which the powers were created. That is to be taken as the intention of Parliament, unless the contrary is clearly apparent.

One submission made was that, even if there is no general power for the SFO to disclose information obtained compulsorily, the SFO does have power to disclose such information to office-holders. The official receiver is one of the persons specified in the list of competent authorities. When a winding-up order is made he becomes the liquidator of the company and he continues in office until another person becomes liquidator in his place. Hence, so it was argued, if the SFO's contention is rejected one would have the curious position that when a winding-up order is made the SFO can disclose information to the official receiver, but as soon as another liquidator is appointed in his place the SFO must stop doing so. Further, the new liquidator could use the information which had been disclosed to the official receiver. In my view the inclusion of the official receiver in the list of competent authorities cuts both ways. By drawing a distinction between the official receiver and other liquidators the Act does produce the results just mentioned. But the presence of the official receiver in the list of competent authorities makes more marked the absence of office-holders. That suggests their omission was deliberate, and not an oversight. The explanation for the inclusion of the official receiver in the list despite the absence of liquidators may well lie in the particular statutory duties imposed on him. For example, he is under a duty to investigate the causes of the failure of a company and generally the business, dealings and affairs of the company (s 132 of the Insolvency Act 1986). I cannot divine here an unexpressed but implicit intention by Parliament that disclosure of information to office-holders was one of the purposes of the 1987 Act. Nor, in my view, is such disclosure reasonably incidental to those purposes.

I appreciate that the SFO's contention would leave the Director with a discretion. He would only make disclosure if satisfied that the case was a proper one to do so. I am not impressed by this. This argument does not advance the SFO's case. I am concerned to construe a statute which confers power to obtain information compulsorily. Plainly, the SFO may use the information for its own investigative purposes. Parliament has also expressly authorised the SFO to disclose the information to specified persons. In respect of those specified persons the Director has a discretion ('may be disclosed'). The issue before me is whether, having regard to the objectives of the Act, it is implicit that the Director has the like discretion in respect of a wider group. In my view it is not.

I pause to note that the matter stands differently if the person from whom the documents were obtained, either by a notice under s 2(3) or a warrant issued under s 2(4), consents to the disclosure sought. In such a case the SFO's authority to disclose the documents to an office-holder, or anyone else, will derive from the consent.

Thus far I have addressed myself to the disclosure by the SFO of information obtained pursuant to an exercise of the powers contained in s 2 of the Act. There remains the position regarding information obtained by the police compulsorily under the Police and Criminal Evidence Act 1984 and disclosed later to the SFO.

In my view the position here is the same as described above. Whatever may be the position regarding information obtained from other sources and disclosed *a* voluntarily to the SFO, in my view information obtained by the police compulsorily under the 1984 Act is, in the hands of the SFO, subject to similar limitations on further disclosure as those applicable to information directly obtained by the SFO pursuant to an exercise of the compulsory powers contained in s 2 of the 1987 Act. I can see no ground for distinguishing these two cases.

b

Section 236 applications: the position of third parties

I turn to the other issue. Section 236(2) of the Insolvency Act 1986 empowers the court, on the application of an office-holder, to summon before it a wide range of persons:

'(*a*) any officer of the company, (*b*) any person known or suspected to have *c* in his possession any property of the company or supposed to be indebted to the company, or (*c*) any person whom the court thinks capable of giving information concerning the . . . business, dealings, affairs or property of the company.'

Such a person can be required by the court to produce any books, papers or *d* records in his possession or under his control relating to the company or its business, dealings, affairs or property.

The present application is not concerned with providing evidence by answering questions. The application is concerned only with the production of documents, and I shall confine my remarks accordingly. Section 236 confers a discretion on the court. When exercising its discretion the court has to weigh the advantages *e* and disadvantages of making the order sought. The court will take into account any prejudice the office-holder may suffer in carrying out his duties if an order for production of the documents is refused. Conversely, the court will have regard to any prejudice the respondent may suffer if an order is made. When the documents whose production is sought belong to or relate to the affairs of a third *f* party, in principle it must be right that the court should also take into account any prejudice the third party may suffer if production is ordered. By a 'third party' I mean a person other than the person who has possession or control of the documents. Otherwise the position would be that a liquidator would be in a better position by bringing an application under s 236 against an agent of a third party than if he had made the application directly against the third party. That *g* cannot be right, and I see nothing in the legislative scheme of which s 236 is part which would lead to that conclusion. Under the section the court has an unfettered discretion. There is no reason why the court should have to wear blinkers when exercising this discretion and be unable to have regard to the interests of a third party who would be adversely affected by an order to produce documents.

The present case affords a striking example of how unsatisfactory and unjust *h* such an artificially narrow approach would be in some circumstances. The documents of which production is sought are in the possession of the SFO. They are copies of documents belonging to third parties. According to the liquidators, the third parties need not be joined as parties to the s 236 application, because the court is not concerned with their interests at all. The court is concerned only to balance the interests of the SFO against production and the interests of the *j* liquidators in favour of production. If an order for production would not be oppressive so far as the SFO is concerned or inimical to the proper functioning of the SFO in this case or generally, production should be ordered regardless of whether this would be oppressive to the third party in question.

I have no hesitation in rejecting this submission. It would mean that the third

party would be worse off than if the liquidators had made their application
a directly against him and that this would be so as a result of the exercise of
compulsory powers having a different objective. I altogether reject the notion
that in the exercise of a discretion, under which the court may and should look at
all relevant circumstances, that can be the position.

There is no reported decision on the point, either concerning s 236 generally or
concerning a case where the documents sought have been acquired under
b compulsory powers. However, in the latter regard there is a compelling analogy
in *Marcel v Comr of Police of the Metropolis* [1992] 1 All ER 72, [1992] Ch 225.
There the police had seized documents under the 1984 Act. A defendant in civil
proceedings issued a subpoena to produce documents against the police officer in
charge of the investigations, requiring production of some of the seized documents
c in court at the trial of the civil proceedings. The police themselves had no
objection to production. The Court of Appeal held that the police officer, like
anyone else, is amenable to produce on subpoena any documents in his possession,
subject to the true owner having the right to challenge the subpoena, or the
production of the documents, on any of the grounds on which a subpoena can be
challenged. That includes the ground of legal professional privilege in favour of
d the true owner. Further, as Dillon LJ observed, that includes objection on the
ground of oppression to those whose documents the police have seized (see [1992]
1 All ER 72 at 82, [1992] Ch 225 at 257–258). The court also held that the police
should not disclose seized documents without the consent of the owner, otherwise
than for the specific purposes mentioned in the 1984 Act, unless a subpoena has
been served and the police have first given the owner of the documents notice of
e the service of the subpoena, and of the wish of the police to produce the
documents, in advance of the attendance at court required by the subpoena and
have given the owner a reasonable opportunity to state any objections he may
have. Nolan LJ said ([1992] 1 All ER 72 at 84, [1992] Ch 225 at 259):

> *f* '. . . I cannot see why the owners of the documents should be able to stop
> the police from producing them to the court in obedience to a subpoena
> duces tecum when the owners themselves, if the documents were in their
> possession, would be bound to obey such a subpoena . . . If it is right that the
> owners of documents seized by the police should be no better off, as regards
> their production on subpoena, than if the documents were in their own
> hands it must also be right that, so far as possible, they should be no worse
> *g* off. I say "so far as possible" because in one respect the owners of such
> documents are inevitably worse off.'

That reasoning is equally applicable in the present case. There is no sound
distinction between production of documents in answer to a subpoena and
production of documents pursuant to an order made under s 236. In both cases,
h those from whom the documents were seized, or the true owners of the
documents, are in general entitled to an opportunity to present to the court any
ground of objection they may have to the production of the documents. The
court will take those matters into account when considering whether to make the
order sought under s 236 or to set aside the subpoena in whole or in part. In a
broad sense, and sometimes also in a very specific sense, there is a public interest
j in seeing that office-holders have the assistance of those who were involved in
running a company's business or had dealings with the company. As Woolf LJ
observed in *Re British and Commonwealth Holdings plc (Nos 1 and 2)* [1992] 2 All ER
801 at 834 [1992] Ch 342 at 384, Parliament has attached importance to office-
holders being able to perform their functions, prescribed by statute, in an effective
and expeditious manner. But office-holders do not have an absolute right to an

order for the production of documents. The court has a discretion, and this head of public interest does not necessitate or justify refusing to afford to those whose *a* documents have been seized an opportunity to advance any proper objections they may have to the court making a s 236 order regarding the documents in question.

These views are in conformity with the practice of the Companies Court on s 236 applications. Usually no question of third party rights arises. If such a question does arise, the rights of the third party are not ignored. What happens *b* in practice is that if, for example, a claim is made by the person having the documents that some of them are the subject of legal professional privilege in favour of a third party the point is argued if necessary and the court does not require production of the documents which are properly the subject of the privilege. (In parentheses I mention in passing that one point touched upon in *c* the course of argument before me was whether legal professional privilege is an answer to an order under s 236. The point was not pursued because it does not arise for decision on this application, so I shall say no more. I am not to be taken as expressing any view, either way, on the point.)

Nor are the views expressed above in conflict with the decision of Buckley J in *Re Rolls Razor Ltd* [1968] 3 All ER 698. The point about third party rights was *d* not argued there, but in any event the witnesses who had given the evidence to the inspectors appointed under the Companies Act 1948 could have had no objection to the production of transcripts of evidence to the liquidators. There is an express statutory provision that answers given by a person to questions put in exercise of powers conferred on the inspectors are admissible in evidence against him in other proceedings. *e*

Accordingly, in the ordinary way when an application is made or proposed to be made against the SFO for an order under s 236 regarding documents acquired by the SFO under compulsory powers, the third party from whom the documents were obtained should be notified of the application or proposed application. He should be told of the SFO's attitude to the production sought, and asked whether he objects to an order being made. If his consent is not forthcoming, steps should *f* be taken to join him as a respondent to the application.

This should be the normal course. There will be exceptional cases. For instance, there may be cases where notice to a third party of the office-holder's application might seriously prejudice the object the office-holder is seeking to achieve in existing or proposed proceedings; or the third party may not be traceable; or the *g* documents may be needed as a matter of dire emergency. This is not intended to be a comprehensive list. There may be cases where for other reasons it is not appropriate or practicable to follow the ordinary route. In such exceptional cases, if it is just to do so the court may make an order under s 236 in the exercise of its discretion even though the third party has not been notified.

I add two further points. In general, it ought not to be necessary for the SFO to *h* be represented on s 236 applications if the Director has no objection to the order sought. The views of the Director can be set out in correspondence which may be formally put in evidence by the office-holder. He need be represented only if there are particular matters arising which cannot be dealt with satisfactorily in his absence. Secondly, nothing I have said is directed at circumstances in which the SFO itself wishes to object to the production of documents. For example, *j* different considerations may well apply to documents created for the purposes of a prosecution, such as witness statements, or documents containing information obtained from abroad where the Director has given an undertaking not to disclose the information except for the purposes of a prosecution. There is no issue under that head on the present application.

The Control group's documents

a   I turn now to apply the principles outlined above, starting with the Control group. The Control group are concerned to be protected on three points. First, many of the documents held by the SFO are irrelevant to the liquidators' investigations. They have nothing to do with BCCI. Had the liquidators served a s 236 application on the Control group in respect of documents in their possession, the Control group would have had the opportunity to segregate the relevant from
b   the irrelevant. They are concerned that they should still have that opportunity. Second, they are concerned about the cost of inspecting the documents in the premises of the SFO. Third, they wish to be supplied with copies of all documents provided by the SFO to the liquidators.

    I shall take these three points in turn. In principle the Control group's
c   contention on the first point is sound. They are entitled, as far as possible, not to be disadvantaged by reason of the liquidators having chosen to make a s 236 application against the SFO rather than directly against the Control group. Nevertheless, the documents are in the possession of the SFO and the order will be directed at the SFO. Accordingly, the SFO will be under an obligation to see that all the documents falling within s 236 are disclosed to the liquidators. The
d   way ahead here is that if there is disagreement between the SFO and the Control group on whether a particular document or class of documents falls within the scope of s 236, the disagreement will have to be resolved by the court.

    I see no reason to anticipate that this course is likely to involve the SFO in significant extra work or expense. The SFO has not suggested that the need for it to separate the documents which fall within s 236 from those which do not would
e   make an order oppressive. Having combed through the documents, the SFO presumably could readily and shortly state its views on relevance if necessary. If a dispute does arise, the SFO should produce the documents to the liquidators unless the Control group make an application to the court supported by an affidavit, verifying that the documents do not relate to BCCI or its affairs. As officers of the court, the Control group's solicitors will have a duty to the court to
f   see that this affidavit is made responsibly.

    As to the second point, I was informed by counsel appearing for the SFO that the copy documents held by the SFO are available for inspection in lever-arch files and are not subject to the (understandably) cumbersome procedure attendant upon inspection of documents in the sealed bags held by the City of London
g   Police. The SFO would not object to a solicitor inspecting these files on behalf of the Control group. If the solicitor needs to take instructions on a document the SFO would not object to his obtaining a copy and showing it to his client. On that footing I see no reason why a special order should be made in this case in respect of legal costs incurred by the Control group in separating the relevant from the irrelevant. In the ordinary way the cost of separating the relevant from the
h   irrelevant in response to a s 236 order falls upon the person to whom the order is addressed.

    As to the third point, I consider that if the Control group wish to have copies of the documents supplied by the SFO to the liquidators they should be entitled to have them but at their own expense. The need for copies stems from the police seizure of the documents; that being so, the liquidators cannot fairly be expected
j   to pay for copies sought by the Control group.

The documents seized from persons not parties to this application

    I turn, finally, to the documents seized from Capcom Financial Services and other persons who are not parties to this application. Mr Bannister QC submitted that there is only a remote chance that any of these persons could object to

production of the documents. The compulsory powers under s 2 of the 1987 Act
and under Pt II of the 1984 Act do not extend to documents which are the subject   *a*
of legal professional privilege. Presumably the police and the SFO have acted
responsibly and properly. Production of the documents will not be physically
burdensome because these persons are not being asked to produce the documents.
All that would remain is an objection that this or that particular document is
irrelevant.

I do not think these considerations justify making an order regarding these   *b*
documents without further ado. I can see no reason why Capcom Financial
Services should not be approached and told of this application and its attitude to
disclosure ascertained. I know nothing about the flight log seized at Stanstead
Airport. Further inquiries should be made about this and its ownership. As to Mr
Abedi, Mr Naqvi and Mr Iqbal, I understand they are all abroad. I need more
information about their present circumstances and the practicability of notifying   *c*
them of this application before I can decide whether notification to them should
be dispensed with.

Conclusion

I have already made an order, in the agreed form, concerning the Price   *d*
Waterhouse documents.

As to the Control group documents, various procedures relating to the
production of the documents have been canvassed between the parties with the
sensible objective of reducing the number of documents which will need to be
inspected. The SFO considers that when the liquidators know more about the
documents they will not wish to have copies of most of the Control group   *e*
documents falling within the scope of the order sought. The principal stumbling-
block seems to have been disagreement on one or more of the three matters
mentioned above. I have now decided these matters. It is to be hoped that
agreement between the parties on a workable practical procedure should now be
possible. I shall therefore leave the form of the order relating to production of
these documents to be agreed between the parties. If agreement cannot be   *f*
reached, the matter can be mentioned again.

I shall adjourn the application so far as it relates to the documents of Capcom
Financial Services and the other persons not parties to this application.

Order accordingly.

Celia Fox   Barrister.

a # R v Crown Court at Manchester, ex parte Director of Public Prosecutions

QUEEN'S BENCH DIVISION

LEGGATT LJ AND PILL J

b 29, 30 JUNE, 2 JULY 1992

Crown Court – Supervisory jurisdiction of High Court – Trial on indictment – High Court having no supervisory jurisdiction in matters relating to trial on indictment – Indictment charging former member of European Parliament with offences of dishonesty relating to expenses received as member of European Parliament – Crown Court quashing *c* *indictment – Whether High Court having jurisdiction to grant judicial review of Crown Court's decision to quash indictment – Whether decision of Crown Court quashing indictment a matter 'relating to trial on indictment' – Supreme Court Act 1981, s 29(3).*

European Economic Community – European Parliament – Sovereignty – Member of European Parliament – Allegations of criminal dishonesty – Whether member of European *d* *Parliament can be prosecuted in respect of expenses dishonestly received as member of European Parliament.*

The defendant, a former member of the European Parliament, was committed for trial in the Crown Court on an indictment charging him with dishonestly obtaining by deception two cheques in respect of expenses from the political *e* group of the European Parliament to which he belonged. The judge quashed the indictment on the ground that the Crown Court had no jurisdiction to entertain proceedings against the defendant because the exercise of jurisdiction would result in an infringement of the sovereignty of the European Parliament and offend the principle of comity since the court would have to interpret the rules of *f* the European Parliament or of political groups within the Parliament relating to the payment of expenses to members of the European Parliament despite the fact that the European Parliament had a procedure of its own, albeit not of a criminal nature, for dealing with the improper payment of expenses. The Director of Public Prosecutions applied for judicial review of the judge's decision. The defendant contended, inter alia, (i) that the judge's decision was a matter 'relating *g* to trial on indictment' and therefore by virtue of s 29(3)^a of the Supreme Court Act 1981 it fell within the exclusive jurisdiction of the Crown Court, (ii) that judicial review of a decision of the European Parliament that a member's claim for expenses was in order and should be refunded would constitute an interference in the internal functioning of the European Parliament and thus an infringement of its sovereignty or autonomy and (iii) that recourse to prosecution by a national *h* authority without the consent of the European Parliament would prejudice the immunity to which the defendant was entitled by virtue of his former status as a member of the European Parliament.

Held – The application would be granted and the judge's order quashed for the following reasons— *j* (1) The High Court had jurisdiction to entertain an application for judicial review of a decision of a judge of that Crown Court to quash an indictment for want of jurisdiction, since the question of the existence of the Crown Court's jurisdiction was not part of the conduct of the trial and s 29(3) of the 1981 Act

a Section 29(3) is set out at p 805 g, post

did not have the effect of rendering immune from judicial review the very
question whether the court had jurisdiction, as distinct from the manner of the   *a*
exercise of that jurisdiction. Furthermore, it was not appropriate that a
determination of an individual judge of the Crown Court that Community law
prohibited criminal proceedings should be immune from challenge and so from
supervision, nor was it appropriate for a court of limited jurisdiction to determine
the limits of that jurisdiction (see p 807 *e*, 809 *g*, p 810 *d*, p 815 *j* and p 816 *a b g*,
post); *Smalley v Crown Court at Warwick* [1985] 1 All ER 769 applied; *R v Central*   *b*
Criminal Court, ex p Randle [1992] 1 All ER 370 and *R v Crown Court at Norwich,*
ex p Belsham [1992] 1 All ER 394 considered.

(2) A review by a national court of an allegation that European Community
funds had been dishonestly appropriated did not constitute an interference with
the internal functioning of the European Parliament, since the fact that national   *c*
proceedings might give rise to the need to interpret the rules of the European
Parliament could not deprive the national court of jurisdiction. In any event what
was in issue was the honesty of a member of the European Parliament in claiming
expenses as provided by rules of the European Parliament, rather than a challenge
to the validity of those rules. It followed that there was nothing about the conduct
of the proposed prosecution which would detract from the autonomy of the   *d*
European Parliament (see p 813 *d e*, p 814 *g h*, p 815 *d e j* p 816 *a* and p 819 *g h*,
post).

(3) Furthermore, in the absence of any provisions of Community law
exempting a member of the European Parliament from criminal liability or of
any sanctions which could be imposed by the European Parliament on a former
member, the question whether expenses in connection with the European   *e*
Parliament had been obtained by dishonesty was a question of national law which
was capable of being raised by a prosecution in criminal proceedings in a national
court. Member states were therefore entitled to prosecute members of the
European Parliament or former members for the criminal offence of obtaining
by dishonesty expenses from the European Parliament (see p 814 *b* to *d j*, p 815 *b*   *f*
j, p 816 *a* and p 819 *j*, post).

Per Leggatt J. (1) There is no concept of 'sovereignty' of the European
Parliament, except in so far as it denotes the autonomy of that Parliament in
relation to the organisation of its internal affairs (see p 814 *h*, post).

(2) Both the validity and interpretation of rules of the European Parliament
may be the subject of proceedings in national courts and the Court of Justice of   *g*
the European Communities. Since the interpretation and validity of those rules
may be referred, if need be, to the European Court, it follows that a national court
cannot be precluded from assuming jurisdiction in a case in which the rules
might be relevant (see p 814 *j* to p 815 *a*, post).

Notes   *h*
For the supervisory jurisdiction of the High Court over the Crown Court, see 10
Halsbury's Laws (4th edn) paras 710, 717, 870, and for cases on the subject, see 16
Digest (Reissue) 229, 2273–2277.

For the direct effect of Community law in the United Kingdom and its
application in English courts, see 51 *Halsbury's Laws* (4th edn) paras 3·41–3·85.

For the European Parliament, see ibid paras 1·71–1·73.   *j*

For the Supreme Court Act 1981, s 29, see 11 *Halsbury's Statutes* (4th edn) (1991
reissue) 990.

Cases referred to in judgments
Bruce of Donington (Lord) v Aspden Case 208/80 [1981] ECR 2205.
EC Commission v Greece Case 68/88 [1989] ECR 2965.

France v European Parliament Joined cases 358/85 and 51/86 [1988] ECR 4821.

a *Parti écologiste 'Les Verts' v European Parliament* Case 294/83 [1986] ECR 1339.

R v Central Criminal Court, ex p Randle [1992] 1 All ER 370, [1991] 1 WLR 1087, DC.

R v Crown Court at Leicester, ex p S (a minor) [1992] 2 All ER 659, DC.

R v Crown Court at Manchester, ex p Cunningham [1992] COD 23, DC.

b *R v Crown Court at Norwich, ex p Belsham* [1992] 1 All ER 394, [1992] 1 WLR 54, DC.

R v Crown Court at Sheffield, ex p Brownlow [1980] 2 All ER 444, [1980] QB 530, [1980] 2 WLR 892, CA.

R v Shoreditch Assessment Committee, ex p Morgan [1910] 2 KB 859, [1908–10] All ER Rep 792, CA.

c *Sampson v Crown Court at Croydon* [1987] 1 All ER 609, [1987] 1 WLR 194, HL.

Smalley v Crown Court at Warwick [1985] 1 All ER 769, [1985] AC 622, [1985] 2 WLR 538, HL.

Wybot v Faure Case 149/85 [1986] ECR 2391.

Cases also cited or referred to in skeleton arguments

d *Anklagemyndigheden v Hansen & Son I/S* Case C-326/88 [1990] ECR I-2911.

Connelly v DPP [1964] 2 All ER 401, [1964] AC 1254, HL.

European Parliament v EC Council Case 302/87 [1988] ECR 5615.

European Parliament v EC Council Case C-70/88 [1990] ECR I-2041.

Factortame Ltd v Secretary of State for Transport (No 2) Case C-213/89 [1991] 1 All ER 70, [1991] AC 603, CJEC and HL.

e *Foto-Frost v Hauptzollamt Lübeck-Ost* Case 314/85 [1987] ECR 4199.

Garland v British Rail Engineering Ltd Case 12/81 [1982] 2 All ER 402, [1983] 2 AC 751, CJEC and HL.

Group of European Right and National Front Party v European Parliament Case 221/86R [1986] ECR 2969.

f *Litster v Forth Dry Dock and Engineering Co Ltd* [1989] 1 All ER 1134, [1990] 1 AC 546, HL.

Luxembourg v European Parliament Case 230/81 [1983] ECR 255.

Marleasing SA v La Comercial Internacional de Alimentación SA Case C-106/89 [1990] ECR I-4135.

Meredith, Ex p [1973] 2 All ER 234, [1973] 1 WLR 435, DC.

g *Pickstone v Freemans plc* [1987] 3 All ER 756, [1989] AC 66, CA; *affd* [1988] 2 All ER 803, [1989] AC 66, HL.

R v Central Criminal Court, ex p Raymond [1986] 2 All ER 379, [1986] 1 WLR 710, DC.

R v County of London Quarter Sessions (Chairman), ex p Downes [1953] 2 All ER 750, [1954] 1 QB 1, DC.

h *R v Crown Court at Cardiff, ex p Jones* [1973] 3 All ER 1027, [1974] QB 113, DC.

R v Crown Court at Chichester, ex p Abodunrin and Sogbanmu (1984) 79 Cr App R 293, DC.

R v Crown Court at Maidstone, ex p Gill [1987] 1 All ER 129, [1986] 1 WLR 1405, DC.

R v Smith (Martin) [1974] 1 All ER 651, [1975] QB 531, CA.

j *Wagner v Fohrmann* Case 101/63 [1964] ECR 195.

Application for judicial review

The acting Director of Public Prosecutions applied, with leave of Macpherson J given on 25 March 1992, for judicial review by way of (i) an order of certiorari to quash the order of Morland J on 4 September 1991 sitting in the Crown Court at Manchester whereby he quashed the indictment in *R v Huckfield, Ennis and Dowd*

and made a declaration that the prosecution and proceedings in the Crown Court
and in the magistrates' court were invalid and of no effect, (ii) declarations that   *a*
the Crown Court possessed jurisdiction to try the defendants for offences of the
kind charged in the indictment, that the Crown Court lacked jurisdiction to grant
any declaration of the kind granted by the judge, and that the Crown Court
lacked jurisdiction to quash the proceedings in the magistrates' court or to declare
the same invalid, and (iii) an order of mandamus directed to the Crown Court
requiring it to exercise the jurisdiction conferred on it by s 46 of the Supreme   *b*
Court Act 1981 and directing it to hear and determine the indictment according
to law. The facts are set out in the judgment of Leggatt LJ.

Gerald Barling QC, Presiley Baxendale QC and *Stephen Richards* (instructed by the
     Crown Prosecution Service, Headquarters) for the applicant.
Richard Plender QC, Geoffrey Robertson QC and *Gavin Millar* (instructed by *David*   *c*
     Phillips & Partners, Liverpool) for Mr Dowd and Mr Ennis as interested parties.
Richard Plender QC and *Edward Fitzgerald* (instructed by *Christian Fisher & Co*) for
     Mr Huckfield as an interested party.
The respondent was not represented.

     d

Cur adv vult

2 July 1992. The following judgments were delivered.

LEGGATT LJ. The Director of Public Prosecutions applies by leave for judicial
review of an order made by Morland J on 4 September 1991 in the Crown Court   *e*
at Manchester whereby he quashed an indictment in *R v Huckfield, Ennis and
Dowd,* and made a consequential order and declaration.
     From June 1984 to June 1989 Mr Huckfield was a member of the European
Parliament (an MEP) for the Merseyside East constituency and was a member of
the British Labour Group and of the Socialist Group of the European Parliament   *f*
(the Parliament). On 14 January 1991 Mr Huckfield was committed for trial in
the Crown Court on an indictment which charged him under two counts of
dishonestly obtaining by deception cheques in respect of expenses from Mr Balfe,
the then treasurer of the British Labour Group in the European Parliament. The
judge quashed the indictment in upholding an objection on behalf of Mr Huckfield
to the jurisdiction of the Crown Court to entertain criminal proceedings against   *g*
him, as a former MEP, on the grounds that the exercise of jurisdiction would
result in an infringement of the sovereignty of the European Parliament because
the court would have to interpret rules of the Parliament, or its subordinate
groups, relating to the payment of expenses to MEPs and that the prosecution
would offend the principle of comity because the European Parliament had a
procedure of its own, albeit not of a criminal nature, for dealing with the   *h*
improper payment of expenses.
     The judge held:

     'Not only legitimately but also of necessity in order to present
     Mr Huckfield's defence effectively the defence would have to introduce the
     rules and regulations which in turn would require the court to interpret
     them or give guidance as to their meaning. In my judgment this would   *j*
     involve an infringement by this court of the sovereignty of the European
     Parliament. For this reason this court declines jurisdiction. I also accept
     Mr Carman's submission [on behalf of Mr Huckfield] that the prosecution
     offends the principle of comity. This prosecution concerns the payment by
     an authorised constituent organ of the European Parliament of moneys for

expenses to a member of the European Parliament in accordance with European Parliament budget lines and rules of the Parliament and of subordinate regulations. The European Parliament, a sovereign body, has a regular procedure, albeit not of a criminal nature, for dealing with irregular or improper payments of expenses. In my judgment it would be wholly improper for this court to supplement that procedure by allowing a criminal prosecution.'

At the end of his judgment the judge declined jurisdiction in this case and counsel adopted his suggestion that the proper form of order was to quash the indictment and also to make an order and declaration that the prosecution and the proceedings, both in the Crown Court and in the magistrates' court, were invalid and of no effect.

The issues in this court are: (1) whether the court has jurisdiction to review the judge's decision to quash the indictment; (2) whether there has been undue delay in making the application for judicial review and, if so, whether the granting of the relief sought would be likely to cause substantial hardship to, or substantially prejudice the rights of, any of the defendants; and (3) whether the judge was right to decline jurisdiction on the ground that trial of the defendants on indictment

would have entailed a contravention of European Community law in either of the respects specified by the judge.
It is convenient to consider these issues in that order.

Jurisdiction

The issue under this head is whether this court has jurisdiction to entertain this application in the light of the provisions of the Supreme Court Act 1981.
Section 46, so far as material, provides:

'(1) All proceedings on indictment shall be brought before the Crown Court.

(2) The jurisdiction of the Crown Court with respect to proceedings on indictment shall include jurisdiction in proceedings on indictment for offences wherever committed . . .'

Section 29(3) provides:

'In relation to the jurisdiction of the Crown Court, other than its jurisdiction

in matters relating to trial on indictment, the High Court shall have all such jurisdiction to make orders of mandamus, prohibition or certiorari as the High Court possesses in relation to the jurisdiction of an inferior court.'

In *R v Crown Court at Sheffield, ex p Brownlow* [1980] 2 All ER 444, [1980] QB 530 the Court of Appeal was concerned with an application by a chief constable

for an order to quash the judge's pre-trial order for disclosure of criminal convictions recorded against members of the jury panel. Shaw LJ said ([1980] 2 All ER 444 at 454, [1980] QB 530 at 544):

'The closeness or remoteness of the relationship of the decision in question to the jurisdiction to try cases on indictment is wholly irrelevant ... Any decision as to a matter which arises out of or incidentally to or in the course

of that jurisdiction whether it relates to a proximate trial or a remote one falls, as I see it, inescapably and inevitably into the immunity from review by the High Court.'

Lord Denning MR, on the other hand, equated the determinative phrase 'relating to trial on indictment' with 'in the course of trial on indictment' (see [1980] 2 All ER 444 at 451–452, [1980] QB 530 at 540).

This case was reviewed by the House of Lords in *Smalley v Crown Court at Warwick* [1985] 1 All ER 769 at 779, [1985] AC 622 at 642–643, in which Lord ***a*** Bridge said:

> 'It is, of course, obvious that the phrase "relating to trial on indictment" in ss 28(2)(a) and 29(3) is apt to exclude appeal or judicial review in relation to the verdict given or sentence passed at the conclusion of a trial on indictment, both of which are subject to appeal as provided by the Criminal Appeal Act ***b*** 1968. I accept the submission of counsel for the respondents that in this context, as in ss 76 and 77 of the 1981 Act, the words "trial on indictment" must include the "trial" of a defendant who pleads guilty on arraignment. Beyond this it is not difficult to discern a sensible legislative purpose in excluding appeal or judicial review of any decision affecting the conduct of a trial on indictment, whether given in the course of the trial or by way of pre- ***c*** trial directions. In any such case to allow an appellate or review process might, as Shaw LJ pointed out in *Brownlow's* case [1980] 2 All ER 444 at 455, [1980] QB 530 at 544–545, seriously delay the trial. If it is the prosecutor who is aggrieved by such a decision, it is in no way surprising that he has no remedy, since prosecutors have never enjoyed rights of appeal or review ***d*** when unsuccessful in trials on indictment. If, on the other hand, the defendant is so aggrieved, he will have his remedy by way of appeal against conviction under the Criminal Appeal Act 1968 if he has suffered an injustice in consequence of a material irregularity in the course of the trial, which, I apprehend, may well result not only from a decision given during the trial, but equally from a decision given in advance of the trial which affects the ***e*** conduct of the trial, eg a wrongful refusal to grant him legal aid. I can, however, discover no intelligible legislative purpose which would be served by giving to the words "relating to trial on indictment" a wider operation than indicated in the foregoing paragraph. An order estreating the recognisance of surety for a defendant who fails to surrender to his bail at the Crown Court to which he was committed for trial cannot affect the conduct ***f*** of any trial on indictment in any way ... If, therefore, the phrase "relating to trial on indictment" may be construed broadly or narrowly, a purposive approach points, to my mind, unmistakably to a construction sufficiently narrow, at all events, to avoid the exclusion of judicial review in such a case as this.'
> ***g***

Having commented in relation to *Brownlow's* case that Lord Denning MR took too narrow a view and that he could find nothing in the language or the policy of the legislation to support what he called the 'sweeping statements' of Shaw LJ, which I have cited, Lord Bridge said ([1985] 1 All ER 769 at 780, [1985] AC 622 at 643–644): ***h***

> 'It must not be thought that in using the phrase "any decision affecting the conduct of a trial on indictment" I am offering a definition of a phrase which Parliament has chosen not to define. If the statutory language is, as here, imprecise, it may well be impossible to prescribe in the abstract a precise test to determine on which side of the line any case should fall and, therefore, ***j*** necessary to proceed, as counsel for the appellant submitted that we should, on a case by case basis. But it is obviously desirable that your Lordships' House should give as clear guidance as the statutory language permits, and I hope the criterion I have suggested may provide a helpful pointer to the right answer in most cases.'

The House reverted to this topic in *Sampson v Crown Court at Croydon* [1987] 1
a All ER 609 at 611, [1987] 1 WLR 194 at 196 in which Lord Bridge said:

> 'It is in any event clear, I apprehend, that certain orders made at the
> conclusion of a trial on indictment are excluded from judicial review as
> "relating to trial on indictment" not because they affect the conduct of the
> trial, but rather because they are themselves an integral part of the trial
b > process. This is obviously true of the verdict and sentence.'

In the light of these authorities this court has had to consider in two recent
cases whether it had jurisdiction to entertain an application for judicial review of
the refusal by a judge of the Crown Court to order a stay of proceedings on the
ground of delay amounting to an abuse of the process. The court held in *R v*
c *Central Criminal Court, ex p Randle* [1992] 1 All ER 370, [1991] 1 WLR 1087 and
reaffirmed in *R v Crown Court at Norwich, ex p Belsham* [1992] 1 All ER 394, [1992]
1 WLR 54 that an application to stay an indictment on grounds of abuse of process
did not affect the conduct of the trial because, if granted, it would permanently
prevent the trial taking place or continuing, that such an application was not
therefore a matter 'relating to trial on indictment' under s 29(3) of the 1981 Act
d and that, accordingly, the High Court in the exercise of its supervisory jurisdiction
had jurisdiction to entertain the application for judicial review.

For the DPP in the present case Mr Barling QC submitted that the orders and
declaration made by Morland J were neither themselves an integral part of the
trial nor did they affect the conduct of the trial. They were directed to the
question of the existence of the court's jurisdiction rather than the exercise of that
e jurisdiction. He submitted that Parliament cannot have intended to exclude
judicial review in relation to such a question and that s 29(3) is not to be construed
as having that effect. He supported this submission by citing *Randle*'s case [1992]
1 All ER 370 at 386, [1991] 1 WLR 1087 at 1103, where Watkins LJ, giving the
judgment of the court, said:

f > 'If approaching the matter in the way Lord Bridge indicates is appropriate,
> we are inclined to the view that a decision on an application to stay on
> grounds of abuse of process does not affect the *conduct* of a trial on indictment,
> because what is being determined is whether there should ever *be* a trial.'
> (Watkins LJ's emphasis.)

g That case was expressly upheld in *Belsham*'s case; and in the similar case of *R v*
Crown Court at Manchester, ex p Cunningham [1992] COD 23 this court drew a
distinction between cases relating to an actual trial on indictment and those where
'consideration is being given as to whether there should be a trial at all'.

Mr Barling sought to distinguish the motion to quash in the present case from
the type envisaged by Watkins LJ in the cases cited. He also contended that it
h would be contrary to principle for the Crown Court's determination of the
boundaries of its own jurisdiction to be conclusive. Finally, he invoked art 5 of
the EEC Treaty for the duty it confers on the United Kingdom to take all measures
necessary to guarantee the application and effectiveness of Community law.

Mr Robertson QC, who presented the argument for the defendants on this
issue, argued that the judge's decision to quash the indictment was valid in form,
j and that it was a matter 'relating to trial on indictment' both literally and in the
purposive sense adopted by the House of Lords. A decision to quash an indictment
affects the conduct of a trial and is part of the trial process. Lord Bridge's use of
these expressions was intended to exclude peripheral matters from immunity
from review. By controlling the immunity Parliament intended to avoid delay,
to give the defendant (but not the prosecution) a right of appeal, and also to give

the defendant a right to treat the judge's decision as final. The defendants relied on *Randle*'s case and *Belsham*'s case for their assumption that a motion to quash is *a* part of trial on indictment and proposed as a test that, wherever a decision is made on the merits or legality of the indictment and the allegation it contains, that decision is unreviewable.

Mr Robertson further supported his submission by an eloquent plea that a motion to stay for abuse is an invitation to a court to exercise its inherent power to stop a proceeding because it is per se oppressive and unfair. Such an order does *b* not relate to trial on indictment in any procedural sense at all: it is not part of a trial nor does it have any impact on the way the trial is conducted. A motion to quash, on the other hand, is concerned with the form of the indictment. This may be a technical form (such as duplicity) or substantive form (such as the charging of an offence unknown to English law, or an offence which the court *c* has no jurisdiction to try). He submitted that it is plain from the cases in the House of Lords that an order to quash the indictment, or any count thereof, is unreviewable. There is no decision which is more closely related to trial on indictment than a decision as to whether the indictment is good or bad. It relates to the legal foundation for the trial itself. The soundness of the indictment is integral to the trial process. It affects the conduct of the trial in that it decides on *d* what counts, if any, the trial shall be conducted. In so far as it results in delay, it offends both public policy and legislative intent. In asserting the distinction between a motion to stay a trial on the ground of abuse of process and a motion to quash an indictment, Mr Robertson urged that the distinction is in reality between an order that an unjust trial should not take place and an order that an indictment is so deficient that it cannot form the basis for a trial. He supported *e* this distinction by the submission that abuse decisions are reviewable because the jurisdiction to stay for abuse is independent of the statutory jurisdiction to try a case on indictment and arises at common law.

Looking at the words of the subsection without the benefit of authority, it would be difficult to say that the quashing of an indictment is not a matter *f* 'relating to trial on indictment'. The use of the expression 'trial on indictment' as distinct from 'a trial on indictment' might have been thought to indicate an intention to distinguish it from other aspects of the court's jurisdiction, such as appeals from magistrates' courts. But the stress laid by the House of Lords in *Smalley*'s case and in *Sampson*'s case on 'the conduct of the trial' and 'the trial process' shows that weight must be given to the actual trial. Thus the forfeiture *g* of a surety's recognisance is not within the exception, but an order that an acquitted defendant should make a legal aid contribution is within it.

This accounts for the decisions of the Divisional Court which have held that applications to stay are outwith the exception and are therefore amenable to judicial review. The court has held that such applications do not affect the conduct of a trial, and so do not relate to trial on indictment because, if granted, they *h* would permanently prevent the trial from taking place.

It was conceded by counsel in both cases that a motion to quash was a matter relating to the conduct of the trial and thus within the exception. The court remarked in *Belsham*'s case [1992] 1 All ER 394 at 402, [1992] 1 WLR 54 at 62–63 that—

j

'a motion to quash is part and parcel of the trial process invariably made at the court of trial on the day fixed for the hearing while an application for a stay is designed to stop the trial taking place on grounds unrelated to the indictment and to the conduct of a trial, namely that it would be unfair for the trial to take place at all.'

But the court at once specified what sort of motion to quash it had in mind
a ([1992] 1 All ER 394 at 402, [1992] 1 WLR 54 at 63):

> 'We would indorse that court's reasoning and emphasise that a motion to
> quash an indictment is made to ensure that the defendant be tried on a count
> that is properly framed. Such a motion, is, we think, inseparable from the
> conduct of the trial. It relates directly to the question of whether there exists
> *b* a properly framed indictment which is essential to the launch of the trial
> itself.'

Similarly, in *Randle's* case [1992] 1 All ER 370 at 386, [1991] 1 WLR 1087 at
1103 the court said:

> *c* 'An application to stay on the grounds that the proceedings are an abuse of
> process seems to us to be in an altogether different category. It is an attempt
> to stop the trial taking place, not by reason of some defect in the indictment,
> but on grounds quite separate and distinct. It is an application based on
> principles of fairness and justice, and the contention is that it would be unjust
> that there should be a trial at all. It is not, in the sense that an application to
> *d* quash is, part of the trial process.'

It had earlier remarked ([1992] 1 All ER 370 at 379–380, [1991] 1 WLR 1087
at 1096):

> '. . . it can undoubtedly be said that an application made before a trial
> commences for an order in effect to prohibit that trial from taking place does
> *e* not affect the conduct of the trial and is not an integral part of the trial
> process. Of course, the application may, as it did in this case, fail, in which
> case the trial proceeds. Here again, however, the dismissal of the order
> determines merely that there shall be a trial, not how it shall take place. In
> that sense the dismissal of the application neither affects the conduct of the
> *f* trial nor is it an integral part of it.'

The type of motion to quash that was being distinguished was one directed to
the framing of the indictment. Here the application to the court was that it
should decline jurisdiction on the ground that the exercise of it would infringe
what the judge called the 'sovereignty' of the European Parliament. In my
g judgment, the 1981 Act does not have the effect of rendering immune from
judicial review the very question whether the court has jurisdiction as distinct
from the manner of its exercise. It would not make for the orderly conduct of the
law if the determination of individual judges of the Crown Court that Community
law prohibits criminal proceedings of a particular kind were immune from
challenge and so from supervision.

h Mr Barling helpfully referred us to various passages from Sir William Wade's
work on *Administrative Law* (6th edn, 1988) esp at p 297 where there is a citation
from Farwell LJ in *R v Shoreditch Assessment Committee, ex p Morgan* [1910] 2 KB
859 at 880 where he said:

> 'No tribunal of inferior jurisdiction can by its own decision finally decide
> on the question of the existence or extent of such jurisdiction: such question
> is always subject to review by the High Court, which does not permit the
> inferior tribunal either to usurp a jurisdiction which it does not possess . . .
> or to refuse to exercise a jurisdiction which it has . . . Subjection in this
> respect to the High Court is a necessary and inseparable incident to all
> tribunals of limited jurisdiction; for the existence of the limit necessitates an

authority to determine and enforce it; it is a contradiction in terms to create
a tribunal with limited jurisdiction and unlimited power to determine such *a*
limit at its own will and pleasure—such a tribunal would be autocratic, not
limited—and it is immaterial whether the decision of the inferior tribunal
on the question of the existence or non-existance of its own jurisdiction is
founded on law or fact . . .'

It is pointed out that this was said about administrative tribunals. But in my *b*
judgment it applies equally to courts of limited jurisdiction which are otherwise
amenable to judicial review. It would equally be a contradiction in terms to create
a court with limited jurisdiction, and unlimited power to determine such limits
at its own will and pleasure, whether the existence or otherwise of its own
jurisdiction was founded on law or fact.

To Mr Plender QC's point that it would be anomalous if an objection to *c*
jurisdiction taken at the close of the prosecution case were immune from review
whereas the same objection taken before the trial began would not be, the answers
must be that a defendant who is not acquitted until the close of the prosecution
case will have been in jeopardy and that, following his acquittal, the Attorney
General could still test the point of law by reference to the Court of Appeal.

I have therefore come to the conclusion that this court has jurisdiction to *d*
entertain the motion for judicial review.

Delay

Mr Robertson also relied on such delay as has occurred in these proceedings as
relevant to the court's discretion to refuse the relief sought. The offences charged *e*
were alleged to have been committed in May 1986 and May 1987. The police
became aware of the allegations in 1987, and then began an investigation which
included the search of Mr Huckfield's home in 1988, visits to Strasbourg in 1989,
and the arrest of the defendants on 4 June 1990. It is also said that the police must
have become aware during this time of what may be termed 'the European
connection', and that that placed them under a statutory duty to report the matter *f*
to the Director of Public Prosecutions: see the Prosecution of Offences Regulations
1978, SI 1978/1357, reg 6(1)(*f*). It is said that at the hearing of the pre-trial review
on 15 July 1991 prosecuting counsel was told about the argument of Community
law and the authorities on which the defendants would rely. On any view, after
the application which resulted in the quashing of the indictment on 4 September
1991, the Crown knew in fullest detail what the defendants' case was. The *g*
essential question is whether the Crown acted promptly to seek judicial review of
the judge's order thereafter. The application for leave to move was not lodged
until 3 December 1991, only one day within the time allowed.

Mr Dowd is aged 73; Mr Ennis has received a suspended sentence for similar
offences; and Mr Huckfield is not alleged to have made any personal gain from *h*
his involvement in these matters. In those circumstances it is submitted that the
lack of promptness shown by the Crown after the judge's order of 4 September
1991 was made was such as would be likely to cause them substantial hardship.

In an affidavit submitted in draft during the hearing against an undertaking to
file it at once, the Crown Prosecutor has deposed that the judge's decision—

'raised novel, important and complex issues of law and policy which had *j*
to be considered by a number of different Government Departments and on
which legal advice had to be obtained and considered.'

This process was impeded by the fact that the transcript of the judgment was not
available for over five weeks after it had been given. After legal advice had been

obtained from leading and junior counsel one of the law officers had to be
a consulted.

Whilst I regard the difficulties by which the Crown say they were confronted
as exaggerated, I do not consider that such delay as can be said to have occurred in
making the application was 'undue' within the meaning of s 31(6) of the Supreme
Court Act 1981, nor do I consider that such delay as has occurred should affect the
court's willingness to grant relief, should it otherwise be so minded.
b

Community law

As I have earlier indicated, the judge upheld the respondents' objection to the
court's jurisdiction on two grounds: first, because the need for the court to
interpret the rules of a political group of the European Parliament would involve
c an infringement of what he called the 'sovereignty' of the Parliament; and,
secondly, because it would be improper for the court, by allowing criminal
prosecution, to supplement the European Parliament's own procedure, albeit not
of a criminal nature, for dealing with improper payments of expenses. It is
common ground that the European Parliament is not sovereign, but is
autonomous. In dealing succesively with these issues I shall therefore refer to
d them as 'autonomy' and 'comity'.

(a) *Autonomy*

Mr Plender, who presented the arguments of Community law on behalf of the
defendants, advanced as his main submission the proposition that as a matter of
Community law, national authorities are bound to respect the decision by the
e European Parliament to refund to MEPs expenses for political activities or for
information campaigns, and the decision taken by the European Parliament that
a claim for such expenses is in order. He contended that a review carried out in
this area by the national authorities, without the consent of the European
Parliament, including a review conducted in the courts of criminal proceedings
against a person who claims expenses in his capacity as an MEP, constitutes an
f interference in the internal functioning of the European Parliament resulting in
a substitution by the national authorities of their appraisal of an MEP's claim for
the appraisal undertaken by the European Parliament in the exercise of its powers.
Each side relied as its main authority on the decision of the Court of Justice of the
European Communities in *Lord Bruce of Donington v Aspden* Case 208/80 [1981]
g ECR 2205. That case raised the issue whether a member state may tax payments
made to an MEP from Community funds as travel and subsistence expenses.
Lord Bruce contended that by reason of art 142 of the EEC Treaty and the first
para of art 8 of the Protocol on the Privileges and Immunities of the European
Communities, which guarantees the free movement of MEPs, the authorities of
the member states were precluded from reviewing the performance by an MEP
h of his duties, including his travel and his related expenditure, in order to see
whether there existed any excess of reimbursement over actual expenses, with a
view to taxing such excess. Lord Bruce contended that member states were not
entitled to tax payments made by the European Parliament for these purposes.
By its judgment the court confirmed that the rules adopted by the Euroepan
Parliament governing subsistence and travelling expenses of MEPs fell within the
j scope of measures of internal organisation the adoption of which was a matter for
the European Parliament pursuant to the first para of art 142 of the EEC Treaty.

After remarking that the appropriations available to the European Parliament
for the reimbursement of expenses of MEPs are subject to the budgetary
procedures provided for by Community law, the court continued (at 2220
(para 19)):

'It is clear from the foregoing that the national authorities are bound to respect the decision taken by the European Parliament to refund travel and *a* subsistence expenses to its Members on a lump-sum basis. A review carried out in this area by the national revenue authorities, such as the one provided for by the United Kingdom legislation, constitutes an interference in the internal functioning of the Parliament resulting in a substitution by the national authorities of their appraisal of the system of allowances for the one undertaken by the Parliament in the exercise of its powers. It would therefore *b* be likely to impair the effectiveness of the action of the Parliament and be incompatible with its autonomy.'

The court concluded that it would be incompatible with this system for revenue authorities to demand from an MEP vouchers for expenses actually incurred. The court added (at 2220–2221 (para 21)): *c*

'In so far as the lump sum fixed for the allowances is excessive and in reality constitutes in part disguised remuneration and not reimbursement of expenses, the Member States are entitled to charge such remuneration to national income tax, given that in the present state of Community law the remuneration of Members of the Parliament is a matter of national law and *d* is not the responsibility of the institutions of the Community. However, an assessment of whether the lump sums fixed by the Parliament are excessive, which is, moreover, a matter of Community law alone, was not requested by the national tribunal, before which it was not alleged that at the time the allowances were unreasonably high.' *e*

Mr Plender invoked art 5 of the EEC Treaty in support of his submission that the obligation to respect decisions made by the European Parliament, and to refrain from reviewing them (or to co-operate with the Parliament), is a duty owed by the United Kingdom to the European Parliament and to other member states pursuant to that article. It provides: *f*

'Member States shall take all appropriate measures, whether general or particular, to ensure fulfilment of the obligations arising out of this Treaty or resulting from action taken by the institutions of the Community. They shall facilitate the achievement of the Community's tasks. They shall abstain from any measure which could jeopardise the attainment of the objectives of *g* this Treaty.'

Mr Plender argued that the claims in respect of which the indictment was laid were for expenses which the European Parliament had decided to make available for political activities or for information campaigns, and that both that decision and the decisions to accept the claims were made by the European Parliament in *h* respect of its internal functioning with which any review by the police and the criminal courts, conducted without the consent of the Parliament, would constitute an interference. This was apparently the view taken by the President of the European Parliament as well as by the chairman of the British Labour Group.

Mr Barling, however, emphasised the court's recognition in *Lord Bruce of* *j* *Donington v Aspden* that in the absence of any provision conferring a tax exemption on MEPs, the member states were entitled to tax any emoluments derived by them from the exercise of their mandate, that in so far as the lump sum fixed by the European Parliament was excessive in relation to expenses actually incurred, so as to constitute disguised remuneration, member states were entitled to subject the excess to national income tax, and that the question whether a lump sum was

a excessive was a question of Community law capable of being raised by the competent national authority in the course of proceedings in the national court. These features are at variance with the judge's reasoning because they show that a national court is entitled to proceed with a case that involves the need to interpret the European Parliament's rules. It seems to me that the reference (see [1981]

b ECR 2205 at 2220–2221 (para 21)) to an assessment of whether the lump sums fixed by the European Parliament are excessive, being a matter of Community law alone, is to the principle that a measure adopted by a Community institution can only be declared invalid by the European Court itself.

As Mr Barling has pointed out, the validity of the rules of the European Parliament and of its political groups about expenses is not challenged. What is

c alleged is that Community funds were dishonestly appropriated without the European Parliament or the relevant political group being aware of the dishonesty.

Since the European Court has in several cases, such as *Wybot v Faure* Case 149/ 85 [1986] ECR 2391 and *Parti écologiste 'Les Verts v European Parliament* Case 294/ 83 [1986] ECR 1339, considered questions not only about the interpretation but also about the validity of rules of the European Parliament upon reference in the

d course of proceedings before national courts, it seems to me to follow ineluctably that the judge's notion that the need to interpret the relevant rules precluded the assumption of jurisdiction by a Crown Court was based upon a fundamental misconception. Since such rules can be referred for interpretation to the European Court, the fact that national proceedings may give rise to the need to interpret them cannot deprive the national court of jurisdiction. In my judgment there is

e nothing that this court has been told about the conduct of the proposed prosecution which would or might detract from the autonomy of the European Parliament; and I do not accept that art 5 imports a duty to respect decisions of the European Parliament of which the United Kingdom would be in breach if the defendants were prosecuted.

f

(b) *Comity*

In this court Mr Plender did not use the word 'comity'. Instead, he seemed to rely upon the argument that recourse to prosecution by a national authority without consent would in some way prejudice immunity to which his former status as an MEP entitled him. Mr Plender speculated that the reason why there

g is apparently no precedent for an attempt by national police to prosecute an MEP for a claim made to the European Parliament for expenses may be that in most member states such proceedings would not be initiated at all, without a waiver of the immunity given to all MEPs. He submits that the conclusion of the European Parliament's Committee on Rules, Powers and Immunities that an MEP enjoys a

h parliamentary immunity from prosecution in respect of political acts is itself an essay in autonomy. This, he says, may be justified on the practical ground that differences should be eliminated between the immunities, and so the risks of prosecution, which MEPs enjoy and to which they are subject, according to which member state they represent. Mr Plender argues that in this context it is for the European Parliament to give or withhold consent to the bringing of a prosecution.

j Relevant to the exercise of the court's discretion, though not to its jurisdiction, is the fact that Mr Balfe, from whom Mr Huckfield is alleged to have obtained the two cheques the subject of the indictment, is apparently an unwilling witness, and is not compellable. Even if the court could compel his attendance, and even though the European Parliament could waive his immunity, no application has been made for either purpose.

On this latter issue this court does not have sufficient information to enable it to evaluate either the importance of Mr Balfe's evidence or the likelihood that he would not give it.

On the main issue of comity I have great difficulty in understanding how it can be said that in circumstances where there is no provision of Community law which exempts an MEP from criminal liability, and there is no way in which the European Parliament could take criminal proceedings against him, prosecution by a national authority can be said to be unwarranted or exceptionable, let alone 'wholly improper'. The Protocol on the Privileges and Immunities of the European Communities defines precisely the immunities from legal proceedings, including criminal proceedings, to which an MEP is entitled. Since an immunity cannot be enjoyed which has not been expressly granted, and since it has not been suggested that any express provision for immunity applies in this case, there is no exemption which the defendants can invoke. If there was any dishonest obtaining of expenses I am not myself persuaded that the European Parliament can impose even disciplinary sanctions against a former MEP. Certainly there is no provision which makes the initiation of prosecutions for criminal offences connected with expenses the sole prerogative of the European Parliament. But I do not find much more compelling than Mr Plender's argument on art 5 of the EEC Treaty Mr Barling's corresponding submissions that, irrespective of the attitude of the European Parliament, the member state concerned owes a duty under art 5 to take criminal proceedings in order to penalise misuse of Community funds. That there is imposed by art 5 of the Treaty 'a duty to prosecute and impose appropriate penalties on those who infringe Community law in such a way as to prejudice its effectiveness' was explained by Advocate General Tesauro in *EC Commission v Greece* Case 68/88 [1989] ECR 2965 at 2977. This opinion was expressly confirmed by the European Court itself which said (at 2985 (para 24)):

'... whilst the choice of penalties remains within their discretion, [the member states] must ensure in particular that infringements of Community law are penalized under conditions, both procedural and substantive, which are analogous to those applicable to infringements of national law of a similar nature and importance and which, in any event, make the penalty effective, proportionate and dissuasive.'

It is, however, unnecessary for present purposes to decide whether the United Kingdom would be in breach of this duty were it to refrain from taking criminal proceedings in respect of the offences alleged against the defendants. It is sufficient that the adoption of that course is not shown to be incompatible with any provision of Community law, from which it follows that maintenance of the prosecution cannot be said to be in disharmony with proceedings of the European Parliament so as to offend the principle of comity.

Conclusion

In summary, there is no concept of 'sovereignty', except in so far as it denotes the autonomy of the European Parliament in relation to the organisation of its internal affairs. Member states are entitled to prosecute an MEP (or former MEP) for criminal offences of obtaining by dishonesty expenses from the Parliament. The question whether they were obtained by dishonesty is a question of *national* law which is capable of being raised by a prosecutor in criminal proceedings in a national court.

Neither the validity nor the interpretation of the European Parliament's rules is here in question, though both can be the subject of proceedings in national

courts or the Court of Justice. Since the interpretation and even the validity of the
a European Parliament's rules can be referred, if need be, to the Court of Justice,
the national courts cannot be precluded from assuming jurisdiction in a case in
which the rules might be relevant.

No provision of Community law exempts an MEP (or former MEP) from
criminal liability. An MEP enjoys no immunities except such as are specified in
the protocol. Since irregular payments can only be deducted from a group's
b appropriation, and no sanctions can be imposed on a former MEP, the only way
of bringing criminal proceedings against him is in a national court, whether or
not art 5 imports a duty to do so.

It should not be a matter of surprise that an MEP is liable to criminal
proceedings in this country in respect of offences connected with his membership.
c It might be thought sensible if all MEPs were dealt with alike, and if the outcome
of such criminal proceedings did not depend upon the immunities accorded, and
the penalties imposed, by the particular member state they happened to represent.
But that result could only be achieved by an appropriate provision of Community
law. That is why the first step, disavowing preconceptions, is to inquire whether
any provision of Community law accords to a former MEP immunity from
d criminal prosecution. None does. There is then no inhibition on the prosecution
of the former MEP unless the review by national authorities of this alleged offence
constitutes an interference with the internal functioning of the Parliament. In
this case that could only occur if the process of review involved any challenge to
the validity or to the interpretation of the rules of the Parliament or one of its
groups. Neither is challenged. What is called in question is the honesty of the
e defendants in claiming expenses as provided by the rules. Whether cheques in
payment of such expenses were obtained dishonestly is peculiarly a matter for
resolution by prosecution in a national court. What would be surprising would
be if no criminal proceedings could be brought at all against a dishonest person
simply because he was a former MEP.

f In these circumstances Mr Plender argues that if the court is against the
defendants on jurisdiction and on discretion, as well as on art 5, the court should
refer to the Court of Justice of the European Communities the questions of
Community law arising in this case, and he has proffered draft questions for
reference, which I need not particularise. In a remarkable about-face to the
Crown's attitude adopted in the Crown Court Mr Barling has also, though less
g forcefully, urged a reference at this stage. From these submissions it seems to
follow that whilst the Crown would be interested, for the clarification of the law
in this important context, to obtain the definitive ruling of the European Court,
the defendants must wish to take that course only if there remains no other means
of avoiding prosecution. In circumstances where it has seemed to this court that
the determination of sensitive issues of Community law admits of only one
h sensible solution, and where the prosecution of the defendants has already been
subject to delays longer than are normally regarded as tolerable in criminal cases,
I do not consider that the court should at this stage introduce into the process a
procedure which would inevitably cause further delay that would, we are told, be
of the order of 18 months. I would accordingly decline to order any reference to
the European Court.
j I would quash the orders and the declaration made by the judge.

As a footnote I add that the quality of counsel's skeleton arguments and pre-
reading by the court in its own time enabled the oral arguments of three leading
counsel to be presented in no more than 1½ days, after which the urgency of the
matter (as we see it) has moved us to give judgment at once without the further
consideration that the main issues raised no doubt deserve.

PILL J. I agree with the order proposed. For the purpose of considering whether a matter comes within the words of exception in s 29(3) of the Supreme Court *a* Act 1981, as relating to 'trial on indictment', not all motions to quash fall on the same side of the line indicated by Lord Bridge in *Smalley v Crown Court at Warwick* [1985] 1 All ER 769 at 780, [1985] AC 622 at 643. The application to quash in the present case did not depend on whether the indictment was properly framed but upon whether, in the light of Community law, the court had jurisdiction.

I agree with Leggatt LJ that the case did not come within the exception in *b* s 29(3) and with Leggatt LJ's reasoning. I cannot accept Mr Robertson QC's submission that Watkins LJ, giving the judgment of the court in *R v Central Criminal Court, ex p Randle* [1992] 1 All ER 370, [1991] 1 WLR 1087 and in *R v Crown Court at Norwich, ex p Belsham* [1992] 1 All ER 394, [1992] 1 WLR 54, was laying down that the distinction to be drawn in this context is always the distinction between an order that an unjust trial should not, on grounds of *c* morality, take place and an order that an indictment is, for whatever reason, so deficient that it cannot form the basis for a trial. Watkins LJ was not deciding that an order in the second category must inevitably be an order relating to trial on indictment. The court in *Randle's* case was considering questions of fairness and justice because it was considering an application based on an alleged abuse of *d* process.

That one factor to be considered, in applying s 29(3), is whether a trial should take place at all, emerges clearly from the extracts from the judgment in *Randle's* case cited by Leggatt LJ. More recently in *R v Crown Court at Leicester, ex p S (a minor)* [1992] 2 All ER 659 at 661 Watkins LJ stated:

> 'The leading principle of law which arises from the authorities can be said *e* to be that if the matter in contention, be it an act, decision or order, is either an integral part of the trial process or it affects the course of the trial, the matter comes within the words of exception in s 29(3) of the 1981 Act and judicial review is not available in respect of it; otherwise it is reviewable.'

We are not constrained by decisions of this court from approaching the statute *f* in the manner indicated by Lord Bridge in *Smalley's* case and *Sampson v Crown Court at Croydon* [1987] 1 All ER 609, [1987] 1 WLR 194 which is what, in my judgment, the court in *Randle's* case did. For the reasons given by Leggatt LJ, the court has jurisdiction to entertain the application for judicial review of Morland J's decision to quash the indictment against Mr Huckfield (the defendant) and *g* others.

The defendant was charged on an indictment containing two alleged offences of obtaining property by deception contrary to s 15(1) of the Theft Act 1968. Other defendants were also charged. The charge includes allegations that the defendant dishonestly obtained cheques from R A Balfe by deception, namely by falsely representing that the documents which were sent to Mr Balfe were all *h* genuine and original documents and related to actual or proposed expenditure in respect of which the defendant was entitled to payment from the British Labour Group of the European Parliament.

Morland J, in the course of his judgment, stated that there was a clear prima facie case that the supporting documents were 'utterly bogus and the proceeds of the cheques were improperly paid'. I accept the contention of both parties to this *j* application that, for present purposes, the actual documents do not require further consideration.

The Crown's case, as noted by the learned judge, was that the proceeds went into legal defence funds to support certain suspended Labour Party members. The learned judge also noted that the defendant's case was that he honestly

believed that the supporting documents were genuine and that he was the
a innocent conduit pipe for the frauds of others. It was not suggested by the Crown
that the defendant had benefited personally.

Morland J declined jurisdiction on the ground that the issues in the case were
such that the court would be required to interpret rules of the European
Parliament and that to do so would be an infringement of its sovereignty. A
prosecution would also offend the principles of comity. The learned judge stated
b that it would be wholly improper for the court to supplement the European
Parliament's procedures for dealing with irregular or improper payment of
expenses by allowing a criminal prosecution.

The learned judge obviously attached importance to the contents of letters
written by parliamentary figures and cited extensive extracts from them. The
letters included those from Mr Ramsay, director of the private office of the
c European Parliament, on 6 October 1988, Mr Rudi Arndt, chairman of the
Socialist Group in the European Parliament, on 10 November 1988 and 14 March
1989 and Lord Plumb, former President of the European Parliament, on
30 August 1991. We also have before us a letter from the current President of the
European Parliament, Dr Egan Klepoh, sent in June 1992 to the Attorney General
d and indorsing the views of Lord Plumb.

Mr Arndt stated on 14 March 1989:

'I would inform you again that, in as far as Leslie Huckfield has submitted
accounts to us for monies from the information campaign fund, these have
been checked in London and Brussels and found to be in order before
reimbursement was made. These accounts are available for inspection by the
e Court of Auditors in accordance with the regulations of our Institution. If
you have the slightest indication that the regulations of the European
Parliament have been contravened in any way, I would ask you to let me
know.'

f Lord Plumb stated:

'I was of the view then and remain of the view, that any alleged irregularity
or alleged dishonesty in a claim for expenses made by a serving member of
the European Parliament lies within the exclusive jurisdiction of the
European Parliament and is to be determined by that Parliament in
accordance with its own Rules. Therefore, I am of the view respectfully that
g any domestic national Court hearing of a Member State of the European
Community prima facie infringes upon the Sovereignty of the European
Parliament.'

It is not suggested in this court that the Protocol on the Privileges and
Immunities of the European Communities confers immunity from prosecution
h upon the defendant. It is accepted on behalf of the defendant that the question
whether the European Parliament is sovereign, or the sovereign legislative
authority, does not arise upon this application. What is at issue, it is submitted, is
the European Parliament's autonomy with respect to its internal functioning. It
is also common ground that the proposed prosecution does not involve a challenge
to the rules of the European Parliament or to the internal rules of the Socialist
j Group.

The defendant's submission is that his prosecution constitutes an interference
in the internal functioning of the European Parliament resulting in a substitution
of the English court's appraisal of the member's claim for expenses for the
appraisal undertaken by the European Parliament in the exercise of its powers. It
is accepted that the Parliament could consent to the bringing of a prosecution, or

even request the national authorities to take appropriate action, in the event of a misappropriation of the Community's funds. It is submitted, by reference to *EC* *a* *Commission v Greece* Case 68/88 [1989] ECR 2965, that, if the European Parliament requests the national authorities to do so, member states must take such action as may be necessary to guarantee the effectiveness of Community law.

What does not follow, it is submitted, is that the national authorities have a duty, or indeed a power, to prosecute where the Community institution has not concluded that it has been a victim of fraud and has not called on the member *b* state to act but, indeed, has protested against the initiation of proceedings.

Mr Plender QC for the defendant accepts that if the relevant claim for, and payment of, expenses had been made by and to a member of an English institution, such as a county council, views expressed by the chairman or officers of the council that payments were 'in order' would not be conclusive of the question whether the claim was an honest one. The issues arising upon a deception *c* charge could properly be investigated by the courts. He submits, however, that by reason of arts 5 and 142 of the EEC Treaty and the decision of the Court of Justice of the European Communities in *Lord Bruce of Donington v Aspden* Case 208/80 [1981] ECR 2205, the United Kingdom and its authorities are under an obligation to respect the decision of the European Parliament and indeed the *d* European Parliament's views as expressed by officers. There has been no formal resolution or decision of the European Parliament that the relevant payments were in order. What is relied on, as excluding the jurisdiction of the English court, are the statements of the president and relevant officers of the Socialist group considered in the context of the EEC Treaty obligation in art 5. The expenses claim has been checked on behalf of the European Parliament, it is *e* submitted, and found to be in good order and that is the end of the matter.

Articles 4(1) and 5 of the EEC Treaty provide:

'*Article 4*
1. The tasks entrusted to the Community shall be carried out by the *f* following institutions: a European Parliament, a COUNCIL, a COMMISSION, a COURT OF JUSTICE.

Each institution shall act within the limits of the powers conferred upon it by this Treaty . . .

Article 5 *g*
Member States shall take all appropriate measures, whether general or particular, to ensure fulfilment of the obligations arising out of this Treaty or resulting from action taken by the institutions of the Community. They shall facilitate the achievement of the Community's tasks.

They shall abstain from any measure which could jeopardise the attainment *h* of the objectives of this Treaty.'

We have been referred to a decision of the European Court upon the meaning of art 5 in *France v European Parliament* Joined cases 358/85 and 51/86 [1988] ECR 4821. The court stated (at 4855 (para 34)):

'With a view to determining the significance of the decisions of the *j* governments of the Member States, attention should also be drawn to the rule imposing reciprocal obligations of bona fide cooperation on the Member States and the Community institutions, as embodied in particular in Article 5 of the EEC Treaty. As regards the working conditions of the Parliament, that rule is of particular importance in a situation where the governments of the Member States have not yet fulfilled their obligation to establish the seat of *a*   the institutions or even decided on a single provisional working place for the Parliament.'

Article 142 provides in its first sentence: 'The European Parliament shall adopt its rules of procedure, acting by a majority of its members.' It is not suggested that the article confers a general power to exempt members of the Parliament from criminal proceedings in member states.

b   In *Lord Bruce of Donington's* case, the United Kingdom Commissioners for the Special Purposes of the Income Tax Acts referred to the European Court the question whether any rule of European law, including art 142, should be interpreted as precluding member states from taxing any part of the expenses and allowances paid from Community funds to members of the European Parliament. The court's ruling was that Community law prohibits the imposition of national

c   tax on lump sum payments made by the European Parliament to its members from Community funds by way of reimbursement of travel and subsistence expenses, unless it can be shown in accordance with Community law that such lump sum reimbursement constitutes in part remuneration.

The European Court stated ([1981] ECR 2205 at 2219 (para 15)):

d   'Rules such as those adopted by the Parliament governing subsistence and travel expenses and allowances therefore fall within the scope of measures of internal organization whose adoption is a matter for the Parliament pursuant to . . .'

and there is a reference to several articles including art 142 of the EEC Treaty.

e   The court concluded (at 2220 (para 19)):

      'It is clear from the foregoing that the national authorities are bound to respect the decision taken by the European Parliament to refund travel and subsistence expenses to its Members on a lump-sum basis.'

f   The court went on to hold that it was open to member states to challenge whether, as a matter of Community law, the lump sum payments were excessive. The European Parliament's decision to refund expenses on a lump sum basis, rather than on some other basis, cannot however be challenged by national authorities.

It does not follow that the jurisdiction of the English courts to consider whether the defendant obtained valuable securities from the commission in the dishonest

g   manner alleged in the indictment is excluded. The prosecution does not involve a challenge to the validity or the reasonableness of the expenses rules of the European Parliament or of a political grouping. Those rules can be construed in an English court if the need arises and subject to the powers and duties of the court under art 177 of the Treaty. For the purposes of the present application, I

h   see no valid distinction between the rules of the European Parliament and those of a political grouping within the European Parliament.

Having considered the EEC Treaty and the decision in *Lord Bruce of Donington's* case, I am unable to read into the Treaty obligations of the United Kingdom anything excluding the jurisdiction of the English court in a case in which specific claims for expenses are alleged to have been made dishonestly. Neither can I read

j   the Treaty as conferring upon the European Parliament, or individual officers, an exclusive jurisdiction to determine the honesty of members' claims for expenses out of community funds. I also agree with the decisions of Leggatt LJ upon the questions of delay, discretion and referral.

Application allowed. Order of certiorari granted to quash orders and declaration of Crown Court. Order of mandamus refused.

The court refused leave to appeal to the House of Lords but certified, under s 1(2) of the Administration of Justice Act 1960, that the following points of law of general public importance were involved in the decision. (1) Whether, in the light of s 29(3) of the Supreme Court Act 1981, the High Court has jurisdiction to entertain an application for judicial review seeking any one or more of the following orders, namely certiorari, mandamus and declarations in respect of: (a) an order of the Crown Court quashing an indictment on the ground that the court lacks jurisdiction to entertain the proceedings in question; (b) an order and declaration by the Crown Court that, for like reasons, a prosecution and proceedings in the Crown Court and in the magistrates' court are invalid and of no effect. (2) If and to the extent that the answer to (1) is Yes: (a) whether the Crown Court had jurisdiction to entertain the proceedings here in question; (b) whether the Crown Court had jurisdiction to make and was right in law to make the order and declaration referred to in (1)(b) above.

Dilys Tausz   Barrister.

Practice Direction

FAMILY DIVISION

Family proceedings – Orders in family proceedings – Application for order – Application by child concerned – Application to be determined in High Court – Application to be transferred to High Court for hearing – Children Act 1989, ss 8, 10 – Family Proceedings Rules 1991, r 4.3 – Family Proceedings Courts (Children Act 1989) Rules 1991, r 3.

Under s 10 of the Children Act 1989 the prior leave of the court is required in respect of applications by the child concerned for s 8 orders (contact, prohibited steps, residence and specific issue orders). Rule 4.3 of the Family Proceedings Rules 1991, SI 1991/1247, and r 3 of the Family Proceedings Courts (Children Act 1989) Rules 1991, SI 1991/1395, set out the procedure to be followed when applying for leave.

Such applications raise issues which are more appropriate for determination in the High Court and should be transferred there for hearing.

Issued with the concurrence of the Lord Chancellor.

22 February 1993   STEPHEN BROWN P

Airedale NHS Trust v Bland

a

FAMILY DIVISION
SIR STEPHEN BROWN P
12, 13, 19 NOVEMBER 1992

b COURT OF APPEAL, CIVIL DIVISION
SIR THOMAS BINGHAM MR, BUTLER-SLOSS AND HOFFMANN LJJ
1, 2, 3, 9 DECEMBER 1992

HOUSE OF LORDS
LORD KEITH OF KINKEL, LORD GOFF OF CHIEVELEY, LORD LOWRY, LORD BROWNE-
c WILKINSON AND LORD MUSTILL
14, 15, 16 DECEMBER 1992, 4 FEBRUARY 1993

Medical treatment – Withdrawal of treatment – Insensate patient – Patient in persistent vegetative state with no hope of recovery – Whether in patient's best interests not to prolong his life – Whether continuance of medical care would confer any benefit on patient
d *– Whether lawful to withdraw life support and allow patient to die.*

Declaration – Procedure – Declaration as to lawfulness of proposed conduct – Proposed medical treatment – Withdrawal of treatment – Insensate patient – Patient in persistent vegetative state with no hope of recovery – Guidance of court to be sought in all cases by
e *way of application for declaration before life-prolonging treatment withheld from patient.*

A 21-year-old patient, AB, in the care of the applicant health authority had been in a persistent vegetative state for three and a half years after suffering a severe crushed chest injury which caused catastrophic and irreversible damage to the higher functions of his brain. He was being fed artificially and mechanically by a
f nasogastric tube which had been inserted through his nose and down into his stomach. The unanimous opinion of all the doctors who had examined him was that there was no hope whatsoever of recovery or improvement of any kind in his condition and that there was no reasonable possibility of his ever emerging to a cognitive sapient state from his existing persistent vegetative state in which, although he continued to breathe unaided and his digestion continued to function,
g he could not see, hear, taste, smell, speak or communicate in any way, was incapable of involuntary movement, could not feel pain and had no cognitive function. In those circumstances the consultant geriatrician at the hospital where AB was being cared for reached the clear conclusion that it would be appropriate to cease further treatment, which would involve withdrawing the artificial
h feeding through the nasogastric tube and declining antibiotic treatment if and when infection appeared. If such a course were adopted the lack of sustenance would bring to an end the physical functioning of AB's body within one to two weeks and he would die by starvation. The consultant's view was supported by other distinguished medical experts. The health authority responsible for AB's care applied to the court for declarations that it and the responsible physicians
j could lawfully discontinue all life-sustaining treatment and medical support measures designed to keep AB alive in his existing persistent vegetative state including the termination of ventilation, nutrition and hydration by artificial means and that they could lawfully discontinue and thereafter need not furnish medical treatment to him except for the sole purpose of enabling him to end his life and die peacefully with the greatest dignity and the least pain, suffering and

distress. The plaintiffs' action was supported by the parents and family of AB. The judge granted the declarations sought. The Official Solicitor appealed to the *a* Court of Appeal, which affirmed the judge's decision. The Official Solicitor appealed to the House of Lords, contending that the withdrawal of life support was both a breach of the doctor's duty to care for his patient, indefinitely if need be, and a criminal act.

Held – A doctor who had in his care a patient who was incapable of deciding whether or not to consent to treatment was under no absolute obligation to prolong the patient's life regardless of the circumstances or the quality of the patient's life. Medical treatment, including artificial feeding and the administration of antibiotic drugs, could lawfully be withheld from an insensate patient with no hope of recovery when it was known that the result would be that the *c* patient would shortly thereafter die, provided responsible and competent medical opinion was of the view that it would be in the patient's best interests not to prolong his life by continuing that form of medical treatment because such continuance was futile and would not confer any benefit on him. Furthermore, discontinuance of life support by the withdrawal of artificial feeding or other means of support did not amount to a criminal act because if the continuance of *d* an intrusive life support system was not in the patient's best interests the doctor was no longer under a duty to maintain the patient's life but was simply allowing his patient to die of his pre-existing condition and his death would be regarded in law as exclusively caused by the injury or disease to which his condition was attributable. Having regard to AB's condition it followed the declaration had been properly granted and that the appeal would therefore be dismissed (see *e* p 861 *f g j*, p 862 *d*, p 865 *e f*, p 866 *b h j*, p 868 *d* to *j*, p 869 *c* to *f h j*, p 870 *f* to *h*, p 871 *c e g*, p 872 *c d j* to p 873 *a g* to *j*, p 875 *d e*, p 876 *g j* to p 877 *a f*, p 881 *g*, p 882 *j* to p 883 *c g j* to p 884 *c*, p 885 *d*, p 894 *g* to *j*, p 895 *d e g* and p 896 *f*, post).

Bolam v Friern Hospital Management Committee [1957] 2 All ER 118 and *F v West Berkshire Health Authority* (*Mental Health Act Commission intervening*) [1989] 2 All *f* ER 545 applied.

Per curiam. (1) Euthanasia by means of positive steps to end a patient's life, such as administering a drug to bring about his death, is unlawful (see p 861 *h j*, p 862 *d*, p 867 *c d f*, p 875 *e*, p 884 *g*, p 885 *d* and p 890 *e* to *h*, post).

(2) Doctors should for time being, as a matter of practice, seek the guidance of the court in all cases before withholding life-prolonging treatment from a patient *g* in a persistent vegetative state. The appropriate means of seeking such guidance is by way of an application for declaratory relief. It is to be hoped that with the passage of time a body of experience and practice will build up which will enable the President of the Family Division to relax that requirement so as to limit applications for declarations to those cases in which there is a special need for the procedure to be invoked (see p 862 *b* to *d*, p 874 *j*, p 876 *a b*, p 880 *c e*, p 884 *e* and *h* p 885 *d*, post); *F v West Berkshire Health Authority* (*Mental Health Act Commission intervening*) [1989] 2 All ER 545 considered.

Per Lord Browne-Wilkinson and Lord Mustill. It is imperative that the moral, social and legal issues raised by the witholding of treatment from an insensate patient with no hope of recovery should be considered by Parliament (see p 879 *j* *j* and p 889 *b c*, post).

Notes

For consent to medical treatment, see 30 *Halsbury's Laws* (4th edn reissue) para 38, and for cases on the subject, see 33 *Digest* (Reissue) 273–275, 2242–2246.

Cases referred to in judgments and opinions

a   *Auckland Area Health Board v A-G* [1993] 1 NZLR 235, NZ HC.

B (a minor) (wardship: medical treatment), Re (1981) [1990] 3 All ER 927, [1981] 1 WLR 1421, CA.

B (a minor) (wardship: sterilisation), Re [1987] 2 All ER 206, [1988] AC 199, [1987] 2 WLR 1213, HL.

b   *Barber v Superior Court of Los Angeles County* (1983) 147 Cal App 3d 1006, Cal CA (2nd Dist).

Belchertown State School Superintendent v Saikewicz (1977) 373 Mass 728, Mass Sup Jud Ct.

Bolam v Friern Hospital Management Committee [1957] 2 All ER 118, [1957] 1 WLR 582.

c   *C (a minor) (wardship: medical treatment), Re* [1989] 2 All ER 782, [1990] Fam 26, [1989] 3 WLR 240, CA.

Clarke v Hurst (30 July 1992, unreported), SA SC.

Conroy, Re (1985) 98 NJ 321, NJ SC.

Cruzan v Director, Missouri Dept of Health (1990) 497 US 261, 110 S Ct 2841, US SC.

d   *Doe (Jane), Guardianship of* (1992) 411 Mass 512, Mass Sup Jud Ct.

F v West Berkshire Health Authority (Mental Health Act Commission intervening) [1989] 2 All ER 545, sub nom *Re F (mental patient: sterilisation)* [1990] 2 AC 1, [1989] 2 WLR 1025, HL.

Finlayson v HM Advocate 1979 JC 33, HC of Just.

Gardner, Re (1987) 534 A 2d 947, Me Sup Jud Ct.

e   *Imperial Tobacco Ltd v A-G* [1980] 1 All ER 866, [1981] AC 718, [1980] 2 WLR 466, HL.

J (a minor) (wardship: medical treatment), Re [1990] 3 All ER 930, [1991] Fam 33, [1991] 2 WLR 140, CA.

J (a minor) (wardship: medical treatment), Re [1992] 4 All ER 614, [1993] Fam 15, *f*   [1992] 3 WLR 507, CA.

Jobes, Re (1987) 108 NJ 394, NJ SC.

Malette v Shulman (1990) 72 OR (2d) 417, Ont CA.

Nancy B v Hôtel-Dieu de Québec (1992) 86 DLR (4th) 385, Que Superior Ct.

Quinlan, Re (1976) 70 NJ 10, NJ SC.

R v Adams (Bodkin) [1957] Crim LR 365, CCC.

g   *R v Arthur* (1981) Times, 6 November, pp 1, 12.

R v Blaue [1975] 3 All ER 446, [1975] 1 WLR 1411, CA.

R v Cox (18 September 1992, unreported), Crown Ct at Winchester.

R v Gibbins (1918) 13 Cr App R 134, CCA.

R v Laskey and ors (1993) pending, HL.

R v Malcherek [1981] 2 All ER 422, [1981] 1 WLR 690, CA.

h   *R v Stone* [1977] 2 All ER 341, [1977] QB 354, [1977] 2 WLR 169, CA.

Royal College of Nursing of the UK v Dept of Health and Social Security [1981] 1 All ER 545, [1981] AC 800, [1981] 2 WLR 279, HL.

S v S, W v Official Solicitor [1970] 3 All ER 107, [1972] AC 24, [1970] 3 WLR 366, HL.

Schloendorff v Society of New York Hospital (1914) 211 NY 125, NY Ct of Apps.

j   *Sidaway v Bethlem Royal Hospital Governors* [1985] 1 All ER 643, [1985] AC 871, [1985] 2 WLR 480, HL.

Storar, Re, re Eichner (1981) 52 NY 2d 363, NY Ct of Apps; *certiorari denied* 454 US 858, US SC.

T (adult: refusal of medical treatment), Re [1992] 4 All ER 649, [1992] 3 WLR 782, CA.

Originating summons

By an originating summons dated 25 September 1992 the plaintiffs, Airedale *a*
NHS Trust, sought in relation to the future medical care and treatment of the
defendant, Anthony Bland, a patient at Airedale General Hospital, Skipton Road,
Steeton, Keighley, West Yorkshire, acting by the Official Solicitor as his guardian
ad litem, declarations in the form of a draft order that, despite the inability of the
defendant to consent thereto, the plaintiffs and the responsible physicians (1)
might lawfully discontinue all life-sustaining treatment and medical support *b*
measures designed to keep the defendant alive in his existing persistent vegetative
state including the termination of ventilation, nutrition and hydration by artificial
means, (2) might lawfully discontinue and thereafter need not furnish medical
treatment to him except for the sole purpose of enabling him to end his life and
die peacefully with the greatest dignity and the least of pain, suffering and distress,
(3) that if death should occur following such discontinuance or termination the *c*
cause of death should be attributed to the natural and other causes of the
defendant's said persistent vegetative state and (4) that such discontinuance or
termination and any other things done or omitted to be done in good faith in
accordance with the order should not give rise to and should be without any civil
or criminal liability therefor on the part of the plaintiffs or any participant *d*
whether physician, hospital or others. The facts are set out in the judgment.

Robert Francis QC and *M R Taylor* (instructed by *Penningtons*, agents for *W J M
   Lovel*, Harrogate) for the plaintiffs.
James Munby QC (instructed by the *Official Solicitor*) for the Official Solicitor as
   guardian ad litem.   *e*
Anthony Lester QC and *Stephen Richards* (instructed by the *Treasury Solicitor*) for the
   Attorney General as amicus curiae.

Cur adv vult

19 November 1992. The following judgment was delivered.   *f*

SIR STEPHEN BROWN P. Anthony Bland became 21 on 21 September 1992
but for the past three and a half years he has been totally unaware of the world
around him. As a keen supporter of Liverpool Football Club he was at the
Hillsborough football ground on 15 April 1989. He was then 17½. He was one of *g*
the victims of the disaster. He suffered a severe crushed chest injury which gave
rise to hypoxic brain damage. His condition rapidly deteriorated and despite the
intensive and heroic efforts of doctors and nurses he has remained ever since in a
state of complete unawareness. This is known to the medical profession as a
'persistent vegetative state'. Although his brain stem is intact he suffered
irreparable damage to the cortex. All the higher functions of Anthony Bland's *h*
brain have been destroyed. There is no hope whatsoever of recovery or
improvement of any kind. That is the unanimous opinion of all the distinguished
doctors who have examined Anthony Bland.

Since 12 May 1989 he has been under the care of Dr J G Howe FRCP, a
consultant geriatrician at the Airedale General Hospital. Dr Howe has very
considerable experience of patients suffering from what is described as persistent *j*
vegetative state. After his transfer to the Airedale General Hospital prolonged and
persistent attempts were made to revive Anthony Bland. The skilled hospital staff
including senior physiotherapists assisted by the parents and sister of Anthony
Bland made exhaustive attempts to achieve some sign of revival. Although
Anthony Bland's body breathes and reacts in a reflex manner to painful stimuli it

is quite clear that there is no awareness on his part of anything that is taking place
a around him. EEG and CT scans reveal no evidence of cortical activity. Indeed
recent scans which have been photographed and produced to the court show that
there is more space than substance in the relevant part of Anthony Bland's brain.
There is simply no possibility whatsoever that he has any appreciation of anything
that takes place around him. He is fed artificially and mechanically by a nasogastric
tube which has been inserted through his nose and down into his stomach. All
b the natural bodily functions have to be operated with nursing intervention. He is
fitted with a catheter which has given rise to infection necessitating surgical
intervention. It is to be noted that the necessary surgical incision was made
without any anaesthetic because Anthony Bland is utterly devoid of feeling of any
kind. He requires four to five hours' nursing attention by two nurses every day.
c No complaint is made by the hospital authorities of the fact that they have to
allocate substantial resources to this particular case—that is not a factor which has
been prayed in aid of the course which the plaintiffs now seek to be allowed to
follow. By August 1989, supported by the opinion of Dr Michael Johnson, a
consultant neurologist of St James's University Hospital, Leeds, Dr Howe had
reached the clear conclusion that there was absolutely no hope of any improvement.
d He felt that it would be appropriate to cease further treatment. This would
involve withdrawing the artificial feeding through the nasogastric tube and
declining antibiotic treatment if and when infection appeared. If this course were
to be adopted then within some 10 to 14 days the lack of sustenance would bring
an end to the physical functioning of the body of Anthony Bland and he would
in terms 'die'. The process would be that of 'starvation'. This would be unpleasant
e for those who had to observe it but Anthony Bland himself would be totally
unaware of what was taking place.

In August 1989 Dr Howe got into touch with the Sheffield coroner who was
responsible for dealing with the fatal cases arising from the Hillsborough disaster.
The coroner, who is both medically and legally qualified, alerted Dr Howe to the
risks which he considered he might run if he took the proposed course of
f withdrawing treatment. The coroner pointed out that as the law stood it was his
understanding that Dr Howe would run the risk of criminal proceedings if he
took a course which brought to an end the existence of Anthony Bland, even
though that existence could be regarded as being wholly pointless. He suggested
that Dr Howe should consult his legal advisers. Heeding the warning of the
coroner Dr Howe did indeed consult legal advisers and as a result the Airedale
g NHS Trust, which is responsible for administering the Airedale General Hospital,
issued the originating summons which is now before the court. This seeks
declarations that the trust and their responsible physicians may lawfully
discontinue all life-sustaining treatment and medical support measures designed
to keep Anthony Bland alive in his existing persistent vegetative state including
h the termination of ventilation, nutrition and hydration by artificial means and
that they may lawfully discontinue and thereafter need not furnish medical
treatment to Anthony Bland except for the sole purpose of enabling Anthony
Bland to end his life and die peacefully with the greatest dignity and the least of
pain, suffering and distress. The plaintiffs' action is fully supported by the parents
and family of Anthony Bland. Because Anthony Bland himself is wholly incapable
j of taking any step with regard to this matter the Official Solicitor of the Supreme
Court has been appointed to act as his guardian ad litem. He has instructed
counsel to appear on the hearing of this summons. Whilst not disputing the
completely insensate condition of Anthony Bland, he opposes the plaintiffs'
application, contending that if the action proposed by Dr Howe and the plaintiff
hospital authority were to be implemented it would in terms amount in law to

the crime of murder. Because of the public importance of this case the court invited the assistance of the Attorney General and he has instructed counsel to *a* appear as amicus curiae.

This case clearly raises serious moral, medical and ethical issues. However, none of the facts relating to the circumstances and the condition of Anthony Bland are in dispute. The court has been assisted by expert medical evidence from witnesses of the highest calibre and of the very greatest experience. All agree that Anthony Bland is now, and has been ever since the date of the Hillsborough disaster, in *b* what is known to the medical profession now as a persistent vegetative state. The condition is irreversible and is not susceptible of any improvement. He is completely insensate and no medical procedure or treatment can bring about any beneficial change in his condition. All the witnesses have stated that the standard of care which has been afforded to Anthony Bland at the Airedale General Hospital is of the highest character. His parents have visited him daily and his sister has *c* also been present frequently. The anguish which they continue to experience is self-evident. His father has given oral evidence before me and I also have a statement from Anthony Bland's mother. The father is a splendid straightforward Yorkshireman. He has faced the terrible tragedy which has befallen his family with remarkable realism and dignity. He has not allowed emotion to influence *d* his judgment. He traced for me Anthony's brief life—explaining how he was a thoroughly normal boy. He described him as not a very clever boy but with a good personality—sensitive and willing. His great interest was football and Liverpool his chosen team. He said that he was not religious but that he had attended Sunday School in the Church of England. His assessment of Anthony Bland's situation was expressed in these clear terms: *e*

> 'He certainly wouldn't want to be left like he is. I would feel that he should be removed and the family feel the same. I was angry when the advice from the coroner was received. I can see no point whatsoever in continuing treatment.'

Of course Anthony Bland is unable to express views of his own and there had *f* been no occasion for him to express any view as to how he might view his situation if some terrible tragedy such as this befell him.

This case raises for the first time in the English courts the question in what circumstances, if any, can a doctor lawfully discontinue life-sustaining treatment (including nutrition and hydration) without which a patient in Anthony Bland's condition will die. Professor Bryan Jennett CBE, until recently Foundation *g* Professor of Neurosurgery at the Institute of Neurological Science in the University of Glasgow and having the very widest experience as a neurosurgeon, was responsible together with Professor Plum of New York for coining the term 'persistent vegetative state' in 1972. It is intended to describe a syndrome that was being increasingly encountered as the life-saving and life-sustaining technologies *h* of intensive care were securing the survival of some patients with brain damage of a severity that would previously have proved fatal. Professor Jennett told the court that until this descriptive term was proposed, and soon widely adopted, such patients were often referred to as being in a prolonged or irreversible coma. However the word 'coma', he said, implies a continuing sleeplike state due to depression of the brain stem activating systems—whilst the hallmark of the *j* vegetative patient is that after a variable time in coma wakefulness returns, with long periods of spontaneous eye opening. This period in coma commonly lasts 10 to 21 days after head injury which causes concussive depression of brain stem function, but after hypoxic insults patients often begin to open their eyes in two

to three days. Unlike less severely brain damaged patients emerging from coma,
a the vegetative patient fails to regain any cognitive behaviour that would indicate
function in the cerebral cortex—the grey matter responsible for consciousness,
thinking, feeling and responding in meaningful (as distinct from reflex) ways to
stimuli from the surroundings. Because the brain stem and various other
sub-cortical and more primitive parts of the brain are still functioning, the
vegetative patient has a wide range of reflex activity, including breathing and, in
b some patients, a very limited capacity to swallow reflexly. Vegetative patients
must be distinguished from patients in a 'locked in' syndrome—who, because of
a focal lesion in the brain stem that does not affect consciousness, are totally
paralysed in limbs and speech but may communicate by a yes/no code using eye
or eyebrow movements. They are also quite different from patients who have
c suffered 'brain death'—whose brain stem has permanently ceased to function and
who are dependent on a ventilator to maintain respiration, and whose heart
always stops within a week or two at the most. By contrast, vegetative patients
have suffered cognitive death, but can continue to breath for years because the
brain stem is still functioning. The key to the diagnosis is that, on clinical
observation over a prolonged period of time, there is no evidence of a working
d mind. EEG records show a range of abnormal activity with severe depression of
cortical activity obvious only in a minority of cases. Professor Jennett referred to
the very considerable research which has taken place internationally and the
consideration of the problem by the medical ethics committee of the British
Medical Association. He concluded from all the research material that only
exceptional cases have been reported as showing recovery after a year, and none
e of those patients appear to have achieved independence. He gave it as his opinion
that nasogastric feeding is a form of 'medical treatment' just as is a ventilator or a
kidney machine. It is a means of substituting a function that has naturally failed.
He said that tube feeding is accepted as 'medical treatment' in the United States of
America and in Canada. He referred to the Appleton International Conference,
f which accepted that life-sustaining hydration and nutrition is a medical treatment
which may justifiably be withdrawn from persistently vegetative patients for
whom there are no patient-based reasons for continuing to treat. He expressed
the opinion that it has become accepted good practice in this country as elsewhere
to agree in consultation with the families of the vegetative patients to withhold
antibiotics and cardiopulmonary resuscitation in the event of complications that
g would call for such measures in patients with a prospect of recovery. He expressed
the very strong view that it would be in accordance with good medical practice in
the case of Anthony Bland to withdraw the nasogastric artificial feeding. He
stated that he considered there to be no benefit in maintaining life-sustaining
treatment because he could see no prospect of recovery of cognitive function. He,
like the other expert medical witnesses who gave evidence before me, had
h examined Anthony Bland. He stated that in his view this was an extreme and
clear case of the persistent vegetative state. He could see no benefit to the patient
in continuing the treatment of feeding by means of a nasogastric tube.
Dr Cartlidge FRCP is the consultant neurologist to the Newcastle Health Authority
and senior lecturer in neurology at the University of Newcastle-upon-Tyne. He
has very considerable experience of the so-called persistent vegetative state. He
j too examined Anthony Bland and expressed the firm opinion that he was showing
all the signs of this extreme condition. He said there is no possibility whatsoever
that he will recover. He too expressed the opinion that it would be medically
justifiable to withdraw the artificial feeding process for there was no useful
purpose in continuing it and it was not in the patient's best interests to prolong

survival in these circumstances. Professor Peter Behan FRCP of the Department
of Neurology at the Institute of Neurological Sciences at the Southern General *a*
Hospital of Glasgow was instructed by the Official Solicitor to examine Anthony
Bland. The court has the advantage of a report prepared by Professor Behan which
has been accepted in evidence. He was unable to attend court to give oral evidence.
In his report he said:

> '1) What is the diagnosis? This can be confidently answered that on the *b*
> basis of history, physical and neurological examination supplemented by
> laboratory data, this is a classical example of the persistent vegetative state ...
> 2) I am confident that from my knowledge of other patients, neurophysiology,
> previous cases from the literature and from animal experimentation that the
> patient has no awareness nor can he suffer pain or experience pleasure ...
> 3) The prospect of improvement can also confidently be answered since based *c*
> on what we know of the degree of damage to his brain, the comparison of
> his case with those recorded in the literature (particularly considering the
> nature of his damage and the duration of his illness) and the type of symptoms
> and signs he exhibits, there is no hint or hope or any prospect of improvement.
> 4) In my opinion artificial feeding and hydration constitutes medical
> treatment. If a patient was to be admitted under my care and was for one *d*
> reason or another unable to feed him self, the setting up of a nasogastric tube
> for feeding and hydration would constitute beyond any measure of doubt
> medical treatment as opposed to normal feeding.'

He further stated that he was very impressed by the recommendation of the
British Medical Association, that is to say in respect of the consultation and *e*
treatment of patients in the persistent vegetative state, which seemed to him to
be a recommendation that where the diagnosis had been well established, the
differential diagnoses had been ruled out and all the necessary laboratory tests
done, then 'the prognosis could confidently be given as zero if after one year there
was no sign of improvement'.

Dr Keith Andrews FRCP is the Director of Medical Research Services at the *f*
Royal Hospital and Home, Putney. At his hospital there is a 20-bed brain injury
rehabilitation unit. Dr Andrews has had experience of about 50 patients in a
persistent vegetative state. He examined Anthony Bland. He told the court: 'I
regard [him] as being in persistent vegetative state and indeed ... the most severe
case ... I have seen ... I do not consider that Tony Bland will make any recovery
whatsoever.' He went on to say that if the regime continues as at present 'he is *g*
likely to survive a few years ... not more than about five, mainly because he ...
is very prone to develop infections ...' He expressed the view that feeding by
tube was not in his view medical treatment. In amplification he said: 'The use of
the equipment might be thought to be medical treatment but not the supply of
food which is a basic human requirement.' He said he would not favour the *h*
withdrawal of treatment because he would find the means of death worrying. It
would be distressing to watch, although Anthony Bland himself would not
experience any sensation. He agreed that sedative drugs could be given to lessen
the unpleasant features which he felt would inevitably follow from the withdrawal
of the artificial feeding.

The plaintiffs' submissions have been put clearly and succinctly by Mr Francis *j*
QC both in a written skeleton argument and also in oral submissions. He submits
that it is the unanimous opinion of all the expert medical witnesses that Anthony
Bland is in a severe persistent vegetative state. There is no hope of any
improvement. His parents with knowledge of their son say that he would not
wish his present condition to be continued. Although Anthony Bland himself

cannot express any view it should be inferred in the light of the medical evidence
a as well as of the evidence of his own father and mother that the prolongation of
the present treatment is not in his best interests. Good medical practice, accepted
by a large and responsible body of medical opinion, suggests that the course
proposed by Dr Howe, and supported by Professor Jennett and by Dr Cartlidge,
should be followed. Mr Francis referred to a passage in the speech of Lord Bridge
in the leading case of *F v West Berkshire Health Authority (Mental Health Act*
b *Commission intervening)* [1989] 2 All ER 545 at 548–549, [1990] 2 AC 1 at 52 where
he said:

> 'Moreover it seems to me of first importance that the common law should
> be readily intelligible to and applicable by all those who undertake the care
> of persons lacking the capacity to consent to treatment. It would be
c intolerable for members of the medical, nursing and other professions
> devoted to the care of the sick that, in caring for those lacking the capacity to
> consent to treatment, they should be put in the dilemma that, if they
> administer the treatment which they believe to be in the patient's best
> interests, acting with due skill and care, they run the risk of being held guilty
> of trespass to the person, but, if they withhold that treatment, they may be
d in breach of a duty of care owed to the patient. If those who undertake
> responsibility for the care of incompetent or unconscious patients administer
> curative or prophylactic treatment which they believe to be appropriate to
> the patient's existing condition of disease, injury or bodily malfunction or
> susceptibility to such a condition in the future, the lawfulness of that
> treatment should be judged by one standard, not two. If follows that if the
e professionals in question have acted with due skill and care, judged by the
> well-known test laid down in *Bolam v Friern Hospital Management Committee*
> [1957] 2 All ER 118, [1957] 1 WLR 582, they should be immune from
> liability in trespass, just as they are immune from liability in negligence.'

It is acknowledged that the present case is not a similar situation to that of the
f mental patient in *F v West Berkshire Health Authority*. There is no curative or
therapeutic treatment which can be applied to Anthony Bland. However,
Mr Francis submits, the same basic principles should be followed because what is
proposed by Dr Howe is effectively medical treatment and it is in the patient's
best interests. He submits that it would be intolerable if Dr Howe were to be put
at risk of a prosecution for murder if he were to follow what he submits is
g generally regarded now as good medical practice.

In his detailed and erudite submission Mr Munby QC on behalf of the Official
Solicitor challenged the view that the artificial feeding regime could be considered
as 'medical treatment'. He sought support for that submission from the evidence
of Dr Keith Andrews. However, his principal submission was that what is
h proposed by Dr Howe is the doing of an act intended to lead to the death of
Anthony Bland. In the result, he argued, the withdrawal of the feeding regime
would amount to unlawful killing and would in fact be the crime of murder. He
referred to the summing up of Devlin J in *R v Adams (Bodkin)* [1957] Crim LR
365. He picked out a phrase used by the learned judge, 'cutting the thread of life'.
Mr Munby argued that even if the artificial feeding process were to be considered
j to be medical treatment it would nevertheless be unlawful in the instant case to
withdraw that treatment. He referred to what Lord Donaldson MR described as
the 'critical equation' in *Re J (a minor) (wardship: medical treatment)* [1990] 3 All
ER 930 at 938, [1991] Fam 33 at 46. That case concerned the consideration of
potential further treatment to a severely brain damaged child. The problem
raised in the case was what should be done if the child should suffer another

collapse, which might occur at any time. Should resuscitative treatment be given in such a case? Mr Munby, relying upon a passage in the judgment of *a* Lord Donaldson MR, submitted that because of the very strong presumption which exists in favour of preserving life a withholding or withdrawing of treatment could only be justified in the critical case where the pain and suffering likely to be suffered by the patient exceeded the benefit to the patient of preserving life. Lord Donaldson MR said ([1990] 3 All ER 930 at 938, [1991] Fam 33 at 46):

> 'This brings me face to face with the problem of formulating the critical equation. In truth it cannot be done with mathematical or any precision. There is without doubt a very strong presumption in favour of a course of action which will prolong life, but, even excepting the "cabbage" case to which special considerations may well apply, it is not irrebuttable. As this court recognised in *Re B* [*Re B (a minor) (wardship: medical treatment)* (1981) *c* [1990] 3 All ER 927, [1981] 1 WLR 1421], account has to be taken of the pain and suffering and quality of life which the child will experience if life is prolonged. Account has also to be taken of the pain and suffering involved in the proposed treatment itself . . . But in the end there will be cases in which the answer must be that it is not in the interests of the child to subject it to treatment which will cause increased suffering and produce no commensurate *d* benefit, giving the fullest possible weight to the child's, and mankind's, desire to survive.'

In this case however, said Mr Munby, there is no question of suffering because Anthony Bland is totally without feeling or awareness. He went on to speak of 'the slippery slope' which would be embarked upon if the court were to make a *e* declaration in the terms sought by the plaintiffs: a dangerous precedent would be established. He developed in depth his submission that there is an absolute prohibition upon a doctor against taking active steps designed to bring about death. He likened the situation to that of two climbers roped together where one climber deliberately cut the rope which bound his companion to himself, or to switching off an iron lung. *f*

Mr Anthony Lester QC, instructed by the Attorney General to appear as amicus curiae, made submissions which in effect supported the plaintiffs' case. He acknowledged that the subject matter of this case is obviously emotive and difficult. He said that the court would not be assisted by an absolutist or dogmatically legalistic approach. It was not a so-called euthanasia case; it was in terms a case about whether in the view of the doctors and the court a particular *g* treatment decision should be taken which would remove the artificial support for life and allow nature to take its course so that death supervenes. He submitted that the law should strive to be in accordance with contemporary medical ethics and good medical practice. He acknowledged that Anthony Bland's case is difficult because, at first sight, it seems to require the court to reject the vital principle of *h* the sanctity of life in favour of value judgments as to the quality of the further artificial prolongation of the life of Anthony Bland. He submitted however that there is no inherent conflict between having regard to the quality of life and respecting the sanctity of life; on the contrary, they are complementary; the principle of sanctity of life embraces the need for full respect to be accorded to the dignity and memory of the individual human being. The meaning and *j* criteria of quality of life should focus on benefit to the patient. He contended that Anthony Bland had an interest in the way in which his family would remember him after his death and in the manner of his dying and submitted that where one could be medically *sure* on all the evidence that the patient in a persistent

vegetative state is suffering permanently from loss of consciousness, there is no
a legal duty to maintain what remains of his or her 'life' whether by feeding or by
giving medication. It is not in the patient's best interests to do so. In those
circumstances he submitted there would be no breach of duty or criminal liability
in ceasing to feed or otherwise to treat the patient. Such a conclusion, he argued,
is in accordance with existing English case law. If the court declared the treatment
proposed by Dr Howe to be 'lawful' then he said the criminal law would not
b become involved because a basic element of criminal liability, that is to say an
unlawful act (the actus reus) is not made out.

It is correct that there has been no previous case of this nature in this
jurisdiction. Mr Lester referred to a case before the Supreme Court of the United
States, *Cruzan v Director, Missouri Dept of Health* (1990) 110 S Ct 2841. The
headnote of the report reads:
c

> 'Guardians of patient in persistent vegetative state brought declaratory
> judgment action seeking judicial sanction of their wish to terminate artificial
> hydration and nutrition for patient. The Circuit Court, Jasper County,
> Probate Division, Charles E. Teel Jr., J., directed state employees to cause
> request of guardians to be carried out. Appeal was taken. The Missouri
d > Supreme Court reversed. Certiorari was granted. The Supreme Court, Chief
> Justice Rehnquist, held that: (1) the United States Constitution did not forbid
> Missouri from requiring that clear and convincing evidence of an
> incompetent's wishes to the withdrawal of life-sustaining treatment; (2) state
> Supreme Court did not commit constitutional error in concluding that
e > evidence adduced at trial did not amount to clear and convincing evidence of
> patient's desire to cease hydration and nutrition; and (3) due process did not
> require state to accept substituted judgment of close family members absent
> substantial proof that their views reflected those of patient.'

The decision therefore turned on a constitutional point as to the jurisdiction of
f the State of Missouri. However, in dissenting judgments Brennan J and three
other justices referred to what may be regarded as the substantive merits of the
case with regard to the treatment of patients in a persistent vegetative state.
Mr Lester referred to passages in the judgments of Brennan and Stevens JJ. He
drew attention to a passage (at 2883):

> 'Medical advances have altered the physiological conditions of death in
g > ways that may be alarming: highly invasive treatment may perpetuate
> human existence through a merger of body and machine that some might
> reasonably regard as an insult to life rather than as its continuation. But those
> same advances, and the reorganization of medical care accompanying the
> new science and technology, have also transformed the political and social
h > conditions of death: people are less likely to die at home, and more likely to
> die in relatively public places, such as hospitals or nursing homes. Ultimate
> questions that might once have been dealt with in intimacy by a family and
> its physician have now become the concern of institutions.'

Stevens J observed (at 2886–2887):
j

> 'But for patients like Nancy Cruzan, who have no consciousness and no
> chance of recovery, there is a serious question as to whether the mere
> persistence of their bodies is *"life"* as that word is commonly understood . . .
> The State's [Missouri's] unflagging determination to perpetuate Nancy
> Cruzan's physical existence is comprehensible only as an effort to define life's

meaning, not as an attempt to preserve its sanctity . . . In any event, absent
some theological abstraction, the idea of life is not conceived separately from   *a*
the idea of a living person.' (Stevens J's emphasis.)

Brennan J used a phrase (at 2864) to which Mr Lester also pointed when he
described the subject in that case as 'a passive prisoner of medical technology'.

Mr Lester also drew attention to the Canadian Law Reform Commission
Working Paper of July 1983. I do not need to comment in detail upon it but in it   *b*
the Law Reform Commission of Canada recommended that the cessation of life-
sustaining treatment in such cases should not attract criminal liability. There are
a number of other decisions of state courts in the United States in which
applications for a declaration, or for leave to withdraw life-sustaining treatment
have been granted. However they are not strictly comparable to cases in this
jurisdiction because many of them import a consideration of parens patriae in the   *c*
particular states.

In the present case there is no question but that Anthony Bland is in a condition
known as the persistent vegetative state. He has no feeling, no awareness, nor can
he experience anything relating to his surroundings. To his parents and family
he is 'dead'. His spirit has left him and all that remains is the shell of his body.
This is kept functioning as a biological unit by the artificial process of feeding   *d*
through a mechanically operated nasogastric tube. Intensive attention by skilled
nurses assists the continuation of the existence of the body. It is a desperately
tragic situation both for what remains of Anthony Bland and for the devoted
members of his family. The doctor having the responsibility for the care of
Anthony Bland has come to a very clear medical conclusion. He is supported in
his assessment and opinion by doctors of unrivalled experience and professional   *e*
standing. They say in terms that it is in accordance with good medical practice
and in accordance with the true benefit to Anthony Bland himself that the
artificial feeding regime should be withdrawn. The Official Solicitor has made
clear to the court the possible implications of a precedent being established by a
decision in favour of the plaintiffs in this case, although such a decision would   *f*
accord with decisions taken in other common law jurisdictions.

The court must consider this case in the light of its particular facts and upon
the principles of law obtaining in this jurisdiction. In my judgment the provision
of artificial feeding by means of a nasogastric tube is 'medical treatment'. The
court has before it overwhelming medical evidence which supports this view.
I accept it. The clinical judgment of Dr Howe is to the effect that it would be in   *g*
the best interests of Anthony Bland for that artificial feeding regime to be
withdrawn at this stage. He has cogently given his reasons for reaching that
conclusion. After three and a half years he has not lightly made that decision. It
is a clinical decision arrived at in the honest and responsible exercise of his duty
of caring for his patient. The fact that Anthony Bland's existence will terminate
does not in my judgment alter the reality that the true cause of death will be the   *h*
massive injuries which he sustained in what has been described as the Hillsborough
disaster. I am satisfied that there is no reasonable possibility of Anthony Bland
ever emerging from his existing persistent vegetative state to a cognitive sapient
state. I am satisfied that there is no therapeutic, medical or other benefit to
Anthony Bland in continuing to maintain his ventilation, nutrition and hydration   *j*
by artificial means. I am further satisfied that to discontinue the same would
accord with good medical practice as recognised and approved within the medical
profession and finally that the order that I propose to make is in the circumstances
in the best interests of Anthony Bland. His parents and sister concur in the
making of the order which I propose to make and I therefore declare that despite

the inability of Anthony Bland to consent thereto the plaintiffs and the responsible
a attending physicians: (1) may lawfully discontinue all life-sustaining treatment
and medical support measures designed to keep Anthony Bland alive in his
existing persistent vegetative state including the termination of ventilation,
nutrition and hydration by artificial means; and (2) that they may lawfully
discontinue and thereafter need not furnish medical treatment to Anthony Bland
except for the sole purpose of enabling Anthony Bland to end his life and to die
b peacefully with the greatest dignity and the least distress.

I do not consider it appropriate to make any declaration with regard to any
possible consequences so far as the criminal law is concerned. In my judgment
the declaration that the course proposed is lawful is sufficient to give to the doctors
and to the hospital the necessary assurance as to the lawfulness of what is proposed.
c There will of course be liberty to apply in the event of there being any material
change in the existing circumstances before the withdrawal of the artificial
feeding. May his soul rest in peace.

It is understandable that those who are concerned with patients in the persistent
vegetative state should seek assistance as to the appropriate practice in the future.
Because of the gravity of the decision and the likely possible variation in the facts
d of individual cases I consider that the approval of the court should be sought in
cases of a similar nature. In accordance with the procedures indicated by
Lord Brandon of Oakbrook in *F v West Berkshire Health Authority* [1989] 2 All ER
545 at 558, [1990] 2 AC 1 at 65 the appropriate procedure should be by a
summons for a declaration made to the Family Division of the High Court. The
Official Solicitor should in my judgment be invited to act as the guardian ad litem
e of the patient, which would guarantee the fullest possible investigation of all the
facts and circumstances of the individual case. Although essentially the decision
is one for the clinical judgment of responsible medical practitioners, in my
judgment it is desirable as a safeguard and for the reassurance of the public that
the court should be involved in the way that I have indicated. I would expect that
in all similar applications there would be not merely one medical opinion but at
f least two responsible medical opinions. Further, the position of the members of
the family is very important. It may be that there will be cases where there is a
division of opinion among members of a family. In such cases it would be
essential in my judgment for responsible medical carers to seek the authority of
the court.

g *Declarations accordingly. No order as to costs.*

Bebe Chua   Barrister.

Appeal
The defendant, acting by the Official Solicitor as his guardian ad litem, appealed
from so much of the order as declared that, despite the inability of the defendant
h to consent thereto, the plaintiffs and the responsible physicians (1) might lawfully
discontinue all life-sustaining treatment and medical support measures designed
to keep the defendant alive in his existing persistent vegetative state, including
the termination of ventilation, nutrition and hydration by artificial means and (2)
might lawfully discontinue and thereafter need not furnish medical treatment to
the defendant except for the sole purpose of enabling him to end his life and to
j die peacefully with the greatest dignity and the least distress.

James Munby QC (instructed by the *Official Solicitor*) for the Official Solicitor as
guardian ad litem.
Robert Francis QC and *M R Taylor* (instructed by *Penningtons*, agents for *W J M
Lovel*, Harrogate) for the plaintiffs.

Anthony Lester QC and *Pushpinder Saini* (instructed by the *Treasury Solicitor*) for the
Attorney General as amicus curiae.   *a*

At the conclusion of the argument the appeal was dismissed and leave to appeal
to the House of Lords was granted for reasons to be given later.

9 December 1992. The following judgments were delivered.   *b*

SIR THOMAS BINGHAM MR. Mr Anthony David Bland, then aged 17½,
went to the Hillsborough ground on 15 April 1989 to support the Liverpool
Football Club. In the course of the disaster which occurred on that day his lungs
were crushed and punctured and the supply of oxygen to his brain was
interrupted. As a result, he suffered catastrophic and irreversible damage to the
higher centres of the brain. The condition from which he suffers, and has suffered   *c*
since April 1989, is known as a persistent vegetative state (PVS).

PVS is a recognised medical condition quite distinct from other conditions
sometimes known as 'irreversible coma', 'the Guillain-Barré syndrome', 'the
locked-in syndrome' and 'brain death'. Its distinguishing characteristics are that
the brain stem remains alive and functioning while the cortex of the brain loses   *d*
its function and activity. Thus the PVS patient continues to breathe unaided and
his digestion continues to function. But, although his eyes are open, he cannot
see. He cannot hear. Although capable of reflex movement, particularly in
response to painful stimuli, the patient is incapable of voluntary movement and
can feel no pain. He cannot taste or smell. He cannot speak or communicate in
any way. He has no cognitive function and can thus feel no emotion, whether   *e*
pleasure or distress. The absence of cerebral function is not a matter of surmise:
it can be scientifically demonstrated. The space which the brain should occupy is
full of watery fluid.

The medical witnesses in this case include some of the outstanding authorities
in the country on this condition. All are agreed on the diagnosis. All are agreed
on the prognosis also: there is no hope of any improvement or recovery. One   *f*
witness of great experience described Mr Bland as the worst PVS case he had ever
seen.

Mr Bland lies in bed in the Airedale General Hospital, his eyes open, his mind
vacant, his limbs crooked and taut. He cannot swallow, and so cannot be spoon-
fed without a high risk that food will be inhaled into the lung. He is fed by means
of a tube, threaded through the nose and down into the stomach, through which   *g*
liquefied food is mechanically pumped. His bowels are evacuated by enema. His
bladder is drained by catheter. He has been subject to repeated bouts of infection
affecting his urinary tract and chest, which have been treated with antibiotics.
Drugs have also been administered to reduce salivation, to reduce muscle tone
and severe sweating and to encourage gastric emptying. A tracheostomy tube has   *h*
been inserted and removed. Urino-genitary problems have required surgical
intervention.

A patient in this condition requires very skilled nursing and close medical
attention if he is to survive. The Airedale National Health Service Trust has, it is
agreed, provided both to Mr Bland. Introduction of the nasogastric tube is itself a
task of some delicacy even in an insensate patient. Thereafter it must be monitored   *j*
to ensure it has not become dislodged and to control inflammation, irritation and
infection to which it may give rise. The catheter must be monitored: it may cause
infection (and has repeatedly done so); it has had to be resited, in an operation
performed without anaesthetic. The mouth and other parts of the body must be

constantly tended. The patient must be repeatedly moved to avoid pressure sores.
Without skilled nursing and close medical attention a PVS patient will quickly
succumb to infection. With such care, a young and otherwise healthy patient
may live for many years.

At no time before the disaster did Mr Bland give any indication of his wishes
should he find himself in such a condition. It is not a topic most adolescents
address. After careful thought his family agreed that the feeding tubes should be
removed and felt that this was what Mr Bland would have wanted. His father
said of his son in evidence: 'He certainly wouldn't want to be left like that.' He
could see no advantage at all in continuation of the current treatment. He was
not cross-examined. It was accordingly with the concurrence of Mr Bland's
family, as well as the consultant in charge of his case and the support of two
independent doctors, that the Airedale NHS Trust as plaintiff in this action applied
to the Family Division of the High Court for declarations that they might—

> '(1) ... lawfully discontinue all life-sustaining treatment and medical
> support measures designed to keep AB [Mr Bland] alive in his existing
> persistent vegetative state including the termination of ventilation nutrition
> and hydration by artificial means; and (2) ... lawfully discontinue and
> thereafter need not furnish medical treatment to AB except for the sole
> purpose of enabling AB to end his life and die peacefully with the greatest
> dignity and the least of pain suffering and distress.'

After a hearing in which he was assisted by an amicus curiae instructed by the
Attorney General, Sir Stephen Brown P made these declarations (subject to a
minor change of wording) on 19 November 1992. He declined to make further
declarations which were also sought. The Official Solicitor on behalf of Mr Bland
appeals against that decision: in doing so he fulfils his traditional role as the voice
of those who, for reasons of incapacity, cannot speak for themselves, ensuring that
their interests do not go by default because of their involuntary silence.

The present appeal raises moral, legal and ethical questions of a profound and
fundamental nature, questions literally of life and death. The case has naturally
provoked much public discussion and great anxiety. Strong and sincerely held
opinions have been expressed both in favour of the decision under appeal and
against it. The issues are such as inevitably to provoke divisions of opinion. But
they are fairly and squarely before the court, which has had the benefit of eloquent
and erudite argument. It cannot shirk its duty to decide. It is, however, important
to be clear from the outset what the case is, and is not, about. It is not about
euthanasia, if by that is meant the taking of positive action to cause death. It is
not about putting down the old and infirm, the mentally defective or the
physically imperfect. It has nothing to do with the eugenic practices associated
with fascist Germany. The issue is whether artificial feeding and antibiotic drugs
may lawfully be withheld from an insensate patient with no hope of recovery
when it is known that if that is done the patient will shortly thereafter die.

There are certain important principles relevant to this issue which both parties
accept. (1) A profound respect for the sanctity of human life is embedded in our
law and our moral philosophy, as it is in that of most civilised societies in the East
and the West. That is why murder (next only to treason) has always been treated
here as the most grave and heinous of crimes. (2) It is a civil wrong, and may be a
crime, to impose medical treatment on a conscious adult of sound mind without
his or her consent: see *F v West Berkshire Health Authority (Mental Health Act
Commission intervening)* [1989] 2 All ER 545, [1990] 2 AC 1. (3) A medical
practitioner must comply with clear instructions given by an adult of sound mind

as to the treatment to be given or not given in certain circumstances, whether those instructions are rational or irrational: see *Sidaway v Bethlem Royal Hospital Governors* [1985] 1 All ER 643 at 665–666, [1985] AC 871 at 904–905 and *Re T (adult: refusal of medical treatment)* [1992] 4 All ER 649, [1992] 3 WLR 782. This principle applies even if, by the time the specified circumstances obtain, the patient is unconscious or no longer of sound mind. (4) Where an adult patient is mentally incapable of giving his consent, no one (including the court) can give consent on his behalf. Treatment in such a case may lawfully be provided by a doctor where the treatment is in the best interests of the patient: see *F v West Berkshire Health Authority*. (5) Where the patient is a child and a ward of court, it will itself decide (paying appropriate regard to professional medical opinion) whether medical treatment is in the best interests of the patient: see *Re B (a minor) (wardship: medical treatment)* (1981) [1990] 3 All ER 927, [1981] 1 WLR 1421, *Re B (a minor) (wardship: sterilisation)* [1987] 2 All ER 206, [1988] AC 199, *Re C (a minor) (wardship: medical treatment)* [1989] 2 All ER 782, [1990] Fam 26 and *Re J (a minor) (wardship: medical treatment)* [1990] 3 All ER 930, [1991] Fam 33.

It follows from these propositions that, if, presciently, Mr Bland had given instructions that he should not be artificially fed or treated with antibiotics if he should become a PVS patient, his doctors would not act unlawfully in complying with those instructions but would act unlawfully if they did not comply, even though the patient's death would inevitably follow. If Mr Bland were a child and a ward of the court, it would decide what was in his best interests, having regard to the views of his parents but not treating them as conclusive: see *Re B (a minor) (wardship: medical treatment)*. If the ratio of *Re J (a minor) (wardship: medical treatment)* is sound, an issue expressly reserved by Mr Munby QC (for the Official Solicitor) for argument in the House of Lords, the court may judge it to be in a child's best interest that life-saving measures be withheld if of opinion that the life thereby prolonged would be one of intolerable pain and deprivation: see *Re B (a minor) (wardship: medical treatment)* and *Re J (a minor) (wardship: medical treatment)*. This case is novel because Mr Bland is not a child and a ward of the court, he is immune to suffering and, as already stated, he gave no instructions concerning his treatment if he were to become a PVS patient.

There can be no doubt that the administration of antibiotics is medical treatment: they cannot be lawfully obtained in this country without prescription, and the choice of antibiotic to treat a given condition calls for professional skill and knowledge. The overwhelming consensus of medical opinion in this country and the United States is that artificial feeding by nasogastric tube is also medical treatment. This is a readily understandable view. The insertion of the tube is a procedure calling for skill and knowledge, and the tube is invasive of the patient's body to an extent which feeding by spoon or cup is not. An intubated patient certainly looks as if he is undergoing treatment, and the mechanical pumping of food through the tube is a highly unnatural process. It does not, however, seem to me crucial whether this is regarded as medical treatment or not, since whether or not this is medical treatment it forms part of the patient's medical care and I cannot think the answer to this problem depends on fine definitional distinctions.

It is relevant to consider the objects of medical care. I think traditionally they have been (1) to prevent the occurrence of illness, injury or deformity (which for convenience I shall together call 'illness') before they occur, (2) to cure illness when it does occur, (3) where illness cannot be cured, to prevent or retard deterioration of the patient's condition and (4) to relieve pain and suffering in body and mind. I doubt if it has ever been an object of medical care merely to prolong the life of an insensate patient with no hope of recovery where nothing

can be done to promote any of these objects. But until relatively recently the
a question could scarcely have arisen since the medical technology to prolong life
in this way did not exist. That is also a new feature of this case.

There are, however, a number of other jurisdictions in which the question has
arisen and been squarely confronted.

In the United States the issue has been much litigated. Despite variations of
practice and strong expressions of dissent, the courts have in the great majority of
b cases sanctioned the discontinuance of artificial feeding of PVS patients. They
have reached this result in deference to the express wishes of the patient where
there were such and, where there were not, on the basis either that the court
could judge what the patient's wishes would have been if expressed or that such
discontinuance was in all the circumstances in the patient's best interests. The
courts have consistently rejected the suggestion that such discontinuance amounts
c to suicide or criminal homicide. Since US courts exercise a parens patriae
jurisdiction even in relation to adults, these cases must be viewed with reserve,
but the trend of authority is clear.

In the South African case *Clarke v Hurst* (30 July 1992, unreported) there was
evidence of a PVS patient's wish that his life should not be artificially prolonged,
d but the court acted on wider grounds in sanctioning the discontinuance of
nasogastric and other non-natural feeding methods and the withholding of
medical treatment.

In New Zealand the question arose in relation to a victim of the Guillain-Barré
syndrome who had expressed no wishes concerning his treatment: see *Auckland
Area Health Board v A-G* [1993] 1 NZLR 235. Thomas J delivered a comprehensive
e oral judgment in the course of which he said (at 250):

> 'In my view, doctors have a lawful excuse to discontinue ventilation when
> there is no medical justification for continuing that form of medical
> assistance. To require the administration of a life-support system when such
> a system has no further medical function or purpose and serves only to defer
f > the death of the patient is to confound the purpose of medicine. In such
> circumstances, the continuation of the artificial ventilation may be lawful,
> but that does not make it unlawful to discontinue it if the discontinuance
> accords with good medical practice.'

Having considered *Re J (a minor) (wardship: medical treatment)* [1992] 4 All ER 614,
g [1993] Fam 15 he said (at 252):

> 'The point, for present purposes is, as I apprehend it, that a doctor acting
> in good faith and in accordance with good medical practice is not under a
> duty to render life support necessary to prolong life if that is, in his or her
> judgment, contrary to the best interests of the patient.'

h Finally he concluded (at 253):

> 'Medical science and technology has advanced for a fundamental purpose;
> the purpose of benefiting the life and health of those who turn to medicine
> to be healed. It surely was never intended that it be used to prolong biological
> life in patients bereft of the prospect of returning to an even limited exercise
j > of human life. Nothing in the inherent purpose of these scientific advances
> can require doctors to treat the dying as if they were curable. Natural death
> has not lost its meaning or significance. It may be deferred, but it need not
> be postponed indefinitely. Nor, surely, was modern medical science ever
> developed to be used inhumanely. To do so is not consistent with its

fundamental purpose. Take the case of a man riddled with cancer, in constant agony, and facing imminent death. Is he to be placed upon a respirator? On the contrary, it has been generally accepted that doctors may seek to alleviate a patient's terminal pain and suffering even though the treatment may at the same time possibly accelerate the patient's death. As I perceive it, what is involved is not just medical treatment, but medical treatment in accordance with the doctor's best judgment as to what is in the best interests of his or her patient. They remain responsible for the kind and extent of the treatment administered and, ultimately, for its duration. In exercising their best judgment in this regard it is crucial for the patient and in the overall interests of society that they should not be inhibited by considerations pertinent to their own self-interest in avoiding criminal sanctions. Their judgment must be a genuinely independent judgment as to what will best serve the well-being of their dying patients. Conscientious doctors will undoubtedly continue to strive with dedication to preserve and promote the life and health of their patients. That is their primary mission. But with a patient such as Mr L, where "life" is being prolonged for no therapeutic or medical purpose or, in other words, death is merely being deferred, the doctor is not under a duty to avert that death at all costs. If, in his judgment, the proper medical practice would be to discontinue the life-support system, and that would be in the best interests of his patient, he may do so subject to adhering to a procedure which provides a safeguard against the possibility of individual error.'

In *Nancy B v Hôtel-Dieu de Québec* (1992) 86 DLR (4th) 385 the Quebec Superior Court granted the plaintiff, a victim of the Guillain-Barré syndrome whose intellectual faculties were unimpaired but whose survival was dependent on artificial respiration, an order that further treatment be discontinued. That was, however, in response to her express and informed wish. A question closer to the present was addressed by the Law Reform Commission of Canada in its Working Paper 28 on *Euthanasia, Aiding Suicide and Cessation of Treatment* (1982), which stated (at p 65):

'At this stage, it may be useful to summarize the tentative conclusions which the Commission has reached to date. These conclusions are as follows: (1) the law should recognise the competent patient's wishes and respect them as regards the cessation or non-initiation of treatment; (2) the law should clearly state that a physician acts legally when he decides to terminate or not to initiate treatment which is useless or which no longer offers reasonable hope, unless the patient has expressed his wishes to the contrary; (3) the law should recognize that the prolonging of life is not an absolute value in itself and that therefore a physician does not act illegally when he fails to take measures to achieve this end, if these measures are useless or contrary to the patient's wishes or interests; (4) the law should recognize that a physician who continues to treat a patient against his wishes is subject to the provisions of the Criminal Code; (5) the law should recognize that the incapacity of a person to express his wishes is not sufficient a reason to oblige a physician to administer useless treatment for the purpose of prolonging his life; (6) the law should recognize that in the case of an unconscious or incompetent patient, a physician incurs no criminal responsibility by terminating treatment which has become useless.'

After extensive consultation the commission recommended in Report 20 (on the same subject) (at p 27) that—

'a physician should not incur any criminal liability if he decides to discontinue or not initiate treatment for an incompetent person, when that treatment is no longer therapeutically useful and is not in the person's best interest.'

In this country, a discussion paper published by the ethics committee of the British Medical Association (the BMA) in September 1992 recorded (at p 22) that there had been no prosecutions in Scotland in cases where doctors had withdrawn nutrition from PVS patients with the agreement of the patients' families. An earlier BMA report had expressed the view that—

'feeding/gastrostomy tubes for nutrition and hydration are medical treatments and are warranted only when they make possible a decent life in which the patient can reasonably be thought to have a continued interest ... There is no justification for continuing medical intervention in such a state [PVS] and the working party feels that the individual concerned is most appropriately treated as an incompetent patient with a terminal condition.'

In 1991 the Institute of Medical Ethics published a majority view (at p 16) that—

'it can be morally justified to withdraw artificial nutrition and hydration from patients in persistent vegetative state.'

In seeking declarations from the court Mr Francis QC for the plaintiff trust relied on the reasoning underlying this weight of authority, as did Mr Lester QC who supported the plaintiff's application. The central steps in the argument were, I think, these. (1) The question whether artificial feeding and antibiotic treatment of Mr Bland should be discontinued is one to be resolved by the doctors in charge of his case, in consultation with independent medical experts, conscientiously exercising a careful and informed judgment of what the best interests of their patient require. In forming that judgment it is appropriate for them to take full account of the family's wishes, as they have done. (2) While the respect accorded to human life always raises a presumption in favour of prolonging it, that presumption is not irrebuttable. (3) Mere prolongation of the life of a PVS patient such as Mr Bland, with no hope of any recovery, is not necessarily in his best interests, if indeed such prolongation is in his interest at all. (4) In making an objective judgment of Mr Bland's best interests, account can be taken not only of any pain and suffering which prolonged feeding and medication might cause but also of wider, less tangible considerations. (5) The assessment of Mr Bland's best interests, although a matter for his doctors in the first instance, is ultimately subject to the sanction of the court where (as here) its jurisdiction is invoked. There is no ground for overriding their judgment.

Step (1) of this argument is in my view consistent with the English authority already referred to. I do not think there is any English authority inconsistent with it.

If the reasoning of *Re J* [1992] 4 All ER 614, [1993] Fam 15 is sound, step (2) of the argument is also sound. I think that the reasoning in *Re J* is sound. It is also consistent with the reasoning in *Re B (a minor) (wardship: medical treatment)* (1981) [1990] 3 All ER 927, [1981] 1 WLR 1421 and *Re C* [1989] 2 All ER 782, [1990] Fam 26. In any event the ratio of *Re J* is binding on this court.

I would for my part accept step (3). Looking at the matter as objectively as I can, and doing my best to look at the matter through Mr Bland's eyes and not my own, I cannot conceive what benefit his continued existence could be thought to give him. It might be different were it possible to hope that, if he lived long enough, means might be found to restore some part of his faculties, but no grounds have been suggested for cherishing such a hope and the physiological findings appear to preclude it.   *a*

It is of course true that pain and suffering, which may (if the foregoing reasoning is sound) weigh in the balance against the presumption in favour of life, are here to be ignored because of Mr Bland's insensible condition. But I accept the argument in step (4) that account may be taken of wider and less tangible considerations. An objective assessment of Mr Bland's best interests, viewed through his eyes, would in my opinion give weight to the constant *b* invasions and humiliations to which his inert body is subject; to the desire he would naturally have to be remembered as a cheerful, carefree, gregarious teenager and not an object of pity; to the prolonged ordeal imposed on all members of his family, but particularly on his parents; even, perhaps, if altruism still lives, to a belief that finite resources are better devoted to enhancing life than simply averting death.   *c*

I accept step (5). In cases where assessment of the patient's best interests is not undertaken by the court itself (as in wardship), the doctors' assessment is none the less subject to the court's review, where its jurisdiction is invoked. Such review may be of real value in excluding the possibilities of medical error, misapprehension of the correct approach, divisions of opinion, conflicts of interest, improper *d* motives and so on. On the doctors' premises, Sir Stephen Brown P found no reason to impugn the doctors' judgment and none was suggested. Unless their premises can be effectively challenged, there is in my view no ground for withholding the court's sanction.

I have not so far directly addressed the submissions made to the court by Mr Munby for the Official Solicitor. He did, however, challenge, radically and *e* robustly, the premises upon which the doctors' judgment was based. To those submissions I now turn.

Mr Munby's first submission was:

> 'To withdraw Anthony Bland's feeding tube is to do an act which will inevitably cause, and is intended to cause, his death. It is, therefore, necessarily *f* unlawful and criminal. This is so whether or not artificial feeding is medical treatment.'

The submission was a short one. Reliance was placed on Devlin J's famous direction in *R v Adams* (8 April 1957, unreported) that 'no doctor, nor any man, no more in the case of the dying than of the healthy, has the right deliberately to cut the thread of life'. Attention was also drawn to Ognall J's recent direction to *g* the jury in *R v Cox* (18 September 1992, unreported) that there is an 'absolute prohibition on a doctor purposefully taking life as opposed to saving it'. Accordingly it is said that the doctors' proposed course of action (at least in relation to feeding) would amount at least to manslaughter, at most to murder.

I have some difficulty in regarding this as a practical issue, since both *R v Adams* *h* and *R v Cox* concerned drugs said to have been deliberately administered to cause or hasten death and I cannot on the present facts imagine any prosecutor prosecuting, any judge leaving the issue to a jury or any jury convicting. But that does not meet the theoretical argument.

The submission may perhaps be tested by three hypothetical examples.

(1) In compliance with the express instructions of a PVS patient given before *j* onset of the condition, when the patient was adult and of sound mind, a doctor discontinues artificial feeding after three years and the patient dies. Has the doctor aided and abetted suicide? I think the answer plainly is that he has not. Why not? There are several possible answers. One is that it cannot be unlawful to act in accordance with the instructions of an adult patient of sound mind. Another is

that the patient lacked the intent necessary for suicide. A third is that it was not
a the discontinuance of artificial feeding but the patient's condition and its
underlying cause which caused his death. A fourth is that the doctor lacked the
intent necessary for aiding and abetting suicide. It may be all four answers are
correct. But if it was not the discontinuance which caused the death or if the
doctor lacked the intent to kill he would have defences to murder and perhaps
manslaughter also even if the patient had given no instructions.

b   (2) A PVS patient's nasogastric tube becomes defective after years of use and has
to be removed. The doctor has to decide whether to continue artificial feeding
through a replacement nasogastric tube or a newly implanted gastrostomy tube.
He decides that, in all the circumstances, three years after the onset of the
condition and with no hope of improvement, it is not in the patient's best interests
c to do so. He does not do so and the patient dies. Is the doctor guilty of murder or
manslaughter? In my view plainly not. If that is so, and the doctors here were to
be guilty, it could only be because of a distinction between initiating a new
regime of artificial feeding and discontinuing an existing regime. Where the
doctor's duty to the patient (to care for him with ordinary professional skill in the
patient's best interests) is the same in the two cases, I cannot think that criminal
d liability depends on such a distinction. The doctor must be guilty in both cases or
neither.

(3) A PVS patient shows signs of life-threatening failure of, in succession, heart,
lungs, liver, kidneys, spleen, bladder, pancreas. In each case the failure can be
safely rectified by serious surgery, carried out without pain or distress to the
unconscious patient. Is the doctor obliged to undertake these life-saving
e procedures? Although pointing out, correctly, that his first submission related
only to artificial feeding, Mr Munby answered that the doctor was so obliged.
Such a suggestion is in my view so repugnant to one's sense of how one individual
should behave towards another that I would reject it as possibly representing the
law. But if I am right to reject it, the doctors could only be guilty here if some
distinction were to be drawn between the surgical procedures described and
f artificial feeding. But I do not think that criminal liability can depend on the
relative invasiveness of different invasive procedures.

A doctor who discontinues artificial feeding of a PVS patient, after a lapse of
time which entitles him to be sure that there is no hope of recovery, in pursuance
of a conscientious and proper judgment that such discontinuance is in the patient's
g best interests, is in my view guilty of no crime. For present purposes I do not
think it greatly matters whether one simply says that that is not an unlawful act,
or that the doctor lacks criminal intent, or that he breaches no duty or that his act
did not cause death. But even if this first submission were (contrary to my view)
sound, it would leave the doctors free to discontinue antibiotics, with the result
that Mr Bland would die sooner rather than later, perhaps less peacefully than on
h withdrawal of artificial feeding. The factual merits of the submission are not
compelling.

Mr Munby's second submission was:

> 'To withdraw Anthony Bland's feeding tube is a breach of the doctors' duty
> to care for and feed him: discontinuance of mechanical hydration and
j > nutrition involves the withdrawal of food, whether or not it also involves the
> withdrawal of medical treatment. Since it will inevitably cause, and is
> intended to cause, his death, it is necessarily unlawful and criminal.'

I think it is evident from what I have already said that I do not accept any
ingredient of this submission for reasons I have given. Its falsity is in my view
highlighted by an attempted analogy with *R v Stone* [1977] 2 All ER 341, [1977]

QB 354, where the defendant convicted of manslaughter had failed to supply
food or procure medical attention for an elderly and infirm but conscious woman   *a*
who was perfectly capable of feeding herself if food was supplied.

Mr Munby's third submission was:

'In any event, and even assuming that artificial feeding is properly to be
regarded as medical treatment (and it ought not to be), there is no justification
for withdrawing that treatment. To withdraw Anthony Bland's feeding tube   *b*
is a breach of the doctors' duty to treat and nurse him. Since it will inevitably
cause, and is intended to cause, his death, it is necessarily unlawful and
criminal.'

Again, I think it is evident from what I have already said that I do not accept
any ingredient of this submission for reasons I have given.

I turn lastly to the issue of procedure, on the assumption that the plaintiff trust   *c*
is entitled to the declarations made. There was only limited dispute about this.
At the end of his judgment Sir Stephen Brown P held that in cases of this kind
application should be made to the court to obtain its sanction for the course
proposed. This was in my respectful view a wise ruling, directed to the protection
of patients, the protection of doctors, the reassurance of patients' families and the   *d*
reassurance of the public. The practice proposed seems to me desirable. It may
very well be that with the passage of time a body of experience and practice will
build up which will obviate the need for application in every case, but for the
time being I am satisfied that the practice which Sir Stephen Brown P described
should be followed.

I would dismiss the appeal. I have read in draft the judgments of Butler-Sloss   *e*
and Hoffmann LJJ and agree also with their reasons for reaching this conclusion.

BUTLER-SLOSS LJ. This is a tragic case and the necessary dispassionate
consideration of all the necessary components of the issues before us should not
blind us to the anguish of the family for whom everyone feels the greatest   *f*
sympathy.

Each court seised of these issues has an awesome task to face. In doing so we
have to rid ourselves of emotional overtones and emotive language which do not
assist in elucidating the profound questions which require to be answered.

The facts are not in dispute. The present condition of Tony Bland has been
described by Sir Thomas Bingham MR. He is at the extreme end of the spectrum   *g*
of those suffering from the condition of persistent vegetative state (PVS). He has
been in that state for three and a half years and there is, while he lives, no release
from it. He is in a 'state of chronic wakefulness without awareness' (American
Medical Association Council Report, January 1990), and has irreversible loss of
cognition. A recent surgical operation was carried out on him without anaesthetic,
and his future care and whether he does or does not receive nutrition and   *h*
hydration, or the manner in which he will die will be a matter of indifference to
him in his present state.

His ability to survive with artificial support is a product of the medical advances
in recent years. Medical science and technology have provided for many a cure or
alleviation of injury or disease but have also created conditions which allow
Anthony Bland to exist in a twilight world. Twenty years ago he would not have   *j*
survived.

Self-determination

The starting point for consideration, in my view, is the right of a human being
to make his own decisions and to decide whether to accept or reject treatment,

the right of self-determination. Such a decision may be rational or irrational (see

a *Sidaway v Bethlem Royal Hospital Governors* [1985] 1 All ER 643 at 665–666, [1985] AC 871 at 904–905). Counsel all agree that the right to reject treatment extends to deciding not to accept treatment in the future by way of advance directive or 'living will'. A well-known example of advance directive is provided by those subscribing to the tenets of the Jehovah's Witnesses, who make it clear that they will not accept blood transfusions (see for example *Malette v Shulman* (1990) 72

b OR (2d) 417). The provision of treatment by a doctor without the consent of the patient other than in an emergency is likely to be a trespass (see *F v West Berkshire Health Authority (Mental Health Act Commission intervening)* [1989] 2 All ER 545 at 562, [1990] 2 AC 1 at 71 per Lord Goff of Chieveley and *Schloendorff v Society of New York Hospital* (1914) 211 NY 125 at 129 per Cardozo J).

c In this case Anthony Bland has not given a clear indication of his views. His family are unable to consent on his behalf (see *Re T (adult: refusal of medical treatment)* [1992] 4 All ER 649 at 653, [1992] 3 WLR 782 at 787 per Lord Donaldson MR). His father expressed in evidence his view that his son would not have wished to live in his present state. As Lord Donaldson MR said the views of relatives may reveal that the patient had made an anticipatory choice

d which does not arise here. The views of the family must always be treated with respect and will be an important consideration in the overall assessment. In some cases the evidence of relatives will require to be treated with great caution since there may be hidden motives. There is no suggestion that such concerns arise in this family.

e

Lack of consent

Mr Bland is both by medical and legal standards incompetent in that he lacks the capacity to give valid consent to medical treatment. No one can consent on his behalf. The parens patriae jurisdiction of the High Court no longer exists and

f in *F v West Berkshire Health Authority* the House of Lords held that at common law there was no jurisdiction in the court to approve or disapprove the giving of medical treatment to such a patient. The lawfulness of the action depended upon whether the treatment was in the best interests of the patient. The House of Lords then devised a procedure in cases of proposed sterilisation of those unable to consent that a declaration might be made by the High Court as to whether

g such an operation was in the best interests of the patient.

Two possible approaches have been suggested to us, the United States preferred route of substituted judgment or the objectively ascertained best interests of the patient. The majority of state superior courts (of the United States) have, in the absence of expressed wishes, founded their decisions on similar issues on the exercise of a substituted judgment based upon ascertaining the patient's known

h views, beliefs, philosophy and lifestyle. In the absence of sufficient information many of the American courts have made decisions based upon the patient's 'best interests'.

Although it appears in origin derived from the English common law, the American approach based on substituted judgment appears to have little in common with the trend discernible in recent English decisions, all of which

j consider the objective best interests of the patient (see for example *F v West Berkshire Health Authority* and *Re T*). I can see no reason to extend the test of substituted judgment beyond the Court of Protection. In assessing the best interests of Anthony Bland, however, his views, personality, how others including his family saw him before his accident will form part of that assessment, although that evidence has a subjective element.

Medical treatment

Before considering the duty of care of the doctor towards his patient, it is   *a*
necessary to deal with the argument of Mr Munby QC that the method of
providing nutrition to Anthony Bland is not 'medical treatment'. All but one of
the doctors who gave evidence to Sir Stephen Brown P treated it as such, and even
Dr Andrews, who disagreed, accepted that, if asked to do so by a patient who was
capable of making a decision, he would remove the nasogastric tube. The evidence
of the doctors was supported by a wealth of medical expertise that it is medical   *b*
treatment, the report of the British Medical Association, the American Medical
Association, the medical ethics committees of England and of the United States.
It is also the conclusion of the Supreme Courts of many of the states of the United
States and, even more persuasive, of the Supreme Court of the United States in
Cruzan v Director, Missouri Dept of Health (1990) 497 US 261. Interestingly, the   *c*
Mental Health Act 1983 includes nursing in its definition of 'medical treatment'.

Although Mr Munby for the Official Solicitor argued that it is not 'medical
treatment' there was overwhelming evidence upon which Sir Stephen Brown P
was entitled to conclude that it is.

If we describe what is being done by the doctors and nurses for Anthony Bland
and others in his condition as medical care rather than treatment, it may to the   *d*
layman make more sense and avoid the uncomfortable attempt to draw a line
between different forms of feeding such as spoon-feeding a helpless patient or
inserting a tube through the nose or direct into the stomach.

The definition of medical treatment does not, in my view, of itself resolve the
problem. The underlying issue is whether, under the extreme circumstances of
this case, there is a duty upon his doctor to continue to provide to Anthony Bland   *e*
nutrition and hydration by an artificial method. Mr Munby argued that there are
basic needs which are the right of a patient, the need for air and the need for
nutrition. That is in my view too narrow an expression of basic needs, which
cannot be seen in isolation from general care including for instance warmth and
hygiene.   *f*

Duty of care

A doctor owes a duty of care towards his patient and in the case of a patient
unable to give instructions or consent to treatment, a duty to treat him in the
patient's best interests (see *F v West Berkshire Health Authority*). The general duty
of a doctor is to act in accordance with a responsible and competent body of   *g*
relevant professional opinion based upon the principles laid down in *Bolam v
Friern Hospital Management Committee* [1957] 2 All ER 118, [1957] 1 WLR 582
(the *Bolam* test). In carrying out his duty towards his patient a doctor is faced all
the time with a series of decisions each of which requires choices—a choice
whether to operate, whether to initiate other invasive treatment such as
chemotherapy, whether to give antibiotics. As his care of the patient progresses   *h*
he may have to decide whether to discontinue a process conscious that such a
choice marks not only the cessation of effective treatment but also brings closer
the end of his patient's life. Medical ethics draw no distinction between the
withholding of treatment and the withdrawing of treatment. It is accepted by
Mr Munby that in making those decisions and choosing one course rather than
another the doctor is rightly guided by the value of the treatment given and the   *j*
lack of value of other treatment proposed and from time to time the futility of
giving any further treatment which will not benefit the patient. The assessment
of the futility of the treatment is in his view justification for ceasing the treatment.
He argued none the less that, since feeding is not treatment, the futility of

continuing useless treatment does not arise, and in any event it is never futile to
a feed. None the less decisions have to be made about future treatment which
involve choices such as whether to provide antibiotics. Sir Stephen Brown P found
that it was the unanimous opinion of all the distinguished doctors who have
examined Mr Bland that there is no hope whatsoever of recovery or improvement
of any kind. The only purpose of the present care is to keep him artificially alive
within his present condition. The medical team caring for Mr Bland have formed
b the medical opinion that it is in his best interests to discontinue all forms of
treatment including the provision of nutrition and hydration.

The question then arises as to the extent or limit of the duty of care of the
doctor towards a PVS patient. The formulation of the duty of care within the
Bolam test may not by itself be an adequate basis for this grave decision which
c requires more than the decision as to the uselessness of future treatment. The
principle of the best interests of an incompetent patient in the present
circumstances encompasses wider considerations, including some degree of
monitoring of the medical decision.

There is a conflict between the principle of self-determination and whatever
may be the equivalent right of those who cannot choose and another basic
d principle of our society, the preservation of life. Lord Donaldson MR spoke in *Re
J (a minor) (wardship: medical treatment)* [1990] 3 All ER 930 at 938, [1991] Fam 33
at 46 of the vast importance of the sanctity of the human life. I respectfully agree
with him. Its importance cannot be overemphasised. He said:

> 'The decision on life and death must and does remain in other hands.
e What doctors and the court have to decide is whether, in the best interests of
> the child patient, a particular decision as to medical treatment should be
> taken which *as a side effect* will render death more or less likely. This is not a
> matter of semantics. It is fundamental. At the other end of the age spectrum,
> the use of drugs to reduce pain will often be fully justified, notwithstanding
> that this will hasten the moment of death. What can never be justified is the
f use of drugs or surgical procedures with the primary purpose of doing so.'
> (Lord Donaldson MR's emphasis.)

Lord Donaldson MR then set out the balancing exercise to be performed:

> 'This brings me face to face with the problem of formulating the critical
> equation. In truth it cannot be done with mathematical or any precision.
g There is without doubt a very strong presumption in favour of a course of
> action which will prolong life, but, even excepting the "cabbage" case to
> which special considerations may well apply, it is not irrebuttable.'

Mr Munby argued in *Re J* the fundamentalist or absolutist approach, that the
pain and suffering experienced and to be experienced by that child should not
h displace the sanctity of life, including the preservation of the life of that child,
whatever it was to be. This court rejected that approach and placed on the other
side of the critical equation the tragic situation of the child concerned and the
quality of her life. Lord Donaldson MR did not feel bound to follow the views
expressed (obiter) in *Re B (a minor) (wardship: medical treatment)* (1981) [1990] 3
i All ER 927, [1981] 1 WLR 1421 as to the degree of awfulness or intolerability of
treatment which might be proposed as providing a quasi-statutory yardstick. He
left the door open. Apart from preferring to use a word other than 'cabbage', I
respectfully agree with him. In *Re B* this court was considering a simple operation
to clear an intestinal obstruction of a Down's syndrome baby. The circumstances
of *Re J* or of this appeal were not considered by the members of the court. Dunn

LJ pointed out that there was no reliable prognosis as to the life expectancy of the child and no evidence at all about the quality of life the child might expect (see   *a* [1990] 3 All ER 927 at 929–930, [1981] 1 WLR 1421 at 1424)

Although this court in *Re J* was exercising the parens patriae jurisdiction, the approach is equally apposite to an incompetent adult, since the consideration of best interests has to import a balancing exercise which Mr Munby recognised. His answer was that severe pain and suffering as experienced by the child in *Re J*   *b* is the only factor which can be put on the other side of the equation to the sanctity of life. He reserved his position to argue elsewhere that *Re J* was wrongly decided and there was nothing to place in the balance against the sanctity of life. In his argument to this court the interests of the PVS patient are limited to that sole consideration.

To place pain and suffering in a unique category, the existence of which may   *c* justify foregoing the preservation of the sanctity of life, does not appear to me to be justifiable. Two reasons come immediately to mind. First, on a practical level, according to Mr Munby the exception of extreme pain can be justified on the basis that it can be objectively verified. The degree of resistance to pain varies enormously from person to person and is intensively subjective however its existence as such may be objectively verified. It is not an absolute state and it will   *d* always be a matter of degree as to whether the state of pain of an incompetent patient is sufficiently severe to meet the necessary criterion. If it is to be the only criterion, excluding all other considerations, the lack of clarity in formulating when it comes into play, creates for me a logical problem in accepting it alone on the other side of the equation.

There is however a second and more fundamental objection. The case for the   *e* universal sanctity of life assumes a life in the abstract and allows nothing for the reality of Mr Bland's actual existence. There are clearly dangers in departing from the fundamental approach to the preservation of life, but in the American decisions it is not conclusive. Two exceptions are already recognised in English common law, the right of self-determination and the *Re J* situation of extreme pain and suffering. The quality of life has already been recognised as a factor and   *f* placed in the equation to allow a life not to be prolonged at all costs. Taylor LJ said in *Re J* [1990] 3 All ER 930 at 945, [1991] Fam 33 at 55: 'Once the absolute test is rejected, the proper criteria must be a matter of degree.' To limit the quality of life to extreme pain is to take a demeaning view of a human being. There must be something more for the humanity of the person of a PVS patient. He remains   *g* a person and not an object of concern. In *Re Conroy* (1985) 98 NJ 321 at 396 Handler J supports this approach:

> 'Clearly, a decision to focus exclusively on pain as the single criterion ignores and devalues other important ideals regarding life and death. Consequently, a pain standard cannot serve as an indirect proxy for additional   *h* and significant concerns that bear on the decision to forego life-prolonging treatments.'

The concentration exclusively upon pain is to me an unacceptable approach to a patient in Anthony Bland's extreme situation. There are other factors to be placed in the critical equation.   *j*

Those other factors have not so far been explored in English decisions but they have been considered extensively in the United States and in a recent case in New Zealand. In *Cruzan v Director, Missouri Dept of Health* (1990) 110 S Ct 2841 at 2885–2886 (a PVS case) Stevens J (in a dissenting opinion) said:

a   'But Nancy Cruzan's interest in life, no less than that of any other person, includes an interest in how she will be thought of after her death by those whose opinions mattered to her. There can be no doubt that her life made her dear to her family, and to others. How she dies will affect how that life is remembered.'

b   In *Guardianship of Jane Doe* (1992) 411 Mass 512 the Supreme Judicial Court of Massachusetts (in a PVS case where the patient had always been incompetent) held that incompetent individuals have the same rights as competent individuals to refuse and terminate medical treatment. Abrams J, giving the majority opinion, accepted the rights of the patient to bodily integrity and privacy and upheld the judge's decision to terminate nasoduodenal feeding and hydration. *Re Jobes* (1987) 108 NJ 394 (a PVS patient) following *Re Quinlan* (1976) 70 NJ 10

c   upheld the principle of self-determination for the incompetent. The views of the family were accepted in each of those cases. Handler J in a concurring opinion considered the best interests test and, after describing the extreme physical condition of Mrs Jobes (very similar to Mr Bland), quoted a passage in his opinion in *Re Conroy* (1985) 98 NJ 321 at 398–399:

d   '"The medical and nursing treatment of individuals in extremis and suffering from these conditions entails the constant and extensive handling and manipulation of the body. At some point, such a course of treatment upon the insensate patient is bound to touch the sensibilities of even the most detached observer. Eventually, pervasive bodily intrusions, even for the best motives, will arouse feelings akin to humiliation and mortification for the

e   helpless patient. When cherished values of human dignity and personal privacy, which belong to every person living or dying, are sufficiently transgressed by what is being done to the individual, we should be ready to say: enough." Based upon such factors it should be possible to structure critical treatment decisions that are reliable, understandable and acceptable.'

f   (See 108 NJ 394 at 443–444.)

Auckland Area Health Board v A-G [1993] 1 NZLR 235 was an extreme example of a Guillain-Barré syndrome, causing a condition somewhat similar to a PVS patient, where the doctors sought a declaration that to withdraw artificial ventilation would not constitute culpable homicide. Thomas J granted the declaration and in doing so considered decisions from a number of common law

g   jurisdictions including the American and our own. He referred (at 245) to—

    'values of human dignity and personal privacy . . . Human dignity and personal privacy belong to every person, whether living or dying. Yet, the sheer invasiveness of the treatment and the manipulation of the human body which it entails, the pitiful and humiliating helplessness of the patient's state,

h   and the degradation and dissolution of all bodily functions invoke these values . . .'

The judge based his decision upon the best interests test. Mr Munby accepted that there was no difference in principle between the ventilator and the nasogastric tube.

    Although the American decisions are often based upon the principle of achieving the right of an incompetent patient to make decisions as if competent through the device of the substituted judgment, in many cases the distinction from best interests is blurred, as Handler J pointed out in *Re Jobes* (1987) 108 NJ 394 at 436, and in some cases it is clearly an objective assessment of best interests

and the decisions are persuasive support for considerations far wider than the
factor of pain to be taken into account in balancing the critical equation.

We all of course recognise that a patient unable to choose cannot himself
exercise his right of self-determination and he cannot make the irrational decision
he might notionally have made if in possession of his faculties. But not to be able
to be irrational does not seem to me to be a good reason to be deprived of a
rational decision which could be taken on his behalf in his best interests.
Otherwise, if, as I believe they are, other factors as well as pain are relevant
considerations, he is put at an unfair disadvantage.

A mentally incompetent patient has interests to be considered and protected,
the basic one being the right to be properly cared for by others. He retains the
right to have proceedings taken on his behalf, for instance to claim damages for
negligence, or to have his estate or other property managed for him, or to respond
to actions or proceedings taken against him, such as divorce proceedings. He
retains in my view the right to be well regarded by others, and to be well
remembered by his family. That right is separate from that of his family to
remember him and to have the opportunity to grieve for him when he is dead.
He has the right to be respected. Consequently he has a right to avoid unnecessary
humiliation and degrading invasion of his body for no good purpose. I was
dismayed to hear the argument of the Official Solicitor that, if Mr Bland suffered
a cardiac arrest or a renal failure, it would be the duty of the doctors to perform a
heart bypass operation or a kidney transplant. I cannot believe that a patient in
the situation of Mr Bland should be subjected to therapeutically useless treatment
contrary to good medical practice and medical ethics which would not be inflicted
upon those able to choose. It is an affront to his right to be respected.

The considerations as to the quality of life of Mr Bland now and in the future
in his extreme situation are in my opinion rightly to be placed on the other side
of the critical equation from the general principle of the sanctity and inviolability
of life. In this appeal those factors which include the reality of Mr Bland's
existence outweigh the abstract requirement to preserve life. The doctors charged
with his care have balanced that equation from the medical standpoint and, after
consultation with the family, who are in agreement, have concluded that his best
interests lie in not artificially prolonging his life. Sir Stephen Brown P reconsidered
all the relevant matters and came to the conclusion that to discontinue the
artificial feeding would be in accordance with good medical practice and was in
the best interests of Mr Bland. In my respectful view he was right and I entirely
agree with his conclusion. The duty of the doctors towards a PVS patient at the
extreme end of the spectrum does not extend to prolonging his life at all costs.
Where they can be medically certain on all the evidence that he has been suffering
from loss of consciousness without hope of recovery for a substantial period of
time, in my judgment they are not in breach of their duty of care if they
discontinue the artificial nutrition and hydration.

The criminal law

The thrust of Mr Munby's argument has been that it is unlawful to discontinue
artificial feeding and consequently the doctors would be at risk of criminal
proceedings. If a doctor owes a duty to continue to treat or to provide artificial
nutrition, his failure to do so is a breach of his duty to the patient and may not
only be actionable, but also a criminal act. In my view, as I have already set out in
this judgment, I do not consider that there remains a duty of care upon the
doctors to continue the artificial feeding and I agree with Mr Lester QC that there
is no actus reus and no unlawful act or omission. The issue of mens rea does not
arise.

There has been no criminal prosecution on these facts in England. My view is *a* supported, however, by the decision of the Superior Court of the State of California, in the County of Los Angeles, in *Barber v Superior Court of Los Angeles County* (1983) 147 Cal App 3d 1006. The court held that the doctors' omission to continue treatment though intentional and with knowledge that the patient would die was not unlawful failure to perform a legal duty.

The position of Dr Cox is different (see *R v Cox* (18 September 1992, unreported), *b* Ognall J). He injected a lethal dose, which was designed to cause death and was an external and intrusive act committed by an outsider and was not in accordance with his duty of care as a doctor. The effect of the cessation of artificial feeding is to place the patient in the position he would have been in before the nasogastric tube was inserted. Without the tube he would have died from his medical *c* condition and with it he has been artificially kept alive despite that condition until now. Whether this is an act or omission carries the matter no further. The distinction between Mr Bland's doctors and Dr Cox is between an act or omission which allows causes already present in the body to operate and the introduction of an external agency of death.

The idea of ceasing the artificial feeding is a distressing one for all of us to *d* contemplate. It would no doubt also be distressing for those who are caring for Mr Bland. We know however from the medical evidence that it would not be a distressing or painful experience for him in his state of non-cognition. The manner of his death can be eased for him and those seeing it by appropriate medical and nursing care until the end of his life.

I have anxiously considered whether this is a decision which ought to be taken *e* by the doctors alone. As the House of Lords said in *F v West Berkshire Health Authority* [1989] 2 All ER 545, [1990] 2 AC 1 it is not generally for the courts to intervene in the decision-making process as to whether a course of action is in the best interests of a patient. That process is for the doctors. The BMA have laid down careful guidelines for these cases. None the less in *F v West Berkshire Health Authority* the House of Lords recognised an exceptional situation which required *f* guidance from the High Court. I have been persuaded by the amicus that in a decision-making process of such gravity as whether to continue treating a PVS patient, the intervention of the High Court is a proper safeguard. I respectfully agree with the formulation of the procedures proposed by Sir Stephen Brown P and that, for the time being at least, each application to discontinue treatment *g* should be made to the High Court. The rapid advances of medical technology create problems which may require the intervention of the courts from time to time. Such intervention may also reassure public concern.

I would dismiss the appeal.

HOFFMANN LJ. Anthony Bland was a cheerful teenager from Keighley in *h* Yorkshire. He enjoyed pop music, football and drinking with his friends. In the spectators' pen at Hillsborough football stadium on 15 April 1989 his lungs were crushed by the pressure of the crowd around him. He ceased breathing until resuscitated by first aid. While he could not breathe his brain was deprived of oxygen.

The human brain consists of the cerebral hemispheres and the lower centre of *j* the brain, which is called the brain stem. The cerebral hemispheres, or more precisely their outer layers, which are called the cerebral cortex, contain the function of consciousness. Without them, we cannot see, hear, feel pain or pleasure, or make any voluntary movements. The brain stem controls the body's semi-autonomous movements, like breathing, reflex actions and the beating of the heart.

The cerebral cortex requires a constant supply of oxygen, glucose and blood. An interruption of oxygen for a few minutes can cause extensive damage to the cells of the cortex, which never regenerate. But the brain stem is relatively resistant to being deprived of oxygen. It may therefore continue to function, and enable the heart to beat, the lungs to breathe and the stomach to digest, after the cortex has been irretrievably destroyed. This condition has been called 'persistent vegetative state'.

Since 15 April 1989 Anthony Bland has been in a persistent vegetative state. He lies in Airedale General Hospital in Keighley, fed liquid food by a pump through a tube passing through his nose and down the back of his throat into the stomach. His bladder is emptied through a catheter inserted through his penis, which from time to time has caused infections requiring dressing and antibiotic treatment. His stiffened joints have caused his limbs to be rigidly contracted so that his arms are tightly flexed across his chest and his legs unnaturally contorted. Reflex movements in the throat cause him to vomit and dribble. Of all this, and the presence of members of his family who take turns to visit him, Anthony Bland has no consciousness at all. The parts of his brain which provided him with consciousness have turned to fluid. The darkness and oblivion which descended at Hillsborough will never depart. His body is alive, but he has no life in the sense that even the most pitifully handicapped but conscious human being has a life. But the advances of modern medicine permit him to be kept in this state for years, even perhaps for decades.

The question in this appeal is whether the court should in these circumstances declare that those in charge of caring for Anthony Bland may lawfully stop providing the artificial means of keeping him alive. This is a terrible decision because the consequence is that he will die. It is a question which until relatively recently would never have arisen. A person who had irreversibly lost consciousness would quickly have died: from lack of nutrition or from one of the many complications which have afflicted Anthony Bland's body over the past three years and which medical technology has been able to hold at bay. Modern medicine therefore faces us with fundamental and painful decisions about life and death which cannot be answered on the basis of normal everyday assumptions.

For reasons which I will eventually state quite briefly, I agree with Sir Thomas Bingham MR and Butler-Sloss LJ that in English law it would be lawful for the Airedale Hospital to stop keeping Anthony Bland alive. But this case has caused a great deal of public concern. People are worried, perhaps not so much about this particular case, but about where it may lead. Is the court to assume the role of God and decide who should live and who should die? Is Anthony Bland to die because the quality of his life is so miserable? Does this mean that the court would approve the euthanasia of seriously handicapped people? And what about the manner of his death? Can it ever be right to cause the death of a human being by deliberately depriving him of food? This is not an area in which any difference can be allowed to exist between what is legal and what is morally right. The decision of the court should be able to carry conviction with the ordinary person as being based not merely on legal precedent but also upon acceptable ethical values. For this reason I shall start by trying to explain why I think it would be not only lawful but right to let Anthony Bland die. In the course of doing so I shall also try to explain why the principles upon which this judgment rests do not make it a precedent for morally unacceptable decisions in the future.

To argue from moral rather than purely legal principles is a somewhat unusual enterprise for a judge to undertake. It is not the function of judges to lay down systems of morals and nothing which I say is intended to do so. But it seemed to me that in such an unusual case as this, it would clarify my own thought and perhaps help others, if I tried to examine the underlying moral principles which have lead me to the conclusion at which I have arrived. In doing so, I must acknowledge the assistance I have received from reading the manuscript of Professor Ronald Dworkin's forthcoming book, *Life's Dominion,* and from conversations with him and Professor Bernard Williams.

I start with the concept of the sanctity of life. Why do we think it would be a tragedy to allow Anthony Bland to die? It could be said that the entire tragedy took place at Hillsborough and that the curtain was brought down when Anthony Bland passed into a persistent vegetative state. Until then his life was precious to him and his family. But since then he has had no consciousness of his life and it could be said to be a matter of indifference to him whether he lives or dies. But the fact is that Anthony Bland is still alive. The mere fact that he is still a living organism means that there remains an epilogue of the tragedy which is being played out. This is because we have a strong feeling that there is an intrinsic value in human life, irrespective of whether it is valuable to the person concerned or indeed to anyone else. Those who adhere to religious faiths which believe in the sanctity of all God's creation and in particular that human life was created in the image of God himself will have no difficulty with the concept of the intrinsic value of human life. But even those without any religious belief think in the same way. In a case like this we should not try to analyse the rationality of such feelings. What matters is that, in one form or another, they form part of almost everyone's intuitive values. No law which ignores them can possibly hope to be acceptable.

Our belief in the sanctity of life explains why we think it is almost always wrong to cause the death of another human being, even one who is terminally ill or so disabled that we think that if we were in his position we would rather be dead. Still less do we tolerate laws such as existed in Nazi Germany, by which handicapped people or inferior races could be put to death because someone else thought that their lives were useless.

But the sanctity of life is only one of a cluster of ethical principles which we apply to decisions about how we should live. Another is respect for the individual human being and in particular for his right to choose how he should live his own life. We call this individual autonomy or the right of self-determination. And another principle, closely connected, is respect for the dignity of the individual human being: our belief that quite irrespective of what the person concerned may think about it, it is wrong for someone to be humiliated or treated without respect for his value as a person. The fact that the dignity of an individual is an intrinsic value is shown by the fact that we feel embarrassed and think it wrong when someone behaves in a way which we think demeaning to himself, which does not show sufficient respect for himself as a person.

No one, I think, would quarrel with these deeply rooted ethical principles. But what is not always realised, and what is critical in this case, is that they are not always compatible with each other. Take, for example, the sanctity of life and the right of self-determination. We all believe in them and yet we cannot always have them both. The patient who refuses medical treatment which is necessary to save his life is exercising his right to self-determination. But allowing him, in effect, to choose to die, is something which many people will believe offends the principle of the sanctity of life. Suicide is no longer a crime, but its decriminalisation was a recognition that the principle of self-determination should in that case prevail over the sanctity of life.

I accept that the sanctity of life is a complex notion, often linked to religion, on which differing views may be held. The Jehovah's Witness who refuses a blood transfusion even though he knows this may result in his death, would probably not consider that he was sacrificing the principle of the sanctity of life to his own right of self-determination. He would probably say that a life which involved receiving a transfusion was so defiled as no longer to be an object of sanctity at all. But someone else might think that his death was a tragic waste and did offend against the sanctity of life. I do not think it would be a satisfactory answer to such a person to say that if he could only see it from the point of view of the Jehovah's Witness, he would realise that the principle of the sanctity of life had not been sacrificed but triumphantly upheld. Similarly it is possible to qualify the meaning of the sanctity of life by including, as some cultures do, concepts of dignity and fulfilment as part of the essence of life. In this way one could argue that, properly understood, Anthony Bland's death would not offend against the sanctity of life. But I do not think that this would satisfy the many people who feel strongly that it does. I think it is better to accept this and confront it.

A conflict between the principles of the sanctity of life and the individual's right of self-determination may therefore require a painful compromise to be made. In the case of the person who refuses an operation without which he will certainly die, one or other principle must be sacrificed. We may adopt a paternalist view, deny that his autonomy can be allowed to prevail in so extreme a case, and uphold the sanctity of life. Sometimes this looks an attractive solution, but it can have disturbing implications. Do we insist upon patients accepting life-saving treatment which is contrary to their strongly held religious beliefs? Should one force-feed prisoners on hunger strike? English law is, as one would expect, paternalist towards minors. But it upholds the autonomy of adults. A person of full age may refuse treatment for any reason or no reason at all, even if it appears certain that the result will be his death.

I do not suggest that the position which English law has taken is the only morally correct solution. Some might think that in cases of life and death, the law should be more paternalist even to adults. The point to be emphasised is that there is no morally correct solution which can be deduced from a single ethical principle like the sanctity of life or the right of self-determination. There must be an accommodation between principles, both of which seem rational and good, but which have come into conflict with each other.

It would therefore be in accordance with the English approach to resolving the conflict between the right to self-determination and the sanctity of life that, if Anthony Bland were to be momentarily restored to consciousness with full knowledge that he would shortly revert to his persistent vegetative state, and if he were to instruct those caring for him that he no longer wanted artificially to be kept alive, the doctors and nurses would be obliged to respect his wishes. If he were to give such an instruction, I think that many would feel that his wishes be obeyed, not only because they were his wishes, but because (unlike the case of a person who for religious reasons refuses treatment which could restore him to vigorous health) his wishes were entirely understandable. The horror of his situation is such that few would not think it perfectly reasonable for him to decide that, as he had already lost all sense and consciousness, he would prefer to die.

In this case, however, Anthony Bland has not made such a decision and never will. Some people make it clear in advance that, if they should fall into a state which seems to them in anticipation to be intolerable, they do not want life-sustaining treatment to be continued. The right of self-determination entails that such wishes should be respected. Different jurisdictions have varying requirements about how clearly such wishes should be expressed. But Anthony Bland expressed

none at all. There is nothing to show that in the course of his short life he gave
a the matter any thought. All that his family can say is that from their knowledge
of him and his general attitude to life, the things that interested him and gave
him pleasure, he would not have wanted to survive in his present state.

Does this mean that people who have not expressed their wishes in advance
and are now incapable of expression must lose all right to have treatment
discontinued and that those caring for them are in every case under a
b corresponding duty to keep them alive as long as medical science will allow?
Counsel for the Official Solicitor said that this was so. If they have not chosen, the
court has no right to choose on their behalf. I think that the fallacy in this
argument is that choice cannot be avoided. To continue treatment is as much a
choice as to discontinue it. Why is it not an act of choice to decide to continue to
c invade the privacy of Anthony Bland's body with tubes, catheters, probes and
injections? If on account of his unconsciousness he is obliged to submit to such
treatment, one cannot say that it is because the court is refusing to choose on his
behalf. One way or the other, a choice is being made. It is only if one thinks it
natural and normal to want treatment that continuing to provide it seems not so
much a choice as a given state of affairs. And of course in most cases this would
d be true. In a case in which it was being said that a person should not be given
treatment which would avoid death and restore him to full health, one would
want to know that this was his personal choice and that it had been expressed
very clearly indeed.

But Anthony Bland's is not a normal case. The continuation of artificial
sustenance and medical treatment will keep him alive but will not restore him to
e having a life in any sense at all. It is necessary to emphasise the awful certainty of
his fate. We all know of cases in which doctors have been mistaken and where
people have recovered to live meaningful lives after being given over for dead.
But no one has ever recovered any vestige of consciousness after being in a
persistent vegetative state for more than a year. Anthony Bland has been in this
f state for more than three years. He has been examined by a number of the most
eminent doctors and they are unanimous that there is no hope whatever of any
consciousness being regained. They say that this is the worst case of irreversible
cortex damage that they have seen. Nor is this a case in which one has to make an
assessment of the quality of life which Anthony Bland has. We all know and
admire people who suffer pain and disability, of whom many would think that
g in their position they would rather be dead, and yet who endure their lives and
derive meaning and satisfaction from living. But the very concept of having a life
has no meaning in relation to Anthony Bland. He is alive but has no life at all.

Counsel for the Official Solicitor argued that however vestigial Anthony Bland's
life might be, one could not assume that he would choose to die. Being
unconscious, he felt no pain or humiliation and therefore had no interests which
h suffered from his being kept alive. Anthony Bland was in fact indifferent to
whether he lived or died and there was nothing to put in the balance against the
intrinsic value of his life.

I think that the fallacy in this argument is that it assumes that we have no
interests except in those things of which we have conscious experience. But this
does not accord with most people's intuitive feelings about their lives and deaths.
j At least a part of the reason why we honour the wishes of the dead about the
distribution of their property is that we think it would wrong them not to do so,
despite the fact that we believe that they will never know that their will has been
ignored. Most people would like an honourable and dignified death and we think
it wrong to dishonour their deaths, even when they are unconscious that this is

happening. We pay respect to their dead bodies and to their memory because we think it an offence against the dead themselves if we do not. Once again I am not *a* concerned to analyse the rationality of these feelings. It is enough that they are deeply rooted in our ways of thinking and that the law cannot possibly ignore them. Thus I think that counsel for the Official Solicitor offers a seriously incomplete picture of Anthony Bland's interests when he confines them to animal feelings of pain or pleasure. It is demeaning to the human spirit to say that, being unconscious, he can have no interest in his personal privacy and dignity, in how *b* he lives or dies.

Anthony Bland therefore has a recognisable interest in the manner of his life and death which help the court to apply the principles of self-determination and the value of the individual. We can say from what we have learned of Anthony Bland from those closest to him that, forced as we are to choose, we think it is more likely that in his present state he would choose to die than to live. There is *c* no suggestion that he was, for example, motivated by any religious principles which would have made him want his life in its present state prolonged. We can also say that in allowing him to die, we would be showing more respect to him as an individual than by keeping him alive.

Thus it seems to me that we are faced with conflicting ethical principles. On *d* the one hand, Anthony Bland is alive and the principle of the sanctity of life says that we should not deliberately allow him to die. On the other hand, Anthony Bland is an individual human being and the principle of self-determination says he should be allowed to choose for himself and that, if he is unable to express his choice, we should try our honest best to do what we think he would have chosen. We cannot disclaim this choice because to go on is as much a choice as to stop. *e* Normally we would unquestioningly assume that anyone would wish to live rather than die. But in the extraordinary case of Anthony Bland, we think it more likely that he would choose to put an end to the humiliation of his being and the distress of his family. Finally, Anthony Bland is a person to whom respect is owed and we think that it would show greater respect to allow him to die and be mourned by his family than to keep him grotesquely alive. *f*

There is no formula for reconciling this conflict of principles and no easy answer. It does no good to seize hold of one of them, such as the sanctity of life, and say that because it is valid and right, as it undoubtedly is, it must always prevail over other principles which are also valid and right. Nor do I think it helps to say that these principles are all really different ways of looking at the *g* same thing. Counsel for the Attorney General said that there was—

> 'no conflict between having regard to the quality of life and respecting the sanctity of life; on the contrary they are complementary; the principle of the sanctity of life embraces the need for full respect to be accorded to the dignity and memory of the individual.'
> *h*

To my mind, this is rhetoric intended to dull the pain of having to choose. For many people, the sanctity of life is not at all the same thing as the dignity of the individual. We cannot smooth away the differences by interpretation. Instead, we are faced with a situation which has been best expressed by Sir Isaiah Berlin in 'Two concepts of liberty' in *Four Essays on Liberty* (1969) pp 168, 170:
j

> 'The world that we encounter in ordinary experience is one in which we are faced with choices between ends equally ultimate, and claims equally absolute, the realisation of some of which must inevitably involve the sacrifice of others . . . The knowledge that it is not merely in practice but in principle impossible to reach clear-cut and certain answers, even in an ideal world of

wholly good and rational men and wholly clear ideas—may madden those
a who seek for final solutions and single, all-embracing systems, guaranteed to
be eternal. Nevertheless it is a conclusion that cannot be escaped by those
who, with Kant, have learnt the truth that out of the crooked timber of
humanity no straight thing was ever made.'

In my view the choice which the law makes must reassure people that the
b courts do have full respect for life, but that they do not pursue the principle to
the point at which it has become almost empty of any real content and when it
involves the sacrifice of other important values such as human dignity and
freedom of choice. I think that such reassurance can be provided by a decision,
properly explained, to allow Anthony Bland to die. It does not involve, as counsel
for the Official Solicitor suggested, a decision that he may die because the court
c thinks that his 'life is not worth living'. There is no question of his life being
worth living or not worth living because the stark reality is that Anthony Bland
is not living a life at all. None of the things that one says about the way people
live their lives—well or ill, with courage or fortitude, happily or sadly—have any
meaning in relation to him. This in my view represents a difference in kind from
the case of the conscious but severely handicapped person. It is absurd to conjure
d up the spectre of eugenics as a reason against the decision in this case.

Thus in principle I think it would be right to allow Anthony Bland to die. Is
this answer affected by the proposed manner of his death? Some might say that
as he is going to die, it does not matter how. Why wait for him to expire for lack
of food or be carried off by an untreated infection? Would it not be more humane
e simply to give him a lethal injection? No one in this case is suggesting that
Anthony Bland should be given a lethal injection. But there is concern about
ceasing to supply food as against, for example, ceasing to treat an infection with
antibiotics. Is there any real distinction? In order to come to terms with our
intuitive feelings about whether there is a distinction, I must start by considering
why most of us would be appalled if he was given a lethal injection. It is, I think,
f connected with our view that the sanctity of life entails its inviolability by an
outsider. Subject to exceptions like self-defence, human life is inviolate even if
the person in question has consented to its violation. That is why although suicide
is not a crime, assisting someone to commit suicide is. It follows that, even if we
think Anthony Bland would have consented, we would not be entitled to end his
life by a lethal injection.
g On the other hand, we recognise that, one way or another, life must come to
an end. We do not impose on outsiders an unqualified duty to do everything
possible to prolong life as long as possible. I think that the principle of inviolability
explains why, although we accept that in certain cases it is right to allow a person
to die (and the debate so far has been over whether this is such a case) we hold
h without qualification that no one may introduce an external agency with the
intention of causing death. I do not think that the distinction turns upon whether
what is done is an act or omission. This leads to barren arguments over whether
the withdrawal of equipment from the body is a positive act or an omission to
keep it in place. The distinction is between an act or omission which allows an
existing cause to operate and the introduction of an external agency of death.
j What complicates this distinction, however, is another ethical principle which
demands that we should show kindness and humanity to our fellow human
beings. At the most basic level, this principle insists that we should, if we are able
to do so, provide food and shelter to a human being in our care who is unable to
provide them for himself. If someone allows a small child or invalid in his care to
starve to death, we do not say that he allowed nature to take its course. We think

he has committed a particularly wicked crime. We treat him *as if* he had introduced an external agency of death. It is the same ethical principle which requires doctors and hospitals to provide the patients in their care with such medical attention and nursing as they are reasonably able to give.

In the normal case there is no moral difference between violations of these two principles—the prohibition on violating the person and the positive duty to act with humanity towards the helpless. Starving a child to death is no different from giving him poison. But there are two distinctions between the prohibition on external violation and the duty to provide humane care and assistance. One distinction is that the duty to provide care—for example to provide medical treatment—ceases when such treatment can serve no humane purpose. In cases when further treatment can prolong the life of the patient only for a short period and at the cost of great pain and suffering, the doctor is under no obligation to continue. Indeed, the duty to act with kindness and humanity points in the opposite direction. But the prohibition on violating the person is absolute. Whatever the patient's sufferings, no one is entitled to introduce an external agency of death. It was this prohibition which Dr Cox violated by injecting Mrs Boyes with potassium chloride (see *R v Cox* (18 September 1992, unreported), Ognall J). The debate over euthanasia centres on the agonising conflict which can arise when, as in that case, the duty to act with kindness and humanity comes into conflict with the absolute prohibition on the violation of the person. At the moment English law unequivocally resolves this conflict by giving priority to the latter principle. This is not the place to debate whether this is the only morally or socially acceptable position. In the present case, no such issue arises. This is not a case about euthanasia because it does not involve any external agency of death. It is about whether, and how, the patient should be allowed to die.

It is, I think, the duty to act with kindness and humanity which leads people to say that, whatever may be the position about artificial medical treatment, it cannot be right to deny the patient food. The giving of food to a helpless person is so much the quintessential example of kindness and humanity that it is hard to imagine a case in which it would be morally right to withhold it. If it is right that Anthony Bland should be allowed to die, then refrain from giving antibiotics and let him be carried off by an infection. But do not allow him to starve.

American writers have referred to these qualms about denial of food as the 'sloganism' and 'emotional symbolism' of food. I do not think that one should make light of these deeply intuitive feelings, which derive, as I have said, from a principle of kindness which is a badge of our humanity. But like the principle of the sanctity of life, they cease to provide true guidance in the extreme case. It is of course hard to imagine a case in which it could be humane to deny food to a patient. But this case stretches the imagination. To deny someone food is wrong because it causes suffering and death. But Anthony Bland cannot suffer and his condition is such that it is right that he should be allowed to die. His interest in the manner of his death—and it is a very important one—is that it should not be distressing or humiliating. If therefore, withdrawal of nourishment would produce distressing symptoms of which Anthony Bland was unconscious but which were visible to the nursing staff and family, this would be a good reason for allowing him to die in some other way. But the medical evidence is that suitable sedation can prevent any untoward symptoms and that withdrawal of nourishment is the most gentle and controlled way in which to allow him to die.

Counsel for the Official Solicitor opened this appeal by saying that Sir Stephen Brown P 'had held that it was lawful for a doctor to starve his patient to death'. This is emotive language and by that I do not mean that this is not a proper case for emotion. It certainly is. By emotive language I mean language which evokes

a emotional images which are false, which have no application to the present case. The use of the language is intended to evoke images of cruelty, suffering and unwelcome death. Such images have no part to play in arriving at an answer to the problem, already difficult enough, which this case presents to the court.

I said that there were two distinctions between the prohibition on violating the person and the duty to provide care and assistance. So far I have mentioned only

b one. The second is that while the prohibition on violation is absolute, the duty to provide care is restricted to what one can reasonably provide. No one is under a moral duty to do more than he can, or to assist one patient at the cost of neglecting another. The resources of the national health service are not limitless and choices have to be made. This qualification on the moral duty to provide care did not

c enter into the argument in this case at all. The Airedale NHS Trust invited us to decide the case on the assumption that its resources were unlimited and we have done so. But one is bound to observe that the cost of keeping a patient like Anthony Bland alive is very considerable and that in another case the health authority might conclude that its resources were better devoted to other patients. We do not have to consider such a case, but in principle the allocation of resources

d between patients is a matter for the health authority and not for the courts.

I can deal with the authorities very shortly. The House of Lords decided in *F v West Berkshire Health Authority (Mental Health Act Commission intervening)* [1989] 2 All ER 545, [1990] 2 AC 1 that the duty of a doctor towards a patient who lacks mental capacity to express his own wishes (and has not expressed any at a time when he had such capacity) is to give or withhold treatment according to what

e appears to be the best interests of the patient. The best interests of the patient in my judgment embrace not only recovery or the avoidance of pain (neither of which apply to this case) but also a dignified death. On this issue I respectfully agree with the dissenting judgments of Handler J in *Re Conroy* (1985) 98 NJ 321 and Brennan and Stevens JJ in *Cruzan v Director, Missouri Dept of Health* (1990)

f 497 US 261. The patient's best interests would normally also include having respect paid to what seems most likely to have been his own views on the subject. To this extent I think that what the American courts have called 'substituted judgment' may be subsumed within the English concept of best interests. On the other hand, cases involving minors like *Re J (a minor) (wardship: medical treatment)* [1990] 3 All ER 930, [1991] Fam 33 show that full weight has to be given to the

g principle of the sanctity of life before deciding that a test of best interests justifies a decision to allow the patient to die. In my judgment, however, such a decision is justified here. I agree with what Sir Thomas Bingham MR and Butler-Sloss LJ have said about the procedure to be followed in future cases.

Finally, I must deal with some aspects of the judgment of Sir Stephen Brown P. As will be apparent, I am in agreement with the decision which he reached.

h But there are certain points in his judgment which may have given rise to concern. First, the judgment contains some discussion about whether the administration of liquid food through a tube can properly be called medical treatment. Some have felt that the issues in this case could not depend upon a semantic point like that. I agree. As I see it, there are only two ways in which it may be relevant to call the feeding medical treatment. They are to identify it as

j something upon which, first, the hospital can properly ask for the guidance of the court as to what it should do and, secondly, the medical profession can properly express a view. Once one is clear about why the question is being asked, it does not matter whether one calls it medical treatment, nursing, care or anything else. There is in my view no distinction between medical treatment and other kinds of

care for the purposes of deciding the central issue in this case. This brings me to
the second point of concern. Sir Stephen Brown P laid some emphasis upon the   *a*
fact that according to professional medical opinion and the British Medical
Association's statement on ethics, ending artificial feeding would be in accordance
with good medical practice. Some have felt concern at the suggestion that
questions of whether patients should live or die should be decided according to
what was thought to be good practice by the medical profession. Once again, I
sympathise with this concern.   *b*

I do not think that Sir Stephen Brown P was saying that the views of the
medical profession should determine the legal and moral questions which I have
discussed in this judgment. Nor do I think that the profession would be grateful
to the court for leaving the full responsibility for such decisions in its hands. It
seems to me that the medical profession can tell the court about the patient's
condition and prognosis and about the probable consequences of giving or not   *c*
giving certain kinds of treatment or care, including the provision of artificial
feeding. But whether in those circumstances it would be lawful to provide or
withhold the treatment or care is a matter for the law and must be decided with
regard to the general moral considerations of which I have spoken. As to these
matters, the medical profession will no doubt have views which are entitled to   *d*
great respect, but I would expect medical ethics to be formed by the law rather
than the reverse.

I should emphasise that this is not a case in which some past act on the part of
a doctor is being called into question. If the issue was whether such an act had
given rise to civil or criminal liability, the fact that the doctor has acted in
accordance with responsible professional opinion would usually be determinative.   *e*
But in this case the plaintiff hospital trust is seeking the opinion of the court as to
whether future conduct will be lawful. It has invited the court to decide whether,
on medical facts which are not in dispute, the termination of life-support would
be justified as being in the best interests of the patient. This is a purely legal (or
moral) decision which does not require any medical expertise and is therefore   *f*
appropriately made by the court.

I would dismiss the appeal.

Appeal dismissed. Leave to appeal to the House of Lords granted. No order as to costs.

Francis Rustin   Barrister.   *g*

Appeal

The defendant, acting by the Official Solicitor as his guardian ad litem, appealed
with the leave of the Court of Appeal.

James Munby QC (instructed by the *Official Solicitor*) for the Official Solicitor as
guardian ad litem.   *h*
Robert Francis QC and *M R Taylor* (instructed by *Penningtons*, agents for *W J M
Lovel*, Harrogate) for the plaintiffs.
Anthony Lester QC and *Pushpinder Saini* (instructed by the *Treasury Solicitor*) as
amicus curiae.   *j*

Their Lordships took time for consideration.

4 February 1993. The following opinions were delivered.

LORD KEITH OF KINKEL. My Lords, as a result of injuries sustained in the
a Hillsborough disaster, Anthony Bland has for over three years been in the
condition known as persistent vegetative state (PVS). It is unnecessary to go into
all the details about the manifestations of this state, which are fully set out in the
judgments of the courts below. It is sufficient to say that it arises from the
destruction, through prolonged deprivation of oxygen, of the cerebral cortex,
which has resolved into a watery mass. The cortex is that part of the brain which
b is the seat of cognitive function and sensory capacity. Anthony Bland cannot see,
hear or feel anything. He cannot communicate in any way. The consciousness
which is the essential feature of individual personality has departed for ever. On
the other hand the brain stem, which controls the reflexive functions of the body,
in particular heartbeat, breathing and digestion, continues to operate. In the eyes
c of the medical world and of the law a person is not clinically dead so long as the
brain stem retains its function. In order to maintain Anthony Bland in his present
condition, feeding and hydration are achieved artificially by means of a nasogastric
tube and excretory functions are regulated by a catheter and by enemas. The
catheter from time to time gives rise to infections which have to be dealt with by
appropriate medical treatment. The undisputed consensus of eminent medical
d opinion is that there is no prospect whatever that Anthony Bland will ever make
any recovery from his present condition, but that there is every likelihood that he
will maintain his present state of existence for many years to come, provided that
the medical care which he is now receiving is continued.

In that state of affairs the medical men in charge of Anthony Bland's case
formed the view, which was supported by his parents, that no useful purpose was
e to be served by continuing that medical care and that it was appropriate to stop
the artificial feeding and other measures aimed at prolonging his existence. Since,
however, there were doubts as to whether this course might not constitute a
criminal offence, the responsible hospital authority, the Airedale NHS Trust,
sought in the High Court of Justice declarations designed to resolve these doubts.
f In the result declarations on the lines asked for were granted by judgment of
Sir Stephen Brown P on 19 November 1992. That judgment was affirmed by the
Court of Appeal (Sir Thomas Bingham MR, Butler-Sloss and Hoffmann LJJ) on 9
December 1992. The declarations are in these terms:

> '... that despite the inability of [the defendant] to consent thereto the
> Plaintiffs and the responsible attending physicians: (1) may lawfully
g > discontinue all life-sustaining treatment and medical support measures
> designed to keep [the defendant] alive in his existing persistent vegetative
> state including the termination of ventilation nutrition and hydration by
> artificial means; and (2) may lawfully discontinue and thereafter need not
> furnish medical treatment to [the defendant] except for the sole purpose of
h > enabling [him] to end his life and die peacefully with the greatest dignity
> and the least of pain suffering and distress ...'

Anthony Bland, by the Official Solicitor as his guardian ad litem, now appeals,
with leave given in the Court of Appeal, to your Lordships' House. At the hearing
of the appeal your Lordships were assisted by submissions made by Mr Anthony
Lester QC as amicus curiae instructed by the Treasury Solicitor.
j The broad issue raised by the appeal is stated by the parties to be: 'In what
circumstances, if ever, can those having a duty to feed an invalid lawfully stop
doing so?' The immediate issue, however, is whether in the particular
circumstances of Anthony Bland's case those in charge of it would be acting
lawfully if they discontinued the particular measures, including feeding by

nasogastric tube, which are now being used to maintain Anthony Bland in his existing condition.

The first point to make is that it is unlawful, so as to constitute both a tort and the crime of battery, to administer medical treatment to an adult, who is conscious and of sound mind, without his consent: see *F v West Berkshire Health Authority (Mental Health Act Commission intervening)* [1989] 2 All ER 545, [1990] 2 AC 1. Such a person is completely at liberty to decline to undergo treatment, even if the result of his doing so will be that he will die. This extends to the situation where the person, in anticipation of his, through one cause or another, entering into a condition such as PVS, gives clear instructions that in such event he is not to be given medical care, including artificial feeding, designed to keep him alive. The second point is that it very commonly occurs that a person, due to accident or some other cause, becomes unconscious and is thus not able to give or withhold consent to medical treatment. In that situation it is lawful, under the principle of necessity, for medical men to apply such treatment as in their informed opinion is in the best interests of the unconscious patient. That is what happened in the case of Anthony Bland when he was first dealt with by the emergency services and later taken to hospital.

The object of medical treatment and care is to benefit the patient. It may do so by taking steps to prevent the occurrence of illness, or, if an illness does occur, by taking steps towards curing it. Where an illness or the effects of an injury cannot be cured, then efforts are directed towards preventing deterioration or relieving pain and suffering. In Anthony Bland's case the first imperative was to prevent him from dying, as he would certainly have done in the absence of the steps that were taken. If he had died, there can be no doubt that the cause of this would have been the injuries which he had suffered. As it was, the steps taken prevented him from dying, and there was instituted the course of treatment and care which still continues. For a time, no doubt, there was some hope that he might recover sufficiently for him to be able to live a life that had some meaning. Some patients who have suffered damage to the cerebral cortex have, indeed, made a complete recovery. It all depends on the degree of damage. But sound medical opinion takes the view that if a PVS patient shows no signs of recovery after six months, or at most a year, then there is no prospect whatever of any recovery. There are techniques available which make it possible to ascertain the state of the cerebral cortex, and in Anthony Bland's case these indicate that, as mentioned above, it has degenerated into a mass of watery fluid. The fundamental question then comes to be whether continuance of the present regime of treatment and care, more than three years after the injuries that resulted in the PVS, would confer any benefit on Anthony Bland. It is argued for the respondents, supported by the amicus curiae, that his best interests favour discontinuance. I feel some doubt about this way of putting the matter. In *F v West Berkshire Health Authority* [1989] 2 All ER 545, [1990] 2 AC 1 this House held that it would be lawful to sterilise a female mental patient who was incapable of giving consent to the procedure. The ground of the decision was that sterilisation would be in the patient's best interests because her life would be fuller and more agreeable if she were sterilised than if she were not. In *Re J (a minor) (wardship: medical treatment)* [1990] 3 All ER 930, [1991] Fam 33 the Court of Appeal held it to be lawful to withhold life-saving treatment from a very young child in circumstances where the child's life, if saved, would be one irredeemably racked by pain and agony. In both cases it was possible to make a value judgment as to the consequences to a sensate being of in the one case withholding and in the other case administering the treatment in question. In the case of a permanently insensate being, who if continuing to live

would never experience the slightest actual discomfort, it is difficult, if not
a impossible, to make any relevant comparison between continued existence and
the absence of it. It is, however, perhaps permissible to say that to an individual
with no cognitive capacity whatever, and no prospect of ever recovering any such
capacity in this world, it must be a matter of complete indifference whether he
lives or dies.

Where one individual has assumed responsibility for the care of another who
b cannot look after himself or herself, whether as a medical practitioner or
otherwise, that responsibility cannot lawfully be shed unless arrangements are
made for the responsibility to be taken over by someone else. Thus a person
having charge of a baby who fails to feed it, so that it dies, will be guilty at least
of manslaughter. The same is true of one having charge of an adult who is frail
and cannot look after herself: see R v Stone [1977] 2 All ER 341, [1977] QB 354. It
c was argued for the guardian ad litem, by analogy with that case, that here the
doctors in charge of Anthony Bland had a continuing duty to feed him by means
of the nasogastric tube and that if they failed to carry out that duty they were
guilty of manslaughter, if not murder. This was coupled with the argument that
feeding by means of the nasogastric tube was not medical treatment at all, but
d simply feeding indistinguishable from feeding by normal means. As regards this
latter argument, I am of opinion that regard should be had to the whole regime,
including the artificial feeding, which at present keeps Anthony Bland alive. That
regime amounts to medical treatment and care, and it is incorrect to direct
attention exclusively to the fact that nourishment is being provided. In any event,
the administration of nourishment by the means adopted involves the application
e of a medical technique. But it is, of course, true that in general it would not be
lawful for a medical practitioner who assumed responsibility for the care of an
unconscious patient simply to give up treatment in circumstances where
continuance of it would confer some benefit on the patient. On the other hand a
medical practitioner is under no duty to continue to treat such a patient where a
large body of informed and responsible medical opinion is to the effect that no
f benefit at all would be conferred by continuance. Existence in a vegetative state
with no prospect of recovery is by that opinion regarded as not being a benefit,
and that, if not unarguably correct, at least forms a proper basis for the decision
to discontinue treatment and care: see Bolam v Friern Hospital Management
Committee [1957] 2 All ER 118, [1957] 1 WLR 582.

Given that existence in the persistent vegetative state is not a benefit to the
g patient, it remains to consider whether the principle of the sanctity of life, which
it is the concern of the state, and the judiciary as one of the arms of the state, to
maintain, requires this House to hold that the judgment of the Court of Appeal
was incorrect. In my opinion it does not. The principle is not an absolute one. It
does not compel a medical practitioner on pain of criminal sanctions to treat a
h patient, who will die if he does not, contrary to the express wishes of the patient.
It does not authorise forcible feeding of prisoners on hunger strike. It does not
compel the temporary keeping alive of patients who are terminally ill where to
do so would merely prolong their suffering. On the other hand it forbids the
taking of active measures to cut short the life of a terminally ill patient. In my
judgment it does no violence to the principle to hold that it is lawful to cease to
j give medical treatment and care to a PVS patient who has been in that state for
over three years, considering that to do so involves invasive manipulation of the
patient's body to which he has not consented and which confers no benefit upon
him.

Although this case falls to be decided by the law of England, it is of some

comfort to observe that in other common law jurisdictions, particularly in the
United States where there are many cases on the subject, the courts have with   *a*
near unanimity concluded that it is not unlawful to discontinue medical treatment
and care, including artificial feeding, of PVS patients and others in similar
conditions.

The decision whether or not the continued treatment and care of a PVS patient
confers any benefit on him is essentially one for the practitioners in charge of his
case. The question is whether any decision that it does not and that the treatment   *b*
and care should therefore be discontinued should as a matter of routine be
brought before the Family Division for indorsement or the reverse. The view
taken by Sir Stephen Brown P and the Court of Appeal was that it should, at least
for the time being and until a body of experience and practice has been built up
which might obviate the need for application in every case. As Sir Thomas
Bingham MR said (at p 842, ante), this would be in the interests of the protection   *c*
of patients, the protection of doctors, the reassurance of the patients' families and
the reassurance of the public. I respectfully agree that these considerations render
desirable the practice of application.

My Lords, for these reasons, which are substantially the same as those set out in
the speech to be delivered by my noble and learned friend Lord Goff of Chieveley,   *d*
with which I agree, I would dismiss the appeal.

LORD GOFF OF CHIEVELEY. My Lords, the facts of the present case are
not in dispute. They are fully set out in the judgment of Sir Stephen Brown P at
first instance (see p 824, ante); they have been admirably summarised in the
judgment of Sir Thomas Bingham MR in the Court of Appeal (see p 834, ante);   *e*
and they have been summarised yet again in the agreed statement of facts and
issues prepared by counsel for the assistance of the Appellate Committee of your
Lordships' House. They reveal a tragic state of affairs, which has evoked great
sympathy, both for Anthony Bland himself and for his devoted family, and great
respect for all those who have been responsible for his medical treatment and care
since he was admitted to hospital following the terrible injuries which he suffered   *f*
at Hillsborough in April 1989. For present purposes, I propose simply to adopt
the sympathetic and economical summary of Sir Thomas Bingham MR (see
pp 834–835, ante), which, for convenience of reference, I will now incorporate
into this opinion.

'Mr Anthony David Bland, then aged 17½, went to the Hillsborough   *g*
ground on 15 April 1989 to support the Liverpool Football Club. In the
course of the disaster which occurred on that day his lungs were crushed and
punctured and the supply of oxygen to his brain was interrupted. As a result,
he suffered catastrophic and irreversible damage to the higher centres of the
brain. The condition from which he suffers, and has suffered since April   *h*
1989, is known as a persistent vegetative state (PVS). PVS is a recognised
medical condition quite distinct from other conditions sometimes known as
"irreversible coma", "the Guillain-Barré syndrome", "the locked-in syndrome"
and "brain death". Its distinguishing characteristics are that the brain stem
remains alive and functioning while the cortex of the brain loses its function
and activity. Thus the PVS patient continues to breathe unaided and his   *j*
digestion continues to function. But, although his eyes are open, he cannot
see. He cannot hear. Although capable of reflex movement, particularly in
response to painful stimuli, the patient is incapable of voluntary movement
and can feel no pain. He cannot taste or smell. He cannot speak or
communicate in any way. He has no cognitive function and can thus feel no

a
emotion, whether pleasure or distress. The absence of cerebral function is not a matter of surmise: it can be scientifically demonstrated. The space which the brain should occupy is full of watery fluid. The medical witnesses in this case include some of the outstanding authorities in the country on this condition. All are agreed on the diagnosis. All are agreed on the prognosis also: there is no hope of any improvement or recovery. One witness of great experience describe Mr Bland as the worst PVS case he had every seen.

b
Mr Bland lies in bed in the Airedale General Hospital, his eyes open, his mind vacant, his limbs crooked and taut. He cannot swallow, and so cannot be spoon-fed without a high risk that food will be inhaled into the lung. He is fed by means of a tube, threaded through the nose and down into the stomach, through which liquefied food is mechanically pumped. His bowels are evacuated by enema. His bladder is drained by catheter. He has been

c
subject to repeated bouts of infection affecting his urinary tract and chest, which have been treated with antibiotics. Drugs have also been administered to reduce salivation, to reduce muscle tone and severe sweating and to encourage gastric emptying. A tracheostomy tube has been inserted and removed. Urino-genitary problems have required surgical intervention. A

d
patient in this condition requires very skilled nursing and close medical attention if he is to survive. The Airedale National Health Service Trust have, it is agreed, provided both to Mr Bland. Introduction of the nasogastric tube is itself a task of some delicacy even in an insensate patient. Thereafter it must be monitored to ensure it has not become dislodged and to control inflammation, irritation and infection to which it may give rise. The catheter

e
must be monitored: it may cause infection (and has repeatedly done so); it has had to be resited, in an operation performed without anaesthetic. The mouth and other parts of the body must be constantly tended. The patient must be repeatedly moved to avoid pressure sores. Without skilled nursing and close medical attention a PVS patient will quickly succumb to infection. With such care, a young and otherwise healthy patient may live for many

f
years. At no time before the disaster did Mr Bland give any indication of his wishes should he find himself in such a condition. It is not a topic most adolescents address. After careful thought his family agreed that the feeding tube should be removed and felt that this was what Mr Bland would have wanted. His father said of his son in evidence: "He certainly wouldn't want to be left like that." He could see no advantage at all in continuation of the

g
current treatment. He was not cross-examined. It was accordingly with the concurrence of Mr Bland's family, as well as the consultant in charge of his case and the support of two independent doctors, that the Airedale NHS Trust as plaintiff in this action applied to the Family Division of the High Court for declarations that they might—"(1) . . . lawfully discontinue all life-sustaining

h
treatment and medical support measures designed to keep AB [Mr Bland] alive in his existing persistent vegetative state including the termination of ventilation nutrition and hydration by artificial means; and (2) . . . lawfully discontinue and thereafter need not furnish medical treatment to AB except for the sole purpose of enabling AB to end his life and die peacefully with the greatest dignity and the least of pain suffering and distress." After a hearing

j
in which he was assisted by an amicus curiae instructed by the Attorney General, Sir Stephen Brown P made these declarations (subject to a minor change of wording) on 19 November 1992. He declined to make further declarations which were also sought.'

The Official Solicitor, acting on behalf of Anthony Bland, appealed against that decision to the Court of Appeal, which dismissed the appeal. Now, with the leave of the Court of Appeal, the Official Solicitor has appealed to your Lordships' *a* House.

In so acting, the Official Solicitor has ensured that all relevant matters of fact and law are properly investigated and scrutinised before any irrevocable decision is taken affecting Anthony Bland, for whom he acts as guardian ad litem. This function was performed by Mr James Munby QC, who appeared before your Lordships as he did before the courts below; and he made submissions in the *b* form of a series of propositions any of which, if accepted, would preclude the grant of the declarations granted by Sir Stephen Brown P. Like the courts below, I have come to the conclusion that I am unable to accept Mr Munby's submissions; but I have nevertheless found them to be of great assistance in that they have compelled me to think more deeply about the applicable principles of law and, I hope, to formulate those principles more accurately. Your Lordships were also *c* fortunate to have the assistance of Mr Anthony Lester QC, appearing as amicus curiae, instructed by the Treasury Solicitor, and of the thoughtful argument of Mr Robert Francis QC for the respondents.

On one point there was no disagreement between counsel appearing before your Lordships. This was that proceedings for declaratory relief of the kind *d* considered by this House in *F v West Berkshire Health Authority* (*Mental Health Act Commission intervening*) [1989] 2 All ER 545, [1990] 2 AC 1 provided the most appropriate means by which authoritative guidance could be provided for the respondents to the appeal, the Airedale NHS Trust, and for Dr Howe, who has Anthony Bland in his care, whose wish it is, in agreement with Anthony's parents, to discontinue the artificial feeding of Anthony, with the inevitable result that, *e* within one or two weeks, he will die. There has therefore been no contested argument about the appropriateness of the declaratory remedy in cases such as these, which are in fact concerned with the question whether in the particular circumstances those who discontinue life support (here artificial feeding) will commit a civil wrong or a criminal offence. In *F v West Berkshire Health Authority* *f* the question arose whether it would be lawful for doctors to sterilise an adult woman of unsound mind. In that case, this House was deeply concerned to discover that it was common ground between the parties that, in the case of adult persons of unsound mind, the parens patriae jurisdiction of the courts had been revoked with the effect that the courts could no longer exercise their jurisdiction to give consent on behalf of such persons. On that occasion Mr Munby, who there *g* as here was instructed by the Official Solicitor, was invited to assist this House by advancing such arguments as could be advanced that the jurisdiction had not been abolished. At the end of the argument, your Lordships' House came reluctantly to the conclusion that the jurisdiction no longer existed; but, dismayed by the possibility that the courts might be powerless to provide the necessary guidance to the medical profession in that case, this House had recourse to *h* declaratory relief for that purpose. Speaking for myself, I remain of the opinion that this conclusion was entirely justified. Of course, I recognise that strong warnings have been given against the civil courts usurping the function of the criminal courts, and it has been authoritatively stated that a declaration as to the lawfulness or otherwise of future conduct is 'no bar to a criminal prosecution, no matter the authority of the court which grants it': see *Imperial Tobacco Ltd v A-G* *j* [1980] 1 All ER 866 at 875, 884, [1981] AC 718 at 741, 752 per Viscount Dilhorne, and see also per Lord Lane. But it is plain that the jurisdiction exists to grant such a declaration, and on occasion that jurisdiction has been exercised, as for example by your Lordships' House in *Royal College of Nursing of the UK v Dept of Health and*

Social Security [1981] 1 All ER 545, [1981] AC 800. It would, in my opinion, be a
a deplorable state of affairs if no authoritative guidance could be given to the
medical profession in a case such as the present, so that a doctor would be
compelled either to act contrary to the principles of medical ethics established by
his professional body or to risk a prosecution for murder. As Compton J said in
Barber v Superior Court of Los Angeles County (1983) 147 Cal App 3d 1006 at 1011:
'... a murder prosecution is a poor way to design an ethical and moral code for
b doctors who are faced with decisions concerning the use of costly and extraordinary
"life support" equipment.' In practice, authoritative guidance in circumstances
such as these should in normal circumstances inhibit prosecution or, if (contrary
to all expectation) criminal proceedings were launched, justify the Attorney
General in entering a nolle prosequi. In the present case it is to be remembered
that an amicus curiae has been instructed by the Treasury Solicitor; yet no
c representations have been made on behalf of the Attorney General that declaratory
relief is here inappropriate. In expressing this opinion, I draw comfort from the
fact that declaratory rulings have been employed for the same purpose in other
common law jurisdictions, such as the United States of America (in a number of
cases, of which the most recent appears to be *Re Gardner* (1987) 534 A 2d 947 at
d 949), New Zealand *Auckland Area Health Board v A-G* [1993] 1 NZLR 235 at 241–
244, 255 per Thomas J, to whom submissions had been addressed upon the point)
and South Africa (*Clarke v Hurst* (30 July 1992, unreported) per Thirion J).

The central issue in the present case has been aptly stated by Sir Thomas
Bingham MR to be whether artificial feeding and antibiotic drugs may lawfully
be withheld from an insensate patient with no hope of recovery when it is known
e that if that is done the patient will shortly thereafter die. The Court of Appeal,
like Sir Stephen Brown P, answered this question generally in the affirmative, and
(in the declarations made or approved by them) specifically also in the affirmative
in relation to Anthony Bland. I find myself to be in agreement with the
conclusions so reached by all the judges below, substantially for the reasons given
by them. But the matter is of such importance that I propose to express my
f reasons in my own words.

I start with the simple fact that, in law, Anthony is still alive. It is true that his
condition is such that it can be described as a living death; but he is nevertheless
still alive. This is because, as a result of developments in modern medical
technology, doctors no longer associate death exclusively with breathing and
heart beat, and it has come to be accepted that death occurs when the brain, and
g in particular the brain stem, has been destroyed (see Professor Ian Kennedy's paper
entitled 'Switching off life support machines: the legal implications' reprinted in
Treat Me Right, Essays in Medical Law and Ethics (1988) esp at 351–352 and the
material there cited). There has been no dispute on this point in the present case,
and it is unnecessary for me to consider it further. The evidence is that Anthony's
h brain stem is still alive and functioning and it follows that, in the present state of
medical science, he is still alive and should be so regarded as a matter of law.

It is on this basis that I turn to the applicable principles of law. Here, the
fundamental principle is the principle of the sanctity of human life—a principle
long recognised not only in our own society but also in most, if not all, civilised
societies throughout the modern world, as is indeed evidenced by its recognition
j both in art 2 of the European Convention on Human Rights (Convention for the
Protection of Human Rights and Fundamental Freedoms (Rome, 4 November
1950; TS 71 (1953); Cmd 8969)) and in art 6 of the International Covenant on
Civil and Political Rights (New York, 19 December 1966; TS 6 (1977);
Cmnd 6702).

But this principle, fundamental though it is, is not absolute. Indeed there are circumstances in which it is lawful to take another man's life, for example by a lawful act of self-defence, or (in the days when capital punishment was acceptable in our society) by lawful execution. We are not however concerned with cases such as these. We are concerned with circumstances in which it may be lawful to withhold from a patient medical treatment or care by means of which his life may be prolonged. But here too there is no absolute rule that the patient's life must be prolonged by such treatment or care, if available, regardless of the circumstances.

First, it is established that the principle of self-determination requires that respect must be given to the wishes of the patient, so that, if an adult patient of sound mind refuses, however unreasonably, to consent to treatment or care by which his life would or might be prolonged, the doctors responsible for his care must give effect to his wishes, even though they do not consider it to be in his best interests to do so (see *Schloendorff v Society of New York Hospital* (1914) 211 NY 125 at 129–130 per Cardozo J, *S v S, W v Official Solicitor* [1970] 3 All ER 107 at 111, [1972] AC 24 at 43 per Lord Reid and *Sidaway v Bethlem Royal Hospital Governors* [1985] 1 All ER 643 at 649, [1985] AC 871 at 882 per Lord Scarman). To this extent, the principle of the sanctity of human life must yield to the principle of self-determination (see p 851 ante, per Hoffmann LJ), and, for present purposes perhaps more important, the doctor's duty to act in the best interests of his patient must likewise be qualified. On this basis, it has been held that a patient of sound mind may, if properly informed, require that life support should be discontinued: see *Nancy B v Hôtel-Dieu de Québec* (1992) 86 DLR (4th) 385. Moreover the same principle applies where the patient's refusal to give his consent has been expressed at an earlier date, before he became unconscious or otherwise incapable of communicating it; though in such circumstances especial care may be necessary to ensure that the prior refusal of consent is still properly to be regarded as applicable in the circumstances which have subsequently occurred (see e g *Re T (adult: refusal of medical treatment)* [1992] 4 All ER 649, [1992] 3 WLR 782). I wish to add that, in cases of this kind, there is no question of the patient having committed suicide, nor therefore of the doctor having aided or abetted him in doing so. It is simply that the patient has, as he is entitled to do, declined to consent to treatment which might or would have the effect of prolonging his life, and the doctor has, in accordance with his duty, complied with his patient's wishes.

But in many cases not only may the patient be in no condition to be able to say whether or not he consents to the relevant treatment or care, but also he may have given no prior indication of his wishes with regard to it. In the case of a child who is a ward of court, the court itself will decide whether medical treatment should be provided in the child's best interests, taking into account medical opinion. But the court cannot give its consent on behalf of an adult patient who is incapable of himself deciding whether or not to consent to treatment. I am of the opinion that there is nevertheless no absolute obligation upon the doctor who has the patient in his care to prolong his life, regardless of the circumstances. Indeed, it would be most startling, and could lead to the most adverse and cruel effects upon the patient, if any such absolute rule were held to exist. It is scarcely consistent with the primacy given to the principle of self-determination in those cases in which the patient of sound mind has declined to give his consent that the law should provide no means of enabling treatment to be withheld in appropriate circumstances where the patient is in no condition to indicate, if that was his wish, that he did not consent to it. The point was put forcibly in the judgment of

the Supreme Judicial Court of Massachusetts in *Belchertown State School*
a *Superintendent v Saikewicz* (1977) 373 Mass 728 at 747 as follows:

> 'To presume that the incompetent person must always be subjected to
> what many rational and intelligent persons may decline is to downgrade the
> status of the incompetent person by placing a lesser value on his intrinsic
> human worth and vitality.'

b   I must however stress, at this point, that the law draws a crucial distinction
between cases in which a doctor decides not to provide, or to continue to provide,
for his patient treatment or care which could or might prolong his life and those
in which he decides, for example by administering a lethal drug, actively to bring
his patient's life to an end. As I have already indicated, the former may be lawful,
either because the doctor is giving effect to his patient's wishes by withholding
c the treatment or care, or even in certain circumstances in which (on principles
which I shall describe) the patient is incapacitated from stating whether or not he
gives his consent. But it is not lawful for a doctor to administer a drug to his
patient to bring about his death, even though that course is prompted by a
humanitarian desire to end his suffering, however great that suffering may be:
d see *R v Cox* (18 September 1992, unreported) per Ognall J in the Crown Court at
Winchester. So to act is to cross the Rubicon which runs between on the one hand
the care of the living patient and on the other hand euthanasia—actively causing
his death to avoid or to end his suffering. Euthanasia is not lawful at common
law. It is of course well known that there are many responsible members of our
society who believe that euthanasia should be made lawful; but that result could,
e I believe, only be achieved by legislation which expresses the democratic will that
so fundamental a change should be made in our law, and can, if enacted, ensure
that such legalised killing can only be carried out subject to appropriate supervision
and control. It is true that the drawing of this distinction may lead to a charge of
hypocrisy, because it can be asked why, if the doctor, by discontinuing treatment,
is entitled in consequence to let his patient die, it should not be lawful to put him
f out of his misery straight away, in a more humane manner, by a lethal injection,
rather than let him linger on in pain until he dies. But the law does not feel able
to authorise euthanasia, even in circumstances such as these, for, once euthanasia
is recognised as lawful in these circumstances, it is difficult to see any logical basis
for excluding it in others.

g   At the heart of this distinction lies a theoretical question. Why is it that the
doctor who gives his patient a lethal injection which kills him commits an
unlawful act and indeed is guilty of murder, whereas a doctor who, by
discontinuing life support, allows his patient to die may not act unlawfully and
will not do so if he commits no breach of duty to his patient? Professor Glanville
Williams has suggested (see *Textbook of Criminal Law* (2nd edn, 1983) p 282) that
h the reason is that what the doctor does when he switches off a life support machine
'is in substance not an act but an omission to struggle' and that 'the omission is
not a breach of duty by the doctor, because he is not obliged to continue in a
hopeless case'.

   I agree that the doctor's conduct in discontinuing life support can properly be
categorised as an omission. It is true that it may be difficult to describe what the
j doctor actually does as an omission, for example where he takes some positive
step to bring the life support to an end. But discontinuation of life support is, for
present purposes, no different from not initiating life support in the first place.
In each case, the doctor is simply allowing his patient to die in the sense that he is
desisting from taking a step which might, in certain circumstances, prevent his

patient from dying as a result of his pre-existing condition; and as a matter of
general principle an omission such as this will not be unlawful unless it constitutes
a breach of duty to the patient. I also agree that the doctor's conduct is to be
differentiated from that of, for example, an interloper who maliciously switches
off a life support machine because, although the interloper may perform exactly
the same act as the doctor who discontinues life support, his doing so constitutes
interference with the life-prolonging treatment then being administered by the
doctor. Accordingly, whereas the doctor, in discontinuing life support, is simply
allowing his patient to die of his pre-existing condition, the interloper is actively
intervening to stop the doctor from prolonging the patient's life, and such conduct
cannot possibly be categorised as an omission.

The distinction appears, therefore, to be useful in the present context in that it
can be invoked to explain how discontinuance of life support can be differentiated
from ending a patient's life by a lethal injection. But in the end the reason for
that difference is that, whereas the law considers that discontinuance of life
support may be consistent with the doctor's duty to care for his patient, it does
not, for reasons of policy, consider that it forms any part of his duty to give his
patient a lethal injection to put him out of his agony.

I return to the patient who, because for example he is of unsound mind or has
been rendered unconscious by accident or by illness, is incapable of stating
whether or not he consents to treatment or care. In such circumstances, it is now
established that a doctor may lawfully treat such a patient if he acts in his best
interests, and indeed that, if the patient is already in his care, he is under a duty
so to treat him: see *F v West Berkshire Health Authority* [1989] 2 All ER 545, [1990]
2 AC 1, in which the legal principles governing treatment in such circumstances
were stated by this House. For my part I can see no reason why, as a matter of
principle, a decision by a doctor whether or not to initiate, or to continue to
provide, treatment or care which could or might have the effect of prolonging
such a patient's life should not be governed by the same fundamental principle.
Of course, in the great majority of cases, the best interests of the patient are likely
to require that treatment of this kind, if available, should be given to a patient.
But this may not always be so. To take a simple example given by Thomas J in
the High Court of New Zealand in *Auckland Area Health Board v A-G* [1993] 1
NZLR 235 at 253, to whose judgment in that case I wish to pay tribute, it cannot
be right that a doctor, who has under his care a patient suffering painfully from
terminal cancer, should be under an absolute obligation to perform upon him
major surgery to abate another condition which, if unabated, would or might
shorten his life still further. The doctor who is caring for such a patient cannot,
in my opinion, be under an absolute obligation to prolong his life by any means
available to him, regardless of the quality of the patient's life. Common humanity
requires otherwise, as do medical ethics and good medical practice accepted in
this country and overseas. As I see it, the doctor's decision whether or not to take
any such step must (subject to his patient's ability to give or withhold his consent)
be made in the best interests of the patient. It is this principle too which, in my
opinion, underlies the established rule that a doctor may, when caring for a
patient who is, for example, dying of cancer, lawfully administer painkilling
drugs despite the fact that he knows that an incidental effect of that application
will be to abbreviate the patient's life. Such a decision may properly be made as
part of the care of the living patient, in his best interests; and, on this basis, the
treatment will be lawful. Moreover, where the doctor's treatment of his patient
is lawful, the patient's death will be regarded in law as exclusively caused by the
injury or disease to which his condition is attributable.

It is of course the development of modern medical technology, and in particular
the development of life support systems, which has rendered cases such as the
present so much more relevant than in the past. Even so, where, for example, a
patient is brought into hospital in such a condition that, without the benefit of a
life support system, he will not continue to live, the decision has to be made
whether or not to give him that benefit, if available. That decision can only be
made in the best interests of the patient. No doubt, his best interests will
ordinarily require that he should be placed on a life support system as soon as
necessary, if only to make an accurate assessment of his condition and a prognosis
for the future. But, if he neither recovers sufficiently to be taken off it nor dies,
the question will ultimately arise whether he should be kept on it indefinitely.
As I see it, that question (assuming the continued availability of the system) can
only be answered by reference to the best interests of the patient himself, having
regard to established medical practice. Indeed, if the justification for treating a
patient who lacks the capacity to consent lies in the fact that the treatment is
provided in his best interests, it must follow that the treatment may, and indeed
ultimately should, be discontinued where it is no longer in his best interests to
provide it. The question which lies at the heart of the present case is, as I see it,
whether on that principle the doctors responsible for the treatment and care of
Anthony Bland can justifiably discontinue the process of artificial feeding upon
which the prolongation of his life depends.

It is crucial for the understanding of this question that the question itself should
be correctly formulated. The question is not whether the doctor should take a
course which will kill his patient, or even take a course which has the effect of
accelerating his death. The question is whether the doctor should or should not
continue to provide his patient with medical treatment or care which, if
continued, will prolong his patient's life. The question is sometimes put in
striking or emotional terms, which can be misleading. For example, in the case
of a life support system, it is sometimes asked: should a doctor be entitled to
switch it off, or to pull the plug? And then it is asked: can it be in the best interests
of the patient that a doctor should be able to switch the life support system off,
when this will inevitably result in the patient's death? Such an approach has
rightly been criticised as misleading, for example by Professor Ian Kennedy (in
his paper in *Treat Me Right, Essays in Medical Law and Ethics* (1988)), and by
Thomas J in *Auckland Area Health Board v A-G* [1993] 1 NZLR 235 at 247. This is
because the question is not whether it is in the best interests of the patient that he
should die. The question is whether it is in the best interests of the patient that
his life should be prolonged by the continuance of this form of medical treatment
or care.

The correct formulation of the question is of particular importance in a case
such as the present, where the patient is totally unconscious and where there is no
hope whatsoever of any amelioration of his condition. In circumstances such as
these, it may be difficult to say that it is in his best interests that the treatment
should be ended. But, if the question is asked, as in my opinion it should be,
whether it is in his best interests that treatment which has the effect of artificially
prolonging his life should be continued, that question can sensibly be answered
to the effect that it is not in his best interests to do so.

Even so, a distinction may be drawn between (1) cases in which, having regard
to all the circumstances (including, for example, the intrusive nature of the
treatment, the hazards involved in it and the very poor quality of the life which
may be prolonged for the patient if the treatment is successful), it may be judged
not to be in the best interests of the patient to initiate or continue life-prolonging

treatment and (2) cases such as the present in which, so far as the living patient is concerned, the treatment is of no benefit to him because he is totally unconscious *a* and there is no prospect of any improvement in his condition. In both classes of case the decision whether or not to withhold treatment must be made in the best interests of the patient. In the first class, however, the decision has to be made by weighing the relevant considerations. For example in *Re J (a minor) (wardship: medical treatment)* [1990] 3 All ER 930 at 945, [1991] Fam 33 at 55 the approach *b* to be adopted in that case was stated by Taylor LJ as follows:

'I consider that the correct approach is for the court to judge the quality of life the child would have to endure if given the treatment and decide whether in all the circumstances such a life would be so afflicted as to be intolerable to that child.'

c

With this class of case, however, your Lordships are not directly concerned in the present case; and, though I do not wish to be understood to be casting any doubt upon any of the reported cases on the subject, nevertheless I must record that argument was not directed specifically towards these cases and for that reason I do not intend to express any opinion about the precise principles applicable in relation to them.

d

By contrast, in the latter class of case, of which the present case provides an example, there is in reality no weighing operation to be performed. Here the condition of the patient, who is totally unconscious and in whose condition there is no prospect of any improvement, is such that life-prolonging treatment is properly regarded as being, in medical terms, useless. As Sir Thomas Bingham MR pointed out in the present case, medical treatment or care may be provided *e* for a number of different purposes. It may be provided, for example, as an aid to diagnosis, for the treatment of physical or mental injury or illness, to alleviate pain or distress, or to make the patient's condition more tolerable. Such purposes may include prolonging the patient's life for example to enable him to survive during diagnosis and treatment. But for my part I cannot see that medical treatment is appropriate or requisite simply to prolong a patient's life when such *f* treatment has no therapeutic purpose of any kind, as where it is futile because the patient is unconscious and there is no prospect of any improvement in his condition. It is reasonable also that account should be taken of the invasiveness of the treatment and of the indignity to which, as the present case shows, a person has to be subjected if his life is prolonged by artificial means, which must cause *g* considerable distress to his family—a distress which reflects not only their own feelings but their perception of the situation of their relative who is being kept alive. But in the end, in a case such as the present, it is the futility of the treatment which justifies its termination. I do not consider that, in circumstances such as these, a doctor is required to initiate or to continue life-prolonging treatment or care in the best interests of his patient. It follows that no such duty rests upon the *h* respondents, or upon Dr Howe, in the case of Anthony Bland, whose condition is in reality no more than a living death, and for whom such treatment or care would, in medical terms, be futile.

In the present case it is proposed that the doctors should be entitled to discontinue both the artificial feeding of Anthony and the use of antibiotics. It is plain from the evidence that Anthony, in his present condition, is very prone to *j* infection and that, over some necessarily uncertain but not very long period of time, he will succumb to infection which, if unchecked, will spread and cause his death. But the effect of discontinuing the artificial feeding will be that he will inevitably die within one or two weeks.

Objection can be made to the latter course of action on the ground that

Anthony will thereby be starved to death, and that this would constitute a breach
a of the duty to feed him which must form an essential part of the duty which
every person owes to another in his care. But here again it is necessary to analyse
precisely what this means in the case of Anthony. Anthony is not merely
incapable of feeding himself. He is incapable of swallowing, and therefore of
eating or drinking in the normal sense of those words. There is overwhelming
evidence that, in the medical profession, artificial feeding is regarded as a form of
b medical treatment; and, even if it is not strictly medical treatment, it must form
part of the medical care of the patient. Indeed, the function of artificial feeding
in the case of Anthony, by means of a nasogastric tube, is to provide a form of life
support analogous to that provided by a ventilator which artificially breathes air
in and out of the lungs of a patient incapable of breathing normally, thereby
c enabling oxygen to reach the bloodstream. The same principles must apply in
either case when the question is asked whether the doctor in charge may lawfully
discontinue the life-sustaining treatment or care; and, if in either case the
treatment is futile in the sense I have described, it can properly be concluded that
it is no longer in the best interests of the patient to continue it. It is true that, in
the case of discontinuance of artificial feeding, it can be said that the patient will
d as a result starve to death; and this may bring before our eyes the vision of an
ordinary person slowly dying of hunger, and suffering all the pain and distress
associated with such a death. But here it is clear from the evidence that no such
pain or distress will be suffered by Anthony, who can feel nothing at all.
Furthermore, we are told that the outward symptoms of dying in such a way,
which might otherwise cause distress to the nurses who care for him or to
e members of his family who visit him, can be suppressed by means of sedatives.
In these circumstances, I can see no ground in the present case for refusing the
declarations applied for simply because the course of action proposed involves the
discontinuance of artificial feeding.

In *F v West Berkshire Health Authority* [1989] 2 All ER 545, [1990] 2 AC 1 it was
f stated that, where a doctor provides treatment for a person who is incapacitated
from saying whether or not he consents to it, the doctor must, when deciding on
the form of treatment, act in accordance with a responsible and competent body
of relevant professional opinion, on the principles set down in *Bolam v Friern
Hospital Management Committee* [1957] 2 All ER 118, [1957] 1 WLR 582. In my
opinion, this principle must equally be applicable to decisions to initiate, or to
g discontinue, life support, as it is to other forms of treatment. However, in a
matter of such importance and sensitivity as discontinuance of life support, it is
to be expected that guidance will be provided for the profession; and, on the
evidence in the present case, such guidance is for a case such as the present to be
found in a discussion paper on *Treatment of Patients in Persistent Vegetative State*,
issued in September 1992 by the medical ethics committee of the British Medical
h Association. Anybody reading this substantial paper will discover for himself the
great care with which this topic is being considered by the profession. Mr Francis
for the respondents drew to the attention of the Appellate Committee four
safeguards in particular which, in the committee's opinion, should be observed
before discontinuing life support for such patients. They are: (1) every effort
should be made at rehabilitation for at least six months after the injury; (2) the
j diagnosis of irreversible PVS should not be considered confirmed until at least 12
months after the injury, with the effect that any decision to withhold life-
prolonging treatment will be delayed for that period; (3) the diagnosis should be
agreed by two other independent doctors; and (4) generally, the wishes of the
patient's immediate family will be given great weight.

In fact, the views expressed by the committee on the subject of consultation

with the relatives of PVS patients are consistent with the opinion expressed by
your Lordships' House in *F v West Berkshire Health Authority* that it is good practice *a*
for the doctor to consult relatives. Indeed the committee recognises that, in the
case of PVS patients, the relatives themselves will require a high degree of support
and attention. But the committee is firmly of the opinion that the relatives' views
cannot be determinative of the treatment. Indeed, if that were not so, the relatives
would be able to dictate to the doctors what is in the best interests of the patient, *b*
which cannot be right. Even so, a decision to withhold life-prolonging treatment,
such as artificial feeding, must require close co-operation with those close to the
patient; and it is recognised that, in practice, their views and the opinions of
doctors will coincide in many cases.

Study of this document left me in no doubt that if a doctor treating a PVS
patient acts in accordance with the medical practice now being evolved by the *c*
medical ethics committee of the British Medical Association he will be acting
with the benefit of guidance from a responsible and competent body of relevant
professional opinion, as required by the *Bolam* test. I also feel that those who are
concerned that a matter of life and death, such as is involved in a decision to
withhold life support in case of this kind, should be left to the doctors would do
well to study this paper. The truth is that, in the course of their work, doctors *d*
frequently have to make decisions which may affect the continued survival of
their patients, and are in reality far more experienced in matters of this kind than
are the judges. It is nevertheless the function of the judges to state the legal
principles upon which the lawfulness of the actions of doctors depend; but in the
end the decisions to be made in individual cases must rest with the doctors
themselves. In these circumstances, what is required is a sensitive understanding *e*
by both the judges and the doctors of each other's respective functions, and in
particular a determination by the judges not merely to understand the problems
facing the medical profession in cases of this kind, but also to regard their
professional standards with respect. Mutual understanding between the doctors
and the judges is the best way to ensure the evolution of a sensitive and sensible *f*
legal framework for the treatment and care of patients, with a sound ethical base,
in the interest of the patients themselves. This is a topic to which I will return at
the end of this opinion, when I come to consider the extent to which the view of
the court should be sought, as a matter of practice, in cases such as the present.

I wish however to refer at this stage to the approach adopted in most American
courts under which the court seeks, in a case in which the patient is incapacitated *g*
from expressing any view on the question whether life-prolonging treatment
should be withheld in the relevant circumstances, to determine what decision the
patient himself would have made had he been able to do so. This is called the
substituted judgment test, and it generally involves a detailed inquiry into the
patient's views and preferences: see e g *Re Quinlan* (1976) 70 NJ 10 and *Belchertown
State School Superintendent v Saikewicz* (1977) 373 Mass 728. In later cases concerned *h*
with PVS patients it has been held that, in the absence of clear and convincing
evidence of the patient's wishes, the surrogate decision-maker has to implement
as far as possible the decision which the incompetent patient would make if he
was competent. However, accepting on this point the submission of Mr Lester, I
do not consider that any such test forms part of English law in relation to
incompetent adults, on whose behalf nobody has power to give consent to medical *j*
treatment. Certainly, in *F v West Berkshire Health Authority* your Lordships' House
adopted a straightforward test based on the best interests of the patient; and I
myself do not see why the same test should not be applied in the case of PVS
patients, where the question is whether life-prolonging treatment should be

withheld. This was also the opinion of Thomas J in *Auckland Area Health Board v*
A-G [1993] 1 NZLR 235, unreported), a case concerned with the discontinuance
of life support provided by ventilator to a patient suffering from the last stages of
incurable Guillain-Barré syndrome. Of course, consistent with the best interests
test, anything relevant to the application of the test may be taken into account;
and, if the personality of the patient is relevant to the application of the test (as it
may be in cases where the various relevant factors have to be weighed), it may be
taken into account, as was done in *Re J (a minor) (wardship: medical treatment)*
[1990] 3 All ER 930, [1991] Fam 33. But, where the question is whether life
support should be withheld from a PVS patient, it is difficult to see how the
personality of the patient can be relevant, though it may be of comfort to his
relatives if they believe, as in the present case, and indeed may well be so in many
other cases, that the patient would not have wished his life to be artificially
prolonged if he was totally unconscious and there was no hope of improvement
in his condition.

I wish to add however that, like the courts below, I have derived assistance and
support from decisions in a number of American jurisdictions to the effect that it
is lawful to discontinue life-prolonging treatment in the case of PVS patients
where there is no prospect of improvement in their condition. Furthermore, I
wish to refer to the section in Working Paper No 28 (1982) on *Euthanasia, Aiding*
Suicide and Cessation of Treatment published by the Law Reform Commission of
Canada concerned with cessation of treatment, to which I also wish to express my
indebtedness. I believe the legal principles as I have stated them to be broadly
consistent with the conclusions summarised in the Working Paper (at pp 65–66),
which was substantially accepted in the Report of the Commission (1983) pp 32–
35. Indeed, I entertain a strong sense that a community of view on the legal
principles applicable in cases of discontinuing life support is in the course of
development and acceptance throughout the common law world.

In setting out my understanding of the relevant principles, I have had very
much in mind the submissions advanced by Mr Munby on behalf of the Official
Solicitor, and I believe that I have answered, directly or indirectly, all his objections
to the course now proposed. I do not, therefore, intend any disrespect to his
argument if I do not answer each of his submissions seriatim. In summary, his
two principal arguments were as follows. First, he submitted that the
discontinuance of artificial feeding would constitute an act which would inevitably
cause, and be intended to cause, Anthony's death; and as such, it would be
unlawful, and indeed criminal. As will be plain from what I have already said, I
cannot accept this proposition. In my opinion, for the reasons I have already
given, there is no longer any duty upon the doctors to continue with this form of
medical treatment or care in his case, and it follows that it cannot be unlawful to
discontinue it. Second, he submitted that discontinuance of the artificial feeding
of Anthony would be a breach of the doctor's duty to care for and feed him; and
since it will (as it is intended to do) cause his death, it will necessarily be unlawful.
I have considered this point earlier in this opinion, when I expressed my view
that artificial feeding is, in a case such as the present, no different from life support
by a ventilator, and as such can lawfully be discontinued when it no longer fulfils
any therapeutic purpose. To me, the crucial point in which I found myself
differing from Mr Munby was that I was unable to accept his treating the
discontinuance of artificial feeding in the present case as equivalent to cutting a
mountaineer's rope, or severing the air pipe of a deep sea diver. Once it is
recognised, as I believe it must be, that the true question is not whether the doctor
should take a course in which he will actively kill his patient, but rather whether

he should continue to provide his patient with medical treatment or care which, if continued, will prolong his life, then, as I see it, the essential basis of Mr Munby's submissions disappears. I wish to add that I was unable to accept his suggestion that recent decisions show that the law is proceeding down a 'slippery slope', in the sense that the courts are becoming more and more ready to allow doctors to take steps which will result in the ending of life. On the contrary, as I have attempted to demonstrate, the courts are acting within a structure of legal principle, under which in particular they continue to draw a clear distinction between the bounds of lawful treatment of a living patient and unlawful euthanasia.

I turn finally to the extent to which doctors should, as a matter of practice, seek the guidance of the court, by way of an application for declaratory relief, before withholding life-prolonging treatment from a PVS patient. Sir Stephen Brown P considered that the opinion of the court should be sought in all cases similar to the present. In the Court of Appeal Sir Thomas Bingham MR expressed his agreement with Sir Stephen Brown P in the following words (see p 842, ante):

'This was in my respectful view a wise ruling, directed to the protection of patients, the protection of doctors, the reassurance of patients' families and the reassurance of the public. The practice proposed seems to me desirable. It may very well be that with the passage of time a body of experience and practice will build up which will obviate the need for application in every case, but for the time being I am satisfied that the practice which Sir Stephen Brown P described should be followed.'

Before the Appellate Committee this view was supported both by Mr Munby for the Official Solicitor and by Mr Lester as amicus curiae. For the respondents, Mr Francis suggested that an adequate safeguard would be provided if reference to the court was required in certain specific cases, ie (1) where there was known to be a medical disagreement as to the diagnosis or prognosis, and (2) problems had arisen with the patient's relatives—disagreement by the next of kin with the medical recommendation; actual or apparent conflict of interest between the next of kin and the patient; dispute between members of the patient's family; or absence of any next of kin to give their consent. There is, I consider, much to be said for the view that an application to the court will not be needed in every case, but only in particular circumstances, such as those suggested by Mr Francis. In this connection I was impressed not only by the care being taken by the medical ethics committee to provide guidance to the profession, but also by information given to the Appellate Committee about the substantial number of PVS patients in the country, and the very considerable cost of obtaining guidance from the court in cases such as the present. However, in my opinion this is a matter which would be better kept under review by the President of the Family Division than resolved now by your Lordships' House. I understand that a similar review is being undertaken in cases concerned with the sterilisation of adult women of unsound mind, with a consequent relaxation of the practice relating to applications to the court in such cases. For my part, I would therefore leave the matter as proposed by Sir Thomas Bingham MR; but I wish to express the hope that the President of the Family Division, who will no doubt be kept well informed about developments in this field, will soon feel able to relax the present requirement so as to limit applications for declarations to those cases in which there is a special need for the procedure to be invoked.

I wish to add one footnote. Since preparing this opinion, I have had the opportunity of reading in draft the speech of my noble and learned friend

Lord Browne-Wilkinson, in which he has expressed the view that a doctor, in
a reaching a decision whether or not to continue, in the best interests of his patient,
to prolong his life by artificial means, may well be influenced by his own attitude
to the sanctity of human life. The point does not arise for decision in the present
case. I only wish to observe that it has implications not only in the case of a
patient who, like Anthony Bland, is totally unconscious, but also one who may be
suffering from great physical pain or (as in the case of one suffering from Guillain-
b Barré syndrome) extreme mental distress; and it would in theory fall to be tested
if the patient's relatives, dismayed by the artificial prolongation of the agony of
their loved one, were to seek to restrain by injunction a doctor who was persisting
in prolonging his life. I cannot help feeling, however, that such a situation is
more theoretical than real. I suspect that it is unlikely to arise in practice, if only
because the solution could be found in a change of medical practitioner. It is not
c to be forgotten, moreover, that doctors who for conscientious reasons would feel
unable to discontinue life support in such circumstances can presumably, like
those who have a conscientious objection to abortion, abstain from involvement
in such work. For present purposes, however, it is enough to state that the best
interests test is broad and flexible in the sense that room must be allowed for the
d exercise of judgment by the doctor as to whether the relevant conditions exist
which justify the discontinuance of life support.

For these reasons, I would dismiss the appeal. Having read in draft the speech
of my noble and learned friend Lord Keith of Kinkel, I can see no significant
difference from the opinion which I have expressed.

e **LORD LOWRY.** My Lords, I have had the advantage of reading in draft the
speeches of my noble and learned friends and, for the reasons given by my noble
and learned friend Lord Goff of Chieveley, with which I understand the remainder
of your Lordships to be generally in agreement, I agree that this appeal should be
dismissed.

I cannot usefully elaborate on your Lordships' careful analysis of the arguments.
f There are, however, four points in relation to your Lordships' reasoning and
conclusions which it may be worth my while to make.

1. I do not believe that there is a valid legal distinction between the omission to
treat a patient and the abandonment of treatment which has been commenced,
since to recognise such a distinction could quite illogically confer on a doctor who
g had refrained from treatment an immunity which did not benefit a doctor who
had embarked on treatment in order to see whether it might help the patient and
had abandoned the treatment when it was seen not to do so.

2. As noted in *F v West Berkshire Health Authority (Mental Health Act Commission
intervening)* [1989] 2 All ER 545, [1990] 2 AC 1 and again in your Lordships'
speeches, the parens patriae jurisdiction over adults who are for whatever reason
h mentally incompetent was abolished by statute. I have never heard a rational, or
indeed any, explanation for this step, which has placed under a further
disadvantage a class of adults who are already handicapped. Parliament has done
nothing since *F v West Berkshire Health Authority* was decided, but I sincerely hope
that the parens patriae jurisdiction over adults will soon be restored. The
corresponding jurisdiction in wardship has continued to prove its value and it is
j most unfortunate that the court's armoury in relation to adults remains thus
depleted. The prospect of restoration of this lost power is not controversial, since
it does not conjure up the spectre of euthanasia; the decisions which can be made
by the courts on behalf of incompetent persons would, as in wardship cases, be
confined within lawful bounds.

3. Procedurally I can see no present alternative to an application to the court such as that made in the present case. This view is reinforced for me when I *a* reflect, against the background of your Lordships' conclusions of law, that, in the absence of an application, the doctor who proposes the cessation of life-supporting care and treatment on the ground that their continuance would not be in the patient's best interests will have reached that conclusion himself and will be judge in his own cause unless and until his chosen course of action is challenged in criminal or civil proceedings. A practical alternative may, however, be evolved *b* through the practice of the Family Division and with the help of the medical ethics committee, which has already devoted so much thought to the problem, and possibly of Parliament through legislation, it will of course be understood that the court has no power to render lawful something which without the court's sanction would have been unlawful. When I take into account that the case now before your Lordships could not be clearer on its facts, I have to say that I am left *c* with the feeling that the general position is not satisfactory.

4. Although entirely satisfied with your Lordships' consensus, I ought finally to touch on the real point in the case. The strength of the Official Solicitor's argument lies in its simplicity. In answer to the respondents' reliance on accepted medical opinion that feeding (nutrition and hydration), particularly by *d* sophisticated artificial methods, is part of the life-supporting medical treatment, he says that the duty to feed a helpless person, such as a baby or an unconscious patient, is something different—an elementary duty to keep the patient alive which exists independently of all questions of treatment and which the person in charge cannot omit to perform: to omit deliberately to perform this duty in the knowledge that the omission will lead to the death of the helpless one, and indeed *e* with the intention, as in the present case, of conducing to that death, will render those in charge guilty of murder. One of the respondents' counter-arguments, albeit not conclusive, is based on the overwhelming verdict of informed medical opinion worldwide, with particular reference to the common law jurisdictions, where the relevant law generally corresponds closely with our own, that therapy and life-supporting care, including sophisticated methods of artificial feeding, are *f* components of medical treatment and cannot be separated as the Official Solicitor contends. In this connection it may also be emphasised that an artificial feeding regime is inevitably associated with the continuous use of catheters and enemas and the sedulous avoidance and combating of potentially deadly infection. I consider that the court, when intent on reaching a decision according to law, ought to give weight to informed medical opinion both on the point now under *g* discussion and also on the question of what is in the best interests of a patient and I reject the idea, which is implicit in the appellant's argument, that informed medical opinion in these respects is merely a disguise for a philosophy which, if accepted, would legalise euthanasia.

The real answer to the Official Solicitor, as your Lordships are already agreed, *h* is that his argument starts from the fallacious premiss, which can be taken as correct in ordinary doctor-patient relationships, namely that feeding in order to sustain life is *necessarily* for the benefit of the patient. But in the prevailing circumstances the opposite view is overwhelmingly held by the doctors and the validity of that view has been accepted by the courts below. The doctors consider that in the patient's best interests they ought not to feed him and the law, as *j* applied by your Lordships, has gone further by saying that they are not entitled to feed him without his consent, which cannot be obtained. So the theory of the 'duty to feed' is founded on a misapprehension and the Official Solicitor's argument leads to a legally erroneous conclusion. Even though the intention to

bring about the patient's death is there, there is no proposed guilty act because, if
a it is not in the interests of an insentient patient to continue the life-supporting
care and treatment, the doctor would be acting unlawfully if he continued the
care and treatment and would perform no guilty act by discontinuing.

I have no difficulty in accepting both this legal conclusion and its practical
effect, but it is not hard to see how the case might appear to a non-lawyer, who
might express himself on the following lines: 'Yes, I understand the point, now
b that you have explained it to me. There is no duty, or indeed right, to feed when
feeding is not in the best interests of the patient. But the real reason for
withdrawing feeding is that the doctors consider that it would be in the patient's
best interests for him to be allowed to die. (I also know that the same result could
be achieved, if not so quickly, by allowing the patient's next infection to go
untreated, but that is not just the point which we have been discussing here.) The
c solution here seems to me to introduce what lawyers call a distinction without a
difference: the intention is to terminate life, but the acceptable way of doing it is
to discontinue a regime which the law has said that the doctors have no duty or
even right to continue. And, incidentally, *F v West Berkshire Health Authority* (not
that I would venture to query your reliance on that authority) was not concerned
d with matters of life and death at all. So might it not be suggested, no doubt quite
wrongly, that this case is, in effect if not in law, an example of euthanasia in
action? I can of course appreciate the arguments in a case like this for indirectly
terminating the patient's life and I believe that very many of my friends would
be in favour of what is now proposed, but equally there must be many people
who, from conviction or simply by virtue of their conventional upbringing, are
e unconvinced that someone who can be kept alive should be allowed to die.'

My Lords, I have used the homely expedient of attributing these words to my
hypothetical non-lawyer in order to demonstrate the possible gap which my noble
and learned friend Lord Mustill sees between old law and new medicine and
perhaps also, I might add, new ethics. It is important, particularly in the area of
criminal law which governs conduct, that society's notions of what is the law and
f what is right should coincide. One role of the legislator is to detect any disparity
between these notions and to take appropriate action to close the gap.

At all events, for the reasons already relied on by your Lordships, I, too, would
dismiss this appeal.

g **LORD BROWNE-WILKINSON.** My Lords, in this case the courts are asked
to give the answer to two questions: whether the Airedale NHS Trust and the
physicians attending Anthony Bland may—

'(1) ... lawfully discontinue all life-sustaining treatment and medical
support measures designed to keep [Mr Bland] alive in his existing persistent
vegetative state including the termination of ventilation nutrition and
h hydration by artificial means; and (2) ... lawfully discontinue and thereafter
need not furnish medical treatment to [Mr Bland] except for the sole purpose
of enabling [Mr Bland] to end his life and die peacefully with the greatest
dignity and the least of pain suffering and distress ...'

Those are questions of law. But behind the questions of law lie moral, ethical,
j medical and practical issues of fundamental importance to society. As Hoffmann
LJ in the Court of Appeal emphasised, the law regulating the termination of
artificial life support being given to patients must, to be acceptable, reflect a moral
attitude which society accepts. This has led judges into the consideration of the
ethical and other non-legal problems raised by the ability to sustain life artificially

which new medical technology has recently made possible. But in my judgment
in giving the legal answer to these questions judges are faced with a dilemma. *a*
The ability to sustain life artificially is of relatively recent origin. Existing law
may not provide an acceptable answer to the new legal questions which it raises.
Should judges seek to develop new law to meet a wholly new situation? Or is this
a matter which lies outside the area of legitimate development of the law by
judges and requires society, through the democratic expression of its views in
Parliament, to reach its decisions on the underlying moral and practical problems *b*
and then reflect those decisions in legislation?

I have no doubt that it is for Parliament, not the courts, to decide the broader
issues which this case raises. Until recently there was no doubt what was life and
what was death. A man was dead if he stopped breathing and his heart stopped
beating. There was no artificial means of sustaining these indications of life for *c*
more than a short while. Death in the traditional sense was beyond human
control. Apart from cases of unlawful homicide, death occurred automatically in
the course of nature when the natural functions of the body failed to sustain the
lungs and the heart.

Recent developments in medical science have fundamentally affected these
previous certainties. In medicine, the cessation of breathing or of heartbeat is no *d*
longer death. By the use of a ventilator, lungs which in the unaided course of
nature would have stopped breathing can be made to breathe, thereby sustaining
the heartbeat. Those, like Anthony Bland, who would previously have died
through inability to swallow food can be kept alive by artificial feeding. This has
led the medical profession to redefine death in terms of brain stem death, ie the
death of that part of the brain without which the body cannot function at all *e*
without assistance. In some cases it is now apparently possible, with the use of the
ventilator, to sustain a beating heart even though the brain stem, and therefore in
medical terms the patient, is dead: 'the ventilated corpse'.

I do not refer to these factors because Anthony Bland is already dead, either
medically or legally. His brain stem is alive and so is he; provided that he is *f*
artificially fed and the waste products evacuated from his body by skilled medical
care, his body sustains its own life. I refer to these factors in order to illustrate the
scale of the problem which is presented by modern technological developments,
of which this case is merely one instance. The physical state known as death has
changed. In many cases the time and manner of death is no longer dictated by
nature but can be determined by human decision. The life of Anthony Bland, in *g*
the purely physical sense, has been and can be extended by skilled medical care
for a period of years.

To my mind, these technical developments have raised a wholly new series of
ethical and social problems. What is meant now by 'life' in the moral precept
which requires respect for the sanctity of human life? If the quality of life of a
person such as Anthony Bland is non-existent since he is unaware of anything *h*
that happens to him, has he a right to be sustained in that state of living death
and are his family and medical attendants under a duty to maintain it? If Anthony
Bland has no such right and others no such duty, should society draw a distinction
(which some would see as artificial) between adopting a course of action designed
to produce certain death, on the one hand through the lack of food, and on the
other from a fatal injection, the former being permissible and the latter *j*
(euthanasia) prohibited? If the withdrawal of life support is legitimate in the case
of Anthony Bland, whose persistent vegetative state (PVS) is very severe, what of
others in this country also in PVS (whom we were told numbered between 1,000
and 1,500) and others suffering from medical conditions having similar impact,

e g the Guillain-Barré syndrome? Who is to decide, and according to what criteria,
a who is to live and who to die? What rights have the relatives of the patient in
taking that decision?

In addition to these ethical questions, the new technology raises practical
problems. Given that there are limited resources available for medical care, is it
right to devote money to sustaining the lives of those who are, and always will be,
unaware of their own existence rather than to treating those who, in a real sense,
b can be benefited, e g those deprived of dialysis for want of resources? Again, the
timing of the patient's death may have a direct impact on the rights of other
parties. In the case of a patient suffering from PVS as a result of a road accident,
the amount of damages recoverable will depend on whether the patient is kept
alive or allowed to die. We were told by the Official Solicitor that there have
c already been cases in which this factor has been taken into account by relatives of
the patient, though there is no question of that in the present case. Again, rights
of succession to the estate of the patient may well depend on the timing of his
death.

On the moral issues raised by this case, society is not all of one mind. Although
it is probably true that the majority would favour the withdrawal of life support
d in the present case, there is undoubtedly a substantial body of opinion that is
strongly opposed. The evidence shows that the Roman Catholic church and
orthodox Jews are opposed. Within the medical profession itself there are those,
including one of the very distinguished doctors who gave evidence in this case,
who draw a distinction between withholding treatment on the one hand and
withholding food and care on the other, the latter not being acceptable. The
e present case is an extreme one, since Anthony Bland can appreciate nothing
whether he is alive or dead; but I have no doubt that less extreme cases will come
before the courts on which public opinion may be more sharply divided.

The position therefore, in my view, is that if the judges seek to develop new
law to regulate the new circumstances, the law so laid down will of necessity
f reflect judges' views on the underlying ethical questions, questions on which
there is a legitimate division of opinion. By way of example, although the Court
of Appeal in this case, in reaching the conclusion that the withdrawal of food and
Anthony Bland's subsequent death would be for his benefit, attaches importance
to impalpable factors such as personal dignity and the way Anthony Bland would
wish to be remembered but does not take into account spiritual values which, for
g example, a member of the Roman Catholic church would regard as relevant in
assessing such benefit. Where a case raises wholly new moral and social issues, in
my judgment it is not for the judges to seek to develop new, all-embracing,
principles of law in a way which reflects the individual judges' moral stance when
society as a whole is substantially divided on the relevant moral issues. Moreover,
it is not legitimate for a judge in reaching a view as to what is for the benefit of
h the one individual whose life is in issue to take into account the wider practical
issues as to allocation of limited financial resources or the impact on third parties
of altering the time at which death occurs.

For these reasons, it seems to me imperative that the moral, social and legal
issues raised by this case should be considered by Parliament. The judges' function
in this area of the law should be to apply the principles which society, through
j the democratic process, adopts, not to impose their standards on society. If
Parliament fails to act, then judge-made law will of necessity through a gradual
and uncertain process provide a legal answer to each new question as it arises. But
in my judgment that is not the best way to proceed.

The function of the court in these circumstances is to determine this particular case in accordance with the existing law, and not seek to develop new law laying down a new regimen. The result of this limited approach may be unsatisfactory, both in moral and practical terms, but it is for Parliament to address the wider problems which the case raises and lay down principles of law generally applicable to the withdrawal of life support systems.

Before turning to the strict legality of what is proposed, I must say something about the procedure adopted in this case. The application asks the court to make declarations as to the legality of proposed future actions, ie, if granted, the declarations will purport to decide whether the proposed discontinuance of life support will constitute a crime. In general the court sets its face against making declarations as to the criminality of proposed future actions. But I agree with my noble and learned friend Lord Goff of Chieveley that in this case it is absolutely necessary to do so. The doctors responsible for Anthony Bland's care have reached the view that it is for his benefit to withdraw life support but have been warned by the coroner that it may constitute a criminal offence if they do so. In the past, doctors exercised their own discretion, in accordance with medical ethics, in cases such as these. To the great advantage of society, they took the responsibility of deciding whether the perpetuation of life was pointless. But there are now present amongst the medical and nursing staff of hospitals those who genuinely believe in the sanctity of human life, no matter what the quality of that life, and report doctors who take such decisions to the authorities with a view to prosecution for a criminal offence. I am not criticising such people: they are acting in accordance with their own moral standards. But their actions have made it extremely risky for a doctor to take a decision of this kind when his action may lie on the borderline of legality. I have no doubt that the courts should, by declaration, provide to doctors faced with such decisions clear rulings whether the course they propose to adopt is or is not lawful.

I turn then to the question whether, under existing law, the proposed discontinuance of the artificial feeding of Anthony Bland would be lawful. Such discontinuance might be unlawful because (a) it would constitute a criminal offence or (b) it will give rise to civil liability to Anthony Bland or his personal representatives after his death.

A. CRIMINAL LIABILITY/MURDER

It is the submission of the Official Solicitor that the withdrawal of artificial feeding would constitute murder. The Official Solicitor has been criticised for using emotive language in this case. In my judgment this criticism is misplaced: much the most difficult question is indeed whether the proposed course of action is, in law, murder notwithstanding the best motives from which everyone concerned is acting.

Murder consists of causing the death of another with intent so to do. What is proposed in the present case is to adopt a course with the intention of bringing about Anthony Bland's death. As to the element of intention, or mens rea, in my judgment there can be no real doubt that it is present in this case: the whole purpose of stopping artificial feeding is to bring about the death of Anthony Bland.

As to the guilty act, or actus reus, the criminal law draws a distinction between the commission of a positive act which causes death and the omission to do an act which would have prevented death. In general an omission to prevent death is not an actus reus and cannot give rise to a conviction for murder. But where the accused was under a duty to the deceased to do the act which he omitted to do, such omission can constitute the actus reus of homicide, either murder (see *R v*

Gibbins (1918) 13 Cr App R 134) or manslaughter (see *R v Stone* [1977] 2 All ER
a 341, [1977] QB 354) depending upon the mens rea of the accused. The Official
Solicitor submits that the actus reus of murder is present on two alternative
grounds, viz (1) the withdrawal of artificial feeding is a positive act of commission
or (2) if what is proposed is only an omission, the hospital and the doctors have
assumed a duty to care for Anthony Bland (including feeding him) and therefore
the omission to feed him would constitute the actus reus of murder.
b

1. *Positive act of commission*

Mr Munby QC, in his powerful but balanced argument for the Official Solicitor,
submits that the removal of the nasogastric tube necessary to provide artificial
feeding and the discontinuance of the existing regime of artificial feeding
c constitute positive acts of commission. I do not accept this. Apart from the act of
removing the nasogastric tube, the mere failure to continue to do what you have
previously done is not, in any ordinary sense, to do anything positive: on the
contrary it is by definition an omission to do what you have previously done.

The positive act of removing the nasogastric tube presents more difficulty. It is
undoubtedly a positive act, similar to switching off a ventilator in the case of a
d patient whose life is being sustained by artificial ventilation. But in my judgment
in neither case should the act be classified as positive, since to do so would be to
introduce intolerably fine distinctions. If, instead of removing the nasogastric
tube, it was left in place but no further nutrients were provided for the tube to
convey to the patient's stomach, that would not be an act of commission. Again,
as has been pointed out (Skegg *Law, Ethics and Medicine* (1985) p 169ff), if the
e switching off of a ventilator were to be classified as a positive act, exactly the same
result can be achieved by installing a time-clock which requires to be reset every
12 hours: the failure to reset the machine could not be classified as a positive act.
In my judgment, essentially what is being done is to omit to feed or to ventilate:
the removal of the nasogastric tube or the switching off of a ventilator are merely
incidents of that omission: see Glanville Williams *Textbook of Criminal Law* (2nd
f edn, 1983) p 282 and *Skegg* p 169ff.

In my judgment, there is a further reason why the removal of the nasogastric
tube in the present case could not be regarded as a positive act causing the death.
The tube itself, without the food being supplied through it, does nothing. The
removal of the tube by itself does not cause the death since by itself it did not
g sustain life. Therefore even if, contrary to my view, the removal of the tube is to
be classified as a positive act, it would not constitute the actus reus of murder
since such positive act would not be the cause of death.

2. *Omission: duty to provide care*

Mr Munby submits that, by starting to treat Anthony Bland as a patient and
h instituting a regime of artificial feeding, the hospital and doctors have undertaken
a duty to provide him with medical care and food for an indefinite period. That
being their duty, the withdrawal of artificial feeding, even though a mere
omission, will be a breach of that duty and therefore constitute murder.

The crux of this submission is the extent of the duty owed by the hospital and
the doctors to Anthony Bland. In order to analyse the nature of that duty, it is
j necessary first to consider the relationship between a doctor and a patient who,
through mental disability, is unable to consent to treatment. Any treatment
given by a doctor to a patient which is invasive (i e involves any interference with
the physical integrity of the patient) is unlawful unless done with the consent of
the patient: it constitutes the crime of battery and the tort of trespass to the

person. Thus, in the case of an adult who is mentally competent, the artificial
feeding regime (and the attendant steps necessary to evacuate the bowels and *a*
bladder) would be unlawful unless the patient consented to it. A mentally
competent patient can at any time put an end to life support systems by refusing
his consent to their continuation. In the ordinary case of murder by positive act
of commission, the consent of the victim is no defence. But where the charge is
one of murder by omission to do an act and the act omitted could only be done
with the consent of the patient, refusal by the patient of consent to the doing of *b*
such act does, indirectly, provide a defence to the charge of murder. The doctor
cannot owe to the patient any duty to maintain his life where that life can only
be sustained by intrusive medical care to which the patient will not consent.

How then does the matter stand in the case of a patient who, by reason of his
being under age or, like Anthony Bland, of full age but mentally disabled, is *c*
unable to give consent to treatment? So far as minors are concerned, the guardian
of the child can consent, failing which the court, exercising the Crown's rights as
parens patriae under the wardship jurisdiction, can consent on the child's behalf.
Until 1960 the court had the same parens patriae jurisdiction over adults who
were mentally incompetent. But by the joint effect of the Mental Health Act
1959 and the revocation of the warrant under the sign manual under which the *d*
jurisdiction of the Crown as parens patriae over those of unsound mind was
conferred on the courts, the courts ceased to have any parens patriae jurisdiction
over the person of a mentally incompetent adult, being left only with the
statutory jurisdiction over his property (as opposed to his person) conferred by
the 1959 Act: see *F v West Berkshire Health Authority (Mental Health Act Commission
intervening)* [1989] 2 All ER 545, [1990] 2 AC 1. Although no one has been able *e*
to explain why Parliament chose to take this course (indeed it has been suggested
that it was an accident) no step has been taken to restore to the courts the parens
patriae jurisdiction over the body of a mentally disabled adult. As a result the
court, even if it thought fit, has no power on Anthony Bland's behalf either to
consent or to refuse consent to the continuation of the invasive procedures *f*
involved in artificial feeding.

Faced with this lacuna in the law, this House in *F v West Berkshire Health
Authority* developed and laid down a principle, based on concepts of necessity,
under which a doctor can lawfully treat a patient who cannot consent to such
treatment if it is in the best interests of the patient to receive such treatment. In
my view, the correct answer to the present case depends on the extent of the right *g*
to continue lawfully to invade the bodily integrity of Anthony Bland without his
consent. If in the circumstances they have no right to continue artificial feeding,
they cannot be in breach of any duty by ceasing to provide such feeding.

What then is the extent of the right to treat Anthony Bland which can be
deduced from *F v West Berkshire Health Authority*? Both Lord Brandon of Oakbrook
and Lord Goff make it clear that the right to administer invasive medical care is *h*
wholly dependent upon such care being in the best interests of the patient (see
[1989] 2 All ER 545 at 557, 565–566, 567, [1990] 2 AC 1 at 64, 75, 77). Moreover,
a doctor's decision whether invasive care is in the best interests of the patient falls
to be assessed by reference to the test laid down in *Bolam v Friern Hospital
Management Committee* [1957] 2 All ER 118, [1957] 1 WLR 582, viz is the decision
in accordance with a practice accepted at the time by a responsible body of medical *j*
opinion? (see [1989] 2 All ER 545 at 559, 567, [1990] 2 AC 1 at 66–67, 78 per
Lord Brandon and Lord Goff). In my judgment it must follow from this that, if
there comes a stage where the responsible doctor comes to the reasonable
conclusion (which accords with the views of a responsible body of medical

a opinion) that further continuance of an intrusive life support system is not in the best interests of the patient, he can no longer lawfully continue that life support system: to do so would constitute the crime of battery and the tort of trespass to the person. Therefore he cannot be in breach of any duty to maintain the patient's life. Therefore he is not guilty of murder by omission.

b *3. What is the correct question?*
    If I am right so far in my analysis, the critical decision to be made is whether it is in the best interests of Anthony Bland to continue the invasive medical care involved in artificial feeding. That question is not the same as, 'Is it in Anthony Bland's best interests that he should die?' The latter question assumes that it is lawful to perpetuate the patient's life; but such perpetuation of life can only be
c achieved if it is lawful to continue to invade the bodily integrity of the patient by invasive medical care. Unless the doctor has reached the affirmative conclusion that it is in the patient's best interest to continue the invasive care, such care must cease.
    The answer to the question must of course depend on the circumstances of each case and there will be no single 'right' answer. Different doctors may take
d different views both on strictly medical issues and the broader ethical issues which the question raises. It follows that the legal question in this case (unlike the question which would arise if there were a parens patriae jurisdiction under which the court has to make the decision) is not whether the court thinks it is in the best interests of Anthony Bland to continue to receive intrusive medical care but whether the responsible doctor has reached a reasonable and bona fide belief
e that it is not. The doctor's answer may well be influenced by his own attitude to the sanctity of human life. In cases where there is no strictly medical point in continuing care, if a doctor holds the view that the patient is entitled to stay alive, whatever the quality of such life, he can quite reasonably reach the view that the continuation of intrusive care, being the only way of preserving such life, is in the patient's best interests. But, in the same circumstances another doctor who
f sees no merit in perpetuating a life of which the patient is unaware can equally reasonably reach the view that the continuation of invasive treatment is not for the patient's benefit. Accordingly, on an application to the court for a declaration that the discontinuance of medical care will be lawful, the court's only concern will be to be satisfied that the doctor's decision to discontinue is in accordance
g with a respectable body of medical opinion and that it is reasonable.

4. The answer to the question
    Anthony Bland has been irreversibly brain damaged: the most distinguished medical opinion is unanimous that there is no prospect at all that the condition will change for the better. He is not aware of anything. If artificial feeding is
h continued, he will feel nothing; if artificial feeding is discontinued and he dies he will feel nothing. Whether he lives or dies he will feel no pain or distress. All the purely physical considerations indicate that it is pointless to continue life support. Only if the doctors responsible for his care held the view that, though he is aware of nothing, there is some benefit to him in staying alive, would there be anything to indicate that it is for his benefit to continue the invasive medical care. In
j Anthony Bland's case, the doctors do not take that view. The discontinuance of life support would be in accordance with the proposals contained in the discussion paper on *Treatment of Patients in Persistent Vegetative State* issued in September 1992 by the medical ethics committee of the British Medical Association. Therefore the *Bolam* requirement is satisfied.

In these circumstances, it is perfectly reasonable for the responsible doctors to conclude that there is no affirmative benefit to Anthony Bland in continuing the *a* invasive medical procedures necessary to sustain his life. Having so concluded, they are neither entitled nor under a duty to continue such medical care. Therefore they will not be guilty of murder if they discontinue such care.

B. CIVIL LIABILITY

The discontinuance of life support could expose the plaintiffs to a liability in *b* tort to Anthony Bland or, more realistically, to his personal representatives. But such liability would have to be founded on a breach of some duty owed by them to Anthony Bland to maintain such life support. For the reasons which I have given in dealing with criminal liability, no such breach of duty can exist in this case. Therefore the discontinuance of life support will also be lawful under civil law.   *c*

I am very conscious that I have reached my conclusions on narrow, legalistic, grounds which provide no satisfactory basis for the decision of cases which will arise in the future where the facts are not identical. I must again emphasise that this is an extreme case where it can be overwhelmingly proved that the patient is and will remain insensate: he neither feels pain from treatment nor will feel pain *d* in dying and has no prospect of any medical care improving his condition. Unless, as I very much hope, Parliament reviews the law, the courts will be faced with cases where the chances of improvement are slight, or the patient has very slight sensate awareness. I express no view on what should be the answer in such circumstances: my decision does not cover such a case. I therefore consider that, for the foreseeable future, doctors would be well advised in each case to apply to *e* the court for a declaration as to the legality of any proposed discontinuance of life support where there has been no valid consent by or on behalf of the patient to such discontinuance.

Finally, the conclusion I have reached will appear to some to be almost irrational. How can it be lawful to allow a patient to die slowly, though painlessly, over a period of weeks from lack of food but unlawful to produce his immediate *f* death by a lethal injection, thereby saving his family from yet another ordeal to add to the tragedy that has already struck them? I find it difficult to find a moral answer to that question. But it is undoubtedly the law and nothing I have said casts doubt on the proposition that the doing of a positive act with the intention of ending life is and remains murder.   *g*

LORD MUSTILL. My Lords, the pitiful state of Anthony Bland and the suffering of his devoted family must attract the sympathy of all. The devotion to duty of the medical staff, and the complete propriety of those who have faced up to the painful dilemma must equally attract the respect of all. This combination of sympathy and respect can but yield an urgent desire to take up the burden, to *h* reach a conclusion on this deep moral issue of life and death, and to put that conclusion into effect as speedily and humanely as possible. The compelling nature of this task does however have its own risks, for it leads to an assumption that the central question of ethics is the only question, and that anything which stands in the way of a solution should be brushed aside as an empty technicality. However natural this impulse may be I believe that it must be resisted, for the *j* authority of the state, through the medium of the court, is being invoked to permit one group of its citizens to terminate the life of another. Thus, although the issues spring from a private grief and the course which is proposed is also private, in the sense that it will not be put into effect by the state, we are nevertheless here in the field of public law. The court must therefore be concerned

a not only to find a humane and morally justified solution to the problems of those directly involved, but also to examine rigorously both the process by which the solution is reached and the legal foundation on which it rests. Otherwise, the pressures created by this very extreme case may distort the law in a way which leads to false conclusions in situations where the issues are similar but more finely balanced, and may in addition create unforeseen anomalies in criminal cases far

b removed from the present. This appeal obviously raises acute problems of ethics, but this should not obscure the fact that it is also exceptionally difficult in point of law, and it is essential that these difficulties should be clearly recognised and objectively analysed, not in a spirit of obstruction or pedantry, but because they are an inescapable part of any decision on whether the declarations made in the

c High Court should be allowed to stand.

Accordingly I shall concentrate in what follows on the legal rather than the ethical aspects of the appeal, although I have of course given the latter the most careful and anxious consideration. The moral issues have already been extensively discussed. I agree with the conclusion of all those who have delivered judgments in the case that the declarations ought to stand and I also agree broadly, although

d not necessarily in every detail, with the way in which that conclusion has been reached. Rather than traverse the same ground again in different language I think it more useful to concentrate on two important matters which received comparatively little attention in the courts below. First, the role of the court, that is the nature of the function which the court is being called upon to perform, and the suitability of the court to perform it. Second, the consistency of the steps

e authorised by the two declarations now under appeal (which I will call 'the proposed conduct') with the existing criminal law. In placing these matters firmly before the House the Official Solicitor, through the medium of Mr Munby QC, has performed a most valuable service.

When performing this task it is essential to face up squarely to the true nature

f of what is proposed, and to have in mind what has been called 'the distinction between the right to choose one's own death and the right to choose someone else's': see 'Medical technology and the law' (1989) 103 Harv LR 1519 at 1665n. Emollient expressions such as 'letting nature take its course' and 'easing the passing' may have their uses, but they are out of place here, for they conceal both the ethical and the legal issues, and I will try to avoid them. I will also abstain

g from debate about whether the proposed conduct will amount to euthanasia. The word is not a term of art, and what matters is not whether the declarations authorise euthanasia, but whether they authorise what would otherwise be murder. I will say only this. The conclusion that the declarations can be upheld depends crucially on a distinction drawn by the criminal law between acts and omissions, and carries with it inescapably a distinction between, on the one hand

h what is often called 'mercy killing', where active steps are taken in a medical context to terminate the life of a suffering patient, and a situation such as the present, where the proposed conduct has the aim for equally humane reasons of terminating the life of Anthony Bland by withholding from him the basic necessities of life. The acute unease which I feel about adopting this way through the legal and ethical maze is I believe due in an important part to the sensation

j that however much the terminologies may differ the ethical status of the two courses of action is for all relevant purposes indistinguishable. By dismissing this appeal I fear that your Lordships' House may only emphasise the distortions of a legal structure which is already both morally and intellectually misshapen. Still, the law is there and we must take it as it stands.

I. THE ROLE OF THE COURT

The issues now before the House fall into three groups. (1) Is it right, as a *a* matter of general ethical principle, that the lives of persons in the position of Anthony Bland should be brought to an end, and if so is it right that they should be brought to an end in the manner proposed? (2) Under the law as it now stands, can the proposed conduct be put into effect without committing a criminal offence, and particularly the offence of murder? (3) If the answer to the second question is 'Yes, provided that certain conditions are shown to exist', do those *b* conditions exist in the case of Anthony Bland?

What is the function of the courts in relation to these groups of issues? It is convenient to begin with the third. If the criteria for the legitimacy of the proposed conduct are essentially factual, a decision upon them is one which the court is well accustomed to perform, and may properly be obtained through the *c* medium of an application for declaratory relief. If however they contain an element of ethical judgment, for example if the law requires the decision-maker to consider whether a certain course is 'in the best interests' of the patient, the skill and experience of the judge will carry him only so far. They will help him to clear the ground by marshalling the considerations which are said to be relevant, eliminating errors of logic, and so on. But when the intellectual part of *d* the task is complete and the decision-maker has to choose the factors which he will take into account, attach relevant weights to them and then strike a balance the judge is no better equipped, though no worse, than anyone else. In the end it is a matter of personal choice, dictated by his or her background, upbringing, education, convictions and temperament. Legal expertise gives no special advantage here. *e*

Questions within the second group are entirely within the province of the courts. It is these questions which have exercised the family and all those in the medical and nursing professions who have cared for Anthony Bland and given advice on his case. (For brevity, I will call these 'the doctors'.) As I understand the position they have all, with heavy hearts, taken the ethical decision that since *f* their efforts have run their course it is better from every point of view that Anthony Bland's life should be brought to an end. But they wish to act within the law, and the very proper warning given by the coroner has been taken to heart. It is therefore natural that they should turn to the court for authority to do what they believe to be best. It is also natural that the court should wish to do everything proper to ensure that the doctors act, as they themselves wish to act, *g* only in accordance with the law. No sensible person could want the doctors to take the risk of having to validate their conduct after the event in the context of a trial for murder.

Because all this is perfectly natural, everyone concerned has pressed ahead without I believe having analysed at all closely just what it is the court is being required to do. Very many applications to the Family Division raise issues of *h* what is essentially social management, as for example where the court decides whether, in the light of guidance given by the appellate courts as to the correct general approach, it is better for a child to go to one parent rather than the other. The present case is quite different, for the declarations under appeal assume the answers to a set of hypothetical questions of criminal law. Not of course hypothetical through being divorced from real life, but hypothetical because they *j* put in suit the criminal consequences of conduct which not only has not happened but never will happen, if the present appeal succeeds. We are thus embarked on a kind of proleptic criminal trial, without charge, jury or verdict.

My Lords, no procedure exists, nor so far as I am aware has one ever been

proposed, for conducting such an inquiry before the criminal courts. Not only
a would the notion that it is a proper function of the criminal courts to provide a
decision, intended to be legally binding as to the future, on the criminality of acts
or omissions as yet only in contemplation be rejected out of hand, but there exists
no mechanism which would enable an application for this purpose even to be
brought before the court. Yet we find that the present proceedings have been
brought in the Family Division without demur, and that the extremely important
b questions of the criminal law to which they give rise have reached your Lordships'
House not through the criminal appellate system but through the civil.

My Lords, by raising this point I am not of course suggesting that your
Lordships should allow this appeal because the procedure adopted was
impermissible. The appeal has reached this House, and your Lordships must
decide it. Anything else would be unthinkable in human terms. Nor do I suggest
c that the grant of declarations as to criminality can never be granted in civil cases.
The principle so strongly urged in *Imperial Tobacco Ltd v A-G* [1980] 1 All ER 866,
[1981] AC 718 is, as was there acknowledged, subject to exception, and this is an
exceptional case. Nor am I troubled by the fact that the decision in the present
case does not create an issue estoppel in the criminal courts and therefore does not
d form a conclusive bar to any future prosecution. I think it a great pity that the
Attorney General did not appear in these proceedings between private parties to
represent the interests of the state in the maintenance of its citizens' lives and in
the due enforcement of the criminal law, for although Mr Munby for the Official
Solicitor and Mr Lester QC as amicus curiae have made invaluable submissions
they were here in a different interest. Nevertheless it would be fanciful to suppose
e that if this appeal is dismissed and the proposed conduct goes ahead the
prosecuting authorities would even think of starting proceedings against the
doctors. What troubles me is very different.

In the first place, whilst the members of the House have all picked a way
through the minefields of the existing law to the conclusion that the proposed
conduct is lawful, it would in my opinion be too optimistic to suppose that this is
f the end of the matter, and that in the future the doctors (or perhaps the judges of
the High Court) will be able without difficulty to solve all future cases by
ascertaining the facts and applying to them the precepts established in the speeches
delivered today. The dozens of cases in the American courts have shown that the
subject is too difficult, and the situations too diverse, for the law to be settled by a
g single appeal. I foresee that the appellate courts will be visited again, and that we
shall find important areas of the criminal law in the course of elaboration through
declaratory relief in the civil courts. Whilst I do not say that this is technically
impossible it may not be the right way ahead. At all events I think it plain that
the court is engaged on an unusual task and that it will be necessary to be sure,
before this procedure becomes firmly established, just how it is that the civil
h courts can do in a criminal matter what the criminal courts themselves cannot
do. The present appeal is not the right vehicle for this task, but since the House is
invited to uphold the declarations granted in the High Court it is I believe
necessary to consider what their effect will be. Three possibilities have been
canvassed.

(1) The effect of the declarations is to change the legal status of the proposed
j conduct *in this particular case*. On this view, even if the proposed conduct would
have been unlawful without the decision of the court the declarations have made
it lawful. This could be accomplished either by enlarging the category of proper
medical treatment, which already stands outside the criminal law, so as to include
a termination of life which the court has sanctioned in advance, or alternatively

(and perhaps it comes to much the same) by altering the content of the doctors' duty to maintain life in cases where declarations such as the present have been *a* made. This proposition would require a change in the law which I would hesitate long before indorsing, but the matter need not be further pursued, since it became plain during argument that none of the counsel were advocating this route.

(2) The effect of the declaration, upheld by your Lordships' House, would be to create, through a binding precedent, a new common law exception to the offence *b* of murder, which in future would not only bind all courts faced with criminal proceedings arising from the termination of life for medical reasons, but would also form a point of growth for the development of the criminal law in new and at present unforeseeable directions. This approach would have the great attraction of recognising that the law has been left behind by the rapid advances of medical technology. By starting with a clean slate the law would be freed from the *c* piecemeal expedients to which courts throughout the common law world have been driven when trying to fill the gap between old law and new medicine. It has however been rightly acknowledged by counsel that this is a step which the courts could not properly take. Any necessary changes would have to take account of the whole of this area of law and morals, including of course all the issues *d* commonly grouped under the heading of euthanasia. The formulation of the necessary broad social and moral policy is an enterprise which the courts have neither the means nor in my opinion the right to perform. This can only be achieved by democratic process through the medium of Parliament.

(3) The declarations will simply apply the law as it now stands to the undisputed facts of the present case. By upholding them the House will bind all courts *e* charged in the future with a similar task to approach it in the same way. The declarations will not however alter the legal status of the proposed conduct from what it would have been even if no declarations had been sought, nor will it make any change in the existing criminal law. The declarations will therefore achieve no more in the present case than the useful but limited function of reassuring the doctors that what they wish to do was lawful when proposed and will be lawful *f* when carried out, and will as a by-product ensure that in practice if the proposed conduct goes ahead no prosecution will ensue. I will not repeat what I have said about the unusual nature of this process, which must I believe be carried out by supposing that the doctors have already put into effect their proposals, have been charged with murder and are now in the course of obtaining a ruling on whether *g* on the undisputed facts they have a good defence.

My Lords, a little while ago I suggested that the present appeal raised three questions. Having discussed the nature of the second and third, I turn to the first, which asks whether it is right to terminate the lives of persons in the position of Anthony Bland, and in particular whether it is right that this should be done in the manner proposed. (I mention the latter question because it is a striking fact *h* that in 20 out of the 39 American states which have legislated in favour of 'living wills' the legislation specifically excludes termination of life by the withdrawal of nourishment and hydration.) These are only fragments of a much wider nest of questions, all entirely ethical in content, beginning with the most general: 'Is it ever right to terminate the life of a patient, with or without his consent?' I believe that adversarial proceedings, even with the help of an amicus curiae, are not the *j* right vehicle for the discussion of this broad and highly contentious moral issue, nor do I believe that the judges are best fitted to carry it out. On the latter aspect I would adopt the very blunt words of Scalia J in *Cruzan v Director, Missouri Dept of Health* (1990) 110 S Ct 2841 at 2859, where a very similar problem arose in a

different constitutional and legal framework. These are problems properly
a decided by the citizens, through their elected representatives, not by the courts.

My Lords, I believe that I have said enough to explain why, from the outset, I
have felt serious doubts about whether this question is justiciable, not in the
technical sense, but in the sense of being a proper subject for legal adjudication.
The whole matter cries out for exploration in depth by Parliament and then for
the establishment by legislation not only of a new set of ethically and intellectually
b consistent rules, distinct from the general criminal law, but also of a sound
procedural framework within which the rules can be applied to individual cases.
The rapid advance of medical technology makes this an ever more urgent task,
and I venture to hope that Parliament will soon take it in hand. Meanwhile, the
present case cannot wait. We must ascertain the current state of the law and see
whether it can be reconciled with the conduct which the doctors propose.
c

II. THE LEGAL FRAMEWORK

Since it is common ground that the function of the court on this appeal is to
apply and if necessary develop the existing law, rather than create entirely new
exceptions to the law of murder, it is convenient to begin by taking stock.

d 1. *Consent to bodily invasion* Any invasion of the body of one person by another
is potentially both a crime and a tort. At the bottom end of the scale consent is a
defence both to a charge of common assault and to a claim in tort. The
concentration in most discussions of this topic on this end of the scale has tended
to divert attention from the fact that whatever the scope of the civil defence of
volenti non fit injuria there is a point higher up the scale than common assault at
e which consent in general ceases to form a defence to a criminal charge. The
precise location of this point is at present under consideration by another
committee of your Lordships' House in *R v Laskey and ors* and I need not explore
it here, but that the point exists is beyond question. If one person cuts off the
hand of another it is no answer to say that the amputee consented to what was
done.

f 2. *Proper medical treatment* How is it that, consistently with the proposition
just stated, a doctor can with immunity perform on a consenting patient an act
which would be a very serious crime if done by someone else? The answer must
be that bodily invasions in the course of proper medical treatment stand
completely outside the criminal law. The reason why the consent of the patient
is so important is not that it furnishes a defence in itself, but because it is usually
g essential to the propriety of medical treatment. Thus, if the consent is absent, and
is not dispensed with in special circumstances by operation of law, the acts of the
doctor lose their immunity.

3. *Paramountcy of the patient's choice* If the patient is capable of making a
decision on whether to permit treatment and decides not to permit it his choice
h must be obeyed, even if on any objective view it is contrary to his best interests.
A doctor has no right to proceed in the face of objection, even if it is plain to all,
including the patient, that adverse consequences and even death will or may
ensue.

4. *Cessation of treatment* Thus it is that the patient who is undergoing life-
maintaining treatment and decides that it would be preferable to die must be
j allowed to die, provided that all necessary steps have been taken to be sure that
this is what he or she really desires.

5. *Emergencies* Although the consent of the patient is normally essential to the
immunity of the doctor from criminal (and also from civil) process there are
occasions when the law permits him to proceed without it. Notably, where

urgent action is imperative in the interests of the patient, and because the patient is unconscious, or disorientated, or for some other reason the consent cannot be   *a* obtained until it is too late.

6. *Necessity* In *F v West Berkshire Health Authority (Mental Health Act Commission intervening)* [1989] 2 All ER 545, [1990] 2 AC 1 your Lordships' House has extended this general exception to the special situation where the patient is permanently incapacitated from making any decision about treatment. In that case, the nature of the bodily invasion was such that unless the acts of the doctors   *b* fell into the special category of proper medical treatment they would have amounted to a most serious crime. If the patient had been capable of deciding whether or not she wished to be treated, and had either not been asked for her consent or had refused it, the doctors would have been criminally liable since consent is normally an essential element in proper medical treatment. As matters   *c* stood, however, the patient was incapable of making a decision, so that to abstain from proceeding without her consent would mean that a decision against treatment would have been taken by default. The necessity for a decision to be made, one way or the other, coupled with her inability to make it enabled treatment to be made in what was considered her best interest.

7. *Murder* It has been established for centuries that consent to the deliberate   *d* infliction of death is no defence to a charge of murder. Cases where the victim has urged the defendant to kill him and the defendant has complied are likely to be rare, but the proposition is established beyond doubt by the law on duelling, where even if the deceased was the challenger his consent to the risk of being deliberately killed by his opponent does not alter the case.

8. *'Mercy killing'* Prosecutions of doctors who are suspected of having killed   *e* their patients are extremely rare, and direct authority is in very short supply. Nevertheless, that 'mercy killing' by active means is murder was taken for granted in the directions to the jury in *R v Adams (Bodkin)* [1957] Crim LR 365, *R v Arthur* (1981) Times, 5 November, Farquharson J) and *R v Cox* (18 September 1992, unreported), was the subject of direct decision by an appellate court in *Barber v Superior Court of Los Angeles County* (1983) 147 Cal App 3d 1006 and has never so   *f* far as I know been doubted. The fact that the doctor's motives are kindly will for some, although not for all, transform the moral quality of his act, but this makes no difference in law. It is intent to kill or cause grievous bodily harm which constitutes the mens rea of murder, and the reason why the intent was formed makes no difference at all.

9. *Consent to 'mercy killing'* So far as I am aware no satisfactory reason has ever   *g* been advanced for suggesting that it makes the least difference in law, as distinct from morals, if the patient consents to or indeed urges the ending of his life by active means. The reason must be that, as in the other cases of consent to being killed, the interest of the state in preserving life overrides the otherwise all-powerful interest of patient autonomy.   *h*

10. *Acts and omissions* The English criminal law, and also it would appear from the cases cited, the law of transatlantic state jurisdictions, draws a sharp distinction between acts and omissions. If an act resulting in death is done without lawful excuse and with intent to kill it is murder. But an omission to act with the same result and with the same intent is in general no offence at all. So also with lesser crimes. To this general principle there are limited statutory exceptions, irrelevant   *j* here. There is also one important general exception at common law, namely that a person may be criminally liable for the consequences of an omission if he stands in such a relation to the victim that he is under a duty to act. Where the result is death the offence will usually be manslaughter, but if the necessary intent is proved it will be murder: see *R v Gibbins* (1918) 13 Cr App R 134.

Precisely in what circumstances such a duty should be held to exist is at present
a quite unclear. No doubt it would be too stern a morality to place human beings
on the same footing as regards criminal responsibility for allowing an undesirable
state of affairs to continue as for bringing that state of affairs into being, but even
if there is sense in the distinction the current state of the law is unsatisfactory
both morally and intellectually, as shown by the troubling case of *R v Stone* [1977]
2 All ER 341, [1977] QB 354. We cannot however try to put it in order here. For
b the time being all are agreed that the distinction between acts and omissions
exists, and that we must give effect to it.

My Lords, this sketch of the law immediately brings forward two very difficult
questions. The first is this. A doctor who kills his patient even with the consent
of the patient is guilty of murder. Plainly a second doctor who kills his patient in
c circumstances where the obtaining of consent is impracticable cannot be in a
better position than the first, even if the termination of life is in the best interests
of the patient; for the combination of necessity and best interests is no more than
a replacement for consent. How then can best interests legitimate the conduct
proposed in the present case? The second question requires a comparison between
this case and *R v Gibbins*. In the latter the appellant had a helpless person in her
d care; because that person was helpless, she could not furnish herself with
nourishment and was dependent for it on the appellant; the appellant intended
to bring about the death of the helpless person by withholding nourishment; she
did so, and the helpless person died. Of course the cases are miles apart from an
ethical standpoint, but where is the difference on the essential facts?

These and kindred questions have given rise to an extensive and understandably
e contentious literature, and to thoughtful discussions in the courts of the United
States, Canada and New Zealand, and no doubt elsewhere. It is impossible to
study it all, but the sources placed before the House, supplemented by a few
others, have been sufficient to bring out the main lines of the possible arguments.
I gratefully acknowledge the great help which this material has furnished, without
f thinking it necessary to give any but the barest of citation in what follows.

It is convenient now to discuss in turn the grounds upon which it might be
held that, under the existing law, and independently of the intervention of the
court, the doctors may lawfully put the proposed conduct into effect.

III. POTENTIAL DEFENCES

g 1. *Attenuation of the interest in preserving life*
The interest of the state in preserving the lives of its citizens is very strong, but
it is not absolute. There are contrary interests, and sometime these prevail; as
witness the over-mastering effect of the patient's refusal of treatment, even where
this makes death inevitable. It has been suggested, for example in *Re Quinlan*
(1976) 70 NJ 10, that the balance may also be tipped, not by the weight of an
h opposing policy but by the attenuation of the interest in preserving life, where
the 'quality' of the life is diminished by disease or incapacity. My Lords, I would
firmly reject this argument. If correct it would validate active as well as passive
euthanasia, and thus require a change in the law of murder. In any event whilst
the fact that a patient is in great pain may give him or her a powerful motive for
wanting to end it, to which in certain circumstances it is proper to accede, that is
j not at all the same as the proposition that because of incapacity or infirmity one
life is intrinsically worth less than another. This is the first step on a very
dangerous road indeed, and one which I am not willing to take.

2. *The patient's choice*
In the majority of cases where the American courts have sanctioned the

withdrawal of life-supporting medical care they have done so by developing the
rule that informed consent can release the doctor from his duty to treat. For this   *a*
purpose they have founded upon the constitutional rights of the patient, either
the express right of due process or the still developing implied right of privacy. It
is unnecessary to explore whether a similar approach would be appropriate in
England, where constitutional rights play a much less theoretically important
role, for I cannot see that the doctrine has anything to offer in the present case. It
is perhaps sufficient to say that it takes two forms. In the first, the court looks for   *b*
the making of an antecedent choice by a patient who can no longer make one, or
communicate one, by the time that the question of termination has arisen. What
is often called a 'living will' has been held sufficient for this purpose. If no explicit
choice has been made, the courts have on occasion felt able to infer from other
evidence what they believe were the general feelings of the patient about   *c*
termination of life in the case of incurable illness. In any event since there is no
evidence that Anthony Bland ever thought or said anything on the subject the
question of making an imputed choice does not arise. Whilst this course is in
many ways attractive there are obvious dangers which may well be felt to justify
the cautious attitude adopted by the courts of New York State in cases such as *Re
Storar, re Eichner* (1981) 52 NY 2d 363.   *d*
    The second method, which is adopted if the evidence is insufficient to justify
an inference of what the patient chose in the past so that it can be projected to the
present, involves the appointment of a surrogate to make on behalf of the patient
the choice which he believes the patient would now make if able to do so. For
this purpose the surrogate builds up a picture of the patient's former character,
feelings, convictions and so on from which the putative choice is deduced. This   *e*
process may perhaps have some justification where the patient is sentient but
unable to communicate a choice, but it breaks down totally in a case such as the
present. To postulate a patient who is in such a condition that he cannot know
that there is a choice to be made, or indeed know anything at all, and then ask
whether he would have chosen to terminate his life because that condition made   *f*
it no longer worth living is surely meaningless, as is very clearly shown by the
lengths to which the court was driven in *Belchertown State School Superintendent v
Saikewicz* (1977) 373 Mass 728. The idea is simply a fiction, which I would not be
willing to adopt even if there were in the case of Anthony Bland any materials
upon which a surrogate could act, which as far as I can see there are not.

g
3. *Causation*
    One argument in support of the conclusion that if the proposed conduct is
carried out and Anthony Bland then dies the doctors will nevertheless be guilty
of no offence depends upon a very special application of the doctrine of causation.
This has powerful academic support: Skegg *Law, Ethics and Medicine* (1985) ch 6,
where it represents the author's chosen solution, and also Glanville Williams   *h*
Textbook of Criminal Law (2nd edn, 1983) pp 282–283 and Professor Ian Kennedy's
paper *Treat me Right, Essays in Medical Law and Ethics* (1988) pp 360–361, where it
is offered by way of alternative. Nevertheless I find it hard to grasp. At several
stages of his discussion Professor Skegg frankly accepts that some manipulation of
the law of causation will be needed to produce the desired result. I am bound to
say that the argument seems to me to require not manipulation of the law so   *j*
much as its application in an entirely new and illogical way. In one form the
argument presented to the House asserts that for the purpose of both civil and
criminal liability the cause of Anthony Bland's death, if and when it takes place,
will be the Hillsborough disaster. As a matter of the criminal law of causation

this may well be right, once it is assumed that the conduct is lawful: see *R v Blaue*
[1975] 3 All ER 446, [1975] 1 WLR 1411, *R v Malcherek* [1981] 2 All ER 422,
[1981] 1 WLR 690 and *Finlayson v HM Advocate* 1979 JC 33. It does not perhaps
follow that the conduct of the doctors is not also causative, but this is of no interest
since if the conduct is lawful the doctors have nothing to worry about. If on the
other hand the proposed conduct is unlawful, then it is in the same case as active
euthanasia or any other unlawful act by doctors or laymen. In common sense
they must all be causative or none; and it must be all, for otherwise euthanasia
would never be murder.

A variant of the argument appears to put the ordinary law of causation into
reverse. Normally, when faced with an act and a suggested consequence one
begins by ascertaining the quality of the act and then, if it is found to be unlawful,
one considers its connection to the consequence. This variant, by contrast, seems
to begin the inquiry with the connection and then by applying a special rule of
causation determine the character of the act. I confess that I cannot understand
what mechanism enables this to be done. If the declarations are wrong and the
proposed conduct is unlawful it is in my judgment perfectly obvious that the
conduct will be, as it is intended to be, the cause of death, and nothing in the
literature or the reported cases from other jurisdictions persuades me to any other
conclusion. I should add that, although part of the thoughtful judgment of
Thomas J in the High Court of New Zealand in *Auckland Area Health Board v A-G*
[1993] 1 NZLR 235 discusses the question of causation, the main thrust of the
reasoning was aimed elsewhere, towards a solution which is broadly in line with
the one which all your Lordships have preferred.

4. Best interests of the community

Threaded through the technical arguments addressed to the House were the
strands of a much wider position, that it is in the best interests of the community
at large that Anthony Bland's life should now end. The doctors have done all they
can. Nothing will be gained by going on and much will be lost. The distress of
the family will get steadily worse. The strain on the devotion of a medical staff
charged with the care of a patient whose condition will never improve, who may
live for years and who does not even recognise that he is being cared for, will
continue to mount. The large resources of skill, labour and money now being
devoted to Anthony Bland might in the opinion of many be more fruitfully
employed in improving the condition of other patients, who if treated may have
useful, healthy and enjoyable lives for years to come.

This argument was never squarely put, although hinted at from time to time.
In social terms it has great force, and it will have to be faced in the end. But this
is not a task which the courts can possibly undertake. A social cost-benefit analysis
of this kind, which would have to embrace 'mercy killing', to which exactly the
same considerations apply, must be for Parliament alone, and the outcome of it is
at present quite impossible to foresee. Until the nettle is grasped we must struggle
on with the existing law, imperfect as it is.

5. Best interests: the termination of life

An alternative approach is to develop the reasoning of *F v West Berkshire Health
Authority* [1989] 2 All ER 545, [1990] 2 AC 1 by concentrating on the best
interests, not of the community at large, but of Anthony Bland himself. Just as in
F v West Berkshire Health Authority, so the argument runs, the best interests of the
patient demand a course of action which would normally be unlawful without
the patient's consent. Just as in *F v West Berkshire Health Authority* the patient is

unable to decide for himself. In practice, to make no decision is to decide that the care and treatment shall continue. So that the decision shall not thus be made by a default it is necessary that someone other than Anthony Bland should consider whether in his own best interests his life should now be brought to an end, and if the answer is affirmative the proposed conduct can be put into effect without risk of criminal responsibility.

I cannot accept this argument, which, if sound, would serve to legitimate a termination by much more direct means than are now contemplated. I can accept that a doctor in charge of a patient suffering the mental torture of Guillain-Barré syndrome, rational but trapped and mute in an unresponsive body, could well feel it imperative that a decision on whether to terminate life could wait no longer and that the only possible decision in the interests of the patient, even leaving out all the other interests involved, would be to end it here and now by a speedy and painless injection. Such a conclusion would attract much sympathy, but no doctrine of best interests could bring it within the law.

Quite apart from this the case of Anthony Bland seems to me quite different. He feels no pain and suffers no mental anguish. Stress was laid in argument on the damage to his personal dignity by the continuation of the present medical regime, and on the progressive erosion of the family's happy recollections by month after month of distressing and hopeless care. Considerations of this kind will no doubt carry great weight when Parliament comes to consider the whole question in the round. But it seems to me to be stretching the concept of personal rights beyond breaking point to say that Anthony Bland has an interest in ending these sources of others' distress. Unlike the conscious patient he does not know what is happening to his body, and cannot be affronted by it; he does not know of his family's continuing sorrow. By ending his life the doctors will not relieve him of a burden become intolerable, for others carry the burden and he has none. What other considerations could make it better for him to die now rather than later? None that we can measure, for of death we know nothing. The distressing truth which must not be shirked is that the proposed conduct is not in the best interests of Anthony Bland, for he has no best interests of any kind.

6. *Best interests: the termination of treatment*

After much expression of negative opinions I turn to an argument which in my judgment is logically defensible and consistent with the existing law. In essence it turns the previous argument on its head by directing the inquiry to the interests of the patient, not in the termination of life but in the continuation of his treatment. It runs as follows. (i) The cessation of nourishment and hydration is an omission not an act. (ii) Accordingly, the cessation will not be a criminal act unless the doctors are under a present duty to continue the regime. (iii) At the time when Anthony Bland came into the care of the doctors decisions had to be made about his care which he was unable to make for himself. In accordance with *F v West Berkshire Health Authority* [1989] 2 All ER 545, [1990] 2 AC 1 these decisions were to be made in his best interests. Since the possibility that he might recover still existed his best interests required that he should be supported in the hope that this would happen. These best interests justified the application of the necessary regime without his consent. (iv) All hope of recovery has now been abandoned. Thus, although the termination of his life is not in the best interests of Anthony Bland, his best interests in being kept alive have also disappeared, taking with them the justification for the non-consensual regime and the correlative duty to keep it in being. (v) Since there is no longer a duty to provide nourishment and hydration a failure to do so cannot be a criminal offence.

My Lords, I must recognise at once that this chain of reasoning makes an
a unpromising start by transferring the morally and intellectually dubious
distinction between acts and omissions into a context where the ethical
foundations of the law are already open to question. The opportunity for anomaly
and excessively fine distinctions, often depending more on the way in which the
problem happens to be stated than on any real distinguishing features, has been
exposed by many commentators, including in England the authors above-
b mentioned, together with Smith and Hogan *Criminal Law* (6th edn, 1988) p 51,
Beynon 'Doctors as murderers' [1982] Crim LR 17 and Gunn and Smith '*Arthur's*
case and the right to life of a Down's syndrome child' [1985] Crim LR 705. All
this being granted, we are still forced to take the law as we find it and try to make
it work. Moreover, although in cases near the borderline the categorisation of
conduct will be exceedingly hard, I believe that nearer the periphery there will be
c many instances which fall quite clearly into one category rather than the other.
In my opinion the present is such a case, and in company with Compton J in
Barber v Superior Court of Los Angeles County (1983) 147 Cal App 3d 1006 at 1017
amongst others I consider that the proposed conduct will fall into the category of
omissions.

d   I therefore consider the argument to be soundly based. Now that the time has
come when Anthony Bland has no further interest in being kept alive, the
necessity to do so, created by his inability to make a choice, has gone; and the
justification for the invasive care and treatment together with the duty to provide
it have also gone. Absent a duty, the omission to perform what had previously
been a duty will no longer be a breach of the criminal law.

e   In reaching this conclusion I have taken into account the fact that, whereas for
almost all concerned the adoption of the proposed course will be a merciful relief,
this will not be so for the nursing staff, who will be called on to act in a way which
must be contrary to all their instincts, training and traditions. They will encounter
the ethical problems, not in a court or in a lecture room, but face to face. As the
United Kingdom Council for Nursing Midwifery and Health Visiting has
f emphasised, for the nurses involved the interval between the initiation of the
proposed conduct and the death of Anthony Bland will be a very stressful period.
Acknowledging this, I hope that the nurses will accept, as I believe, that sadly it is
for the best.

For these reasons I would uphold the declarations. Whilst there is no need to
g go further it is better to mention one further point. The reasoning which I
propose is, I believe, broadly in line with that of your Lordships. But I venture to
feel some reservations about the application of the principle of civil liability in
negligence laid down in *Bolam v Friern Hospital Management Committee* [1957] 2
All ER 118, [1957] 1 WLR 582 to decisions on 'best interests' in a field dominated
by the criminal law. I accept without difficulty that this principle applies to the
h ascertainment of the medical raw material such as diagnosis, prognosis and
appraisal of the patient's cognitive functions. Beyond this point, however, it may
be said that the decision is ethical, not medical, and that there is no reason in logic
why on such a decision the opinions of doctors should be decisive. If there had
been a possibility that this question might make a difference to the outcome of
the appeal I would have wished to consider it further, but since it does not I prefer
j for the moment to express no opinion upon it.

IV. THE ETHICAL QUESTION

After discussing the legal issues at length I will deal only briefly with the ethical
question, which must be for most lay people what the case is really about. With

the general tenor, if not with the details, of what was said in the courts below I
respectfully agree. But, I prefer to advance on a narrower front. In law, if my　*a*
conclusion is right, the way is clear for the doctors to proceed as they and the
family think best. If the principle of *Bolam* applies that is the end of the matter,
since nobody could doubt that a body of reasonable medical opinion would regard
the proposed conduct as right. But, even if *Bolam* is left aside, I still believe that
the proposed conduct is ethically justified, since the continued treatment of
Anthony Bland can no longer serve to maintain that combination of manifold　*b*
characteristics which we call a personality. Some who have written on this subject
maintain that this is too narrow a perspective, so I must make it clear that I do not
assert that the human condition necessarily consists of nothing except a
personality, or deny that it may also comprise a spiritual essence distinct from
both body and personality. But of this we can know nothing, and in particular
we cannot know whether it perishes with death or transcends it. Absent such　*c*
knowledge we must measure up what we do know. So doing, I have no doubt
that the best interests of Anthony Bland no longer demand the continuance of his
present care and treatment. This is not at all to say that I would reach the same
conclusion in less extreme cases, where the glimmerings of awareness may give
the patient an interest which cannot be regarded as null. The issues, both legal　*d*
and ethical, will then be altogether more difficult. As Mr Munby has pointed out,
in this part of the law the court has moved a long way in a short time. Every step
forward requires the greatest caution. Here however I am satisfied that what is
proposed, and what all those who have considered the matter believe to be right,
is in accordance with the law.

My Lords, having said this I must admit to having felt profound misgivings　*e*
about almost every aspect of this case. I will not rehearse them. I need only say
that I entirely agree with and adopt everything said by my noble and learned
friend Lord Browne-Wilkinson at the conclusion of his judgment.

I would dismiss this appeal.

Appeal dismissed. No order as to costs.　　　　　　　　　　　　　　　　　　　　　　　*f*

Mary Rose Plummer　Barrister.

a # Joyce v Sengupta and another

COURT OF APPEAL, CIVIL DIVISION
SIR DONALD NICHOLLS V-C, BUTLER-SLOSS LJ AND SIR MICHAEL KERR
23, 24 JUNE, 31 JULY 1992

b *Malicious falsehood – Libel and slander – Choice of action – Defendant making false statement about plaintiff – Plaintiff choosing to sue for malicious falsehood rather than defamation – Legal aid available for action for malicious falsehood but not for action for defamation – Defendant not entitled to jury trial as of right in action for malicious falsehood – Whether plaintiff having choice of action – Whether malicious falsehood and defamation incompatible causes of action – Defamation Act 1952, s 3.*

c

Malicious falsehood – Damages – Nature of damages recoverable – Damages for anxiety and distress – Aggravated damages – Whether plaintiff who is unable to prove any compensatable pecuniary loss restricted to nominal damages – Whether damages for anxiety and distress or aggravated damages recoverable for malicious falsehood – Defamation Act 1952, s 3.

d

The defendants published on the front page of their newspaper an article written by the first defendant, who was their chief crime correspondent, about the alleged theft of letters from the Princess Royal by a lady's maid employed by her. The article, which was based on police suspicions, clearly referred to the plaintiff and *e* contained several assertions regarding her, in particular that she had stolen the Princess Royal's intimate letters, that she had handed the letters to a national newspaper, that she had been ordered not to go into rooms where there might be confidential papers and that she had been or was about to be dismissed. Those assertions were in fact false. Instead of suing for defamation, for which legal aid was not available, the plaintiff issued a writ against the defendants claiming *f* damages for malicious falsehood and obtained legal aid to pursue her claim. The defendants applied to strike out the statement of claim as an abuse of process. The judge struck out the claim on the ground that the case could not be pleaded properly as malicious falsehood because it was in essence a case of libel. The plaintiff appealed.

g **Held** – Since a plaintiff could choose which cause of action he wished to pursue when more than one cause of action was available to him, a person who was the subject of a defamatory article was entitled to bring an action for malicious falsehood with the assistance of legal aid instead of defamation, notwithstanding that legal aid was not available in defamation cases or that, unlike a defamation *h* action, the defendant was not entitled to jury trial as of right in an action for malicious falsehood, or that the damages recoverable in an action for malicious falsehood could be insignificant compared to the costs involved. In order to succeed in a claim for malicious falsehood the plaintiff had to establish that the defendant had maliciously made a false statement which had caused him damage or in respect of which he was relieved from proving damage by s 3[a] of the *j* Defamation Act 1952 because the words complained of were calculated to cause the plaintiff pecuniary damage. Since the plaintiff's statement of claim raised an arguable claim for malicious falsehood she was entitled to pursue her claim even though had legal aid been available the action would have been a straightforward

---

a   Section 3, so far as material, is set out at p 905 *j* to p 906 *a*, post

defamation action. The appeal would therefore be allowed and the action reinstated (see p 901 *c* to *e*, p 902 *b* to *g j*, p 903 *c d*, p 904 *b e* to *g*, p 905 *a c*, p 908 *d e* and p 910 *d*, post).   **a**

Per curiam. A plaintiff who relies on s 3 of 1952 Act because he is unable to prove any compensatable pecuniary loss is not thereby restricted to nominal damages (see p 906 *d* to *f* and p 908 *e f*, post).

Per Sir Michael Kerr. There is no reason why aggravated damages should not be recoverable for the tort of malicious falsehood either in addition to special **b** pecuniary loss where that has been pleaded and proved or as general damages where the plaintiff relies on s 3 of 1952 Act (see p 910 *c* and p 911 *h j*, post).

Quaere. Whether damages for anxiety and distress are recoverable for malicious falsehood (see p 907 *c d g* to *j*, p 908 *c e*, p 910 *e f*, p 911 *j* to p 912 *a*, post).

Notes   **c**
For malicious falsehood, see 28 *Halsbury's Laws* (4th edn) paras 265, 272.

For the Defamation Act 1952, s 3, see 24 *Halsbury's Statutes* (4th edn) (1989 reissue) 109.

Cases referred to in judgments   **d**
Associated Provincial Picture Houses Ltd v Wednesday Corp [1947] 2 All ER 680, [1948] 1 KB 223, CA.
Bracegirdle v Orford (1813) 2 M & S 77, 105 ER 311.
Calvet v Tomkies [1963] 3 All ER 610, [1963] 1 WLR 1397, CA.
Davis v Bromley UDC (1903) 67 JP 275, CA.
Fielding v Variety Inc [1967] 2 All ER 497, [1967] 2 QB 841, [1967] 3 WLR 415, **e**
   CA.
Huxley v Berg (1815) 1 Stark 98, 171 ER 413.
Lynch v Knight (1861) 9 HL Cas 577, 11 ER 854.
Marshall (W F) Ltd v Barnes & Fitzpatrick (a firm) [1953] 1 All ER 970, [1953] 1
   WLR 639.
Pratt v British Medical Association [1919] 1 KB 244, [1918–19] All ER Rep 104.   **f**
Quinn v Leathem [1901] AC 495, [1900–3] All ER Rep 1, HL.
Rookes v Barnard [1964] 1 All ER 367, [1964] AC 1129, [1964] 2 WLR 269, HL.
Rothermere v Times Newspapers Ltd [1973] 1 All ER 1013, [1973] 1 WLR 448, CA.
Royal Baking Powder Co v Wright Crossley & Co (1900) 18 RPC 95, HL.
Sutcliffe v Pressdram Ltd [1990] 1 All ER 269, [1991] 1 QB 153, [1990] 2 WLR 271,
   CA.   **g**

Cases also cited or referred to in skeleton arguments
Ashmore v British Coal Corp [1990] 2 All ER 981, [1990] 2 QB 338, CA.
Balden v Shorter [1933] Ch 427, [1933] All ER Rep 249.
Derbyshire CC v Times Newspapers Ltd [1992] 3 All ER 65, [1992] QB 770, CA. **h**
Goldsmith v Sperrings Ltd [1977] 2 All ER 566, [1977] 1 WLR 478, CA.
Greers Ltd v Pearman & Corder Ltd (1922) 39 RPC 406, KBD and CA.
Halsey v Brotherhood (1881) 19 Ch D 386, CA.
Horrocks v Lowe [1974] 1 All ER 662, [1975] AC 135, HL.
Kaye v Robertson [1991] FSR 62, CA.
Lawrance v Lord Norreys (1890) 15 App Cas 210, [1886–90] All ER Rep 858, HL. **j**
Ratcliffe v Evans [1892] 2 QB 524, [1891–4] All ER Rep 699, CA.
Remmington v Scoles [1897] 2 Ch 1, [1895–99] All ER Rep 1095, Ch D and CA.
Shapiro v La Morta (1923) 40 TLR 39; *affd* 130 LT 622, [1923] All ER Rep 378,
   CA.

Slipper v BBC [1991] 1 All ER 165, [1991] 1 QB 283, CA.
a *Smith & Fawcett Ltd, Re* [1942] 1 All ER 542, [1942] Ch 304, CA.
Steamship Mutual Underwriting Association Ltd v Trollope & Colls (City) Ltd (1986) 6 Con LR 11, CA.
Strix Ltd v Otter Controls Ltd [1991] FSR 354, CA.
Wenlock v Moloney [1965] 2 All ER 871, [1965] 1 WLR 1238, CA.
Willis v Earl Howe [1893] 2 Ch 545, CA.
b

Interlocutory appeal

The plaintiff, Linda Karen Joyce, appealed from the judgment of Gilbert Gray QC sitting as a deputy judge of the High Court in the Queen's Bench Division on 12 December 1990 whereby he struck out the plaintiff's statement of claim in her *c* action claiming damages against the defendants, Kim Sengupta and News (UK) Ltd, for malicious falsehood and dismissed the action. The facts are set out in the judgment of Sir Donald Nicholls V-C.

Geoffrey Robertson QC and *Andrew Nicol* (instructed by *Stephens Innocent*) for the plaintiff.
d *Desmond Browne QC* (instructed by *Theodore Goddard*) for the defendants.

Cur adv vult

31 July 1992. The following judgments were delivered.

e **SIR DONALD NICHOLLS V-C.** In 1989 Miss Linda Joyce was employed by Her Royal Highness the Princess Royal as her lady's maid. On 25 April the Today newspaper published an eye-catching article written by its chief crime correspondent, Mr Kim Sengupta. The banner headlines on the front page read 'ROYAL MAID STOLE LETTERS' and 'Sacked as Anne names the culprit'. The material *f* part of the article read:

> 'The thief who stole Princess Anne's intimate letters has been tracked down by police. She is a royal maid who has been interviewed by detectives four times. The Princess had told police that she believed the maid was the culprit and that she acted out of spite when she handed the four letters, written by the Queen's Equerry, to a national newspaper. After the theft, Anne *g* immediately ordered that the maid should not go into rooms where there might be confidential papers. The servant, who is unmarried, will now be dismissed from royal service. As TODAY revealed two weeks ago, she will not be prosecuted. Buckingham Palace has told Scotland Yard that the Queen does not want the adverse publicity a court case will inevitably bring. But *h* the maid will have to give a written guarantee that she will not discuss the sensitive letters from Commander Tim Laurence either in Britain or abroad. The woman, who has travelled abroad on royal tours, has repeatedly denied the allegation despite intense grilling by the Yard's Serious Crime Squad under Det Chief Supt Roy Ramm. Her fingerprints were taken at Anne's home, Gatcombe Park in Gloucestershire, and will now be compared with *j* forensic clues from the intimate notes. The results will be known within a week. Police have discovered that the maid had been on bad terms with the Princess for a long time. Anne had told her off several times. The maid has also complained to colleagues about poor pay and conditions. A senior detective said: "This appears to be a classic case of a woman who feels she has

been wronged. We have little doubt she is the guilty party and are now
awaiting forensic confirmation. Even if we get the proof we cannot prosecute.
The matter will be decided behind closed doors by the Palace."'

The article clearly referred to the plaintiff, and it contained several assertions
regarding her. In particular, the article said she had stolen her royal employer's
intimate letters, she had handed the letters to a national newspaper, she had been
ordered not to go into rooms where there might be confidential papers and she
had been or was about to be dismissed.

One might expect that proceedings for libel would have followed. The article
was grossly defamatory. The newspaper did not publish any retraction or
apologise, although it has not sought to say that the assertions of fact were true.
However, there was a difficulty confronting the plaintiff. She did not have the
money needed to pursue proceedings at her own expense, and legal aid is not
available for defamation proceedings. There is an express provision to this effect
in the Legal Aid Act 1988 (see Sch 2, Pt II, para 1).

Nothing daunted, the plaintiff's legal advisers formulated a claim against Mr
Sengupta and News (UK) Ltd, the publisher of the newspaper, for malicious
falsehood. In law this is a different cause of action, with different ingredients,
from a claim for defamation. Unlike defamation, malicious falsehood is a type of
proceedings for which legal aid is available. Legal aid to bring proceedings for
malicious falsehood was granted to the plaintiff, and this action followed. A writ
was issued on 31 August 1990, and the statement of claim was served on 21
September. The defendants then applied to strike out the statement of claim as
an abuse of the process of the court. On 12 December 1990 Mr Gilbert Gray QC,
sitting as a deputy judge of the High Court in the Queen's Bench Division,
acceded to that application. He decided that a case of defamation had been forced
into the ill-fitting garb of an action for malicious falsehood. The case could not be
pleaded properly as malicious falsehood because it was in essence a case of libel.
From that decision the plaintiff has now appealed.

The plaintiff's claim
The plaintiff seeks an opportunity to amend her statement of claim, so I work
from the latest version of the proposed amendments. Miss Joyce's case is that the
article contains several serious untruths regarding her: contrary to what is said in
the article, she did not steal the letters, she was not banned from rooms containing
confidential documents, she was not dismissed in consequence, she was not
required to undertake that she would not discuss the letters and she was not on
bad terms with the Princess. She has left her employment with Princess Anne.
She did so on 5 May 1989, following a letter of resignation written months earlier
in January 1989, but her resignation was for personal reasons unconnected with
the statements in the Today article.

Miss Joyce asserts that the article was published maliciously: Mr Sengupta who
wrote the article and the sub-editor who chose the headline 'ROYAL MAID STOLE
LETTERS' were recklessly indifferent about the truth or falsity of the serious
allegations. Mr Sengupta took no steps to check the police suspicions on which he
says he relied; he did not speak to the plaintiff, he made no independent
investigations, he did not even await the outcome of the fingerprint tests
mentioned in the article.

Miss Joyce claims damages. The article falsely portrays her as untrustworthy.
This has damaged her future employment prospects. She also claims exemplary
damages, and an injunction against repetition.

Malicious falsehood and defamation

a   Before turning to the issues raised by the appeal I should comment briefly on the difference between defamation and malicious falsehood. The remedy provided by the law for words which injure a person's reputation is defamation. Words may also injure a person without damaging his reputation. An example would be a claim that the seller of goods or land is not the true owner. Another example would be a false assertion that a person has closed down his business. Such claims

b   would not necessarily damage the reputation of those concerned. The remedy provided for this is malicious falsehood, sometimes called injurious falsehood or trade libel. This cause of action embraces particular types of malicious falsehood such as slander of title and slander of goods, but it is not confined to those headings.

c   Falsity is an essential ingredient of this tort. The plaintiff must establish the untruth of the statement of which he complains. Malice is another essential ingredient. A genuine dispute about the ownership of goods or land should not of itself be actionable. So a person who acted in good faith is not liable. Further, since the object of this cause of action is to provide a person with a remedy for a false statement made maliciously which has caused him damage, at common law

d   proof of financial loss was another essential ingredient. The rigour of this requirement was relaxed by statute. I shall have to return to the question of damages at a later stage. For present purposes it is sufficient to note that if a plaintiff establishes that the defendant maliciously made a false statement which has caused him financial damage, or in respect of which he is relieved from proving damage by the Defamation Act 1952, the law gives him a remedy. The

e   false statement may also be defamatory, or it may not. As already mentioned, it need not be defamatory. Conversely, the fact that the statement is defamatory does not exclude a cause of action for malicious falsehood, although the law will ensure that a plaintiff does not recover damages twice over for the same loss.

f   *Abuse of process: (1) no right to trial by jury*

It is as plain as a pikestaff that, had legal aid been available for libel, this action would have been a straightforward defamation action. In an action for malicious falsehood the plaintiff has to take on the burden of proving that the words were false and that in publishing them the defendant was actuated by malice. It would make no sense for Miss Joyce to take on this burden. If this had been a defamation

g   action she would not have to prove malice, and if the newspaper wished to put in issue the truth of the defamatory assertions it would have to plead and prove justification as a defence.

One consequence of this action being a claim for malicious falsehood and not defamation is that there is no absolute right to a trial by jury. With certain

h   exceptions not applicable to this case, either party to an action has a right to have the action tried with a jury where there is in issue a claim in respect of libel, slander, malicious prosecution or false imprisonment (see s 69(1) of the Supreme Court Act 1981). In cases outside s 69(1) there is no such right, although the court retains a discretion to order trial with jury. Counsel for the defendants submitted that trial by jury in defamation actions is a constitutional right of newspapers. He

j   reminded us of the observation of Lord Denning MR in *Rothermere v Times Newspapers Ltd* [1973] 1 All ER 1013 at 1017, [1973] 1 WLR 448 at 452 that every defendant who is charged with libel, either in criminal or civil proceedings, has a 'constitutional right to have his guilt or innocence determined by a jury'. In *Sutcliffe v Pressdram Ltd* [1990] 1 All ER 269 at 286, [1991] 1 QB 153 at 181

Nourse LJ referred to 'the primacy of the jury' in defamation cases and that this
had been settled by the Libel Act 1792 (Fox's Act).   *a*

Against this background counsel submitted that the present action should be
struck out by the court as an abuse of process because it is based on a secondary
tort which deprives the defendants of their absolute right to have a jury trial.
This right is a legitimate juridical advantage they would have had if the plaintiff
had relied on the primary tort. By a 'secondary tort' was meant a tort which
would not be relied upon save for the plaintiff's need to secure a collateral purpose   *b*
unrelated to the merits of her claim.

I am not able to accept this submission. The concept of a legitimate juridical
advantage has been taken from the field of conflict of laws where an issue arises
over the country in which a dispute between the parties should be determined.
The issue there concerns which of two countries, with their different laws and
legal systems, would be the more appropriate forum.   *c*

I can see no place for that concept in wholly domestic proceedings. English law
has marked out causes of action on which plaintiffs may rely. Many causes of
action overlap. On one set of facts a plaintiff may have more than one cause of
action against a defendant. He may have a cause of action in tort and also for
breach of contract. This is an everyday occurrence with some claims for   *d*
negligence, or with claims for breach of confidence. Again, a plaintiff may have a
cause of action for breach of contract and for breach of fiduciary duty. This also is
a frequent occurrence with claims against directors of companies. Or a plaintiff
may have more than one cause of action in tort: a factory accident may give rise
to a claim in negligence and for breach of statutory duty. These instances could
be multiplied. When more than one cause of action is available to him, a plaintiff   *e*
may choose which he will pursue. Usually he pursues all available causes of
action, but he is not obliged to do so. He may pursue one to the exclusion of
another, even though a defence available in one cause of action is not available in
another. Indeed, the availability of a defence in one cause of action but not
another may be the very reason why a plaintiff eschews the one and prefers the
other. Limitation is an example of such a defence. I have never heard it suggested   *f*
before that a plaintiff is not entitled to proceed in this way, and take full advantage
of the various remedies English law provides for the wrong of which he complains.
I have never heard it suggested that he must pursue the most appropriate remedy,
and if he does not do so he is at risk of having his proceedings struck out as a
misuse of the court's procedures. In my view those suggestions are as unfounded   *g*
as they are novel.

I add one further comment regarding the particular context of defamation
actions and trial by jury. I shall return to the question of legal aid. Legal aid apart,
there is no reason to suppose that in future persons who are the subject of
defamatory articles in newspapers will be queuing up to issue writs for malicious
falsehood. It would make no sense for them to do so, and take on the burden of   *h*
proving malice and, if successful, still not be able to recover damages for loss of
reputation.

I return to the present case and add this. The plaintiff is not seeking to avoid a
trial by jury. That is not the reason why there is no claim for defamation. As it is,
the court retains a discretion to order that the action be tried with a jury. Through
her counsel the plaintiff has said she would not oppose any application the   *j*
defendants may wish to make for a jury in this case. I can detect no improper use
of the court's process by the plaintiff.

Abuse of process: (2) 'economic lunacy' and legal aid
Mr Browne QC's second submission was as bold as his first. He submitted that

another reason why this action is an abuse is that only nominal damages, or at
a best modest damages of a few hundred pounds, will be recoverable by the
plaintiff. The amount she stands to obtain is wholly out of line with the costs each
side will incur. In practice the defendants will never recover their costs even if
they are successful in defending the action and even if they make a payment into
court of an amount in excess of any damages awarded at the trial. Mr Browne
submitted that, so far as the plaintiff is concerned, the action is 'economic lunacy',
b given that any damages awarded to her will be swallowed up by the Legal Aid
Board's charge over them as property recovered in the proceedings. Public funds
are being used to support the plaintiff in a wholly uneconomic way.

With all respect to counsel, this a hopeless submission. I shall consider later the
question of damages. For the moment let me assume that the defendants are
c correct in submitting that the plaintiff is unlikely to recover more than a few
hundred pounds in damages. I shall make that assumption although I am not to
be taken as indorsing it. Even so I do not see how it follows that this action should
be struck out as an abuse. The plaintiff's main purpose in bringing this action is
to clear her name. If she wins, she will succeed in doing so. Compared with a
libel action, the amount of damages she may recover in malicious falsehood may
d be small, but there is no reason why she should not be entitled to pursue such a
claim. I see no justification for the court stopping her action. The defendants, it
must be borne in mind, are resisting her claim in its entirety. The prospect that
they are unlikely to recoup their costs even if their defence is wholly successful is
an unfortunate fact of everyday life for many defendants when sued by legally
aided plaintiffs.

e The reality here is that the defendants are unhappy that the plaintiff has
obtained legal aid to pursue the action. They fear that if this action is permitted
to proceed, the floodgates will be opened. The Legal Aid Board will be flooded
with applications for legal aid to pursue claims for malicious falsehood against
newspapers. Newspapers will be faced with the prospect, not intended by
Parliament, of legally aided plaintiffs pursuing claims against them founded on
f defamatory articles.

As to these fears, it is vital to keep in mind that the decision on whether or not
to grant legal aid has been entrusted by Parliament to the Legal Aid Board, not
the court. Parliament has prescribed a framework of limitations and conditions
but the Legal Aid Board retains a discretion. A person whose financial resources
g make him eligible for legal aid must satisfy the board that he has reasonable
grounds for taking, defending or being a party to the proceedings (see s 15(2) of
the Legal Aid Act 1988). He may be refused representation if in the particular
circumstances of the case it appears to the board unreasonable he should be
granted representation (see s 15(3)). Representation may be granted with or
without limitations and may be amended, withdrawn or revoked (see s 15(4)).
h Regulation 28 of the Civil Legal Aid (General) Regulations 1989, SI 1989/339, as
substituted by reg 10 of the Civil Legal Aid (General) (Amendment) (No 2)
Regulations 1991, SI 1991/2036, underscores the duty of the area director to
consider the overall merits of each case:

> '(1) Without prejudice to the generality of sections 15(2) . . . of the Act . . .
j an application for a certificate shall only be approved after the Area Director
> has considered all the questions of fact or law arising in the action, cause or
> matter to which the application relates and the circumstances in which the
> application was made . . .'

These provisions show that in reaching its decision the board takes into account
a wide range of factors. One factor is the probable cost of the proceedings (see

W F Marshall Ltd v Barnes & Fitzpatrick (a firm) [1953] 1 All ER 970 at 978, [1953] a
1 WLR 639 at 649). Another is that it may be unreasonable for legal aid to be
continued if a legally assisted plaintiff refuses to accept a reasonable offer or a
payment made into court by a defendant. In the present case a further factor to
be taken into account by the board is the policy underlying the legislature's
exclusion of proceedings wholly or partly in respect of defamation from the scope
of civil legal aid. These factors are material to the board's decision, but they are
not material to a decision by the court on whether to permit a properly constituted b
action to proceed to trial or to stop it summarily as a misuse of the court's
processes.

If the defendants consider legal aid should not have been granted in this case
one course open to them is to take up the matter with the Legal Aid Board. This
is commonly done by unassisted parties. Frequently an unassisted defendant goes c
to the board and asks for a legal aid certificate to be revoked when a legally assisted
plaintiff has declined a reasonable offer. Further, if these defendants consider they
have grounds for contending that the board misdirected itself or that the decision
to grant legal aid was unreasonable in the *Wednesbury* sense (see *Associated
Provincial Picture Houses Ltd v Wednesbury Corp* [1947] 2 All ER 680, [1948] 1 KB
223), an application for judicial review of the board's decision is another course d
open to them. Those are remedies available to the defendants with regard to the
board's decision.

I hasten to add that I do not mention these points with a view to encouraging
the defendants to challenge the board's decision. I am not to be taken as hinting
that the board's decision was erroneous. I express no view either way on that
matter. I mention these points only because it is important to appreciate that the e
defendants' submission raises two distinct questions; one of these questions is
before us on this appeal and the other is not. One question is whether legal aid
should have been granted. That question is not before us. The other question is
whether, legal aid having been granted, this action should be permitted to
continue even if, as the defendants assert, at most only modest damages will be f
recoverable. On this second question the fact that the plaintiff is legally aided is
neither here nor there. In general the rights conferred on assisted persons by the
Legal Aid Act 1988—

> 'shall not affect the rights or liabilities of other parties to the proceedings
> or the principles on which the discretion of any court or tribunal is normally
> exercised.' (See s 31(1)(*b*).) g

Once this is appreciated, there is nothing left of the defendants' second submission.

Abuse of process: (3) the action is bound to fail
The defendant's third submission was that the action is incapable of success and
should be struck out summarily. The jurisdiction the defendants invoke here is h
well established. The court will not permit an action to go to trial if plainly and
obviously it cannot succeed. But when exercising this jurisdiction the court is
careful not to conduct a summary trial on affidavit evidence without the benefit
of discovery of documents and cross-examination of witnesses on disputed
questions of fact. If there is an issue or dispute that ought to be tried, the action
must go to trial. j

Whether this action is bound to fail turns on a consideration of the statement
of claim and the affidavit evidence. I approach this issue having in mind that, but
for the legal aid complication, this would be a defamation action. It is right to
scrutinise the allegations of malice and damage with particular care.

So far as the statement of claim is concerned I am satisfied that, although open
a to criticism here and there, it does disclose the essentials of a cause of action for
malicious falsehood. It is susceptible to a request for further particulars in some
respects, but the omissions are not so serious or incapable of being made good
that the defendants will be embarrassed in the conduct of their defence.

The judge took a different view. He considered that the particulars of malice
were hopelessly inadequate, but he had before him an earlier version of the
b statement of claim. The draftsman of the pleading has taken note of the criticisms,
and the draft before us reflects this. Essentially, the plaintiff's case on malice is
that the defendants went ahead and published the police suspicions as though
they were fact and did so without taking any steps to check or verify them. This
showed a calculated, reckless indifference to the truth or falsity of the allegations.
Malice is to be inferred from the grossness and falsity of the assertions and the
c cavalier way they were published. In my view the pleading raises an arguable
issue, and it does so in terms sufficient to inform the defendants of the case against
them.

I turn to the evidence. Mr Sengupta has made an affidavit setting out the
circumstances in which he wrote the article. He refers to conversations with
d senior police officers. The police told him they were convinced Miss Joyce had
stolen the letters. Mr Sengupta tried to reach her on the telephone but was unable
to do so. He had no antipathy to her. He honestly believed that what he wrote
was true. There are other affidavits produced by the defendants, including one
from the editor of Today. The judge seems to have proceeded on the footing that
he should accept this affidavit evidence when there was no affidavit evidence on
e the other side about Mr Sengupta's state of mind. I think the judge fell into error
on this. The plaintiff does not accept the accuracy of Mr Sengupta's evidence. In
the nature of things she is not in a position to produce evidence to the contrary
effect. That should not deprive her of the opportunity to question Mr Sengupta,
with a view to persuading the judge or jury that he is not to be believed. In some
cases a plaintiff's case will be so weak that a trial is not necessary, but that is not
f this case. Indeed, had this been a libel action in which a plea of malice had been
raised, I do not believe the defendants would have attempted to strike out the plea
summarily as one which was bound to fail at trial.

The other matter which weighed with the judge concerned the damage alleged
in the statement of claim. He was impressd by the plaintiff's letter of resignation.
g It was clear she had decided that her days as a private personal maid to other
ladies, no matter of what status or high degree, were finished. She had indicated
her desire to leave service as a ladies' maid before the article was published. This
was inconsistent with publication of the article having caused her any special
damage. As to this, all I need say is that the damages allegation has now been
amended. I did not understand Mr Browne to contend that in its present form
h the damages claim is bound to fail.

Damages

I turn to the points raised regarding damages. The plaintiff claims, first, that
she suffered financial loss in consequence of the Today article. Having regard to
j the nature and prominence of the assertions in the article, her chances of finding
work in any employment requiring trust and confidence have been diminished.
Secondly, she relies on s 3 of the Defamation Act 1952, which provides:

'(1) In an action for slander of title, slander of goods or other malicious
falsehood, it shall not be necessary to allege or prove special damage—(*a*) if

the words upon which the action is founded are calculated to cause pecuniary
damage to the plaintiff and are published in writing or other permanent
form; or (b) if the said words are calculated to cause pecuniary damage to the
plaintiff in respect of any office, profession, calling, trade or business held or
carried on by him at the time of the publication . . .'

The plaintiff relies on para (a). She alleges that the article was likely to cause
pecuniary damage to her by seriously prejudicing her opportunity to obtain other
employment requiring trust and confidence.

On this interlocutory appeal it would be wholly inappropriate for us to attempt
to go into the detail of the evidence which may properly be called in support of
these claims. Suffice to say, on the first claim the plaintiff will need to give
particulars of the financial loss she claims to have suffered sufficient to ensure that
the defendants will not be taken by surprise by any evidence she may adduce on
the amount of her loss.

As to the second claim, this is an allegation of general damage. In support of
this claim the plaintiff cannot adduce evidence of actual loss (see Lord Denning
MR in *Calvet v Tomkies* [1963] 3 All ER 610 at 611, [1963] 1 WLR 1397 at 1399).
I do not accept, however, that in consequence the award under this head must
necessarily be nominal only. In *Fielding v Variety Inc* [1967] 2 All ER 497, [1967]
2 QB 841 the malicious falsehood lay in falsely describing the 'Charlie Girl' show
in London as a disastrous flop. Only nominal damages of £100 were awarded in
that case because there was no likelihood of the words damaging the success of
the show in London or prejudicing the chances of a production in the United
States. That case is not authority for the proposition that, in the absence of
evidence of actual loss, a plaintiff who relies on s 3 can recover only nominal
damages. The whole purpose of s 3 was to give the plaintiff a remedy in malicious
falsehood despite the difficulty of proving actual loss. A plaintiff is seldom able to
call witnesses to say they ceased to deal with him because of some slander that had
come to their ears. In consequence actions for malicious falsehood had become
extremely rare (see the Report of Lord Porter's Committee on Defamation (1948
(Cmd 7535 (1948), paras 50–54)). Section 3 was enacted to right this injustice.
The section would fail in its purpose if, whenever relied on, it could lead only to
an award of nominal damages.

Damages for distress and injury to feelings

The plaintiff claims, thirdly, that as a consequence of the article she suffered
anxiety, distress and injury to her feelings. Mr Browne submitted that this third
head of damages is irrecoverable as a matter of law and should be struck out. Mr
Robertson QC contended that, although at common law proof of pecuniary
damage was an essential ingredient of the tort, once pecuniary loss is established,
or a claim under s 3 is made out, a plaintiff is entitled to recover his whole loss. If
he suffered mental distress, the law will include an award of damages under this
head also.

The point seems never to have been decided. As already noted, it is well settled
that at common law proof of 'special damage' is an essential ingredient in this
cause of action. At common law if such damage is not established the action will
fail. Lord Robertson emphasised this in *Royal Baking Powder Co v Wright Crossley
& Co* (1900) 18 RPC 95 at 103:

'Unless the Plaintiff has in fact suffered loss which can be and is specified,
he has no cause of action. The fact that the Defendant has acted maliciously
cannot supply the want of special damage, nor can a superfluity of malice eke
out a case wanting in special damage.'

With one exception there is no authority dealing expressly with the question

a whether, if pecuniary loss is established, a plaintiff can also recover damages for anxiety and distress. The authorities are silent on the point. Thus, so far as the reported decisions go, they show that an award of 'parasitic' damages under this head has never been made for malicious falsehood. The one exception is an observation of high authority. In *Fielding v Variety Inc* [1967] 2 All ER 497 at 499, [1967] 2 QB 841 at 850 Lord Denning MR stated, in the context of a case where

b s 3 was being relied on, that the plaintiffs could only recover damages for their probable money loss and not for their injured feelings.

This state of the authorities suggests that damages for anxiety and distress are not recoverable for malicious falsehood. If that is the law it could lead to a manifestly unsatisfactory and unjust result in some cases. Take the example I

c gave earlier of a person who maliciously spreads rumours that his competitor's business has closed down. Or the rumour might be that the business is in financial difficulty and that a receiver will soon be appointed. The owner of the business suffers severe financial loss. Further, because of the effect the rumours are having on his business he is worried beyond measure about his livelihood and his family's future. He suffers acute anxiety and distress. Can it be right that the law is unable

d to give him any recompense for this suffering against the person whose malice caused it? Although injury to feelings alone will not found a cause of action in malicious falsehood, ought not the law to take such injury into account when it is connected with financial damage inflicted by the falsehood?

One turns to analogous torts for guidance. Inducement of breach of contract is another tort in which proof of damage is an essential ingredient. In *Pratt v British*

e *Medical Association* [1919] 1 KB 244 at 282, [1918–19] All ER Rep 104 at 122 McCardie J took humiliation and menace into account when assessing the damages. Likewise in conspiracy (see the direction to the jury in *Quinn v Leathem* [1901] AC 495 at 498). A close analogy is that of slander in a case where it is actionable only on proof of pecuniary damage. In *Lynch v Knight* (1861) 9 HL Cas

f 577 at 598, 11 ER 854 at 863 Lord Wensleydale said:

'Mental pain or anxiety the law cannot value, and does not pretend to redress, when the unlawful act complained of causes that alone; though where a material damage occurs, and is connected with it, it is impossible a jury, in estimating it, should altogether overlook the feelings of the party interested.'

g

The point bristles with problems, not all of which were explored in argument. One possibility is that in an action for malicious falsehood damages are limited to financial loss. That would mark out a clear boundary, but it would suffer from the drawback of failing to do justice in the type of case I have mentioned. I

h instinctively recoil from the notion that in no circumstances can an injured plaintiff obtain recompense from a defendant for understandable distress caused by a false statement made maliciously. However, once it is accepted there are circumstances in which non-pecuniary loss, or some types of non-pecuniary loss, can be recovered in a malicious falsehood action, it becomes extremely difficult to define those circumstances or those types of loss in a coherent manner. It would

j be going too far to hold that all non-pecuniary loss suffered by a plaintiff is recoverable in a malicious falsehood action, because that would include injury to reputation at large. The history of malicious falsehood as a cause of action shows it was not designed to provide a remedy for such injury: the remedy for such loss is an action for defamation in which, incidentally, damages for injury to feelings may be included in a general award of damages (see *Fielding v Variety Inc* [1967] 2

All ER 497 at 500, 502, [1967] 2 QB 841 at 851, 855 per Lord Denning MR and
Salmon LJ).

Nor would these difficulties be solved by rejecting damages for distress as a
separate head of loss in a malicious falsehood action but permitting distress to be
taken into account as an aggravating factor. On this footing the judge or jury
could take injury to feelings into account when awarding a lump sum of damages
'in the round'. I do not see how, *if only pecuniary loss is recoverable*, the amount
awarded can be increased to reflect the plaintiff's distress. That would be a
contradiction in terms. It would be to award damages for distress in a disguised
fashion. If distress can inflame the damages recoverable for pecuniary loss, the
difference between awarding aggravated damages for that reason and awarding
damages for distress as a separate head of loss is a difference of words only.

My conclusion is that, on the limited argument addressed to us, it would be
undesirable to decide this point. It is an important point of law but only a minor
point in the present application. The pleading should be left as it stands and, if
need be, this issue can be pursued further at the trial. Taking this course will not
significantly affect the preparation of the evidence for the trial.

Conclusion

I would allow this appeal, discharge the judge's order, and give the plaintiff
leave to amend her statement of claim.

BUTLER-SLOSS LJ. I agree.

SIR MICHAEL KERR. I agree with the judgment of Sir Donald Nicholls V-C
and the order which he proposes. I only add a few words on the issues relating to
damages. However, I do so with some hesitation, since my remarks refer to
authorities which were not canvassed in the arguments before us. I therefore
mention them merely as an aide-mémoire for the sake of completeness.

The first aspect concerns the recoverability of general damages in cases where a
plaintiff relies on s 3 of the Defamation Act 1952 because he or she is unable to
prove any compensatable pecuniary loss. I agree that in such cases it does not
follow at all that he will only recover nominal damages. As it seems to me, this
conclusion flows from a general principle of the law of torts. As shown by the
speech of Lord Devlin in *Rookes v Barnard* [1964] 1 All ER 367 at 407, [1964] AC
1129 at 1221, with which the other members of the House agreed, there are
many illustrations of circumstances in which torts are committed which may
justify an award of damages beyond mere pecuniary compensation. He said:

> 'It must be remembered that in many cases of tort damages are at large,
> that is to say, the award is not limited to the pecuniary loss that can be
> specifically proved. In the present case, for example, and leaving aside any
> question of exemplary or aggravated damages, the appellant's damages would
> not necessarily be confined to those which he would obtain in an action for
> wrongful dismissal. He can invite the jury to look at all the circumstances,
> the inconvenience caused to him by the change of job and the unhappiness
> maybe by a change of livelihood. In such a case as this, it is quite proper
> without any departure from the compensatory principle to award a round
> sum based on the pecuniary loss proved.'

Pausing there, it seems to me that in referring to 'a round sum based on the
pecuniary loss proved' Lord Devlin was using the word 'based' in the sense that
the pecuniary loss would provide the core or starting point for the assessment of

the ultimate award, not that this must be limited to, or reflect no more than, the
a proved pecuniary loss. Perhaps this goes without saying, having regard to the
context. He went on ([1964] 1 All ER 367 at 407, [1964] AC 1129 at 1221):

> 'Moreover, it is very well established that in cases where the damages are
> at large the jury (or the judge if the award is left to him) can take into account
> the motives and conduct of the defendant where they aggravate the injury
> *b* done to the plaintiff. There may be malevolence or spite or the manner of
> committing the wrong may be such as to injure the plaintiff's proper feelings
> of dignity and pride. These are matters which the jury can take into account
> in assessing the appropriate compensation. Indeed, when one examines the
> cases in which large damages have been awarded for conduct of this sort, it is
> not at all easy to say whether the idea of compensation or the idea of
> *c* punishment has prevailed. There are also cases in the books where the awards
> given cannot be explained as compensatory, and I propose therefore to begin
> by examining the authorities in order to see how far and in what sort of cases
> the exemplary principle has been recognised.'

Lord Devlin then proceeded to review a long line of cases in which damages of
d this nature have been awarded, but wrongly, as he held, under the categorisation
of exemplary damages. He then stated that exemplary damages may only be
awarded in three categories of cases (see [1964] 1 All ER 367 at 410–412, [1964]
AC 1129 at 1226–1228). These do not matter for present purposes save that it
should be mentioned, for completeness, that in the present action there is also a
claim for exemplary damages under the second of these categories, 'in which the
e defendant's conduct has been calculated by him to make a profit for himself
which may well exceed the compensation payable to the plaintiff'. However, we
are not concerned with that aspect today.

Lord Devlin then proceeded to deal with the category of damages to which he
had referred, which should properly be described as aggravated damages. He said
f ([1964] 1 All ER 367 at 411–412, [1964] AC 1129 at 1228):

> 'As I have said, damages that are at large can always be fixed as a round
> sum. Some juries have in the past been very liberal in their ideas of what a
> round sum should be and the courts which have always been very reluctant
> to interfere with awards of damages by a jury, have allowed very liberal
> awards to stand.'

g
After referring to some of the epithets which have been used to describe such
damages, he went on ([1964] 1 All ER 367 at 412, [1964] AC 1129 at 1229):

> 'When this has been said, there remains one class of case for which the
> authority is much more precise. It is the class of case in which the injury to
> *h* the plaintiff has been aggravated by malice or by the manner of doing the
> injury, that is, the insolence or arrogance by which it is accompanied. There
> is clear authority that this can justify exemplary damages, though ... it is
> not clear whether they are to be regarded as in addition to, or in substitution
> for, the aggravated damages that could certainly be awarded.'

j He then reviewed a number of further authorities and concluded that exemplary
damages could not be awarded in addition to aggravated damages. He said ([1964]
1 All ER 367 at 412, [1964] AC 1129 at 1230):

> 'This conclusion will, I hope, remove from the law a source of confusion
> between aggravated and exemplary damages which has troubled the learned

commentators on the subject. Otherwise, it will not, I think, make much
difference to the substance of the law or rob the law of the strength which it   *a*
ought to have. Aggravated damages in this type of case can do most, if not
all, of the work that could be done by exemplary damages.'

Many illustrations of cases in which aggravated general damages have been
recovered for the commission of various kinds of torts can be found in the
textbooks. They have been considered, for instance, in the context of the torts of   *b*
assault, conversion, deceit, false imprisonment, malicious prosecution, trespass
and others, and Sir Donald Nicholls V-C has already referred to conspiracy and
inducing breaches of contract. There is therefore no reason whatever why such
damages should not also be recoverable for the tort of malicious falsehood, either
in addition to special pecuniary loss where this has been pleaded and proved or as
general damages where a plaintiff relies on s 3 of the Defamation Act 1952.   *c*

I need hardly add that, in drawing attention to this line of authority, I am not
for one moment suggesting that an award of aggravated damages would be
appropriate in the present case, even if the plaintiff establishes the necessary
ingredients of falsity and malice. That will of course be a matter for the judge or
jury if the case goes to trial. My object is solely to demonstrate why there could   *d*
in my view be no question of striking out this action on the ground that no more
than nominal damages could be recovered in any event.

However, while the authorities go thus far in favour of the plaintiff, they
conflict with her contention that damages for distress and injury to her feelings
can also be recovered as an additional or separate head of damage, and there is
certainly no support for such a contention where the alleged malicious falsehood   *e*
is defamatory, as in the present case. However, for the sake of completeness, and
although the authorities are somewhat confused (see *McGregor on Damages* (15th
edn, 1988) paras 1403–1406), it is worth noting two old cases which support the
conclusion that in claims other than for defamation damages for distress and
injury to feelings are not recoverable as a separate head of damage, but only in
appropriate cases as an ingredient of aggravated damages.   *f*

The first is the decision of the King's Bench in *Bracegirdle v Orford* (1813) 2
M & S 77, 105 ER 311. That was an action for trespass to the plaintiff's dwellinghouse by searching and ransacking it, and it was also alleged that the circumstances
implied a false charge to her credit and character that she was a receiver of stolen
goods. The jury awarded £50 as general damages, a very large sum at that time,
and there was a motion for a new trial. The argument for the defendants was that   *g*
the allegation of injury to the plaintiff's credit and character was effectively one
which lay in slander, for which there was a different limitation period, and there
was also a complaint that the judge should not have directed the jury that 'the
damages undoubtedly ought not to be merely nominal' if they found that the
defendant's conduct implied that the plaintiff had had stolen property on the   *h*
premises. However, Lord Ellenborough CJ and Le Blanc J upheld the verdict.
Lord Ellenborough CJ said that the alleged false charge of receiving stolen goods
had been 'laid as matter of aggravation only', and not 'as a distinct and substantive
ground of damage'. Le Blanc J added: 'It is always the practice to give in evidence
the circumstances which accompany and give a character to the trespass.'

It seems to me that this decision clearly supports the conclusion that in claims   *j*
for torts other than defamation damages for distress and injury to the plaintiff's
feeling are not recoverable as an additional head of damages. The second old case
may also be taken to lend some weight to this conclusion, but it is less compelling
since the alleged injury was not caused to the plaintiff but to his wife. That was

Huxley v Berg (1815) 1 Stark 98, 171 ER 413. The claim was again for trespass for
a breaking and entering the plaintiff's house, and also for battery. The report is
contained in a single paragraph as follows:

> 'The plaintiff was allowed to give in evidence that his wife was so terrified
> by the conduct of the defendants, that she was immediately taken ill, and
> soon afterwards died; but this was held to be admissible for the purpose only
b of shewing how outrageous and violent the breaking, &c. was, and not as a
> substantive ground of damage.'

Finally, a decision of this court may also be worth noting, since it provides a
good example of a case in which general aggravated damages were held to be
recoverable in addition to a claim for pecuniary loss. In *Davis v Bromley UDC*
c (1903) 67 JP 275 the plaintiff brought a claim for damages for trespass against his
local authority on the ground that they had wrongfully demolished a wall which
he had built on his property. The circumstances showed that the authority had
done so in a high-handed and arrogant manner, without respect to his rights. The
trial judge directed the jury that the measure of damages was the amount of the
out-of-pocket expenses to which the plaintiff had been put by reason of the
d trespass, and the jury assessed the damages at £20. But the plaintiff successfully
appealed on the ground that this was a misdirection, and a new trial was ordered.
Collins MR said that there must be a new trial because there had been a
miscarriage of justice. He said (at 276):

> 'It seems to me that the local authority had taken the law into their own
> hands, and had done it in such a way as to aggravate the insult to the plaintiff.
e They acted in a way which had the effect of branding him as a person who
> was interfering with their rights . . . The action was brought for an injunction
> and damages, and in my opinion the learned judge ought to have drawn the
> attention of the jury to the fact that the defendants had acted in an arbitrary
> and high-handed manner and without any real justification whatever. I do
f not think it was fair to treat the matter, as the learned judge appears to have
> treated it, as a mere question of costs out of pocket. On the contrary, it seems
> to me that the gist of the case was the aggravation by reason of the
> circumstances under which the act was done . . . The learned judge at the
> trial dealt with the action as if it had been one for the recovery of money out
> of pocket, and I am bound to say that his dealing with it in that way led to a
g miscarriage of justice.'

Stirling LJ agreed and Mathew LJ said (at 276):

> 'In my opinion, a material part of the plaintiff's case was the insult which
> he had suffered, and I think the learned judge was wrong in dealing with the
h expenses out of pocket as the proper measure of damages.'

As already mentioned, in my view all these authorities must be equally
applicable to claims for malicious falsehood. Furthermore, I can see no reason
why they should apply any differently according to whether the plaintiff pleads
that he has suffered special damage in the form of some pecuniary loss, as he had
to before 1952, or whether he now takes advantage of s 3 of the Defamation Act
j 1952, as in the present case. But they only support the possibility of an award for
aggravated general damages, not for an additional claim for distress and injury to
feelings, as is expressly claimed in the present case.

I would accordingly strike out this claim as such, although I recognise that
something of the same nature could still be recovered as an ingredient of a possible

award of aggravated damages. However, since none of the foregoing authorities were considered in the arguments before us and the issue was not explored in *a* depth, I agree that it would be undesirable to decide this point at the present stage and that the pleading should be left as it stands.

Appeal allowed.

b

Celia Fox   Barrister.

Director of Public Prosecutions v Corcoran

QUEEN'S BENCH DIVISION
McCOWAN LJ AND PILL J
23 JUNE 1992

c

Road traffic – Failure to provide specimen for analysis or laboratory test – Offence – Information – Driving or being in charge of vehicle when under influence of drink or with blood-alcohol proportion above prescribed limit – Different penalties depending on whether *d* *accused driving or being in charge of vehicle – Information – Accused charged with failing without reasonable excuse to provide specimen – Information not specifying whether specimen was required in connection with driving or being in charge of vehicle – Whether information containing two offences – Whether information duplicitous – Road Traffic Act 1988, ss 4(1)(2), 5(1)(a)(b), 7(6).*

e

The respondent was seen by police officers in uniform on mobile patrol to be driving his car erratically. After being chased by the police patrol the respondent drove his car into a driveway and left the vehicle. The officers apprehended the respondent and, suspecting that he had committed the offence of driving with excess alcohol, requested him to provide a specimen of breath for testing but he failed to provide the specimen requested. He was arrested and taken to a police *f* station where the drink/driving procedure was followed. He was subsequently charged with failing without reasonable excuse to provide a specimen of breath for analysis in pursuance of a requirement by a constable, contrary to s 7(6)[a] of the Road Traffic Act 1988. At the hearing of the charge the justices found that he had been charged on the basis that he had been driving his vehicle but dismissed the information on the ground that it was bad for duplicity. The prosecution *g* appealed.

Held – An information charging the offence of failing without reasonable excuse to provide a specimen of breath, blood or urine for analysis when required to do so by a constable, contrary to s 7(6) of the Road Traffic Act 1988, had to specify whether at the time the request for a specimen was made the specimen was *h* required in connection with an offence with respect to driving or attempting to drive a vehicle contrary to s 4(1)[b] or s 5(1)(a)[c] of the Road Traffic Act 1988 or whether it was required in connection with an offence with respect to being in charge of a vehicle contrary to s 4(2) or s 5(1)(b) of that Act, since offences with respect to driving or attempting to drive and offences with respect to being in charge of a vehicle carried different penalties. Accordingly, s 7(6) created two *j* offences with different penalties under the Road Traffic Offenders Act 1988, Sch 2[d], and if the charge did not state in respect of which offence the specimen

---

a Section 7(6) is set out at p 915 *a*, post
b Section 4, so far as material, is set out at p 914 *g h*, post
c Section 5(1), so far as material, is set out at p 914 *j*, post
d Schedule 2, so far as material, is set out at p 915 *c*, post

had been required it was bad for duplicity. Since the information preferred
a against the respondent did not specify the purpose for which the specimen had
been required it was duplicitous and had rightly been dismissed. The prosecution's
appeal would therefore be dismissed (see p 917 *g h*, post).

R v Courtie [1984] 1 All ER 740 applied.

Notes

b For the scope of an information, see 29 *Halsbury's Laws* (4th edn) para 318, and
for cases on the subject, see 33 *Digest* (Reissue) 116–122, 739–805.

For failure to provide a specimen of breath, blood or urine for analysis, see 40
Halsbury's Laws (4th edn) paras 492–493, and for cases on the subject, see 39(1)
Digest (Reissue) 503–508. 3721–3747.

For the Road Traffic Act 1988, ss 4, 5, 7, see 38 *Halsbury's Statutes* (4th edn) 834,
c 836, 842.

For the Road Traffic Offenders Act 1988, Sch 2, see ibid 1137.

Cases referred to in judgments

Gardner v DPP (1989) 89 Cr App R 229, DC.
d *George v DPP* [1989] RTR 217, DC.
R v Courtie [1984] 1 All ER 740, [1984] AC 463, [1984] 2 WLR 330, HL.
R v Newton (1982) 77 Cr App R 13, CA.
R v Waltham Forest Justices, ex p Barton [1990] RTR 49, DC.

Case stated

e The Director of Public Prosecutions appealed by way of a case stated by the Justices
for the County of Merseyside acting in and for the Petty Sessional Division of
South Sefton, in respect of their adjudication as a magistrates' court sitting at
Bootle on 31 January 1991 whereby they dismissed for duplicity an information
laid by the Crown Prosecution Service against the respondent, Terence Michael
Corcoran, that he had on 19 May 1990 in the course of an investigation whether
f he had committed an offence under ss 4 or 5 of the Road Traffic Act 1988 without
reasonable excuse failed to provide a specimen of breath for analysis in pursuance
of a requirement by a constable under s 7 of that Act, contrary to s 7(6). The
ground on which the justices dismissed the information was that as it did not
specify the purpose for which the specimen was required it contained two offences
and was therefore duplicitous. The questions for the opinion of the court are set
g out at p 915 *f*. The facts are set out in the judgment of Pill J.

Stuart Baker (instructed by the *Crown Prosecution Service*, Bootle) for the prosecutor.
Alison Hewitt (instructed by *Moore Sexton Bibby*, Liverpool) for the respondent.

h **PILL J** (giving the first judgment at the invitation of McCowan LJ). This is a
prosecutor's appeal by way of case stated from an adjudication of the justices for
the petty sessional division of South Sefton sitting at Bootle on 31 January 1991.
On 19 May 1990 an information had been preferred by the prosecutor against
Terence Michael Corcoran that he, on 19 May 1990 in the course of an
investigation whether he had committed an offence under ss 4 or 5 of the Road
j Traffic Act 1988, did, without reasonable excuse, fail to provide a specimen of
breath for analysis in pursuance of a requirement by a constable under the
provisions of s 7 of Road Traffic Act 1988 contrary to s 7(6) of the Road Traffic
Act 1988.

The respondent did not appear at the hearing on 31 January but nothing turns
upon that. He was represented. The facts as found by the justices, in so far as they
are material, were that on 19 May 1990 police officers in uniform on mobile

patrol saw a BMW motor car being driven erratically in Altway. They followed
the car, which accelerated away. They gave chase. Eventually the car was driven   *a*
into a driveway and the respondent left the vehicle from the driver's door. There
were no other persons in the vehicle or at the scene.

The officers found that the respondent's breath smelt of intoxicants and they
suspected that he had committed an offence of driving with excess alcohol in his
body. He was requested to go to the police vehicle and provide a specimen of
breath for test. The kit was assembled but he failed to provide the specimen   *b*
requested. He was arrested and taken to the police station. There the procedure
in the drink/drive check sheet, known as AOJ17, was followed and questions were
put to the respondent. It is clear that the justices found that it had been alleged
that the respondent was arrested on the basis that he had been driving his vehicle.

On behalf of the respondent it was submitted to the justices at the close of the   *c*
prosecution case that the information was bad for duplicity. The justices upheld
that submission. They stated that they—

> 'were satisfied that the offence of failing to provide a specimen under
> Section 7(6) Road Traffic Act 1988 did create two offences, one of failing to
> provide a specimen after driving and one after being in charge of a motor
> vehicle and that in fairness to the offender he should be aware of the   *d*
> prosecution case as to what purpose the specimen was required for in the
> information at the outset of the case. As the information in the above case
> did not specify the purpose for which the specimen was required it therefore
> contained two offences and was therefore duplicitous.'

The questions for the opinion of this court are whether: *e*

> '(a) A charge under Section 7(6) of the Road Traffic Act 1988 creates two
> offences depending on whether the defendant is alleged to have been driving
> a vehicle or in charge of a vehicle at the time a request for a specimen was
> made and (b) whether a charge under Section 7(6) Road Traffic Act 1988
> which does not distinguish the purpose [for] which the request was made is   *f*
> therefore bad for duplicity.'

I refer to the statutory framework. Section 4 of the Road Traffic Act 1988
provides:

> '(1) A person who, when driving or attempting to drive a motor vehicle on
> a road or other public place, is unfit to drive through drink or drugs is guilty   *g*
> of an offence.
> (2) Without prejudice to subsection (1) above, a person who, when in
> charge of a motor vehicle which is on a road or other public place, is unfit to
> drive through drink or drugs is guilty of an offence . . .'

Section 5 provides: *h*

> '(1) If a person—(a) drives or attempts to drive a motor vehicle on a road
> or other public place, or (b) is in charge of a motor vehicle on a road or other
> public place, after consuming so much alcohol that the proportion of it in his
> breath, blood or urine exceeds the prescribed limit he is guilty of an offence
> . . .'   *j*

It will be noted that ss 4(1) and 5(1)(a) deal with persons who are driving or
attempting to drive a motor vehicle, whereas ss 4(2) and 5(1)(b) deal with persons
in charge of a motor vehicle. Section 7 provides, inter alia:

> '(1) In the course of an investigation into whether a person has committed
> an offence under section 4 or 5 of this Act a constable may, subject to the . . .

a provisions of this section . . . require him—(*a*) to provide two specimens of breath for analysis . . .'

Section 7(6) provides:

'A person who, without reasonable excuse, fails to provide a specimen when required to do so in pursuance of this section is guilty of an offence.'

b The appropriate punishments are set out in Sch 2 to the Road Traffic Offenders Act 1988. That refers in a table first to the provision creating the offence, in this case s 7 of the Road Traffic Act 1988 defined as 'Failing to provide specimen for analysis or laboratory test.' The table provides in col 3 that the offence is triable summarily. Under the heading 'Punishment' in col 4 it is stated:

c '(*a*) Where the specimen was required to ascertain ability to drive or proportion of alcohol at the time offender was driving or attempting to drive, 6 months or level 5 on the standard scale or both. (*b*) In any other case, 3 months or level 4 on the standard scale or both.'

d In the column headed 'Disqualification' it appears that where para (*a*) under the heading 'Punishment' applies it is obligatory to disqualify, whereas where para (*b*) applies it is discretionary.

The sentencing powers of the justices upon a s 7(6) offence depend therefore upon whether the offence being investigated is a s 4(1) or s 5(1)(*a*) offence, on the one hand, or a s 4(2) or s 5(1)(*b*) offence, on the other hand. Heavier sentences can be imposed in the former case and disqualification is obligatory.

e Miss Hewitt for the respondent submits that there are two offences. She relies upon the statement of Lord Diplock in *R v Courtie* [1984] 1 All ER 740, [1984] AC 463. In that case consideration was given to offences created by the Sexual Offences Act 1967. The House of Lords held that the 1967 Act created a number of specific offences for which the maximum punishment prescribed varied upon a descending scale according to the existence or absence of particular factual

f ingredients. A material ingredient under consideration was the presence or absence of consent.

In that context Lord Diplock stated ([1984] 1 All ER 740 at 744, [1984] AC 463 at 471):

g 'My Lords, where it is provided by a statute that an accused person's liability to have inflicted on him a maximum punishment which, if the prosecution is successful in establishing the existence in his case of a particular factual ingredient, is greater than the maximum punishment that could be inflicted on him if the existence of that particular factual ingredient were not established, it seems to me to be plain beyond argument that Parliament has thereby created two distinct offences, whether the statute by which they are

h created does so by using language which treats them as being different species of a single genus of offence or by using language which treats them as separate offences unrelated to one another.'

Mr Baker on behalf of the appellant submits that, if the factual ingredient goes to sentence only and not to the question of guilt, one offence only is created. The

j lack of particulars in a charge does not render that charge bad for duplicity. Where the factual ingredient goes only to punishment, there is no duplicity. He submits that in the present situation there is only one type of misconduct specified and that is the failure to provide a specimen.

Miss Hewitt accepts that the basic act charged is the refusal to give a specimen. However, she submits that the extent of the penalty and the powers to impose a penalty depend also upon the surrounding circumstances. The circumstances and

in particular the nature of the default are relevant. Whether or not the defendant
was driving at the time is a material fact and ingredient. That matter should be *a*
charged and decided, she submits, upon the trial of the issue of conviction and
not at the stage of sentence. A defendant would be entitled to an acquittal on a
charge where driving is alleged if the driving is not proved. She makes the further
point that, if the offence is charged in the form it was charged in this case, then
upon a guilty plea, it will not be apparent to the magistrates what their powers of
sentence are.   *b*

Mr Baker also submits that no injustice has been done in the present case. It
was made plain by the prosecutor that what was being alleged was that the
defendant had driven. The defendant can have been in no doubt as to what case
he had to meet.

We were referred to three decisions of this court made under similar provisions
in the Road Traffic Act 1972. *George v DPP* [1989] RTR 217, *Gardner v DPP* (1989) *c*
89 Cr App R 229 and *R v Waltham Forest Justices, ex p Barton* [1990] RTR 49.
Gardner's case was a defendant's appeal against the justices' opinion on
disqualification on the question whether, where a motorist was charged with
having failed to provide a breath specimen on being required so to do to assess his
ability to be in charge of a vehicle, the justices could sentence on the factual basis *d*
that he was driving in circumstances where the constable requiring the screening
breath test stated in evidence that he required such a test to be taken only so as to
ascertain the ability of the defendant to be in charge of the vehicle.

Leggatt J stated (89 Cr App R 229 at 234):

> 'Where the investigating officer does not specify the offence which he is *e*
> investigating, it will be a question of fact no doubt for resolution by the
> justices for what purpose he was requiring the specimen of breath. But
> where, as here, a particular offence is specified by the officer, there is no room
> for dispute which offence was under investigation.'

Leggatt J added (at 234–235):   *f*

> 'Before leaving the case it is right to refer to the decision of the House of
> Lords in *R v Courtie* ([1984] 1 All ER 740, [1984] AC 463) to which our
> attention has helpfully been drawn by Mr. Lyons who has appeared before
> us, though not before the justices, on behalf of the defendant. In that case it
> was held by the House of Lords that where a statute provided that a
> defendant's liability to have inflicted upon him a maximum punishment *g*
> which, if the prosecution was successful in establishing the existence in this
> case of a particular factual ingredient was greater than the maximum
> punishment that could have been inflicted upon him in its absence, it was
> manifest that Parliament had thereby created two distinct offences. It was
> suggested by their Lordships that this difficulty could be overcome either by *h*
> charging the more serious offence (and thereby leaving it open to the jury to
> convict of either offence), or more suitably by charging both offences in the
> alternative. It seems to me that similar considerations may apply to offences
> charged under section 8(7) of the Road Traffic Act 1972, since upon the
> interpretation which I would adopt of Schedule 4, the question whether the
> disqualification which is to be imposed by justices is obligatory or discretionary *j*
> will be determined by the purpose for which the specimen was originally
> required. If the prosecution allege that the specimen was required to ascertain
> ability to drive or proportion of alcohol at the time the offender was driving
> or attempting to drive, that information should in fairness to the person
> charged be made plain by the summons.'

In *R v Waltham Forest Justices, ex p Barton* [1990] RTR 49 a sentence of
a disqualification was quashed upon an application for judicial review. Woolf LJ
stated (at 58):

> *b*   'In order to assist those who are responsible for prosecuting these matters
> to avoid this sort of catalogue of errors occurring again in the future, I would
> make the following suggestions. First of all, having regard to the two sets of
> penalties contained in Schedule 4 with regard to section 8(7) offences, the
> charge itself should allege that the case comes within paragraph (*a*) of
> Schedule 4 on the basis that it is alleged that the specimen was required to
> ascertain the ability of the defendant at the time that he was driving or
> attempting to drive. If that is done, then if the defendant wishes to plead
> guilty to a charge in that form, it will make it clear that he is accepting that
> *c*   he has committed an offence to which the heavier penalty applies. If he is
> not prepared to accept that that paragraph is applicable to his case, then there
> can be a hearing to determine whether or not the case is properly alleged to
> involve an offence to which the heavier sentence applies. In order to establish
> that matter, the procedure laid down in *Reg. v Newton* ((1982) 77 Cr App R
> *d*   13) will be perfectly appropriate. It will be for the prosecution to call the
> evidence to show that they are entitled to rely on the greater powers of
> punishment imposed by paragraph (*a*). It will be open to the defendant to
> call evidence in rebuttal. If the justices are not satisfied at the end of that
> evidence that the case does fall within paragraph (*a*), then their powers of
> punishment will be those which are applicable to cases falling within
> *e*   paragraph (*b*). In cases where the charge does not include the allegations
> which would make it appropriate for the heavier penalties to be available,
> then again there can be a hearing. However, although the procedure to that
> extent will be the same, in my view it certainly is at least preferable that the
> charge itself should make the position clear so that the defendant knows
> exactly the penalty which he faces.'

f   Mr Baker accepts that in those judgments adverse comments are made upon
procedure which the prosecution followed in this case. Mr Baker, however, points
out that in none of the three cases was the charge held to be bad for duplicity. It
appears that the point was not argued in those cases. Indeed the Divisional Court
proceedings took a form in which it may have been inappropriate to argue the
g point.

In my judgment the charge is bad for duplicity. There are two offences. Lord
Diplock's statement in *R v Courtie* [1984] 1 All ER 740, [1984] AC 463 covers the
present situation. Further, the good sense of the approach he lays down, if I may
say so with respect, is illustrated by the difficulties which have arisen in other
cases where informations have been laid upon a different basis, namely the basis
h of the information in the present case.

There must be a single rule covering this point and its application cannot
depend upon whether the defendant has been given notice of how the prosecution
put their case. I would answer the questions posed in the affirmative and dismiss
this appeal.

j **McCOWAN LJ.** I agree.

Appeal dismissed.

Dilys Tausz   Barrister.

Shaw v Director of Public Prosecutions   a
and other cases

QUEEN'S BENCH DIVISION
WATKINS LJ, MACPHERSON AND ROCH JJ
8 OCTOBER, 12 NOVEMBER 1992   b

*Road traffic – Failure to provide specimen for analysis or laboratory test – Offence –
Information – Driving or being in charge of vehicle when under influence of drink or with
blood-alcohol proportion above prescribed limit – Different penalties depending on whether
accused driving or being in charge of vehicle – Information – Accused charged with failing
without reasonable excuse to provide specimen – Information not specifying whether*   c
*specimen was required in connection with driving or being in charge of vehicle – Whether
information containing two offences – Whether information duplicitous – Road Traffic
Act 1988, ss 4(1)(2), 5(1)(a)(b), 7(6).*

Section 7(6)[a] of the Road Traffic Act 1988, which provides that it is an offence to
fail without reasonable excuse to provide a specimen of breath, blood or urine for   d
analysis when required to do so by a constable, does not create two offences
notwithstanding that under Sch 2[b] to the Road Traffic Offenders Act 1988 the
maximum punishment for failing to provide a specimen pursuant to s 7(6) is
higher where the specimen was required to be provided by a defendant who was
alleged to have been driving or attempting to drive a vehicle than where it was
alleged that the defendant was in charge of a vehicle. Section 7(6) creates the   e
single offence of failing without reasonable excuse to provide a specimen when
required to do so and the particular purpose for which the specimen is required,
which is not referred to in s 7(6) but only in Sch 2 to the Road Traffic Offenders
Act 1988, is relevant only to the question of sentence. Accordingly, an information
charging a failure to provide a specimen for analysis contrary to s 7(6) without   f
specifying whether at the time a request for a specimen was made it was required
in connection with an offence with respect to driving or attempting to drive a
vehicle contrary to s 4(1)[c] or s 5(1)(a)[d] of the Road Traffic Act 1988 or whether it
was required in connection with an offence with respect to being in charge of a
vehicle contrary to s 4(2) or s 5(1)(b) of that Act, is not bad for duplicity (see
p 922 f g, p 926 c d and p 930 d e, post).   g
   Metropolitan Police Comr v Curran [1976] 1 All ER 162 applied.
   R v Courtie [1984] 1 All ER 740 distinguished.
   DPP v Corcoran [1993] 1 All ER 912 doubted.

Notes
For the scope of an information, see 29 *Halsbury's Laws* (4th edn) para 318, and   h
for cases on the subject, see 33 *Digest* (Reissue) 116–122, 739–805.

a   Section 7(6) is set out at p 922 a, post
b   Schedule 2, so far as material, is set out at p 928 f to h, post
c   Section 4, so far as material, provides:
      '(1) A person who, when driving or attempting to drive a motor vehicle on a road or other   j
   public place, is unfit to drive through drink or drugs is guilty of an offence.
      (2) Without prejudice to subsection (1) above, a person who, when in charge of a motor vehicle
   which is on a road or other public place, is unfit to drive through drink or drugs is guilty of an
   offence . . .'
d   Section 5(1) provides: 'If a person—(a) drives or attempts to drive a motor vehicle on a road or
   other public place, or (b) is in charge of a motor vehicle on a road or other public place, after
   consuming so much alcohol that the proportion of it in his breath, blood or urine exceeds the
   prescribed limit he is guilty of an offence.'

For failure to provide a specimen of breath, blood or urine for analysis, see 40
a *Halsbury's Laws* (4th edn) paras 492–493, and for cases on the subject, see 39(1)
Digest (Reissue) 503–508, 3721–3747.

For the Road Traffic Act 1988, ss 4, 5, 7, see 38 *Halsbury's Statutes* (4th edn) 834,
836, 842.

For the Road Traffic Offenders Act 1988, Sch 2, see ibid 1137.

b **Cases referred to in judgment**
Bastin v Davies [1950] 1 All ER 1095, [1950] 2 KB 579, DC.
DPP v Corcoran [1993] 1 All ER 912, DC.
Edwards v Jones [1947] 1 All ER 830, [1947] KB 659, DC.
Gardner v DPP (1989) 89 Cr App R 229, DC.
George v DPP [1989] RTR 217, DC.
c *Mallon v Allon* [1963] 3 All ER 843, [1964] 1 QB 385, [1963] 3 WLR 1053, DC.
Metropolitan Police Comr v Curran [1976] 1 All ER 162, [1976] 1 WLR 87, HL.
R v Courtie [1984] 1 All ER 740, [1984] AC 463, [1984] 2 WLR 330, HL.
R v Crown Court at Norwich, ex p Belsham [1992] 1 All ER 394, [1992] 1 WLR 54,
DC.
d *R v Greater Manchester Coroner, ex p Tal* [1984] 3 All ER 240, [1985] QB 67, [1984]
3 WLR 643, DC.
R v Greenfield [1973] 3 All ER 1050, [1973] 1 WLR 1151, CA.
R v Newton (1982) 77 Cr App R 13, CA.
R v Richardson (John) [1975] 1 All ER 905, [1975] 1 WLR 321, CA.
R v Surrey Justices, ex p Witherick [1932] 1 KB 450, [1931] All ER Rep 807, DC.
e *R v Waltham Forest Justices, ex p Barton* [1990] RTR 49, DC.
Roberts v Griffiths [1978] RTR 362, DC.

Cases also cited or referred to in skeleton arguments
Amos v DPP [1988] RTR 198, DC.
Anderton v Lythgoe [1985] 1 WLR 222, DC.
f *Bunyard v Hayes* [1985] RTR 348, DC.
Cassell & Co Ltd v Broome [1972] 1 All ER 801, [1972] AC 1027, HL.
Cotterill v Lempriere (1890) 24 QBD 634, DC.
Dillon v R [1982] 1 All ER 1017, [1982] AC 484, PC.
Foulkes v Baker [1975] 3 All ER 651, [1975] 1 WLR 1551, HL.
g *Griffiths v Freeman* [1970] 1 All ER 117, [1970] 1 WLR 659, DC.
Halls Construction Services v DPP [1989] RTR 399, DC.
Hargreaves v Alderson [1962] 2 All ER 1019, [1964] 2 QB 159, DC.
Huddersfield Police Authority v Watson [1947] 2 All ER 193, [1947] KB 842, DC.
Jemmison v Priddle [1972] 1 All ER 539, [1972] 1 QB 489, DC.
Jones v Sherwood [1942] 1 KB 127, DC.
h *Meek v Powell* [1952] 1 All ER 347, [1952] 1 KB 164, DC.
Morelle Ltd v Wakeling [1955] 1 All ER 708, [1955] 2 QB 379, CA.
Newton (G) Ltd v Smith [1962] 2 All ER 19, [1962] 2 QB 278, DC.
Note [1966] 3 All ER 77, [1966] 1 WLR 1234, HL.
O'Reilly v Mackman [1982] 2 All ER 1124, [1983] AC 237, HL.
Pearson v Comr of Police for the Metropolis [1988] RTR 276, DC.
j *Practice Direction* [1982] 2 All ER 704, [1982] 1 WLR 979, DC.
R v Bolton Justices, ex p Scully [1991] 2 All ER 619, [1991] 1 QB 537, DC.
R v Bove [1970] 2 All ER 20, [1970] 1 WLR 949, CA.
R v Clow [1963] 2 All ER 216, [1965] 1 QB 598, CCA.
R v Dairy Produce Quota Tribunal, ex p Caswell [1990] 2 All ER 434, [1990] 2 AC
738, HL.
R v Gould [1968] 1 All ER 849, [1968] 2 QB 65, CA.

R v Greenwich London BC, ex p Lovelace (No 2) [1992] 1 All ER 679, [1992] QB 155, CA.

R v Harrow Justices, ex p Osaseri [1985] 3 All ER 185, [1986] QB 589, DC.

R v Jones, ex p Thomas [1921] 1 KB 632, DC.

R v Leeds County Court, ex p Morris [1990] 1 All ER 550, [1990] 1 QB 523, DC.

R v Mitchell [1977] 2 All ER 168, [1977] 1 WLR 753, CA.

R v Newsome [1970] 3 All ER 455, [1970] 2 QB 711, CA.

R v Ramsden [1972] Crim LR 547, CA.

R v Shivpuri [1986] 2 All ER 334, [1987] AC 1, HL.

R v Spencer [1985] 1 All ER 673, [1985] QB 771, CA.

R v Surrey Coroner, ex p Campbell [1982] 2 All ER 545, [1982] QB 661, DC.

R v Taylor [1950] 2 All ER 170, [1950] 2 KB 368, CCA.

R v Whitehouse [1977] 3 All ER 737, [1977] QB 868, CA.

R v Wilson (1979) 69 Cr App R 83, CA.

Royal Society for the Prevention of Cruelty to Animals v Fishwick (31 January 1991, unreported), DC.

Thomson v Knights [1947] 1 All ER 112, [1947] 1 KB 336, DC.

Ware v Fox [1967] 1 All ER 100, [1967] 1 WLR 379, DC.

Young v Bristol Aeroplane Co Ltd [1944] 2 All ER 293, [1944] KB 718, CA; *affd* [1946] 1 All ER 98, [1946] AC 163, HL.

Younghusband v Luftig [1949] 2 All ER 72, [1949] 2 KB 354, DC.

Case stated and applications for judicial review

Shaw v DPP

Christopher Shaw appealed by way of a case stated by the Crown Court at Leeds in respect of its adjudication sitting on appeal from the justices for the county of West Yorkshire in and for the petty sessional division of Wetherby on 21 February 1992 whereby it dismissed his appeals against his conviction by the justices on 14 November 1991 on an information charging him with failure without reasonable excuse to provide a specimen of breath when required to do so contrary to s 7(6) of the Road Traffic Act 1988 on the ground that, following the decision in *DPP v Corcoran* [1993] 1 All ER 912 the information was duplicitous, and against sentence passed by the justices on 9 January 1992 of two months' imprisonment, disqualification from holding or obtaining a licence to drive for four years, and endorsement of his licence. The facts are set out in the judgment of the court.

Applications for judicial review

R v Crown Court at Bournemouth, ex p Yates

James Richard Yates applied out of time with the leave of Macpherson J given on 5 August 1992 for judicial review by way of an order of certiorari to quash the decision of the Crown Court at Bournemouth on 27 March 1992 to dismiss his appeal against conviction by the Ringwood Magistrates' Court on 13 February 1992 on an information charging him with failure without reasonable cause to provide a specimen of blood for analysis when required to do so contrary to s 7(6) of the Road Traffic Act 1988 and an order of mandamus requiring the Crown Court at Bournemouth to allow the appeal, on the ground that, in the light of the subsequent decision of the Divisional Court in *DPP v Corcoran* [1993] 1 All ER 912, the information was bad for duplicity. The facts are set out in the judgment of the court.

R v Vale of Glamorgan Magistrates' Court, ex p Boundford

Graham Percival Boundford applied out of time with the leave of Rose J given on 25 September 1992 for judicial review by way of an order of certiorari to quash

his conviction by the Vale of Glamorgan Magistrates' Court on 9 December 1991
on an information charging him with failure without reasonable excuse to
provide a specimen of breath for analysis contrary to s 7(6) of the Road Traffic Act
1988 and Sch 2 to the Road Traffic Offenders Act 1988 on the ground that,
following the decision in *DPP v Corcoran* [1993] 1 All ER 912 the information
was duplicitous. The facts are set out in the judgment of the court.

R v Coventry Magistrates' Court, ex p Bolton

William George Bolton applied out of time with the leave of Rose J given on 25
September 1992 for judicial review by way of an order of certiorari to quash his
conviction by the Coventry Magistrates' Court on 1 May 1992 on an information
charging him with failure without reasonable excuse to provide a specimen of
breath for analysis when required to do so contrary to s 7(6) of the Road Traffic
Act 1988 on the ground, inter alia, that following the decision in *DPP v Corcoran*
[1993] 1 All ER 912 the information was duplicitous. The facts are set out in the
judgment of the court.

R v Cheshire Justices, ex p White

Paul White applied out of time with the leave of Rose J given on 25 September
1992 for judicial review by way of an order of certiorari to quash his conviction
by the Cheshire Justices on 5 February 1992 on an information charging him
with failure without reasonable excuse to provide a specimen for analysis when
required to do so contrary to s 7(6) of the Road Traffic Act 1988 on the ground
that, following the decision in *DPP v Corcoran* [1993] 1 All ER 912 the information
was duplicitous. The facts are set out in the judgment of the court.

R v Marylebone Magistrates' Court, ex p Garcia

Gabriel Gus Garcia applied out of time with the leave of Rose J given on 25
September 1991 for judicial review by way of an order of certiorari to quash his
conviction by the Marylebone Magistrates' Court on 21 August 1991 on an
information charging him with failure without reasonable excuse to provide a
specimen for analysis when required to do so, contrary to s 7(6) of the Road Traffic
Act 1988 and Sch 2 to the Road Traffic Offenders Act 1988, on the ground that,
following the decision in *DPP v Corcoran* [1993] 1 All ER 912 the information
was duplicitous. An appeal by way of case stated, on other grounds, was pursued
separately from the application for judicial review. The facts are set out in the
judgment of the court.

Stuart Brown QC and *David Hall* (instructed by *Ian Bosley & Co*, Leeds) for the
　appellant Shaw.
Graham J Davies (instructed by *Cordell Tibber & Co*) for the applicants Yates and
　Garcia.
Nigel Joseph Ley (instructed by *Passmore Walters & Hopkins*, Cardiff) for the
　applicant Boundford, (instructed by *Hughes & Masser*, Coventry) for the
　applicant Bolton and (instructed by *Byrne Frodsham & Co*, Widnes) for
　the applicant White.
R Alun Jones QC and *James Lewis* (instructed by the *Crown Prosecution Service*,
　Headquarters) for the respondents.
Stephen Richards (instructed by the *Treasury Solicitor*) as amicus curiae.

　　　　　　　　　　　　　　　　　　　　　　　　　　　Cur adv vult

12 November 1992. The following judgment of the court was delivered.

WATKINS LJ. On 7 and 8 October 1992 this court heard arguments in six cases
concerning s 7(6) of the Road Traffic Act 1988, which provides:

'A person who, without reasonable excuse, fails to provide a specimen when required to do so in pursuance of this section is guilty of an offence.'   *a*

The maximum punishment for failing to provide a specimen pursuant to s 7(6) is higher—

'where the specimen was required to ascertain ability to drive or proportion of alcohol at the time the offender was driving or attempting to drive'   *b*

than it is 'in any other case' (see the Road Traffic Offenders Act 1988, Sch 2).

It was held by the Divisional Court (McCowan LJ and Pill J) on 23 June 1992, in *DPP v Corcoran* [1993] 1 All ER 912, that (a) by reason of that difference in maximum punishment s 7(6) creates two offences and (b) an information in terms of s 7(6) alone is therefore bad for duplicity.

All the six cases before this court concern convictions under s 7(6) which the   *c* applicants seek to have quashed in accordance with the decision in *DPP v Corcoran*. They are but a few of very many decided cases which are affected by that decision. The persons convicted in those cases, either by the court or upon confession, await with very much interest the resolution of the issues which we have been called upon to determine.   *d*

The respondents, represented by Mr Alun Jones QC, argue that *DPP v Corcoran* was wrongly decided. Anyhow, he said, the decision was per incuriam and, therefore, not binding upon us. Even if the decision was not per incuriam we should, he claimed, depart from it regardless of precedent. The respondents' contentions, indorsed in essential parts in the submissions of Mr Stephen Richards, for whose helpful argument as amicus curiae we are most grateful, are said to be   *e* supported by an examination of the framework of the road traffic legislation of 1988, the legislative history of s 7(6) thereof, the applicable sentencing provisions and by the words of those sentencing provisions themselves.

In its starkest form the argument for the respondents is that as a matter of simple construction by reference to the language of its own provisions, s 7(6) of the Road Traffic Act 1988 defines a single offence, while Sch 2 of the Road Traffic   *f* Offenders Act 1988 separately defines the varying punishment for offences under s 7(6). This section makes no reference to the particular purpose for which the specimen is required; that comes into play only in the context of sentence and that is referred to only in Sch 2 of the latter Act.

This construction and argument is strongly supported, it was submitted, by the   *g* decision in *Metropolitan Police Comr v Curran* [1976] 1 All ER 162, [1976] 1 WLR 87, which was not cited to the court in *DPP v Corcoran*. If *Curran's* case had been cited to the court in *Corcoran* the court's conclusion would, Mr Alun Jones maintained, surely have been different.

Five of the cases before this court are applications for judicial review. One is by   *h* way of appeal by case stated from the Crown Court.

The procedural circumstances of each individual case are as follows.

Shaw is an appeal by way of case stated from the Crown Court. The points raised are the same as those in *DPP v Corcoran* but were taken prior to the decision in *DPP v Corcoran* and were indeed argued both before the justices and on appeal before the Crown Court. The appeal was brought within the relevant time limit.

Yates is an application for judicial review to quash a decision of the Crown   *j* Court dismissing an appeal against conviction. The application was made out of time following the decision in *DPP v Corcoran*. The conviction was on an appeal after a plea of not guilty, but it would seem that the points argued before the magistrates' court and the Crown Court were not the same as those in *DPP v Corcoran*.

a *Boundford, Bolton* and *White* are applications for judicial review to quash convictions by magistrates' courts. The applications were made out of time following the decision in *DPP v Corcoran*. The convictions were on a plea of guilty and the points in *DPP v Corcoran* were not argued below. (*Bolton* also raises a separate issue unconnected with *DPP v Corcoran*.)

b *Garcia* is an application for judicial review to quash a conviction by the magistrates' court. The application was made out of time following the decision in *DPP v Corcoran*. The conviction followed a plea of not guilty, but the points argued were entirely different from those in *DPP v Corcoran*. The points argued were the subject of a case stated which is to be heard separately from the present applications.

c It is unnecessary in our judgment to set out the individual details of each case. In all of them the fact was that there was failure to provide a specimen of breath or blood, and each applicant was sentenced after conviction.

If *DPP v Corcoran* was wrongly decided all the convictions will stand, and the questions posed by the case stated will be answered in the negative. The questions posed by the case stated are: (i) does s 7(6) of the Road Traffic Act 1988 create two offences? (ii) should a charge alleging an offence under s 7(6) of the Road Traffic *d* Act 1988 state on its face whether the appellant was being investigated for an offence under either s 4(1) of the Road Traffic Act 1988 or s 4(2) of the Road Traffic Act 1988 or s 5(1)(*a*) of the Road Traffic Act 1988 or s 5(1)(*b*) of the Road Traffic Act 1988? (iii) does a failure on its face of a charge under s 7(6) of the Road Traffic Act 1988 to specifically identify which other sections of the Act are said to apply so that the appellant cannot determine the penalty for the offence which he *e* is charged mean that the charge is defective as being in breach of r 100 of the Magistrates' Courts Rules 1981, SI 1981/552?

Each case will effectively be resolved by this court's conclusions as to the proper construction of s 7(6) and the argument as to duplicity, to which we now turn.

Rule 12(1) of the Magistrates Court Rules 1981, provides:

f 'Subject to any Act passed after 2nd October 1848, a magistrates' court shall not proceed to the trial of an information that charges more than one offence.'

Where, however, an information contains more than a single offence, the justices must decline to allow the prosecutor to proceed on both, but if one charge is *g* discarded, the other can be proceeded with: see *Edwards v Jones* [1947] 1 All ER 830, [1947] KB 659. Section 123 of the Magistrates' Courts Act 1980 provides:

'(1) No objection shall be allowed to any information or complaint, or to any summons or warrant to procure the presence of the defendant, for any defect in it in substance or in form, or for any variance between it and the evidence adduced on behalf of the prosecutor or complainant at the hearing *h* of the information or complaint.

(2) If it appears to a magistrates' court that any variance between a summons or warrant and the evidence adduced on behalf of the prosecutor or complainant is such that the defendant has been misled by the variance, the court shall, on the application of the defendant, adjourn the hearing.'

j Mr Alun Jones conceded that s 123 could not be used to cure an information bad for duplicity once the trial of the defendant had started in the magistrates' court.

The nature of 'duplicity' was considered by the Court of Appeal, Criminal Division, in *R v Greenfield* [1973] 3 All ER 1050, [1973] 1 WLR 1151 by a court consisting of Lord Widgery CJ, Lawton LJ and Milmo J. In the judgment of the court delivered by Lawton LJ it was said ([1973] 3 All ER 1050 at 1054, [1973] 1 WLR 1151 at 1156):

'Duplicity in a count is a matter of form; it is not a matter relating to the evidence called in support of the count.'

The word 'duplicity' is applied to more than one kind of defect in an information. The first is where the information charges two separate offences. An example is *Edwards v Jones*, where the information charged the defendant with unlawfully driving a motor car in a manner dangerous to the public having regard to all the circumstances, contrary to s 11 of the Road Traffic Act 1930, and with having on the same date and at the same place unlawfully driven a motor car without due care and attention contrary to s 12(1) of the 1930 Act. In such a case the information purports to charge the defendant with two distinct offences. The fact that the two distinct offences are contained within the same section of the Act does not prevent the information being duplicitous: see *R v Surrey Justices, ex p Witherick* [1932] 1 KB 450, [1931] All ER Rep 807, where the information charged a defendant with driving a motor vehicle on a road without due care and attention or without reasonable consideration for other persons using the road contrary to s 12 of the 1930 Act.

The second kind of duplicity is where an offence can be committed in several different ways and the charge specifies more than one of the alternative ways of committing that offence. That occurred in *Mallon v Allon* [1963] 3 All ER 843, [1964] 1 QB 385, where para 2 of Sch 2 to the Betting and Gaming Act 1960 provided that no person apparently under the age of 18 years or who is known to any person connected with the licensee's business and present on the licensed premises to be under that age should be admitted to or allowed to remain on those premises. An information charging the manager of the betting office that he did unlawfully admit and allow to remain in the licensed betting office a person apparently under the age of 18 was held to be bad for duplicity and the manager's convictions were quashed because the justices had had no jurisdiction to hear the information. In the second category of case the vice is ambiguity and uncertainty rather than the charging of two separate offences. The defendant does not know which case he has to meet. In *Bastin v Davies* [1950] 2 KB 579 at 581 Lord Goddard CJ, in respect of such an information, said:

'The blemish, however, if any, is not duplicity but uncertainty. Duplicity consists in charging two or more separate offences in one information or count conjunctively: uncertainty arises when two or more offences are so charged in the alternative or disjunctively, for obviously such a procedure leaves it quite uncertain with which of those offences the defendant is charged, and the conviction, which must follow the information, would also leave it in doubt of which offence the defendant had been found guilty. The question therefore is whether this information did in fact charge three offences in the alternative, or disjunctively, or whether it disclosed only one offence.'

The information had charged the sale of an article of food which was not of the nature or not of the substance or not of the quality of the article demanded, contrary to s 3(1) of the Food and Drugs Act 1938.

The charges in the cases before us were these.

Shaw

'That you at Garforth Police Station on Monday 10th June 1991 without reasonable excuse failed to provide a specimen of breath when required to do so, contrary to section 7(6) of the Road Traffic Act 1988.'

Yates

> 'At Ringwood in Hampshire on Friday 29th November 1991 having been required to provide a specimen of blood for analysis pursuant to section 7 of the Road Traffic Act 1988 failed without reasonable excuse to do so contrary to section 7(6) Road Traffic Act 1988.'

Boundford

> 'For that you at Barry in the County of South Glamorgan on Saturday 9th November 1991, having been required to provide a specimen of breath for analysis pursuant to section 7 of the Road Traffic Act 1988 failed without reasonable excuse to do so contrary to section 7(6) of the Road Traffic Act 1988 and Schedule 2 to the Road Traffic Offenders Act 1988.'

Bolton

> 'On Friday 28/2/92 in Coventry having been required by a constable to provide a specimen of breath for analysis under section 8 of the Road Traffic Act 1972 without reasonable excuse you failed to do so contrary to section 7(6) of the Road Traffic Act 1988.'

It will be observed that in the wording of this charge an incorrect reference was made to s 8 of the Road Traffic Act 1972 but nothing now turns upon that error.

White

> 'That you did at Widnes in the County of Cheshire on Sunday 16th December 1990 in the course of an investigation into whether you had committed an offence under section 4/5 of the Road Traffic Act 1988, did fail without reasonable excuse, whilst at the police station, to provide two specimens of breath when required to do so by a constable, contrary to section 7, Road Traffic Act 1988.'

Garcia

> '. . . at Notting Hill police station being a person who was required in pursuance of section 7 Road Traffic Act 1988 to provide a specimen you did without reasonable excuse fail to provide such a specimen contrary to section 7(6) Road Traffic Act 1988 and Schedule 2 to the Road Traffic Offenders Act 1988.'

The information charged each defendant with a single omission or course of conduct, namely failure to provide a specimen when requested to do so. The request would have to be lawful, that is to say made in accordance with the provisions of ss 7 and 9 of the Road Traffic Act 1988. Section 9 provides for the protection of hospital patients and has no relevance to these appeals. Thus the request would have to be made at a police station or a hospital and in the course of an investigation into whether a person has committed an offence under s 4 or s 5 of the Road Traffic Act 1988. Only one information, namely that in *White*, referred to an investigation under s 4 or s 5.

The purpose of empowering a constable to require a person to provide a specimen is to enable the police to obtain evidence of blood alcohol level without delay which would cause such evidence to be lost for ever. Common sense would suggest that provided there is a bona fide investigation into the existence of an offence under s 4 or s 5 of the Road Traffic Act 1988, that is an offence of driving a vehicle on a road whilst unfit to drive through drink or drugs, attempting to drive a vehicle in such circumstances, being in charge of a vehicle in such circumstances, driving a vehicle on a road after consuming so much alcohol that the proportion of the alcohol in the breath, blood or urine exceeds the prescribed limit, attempting to drive a motor vehicle in such circumstances and being in charge of a motor vehicle in such circumstances, then the request is within s 7.

Part of the investigation may be to discover whether the person asked for the specimen was driving or attempting to drive or in charge of a vehicle whilst unfit or with more than the prescribed limit of alcohol in his blood, breath or urine. At the time the specimen is required, however, the investigating officer may well have no or no sufficient evidence as to these matters and will have no or no sufficient evidence until the investigation is complete. At that stage the officers may well not know if they are investigating an offence vis-à-vis the person of whom the request is being made under s 4 or s 5 of the Road Traffic Act 1988, and within each of those sections precisely which of the three possible offences, or variation of them.

Having regard to the provisions of s 7(6), provided the requirement for the specimen is properly made, there is unquestionably, in our view, a single course of conduct which constitutes the offence, namely the failing to provide the specimen without reasonable excuse.

On this analysis no one of the informations or charges we have set out could possibly be bad for duplicity. The appellants collectively argue that if s 7(6) is read together with Pt 1 of Sch 2 of the Road Traffic Offenders Act 1988, it will be seen that Parliament has created more than one offence or alternatively more than one way of committing the offence of failing to provide a specimen.

In *Metropolitan Police Comr v Curran* [1976] 1 All ER 162, [1976] 1 WLR 87 the ingredients of an offence under s 9(3) of the Road Traffic Act 1972, which was a predecessor of s 7(6), were considered by their Lordships' House. Section 9(3) provided:

> 'A person who, without reasonable excuse, fails to provide a specimen for a laboratory test in pursuance of a requirement imposed under this section shall be guilty of an offence.'

Their Lordships held that the language of s 9(3) of the 1972 Act was simple, clear and unambiguous and nothing in it suggested that the offence thereby created was in any way connected with the suspect's guilt or innocence of the offence which he was suspected of having committed when he was arrested. The offence under s 9(3) could be established without establishing that the defendant was a person in charge of, or driving, or attempting to drive a motor vehicle on a road or other public place. Lord Diplock in his speech said ([1976] 1 All ER 162 at 165, [1976] 1 WLR 87 at 91–92):

> 'What these sections provide is a procedure by which a person who is reasonably suspected by a policeman of having committed an offence under s 5 or s 6 [the predecessors of ss 4 and 5 of the 1988 Act] can be required to provide material evidence in the form of a specimen of his blood or urine which may be used against him at his trial for an offence under either section, and without which, in the case of an offence under s 6, no prosecution could ever be brought against him. So the procedure under ss 8 and 9 applies to persons when they are suspects only. They may not in fact have committed the offence under s 5 or s 6 of which they are suspected; but, if they have, their refusal to provide a specimen of blood or urine would prevent their being prosecuted for any offence under s 6 and would enhance their prospects of escaping conviction for an offence under s 5. If the procedure is to achieve its evident purpose it is essential that a refusal without reasonable excuse to provide a specimen of blood or urine should attract penal sanctions

a   irrespective of whether or not it ultimately proved that the person refusing to provide the specimen had been guilty of the offence of which he was suspected. In my opinion this is what s 9(3) quite plainly does . . . There is nothing in that language to suggest that the offence thereby created is in any way connected with the suspect's guilt or innocence of the offence which he was suspected of having committed when he was arrested.'

b   Lord Hailsham in his speech said ([1976] 1 All ER 162 at 171, [1976] 1 WLR 87 at 98):

> 'We must now, therefore, consider whether a refusal to provide the required laboratory specimen, made in such circumstances without reasonable excuse, gives rise of itself to an offence under s 9(3) of the 1972 Act. If it does, *c*   it is because it is not necessary for the prosecution to establish, if the fact be challenged, to the satisfaction of the jury that the suspect was at the time of the alleged offence in actual physical charge of the vehicle in question. The question of reasonable excuse hardly arises in this connection. If being in charge is an essential ingredient of the offence, no reasonable excuse is required. The prosecution fails because it has failed to prove what is necessary. *d*   If it succeeds, it is because the essential ingredients do not include that the accused should actually have been in charge.'

The appellant Curran had been indicted with being unfit to drive through drink when in charge of a motor vehicle on a road, in respect of which the jury had acquitted him, and of failing without reasonable excuse to provide the *e*   required specimen of blood or urine for the prescribed laboratory test, an offence of which he was convicted. His case was that the two verdicts were inconsistent, and that submission depended upon it being a necessary ingredient of the offence of failing to provide a specimen that it should be proved that he had been in charge of the motor vehicle. The punishment for the offence was set out in Pt I of Sch 4 to the 1972 Act. The relevant part of that read:

f

4 Punishment	5 Disqualification
(i) Where it is shown that at the relevant time . . . the offender was driving or attempting to drive a motor vehicle on a road or other public place, 4 months or £100 or both . . . (ii) Where in any other case it is shown that at that time the offender was in charge of a motor vehicle on a road or other public place, 4 months or £100 or both.	(*a*) Obligatory if it is shown as mentioned in paragraph (i) of column 4. (*b*) Discretionary if it is not so shown.

h   It was submitted to the House of Lords that that provision in Sch 4 meant that there were at least two separate offences in respect of which there were different punishments. Lord Hailsham closed his speech with these words ([1976] 1 All ER 162 at 174, [1976] 1 WLR 87 at 101):

j   'It follows, moreover, from what I have said about the decision in *R v Richardson* [1975] 1 All ER 905, [1975] 1 WLR 321, that I agree with the opinion expressed by my noble and learned friends to the effect that, on a charge under s 9(3), the matters of fact on which the decision as to penalty under cols 4 and 5 of Sch 4 depend are matters of fact for the court after verdict and not matters of fact for the jury at the trial.'

The House of Lord's decision in *Metropolitan Police Comr v Curran* was referred to by the Divisional Court in *Roberts v Griffiths* [1978] RTR 362. In that case justices dismissed an information charging a defendant with contraventions of ss 5(2) and 9(3) of the 1972 Act. As in *Metropolitan Police Comr v Curran* the justices found that it was not established that the defendant had been in charge of the motor vehicle. However, the justices found that the defendant had been properly arrested and that the requirement for the laboratory test specimen had been properly made under s 9, and that he had failed without reasonable excuse to provide a specimen. The particulars in the information relating to contravention of s 9(3) had referred to the defendant being in charge of the motor vehicle. The justices invited the prosecutor to amend the information by deleting that reference and the prosecutor refused. The justices then dismissed the information. On appeal the Divisional Court held that it was irrelevant that he had not been proved to have been in charge of the vehicle or committing an offence under s 5(2), that consequently the reference in the information to the defendant being a person in charge of a motor vehicle was surplusage, that the defendant would not have been misled by the superfluous words and that consequently the justices should have disregarded them and convicted the defendant. The case was sent back to the justices with a direction to convict. The Divisional Court followed the House of Lords in *Metropolitan Police Comr v Curran*.

It is true that in neither of those cases was the question of duplicity raised, but it is conceded by counsel for the appellants that if the punishment provisions are not to be looked at in deciding what are the essential ingredients of the offence of failing to provide a specimen, then no question of duplicity can arise.

Since those two decisions the 1972 Act has been repealed and the offence is now contained in s 7(6) of the Road Traffic Act 1988 and the penalties in Pt I of Sch 2 to the Road Traffic Offenders Act 1988. The relevant part of that schedule reads:

(2) General nature of offence	...	(4) Punishment	(5) Disqualification
Failing to provide specimen for analysis or laboratory test.		(a) Where the specimen was required to ascertain ability to drive or proportion of alcohol at the time offender was driving or attempting to drive, 6 months or level 5 on the standard scale or both.	(a) Obligatory in case mentioned in column 4(a).
		(b) In any other case, 3 months or level 4 on the standard scale or both.	(b) Discretionary in any other case.

Since the decision in *Metropolitan Police Comr v Curran* there have been further decisions of the courts and in particular *R v Courtie* [1984] 1 All ER 740, [1984] AC 463 and *Gardner v DPP* (1989) 89 Cr App R 229. The question which arises is whether the changes in the statutory wording or decisions such as *R v Courtie* [1984] 1 All ER 740, [1984] AC 463 and *Gardner v DPP* have overruled or substantially affected the decision in *Metropolitan Police Comr v Curran*? If not, we consider ourselves bound by *Curran's* case. The authorities of *Curran's* case and *Roberts v Griffiths* [1978] RTR 362 were not cited to the Divisional Court in *DPP v*

Corcoran [1993] 1 All ER 912, whereas the most recent authorities, and particularly

a those of *R v Courtie* and *Gardner v DPP* were relied upon by the Divisional Court in *DPP v Corcoran* in reaching their conclusion that an information which charged Corcoran with failing to provide a specimen of breath for analysis in pursuance of a requirement by a constable under the provisions of s 7 of the Road Traffic Act 1988 contrary to s 7(6) of that Act was bad for duplicity because the court was satisfied that s 7(6) of the 1988 Act read together with Pt I of Sch 2 to the Road

b Traffic Offenders Act 1988 created at least two offences.

Pill J, with whose judgment McCowan LJ agreed, quoted what was said by Lord Diplock in *R v Courtie* [1984] 1 All ER 740 at 744–745, [1984] 1 AC 463 at 471:

> *c*   'My Lords, where it is provided by a statute that an accused person's liability to have inflicted on him a maximum punishment which, if the prosecution is successful in establishing the existence in his case of a particular factual ingredient, is greater than the maximum punishment that could be inflicted on him if the existence of that particular factual ingredient were not established, it seems to me to be plain beyond argument that Parliament has thereby created two distinct offences, whether the statute by which they are
> *d*   created does so by using language which treats them as being different species of a single genus of offence, or by using language which treats them as separate offences unrelated to one another.'

And ended his judgment by saying 'Lord Diplock's statement . . . covers the present situation' (see *DPP v Corcoran* [1993] 1 All ER 912 at 917).

e   The failure to refer that court to *Metropolitan Police Comr v Curran* [1976] 1 All ER 162, [1976] 1 WLR 87 and *Roberts v Griffiths* [1978] RTR 362 denied it the opportunity, most unfortunately we think, to consider a comparison between the class or classes of criminal offence which Lord Diplock had in mind in *R v Courtie* and the very different road traffic legislation considered by the House of Lords, Lord Diplock included of course, in *Metropolitan Police Comr v Curran*.

f   Mr Richards submitted, very cogently in our opinion, as follows. We quote from his written submissions:

> 'The weight of the decision in *Corcoran* is placed on *R. v. Courtie* ([1984] 1 All ER 740 esp at 744, [1984] AC 463 esp at 471) per Lord Diplock. It is submitted, however, that *Courtie* does not have the effect that the court in
> *g*   *Corcoran* considered it to have. The case was not concerned with a statutory context comparable with that of the Road Traffic Act 1988; *Curran* and the reasoning in that case were not even raised for consideration; and Lord Diplock's dicta as to the effect of differences in maximum punishment have to be placed in their particular context and must not be treated as being of universal application. The reasoning in *Courtie* was that the *statutory definition*
> *h*   of the offences under consideration involved the existence of at least one of several necessary factual ingredients which differed from one another; it did not necessarily follow that as many different statutory offences were created as there were necessary factual ingredients; but where there were different maximum punishments according to the existence or absence of particular factual ingredients, it was plain that distinct offences were created (see [1984]
> *j*   1 All ER 740 at 743–745, [1984] AC 463 at 470–471). That reasoning does not apply to the present context, where the *statutory definition* of the offence is in the simple terms of s. 7(6) and does *not* involve the existence of different factual ingredients. (Only if one assumes that Sched. 2 to the Road Traffic Offenders Act 1988 is *part of* the statutory definition of the offence do

different factual ingredients exist. But that is to fly in the face of the straightforward language of s. 7(6) and/or to engage in circularity by assuming *a* the very point that falls to be determined.) [We interpolate here that in oral argument the telling point was made that offence and punishment are now in different Acts.] *George v. DPP* ([1989] RTR 217), *Gardner v. DPP* ((1989) 89 Cr App R 229) and *R. v. Waltham Forest Justices, ex p. Barton* ([1970] RTR 49), all of which are referred to in *Corcoran*, do not focus on the material issue and do not support the decision in *Corcoran*. On the contrary, they presuppose *b* that the factual issues raised by the differences in maximum punishment can properly be investigated at the sentence stage and do not *have* to be determined through the formulation of the offence.' (Mr Richard's emphasis.)

It is of relevance to observe that in each of the three cases to which Mr Richards *c* referred at the end of that extract the issues involved sentence only, conviction was not questioned. None of those courts had, therefore, to consider *Metropolitan Police Comr v Curran* and *Roberts v Griffiths*, nor so far as we can discover did they.

We agree entirely with the submissions of Mr Richards and are, therefore, driven with respect to differ from the decision in *DPP v Corcoran*, which, in our opinion, was erroneous and reached per incuriam. *d*

It is, of course, understandable that a defendant should wish to be aware as precisely as possible of the likely consequences in terms of punishment of his admitted conduct or that found by the court to have been committed. But that cannot affect the construction of a plain straightforward provision creating an uncomplicated offence, as s 7(6) undoubtedly does. It stands in isolation from other circumstances prior to and succeeding its commission. The matter of *e* penalty and the other circumstances which may affect it are for independent ascertainment by 'Newton' style hearing (see *R v Newton* (1982) 77 Cr App R 13) if they have not been admitted, or have not emerged during a trial of a not guilty plea. Whether it would be more just that the prosecution at some early stage inform a defendant of relevant circumstances sought to be relied upon is a matter which goes to procedural fairness and is, we think, easily resolved by a suitable *f* procedure.

Finally, we turn to the precedent issue. Should we be wrong in regarding the decision in *DPP v Corcoran* as being reached per incuriam we recognise, of course, the rareness of departing from a previous decision of this court. In this context we have naturally reminded ourselves of *R v Greater Manchester Coroner, ex p Tal* [1984] 3 All ER 240, [1985] QB 67 and *R v Crown Court at Norwich, ex p Belsham* *g* [1992] 1 All ER 394, [1992] 1 WLR 54.

We agree with Mr Richards for the reasons he advanced that it would be highly artificial to adopt different tests according to whether we are in the context of the cases before us considering an appeal by case stated or judicial review.

We are persuaded that we should depart from *DPP v Corcoran* on the basis that *h* it was wrongly decided, though we infinitely prefer the view that it was decided per incuriam.

Therefore, we dismiss the appeal by case stated and answer the questions posed in the negative and dismiss all applications for judicial review.

We think it right to add that, if we had concluded that *DPP v Corcoran* should be followed, we would have allowed Shaw's appeal which was brought in time *j* following a hearing in the Crown Court in which the points of relevance considered in this judgment were argued. However, we would not in our discretion grant relief to any one of the applicants notwithstanding that leave to move was granted. Their applications were made well outside the normal time limit for judicial review either following a plea of guilty or a contest upon a *a* different point. In none of the applications is it alleged that the applicant did not know the case he had to meet. As Mr Richards pointed out, the applications were based on a procedural technicality which could have been raised and cured at the time. We agree with that. It is, moreover, absolutely plain that none of the applicants has suffered any injustice whatsoever as a consequence of the decision in *DPP v Corcoran*.

b *Appeal dismissed. Applications for judicial review refused.*

The court refused leave to appeal to the House of Lords and refused to certify, under s 1(2) of the Administration of Justice Act 1960, that a point of law of general public importance was involved in the decision.

c   Kate O'Hanlon   Barrister.

---

d # Re B (a minor) (disclosure of evidence)

COURT OF APPEAL CIVIL DIVISION
GLIDEWELL, BALCOMBE LJJ AND BOREHAM J
17, 18 JUNE, 16 JULY 1992

e
Family proceedings – Orders in family proceedings – Residence or contact orders – Evidence – Disclosure – Application by mother to revoke father's access to son – Affidavit by mother supporting application – Affidavit containing allegations against father of sexual abuse of daughter – Whether court having power to prohibit disclosure of mother's affidavit to father – Children Act 1989, ss 8, 10.

f
The parties were divorced in 1991. In July and November 1991 consent orders were made granting custody, care and control of the mother's daughter by a previous marriage, L, to the mother, and joint custody of the son of the marriage, T, to both parents, with care and control to the mother and reasonable access to the father. Subsequently, the mother applied under s 10(1)[a] of the Children Act *g* 1989 for an order under s 8[b] of that Act varying the joint custody order, revoking the order for reasonable access and prohibiting the father from communicating with T. The application was supported by an affidavit sworn by the mother which contained allegations that L had been sexually abused by the father and that since T had become aware of his sister's allegations the mother wished to *h* ensure that T did not, during access, inadvertently tell his father of L's complaints. When the matter came on for hearing ex parte the judge ordered that T should

---

a   Section 10(1), so far as material, provides: 'In any family proceedings in which a question arises with respect to the welfare of any child, the court may make a section 8 order with respect to the child if—(a) an application for the order has been made by a person who—(i) is entitled to apply for a section 8 order with respect to the child; or (ii) has obtained the leave of the court to make *j*   the application . . .'
b   Section 8, so far as material, provides:
          (1) . . . "a contact order" means an order requiring the person which whom a child lives . . . to allow the child to visit or stay with the person named in the order . . . "a residence order" means an order settling the arrangements to be made as to the person with whom a child is to live . . .
          (2) . . . "a section 8 order" means any of the orders mentioned in subsection (1) and any order varying or discharging such an order . . .'

have no contact with his father until the full directions hearing of the application
and that the mother should not disclose to the father the affidavit filed by her in *a*
connection with her application. The father applied for orders discharging the
prohibition of contact with T and requiring disclosure of the mother's affidavit.
The judge held that he had had no power to order that the affidavit was not to be
disclosed and ordered that the affidavit be supplied forthwith to the father's
solicitors. The mother appealed.

b

Held – For the purposes of applications under ss 8 and 10 of the 1989 Act the
court had power to order that evidence filed by one party in support of the
application or in opposition to the application, or any part of the material
contained in the application form should not be disclosed to the other party if the
court was satisfied, having balanced the interests of the child, which were
paramount, against the requirements of natural justice, that such disclosure *c*
would be so detrimental to the welfare of the child or children under consideration
as to outweigh the normal requirement for a fair trial that all evidence must be
disclosed so that all parties could consider it and if necessary seek to rebut it.
However, the power to prohibit disclosure should only be exercised in exceptional
circumstances and then only for the shortest possible period consonant with *d*
preserving the welfare of the child or children. Since the order had been sought
for the protection of the daughter, whereas it was the son's welfare which was the
paramount consideration when considering whether he should continue to have
access to his father, the interests of justice to the father greatly outweighed any
possible detriment to the son. It followed that disclosure of the mother's affidavit
to the father should not be prohibited and that the appeal would be dismissed (see *e*
p 936 *d e h*, p 941 *e f*, p 942 *g* to *j* and p 943 *a* to *h*, post).

Official Solicitor v K [1963] 3 All ER 191 followed.

Notes
For the principle that judgment should only be given on the basis of evidence
made known to all the parties, see 10 *Halsbury's Laws* (4th edn) para 722. *f*

For orders with respect to children in family proceedings, see Supplement to
24 *Halsbury's Laws* (4th edn) para 541A.

For the Children Act 1989, ss 8, 10, see 6 *Halsbury's Statutes* (4th edn) (1992
reissue) 400, 403.

Cases referred to in judgments *g*
C (a minor: irregularity of practice), Re [1991] 2 FLR 438, CA.
Fowler v Fowler and Sines [1963] 1 All ER 119, [1963] P 311, [1963] 2 WLR 155,
CA.
Official Solicitor v K [1963] 3 All ER 191, [1965] AC 201, [1963] 3 WLR 403, HL,
rvsg sub nom *Re K (infants)* [1962] 3 All ER 1000, [1963] Ch 381, [1962] 3 WLR
1517, CA; *rvsg* [1962] 3 All ER 178, [1963] Ch 381, [1962] 3 WLR 752. *h*
Russell v Duke of Norfolk [1949] 1 All ER 109, CA.
Scott v Scott [1913] AC 417, [1911–13] All ER Rep 1, HL.

Cases also cited or referred to in skeleton arguments
A (minors) (residence order), Re [1992] 3 All ER 872, [1992] 3 WLR 422, CA.
A (minors) (wardship: child abuse: guidelines), Re [1992] 1 All ER 153, [1991] 1 WLR *i*
1026.
B v B (child abuse: evidence) [1991] 2 FLR 487.
Boatman v Boatman (1980) 10 Fam Law 120, DC.
Brinkley v Brinkley [1963] 1 All ER 493, [1965] P 75, DC.
D v National Society for the Prevention of Cruelty to Children [1977] 1 All ER 589,
[1978] AC 171, HL.

DF (a minor), Re (1977) 76 LGR 133.

a *Eaton (decd), Re, Shaw v Midland Bank Executor and Trustee Co Ltd* [1964] 3 All ER 229, [1964] 1 WLR 1269.

Elder v Elder [1986] 1 FLR 610, CA.

H v H and C [1969] 1 All ER 262, [1969] 1 WLR 208, CA.

J v C [1969] 1 All ER 788, [1970] AC 668, HL.

b *M (an infant) (adoption: parental consent), Re* [1972] 3 All ER 321, [1973] QB 108, CA.

M (a minor) (disclosure of material), Re [1990] 2 FLR 36, CA.

M (minors) (wardship: freedom of publication), Re, [1990] 1 All ER 205, [1990] Fam 211, CA.

Moritz (decd), Re, Midland Bank Executor and Trustee Co Ltd v Forbes [1959] 3 All

c ER 767, [1960] Ch 251.

R v Hampshire CC, ex p K [1990] 2 All ER 129, [1990] 2 QB 71, DC.

R v West Malling Juvenile Court, ex p K [1986] 2 FLR 405.

R v Worcester City Juvenile Court, ex p F [1989] 1 All ER 500.

S (minors) (wardship: police investigation), Re [1987] 3 All ER 1076, [1987] Fam 199.

Suter v Suter and Jones [1987] 2 All ER 336, [1987] Fam 111, CA.

d *T (an infant), Re* (1974) 118 SJ 78.

T (a minor) (adoption: parental consent), Re [1986] 1 All ER 817, [1986] Fam 160, CA.

W (a minor), Re (1980) 10 Fam Law 120.

WLW, Re [1972] 2 All ER 433, [1972] Ch 456.

e **Interlocutory appeal**

By notice of appeal dated 28 April 1992 the mother of two children appealed from the order of Judge John Wilson made in the Northampton County Court on 15 April 1992 whereby he ordered, inter alia, (i) than an earlier order made by the judge dated 27 March 1992 that the mother do not disclose to the father the affidavit filed by her in support of her application under ss 8 and 10 of the

f Children Act 1989 be discharged and (ii) that the mother serve on the father's solicitors a copy of the affidavit. The facts are set out in the judgment of Glidewell LJ.

Jeremy Posnansky (instructed by *Toller Hales & Collcutt,* Wellingborough) for the mother.

g *Richard Vain* (instructed by *Woolley & Weston,* Welwyn Garden City) for the father.

At the conclusion of the argument the court ordered that the mother's affidavit be disclosed 36 hours thereafter and that it would give its reasons later.

h 16 July 1992. The following judgments were delivered.

GLIDEWELL LJ. This is an appeal against part of an order made on 15 April 1992 by Judge John Wilson in the Northampton County Court on an application made on behalf of the father to vary an order made by the learned judge on 27 March 1992 on an ex parte application by the mother.

j The father and the mother were married on 2 June 1979. The mother already had a daughter by her previous marriage, L, who was born on 16 December 1976 and is thus now 15 years of age. On 16 April 1980 she gave birth to a son, T. He is now 12 years old.

The father, the mother and the two children lived together in the matrimonial home until 27 October 1990 when, as a result of disagreements between the mother and the father, the father left at the mother's request. They have not lived

together since. On 31 January 1991 the mother filed a petition for divorce and on   *a*
19 April 1991 a decree nisi was pronounced.

On 15 July 1991 Judge Wilson made an order by consent, after the giving of a
number of undertakings by the father, which included: (1) a prohibition on the
exercise by the father of his right to occupy the former matrimonial home; (2)
the grant of custody, care and control of L to the mother; (3) the grant of interim
custody, care and control of T to the mother; (4) a provision that there should be
no access by the father to L; and (5) an order that the applications concerning the   *b*
custody of, and access to, T should be adjourned to a date to be fixed, with interim
access to T to the father, and directions as to the steps to be taken before the
hearing of the application.

The undertakings given by the father on that occasion included undertakings
that he would not assault, molest or interfere with the mother or either of the   *c*
children, that he would not communicate with L in any way, that he would not,
save in one respect, go within 100 yards of the former matrimonial home, and
that he would not remove the children from the care of the mother save for access
to T.

On 27 November 1991 the application regarding the custody and access of T
came before the learned judge. He granted by consent joint custody of T to both   *d*
parents, with care and control to the mother and reasonable access to the father.
In certain respects not relevant to this appeal the father's undertakings were
amended.

On 27 November 1991 the divorce decree was made absolute.

On 27 December 1991 the father moved to a new home in Oxfordshire. Over
the weekend of 17–19 January 1992 the father remarried. T stayed with his father   *e*
over that weekend and attended the wedding. This was the last occasion on which
there was contact between T and his father.

On the morning of 31 January 1992 the mother's solicitors sent to the father's
solicitors by fax a letter giving notice that T would not have access to his father
that weekend, the access being due to start on the evening of that day. By letter   *f*
dated 7 February 1992 the mother's solicitors said:

> 'For the record we do confirm all parties in contact with [T], his School, his
> Doctor and of course our Client, his mother, have become increasingly aware
> [T] has been under a good deal of stress recently, it would seem as a result of
> his father's sudden move to Oxford having told his son the reason for this
> was a secret and the fact that his father has remarried so quickly and to   *g*
> someone his father had not taken the time to ensure his son knew.'

On 26 March 1992 application was made on behalf of the mother under s 10
of the Children Act 1989. The form of application said that it was made in respect
of both T and L. Orders were sought (1) varying the joint custody order and
ordering that T should reside with his mother, (2) revoking the order for the   *h*
father to have reasonable access to T and for an order that there be no contact
between them, (3) prohibiting the father from communicating with T and (4)—

> 'That no part of the evidence produced to the court be disclosed to the
> [father] whilst the present investigations remain to be completed and that a
> specific issue order be made directing the [father's] solicitors as officers of the   *j*
> court not to disclose to the [father] the nature of the matters under
> investigation and the information now laid before the court.'

The reason for the making of the application was expressed in the following
terms:

> 'I am fearful of the consequences for both children of the family in the

a event of the [father] becoming aware of the allegations now being made against him and I refer to my affidavit of even date filed in connection with this my application together with the exhibits thereto in support.'

As there said, the application was supported by an affidavit sworn by the mother.

This application came on for hearing ex parte in the Northampton County b Court before Judge Wilson on 27 March 1992. The judge ordered: (1) that the father should not have any contact with T until the full directions hearing of the application or further order; (2) that the father's access to T should be suspended until further order; and (3) that the mother should not disclose to the father the affidavit filed by her in connection with her application.

Although it seems that the judge had not specifically so ordered, the form of c application then served upon the father was amended by deleting parts of it. The fourth order sought was truncated so that it read only: 'That no part of the evidence produced to the court be disclosed to the [father].' The reason why the application was made was wholly deleted, so that this part of the form was simply left blank.

d On 10 April 1992 the father applied for orders discharging the prohibition of contact with T, requiring the mother to complete her application form, and requiring her to supply him forthwith with a copy of her affidavit and exhibits. It was this application which came before the learned judge on 15 April 1992.

At the hearing the father was represented by Mr Vain of counsel who appears before us. The mother was represented by her solicitor, Mr Mitchell. At the e hearing Mr Vain, without any objection from Mr Mitchell, referred the judge to two previous decisions of this court, of which the first was *Re K (infants)* [1962] 3 All ER 1000, [1963] Ch 381, in which the decision of this court was given on 30 October 1962. In that case two children had been made wards of court, and the Official Solicitor was ordered to be their guardian ad litem. At two stages during the course of the proceedings the Official Solicitor lodged statements of fact, f accompanied by confidential reports, and on the second occasion the report of a medical specialist on the children. He did not serve copies either of the confidential reports or of the specialist's report on either the mother or the father.

The mother took a preliminary point that she was entitled as of right to see the whole of the material filed by the Official Solicitor, including the confidential reports and the medical report. Ungoed-Thomas J rejected her contention. On g appeal, this court allowed the appeal on the principle that the determination of the question what was best to be done for the welfare of the children was a judicial inquiry, and that it is fundamental to any such inquiry that an interested party has the right to see all information put before the judge to enable him or her to comment on it and if need be to seek to challenge it.

h The second decision to which the judge was referred was that in *Fowler v Fowler and Sines* [1963] 1 All ER 119, [1963] P 311. In that case this court, in a judgment given on 7 December 1962, followed its previous decision in *Re K (infants)*.

Judge Wilson concluded that he was bound by the decision of this court in *Re K (infants)* to hold that in the present case the father was entitled to see the mother's affidavit. He recognised that such disclosure might cause some harm to the children, but nevertheless concluded that only if there is a specific statutory j power to order non-disclosure to a party of material which is placed before the court itself can the court make such an order. He therefore discharged his ex parte order that the mother should not disclose her affidavit to the father, required her forthwith to serve upon the father's solicitors a copy of her affidavit together with the exhibits and a copy of the completed application form, adjourned the application to a date to be fixed and agreed to stay his order pending consideration by the mother of an appeal to this court. On 14 May 1992 he extended his stay until the hearing of the appeal.

Most unfortunately, when they appeared before the judge, neither Mr Vain nor Mr Mitchell was aware that the Official Solicitor had appealed to the House of Lords against the decision of this court in *Re K (infants)* and that the appeal had been allowed. Thus the decision upon which the judge had based himself had been reversed: see sub nom *Official Solicitor v K* [1963] 3 All ER 191, [1965] AC 201. We need not consider at this stage how this most regrettable state of affairs came about. It suffices to say that the judge's understandable ignorance of the decision of the House of Lords invalidated the basis of his judgment.

Before us the following issues arose. (1) On an application relating to the custody or care and control of and/or access to a child, has a court any power to order that evidence filed by one party in support of the application or in opposition to the application, or any part of the material contained in the form of application shall not be disclosed to the other party? (2) If so, should this court decide whether in the circumstances it was right to make such an order in this case, or should it remit that question for rehearing? (3) If this court is prepared to decide this second issue itself, should such an order be made?

At the hearing we considered the first issue, which obviously raises a question of general importance. We announced our decision that in our opinion in proceedings such as these, affecting the welfare of children, the court does have power to make an order for non-disclosure of the kind sought by the mother, but that such power is only to be exercised in the most exceptional circumstances. Having announced that decision, we also concluded without any objection from the parties that we were in as good a position as a lower court would be to decide whether in the circumstances of this case such an order should be made. At that stage in the hearing, at our request, we were supplied with copies of the mother's affidavit and of the text of the words deleted from her form of application when it was served on the father. We were told that the words of the application form had been shown to Mr Vain at the hearing before the judge, but neither he nor his client was as yet aware of the content of the affidavit filed on behalf of the mother.

We decided that the proper way in which to hear submissions on the question whether the affidavit should be disclosed was to hear submissions first from Mr Posnansky, counsel for the mother, in the absence of the father, his solicitors and his counsel, Mr Vain. We made it clear that, if we were minded to be persuaded by Mr Posnansky's arguments, we would then require disclosure on terms of the affidavit to Mr Vain (but not to his client at that stage) for him to be able to argue against an order for non-disclosure. However, at the conclusion of Mr Posnansky's argument we had no doubt that it would be wrong for us to make an order that the affidavit should remain undisclosed for more than a very short time. Indeed Mr Posnansky in effect conceded that at this stage the affidavit must be disclosed, only asking for a short delay to enable appropriate steps to be taken to inform one of the children that this was to be done. We therefore ordered disclosure of the affidavit and of the material contained in the application form to take effect some 36 hours after the conclusion of our hearing.

We now give our reasons for our decision.

Does the court have power to order that evidence filed by one party be not disclosed to the other party?

The main authority on this issue is the decision of the House of Lords in *Official Solicitor v K* [1963] 3 All ER 191, [1965] AC 201. I have already set out the facts of that case, and the way in which the issue came, on an appeal on a preliminary point, before the House of Lords.

In his speech, Lord Evershed quoted the well-known dictum of Tucker LJ in
a *Russell v Duke of Norfolk* [1949] 1 All ER 109 at 118 as follows:

> 'There are, in my view, no words which are of universal application to
> every kind of inquiry and every kind of domestic tribunal. The requirements
> of natural justice must depend on the circumstances of the case, the nature
> of the inquiry, the rules under which the tribunal is acting, the subject-
> *b* matter that is being dealt with, and so forth.'

Lord Evershed continued ([1963] 3 All ER 191 at 196–197, [1965] AC 201 at
218–219):

> *c* 'My lords, I would adopt Tucker, L.J.'s language and apply it to the present
> case. It is not in doubt that a judicial inquiry concerning the proper steps to
> be taken for the care and maintenance of a ward of court is subject—and
> necessarily subject because of the nature and purpose of the inquiry—to a
> procedure in many respects quite special. The case is normally heard in
> private and it is conceded that the judge may properly see—that it may be
> *d* his duty to see—the infant (and perhaps one or other or both parents) in
> private; and it is important to have in mind that in ordinary circumstances
> no final order is ever made. I venture to repeat and to emphasise that the aim
> and purpose of the judicial inquiry is the benefit of the infant, and for such
> purpose to make a decision about his or her immediate future upbringing or
> control. For such purpose also the infant is in relation to the court in a special
> *e* position distinct from that of other parties—for he or she is a ward of the
> court, a "child-in-law" of the court exercising the ancient prerogative and
> parental jurisdiction. If this be so, then it cannot, as it seems to me, be right
> that the court is always compelled in circumstances such as have arisen in the
> present case, to choose the lesser of two evils, to do that which in the court's
> view will be against the infant's interest and to console itself in so doing by
> *f* regarding the result as a distressing consequence of a broken home. If the
> court is compelled so to act, then it is surely disqualifying and disabling itself
> from exercising the judicial function with which it is invested . . . It follows,
> therefore, in my opinion, that there cannot be in circumstances such as exist
> or as are suggested in the present case, an absolute right on the mother's part
> to see the report of the Official Solicitor. On the other hand I have equally no
> *g* doubt that the judge must give very great weight indeed to the principle that
> he should not base a conclusion adverse to a proper party to the proceedings
> (and particularly a parent) on information which that party has not seen and
> has had no opportunity of challenging or contesting. When a situation arises
> such as has in the present case arisen, there may well indeed have to be, in
> *h* the language of Russell, L.J. ([1962] 3 All ER 1000 at 1016, [1963] Ch 381 at
> 417), a "balancing" of the generally accepted right of a properly interested
> party, particularly a parent, to disclosure of information submitted to the
> judge on which he proposes in some measure to base his conclusion (on the
> one hand) and the paramount interest of the ward of court (on the other
> hand). It may, however, be that, in such a situation, the latter consideration
> *j* on the balance should outweigh the former. But in reaching such a conclusion
> the judge must in the first place be well satisfied that the confidential
> information to which he proposes to pay regard is in truth reliable . . . It
> must, therefore, follow that a judge should not reach such a conclusion
> without the relevant disclosure to the party or parent save in rare cases and
> where he is fully satisfied judicially that real harm to the infant must
> otherwise ensue.'

Lord Evershed ([1963] 3 All ER 191 at 197, [1965] AC 201 at 220):

'I am concerned only to express my view that, though the judge must *a*
indeed attach very great weight to the principle which I have stated, yet there
can be no unqualified right on the part of a parent or other proper party to
disclosure of information supplied to the judge, unless the judge wholly
rejects such information in arriving at his conclusion. I accept entirely the
view of UPJOHN, L.J. ([1962] 3 All ER 1000 at 1007, [1963] Ch 381 at 403), *b*
that "the rights, claims or wishes (however one likes to describe them) of the
parents or other proper parties must be . . . given such weight as the judge
may consider proper, in forming his final view." But I cannot deduce from
that premise the conclusion that, if the conflict arises, the "right" of the
parent to disclosure must inevitably override what the judge regards as the
best interest of the ward. The interest of the infant is the paramount interest *c*
and purpose of the jurisdiction. Disclosure or no disclosure therefore must
in the end remain a matter for the judge's discretion . . .'

Lord Jenkins said ([1963] 3 All ER 191 at 205, [1965] AC 201 at 232):

'I must now return to the specific question whether the mother is entitled *d*
as of right to disclosure of the two reports made by the Official Solicitor as
guardian ad litem of the children. It seems to me, as it did to UNGOED-
THOMAS, J., that this question must be answered in the negative, the disclosure
(if any) to be allowed in any particular case being essentially a matter to be
determined by the judge in the exercise of his discretion. If it were not so,
there, so far as I can see, would be an end of any effective control of wards by *e*
the court. If the mother is to be entitled as of right to disclosure of the two
reports with which the present application is concerned, I do not see why, by
parity of reasoning, she should not equally be entitled to insist on like
disclosure of information from other sources however damaging to the ward
such disclosure might be. I appreciate that the welfare of the infant is the
paramount consideration, but surely this requirement can only be complied *f*
with if the judge, or the master on his behalf, is given a wide discretion to
determine whether the disclosure sought by the parent in the particular case
is in the best interests of the ward. It is objected that the use by the court of
undisclosed documents or information in wardship cases is objectionable as
offending against the fundamental principle of justice to the effect that
anyone against whom a charge is made must be given a fair opportunity of *g*
knowing and understanding what the charge is and on what evidence it is
based. The question whether in a particular case compliance with that
principle should be accorded greater or less importance than the probability,
whatever it may be, of damage (if any) to the infant ensuing from such
compliance, depends on the facts of that particular case; and any attempt to *h*
formulate general pronouncements applicable in all cases will be likely to
create more difficulties than it solves.'

Lord Hodson said ([1963] 3 All ER 191 at 206–207, [1965] AC 201 at 234–235):

'I agree with the Court of Appeal that this appeal raises an acute conflict
between two principles. It is said with force, as RUSSELL, L.J., remarked *j*
([1962] 3 All ER 1000 at 1015, [1963] Ch 381 at 416), that it is contrary to
natural justice that the contentions of a party in a judicial proceeding may be
overruled by considerations in the judicial mind which the party has no
opportunity of criticising or controverting because he or she does not know
what they are: that moreover the judge may (without the inestimable benefit

a

of critical argument) arrive at a wrong conclusion on the undisclosed material, and that even worse the undisclosed evidence may, if subjected to criticism, prove to be misconceived or based on false premises. On the other hand the substantive law governing proceedings of this character is summarised in the Guardianship of Infants Act, 1925, of which s. 1 says that the first and foremost consideration is the welfare of the infant. How then, it is said, can it be right to insist on the application of a view of natural justice over procedural law in a manner which in the view of the judge will do harm to the infant? ... There is no doubt that, although its origin lies in the prerogative of the Crown as parens patriae, the jurisdiction over infants has long been exercised by the judges of the Chancery Division in accordance with the principle to which VISCOUNT HALDANE, L.C., referred in *Scott* v. *Scott* ([1913] AC 417, [1911–13] All ER Rep 1) when he said ([1913] AC 417 at 437, [1911–13] All ER Rep 1 at 9): "There the judge who is administering their affairs in the exercise of what has been called a paternal jurisdiction, delegated to him from the Crown through the Lord Chancellor, is not sitting merely to decide a contested question. His position as an administrator as well as judge may require the application of another and overriding principle to regulate his procedure in the interests of those whose affairs are in his charge ... In the two cases of wards and lunatics the court is really sitting primarily to guard the interests of the ward or the lunatic. Its jurisdiction is in this respect paternal and administrative, and the disposal of controverted questions is an incident only in the jurisdiction. It may often be necessary, in order to attain its primary object, that the court should exclude the public. The broad principle which usually governs it, therefore, yields to the paramount duty, which is the care of the ward or lunatic." As the passage which I have read shows, the subject under consideration in *Scott's* case was the jurisdiction of courts to exclude the public, not as here one of the primary rules of natural justice expressed by the phrase audi alteram partem, but the conclusion that I have reached after long hesitation is that one must approach the question now under consideration from the point of view expressed by LORD HALDANE when discussing hearings in camera. In the last resort the welfare of the child must dominate and in those rare cases, of which this is one, where the judge has found himself unable to disregard a secret and unverified report yet has thought the report must not in the child's interest be shown to the parents, his view must prevail.'

Lord Devlin said ([1963] 3 All ER 191 at 209–210, [1965] AC 201 at 238–241):

'But a principle of judicial inquiry, whether fundamental or not, is only a means to an end. If it can be shown in any particular class of case that the observance of a principle of this sort does not serve the ends of justice, it must be dismissed; otherwise it would become the master instead of the servant of justice. Obviously, the ordinary principles of judicial inquiry are requirements for all ordinary cases and it can only be in an extraordinary class of case that any one of them can be discarded. This is what was so clearly decided in *Scott* v. *Scott* ([1913] AC 417, [1911–13] All ER Rep 1). That case offers much more than authority for the view, not challenged before your Lordships, that wardship proceedings are an exception to the general principle that justice cannot be done in camera. VISCOUNT HALDANE, L.C. sets out the terms on which such exceptions are to be made. After he had considered two exceptions to the general rule that justice must be done in public, namely, wardship proceedings and a case involving a secret process, he states the test which is applicable to both. He says ([1913] AC 417 at 437, [1911–13] All ER

Rep 1 at 9): "As the paramount object must always be to do justice, the
general rule as to publicity, after all only the means to an end, must   *a*
accordingly yield. But the burden lies on those seeking to displace its
application in the particular case to make out that the ordinary rules must as
of necessity be superseded by this paramount consideration. The question is
by no means one which, consistently with the spirit of our jurisprudence,
can be dealt with by the judge as resting in his mere discretion as to what is
expedient. The latter must treat it as one of principle, and as turning, not on   *b*
convenience, but on necessity." ... That test is not easy to pass. It is not
enough to show that dispensation would be convenient. It must be shown
that it is a matter of necessity in order to avoid the subordination of the ends
of justice to the means. I think that the learned judge in this case stated and
applied the test correctly, and I cannot do better than quote from what he
said ([1962] 3 All ER 178 at 180, [1963] Ch 381 at 386): "The jurisdiction   *c*
regarding wards of court which is now exercised by the Chancery Division is
an ancient jurisdiction deriving from the prerogative of the Crown as parens
patriae. It is not based on the rights of parents, and its primary concern is not
to ensure their rights but to ensure the welfare of the children ... and now
the legislature, by the Guardianship of Infants Act, 1925, s. 1, has expressly   *d*
enacted that where, in any proceedings before any court, the custody or the
upbringing of an infant is in question, the court in deciding that question
shall regard the welfare of the infant as the first and paramount consideration.
A ward of court case is not, therefore, an ordinary lis between the parties but
partakes of an administrative character ... In the ordinary lis between
parties, the paramount purpose is that the parties should have their rights   *e*
according to law, and in such cases the procedure, including the rules of
evidence, is framed to serve that purpose. Where, however, the paramount
purpose is the welfare of the infant, the procedure and rules of evidence
should serve and certainly not thwart that purpose. Over a very large field in
infant cases, the procedure and rules of evidence applicable to a lis between
parties serve that purpose admirably and are habitually applied, but they   *f*
should never be so rigidly applied as of inflexible right as to endanger or
prejudice the very purpose which they should serve. In general, publicity is
vital to the administration of justice. Disclosure to parties not only enables
them to present their case fully but it provides in some degree the advantages
of publicity; and it further ensures that the court has the assistance of those   *g*
parties in arriving at the right decision. So when full disclosure is not made,
it should be limited only to the extent essential to achieve the object of the
jurisdiction and no further." This is the essence of the matter. Where the
judge sits as an arbiter between two parties, he need consider only what they
put before him. If one or other omits something material and suffers from
the omission, he must blame himself and not the judge. Where the judge   *h*
sits purely as an arbiter and relies on the parties for his information, the
parties have a correlative right that he should act only on information which
they have had the opportunity of testing. Where the judge is not sitting
purely or even primarily as an arbiter but is charged with the paramount
duty of protecting the interests of one outside the conflict, a rule that is
designed for just arbitrament cannot in all circumstances prevail.'   *j*

Mr Vain argues that the principle embodied in *Official Solicitor v K* applies only
to wardship proceedings, and is therefore not applicable to the present case. I see
no reason why this should be so. Section 1 of the Children Act 1989 required the
judge, when considering the mother's application for custody of and for the

revocation of the father's access to T, to treat the child's welfare as the paramount
a consideration. As is clear from the passages I have quoted from the speeches in
Official Solicitor v K, the application of that principle was the whole basis of their
Lordships' decision that the mother was not entitled as of right to disclosure of
the Official Solicitor's confidential reports and the medical report.

My conclusion that the principles laid down in *Official Solicitor v K* applied to
cases relating to children who are not wards of court is confirmed by the decision
b of this court in *Re C (a minor: irregularity of practice)* [1991] 2 FLR 438. In that
case this court held that it was permissible for a judge in the exercise of his
discretion and acting in the paramount interests of the child, to see a court welfare
officer privately in his chambers during a trial, and that there was no absolute
objection to the receipt of a confidential report, but that the judge should only
c exercise his discretion to adopt either of these courses in exceptional circumstances.
In his judgment, with which Thorpe J agreed, Dillon LJ applied the principles to
be derived from *Official Solicitor v K*. He said (at 444): 'In my judgment, all
questions need to be decided by reference to what the House of Lords held in
Re K.'

It is right to say that he records that counsel for the appellant, the father, had
d accepted there can be no distinction between the wardship jurisdiction and the
jurisdiction under the Guardianship of Minors Act 1971 (now the Children Act
1989). However, it is clear that the court considered and adopted this concession
as part of its reasoning.

In my opinion, therefore, a court which is considering an application for an
order under ss 8 and 10 of the Children Act 1989 has the power, in its discretion,
e to receive and act on evidence adduced by one party, or emanating from a welfare
officer, which is not disclosed to the other party. That power is, however, only to
be exercised in most exceptional circumstances, in accordance with the principles
laid down in *Official Solicitor v K* [1963] 3 All ER 191, [1965] AC 201. Before
ordering that any such evidence be not disclosed to another party, the court will
f have to consider it in order to satisfy itself that the disclosure of the evidence
would be so detrimental to the welfare of the child or children under consideration
as to outweigh the normal requirements for a fair trial that all evidence must be
disclosed, so that all parties can consider it and if necessary seek to rebut it.

On this issue we were referred to other decisions of the courts. I have not found
it necessary to cite them in this judgment because, without disrespect to counsel,
g I did not find that they assisted me to arrive at a conclusion on the issue of
principle.

On the second issue, should this court then exercise its discretion to decide
whether the evidence should not be disclosed, or order the question to be reheard,
both counsel agreed that this court would be in as good a position to consider the
matter as would a court of first instance, and that if we did so there would be a
h saving of time. We therefore agreed to this course, which involved us reading
and considering the evidence which had not hitherto been disclosed.

*Should an order be made that the mother's evidence in support of her application,
or any part of it, should not be disclosed to the father?*

The evidence consists of an affidavit sworn by the mother on 26 March 1992,
j to which are exhibited reports by a consultant in child and family psychiatry, a
social worker and a police officer. We have also been supplied with a psychiatric
report dated 11 June 1992 from Dr McCann of the adolescent unit where L is at
present staying.

The information and advice contained in these documents can be summarised
as follows.

In the latter part of 1991 L's emotional condition gave grave cause for concern. On 30 December 1991 L informed a friend that her stepfather (the father in these *a* proceedings) had sexually abused her. She expressed the fear that, if the father learnt that she had made this complaint, he would kill her.

These complaints were investigated by the social services department of Bedfordshire County Council in January 1992. L complained of indecent assaults and of the use of force—punching, kicking and holding her down—by the father. Since these disclosures, L has taken overdoses of paracetamol and cut her arms. *b*

T became aware of the general nature of the complaints his sister was making, and of her fears for her life if the father should learn that she had made the complaints.

The mother terminated T's access to the father in order to ensure that he did not, during such access inadvertently tell his father something of L's complaints. This decision was made on the advice of the social services, mainly to protect L. *c*

The report dated 11 June 1992 from Dr McCann includes the following recommendation, which I regard as extremely sensible:

'I have been asked to consider whether I believe that it would be detrimental to [L's] mental state if [the father] were to see [the mother's] affidavit. In my opinion, the fear that [L] is currently experiencing about *d* this issue is increasing steadily. The longer this fear is avoided, the greater it will become in [L's] mind. [L] currently sees [the father] as very powerful but I believe part of this power lies in the "secret" that exists between [the father] and [L], i.e. the sexual abuse that has occurred to [L]. I do not believe that it would necessarily be detrimental to [L] if [the father] were to see [the *e* mother's] affidavit. It may be therapeutic for the abuse victim to confront the fear and progress forward thereafter. However, were this to happen, I feel strongly that it would need to occur while [L] was still an inpatient as she would need to feel that she was in a safe, containing environment to help her with her very real fear. For these reasons, I do not feel this step could have been taken while [L] was at home.' *f*

Conclusion

If, at the inter partes hearing on 15 April 1992, Judge Wilson had been made aware of the decision of the House of Lords in *Official Solicitor v K* [1963] 3 All ER 191, [1965] AC 201, and thus that he had the power to continue in force his ex parte order that the mother's affidavit should not be disclosed, I have no doubt at *g* all that it would have been wrong for him to exercise his discretion so as to continue the order in force. The order was sought, mainly if not entirely, for the protection of L, and it was T's welfare which was the paramount consideration when considering whether he should continue to have access to his father. Even if it were suggested that in some way T might be harmed, e g by being put in a *h* position where he had to try to conceal L's allegations from his father, that possibility had to be weighed against the grave injustice to the father which resulted from non-disclosure. L's allegations are, of course, extremely serious. It is quite wrong that, for an indefinite period, the father should not know of them and be given the opportunity to deny them if they are untrue or explain them if they are true in part. Balancing these factors, in my view the interests of justice *j* to the father greatly outweighed any possible detriment to T.

But there is another aspect of the matter which is reflected in Dr McCann's report. Having made these grave allegations, L must somehow be persuaded to overcome her expressed fear, and this can only be done when the allegations are disclosed to the father. I can understand that, while L was still at home, the *a* mother would not wish the allegations to be disclosed. But, once L was staying at the adolescent unit, this ceased to be a valid reason for non-disclosure. I am far from sure that it was right to make the order for non-disclosure ex parte in the first place, though I well understand the judge's anxiety to avoid what was presented to him as a real risk of harm to both children. But by the time the husband's application for discharge of the ex parte order came to be heard, there was in my view no justification for continuing the order in force.

b Although I have concluded that the learned judge made his decision of 15 April 1992 for reasons which, through no fault of his, were unsound, I am confident that the decision itself was correct. These are my reasons for the dismissal of the appeal.

c **BALCOMBE LJ.** I have had the advantage of reading in draft the judgment of Glidewell LJ in this case. I agree with him that the effect of the decisions of the House of Lords in *Official Solicitor v K* [1963] 3 All ER 191, [1965] AC 201 and of this court in *Re C (a minor: irregularity of practice)* [1991] 2 FLR 438 is that in any case which is directly concerned with the welfare of a child the court has power to direct that material, the disclosure of which may be damaging to the child,

d shall not be disclosed to a party to the case. However, the jurisdiction should only be exercised in exceptional circumstances, and then only for the shortest period possible consonant with preserving the welfare of the child.

In the present case the relevant facts are set out in the judgment of Glidewell LJ and I do not repeat them. In my judgment it was quite impossible that the father should be kept in indefinite ignorance of the allegations made against him

e by L, since those allegations were the basis of the mother's application that he be denied contact with his son T. If it was at any time proper to withhold from the father the nature of the allegations being made against him, it could only have been for such period as might have been necessary for L to be moved to a place of safety, so that the father did not know, and she knew that the father did not know, where she was. In my judgment the ex parte order of 27 March 1992

f should have been limited accordingly. Equally, by the time of the inter partes hearing on 15 April 1992 it would have been clearly wrong to continue further the ban on the father being shown material containing L's allegations against him, as the judge was minded to do had he not been convinced, wrongly, that he had no power to continue the ban.

g For these reasons, as well as those given by Glidewell LJ with which I agree, it was inevitable that this appeal should be dismissed.

BOREHAM J. I have had the advantage of reading the judgments of Glidewell and Balcombe LJJ. I agree, for the reasons they have given, that this appeal must be dismissed.

h
Appeal dismissed.

L I Zysman Esq   Barrister.

Hampshire County Council v S   *a*

FAMILY DIVISION
CAZALET J
17 SEPTEMBER, 13 OCTOBER 1992

Family proceedings – Orders in family proceedings – Contact order – Variation – **b**
Hearing – Local authority applying for variation of contact order – Justices varying
contact order without reading documents filed – Justices dealing with application on basis
of submissions only – Justices failing to give proper reasons and findings of fact for
variation of order – Procedure to be followed by justices on interim applications – Children
Act 1989, s 34(2) – Family Proceedings Courts (Children Act 1989) Rules 1991,
r 21(1)(6).   **c**

On 19 March 1992 the parents of a five-year-old boy agreed to the making of an
order under s 31 of the Children Act 1989 placing the child in the care of the local
authority and a contact order under s 34(2)[a] under which the child and the parents
were to have contact with a view to rehabilitation. The local authority
subsequently became concerned at the effect of contact on the boy and suspended   **d**
contact for seven days under s 34(6)[b] and applied for a variation of the contact
order. At a hearing for directions on 18 June 1992 the matter was adjourned for
an interim hearing on 25 June to decide only those matters relating to the
reduction of contact, if any, pending the final hearing. Although no specific
directions were given on 18 June as to the filing of evidence, the local authority   **e**
filed statements from four different deponents and the guardian ad litem filed
her report but the mother and father did not file any statements. On 25 June
1992 the justices, after seeking the views of the parties' legal representatives as to
how best to proceed given that there would not be enough time for evidence to
be called and without having read any of the evidence filed, decided, contrary to
the wishes of the local authority and guardian ad litem, to determine the question **f**
of interim contact on the basis of the parties' submissions rather than reading all
the statements. At the end of the hearing the justices made on order reducing the
parents' contact pending the final hearing and stated that their reasons would be
given within one week. The parents appealed on the ground that the justices had
acted contrary to r 21(1)[c] of the Family Proceedings Courts (Children Act 1989)
Rules 1991, which required justices to read before the hearing any documents   **g**
filed in respect of the hearing, and r 21(6), which provided that the justices had to
state any findings of fact and the reasons for the court's decision when making
their order.

Held – (1) Although concerned with an interim application, the hearing on 25   **h**
June 1992 was a 'hearing' within r 21(1) of the 1991 rules involving the making
of a judicial decision and the justices had failed to comply with the mandatory
requirements of r 21(1) that before the hearing they had to read the documents
which had been filed. Furthermore, since r 21(2) gave the justices a discretion to
make directions as to the order of speeches and evidence, at the 18 June hearing

j

---

a Section 34(2) provides: 'On an application made by the authority or the child, the court may make
   such order as it considers appropriate with respect to the contact which is to be allowed between
   the child and any named person.'
b Section 34(6) is set out at p 946 *f*, post
c Rule 21, so far as material, is set out at p 948 *h* and p 949 *b f*, post

a for directions they could and should have ordered the parents to file written statements before the hearing on 25 June. It followed that the justices' decision to deal with the interim application on the basis of submissions only without having read the filed statements was erroneous (see p 948 *f j*, p 949 *b c* and p 950 *g*, post).

(2) The limited statement given by the justices when making their order was a clear breach of r 21(6) since, although they were dealing with an interim application, the justices were not absolved from stating their findings of fact and
b giving proper reasons for their decision. The appeal would therefore be allowed and the justices' order set aside (see p 948 *f*, p 949 *g*, p 950 *g h* and p 952 *b*, post).

Observations on the way in which justices should deal with interim applications in family proceedings courts (see p 950 *j* to 952 *a*, post).

c **Notes**

For the making of care orders on the application of the local authority, see Supplement to 24 *Halsbury's Laws* (4th edn) para 732A.

For the Children Act 1989, ss 31, 34, see 6 *Halsbury's Statutes* (4th edn) (1992 reissue) 431, 437.

For the Family Proceedings Courts (Children Act 1989) Rules 1991, r 21, see 4
d *Halsbury's Statutory Instruments* (1992 reissue) 338.

Cases referred to in judgment

Hillingdon London BC v H [1993] 1 All ER 198, [1993] Fam 43, [1992] 3 WLR 521.
W (minors) v Hertfordshire CC (1992) Times, 1 September.

e **Appeal**

The parents of a child, S, who was in the care of the respondent, Hampshire County Council, appealed from the order of the Andover Family Proceedings Court made under s 34(9) of the Children Act 1989 and dated 25 June 1992, whereby it ordered that a contact order made on 19 March 1992 defining contact
f between S and the parents be varied so that the parents be limited to one two-hour supervised visiting contact each week. The facts are set out in the judgment.

Mark Johnstone (instructed by *Houghton Russell-Smith & Coward*, Andover and *Lemon Felton*, Salisbury) for the parents.
Patricia Kelly (instructed by *P C B Robertson*, Winchester) for the local authority.
g *Roberta Holland* (instructed by *Dutton Gregory & Williams*, Winchester) for the guardian ad litem.

Cur adv vult

h 13 October 1992. The following judgment was delivered.

CAZALET J. This appeal concerns a child, S, who is now nearly five years of age.

The first appellant is the mother of S. The second appellant is the father of S. I shall hereafter refer to the first and second appellants as 'mother' and 'father'
j respectively. They are jointly represented before me. The first respondent is the Hampshire County Council and the second respondent is S himself, who is represented by his guardian ad litem.

The mother and father appeal from an interim order made by the Andover Family Proceedings Court on 25 June 1992 when the court varied an order made by the family proceedings court on 19 March 1992.

The order of 19 March 1992 had been made by consent and was to the effect that S, having already been moved from his parents' home, should be placed in *a* the care of the local authority, but with arrangements building up from visiting to staying contact with a view to there being a rehabilitation of S to his parents. The consent order of 19 March 1992 established a pattern which was to lead on to staying contact starting at about mid-April for one night each week.

This plan was set in train. However, soon after the staying contact of once a week had started the local authority became concerned as to its effect on S. As a *b* result the local authority, in what appeared to it to be a worsening situation from S's standpoint, resolved to apply to the family proceedings court for an order substantially reducing contact, and in particular prohibiting staying contact.

In the event, on 25 June 1992, when the court was first required to make an order, the matter had to be dealt with on an interim basis. An interim order was *c* made to the effect that the mother's and father's contact to S should be reduced from 32 hours contact per week (which included unsupervised and staying contact) to two hours supervised contact once per week. It is against this interim order that the mother and father appeal.

Both the local authority and the guardian ad litem have been represented before me. For reasons to which I will turn in a moment they have indicated *d* through counsel that because of the course which was followed in the lower court they are not in a position to oppose this appeal being allowed.

The consent care order made on 19 March 1992 was made under s 31 of the Children Act 1989. It was coupled with the contact order, to which I have referred, made under s 34(2) of that Act.

S had visiting contact to his parents on 30 May 1992; his next contact was due *e* on 2 June 1992. In the light of their concern the local authority elected to exercise their powers under s 34(6) of the Act, which provides as follows:

'An authority may refuse to allow the contact which would otherwise be required by virtue of subsection (1) or an order under this section if—(*a*) they are satisfied that it is necessary to do so in order to safeguard or promote the *f* child's welfare; and (*b*) the refusal—(i) is decided upon as a matter of urgency; and (ii) does not last for more than seven days.'

Because the next contact date was 2 June 1992 the local authority was entitled under this section, subject to being satisfied as to the other provisions required by the section, to suspend contact for up to seven days. After the seven-day period *g* had almost elapsed the local authority issued its application, on 8 June 1992, to the family proceedings court, for a variation of contact. There was no hearing, interim or otherwise, at this stage, but it was agreed between the parties that pending the matter first coming before the court on 18 June 1992 some visiting, but not staying contact, should continue.

On 18 June 1992 the matter was listed for hearing before the Andover Family *h* Proceedings Court. All parties were present. It was accepted by all concerned that that hearing day should be treated as being for directions only, with the matter to go over to 25 June 1992 on the basis that, as was indicated by the court clerk, the justices would then only have time to hear the 'emergency' issues and an interim order could only then be made. Two visiting contact visits were agreed during the intervening week. *j*

The parties have agreed that there should be put before this court affidavits sworn to on behalf of the father and mother by the solicitors who represented them at the family proceedings court. At that stage the father and mother, although they had lived together for many years and continue so to do, were separately represented as it was thought that there might be a conflict of interest between them. The father's representative swore to an affidavit on 4 August 1992

a and an affidavit on behalf of the mother was sworn on 3 August 1992. The two deponents were present at court on both 18 and 25 June 1992. The mother's representative exhibits to her affidavit a full note which she took of the proceedings before the justices and that is confirmed by the father's representative. The court clerk took a very short note of the proceedings.

It is apparent from the evidence before me that, following the directions

b hearing on 18 June 1992, it was the understanding of all concerned that the hearing on 25 June was to be an interim hearing, with the afternoon set aside for it, and that only 'emergency issues' would be considered. It was understood that the 'emergency issues' were those matters which related to any reduction of contact pending the final hearing.

c No specific directions were given on 18 June 1992 as to the filing of evidence. However by that time the local authority had filed, pursuant to r 17 of the Family Proceedings Courts (Children Act 1989) Rules 1991, SI 1991/1395, statements running to 31 pages from four different deponents, namely the maternal grandmother (with whom S was living), the social worker, the health visitor and a resource centre worker. It was however envisaged that the local authority would

d cause the four witnesses from whom the filed statements had been taken to attend at court on 25 June 1992 so that they would be available for the purpose of cross-examination.

Prior to the resumed hearing on 25 June 1992 the solicitors for the father sought by letter to obtain from the local authority an outline of those matters in the filed statements upon which the local authority would rely at the resumed

e hearing in support of the 'emergency issues'. The local authority answered by stating the substance of the local authority's case and that the witnesses concerned would be available for cross-examination.

In fact the hearing on 25 June 1992 did not start until about 3.40 pm. Because of the shortage of time views were sought of the legal representatives concerned

f as to how the matter could best proceed on the basis that there would not be time for evidence to be called. The mother and father had not by then filed any statements and so the only written material before the court comprised that filed by the local authority, and a report from the guardian ad litem dated 24 June 1992. For the reasons set out in her report the guardian ad litem advised that there should be an immediate change in the contact arrangements with a

g reduction to two supervised contacts each week of one to two hours duration.

At the start of the hearing the justices indicated that they were not in a position to hear evidence. They had not read any of the statements filed. Those appearing on behalf of the local authority and the guardian ad litem required the justices to read the filed statements. Those appearing on behalf of the mother and father submitted that it would be most unfair to the mother and father if such statements

h were to be read because there were no statements as yet filed by the mother and father, and the court would, in such circumstances, obtain a wholly one-sided view of the matter. This procedural point was argued and the justices retired in order to decide what course to adopt. The notes of evidence prepared by the clerk of the court indicate that they decided to determine the question of interim contact 'on the basis of representation by parties rather than reading all the

j statements.' The matter proceeded on this basis and submissions were made by all concerned. Because the justices had not read the guardian ad litem's report, the representative on behalf of the guardian ad litem then told the justices that she felt so strongly about the matter that she intended to make her own submissions and that would include reading the guardian's statement to the court.

The hearing proceeded, with counsel on behalf of the local authority putting

the case for reduced contact. This inevitably meant that counsel was obliged to
make quite extensive reference to the detailed factual evidence in the statements   *a*
filed by the local authority.

In answer to this, submissions were made to the court on behalf of the mother
and father. Submissions were then made on behalf of the guardian ad litem and
at the conclusion of the submissions the guardian herself addressed the court. She
summarised the content of her report and recommended substantially reduced
contact.   *b*

At about 5.40 pm the bench retired. At 6.15 pm when the bench returned the
substance of what was then said by or on behalf of the chairman was as follows:

> 'The welfare of the child must come first. We are aware of the need to do
> something urgently and have therefore decided to make the following
> interim order: one session per week from 2–4 pm at the Family Resources   *c*
> Centre until final order. The reasons should be given in writing within one
> week.'

There was a discussion as to a date for a directions hearing. The justices were told
that witnesses required for the hearing would, for reasons of holiday, be in a
difficulty in attending after 7 July until a date into September. The justices   *d*
directed the parents to file their written statements of evidence by 9 July 1992.

The matter came back for a directions appointment on 9 July 1992. By that
time the parents had filed their evidence. The matter was put over to 23 July for
a further directions hearing. When the matter then came back before the justices
on 23 July 1992 they transferred the case to the county court.

On 10 August 1992, on application, the county court certified that the hearing   *e*
of the appeal was fit for vacation business. On 17 August 1992 leave to appeal out
of time was given to the parents and directions were given as to the hearing at the
care centre. On 7 and 8 September the care centre court at Portsmouth, at the end
of a two-day hearing, gave directions as to interim contact pending the final
hearing. This final hearing is now to take place at the care centre starting on 23   *f*
November next.

Although the court procedure on how to deal with interim applications of the
kind raised in the present case has not as yet been fully clarified, it is apparent that
the justices in the present case made a number of serious errors.

When the matter came back before them on 25 June 1992 it was envisaged
that the limited time available would only permit an interim order to be made.   *g*
The statements of the four witnesses to be called on behalf of the local authority
had in fact been filed pursuant to r 17 by 18 June 1992; yet at no time had the
justices read them. Rule 21(1) provides as follows:

> 'Before the hearing, the justice or justices who will be dealing with the case
> shall read any documents which have been filed under rule 17 in respect of   *h*
> the hearing.'

Although concerned with an interim application, this hearing involved the
making of a judicial decision and was a hearing within the meaning of r 21(1).
The justices therefore failed to comply with the mandatory provisions of r 21(1),
which required that, before the hearing, they must read those documents which
had been filed. Accordingly they should not have permitted any argument as to   *j*
whether they were required to read them; put quite simply they were obliged to
read these statements, including the report filed on behalf of the guardian ad
litem before the hearing began. I would add that, in my view, the justices should,
on 18 June 1992, have directed that the parents file written statements before the
hearing on 25 June 1992. These statements could have been short and to the

point, dealing only with the immediate issues. Fuller statements could later have
a been filed on their behalf prior to the final hearing. Had this course been taken
the justices would have had before them the substance of each party's case in
writing. Rule 21(2) provides as follows:

> 'The justices' clerk at a directions appointment, or the court at a hearing or
> directions appointment, may give directions as to the order of speeches and
> *b* evidence.'

Under this rule justices have a discretion, which must always be exercised
judicially, to give directions as to the order of speeches and evidence. However
because the justices in this case had not read the filed statements they were not, in
my view, in a position properly to exercise their discretion under this rule;
c accordingly any direction to deal with the interim application on the basis of
submissions only without having read the filed statements was wholly erroneous.
If, because of the shortage of time on that date, they had decided after reading the
filed statements to hear submissions only, they should, bearing in mind the
substantial change of direction arising from the interim order which they
proposed to make, have taken much more positive steps to ensure that the final
d hearing took place at an earlier stage, notwithstanding the difficulties that certain
witnesses had in attendance at court. A timetable to lead to an early hearing
should have been devised. Furthermore, in my view, given that the justices were
to permit the guardian ad litem to give her advice, they should also have permitted
her to have been cross-examined at that stage.

I turn now to the justices' reasons. Rule 21(5) and (6) provides as follows:
e

> '(5) Before the court makes an order or refuses an application or request,
> the justices' clerk shall record in writing—(*a*) the names of the justice or
> justices constituting the court by which the decision is made, and (*b*) in
> consultation with the justice or justices, the reasons for the court's decision
> and any findings of fact.
> *f* (6) When making an order or when refusing an application, the court, or
> one of the justices constituting the court by which the decision is made, shall
> state any findings of fact and the reasons for the court's decision.'

I have already referred to the short statement given by the bench when making
its order. This limited statement was, in my view, a clear breach of r 21(6).
g Although this was an interim application, the court was not absolved from stating
its findings of fact and giving proper reasons for the basis of its decision.

Furthermore, it does not appear that the appropriate record was made by the
justices' clerk, at that time, in compliance with r 21(5). Such a record must be
prepared before the court makes its order.

On 2 July 1992 I was told that a statement of the justices' reasons was served on
h the parties concerned. In *W (minors) v Hertfordshire CC* (1992) Times, 1 September
Booth J held as follows:

> 'Rule 21 was mandatory. In every case the decision-making process was
> the same. Parties were entitled to know the reasons and the findings. On
> July 28 a document purporting to contain the justices' reasons became
> *j* available to the parties. However, in view of the failure to comply with the
> provisions of rule 21 the reasons could not be admitted to the appellate court:
> see *Hillingdon London BC v H* ([1993] 1 All ER 198, [1993] Fam 43).'

The question accordingly arises as to whether in fact the justices' reasons are
admissible on this appeal. No point was taken before me in regard to this,
doubtless because no party opposes this appeal. However the reasons themselves

do not appear to comply with the formal requirements of r 21(5)(*a*), namely that of setting out the names of the justices concerned, although the substance of the *a* decision is then, in my view, adequately set out. Had reasons in this form, or substantially in this form been given on 25 June 1992, then no question could have been raised as to a breach of r 21(6). Nevertheless this was not the course which was followed. No proper reasons were given prior to the order being made. Accordingly following *W (minors) v Hertfordshire CC* the justices' reasons are not strictly admissible before me on this appeal. *b*

It is not suggested in the present case that the justices did not take a great deal of care in reaching their decision. However, it is inevitable that the drafting of findings and reasons can, particularly when a number of individuals are concerned, take much time even when the actual decision has been made following full discussion. In the present case the justices, as permitted by r 21(6), would have *c* been well advised to have required one of their number to come back the following court day and at that stage (and not before) give their decision. This would have avoided the time pressure to which they must have felt subjected and would have enabled the appropriate written record to have been completed before the order was made.

I turn now to the note of the hearing made by the clerk to the court. Rule 20 *d* reads as follows:

'The justices' clerk or the court shall keep a note of the substance of the oral evidence given at the hearing of, or directions appointment in, relevant proceedings.'

It is plain that the note made by the clerk is extremely short, omitting reference *e* to a number of the main submissions. Furthermore there is no reference in the note to the fact that submissions were made on behalf of the guardian ad litem, nor indeed that the guardian ad litem herself gave oral advice to the court.

Under r 20 the justices' clerk is required to keep a note of the *oral* evidence. However, in the present case, where competing submissions, in the absence of oral evidence, on matters of substances are made by the different parties, I consider *f* that it is desirable that the justices' clerk should, as a matter of practice, keep a much fuller note than was taken in the present case. Further and in any event, the note should have made reference to the fact that the guardian ad litem had given advice to the court and to the nature of that advice (see r 11(5)). In fact the disadvantages arising from the paucity of the note by the clerk have been *g* alleviated by the full note taken by the legal representatives who were at court.

For the reasons which I have given the hearing before the justices was, in my view, fatally flawed on the grounds of the improper and erroneous procedures adopted. However, as a result of the justices transferring this case to the care centre on 23 July 1992 matters have, happily, proceeded satisfactorily from there and, as I have indicated, an interim order has already been made with the hearing *h* date for the substantive application fixed. It follows therefore that it is not necessary for me to make any order on the appeal other than that of setting aside the interim order which the justices made on 18 June 1992.

I have been told that, in the light of the procedural problems which have arisen in the present case, it would help if I was to give some guidance as to the way in which justices should deal with interim applications of the nature raised in these *j* proceedings. Accordingly with the President's approval I make the following observations.

1. Justices should bear in mind that they are not, at an interim hearing, required to make a final conclusion; indeed it is because they are unable to reach a final conclusion that they are empowered to make an interim order. An interim

order or decision will usually be required so as to establish a holding position,

a after weighing all the relevant risks, pending the final hearing. Nevertheless justices must always ensure that the substantive issue is tried and determined at the earliest appropriate date. Any delay in determining the question before the court is likely to prejudice the welfare of the child (see s 1(2) of the 1989 Act).

2. If justices find that they are unable to provide the appropriate hearing time,

b be it through pressure of work or for some other reason, they must, when an urgent interim order may have to be made, consider taking steps pursuant to r 14(2)(h) to transfer the proceedings laterally to an adjacent family proceedings court.

3. At the start of a hearing which is concerned with interim relief, justices will usually be called upon to exercise their discretion under r 21(2) as to the order of

c speeches and evidence. The circumstances prevailing will almost certainly not permit full evidence to be heard. Accordingly, in such proceedings, justices should rarely make findings as to disputed facts. These will have to be left over to the final hearing.

4. Justices must bear in mind that the greater the extent to which an interim order deviates from a previous order or the status quo the more acute the need is

d likely to be for an early final hearing date. Any disruption in a child's life almost invariably requires early resolution. Justices should be cautious about changing a child's residence under an interim order. The preferred course should be to leave the child where it is with a direction for safeguards and the earliest possible hearing date.

5. When an interim order may be made which will lead to a substantial change

e in a child's position, justices should consider permitting limited oral evidence to be led and challenged by way of cross-examination. However, it will necessarily follow that, in cross-examination, the evidence will have to be restricted to the issues which are essential at the interim stage. To this end the court may well have to intervene to ensure that this course is followed and that there is not a

f 'dress rehearsal' of the full hearing.

6. Justices should, if possible, ensure that they have before them written advice from the guardian ad litem. When there are substantial issues between the parties the guardian should, if possible, be at court to give oral advice. A party who is opposed to a recommendation made by the guardian should normally be given an opportunity to put questions to him/her in regard to advice given to the court.

g 7. Justices must always comply with the mandatory requirements of the 1991 rules. These include compliance with: (a) r 21(1), which requires the justices to read, before the hearing, any documents which have been filed under r 17; (b) r 21(5), which requires the justices' clerk to make the appropriate written record of the hearing and in consultation with the justices to record the reasons for the court's decision and any findings of fact; and (c) r 21(6), which requires the court,

h when making its order, or giving its decision, to state any findings of fact and the reasons for the court's decision.

8. If shortage of time or some other circumstance delays the court in the preparation of its written findings of fact and reasons, justices should adjourn the making of their order or the giving of their decision until the following court day or the earliest possible date. At that further hearing it is permissible for one of

j their number to return to court and state the decision, findings of fact and reasons (see r 21(6)). When the length of a hearing lasts beyond normal hours it will often be sensible for the court to take this course so that it is not formulating its reasons and making perhaps a difficult decision under the sort of pressure which can arise when a sitting runs late into the day.

9. When justices grant interim relief, they should state their findings and

reasons concisely. Although it will not normally be open to them to make findings on disputed facts (because the court will not have heard the full evidence) *a* it may assist if justices summarise briefly the essential factual issues between the parties.

I return now to the instant appeal. For the reasons which I have already given, I allow this appeal but make no other order save that of setting aside the order made by the justices on 25 June 1992.

b

Appealed allowed.

Bebe Chua Barrister.

c

Costellow v Somerset County Council

COURT OF APPEAL, CIVIL DIVISION

SIR THOMAS BINGHAM MR, STUART-SMITH AND SIMON BROWN LJJ

28 OCTOBER, 9 NOVEMBER 1992

d

Action – Dismissal – Failure to serve statement of claim – Application to dismiss action for want of prosecution – Plaintiff failing to deliver statement of claim within time specified in rules of court – Plaintiff guilty of inexcusable but not inordinate delay – Defendant not prejudiced by delay – Appropriate practice to be followed in deciding whether action should be dismissed.

e

On 15 September 1987 the plaintiff suffered personal injuries when he slipped on loose gravel thrown onto a pavement during road resurfacing works. He consulted solicitors but no claim was intimated to the defendant highway authority until a letter before action dated 13 September 1990. The following day a writ was issued, just within the three-year limitation period, against the defendants claiming damages for personal injuries but it was not served on the defendants until 11 January 1991, just within the four-month period allowed for service. On 24 May 1991, by which time no statement of claim had been served despite repeated reminders and threats to apply for the action to be dismissed, the defendants issued a summons to dismiss the plaintiff's action for failure to comply *g* with RSC Ord 18, r 1 by serving a statement of claim, failure to serve a medical report or schedule of loss in breach of RSC Ord 18, r 12(4)(a) or for want of prosecution. The district judge made the order sought and his decision was affirmed on appeal by the judge, who also dismissed an application by the plaintiff for leave to serve the statement of claim out of time on the ground that the plaintiff had not shown good reason for the delay. The plaintiff appealed, *h* contending that the delay complained of after the issue of proceedings had caused no prejudice or serious risk of prejudice to the defendant, that although it was inexcusable it was not inordinate and that therefore the action should be allowed to proceed.

Held – In the ordinary way and in the absence of special circumstances, such as *j* procedural abuse, questionable tactics, contumelious and intentional default or where a default was repeated or persisted in after a peremptory order, the court should not exercise its inherent jurisdiction to dismiss a plaintiff's action for want of prosecution unless the delay complained of after the issue of the proceedings

had caused at least a real risk of prejudice to the defendant. A similar approach
should govern applications to dismiss on failure to comply with a time limit
under Ords 19, 24, 25, 28 and 34. Furthermore, the approach to applications to
extend the time limit under Ord 3, r 5 should in most cases not be very different
and save in special cases or exceptional circumstances it would rarely be appropriate
to refuse the plaintiff an extension because of a procedural fault where the overall
justice of the case required that the action be allowed to proceed. Although the
plaintiff's case was not very strong there was no ground for dismissing the action
for want of prosecution in the absence of prejudice to the defendants. The appeal
would therefore be allowed and the plaintiff's application for an extension of time
in which to serve the statement of claim would be granted (see p 960 *a* to *h*, post).

Per curiam. There is no general rule that where the defendant seeks to dismiss
an action and the plaintiff seeks an extension of time the plaintiff's application
should be heard first, with dismissal being the inevitable consequence if he fails
to show good reason for his procedural default. In most cases it is appropriate for
the court to hear both summonses together, since in considering what justice
requires the court is concerned to do justice to both parties, and the case is best
viewed in the round (see p 959 *h j* and p 960 *g h*, post).

Notes

For judgment in default of service of statement of claim, see 37 *Halsbury's Laws*
(4th edn) para 404, and for cases on the subject, see 37(1) *Digest* (Reissue) 246,
1644–1645 and 37(3) *Digest* (Reissue) 27, 3092.

Cases referred to in judgments

Allen v Sir Alfred McAlpine & Sons Ltd [1968] 1 All ER 543, [1968] 2 QB 229,
[1968] 2 WLR 366, CA.
Birkett v James [1977] 2 All ER 801, [1978] AC 297, [1977] 3 WLR 38, HL.
Erskine Communications Ltd v Worthington (1991) Times, 8 July, [1991] CA
Transcript 725.
Hytrac Conveyors Ltd v Conveyors International Ltd [1982] 3 All ER 415, [1983] 1
WLR 44, CA.
Price v Dannimac Ltd (1990) Independent, 3 August, [1990] CA Transcript 579.
Revici v Prentice Hall Inc [1969] 1 All ER 772, [1969] 1 WLR 157, CA.

Cases also cited or referred to in skeleton arguments

Abouchalache v Hilton International Hotels (UK) Ltd (1982) 126 SJ 857, CA.
Boys v Chaplin [1968] 1 All ER 283, [1968] 2 QB 1, CA; affd [1969] 2 All ER 1085,
[1971] AC 356, HL.
Clough v Clough [1968] 1 All ER 1179, [1968] 1 WLR 525, CA.
Dept of Transport v Chris Smaller (Transport) Ltd [1989] 1 All ER 897, [1989] AC
1197, HL.
Dutton v Spink & Beeching (Sales) Ltd [1977] 1 All ER 287, CA.
Greek City Co Ltd v Demetriou (trading as Spectron Electronics), Greek City Co Ltd v
Athanasiou (trading as Alpha Electrical Contractors) [1983] 2 All ER 921.
Halls v O'Dell [1992] 2 QB 393, CA.
Marlton (an infant) v Lee-Leviten [1968] 2 All ER 874, [1968] 1 WLR 1214, CA.
Martin v Turner [1970] 1 All ER 256, [1970] 1 WLR 82, CA.
Morelle Ltd v Wakeling [1955] 1 All ER 708, [1955] 2 QB 379, CA.
Rowe v Tregaskes [1968] 3 All ER 447, [1968] 1 WLR 1475, CA.
Young v Bristol Aeroplane Co Ltd [1944] 2 All ER 293, [1944] KB 718, CA; affd
[1946] 1 All ER 98, [1946] AC 163, HL.

Interlocutory appeal

The plaintiff, Joseph Henry William Costellow, appealed with the leave of the   *a*
judge from the decision of Sir Gervase Sheldon sitting as a judge of the High
Court in the Queen's Bench Division on 11 November 1991 dismissing the
plaintiff's appeal from the decision of District Judge Turner sitting in chambers
at Taunton given on 6 August 1991 striking out the plaintiff's claim pursuant to
RSC Ord 19, r 1 for failure to serve a statement of claim within the time limited
by RSC Ord 18, r 1 and refusing to extend the time for serving the statement of   *b*
claim in an action in which the plaintiff claimed from the defendants, Somerset
County Council, as the highway authority responsible for the maintenance and/
or repair of St Augustine Street, Taunton, Somerset, (1) damages for personal
injuries and consequential losses sustained on 15 September 1987 by reason of the
negligence and/or breach of duty of the defendants, their servants or agents with
regard to the carrying out of the maintenance and/or repair of the highway and   *c*
(2) interest pursuant to s 35A of the Supreme Court Act 1981. The facts are set out
in the judgment of Sir Thomas Bingham MR.

Dermod O'Brien QC and *Stephen Archer* (instructed by *Clarke Willmott & Clarke,*
    Taunton) for the plaintiff.   *d*
Timothy Preston QC and *Henry de Lotbiniere* (instructed by *Porter Bartlett & Mayo,*
    Yeovil) for the defendants.

Cur adv vult

9 November 1992. The following judgments were delivered.   *e*

SIR THOMAS BINGHAM MR. On 6 August 1991 District Judge Turner,
sitting in Taunton, struck out the plaintiff's action for failure to serve a statement
of claim. That decision was affirmed on 11 November 1991 by Sir Gervase
Sheldon, sitting as a judge of the High Court in Exeter, who also refused an
application by the plaintiff for an extension of time to serve a statement of claim.   *f*
The plaintiff challenges the judge's decision with leave granted by the judge.

The facts giving rise to the appeal are of the simplest. The plaintiff says that on
15 September 1987 he slipped on loose gravel thrown onto a pavement in Taunton
during road resurfacing works. He suffered personal injuries as a result. He
consulted solicitors but no claim was intimated to the defendants until a letter   *g*
before action dated 13 September 1990. A writ was issued against the defendants
on the following day, just within the three-year limitation period.

In October the defendants called for a statement of claim, although the writ
had not been served, and the plaintiff's solicitors said they would serve one. But
they did not do so. The writ was served on 11 January 1991, just within the four-
month period allowed for service.   *h*

The statement of claim became due on 2 February 1991. The plaintiff's
solicitors invited the defendants' solicitors on 11 February to agree to a moratorium
in service of the statement of claim, but the defendants' solicitors refused to agree
and spoke of applying to dismiss for want of prosecution. On 1 March 1991 the
plaintiff's solicitors sought to explain their reasons for delay in serving the
statement of claim, but the defendants' solicitors again threatened to apply for   *j*
dismissal of the action. On 24 May 1991, no statement of claim having been
served, the defendants duly issued a summons. In this they asked that the
plaintiff's claim be dismissed for failure to comply with RSC Ord 18, r 1 by
serving a statement of claim, and alternatively on the ground that no medical
report or schedule of loss had been served, in breach of Ord 18, r 12(4)(*a*), and,

alternatively, for want of prosecution. When the summons was heard by the
a district judge he had no evidence before him other than an affidavit of the
defendants exhibiting the correspondence. He made the order asked. The
plaintiff's solicitors had by then, on 25 June 1991, tried to serve a statement of
claim together with a medical report and schedule of special damage, which the
defendant had refused to accept.

By the date of the appeal to the judge on 11 November 1991 there had been
b two changes. First, the plaintiff's solicitors had issued a summons seeking leave
to serve the statement of claim out of time. Secondly, the plaintiff's solicitor had
sworn an affidavit seeking to explain and excuse the delay. He advanced three
reasons. Following the accident in September 1987 the plaintiff had suffered
another accident and had instructed his solicitors to concentrate on that. There
had been doubt as to the local authority responsible for the pavement where the
c original accident had occurred. And, most importantly, there had been difficulty
in arranging an appointment for the medical examination of the plaintiff and
obtaining a medical report.

On the appeal, the judge directed himself in accordance with a recent decision
of the Court of Appeal in *Price v Dannimac Ltd* (1990) Independent, 3 August,
d which I discuss below. With reference to that case he said, according to the
approved note of his judgment:

'It is for the plaintiff as applicant in that application [for an extension of
time to serve the statement of claim] to satisfy the court that time should be
extended. The plaintiff was very seriously in default and had to tender a good
e reason for the delay.'

On the instant case, he said:

'I am conscious of the fact that greater delay occurred in the three years
and the delay since then has been relatively minor. I approach the matter on
the basis that in order to extend time, the plaintiff has to satisfy me there is
f good reason for the delay. I have read the affidavit by [the plaintiff's solicitor]
and I am not persuaded there was good reason.'

This last conclusion of the judge is not challenged. The plaintiff accepts there was
no good reason for delay in serving the statement of claim. If the medical report
and schedule of special damage were not ready, application could have been made
g to the court under Ord 18, r 12(1B).

In conclusion, the judge held that he should exercise his discretion to extend
time, as under Ord 6, r 8, only if the plaintiff showed a good reason for his delay:

'That is the principle which should apply in the present instance although
the rules are not identical. I am not persuaded to grant leave. That is the end
h of the matter. Dismissal is a formality. I would in any event have taken the
view that I would have complied with the application of the defendant and
would have dismissed the action and upheld the decision of District Judge
Turner.'

In *Price v Dannimac Ltd* a personal injuries plaintiff delayed in issuing her writ
j and delayed in serving it. There was then a delay of some 22 months in serving a
statement of claim. The plaintiff sought an extension of time to serve it. The
defendant applied to dismiss for want of prosecution. When the matter reached a
deputy judge on appeal he directed himself:

'If the defendants are unable to persuade me that this action should be
dismissed for want of prosecution then there is no reason to refuse the leave

which the plaintiff seeks. Such a conclusion of fact on that issue would make
this an appropriate case to go forward to trial.'   a

Commenting on this direction, Fox LJ said (and I read from the transcript):

'That may have the effect of reversing the burden of proof in relation to
the application for extension of time. It is for the plaintiff as applicant in that
application to satisfy the court that time should be extended. If the plaintiff
fails to discharge that burden, then the action is defunct. It can go no further.   b
Striking out would follow as a formality. If the application to extend time
failed, there would be no action to go to trial. The result is that the decision
on either application may have the practical effect of deciding the whole
matter. If, however, the application to dismiss the action for want of
prosecution fails, the plaintiff still has to persuade the court that it is a proper   c
case to extend time for delivery of the statement of claim. The position here
is that the plaintiff is very seriously in default. She was no less than 22
months out of time in serving the statement of claim. In order to justify an
extension of time she must tender a good reason for the delay.'

It is evident that in the present case the learned judge based himself in particular   d
on that last sentence.

Later in his judgment Fox LJ said:

'This is a case of very serious delay amounting almost to two years before
the statement of claim was attempted to be served. In my view, the evidence
comes nowhere near justifying that delay. The evidence is thin in the
extreme. One is given little or no information at all as to what was actually   e
done, what inquiries were made and when they were made to enable the
claim to be proceeded with. The result, in my view, is that the evidence is
quite inadequate to explain the delay and does not justify an order extending
time under Ord 3, r 5. I would, therefore, dismiss the application to extend
time. That is really enough to dispose of the case but for completeness let me   f
consider the application to dismiss for want of prosecution.'

He went on to hold that the plaintiff's delay had been prejudicial to the defendant
and that the action should be dismissed for want of prosecution. Johnson J, the
other member of the court, took the same view on both points.

Price v Dannimac Ltd is relied on by the editors of *The Supreme Court Practice
1993* Vol 1, para 19/1/4 as authority for this proposition: g

'When the court is faced with an application by the plaintiff for an
extension of time in which to serve a statement of claim under O. 3, r. 5 and
O. 18, r. 1, and a cross-application by the defendant to dismiss the action for
want of prosecution under O. 19, r. 1, it should consider the plaintiff's
application first, since it is for the plaintiff to satisfy the court that time   h
should be extended, and, if he fails to discharge that burden, the cross-
application becomes a mere formality . . .'

On the hearing of this appeal our attention was drawn (as that of the judge
below was not) to a decision of the Court of Appeal given on 22 May 1991, *Erskine
Communications Ltd v Worthington* (1991) Times, 8 July. The facts and procedural   j
history of that case were very different from those of *Price v Dannimac Ltd* and the
present case. The common features were delay (of about three months) in service
of a statement of claim and application by the defendants to dismiss the action for
want of prosecution. At first instance the judge declined to dismiss for want of
prosecution and gave the plaintiffs leave to serve a statement of claim out of time.

The Court of Appeal affirmed that decision, and in doing so made valuable
a observations on the correct approach to issues of this kind. In argument in that
case, the defendants had relied on *Hytrac Conveyors Ltd v Conveyors International
Ltd* [1982] 3 All ER 415, [1983] 1 WLR 44 and also *Price v Dannimac Ltd*. Mustill
LJ, in a leading judgment with which Balcombe and Woolf LJJ agreed, said (and
I read from the transcript):

b   'On these authorities the appellants based a number of propositions. It is
convenient to take the first three together. They are:—(1) there is a difference
between the standards to be applied when the plaintiff requires an extension
of the time for delivering his statement of claim and when the defendant
seeks to have the action dismissed under the general jurisdiction; (2) the
burden of proof is different in the two cases; (3) whereas in the present case
c   there are cross-applications the question of extending the time for service
should be considered first. As regards the first and second of these
propositions, I am willing to accept that an application to extend time in the
context of a failure to comply with rules of court may be approached in a
rather different light from an application to dismiss for want of prosecution.
In the one instance the plaintiff has by instituting his action submitted
d   himself to an explicit and mandatory regime, set out in the rules. If he wishes
his action to continue notwithstanding his transgression of these rules, he has
some work to do, in the sense of persuading the court that in the interests of
justice the action ought to go ahead, whereas in the case of an application to
dismiss under the general jurisdiction, where often the plaintiff's lack of
e   progress does not directly infringe any rule of court, the defendant must
make the running so as to show that there is good reason why the proceedings,
apparently well constituted, should be brought to a halt. Thus, I am ready to
go this far with the appellants that the principles, so far as there are any,
governing the application to extend and the application to dismiss may on
occasion require the facts to be looked at in a rather different perspective. So
f   that, for example, the inability of the defendant to prove that he has suffered
detriment through the delay, or the fact that a fresh action may be started
within the time limit, are now regarded as almost inevitably fatal to an
attempt to dismiss, whereas in the context of a long overdue statement of
claim, which is not only a breach of the rules but may leave the defendant
without any clear idea of the case which he has to meet, may call for an
g   assessment which treats the plaintiff more severely. Nevertheless, these are
only shades of emphasis. For my part, I deprecate the attempts which are
constantly made to cram the general discretions conferred by the rules of
court into a set of rigid formulae, expressed in terms of the burden of proof,
and so on. The rules are an indispensable framework for the orderly
administration of justice. But they are no more. They should not be a prison
h   restricting the free exercise by the court of its powers to conduct the litigation
brought before it in whatever way, consistently with rules, seems [most] fair
in the circumstances of the individual case. Thus, when one comes to regard
the appellants' third proposition, its artificiality is easily seen. In some cases,
for example where the real vice is not the plaintiff's breach of a rule, but his
consistent delay in prosecuting the action, it will be sensible to look at the
j   dismissal first. In others, the total delay may not be long, so that a fair hearing
is still feasible; and yet the plaintiff's breach of the rules may be serious
enough, and the immediate consequences sufficiently damaging, to justify a
course which enables the defendant to have the action disposed of with all
the attendant costs, even if at some later date a properly prepared and

conducted action can be started afresh. In still other cases, the factors
weighing in the scales of justice may be substantially the same, whichever of *a*
the cross-applications is considered. It is true that in *Price v Dannimac Ltd* the
court started with the application to extend; but it does not follow that this
is the only permissible point of entry. It is also true that the court disapproved
of the judge's formulation, quoted above, which entailed that failure on
dismissal inevitably led to the granting of an extension. But this does not
imply that, because in one case it is the defendant and in the other the *b*
plaintiff who makes the application, the nature of the inquiry to be
performed, and the outcome of it, will necessarily be different. In some
instances it will be sensible to start with the extension; in others with the
dismissal; and in the remainder the best course will be to look at the merits
of both applications together. The appellants' next proposition is also founded *c*
on *Price v Dannimac Ltd,* and is to the effect that a plaintiff who is late in
tendering a statement of claim must furnish a convincing excuse for the
delay if his application for an extension of time is to succeed. I do not agree.
I go this far with the appellants, that the reference to an "excuse" in *Price v
Dannimac Ltd* must have meant "an acceptable explanation", not a mere
assertion that the person in charge of the action forgot the statement of claim *d*
or was too busy to get on with it. I also accept, what is obvious, that the
tendering of an acceptable excuse, such as illness, will prompt a more
sympathetic response to the application than if the omission was caused by
neglect. Furthermore, there is no doubt, as I have already said, that the party
guilty of inexcusable delay in complying with the rules, rather than his
opponent, has to make the running when the court is asked to exercise a *e*
discretion. This is, I believe, all that can be extracted by way of principle
from *Revici v Prentice Hall Inc* [1969] 1 All ER 772, [1969] 1 WLR 157, a case
in which, it may be noted, the applicant sought an extension of time for
appealing, and was therefore in a situation in which his opponent had
obtained an order which on the face of it was final. But it would be absurd to *f*
say that every instance of overstepping the time limit without excuse,
however short and however lacking in harmful consequence to the defendant,
should be punished by the loss of the action. I am confident that the court in
Price v Dannimac Ltd intended no such result.'

It is plain that the court would not have accepted the stark proposition quoted *g*
from the current *Supreme Court Practice.* The difference of approach between *Price
v Dannimac Ltd* and *Erskine Communications Ltd v Worthington* is, indeed, referred
to in *The Supreme Court Practice 1993* vol 1, para 3/5/6.

On the hearing of this appeal, counsel for the appellant plaintiff criticised the
decision in *Price v Dannimac Ltd.* It was, he argued, inconsistent with the line of
authority established by leading cases such as *Allen v Sir Alfred McAlpine & Sons* *h*
Ltd [1968] 1 All ER 543, [1968] 2 QB 229 and *Birkett v James* [1977] 2 All ER 801,
[1978] AC 297 to dismiss actions where, as here, the plaintiff's delay complained
of after the issue of proceedings had caused no prejudice or serious risk of
prejudice to the defendant. Put shortly, he submitted that the delay involved in
almost every application to strike out for want of prosecution carries with it a
failure by the plaintiff to comply with a procedural time limit and thus his need *j*
to apply for an extension of time. To refuse an extension and therefore dismiss
the action merely because the delay is inexcusable is, he submits, wholly
inconsistent with the great body of jurisprudence recognising that actions are not
ordinarily dismissed for want of prosecution unless the delay is not merely

inexcusable but also inordinate and, more pertinently to this appeal, such as to
a cause prejudice. It is a powerful argument.

Counsel for the defendants did not argue for a rigid approach along the lines
suggested by *The Supreme Court Practice* but did point to the plaintiff's four and a
half month delay in serving his statement of claim, following a long delay in
telling the defendants of his claim and issuing proceedings, and following
repeated reminders and threats by the defendants. He could not, however, point
b to any prejudice the defendants might have suffered as a result of the plaintiff's
failure to serve a statement of claim in time.

We are told that there is some uncertainty among practitioners and judges as
to the appropriate practice in situations such as this. It is plainly desirable that we
should give such guidance as we can.

c As so often happens, this problem arises at the intersection of two principles,
each in itself salutary. The first principle is that the rules of court and the
associated rules of practice, devised in the public interest to promote the
expeditious dispatch of litigation, must be observed. The prescribed time limits
are not targets to be aimed at or expressions of pious hope but requirements to be
met. This principle is reflected in a series of rules giving the court a discretion to
d dismiss on failure to comply with a time limit: Ord 19, r 1, Ord 24, r 16(1), Ord
25, r 1(4) and (5), Ord 28, r 10(1) and Ord 34, r 2(2) are examples. This principle
is also reflected in the court's inherent jurisdiction to dismiss for want of
prosecution.

The second principle is that a plaintiff should not in the ordinary way be denied
an adjudication of his claim on its merits because of procedural default, unless the
e default causes prejudice to his opponent for which an award of costs cannot
compensate. This principle is reflected in the general discretion to extend time
conferred by Ord 3, r 5, a discretion to be exercised in accordance with the
requirements of justice in the particular case. It is a principle also reflected in the
liberal approach generally adopted in relation to the amendment of pleadings.

f Neither of these principles is absolute. If the first principle were rigidly
enforced, procedural default would lead to dismissal of actions without any
consideration of whether the plaintiff's default had caused prejudice to the
defendant. But the court's practice has been to treat the existence of such prejudice
as a crucial, and often a decisive, matter. If the second principle were followed
without exception, a well-to-do plaintiff willing and able to meet orders for costs
g made against him could flout the rules with impunity, confident that he would
suffer no penalty unless or until the defendant could demonstrate prejudice. This
would circumscribe the very general discretion conferred by Ord 3, r 5, and
would indeed involve a substantial rewriting of the rule.

The resolution of problems such as the present cannot in my view be governed
by a single universally applicable rule of thumb. A rigid, mechanistic approach is
h inappropriate. Where, as here, the defendant seeks to dismiss and the plaintiff
seeks an extension of time, there can be no general rule that the plaintiff's
application should be heard first, with dismissal of his action as an inevitable
consequence if he fails to show a good reason for his procedural default. In the
great mass of cases, it is appropriate for the court to hear both summonses
together, since, in considering what justice requires, the court is concerned to do
j justice to both parties, the plaintiff as well as the defendant, and the case is best
viewed in the round. In the present case, there was before the district judge no
application by the plaintiff for extension, although there was before the judge. It
is in my view of little or no significance whether the plaintiff makes such an
application or not: if he does not, the court considering the defendant's application

to dismiss will inevitably consider the plaintiff's position and, if the court refuses
to dismiss, it has power to grant the plaintiff any necessary extension whether *a*
separate application is made or not.

Cases involving procedural abuse (such as *Hytrac Conveyors Ltd v Conveyors
International Ltd* [1982] 3 All ER 415, [1983] 1 WLR 44) or questionable tactics
(such as *Revici v Prentice Hall Inc* [1969] 1 All ER 772, [1969] 1 WLR 157) may call
for special treatment. So, of course, will cases of contumelious and intentional
default and cases where a default is repeated or persisted in after a peremptory *b*
order. But in the ordinary way, and in the absence of special circumstances, a
court will not exercise its inherent jurisdiction to dismiss a plaintiff's action for
want of prosecution unless the delay complained of after the issue of proceedings
has caused at least a real risk of prejudice to the defendant. A similar approach
should govern applications made under Ords 19, 24, 25, 28 and 34. The approach *c*
to applications under Ord 3, r 5 should not in most cases be very different. Save
in special cases or exceptional circumstances, it can rarely be appropriate, on an
overall assessment of what justice requires, to deny the plaintiff an extension
(where the denial will stifle his action) because of a procedural default which,
even if unjustifiable, has caused the defendant no prejudice for which he cannot
be compensated by an award of costs. In short, an application under Ord 3, r 5 *d*
should ordinarily be granted where the overall justice of the case requires that the
action be allowed to proceed.

In the present case, the judge was in my view misled by *Price v Dannimac Ltd*
and by reliance on an inappropriate analogy with Ord 6, r 8 into taking much too
narrow a view of the task before him. Had he viewed the case in the round, he
would have been bound to hold that there was no ground for dismissing the *e*
action for want of prosecution in the absence of prejudice to the defendants. He
would also have felt it unjust to stifle the plaintiff's claim on the basis of a delay
which he described as 'relatively minor', however lame the excuses for it, in the
absence of such prejudice. The plaintiff's case may not be very strong, but on a
proper direction in law the conclusion is in my view inescapable that he should
not be precluded from pursuing it for whatever it is worth. Since the judge's *f*
exercise of discretion was in my judgment vitiated by misdirection, it is for this
court to exercise its discretion afresh. I would do so by granting the plaintiff the
extension he seeks and refusing the defendants' application to dismiss for want of
prosecution.

I would accordingly allow the appeal. *g*

STUART-SMITH LJ. I agree.

SIMON BROWN LJ. I also agree.

Appeal allowed. Order of judge set aside; plaintiff to have necessary extension of time to *h*
serve statement of claim; defendants' application to dismiss for want of prosecution
dismissed; plaintiff's solicitors personally to pay costs of hearing before district judge;
defendants to pay plaintiff's costs of hearing before judge and of appeal.

Mary Rose Plummer   Barrister.

a   Trill and another v Sacher and others

COURT OF APPEAL, CIVIL DIVISION
NEILL AND GLIDEWELL LJJ
18, 19 MARCH, 6 MAY 1992

b *Practice – Dismissal of action for want of prosecution – Inordinate delay without excuse – Three periods of delay after issue of writ – First two periods of delay occurring before expiry of limitation period – Third period of delay occurring after expiry of limitation period – Periods of delay amounting to three years in total out of a period of six years five months between issue of writ and application to dismiss action – Whether first two periods of delay relevant – Whether court entitled to take account of all three periods of delay on*
c *application to dismiss action for want of prosecution – Whether delay inordinate and inexcusable.*

In September 1983 the plaintiffs issued a writ and shortly thereafter served a statement of claim against the defendants alleging, inter alia, breach of contract
d and conspiracy to defraud and claiming rescission of the contract, the return of shares in a private company which the plaintiffs had agreed under the contract to sell to one of the defendants for a nominal sum, and damages. In December 1983 the defendants applied to strike out the writ and statement of claim as disclosing no reasonable cause of action, but that application was substantially dismissed, as was an appeal to the Court of Appeal on 3 September 1984. On 20 May 1985 the
e statement of claim was amended and re-served. On 15 April 1986 an order was made laying down a timetable for the remaining steps in the action prior to trial, including service of lists of documents by 25 April. The order was ignored by both parties and nothing further happened in the action until 24 April 1987, when the plaintiffs' solicitors purported to serve a list of documents on the defendants' solicitors. Following service by the defendants of their own list of
f documents, the parties entered into negotiations with a view to reaching a settlement, but by 11 January 1989 it was apparent that those negotiations had not been successful. In July 1989 the limitation period relating to the plaintiffs' claim expired. No further steps in the action were taken until 12 June 1990, when the plaintiffs served an amended list of documents. On 11 September the plaintiffs served notice of intention to proceed pursuant to RSC Ord 3, r 6*a*, which
g provided that, where a year or more had elapsed since the last proceeding in a cause or matter, the party desiring to proceed was required to give to every other party not less than one month's notice of his intention to proceed. On 4 February 1991 the defendants applied to have the action dismissed for want of prosecution. The judge dismissed the application on the grounds, inter alia, that the periods of
h delay from 3 September 1984 to 20 May 1985 and from 15 April 1986 to 24 April 1987 were not relevant since they had occurred before the expiration of the limitation period, and were in any event not inordinate and inexcusable, and that the period of delay from 11 January 1989 to 12 June 1990 had not prejudiced the chances of a fair trial. The defendants appealed to the Court of Appeal, where the questions arose (i) whether there had been inordinate and inexcusable delay since
j the issue of the writ on the part of the plaintiffs in the conduct of the action, (ii) if so, whether the defendants were estopped from relying on that delay by their

---

a Rule 6, so far as material, provides: 'Where a year or more has elapsed since the last proceeding in a cause or matter, the party who desires to proceed must give to every other party not less than one month's notice of his intention to proceed . . .'

own conduct in not applying to dismiss the action for want of prosecution within one month following the plaintiffs' service of notice of intention to proceed and *a* (iii) if they were not so estopped, whether the delay had caused serious prejudice to the defendants.

Held – (1) RSC Ord 3, r 6 placed no obligation on a defendant who wished to apply to strike out an action for want of prosecution to do so within the one month period of notice under that rule and since the defendants had taken no *b* active step to induce in the plaintiffs a belief that the defendants consented to the action continuing the defendants were not estopped from applying to have the action dismissed for want of prosecution because of the plaintiffs' delay (see p 972 *a* to *d*, p 975 *c d* and p 981 *a b*, post).

(2) Where a defendant applied after the expiry of the limitation period to strike *c* out an action for want of prosecution, inordinate and inexcusable delay by the plaintiff after the issue of the writ but within the limitation period could be relied upon to support the application. It followed that all three periods of delay were relevant and could be taken into account by the court in deciding whether to strike out the action. Moreover, those periods, amounting together to three years in total, out of a period of six years and five months between the issue of the writ *d* and the application to strike out, constituted inordinate and, for the most part, inexcusable delay on the part of the plaintiffs. However, since that delay had not given rise to a substantial risk that it would not be possible to have a fair trial, nor had it caused serious prejudice to the defendants, the application to strike out had been rightly dismissed. The appeal would therefore be dismissed (see p 970 *d e j* to p 971 *a*, p 974 *e* to *g*, p 975 *b* to *d*, p 980 *j* to p 981 *d*, post); dicta of Diplock LJ *e* in *Allen v Sir Alfred McAlpine & Sons Ltd* [1968] 1 All ER 543 at 556, of Lord Diplock in *Birkett v James* [1977] 2 All ER 801 at 805 and *Rath v C S Lawrence & Partners (a firm) (P J Cook & Co (a firm), third party)* [1991] 3 All ER 679 applied.

Per Neill LJ. Principles and guidelines to be applied on an application to strike out for want of prosecution where it is not suggested that the plaintiff has been *f* guilty of intentional and contumelious default (see p 978 *f* to p 980 *h*, post).

Notes

For dismissal of actions for want of prosecution, see 37 *Halsbury's Laws* (4th edn) paras 447–450, and for cases on the subject, see 37(3) *Digest* (Reissue) 67–78, *g* 3293–3341.

Cases referred to in judgments

Allen v Sir Alfred McAlpine & Sons Ltd, Bostic v Bermondsey and Southwark Group Hospital Management Committee, Sternberg v Hammond [1968] 1 All ER 543, *h* [1968] 2 QB 229, [1968] 2 WLR 366, CA.

Birkett v James [1977] 2 All ER 801, [1978] AC 297, [1977] 3 WLR 38, HL.

County and District Properties Ltd v Lyell (1977) [1991] 1 WLR 683, CA.

Dept of Transport v Chris Smaller (Transport) Ltd [1989] 1 All ER 897, [1989] AC 1197, [1989] 2 WLR 578, HL.

Eagil Trust Co Ltd v Pigott-Brown [1985] 3 All ER 119, CA. *j*

Fitzpatrick v Batger & Co Ltd [1967] 2 All ER 657, [1967] 1 WLR 706, CA.

Hollis v Islington London BC [1989] CA Transcript 67.

Rath v C S Lawrence & Partners (a firm) (P J Cook & Co (a firm), third party) [1991] 3 All ER 679, [1991] 1 WLR 399, CA.

Reynolds v British Leyland Ltd [1991] 2 All ER 243, [1991] 1 WLR 675, CA.

Cases also cited or referred to in skeleton arguments

a   *Austin Securities Ltd v Northgate and English Stores Ltd* [1969] 2 All ER 753, [1969] 1 WLR 529, CA.

Banca Popolare di Novara v John Livanos & Sons Ltd (1973) 117 SJ 509, CA.

Dexters Ltd v Hillcrest Oil Co (Bradford) Ltd [1926] 1 KB 348, [1925] All ER Rep 273, CA.

Dutton v Spink & Beeching (Sales) Ltd [1977] 1 All ER 287, CA.

b   *Greek City Co Ltd v Demetriou (trading as Spectron Electronics), Greek City Co Ltd v Athanasiou (trading as Alpha Alpha Electrical Contractors)* [1983] 2 All ER 921.

Instrumatic Ltd v Supabrase Ltd [1969] 2 All ER 131, [1969] 1 WLR 519, CA.

Lissenden v Bosch (CAV) Ltd [1940] 1 All ER 425, [1940] AC 412, HL.

National Insurance and Guarantee Corp Ltd v Robert Bradford & Co Ltd, City General Insurance Co Ltd v Robert Bradford & Co Ltd (1970) 114 SJ 436, CA.

c   *Tinkler v Hilder* (1849) 4 Exch 187, 154 ER 1176.

Tsangaris v Tzortzis (1976) Times, 17 December, [1976] CA Transcript 448.

Wallersteiner v Moir [1974] 3 All ER 217, [1974] 1 WLR 991, CA.

Interlocutory appeal

d   The defendants, Elizabeth Sacher, Simon Sacher, Steinberg & Sons Ltd, Christopher Trill Ltd and Anthony Stanbury, appealed with the leave of the deputy judge from the decision of Philip Cox QC sitting as a deputy judge of the High Court in the Queen's Bench Division on 30 April 1991 dismissing their application to dismiss the action brought against them by the plaintiffs, Christopher Trill and Patricia Glanville, for want of prosecution. The facts are set out in the judgment
e   of Glidewell LJ.

Gordon Pollock QC and *Joseph Smouha* (instructed by *S J Berwin & Co*) for the defendants.

Michael Burke-Gaffney QC and *Anthony Connerty* (instructed by *Beor Wilson & Lloyd*, Swansea) for the plaintiffs.

f

Cur adv vult

6 May 1992. The following judgments were delivered.

g   **GLIDEWELL LJ** (giving the first judgment at the invitation of Neill LJ). This is an appeal against a decision of Mr Philip Cox QC sitting as a deputy judge of the High Court, who, on 30 April 1991, dismissed an application by the defendants to dismiss this action for want of prosecution. The judge then made consequential orders, to some of which I shall refer later.

h   *The history*

The plaintiffs, Mr Trill and Miss Glanville, are designers of high fashion handbags, belts and other fashion accessories. Before 1982 they had both achieved considerable success and reputation in that field. They wished to form a new company to manufacture and sell articles designed by them. For this purpose they needed financial backing. They therefore entered into discussions with the
i   first defendant, Mrs Sacher, who was the controlling director of a company called Argohome Ltd. Mrs Sacher is the wife of the second defendant, Mr Simon John Sacher, who is, or was at the material time, a director of Marks & Spencer plc.

By a written agreement made on 15 July 1982 between the two plaintiffs, Mrs Sacher, Argohome Ltd, Mr Jasper Conran (a fashion designer) and his company Jasper Conran Ltd, the parties agreed to form a new company, Christopher Trill

Ltd, which is now the fourth defendant. All four individuals, parties to the agreement, became directors of the new company. The company had 1,000 issued shares, of which 750 were issued to Argohome Ltd and 250 were agreed to be issued to the plaintiffs to be shared between them in such proportions as they should decide. The agreement was expressed to last for five years in the first instance. The plaintiffs agreed to work full-time for the company, in return for salaries and commission. Argohome Ltd agreed to provide finance by guaranteeing bank borrowing by the company, together with management services, in return for a management fee.

The company was formed and in July 1982 started to trade. Its products were shown for the first time at the London Designer Collection in October 1982.

In their statement of claim in this action, the plaintiffs make the following allegations about Mrs Sacher's conduct from October 1982 onwards. (a) In or about October 1982 Mrs Sacher represented to the plaintiffs that she would be unable to obtain further overdraft facilities, which was untrue. As a result Mr Trill obtained a loan of £10,000 from his father and himself loaned this amount to the company. Mrs Sacher also loaned £10,000 to the company. (b) In May 1983 Mrs Sacher made it clear to the plaintiffs that neither she nor Argohome Ltd was prepared to invest any more in the company, which the plaintiffs allege was a breach of the agreement of 15 July 1982. (c) Also in breach of that agreement, Mrs Sacher refused to devote sufficient time to the management of the company.

It is common ground that the plaintiffs were then introduced to Mr Stanbury, the fifth defendant, a friend of Mr Sacher. Mr Stanbury controlled the third defendant, Steinberg & Sons Ltd. Steinberg & Sons Ltd was a major supplier to Marks & Spencer plc.

On 8 July 1983 the plaintiffs entered into a new agreement to sell their shares in Christopher Trill Ltd to Argohome Ltd at a nominal price and to resign as directors of the company. In return it was agreed that both plaintiffs would be employed as senior designers by the third defendant, Steinberg & Sons Ltd, at a salary subject to six months' notice, and would be paid compensation for loss of their offices in Christopher Trill Ltd.

The plaintiffs allege that on 25 August 1983 they were summarily dismissed from their employment with Steinberg by the fifth defendant, Mr Stanbury, and paid six months' salary in lieu of notice. In addition to the allegations of breach of contract against Mrs Sacher, the plaintiffs in their statement of claim as amended allege that they entered into the agreement of 8 July 1983 as the result of an inducement held out to them by all the defendants except Christopher Trill Ltd, and that these defendants had conspired together to defraud them. The nub of the allegation is that the offers of employment by Steinberg & Sons Ltd were sham offers which Steinberg and Mr Stanbury never intended to honour or be bound by.

In the statement of claim as pleaded and indeed after amendment in May 1985, the plaintiffs claimed rescission of the agreement of 8 July 1983, an order for the return to the plaintiffs of their shares in Christopher Trill Ltd, and damages including exemplary and aggravated damages. However, this claim for damages was not quantified in any way in the statement of claim.

The progress of the action

The action got off to a speedy start. The cause of action as alleged arose on or about 8 July 1983. On 26 September 1983 the writ was issued against the first, second and third defendants. The fourth defendant was added on 3 November 1983. On 23 November 1983 the statement of claim was served.

On 5 December 1983 the defendants took out a summons to strike out the writ
a and statement of claim as disclosing no reasonable cause of action. This application
was heard by Master Topley on 16 March 1984. He dismissed the application,
gave leave to add Mr Stanbury as the fifth defendant, and extended time for
service of the defence until after any appeal against his order.

The first four defendants duly appealed, and the appeal was heard on 13 June
1984 by Mustill J. He allowed it to the limited extent of striking out two
b paragraphs alleging fraudulent misrepresentation, but otherwise dismissed the
appeal.

The defendants appealed to this court, which heard the appeal on 3 September
1984. Griffiths LJ, in a judgment with which May LJ agreed, referred to the
separate causes of action alleged in the statement of claim as originally drafted,
c and said:

> 'What has been submitted by Mr Lightman QC is that nowhere on the
> face of the pleadings does that allegation, namely, "You induced us to waive
> all our rights under the 1982 agreement by a bogus promise of employment
> by Steinberg Ltd" appear clearly set out. I am bound to agree with Mr
> Lightman that this pleading is not an elegant document. It does appear to
d > me to have shied away from setting out the real gravamen of the complaint.
> Nevertheless, at the end of the day, I have arrived at the same conclusion as
> did Mustill J, which is that, reading the pleading as a whole, the nature of the
> allegation does emerge. As Mr Lightman has said, this being a serious matter
> the defendants are very anxious that it should be brought to trial as quickly
e > as possible, because of course he points out that he is arguing this case upon
> the basis that he must accept what appears in the statement of claim, whereas
> in fact it will be seriously contested. That being so, it seems to me that it is
> preferable that this action should proceed on the pleading as it stands at the
> moment, rather than that we should take the alternative course suggested by
> Mr Lightman, namely, to strike out the pleading in its present form and
f > allow Mr Godfrey to recast it, setting out, certainly with greater clarity, the
> true nature of the allegation that the defendants have to meet.'

The appeal to this court was therefore dismissed.

So, a year had passed since the issue of the writ, nine months of it on the
defendants' application to strike out and subsequent appeals. At least those
g proceedings had the effect of clarifying the plaintiffs' allegations.

On 20 May 1985 the statement of claim was amended to reflect what Griffiths
LJ had said, and re-served. We have had no explanation why, after the judgment
of this court, it took over eight months to make this amendment, save that during
this period the plaintiffs applied for legal aid.

On 2 July 1985, on an application by the plaintiffs for judgment against the
h defendants for failing to serve their defences (or in the case of the fifth defendant
for failing to serve notice of intention to defend), the application was dismissed.
The time for service of defence was extended to 2 July 1985, the date on which a
defence and counterclaim had already been served. A timetable for further steps
in the action was then laid down. This provided for service of a reply to the
defence within 21 days, exchange of lists of documents within 28 days, inspection
j 7 days thereafter, and setting down for trial within 42 days thereafter.

On 31 October 1985 legal aid was granted to the plaintiffs.

On 12 December 1985 a defence to the counterclaim was served, four months
outside the period limited by the order of 2 July 1985.

On 11 February and again on 15 April 1986 further orders were made for a
timetable for the remaining steps in the action. The order of 15 April 1986

provided for lists of documents by 25 April 1986, inspection 7 days thereafter, and setting down within 42 days thereafter. This timetable required the action to *a* be set down not later than 14 June 1986.

The solicitors seem not to have taken the slightest notice of the order of 15 April 1986. Nothing more happened between the parties until 24 April 1987, when the plaintiffs' solicitors purported to serve a list of documents on the defendants' solicitors. The defendants' solicitors wrote pointing out that under RSC Ord 3, r 6 notice of intention to proceed was required. On 30 April 1987 the *b* plaintiffs' solicitors therefore served such a notice, and on 30 May 1987 again served the plaintiffs' list of documents.

As to the defendants, they finally served their list of documents on 6 August 1987.

On 28 October 1987 there were without prejudice negotiations between the respective solicitors which were not successful. For the next three months the *c* parties were engaged in exchanging documents. Up to this time the plaintiffs had changed solicitors on two occasions. In June 1988 there was a further change of solicitors to Messrs Beor Wilson & Lloyd, the plaintiffs' present solicitors. Shortly after they were appointed, the defendants' solicitors made a further approach for a discussion of a possible settlement. Without prejudice negotiations then ensued *d* which continued until 11 January 1989, when it became apparent that they had failed.

From that date until 12 June 1990 there was no further exchange of correspondence or activity between the parties. Affidavits filed on behalf of the plaintiffs disclose what the plaintiffs' advisers were doing during this time, but the action itself made no progress. During this period to June 1990, namely in *e* July 1989, the limitation period expired.

The action awoke from its sleep when, on 12 June 1990, the plaintiffs purported to serve an amended list of documents. However, the plaintiffs' solicitors had again failed to serve the necessary notice of intention to proceed required under RSC Ord 3, r 6. Such a notice was finally served on 11 September 1990. On the following day, the limitation on the plaintiffs' legal aid certificate, which until *f* then had covered the proceedings up to the end of discovery plus counsel's advice, was removed.

On 30 October 1990, the plaintiffs' solicitors issued summonses relating to applications for leave to reamend the statement of claim and for interrogatories, both returnable on 25 February 1991. On 4 December 1990 they issued a further summons seeking specific discovery. *g*

On 4 February 1991 the defendants' solicitors issued the application to dismiss for want of prosecution, for hearing on the same day as the plaintiffs' applications. It was then agreed that all the matters should be put in front of a judge.

There is unfortunately a disagreement between the respective parties' solicitors as to what occurred before the defendants issued their application to dismiss. The *h* defendants' solicitor asserts that he informed his opposite number early in November 1990 of his intention to issue an application to dismiss for want of prosecution. The plaintiffs' solicitor does not recollect receiving this notification until shortly before the issue of the summons in February 1991. Whichever be correct, the plaintiffs had already issued their two summonses on 30 October 1990 before any such conversation took place. For the purposes of this appeal we *j* cannot resolve this dispute, and in my view must therefore proceed on the basis that there was no notification of intention to apply to strike out until shortly before the application itself was made.

The deputy judge delivered his judgment on 30 April 1991, but the resulting order was not drawn up until 22 May 1991 or sealed until 3 June 1991. Meanwhile

on 13 May 1991 the plaintiffs' solicitors set down the action for trial. In addition
a to refusing to dismiss the action for want of prosecution, the judge gave the
plaintiffs leave to reamend the statement of claim with leave to the defendants to
make consequential amendments to the defence. The judge also made two 'unless'
orders requiring the plaintiffs to serve full and proper particulars of the quantum
of their claim by 11 June 1991 provided that if such particulars be not served by
midnight on that date the plaintiffs' claim should be struck out and judgment be
b entered for the defendants with costs, and also requiring the plaintiffs to serve by
the same time any accountant's report in support of their claim for damages,
failing which they would be barred from calling or relying upon expert evidence
at the trial.

Within the time-scale a copy of an accountant's report was served by the
c plaintiffs, with a letter indicating that they took the view that this served as
further and better particulars. The defendants took the opposite view and the
parties made their positions clear in correspondence. On the plaintiffs failing to
serve any different form of further and better particulars, the defendants entered
judgment in default on 12 June 1991. On 17 July 1991 on the plaintiffs'
application it was ordered by Macpherson J that the judgment should be set aside
d if particulars were served by 22 July 1991.

On 25 July 1991 the defendants' notice of appeal was served, with a respondent's
notice being served on 13 August 1991.

The issues

e The principles to be applied are those set out in the speech of Lord Diplock in
Birkett v James [1977] 2 All ER 801 at 805, [1978] AC 297 at 318:

> 'The power [to strike out for want of prosecution] should be exercised only
> where the court is satisfied either (1) that the default has been intentional and
> contumelious, eg disobedience to a peremptory order of the court or conduct
> amounting to an abuse of the process of the court; or (2) (a) that there has
f > been inordinate and inexcusable delay on the part of the plaintiff or his
> lawyers, and (b) that such delay will give rise to a substantial risk that it is not
> possible to have a fair trial of the issues in the action or is such as is likely to
> cause or to have caused serious prejudice to the defendants . . .'

These principles were derived from the decision of this court in *Allen v Sir*
g *Alfred McAlpine & Sons Ltd* [1968] 1 All ER 543, [1968] 2 QB 229, which was
expressly approved in *Birkett v James*. In particular in his judgment in that case
Diplock LJ (as he then was) explained the reasons which led him to the conclusion
([1968] 1 All ER 543 at 555, [1968] 2 QB 229 at 258):

> 'It is thus inherent in an adversary system which relies exclusively on the
h > parties to an action to take whatever procedural steps appear to them to be
> expedient to advance their own case, that the defendant, instead of spurring
> the plaintiff to proceed to trial, can with propriety wait until he can
> successfully apply to the court to dismiss the plaintiff's action for want of
> prosecution on the ground that so long a time has elapsed since the events
> alleged to constitute the cause of action that there is a substantial risk that a
j > fair trial of the issues will not be possible.'

After setting out the principles to which I have already referred, Diplock LJ said
([1968] 1 All ER 543 at 556, [1968] 2 QB 229 at 260):

> 'Since the power to dismiss an action for want of prosecution is only
> exercisable on the application of the defendant his previous conduct in the

action is always relevant. So far as he himself has been responsible for any
unnecessary delay, he obviously cannot rely on it. Moreover, if after the a
plaintiff has been guilty of unreasonable delay the defendant so conducts
himself as to induce the plaintiff to incur further costs in the reasonable belief
that the defendant intends to exercise his right to proceed to trial
notwithstanding the plaintiff's delay, he cannot obtain dismissal of the action
unless the plaintiff has thereafter been guilty of further unreasonable delay.
For the reasons already mentioned, however, mere non-activity on the part b
of the defendant where no procedural step on his part is called for by the
rules of court is not to be regarded as conduct capable of inducing the plaintiff
reasonably to believe that the defendant intends to exercise his right to
proceed to trial. It must be remembered, however, that the evils of delay are
cumulative, and even where there is active conduct by the defendant which c
would debar him from obtaining dismissal of the action for excessive delay
by the plaintiff anterior to that conduct, the anterior delay will not be
irrelevant if the plaintiff is subsequently guilty of further unreasonable delay.
The question will then be whether as a result of the whole of the unnecessary
delay on the part of the plaintiff since the issue of the writ, there is a
substantial risk that a fair trial of the issues in the litigation will not be d
possible.'

The main issue in *Birkett v James* was whether the court should strike out an
action on the ground of inordinate delay (as opposed to disobedience to a court
order) when the application to strike out is made before the period of limitation
has expired. The House of Lords decided that normally in such circumstances the e
action should not be struck out. To quote Lord Diplock again ([1977] 2 All ER
801 at 806, [1978] AC 297 at 320):

'So in such a case, at any rate, time elapsed before issue of the writ which
does not extend beyond the limitation period cannot be treated as inordinate
delay; the statute itself permits it.' f

Lord Diplock added ([1977] 2 All ER 801 at 808, [1978] AC 297 at 322):

'It follows a fortiori from what I have already said in relation to the effect
of statutes of limitation on the power of the court to dismiss actions for want
of prosecution, that time elapsed before the issue of a writ within the
limitation period cannot of itself constitute inordinate delay however much g
the defendant may already have been prejudiced by the consequent lack of
early notice of the claim against him, the fading recollections of his potential
witnesses, their death or their untraceability. To justify dismissal of an action
for want of prosecution the delay relied on must relate to time which the
plaintiff allows to lapse unnecessarily after the writ has been issued.'

h

In the present case, there was argument in the court below as to whether the
plaintiffs had been guilty of intentional and contumelious delay. The judge held
that the delay could not properly be described as contumelious. In this court Mr
Pollock QC for the defendants, rightly, in my view, does not seek to reopen this
question.

The issues for this court's decision can therefore be summarised as follows. j
(1) Has there been inordinate and inexcusable delay since the issue of the writ on
the part of the plaintiffs in the conduct of the action? (2) If so, are the defendants
estopped by their own conduct from relying on that delay? (3) If not, does the
delay give rise to a substantial risk that it will not now be possible to have a fair

trial of the action, or is it likely to cause, or has it caused, serious prejudice to the
a defendants?

I will deal with each of these matters in turn. In doing so, I remind myself of
Lord Diplock's words in *Birkett v James* [1977] 2 All ER 801 at 804, [1978] AC 297
at 317 about the approach which this court should adopt to such questions:

b
'It is only very exceptionally that an appeal on an interlocutory order is
allowed to come before this House. These are matters best left to the decision
of the masters and, on appeal, the judges of the High Court whose daily
experience and concern is with the trial of civil actions. They are decisions
which involve balancing against one another a variety of relevant
considerations on which opinions of individual judges may reasonably differ
as to their relative weight in a particular case. That is why they are said to
c
involve the exercise by the judge of his "discretion". That, and the consequent
delay and expense which appeals in interlocutory matters would involve, is
also why no appeal to the Court of Appeal from his decision is available
except with the judge's leave or that of the Court of Appeal. Where leave is
granted, an appellate court ought not to substitute its own "discretion" for
that of the judge merely because its members would themselves have
d
regarded the balance as tipped against the way in which he had decided the
matter. They should regard their function as primarily a reviewing function
...'

Delay

e As the history I have summarised reveals, during the course of this action there
have been three substantial periods of delay for which the plaintiffs or their legal
advisers were responsible. They were: (i) from 3 September 1984 to 20 May 1985
when the statement of claim was amended; (ii) from 15 April 1986 to 24 April
1987; (iii) from 11 January 1989 to 12 June 1990.

f The defendants could not seek to strike out during the first or second periods
of delay since both fell within the limitation period. The question therefore arises,
as a result of the third period of delay, should the court now take account of all
three periods in deciding whether to strike out?

In *Rath v C S Lawrence & Partners (a firm)* [1991] 3 All ER 679, [1991] 1 WLR
399 this court held that inordinate and inexcusable delay by the plaintiffs after
g the issue of a writ but within the limitation period could be relied upon to support
the defendant's application to strike out after the expiry of the limitation period.
Farquharson LJ said ([1991] 3 All ER 679 at 684, [1991] 1 WLR 399 at 406):

'Once a plaintiff has issued his writ and set the treadmill of litigation into
motion, he is bound to observe the rules of the court. If he flouts them to the
h extent that the plaintiffs have in the present case I can see no reason why the
defendants should not rely upon it, after the limitation period has expired, to
support an application to strike out.'

Slade LJ, with whom Nicholls LJ expressly agreed, said ([1991] 3 All ER 679 at
688–689, [1991] 1 WLR 399 at 411):

j 'Having once again studied *Birkett v James*, however, I can find no support
for the proposition that time elapsed *after the issue of a writ but before the
expiration of the limitation period* cannot constitute inordinate delay for the
relevant purpose. The late issue of a writ is one thing; by itself if cannot be
regarded as culpable. The casual and dilatory conduct of proceedings in

breach of the rules, after a writ has been issued, is another thing. If a person
who claims to have a cause of action chooses to take advantage of the process *a*
of the court by issuing a writ at whatever time during the limitation period,
he has, in the words of Lord Diplock ([1977] 2 All ER 801 at 809, [1978] AC
297 at 323), "a corresponding right to continue to prosecute it to trial and
judgment *so long as he does so with reasonable diligence*. Though I do not think
they bind this court, I respectfully agree with the observations of Stuart-
Smith LJ in *Hollis v Islington London BC* [1989] CA Transcript 67 quoted by *b*
Farquharson LJ, in which he found—"no warrant for equating the effect of
prejudice due to delay which inevitably is caused by permitted and non-
culpable delay in issuing proceedings, with prejudice caused by culpable
delay, even though the right to strike out has not yet arisen because the
limitation period has not expired." In my judgment, therefore, the full *c*
period of inordinate and inexcusable delay in the plaintiffs' conduct of their
action running between about October 1984 and February 1989 falls to be
taken into account for the purpose of applying the principle of *Birkett v James*
referred to above.' (Slade LJ's emphasis)

It follows that in the present case all three periods are relevant. Together they *d*
amount to three years in total, out of a period of six years five months between
the issue of the writ and the application to strike out. I have no doubt that all this
delay was inordinate. It may be said that there was some excuse for the first
period, since during it the plaintiffs (in January 1985) applied for legal aid. But
this cannot have been a major reason for not amending the statement of claim in
accordance with the suggestions made by Griffiths LJ, since an amended statement *e*
of claim was finally served on 20 May 1985, although legal aid was not granted to
the plaintiffs until October of that year. Most, if not all, of this three years' delay
was therefore inexcusable.

In his judgment, the judge said of the earlier periods of delay:

'On any view, the case did not proceed as expeditiously as one would have *f*
wished, and it is accepted by Mr Beveridge on behalf of the plaintiffs that
proper particulars of the way in which the plaintiffs' claim is calculated have
not even today been given. However, this is far from saying that there has
been inordinate and inexcusable delay on the part of the plaintiffs or their
solicitors in the prosecution of this case. As Mr Beveridge pointed out in the
course of his argument, this is not a case, as is so often before the courts, *g*
where nothing is done for years. This is a case where something was being
done, unfortunately not always very effectively, and it is that picture which
really prevails throughout the chronology in this case. It is not, however,
necessary, in my judgment, for me to analyse in detail the history of this
action up to the end of 1988, because between October 1987 and early *h*
January 1989, it is clear that without prejudice negotiations for a settlement
were going on between the parties. Sometimes the defendants themselves
were seeking information with a view to the possibility of a settlement. I
find, therefore, that the defendants, by taking part in these negotiations,
acquiesced in the slow progress of the case, and when the negotiations were
broken off, they must have contemplated that the case would then proceed *j*
to trial. I have to bear in mind that had an application to dismiss the action
for want of prosecution been made before the expiry of the limitation period
in July 1989, the plaintiff would have had the right to issue a fresh writ. This
was made clear by the House of Lords in *Birkett v James*.'

a It is clear, therefore, that the judge did not regard the earlier periods of delay as relevant. For the reasons I have already explained, he was wrong not to do so.

As to the last period of delay, the judge said simply:

'Since July 1989 it is clear that progress has still been somewhat slow. But again, in my judgment, the additional lapse of time has not prejudiced the chances of a fair trial . . .'

b The judge made no finding whether this period of delay was inordinate or inexcusable. In concluding that this delay deserves both adjectives, I am thus not trespassing on any exercise of the judge's discretion.

Estoppel

c Mr Burke-Gaffney QC for the plaintiffs argues that even though his clients' solicitors may have been guilty of inordinate and inexcusable delay, at the time when they issued the application to dismiss for want of prosecution in February 1991 the defendants were estopped by their own previous conduct from relying on that delay.

I have already quoted the passage from the judgment of Diplock LJ in *Allen v*
d *Sir Alfred McAlpine & Sons Ltd* [1968] 1 All ER 543 at 556, [1968] 2 QB 229 at 260 which referred to this question. In a more recent decision of this court, *County and District Properties Ltd v Lyell* (1977) [1991] 1 WLR 683 at 688–689, both Stephenson and Roskill LJJ said that they preferred to regard the concept as one of estoppel. Bridge LJ, agreeing with them both, said (at 690):

e 'I share the opinion of both Stephenson and Roskill L.JJ. that the principle with which we are concerned in this appeal may not be altogether aptly labelled by the terms "waiver" or "acquiescence." If one looks to the classic and precise expressions of principle in the two passages from the judgments of Diplock and Salmon L.JJ. cited by Stephenson L.J. from *Allen v. Sir Alfred*
f *McAlpine & Sons Ltd.* ([1968] 1 All ER 543 at 556, 563–564, [1968] 2 QB 229 at 260, 272), one finds that the elements which are present are the familiar elements of the principle of estoppel understood in its broadest sense. To disentitle a defendant from relying upon inordinate and inexcusable delay which has caused substantial prejudice to secure the dismissal of an action for want of prosecution, two things must be shown: first, that the defendant's own conduct has reasonably induced in the plaintiff a belief that the action is
g to be allowed to proceed; secondly, action taken upon that reasonable belief by the plaintiff to alter his position or to act to his detriment, action which will take the form in the ordinary case of incurring expense.'

This decision has recently been relied upon and applied by Russell and Staughton LJJ in *Reynolds v British Leyland Ltd* [1991] 2 All ER 243, [1991] 1 WLR
h 675.

Mr Burke-Gaffney makes the point that, after the plaintiffs' solicitors had given notice of intention to proceed on 11 September 1990, the defendants' solicitors did not at once make an application to dismiss for want of prosecution. RSC Ord 3, r 6 requires one month's notice, so the plaintiffs could not take any further steps in the action until a month had elapsed. In the ordinary way the application
j to dismiss would be made within that month. As it was not made, Mr Burke-Gaffney continues, the plaintiffs on 30 October 1990 issued summonses for leave to reamend the statement of claim and for leave to interrogate some of the defendants, and on 4 December 1990 a further summons seeking specific discovery. It was not until 4 February 1991 that the defendants' solicitors issued

the application to dismiss for want of prosecution. By this time they were estopped, since the plaintiffs had incurred further costs in issuing the summonses *a* in the belief that the defendants were content that the action should continue.

In reply Mr Pollock argues that RSC Ord 3, r 6 places no obligation on a defendant to apply to strike out within the period of notice under that rule. He accepts that if such an application is not made within the month the plaintiff at the end of that time may set down the action for trial, after which it will of course *b* be too late to apply to dismiss for want of prosecution. But, provided that the defendant takes no active step which induces in the plaintiff a belief that he consents to the action continuing, he is not estopped. While it is true that the plaintiffs' solicitors did issue the summonses, between September 1990 and 4 February 1991 the defendants had taken no steps at all to induce such a belief. Therefore although they had waited a long time to issue their application, they *c* were not estopped.

In my view, the defendants' advisers were taking a risk in not issuing the application to dismiss for want of prosecution within the month following the service of notice of intention to proceed, but nevertheless I would hold that Mr Pollock's argument is correct. I therefore conclude that the defendants were not estopped from applying to dismiss for want of prosecution. *d*

Mr Burke-Gaffney also argues that, by their conduct following the judgment of the judge, the defendants are estopped from pursuing this appeal. He advances this argument under two heads.

(a) I have already said that the judge not merely ordered that the application to dismiss for want of prosecution should be dismissed, but ordered that, unless the plaintiffs served certain further and better particulars of this claim by midnight *e* on 11 June 1991, their claim should be struck out and judgment be entered for the defendants. In the event the plaintiffs served an accountant's report within this time-scale, and sought to have it treated as further and better particulars. The defendants said that they were not prepared to accept it as compliance with the order for further and better particulars. On the plaintiffs' failure to serve *f* particulars as such, the defendants entered judgment in default on 12 June 1991. On 17 July 1991 this judgment was set aside by Macpherson J on condition that the particulars requested were served by 22 July 1991, as they were.

The point made by Mr Burke-Gaffney is that, by entering judgment, the defendants estopped themselves from appealing against the judge's decision when that judgment was set aside. Mr Pollock's answer to this is that the defendants' *g* entry of judgment, although very likely to be set aside in the circumstances, did not induce the plaintiffs to do anything to their detriment. In my view this argument is also correct.

(b) There then followed some correspondence between the parties about the possibility of splitting the trial on liability from the issue of damages. It commenced with a 'without prejudice' letter from the defendants' solicitors dated *h* 22 July 1991 making the suggestion. The letter however says:

'Our present advice to our clients would be to appeal the order of [the judge] and to apply to strike out the Particulars but, if we can hear from you before Notice of Appeal is given on the issue of a split trial, we can take instructions as to whether that alternative course could be taken.' *j*

The plaintiffs' solicitors replied by fax on 23 July 1991 saying they were taking instructions and giving an estimate of time. On the same day the defendants' solicitors wrote saying that they had been instructed to appeal the order of the judge and a notice of appeal would be served shortly. On 25 July 1991 the plaintiffs' solicitors sent a letter by fax agreeing to a split trial, but on the same day the defendants' solicitors served notice of appeal against the judge's decision. There followed some further correspondence about a split trial, but in their letters the defendants' solicitors made it clear that this was without prejudice to the appeal to this court.

I can find nothing here that estops the defendants from pursuing this appeal. On the contrary, I think it was sensible to seek to deal with issues leading to the trial of this action at the same time as giving notice of appeal but without prejudice to that appeal.

Prejudice

I use this as a title for the last issue, namely have the defendants shown that the—

> 'delay will give rise to a substantial risk that it is not possible to have a fair trial of the issues in the action or is such as is likely to cause or to have caused serious prejudice to the defendants . . .' (See *Birkett v James* [1977] 2 All ER 801 at 805, [1978] AC 297 at 318.)

I have found this in some ways the most difficult of the issues to decide. In his judgment the judge referred to the speech of Lord Griffiths in *Dept of Transport v Chris Smaller (Transport) Ltd* [1989] 1 All ER 897 at 905, [1989] AC 1197 at 1209, where he said:

> 'I would, however, express a note of caution against allowing the mere fact of the anxiety that accompanies any litigation being regarded as of itself a sufficient prejudice to justify striking out an action. Counsel for the defendants did not seek to argue that the anxiety occasioned by the extra 13 months in this case should be regarded as a sufficient ground of prejudice to justify making a striking out order. There are, however, passages in some of the judgments that suggest that the mere sword of Damocles, hanging for an unnecessary period, might be a sufficient reason of itself to strike out. On this aspect I repeat the note of caution I expressed in the Court of Appeal in *Eagil Trust Co Ltd v Pigott-Brown* [1985] 3 All ER 119 at 124, where I said: "Any action is bound to cause anxiety, but it would as a general rule be an exceptional case where that sort of anxiety alone would found a sufficient ground for striking out in the absence of any particular prejudice . . ." '

The allegations of fraud and conspiracy made in the statement of claim against these defendants are extremely serious, and it is wholly wrong that they should have not been able to have them brought to trial as soon as could be done. The delay must therefore have caused them anxiety. Nevertheless, Mr Pollock on their behalf, no doubt having Lord Griffiths's words in mind, has not sought to argue that this of itself amounts to sufficient prejudice to justify striking out.

In his judgment the judge gave the following reason for not striking out:

> 'In my judgment, this is not a case which will depend upon the witnesses' recollection of fine points of detail such as frequently occurs in road accident cases and cases involving personal injury at work and so forth . . . If this case proceeds to trial, it will be essentially a case where the judge will have to decide which of two entirely conflicting accounts is the truth. Even after the passing of many years, it seems to me that each of the parties present at the various meetings who are likely to be witnesses at the trial will retain a pretty

clear recollection of the essentials of what took place, and indeed affidavits of these witnesses were sworn on behalf of the plaintiffs and on behalf of the *a* defendants at a comparatively early stage in this history.'

It is true that when he said this, the judge was considering only the period of delay from January 1989 onwards. Nevertheless, we have to decide whether the same considerations apply to the whole of the delay. On the one hand, it is true that the trial of this issue will depend to a considerable extent upon the oral *b* evidence of the parties and perhaps some other supporting witnesses. No doubt, some of them will be subjected to substantial cross-examination. Moreover, the plaintiffs' solicitors, for reasons I do not understand, have sought to administer interrogatories to some of the defendants, thus showing that they seek to go into a fair amount of detail.

On the other hand, in the end the main question which the court of trial is *c* going to have to decide is: does the evidence prove that these defendants conspired together to defraud or damage the plaintiffs? It is unlikely that the plaintiffs will be able to produce direct evidence of such a conspiracy. They will presumably ask the court to infer it from the circumstances, and in particular from the fact that they were dismissed from what they had been led to believe would be secure, profitable and interesting employment so soon after being engaged. In order for *d* the plaintiffs to succeed, it will be necessary for the court to find that Mr Stanbury, of his own volition or persuaded by Mr and Mrs Sacher, offered the plaintiffs employment when, in truth, he knew perfectly well that he did not intend to retain them as employees of his company. In other words, it must be shown that the entire offer of employment was a sham. This is the essence of the plaintiffs' *e* case.

Although after the passage of so many years the memories of all the witnesses, whether for the plaintiffs or the defendants, will undoubtedly be less clear than they would have been nearer the time about the detail of particular events or conversations, it is in my view unlikely in the extreme that any of the defendants will not remember whether they did enter into a fraudulent agreement. In *f* particular, I find it inconceivable that Mr Stanbury will not have a clear recollection of the truth or falsity of the plaintiffs' allegations. In the end, therefore, I have concluded that the judge's evaluation of this issue was correct.

As I have said, the plaintiffs on 3 June 1991, pursuant to the order of the judge, served on the defendants their accountants' report, and later served particulars of their claim for damages based upon that report. The plaintiffs claim loss of *g* earnings from 30 November 1982 to 30 November 1987 in the sum of £83,060, and loss of the share value in Christopher Trill Ltd in the sum of £792,000, together with interest on both sums.

These claims are both based on the opinion expressed in the accountants' report that if the defendants had not fraudulently persuaded the plaintiffs to dispose of *h* their shares in Christopher Trill Ltd, that company would have traded successfully and profitably and would have expanded its turnover and profits year by year, to the benefit of both plaintiffs. The accountants' report contains for each of the five years ending 30 November 1987 projected balance sheets, profit and loss accounts and cash flow projections for Christopher Trill Ltd.

Mr Pollock submits that, as a result of the delay, it will be difficult, if not *j* impossible, for the defendants to counter this evidence properly. Doing so will involve a consideration of the trading conditions for such companies at the relevant time which will now be extremely difficult to make. Moreover, it may prove impossible to check some of the assumptions in the accountants' report.

I do not accept this submission. Whilst consideration of the plaintiffs' accountants' report may well involve a considerable amount of detailed work, the majority of the assumptions in it must be based upon documentary material—documents in the action or other published material—which will be equally available to accountants instructed by the defendants. Moreover, it is for the plaintiffs to prove the case they seek to make. If some of the assumptions in the accountants' report cannot be checked, it must follow that they cannot be justified. If anybody will suffer prejudice in this situation, it will be the plaintiffs.

Although I think that the delays in the conduct of this litigation are deserving of very considerable censure, I cannot find that there is a substantial risk that a fair trial of the central issue will not be possible, or that the defendants have been prejudiced in relation to that issue by this delay.

For this reason, despite the view I have formed about the other issues, I would dismiss this appeal.

NEILL LJ. I agree that this appeal should be dismissed for the reasons given by Glidewell LJ. As, however, we had the benefit of detailed arguments as to the practice to be followed on an application to strike out for want of prosecution, I have decided to add a short judgment of my own.

The power of the court to dismiss an action for want of prosecution is not based on any statute or any rule of court but on the inherent jurisdiction of the court to control its own procedure.

It was in 1967, following the decision of the Court of Appeal in *Fitzpatrick v Batger & Co Ltd* [1967] 2 All ER 657 at 659, [1967] 1 WLR 706 at 710, that this power began to be exercised with any frequency. Since then countless cases involving delay have been decided. Many of these cases have been reported. For the purpose of formulating the relevant principles, however, it is sufficient to refer to only a few authorities.

In December 1967 three cases which had been dismissed for want of prosecution came before the Court of Appeal. In judgments which were delivered in January 1968 the court laid down the principles to be applied. The leading case was *Allen v Sir Alfred McAlpine & Sons Ltd* [1968] 1 All ER 543, [1968] 2 QB 229. Diplock LJ set out the principles as follows ([1968] 1 All ER 543 at 555–556, [1968] 2 QB 229 at 259–260):

'What then are the principles which the court should apply in exercising its discretion to dismiss an action for want of prosecution on a defendant's application? The application is not usually made until the period of limitation for the plaintiff's cause of action has expired. It is then a Draconian order and will not be lightly made. It should not in any event be exercised without giving the plaintiff an opportunity to remedy his default, unless the court is satisfied either that the default has been intentional and contumelious, or that the inexcusable delay for which the plaintiff or his lawyers have been responsible has been such as to give rise to a substantial risk that a fair trial of the issues in the litigation will not be possible at the earliest date at which, as a result of the delay, the action would come to trial if it were allowed to continue. It is for the defendant to satisfy the court that one or other of these two conditions is fulfilled. Disobedience to a peremptory order of the court would be sufficient to satisfy the first condition. Whether the second alternative condition is satisfied will depend on the circumstances of the particular case; but the length of the delay may of itself suffice to satisfy this condition if the relevant issues would depend on the recollection of witnesses of events which happened long ago. Since the power to dismiss an action for want of prosecution is only exercisable on the application of the defendant his previous conduct in the action is always relevant. So far as he himself has been responsible for any unnecessary delay, he obviously cannot rely on it. Moreover, if after the plaintiff has been guilty of unreasonable delay the defendant so conducts himself as to induce the plaintiff to incur further costs in the reasonable belief that the defendant intends to exercise his right to proceed to trial notwithstanding the plaintiff's delay, he cannot obtain dismissal of the action unless the plaintiff has thereafter been guilty of further unreasonable delay. For the reasons already mentioned, however, mere non-activity on the part of the defendant where no procedural step on his part is called for by the rules of court is not to be regarded as conduct capable of inducing the plaintiff reasonably to believe that the defendant intends to exercise his right to proceed to trial. It must be remembered, however, that the evils of delay are cumulative, and even where there is active conduct by the defendant which would debar him from obtaining dismissal of the action for excessive delay by the plaintiff anterior to that conduct, the anterior delay will not be irrelevant if the plaintiff is subsequently guilty of further unreasonable delay. The question will then be whether as a result of the whole of the unnecessary delay on the part of the plaintiff since the issue of the writ, there is a substantial risk that a fair trial of the issues in the litigation will not be possible.'

Ten years later the principles laid down in *Allen v Sir Alfred McAlpine & Sons Ltd* were approved by the House of Lords in *Birkett v James* [1977] 2 All ER 801, [1978] AC 297. Lord Diplock sets out the circumstances in which the power should be exercised in these terms ([1977] 2 All ER 801 at 805, [1978] AC 297 at 318):

'The power should be exercised only where the court is satisfied either (1) that the default has been intentional and contumelious, eg disobedience to a peremptory order of the court or conduct amounting to an abuse of the process of the court; or (2) (a) that there has been inordinate and inexcusable delay on the part of the plaintiff or his lawyers, and (b) that such delay will give rise to a substantial risk that it is not possible to have a fair trial of the issues in the action or is such as is likely to cause or to have caused serious prejudice to the defendants either as between themselves and the plaintiff or between each other or between them and a third party.'

In *Birkett v James* the House of Lords considered three further questions which had not arisen for decision in *Allen v Sir Alfred McAlpine & Sons Ltd*: (1) whether an action should be struck out on the ground of delay before the expiration of the limitation period; (2) where the plaintiff has delayed bringing an action, whether the defendant has to show that he has suffered prejudice additional to that caused by the tardy commencement of proceedings; (3) whether it is relevant that the plaintiff may have an alternative remedy against his solicitor.

In addition the House of Lords gave guidance as to how in an interlocutory matter an appellate court should approach the decision of the court of first instance.

On the first of these questions it is sufficient to refer to a passage in the speech of Lord Diplock ([1977] 2 All ER 801 at 806–807, [1978] AC 297 at 320–321):

'There may be exceptional cases . . . where the plaintiff's conduct in the previous proceedings has induced the defendant to do something which will create more difficulties for him in presenting his case at the trial than he

would have had if the previous proceedings had never been started. In such
a case it may well be that the court, in the exercise of its inherent jurisdiction,
should stay the second proceedings on the ground that, taken as a whole, the
plaintiff's conduct amounts to an abuse of the process of the court. But such
exceptional cases apart, where all that the plaintiff has done has been to let
the previous action go to sleep, the court in my opinion would have no power
to prevent him starting a fresh action within the limitation period and
proceeding with it with all proper diligence notwithstanding that his previous
action had been dismissed for want of prosecution. If this be so, it follows
that to dismiss an action for want of prosecution before the limitation period
has expired does not, save in the exceptional kind of case to which I have
referred, benefit the defendant or improve his chances of obtaining a fair
trial; it has the opposite tendency.'

On the second question I can again take a short passage from the speech of Lord
Diplock. He said ([1977] 2 All ER 801 at 809, [1978] AC 297 at 323):

'To justify dismissal of an action for want of prosecution some prejudice to
the defendant additional to that inevitably flowing from the plaintiff's
tardiness in issuing his writ must be shown to have resulted from his
subsequent delay (beyond the period allowed by rules of court) in proceeding
promptly with the successive steps in the action. The additional prejudice
need not be great compared with that which may have been already caused
by the time elapsed before the writ was issued; but it must be more than
minimal; and the delay in taking a step in the action if it is to qualify as
inordinate as well as prejudicial must exceed the period allowed by rules of
court for taking that step.'

On the third question Lord Diplock, Lord Edmund-Davies and Lord Russell of
Killowen expressed the opinion that the fact that the plaintiff may or may not
have an alternative remedy against his solicitor is not a relevant consideration in
considering whether to dismiss an action for want of prosecution.

In the light of some of the arguments which were addressed to this court, I
should refer also to an earlier passage in the speech of Lord Diplock ([1977] 2 All
ER 801 at 804, [1978] AC 297 at 317):

'It is only very exceptionally that an appeal on an interlocutory order is
allowed to come before this House. These are matters best left to the decision
of the masters and, on appeal, the judges of the High Court whose daily
experience and concern is with the trial of civil actions. They are decisions
which involve balancing against one another a variety of relevant
considerations on which opinions of individual judges may reasonably differ
as to their relative weight in a particular case. That is why they are said to
involve the exercise by the judge of his "discretion". That, and the consequent
delay and expense which appeals in interlocutory matters would involve, is
also why no appeal to the Court of Appeal from his decision is available
except with the judge's leave or that of the Court of Appeal. Where leave is
granted, an appellate court ought not to substitute its own "discretion" for
that of the judge merely because its members would themselves have
regarded the balance as tipped against the way in which he had decided the
matter. They should regard their function as primarily a reviewing function
and should reverse his decision only in cases either (1) where they are satisfied
that the judge has erred in principle by giving weight to something which
he ought not to have taken into account or by failing to give weight to
something which he ought to take into account; or (2) . . . in order to promote

consistency in the exercise of their discretion by the judges as a whole where there appear, in closely comparable circumstances, to be two conflicting *a* schools of judicial opinion as to the relative weight to be given to particular considerations.'

Finally I should refer to the decision of the Court of Appeal in *Rath v C S Lawrence & Partners (a firm)* [1991] 3 All ER 679, [1991] 1 WLR 399. In that case the causes of action accrued in January 1983 and the limitation period expired in *b* January 1989. The writ was issued on 22 May 1984 and reasonable progress was made until about the end of that year. There then followed, however, a delay by the plaintiffs in proceeding with the action which extended to a period in excess of four years. In March 1989 the defendants took out summonses to dismiss the action for want of prosecution. The question which arose for decision was whether the defendants could rely on the long period of delay which, except for the few *c* weeks between January and March 1989, had taken place exclusively during the limitation period. The Court of Appeal held unanimously that the defendants were entitled to rely on this delay. Slade LJ said ([1991] 3 All ER 679 at 688–689, [1991] 1 WLR 399 at 411):

> 'The late issue of a writ is one thing; by itself it cannot be regarded as *d* culpable. The casual and dilatory conduct of proceedings in breach of the rules, after a writ has been issued, is another thing. If a person who claims to have a cause of action chooses to take advantage of the process of the court by issuing a writ at whatever time during the limitation period, he has, in the words of Lord Diplock ([1977] 2 All ER 801 at 809, [1978] AC 297 at 323), "a corresponding right to continue to prosecute it to trial and judgment *so long* *e* *as he does so with reasonable diligence"* . . . In my judgment, therefore, the full period of inordinate and inexcusable delay in the plaintiffs' conduct of their action running between about October 1984 and February 1989 falls to be taken into account for the purpose of applying the principle of *Birkett v James* . . .' (Slade LJ's emphasis.) *f*

From these and the other relevant authorities, I would extract the following principles and guidelines for use on an application to strike out for want of prosecution where it is not suggested that the plaintiff has been guilty of intentional and contumelious default.

(1) The basic rule is that an action may be struck out where the court is satisfied— *g*

> '(a) that there has been inordinate and inexcusable delay on the part of the plaintiff or his lawyers, and (b) that such delay will give rise to a substantial risk that it is not possible to have a fair trial of the issues in the action or is such as is likely to cause or to have caused serious prejudice to the defendants either as between themselves and the plaintiff or between each other or *h* between them and a third party.' (See *Birkett v James* [1977] 2 All ER 801 at 805, [1978] AC 297 at 318.)

(2) The general burden of proof on an application to strike out for want of prosecution is on the defendant.

(3) 'Inordinate' delay cannot be precisely defined. 'What is or is not inordinate *j* delay must depend on the facts of each particular case' (see *Allen's* case [1968] 1 All ER 543 at 561, [1968] 2 QB 229 at 268). It is clear, however, (a) that for delay to be inordinate it must exceed, and probably by a substantial margin, the times prescribed by the rules of court for the taking of steps in the action and (b) that delay in issuing the writ cannot be classified as 'inordinate' provided the writ is issued within the relevant period of limitation.

(4) Delay which is inordinate is prima facie inexcusable (see *Allen*'s case [1968]
1 All ER 543 at 561, [1968] 2 QB 229 at 268). It is for the plaintiff to make out a
credible excuse. For example, difficulties with regard to obtaining legal aid *may*
provide such an excuse.

(5) Where a plaintiff delays issuing proceedings until towards the end of the
period of limitation he is then under an obligation to proceed with the case with
reasonable diligence (see *Birkett v James* [1977] 2 All ER 801 at 809, [1978] AC 297
at 323). Accordingly, a court is likely to look strictly at any subsequent delay
which is in excess of the period allowed by rules of court for taking the relevant
step, and may regard such subsequent delay as inordinate even though a similar
lapse of time might have been treated less strictly had the action been started
earlier.

(6) A defendant cannot rely on a period of delay for which he has himself been
responsible.

(7) A defendant cannot rely on a period of delay if at the end of the period he—

> 'so conducts himself as to induce the plaintiff to incur further costs in the
> reasonable belief that the defendant intends to exercise his right to proceed
> to trial notwithstanding the plaintiff's delay . . .' (See *Allen*'s case [1968] 1 All
> ER 543 at 556, [1968] 2 QB 229 at 260.)

It has been said that this rule is based on waiver or acquiescence, but the better
view appears to be that the defendant is estopped (see *County and District Properties
Ltd v Lyell* (1977) [1991] 1 WLR 683 at 690).

(8) Save in exceptional cases an action will not be struck out for want of
prosecution before the expiry of the relevant limitation period (see *Birkett v James*
[1977] 2 All ER 801 at 807, [1978] AC 297 at 321). It is not altogether clear how
this rule is best explained. It may be that before the limitation period has expired
the delay cannot properly be regarded as 'inordinate' (cf *Birkett v James* [1977]
2 All ER 801 at 807, [1978] AC 297 at 321). Alternatively, it may be that, though
the delay is both inordinate and inexcusable, the court would not in the ordinary
case exercise its discretion to strike the action out if a fresh writ could be issued at
once. To do so would only delay the trial.

(9) Once the limitation period has expired the court is entitled to take account
of all the earlier periods of inexcusable delay since the issue of the writ. These
periods can include: (a) periods of delay occurring before the expiry of the
limitation period which at an earlier stage could not be *treated* as 'inordinate' (see
8 above); (b) periods of delay on which at an earlier stage the defendant could not
rely because he was estopped from doing so by inducing the plaintiff to incur
further costs in the reasonable belief that the action was going to proceed to trial,
but which have been revived by subsequent inordinate and inexcusable delay.
This proposition seems to follow from Diplock LJ's proviso in *Allen*'s case [1968]
1 All ER 543 at 556, [1968] 2 QB 229 at 260: '. . . unless the plaintiff has thereafter
been guilty of further unreasonable delay'. It is also supported by a later passage
in his judgment in *Allen*'s case [1968] 1 All ER 543 at 556, [1968] 2 QB 229 at 260
where he said:

> 'It must be remembered, however, that the evils of delay are cumulative,
> and even where there is active conduct by the defendant which would debar
> him from obtaining dismissal of the action for excessive delay by the plaintiff
> anterior to that conduct, the anterior delay will not be irrelevant if the
> plaintiff is subsequently guilty of further unreasonable delay.'

(10) A defendant cannot rely on any prejudice caused to him by the late issue
of a writ. Thus such prejudice is not due to delay which can be characterised as

inordinate or inexcusable. Some additional prejudice after the issue of the writ must be shown:

'The additional prejudice need not be great compared with that which may have been already caused by the time elapsed before the writ was issued; but it must be more than minimal; and the delay in taking a step in the action if it is to qualify as inordinate as well as prejudicial must exceed the period allowed by rules of court for taking that step.' (See *Birkett v James* [1977] 2 All ER 801 at 809, [1978] AC 297 at 323.)

(11) Prejudice to the defendant may take different forms. In many cases the lapse of time will impair the memory of witnesses. In other cases witnesses may die or move away and become untraceable.

(12) The prejudicial effect of delay may depend in large measure on the nature of the issues in the case. Thus the evidence of an eye witness or of a witness who will testify to the words used when an oral representation was made is likely to be much more seriously impaired by the lapse of time than the evidence of someone who can rely on contemporary documents. A defendant may also suffer some prejudice from prolonged delay in an action which involves imputations against his reputation, though this factor by itself is unlikely to provide a ground for striking out.

(13) When considering the question of prejudice and, if it is raised, the question whether there is a substantial risk that it will not be possible to have a fair trial of the issues in the action, the court will look at all the circumstances. It will look at the periods of inordinate and inexcusable delay for which the plaintiff or his advisers are responsible and will then seek to answer the questions: has *this* delay caused or is it likely to cause serious prejudice, or is there a substantial risk that because of *this* delay it is not possible to have a fair trial of the issues in the action? As Slade LJ stressed in *Rath's* case [1991] 3 All ER 679 at 688, [1991] 1 WLR 399 at 410:

'. . . a causal link must be proved between the delay and the inability to have a fair trial or other prejudice, as the case may be.'

(14) An appellate court should regard its function as primarily a reviewing function and should recognise that the decision below involved a balancing of a variety of different considerations upon which the opinion of individual judges may reasonably differ as to their relative weight. Accordingly, unless intervention is necessary or desirable in order to achieve consistency where there appear to be conflicting schools of judicial opinion, the appellate court should only interfere where the judge has erred in principle (see *Birkett v James* [1977] 2 All ER 801 at 804, [1978] AC 297 at 317).

I return to the facts of the present case. The writ against the first three defendants was issued as long ago as 26 September 1983. At that point, in the words of Farquharson LJ in *Rath's* case [1991] 3 All ER 679 at 684, [1991] 1 WLR 399 at 406, the plaintiffs 'set the treadmill of litigation into motion' and thereafter became bound to observe the rules of court. This is not a case where the plaintiffs can place any reliance on the principle that delay in the issue of the writ cannot constitute inordinate delay provided it is issued within the limitation period.

Glidewell LJ has identified the three relevant periods of delay: (a) 3 September 1984 to 20 May 1985; (b) 15 April 1986 to 24 April 1987; (c) 11 January 1989 to 12 June 1990. The period of limitation expired in July 1989 so the first two periods of delay occurred before the date of expiry. The third period spanned that date. I am satisfied, applying the principles I have set out above, that the *a* defendants can rely on all three periods. They amount in aggregate to about three years. The earlier periods of delay were revived by the last period.

One comes therefore to the questions of estoppel and prejudice. I have had the advantage of reading in draft the judgment of Glidewell LJ on the issue of estoppel. I agree with his analysis of the matter and do not wish to add anything.

I also agree with Glidewell LJ's conclusion on the more difficult question of prejudice. Furthermore, though I consider that the judge went wrong when *b* dealing with the issue of delay, I attach some importance to the reasons which he gave for not striking the action out. I agree with him that the case at trial will not depend upon the witnesses' recollection of fine points of detail. The central issue is stark and clear: did these defendants conspire together to defraud or damage the plaintiffs? Or, to put the matter even more simply, was the offer of employment by Mr Stanbury a dishonest trick?

c The delay is serious and deplorable, but in the end I have reached the same conclusion as Glidewell LJ and the judge. I am not persuaded that by reason of the delay there is a substantial risk that a fair trial will not be possible or that the defendants have been seriously prejudiced in relation to the trial of the central issue of conspiracy.

d I too would dismiss the appeal.

Appeal dismissed.

L I Zysman Esq   Barrister.

McAllister v General Medical Council   *a*

PRIVY COUNCIL,
LORD KEITH OF KINKEL, LORD GRIFFITHS AND LORD JAUNCEY OF TULLICHETTLE
23, 24 NOVEMBER, 14 DECEMBER 1992

Medical practitioner – Professional misconduct – Charge of serious professional *b*
misconduct – Evidence – Corroboration – Acts of dishonesty – Committee sitting in
Scotland – Whether English or Scots law applicable – Whether acts of dishonesty required
to be proved by corroborated evidence – Civil Evidence (Scotland) Act 1988, ss 1(1), 9.

The appellant, a Scottish registered medical practitioner practising in Scotland,
was charged by the Professional Conduct Committee of the General Medical   *c*
Council with serious professional misconduct by, inter alia, acting dishonestly in
persuading a company to give him cheque for £38,000 as a donation to the
hospital where he was a consultant for the purchase of specific equipment and
then inducing the hospital finance officer to give him a replacement cheque for
the same amount, part of which he put into his personal account. Because of the
state of the appellant's health the committee sat for the first time in Scotland   *d*
rather than London to hear the charges. Both the appellant and the council were
represented by English counsel and an English Queen's Counsel assisted the
committee as legal assessor. The appellant was found guilty and his name was
ordered to be erased from the register of medical practitioners. The appellant
appealed to the Privy Council, contending that since no specific provision had   *e*
been made for the law to be applied by the committee Scots law applied to the
proceedings as the lex fori, not English law, and that since the Scots criminal law
of evidence required corroboration, of which there was none, the legal assessor's
failure to draw the committee's attention to the need for corroboration vitiated
the proceedings.

f

Held – (1) The law of England applied to all proceedings before the Professional
Conduct Committee of the General Medical Council wherever the committee sat
in the United Kingdom. Even if the law of Scotland had applied there was ample
evidence to corroborate the hospital finance officer's evidence that the appellant
had dishonestly induced him to provide a replacement cheque. In any event no
corroboration of that evidence would have been required because the relevant   *g*
law of evidence would have been Scots civil rather than criminal law since no
specific provision had been made pursuant to para (c) of the definition of 'civil
proceedings' in s 9ᵃ of the Civil Evidence (Scotland) Act 1988 as regards the rules
of evidence which were to apply and under s 1(1)ᵇ of that Act a Scottish civil court
was entitled to find a fact proved notwithstanding that the evidence was not   *h*
corroborated (see p 987 g h and p 988 e to p 989 d, post).
     (2) When a charge of serious professional misconduct was brought against a
doctor by the Professional Conduct Committee of the General Medical Council, it
was of prime importance that the charge and the conduct of the proceedings
should be fair to the doctor in question. However, the rules of evidence applicable
to a criminal trial did not necessarily apply in all cases before the committee since   *j*
although it might be appropriate to apply the criminal onus and standard of proof
where the charges would found serious criminal charges it might not be

---

a   Section 9, so far as material, is set out at p 986 j to p 987 a, post
b   Section 1(1) is set out at p 987 a, post

a appropriate to do so if the charges could not be the subject of serious or criminal charges. In the circumstances the committee was entitled to find the appellant guilty of serious professional misconduct and the appeal would be dismissed (see p 987 *j* to p 988 *c* and p 989 *d*, post); dictum of Lord Lowry in *Lanford v General Medical Council* [1989] 2 All ER 921 at 925 disapproved.

b **Notes**

For procedure on an inquiry by the Professional Conduct Committee of the General Medical Council into professional misconduct, see 30 *Halsbury's Laws* (4th edn reissue) paras 144–153, and for cases on the subject, see 33 *Digest* (Reissue) 289–292, 2335–2348.

c **Case referred to in judgment**

Lanford v General Medical Council [1989] 2 All ER 921, [1990] 1 AC 13, [1989] 3 WLR 665, PC.

Appeal

d Dr Thomas Anderson McAllister appealed from the determination of the Professional Conduct Committee of the General Medical Council on 8 May 1992 that by reason of serious professional misconduct his name be erased from the register of medical practitioners. The hearing was in Glasgow and the committee was assisted by an English Queen's Counsel as legal assessor. The facts are set out in the judgment of the Board.

e *Jonathan Mitchell QC* (of the Scottish Bar) (instructed by *Le Brasseurs*) for the appellant.

Julian Bevan QC and *Rosalind Foster* (instructed by *Field Fisher Waterhouse*) for the General Medical Council.

f 14 December 1992. The following judgment of the Board was delivered.

LORD JAUNCEY OF TULLICHETTLE. This appeal arises from a decision of the Professional Conduct Committee (the committee) of the General Medical Council (the council) on 8 May 1992 that the appellant, Dr Thomas Anderson McAllister, was guilty of serious professional misconduct and a direction by the

g committee that his name be erased from the register of medical practitioners. The charges against the appellant, all of which were found by the committee to be proved, were in these terms:

'That being registered under the Medical Act, 1(a) On various occasions between 1 January 1988 and 12 May 1989 you suggested to representatives

h of John Laing Construction Ltd (JLCL) that JLCL might donate money for the purchase of a Blood Culture System machine (known as a Bactec machine) for the Royal Hospital for Sick Children, Yorkhill, Glasgow; (b) On about 10 May 1989 you took possession of a cheque for £38,000 made payable to the Royal Hospital for Sick Children by JLCL; (c) At the time you took possession of the said cheque you knew that JLCL had donated a cheque in

j the belief that the proceeds of the said cheque would be used to enable the said hospital to pay for the Bactec machine, then installed in the said hospital; (d) Prior to 10 May (i) the said Bactec machine had been paid for by the Greater Glasgow Health Authority; (ii) you knew that the said Bactec machine had been paid for as described in (i) above; (e) In May 1989 you induced the Unit Finance Officer of the said hospital to pay the said £38,000 cheque into a hospital account and to provide you with a replacement cheque in the sum of £38,000 made payable to the Interferon Fund; (f) In June 1989 you (i) *a* caused £30,000 of the £38,000 replacement cheque to be credited to an account number 057720 held at the Clydesdale Bank plc, Bearsden bearing the title "Dr T McAllister for the Interferon High Interest Cheque Account", you being a signatory to the said account; (ii) caused £8,000 of the said £38,000 replacement cheque to be credited to an account number (7)0055076 held at the Clydesdale Bank plc, Bearsden, bearing the title "Dr Thomas *b* Anderson McAllister and Mrs Catherine M McAllister", you being a signatory to the said account, which at the material time was your personal account; (g) On about 3 June 1989 you caused £8,000 to be withdrawn from account number (7)0055076 and to be deposited in an Abbey National account number K665604McA, bearing the title "Dr T A and Mrs C M McAllister", *c* being an account to which you were a signatory; (h) after being informed in mid-June 1989 of allegations regarding your financial dealings, you caused £8,000 to be transferred from the said Abbey National Account to the Interferon account number 057720. 2(a) You acted dishonestly in deliberately misleading JLCL into believing that it was your intention to use the proceeds of the said £38,000 cheque provided by JLCL towards paying for the said *d* Bactec machine then installed at the said hospital; (b) You acted dishonestly in inducing the Unit Finance Officer to provide you with a replacement cheque for £38,000, knowing that JLCL had donated the money to the said hospital; (c) You acted dishonestly in using the proceeds of the replacement cheque provided by the Unit Finance Officer to credit accounts held under your control and outside the control of the said hospital, thereby removing *e* the money from the said hospital. And that in relation to the facts alleged you have been guilty of serious professional misconduct.'

A hearing took place before the committee in Glasgow from 4 to 8 May 1992 at which both parties were represented by English counsel and at which an English Queen's Counsel attended as legal assessor.   *f*

At the time of the events referred to in the charges the appellant was a consultant microbiologist at the Royal Hospital for Sick Children and Queen Mother's Hospital, Yorkhill, Glasgow. The charges arose out of circumstances summarised by him as 'the case against him' in his original printed case to this Board:

g

'In 1988 John Laing Construction Company ("Laings") decided to raise money for charity. Laings were put in touch with the Appellant who had a reputation going back many years for raising charity money. Eventually, by letter dated 3rd April 1989, Laings wrote to the Appellant indicating that they intended to hold a cheque handing-over ceremony in the Glasgow City Chambers banqueting hall on 10th May 1989. The letter included the *h* sentence "An indication of specific areas where the money could be used would also be appreciated". By letter dated 12th April 1989, the Apellant wrote back indicating, inter alia, that there was situate in the hospital and on approval a "Bactec" machine which "would be top of our shopping list. It is also photogenic". The machine had in fact already been paid for in March 1989 by the Greater Glasgow Health Authority and this fact was known to *j* the Appellant. (The Appellant disputed this). Under the impression that their charity money was going to be used for the purchase of this machine, at a public ceremony on 10th May 1989 at The City Hall, Laings handed over the Appellant a cheque for £38,000 payable to The Royal Hospital for Sick Children, Glasgow. On 11th May 1989 representatives of Laings made a tour of the hospital and inspected a plaque which had been affixed to the machine by Mr. Roud, the Chief Medical Laboratory Scientific Officer, at the request of the Appellant indicating that the machine had been presented by Laings. On the same day the Appellant asked the Unit Finance Officer [Mr Paterson] of the hospital to bank the Laings cheque and issue him with a replacement cheque made payable to The Interferon Fund, a fund set up in the late 1970s by the Appellant for research purposes. On 31st May 1989 the Unit Finance Officer provided a replacement cheque to the Appellant in the sum of £38,000 payable to The Interferon Fund. The Appellant split the £38,000, paying £30,000 into a newly opened High Interest Account named The Interferon Fund and £8,000 into a current non-interest bearing personal account in the name of himself and his wife, both accounts being at The Clydesdale Bank. He then transferred the £8,000 from the current personal account to an interest bearing personal account at The Abbey National Building Society in the name of himself and his wife. In about mid-June 1989 the Appellant was formally told he was the subject of an investigation in relation to the Laing charity gift and he gave instructions for the £8,000 to be transferred from The Abbey National Building Society to The Interferon Fund High Interest Account, where it thereafter remained.'

All the matters in the summary were matter of admission or the subject of evidence. In his original printed case, which was signed by English counsel who had represented him before the committee, he advanced three reasons why the appeal should be allowed, which were as follows:

'1. Because a material irregularity with regard to disclosure of documents prejudiced the Appellant. 2. Because the Committee failed to apply the correct test in relation to jurisdiction to order disclosure of documents. 3. Because of the way the case was put to the Committee on the ingredients and meaning of the word "dishonestly".'

The documents referred to in the first and second reasons were precognitions taken by the Procurator Fiscal in Glasgow.

When the case came before this Board, Scottish counsel appeared on behalf of the appellant and sought leave to lodge a supplementary case which departed entirely from the reasons in the original case and sought to introduce fresh reasons attributable to the fact that the proceedings before the committee had taken place in Scotland rather than in England. The case also accepted that there was evidence in relation to charges 2(a) and (c) which, if accepted as credible and reliable, was sufficient to entitle the committee to find those charges proved. The new reasons were in the following terms:

'1. Because the proceedings were subject to Scots law and not to English law. 2. Because there was insufficient evidence to entitle the Committee to find the allegations in paragraphs 1(e) and 2(b) proved. 3. Because the entire decision of the Committee was vitiated by its failure to appreciate the existence and importance of the requirement for corroboration on all charges. 4. Because the Committee were materially misdirected by omission on a matter of central significance to the case and which they required a direction upon, causing a material risk that there was a miscarriage of justice. 5. Because the legal assessor's failure to advise on the question of sufficiency of evidence and of corroboration amounted to a material misdirection causing a material risk that there was a miscarriage of justice, and accordingly invalidated the decision of the Committee.'

Although the questions raised in the grounds of appeal in the supplementary case had never been argued before the committee their Lordships allowed Mr _a_ Mitchell QC, for the appellant, to lodge the supplementary case and develop an argument thereupon. This he did with considerable skill and ingenuity, maintaining that, in the absence of any direction in the statutory rules as to which system of law should apply to hearings before the committee, the lex fori must apply and that there was insufficient corroboration by the law of Scotland to entitle the committee to find charge 2(b) proved. Before considering this _b_ argument in more detail it is necessary to examine the statutory background against which the committee operates.

The Medical Act 1983, which was a consolidation Act, provided by s 1(3) for the continued existence of four committees of the council including the professional conduct committee. Schedule 4 dealt, inter alia, with proceedings _c_ before the committee and provided by para 1 that the council should make rules with respect, inter alia, to the procedure to be followed and the rules of evidence to be observed in proceedings before the committee. Paragraph 2 of the schedule referred specifically to proceedings which might take place not only in England and Wales but also in Northern Ireland and in Scotland. Paragraph 7 of the schedule provided that the committee should sit with a legal assessor who should _d_ be either a barrister, advocate or solicitor of not less than ten years' standing and made further reference to proceedings taking place in Scotland.

In accordance with their duty under para 1 of Sch 4 to the 1983 Act the council made rules which were approved in the General Medical Council Preliminary Proceedings Committee and Professional Conduct Committee (Procedure) Rules Order of Council 1988, SI 1988/2255. Two of these rules were relied upon by the _e_ appellant, namely r 27(1)(e), which provides:

> 'In cases relating to conduct, the following order of proceedings shall be observed as respects proof of the facts alleged in the charge or charges . . . (e) At the close of the case against him the practitioner may make either or both of the following submissions, namely: (i) in respect of any or all of the facts _f_ alleged and not admitted in the charge or charges, that no sufficient evidence has been adduced upon which the Committee could find those facts proved; (ii) in respect of any charge, that the facts of which evidence has been adduced or which have been admitted are insufficient to support a finding of serious professional misconduct; and where any such submission is made, the Solicitor or the complainant, as the case may be, may answer the submission _g_ and the practitioner may reply thereto.'

And r 50(1), which was in the following terms:

> 'The Professional Conduct Committee may receive oral, documentary or other evidence of any fact or matter which appears to them relevant to the inquiry into the case before them: Provided that, where any fact or matter is _h_ tendered as evidence which would not be admissible as such if the proceedings were criminal proceedings in England, the Committee shall not receive it unless, after consultation with the legal assessor, they are satisfied that their duty of making due inquiry into the case before them makes its reception desirable.' _j_

Two further statutory provisions are relevant to this appeal, namely ss 1(1) and 9(c) of the Civil Evidence (Scotland) Act 1988, which provide respectively:

> '**1.**—(1) In any civil proceedings the court or, as the case may be, the jury, if satisfied that any fact has been established by evidence in those proceedings,

a   shall be entitled to find that fact proved by that evidence notwithstanding that the evidence is not corroborated . . .

9 . . . "civil proceedings" includes . . . (*c*) any proceedings before a tribunal or inquiry, except in so far as, in relation to the conduct of proceedings before the tribunal or inquiry, specific provision has been made as regards the rules of evidence which are to apply . . .'

b   Mr Mitchell submitted that, the Medical Act 1983 and r 50 of the 1988 rules having made no specific provision for the law to be applied by the committee, the lex fori must determine questions of substantive law, evidence and procedure. Rule 50, although referring questions of admissibility of evidence to English law, left all other evidential matters to be dealt with by the lex fori. Scots law required corroboration of which there was none in relation to the dishonesty referred to in *c*   charge 2(b), the only relevant evidence being that of Mr Paterson the unit finance officer. The failure of the legal assessor to draw the attention of the committee to the need for corroboration vitiated the whole proceedings and accordingly the case should be remitted back to the committee for a rehearing. This argument presented Mr Mitchell with some difficulty in relation to the Civil Evidence (Scotland) Act 1988 since he accepted that the proceedings before the committee *d*   albeit analogous to criminal proceedings were in fact civil rather than criminal. However he sought to overcome this difficulty by submitting that the reference in r 50 to the application of English criminal law to questions of admissibility of evidence constituted 'specific provision' for the purposes of the exception in s 9(*c*), thereby removing proceedings before the committee from the ambit of the 1988 *e*   Act. He further submitted that a dictum in the judgment of this Board in *Lanford v General Medical Council* [1989] 2 All ER 921 at 925, [1990] 1 AC 13 at 19–20 required that notwithstanding the provision of the 1988 Act corroboration was necessary. That passage was in the following terms:

'Counsel for the appellant (rightly, as their Lordships consider) submitted that the onus and standard of proof in these disciplinary proceedings and the *f*   relevant legal principles were those applicable to a criminal trial.'

If it be the case that Scots law of evidence, as the lex fori, applied to the proceedings of the committee in Glasgow, there are two reasons why their Lordships consider that the appeal must fail. In the first place s 1(1) of the 1988 Act applies to any civil proceedings or a tribunal unless specific provision has been *g*   made as regards the rules of evidence which are to apply (s 9(*c*)). Rule 50 deals with admissibility of evidence in certain circumstances but makes no reference to corroboration which has therefore not been made the subject of a provision. As a matter of construction the exception to s 9(*c*) can apply only where there exist rules which specifically deal with corroboration in a manner which supersedes *h*   the application of s 1(1). There being no such provision in the 1988 rules, it follows that if the Scots law of evidence applied to the proceedings the rules did not exclude the application of s 1(1) of the 1988 Act.

It remains to consider the above quoted dictum in *Lanford v General Medical Council*. That case concerned two separate complaints by women patients of indecent conduct and speech towards them on the part of a doctor. The passage *j*   therefore related to events which, had they been the subject of criminal charges in England, would have required to be proved by corroborated evidence. The appellant argued that in the particular circumstances of the case the evidence of one patient did not corroborate that of the other. The council did not traverse this argument by submitting that corroboration was not necessary and the issue of the need for corroboration was therefore not before the Board. Their Lordships do not consider that the above dictum can be treated as having universal application in all cases arising before the committee. In charges brought against a doctor where the events giving rise to the charges would also found serious criminal charges it may be appropriate that the onus and standards of proof should be those applicable to a criminal trial. However there will be many cases where the charges which a doctor has to face before the committee could not be the subject of serious or any criminal charges at all. The committee is composed entirely of medical men and women learned in their profession and to require that every charge of professional misconduct has to be proved to them just as though they were a jury of laymen is, in their Lordships' view, neither necessary nor desirable. What is of prime importance is that the charge and the conduct of the proceedings should be fair to the doctor in question in all respects. It is not without significance (i) that r 50 clearly contemplates that the committee may consider evidence which would not be admissible in criminal proceedings and (ii) that the rules nowhere provide that criminal standards of proof and corroboration must at all times apply.

Neither r 50 nor any other rule required to be considered by this Board in *Lanford v General Medical Council* and their Lordships doubt whether the above dictum would have been couched in such wide terms had it been drawn to the attention of the Board. Indeed if Parliament had intended that rules of evidence appropriate to criminal proceedings should apply in all proceedings before the committee, it is surprising that the council were not directed to make such rules in para 1(1) of Sch 4 to the 1983 Act. In all the circumstances their Lordships do not consider that, if Scots law applied to proceedings in Glasgow, the council would have been obliged to disregard the provision of s 1(1) of the 1988 Act and to apply the criminal law of evidence instead.

In the second place, even if corroboration of the fact that the appellant dishonestly induced Mr Paterson to provide him with a replacement cheque were necessary, their Lordships are satisfied that there was ample evidence to corroborate that of Mr Paterson. The provision of a replacement cheque by Mr Paterson was admitted by the appellant, as were his subsequent dealings with that cheque through the accounts in the Clydesdale Bank, Bearsden. The committee found, as the appellant accepts that they were entitled to find, that he acted dishonestly in deliberately misleading John Laing Construction Ltd into believing that he intended to use their cheque towards payment for the Bactec machine. There was accordingly ample evidence on which the committee were entitled to infer that when the appellant induced Mr Paterson to provide him with a replacement cheque he was acting dishonestly.

That is sufficient for the disposal of this appeal but their Lordships think it right to consider whether Scots law was applicable at all to the proceedings. This is the first occasion, so this Board was informed, on which the committee had sat in Scotland. It did so because of the state of health of the appellant. Cases involving Scots doctors have to date always been heard in London and it has never been suggested that any law other than that of England applied to the proceedings. The council and the committee are United Kingdom bodies and it is highly desirable that the same rules of evidence and procedure should apply throughout the United Kingdom wherever the committee sits. Conversely it is highly undesirable that the committee should apply different standards of proof to different doctors depending upon where they elect to sit. Although the 1983 Act makes reference to the Court of Session in the context of termination or suspension of a person's registration in the register (s 38(6) and (7)) and to the appointment of an advocate as a legal assessor to the committee in relation to proceedings in Scotland (paras 7(1) and (3) of Sch 4), these provisions do not necessarily point to

Scots law being applied by the committee. It is possible to envisage situations
a where a doctor had been convicted of offences in Scotland in circumstances in
which it would be desirable for the committee to be advised as to what were the
necessary components of that offence. More significant matters are: (1) that in
para 1(1) of Sch 4 to the 1983 Act no direction is given to the General Medical
Council to make different sets of rules of evidence for Scotland and England, and
(2) that in r 50 admissibility of evidence is in certain circumstances to be tested
b by English law.

This latter provision suggests that the council as rule makers contemplated that
English law should apply to all proceedings before the committee wherever they
might take place. Given the desirability of a single code of evidence being applied
in the committee's proceedings throughout the United Kingdom and given the
aforementioned indications in r 50, their Lordships are satisfied that the law of
c England was the correct law to have been applied in these proceedings.

In summary the appeal fails for the following reasons: (1) because the law of
England applied to the proceedings before the committee; (2) even if the law of
Scotland had applied (a) there was ample evidence to corroborate that of
Mr Paterson in relation to charge 2(b), and (b) in any event no corroboration of
d that evidence was required having regard to the provision of s 1(1) of the Civil
Evidence (Scotland) Act 1988.

Their Lordships will therefore humbly advise Her Majesty that the appeal
should be dismissed. The appellant must pay the respondent's costs.

Appeal dismissed.
e
Mary Rose Plummer   Barrister.

f # Lawson v Midland Travellers Ltd and another

COURT OF APPEAL, CIVIL DIVISION
SIR THOMAS BINGHAM MR, STUART-SMITH AND SIMON BROWN LJJ
11 NOVEMBER, 2 DECEMBER 1992

g *Practice – Acknowledgment of service – Notice of intention to contest proceedings – Oral
agreement extending time for service of defence – Oral agreement not confirmed in
writing until after expiry of time limit for service of defence – Defendant allowing time
for service of defence to expire without issuing summons to set aside writ – Whether
defendant irrevocably submitting to jurisdiction and waiving any irregularity in writ –*
h *Whether service of writ should be set aside – RSC Ord 3, r 5, Ord 12, r 8(1)(7).*

The plaintiff, a disabled person who had to use crutches or a wheelchair to get
about, booked a holiday at a hotel in Spain organised by the second defendant, a
tour operator, through the first defendant, a travel agent. On 26 September 1987,
while on holiday, the plaintiff accidently fell while walking up some steps at the
j hotel recommended by the defendants. On 31 August 1990 he issued a writ
against the defendants alleging negligence and/or breach of statutory duty and
claiming damages for personal injuries. The limitation period for the plaintiff's
claim expired on 25 September 1990. On 8 November the writ was amended to
include a claim for breach of contract. The writ was not served within the four
months permitted by the rules of court. On 7 March 1991 the plaintiff served the

writ and statement of claim but the statement of claim was not accompanied by
a medical report or statement of special damages as required by RSC Ord 18,   *a*
r 12(1A). On 8 March the second defendant filed an acknowledgment of service
and on 28 March there was an oral agreement between the parties' solicitors
extending the time for service of the defence until 14 days after the plaintiff
served a medical report and schedule of special damages. That agreement was
confirmed in writing on 8 April. The time for service of the defence would have
expired on 3 April but for the agreement to extend the time, assuming the   *b*
agreement was valid. On 19 April the plaintiff served his medical evidence but
not a schedule of special damages. On 4 July the second defendant issued
summonses (i) to set aside service of the writ, (ii) for an extension of time to serve
their defence if there had been no valid extension by agreement and (iii) for leave
to withdraw their acknowledgment of service. The district judge dismissed the
summonses. The second defendant appealed to the judge, who dismissed the   *c*
appeal on the ground that under Ord 12, r 8(7)[a] the second defendant had
submitted to the jurisdiction by acknowledging service of the writ and not
applying under Ord 12, r 8(1)[b] to have the service of the writ set aside before the
time limited for service of the defence on 3 April 1992. The judge further held
that the written consent given by the plaintiff on 8 April 1991 confirming the   *d*
previous oral consent, after the time for service of the defence had expired, was
ineffective to extend the time limited by the rules for service of the defence
because although there could be a retrospective extension of the time for service
of a defence by the court under Ord 3, r 5(2)[c] there could be no retrospective
extension by consent under Ord 3, r 5(3). The second defendant appealed.

                                                                                 e
Held – RSC Ord 3, r 5(3) enabled the parties to do by consent that which the
court could do on an application under r 5(2), thereby avoiding the need for an
application to the court, since there was no fetter on the power of the court under
Ord 3, r 5 to grant a retrospective extension of time. Accordingly, the written
consent given by the plaintiff on 8 April 1991 had validly extended the time for
service of the defence. Furthermore, an extension of time for service of the   *f*
defence automatically involved an extension of time for making an application
under Ord 12, r 8(1) to set aside service of the writ, since the defendant was
entitled to see the nature of the claim properly pleaded in the statement of claim
before deciding whether to challenge the jurisdiction or deal with the case on the
merits. Accordingly, since the application to set aside the service had been made
within the extended period the second defendant was not deemed irrevocably to   *g*
have submitted to the jurisdiction by failing to apply within the prescribed time.
It followed that, since the statement of claim was defective because it did not
comply with Ord 18, r 12(1A), the second defendant was not to be taken, simply
by taking a step in the action by inviting the plaintiff or the court to extend the
time for service of the defence, to have waived its right to apply under Ord 12,   *h*
r 8(1) to set aside the writ until the plaintiff had made good the defective service
of the statement of claim. The appeal would therefore be allowed and service of
the writ set aside (see p 994 *g* to *j*, p 995 *d*, p 996 *f g* and p 997 *b g*, post).
    Per curiam. A plaintiff who wishes only to grant an extension of time for
service of the defence but not to apply to set aside the writ must expressly say so
when granting his consent (see p 996 *e g* and p 997 *b g*, post).   *j*

---

a   Rule 8(7) is set out at p 993 *d*, post
b   Rule 8(1), so far as material, is set out at p 994 *b*, post
c   Rule 5, so far as material, is set out at p 994 *d e*, post

Notes

a For extension or abridgment of time, see 37 *Halsbury's Laws* (4th edn) paras 30–31, and for cases on the subject, see 37(2) *Digest* (Reissue) 200–203, 1319–1344.

For effect of non-compliance with the rules of court, see 37 *Halsbury's Laws* (4th edn) para 36, and for cases on the subject, see 37(2) *Digest* (Reissue) 205–212, 1355–1390.

For disputing jurisdiction of court, see 37 *Halsbury's Laws* (4th edn) paras 209–
b 211 and for cases on the subject, see 37(2) *Digest* (Reissue) 341, 2123–2127.

Cases referred to in judgments

Carmel Exporters (Sales) Ltd v Sea-Land Services Inc [1981] 1 All ER 984, [1981] 1 WLR 1068.

c *Sage v Double A Hydraulics Ltd, Chambers v Starkings* (1992) Times, 2 April, CA.

Cases also cited or referred to in skeleton arguments

Bernstein v Jackson [1982] 2 All ER 806, [1982] 1 WLR 1082, CA.
Rein v Stein [1892] 1 QB 753, CA; *affg* 66 LT 469, DC.
Somportex Ltd v Philadelphia Chewing Gum Corp [1968] 3 All ER 26, CA.
d *Williams & Glyn's Bank plc v Astro Dinamico Cia Naviera SA* [1984] 1 All ER 760, [1984] 1 WLR 438, HL.

Interlocutory appeal

The second defendant, Thomson Holidays Ltd, appealed with leave of the judge given on 14 April 1992 from the order of Laws J sitting at Birmingham on 6
e March 1992 dismissing its appeal from the order of District Judge Hargreaves dated 11 November 1991 dismissing the second defendant's application for an order that service of the writ issued on 31 August 1990 by the plaintiff, Michael Roderick Lawson, claiming damages for personal injury, loss and expense from the first defendant, Midland Travellers Ltd, and the second defendant, arising out
f of an accident allegedly caused by the negligence and/or breach of statutory duty of the defendants, and damages for breach of contract, be set aside and the action be dismissed, and dismissing the second defendant's application for an extension of the time for service of the defence and/or for leave to withdraw acknowledgment of service. Service of the writ against the first defendant was set aside pursuant to the order of District Judge Cole made in Birmingham district registry on 27 June
g 1991. The facts are set out in the judgment of Stuart-Smith LJ.

Dermod O'Brien QC (instructed by *Lawrence Graham*) for the second defendant.
Julia Smith (instructed by *Howell & Co*, Birmingham) for the plaintiff.

Cur adv vult

h
2 December 1992. The following judgments were delivered.

STUART-SMITH LJ (giving the first judgment at the invitation of Sir Thomas Bingham MR). This appeal raises a question of some interest and general importance on the interpretation of RSC Ord 12, r 8 relating to disputes as to
j jurisdiction and in particular applications to set aside service of a writ, and Ord 3, r 5 relating to extensions of time within which such an application can be made.

The facts are these. The plaintiff is crippled and has to use crutches or a wheelchair to get about. He booked a holiday at a hotel in Spain through the agency of the first and/or second defendant. On 26 September 1987 he suffered an accident when he fell while walking up some steps at the hotel recommended by the defendants. On 31 August 1990 he issued a writ against both defendants claiming damages for personal injuries caused by their negligence and/or breach of statutory duty. On 25 September 1990 the limitation period expired. On 8 November the writ was amended to include a claim for breach of contract. The writ was not served within the four months permitted by the rules (see Ord 6, r 8(1)(b)).

On 7 March 1991 the plaintiff's solicitors prepared to serve the writ and a statement of claim by fax. No point is taken by the defendants that the purported service was by fax. The statement of claim was not accompanied, as it should have been, with a medical report or statement of the special damages claimed (see Ord 18, r 12(1A)). But Mr O'Brien does not contend that the statement of claim is a nullity because of non-compliance with this rule. On 8 March the second defendant's solicitors filed an acknowledgment of service. On 28 March there was an oral agreement between solicitors extending the time for service of the defence until 14 days after the plaintiff served a medical report and schedule of special damages. On 2 April 1991 the second defendant's solicitors wrote to the plaintiff's solicitors as follows:

> 'We also confirm our telephone conversation with Mr Williams of the 28 March when we pointed out that when serving the Statement of Claim you had failed to comply with the revised provisions of RSC Order 18 Rule 12 in that you had not served with the pleading your medical evidence and a Schedule of Special Damages. In these circumstances we confirm your agreement to extend our time for service of the Defence until 14 days after you have remedied this omission.'

On 8 April by letter the plaintiff's solicitors confirmed their agreement in those terms. But for that extension of time, if it was valid, time for service of the defence would have expired on 3 April. On 19 April the plaintiff served medical evidence, but not a schedule of special damages. On 4 July the second defendant issued a summons to set aside service of the writ. On 11 November District Judge Hargreaves dismissed the application. The second defendant appealed on 15 November and on the same day issued a summons returnable before the judge asking for an order for extension of time to serve the defence (if there had been no valid extension by agreement) and leave to withdraw the acknowledgment of service. On 6 March 1992 Laws J dismissed the second defendant's appeal and summons; on 14 April 1992 he gave leave to the second defendant to appeal his order. The second defendant now appeals pursuant to that leave. For the sake of completeness I should add that the first defendant had successfully applied to have the service of the writ set aside against it. Furthermore, the plaintiff had applied to the district judge for an extension of the writ; that was refused and the plaintiff did not appeal.

Before coming to Ord 12, r 8 as it is presently drafted, it is desirable to consider briefly the legislative history of this rule. Before 1979 a defendant had to enter an appearance; by so doing he not only showed his intention to defend, but he submitted to the jurisdiction of the court. If he wished to challenge the jurisdiction, he could either obtain leave to enter a conditional appearance and then apply to set aside service of the writ, or make that application forthwith. In 1979 the rules were changed and the defendant no longer had to enter an appearance (see RSC (Writ and Appearance) 1979, SI 1979/1716). Instead he had to file an acknowledgment of service.

Order 12, r 7 was in substantially the same terms as it now is. The current rule provides:

'The acknowledgment by a defendant of service of a writ shall not be treated as a waiver by him of any irregularity in the writ or service thereof or in any order giving leave to serve the writ out of the jurisdiction or extending the validity of the writ for the purpose of service.'

Order 12, r 8(1) of the 1979 rules was as follows:

'A defendant who wishes to dispute the jurisdiction of the court in the proceedings by reason of any such irregularity as is mentioned in rule 7 or on any other ground shall give notice of intention to defend the proceedings and shall, within 14 days thereafter, apply to the Court for—(a) an order setting aside the writ or service of the writ or notice of the writ on him . . . '

Sub-paragraphs (b) to (h) are not material to this appeal and are in substantially the same terms as in the current rule. Paragraph (2) provided:

'Order 3, rule 5 shall apply in relation to the period of 14 days mentioned in paragraph (1) with the modification that the said period may be extended by the Court only on an application made before the expiration of the period.'

Paragraphs (3) to (6) are not material. Paragraph (7) was as follows:

'Except where the defendant makes an application in accordance with paragraph (1), the acknowledgment by a defendant of service of a writ [or notice of a writ] shall, unless the acknowledgment is withdrawn by leave of the Court under Order 21, rule 1, be treated as a submission by the defendant to the jurisdiction of the Court in the proceedings.'

The effect of paras (2) and (7) was that, if the defendant failed to make an application to extend the 14 days provided by para (1) within that time, he was to be treated as having submitted to the jurisdiction. This was so held by Robert Goff J in *Carmel Exporters (Sales) Ltd v Sea-Land Services Inc* [1981] 1 All ER 984, [1981] 1 WLR 1068. But the judge drew attention to the difficulties caused by this rigid time limit. He said ([1981] 1 All ER 984 at 993, [1981] 1 WLR 1068 at 1079):

'Second, I wish to return to the requirement in the new Ord 12, r 8(2), that an application under Ord 3, r 5, for an extension of the 14-day period within which an application to the court under r 8(1) has to be made, must be made before the expiration of the 14-day period. The exceptional rigidity of this requirement contrasts forcibly with the flexibility which is now generally characteristic of the Rules of the Supreme Court, and which enables the court to ensure that justice is done. No doubt short time limits are sometimes desirable; a recent example of this is the period of 21 days now required under Ord 73, r 5 for the commencement and service of proceedings to challenge arbitration awards. But the imposition of the guillotine in Ord 12, r 8(2) appears to be contrary to the trend in our rules, which is to ensure so far as possible that parties do not fall into procedural traps, and to give the court power to deal with the situation if they do so. The widening some years ago of the court's powers under Ord 2, r 1 to deal with failures to comply with the rules, provides a vivid illustration of this trend. It is not difficult to see how, due to error, oversight or even illness in a busy solicitor's office, the 14-day period in r 8(1) might be allowed to pass without an application being made under Ord 3, r 5 for an extension of time. I must confess that it seems strange that the court should be deprived of any power to remedy the situation, especially where the plaintiff has suffered no prejudice, as for example where the point at issue has already been developed in correspondence.'

He expressed the hope that the Rule Committee might remedy the situation. The committee responded and produced the current rule in 1983.

Order 12, r 8(1) now reads, so far as is material:

'A defendant who wishes to dispute the jurisdiction of the court in the proceedings by reason of any such irregularity as is mentioned in rule 7 or on any other ground shall give notice of intention to defend the proceedings and shall, within the time limited for service of a defence, apply to the Court for—(a) an order setting aside the writ or service of the writ on him . . .'

Paragraph (2) has now been revoked.

Save for reference to the notice of the writ which has been deleted para (7) is in the same terms as the 1979 rule.

I must now refer to Ord 3, r 5. This provides:

'(1) The Court may, on such terms as it thinks just, by order extend or abridge the period within which a person is required or authorised by these rules, or by any judgment, order or direction, to do any act in any proceedings.

(2) The Court may extend any such period as is referred to in paragraph (1) although the application for extension is not made until after the expiration of that period.

(3) The period within which a person is required by these rules, or by any order or direction, to serve, file or amend any pleading or other document may be extended by consent (given in writing) without an order of the Court being made for that purpose . . .'

Laws J held that although there could be a retrospective extension of time for delivery of defence by the court under Ord 3, r 5(2) there could be no such retrospective extension by consent under para (3). Accordingly, since the written consent was not given until after the time for service of the defence had expired, there was no valid extension and the second defendant had not made its application in time.

In my judgment the judge was wrong in adopting this construction. Paragraph (3) enables the parties to do by consent what the court can do on application under para (2), thereby avoiding the need for an application to the court. This being so, Mr O'Brien QC on behalf of the second defendant submits that the written consent validly extended time for service of the defence and the application to set aside the service was made within the extended period.

Miss Smith for the plaintiff sought to counter this argument in four ways. First, she submitted that the effect of Ord 12, r 8(7) is that, as soon as the primary time limit set out in r 8(1) has expired, unless it is extended during the currency of that period, the defendant is to be treated as having submitted to the jurisdiction and he cannot apply under r 8(1). In other words, she submits that the revocation of para (2) makes no difference. I cannot accept that submission; the only effect of the old para (2) was to place a fetter on the power of the court which otherwise existed under Ord 3, r 5 to grant a retrospective extension of time. That fetter has now been removed. It cannot be reintroduced by a sidewind.

The second argument, which was not advanced before Laws J and was prompted by a suggestion from the court and was then the subject of an amended respondent's notice, was to this effect: it is not sufficient for the defendant to obtain an extension of time for service of the defence whether by order of the court or by consent; he must apply in terms for an extension of time in which to

make the application under Ord 12, r 8(1). In other words the reference to the
a time limited for service of the defence is simply shorthand for the times specified
in Ord 18, r 2(1). If the rule therefore is set out in full it would read:

> 'A defendant who wishes to dispute the jurisdiction of the court . . . shall,
> within 14 days after the time limited for acknowledgment of service of the
> writ or after the statement of claim is served on him, whichever is the later,
b > apply to the court for an order.'

I cannot accept this submission for three reasons. (1) If that is what is intended,
there is no difficulty in saying so, or if the language is thought cumbersome, a
fixed period of say 28 days could have been specified as in the older Ord 12, r 8(1).
(2) While the new rule may have removed one trap for a defendant, it would have
c introduced an equally fatal but more subtle one. If he follows precisely the word
of the rule and applies to extend time for service of the defence, he does not
thereby automatically extend his time for making the application under Ord 12,
r 8(1); but he has to make a separate application in that behalf. I cannot believe
that was the intention of the Rule Committee. (3) In my judgment there has
been a deliberate change of policy to enable the defendant to see the nature of the
d claim properly pleaded in the statement of claim before he has to decide whether
to challenge the jurisdiction or deal with the case on the merits. There may be
cases where the grounds for setting aside the service are less clear cut than in this
case, where the defendants' insurers may prefer to buy off for a modest sum what
appears to be a weak case made at the end of the limitation period, rather than
contest the court's jurisdiction.
e Miss Smith relied upon a recent decision of this court in *Sage v Double A
Hydraulics Ltd, Chambers v Starkings* (1992) Times, 2 April, of which we have seen
a transcript. The facts of that case were unusual. The plaintiff had served the writ
after its expiry and after the limitation period. The defendants applied within the
primary time limited by Ord 12, r 8(1) to set aside service; however they failed to
f turn up on the summons and it was dismissed. Instead of applying to reinstate
the summons they applied retrospectively for an order to extend time for delivery
of defence and only after that applied to reinstate the summons to set aside service.
   The question in that case was whether by issuing a summons for extension of
time for serving the defence at a time when they had not either appealed the
dismissal of the application to set aside or applied to reinstate that summons, the
g defendants had waived their right to challenge the writ or the court's jurisdiction.
Farquharson LJ, with whose judgment Lord Donaldson MR and Stocker LJ
agreed, said in answer to this question:

> 'What in my judgment is conclusive against the defendants is the issue of
> the time summons on 22 March 1991 and its service. This was done at a time
h > when the writ was not apparently being challenged as the application for
> reinstatement of the original summons to set aside was not made until 26
> March 1991. It is appreciated that the steps taken to extend time were to
> protect the defendants' position in the event of the failure of the summons to
> set the writ aside, but as already observed the acts of the defendant and his
> solicitors must be regarded objectively. So regarded, in my judgment, the
j > defendants did take a step in the action inconsistent with their challenge and
> thus waived their right to object to the writ.'

In my judgment that case depends on its particular facts. The present argument
was not addressed to the court. It is no authority for the proposition that if the
defendant merely applies for an extension of time for service of the defence,

which automatically carries with it the extension of time in which to apply under Ord 12, r 8(1), that this is to be taken as a waiver.

Thirdly, Miss Smith submitted that the second defendant's solicitors' letter of 2 April 1991, the material part of which I have already set out, constituted a step in the action and hence a waiver. She submitted that by asking for service of the medical evidence and schedule of special damage the second defendant was inviting the plaintiff to incur further expense in the belief that the matter would be defended on the merits.

In my judgment there are a number of answers to this submission. First, the second defendant did not call for those documents at all, it merely asked for an extension of time until they were served. Secondly, there is no evidence that the plaintiff incurred any expense after the letter of 2 April; they may or may not have done. Those reasons are peculiar to this case. But the real objection in my opinion is that the service of the statement of claim was defective (although not a nullity) because it did not comply with Ord 18, r 12(1A). This did not prevent time for service of the defence running. But, having regard to the policy to which I have earlier referred, I do not think the second defendant should be taken to have waived his right to apply under Ord 12, r 8(1) simply because he has invited the plaintiff or the court to extend time for service of the defence until the plaintiff has made good the defective service of the statement of claim.

Finally, Miss Smith submitted that the exchange of letters between the solicitors should be construed as granting an extension of time for service of the defence, but not for applying to set aside the writ. I can see no basis for this construction. If, as in my opinion is the case, an extension of time for service of the defence automatically involves an extension of time for applying under Ord 12, r 8(1) a plaintiff who wishes only to extend the time for the former but not the latter purpose, must expressly say so in granting his consent. I see no reason why he should not do so, if he is so minded; though this will draw attention to the defective service which he may hope, perhaps forlornly, that the defendant has overlooked. Equally it would I think be possible for the court, on an application under Ord 3, r 5(2) to grant a longer extension for service of the defence in contradistinction to making the application to set aside. But if no such distinction is made, the extension of time for service of the defence carries with it the extension of time to apply to set aside service of the writ.

For these reasons I would allow the appeal and set aside service of the writ.

SIMON BROWN LJ. I am in full agreement with the judgment of Stuart-Smith LJ.

Recognising, however, the force of the concern expressed by Sir Thomas Bingham MR in his draft judgment, which I have also had the advantage of reading, I venture to advance these two thoughts.

First, that, following upon this decision, plaintiff's solicitors will know that one of the consequences of consenting to an extension of time for the defence is, unless otherwise stipulated, that time is also extended for RSC Ord 12, r 8 purposes. Where appropriate, therefore, they should stipulate the contrary and, indeed, invite the court so to do if extension is being sought under Ord 3, r 5(1) or (2). If, of course, as here, the defendant is virtually entitled to an extension of time because of the plaintiff's failure to serve his medical evidence and schedule of special damage with the statement of claim, such stipulation is unlikely to be accepted. Assuming, however, that the plaintiff is not in default, it doubtless would be.

Second, that, in any case where the consequence of obtaining extensions of time for the service of the defence and thus for the making of a setting aside *a* application under Ord 12, r 8 is to put the plaintiff outside the limitation period for the institution of fresh proceedings, the court would be alert to find wherever appropriate that the defendant by his conduct had waived any rights under Ord 12, r 8, in particular where the defendant appeared to have sought extensions of time for that very purpose.

For the reasons given by Stuart-Smith LJ I too would allow this appeal and set aside service of the writ.

b

SIR THOMAS BINGHAM MR. I have felt more difficulty about this case than Stuart-Smith and Simon Brown LJJ.

I do not doubt that the amendments made to RSC Ord 12, r 8 following *Carmel Exporters (Sales) Ltd v Sea-Land Services Inc* [1981] 1 All ER 984, [1981] 1 WLR 1068 were intended to allow extensions of time for applying to set aside service to be applied for or agreed after expiry of the time allowed for making such applications, and I see no reason to distinguish between extensions granted by the court under Ord 3, r 5(2) and extensions agreed in writing between the parties under Ord 3, r 5(3). I think that the judge was wrong to draw that distinction. I cannot, therefore, accept the plaintiff's argument that if a defendant fails to

d apply for, or agree, an extension of time for setting aside service within the time prescribed he is deemed irrevocably to have submitted to the jurisdiction.

What troubles me is the proposition that any extension of time for serving a defence, whether granted by the court or agreed in writing between the parties, carries with it an extension of time for applying to set aside service, even though no reference is made to setting aside and even though the plaintiff and the court

e may be quite unaware of the possibility of such an application.

If 'the time limited for service of a defence' in Ord 12, r 8 means 'the time limited by Ord 18, r 2 as extended by any order of the court or agreement in writing between the parties', then the proposition noted above must follow. If, on the other hand, it means 'the period prescribed by Ord 18, r 2', I do not think

f it would follow.

I do not find it altogether easy to choose between these constructions, and the first construction would make it possible for a defendant to obtain extensions of time for defence until after a limitation period had expired and then spring an application to set aside service on the grounds of some default of which he had been aware all along. The plaintiff's counsel in this case did not, however, at first

g advance the second construction as part of her case, it was never considered by the judge, it does not find favour with Stuart-Smith and Simon Brown LJJ and I do not find any clear pointer to the rule-makers' intentions in the rules themselves.

In these circumstances, although with some unease, I agree that the appeal should be allowed and the service of the writ set aside.

Appeal allowed.

Mary Rose Plummer   Barrister.

The Indian Endurance
Republic of India and others v India
Steamship Co Ltd

HOUSE OF LORDS

LORD TEMPLEMAN, LORD GOFF OF CHIEVELEY, LORD JAUNCEY OF TULLICHETTLE, LORD
MUSTILL AND LORD SLYNN OF HADLEY

26, 27 OCTOBER 1992, 18 FEBRUARY 1993

Pleading – Striking out – Estoppel per rem judicatam – Claim for damage to and loss of cargo – Judgment obtained in India in respect of part of goods – Action brought in England in respect of whole of loss – Whether cause of action in England identical to that in India – Whether English action barred – Whether action should be struck out – Civil Jurisdiction and Judgments Act 1982, s 34.

The appellants, the Republic of India and the Indian Ministry of Defence, were the owners of a cargo of munitions carried on board the respondents' vessel in September 1987 pursuant to bills of lading for a voyage from Sweden to India. The munitions, which included a small number of artillery shells, were loaded in no 3 hold above wood pulp destined for other consignees. In the course of the voyage a fire was discovered in the hold and it was extinguished with water. The vessel diverted to Cherbourg for a survey and the cargo was repacked and restowed. Fifty-one artillery shells were jettisoned as damaged and compression damage to some of the boxes of munitions, caused by the swelling of the wood pulp in the hold after it had been flooded with water, was noted. The vessel then continued its voyage to India, where the cargo was unloaded from the vessel. Following correspondence between the Ministry of Defence and the respondents about the damage to the cargo, the ministry made a claim against the respondents for the total loss of their cargo. In early August 1988 agreement was reached to extend time for commencement of proceedings for a year. On 1 September 1988 the Union of India as plaintiff brought proceedings in India against the respondents claiming damages for the 51 shells which had not been delivered, alleging negligence while the cargo was in transit. Judgment was given against the respondents in December 1989. However, before judgment was given the appellants issued out of the Admiralty Court in England a writ in rem against the respondents claiming total loss of the munitions, including the 51 shells which had been the subject of the Indian action, and alleging (i) breach of contract and/or duty as a carrier by sea for reward to deliver the goods in like good order and condition as when shipped, (ii) negligence and breach of duty as carriers and/or bailees for reward, and (iii) breach of their obligations under the Hague Visby Rules (as set out in the schedule to the Carriage of Goods by Sea Act 1971). The respondents by their defence asserted that the claim was barred by res judicata and relied on s 34[a] of the Civil Jurisdiction and Judgments Act 1982. The judge upheld that contention and struck out the claim. On appeal by the appellants the Court of Appeal affirmed his decision. The appellants appealed to the House of Lords, contending, inter alia, that there was no identity between the subject matters of the two sets of proceedings and, in any event, there was an arguable case that the respondents had waived or were estopped from relying on their right

a   Section 34 is set out at p 1004 d, post

to invoke s 34 of the 1982 Act and that, therefore, the case should be remitted to
a the Admiralty Court to determine that issue on the evidence.

Held – (1) Since the contract of carriage under which the goods were shipped
regulated the respective rights and obligations of the parties regarding the
seaworthiness of the ship and the care of the goods, the mere fact that an action
could be raised by pleading short delivery or delivery of the goods not in the like
b good order and condition as when shipped was irrelevant because the cause of
action arose under the contract. Since the factual basis relied on by the appellants,
ie the fire during transit resulting in the damage to and loss of the consignment,
as giving rise to the two breaches of contract was the same in both actions there
was identity of the causes of action in the two proceedings and s 34 of the 1982
Act applied (see p 1000 *f*, p 1007 *b* to *e* and p 1010 *f* to *h*, post).
c
  (2) However, s 34 of the 1982 Act on its true construction provided no more
than a bar against proceedings by a plaintiff and did not exclude the jurisdiction
of the court, its function being to give effect to the policy underlying the principle
of res judicata in the circumstances specified therein. It was therefore open to the
appellants to raise the plea of waiver or estoppel. In the circumstances the plea of
d waiver or estoppel should not be rejected summarily; whether the respondents
were estopped from raising the plea of res judicata was a matter to be decided on
the evidence. The appeal would therefore be allowed and the case remitted to the
judge to order pleadings and determine the issue in the ordinary way (see p 1000
f, p 1009 *f* to *j* and p 1010 *b c f* to *h*, post).

e **Notes**
For the doctrine of res judicata and issue estoppel, see 16 *Halsbury's Laws* (4th edn
reissue) paras 974–983, and for cases on the subject, see 21 *Digest* (Reissue) 56–62,
368–390.
  For the Civil Jurisdiction and Judgments Act 1982, s 34, see 22 *Halsbury's
Statutes* (4th edn) (1991 reissue) 402.
f   For the Carriage of Goods by Sea Act 1971, Sch, see 39 *Halsbury's Statutes* (4th
edn) 836.

Cases referred to in opinions
Arnold v National Westminster Bank plc [1991] 3 All ER 41, [1991] 2 AC 93, [1991]
  2 WLR 1177, HL.
g *Brunsden v Humphrey* (1884) 14 QBD 141, [1881–5] All ER Rep 357, CA.
Carl-Zeiss-Stiftung v Rayner & Keeler Ltd (No 2) [1966] 2 All ER 536, [1967] 1 AC
  853, [1966] 3 WLR 125, HL.
Conquer v Boot [1928] KB 336, [1928] All ER Rep 120, DC.
Henderson v Henderson (1843) 3 Hare 100, [1843–60] All ER Rep 378, 67 ER 313,
h   V-C.
Kammins Ballrooms Co Ltd v Zenith Investments (Torquay) Ltd [1970] 2 All ER 871,
  [1971] AC 850, [1970] 3 WLR 287, HL.
Kendall v Hamilton (1879) 4 App Cas 504, [1874–80] All ER Rep 932, HL.
King v Hoare (1844) 13 M & W 494, 153 ER 206.
Langdon v Richards (1917) 33 TLR 325.
j *Letang v Cooper* [1964] 2 All ER 929, [1965] 1 QB 232, [1964] 3 WLR 573, CA.
Litchfield v Ready (1850) 5 Exch 939, 155 ER 409.
Lothian v Henderson (1803) 3 Bos & P 499, 127 ER 271, HL
Magrath v Hardy (1838) 4 Bing NC 782, 132 ER 990.
New Brunswick Rly Co v British and French Trust Corp Ltd [1938] 4 All ER 747,
  [1939] AC 1, HL.

Ricardo v Garcias (1845) 12 Cl & Fin 368, 8 ER 1450, HL.
Thoday v Thoday [1964] 1 All ER 341, [1964] P 181, [1964] 2 WLR 371, CA.
Yat Tung Investment Co Ltd v Dao Heng Bank Ltd [1975] AC 581, [1975] 2 WLR 690, PC.

Appeal

The Republic of India and the Government of India (Ministry of Defence), being the owners of the cargo lately laden on board the vessel Indian Grace, appealed with the leave of the Appeal Committee of the House of Lords given on 30 January 1992 from the decision of the Court of Appeal (Glidewell, McCowan and Leggatt LJJ) (sub nom *Republic of India and the Government of the Republic of India (Ministry of Defence) v India Steamship Co Ltd, The Indian Grace* [1992] 1 Lloyd's Rep 124) on 26 September 1991 dismissing their appeal from the order of Sheen J dated 12 December 1990 striking out their action in rem against the respondents, India Steamship Co Ltd, the owners of the vessel Indian Endurance, a sister ship of the Indian Grace, on the ground that the cause of action was the same as the cause of action on which the appellants had relied when they obtained judgment in India for damage to part of the cargo which had been carried on the respondents' vessel from Sweden to India. The facts are set out in the opinion of Lord Goff.

Jonathan Sumption QC and *Timothy Charlton* (instructed by *Clyde & Co*) for the appellants.
Stewart Boyd QC and *Jeffrey Gruder* (instructed by *Ince & Co*) for the respondents.

Their Lordships took time for consideration.

18 February 1993. The following opinions were delivered.

LORD TEMPLEMAN. My Lords, for the reasons given by my noble and learned friend Lord Goff of Chieveley I would allow this appeal.

LORD GOFF OF CHIEVELEY. My Lords, there is before your Lordships' House an appeal by the appellants, the Republic of India and the Government of India (Ministry of Defence), against the dismissal by the Court of Appeal of an appeal from a decision by Sheen J ordering that the appellants' claim against the respondents, the India Steamship Co Ltd (the owners of the vessel Indian Endurance) be struck out.

The following account of the facts of the case is largely taken from the agreed statement of facts helpfully prepared by the parties' counsel. The appellants claim to be entitled to sue for damage suffered by a consignment of munitions carried on board the respondents' vessel (Indian Grace) on a voyage from Uddevala in Sweden to Cochin in India between 26 June and 4 September 1987. The munitions were loaded in no 3 hold, above wood pulp destined for other consignees. On 1 July, a fire was discovered in no 3 hold; this was extinguished with water. The vessel put in to Cherbourg for survey, and to repack and restow the cargo in no 3 hold. At about this time a small number of artillery shells, probably 51, were jettisoned as damaged. In addition, compression damage to some of the boxes of munitions was noted. This was caused by the swelling of the wood pulp in the hold after it had been flooded with water.

The vessel resumed her voyage to India on 6 August 1987, arriving at Cochin in early September, and the cargo was cleared by 4 September. The appellants contend that they have not only lost the shells jettisoned and those damaged by

crushing in the hold, but that they have also lost the value of the remaining
a munitions because of the effect of radiant heat upon them. It is accordingly
contended that the cargo was a total loss. The claim amounts to just over
SwKr27m the equivalent of £2·6m at the time of the appeal before this House.

The damage became the subject of correspondence (the record of which appears
to be incomplete at present). On 9 December 1987 the Ministry of Defence in
b New Delhi wrote to the respondents making a claim for the total loss of the cargo
in the sum of Rs136m—the sterling equivalent is £2·6m. The respondents
replied on 2 January 1988 asking, in effect, for further particulars of the loss. It
appears that on 3 February 1988 a notice of claim in the sum of Rs189,508, the
equivalent of £6,000, was lodged with the vessel's agents by the appellants 'as per
directions from Army headquarters'. At all events, correspondence between the
c Ministry of Defence in New Delhi and the respondents resumed on 5 July 1988,
when the Ministry of Defence repeated its demand for payment of the full claim
for Rs136m. This was followed on 21 July 1988 by a request for an extension of
the Hague Rules time limit (due to expire on 31 August 1988) and notice that the
appellants' underwriters, Oriental Insurance Co Ltd, were authorised to pursue
the claim. Thereafter, there were telex exchanges between W E Cox (Recoveries)
d Ltd, who were instructed to handle the claim for recovery of the loss, and the
respondents, in which agreement was reached to extend time for commencement
of proceedings for one year with effect from 1 September 1988. It was also agreed
that English law and jurisdiction should apply. These agreements were concluded
in early August 1988.

On 1 September 1988 the 'Union of India represented by the Madras
e Commandant as plaintiff' issued a plaint in the Subordinate Judge's Court in
Cochin, India, seeking damages for the 51 shells which were not delivered. By
para 4 of the plaint the plaintiff purported to confine the suit to a claim for
Rs189,508·67 in respect of the 51 shells only. No application was made to amend
the pleading to bring forward a larger claim. This suit came on for final hearing
f on 7 December 1989, and judgment was given on 16 December 1989 by the
principal sub-judge in the Subordinate Judge's Court, Cochin. The plaintiff was
awarded the full amount of its claim against the respondents. The respondents
have appealed against this judgment, and the appeal is still pending in India.

On 25 August 1989 (ie before judgment was given in the action in Cochin) the
writ in rem in the present action was issued. It was served on 4 May 1990 upon
g the Indian Endurance at Tees Dock, Middlesborough. Exchanges then ensued
between the appellants' solicitors, Clyde & Co, the respondents' P & I club,
Steamship Mutual Underwriting Association Ltd, and the respondents' solicitors,
Ince & Co. On 8 May these resulted in a (repeated) agreement to the application
of English law and jurisdiction, and in the provision of a letter of undertaking by
Steamship Mutual to pay the claim (if proved).

h The statement of claim was served on 25 May 1990. In its original form, it
makes claim for the total loss of the munitions cargo, including the 51 shells and
10 charges which had been the subject of the action in Cochin. The defence was
served on 16 August 1990 and, in its original form, it pleaded issue estoppel as a
defence to the claim, upon the ground that the appellants were capable of
bringing the whole claim in Cochin but decided not to do so. The respondents
j issued a summons on 16 August 1990 seeking to strike out the appellants' claim
upon the grounds that it was frivolous, vexatious or abusive, pursuant to RSC Ord
18, r 19.

At the hearing of this summons before Sheen J the respondents amended their
defence (and therefore the grounds for their application by the summons) to

allege that the appellants' claim was barred by res judicata and to rely upon s 34 of the Civil Jurisdiction and Judgments Act 1982. By order dated 12 December *a* 1990, Sheen J acceded to the respondents' application, and struck out the appellants' claim on that ground. The appellants' appeal to the Court of Appeal against this order was dismissed (see [1992] 1 Lloyd's Rep 124).

There is no doubt that the effect, in financial terms, of the decision of the courts below is most striking. The successful claim of the appellants in Cochin in respect of part of the consignment yielded only £6,000. The remainder of their claim, *b* pursued in the English courts, is for over £2·5m. Yet the effect of invocation by the respondents of the principle of res judicata, as embodied in s 34 of the 1982 Act is, if the courts below are correct, to exclude any adjudication on the merits of this very substantial claim in the courts of this country. This result was regarded with dismay by Sheen J, who reached his decision only because he felt *c* that he was compelled to do so on the basis of s 34. Similar sentiments were expressed by Glidewell LJ in the Court of Appeal (see [1992] 1 Lloyd's Rep 124 at 133), but he, together with Leggatt LJ (who delivered the principal judgment) and McCowan LJ, reached the same conclusion. Indeed, it has to be recognised that consequences of this kind may result from the application of the principle, which is founded upon the public interest in finality of litigation rather than the *d* achievement of justice as between the individual litigants. What is startling about the present case is the extreme disparity between the very small size of the appellants' recovery in the courts of Cochin and the very large size of their claim in the English courts which has been held to be excluded by reason of the judgment obtained by them in Cochin.

Apart from one argument not raised in the courts below which the appellants *e* sought to raise before your Lordships (to which I will refer later), the appellants challenged the correctness of the decision below on three grounds. First, they submitted that there was no identity between the cause of action which was the subject matter of the Cochin judgment, and that which is the subject matter of the proceedings in this country. Second, they submitted that the issue in the present case fell to be decided not under s 34, but on the principle of issue *f* estoppel; and that on that basis it was not appropriate to strike out the appellants' claim at the present stage, since there were matters which required examination before any conclusion could be reached on that issue. Third, in any event, the appellants had raised the issue that the respondents' plea of res judicata was not open to them, since arguably they had waived their right to rely upon it or were *g* estopped from doing so, and the resolution of this issue too depended upon a full investigation of the relevant facts.

Central to the consideration of these issues is the impact of s 34 of the 1982 Act, upon which Sheen J and the Court of Appeal based their conclusion that the appellants' claim should be struck out. Indeed Sheen J expressed the view that, if s 34 did not apply, and the case was to be decided upon the basis of the common *h* law principle of issue estoppel, further investigation of the facts would be necessary. I propose therefore to turn first to consider the legislative purpose underlying s 34, and the effect of the section in the light of that legislative purpose; and in order to carry out that task it will, in my opinion, be necessary to set the section against the background of the common law principle of res judicata. *j*

In *Thoday v Thoday* [1964] 1 All ER 341 at 352, [1964] P 181 at 197–198 Diplock LJ explained that estoppel per rem judicatam is a generic term which in modern law includes two species. He continued:

'The first species, which I will call "cause of action estoppel", is that which *a* prevents a party to an action from asserting or denying, as against the other party, the existence of a particular cause of action, the non-existence or existence of which has been determined by a court of competent jurisdiction in previous litigation between the same parties. If the cause of action was determined to exist, i.e., judgment was given on it, it is said to be merged in the judgment, or, for those who prefer Latin, transit in rem judicatam. If it

b was determined not to exist, the unsuccessful plaintiff can no longer assert that it does; he is estopped per rem judicatam. This is simply an application of the rule of public policy expressed in the Latin maxim "nemo debet bis vexari pro una et eadem causa". In this application of the maxim causa bears its literal Latin meaning. The second species, which I will call "issue estoppel", is an extension of the same rule of public policy. There are many causes of

c action which can only be established by proving that two or more different conditions are fulfilled. Such causes of action involve as many separate issues between the parties as there are conditions to be fulfilled by the plaintiff in order to establish his cause of action; and there may be cases where the fulfilment of an identical condition is a requirement common to two or more different causes of action. If in litigation on one such cause of action any of

d such separate issues whether a particular condition has been fulfilled is determined by a court of competent jurisdiction, either on evidence or on admission by a party to the litigation, neither party can, in subsequent litigation between them on any cause of action which depends on the fulfilment of the identical condition, assert that the condition was fulfilled if the court has in the first litigation determined that it was not, or deny that it

e was fulfilled if the court in the first litigation determined that it was.'

I wish to add that—

> 'there is a wider sense in which the doctrine [of res judicata] may be appealed to, so that it becomes an abuse of process to raise in subsequent proceedings matters which could and therefore should have been litigated in
f earlier proceedings.' (See *Yat Tung Investment Co Ltd v Dao Heng Bank Ltd* [1975] AC 581 at 590 per Lord Kilbrandon, citing the locus classicus of *Henderson v Henderson* (1843) 3 Hare 100 at 115, [1843–60] All ER Rep 378 at 381–382 per Wigram V-C.)

g There is one observation which I wish to make upon the passage from the judgment of Diplock LJ which I have just quoted. This is that the principle of merger to which Diplock LJ refers as applying where the cause of action was determined to exist, in the sense that judgment was given upon it, cannot be described simply as a species of estoppel. The principle, which is sometimes called the doctrine of merger in judgment, is that a person—

h 'in whose favour an English judicial tribunal of competent jurisdiction has pronounced a final judgment . . . is precluded from afterwards recovering before any English tribunal a second judgment for the same civil relief on the same cause of action . . .'

(See *Spencer Bower and Turner on the Doctrine of Res Judicata* (2nd edn, 1969) p 355,
j para 423.)

The basis of the principle is that the cause of action, having become merged in the judgment, ceases to exist, as is expressed in the Latin maxim transit in rem judicatam: see *King v Hoare* (1844) 13 M & W 494 at 504, 153 ER 206 at 210 per Parke B, cited by Lord Penzance and Lord Blackburn in *Kendall v Hamilton* (1879) 4 App Cas 504 at 526, 542, [1874–80] All ER Rep 932 at 941, 950.

The distinction between cause of action estoppel and issue estoppel on the one
hand, and the principle of merger in judgment on the other hand, has been of   *a*
great importance where the judgment in question is the judgment of a foreign
court in the sense of a non-English court. This is because, whereas it has been
recognised that the judgment of a non-English court may give rise to a cause of
action estoppel where the judgment is in favour of the defendant (see e g *Ricardo
v Garcias* (1845) 12 Cl & Fin 368, 8 ER 1450), and more recently to an issue
estoppel (see *Carl-Zeiss-Stiftung v Rayner & Keeler Ltd (No 2)* [1966] 2 All ER 536,   *b*
[1967] 1 AC 853), nevertheless such a judgment, in favour of the plaintiff, did not
at common law constitute a bar against proceedings in England founded upon
the same cause of action. This was because the principle of merger in judgment
did not apply in the case of a non-English judgment: see *Spencer Bower and Turner*
pp 363–364, and cases there cited. It was to remove this anomaly that s 34 of the   *c*
Civil Jurisdiction and Judgments Act 1982 was enacted. This provides:

> 'No proceedings may be brought by a person in England and Wales or
> Northern Ireland on a cause of action in respect of which a judgment has
> been given in his favour in proceedings between the same parties, or their
> privies, in a court in another part of the United Kingdom or in a court of an
> overseas country, unless that judgment is not enforceable or entitled to   *d*
> recognition in England and Wales or, as the case may be, in Northern Ireland.'

In Dicey and Morris *The Conflict of Laws* (11th edn, 1987) p 431 the effect of the
section is described as being that it 'reverses in part the rule that a foreign
judgment does not of itself extinguish the original cause of action in respect of
which the judgment was given.'   *e*

Such is the common law background to s 34. This will be of particular relevance
when I come to consider the third submission of the appellants, concerned with
their plea of waiver or estoppel by representation. However I propose to turn
next to their first submission, which was that there was no identity between the
cause of action which was the subject matter of the Cochin judgment, and that   *f*
which is the subject matter of the proceedings in this country; and that on that
basis s 34 of the 1982 Act does not apply in the present case.

It is necessary for this purpose to examine the two sets of proceedings. I take
first the present proceedings in this country. There, the statement of a claim is in
the ordinary form for a damage to cargo claim, alleging against the shipowners
(1) breach of contract and/or duty as carrier by sea for reward to deliver the goods   *g*
in like good order and condition as when shipped, (2) negligence, in breach of
duty as carriers and/or as bailees for reward, and (3) breach of their obligations
under art III(1) and (2) of the Hague Visby Rules (set out in the schedule to the
Carriage of Goods by Sea Act 1971), which apply to the contracts contained in or
evidenced by the two bills of lading under which the goods were shipped. Article
III(1) provides: *h*

> 'The carrier shall be bound before and at the beginning of the voyage to
> exercise due diligence to—(*a*) Make the ship seaworthy . . . (*c*) Make the holds
> . . . fit and safe for [the] reception, carriage and preservation [of the goods].'

Article III(2) provides: *j*

> 'Subject to the provisions of Article IV, the carrier shall properly and
> carefully load, handle, stow, carry, keep, care for, and discharge the goods
> carried.'

Article IV(2) sets out a list of circumstances in which neither the carrier nor the
ship shall be responsible for loss or damage. These include: '(*a*) Act, neglect, or

default of the master, mariner, pilot, or the servants of the carrier in the navigation

a or in the management of the ship. '(*b*) Fire, unless caused by the actual fault or privity of the carrier . . .'

It will be observed that, among the allegations pleaded against the shipowners is a failure to deliver the goods in like good order and condition as when shipped. This reflects the fact that such a failure is prima facie evidence of breach of contract, and probably also of negligence (ie breach of duty as bailee), with the

b effect that the onus then passes to the shipowner to exonerate himself from liability, which is normally done by invoking one of the excepted perils. However in a case like the present, in which the Hague Visby Rules apply, it is inevitable that attention will be focused upon the applicable obligations and exceptions in arts III and IV of the rules, and that the dispute will be decided on the basis of

c those provisions.

I turn to the proceedings in India. As appears from the plaint in the Cochin action, the claim was in respect of deficiencies in (or, as we usually call it, short delivery of) the cargo delivered at Cochin, viz 51 shells (and a small item described as 'charge green bag'). According to the agreed statement of facts before your Lordships, the 51 shells had been jettisoned at Cherbourg. The claim was

d advanced under one of the two bills of lading under which the consignment was shipped. Your Lordships were, however, informed that no point was taken on this, presumably because some of the 51 shells had in fact been shipped under each of the two bills of lading (see the particulars of loss under para 10 of the amended statement of claim in the present proceedings ([1992] 1 Lloyd's Rep 124 at 128). In the plaint, it was alleged that the shipowners had been guilty of

e negligence while the cargo was in transit in the vessel, which presumably refers to a breach of their duty as bailees (carriers for reward). However, in the judgment, the learned judge stated that it was 'more or less not in dispute' that the law applicable to the carriage of the goods was the Indian Carriage of Goods by Sea Act 1925. That must have incorporated the old Hague Rules into the bill

f of lading contract; they are not for present purposes different from the Hague Visby Rules. Further, the judge made an express finding that the ship was seaworthy and cargoworthy. He then considered whether the shipowners were entitled to be relieved from liability (presumably under art III(2)) by virtue of art IV(2)(*a*) or (*b*) of the Hague Visby Rules, and decided that they were unable to do so on the facts of the case. Accordingly, he held the shipowners liable for the

g value of the undelivered cargo.

The argument advanced by the appellants before your Lordships was that, for the purposes of ascertaining whether there was identity between the causes of action in the two sets of proceedings, a distinction had to be drawn between an action for damage to cargo (as in the present proceeding) and an action for short delivery (as in the Cochin proceedings). The submission was that, in accordance

h with the principle stated by Diplock LJ in *Letang v Cooper* [1964] 2 All ER 929 at 935, [1965] 1 QB 232 at 243, a cause of action consists of the minimum facts which a plaintiff is required in law to plead and (if traversed) prove in order to obtain the relief which he claims. The minimum facts which, it was submitted, have to be proved in a damage to cargo claim are (1) the condition of goods on shipment and (2) their damaged condition on delivery; whereas in a short delivery

j claim they are (1) the quantity of the goods shipped and (2) the lesser quantity delivered. It follows, ran the submission, that there was no identity between the causes of action in the two sets of proceedings. Furthermore, the appellants submitted, the Court of Appeal had in truth confused the principle of res judicata, under which the same cause of action cannot be litigated twice, with the wider principle in *Henderson v Henderson* (1843) 3 Hare 100, [1843–60] All ER Rep 378, under which a point which could and should have been but was not raised in certain proceedings is barred in subsequent proceedings in which the same issue *a* arises. On this basis, the appellants were able to argue, first, that s 34 of the 1982 Act did not apply, and second, that on the principle in *Henderson v Henderson*, which does not apply in certain special circumstances, arguments were open to them which required investigation and which rendered it inappropriate to strike out their statement of claim in the present case.

Now the difficulty with this argument is that it ignores the fact that the goods *b* in question were shipped under a contract of carriage the terms of which (as set out in the Hague Rules or the Hague Visby Rules) regulate the respective rights and obligations of the parties. In these circumstances, the mere fact that the pleader can, so to speak, get the case on its feet by alleging short delivery or delivery of the goods not in the like good order and condition as when shipped, *c* does not in my opinion assist. For it is wholly unrealistic to regard the cause of action as being other than a cause of action arising under the contract, which provides for the relevant duties of the shipowners regarding the seaworthiness of the ship and the care of the goods. Even if attention is concentrated on the liability of the shipowner as bailee, the fact remains that he is a bailee for reward, and that accordingly his liability will be governed by the terms of the contract of *d* carriage.

In these circumstances, the case is very different from a simple action in negligence, as for example a running down action, where damage is of the essence of the claim in the sense that damage must be proved to establish the cause of action. In such a case, it is theoretically possible to segregate different causes of action by reference to different heads of damage. Thus in *Brunsden v Humphrey* *e* (1884) 14 QBD 141, [1881–5] All ER Rep 357, a case concerned with res judicata, a distinction was drawn between damage to the plaintiff's carriage and damage to his person arising out of the same incident, and it was held that an earlier action by the plaintiff for the former constituted no bar to a subsequent action for the latter. The decision has not been without its critics, who prefer the dissenting *f* judgment of Lord Coleridge CJ; but so narrow an approach is not in any event possible in a contractual context, where proof of damage is not necessary to establish the cause of action. Here, as is shown by *Conquer v Boot* [1928] 2 KB 336, [1928] All ER Rep 120, it is necessary to identify the relevant breach of contract; and if it transpires that the cause of action in the first action is a breach of contract which is the same breach of contract which constitutes the cause of action in the *g* second, then the principle of res judicata applies, and the plaintiff cannot escape from the conclusion by pleading in the second action particulars of damage which were not pleaded in the first. In *Conquer v Boot* the relevant breach of contract was identified as being breach of a promise to complete a bungalow which the defendant was building for the plaintiff. Talbot J said ([1928] 2 KB 336 at 344–345, [1928] All ER Rep 120 at 124):	*h*

'Here there is but one promise, to complete the bungalow; and the question whether or not it has been performed is to be decided by the state in which the bungalow was when it was handed over by the defendant to the plaintiff as complete. From that moment the Statute of Limitations began to run as to the whole. The plaintiff could not alter the fact that he was recovering *j* damages for the breach of this single promise by failing to specify in his action all the particulars of the breach and all the damages to which he was entitled. The test whether a previous action is a bar is not whether the damages sought to be recovered are different, but whether the cause of action is the same . . .'

Talbot J expressed his conclusion as follows ([1928] 2 KB 336 at 346, [1928] All
a ER Rep 120 at 125):

> 'I think therefore that the plea of res judicata or judgment recovered is an
> answer to the whole of this action, and that the defendant is entitled to
> judgment.'

If I turn to the present case, I find that the situation is not precisely the same.
b The present case is not concerned with the failure to construct a building in
accordance with a certain specification, which can result in a whole series of
defects which may nevertheless lead to a single breach of contract, ie the failure
to hand over the building constructed in accordance with the terms of the
contract. It is rather concerned with a single incident, ie the fire during transit
c which broke out in the cargo over which the appellants' consignment of
munitions was stowed, which resulted in the damage to that consignment and to
loss (by jettison) of a small part of it. Furthermore, as appears from the pleadings,
that loss or damage might have resulted from breach of more than one term of
the contract, for example breach of the obligation to make the vessel seaworthy
under art III(1) of the Hague Visby Rules, or breach of the obligation to load and
d stow etc the vessel carefully under art III(2). However, for present purposes, there
is no need to distinguish between the two breaches, because the factual basis relied
upon by the appellants as giving rise to the two breaches is the same, and indeed
was referred to compendiously by the appellants in the Cochin action as
'negligence'. In these circumstances, I am satisfied that there is identity between
the causes of action in the two sets of proceedings.
e In these circumstances the appellants' second submission, which was founded
upon the assumption that s 34 of the 1982 Act is inapplicable, does not arise. I
turn therefore to their third submission which was that there was an arguable
case that the respondents had waived, or were estopped from relying upon, their
right to invoke s 34; and that, if so, the matter should be remitted to the
Admiralty judge to determine the question on the evidence. It was however
f recognised by the appellants that, before your Lordships, the issue really turned
on the question whether s 34 is (as the Court of Appeal held) a mandatory
provision limiting the jurisdiction of the English courts, or simply makes available
a defence. It was common ground between the parties that if the section imposed
a mandatory limitation on the jurisdiction of the English courts, then the parties
g could not enlarge that jurisdiction by any agreement between themselves.
Before considering the wording of s 34 itself, I think it desirable first to return
to the background to the section, which I have already set out, with the purpose
of considering whether, and if so how far, the principles of waiver or estoppel
apply to the common law principle of res judicata. I put on one side for the
moment the doctrine of merger in judgment, and take first estoppel per rem
h judicatam. In *Spencer Bower and Turner on the Doctrine of Res Judicata* (2nd edn,
1969) pp 331–332 the opinion is expressed that in such cases it is open to a party,
against whom a plea of res judicata is raised, to invoke an estoppel by
representation, and a fortiori by agreement, in answer to that plea. The reasoning
runs as follows:

j

> '385 ... where an estoppel *per rem judicatam* meets an estoppel by
> representation, there is a genuine cross-estoppel, in the strictest sense of the
> word. For here, A. having established a good estoppel by *res judicata* against
> B., B. confesses and avoids such estoppel by alleging and proving that A., by
> representation, has precluded himself from relying upon the *res judicata*. B.

does not deny that he is estopped, but insists that A. is estopped from saying
so . . .

387　It is scarcely necessary to add that, if a party can by conduct or inaction
estop himself from setting up estoppel *per rem judicatam*, an express contract
to disregard any judicial decision which may be given on a specified point
affords, *a fortiori*, a complete affirmative answer to an estoppel based upon
such decision.'

The line of authority cited in support of these propositions includes *Lothian v
Henderson* (1803) 3 Bos & P 499 at 547–548, 127 ER 271 at 546–547, per Lord
Eldon LC and Lord Alvanley (a Scottish appeal); *Magrath v Hardy* (1838) 4 Bing
NC 782, 132 ER 980; *Litchfield v Ready* (1850) 5 Exch 939 at 945, 155 ER 409 at
412 per Parke B; and *Langdon v Richards* (1917) 33 TLR 325. I do not propose to
examine these cases in detail. The line of authority is not particularly strong.
Apart from *Langdon v Richards*, the cases are of some antiquity. *Lothian v Henderson*
was concerned with the effect to be given to the decision of a French court which
determined that cargo on a ship was lawful prize. *Magrath v Hardy* decided that
a party who took issue on a fact relevant to the estoppel had waived any benefit
which might have derived from the estoppel. *Litchfield v Ready* is doubtfully
relevant. *Langdon v Richards* was a case in which the Crown took no objection to
the fact that an issue had been determined previously by another tribunal.
Furthermore, the point was not investigated in argument before your Lordships.
I propose therefore to content myself with the observation that, as a matter of
justice, there is much to be said for the opinion so expressed by *Spencer Bower and
Turner*; and, especially since *Arnold v National Westminster Bank plc* [1991] 3 All
ER 41, [1991] 2 AC 93, in which your Lordships' House evinced a readiness to
adopt a less technical approach than has been adopted in the past to this most
technical subject, it may very well be recognised that what *Spencer Bower and
Turner* call a 'cross-estoppel' may be pleaded in answer to a plea of estoppel per
rem judicatam. Moreover such an approach appears to be consistent with the
view of *Spencer Bower and Turner* p 13 that the principle of estoppel per rem
judicatam is no more than a rule of evidence, with the view of Lord Maugham
LC that the basis of the principle is that 'it is unjust and unreasonable to permit
the same issue to be litigated afresh between the same parties, or persons claiming
under them' (see *New Brunswick Rly Co v British and French Trust Corp Ltd* [1938] 4
All ER 747 at 754, [1939] AC 1 at 20) and with the view of Diplock LJ in *Thoday
v Thoday* [1964] 1 All ER 341 at 351, [1964] P 181 at 197 that here, as elsewhere,
an estoppel merely means that—

> 'a party is not allowed, in certain circumstances, to prove in litigation
> particular facts and matters which, if proved, would assist him to succeed as
> plaintiff or defendant in an action.'

I strongly suspect that, in practice, the point seldom arises, except where in
litigation the principle of estoppel per rem judicatam is not invoked and the party
who might have taken it but does not do so thereby waives his right to rely upon
it, and that this is the explanation for the dearth of authority on the matter.
However, it is perhaps more difficult for a plea of waiver or estoppel to be effective
in a case where the doctrine of merger in judgment applies, since the effect of the
merger is that the cause of action ceases to exist; and indeed in *Spencer Bower and
Turner* pp 398–399, para 491 it is pointed out that the only instances of estoppel
as an affirmative answer to a case of this kind are to be found in cases of waiver or
estoppel by omission to plead the former recovery. Even so, I hesitate to conclude

that estoppel or waiver can otherwise have no application in such a case. However once again your Lordships did not have the benefit of argument on the point; and I will assume, in favour of the respondents, that generally a plea of estoppel or waiver will not be effective where the doctrine of merger in judgment applies at common law.

Now it can be argued that, since the function of s 34 was to overcome the anomaly created by the fact that the doctrine of merger in judgment did not apply in the case of foreign, ie non-English, judgments, s 34 should be read as having the same effect as that doctrine, and that upon that basis it would not be open to the appellants in the present case to plead either waiver or estoppel by representation. However it is important to observe that s 34 does not expressly apply the doctrine of merger in judgment to foreign judgments. It simply provides that 'No proceedings may be brought' on a cause of action in respect of which a foreign judgment of the relevant kind has been given. Founding themselves upon these words, the appellants submitted that the intention of Parliament was to do no more than create a defence, which was capable of being defeated by estoppel or waiver. A similar view was expressed in a note on the present case in the *Law Quarterly Review* by Mr Lawrence Collins, the general editor of *Dicey and Morris on the Conflict of Laws* (see 'Illogical survivals and astonishing results' (1992) 108 LQR 393).

Taking the section in isolation, the words of the statute are certainly amenable to this approach. Indeed, similar provisions in statutes of limitation (for example ss 2 and 5 of the Limitation Act 1980 'An action shall not be brought after . . .') have been held to be capable of waiver. Furthermore, in *Kammins Ballrooms Co Ltd v Zenith Investments (Torquay) Ltd* [1970] 2 All ER 871, [1971] AC 850, which was concerned with s 29(3) of the Landlord and Tenant Act 1954, in which it was provided that 'No application under subsection (1) of section twenty-four of this Act shall be entertained' unless made within a certain period, not only did this House hold that the words in question did not have the effect of ousting the jurisdiction of the court, but Lord Reid relied upon the 'well-established principle that any provision ousting the jurisdiction of the court must be construed strictly' (see [1970] 2 All ER 871 at 875, [1971] AC 850 at 860). On this approach, the words of s 34 can appropriately be read as providing no more than a bar against proceedings by the plaintiff rather than excluding the jurisdiction of the court.

I then ask myself: does the fact that the function of s 34 is to overcome the difficulty created by the old rule that the doctrine of merger in judgment does not apply to foreign judgments require any different conclusion? For my part, I do not think so. To achieve the requisite result of giving effect to the policy underlying the principle to res judicata in the circumstances specified in s 34, there was no need for Parliament to invoke the highly technical doctrine of merger in judgment; the same practical result could be achieved by the simple words chosen in the section. And if the effect is that the statutory bar created by the section may be the subject of waiver or estoppel or contrary agreement, the result is only that in a case such as this the general rule of public policy enshrined in the principle of res judicata is subject to a particular exception which enables practical justice to be done in rare cases, without any harm being done to the rule of public policy.

For these reasons, I am of the opinion that it is open to the appellants to raise the plea of waiver or estoppel in the present case.

Before your Lordships, it was urged by the respondents that the matters invoked by the appellants as giving rise to a waiver or estoppel could not have any such effect; and accordingly, even if such a plea was open to them, your Lordships should nevertheless not disturb the order that the appellants' statement of claim

be struck out. I must confess that I would be most reluctant, as a matter of
principle, to strike out a pleading which raises an issue of this kind, which is *a*
essentially one that should be decided on the evidence. The present claim is for a
very large sum of money, and the defence of res judicata is a highly technical
defence which has the effect, where it applies, of precluding a decision on the
merits. The appellants' plea of waiver or estoppel has not yet been pleaded; but it
is plain that it relates to events in India as well as in this country. I for my part do
not think it would be right for this plea to be rejected summarily in the way *b*
suggested by the respondents. I would therefore allow the appeal, and remit the
action generally to the Admiralty judge, with the effect that he will be able to
order the necessary pleadings and determine the issue in the ordinary way.

Finally, I wish to refer to the argument which the appellants sought to raise for
the first time before your Lordships, which was to the effect that the judgment of
the Cochin court was not a judgment on the same cause of action as the appellants *c*
assert in the present action, because it was a judgment in personam, whereas the
present action is an Admiralty action in rem. This point was explained to your
Lordships, and it became plain that it involved examination of matters of
Admiralty law and practice of a fundamental kind. Your Lordships were put in
the position that, on the one hand they were most reluctant to shut out an *d*
argument on a point of pure law of this kind, but on the other hand they were
also more reluctant to determine, as a court of last resort, fundamental questions
of Admiralty law and practice without having the benefit of the opinions of the
Admiralty judge and the Court of Appeal on those questions. However, if the
case is in any event to be remitted to the Admiralty judge, this matter too can be
raised before him in the ordinary way, subject to any order which he may think *e*
fit to make on the question of costs when giving leave to amend.

The costs already incurred in your Lordships' House and in the courts below
will be costs in the cause in so far as it relates to the issue raised by the respondents'
plea of res judicata.

LORD JAUNCEY OF TULLICHETTLE. My Lords, for the reasons given *f*
by my noble and learned friend Lord Goff of Chieveley I too would allow this
appeal.

LORD MUSTILL. My Lords, I have had the advantage of reading in draft the
speech prepared by my noble and learned friend Lord Goff of Chieveley. For the
reasons he gives I too would allow the appeal and remit the matter as he proposes. *g*

LORD SLYNN OF HADLEY. My Lords, I have had the advantage of reading
in draft the speech prepared by my noble and learned friend Lord Goff of
Chieveley. For the reasons he gives I too would allow the appeal and remit the
matter as he proposes. *h*

Appeal allowed.

Mary Rose Plummer   Barrister.

Derbyshire County Council v Times Newspapers Ltd and others

HOUSE OF LORDS

LORD KEITH OF KINKEL, LORD GRIFFITHS, LORD GOFF OF CHIEVELEY, LORD BROWNE-WILKINSON AND LORD WOOLF

7–10 DECEMBER 1992, 18 FEBRUARY 1993

Libel and slander – Parties – Right to sue – Corporation – Local government corporation – Right of local authority to sue – Publication relating to administration by local authority of its superannuation fund – Local authority alleging publication defamatory of it – Whether organs of central or local government entitled to sue for libel.

The plaintiff local authority brought an action against the publishers of a Sunday newspaper, its editor and two journalists claiming damages for publishing articles about the authority's investment and control of its superannuation fund which were alleged to be defamatory of the local authority. The defendants applied to have the action struck out as disclosing no cause of action against them on the grounds, inter alia, that a local authority, being a non-trading statutory corporation, could not maintain an action for a libel which reflected on its administrative reputation when no actual financial loss was pleaded. The judge dismissed the defendants' application, holding that a local authority could sue for libel in respect of its governing or administrative reputation even though no actual financial loss was pleaded or alleged, since it was an ordinary incident of all corporations, whether trading or municipal, that they could sue for libel. The defendants' appeal to the Court of Appeal was allowed on the grounds that a local authority could not sue for libel in respect of its governing or administrative reputation if no actual financial loss was pleaded or alleged because if it were to have that right it would be able to stifle legitimate public criticism of its activities. The local authority appealed to the House of Lords.

Held – Under common law a local authority did not have the right to maintain an action for damages for defamation as it would be contrary to the public interest for the organs of government, whether central or local, to have that right. Not only was there no public interest favouring the right of government organs to sue for libel but it was of the highest public importance that a governmental body should be open to uninhibited public criticism, and a right to sue for defamation would place an undesirable fetter on freedom of speech. The appeal would therefore be dismissed (see p 1017 *j*, p 1019 *d*, p 1020 *e*, p 1021 *g* to p 1022 *a*, post).

City of Chicago v Tribune Co (1923) 307 Ill 595 and dicta of Watermeyer CJ and Schreiner JA in *Die Spoorbond v South African Railways* [1946] AD 999 at 1009, 1012–1013 applied.

Bognor Regis UDC v Campion [1972] 2 All ER 61 overruled.

Decision of the Court of Appeal [1992] 3 All ER 65 affirmed.

Notes

For actions for libel and slander by corporations, see 9 *Halsbury's Laws* (4th edn) para 1378 and 28 *Halsbury's Laws* (4th edn) para 25, and for cases on the subject, see 13 *Digest* (Reissue) 349–350, 2972–2977.

Cases referred to in opinions

A-G v Guardian Newspapers Ltd [1987] 3 All ER 316, [1987] 1 WLR 1248, HL.   *a*

A-G v Guardian Newspapers Ltd (No 2) [1988] 3 All ER 545, [1990] 1 AC 109, [1988] 2 WLR 805, CA and HL.

Barthold v Germany (1985) 7 EHRR 383, E Ct HR.

Bognor Regis UDC v Campion [1972] 2 All ER 61, [1972] 2 QB 169, [1972] 2 WLR 983.

Brind v Secretary of State for the Home Dept [1991] 1 All ER 720, [1991] 1 AC 696,   *b*
[1991] 2 WLR 588, HL.

Chicago (City) v Tribune Co (1923) 307 Ill 595, Ill SC.

Die Spoorbond v South African Railways [1946] AD 999, SA SC.

Hector v A-G of Antigua and Barbuda [1990] 2 All ER 103, [1990] 2 AC 312, [1990] 2 WLR 606, PC.

Lingens v Austria (1986) 8 EHRR 407, E Ct HR.   *c*

Manchester Corp v Williams [1891] 1 QB 94, 63 LT 805, DC.

Metropolitan Saloon Omnibus Co Ltd v Hawkins (1859) 4 H & N 87, [1843–60] All ER Rep 430, 157 ER 769.

National Union of General and Municipal Workers v Gillian [1945] 2 All ER 593, [1946] KB 81, CA; affg [1945] 2 All ER 593.   *d*

New York Times Co v Sullivan (1964) 376 US 254, US SC.

South Hetton Coal Co Ltd v North-Eastern News Association Ltd [1894] 1 QB 133, [1891–4] All ER Rep 548, CA.

Sunday Times v UK (1979) 2 EHRR 245, E Ct HR.

W (a minor) (wardship: freedom of publication), Re [1992] 1 All ER 794, [1992] 1 WLR 100, CA.   *e*

Warner Instrument Co v Ingersoll (1907) 157 F 311, US CC SD NY.

Willis v Brooks [1947] 1 All ER 191.

Appeal

The plaintiffs, the Derbyshire County Council, appealed with the leave of the   *f*
Court of Appeal from the decision of that court (Balcombe, Ralph Gibson and Butler-Sloss LJJ) ([1992] 3 All ER 65, [1992] 1 QB 770) on 19 February 1992 allowing the appeal of the defendants, Times Newspapers Ltd, the publishers of the Sunday Times newspaper, Andrew Neil, the editor of the newspaper, and Peter Hounam and Rosemary Collins, two journalists employed on the newspaper, from the judgment of Morland J ([1991] 4 All ER 795, [1992] 1 QB 770) given on   *g*
15 March 1991 after the trial of a preliminary issue ordered by Master Miller on 2 November 1990 whereby, on an application by the defendants to strike out the action brought by the plaintiffs against the defendants claiming damages for libel and an injunction in respect of articles published in the Sunday Times on 17 and 24 September 1989 relating to the investment of the council's superannuation fund, the judge held (i) that a local authority could sue for libel in respect of its   *h*
governing or administrative reputation, when no actual damage was alleged, and (ii) that the plaintiffs had a cause of action in libel against the defendants on the basis of the pleaded statement of claim. The facts are set out in the opinion of Lord Keith.

    j

Charles Gray QC and Heather Rogers (instructed by Kingsford Stacey, agents for David Tysoe, Matlock) for the plaintiffs.

Anthony Lester QC and Desmond Browne QC (instructed by Biddle & Co) for the defendants.

Their Lordships took time for consideration.

18 February 1993. The following opinions were delivered.

a

LORD KEITH OF KINKEL. My Lords, this appeal raises, as a preliminary issue in an action for damages for libel, the question whether a local authority is entitled to maintain an action in libel for words which reflect on it in its governmental and administrative functions. That is the way the preliminary point of law was expressed in the order of the master, but it has opened out into *b* an investigation of whether a local authority can sue for libel at all.

Balcombe LJ, giving the leading judgment in the Court of Appeal, summarised the facts thus ([1992] 3 All ER 65 at 69, [1992] QB 770 at 802):

> 'The facts in the case are fortunately refreshingly simple. In two issues of the Sunday Times newspaper on 17 and 24 September 1989 there appeared *c* articles concerning share deals involving the superannuation fund of the Derbyshire County Council. The articles in the issue of 17 September were headed "REVEALED: SOCIALIST TYCOON'S DEALS WITH A LABOUR CHIEF" and "BIZARRE DEALS OF A COUNCIL LEADER AND THE MEDIA TYCOON": that in the issue of 24 September was headed "COUNCIL SHARE DEALS UNDER SCRUTINY". The council leader was Mr David Melvyn Bookbinder; the "media tycoon" was *d* Mr Owen Oyston. It is unnecessary for the purposes of this judgment to set in any detail the contents of these articles: it is sufficient to say that they question the propriety of certain investments made by the council of moneys in its superannuation fund, with Mr Bookbinder as the prime mover, in three deals with Mr Oyston or companies controlled by him. Excerpts from the articles giving the flavour of the allegations made will be found in the *e* judgment at first instance to which those interested may refer (see [1991] 4 All ER 795 at 798, [1992] QB 770 at 776–777). The council is the "administering authority" of its superannuation fund under the Superannuation Act 1972 and the regulations made thereunder.'

Following the publication actions for damages for libel were brought against *f* the publishers of the Sunday Times, its editor and the two journalists who wrote the articles, by Derbyshire County Council (the appellants), Mr Bookbinder and Mr Oyston. Mr Oyston's action was settled by an apology and payment of damages and costs. The statements of claim in this action by the appellants and in that by Mr Bookbinder are for all practical purposes in identical terms. That of the appellants asserts in para 6 that there were written and published 'of and *g* concerning the council and of and concerning the council in the way of its discharge of its responsibility for the investment and control of the superannuation fund' the words contained in the article of 17 September, and para 8 makes a similar assertion in relation to the article of 24 September. Paragraph 9 states:

> 'By reason of the words published on the 17th September 1989 and the *h* words and graph published on the 24th September 1989 the Plaintiff Council has been injured in its credit and reputation and has been brought into public scandal, odium and contempt, and has suffered loss and damage.'

No special damage is pleaded. On 31 July 1991 French J refused an application by the appellants to amend the statement of claim so as to plead a certain specific *j* item of special damage.

The preliminary point of law was tried at first instance before Morland J, who on 15 March 1991 decided it in favour of the appellants ([1991] 4 All ER 795, [1992] QB 770). However, on appeal by the present respondents his judgment was reversed by the Court of Appeal (Balcombe, Ralph Gibson and Butler-Sloss LJJ) on 19 February 1992 (see [1992] 3 All ER 65, [1992] QB 770). The appellants now appeal, with leave given in the Court of Appeal, to your Lordships' House.

There are only two reported cases in which an English local authority has sued for libel. The first is *Manchester Corp v Williams* [1891] 1 QB 94, 63 LT 805. The defendant had written a letter to a newspaper alleging that 'in the case of two if not three departments of our Manchester city council, bribery and corruption have existed and done their nefarious work'. A Divisional Court consisting of Day and Lawrance JJ held that the statement of claim disclosed no cause of action. The judgment of Day J is in these terms (as reported in [1891] 1 QB 94 at 96):

> 'This is an action brought by a municipal corporation to recover damages for what is alleged to be a libel on the corporation itself, as distinguished from its individual members or officials. The libel complained of consists of a charge of bribery and corruption. The question is whether such an action will lie. I think it will not. It is altogether unprecedented, and there is no principle on which it can be founded. The limits of a corporation's right of action for libel are those suggested by Pollock, C.B., in the case which has been referred to. A corporation may sue for a libel affecting property, not for one merely affecting personal reputation. The present case falls within the latter class. There must, therefore, be judgment for the defendant.'

Lawrance J said that he was of the same opinion.

The Law Times report contains a somewhat longer judgment of Day J in these terms (63 LT 805 at 806–807):

> 'This action is brought by the mayor, aldermen, and citizens of the city of Manchester to recover damages from the defendant in respect of that which is alleged by them to be a libel on the corporation. The alleged libel is contained in a letter written by the defendant to the editor of the *Manchester Examiner and Times*, which charged, as alleged by the statement of claim, that bribery and corruption existed or had existed in three departments of the Manchester City Council, and that the plaintiffs were either parties thereto or culpably ignorant thereof, and that the said bribery and corruption prevailed to such an extent as to render necessary an inquiry by a Parliamentary Commission. Now it is for us to determine whether a corporation can bring such an action, and I must say that, to my mind, to allow such a thing would be wholly unprecedented and contrary to principle. A corporation may sue for a libel affecting property, not for one merely affecting personal reputation. This does not fall within the class of cases in respect of which a corporation can maintain an action, but does fall within the second class commented on by Pollock, C.B. in his judgment in the case of the *Metropolitan Saloon Omnibus Company* v. *Hawkins* ((1859) 4 H & N 87, [1843–60] All ER Rep 430) with which I fully agree [a quotation follows]. The charge in the present case is one of bribery and corruption, of which a corporation cannot possibly be guilty, and therefore, in my opinion, this action will not lie.'

It is likely that the Law Reports version of his judgment was one revised by Day J, in which he omitted the sentence which ends the Law Times report, so that the true and only ratio of the decision is that a corporation may sue for a libel affecting property, but not for one merely affecting personal reputation.

Metropolitan Saloon Omnibus Co Ltd v Hawkins (1859) 4 H & N 87, [1843–60] All ER Rep 430 was an action by a company incorporated under the Joint Stock Companies Act 1856 in respect of a libel imputing to it insolvency, mismanagement and dishonest carrying on of its affairs. The Court of Exchequer held the action to be maintainable. Pollock CB, in the passage referred to by Day J, said (4 H & N 87 at 90, [1843–60] All ER Rep 430 at 431):

'That a corporation at common law can sue in respect of a libel there is no
doubt. It would be monstrous if a corporation could maintain no action for
slander of title through which they lost a great deal of money. It could not
sue in respect of an imputation of murder, or incest, or adultery, because it
could not commit those crimes. Nor could it sue in respect of a charge of
corruption, for a corporation cannot be guilty of corruption, although the
individuals composing it may. But it would be very odd if a corporation had
no means of protecting itself against wrong; and if its property is injured by
slander it has no means of redress except by action. Therefore it appears to
me clear that a corporation at common law may maintain an action for a
libel by which its property is injured.'

In *South Hetton Coal Co Ltd v North-Eastern News Association Ltd* [1894] 1 QB 133,
[1891–4] All ER Rep 548 a newspaper had published an article alleging th⁀t the
houses in which the company accommodated its colliers were in a highly
insanitary state. The Court of Appeal held that the company was entitled to
maintain an action for libel without proof of special damage, in respect that the
libel was calculated to injure the company's reputation in the way of its business.
Lord Esher MR said ([1894] 1 QB 133 at 138, [1891–4] All ER Rep 548 at 550):

'I have considered the case, and I have come to the conclusion that the law
of libel is one and the same as to all plaintiffs; and that, in every action of
libel, whether the statement complained of is, or is not, a libel, depends on
the same question—viz., whether the jury are of opinion that what has been
published with regrd to the plaintiff would tend in the minds of people of
ordinary sense to bring the plaintiff into contempt, hatred, or ridicule, or to
injure his character. The question is really the same by whomsoever the
action is brought—whether by a person, a firm, or a company. But though
the law is the same, the application of it is, no doubt, different with regard to
different kinds of plaintiffs. There are statements which, with regard to some
plaintiffs, would undoubtedly constitute a libel, but which, if published of
another kind of plaintiffs, would not have the same effect.'

He went on to say that certain statements might have the same effect, whether
made with regard to a person, or a firm, or a company, for example statements
with regard to conduct of a business, and, having elaborated on the question
whether or not a particular statement might reflect on the manner of conduct of
a business, he continued ([1894] 1 QB 133 at 139, [1891–4] All ER Rep 548 at
551):

'With regard to a firm or a company, it is impossible to lay down an
exhaustive rule as to what would be a libel on them. But the same rule is
applicable to a statement made with regard to them. Statements may be
made with regard to their mode of carrying on business, such as to lead
people of ordinary sense to the opinion that they conduct their business badly
and inefficiently. If so, the law will be the same in their case as in that of an
individual, and the statement will be libellous. Then, if the case be one of
libel—whether on a person, a firm, or a company—the law is that the
damages are at large. It is not necessary to prove any particular damage; the
jury may give such damages as they think fit, having regard to the conduct
of the parties respectively, and all the circumstances of the case.'

In *National Union of General and Municipal Workers v Gillian* [1945] 2 All ER 593,
[1946] KB 81 the Court of Appeal held that a trade union could, in general,

maintain an action in tort, and that an action for libel was no exception to that rule. No detailed consideration was given to the nature of the statements in respect of which the action might lie, though Scott LJ referred to the disintegration of a trade union which might result from a libel (see [1945] 2 All ER 593 at 604, [1946] KB 81 at 87), and Uthwatt J said that he saw no reason why a non-trading corporation should not have the same rights as a trading corporation as respects inputations on the conduct by it of its activities (see [1945] 2 All ER 593 at 605, [1946] KB 81 at 88).

The second case involving proceedings by a local authority is *Bognor Regis UDC v Campion* [1972] 2 All ER 61, [1972] 2 QB 169, a decision of Browne J. Mr Campion had distributed at a meeting of a ratepayers' association a leaflet savagely attacking the council, which sued him for libel. At the trial Mr Campion conducted his own case without the assistance of solicitors or counsel. Browne J found in favour of the council and awarded it damages of £2,000. He stated his intention to apply a principle to be found in *National Union of General and Municipal Workers v Gillian*, from which he quoted extensively. He continued ([1972] 2 All ER 61 at 66, [1972] 2 QB 169 at 175):

> 'Just as a trading company has a trading reputation which it is entitled to protect by bringing an action for defamation, so in my view the council, as a local government corporation, have a "governing" reputation which it is equally entitled to protect in the same way—of course, bearing in mind the vital distinction between defamation of the corporation as such and defamation of its individual officers or members. I entirely accept the statement made in *Gatley on Libel and Slander* (6th edn, 1967) p 409, para 890): "A corporation or company cannot maintain an action of libel or slander for any words which reflect, not upon itself, but solely upon its individual officers or members." Then there is a quotation: "To merely attack or challenge the rectitude of the officers or members of a corporation, and hold them or either of them up to scorn, hatred, contempt, or obloquy for acts done in their official capacity, or which would render them liable to criminal prosecution, does not give the corporation a right of action for libel." I stress the words "solely" and "merely" in those passages. The quotation given in Gatley there is from a United States case (*Warner v Ingersoll* (1907) 157 F 311).'

Browne J then proceeded to consider *Manchester Corp v Williams*, and after quoting from the judgment of Day J (63 LT 805 at 806) said ([1972] 2 All ER 61 at 68, [1972] 2 QB 169 at 177):

> 'Day J seems to put his judgment on two grounds; first, that a corporation may sue for a libel affecting property and not for one merely affecting personal reputation. If this was ever right, it has in my view been overruled by the *South Hetton* case [1894] 1 QB 133, [1891–4] All ER Rep 548 (where substantially this argument was used by the defendants (see [1894] 1 QB 133 at 134–135)) and by *National Union of General and Municipal Workers v Gillian* [1945] 2 All ER 593 at 601 (where the *Manchester* case [1891] 1 QB 94 was cited). The other ground seems to have been that a corporation cannot be guilty of corruption and therefore it cannot be defamatory to say or write that it has been guilty of corruption. This was based on the obiter dictum of Pollock CB in the *Metropolitan Saloon Omnibus* case (1859) 4 H & N 87, [1843–60] All ER Rep 430 and was repeated later by Lopes LJ in the *South Hetton* case [1894] 1 QB 133 at 141, [1891–4] All ER Rep 548 at 552. The *Manchester* case is severely criticised in Spencer on Bower on Actionable Defamation

(2nd edn, 1923) pp 245–246, in Fraser on Libel and Slander (7th edn, 1936) pp 89–90, and by Oliver J in *Willis v Brooks* [1947] 1 All ER 191 at 192 (another trade union case) where he said after reading the *National Union of General and Municipal Workers* case that he agreed with the editors of Fraser, who say (p 90): "It is respectfully submitted that the above statement of the law by Mr. Justice Day . . . is unsound in principle and would not be upheld in the Court of Appeal." Oliver J in *Willis v Brooks* [1947] 1 All ER 191 at 192 said: "Counsel for the defendants [who incidentally were Sir Valentine Holmes KC and Mr H P J Milmo (as he then was)] did not seriously contend that an action for libel imputing something very like corruption, as in this case, would not lie in any circumstances at the suit of a trade union," and he awarded the plaintiffs £500 damages. As I have said, the *Manchester* case was cited in the *General and Municipal Workers* case and the libel in that case seems to have imputed among other things something very like corruption.'

Finally, he said ([1972] 2 All ER 61 at 69, [1972] 2 QB 169 at 178):

'The actual decision in the *Manchester* case can perhaps be supported, as counsel for the council suggested, on the argument that the libel there was not capable of referring to a corporation consisting (as the plainitiffs did) of the mayor, aldermen and *citizens*, and not, as here, of the chairman and councillors. I think that that case is distinguishable from this on that ground, and also on the ground that in my view none of the statements in the leaflet in this case actually impute corruption. But I hope that the Court of Appeal will soon have occasion to consider the *Manchester* case.' (Browne J's emphasis.)

It is to be observed that Browne J did not give any consideration to the question whether a local authority, or any other body exercising governmental functions, might not be in a special position as regards the right to take proceedings for defamation. The authorities cited above clearly establish that a trading corporation is entitled to sue in respect of defamatory matters which can be seen as having a tendency to damage it in the way of its business. Examples are those that go to credit such as might deter banks from lending to it, or to the conditions experienced by its employees, which might impede the recruitment of the best qualified workers, or make people reluctant to deal with it. The *South Hetton Coal Co* case would appear to be an instance of the latter kind, and not, as suggested by Browne J, an authority for the view that a trading corporation can sue for something that does not affect it adversely in the way of its business. The trade union cases are understandable upon the view that defamatory matter may adversely affect the union's ability to keep its members or attract new ones or to maintain a convincing attitude towards employers. Likewise in the case of a charitable organisation the effect may be to discourage subscribers or otherwise impair its ability to carry on its charitable objects. Similar considerations can no doubt be advanced in connection with the position of a local authority. Defamatory statements might make it more difficult to borrow or to attract suitable staff and thus affect adversely the efficient carrying out of its functions.

There are, however, features of a local authority which may be regarded as distinguishing it from other types of corporation, whether trading or non-trading. The most important of these features is that it is a governmental body. Further, it is a democratically elected body, the electoral process nowadays being conducted almost exclusively on party political lines. It is of the highest public importance that a democratically elected governmental body, or indeed any governmental body, should be open to uninhibited public criticism. The threat of a civil action for defamation must inevitably have an inhibiting effect on freedom of speech.

In *City of Chicago v Tribune Co* (1923) 307 Ill 595 the Supreme Court of Illinois held that the city could not maintain an action of damages for libel. Thompson CJ said (at 606–607):

> 'The fundamental right of freedom of speech is involved in this litigation and not merely the right of liberty of the press. If this action can be maintained against a newspaper it can be maintained against every private citizen who ventures to criticise the ministers who are temporarily conducting the affairs of his government. Where any person by speech or writing seeks to persuade others to violate existing law or to overthrow by force or other unlawful means the existing government he may be punished ... but all other utterances or publications against the government must be considered absolutely privileged. While in the early history of the struggle for freedom of speech the restrictions were enforced by criminal prosecutions, it is clear that a civil action is as great, if not a greater, restriction than a criminal prosecution. If the right to criticise the government is a privilege which, with the exceptions above enumerated, cannot be restricted, then all civil as well as criminal actions are forbidden. A despotic or corrupt government can more easily stifle opposition by a series of civil actions than by criminal prosecutions ...'

After giving a number of reasons for this, he said (at 607–608):

> 'It follows, therefore, that every citizen has a right to criticise an inefficient or corrupt government without fear of civil as well as criminal prosecution. This absolute privilege is founded on the principle that it is advantageous for the public interest that the citizen should not be in any way fettered in his statements, and where the public service or due administration of justice is involved he shall have the right to speak his mind freely.'

These propositions were indorsed by the Supreme Court of the United States in *New York Times Co v Sullivan* (1964) 376 US 254 at 277. While these decisions were related most directly to the provisions of the American Constitution concerned with securing freedom of speech, the public interest considerations which underlaid them are no less valid in this country. What has been described as 'the chilling effect' induced by the threat of civil actions for libel is very important. Quite often the facts which would justify a defamatory publication are known to be true, but admissible evidence capable of proving those facts is not available. This may prevent the publication of matters which it is very desirable to make public. In *Hector v A-G of Antigua and Barbuda* [1990] 2 All ER 103, [1990] 2 AC 312 the Judicial Committee of the Privy Council held that a statutory provision which made the printing or distribution of any false statement likely to undermine public confidence in the conduct of public affairs a criminal offence contravened the provisions of the constitution protecting freedom of speech. Lord Bridge of Harwich said ([1990] 2 All ER 103 at 106, [1990] 2 AC 312 at 318):

> 'In a free democratic society it is almost too obvious to need stating that those who hold office in government and who are responsible for public administration must always be open to criticism. Any attempt to stifle or fetter such criticism amounts to political censorship of the most insidious and objectionable kind. At the same time it is no less obvious that the very purpose of criticism levelled at those who have the conduct of public affairs by their political opponents is to undermine public confidence in their

a   stewardship and to persuade the electorate that the opponents would make a better job of it than those presently holding office. In the light of these considerations their Lordships cannot help viewing a statutory provision which criminalises statements likely to undermine public confidence in the conduct of public affairs with the utmost suspicion.'

b   It is of some significance to observe that a number of departments of central government in the United Kingdom are statutorily created corporations, including the Secretaries of State for Defence, Education and Science, Energy, Environment and Social Services. If a local authority can sue for libel there would appear to be no reason in logic for holding that any of these departments (apart from two which are made corporations only for the purpose of holding land) were not also entitled to sue. But as is shown by the decision in *A-G v Guardian Newspapers Ltd*

c   *(No 2)* [1988] 3 All ER 545, [1990] 1 AC 109, a case concerned with confidentiality, there are rights available to private citizens which institutions of central government are not in a position to exercise unless they can show that it is the public interest to do so. The same applies, in my opinion, to local authorities. In both cases I regard it as right for this House to lay down that not only is there no

d   public interest favouring the right of organs of government, whether central or local, to sue for libel, but that it is contrary to the public interest that they should have it. It is contrary to the public interest because to admit such actions would place an undesirable fetter on freedom of speech. In *Die Spoorbond v South African Railways* [1946] AD 999 the Supreme Court of South Africa held that the South African Railways and Harbours, a governmental department of the Union of

e   South Africa, was not entitled to maintain an action for defamation in respect of a publication alleged to have injured its reputation as the authority responsible for running the railways. Schreiner JA said (at 1012–1013):

> 'I am prepared to assume, for the purposes of the present argument, that
> the Crown may, at least in so far as it takes part in trading in competition
f > with its subjects, enjoy a reputation, damage to which could be calculated in
> money. On that assumption there is certainly force in the contention that it
> would be unfair to deny to the Crown the weapon, an action for damages for
> defamation, which is most feared by calumniators. Nevertheless it seems to
> me that considerations of fairness and convenience are, on balance, distinctly
> against the recognition of a right in the Crown to sue the subject in a
g > defamation action to protect that reputation. The normal means by which
> the Crown protects itself against attacks upon its management of the country's
> affairs is political action and not litigation, and it would, I think, be
> unfortunate if that practice were altered. At present certain kinds of criticism
> of those who manage the State's affairs may lead to criminal prosecutions,
h > while if the criticism consists of defamatory utterances against individual
> servants of the State actions for defamation will lie at their suit. But subject
> to the risk of these sanctions and to the possible further risk, to which
> reference will presently be made, of being sued by the Crown for injurious
> falsehood, any subject is free to express his opinion upon the management of
> the country's affairs without fear of legal consequences. I have no doubt that
j > it would involve a serious interference with the free expression of opinion
> hitherto enjoyed in this country if the wealth of the State, derived from the
> State's subjects, could be used to launch against those subjects actions for
> defamation because they have, falsely and unfairly it may be, criticised or
> condemned the management of the country. Such actions could not, I think,

be confined to those brought by the Railways Administration for criticism of the running of the railways. Quite a number of Government departments, as appeared in the course of the argument, indulge in some form of trading on a greater or a lesser scale. Moreover, the Government, when it raises loans, is interested in the good or bad reputation that it may enjoy among possible subscribers to such loans. It would be difficult to assign any limits to the Crown's right to sue for defamation once its right in any case were recognised.'

These observations may properly be regarded as no less applicable to a local authority than to a department of central government. In the same case Watermeyer CJ observed that the reputation of the Crown might fairly be regarded as distinct from that of the group of individuals temporarily responsible for the management of the railways on its behalf (at 1009). In the case of a local authority temporarily under the control of one political party or another it is difficult to say that the local authority as such has any reputation of its own. Reputation in the eyes of the public is more likely to attach itself to the controlling political party, and with a change in that party the reputation itself will change. A publication attacking the activities of the authority will necessarily be an attack on the body of councillors which represents the controlling party, or on the executives who carry on the day-to-day management of its affairs. If the individual reputation of any of these is wrongly impaired by the publication any of these can himself bring proceedings for defamation. Further, it is open to the controlling body to defend itself by public utterances and in debate in the council chamber.

The conclusion must be, in my opinion, that under the common law of England a local authority does not have the right to maintain an action of damages for defamation. That was the conclusion reached by the Court of Appeal, which did so principally by reference to art 10 of the European Convention on Human Rights (Convention for the Protection of Human Rights and Fundamental Freedoms (Rome, 4 November 1950; TS 71 (1953); Cmd 8969), to which the United Kingdom has adhered but which has not been enacted into domestic law. Article 10 is in these terms:

'(1) Everyone has the right to freedom of expression. This right shall include freedom to hold opinions and to receive and impart information and ideas without interference by public authority and regardless of frontiers . . .
(2) The exercise of these freedoms, since it carries with it duties and responsibilities, may be subject to such formalities, conditions, restrictions or penalties as are prescribed by law and are necessary in a democratic society, in the interests of national security, territorial integrity or public safety, for the prevention of disorder or crime, for the protection of health or morals, for the protection of the reputation or rights of others, for preventing the disclosure of information received in confidence, or for maintaining the authority and impartiality of the judiciary.'

As regards the words 'necessary in a democratic society' in connection with the restrictions on the right to freedom of expression which may properly be prescribed by law, the jurisprudence of the European Court of Human Rights has established that 'necessary' requires the existence of a pressing social need, and that the restrictions should be no more than is proportionate to the legitimate aim pursued. The domestic courts have 'a margin of appreciation' based upon local knowledge of the needs of the society to which they belong (see *Sunday Times v UK* (1979) 2 EHRR 254, *Barthold v Germany* (1985) 7 EHRR 383 and *Lingens v*

part-time workers as compared with full-time workers in the respective qualifying
a periods for eligibility for statutory employment rights had the effect of
discriminating against women and conflicted with the obligations of the United
Kingdom under EEC law, namely art 119[a] of the EEC Treaty and Council
Directives (EEC) 75/117 (the equal pay directive) and 76/207 (the equal treatment
directive), to provide men and women with the right to receive equal pay for
equal work. In correspondence with the commission the Secretary of State
b declined to accept that the United Kingdom was in breach of its obligations under
Community law by providing less favourable treatment in the conditions of
employment of full-time and part-time workers. The commission and a part-
time worker who had been made redundant by her employer after less than five
years' employment applied for judicial review of the Secretary of State's decision
c and sought a declaration that the Secretary of State and the United Kingdom were
in breach of Community law obligations. They also sought an order of mandamus
requiring the Secretary of State to introduce legislation to provide for the right of
men and women to receive equal pay for equal work. The commission also
sought a declaration and mandamus in respect of the Secretary of State's failure to
amend the 1978 Act so as to provide that part-time workers who had previously
d worked full-time should have their period of full-time work taken into account
in the calculation of statutory redundancy pay. The Divisional Court rejected the
Secretary of State's contention that he had not made any 'decision' susceptible to
judicial review and held that the commission had locus standi to bring the
proceedings, that it was appropriate that the proceedings should be brought by
way of judicial review, both by the individual applicant and the commission, and
e that it was appropriate for the commission to bring proceedings in the national
court rather than wait for the European Commission to bring proceedings in the
European Court, but further held that the Divisional Court only had jurisdiction
to declare rights and obligations under the existing state of the law which were
enforceable and that it had no jurisdiction to grant mandamus requiring the
Secretary of State to introduce legislation to amend the 1978 Act or to declare that
f he was under a duty to do so. On the substantive issue the court held that the fact
that the less favourable treatment of part-time workers under the 1978 Act was
discriminatory against women did not constitute an infringement of art 119 of
the EEC Treaty and was in any event justifiable. The commission and the
individual applicant appealed.

g **Held** – The appeals would be dismissed for the following reasons—

(1) The individual applicant's application was essentially a private law claim
and the natural respondent to such a claim was the individual applicant's
employer, not the Secretary of State. The appropriate forum for her claim was
therefore an industrial tribunal and not the Divisional Court. Accordingly,
h without prejudice to the continuation of her proceedings in the industrial
tribunal, the individual applicant's appeal would be dismissed (see p 1029 *e f j*,
p 1030 *a*, p 1038 *h*, p 1050 *b c* and p 1056 *a b*, post); *R v East Berkshire Health
Authority, ex p Walsh* [1984] 3 All ER 425 applied.

(2) (Dillon LJ dissenting) The commission's appeal would also be dismissed
because the nature and subject matter of the application and the commission's
j position, coupled with the impossibility of granting remedies to force the
Secretary of State to comply with the directives if he was wrong in his view that
the United Kingdom was not in breach of Community law, or to force him to
introduce legislation to amend the 1978 Act, together with the availability of

---

a Article 119, so far as material, is set out at p 1033 *a*, post

remedies elsewhere, meant not only that there was no justiciable issue suitable
for consideration by means of judicial review but also that the commission had *a*
no locus standi to bring proceedings for judicial review against the Secretary of
State. The Secretary of State's statement in his correspondence with the
commission that the United Kingdom was not in breach of its obligations under
Community law and that he did not intend to bring in legislation to amend the
1978 Act was not, as such, a decision or expression of view which could be
challenged by means of judicial review since it did not alter any person's rights or *b*
obligations or deprive anyone of any benefit or advantage and did not infringe or
affect any right belonging to the commission, but merely sought to preserve the
status quo. Moreover, the directives were obligations under Community law and
not only could the courts not directly enforce their implementation in the United
Kingdom but also there were alternative procedures available for challenging
either the compatibility of the United Kingdom's domestic legislation relating to *c*
sex discrimination with Community law or any alleged failures of the United
Kingdom to comply with its Community obligations, namely by individuals
before an industrial tribunal, supported by the commission if it so wished, or by
the EC Commission before the Court of Justice of the European Communities.
Furthermore, as between the commission and the Secretary of State, the issue *d*
raised by the commission was one of public and not private law and the
commission did not have a sufficient interest within RSC Ord 53, r 3(7) to bring
proceedings for judicial review either to challenge the Secretary of State's view of
the law or to require him to introduce legislation reflecting the commission's
proposals (see p 1040 g to j, p 1042 g to p 1043 b e h, p 1044 d e h j, p 1045 g,
p 1047 b c, p 1048 g h, p 1050 j, p 1055 d to h and p 1056 a b, post); dictum of *e*
Lord Diplock in *Council of Civil Service Unions v Minister for the Civil Service* [1984]
3 All ER 935 at 949 followed; *Gillick v West Norfolk and Wisbech Area Health
Authority* [1985] 3 All ER 402 and *Equal Opportunities Commission v Birmingham
City Council* [1989] 1 All ER 769 considered.

Per Dillon and Hirst LJJ. Compensation for unfair dismissal, being
compensation payable by the employer for the unfair premature determination *f*
of the contract of employment, falls within the definition of 'pay' in art 119 of
the EEC Treaty as being part of 'the ordinary basic or minimum wage or salary
and any other consideration, whether in cash or in kind, which the worker
receives, directly or indirectly, in respect of his employment' (see p 1033 d and
p 1053 a b, post); *Arbeiterwohlfahrt der Stadt Berlin eV v Bötel* Case C-360/90 [1992]
IRLR 423 at 425 (para 12) and *Barber v Guardian Royal Exchange Assurance Group* *g*
Case C-262/88 [1990] 2 All ER 660 at 700–701 (paras 12–18) followed.

Per Kennedy and Hirst LJJ. The United Kingdom complies with its Community
obligations under art 6 of Council Directive 76/207 (the equal treatment directive)
by providing industrial tribunals and the corresponding appellate procedure to
protect individuals' rights in respect of sex discrimination (see p 1045 e f and *h*
p 1051 e, post).

Quaere (per Dillon and Hirst LJJ). Whether the fact that less favourable
treatment in the conditions of employment of full-time and part-time workers
under the 1978 Act discriminates against women is objectively justified (see
p 1035 f g, p 1038 a to d and p 1052 e to p 1053 a, post); *Bilka-Kaufhaus GmbH v
Weber von Hartz* Case 170/84 [1986] ECR 1607 considered. *j*

Appeal from the Divisional Court of the Queen's Bench Division [1992] 1 All
ER 545 dismissed.

Notes

For the Equal Opportunities Commission, see 16 *Halsbury's Laws* (4th edn)
paras 771:21–771:22, and for a case on the subject, see 20 *Digest* (Reissue) 594,
4520.

For the requirement in United Kingdom legislation of equal treatment of men
a and women regarding terms and conditions of employment, see 16 *Halsbury's Laws* (4th edn) para 767, and for cases on the subject, see 20 *Digest* (Reissue) 579–593, 4466–4515.

For the principle of equal pay for equal work in Community law, see 52 *Halsbury's Laws* (4th edn) paras 21.11–21.13.

For the nature and scope of judicial review, mandamus and declarations and
b locus standi therefor, see 1(1) *Halsbury's Laws* (4th edn reissue) paras 60, 64, 128, 132, 134, 155, 157, and for cases on the subject, see 16 *Digest* (Reissue) 321–366, 3362–3874 and 30 *Digest* (2nd reissue) 254–264, 2971–3025.

For the Employment Protection (Consolidation) Act 1978, see 16 *Halsbury's Laws* (4th edn) (1990 reissue) 232.

c For the EEC Treaty, arts 119, see 50 *Halsbury's Statutes* (4th edn) 306.

Cases referred to in judgments

Amministrazione delle Finanze dello Stato v SpA San Giorgio Case 199/82 [1983] ECR 3595.

Arbeiterwohlfahrt der Stadt Berlin eV v Bötel Case C-360/90 [1992] IRLR 423, CJEC.

d *Associated Provincial Picture Houses Ltd v Wednesbury Corp* [1947] 2 All ER 680, [1948] 1 KB 223, CA.

Barber v Guardian Royal Exchange Assurance Group Case C-262/88 [1990] 2 All ER 660, [1991] 1 QB 344, [1991] 2 WLR 72, [1990] ECR I-1889, CJEC.

Bilka-Kaufhaus GmbH v Weber von Hartz Case 170/84 [1986] ECR 1607.

Coenen v Sociaal-Economische Raad Case 39/75 [1975] ECR 1547.

e *Council of Civil Service Unions v Minister for the Civil Service* [1984] 3 All ER 935, [1985] AC 374, [1984] 3 WLR 1174, HL.

EC Commission v Belgium Case 155/82 [1983] ECR 531.

Emmott v Minister for Social Welfare Case C-208/90 [1991] 3 CMLR 894, CJEC.

Enderby v Frenchay Health Authority [1991] ICR 382, EAT.

Equal Opportunities Commission v Birmingham City Council [1989] 1 All ER 769,
f [1989] AC 1155, [1989] 2 WLR 520, HL.

Francovich v Italy, Bonifaci v Italy Joined cases C-6/90 and C-9/90 [1992] IRLR 84, CJEC.

Gillick v West Norfolk and Wisbech Area Health Authority [1985] 3 All ER 402, [1986] AC 112, [1985] 3 WLR 830, HL.

g *Handels- og Kontorfunktionærernes Forbund i Danmark v Dansk Arbejdsgiverforening (acting on behalf of Danfoss)* Case C-109/88 [1989] ECR I-3199.

IRC v National Federation of Self-Employed and Small Businesses Ltd [1981] 2 All ER 93, [1982] AC 617, [1981] 2 WLR 722, HL.

Marshall v Southampton and South West Hampshire Area Health Authority (Teaching) Case 152/84 [1986] 2 All ER 584, [1986] QB 401, [1986] 2 WLR 780, [1986]
h ECR 723, CJEC.

Nakkuda Ali v Jayaratne [1951] AC 66, PC.

Netherlands v Federatie Nederlandse Vakbeweging Case 71/85 [1986] ECR 3855.

Nimz v Freie und Hansestadt Hamburg Case C-184/89 [1991] ECR I-297.

R v Chief Constable of the Merseyside Police, ex p Calveley [1986] 1 All ER 257, [1986] QB 424, [1986] 2 WLR 144, CA.

j *R v East Berkshire Health Authority, ex p Walsh* [1984] 3 All ER 425, [1985] QB 152, [1984] 3 WLR 818, CA.

Rainey v Greater Glasgow Health Board [1987] 1 All ER 65, [1987] AC 224, [1987] 3 WLR 1017, HL.

Rewe-Zentralfinanz eG v Landwirtschaftskammer für das Saarland Case 33/76 [1976] ECR 1989.

Rinner-Kühn v FWW Spezial-Gebäudereinigung GmbH & Co KG Case 171/88 [1989] ECR 2743.

Roy v Kensington and Chelsea and Westminster Family Practitioner Committee [1992]
1 All ER 705, [1992] 1 AC 624, [1992] 2 WLR 239, HL.   *a*
Royal College of Nursing of the UK v Dept of Health and Social Security [1981] 1 All ER
545, [1981] AC 800, [1981] 2 WLR 279, QBD, CA and HL.
Ruzius-Wilbrink v Bestuur van de Bedrijfsvereniging voor Overheidsdiensten Case
C-102/88 [1989] ECR 4311.
Thomas v Adjudication Officer [1991] 3 All ER 315, [1991] 2 QB 164, [1991] 2 WLR
886, CA.   *b*

Cases also cited
Amministrazione delle Finanze dello Stato v Simmenthal SpA Case 106/77 [1978] ECR
629.
Brind v Secretary of State for the Home Dept [1991] 1 All ER 720, [1991] 1 AC 696,
HL.   *c*
Costa v ENEL Case 6/64 [1964] ECR 585.
Cotter v Minister for Social Welfare Case C-377/89 [1991] ECR I-1155.
Defrenne v Sabena Case 43/75 (1976) [1981] 1 All ER 122, [1976] ECR 455, CJEC.
Dik v College van Burgemeester en Wethouders Arnhem Case 80/87 [1988] ECR 1601.
Factortame Ltd v Secretary of State for Transport [1989] 2 All ER 692, [1990] 2 AC   *d*
85, HL.
Factortame Ltd v Secretary of State for Transport (No 2) Case C-213/89 [1991] 1 All
ER 70, [1991] 1 AC 603, CJEC and HL.
Johnston v Chief Constable of the Royal Ulster Constabulary Case 222/84 [1986] 3 All
ER 135, [1987] QB 129, [1986] ECR 1651, CJEC.
Kowalska v Freie und Hansestadt Hamburg Case C-33/89 [1990] ECR I-2591.   *e*
Marleasing SA v Comercial Internacional de Alimentación SA Case C-106/89 [1990]
ECR I-4135.
Orphanos v Queen Mary College [1985] 2 All ER 233, [1985] AC 761, HL.
Pickstone v Freemans plc [1988] 2 All ER 803, [1989] AC 66, HL.
Preston v IRC [1985] 2 All ER 327, [1985] AC 835, HL.
Stevens v Bexley Health Authority [1989] ICR 224, EAT.   *f*

Appeals
The Equal Opportunities Commission and Patricia Elizabeth Day (the individual
applicant) appealed from the decision of the Divisional Court of the Queen's
Bench Division (Nolan LJ and Judge J) ([1992] 1 All ER 545) given on 10 October
1991 refusing the application of the commission and the individual applicant for *g*
judicial review of a decision of the Secretary of State for Employment dated 23
April 1990 declining to accept that the United Kingdom was in breach of its
obligations under EEC law by providing less favourable treatment of part-time
workers than of full-time workers in relation to the conditions for the right not
to be unfairly dismissed and for receipt of statutory redundancy pay and   *h*
compensation for unfair dismissal and refusing to introduce amending legislation
to make the Employment Protection (Consolidation) Act 1978 comply with the
relevant provisions of Community law. The facts are set out in the judgment of
Dillon LJ.

Anthony Lester QC and *Monica Carss-Frisk* (instructed by *J Alan Lakin,* Manchester) *j*
for the appellants.
Michael Beloff QC and *Stephen Richards* (instructed by the *Treasury Solicitor*) for the
Secretary of State.

Cur adv vult

6 November 1992. The following judgments were delivered.

a

DILLON LJ.

General

The court has before it appeals, in the one case by the Equal Opportunities Commission (the EOC) and a Mrs Patricia Day (the first application) and in the other case by the EOC alone (the second application), against orders of a Divisional
b Court of the Queen's Bench Division (Nolan LJ and Judge J) ([1992] 1 All ER 545), which on 10 October 1991 rejected two substantive applications for relief by way of judicial review. Leave to move had in each case been duly granted earlier. The respondent to each of the applications was the Secretary of State for Employment, who is the sole respondent to the appeals.

c The relief sought by each of the appeals is merely declaratory, viz declarations to the effect that the United Kingdom is in breach of its obligations under art 119 of the EEC Treaty and Council Directive (EEC) 75/117 (the equal pay directive) or, alternatively, Council Directive (EEC) 76/207 (the equal treatment directive), by providing less favourable treatment of part-time workers (most of whom are women) than of full-time workers (most of whom are men) in relation, under the
d first application, to the conditions for receipt of statutory redundancy pay and compensation for unfair dismissal and in relation, under the second application, to the method of calculation of statutory redundancy pay. In essence the claim is in each case that provisions at present contained in the Employment Protection (Consolidation) Act 1978 are inconsistent with and overriden by EC law under art 119 and the two directives.

e
In the court below, and at the suggestion of the court, the appellants amended their forms of application to claim additionally relief by way of mandamus, viz mandamus to compel the Secretary of State to introduce the necessary legislation to amend the 1978 Act to ensure that provisions contrary to art 119 and the two directives are eliminated. In this court Mr Lester QC for the appellants disclaimed
f seeking relief by way of mandamus, and said that he had not in fact sought it in the court below. He realises, as no doubt he realised below, that mandamus in that form is a relief which the court could not or would not grant. But the nature of what would be required if there were to be enforcement by mandamus is relevant to one of the arguments as to whether the court can or should grant the declarations sought. I will come to that later.

g Apart from the substantive questions as to whether the relevant provisions of the 1978 Act are discriminatory or justifiable under EC law, the appeals raise important questions of national law as to the procedures available under English law to raise a question in the English courts whether a statutory provision enacted by the United Kingdom Parliament is valid or not under EC law and as to the capacity of the EOC to raise a general question of alleged sexual discrimination
h by bringing an application in its own name for judicial review, as opposed to merely sponsoring an application in the appropriate English court—be it the Divisional Court, an industrial tribunal or some other court—by a person who is an actual victim of the alleged discrimination.

I find it convenient to deal with the two appeals separately, and I take first the
j appeal against the refusal of relief on the first application.

The first application

The provisions in the 1978 Act complained of on this appeal are the provisions as to the qualifying periods for entitlement to the right to statutory redundancy pay and the right to compensation for unfair dismissal. Under the 1978 Act the qualifying period for employees who work for 16 or more hours a week is two years of continuous employment, but the qualifying period for employees who work for between 8 and 16 hours a week is five years of continuous employment, and employees who work for fewer than 8 hours a week cannot qualify at all for either of the rights in question. It is convenient in this part of this judgment to refer to employees who work for 16 or more hours a week as 'full-time employees' and to employees who work for between 8 and 16 hours a week as 'part-time employees'; these are ad hoc definitions only.

Since it is common ground that a very large majority of part-time employees are women and a majority of full-time employees are men, and it is common ground also that the main reason why women seek part-time employment rather than full-time employment is their responsibility as carers for children or elderly relatives, it is accepted by the Secretary of State that the difference in thresholds between two years for full-time employees and five years for part-time employees involves indirect discrimination on grounds of sex, but it is said that that discrimination is 'objectively justifiable' by factors unrelated to any discrimination on grounds of sex, and is therefore not offensive to EC law.

The essential question on this appeal is therefore the question of objective justification.

In relation to the provision that employees who work for fewer than eight hours a week cannot qualify for any of the rights, it is to be noted that the EC Social Affairs Commissioner issued, apparently on grounds of administrative convenience, a form of directive which recognised that it was appropriate that employees who had only worked for very short periods every week should not be entitled to every right or benefit to which employees who worked for much longer periods would be entitled; it was recognised therefore that there could be a threshold, which was set at eight hours per week. In the light of this, I would despite Mr Lester's arguments hold that the provision that employees who work for fewer than eight hours a week cannot qualify for the rights in question is objectively justified on the ground of administrative convenience and is not offensive to EC law. This was not a matter to which any great length of argument was directed, and I do not propose to refer to it further.

Apart from the essential question of objective justification of the differential thresholds of two or five years for full-time or part-time employees as above defined, Mr Beloff QC for the Secretary of State takes a number of points on which he contends that these proceedings for judicial review are misconceived. In his skeleton argument he has classified these points as 'the decision issue', 'the locus issue', 'the forum issue' and 'the relief issue'. In the Divisional Court the appellants succeeded on the decision issue, the locus issue and the forum issue, but the Secretary of State succeeded on the relief issue. All these issues go to the ability and readiness of the court to grant relief by way of judicial review and there is considerable overlap between several of them. I propose therefore to deal with the issues in a somewhat different order.

There is a further subordinate issue referred to by Mr Beloff as 'the pay issue'. This is whether compensation for unfair dismissal is 'pay' within the meaning of art 119 and the equal pay directive. (It has been held that redundancy pay counts as pay within that meaning—*Barber v Guardian Royal Exchange Assurance Group* Case C-262/88 [1990] 2 All ER 660, [1991] 1 QB 344—and it is accepted that the conditions for receiving compensation for unfair dismissal fall within the scope of the equal treatment directive even if the compensation is not pay.) I propose to deal first with the locus forum and relief issues, then with the decision issue and then with the pay issue before turning to the substantive question of objective justification.

The locus and forum issues and Mrs Day

a   Has Mrs Day standing to make a claim against the Secretary of State, and is the Divisional Court the, or an, appropriate forum for her to proceed in?

Mrs Day was joined as a co-applicant in the first application during the hearing in the Divisional Court. The application was initially brought by the EOC alone. Mrs Day was employed by the Hertfordshire Area Health Authority as a part-time employee, but was made redundant shortly before she had completed five
b   years' continuous employment. She did not therefore pass the threshold under the 1978 Act as it stands, but claims that as a result of EC law she has none the less a directly enforceable right to recover redundancy pay. On the facts she does not assert any claim to compensation for unfair dismissal. She has brought proceedings for redundancy pay against her employers in the appropriate industrial tribunal, and these stand adjourned pending the outcome of the present proceedings.
c
Since Mrs Day's former employer is a public body, it is regarded in EC law as an emanation of the state and so is not entitled to set up against Mrs Day any failure of the state to amend its legislation to comply with art 119 and the equal pay directive; any offending provisions of the national statute can be disapplied by the national court—*Marshall v Southampton and South West Hampshire Area*
d   *Health Authority (Teaching)* Case 152/84 [1986] 2 All ER 584, [1986] QB 401.

It is therefore conceded by the Secretary of State that if the five-year threshold for part-time employees is not objectively justified Mrs Day is entitled to recover her redundancy pay from her former employers.

But the appropriate forum for that is the industrial tribunal, in which she has already started proceedings, and not the Divisional Court. Moreover, the party
e   liable to pay her the redundancy pay would be her former employer and not the Secretary of State, although the Secretary of State would be entitled to apply to be heard on her proceedings in the industrial tribunal.

It follows that, there being the remedy available to her in the industrial tribunal, it is not right that Mrs Day should bring proceedings in the Divisional Court. I respectfully agree with the statement of the law by May LJ in *R v East*
f   *Berkshire Health Authority, ex p Walsh* [1984] 3 All ER 425 at 434, [1985] QB 152 at 169–170. The industrial tribunal has ample jurisdiction to decide the question of objective justification; analogous issues arising from EC law were decided by the industrial tribunal in *Marshall's* case. Although the success of Mrs Day's claim depends on the effect of EC law it is essentially a private law claim to be enforced in the appropriate tribunal for private claims, and not in the Divisional Court;
g   compare also *Roy v Kensington and Chelsea and Westminster Family Practitioner Committee* [1992] 1 All ER 705, [1992] 1 AC 624.

There may be cases in which it is appropriate for proceedings for judicial review to be brought before a private law claim can be launched, e g where a statute or a certificate of a minister apparently precludes a person from bringing proceedings
h   in the private tribunal which would otherwise be appropriate. It is not necessary to pursue such possibilities in the present case.

I do not however agree with the views expressed by the Divisional Court in its judgment (see [1992] 1 All ER 545 at 557–558) as to the justification for Mrs Day proceeding in the Divisional Court. Since Mrs Day has directly enforceable rights—if she is correct in her contentions on objective justification—the natural
j   respondent to her complaints is indeed her employer, and not the Secretary of State as the designated minister for the purpose of s 2(2) of the European Communities Act 1972 in relation to measures to prevent discrimination between men and women as regards terms and conditions of employment. That aspects of the facts may be difficult to decide does not warrant trying issues of fact in a claim for redundancy pay in a tribunal other than the tribunal to which such claims are

by statute allocated. Moreover, if certain types of claim are by statute allocated to the industrial tribunals, the fact that legal aid is not available in those tribunals cannot warrant having issues raised by those claims tried in other courts where legal aid may be available.

I would accordingly dismiss Mrs Day's appeal, without prejudice to the continuation of her proceedings in the industrial tribunal.

The locus, forum and relief issues and the EOC

There can be no doubt that if the EOC is, on the locus and relief issues, entitled at all to bring proceedings in its own name against the Secretary of State the only possible forum is the Divisional Court. The EOC has no locus to bring any claim in its own name in an industrial tribunal and as between the EOC and the Secretary of State the issue raised by the EOC is an issue of public, and not private, law.

So far as the EOC is concerned, therefore, the question is essentially one of locus, having regard also to the nature of the relief claimed.

The EOC was established by the Sex Discrimination Act 1975. Its duties are set out in s 53(1) of that Act. So far as, in my judgment, they are relevant to the present case, they are: '(a) to work towards the elimination of discrimination, and (b) to promote equality of opportunity between men and women generally . . .'

Subsequent sections give the EOC specific powers, including in s 75 power to grant assistance, including payment of legal expenses, to any actual or prospective claimant or complainant if the case raises a question of principle, or it is unreasonable, having regard, inter alia, to the complexity of the case, to expect the claimant to deal with the case unaided.

Mr Beloff tended to the submission that the powers of the EOC should, in general, be limited to the powers expressly conferred by the 1975 Act. But I see nothing to make the maxim expressio unius est exclusio alterius applicable, and I note that s 57, which gives power to the EOC to conduct a formal investigation for any purpose connected with the carrying out of its duties, is prefaced with the words 'Without prejudice to their general power to do anything requisite for the performance of their duties under section 53(1), the Commission may if they think fit . . .' In my judgment, the EOC has such a general power and it is therefore, in my judgment, in general at any rate, authorised to apply for judicial review where the application, if successful, would be requisite in working towards the elimination of some particular instance of discrimination.

No doubt if the case did not raise a question of principle—see s 75(1)(a)—leave to move would not be granted.

An instance unconnected with EC law in which the EOC made a successful application for judicial review to establish that a public authority was in continuing breach of its obligations under the Sex Discrimination Act 1975 is *Equal Opportunities Commission v Birmingham City Council* [1989] 1 All ER 769, [1989] AC 1155. There the city council, as education authority, was held to be in breach of its obligations under that Act because it had failed to provide as many grammar school places for girls as for boys; it was not absolved from liability by the fact that the disparity had come about because the city council had inherited a number of grammar schools founded long ago which were by their constitutions legitimately single sex schools for boys only. In the *Birmingham City Council* case there was no suggestion at any stage that the EOC had no locus to bring the proceedings; had such a suggestion been made, it should, in my judgment, have been rejected by the courts.

a I do not regard the jurisdiction of the Divisional Court as so limited that in such a context all that the EOC can do to combat discrimination is to sponsor claims for compensation by individual girls who have wrongly been denied grammar school places which they would have obtained had they been boys.

Mr Beloff submits that the limits to define the requisites for locus standi for a person to bring proceedings for judicial review have been authoritatively considered by Lord Diplock in *IRC v National Federation of Self-Employed and Small* *b* *Businesses Ltd* [1981] 2 All ER 93 at 105–107, [1982] AC 617 at 642–644. He submits that the EOC does not qualify because it has no right, interest, privilege or legitimate expectation at stake, and would not itself be the beneficiary of any changes to the domestic law which might result from the establishment of the incompatibility of such law in its present state with EC law.

c But Mr Beloff concedes that the criteria indicated in his submissions were extended in *Gillick v West Norfolk and Wisbech Area Health Authority* [1985] 3 All ER 402, [1986] AC 112, where Mrs Gillick was held to have locus standi to challenge advice issued to the public by a public body which she claimed was wrong in law. A fortiori the EOC which was established by statute for the statutory purpose of eliminating discrimination has locus standi to apply for *d* judicial review on a point of public law when a public body such as the Birmingham City Council is perpetuating discrimination by its policies, and is denying that it is under any obligation to act otherwise.

Does it then make any difference that the present case involves EC law?

Mr Beloff submits that it is not the function of the courts to enforce treaty obligations against the Crown. Indeed the courts do not even have the power to *e* construe a treaty if the treaty has not been given statutory effect by Parliament.

But s 2 of the European Communities Act 1972 expressly provides:

'(1) All such rights, powers, liabilities, obligations and restrictions from time to time created or arising by or under the Treaties, and all such remedies and procedures from time to time provided for by or under the Treaties, as *f* in accordance with the Treaties are without further enactment to be given legal effect or used in the United Kingdom shall be recognised and available in law, and be enforced, allowed and followed accordingly . . .'

But matters arising under art 119 of the Treaty and the two directives are directly enforceable against the Crown. That is the basis of *Marshall's* case and the *g* earlier decisions of the European Court on which it is founded. Moreover, quoad the points in the 1978 Act with which the appeal in relation to the first application is concerned, it is, as in *Marshall's* case, merely a question of disapplying the five-year threshold, and applying the two-year threshold which (in the phrase used in the EC cases of *Ruzius-Wilbrink v Bestuur van de Bedrijfsvereniging voor Overheidsdiensten* Case C-102/88 [1989] ECR 4311 and *Nimz v Freie und Hansestadt* *h* *Hamburg* Case C-184/89 [1991] ECR I-297) will remain the only valid reference point. In addition it appears from the recent EC decision of *Francovich v Italy, Bonifaci v Italy* Joined cases C-6/90 and C-9/90 [1992] IRLR 84—though Mr Richards disputes this on behalf of the Secretary of State and it is not necessary to form a final conclusion—that, though the two directives are not directly enforceable against a private employer, a part-time employee of a private employer *j* who is deprived of redundancy pay or compensation for unfair dismissal as against his private employer because his or her employment is terminated after less than five but more than two years of continuous employment will have an action for damages against the Crown to be enforced by action by writ against the Attorney General.

I see no basis, therefore, for denying locus to the EOC to bring the application for judicial review in the first application in its own name, notwithstanding that matters of EC law are involved. The EC aspect does not render this application distinguishable from the *Birmingham City Council* case so far as locus is concerned.

Moreover, so far as the relief issue is concerned, the fact that relief will not be granted against the Secretary of State by way of mandamus requiring him to introduce new legislation in Parliament to amend the 1978 Act (or to amend it himself by exercise of the powers delegated to him under s 2 of the European Communities Act 1972) will not render the declarations sought brutum fulmen, or of no practical effect. The making of the declarations in these proceedings would further the statutory duties of the EOC by providing an authoritative ruling by a competent national court which can form the basis for claims by persons otherwise discriminated against by the five-year threshold, in industrial courts, or by actions for damages on the basis of *Francovich's* case.

The decision issue

This is the label used in argument to describe the question whether, even if the EOC has locus to bring these proceedings, there is anything for the court to review. It is of course accepted by the EOC that not every expression of an opinion on a point of law by a department of state or other public authority in a correspondence with some other person or body automatically warrants that other person or body rushing to the Divisional Court to determine whether the opinion expressed is or is not erroneous in law. Mr Beloff submits that there is no basis for judicial review unless there has been a decision founded on error of law or a refusal to make a decision—see per Lord Diplock in *Council of Civil Service Unions v Minister for the Civil Service* [1984] 3 All ER 935 at 949, [1985] AC 374 at 408—or, presumably in the light of *Gillick's* case, a public promulgation for the public to act on of a policy founded on error of law.

What actually happened so far as regards the first application is as follows. On 21 March 1990 the chief executive of the EOC wrote to the Secretary of State. The letter referred to a certain decision of the European Court and suggested in effect that certain provisions of the 1978 Act, and in particular the five-year qualifying period for part-time employees (working for between 8 and 16 hours per week) to qualify for redundancy pay or compensation for unfair dismissal, constituted indirect discrimination against women employees, contrary to the relevant rules of Community law. The Secretary of State was accordingly asked to consider these matters as a matter of urgency and to inform the EOC whether the government would be willing to introduce the necessary legislation to remove the discrimination from the 1978 Act, giving reasons for his decision if the reply was in the negative.

The Secretary of State gave his considered reply in a letter of 23 April 1990. He stated that 'we do not accept that statutory redundancy pay and statutory compensation for unfair dismissal constitutes pay within the meaning of Article 119, or that they fall within the equal treatment directive'—a position that in a large part Mr Beloff has not sought to defend. He further stated that, for reasons briefly touched on, 'we' believe that the current statutory thresholds are entirely justifiable, and ended by stating that 'we' have no plans to change the thresholds.

I have no doubt that, given that the EOC is a statutory body and that its statutory duties include the elimination of discrimination, and given the clarity of the Secretary of State's statement of the government's position, the EOC was on receipt of that letter fully entitled to apply for judicial review to challenge the government's position, thus clearly stated, as erroneous in law.

The pay issue

a 'Pay' is defined in art 119 as—

> 'the ordinary basic or minimum wage or salary and any other consideration, whether in cash or in kind, which the worker receives, directly or indirectly, in respect of his employment . . .'

That has been broadly interpreted by the European Court. Thus in the decision
b of the court in *Arbeiterwohlfahrt der Stadt Berlin eV v Bötel* Case C-360/90 [1992] IRLR 423 at 425 (para 12) it is stated:

> 'According to the case law of the Court . . . the concept of "pay" within the meaning of Article 119 of the Treaty comprises any consideration whether in cash or in kind, whether immediate or future, provided that the employee
c receives it, albeit indirectly, in respect of his employment from his employer, whether under a contract of employment, legislative provisions or made ex gratia by the employer.'

See also the decision of the European Court in *Barber v Guardian Royal Exchange Assurance Group* Case C-262/88 [1990] 2 All ER 660 at 700–701, [1991] 1 QB 344
d at 399–400 (paras 12–18), which established that redundancy pay was pay.

By this test compensation for unfair dismissal, which is compensation payable by the employer for the unfair premature determination of the contract of employment, must, in my judgment, fall within the definition of 'pay'.

Objective justification

e This is the substantive, as opposed to procedural, point in the appeal against the refusal of relief on the first application. The EC law on the subject is well settled and has been many times stated. It is conveniently summed up in the decision of the European Court in *Bilka-Kaufhaus GmbH v Weber von Hartz* Case 170/84 [1986] ECR 1607 at 1628–1629 (paras 36–37), which were cited by Lord Keith of Kinkel in *Rainey v Greater Glasgow Health Board* [1987] 1 All ER 65 at 72, [1987] AC 224
f at 238:

> '36. It is for the national court, which has sole jurisdiction to make findings of fact, to determine whether and to what extent the grounds put forward by an employer to explain the adoption of a pay practice which applies independently of a worker's sex but in fact affects more women than men
g may be regarded as objectively justified economic grounds. If the national court finds that the measures chosen by Bilka correspond to a real need on the part of the undertaking, are appropriate with a view to achieving the objectives pursued and are necessary to that end, the fact that the measures affect a far greater number of women than men is not sufficient to show that they constitute an infringement of Article 119.
h 37. The answer to question 2(a) must therefore be that under Article 119 a department store company may justify the adoption of a pay policy excluding part-time workers, irrespective of their sex, from its occupational pension scheme on the ground that it seeks to employ as few part-time workers as possible, where it is found that the means chosen for achieving that objective
j correspond to a real need on the part of the undertaking, are appropriate with a view to achieving the objective in question and are necessary to that end.'

Although, however, the law is clear, its application by the national court can in some cases be difficult, and there can be questions of EC law as to what is capable of amounting to an objective justification of an otherwise discriminatory practice. Thus it is stated in the judgment of the European Court in *Rinner-Kühn v FWW*

Spezial-Gebäudereinigung GmbH & Co KG Case 171/88 [1989] ECR 2743 at 2761 (para 15) that considerations which only represent generalised statements concerning certain categories of worker do not admit the conclusion of objective criteria unrelated to any discrimination on grounds of sex; the member state must be in a position to establish that the means selected correspond to an objective necessary for its social policy and are appropriate and necessary to the attainment of that objective.

It appears from the evidence given by an official of the Department of Employment to the House of Commons Employment Committee in 1989 that the original rationale for having the differential five-year threshold for part-time employees who worked less than 16 hours a week was the view that there is a difference in the commitment of a part-timer and a full-timer to their employer. That is not now relied on as a justification for the discriminatory threshold, and it could not be in the light of the decisions of the European Court.

In the letter of 23 April 1990 the Secretary of State, after asserting that the statutory thresholds were entirely justifiable, said:

> 'These thresholds have existed in one form or another ever since employment protection legislation was first introduced. Their purpose is to ensure that a fair balance is struck between the interests of employers and employees.'

That again is not good enough to establish objective justification. It does not indicate what the objective or real need is that the differential threshold is said to satisfy nor does it offer any evidence that the differential threshold is necessary—in any sense of that word—to achieve that objective or satisfy that real need.

What is now said is that the objective is that there should be as much part-time work as possible available for those who want to work part-time, rather than full-time, and that to achieve that it is necessary that the qualifying period of continuous employment for these particular benefits should be longer for part-time workers than for full-time workers; otherwise employers will engage full-time workers rather than part-time workers and there will be (significantly) less part-time work available.

That appears to me to be the surviving shadow of the thinking that was once prevalent and is now discarded in this country that, unless the basic rate of pay of part-time workers was less than the basic rate of pay for full-time workers, employers would engage full-time workers rather than part-time workers and there would be less part-time work available.

It appears from the evidence given to the House of Commons Employment Committee in 1989 that representatives of employers' organisations were of the opinion that if there were no differential thresholds for part-time workers to qualify for redundancy pay and compensation for unfair dismissal there would be less part-time work available, because employers would prefer to engage full-time employees; but representatives of the trade union movement and of certain corporate employers were of the opposite opinion, viz that the absence of the differential threshold would have no significant effect on the amount of part-time work available. What emerges to my mind from the expression of these differing views is that there was no factual evidence to support either view.

The Divisional Court accepted, as would anyone, that any reduction in the number of employment opportunities would be socially undesirable. It added—

in words eerily apposite to the particular events of the week in which this appeal
a happened to be argued ([1992] 1 All ER 545 at 565):

> 'Some would put it higher and suggest that any deliberate step which
> might have the effect of reducing employment opportunities would be
> socially unacceptable.'

But the essence of the Divisional Court's decision rests, as I understand it, on
b two propositions, namely firstly that the submissions of the Secretary of State
appear to be 'inherently logical', and secondly that, even if it cannot be positively
established that the high rate of employment of women in the United Kingdom
is a direct consequence of the provisions of the 1978 Act, 'it is not unreasonable
for the Secretary of State for Employment to conclude that amendments to the
legislation might have adverse consequences for women seeking part-time
c employment' (at 565).

Mr Lester submits that in these passages the Divisional Court is setting up a
Wednesbury test, as the criterion for testing an assertion by the Crown of objective
justification (see *Associated Provincial Picture Houses Ltd v Wednesbury Corp* [1947]
2 All ER 680, [1948] 1 KB 223). The word 'Wednesbury' has emotive connotations,
d and I prefer not to use it. The essential point to my mind is the distinction to
which Lord Radcliffe drew attention in *Nakkuda Ali v Jayaratne* [1951] AC 66 at
76 between the Secretary of State having reasonable cause to believe something or
other and the Secretary of State honestly supposing that he has reasonable cause
to believe whatever it is. In the present case objective justification has to be
shown, and it is not shown by showing that the Secretary of State honestly and
e not unreasonably believes that there is objective justification.

I can see no *evidence* that abolishing the five-year threshold of continuous
employment for part-time workers to be able to claim redundancy pay or
compensation for unfair dismissal will cause any significant reduction in the
availability of part-time employment. On the contrary, recent history in relation
f to other discriminatory measures underlines that according women the equal
status which is justly their due has not led to the dire results which were foretold
by the prophets of doom. In addition I am much impressed by the fact that no
other member state of the European Community has a comparable threshold for
workers working not more than 16 hours a week or thereabouts who want to
claim such benefits. The Republic of Ireland did have an 18 hour per week
threshold for entitlement to such benefits, but this has been reduced by the Irish
g Parliament to 8 hours per week.

The Divisional Court attached importance to the fact that the European
Commission had accepted that there could be a threshold before part-time
employees may qualify for the same benefits and advantages as full-time
employees. That is a reference to the draft directive put forward by the Social
h Affairs Commissioner. But the justification for the 8 hours per week threshold in
the document was to rule out disproportionate administrative costs and take into
account firms' economic needs. That is not the justification put forward by the
Secretary of State for the five years' continuous employment threshold for
employees who work between 8 and 16 hours per week. 'Administrative costs' to
the employer cannot justify having the two thresholds, one at 8 hours per week
j and the other at 16. Extra cost to the employer, from having to pay higher
benefits to women so as to bring their benefits in line with the benefits paid to
men, is inherent in the concepts of equal pay and equal treatment, and so cannot,
per se, justify failure to accord a class which is predominantly female equality
with a class which is predominantly male.

The onus is on the Secretary of State and, in my judgment, he has not discharged it. Therefore I would, for my part, allow the appeal of the EOC in relation to the *a* the first application, and I would make a declaration to the effect of the first two of the declarations sought.

I would add one point.

Mr Lester has stressed that the EC doctrine of proportionality applies to the question of objective justification, ie even if a particular objective is legitimate and desirable, and some restriction on the free movement of goods, or some *b* discriminatory measure, is therefore warranted, the particular restriction or discriminatory measure imposed by the national state will none the less not be justified if a lesser restriction or less discriminatory measure would have sufficed: see the decision of the European Court in *EC Commission v Belgium* Case 155/82 [1983] ECR 531 at 543 (para 12) and in *Coenen v Sociaal-Economische Raad* Case 39/ *c* 75 [1975] ECR 1547 at 1556 (para 12). But in the application of that rule there must, I apprehend, be a margin of appreciation (to adopt a phrase from the jurisprudence of the European Court of Human Rights) or balance of discretion allowed to the national authority. It is not enough to say that the Secretary of State has not directed his attention to showing that a four-year threshold, rather than a five-, or 14 hours per week of employment rather than 16, would not be *d* enough to achieve his purpose.

The second application

This application is concerned with the method of calculation of statutory redundancy pay. It is not concerned with compensation for unfair dismissal. The particular point in the 1978 Act which is challenged as being offensive to art 119 *e* and the directives is that under the 1978 Act as it stands redundancy pay is calculated by reference to the rate of pay of an employee at the time when he or she is made redundant without regard to the rate of his or her pay at any earlier stage of his or her employment. It is said that this requirement is unfair to employees who work full-time and then work part-time, because it gives them no credit, in the calculation of their redundancy pay, for the higher wages that *f* they would have been earning while they were working full-time, as compared with the wages they would have been earning when working part-time.

The evidence shows that a higher proportion of those switching from full-time to part-time work are women, and the proportion of men so switching is lower. Typically a woman who worked full-time would switch to part-time work when *g* she became subject to responsibilities as a carer for a newborn child or an elderly relative. It is therefore submitted that there is unfair discrimination against women in breach of art 119 and the directives.

This application is brought by the EOC alone. Mrs Day is not concerned, since she never worked full-time for the Hertfordshire Area Health Authority. We are only concerned with the employees who, having worked full-time for an *h* employer, switch to working part-time for the same employer. We are not concerned for example with women who, having worked full-time for an employer, switch to part-time work for a different employer because of calls on them as carers.

For the purposes of this application and this appeal, the definition of part-time employees is taken to be those who work for less than 30 hours per week, which *j* was the definition used in a memorandum submitted by the Department of Employment to the House of Commons Employment Committee in 1989. It was said by the author of that memorandum to be the normal definition. (The 16 hours per week and 8 hours per week figures discussed in my judgment in

relation to the first application are relevant to the thresholds for qualifying for
a redundancy pay; they are not relevant to the calculation of the redundancy pay of
those who do qualify, and thus are not relevant to the second application).

As to the facts, on 16 May 1990 the chief executive of the EOC wrote to the
Secretary of State for Employment a letter on substantially the same lines as the
letter of 21 March 1990 to which I have referred in relation to the first application,
and asking at the end the same question, but in relation to discrimination as I
b have indicated in the calculation of redundancy payments for those who qualify
for such payments. The Secretary of State replied by a letter of 2 June 1990; he
did not agree that the legislation was unfairly discriminating against women, he
referred to the earlier correspondence and he maintained that the statutory
thresholds were justified.

c So far as the 'decision issue', discussed above, is concerned, I see no significant
distinction between this appeal and that in respect of the first application.
Likewise much that I said in the earlier part of this judgment in relation to the
locus standi of the EOC applies to this appeal. There are, however, three separate
points which arise on the second application.

(1) Apart altogether from any question of objective justification, the Secretary
d of State does not accept that the provisions of the 1978 Act which are attacked by
the second application involve any discrimination against women (the discrimination issue).

(2) Even if there would otherwise be unlawful discrimination, the Secretary of
State submits that there is objective justification for the statutory provisions, but
the objective justification put forward is, of course, not the same as that put
e forward in relation to the provisions attacked by the the first application (the
objective justification issue).

(3) On the question of the relief sought, the Secretary of State seeks to
distinguish the provisions considered in relation to the the first application on the
ground that, even if anything, illegal by EC law, in those provisions can be cured
by disapplying the offending threshold, any cure for anything illegal in the
f provisions to be considered in respect of the second application must involve
writing in some new statutory provision (the relief issue). The distinction drawn
by the Secretary of State on the discrimination issue is that, in the provisions of
the 1978 Act which had to be considered in relation to the first application, there
were on the face of the statute two rival thresholds to be compared, the five-year
g threshold for part-time employees and the two-year threshold for full-time
employees. Since therefore the more onerous five-year threshold was imposed for
part-time employees, who are mainly women, and the less onerous two-year
threshold was imposed for full-time employees, who are mainly men, there was
plainly indirect sexual discrimination against women unless the distinction in
treatment could be objectively justified. But in relation to the provisions to be
h considered on the second application there are no two criteria laid down by the
statute and there is no comparison invited by the terms of the statute. There is
merely a single factor—not even a condition—to be taken into account, in relation
to pay, namely the rate of pay at the date the employee was made redundant, and
that is to apply to all employees, whether male or female and whether they
worked full-time throughout their employment, or part-time throughout, or
j full-time and then part-time or part-time and then full-time. Essentially, the
Secretary of State submits that there can be no discrimination if all are treated
alike.

Apart from its relevance to the discrimination issue, this distinction is, to my
mind, highly relevant to the relief issue.

(4) In this section "the relevant statutory provisions" has the meaning given by section 53 of the Health and Safety at Work etc. Act 1974.'

Section 53(1) of the 1974 Act defines 'the relevant statutory provisions' as:

'(a) the provisions of this Part and of any health and safety regulations . . . and (b) the existing statutory provisions . . .'

Returning to Pt VI of the Sex Discrimination Act 1975, s 57(1) provides:

'Without prejudice to their general power to do anything requisite for the performance of their duties under section 53(1), the Commission may if they think fit, and shall if required by the Secretary of State, conduct a formal investigation for any purpose connected with the carrying out of those duties.'

Part VII of the 1975 Act is entitled 'Enforcement' and s 62, so far as material, provides:

'(1) Except as provided by this Act no proceedings, whether civil or criminal, shall lie against any person in respect of an act by reason that the act is unlawful by virtue of a provision of this Act.
(2) Subsection (1) does not preclude the making of an order of certiorari, mandamus or prohibition . . .'

Mr Lester QC for the EOC makes the obvious point that the wording of s 62(2) clearly contemplates the possibility of an application for judicial review, and at the end of Pt VII s 75(1) provides:

'Where, in relation to proceedings or prospective proceedings either under this Act or in respect of an equality clause, an individual who is an actual or prospective complainant or claimant applies to the Commission for assistance under this section, the Commission shall consider the application and may grant it if they think fit to do so on the ground that—(a) the case raises a question of principle, or (b) it is unreasonable, having regard to the complexity of the case or the applicant's position in relation to the respondent or another person involved or any other matter, to expect the applicant to deal with the case unaided, or by reason of any other special consideration.'

The rest of s 75 specifies how assistance can be provided.

I can find nothing in the sections which I have cited which would enable me to conclude that the EOC is entitled to proceed against the Secretary of State, either to challenge his interpretation of the law, or to induce him to introduce fresh legislation. Certainly the EOC is required to work towards the elimination of discrimination and to promote equality of opportunity between men and women generally (s 53(1)(a) and (b)). If those provisions are considered in isolation it can be argued that the present proceedings are within their scope, but the subsequent provisions of the 1975 Act which I have cited, in particular ss 53(1)(c), 55(1) and (2), make it clear to me that, vis-à-vis the Secretary of State, the role of the EOC is that of adviser and, as the Divisional Court pointed out, there is nothing in the 1975 Act which suggests that the Secretary of State is under any obligation to accept the proposals made to him by the EOC or to introduce legislation on its recommendations (see [1992] 1 All ER 545 at 553). It is surprising that if Parliament intended to vest the EOC with authority to compel the Secretary of State to act it did not say so. Accordingly I conclude that the EOC does not have the capacity to initiate either of these applications, and in my judgment it is of no significance that on other occasions the EOC has initiated or taken part in

proceedings for judicial review, not only because, as is conceded, the issue of locus
standi was not argued, but also because the proceedings themselves were of a
different character. In *Equal Opportunities Commission v Birmingham City Council*
[1989] 1 All ER 769, [1989] AC 1155 the respondent was a local authority which
was found to have treated girl pupils less favourably than boys. In *Thomas v
Adjudication Officer* [1991] 3 All ER 315, [1991] 2 QB 164 the EOC was simply,
without opposition, joined as a party to resist an appeal by the Secretary of State
from a decision of social security commissioners.

In order to complete my consideration of locus standi I must also look, as the
Divisional Court pointed out, at the subject matter of the application. I must
consider the remedies sought, and the available alternatives. Those are matters to
which I turn in the ensuing paragraphs of this judgment.

3. Justiciable issues

In *Council of Civil Service Unions v Minister for the Civil Service* [1984] 3 All ER
935 at 949, [1985] AC 374 at 408–409 Lord Diplock said:

> 'The subject matter of every judicial review is a decision made by some
> person (or body of persons) whom I will call the "decision-maker" or else a
> refusal by him to make a decision. To qualify as a subject for judicial review
> the decision must have consequences which affect some person (or body of
> persons) other than the decision-maker, although it may affect him too. It
> must affect such other person either (a) by altering rights or obligations of
> that person which are enforceable by or against him in private law or (b) by
> depriving him of some benefit or advantage ... For a decision to be
> susceptible to judicial review the decision-maker must be empowered by
> public law (and not merely, as in arbitration, by agreement between private
> parties) to make decisions that, if validly made, will lead to administrative
> action or abstention from action by an authority endowed by law with
> executive powers, which have one or other of the consequences mentioned
> in the preceding paragraph.'

It may well be that if those words are read in isolation too much emphasis can be
given to the concept of a decision. In *Gillick v West Norfolk and Wisbech Area Health
Authority* [1985] 3 All ER 402 at 427, [1986] AC 112 at 193 a government
department's circular dealing with contraceptive advice to young people was
under consideration in an action commenced by writ, and Lord Bridge, after
referring to the decision of the House of Lords in *Royal College of Nursing of the UK
v Dept of Health and Social Security* [1981] 1 All ER 545, [1981] AC 800, said:

> '... if a government department, in a field of administration in which it
> exercises responsibility, promulgates in a public document, albeit non
> statutory in form, advice which is erroneous in law, then the court, in
> proceedings in appropriate form commenced by an applicant or plaintiff who
> possesses the necessary locus standi, has jurisdiction to correct the error of
> law by an appropriate declaration.'

In each of the present applications the decision complained of is to be found in
an exchange of correspondence between the EOC and the Secretary of State for
Employment, and it is of some importance to look at what was said. To my mind
there is for present purposes no significant difference between the two sets of
correspondence, so I need deal only with the correspondence which is relevant to
the first application. It begins with a letter from the chief executive of the EOC
dated 21 March 1990. The letter refers to a decision of the Court of Justice of the

European Communities, and to the qualifying periods prescribed by the
Employment Protection (Consolidation) Act 1978 before benefits such as *a*
redundancy payments can be obtained. The period is longer for those who work
only part-time, and as those who work part-time are mostly women it is suggested
in the letter that the qualification provisions offend against European law because
they are discriminatory. The letter ends:

> 'We should be grateful if you would consider these matters as a matter of *b*
> urgency, and inform the Commission whether the government will be
> willing to introduce the necessary legislation to remove this discrimination
> from the 1978 Act. If your answer is in the negative, we would ask you to
> give reasons for your decision.'

On 23 April 1990 the Secretary of State replied. He challenged the assertion that
redundancy payments and compensation for unfair dismissal constitute 'pay' *c*
within the meaning of art 119 of the EEC Treaty or within the equal treatment
directive, and concluded:

> 'Whether or not such payments were ever held to be pay, or to come
> within the Directive, we believe that our current statutory thresholds are
> entirely justifiable. These thresholds have existed in one form or another *d*
> ever since employment protection legislation was first introduced. Their
> purpose is to ensure that a fair balance is struck between the interests of
> employers and employees. We have no plans to change the thresholds.'

In the amended notice of application for leave to move for judicial review the
decision in respect of which relief was sought was identified as: *e*

> 'The decision of the Secretary of State for Employment dated 23 April
> 1990 declining to accept that the United Kingdom is in breach of its
> obligations under Community law by providing less favourable treatment of
> part-time workers than of full-time workers in relation to the conditions for
> the right not to be unfairly dismissed and for receipt of statutory redundancy *f*
> pay and compensation for unfair dismissal and refusing to introduce
> amending legislation to make the Employment Protection (Consolidation)
> Act 1978 comply with the relevant provisions of Community law.'

So what is complained of is, first, a refusal by a minister to accept that the
United Kingdom is in breach of Community law, and, secondly, his refusal to *g*
introduce legislation to amend the 1978 Act.

I accept of course that the Secretary of State's letter of 23 April 1990 was a
considered reply to a letter from a responsible body, but I do not see why it should
be regarded as a decision subject to challenge by means of judicial review. It does
not satisfy the criteria suggested by Lord Diplock in *Council of Civil Service Unions
v Minister for the Civil Service*. It did not alter any rights or obligations of any *h*
person, or deprive anyone of any benefit or advantage. On the contrary it sought
to preserve the status quo. If, by reason of the admitted supremacy of Community
law, a part-time employee whose employment was terminated was entitled by
virtue of art 119 of the Treaty or (if she was a state employee) by virtue of Council
Directive (EEC) 76/207 (the equal treatment directive) to require an industrial
tribunal to disapply the qualifying period of five years in the 1978 Act, her right *j*
to have that period disapplied was the same after the Secretary of State wrote his
letter as it was before it. Furthermore, the decision required of the Secretary of
State did not satisfy Lord Diplock's further criteria. It was not a decision which if
validly made would lead to administrative action or abstention from action by an

authority endowed by law with executive powers which altered rights or
obligations or deprived persons of some benefit or advantage. The action in
contemplation was the introduction of proposals to amend the 1978 legislation,
which proposals Parliament might or might not accept. Turning to what was said
by Lord Bridge in *Gillick's* case, I cannot regard the letter of 23 April 1990 as a
public document promulgating advice, comparable with a ministry circular, and,
as I have already indicated, if it expressed an erroneous view of the law that could
easily be tested in relation to an individual claimant before an industrial tribunal.
No right belonging to the EOC was infringed by the letter of 23 April 1990, nor
so far as the EOC was concerned was the Secretary of State on 23 April 1990 under
any obligation to act in any other way, which is another reason for saying that the
EOC in these proceedings in my view lacks locus standi.

On behalf of the EOC the case was put in different ways. It was submitted that,
if the letter of 23 April 1990 could not be regarded as a decision, it could be
regarded as a challengeable expression of view in relation to which the EOC is
entitled to launch a challenge by means of judicial review so as to clarify the law
for the public benefit. But it is not the function of judicial review simply to
pronounce upon the law in order to clarify it, especially when in the normal
course of events an industrial tribunal would have to pronounce upon it in order
to decide a specific claim. If the tribunal is wrong the decision can be tested
through the usual appellate channels. In his reply Mr Lester submitted that this
is a very exceptional case because it attacks the alleged non-implementation of
directives. In my judgment that is, as Mr Beloff QC submitted, what the case is
really about. It is an attempt to enforce obligations which if they exist do so only
under international law, and even the implementation of the European
Communities Act 1972 does not entitle the courts of this country to enforce
obligations of that kind. As the Divisional Court said in the present case ([1992] 1
All ER 545 at 561):

> '. . . the 1972 Act alters the traditional relationship between the courts and
> Parliament in this country in that it obliges the courts to disregard the laws
> made by Parliament in so far as they conflict with directly enforceable
> Community law. Further than that it does not go. Domestic legislation
> remains a matter for Parliament, not for the courts. How could it be right
> for us to tell the Secretary of State that he must introduce legislation
> amending the 1978 Act, when so far as we can see it would equally be open
> to him as a member of Parliament to introduce legislation amending or
> repealing the 1972 Act? If it would be wrong and unconstitutional, as we
> believe, for the courts to give him an order in these terms, it must equally be
> wrong for the courts to make a declaration that such was his duty.'

I recognise that the EOC does not now seek an order of mandamus, and only did
so by amendment at the invitation of the Divisional Court, but for the reasons
given by the Divisional Court it is my conclusion that the EOC is not entitled to
the principal declaration which it seeks.

In attempting to deal with the decision issue I have been to some extent
concerned with the remedies sought, but before I turn to other aspects of that
topic it is worth noting that whereas, as it seems to me, Mr Lester had considerable
and understandable difficulty in defining in a compelling way the justiciable issue
or the decision issue so as to fit the EOC's complaint within the framework of
judicial review, no such problem would arise in the case of Mrs Day. If there were
not another forum for her she could simply rely on the refusal to make
redundancy payments without regard to the threshold requirement of employ-

ment for five years. There is a decision which to my mind contrasts sharply with the absence of any well-defined justiciable issue in the case of the EOC.

4. Remedies

In the first application the EOC seeks four declarations as well as an order for mandamus and costs. The court is invited to declare that by reason of the operation of the qualifying provisions in the 1978 Act the United Kingdom is: (1) in breach of its obligations under art 119 of the EEC Treaty and Council Directive 75/117 (the equal pay directive), (2) in breach of its obligations under the equal treatment directive.

The third declaration sought is that the United Kingdom is in breach of its obligations under the Treaty and the directives by failing to introduce legislation to amend the 1978 Act. Finally, the fourth declaration sought is to the effect that—

'employees who work for fewer than sixteen hours per week are subject to the same conditions for the right not to be unfairly dismissed and for entitlement to compensation for unfair dismissal and redundancy pay pursuant to the Employment Protection (Consolidation) Act 1978 as employees who work for more than sixteen hours per week.'

For the reasons given by the Divisional Court, and which I have already cited, it is my conclusion that the EOC cannot be entitled to any of the first three declarations which are sought. It is not for the Divisional Court or for this court to pronounce upon whether the United Kingdom is or is not in breach of international obligations, although it is for the court to apply directly effective European law in preference to domestic law if the laws conflict. As the Divisional Court said ([1992] 1 All ER 545 at 561):

'Rights and duties which have become part of English law by virtue of s 2 of the 1972 Act, or by virtue of subordinate legislation made under that section, are matters for us; the obligations of the United Kingdom under the EEC Treaty are not ... declarations by the court should not in our view go beyond defining the present state of the law as a matter of practical reality. They should be limited to rights and obligations which the national courts can and will, if necessary, enforce.'

That leaves only the fourth declaration, which does no more than recite what, if the EOC's arguments are correct, an individual claimant such as Mrs Day can prove before an industrial tribunal. In saying that I recognise that an employee who is not an employee of an organ of the state cannot claim that she has directly effective rights arising out of the directive, but such a person may be able to obtain damages from the state if the directive is not acted upon (*Francovich v Italy, Bonifaci v Italy* Joined cases C-6/90 and C-9/90 [1992] IRLR 84). As Mr Beloff put it, relief confined to the fourth declaration sought would not have any immediate connection with the exchange of letters between the EOC and the Secretary of State, and would really amount to no more than a declaration of private rights arising under Community law. If that is the only remedy that can properly be claimed it casts further doubt upon the standing of the EOC in these proceedings, and upon the question of whether there ever was a justiciable issue suitable for consideration by means of judicial review.

5. Alternative remedies

I have already given some consideration to the existence of alternative remedies, but I must say a little more because it is in the forefront of Mr Beloff's case that the availability of alternative remedies which cover most of the ground makes

a judicial review unnecessary. In *R v Chief Constable of the Merseyside Police, ex p Calveley* [1986] 1 All ER 257, [1986] QB 424 all three members of the Court of Appeal emphasised that judicial review will very rarely be available where there is an alternative remedy. Here it is common ground that employees such as Mrs Day can go to an industrial tribunal, and arts 169 and 170 of the EEC Treaty provide the means by which the European Commission can take steps to ensure

b that the United Kingdom complies with its obligations under the Treaty, such as its obligation to give effect to directives. I accept that the art 169 procedure may be slow and cumbersome, and that, subject to the decision in *Francovich's* case, until that procedure is complete an employee not employed by an organ of the state is at some disadvantage, because directives until implemented have no direct

c effect. But nevertheless, for the reasons I have attempted to outline, I do not accept that it is possible to use the procedure of judicial review as a form of fast track to give European directives full and immediate effect in English law. As Mr Beloff submitted, if that route is available there is really little left of the Community law concept of direct effect. Even where there is no direct effect the rights will be enforceable. Of course it would be convenient, and possibly cost

d effective, for the EOC to be able to obtain a declaratory judgment rather than support one or more litigants before an industrial tribunal and proceed from there, but it seems to me that convenience cannot be even a persuasive factor in the present case.

I accept, as I said at the outset, that if the EOC cannot proceed in the Divisional Court it cannot proceed at all, but its only object in bringing proceedings is to

e protect part-time workers from discrimination, and as I have indicated if they are discriminated against they can at least to a very large extent protect themselves. Although not directly in issue in the present case it is my conclusion that the United Kingdom complies with its obligations under art 6 of the equal treatment directive by providing industrial tribunals and the appellate structure that goes

f with them.

6. Conclusion

The conclusions which I have reached in relation to the various issues which I have canvassed, namely, locus standi, the decision issue, the remedies sought and the remedies available elsewhere, lead me to decide against the EOC in relation to

g both applications. I find it unnecessary to consider the remaining issues and I would dismiss the EOC's appeals.

h **HIRST LJ.** I gratefully adopt Dillon LJ's recital of the facts, and of the relevant framework of EC law and United Kingdom legislation. I propose to consider the issues under similar headings to those used in the Divisional Court, though, if I am right in my conclusion in favour of the Secretary of State on the jurisdictional issues, the substantive issues are academic.

j *The remedies sought*

These are as follows, using the same numbering as the Divisional Court ([1992] 1 All ER 545 at 560):

'... (1) declarations to the effect that employees who work for fewer than 16 hours per week (most of whom are women) are subject to the same conditions as employees who work for 16 or more hours per week (most of

whom are men) as regards the right not to be unfairly dismissed, the right to
compensation for unfair dismissal, the right to redundancy pay and the   *a*
method of calculation of redundancy pay in respect of those part-time
workers who have previously worked full time, (2) declarations to the effect
that the Secretary of State is in breach of the obligations imposed upon the
United Kingdom by art 119 of the EEC Treaty and the equal pay and equal
treatment directives [Council Directives (EEC) 75/117 and 76/207] by failing
to introduce legislation to amend the [Employment Protection (Consolida-   *b*
tion) Act 1978] so as to bring it into line with the Treaty and the directives,
(3) mandamus to compel the Secretary of State to introduce such legislation
and (4) a declaration that the United Kingdom is in breach of its obligations
under art 119 and the directives.'

During the hearing Mr Lester QC made it clear that he was not pressing for the   *c*
order of mandamus.

The 'decisions' issue
   The request of the Equal Opportunities Commission (the EOC) and the
Secretary of State's reply so far as relevant were in the following terms: *d*

   'We should be grateful if you would consider these matters as a matter of
   urgency, and inform the Commission whether the Government will be
   willing to introduce the necessary legislation to remove this discrimination
   from the 1978 Act. If your answer is in the negative, we would ask you to
   give reasons for your decision.'
                                                                               e
   'Whether or not such payments were ever held to be pay, or to come
   within the Directive, we believe that our current statutory thresholds are
   entirely justifiable. These thresholds have existed in one form or another
   ever since employment protection legislation was first introduced. Their
   purpose is to ensure that a fair balance is struck between the interests of
   employers and employees. We have no plans to change the thresholds.'   *f*

The Divisional Court held that this amounted to a decision or decisions susceptible
to judicial review on ordinary principles, as embodying the Secretary of State's
considered view on the question of employment law, and constituting a refusal
to carry out what the EOC contended was his legal duty.
   In *Council of Civil Service Unions v Minister for the Civil Service* [1984] 3 All ER   *g*
935 at 949, [1985] AC 374 at 408 Lord Diplock stated, in a passage with which
Lord Scarman agreed, as follows:

   'To qualify as a subject for judicial review the decision must have
   consequences which affect some person (or body of persons) other than the
   decision-maker, although it may affect him too. It must affect such other   *h*
   person either (a) by altering rights or obligations of that person which are
   enforceable by or against him in private law or (b) by depriving him of some
   benefit or advantage which either (i) he has in the past been permitted by the
   decision-maker to enjoy and which he can legitimately expect to be permitted
   to continue to do until there has been communicated to him some rational
   ground for withdrawing it on which he has been given an opportunity to   *j*
   comment or (ii) he has received assurance from the decision-maker will not
   be withdrawn without giving him first an opportunity of advancing reasons
   for contending that they should not be withdrawn.'

Only para (a) is relevant in the present case.

Mr Lester supported the Divisional Court's conclusion, and submitted that the
a Secretary of State's reply amounted to a statement that he had no intention to
amend the 1978 Act, because he did not regard Community law as requiring the
United Kingdom to change it, and that this was an official decision by the
responsible minister in relation to the performance of his public duties in the
exercise of his public powers.

Mr Beloff QC relied on Lord Diplock's statement, and submitted that this was
b not a decision at all, but rather no more than a deliberately solicited expression of
the Secretary of State's view as to the scope of Community law.

I accept Mr Beloff's construction of the Secretary of State's reply, and am unable
to accept Mr Lester's argument that it amounted to a refusal in effect to carry out
a legal duty, since it is plain that, when stating that he did not plan to change the
thresholds, he was saying no more than that he had no plans to exercise his power
c under s 2(2) of the European Communities Act 1972 to introduce subordinate
legislation. This seems to me a far cry from the test laid down by Lord Diplock
above. There was not, therefore, in my judgment a decision susceptible of judicial
review.

This still leaves open the question whether it constituted a 'view' susceptible of
d judicial review under the principles laid down by the House of Lords in *Gillick v
West Norfolk and Wisbech Area Health Authority* [1985] 3 All ER 402, [1986] AC
112.

In that case Lord Bridge of Harwich laid down the limitations of this extension
of the scope of judicial review, in a statement with which Lord Templeman
agreed, as follows ([1985] 3 All ER 402 at 426–427, [1986] AC 112 at 193–194):

e
> 'The question whether the advice tendered in such non-statutory guidance
> is good or bad, reasonable or unreasonable cannot, as a general rule, be subject
> to any form of judicial review. But the question arises whether there is any
> exception to that general rule. Your Lordships have been referred to the
> House's decision in *Royal College of Nursing of the UK v Dept of Health and Social
f > Security* [1981] 1 All ER 545, [1981] AC 800. The background to that case
> was exceptional, as only becomes fully clear when one reads the judgment of
> Woolf J at first instance (see [1981] 1 All ER 545). The Royal College of
> Nursing (the RCN) and the DHSS had received conflicting legal advice
> whether or not it was lawful, on the true construction of certain provisions
> of the Abortion Act 1967, for nurses to perform particular functions in the
g > course of a novel medical procedure for the termination of pregnancy, when
> acting on the orders and under the general supervision of a registered medical
> practitioner but not necessarily in his presence. The RCN had issued a
> memorandum and a later circular to its members to the effect that it was not
> lawful. The DHSS had issued a circular advising that it was lawful. The
> desirability of an authoritative resolution of this dispute on a pure question
h > of law was obvious in the interests both of the nursing profession and of the
> public. The proceedings took the form of a claim by the RCN against the
> DHSS for a suitable declaration and the DHSS in due course counterclaimed
> a declaration to the opposite effect. As Woolf J pointed out, neither side took
> any point as to the jurisdiction of the court to grant a declaration. Woolf J
> himself felt it necessary to raise and examine certain questions as to the locus
j > standi of the RCN to bring the proceedings and as to the propriety of their
> form. He answered these questions in a favourable sense to enable him to
> decide the disputed question of law on its merits. No technical question
> bearing on jurisdiction attracted any mention in the Court of Appeal (see
> [1981] 1 All ER 545, [1981] AC 800) or in this House. In the litigation the

original conflict between the parties was reflected in a conflict of judicial opinion. On a count of judicial heads a majority of five to four favoured the RCN. But by a majority of three to two in your Lordships' House the DHSS carried the day and obtained the declaration they sought. Against this background it would have been surprising indeed if the courts had declined jurisdiction. But I think it must be recognised that the decision (whether or not it was so intended) does effect a significant extension of the court's power of judicial review. We must now say that if a government department, in a field of administration in which it exercises responsibility, promulgates in a public document, albeit non-statutory in form, advice which is erroneous in law, then the court, in proceedings in appropriate form commenced by an applicant or plaintiff who possesses the necessary locus standi, has jurisdiction to correct the error of law by an appropriate declaration. Such an extended jurisdiction is no doubt a salutary and indeed a necessary one in certain circumstance, as the *Royal College of Nursing* case itself well illustrates. But the occasions of a departmental non-statutory publication raising, as in that case, a clearly defined issue of law, unclouded by political, social or moral overtones, will be rare. In cases where any proposition of law implicit in a departmental advisory document is interwoven with questions of social and ethical controversy, the court should, in my opinion, exercise its jurisdiction with the utmost restraint, confine itself to deciding whether the proposition of law is erroneous and avoid either expressing ex cathedra opinions in areas of social and ethical controversy in which it has no claim to speak with authority or proffering answers to hypothetical questions of law which do not strictly arise for decision.'

The Divisional Court held that this alternative basis of jurisdiction did apply if, contrary to its view, no decision had been made, and Mr Lester supported this conclusion by submitting that the present case is comparable, seeing that the EOC has to regulate its own affairs, i e its duties and powers, in the light of ministerial statements.

I am unable to accept this submission. The passage I have quoted from Lord Bridge's speech above plainly shows that the extended jurisdiction applied in *Gillick*'s case is the exception rather than the rule.

In the present case, as the evidence shows, the legal issue is closely interwoven with questions of social and political controversy, and does not in my judgment qualify as an exception to the general rule.

I would therefore hold that the Secretary of State's letter was neither a decision nor an expression of view susceptible of judicial review.

This conclusion is reinforced by the Divisional Court's analysis of available remedies in which it held (rightly in my judgment) that declarations (2) and (4), which went to the Secretary of State's duties and powers, were outside its jurisdiction.

Declaration (1), which it did grant, is not declaratory of the Secretary of State's duties and powers, but of employees' rights under the employment legislation. In the end, therefore, the application, which Mr Lester submits was the proper means of reviewing the Secretary of State's decision, resulted in no express declaration on that topic. I shall refer to this aspect in more detail in the final section of this judgment.

The locus standi issue

The issue here is as to the EOC's locus standi, it not being in dispute that Mrs Day, for the purpose of the first application only, has the necessary locus

standi. It is common ground that the crucial question is whether the EOC has a
a   sufficient interest, which, as the Divisional Court rightly stated, depends in part
on the nature of its duties as defined by the statute which created it, and in part
by consideration of the particular subject matter of the application itself.

So far as the first limb of the test is concerned, Mr Beloff submitted that the
EOC has no right, interest, privilege or legitimate expectation at stake, and that
nothing in the Sex Discrimination Act 1975 expressly gives it locus standi in
b   matters of this kind. On the contrary, he submitted, its duties quoad the Secretary
of State are no more than to advise on the working of the 1975 Act and the Equal
Pay Act 1970 under s 53(1)(c) of the former.

In my judgment Mr Lester is right in submitting that this approach is much
too narrow in view of the EOC's duty under s 53(1)(a) to work toward the
elimination of discrimination. This is a very wide power, which is sufficient to
c   embrace applications for judicial review, and which is not cut down by para (c).

It follows that the EOC has locus standi to bring judicial review proceedings
provided the second limb of the Divisional Court's test is also fulfilled, and
provided also that the other necessary criteria (reviewable decision, appropriate
forum etc) are met, as no doubt they were in, for example, *Equal Opportunities
d   Commission v Birmingham City Council* [1989] 1 All ER 769, [1989] AC 1155, though
there appears to have been no contest on this issue there.

The forum issue

It is not in dispute that there are clearly established procedures for challenging
either the compatibility of domestic legislation with Community law, or alleged
e   failures by the United Kingdom to comply with its Community obligations, viz
(a) by individuals enjoying directly effective rights under Community law (in this
case under art 119 of the EEC Treaty), who are entitled to enforce such rights in
the appropriate court or tribunal, which will be bound under s 2(1) of the 1972
Act to disapply domestic legislation if and so far as it is inconsistent with those
f   rights, and (b) by the EC Commission and other member states, who can invoke
the machinery laid down by the Treaty, particularly in art 169, for bringing
proceedings against a member state in the European Court for failure to fulfil its
obligations under the Treaty.

To this may be added a third method, as laid down in the decision of the
European Court in *Francovich v Italy, Bonifaci v Italy* Joined cases C-6/90 and C-9/90
g   [1992] IRLR 84, namely a claim by individuals not enjoying directly enforceable
rights under EC law for damages against the government for failure to implement
EC directives; however, Mr Richards in his final reply invited the court to
approach this case with caution, seeing that the scope of the remedy is as yet not
clearly delimited.

Mr Lester, supporting the conclusion of the Divisional Court, submitted that
h   the central issues in the present case do not depend on the 'adjudicative facts' of
individual cases involving private disputes between employees and their
employers, but rather the 'legislative and governmental facts, information, and
opinion' about the operation of the statutory scheme upon the labour market in
the United Kingdom and elsewhere in the Community, and the law and practice
in other member states, and that it is obvious that the Divisional Court is more
j   expert in tackling such issues and more capable of granting appropriate relief
than an industrial tribunal; consequently the Divisional Court is the appropriate
forum for both Mrs Day and the EOC.

Mr Beloff submitted that, so far as Mrs Day is concerned, she enjoys directly
effective rights both under art 119, and, because her employer is a public

authority, under the directives, and that these are private rights which she should seek to enforce against her employers in the industrial tribunal in the proceedings which are already in progress.

So far as the EOC is concerned, Mr Beloff submitted that it is seeking impermissibly to use the machinery of judicial review as a means of enforcing the alleged obligation of the United Kingdom under the Treaty, and is not asserting any directly effective rights of its own.

In my judgment, for the reasons given by Dillon LJ, where an individual like Mrs Day is seeking to enforce directly effective rights under art 119, the appropriate forum for their enforcement is unquestionably the industrial tribunal. This tribunal will be obliged under s 2(1) of the 1972 Act to disapply domestic legislation if and in so far as it is inconsistent with Community law, thus ensuring that Community law will prevail.

The industrial tribunal, rather than the Divisional Court, is moreover in my judgment the appropriate forum for the determination of the factual issues which arise in relation to the objective justification of any discriminatory law or practice. In *R v East Berkshire Health Authority, ex p Walsh* [1984] 3 All ER 425 at 434, [1985] QB 152 at 169–170 May LJ stated as follows:

'Further, I think that at the present time, in at least the great majority of cases involving disputes about the dismissal of an employee by his employer, the most appropriate forum for their resolution is an industrial tribunal. In my opinion the courts should not be astute to hold that any particular dispute is appropriate for consideration under the judicial review procedure provided for by RSC Ord 53. Employment disputes not infrequently have political or ideological overtones, or raise what are often described as "matters of principle"; these are generally best considered not by the Divisional Court but by an industrial tribunal to the members of which, both lay and legally qualified, such overtones or matters of principle are common currency.'

These words seem to me entirely apposite to the present case, since, as already observed, objective justification has significant political and ideological overtones. So far as the EOC is concerned, it will always be open to it to support Mrs Day, or any other suitable claimant with directly enforceable rights, in industrial tribunal proceedings under its powers contained in s 75 of the Sex Discrimination Act 1975. This will ensure that cases in which the EOC wishes to obtain a ruling are brought in the appropriate forum.

Mr Lester raised the spectre of hundreds of industrial tribunal cases being mounted at inordinate expense, and contrasted what he submitted are the much more convenient and expeditious alternative proceedings by way of judicial review in the Divisional Court. This seems to me to be unduly alarmist. It is always open to the EOC to select one or a very small number of suitable test cases, which can be brought conveniently in the industrial tribunal, without undue expense, and if necessary carried through to appeal within the equivalent time-scale (two and a half years) to the present case.

Proceedings aimed at impleading the government, or a minister, for failure to fulfil their obligations under the Treaty to amend legislation inconsistent with the EC law or directives should in my judgment be brought not by the EOC or any equivalent body in the English courts, but by the commission, who are the guardians of the Treaty, in the European Court under the machinery laid down in the Treaty itself in art 169. In the light of the past record of the United Kingdom government, so we were assured by Mr Richards, any adverse ruling by a the European Court will quickly result in the introduction of amending legislation.

The Divisional Court reached the opposite conclusion on the ground that women in the United Kingdom should not have to wait upon a decision of the commission to invoke art 169, and that the directly enforceable rights which the EOC seeks to enforce are rights under English law as well as under Community law which the EOC is entitled to have determined by the English courts.

b This reasoning seems to me to overlook the fact that the EOC will not have to wait for the commission to act, but can achieve the result sought in English proceedings by supporting Mrs Day's case in the industrial tribunal, and if necessary carrying it to appeal.

In this connection the recent ruling of the European Court in *Emmott v Minister for Social Welfare* Case C-208/90 [1991] 3 CMLR 894 at 914–915 (para 16) is highly
c pertinent. The court in that case ruled as follows:

> 'As the Court has consistently held (see, in particular, Case 33/76 REWE-ZENTRALFINANZ eG AND REWE-ZENTRAL AG V. LANDWIRTSCHAFTSKAMMER FÜR DAS SAARLAND ([1976] ECR 1989) and Case 199/82 AMMINISTRAZIONE DELLE FINANZE DELLO STATO V. SAN GIORGIO SPA ([1983] ECR 3595)) in the absence of
> d Community rules on the subject, it is for the domestic legal system of each member-State to determine the procedural conditions governing actions at law intended to ensure the protection of the rights which individuals derive from the direct effect of Community law, provided that such conditions are not less favourable than those relating to similar actions of a domestic nature nor framed so as to render virtually impossible the exercise of rights conferred
> e by Community law.'

In the United Kingdom industrial tribunal proceedings meet this criterion.

The first application

It is common ground that the thresholds laid down under the 1978 Act are
f discriminatory against part-time employees, 90% of whom are women.

It follows that it is incumbent on the Secretary of State to satisfy the court that this discrimination is objectively justifiable.

A great deal of time was spent in argument debating the requirements which have to be satisfied in the light of *Bilka-Kaufhaus GmbH v Weber von Hartz* Case 170/84 [1986] ECR 1607. The key passage in the judgment in the European
g Court in that case is as follows (at 1628 (para 36)):

> 'It is for the national court, which has sole jurisdiction to make findings of fact, to determine whether and to what extent the grounds put forward by an employer to explain the adoption of a pay practice which applies independently of a worker's sex but in fact affects more women than men
> h may be regarded as objectively justified economic grounds. If the national court finds that the measures chosen by Bilka correspond to a real need on the part of the undertaking, are appropriate with a view to achieving the objectives pursued and are necessary to that end, the fact that the measures affect a far greater number of women than men is not sufficient to show that they constitute an infringement of Article 119.'

i Mr Lester in effect invited the court to treat these words as if they are equivalent to a statutory definition, though he did not go so far as to submit that the word 'necessary' is equivalent to 'indispensable'.

In my judgment Mr Beloff is right in his submission that these words are not definitive, but illustrative of the stringency of the criterion, which goes well beyond reasonableness, let alone the *Wednesbury* test (see *Associated Provincial Picture Houses Ltd v Wednesbury Corp* [1947] 2 All ER 680, [1948] 1 KB 223).   *a*

This I think is supported by the formulation of the test by the European Court in *Handels- og Kontorfunktionærernes Forbund i Danmark v Dansk Arbejdsgiverforening (acting on behalf of Danfoss)* Case C-109/88 [1989] ECR I-3199 at 3228 (para 22) where the court stated as follows:

> 'In its judgment of 13 May 1986 in Case 170/84 *Bilka v Weber von Hartz*   *b*
> [1986] ECR 1607, the Court took the view that an undertaking's policy of
> generally paying full-time employees more than part-time employees who
> were excluded from the undertaking's pension scheme, could affect far more
> women than men in view of the difficulties which women encountered in
> working full-time. It nevertheless held that the undertaking might show
> that its wages practice was based on objectively justified factors unrelated to   *c*
> any discrimination on grounds of sex and if the undertaking did so there was
> no infringement of Article 119 of the Treaty. Those considerations also apply
> in the case of a wages practice which specially remunerates the employee's
> adaptability to variable hours and varying places of work. The employer may
> therefore justify the remuneration of such adaptability by showing it is of
> *importance* for the performance of specific tasks entrusted to the employee.'   *d*
> (My emphasis.)

In its answers to the questions posed under art 177 by the Danish Industrial Arbitration Board, the European Court repeated the same test ('of importance for the performance of the specific tasks . . .').

The Divisional Court cited the *Bilka-Kaufhaus* case and, despite Mr Lester's   *e* submission to the contrary, I am satisfied that it applied the correct test (see [1992] 1 All ER 545 at 562–563).

I am also satisfied that its careful and thorough analysis of the evidence was sound, and that it was correct to conclude that the Secretary of State had objectively justified the thresholds.

I do not propose to repeat its analysis, but wish to emphasise the following   *f* points.

(i) Mr Lester set great store by the Department of Employment's own survey, but in my judgment this survey does not carry the weight which he sought to attach to it, both because it does not concentrate on the relevant class (ie those working between 0 and 16 hours per week) but rather upon those working up to   *g* 30 hours per week, and because the respondents from the comparatively small sample (under 1,000) comprised mostly those working over 16 hours per week.

(ii) Mr Lester also laid stress on the arrangements in other member states, especially Ireland and the Netherlands. These do not, however, seem to me to have much force, since Ireland has reduced its thresholds not abolished them, and the Netherlands has no minimum wage requirements for a substantial proportion   *h* of part-time workers.

(iii) The evidence accepted by the Divisional Court seems to me to give ample support for the proposition that the application of the same conditions for all part-timers, irrespective of their hours of work, would impose significant administrative burdens and costs on employers, and would tend to reduce the availability of part-time work.   *j*

(iv) Mr Beloff was in my view fully entitled to lay stress on the commission's proposals for an 8-hour threshold, which gives powerful independent support for the conclusion that a threshold is in principle objectively justifiable, derived from a body which presumably applied the *Bilka* test. Once it is established that a

threshold as such is in principle objectively justifiable under EC law, it seems to
a me that a margin of appreciation must be allowed to the national legislature in
fixing at which precise hour or hours the line is to be drawn.

The pay issue
    I agree with Dillon LJ.

b *The second application—discrimination*
    Mr Lester submitted that the Divisional Court was correct to hold that the
mode of calculation, based on salary at date of redundancy, was discriminatory
against part-time workers, seeing that indirect sex discrimination arises where
there is an equal rule which has a disproportionate adverse impact on women,
since the concept of indirect discrimination looks at the consequences, ie
c inequality of result.
    He relied strongly on *Arbeiterwohlfahrt der Stadt Berlin eV v Bötel* Case C-360/90
[1992] IRLR 423, where the European Court held that there was discrimination
against a part-time nurse in respect of her participation in training courses, since
the provisions in force only entitled her to compensation for time spent on the
d course up to the limit of her own working hours, whereas full-time employees
were fully compensated. The European Court stated as follows (at 426 (para 17)):

> 'It appears that the two categories of members of Staff Committees devote
> the same number of hours to participation in the training courses in question.
> Nevertheless, as the length of the courses organised within the full-time
> working hours applicable in the undertaking exceeds the working hours of
e > members who are part-time employees, the latter receive less by way of
> compensation from their employer than those employees who are employed
> full-time and are, in consequence, treated differently.'

    Mr Beloff submitted that the present method of calculation treats all workers
identically, namely by reference to their pay at the date of termination of
f employment, and that there is no discrimination against any definable group of
workers, since the system operates in exactly the same way in respect of part-time
workers and full-time workers.
    He relied on the statement in *Ruzius-Wilbrink v Bestuur van de Bedrijfsvereniging
voor Overheidsdiensten* Case C-102/88 [1989] ECR 4311 at 4333 (para 20) as follows:

g > 'It is apparent from the judgment of 4 December 1986 in Case 71/85
> *Netherlands v Federatie Nederlandse Vakbeweging* [1986] ECR 3855 that, in a
> case of direct discrimination, women are entitled to be treated in the same
> manner, and to have the same rules applied to them, as men who are in the
> same situation, since, where the directive has not been correctly implemented,
> those rules remain the only valid point of reference. By analogy, in a case of
h > indirect discrimination such as that in the main proceedings, the members
> of the group placed at a disadvantage, be they men or women, are entitled to
> have the same rules applied to them as are applied to the other recipients of
> the allowance.'

    Here, he submitted, application of the same rules as are applied to the other
j recipients of the benefit would produce exactly the same result as at present, since
identical rules are already applied to both classes, drawing no distinction between
either class.
    He further submitted that a practice could only be assumed to have an adverse
disproportionate impact on part-time workers if it was a precondition for

acquiring a particular benefit that a worker was in full-time employment. This applied in *Bötel's* case, seeing that, as the above quoted passage shows, it was a condition, which the part-time workers could not meet, that the entire course took place in working hours.

In my judgment Mr Beloff's submissions are correct. This particular pay practice lays down precisely identical rules for both full-time and part-time workers, and there is no condition which part-timers (unlike full-timers) are unable to meet. Mr Lester gave the following example to illustrate his case. A woman who has been in continuous full-time employment for six years between the ages of 22 and 28 (earning £160 per week), who changes to part-time work at the age of 28 (working 16 hours per week, earning £64 per week) and is then made redundant at the age of 30, will under the present scheme be entitled to a redundancy payment of only £512 (8 × £64), whereas if she were given credit for her years of full-time service she would be entitled to a payment of £1,088 (6 × £160 + 2 × £64). In my judgment this example vividly demonstrates that Mr Lester is not seeking to redress a discriminatory disadvantage affecting part-time workers, but rather impermissibly to substitute an entirely new set of rules for the present system.

I should add that if the European Court upholds the decision of the Employment Appeal Tribunal in *Enderby v Frenchay Health Authority* [1991] ICR 382, which has been referred by the Court of Appeal to the court under art 177, this would place a further obstacle in the EOC's path, since the Employment Appeal Tribunal concluded, in the words of the headnote (at 383):

> 'Held, (1) dismissing the appeal, that where unintentional indirect discrimination was alleged it was necessary to identify a requirement or condition and to consider whether it had a disparate adverse impact on women because fewer women than men in the appropriate pool were able to comply with it; that the mere fact of a difference in pay, with a predominantly female group earning less than another group which at the time happened to be predominantly male, was not sufficient to raise a prima facie case of indirect discrimination; that if the difference in pay came about from a factor which was not tainted by gender the question of justification did not arise; that since either no requirement or condition had been shown in the present case or, alternatively, that the suggested requirement, the Whitley Council collective bargaining arrangements, was not tainted by sex discrimination, the requirement for the respondents to justify their policy did not arise . . .'

The second application—justification

Mr Beloff supported the conclusion of the Divisional Court, and submitted that it was right to place weight on the fact that it was a clear, direct and simple rule, calculated on a straightforward formula which is applicable to all employees without distinction, and in a manner which avoids administrative complexities and costs to which an alternative system of the kind proposed by the EOC would give rise.

Mr Lester submitted that it was the main objective of the redundancy payments scheme to compensate for length of service, and that the calculation by reference to final pay failed adequately to compensate for length of service those part-time employees who have switched from full-time to part-time work at the date of redundancy.

In my judgment Mr Lester placed too much weight on one of a number of factors underlying the redundancy scheme, which include not only reward for length of service, but also the facilitation of the employee's adjustment to the new

circumstances resulting from the loss of his employment, and the provision of a
a source of income during the period in which he is seeking new employment
(*Barber v Guardian Royal Exchange Assurance Group* Case C-262/88 [1990] 2 All ER
660, [1991] 1 QB 344). I accept Mr Beloff's submissions and consider that the
Divisional Court was right for the reasons it gave in holding that the Secretary of
State had made good his objective justification in relation to the second application.

b
Remedies
   Although Mr Lester no longer presses for an order of mandamus, it is plain
from declarations (2) and (4) that the main purpose of both these applications is,
as stated by the Divisional Court, to establish as a matter of law that the Secretary
of State is bound to introduce amending legislation under s 2(2) of the 1972 Act
c in his capacity as the designated minister. This was confirmed by Mr Lester in his
reply submissions when he stated that the Divisional Court is the only forum able
to determine whether the minister acted or failed to act lawfully. The Divisional
Court proceeded as follows ([1992] 1 All ER 545 at 561):

> '. . . we are of the opinion that it is not open to us to grant relief of the kind
d   sought under the second and third headings. It is plain enough that s 2 of the
> 1972 Act alters the traditional relationship between the courts and Parliament
> in this country in that it obliges the courts to disregard the laws made by
> Parliament in so far as they conflict with directly enforceable Community
> law. Further than that it does not go. Domestic legislation remains a matter
> for Parliament, not for the courts. How could it be right for us to tell the
e   Secretary of State that he must introduce legislation amending the 1978 Act,
> when so far as we can see it would equally be open to him as a member of
> Parliament to introduce legislation amending or repealing the 1972 Act? If
> it would be wrong and unconstitutional, as we believe, for the courts to give
> him an order in these terms, it must equally be wrong for the courts to make
f   a declaration that such was his duty. Declarations are intended to have
> practical consequences and not merely to be of academic interest. Further, it
> goes without saying that, even if, contrary to our view, it were right for us to
> exert the legal pressure of mandamus or the moral pressure of a declaration
> upon the Secretary of State to introduce legislation amending the 1978 Act,
> the last word would lie with Parliament. At one point in his argument
g   Mr Lester appeared to envisage that Parliament itself could be made a
> respondent to these proceedings and directed in effect to mend its ways, but
> at the end we understood him to resile from this revolutionary proposition.
> It follows from what we have said that in our judgment it is equally not open
> to us to contemplate the granting of relief under the fourth heading. We
> accept Mr Beloff's submissions upon this aspect of the case. Rights and duties
h   which have become part of English law by virtue of s 2 of the 1972 Act, or
> by virtue of subordinate legislation made under that section, are matters for
> us; the obligations of the United Kingdom under the EEC Treaty are not.'

This is entirely consistent with para 2 of Sch 2 to the 1972 Act, which provides:

> '(1) Subject to paragraph 3 below, where a provision contained in any
j   section of this Act confers power to make regulations (otherwise than by
> modification or extension of an existing power), the power shall be exercisable
> by statutory instrument.
>   (2) Any statutory instrument containing an Order in Council or regulations
> made in the exercise of a power so conferred, if made without a draft having

been approved by resolution of each House of Parliament, shall be subject to annulment in pursuance of a resolution of either House.'

This analysis by the Divisional Court of the constitutional position seems to me strongly to reinforce my conclusion on the jurisdictional issues.

For all the above reasons I would dismiss the appeals of both appellants.

Appeals dismissed. Leave to appeal to the House of Lords refused.

25 February 1993. The Appeal Committee of the House of Lords gave leave to appeal.

Carolyn Toulmin   Barrister.

End of Volume 1